T5-COB-585

Catalogue of Books from the Low Countries 1601–1621 in the British Library

Catalogue of Books from the Low Countries 1601–1621 in the British Library

Compiled by Anna E.C. Simoni

THE BRITISH LIBRARY
1990

First published 1990
by The British Library
Great Russell Street, London WC1B 3DG

British Library Cataloguing in Publication Data
British Library
Catalogue of books from the Low Countries 1601–1621
in the British Library.
1. Books with Benelux countries imprints. Catalogues, indexes
I. Title II. Simoni, Anna E.C.
015.492'03

ISBN 0-7123-0066-X

Titlepage illustration: The device has been taken from Adrianus Toll, *Disputatio inauguralis, de palpitatione Cordis,* Lugduni Batavorum [Leiden], 1615

Designed by John Mitchell
Typeset in Linotron 202 Bembo
by Bexhill Phototypesetters, Bexhill-on-Sea
Printed in England on long-life ∞ paper in an edition of 500 copies
by Redwood Press Ltd, Melksham, Wiltshire

CONTENTS

PREFACE

For some time now a new series of catalogues devoted to the British Library's holdings of seventeenth-century books from various linguistic-geographical areas has been appearing, in succession to the well-known short-title catalogues of books printed before 1601 in the British Museum/British Library. The present volume of books from the Low Countries held in the British Library is one of these. The area it covers is roughly the same as that of its predecessor, the *Short-title catalogue of books printed in the Netherlands and Belgium and of Dutch and Flemish books printed in other countries from 1470 to 1600 now in the British Museum* of 1965, but its timespan is very much shorter, embracing no more than the years from 1601 to 1621. The reason for this limitation is very simple: the compiler undertook her task as she was approaching retirement and thought it prudent not to attempt a catalogue of Dutch books throughout the seventeenth century.

The resulting volume is nevertheless much more substantial than its fifteenth and sixteenth-century forerunner. This is due not only to the greater output of Dutch presses as time went on, but also to the compiler's different views of the scope and purpose of this catalogue which should bring the Library's holdings in these varied and interesting books to the notice of the scholarly public in a way that is informative and, perhaps, challenging.

October 1989

J.M. Smethurst
Director General
Humanities and Social Sciences
The British Library

INTRODUCTION

Like the *Short-title catalogue of books printed in the Netherlands and Belgium and of Dutch and Flemish books printed in other countries from 1470 to 1600 now in the British Museum,* more generally known as the 'Dutch STC' or 'STC Dutch', which it follows chronologically, this new catalogue lists books now in the British Library whose text is either wholly or to a large extent in Dutch or which, though in other languages, were printed or published in the Low Countries. These are understood to comprise the present-day Netherlands, Belgium and Luxemburg, with the inclusion of the areas then under Spanish rule but ceded to France later in the seventeenth century.

The dates of the books here listed range from 1601 to 1621, the latter date chosen so as to record all the pamphlet literature in so far as it is represented in the British Library, connected with the Twelve-Year Truce which ended in 1621. Occasionally the period has been extended back into the final years of the sixteenth century or beyond 1621 in order to preserve the completeness of multi-volume books produced across these arbitrary limits. The same principle of describing items in their totality has been applied in the case of the series of news reports issued by Abraham Verhoeven at Antwerp. These went on being published well beyond 1621, but as the British Library's recognised set ends with a small number bearing the date 1622, these have been included.

Books wholly in oriental languages have been excluded: they are placed in Oriental Collections and are described in the catalogues of that department. Books combining these with a European language, usually Latin, such as editions of the Bible or grammars and dictionaries of oriental languages, whether in the British Library's Western European or Oriental Collections, will be found here, the shelfmarks of the latter being preceded by the distinguishing letters 'Or.'. Works in the Music Library and the Map Library are included, with the exception of single maps. Also included are printed items found in the Department of Manuscripts. All these are easily recognised by their shelfmark prefixes. Material belonging to the British Museum's Department of Prints & Drawings, once described in the General Catalogue and in the short-title catalogues, had to be omitted.

The catalogue attempts to encompass not only books plainly identifiable as belonging within the geographical and chronological limits defined above, but also those publications which bear other imprints or none, other dates or none, but which can with certainty or at least a fair measure of probability be laid at the door of a Dutch printer or publisher within the specified period. For instance, the work of the pseudonymous writer Nicocles Catholicus (N196), written in Latin, bears no imprint, but betrays such detailed knowledge of local circumstances and offers such strong political opinions that it merited an ascription to a printer in the Southern Netherlands and probably one at Antwerp.

These were years of political and religious upheavals and persecutions, when not only established governments and churches, but also their opponents and dissenters availed themselves to the utmost of the possibilities offered by the printing press, and anonymity and pseudonymity were practised not only by authors, but equally by printers and publishers. The withholding or falsification of a date of publication was another part of this need to mislead. The resulting imprints have been adding spice to the cataloguer's fare ever since and will continue to do so, since many have proved successful beyond the reasonable expectations of their makers. Many solutions are found in reference books and other scholarly publications on which this catalogue has drawn freely and gratefully. Some may be incorrect and need further investigation; others appeared doubtful to me and are so qualified in footnotes.

Some books without a date of publication on their titlepage or in the colophon, without any internal reference to a likely date, or deprived of their titlepage by some misfortune, have been described in the hope that more closely argued definitions will eventually be forthcoming from a reader. As an example, the British Library owns an imperfect copy of an otherwise apparently unrecorded Dutch translation of Jean de Carthenay's *Le voyage du chevalier errant* (Antwerp 1572), wanting the titlepage, any preliminary matter and all after part one. Even the author's name had been unknown to the General Catalogue until the book was examined for a possible entry in this new catalogue. An appeal to Leiden University then uncovered the author, but not the date of publication. A suggested one of circa 1620, allowing its inclusion (C34), can be justified as only by presenting it to scholars in this way may it elicit from one of them the details so far lacking.

Users of this catalogue checking on items previously encountered in the General Catalogue or expecting similar forms of entries to the short-title catalogues will find that this catalogue has been compiled according to rules that differ in some respects. Some books previously described as of Dutch origin and dating from the 1601–1621 period were on closer inspection found to be ineligible for inclusion. Other books have been moved to a different heading, be it to conform with more recent findings regarding their authorship, be it to make use of a simpler system of cataloguing anonymous titles.

Titlepages, including author statements and imprints, are transcribed with a faithfulness extending to the use of upper and lower case letters, punctuation, contractions and abbreviations, though all typefaces are represented as roman and variations in size and colour are not described. Round brackets and dates in roman numerals are maintained. Omissions are indicated and additions are made in the footnotes. In the imprint the address is normally omitted and only transcribed where it gives a clue to an unnamed printer or publisher. Also omitted are phrases referring to a privilege or licence unless to distinguish one issue from another or otherwise identify an edition.

Entries for books destroyed in World War II have been given their normal place in the alphabetical sequence, but are enclosed in square brackets. They include, where available, information in the footnote on other copies or descriptions that were drawn upon in arriving at as exact a title as possible. It has been the Library's experience that some books formerly necessarily described as 'destroyed' were replaceable and it is hoped that this process will go on.

Headings are arranged alphabetically, with finding references from non-standard forms of names. Names of sovereigns, princes of sovereign houses and of saints are given in English, e.g. 'WILLIAM I; Prince of Orange'; 'PETER Canisius; Saint'. Names of French origin beginning with the definite article whether in its plain form or contracted with a preposition are considered as indivisible units together with this article, i.e. 'L'APOSTRES, George'; 'LE BOUCQ, Simon'; DU JON, François'; 'LA MARCHE, Olivier de'. Theses other than doctoral dissertations are entered under the 'praeses' in recognition of the fact that in general they do not so much represent the student's original work as a repetition of the lectures delivered by the professor.

Under an author's name, his or her books are normally arranged in the alphabetical order of their titles. However, editions of collected works, of more than one work not originally jointly published and of genuine letters precede those of single works. A single work has its own various editions entered chronologically, regardless of any change of title, first in its original language, then in translations which, if there are translations into different languages, themselves follow a fixed order: an English version first, followed by those into other languages in the alphabetical order of their names in English. At the end of an author's list of books will be found editions of selections from all or several of his or her works, just as selections from a single work will be found at the end of the entries relating to that work.

Where necessary collective titles ('[Works]', '[Letters]' or '[Selections]') or filing-titles (the original titles of books) in square brackets precede the titlepage titles.

An author's anonymous or pseudonymous works are part of this arrangement, with finding references from the anonymous title or the pseudonym. Books published under initials or under a descriptive phrase of more than one word are treated as anonymous. Definite and indefinite articles and ordinal numbers at the beginning of a title, including the Latin 'alter' in the meaning of 'second', are disregarded in filing. Lists of theses qualified by ordinal numbers are however entered in numerical order.

The publications of state, provincial or municipal governments are entered under the English names of these countries, provinces and towns, the Netherlands being divided into 'Southern Provinces' and 'United Provinces'. Within these headings the arrangement is chronological. Some bodies, e.g. the Schola Publica at Alkmaar, have been entered under the name of the relevant town, but private institutions like the Chambers of Rhetoric have not been treated as authors of books connected with them but written by individuals. Religious orders are credited with editions of their rules and collected works of their members. They too are entered under the English form of their name, e.g. 'JESUITS'.

The most substantial conventional headings are 'BIBLE' and 'LITURGIES', each of these being preceded by an explanation of its arrangement. One Jewish service book is entered under 'JEWS'. Among other conventional headings are those for famous romances such as 'AMADÍS de Gaula' and 'LAZARILLO de Tormes'. Otherwise anonymous books are entered under the first word of their titles other than an article or ordinal number, whatever its grammatical form or spelling. There are no cross-references from secondary authors, editors, translators, etc. to the full entry: these names as well as initials used to hide authors or other persons concerned in the writing of the text are listed in the general index to be described below.

Where a book consists of several volumes or has constituent parts each preceded by its own internal titlepage, these have been transcribed in the same manner as the main titlepage. Colophons are likewise transcribed after the qualification '(col.)', whether or not they differ from the information given on the titlepage(s). Misprints are reproduced, followed by '[*sic*]'. The pagination or foliation of a book is supplied after 'pp.' and 'ff.'. It would have taken too much time to provide bibliographical collations and therefore signatures are given (after 'sig.') only for books lacking pagination, for parts of books interrupting paginated sequences or, in addition to pagination, for the Verhoeven news reports in which they often help to determine the sequence of publication.

The pagination (or signatures) for works in several parts is shown continuously, a comma dividing several sequences in one volume, a semicolon dividing the pagination between volumes. Plates, i.e. leaves bearing illustrations inserted into a book separately from text gatherings, are indicated by the word 'plate' or 'plates' or, if numbered, by 'pl.' and the number as it appears in the book. Illustrations which are printed within the text, whether on parts of pages or on whole pages themselves part of a regular gathering, are indicated by 'illus.'. Portraits of persons mentioned in the title are listed as 'port.' or 'ports.'; the terms 'maps' and 'music', if present, are self-explanatory. British Library shelfmarks are given on a separate line. Footnotes add miscellaneous information, first such as would apply to all copies of the book, then as it applies to the copy described. Imperfections are noted, as are provenances (if decipherable), special bindings and other features of interest.

The information supplied in the footnotes is derived wherever possible from the books themselves or, failing this, from secondary sources, which are not specifically mentioned except where necessary for purposes of identification of editions or issues or for other clarification. A list of the abbreviations used for such references is to be found at the foot of this introduction.

Regular news reports bearing individual anonymous titles and early newspapers with variable spelling in theirs, inevitably scattered through the alphabetical catalogue, are listed in an appendix in chronological order under their printers by place of imprint, true or alleged, with more extensive references to the relevant literature.

An index of printers and publishers, the latter term also comprising booksellers named in imprints, is also arranged under their names by the towns of their activity, with an alphabetical list of their names leading to the places of publication as given in imprints. Pseudonymous and fictitious printers together with their true identities where known or presumed are entered in both places and the list ends with references to books whose precise origin has remained unknown.

Lastly, a general index contains all secondary names from the entries in the main alphabetical catalogue, including initials, with those of artists, provenances, etc. There are references also under literary genres and under subjects. These three ancillary sections are each preceded by an explanatory introduction.

The illustrations chosen for this catalogue were selected partly to assist the bibliographical descriptions of the books from which they come, partly to add some examples of less well-known artistic productions from among the catalogued items.

This work could not have been done without the assistance of friends and colleagues both inside and outside the British Library, in this country and abroad. Their advice and expertise has solved innumerable queries and prevented as many errors, whether of fact or opinion. Those that remain are exclusively my own. I cannot individually thank all those who have so greatly helped me over the years: let them be assured of my deep gratitude. There are however a few whose names I cannot for various reasons refrain from mentioning: my colleague David L. Paisey, to whom I am indebted not only for help with German bibliographical problems, but for the discussion also of the general design and scope of the whole catalogue at its outset and for his critical reading of this introduction towards its close; my former colleague Antony F. Allison for allowing me access before publication to what has since become A.F. Allison and D.M. Rogers, *The contemporary printed literature of the English Counter-Reformation between 1558 and 1640.* vol.1. *Works in languages other than English* (Aldershot 1989); my friend Professor Dr. Jan A. van Dorsten of Leiden University who did not live to see completed what he so generously encouraged and supported in its early stages; Mr. David D.H. Way of the British Library's Marketing and Publishing Office for his guidance and cooperation in the process of transferring the manuscript of this catalogue into print; Dr. Theo Hermans of London University College Dutch Department for his help in proof-reading; and last but far from least, my husband William A. Harvey for his constant interest and never ending patience.

Gillingham, Dorset ANNA E.C. SIMONI
October 1989

ABBREVIATIONS OF BOOKS REFERRED TO IN FOOTNOTES

Van der Aa: A.J. van der Aa, *Biographisch woordenboek der Nederlanden,* etc. Haarlem, 1852–78

Adelung: J.C. *Adelung, Fortsetzung und Ergänzungen zu Christian Gottlieb Jöchers allgemeinem Gelehrten-Lexico,* etc. Leipzig, 1784–1819

Albareda: A.M. Albareda, *Bibliografia de la Regla Benedictina.* Montserrat, 1933

Asher: G.M. Asher, *A bibliographical and historical essay on the Dutch books and pamphlets relating to New-Netherland, and to the Dutch West-India Company,* etc. Amsterdam, 1854–67 [reprinted 1960; 1966]

Atlas van Stolk: Katalogus der historie- spot- en zinneprenten betrekkelijk de geschiedenis van Nederland verzameld door A. van Stolk . . . Beschreven door G. van Rijn. Amsterdam, 1895–1923

BB: Bibliotheca Belgica. Bibliographie générale des Pays-Bas. Fondée par Ferdinand van der Haeghen. Rééditée sous la direction de Marie-Thérèse Lenger. Bruxelles, 1964–75

BCNI: Bibliotheca Catholica Neerlandica impressa 1500–1727. Hagae Comitis, 1954

Bibliographie gantoise: Bibliographie gantoise . . . 1483–1850. Par F. Vanderhaeghen. Gand, 1858–69

De Bie & Loosjes: J.P. de Bie and J. Loosjes, *Biographisch woordenboek van protestansche godgeleerden in Nederland.* 's-Gravenhage, 1919–40(?)

Blom: J.M. Blom, *The post-Tridentine Primer.* London, 1982 (Catholic Records Society. Publications. Monograph series. vol.3)

Breugelmans: R. Breugelmans, '*Quaeris quid sit amor?* Ascription, date of publication and printer of the earliest emblem book to be written and published in Dutch', in: *Quaerendo.* vol.3 (Amsterdam 1973), pp.281–90

Briels: J.G.C.A. Briels, *Zuidnederlandse boekdrukkers en boekverkopers in de Republiek der Verenigde Nederlanden omstreeks 1570–1630,* etc., Nieuwkoop, 1974 (Bibliotheca bibliographica neerlandica. vol.6)

Bruckner: J. Bruckner, *A bibliographical catalogue of seventeenth-century German books published in Holland.* The Hague, Paris, 1971 (Anglica Germanica. vol.13)

Carter & Vervliet: H.G. Carter and H.D.L. Vervliet, *Civilité types*. Oxford, 1966 (Oxford Bibliographical Society. Publications. new series. vol.14)

Catalogue de l'histoire de France: Bibliothèque Nationale. Catalogue de l'histoire de France. Ed. J.A. Taschereau. Paris, 1855–95. *Table générale alphabétique des ouvrages anonymes.* Paris, 1905–32

Dijksterhuis: E.J. Dijksterhuis, *Simon Stevin,* etc. 's-Gravenhage, 1943

Dutch STC: Short-title catalogue of books printed in the Netherlands and Belgium and of Dutch and Flemish books printed in other countries from 1470 to 1600 now in the British Museum. London, 1965

Eyffinger: A.C.G.M. Eyffinger, *Grotius poeta. Aspecten van Hugo Grotius' dichterschap.* 's-Gravenhage, 1981

Harris & Jones (1): R. Harris and S.K. Jones, *The Pilgrim Press. A bibliographical & historical memorial of the books printed at Leyden by the Pilgrim Fathers,* etc. Cambridge, 1922

Harris & Jones (2): R. Harris and S.K. Jones, *The Pilgrim Press . . . Partial reprint with new contributions by R. Breugelmans, J.A. Gruys & Keith L. Sprunger. Ed. R. Breugelmans.* Nieuwkoop, 1987 (Bibliotheca bibliographica neerlandica. vol.23)

Hirschel: L. Hirschel, 'Jodocus Hondius en Hugh Broughton', in: *Het Boek*. jaarg. 17 (Den Haag 1928), pp.199–208

Houdoy: J. Houdoy, *Les imprimeurs lillois. Bibliographie des impressions lilloises* 1595–1700. Paris, 1879

Jöcher: C.G. Jöcher, *Allgemeines Gelehrten-Lexicon,* etc. Leipzig, 1750–51

Johnson: A.F. Johnson, 'The exiled English Church and its press', in: *The Library*. ser.5. vol.5 (London 1951), pp.219–42

Kempenaer: A. de Kempenaer, *Vermomde Nederlandsche en Vlaamsche schrijvers,* etc. Leiden, 1928

Kleerkoper Starters werken: M.M. Kleerkoper, *Bibliographie van Starters werken,* etc. 's-Gravenhage, 1911

Knuttel: W.P.C. Knuttel, *Catalogus der pamfletten-verzameling berustende in de Koninklijke Bibliotheek te 'sGravenhage.* 'sGravenhage, 1889–1920

Koeman: C. Koeman, *Atlantes neerlandici.* Amsterdam, 1967–71

Labarre: A. Labarre, *Répertoire bibliographique des livres imprimés en France au XVIIe siècle.* IV. *Douai.* Baden-Baden, 1982

Lacroix Meenen: A. Lacroix and F. Meenen, *Notice historique et bibliographique sur Philippe de Marnix.* Bruxelles, 1858

Landwehr: J. Landwehr, *Emblem books in the Low Countries 1554–1949. A bibliography.* Utrecht, 1970 (Bibliotheca emblematica. vol.3)

Ledeboer: A.M. Ledeboer, *Het geslacht van Waesberghe. 2e vermeerderde uitgave.* 'sGravenhage, Utrecht, 1869

Mauquoix-Hendrickx: M. Mauquoix-Henrickx, *Les estampes des Wierix conservées au Cabinet des estampes de la Bibliothèque Royale Albert I,* etc. Bruxelles, 1978–83

Muller: F. Muller, *De Nederlandsche geschiedenis in platen,* etc. Amsterdam, 1863–82

Muller S: Supplement volume to *Muller* above

Nagler: G.C. Nagler, *Die Monogrammisten,* etc. München, 1858–79

NNBW: Nieuw Nederlandsch biografisch woordenboek. Onder redactie van Dr. P.C. Molhuysen, P. Blok, etc. Leiden, 1911–37

NUC: Library of Congress. The national union catalog: pre-1956 imprints, etc. London, 1968–81

Palau: A. Palau y Dulcet, *Manual del librero hispano-americano. 2a edición,* etc. Barcelona, 1948–77

Petit: L.D. Petit, *Bibliotheek van Nederlandsche pamfletten. Verzamelingen van de Bibliotheek van Joannes Thysius en de Bibliotheek der Rijks-Universiteit te Leiden.* 's-Gravenhage, 1882–1934

Petit Lijst: L.D. Petit, *Bibliographische lijst der werken van de Leidsche hoogleraren,* etc. Leiden, 1894

Rahir: É. Rahir, *Catalogue d'une collection unique de volumes imprimés par les Elzeviers et divers typographes hollandais du XVIIe siècle,* etc. Paris, 1896

Rogers: D.M. Rogers, 'Henry Jaye (15?–1643)', in: *Biographical studies,* vol. 1 (Bognor Regis 1951), pp. 86–111

Rogge: H.C. Rogge, *Beschryvende catalogus der verzameling van de boekerij der Remonstrantsche Kerk te Amsterdam.* Amsterdam, 1862–63

Rogge Taurinus: H.C. Rogge, 'Jacobus Taurinus en de Utrechtsche kerk in het begin der 17de eeuw', in: *Archief voor Nederlandsche kerkgeschiedenis,* vol. 3 ('s-Gravenhage 1889), pp. 105–264

Sabbe: M. Sabbe, *De Moretussen en hun kring. Verspreide opstellen.* Antwerpen, 1928

Scheurleer: D.F. Scheurleer, *Nederlandsche liedboeken. Lijst der in Nederland tot 1800 uitgegeven liedboeken.* 's-Gravenhage, 1912–23

Schuytvlot: A.C. Schuytvlot, *Catalogus van werken van en over Vondel gedrukt vóór 1801 en aanwezig in de Universiteitsbibliotheek van Amsterdam,* etc. Nieuwkoop, 1987 (Bibliotheca bibliographica neerlandica. vol. 25)

Sellin: P.R. Sellin, *Daniel Heinsius and Stuart England. With a short check list of the works of Daniel Heinsius.* Leiden, Oxford, 1968 (Publications of the Sir Thomas Browne Institute, Leiden. General series. vol. 3)

Van Someren Portretten: J.F. van Someren, *Beschrijvende catalogus van gegraveerde portretten van Nederlanders,* etc. Amsterdam, 1888–91

Sommervogel: C. Sommervogel, *Bibliothèque des écrivains de la Compagnie de Jésus . . . Par les pères Augustin et Aloys de Backer . . . Nouvelle édition par Carlos Sommervogel.* Bruxelles, Paris, 1890–1917

STC: A.W. Pollard and G.R. Redgrave, *A short-title catalogue of books printed in England, Scotland, & Ireland and of English books printed abroad 1475–1640. Ed.2 revised & enlarged, begun by A.W. Jackson & F.S. Ferguson, Completed by Katharine F. Pantzer.* London, 1976–86

STC (original): A.W. Pollard and G.R. Redgrave, *A short-title catalogue of books printed in England, Scotland, & Ireland and of English books printed abroad, 1475–1640,* etc. London, 1926

De Theux: X. de Theux de Montjardin, *Bibliographie liégeoise,* etc. *Ed.2, augmentée.* Bruges, 1885

Tiele: P.A. Tiele, *Bibliotheek van Nederlandsche pamfletten. Verzameling van Frederik Muller te Amsterdam. Naar tijdsorde gerangschikt en beschreven.* Amsterdam, 1858–61

Tiele Land- en volkenkunde: P.A. Tiele, *Nederlandsche bibliographie van land- en volkenkunde.* Amsterdam, 1884

Tiele Mémoire: P.A. Tiele, *Mémoire bibliographique sur les journaux des navigateurs néerlandais reimprimés dans les collections de De Bry et Hulsius et dans les collections hollandaises du XVIIe siècle, et sur les anciennes éditions hollandaises des journaux de navigateurs étrangers,* etc. Amsterdam, 1867 (reprinted 1960, 1969)

UBA CNL: *Universiteits-Bibliotheek Amsterdam. Catalogus oudere werken op het gebied der Nederlandsche letteren.* [Compiled by B.M. Berg-van der Stempel.] Amsterdam, 1921

Unger Vondel: J.H.W. Unger, *Bibliographie van Vondels werken.* Amsterdam, 1888 (Bijdragen tot eene Nederlandsche bibliographie. vol. 2)

Warmholtz: C.G. Warmholtz, *Bibliotheca historica Sueco-Gothica.* København, 1966–68 [A facsimile of the edition 1782–1817]

Weller Lexicon: E. Weller, *Lexicon Pseudonymorum,* etc. Regensburg, 1886

Willems: A. Willems, *Les Elzeviers.* Bruxelles, 1880

Van der Wulp: J.K. van der Wulp, *Catalogus van de tractaten, pamfletten, enz. over de geschiedenis van Nederland, aanwezig in de bibliotheek van Isaac Meulman.* Amsterdam, 1866–68

ALPHABETICAL CATALOGUE

A

A son Alteze. 1620. *See* AEN zijn Hoocheyt.

A1 AACHEN

[9.9.1614] PLACCAET Van Borghemeesteren ende Raet der Stadt AKEN. Ghepubliceert den 9. Septembris 1614. waerin alle Predicanten/Lesers ende Leeraers/ooc alle Wederdoopers de Stadt verboden wordt . . . Dit is een wreeder Placeaet [*sic*] als oyt Duc Dalf de Tyran heeft laten wtgaen. Na de Copy tot Aken/by des Stadts Drucker. 4° sig. A^2

T.1717(46); T.1727(13).

Without a Dutch imprint. Another edition (or issue?) bears the imprint of Adriaen Leenaertsz at Amsterdam. Probably published in 1614.

A2 ABBAMA, Isaak

[Maechts antwoort tegen, op, en aen, de] aenspraek van een-courtisaen Die haer als een valsch gedrocht,,tong-erg te verleijen socht Door Isaac Abbama . . . tot Rotterdam Bij Dauit Jacopsen van hakendover [etc.] 4° sig. A-C^4; illus.

1578/343.

In verse, replying to the 'Ernstighe aenspraeck' of Jacobus Taurinus. The titlepage is engraved. It is cropped, with the loss of the first seven words which have been supplied from the description in *Knuttel* no.2471. Published in 1617.

A3 ABBILDUNG

[Abbildung der fürnembsten Städt, Schlösser, und Flecken.] Den Omloop Ofte Afbeeldingen der Plaetsen die Marquis Spinola verovert heeft ontrent Franckfoort ende Mentz. (col.) Naer de Copij van Franckfort. Tot Leyden, By Zacharias de Smit/1621. fol. a single sheet

T.2424(10).

A translation from the German, consisting of an engraving in the form of a coiled snake with the portrait of Spinola as its head and added letterpress text.

A4 ABBOT, Robert; Bishop

[De gratia et perseverantia sanctorum.] Van de GENADE GODS, Ende van de VOLHERDINGHE DER VVARE GELOVIGEN, Een Lesse, ende vier Oratien, gedaen inde Vniversiteyt van Oxfort . . . tegen de dwalingen van IACOBVS ARMINIVS, ende zijner Discipulen. Door ROBERTVS ABBOTVS . . . uyt het Latijn overgeset/door DANIEL GYSIVS . . . TOT LEYDEN, By David Jansz. van Ilpendam . . . 1618. 4° pp.79

T.2248(37).

A5 ABRIDGEMENT

AN ABRIDGEMENT OF THAT BOOKE WHICH THE MINISTERS OF LINCOLNE DIOCESSE DEliuered to his Maiestie vpon the first of December 1605. BEING THE FIRST PART OF AN APOLOGIE FOR THEMSELVES AND THEIR BRETHREN THAT REFVSE THE Subscription and Conformitie which is required. WHEREVNTO IS ANNEXED, A Table of sundry Poynts not handled in this Abridgement . . . Reprinted . . . 1617. 8° pp.[102]

851.f.17.

Without imprint; printed by William Brewster at Leiden. Cropped, with loss of pagination. Ownership inscription: G. Doody.

A6 ABUDACNUS, Josephus

SPECVLVM HEBRAICVM, QVO omninò radicum Hebræarum, præcipuorúmque inde deriuatorum significata, facili methodo est intueri. AVCTORE IOSEPHO BARBATO, MEMPHITICO, LINGVARVM ORIENTALIVM PROFESSORE. LOVANII, In Officinâ Typographicâ GERARDI RIVII . . . M.D.C.X.V. [etc.] fol. sig.a^2A-F^4

1505/220.

The author's name supplied on the titlepage in an alternative form.

ACCOORDT ende conditien ghesloten int ouergheuen des H. Rijckx-Stadt Vlm. 1620. *See* GERMANY. League of Würzburg, 1610 [23.6.1620]

ACHABS biddagh. 1621. *See* WTENBOGAERT, Jan

ACHABS treur-spel. 1618. *See* KONING, Abraham de

ACHT voorstellinghen. 1609. *See* WTENBOGAERT, Jan

A7 ACONTIUS, Jacobus

IACOBI ACONTII . . . De methodo, sive Recta investigandarum, tradendarumque artium, ac scientiarum ratione. Libellus . . . nunc iterum editus. LVG. BATAVORVM, Apud Iohannem Maire, 1617. 12° pp.96

526.a.12.

Printed by Henrick Lodewijcxsoon van Haestens at Leiden?

A8 ACRONIUS, Johannes

[Erinneringe van de beropinge der Prediger.] GRONDTLICK BERICHT VANDE BEROEPINGE DER PREDICANTEN . . . door IOHANNEM ACRONIVM . . . Ende nu ghetrouwelick overgheset door IOH. PANNEEL . . . TOT MIDDELBVRGH. By Adriaen vande Vivere . . . M.DC.XV. 4° pp.44

T.2245(11).

ACRONIUS, Ruardus. Bedenckingen, Over de Beroepinghe D. D. Conradi Vorstii. 1611. *See* HOLLAND. Staten [29.4.1611]

A9 ACRONIUS, Ruardus

Christelijcke ende Wettelijcke Beroepinge Der Dienaren Jesu Christi/gelijck die God . . . door zyne Propheten/Apostelen ende Dienaren Christi ingestelt heeft. Ende Tot noch toe . . . inde ware Christelijcke Gereformeerde Kercke

onderhouden is geworden . . . T'AMSTELDAM, Voor MARTEN IANSZ. BRAND . . . 1620. (col.) T'AMSTELDAM, Gedruckt by Paulus van Ravesteyn . . . 1620. 4° pp.39
T.2250(3).

Signed: Ruardus Acronius. Followed by 'Wt die Acta ofte Handelinghen des Provincialen Synodi der Kercken van Holland ende Zeeland' and other documents.

A10 ACRONIUS, Ruardus

ENARRATIONES CATECHETICÆ: Quibus Quæstiones & Responsiones Catechismi Ecclesiarum Belgicarum & Palatinatus, Methodice, compendiose & dilucide, explicantur, ac brevis sed integra purioris doctrinæ Hypotyposis, continetur . . . Auctore RUARDO ACRONIO . . . SCHIEDAMI, Typis & operâ ADRIANI CORNELI & IOHANNIS, germani Fratris . . . M.D.C.VI. 4° ff.244
3504.ee.25.

A11 ACRONIUS, Ruardus

Nootwendich Vertooch/daer in naectelijck wt Godts Woordt/ende de gheloofwaerdige Historien der Kercken aen-ghewesen wort/hoe Godts Ghemeynte . . . in hare regieringhe van de Politike regieringhe onderscheyden is gheweest . . . ende wat na vermoghen des Godtlijcken Woordts . . . der Christelijcker Magistraten Ampt is/int verzorghen ende bevorderen van Kerckelijcke zaken. Door RVARDVM ACRONIVM . . . Voor Adriaen Gerritsz . . . tot Delf . . . M.D.C.X. 4° pp.68
T.2240(11).

With the printer's device of Adriaen and Jan van Delf at Schiedam.

A12 ACROPOLITA, Georgius

[Χρονικὸν.] GEORGII LOGOTHETAE ACROPOLITAE CHRONICON Constantino-politanum, Complectens captæ a Latinis Constantinopoleos & annorum circiter sexaginta Historiam . . . Nunc primùm Græcè & Latinè editum, Notisq; illustratum. Ex Bibliotheca THEODORI DOVSÆ. LVGDVNI BATAVORVM, Ex Officinâ GODEFRIDI BASSON, M.DC.XIV. 8° pp.56,95
1053.a.13(1).

AD Paulum V. . . . epistolae IIII. 1606. *See* LISCA, Alessandro

A13 ADAMS, Yemant

Raedtsel. IEghelijck doet geern wat/Naer dat Discourssen ende verscheyden Droomen op den handel vanden Vrede in Neder-landt zijn uyt ghghaen: [etc.] 4° sig.A^4
106.b.2.

Signed: Den tijdt sal leeren. Yemant Adams. The name is variously interpreted as pseudonym of Simon van Middelgeest or Willem Usselincx. Published in 1608. A copy of the issue with the correction in last line of sig.A1r of 'bebben' to 'hebben', corresponding to the copy described in *Knuttel* no.1422.

An ADIOYNDER to the Supplement of Father Robert Persons his Discussion. 1613. *See* FITZ-HERBERT, Thomas

An ADMONITION to the Parliament holden . . . 1570. and . . . 1571. 1617. *See* FIELD, John

ADRIAENSZ, Cornelis. For the work purporting to be an edition of the sermons of Brother Cornelis Adriaensz (Brouwer), *see* CHRISTIANUS NEUTER

A14 ADRIANI, Henricus

CATHOLYCKE SERMOONEN OP ALLE De Epistelen ende Evangelien vande Sondaghen ende Heylighe daghen vanden gheheelen Jare. De leste Editie, Nu in desen lesten

druck vvederom op een nieu oversien ende nae den Roomschen Text verbetert. DOOR HENRICVM ADRIANI . . . t'ANTWERPEN By Hieronymvs Verdussē . . . 1616. fol. pp.ccccccccxiij; illus.
1471.k.14.

With the texts. The titlepage, which has an engraved border, is mutilated. The illustrations are woodcuts. Ownership inscription: Ick behoore toe aen Gss: Goemaere, Desselghem 1715.

A15 ADRIANI, Henricus

LEGENDE OFT D'LEVEN, WERCKEN, doot end[e m]iraculen ons liefs Heeren IESV CHRISTI, ende vande . . . Moeder Godts ende Maghet Maria, ende alle . . . Heylighen. Eerst vergadert . . . DOOR HENRICVM ADRIANI . . . Ende nu in desen derden druck vermeerdert . . . by last eñ toedoen van H.AVBERT LE MIRE . . . T'ANTWERPEN By Hieronimus Verdussen. 1609. [etc.] fol. ff.398; illus.
1572/173(1).

The titlepage, which has an engraved border, is slightly mutilated. Illustrated with one engraving and numerous woodcuts.

An ADVERTISEMENT or admonition. 1611. *See* HELWYS, Thomas

ADVERTISSEMENT aen alle goede in-woonderen. 1618. *See* PATRIOTA, I.

ADVERTISSEMENT, ofte waerschouwingh. 1621. *See* WTENBOGAERT, Jan

A16 ADVIS

ADVIS FAMILIERS, Proposez par vn Zelateur de la prosperité des Païs-bas: Sur le bruit d'vne Treve ou Paix, proposée par le Roy d'Espaigne (aux Seigneurs Estats des Provinces-vnies) par voye de l'Archiduc Albert d'Austriche . . . l'An 1607. De Savoye, Par G.F. . . . L'An 1608. 8° sig. ( )^6
T.2420(1).

Signed: Ie F.M.N. Esperant mieux, sometimes interpreted as Gabriel Fourmennois. Some copies are described as signed: Ie I.M.N., but this must be a wrong reading of a badly inked 'F'. Probably printed in the Netherlands. The leaves of this copy are mounted and it is imperfect, wanting all after sig.( )^6.

A17 AEGIDIUS; of Liège

[Gesta pontificum Leodiensium.] VIDA DE S.ALBERTO CARDENAL DEL TITVLO DE S.ª CRUZ OBISPO DE LIEIA Y MARTYR. Escrita en Latin por Egidio de Lieja Monge del Conuento de Dorual: con adiciones y notas del Licenciado Auberto Mireo . . . Traducido en Castellano por Fr. Andres de Soto . . . EN BRVSSELAS, Por Roger Velpio y Huberto Antonio . . . 1613.[etc.] 8° pp.229; illus.
862.f.20(2).

The titlepage engraving shows a cardinal's hat and two crossed swords. Ownership inscription: Marguerite Vay Macleod (?).

A18 AELIANUS Tacticus

CLAVDII AELIANI TACTICA, SIVE De instruendis aciebus; GRÆCE ET LATINE. Cum Notis & Animaduersionibus SIXTI ARCERII. Accedunt PRAELIORVM ALIQVOT DESCRIPTIONES, & nonnulla alia; additis TABVLIS AENEIS. LVGDVNI BATAVORVM, Apud Ludouicum Elzeuirium . . . M.DCXIII. 4° pp.214; plates; illus.
C.76.c.5(2).

The illustrations are woodcuts. Reissued the same year in a combined edition with 'Leonis Imp. Tactica', for which see below.

A19 AELIANUS Tacticus

CL. AELIANI, ET LEONIS IMP. TACTICA, sive De instruendis aciebus; Græce & Latine. Quorum hic Græcè primum opera IOHANNIS MEVRSII, ille ex SIXTI ARCERII noua interpretatione Latina: ambo autem NOTIS & ANIMADVERSIONIBVS illustriores in

lucem exeunt. Accedunt PRÆLIORVM ALIQVOT DESCRIPTIONES, & nonnulla alia; additis TABVLIS ÆNEIS, & MODESTI libello de vocabulis militaribus. LVGDVNI BATAVORVM Apud LVDOVICVM ELZEVIRIVM . . . M.D CXIII. (col.) EXCVDEBAT IOANNES BALDVINI, IMPENSIS LVDOVICI ELZEVIRI. LVGDVNI BATAVORVM xii. MART. ANNO M.DC.XII. 4° 3 pt.: pp.214; 447; 7: plates; illus.
717.g.32.
The colophon belongs to pt.2. The whole is a reissue of the separate editions of these two authors published in 1613 and 1612 respectively.

AELTIUS, Godeschalcus. *See* ALTIUS, Godeschalcus

A20 AEMILIUS, Antonius

ANTONII ÆMILII AQVENSIS POEMA ANNIVERSARIUM Ad pubem literariam civium Vltrajectinorum . . . TRAIECT[I] AD RHENVM. Veneunt apud Ioannem à Doorn . . . 1621. 4° sig.A^4
1608/4600.
Partly in Greek. With the printer's device of Herman van Borculo the Younger at Utrecht. The last letter of 'Traiecti' has failed to print.

A21 AEN

Aen zijn HOOCHEYT Op de nieuvve Tydinghen ghecomen int leste van Nouember, op Sinte ALBERTVS auont. Nv eerst ghedruckt den 5. December. T'Hantwerpen/By Abraham Verhoeuen/[etc.] 4° pp.7; sig.Ff^4
1480.aa.15(51); P.P.3444.af(153).
Poems and inscriptions addressed to the Archduke Albert and others in celebration of the victory over Frederick of Bohemia. The inscriptions signed: Liefde doet hopen, motto of Joan Ysermans. Published in 1620.

A22 AEN

[Aen zijn Hoocheyt, etc.] A SON ALTEZE. Sur les nouuelles venues le 23, Nouembre 1620, veille de la Feste de S[t]. Albert. A Anuers, Par Abraham Verhoeuen, [etc.] 4° pp.8; sig. Hh^4; illus.
1480.aa.15(46); P.P.3444.af(154).
A French version of the poems addressed to the Archduke and others published in Dutch in the preceding, with Latin epigraphs in place of the Dutch inscriptions in the above. The titlepage woodcut shows the double portrait of Albert and Isabella. Published simultaneously with the preceding and with the intervening signature Gg.

AENHANGSEL van der kercken-dienarē Remonstranten Naerder bericht. 1612. *See* WTENBOGAERT, Jan

A23 AENIGMATA

AENIGMATA ET GRIPHI VETERVM AC RECENTIVM: Cum Notis Iosephi Castalionis I.C. in Symposium: Adhęc Pythagoræ Symbola. ET Ioan. Ægidij Nuceriensis Adagiorum Gallis vulgarium hac recenti editione auctorum in . . . latinæ linguæ versiculos traductio. DVACI, M DCIIII. Apud Carolum Boscardum [etc.] 8° pp.160
12305.ccc.32.
Partly in Latin only, partly in Latin and French.

A24 AEN-MERCKINGE

Aen-merckinge Op de Propositie vanden Ambassadeur PECKIUS. Inhoudende een kort verhael vande wreedtheyd ende bedriegerije vanden Spaenschen Koning ende zynen Raed aen dese Landen bewesen . . . T'AMSTELREDAM, Voor Marten Jansz Brant . . . 1621. 4° pp.58
T.2251(18).
Printed by Paulus van Ravesteyn, with some use of civilité.

AENMERCKINGHE op de tegenwoordige steert-sterre. 1619. *See* CATS, Jacob

A25 AENSLAGEN

AENSLAGEN Vanden Prince Hendric Frederic vā Orangiē inden Vnions Krijch. Met Tijdinghe wt Vranckrijck van de Hughenotten. Overgeset wt de Hoochduytsche sprake in onse Nederlātsche Tale. Eerst ghedruckt in Januarius. 1621. T'Hantwerpen/By Abraham Verhoeuen/[etc.] 4° pp.8; sig. A^4; illus.
P.P.3444.af(179).

Headed: Ianuarius 1621.10. The titlepage woodcut shows a battle outside a besieged fortress.

AERSSEN, François van. Advertissement aen alle goede in-woonderen. 1618. [By François van Aerssen?] *See* PATRIOTA, I.

AERSSEN, François van. Andere vraech-al. 1618. [By François van Aerssen?] *See* VRAEGH-AL. Andere vraech-al

A26 AERSSEN, François van

CORTE ANTVVOORT, Aen de . . . STATEN GENERAEL. Overgegeven by d'Heer van SOMMELSDIICK Tegens seker Vertooch/geadvoueert/ende getekent CORNELIS vander MYLE. IN 'SGRAVENHAGE, By Aert Meurs . . . 1618. 4° pp.15
T.2422(14).

AERSSEN, François van. Gulden legende van den nieuwen S[t]. Jan. 1618. [By François van Aerssen?] *see* GULDEN

AERSSEN, François van. Naerder openinghe van een hooch-wichtighe sake. 1618. [By François van Aerssen?] *See* NAERDER openinghe

A27 AERSSEN, François van

Noodighe REMONSTRANTIE Aende . . . Staten Generael der vereenichde Nederlanden. Mitsgaders Aende . . . Staten van Gelderlandt, Hollant . . . int particulier. Overghegheven . . . opten 30. Mey: Anno 1618. Door . . . Franchoys van Aerssens. Ghedruckt voor N.N. uwen ootmoedighen Dienaer . . . 1618. 4° pp.24
T.2248(56); T.2422(12).

An attack on Cornelis van der Myle.

AERSSEN, François van. Noodtwendigh ende levendigh discours. 1618. [Sometimes attributed to François van Aerssen.] *See* NOODTWENDIGH

AERSSEN, François van. Oprechte tonge. 1618. [Sometimes attributed to François van Aerssen.] *See* NOODTWENDIGH ende levendigh discours. Oprechte tonge

AERSSEN, François van. Practycke van den Spaenschen raedt. 1618. [By François van Aerssen?] *See* PRACTYCKE

AERSSEN, François van. Provisionele openinghe. 1618. [By François van Aerssen?] *See* PROVISIONELE openinghe

A28 AERTSZ, Geeraert

DE KLEYN GOVDT-BALANS, Al waer in gewogen wort hoe dat met onwaerheyt de oude Gereformeerde Leeraers/diemen nu Contraremonstranten noemt/belogen worden/van datse God den Auteur van quaet maecken; ende wort hier anders bewesen wt haer lieden eygen schriften . . . Maer ter contrarie sulcx eer can bewesen worden wt de Thesibus Jacobi Arminii/hier nevens gestelt . . . Door Geeraert Aertsz. Gedruckt tot Leyden/by Jan Claesz. van Dorp/1618. 4° pp.16
700.h.25(10).

A29 AESOP [Spanish]

LA VIDA Y FABVLAS DEL ESOPO: A las quales se añadieron algunas muy graciosas de

Auieno, y de otros sabios fabuladores. En la oficina PLANTINIANA. 1607. 8° pp.384; illus.
12304.aa.45.
Published at Leiden. The illustrations are woodcuts. With a heraldic bookplate 'Sub robore virtus'.

AETSEMA, Leo. *See* AITZEMA, Lieuwe van

AF-BEELDINGE der Coninghinne Elyzabeth. 1604. *See* BAUDAERT, Willem

A30 AFBEELDINGE
Afbeeldinge/ende corte Beschrijvinghe vanden dolenden Jode. IVDÆI OBERRANTIS EFFIGIES. Iuxta eam quæ olim Malduiæ, & a paucis annis Parisijs fuit efformata. T'hantwerpen/By Abraham verhoeven/ . . . 1620. 4° pp.8; illus.
P.P.3444.af(168).
With a signature mark ¶ on leaf 'iiij' only. The titlepage woodcut shows Christ carrying the Cross in a street, with the 'Jew' looking on, barefoot and in 17th-century costume. The text is in Dutch only.

A31 AFBEELDINGE
Afbeeldinge vande belegeringhe der Stadt Gulich met het . . . Casteel . . . 1610. fol. a single sheet
T.1729(2*).
An unsigned engraving with inscriptions in Dutch.

A32 AFBEELDINGHE
Afbeeldinghe des SYNODI Nationael, Met de sidt plaetsen der . . . Staten Generael/ als in Heemsche ende uyt Heemsche Professoren ende Predicanten/gehouden binnen Dordrecht An.1618. Ghedruct voor Niclaes Geelkerck. 4° sig.A^4B^2; illus.
T.2248(22).
The engraving shows the Synod, in the centre a man is seen walking towards the top table. Published at Leiden in 1618.

AFCONTERFEYTINGHE der stercke stadt Grave. 1602. *See* DOETECHUM, Baptista van

Het AF-SCHEIDT vande . . . Heeren Staten vande Gheunieerde Provintien/gegeven aende Ghecommitteerde vanden Coninck van Spaegnien . . . 1608. *See* NETHERLANDS. United Provinces. Staten Generael [25.8.1608]

AFSCHEYDT den predicanten van Nimmeghen ghegheven. 1618. *See* NIJMEGEN [8.4.1618]

A33 AGAZZARI, Agostino
(tp.1) DI AGOSTINO AGAZZARI . . . MADRIGALI A CINQVE VOCI Con vn Dialogo à Sei, & vn Pastorale à Otto, à l'ultimo, NOVAMENTE STAMPATI ET DATI IN LVCE. TENORE. IN ANVERSA. Appresso Pietro Phalesio. M.D.C.II.
(tp.2) DI AGOSTINO AGAZZARI . . . MADRIGALI A CINQVE VOCI . . . BASSO. IN ANVERSA. Appresso Pietro Phalesio. M.D.C.II. obl.4° 2 pt.: pp.12; 12
Music A.232.a.
The two parts bear the signatures D-F and K-M respectively. The titlepage of the Basso part bears the ownership inscription of 'Giovanni Vatchin Ingles'.

AGNAEUS, Theodorus Bernhardus. Theses medicae de phthisi. 1621. *See* VORSTIUS, Aelius Everardus

A34 AGRIPPA, Henricus Cornelius

[De nobilitate & praecellentia foeminei sexus.] Een Treffelijck ende wonderlijck Vrouwen-lof. Beschreven int Latijn door H.C.A. Rechtsgheleerde. Ende Daer na in duytsch overgeset. TOT ROTTERDAM. By my Matthijs Bastiaenseu [*sic*] . . . 1611. 8° sig. A-D^8

8416.aa.16.

Anonymous.

A35 AGUILAR, Gaspar de

[La venganza honrosa.] T'QUAEDT Syn Meester loondt Bly eynde Spel. 't AMSTERDAM, Ghedruckt by Paulus van Ravesteyn. Voor Dirck Petersz. Voskuyl . . . 1618. 4° sig. A-F^4G^2; illus.

11755.bb.81(4).

Anonymous. The dedication signed by the translator-adaptor Theodore Rodenburgh and with his 'Nobilitas' device on the titlepage.

A36 AGUILONIUS, Franciscus

FRANCISCI AGVILONII . . . OPTICORVM LIBRI SEX Philosophis iuxtà ac Mathematicis vtiles. ANTVERPIÆ, EX OFFICINA PLANTINIANA, Apud Viduam et Filios Io. Moreti. M.DC.XIII. fol. pp.684; illus.

1575/134.

The titlepage and vignettes at the beginning of the individual books engraved by Theodoor Galle after Rubens. From the Old Patent Office Library.

A37 AGUSTÍN, Antonio; Archbishop

[Dialogos de medallas, inscriciones, y otras antiguedades.] (tp.1) ANTONII AVGVSTINI . . . ANTIQVITATVM ROMANARVM HISPANARVMQVE IN NVMMIS VETERVM DIALOGI XI. Latinè redditi Ab ANDREA SCHOTTO . . . Cuius accessit Duodecimus, De prisca Religione, Diisque Gentium. SEORSIM EDITAE NOMISMATVM ICONES A IACOBO BIÆO æri graphicè incisæ ANTVERPIÆ, Apud Henricum Aertsium. M.DC.XVII. [etc.]

(tp.2) NOMISMATA IMPERATORVM ROMANORVM aurea. argentea, aerea . . . OPERA IACOBI BIAEI . . . aeri graphice incisa cum indice copioso ANTVERPIAE M.DC.XVII. [etc.] fol. 2 pt.: pp.182: pl.68

C.45.h.12(2).

The titlepage of pt.2 is engraved.

A38 AINSWORTH, Henry

AN ANIMADVERSION TO Mr RICHARD CLYFTONS Advertisement. Who under pretense of answering Chr. Lawnes book, hath published an other mans private Letter, with Mr Francis Iohnsons answer therto. Which letter is here justified; the answer therto refuted: and the true causes of the lamentable breach that hath lately fallen out in the English exiled Church at Amsterdam, manifested, By HENRY AINSWORTH. Imprinted at Amsterdam, by Giles Thorp . . . 1613. 4° pp.138

4103.d.4.

With a contribution by John Robinson and William Brewster, 'Elders of the Church at Leyden'.

AINSWORTH, Henry. Annotations upon the book of Psalmes. 1617. *See* BIBLE. Psalms. English

A39 AINSWORTH, Henry

(tp.1) ANNOTATIONS Upon the first book of Moses, called GENESIS. Wherin the Hebrew words and sentences, are . . . explayned . . . By H.A. . . . Imprinted in the yeare 1616.

(tp.2) ANNOTATIONS Upon . . . EXODVS . . . By Henry Ainsworth . . . Imprinted . . . 1617.
(tp.3) ANNOTATIONS Upon . . . LEVITICVS . . . By Henry Ainsworth . . . Imprinted . . . 1618.
(tp.4) ANNOTATIONS Upon . . . NUMBERS . . . By Henry Ainsworth . . . Imprinted . . . 1619.
(tp.5) ANNOTATIONS Upon . . . DEVTERONOMIE . . . By Henry Ainsworth . . . Imprinted . . . 1619. 4° 5 pt.: ⁎⁎^{4} ‡‡‡^{2} A-Kk^4; A-Gg^{4}Hh^2; A-Mm^4; A-Qq^4; A-Nn^{4}Oo^2
3155.dd.7(1); 03166.f.13(2).
Containing the texts also. Printed by Giles Thorp at Amsterdam. The copy at 3155.d.7(1) is a made-up set; that at 03166.f.13(2) consists of pt.3 only.

A40 AINSWORTH, Henry
ANNOTATIONS Upon the first book of Moses, called GENESIS. Wherein the Hebrew words and sentences, are . . . explained . . . By H. A. . . . Imprinted . . . 1621. 4° sig. ⁎⁎, ‡‡‡, A-Ii^{4}Kk^3
03166.f.13(1).
Containing the text also. The 'Annotations upon Exodus', 1622, which form part of this edition were printed and published in London. This part printed by Giles Thorp at Amsterdam.

A41 AINSWORTH, Henry
AN APOLOGIE OR DEFENCE OF SVCH TRVE CHRISTIANS as are commonly (but vniustly) called Brovvnists: Against such imputations as are laid vpon them by the Heads and Doctors of the Vniversity of Oxford, In their Ansvver To the humble Petition of the Ministers of the Church of England, desiring reformation of certayne Ceremonies . . . 1604. 4° pp.118
4103.c.53(1); 105.c.46.
Anonymous and without imprint. By Henry Ainsworth and Francis Johnson. Both copies are of the issue with line 1 of sig.⋆3r beginning with 'endlesse'. The copy at 106.c.46 is imperfect, wanting pp.113, 114.

A42 AINSWORTH, Henry
AN APOLOGIE . . . OF SUCH TRUE CHRISTIANS As are . . . called Brownists . . . 1604. 4° pp.118
4139.b.19.
Another edition of the preceding, anonymous and without imprint. By Henry Ainsworth and Francis Johnson. Printed by Giles Thorp at Amsterdam. Line 1 of sig. ⋆3r begins: 'tle in'.

A43 AINSWORTH, Henry
AN ARROW AGAINST IDOLATRIE. Taken out of the quiver of the Lord of hosts. By H. A. . . . Printed. 1611. 8° pp.174
4099.bbb.55(2).
Anonymous and without imprint; printed by Giles Thorp at Amsterdam.

A44 AINSWORTH, Henry
THE COMMVNION of Saincts. A treatise of the fellowship that the faithful have with God, and his Angels, and one with an other; in this present life. Gathered out of the holy Scriptures, by H. A. . . . Imprinted at Amsterdam by Giles Thorp. 1607. 8° pp.487
1506/484.
The preface signed: Henry Ainsworth.

A45 AINSWORTH, Henry

THE COMMVNION OF SAINCTS. A TREATISE OF THE fellowship that the Faithful have with GOD, and his Angels, and one with another; in this present life. Gathered out of the holy Scriptures, by H. A. . . . Reprinted in the yeare 1615. 8° pp.493
4409.bbb.55(1).

The preface signed: Henry Ainsworth. Printed by Giles Thorp at Amsterdam.

A46 AINSWORTH, Henry

THE COMMVNION OF SAINCTS. A Treatise . . . Gathered out of the holy Scriptures, by H. A. . . . REPRINTED . . . 1618. 8° pp.388
4409.b.53.

The preface signed: Henry Ainsworth. Printed by Richard Plater at Amsterdam. The date is a misprint for 1628.

A47 AINSWORTH, Henry

COVNTERPOYSON. CONSIDERATIONS touching the points in difference between the godly Ministers & people of the Church of England, and the seduced Brethren of the Separation. ARGVMENTS That the best assemblies of the present Church of England are true visible Churches. That the Preachers in the best assemblies of Engl. are true Ministers of Christ. M[r] BERNARDS book intituled The Separatists Schisme. M[r] CRASHAWES Questions propounded in his Sermon preached at the Crosse. Examined and Answered by H. A. . . . 1608. 4° pp.155[255]
4103.b.10.

The preface signed: Henry Ainsworth. Printed by Giles Thorp at Amsterdam.

A48 AINSWORTH, Henry

A DEFENCE OF THE HOLY SCRIPTURES, WORSHIP, AND MINISTERIE, used in the Christian Churches separated from Antichrist: Against the challenges, cavils and contradiction of M. Smyth: in his book intituled The differences of the Churches of the Separation. Hereunto are annexed a few observations upon some of M. Smythes Censures; in his answer made to M. Bernard, By Henry Ainsworth . . . Imprinted at Amsterdam by Giles Thorp . . . 1609. 4° pp.121[132]
4103.d.3.

A49 AINSWORTH, Henry

A REPLY TO A PRETENDED CHRISTIAN PLEA FOR THE ANTI-CHISTIAN [*sic*] CHVRCH OF ROME: published by M[r]. Francis Iohnson a°. 1617. Wherin the weakness of the sayd Plea is manifested . . . By Henry Ainsworth. Anno 1618 . . . Printed in the yeare 1620. 4° pp.184
707.a.34(2); 3935.d.20.

Without imprint. Printed by Giles Thorp at Amsterdam.

A50 AINSWORTH, John

THE TRYING OVT OF THE TRVTH: BEGVN AND PROSEQVVTED IN CERTAYN Letters or Passages between Iohn Aynsworth and Henry Aynsworth; the one pleading for, the other against the present religion of the Church of Rome . . . Published for the good of others by E. P. in the yeare 1615. 4° pp.190
4103.d.5.

Printed by Giles Thorp at Amsterdam.

A51 AITZEMA, Lieuwe van

LEONIS AETSEMA . . . POEMATA IVVENILIA. FRANEKERÆ, Excudebat FREDERICUS HEYNSIUS . . . 1617. 4° pp.124
1213.h.18.

AKEN. *See* AACHEN

A52 ALABASTER, William

APPARATVS IN REVELATIONEM IESV CHRISTI. Noua & admirabilis ratio inuestigandi Prophetiarum mysteria ex scriptura seipsam interpretante. Authore Guilielmo Alabastro . . . ANTVERPIÆ, Ex Officina Arnoldi Conincx. 1607. [etc.] 4° pp.307: plate; illus.

1017.h.14.

The titlepage engraving shows the Flood and the Ark.

A53 ALAIS. Synod

[Jugement et canon.] Oordeel ende uytsprake/Met Den Eedt van Approbatie van het Synode Nationael der Gereformeerde Kercken van Vranckryck/gehouden tot ALEZ inde CEVENNES, besloten ende gearresteert den 6. Octobris 1620. Over het Synode Nationael der Gereformeerde Kercken vande Vereenighde Nederlanden, gehouden tot DORDRECHT inde Iaren 1618. ende 1619. Nopende de vyf Artikulen . . . Naer de Copije ghedruckt tot NISMES door Iean Vaguenar, ende nu tot AMSTELDAM, Voor Iacob Pietersz. Wachter . . . 1621. [etc.] 4° pp.11; illus.

T.2251(15).

The titlepage woodcut shows the French royal arms. The copy imprint is that of the original French edition which Wachter also republished. Printed by Paulus van Ravesteyn at Amsterdam.

A54 ALANUS de Insulis; Bishop

CYCLOPÆDIÆ ANTICLAUDIANI SEV DE OFFICIO VIRI BONI LIBRI NOVEM, Heroico carmine conscripti. ANTVERPIÆ APVD IOACH. TROGNÆSIVM. M.DC.XI. [etc.] 8° pp.156

11408.a.21.

Pseudonymous. The editor's dedication signed: Alex. Car. Trognæsius.

A55 ALANUS de Insulis; Bishop

CYCLOPÆDIÆ ANTICLAUDIANI . . . LIBRI NOVEM . . . ANTVERPIÆ APVD IOACH. TROGNÆSIVM. M.DC.XXI. [etc.] 8° pp.156

11408.aa.20.

Pseudonymous. A reissue of the preceding, with different preliminaries and a different device on the titlepage.

ALBERT; Archduke. Official documents issued by Archduke Albert and/or Isabella of Spain are entered under NETHERLANDS. Southern Provinces

A56 ALBERT; Saint [Albertus Magnus]

[Two or more works] THE PARADISE OF THE SOVLE. OR A Treatise of Vertues. Written in Latin, by the Venerable and Learned Man Albertus, surnamed the Great. VVhereunto is adioyned another Treatise of the same Author, Of the Vnion with God. Both translated into English, by a Father of the Society of IESVS . . . M.DC.XVII. 12° pp.372

C.26.gg.9.

Translated by Thomas Everard. Published by the English College press at St. Omer.

A57 ALBERT; Saint [Albertus Magnus]

B. ALBERTI DOCTORIS MAGNI . . . DE ADHÆRENDO DEO LIBELLVS. Accedit eiusdem ALBERTI Vita, DEO ADHAERENTIS exemplar. ANTVERPIÆ, EX OFFICINA PLANTINIANA, Apud Balthasarem Moretum, & Viduam Ioannis Moreti, & Io. Meursium. M.DC.XXI. (col.) ANTVERPIAE, EX OFFICINA PLANTINIANA BALTHASARIS MORETI M.DC.XXI. 12° pp.341

847.l.16.

Pp.61-341: Vita B. Alberti . . . Compilatore . . . Petro de Prussia.

A58 ALCIATI, Andrea

ANDREÆ ALCIATI . . . EMBLEMATA CVM CLAVDII MIÑOIS . . . Commentariis Ad postremam Auctoris editionem auctis & recognitis. EX OFFICINA PLANTINIANA RAPHELENGII. 1608. 8° pp.218, 698; illus., port.
95.a.19, 20.

The engraved portrait of Alciati signed: WS., i.e. Willem Swanenburgh. Published at Leiden.

A59 ÁLDRETE, Bernardo José

VARIAS ANTIGVEDADES DE ESPAÑA AFRICA Y OTRAS PROVINCIAS Por . . . Bernardo Aldrete . . . En Amberes, a costa de Iuan Hasrey . . . M.DC.XIV. (col.) ANTVERPIÆ, Typis GERARDI WOLSSCHATII, ET HENRICI ÆRTSII . . . M.DC.XIV. 4° pp.640; illus., maps.
671.g.17; 178.b.14; G.4494.

The titlepage is engraved. All three copies are of the issue with 8 preliminary leaves.

A60 ALEMÁN, Mateo

PRIMERA PARTE DE LA VIDA DEL PICARO GVZMAN DE Alfarache. COMPVESTO POR MATHEO ALEMAN . . . EN BRVCELLAS En la Enprenta de Iuan Mommarte . . . 1604, [etc.] 8° ff.215
12490.c.14.

The foliation is irregular. ff.6, 7 are mutilated.

ALEXANDER. 1618. *See* RODENBURGH, Theodore

A61 ALKMAAR. Schola Publica

CONSPECTVS SCHOLAE PVBLICAE, IN Civitate Alcmarianâ, SEV Vniversa illius administrandæ NORMA. Volcomene Beschrijvinge van't beleyd der Latijnsche/of Groote Schole binnen Alcmaer. ALCMARIAE, Excudebat . . . Vidua IACOBI MEESTERI. M.D.C.XV. 4° sig.A^4B^5
913.l.4(10).

The dedication signed: F. Osdorpius.

A62 ALMOND, Oliver

THE LIFE AND GATE OF CHRISTIANITIE, ENTREATING OF THE SACRAMENT OF BAPTISME, DEVIDED INTO FIVE BOOKES . . , Composed, gathered, and written by O. A. . . . M.DC.XIIII. (col.) A DOVAY, PAR PIERRE AVROI . . . 1614. 8° pp.202
Cup.403.a.3.

Anonymous.

ALTENA, Johannes. Disputatio medica de hepatis obstructione. 1613. *See* VORSTIUS, Aelius Everardus

A63 ALTHUSIUS, Joannes

IOHANNIS ALTHUSII . . . POLITICA Methodicè digesta atq; exemplis sacris & profanis illustrata; Cui in fine adjuncta est, ORATIO PANEGYRICA, De necessitate & antiquitate scholarum. GRONINGAE, Excudebat IOHANNES RADAEUS, 1610. 4° pp.28, 715
C.74.b.3.

From the library of James I. Misbound, with the 'De Vtilitate, Necessitate & Antiquitate Scholarum, ADMONITIO PANEGYRICA' preceding instead of following the main work and the leaves bearing sig. ⋆⋆, $⋆⋆^2$ with the 'SCHEMA POLITICÆ'-table inserted in reverse order between pp.26 and 27 in it.

A64 ALTIUS, Godeschalcus

Querela Pacis, dat is Vreden-clacht/Aen die vereenichde Nederlanden/Waerinne de Vrede haer beclaecht datse onder dē schijn van Vrede ofte Trevis/beyde uyt die Kerckelijcke ende Burgelijcke regeringhe wort verdreven ende verbannen. Tot navolginghe . . . ERASMI ROTERODAMI, Aldus ghestelt . . . Door GODESCHALCUM

AELTIUM . . . Gedruckt Tot Leeuvvarden, By Abraham vanden Rade . . . 1612. Men vintse te coop by Jan Lamrinck tot Bolswert/ende by Isaac Knoop tot Leeuwaerden. 4° pp.36
1609/6176.
Including passages in Latin. Printed with some civilité.

ALUTARIUS, Henricus. Theses theologicae, de libero . . . arbitrio. 1610. *See* LINDEN, Henricus Antonides van der

A65 ÁLVAREZ DE PAZ, Jacobus
DE QVOTIDIANA VIRTVTVM EXERCITATIONE, Siue DE VITA RELIGIOSE INSTITVENDA, LIBELLVS: Auctore IACOBO ALVAREZ DE PAZ . . . Nunc primùm in lucem ædita. DVACI, Apud LAVRENTIVM KELLAM . . . M.DC.XIII. 12° pp.546
1483.b.32.
The editor's preface signed: Consalvus Barnovius.

A66 ÁLVAREZ DE PAZ, Jacobus
EPITOME I. ALVAREZ DE PAZ . . . In omnes libros DE VITA SPIRITVALI Eiusque PERFECTIONE Per R. IOANNEM A GORCVM . . . collecta. ANTVERPIÆ, Apud Heredes Martini Nutij . . . M.DC.XX. 8° pp.480
847.c.22.
The dedicatory letter signed: Hieronymus Verdussius, and with Verdussen's device on the titlepage. The privilege names Verdussen only.

A67 AMADÍS de Gaula
Het eerste Boec van Amadis van Gaule . . . Wt de Fransoysche in onse Nederduytsche Tale overgezet. Met veel schoone Figueren . . . verciert. TOT ROTTERDAM, By Jan van Waesberghe . . . 1619. 4° ff.107; illus.
12450.d.25(1).
Cropped.

A68 AMADÍS de Gaula
Het tweede Boec van Amadis van Gaule . . . Nu eerst overghezet in onse Nederlantsche sprake. TOT ROTTERDAM, By Jan van Waesberghe . . . 1619. 4° ff.83; illus.
12450.d.25(2).
Cropped.

A69 AMADÍS de Gaula
Het Derde boeck. Vanden vroomen eñ doorluchtigen Ridder Amadis van Gaule . . . Nu eerst overgheset in onse Nederlantsthe [*sic*] sprake . . . T'AMSTERDAM. By Hendrick Barentsz. . . . 1613. (col.) Tot Amstelredam, By Hendrick Barentsz. . . . 1613. 4° ff.112; illus.
12450.d.25(3).
Cropped.

A70 AMADÍS de Gaula
Het vierde Boec van Amadis van Gaule . . . Van nieus overgezet . . . TOT ROTTERDAM, By Jan van Waesberghe . . . 1619. 4° ff.88; illus.
12450.d.25(4).
Cropped.

A71 AMADÍS de Gaula
Het vijfde Boec van Amadis van Gaule . . . Overghezet wt het Fransoys in onse Duytsche tale. TOT ROTTERDAM, By Jan van Waesberge . . . 1607. 4° ff.[93]; illus.
12450.d.25(5).
Cropped, with the loss of the foliation on f.93. The leaf bearing the contents is mutilated.

A72 AMADÍS de Gaula
Het Zeste Boec/Van den doorluchtigen ende vroomen Ridder/Amadis van Gaule . . . Van nieus inde Nederduytsche tale overghezet. TOT ROTTERDAM, By Jan van Waesberghe/1615. 4° ff. 110; illus.
12450.d.26(1).
The foliation is irregular.

A73 AMADÍS de Gaula
Het sevenste Boeck, Van Amadis de Gaule . . . t'AMSTELREDAM, By Broer Jansz . . . 1613. (col.) Ghedruckt by Broer Iansz. 4° pp. 208; illus.
12450.d.26(2).
The translator's dedication signed: G. V., sometimes identified as Gilles Verniers.

A74 AMADÍS de Gaula
Het achtste Boec van Amadis van Gaule . . . TOT ROTTERDAM, By Jan van Waesberghe . . . 1617. 4° ff. 152; illus.
12450.d.26(3).
Translated by G. V., i.e. Gilles Verniers?

A75 AMADÍS de Gaula
Het neghende Boec van Amadis van Gaule . . . TOT ROTTERDAM, By Jan van Waesberghe . . . 1613. 4° ff. 169; illus.
12450.d.26(4).
Translated by G. V., i.e. Gilles Verniers?

A76 AMADÍS de Gaula
Het thiende Boeck/Van Amadis de Gaule . . . nu nieulijcx uyt het Fransoys/int [*sic*] Nederlantsche spraecke . . . Overgheset. T'AMSTELREDAM, Voor Jan Marcussz. . . . 1616. (col.) Ghedruckt by Joris Gerritsz. Nachtegael. 4° pp. 263; illus.
12450.d.27(1).
Translated by G. V., i.e. Gilles Verniers? The pagination is irregular.

A77 AMADÍS de Gaula
Het Elfste Boeck van Amadis van Gaule . . . Nu nieus overgeset uyt de Fransoysche sprake, in onse Neerlantsche Tale . . . T'AMSTELREDAM. By Heyndrick Lauwerensz. . . . M.D.C.XIII. 4° pp. 212[312]; illus.
12450.d.27(2).
Translated by G. V., i.e. Gilles Verniers? The pagination is irregular.

A78 AMADÍS de Gaula
Het twaelfste boeck van Amadis van Gaule . . . t'AMSTELREDAM, By Cornelis Lodewijcxsz van der Plasse . . . 1616. 4° ff. 209; illus.
12450.d.28(1)
Translated by G. V., i.e. Gilles Verniers?

A79 AMADÍS de Gaula
Het XIII.de Boeck Van Amadis de Gaule . . . Nu van nieus uyt de Fransche in onse nederduytsche tale Overgheset. t'AMSTELREDAM, Ghedruckt by Hendrick Barentsz . . . 1618. 4° pp. 188; illus.
12450.d.28(2).
Translated by G. V., i.e. Gilles Verniers?

A80 AMADÍS de Gaula
Het XIIII.de Boeck Van Amadis de Gaule . . . Vyt de Fransche in onse

Nederduytsche Tale over gheset. t'AMSTERDAM. By Hendrick Barentsz . . . 1620. 4° pp.166; illus.
12450.d.28(3).
Translated by G. V., i.e. Gilles Verniers?

A81 AMADÍS de Gaula
Het XV.[de] Boeck Van Amadis de Gaule . . . Nu van nieus uyt de Fransche in onse Nederduytsche Tale overgheset. t'AMSTELREDAM. By Hendrick Barentsz . . . 1609. 4° pp.146; illus.
12450.d.28(4).

A82 AMADÍS de Gaula
Het XVI.[de] Boeck Van Amadis de Gaule . . . VVt de Fransche in onse Nederduytsche Tale overgheset. t'Amstelredam, By Hendrick Barentsz. . . . 1612. 4° pp.94; illus.
12450.d.28(5).

A83 AMADÍS de Gaula
Het XVIII. Boeck Van Amadis van Gaule . . . Nu nieus overgeset uyt de Francoysche in onse Nederlandtsche Tale . . . TOT AMSTERDAM, By Hendrick Barentsz. . . . 1615. 4° pp.402; illus.
12450.d.29(2)
At the end of the preliminaries an ornament combining the letters W I C I AB in a monogram. From book 12 onward illustration is limited to the titlepages only. Books 17, 19-21 in the British Library's set were published after 1621.

A84 AMAMA, Sixtinus
CENSVRA VVLGATAE Atque à Tridentinis Canonizatæ VERSIONIS Quinque Librorum Mosis . . . AUCTORE SIXTINO AMAMA . . . FRANEKERÆ FRISIORUM, Prostant apud Danielem Iohannidem . . . Typis Frederici Heynsii . . . 1620. 4° pp.309
3155.b.35.

A85 AMES, William
GVIL. AMESII ad Responsum NIC. GREVINCHOVII RESCRIPTIO CONTRACTA. Accedunt ejusdem assertiones Theologicæ de Lumine Naturæ & Gratiæ. Prostant LVGDVNI BATAVORVM, Apud Guiljelmum Brewsterum . . .1617. 8° pp.209
4255.aa.9.

A86 AMES, William
CORONIS AD COLLATIONEM HAGIENSEM, Quâ ARGUMENTA PASTORUM HOLLANDIÆ adversus REMONSTRANTIVM Quinque Articulos de Divinâ PRÆDESTINATIONE . . . producta, ab horum exceptionibus vindicantur. Auctore GUILIELMO AMESIO. LUGDUNI BATAVORUM, Ex Officinâ ELZEVIRIANA . . . M D C XVIII. (col.) Typis ISAACI ELZEVIRI, [*sic*] 4° pp.368
1354.f.49.

A87 AMES, William
DISSERTATIO THEOLOGICA DE DVABVS QVAESTIONIBVS HOC TEMpore controversis, Quarum PRIMA EST DE RECONCILIATione per mortem Christi impetrata omnibus ac singulis hominibus: ALTERA: DE ELECTIONE ex fide prævisa. Sermone primùm inchoata, posteà verò scripto continuata, Inter GVILIELMVM AMESIVM . . . & NICOLAVM GREVINCHOVIVM . . . cui accessit ejusdem Grevinchovij responsio ad Amesij Instantias. ROTERODAMI BATAVORVM, Excudebat Mathias Sebastiani . . . M D CXV. 4° pp.438
4226.cc.5.

A88 AMES, William

[Dissertatio theologica.] THEOLOGISCHE VERHANDELINGHE Over Twee Poincten/ huydens-daeghs in gheschil staende/Van welcke Het eerste is: vande Verzoeninge door de Doodt Christi . . . Het andere: Vande Verkiesinge uyt het voorzien Gheloove. Eerst Mondelingh begonnen, maer daer na Schriftelijck achtervolcht: Tusschen Guilhelmum Amesium . . . ende Nicolaum Grevinchovium . . . Waer by noch ghevoecht is/des . . . Grevinchovij Antwoordt/op de Aenhoudinghen Amesij. TOT ROTTERDAM, By Matthijs Bastiaensz . . . 1615. 4° sig. A-G^4, pp.86
T.2245(18).

A89 AMMONIUS Hermeae

VITA ARITOTELIS [*sic*] . . . Per AMMONIVM, seu PHILOPONVM, Addita Vetere interpretatione Latina longe auctiore, nunc primum ex MS. edita, Cum . . . Scholijs V.C. PET. IOAN. NVNNESI . . . LVGDVNI BATAVORVM, Apud IOANNEM DIEPHORST . . . M D CXXI. 8° pp.172
715.b.27.

A separate issue, with its own cancel titlepage, of the edition joined to 'De studio philosophico' by Nunnesius which is entered under that author. With the printer's device of Jan Bouwensz?

A90 AMPSING, Joannes Assuerus

TRES DISPVTATIONES THEOLOGICÆ Adversus Anabaptistas. I. DE INCARNATIONE FILII DEI. II. DE PÆDO-BAPTISMO. III. DE DISCIPLINA ECCLESIASTICA. Quas ex Patris sui Iohannis Assveri Ampsingij lucubrationibus Belgicis paulò locupletiores Latinas fecit SAMVEL AMPSINGIVS . . . Lugduni Batavorum, Apud IOHANNEM MAIRE . . . M.D.C.XIX. 8° pp.395
3925.aaa.5(3).

A91 AMPSING, Samuel

DEN LOF VAN HAERLEM. TOT HAERLEM. Voor Salomon Bogaert . . . 1616. 4° sig.A-C^4
11556.cc.33.

Anoymous. Signed: Consts vyant onverstant. Printed by Adriaen Roman at Haarlem.

A92 AMPSING, Samuel

[Den lof van Haerlem.] HET LOF DER STADT HAERLEM IN HOLLANDT. (col.) TOT HAERLEM. Gedruckt by ADRIAEN ROOMAN . . . 1621. 4° sig.A-E^4F^2: plate
11557.bbb.61(1).

Anonymous. An enlarged edition of the preceding, signed: Sustine, & abstine.

A93 AMSTERDAM

[1613] REGISTER Van allen den Schouten/Burghermeesteren/Schepenen/xxxvj. Raeden/ende allen anderen Regenten der Stede Amstelredamme. Anno/M.DC.XIII. 4° pp.41
1568/2112.

An official publication, usually found attached to the 'Handvesten en privilegien' of Amsterdam. Published in 1613.

A94 AMSTERDAM

[21-23.2.1617] ORDONNANTIE By de Heeren van den Gherechte der Stadt Amstelredam. Ghepubliceert den 21. Februarii Anno 1617 . . . t'AMSTERDAM, By Jan Gerritsz. . . . 1617. 4° sig.A^4
1578/342.

On the Contra-Remonstrant riots. With the text of a supplementary order, issued 23.2.1617, on the pamphlets published by the Remonstrants in their own defence, some of them later known to have been written by Jacobus Taurinus.

A95 AMSTERDAM
[21-23.2.1617] PVBLICATIE Ghedaen binnen Amsterdam den xxj. eñ xxiij. Februarij 1617. tegen de insolentien ende moedtwille aldaer ghepleecht/etc. t'Amsterdam. Ghedruckt by Broer Jansz. . . . 1617. 4° sig.A[2]
T.2247(22).
Another edition of the preceding.

A96 AMSTERDAM
[9.1617] VERCLARINGE Vande Heeren Burgemeesteren/Raden/ende Vroedtschappen der Steden van Amstelredam/Enckhuysen/Edam/en Purmereynde . . . Waer by hare E. E. . . . verthoonen de getrouwe affectie/die zy . . . hebben tot den welstant der Landen/ende Kercken van Hollandt ende West-Vrieslandt/Ende hoe verre d'authoriteyt van een Christelijcke Hooge Overicheyt . . . geexerceert behoort te werden: Ende waeromme hare E. E. niet hebben connen goet vinden/dat de . . . opinie van seeckere vijf poincten op't stuck vande Predestinatie . . . soude werden gemeen gemaeckt . . . TOT AMSTELREDAM, By Marten Jansz. Brant . . . 1617. [etc.] 4° pp.16
T.2247(15); 106.a.53.
Dated September 1617. Printed by Paulus van Ravesteyn.

AMSTERDAMSCHE nouvelles. 1620. *See* SLATIUS, Henricus

ANDERE . . . For anonymous works beginning with 'Andere' in the sense of 'second' *see* the noun qualified by it

ANDERTON, Lawrence. *See* BRERELY, John; sometimes believed to be the pseudonym of Lawrence Anderton

ANDLA, Anchises. Disputatio medica de regio morbo. 1621. *See* VORSTIUS, Aelius Everardus

ANDLA, Anchises. Disputationum anatomicarum tertia . . . de ossibus . . . quam . . . proponit Anchises Andla. 1618. *See* WINSEMIUS, Menelaus

ANDLA, Anchises. Disputationum anatomicarum nona . . . de nervis . . . quam . . . proponit Anchises Andla. 1618. *See* WINSEMIUS, MENELAUS

ANDLA, Anchises. Disputationum anatomicarum decima-quinta . . . de partibus chyli distributioni inservientibus, quam . . . proponit Anchises Andla. 1619. *See* WINSEMIUS, Menelaus

ANDLA, Anchises. Disputationum anatomicarum vicesima . . . de procreatione hominis. Ad quam . . . resp. Anchises Andla. 1620. *See* WINSEMIUS, Menelaus

A97 ANDREAS, Valerius
IMAGINES DOCTORVM VIRORVM E VARIIS GENTIBVS, Elogijs breuibus illustratæ. VALERIVS ANDREAS . . . publicabat. ANTVERPIÆ. Apud Dauidem Martinium . . . M.DC.XI. [etc.] 12° sig. A-D[12]; illus.
10604.aa.4.
The illustrations are woodcuts.

A98 ANDREWES, Lancelot; Bishop
[A sermon preached . . . at Hampton Court.] Een SERMOON, Ghepredickt In de teghenwoordicheyt van zijn Conincklijcke Maijesteyt van Groot Britannien/in zijn Hoff tot Hampton. aengaende t'Recht ende de Macht om Vergaderingen by een te roepen, ende dat met naeme, Kerckelijcke; als Synoden, &c. door den Bischop van Chichester, op den 28. Septemb. 1606. uyt het Enghels overgheset . . . Tot LEYDEN, By Thomas Basson. 1610. 4° pp.28
T.2240(16).
Translated, and with a preface, by Thomas Basson.

A99 ANDRIES, Jodocus

(tp.1) LACRYMAE IN OBITVM . . . HISPANIARVM REGINÆ MARGARETÆ AVSTRIACAE. Collegium Societatis IESV Bruxellæ Anno 1611. Oratio. Elegiæ. Epigrammata. Hieroglyphica. Emblemata. BRVXELLÆ. Ex officina RVTGERI VELPII, & HVBERTI ANTONII . . . 1611.
(tp.2=sig.★4) ORATIO FVNEBRIS IN OBITVM . . . REGINÆ MARGARETÆ . . . Habita in Templo Collegij Societatis Iesu Anno 1611 . . . M.DC.XI.
(tp.3=p.41) IN OBITVM EIVSDEM . . . REGINÆ MARGARETÆ . . . Collegium Societatis IESV Bruxellæ Anno 1611. Elegiæ, Hieroglyphica, Epigrammata, Emblemata . . . M.DC.XII. 8° pp.80
1213.h.16.

Anonymous. The whole published in 1612.

A100 ANDROZZI, Fulvio

[Collections] R.P. FVLVII ANDROTII SOCIETATIS Iesu OPVSCVLA SPIRITVALIA. Ex Italico idiomate à Patre eiusdem Societatis in Latinum conuersa. DVACI, Typis PETRI AVROY . . . 1615. [etc.] 12° pp.312
861.h.11.

Translated by Joannes Busaeus. The preface signed: Richardus Gibbonus.

A101 ANDROZZI, Fulvio

[Opere spirituali. pt.1. Della meditazione della vita e morte del nostro Salvatore Gesù Christo.] MEDITATIONS VPPON THE PASSION OF OVR LORD IESVS CHRIST. MADE By . . . FVLVIVS ANDROTIVS of the Societie. OF IESVS Newlie translated out of Italian into English . . . 1606. 12° pp.94
1112.a.40.

Translated by Thomas Everard. Printed by Pierre Auroi at Douai.

A102 ANDROZZI, Fvlvio

[Opere spirituali. pt.2. Della frequenza della Communione.] CERTAINE DEVOVT CONSIDERATIONS OF FREQVENTING THE BLESSED SACRAMENT: WRITTEN By . . . FVLVIVS ANDROTIVS of the Societie of IESVS. WITH SVNDRIE OTHER PRECEPTES . . . Firste written in Italian: after turned into Latin: and now translated into English . . . Permissu Superiorum. 12° pp.296; illus.
4410.aa.2.

The translator's dedication signed: I. G., i.e. by or jointly with Thomas Everard? With 'Remedies against divers temptations . . . gathered out of sundrie learned writers'. Printed by Pierre Auroi at Douai and published in 1606. Imperfect; wanting the last four leaves of the preliminaries containing the author's address to the reader.

A103 ANESEUS, Jan

De Prophetie, Van den SMET VAN HVYSSE gheheeten Ian Aneseus. Midts-gaders de Prophetie van Abacuch/seer wonderbaer ende nuttelijc om lesen: voor den tijt als nv present wesende. TOT ROTTERDAM, Ghedruckt by Jan van Ghelen . . . 1609. 4° sig.A^4; illus.
T.2420(38).

The woodcut illustrations include an astrologer at the window on the titlepage and a portrait of Habakkuk (?) on A4r.

An ANKER of Christian doctrine. 1618. *See* WORTHINGTON, Thomas

ANNA Rodenburghs trouwen Batavier. 1617. *See* GUARINI, Giovanni Battista [Il Pastor Fido.]

ANNOSUS, Fidelis; Veremontanus (or: Verimentanus) Druinus, pseudonym of John Floyd. *See* FLOYD, John

De Prophetie,

Van den

MET VAN HVYSSE

gheheeten Ian Aneſeus.

Midts-gaders de Prophetie van Abacuch/ ſeer wonderbaer ende nutteliic om leſen: voor den tijt als nv preſent weſende.

TOT ROTTERDAM,

Ghedruckt by Jan van Ghelen / In den witten Haſewint, Anno/ 1609.

ANNOTATIEN op de voor-reden van Cornelis Boogaerts Aendachtighe ghebeden. 1618. *See* KRIJNSZ, Willem

ANRAET, Jacobus. Theses medicae de melancholia hypochondriaca. 1612. *See* VORSTIUS, Aelius Everardus

ANSTA, Johannes Hobbii. Disputationum anatomicarum secunda, de humani corporis divisione . . . quam . . . defendere conabitur Iohannes Hobbii Ansta. 1618. *See* WINSEMIUS, Menelaus

ANSTA, Johannes Hobbii. Disputationum anatomicarum octava . . . de venis et arteriis, quam . . . exagitandam adfert Joannes Hobbii Ansta. 1618. *See* WINSEMIUS, Menelaus

ANSTA, Johannes Hobbii. Disputationum anatomicarum decima-quarta . . . de organis chylificationi inservientibus, quam . . . proponit Ioannes Hobbii Ansta. 1619. *See* WINSEMIUS, Menelaus

ANSTA, Johannes Hobbii. Disputationum anatomicarum decima-nona . . . de procreatione hominis quam . . . proponit Ioannes Hobbii Ansta. 1619. *See* WINSEMIUS, Menelaus

An ANSWER to Thomas Bels late challeng. 1605; 1606. *See* SMITH, Richard; Bishop

A104 ANSWERE

AN ANSVVERE TO A SERMON PREACHED THE 17 OF APRIL ANNO D. 1608, BY GEORGE DOWNAME . . . INTITVLED, A sermon defendinge the honorable function of Bishops; wherein, All his reasons . . . are answered and refuted . . . Imprinted anno 1609. 4° 2 pt.: pp.58,166
110.g.59,59*.
Sometimes wrongly attributed to John Rainolds. Without imprint; the printing of pt.1, containing the preface and 'The answere to his preface', sometimes attributed to Jodocus Hondius; pt.2, containing 'Mr Downames sermon . . . answered and refuted', printed by Giles Thorp, both at Amsterdam.

ANTICLAUDIANUS. *See* ALANUS de Insulis; Bishop

ANTI-COTTON. 1610. *See* COTON, Pierre. Brief dienende tot verclaringe.

An ANTIDOTE or soveraigne remedie. 1615. *See* NORRIS, Sylvester

ANTIDOTUM continens pressiorem declarationem . . . sententiae. 1620. *See* EPISCOPIUS, Simon

ANTIDOTUM, ende naerder openinghe. 1618. *See* EPISCOPIUS, Simon

A105 ANTIGONUS Carystius

ANTIGONI CARYSTII Historiarum Mirabilium Collectanea. IOANNES MEVRSIVS Recensuit, & NOTAS Addidit. LVGDVNI BATAVORVM, Apud ISAACVM ELZEVIRIVM . . . M DC XIX. 4° pp.210
462.a.26(1); 235.e.32(1).
In Greek and Latin, the latter stated to be 'Gulielmo Xylandro interprete'.

ANTIQUITATVM liturgicarum arcana. 1605. *See* HAER, Floris vander

An ANTIQUODLIBET. 1602. *See* FENNER, Dudley

ANTONIDES, Henricus. *See* LINDEN, Henricus Antonides van der

ANTONIUS, Henricus; Nerdenus. *See* LINDEN, Henricus Antonides van der

A106 ANTWERP

[1584] Copye des Sendtbriefs van . . . Borghemeesteren ende Schepenen der Stadt Antwerpen aenden Hooch bailliu/Voorschepen/Schepenen . . . ende Raedt der Stadt van Gendt: Nopende de verhandelinge van Peyse by hen met de Malcontenten voorghenomen . . . Eerst Ghedruckt T'ANTWERPEN Inde druckerije van Christoffel Plantijn. M.D.LXXXIIII. Ende nu tot Franeker By Ian Lamrinck . . . 1618. 4° sig AB^4
700.h.25(9).

Published as a supplement to 'Discours Fr. Campanellæ' where it is mentioned on the titlepage.

A107 ANTWERP

[7.11.1603] Gheboden ende wt-gheroepen van weghen mijnen Heeren den Onder-schouteth, Borgher-meesteren, Schepenen, ende Raedt deser Stadt van Antwerpen, op den vij. Nouembris, 1603. fol. a single sheet
112.f.31(8).

Regulations against an epidemic. Printed by the Officina Plantiniana at Antwerp in 1603.

A108 ANTWERP

[26.3.1605] Gheboden ende wt-gheroepen by mijnen Heeren Onder-schouteth, Borgermeesteren, Schepenen ende Raedt der stadt van Antwerpen, op den xxvj. Martij, 1605. fol. a single sheet
105.f.3(7).

Regulations concerning beggars. Printed by the Officina Plantiniana at Antwerp in 1605. Cropped, with the loss of the Antwerp arms.

A109 ANTWERP

[5.4.1605] Gheboden ende wt-gheroepen van weghen mijnen Heeren Onderschouteth, Borgher-meesteren, Schepenen, ende Raedt der Stadt van Antvverpen, op den vijfden dagh April, 1605. fol. a single sheet
105.f.6(13).

Regulations for the drapers. Printed by the Officina Plantiniana at Antwerp in 1605.

A110 ANTWERP

[31.1.1607] ORDONNANTIE Op't stuck vande Borgherlijcke Wachte der Stadt van Antwerpen. Gheboden ende uytgeroepen by mijnen Heeren, Onderschouteth, Borghermeesteren, Schepenen ende Raedt der seluer stadt, op den xxxj. Ianuarij, M.DC.VII. T'ANTVVERPEN, Inde Plantijnsche Druckerije/By Jan Moerentorf. M.DC.VII. 16° sig. AB^{8}C^6
106.a.47.

A111 ANTWERP

[23.3.1609] Ordonnantie prouisionel Den Buydel-dragers verleent by mijnen Heeren/Schouteth/Borgher-meesteren/Schepenen/ende Raedt deser stadt/op den xxiij. Meert/M.VI^C.IX. T'ANTWERPEN, Inde Plantijnsche Druckerije/By Ian Moerentorf. M.DC.IX. 4° sig. A^4
107.g.23(16).

A112 ANTWERP

[10.12.1611] Vernieuwinghe ende verclaringhe van het STATVT ende ORDONNANTIE op't feyt van de ISSVE DESER STADT VAN ANTVVERPEN: Ghepubliceert by mijne Heeren den Schouteth/Borger-meesteren/Schepenen/ende Raedt der seluer Stadt/ op den x. Decembris/M.DC.XI. T'ANTWERPEN, Inde Plantijnsche Druckerije/By de Weduwe ende Sonen van Ian Moerentorf. M.DC.XI. 8° pp.8
106.a.50(1).

A113 ANTWERP
[10.4.1612] Gheboden ende wt-gheroepen by mijnen Heeren, Onder-Schouteth, Borger-meesteren, Schepenen, ende Raedt der Stadt van Antwerpen, op den x. Aprilis, 1612. fol. a single sheet
105.f.5(9).
Regulations for chandlers. Printed by the Officina Plantiniana at Antwerp in 1612. Cropped, with loss of the woodcut showing the Antwerp arms.

A114 ANTWERP
[8.12.1612] Gheboden ende wt-gheroepen by mijnen Heeren, Onder-Schouteth, Borgermeesteren, Schepenen, ende Raedt der Stadt van Antwerpen, op den viij. December, 1612. 4° a single sheet
Dept. of Manuscripts. King's 179(f.35).
On the establishment of a prison and asking for volunteers to staff it. Printed by the Officina Plantiniana at Antwerp in 1612.

A115 ANTWERP
[28.3.1613] ORDONNANTIE ENDE GHEBODEN, ghemaeckt . . . by mijnen Heeren, Onder-schouteth, Borgermeesteren, Schepenen, ende Raedt der Stadt van Antwerpen, aengaende de Specerije. In date den 28. Martij . . . 1613. fol. a single sheet
112.f.35(7).
Printed by the Officina Plantiniana at Antwerp in 1613.

A116 ANTWERP
[20.9.1613] Gheboden ende wt-gheroepen by mijnen Heeren/Onder-Schouteth, Borgher-meesteren, Schepenen, ende Raedt der Stadt van Antwerpen, opden xx. September, 1613. fol. a single sheet
112.f.31(9).
Regulations for postal charges. Printed by the Officina Plantiniana at Antwerp in 1613.

A117 ANTWERP
[21.8.1614] Gheboden ende wt-gheroepen van weghen mijn Heere den Onder-Schouteth, Borgher-meesteren, Schepenen, ende Raedt der Stadt van Antwerpen, opden xxj. Augusti, 1614. fol. a single sheet
112.f.31(10).
Regulations for lepers. Printed by the Officina Plantiniana at Antwerp in 1614.

A118 ANTWERP
[22.9.1615] Gheboden ende wt-gheroepen by mijnen Heeren, Onder-Schouteth, Borgermeesteren, Schepenen, ende Raedt der Stadt van Antwerpen, op den xij. September, 1615. 4° a single sheet
107.g.24(2).
Regulations for the hospital. Printed by the Officina Plantiniana at Antwerp in 1615.

A119 ANTWERP
[7.11.1615] Gheboden ende wt-gheroepen by mijnen Heeren, Onder-Schouteth, Borgermeesteren, Schepenen, ende Raedt der Stadt van Antwerpen, op den vij. Nouember, 1615. 4° a single sheet
107.g.23(1).
Declaring recently published and allegedly legal posters relating to the guild of secondhand clothes dealers to be illegal. Printed by the Officina Plantiniana at Antwerp in 1615.

A120 ANTWERP

[26.1.1616] TAXATIE VANDE SALARISEN voort-aen te betalen aen de Secretarisen der Stadt van Antwerpen, by mijne Heeren, Borger-meesteren, Schepenen, ende Raedt der seluer Stadt ghearresteert den xxvj. Ianuarij, 1616. fol. a single sheet
112.f.31(11).

Printed, in civilité, by the Officina Plantiniana at Antwerp in 1616.

A121 ANTWERP

[3.4.1617] Gheboden ende wt-gheroepen by mijnen Heeren/Schouteth/Borghermeesteren/Schepenen/ende Raedt der Stadt van Antwerpen, op den iij. Aprilis, 1617. fol. a single sheet
112.f.36(2).

Regulations for the postal service between Antwerp and Brussels. Printed by the Officina Plantiniana at Antwerp in 1617. Cropped, with loss of the Antwerp arms.

A122 ANTWERP

[11.8.1618] Gheboden ende wt-gheroepen by mijnen Heeren, Schouteth, Borghermeesteren, Schepenen, ende Raedt der Stadt van Antwerpen, op den xj. Augusti, 1618. 4° a single sheet
107.g.23(2).

A warrant against Marten Vermanden on a charge of wounding. Printed by the Officina Plantiniana at Antwerp in 1618.

A123 ANTWERP

[11.8.1618] Gheboden ende wt-gheroepen by mijnen Heeren, Schouteth, Borghermeesteren, Schepenen, ende Raedt der Stadt van Antwerpen, op den xj. Augusti, 1618. 4° a single sheet
107.g.23(3).

A warrant against Quirijn vanden Wijngaerde on a charge of murder. Printed by the Officina Plantiniana at Antwerp in 1618.

A124 ANTWERP

[29.7.1621] Gheboden ende wt-gheroepen by mijnen Heeren/Schouteth/Borgermeesteren/Schepenen, ende Raedt der Stadt van Antwerpen, op den xxix. Iulij, 1621. fol. a single sheet
112.f.21(2).

Regulations for beggars. Printed by the Officina Plantiniana at Antwerp in 1621.

A125 ANTWERP

[18.8.1621] Gheboden ende wt-gheroepen by mijnen Heeren/Schouteth/Borghermeesteren, Schepenen, ende Raedt der Stadt van Antwerpen, op den xviij. Augusti, 1621. fol. a single sheet
112.f.31(12).

On the price of bread. Printed by the Officina Plantiniana at Antwerp in 1621. Cropped, with loss of the woodcut showing the Antwerp arms.

A126 ANTWERP. Diocese

[22.12.1611] *Begin.* Men ghebiedt eenen yegelijcken. *End.* Actum den twee-entwintighsten Decembris/M.DC.XI. obl. fol. a single sheet
Dept. of Manuscripts. King's 179(f.32).

Prohibiting the carrying of parcels or sacks into churches. Printed by the Officina Plantiniana at Antwerp in 1611?

A127 ANTWERP. Diocese

[5.5.1617] IOANNES MALDERVS . . . Bisschop van Antwerpen/Allen den ghenen die dese sullen sien/saligheyt inden Heere. fol. a single sheet
112.f.37(1).

Regulations for church attendance. Dated 5 May 1617. Printed by the Officina Plantiniana at Antwerp in 1617?

A128 ANTWERP. Diocese. Synod

DECRETA SYNODI DIOECESANÆ ANTVERPIENSIS Mense Maio anni M.DC.X. celebratæ: Præsidente . . . IOANNE MIRÆO Episcopo Antuerpiensi. ANTVERPIÆ, Ex OFFICINA PLANTINIANA, Apud Ioannem Moretum. M.DC.X. (col.) ANTVERPIÆ, Ex OFFICINA PLANTINIANA, Apud Viduam & Filios Io. Moreti. M.DC.X. 8° 2 pt.: pp.154, sig.★[8]

1607/1072(5,6).

With documents reproduced in Dutch or French. With 'IOANNIS MIRÆI . . . ORATIO Ad Clerum habita in Synodo Diœcesana, Antuerpiæ, M DC.X.'. Edited by Joannes Miraeus.

A129 ANTWOORDE

Antwoorde op den Brief van C. P. H. [*sic*] gheschreven AEN HELENAM, Waer in Helena haer ontschuldight . . . 1616. 4° sig.AB[4]

11555.aaa.20.

A reply in verse to Pieter Corneliszoon Hooft's 'Brief van Menelaus aen Helena'. Signed: Tandem fit surculus arbor.

ANTWOORDE op dry vraghen. 1615. *See* LA BASSECOURT, Fabrice de; the Elder

ANTWOORDT op de malitieuse calumnie. 1620. *See* POPPIUS, Eduardus

A130 ANTWOORT

Antwoort Op de Vraghe/uytghegeven by de Brabandsche Reden-rijck Camer 'tWit Lavender, UYT LEVENDER IONST tot Amsterdam. Vrage. Wat's d'Oorsaeck meest, waerom 'tverkeerde Werelts Rond, Sich Waenwijs so bedrieght, en bloeyd in alle sond? Ende op den Reghel: De sulcke die zijn dwaes, en d'Werelt achtse wijs. 't AMSTERDAM, Ghedruckt by Paulus van Ravesteyn. Voor Abraham Huybrechtsz . . . 1613. (col.) 't AMSTERDAM, Ghedruckt by Paulus van Ravesteyn . . . 1613. 4° sig.★,★★, A-Y[4]; illus.

11555.d.1; 11556.ccc.6(1).

The two illustrations are both the same woodcut device of the Chamber.

A131 ANTWOORT

ANTVVOORT, Tot wederlegginghe van het monstreus/oproerich Discours en Pasquil Iacobi Taurini en der sijner/het welcke in Vergaderinge der . . . Staten van Hollant . . . is ghecondemneert. Gestelt door een Lief-hebber der Waerheyt . . . De tweede Editie. Ghedruckt . . . 1617. 4° pp.61

T.2247(21).

Part of the controversy after the Amsterdam riots in February 1617.

A132 APIANUS, Petrus

[Cosmographia.] Cosmographie. Ofte beschrijvinge der gheheelder Werelt . . . gheschreven in Latijn door Petrus Apianus. Gecorrigeert ende vermeerdert door M. Gamma Frisius . . . met sommighe andere tractaten van de selve materie, ghemaect van den voorseyden Gamma . . . TOT AMSTELREDAM, By Cornelis Claesz. . . . 1609. (col.) Tot Amstelredam/by Cornelis Claesz. . . . M.VJ.C.ende JX. 4° ff.121; illus., maps

C.142.cc.31.

Also with 'De gheleghentheyt ende Beschrijvinghe van Indien . . . ghetrocken uyt de generale Historie van Indien . . . Door . . . Francisque Lopez de Gomara' and 'De gheleghentheyt ende Beschrijvinghe van Indien . . .ghetrocken uyt die Cosmographie vande Heere Jeronymus Girana Arragonoys'. The titlepage illustration is an engraving of Jodocus Hondius's world map. The woodcut illustrations include several volvelles fastened with engraved roses. The colophon contains an acrostic on the name Cornelis Claeszoon.

APOCALYPSIS insignium aliquot haeresiarcharum. 1608. *See* SICHEM, Christoffel van

APOLLO of ghesangh der Musen. 1615. *See* BREDERO, Gerbrand

A133 APOLLONIUS Alexandrinus Dyscolus

APOLLONII DYSCOLI, Alexandrini . . . Historiæ Commentitiæ Liber. IOANNES MEVRSIVS Recensuit, SYNTAGMA De eius nominis Scriptoribus, & COMMENTARIVM, addidit. LVGDVNI BATAVORVM, Apud ISAACVM ELZEVIRIVM . . . M D CXX. 4° pp.174
235.e.32(2).
In Greek and Latin.

APOLLONIUS Pergaeus. Reconstructions of lost works. De sectione determinata. 1608. *See* SNELLIUS, Willebrordus. Apollonius Batavus.

APOLOGIA ofte volcomen verantwoordinghe. 1618. *See* BOHEMIA. States [25.5.1618]

APOLOGIA Ordinum inclyti Regni Bohemię. 1618. *See* BOHEMIA. States [25.5.1618]

APOLOGIA pro hierarchia ecclesiastica. 1601. *See* PERSONS, Robert

An APOLOGICALL epistle. 1601. *See* BROUGHTON, Richard, Historian

An APOLOGIE or defence of such true Christians. 1604. *See* AINSWORTH, Henry

APOLOGIE ou declaration des raisons pour lesquelles les trois estats du Royaume de Boheme . . . ont esté contraints de prendre les armes. 1619. *See* BOHEMIA. States [25.5.1618]

THE APOLOGIES of the most Christian Kinges of France and Navar . . . for the Fathers of the Society of Jesus. 1611. *See* FRANCE [1603–1610]

AN APOLOGY of T.F. in the defence of him-self. 1602. *See* FITZ-HERBERT, Thomas. A defence of the Catholyke cause.

APOSTOLICAE Sedis definitiones veteres, de gratia Dei. 1616. *See* PEETERS, Bartholomaeus

A134 APOSTOLIOS, Michael

ΜΙΧΑΗΛΟΥ ΑΠΟΣΤΟΛΙΟΥ ΠΑΡΟΙΜΙΑΙ. MICHAELIS APOSTOLII PAROEMIÆ: Nunc demum . . . integræ, cum Petri Pantini versione, ejusque & Doctorum notis, in lucem editæ. LVGDVNI BATAVORVM, Ex Officinâ ELZEVIRIANA . . . M D C XIX. (col.) LVGDVNI BATAVORVM, Typis ISAACI ELZEVIRII . . . M D C XIX. 4° pp.387
634.k.1.
In Greek and Latin.

APPART, Abraham. Disputationum theologicarum decima-quinta, de lege Dei. 1603. *See* GOMARUS, Franciscus

APPART, Abraham. Theses theologicae de primo primi hominis peccato. 1604. *See* ARMINIUS, Jacobus

APPENDIX oft by-voechsel achter Journael vande reyse der Hollantsche schepen op Iava. 1618 [1598]. *See* HOUTMAN, Cornelis de

An APPENDIX to the Antidote. 1621. *See* NORRIS, Sylvester

A135 [*AP-ROBERT, J.

THE YOUNGER BROTHER HIS APOLOGY BY IT SELFE. OR A Fathers free power disputed, for the disposition of his lands, or other his fortunes to his Sonne, Sonnes, or any one of them . . . By I. AP-ROBERT Gent . . . M.DC.XVIII. 4° pp.62
6355.a.1.]

*Destroyed. Transcribed from the facsimile made from a copy at Cambridge University Library, published in vol. 103 of *English recusant literature*, 1972. Copies of later editions in the British Library were not destroyed. The 1618 edition was printed by the English College press at St. Omer.

A136 APULEIUS, Lucius; Madaurensis
[Asinus aureus.] De Elf Boecken Van LVCIVS APVLEIVS, Handelende Van den Gulden Esel . . . tot ANTWERPEN, By Guilliame van Parijs, woonende op de Catalijne Veste. 12° pp.285
12431.a.15.
The date of publication is uncertain and has been variously suggested as ca. 1590, ca. 1610 and between 1608 and 1636. The date 1610–11 is given for an Antwerp bookseller Willem Parys, without an address, perhaps this should be Willem van Parijs.

A137 ARIAS, Francisco
[Libro de la imitacion de Christo nuestro Señor.] THE IUDGE WHEREIN IS SHEWED, how Christ our Lord is to Iudge the World at the last Day . . . Translated into English . . . 1621. 8° pp.253
4378.a.2; C.26.h.14.
Anonymous. An extract from the work of Francisco Arias. The translator's dedication signed: G.M., i.e. Sir Tobias Matthew. Without imprint; published by the English College press at St. Omer. The copy at 4378.a.2 has the bookplate of Henry Stevens of Vermont 1882, that at C.26.h.14 has the initials AVR (?) on the binding and ownership inscriptions: Eliz Hales; Bark (or:Barr).

A138 ARIAS MONTANUS, Benedictus
NATVRAE HISTORIA, PRIMA IN MAGNI OPERIS CORPORE PARS, Benedicto Aria Montano descriptore . . . ANTVERPIÆ, EX OFFICINA PLANTINIANA, Apud Ioannem Moretum. M.DCI. (col.) ANTVERPIÆ, EX OFFICINA PLANTINIANA, APVD IOANNEM MORETVM. M.DCI. 4° pp.525; illus.
446.d.9.
A posthumously published continuation of the 'Liber generationis et regenerationis Adam' of 1593, both volumes intended to form the first part of an unfinished work. The illustrations are woodcuts.

A139 ARIOSTO, Lodovico
[Orlando Furioso.] IL DIVINO ARIOSTO oft ORLANDO Furioso . . . Ouergeset wyt Italiaensche veersen In Nederlantsche Rymen door Euerart Siceram van Brussel . . . By Dauid Mertens Thãtwerpẽ 1615. 8° pp.623; illus., ports.
11426.b.10.
The titlepage is engraved; the illustrations are engraved, the portraits of author and translator appear on the last of the preliminaries.

A140 ARISTOTELES
[Ethica Nicomachea. Summaries and Paraphrases.] ARISTOTELIS ETHICORVM NICOMACHIORVM PARAPHRASIS, Incerto Auctore, antiquo & eximio peripatetico; Ex BIBLIOTHECA LUGDUNOBATAVA nunc primum Græce edita, emendata & Latine reddita a DANIELE HEINSIO. LUGD. BAT. Ex officina Johannis Patij . . . M.D.CVII. 4° pp.418, 524: plate; illus.
30.h.1.
Compiled by Andronicus Rhodius. The titlepage is engraved, signed: W. Swanenburg fecit. The portrait of Aristotle signed: WS. With the ownership inscription: Theodorus Zuylenus 1615.

A141 ARISTOTELES

[Ethica Nicomachea. Summaries and Paraphrases.] (tp.1) ANDPONIKOY ΡΟΔΙΟΥ . . . Παράφρασις τῶν ἠθικῶν Νικομαχείων. ANDRONICI RHODII Ethicorum Nicomacheorum PARAPHRASIS. Cum interpretatione DANIELIS HEINSII, hac editione plurimis . . . mendis ab autore vindicata. LVGDVNI BATAVORVM, Excudit Ioannes Patius . . . 1617.
(tp.2=sig.Zz1, unnumbered leaf between pp.729, 730) ANDRONICI RHODII . . . libellus ΠΕΡΙ ΠΑΘΩΝ, ID EST, De animi affectionibus. ET Anonymus de virtutibus & vitijs. Editi operâ Davidis Hœschelij . . . LVGDVNI BATAVORVM, Excudit Ioannes Patius . . . 1617. 8° pp.775
524.g.24.

Pp.762–775: EXCERPTA E LIBRO Maximi Monachi . . . ad S. Marinum presbyterum. Inscribed: bequeathed by Thomas Tyrwhitt 1786.

A142 ARISTOTELES

[Poetica.] (tp.1) ARISTOTELIS DE POETICA LIBER. DANIEL HEINSIVS recensuit, ordini suo restituit, Latine vertit, Notas addidit. Accedit eiusdem DE TRAGICA CONSTITVTIONE LIBER . . . LVGDVNI BATAVORVM, Apud IOANNEM BALDUINUM. Prostat in Bibliopolio Ludouici Elzevirij . . . M.D.C.XI.
(tp.2) DANIELIS HEINSII DE TRAGOEDIÆ constitutione liber . . . LVGDVNI BATAVORVM, apud IOANNEM BALDUINUM. Prostat in Bibliopolio Ludouici Elzevirij . . . M.D.C.XI. 8° pp.104, 251
714.b.2.

The first part in Greek and Latin.

A143 ARISTOTELES

[Politica.] ΑΡΙΣΤΟΤΈΛΟΥΣ ΠΟΛΙΤΙΚΩ͂Ν ΒΙΒ. Θ. ARISTOTELIS POLITICORVM LIBRI VIII. Cum perpetua DANIELIS HEINSII in omnes libros Paraphrasi. Accedit accuratus rerum Index. LVGDVNI BATAVORVM, Ex Officinâ ELZEVIRIANA . . . M D C XXI. (col.) LVGDVNI BATAVORVM, TYPIS ISAACI ELZEVIRI . . . M D CXXI. 8° pp.1045
520.e.10; 160.k.2, 3; G.7928.

A144 ARISTOXENUS

ARISTOXENVS. NICOMACHVS. ALYPIVS. Auctores Musices antiquissimi, hactenus non editi. IOANNES MEVRSIVS Nunc primus vulgavit, & NOTAS addidit. LUGDUNI BATAVORUM, Ex Officinâ LVDOVICI ELZEVIRI. Typis GODEFRIDI BASSON . . . M.DC.XVI. 4° pp.160[196]
519.b.27; 52.d.29.

In Greek and Latin.

A145 ARMINIAENS

t'Arminiaens Testament. fol. a single sheet
1790.b.29(100).

An engraving bearing the above title in Dutch, made after the plate attributed to Simon Frisius, with accompanying text in German, entitled 'Der Arminianer Testament/vnd Inventaris dero nachgelassenen Meubelen zu oberlieberen denen es von rechts halben zugehört'. Printed in the Netherlands in 1618?

A146 ARMINIAENSCHE

d'ARMINIAENSCHE SCHANS TOT LEYDEN . . . Ghedruckt . . . 1618. 4°? a single sheet
1889.d.3(304).

An unsigned engraving, by Claes Jansz Visscher? with explanatory text and with French and Dutch verses directed against Johan van Oldenbarnevelt. With the additional text of 'd'Arminiaensche Bulleback' at the foot of the sheet. Printed at Amsterdam by C. J. Visscher? This copy has been mounted.

A147 ARMINIAENSCHE

[d'Arminiaensche schans.] 'd ARMINIANZE SCHANS TOT LEYDEN . . . J. Tangena Excud. . . . Gedrukt . . . 1618. 4° a single sheet

Maps C.9.d.4(96).

One of the 1618 engravings entitled 'd'Arminiaensche schans', reprinted by Johannes Tangena at Leiden, ca. 1690. With the original engraved French verses and the explanatory letterpress text in Dutch. Part of the Beudeker collection.

A148 ARMINIAENSCHE

DE ARMINIAENSCHE VAERT NAER SPAEGNIEN. Wy spoeden lustich voort, [etc.] 4° sig. AB^4; illus.

T.2422(23).

In verse. The continuation promised in 'Wonderlijcken droom van de schoolhoudinghe van Mr. Jan van Oldenbarnevelt'. The titlepage contains an engraved illustration of the subject. Published in 1618.

A149 ARMINIANEN

Der Arminianen Troost. 8° a single sheet

T.2249(32).

A satirical poem. Published in 1619.

Der ARMINIANER Testament. 1618? *See* ARMINIAENS

'd ARMINIANZE schans. 1618[ca.1690]. *See* ARMINIAENSCHE

A150 ARMINIUS, Jacobus

[Collections] IACOBI ARMINII . . . DISPVTATIONES Magnam partem S. Theologiæ complectentes, PVBLICÆ & PRIVATÆ. Priores cum accessione aliqua, & correctiores . . . Alteræ vero totæ novæ . . . Præmittitur Oratio de Vita & Obitu Auctoris, recitata à D. Petro Bertio . . . LVGDVNI BATAVORVM, Ex Officina THOMÆ BASSON. M.D.CX. 8° pp.247[248], 191

1010.a.6.

A151 ARMINIUS, Jacobus

[Collections] IACOBI ARMINII . . . ORATIONES, itemque TRACTATVS insigniores aliquot . . . LVGDVNI BATAVORVM, Ex Officina THOMÆ BASSON. M.D.CXI. 8° pp.136, 176

4375.aa.2.

A152 ARMINIUS, Jacobus

EEN Cleyn Tractaetgen/vervatende seeckere Articulen teghens den Aflaet ende Vaghevier. Ghedisputeert onder Iacobo Arminio . . . tot Leyden/anno 1606. den 22. Februarij. VVt het Latijn . . . overgheset. Nae de Copye, By Jan Paets ghedruckt/ende nu tot Amstelredam/by Dirck Pietersz. . . . 1609. 4° sig. A^4; illus.

T.2239(14).

The illustration shows a cardinal's hat and a parchment scroll inscribed 'MANDATA' with six seals. The original was printed at Leiden.

A153 ARMINIUS, Jacobus

EEN Cort/ende bundich Tractaetgen/vervatende seeckere Theses off Articulen daer inne bewesen wort/Dat de Gereformeerde Kercken vande Roomsche Kercke niet affgheweecken en zijn/Ende Dat sy wel doen/weygerende mette selve Kercke eenighe ghemeynschap te houden . . . Ghestelt Door IACOBVM ARMINIVM . . . Wten Latijne . . . overgheset . . . IN S'GRAVEN-HAGHE, By Hillebrandt Jacobssz . . . 1609. 4° sig. $A\text{-}C^4D^1$

T.2239(13).

A translation of 'Disputatio publica' no. 22, not published in Latin until 1610.

A154 ARMINIUS, Jacobus

Corte ende grondighe verclaringhe uyt de Heylighe Schrift Over het swaerwichtighe poinct VANDE Cracht ende Rechtvaerdicheyt der Voorsienicheyt Godts ontrent het quade: Wesende eerstmael int Iaer 1605. andermael int Iaer 1607 . . . openbaerlick om te disputeren voorghestelt door D. IACOBVM ARMINIVM . . . Ende nu . . . by malcanderen ghebracht ende int Nederduyts overgheset. Tot Leyden, By IAN PAETS IACOBSZOON . . . 1609. 4° sig. A-C^4D^3
T.2239(10).

Compiled and translated from 'Disputationes publicae' no. 9, 10, not published in Latin until 1610.

A155 ARMINIUS, Jacobus

IACOBI ARMINII . . . De vero & genuino sensu CAP. VII. EPISTOLAE AD ROMANOS DISSERTATIO. LUGDUNI BATAVORUM. Ex Officinâ GODEFRIDI BASSON. M.D.CXII. 8° pp. 199: plate; illus.
4256.bb.59(2).

The plate is a synoptical chart of the argument.

A156 ARMINIUS, Jacobus

DISPVTATIONVM THEOLOGICARVM QVARTO REPETITARVM QVINTA DE PERSONA PATRIS, ET FILII, Quam . . . Sub Præsidio . . . D. IACOBI ARMINII . . . publicè discutiendam proponit PETRVS DE LA FITE . . . LVGDVNI BATAVORVM, Ex Officinâ Ioannis Patii . . . M.D.C.V. 4° sig. F^4
4376.de.16(75).

A157 ARMINIUS, Jacobus

DISPVTATIONVM THEOLOGICARVM QVARTO REPETITARVM VIGESIMA. TERTIA DE FIDE. Quam . . . Præside . . . D. IACOBO ARMINIO . . . publicè examinandam proponit RICARDUS IANUS NERÆUS . . . LVGDVNI BATAVORVM, Ex Officinâ Ioannis Patii . . . M.D.CV. 4° 4 leaves
4376.de.16(67).

Cropped, with loss of signatures.

A158 ARMINIUS, Jacobus

IACOBI ARMINII . . . EXAMEN MODESTVM Libelli, quem D. GVLIELMVS PERKINSIVS . . . edidit ante aliquot annos De Prædestinationis modo & ordine, itemque de Amplitudine gratiæ divinæ. Addita est . . . ANALYSIS CAP. IX. AD ROMAN. ante multos annos ab eodem . . . Arminio delineata . . . LUGDUNI BATAVORUM Ex Officinâ GODEFRIDI BASSON. M.D.CXII. 8° pp. 312
4256.bb.59(1).

A159 ARMINIUS, Jacobus

THESES THEOLOGICÆ DE NATVRA DEI . . . PRO PUBLICO DOCTURÆ TESTIMONIO . . . AD DISPVTANDVM PROPOSITAE . . . A IACOBO ARMINIO . . . LUGDUNI BATAVORUM, Ex Officinâ Ioannis Patii . . . M.D.CIII. 4° sig. AB^4C^6
4376.de.16(40).

Cropped.

A160 ARMINIUS, Jacobus

THESES THEOLOGICÆ DE Primo primi hominis peccato, Ad quas . . . Sub Præsidio . . . D. IACOBI ARMINII . . . respondebo ABRAHAM G.F. APPART . . . LUGDUNI BATAVORUM, Ex Officinâ Ioannis Patii . . . M D CIV. 4° sig. A^4
4376.de.16(80).

A161 ARMINIUS, Jacobus

VERCLARINGHE IACOBI ARMINII . . . Aengaende zijn ghevoelen, so van de Predestinatie, als van eenige andere poincten der Christelicker Religie . . .

Wtghegheven/by de Weduwe . . . ende haere Broeders. TOT LEYDEN, Ghedruckt by Thomas Basson . . . 1610. 4° pp.52
T.2240(5).
With manuscript notes and with a drawing dated 1615 on the titlepage verso.

A162 ARMINIUS, Jacobus
VIERDERLEY Theses of Articulen/teghen 't Pausdom . . . Ghestelt ende ghedisputeert binnen Leyden/by . . . Iacobum Arminium . . . Wt den Latijne in Nederlandtsche Tale . . . overgheset. IN S'GRAVEN-HAGHE, By Hillebrant Iacobsz. . . . 1610. 4° pp.47
T.2240(6).

A163 ARMINIUS, Jacobus
[Supposititious works] Vertaelde THESES Inhoudende een corte ondervvijsinghe Vande oprechte Regeeringhe der Kercke Christi, ende vande oeffeninghe der Discipline inde selve. Eertijdts door . . . Jacobum Arminium . . . int Latijn beschreven, doch met versvvijghen van zijnen name doenmael uytghegheven. TOT DELF, Ghedruckt by Ian Andriesz. . . . 1612. 4° pp.68
T.2242(3).
Falsely attributed to Arminius. A manuscript note names Abraham van M. as the true author.

A164 ARNAULD, Antoine; Avocat-général
[Premiere Sauoisienne.] IVS BELLI SABAVDICI deductum declaratumque RELATIONE VERA, AC SVFFICIENTI ENARRATIONE, QVIBVS DE CAVSIS BELLVM INTER FRANCIAE & Nauarræ Regem, Henricum IV. & . . . Carolum Emanuelem, Ducem Sabaudiæ, anno 1600. exortum sit: quo bello, Franciæ Rex, tota Sabaudia Ducem exuit, nec expedire, vt eam reddat, libelli Gallicè æditi author . . . multis rationibus Regi persuadere studet. ACCESSIT ELENCHVS . . . COMITVM ET DVCVM SABAVDIAE . . . NEC OMISSA. HISTORICA RELATIO BELLI, QVOD REX FRANCIAE . . . Henricus tertius intulit . . . Carolo Emmanueli Duci Sabaudiæ, ob Anno 1588. occupatum Marchionatum Salussanum, quod bellum continuauit Rex . . . Henricus quartus, donec pace Anno 1598 . . . conclusa sopitum fuit, sed recruduit bellum anno 1600, quo Rex Franciæ Sabaudiam occupauit. Hi tractatus ex lingua Francica Latini facti sunt. AMSTELREDAMI, Sumptibus Zachariæ Heinss. . . . M.DCI. 4° pp.35,15,64: plates; maps, port.
1057.g.2.
Anonymous. The preface preceding the titlepage mentions the original title as 'Savoisienne', a work by Antoine Arnauld. Originals of pt.2 and 3 not traced. The main body of the work probably printed in Germany, with titlepage and preface only printed at Amsterdam? The portrait of Henry IV is accompanied by German verses, dated 1595.

A165 ARNOBIUS Afer
ARNOBII DISPVTATIONVM ADVERSVS GENTES LIBRI SEPTEM CVM GODESCALCI STEVVECHII ELECTIS. ANTVERPIÆ APVD IOACH. TROGNÆSIVM. M.DCIV. 8° pp.431
846.e.5.

ARNOLDUS, Joannes; Lugdunensis. Theses theologicae de remissione debitorum. 1601. *See* KUCHLINUS, Joannes; Theologian

ARREST ende sententie op ende teghens eenen Guilaume Pingre. 1609. *See* PARIS. Parlement

An ARROW against idolatrie. 1611. *See* AINSWORTH, Henry

ARTICULEN eñ conditien besloten op den Neder-Oostenrijckschen Landtdach. 1621. *See* AUSTRIA. Lower Austria. Landtag

ARTICULEN, ende inneminghe . . . der stadt van S. Ian d'Angely. 1621. *See* PRISE et reduction de la ville de S. Iean d'Angely

ARTIJCULEN van t'verdrach . . . tusschen den . . . Marquis Spinola . . . ende . . . Ioachim Ernest Marquis van Brandenborch. 1621. *See* GERMANY [12.4.1621]

ARTYCKELEN van het bestandt. 1609. *See* NETHERLANDS. Southern Provinces [9.4.1609]

A166 ASSCHE, Judocus van

Den Schadt DES HEYLIGHEN SCAPVLIERS, Inhoudende Den Oorspronck/Voordelen/ende Aflaten van het Broederschap/der suyvere Maghet ende Moeder Godts MARIA des Berghs Carmeli. door F. IVDOCVM VAN ASSCHE . . . T'ANTVVERPEN, By Cornelis Verschueren . . . 1619. (col.) Typus [*sic*] Ieremiæ van Ghelen. 8° pp.224[225]; illus.

1568/5689.

The pagination is very irregular. The titlepage engraving shows saints, the titlepage verso the engraved arms of the dedicatee. Ownership inscription: Arthur Day 1884.

ASSERTIO Lipsiani Donarii adversus gelastorum suggillationes. 1607. *See* WOVERIUS, Joannes; of Antwerp

A167 ASTERIUS; Saint, Bishop

S. ASTERII . . . HOMILIAE Græcè & Latinè nunc primùm editæ PHILIPPO RVBENIO interprete. EIVSDEM RVBENI Carmina, Orationes, & Epistolæ selectiores: itemque AMICORVM in vitâ functum Pietas. ANTVERPIÆ, EX OFFICINA PLANTINIANA, Apud Viduam & Filios Ioannis Moreti. M.DC.XV. (col.) ANTVERPIÆ, EX OFFICINA PLANTINIANA, APVD VIDVAM ET FILIOS IOANNIS MORETI. M.DC.XV. 4° pp.284; illus., port.

C.82.e.1.

Edited by Joannes Brantius. The engraved portrait of Philips Rubens, by Pieter Paul Rubens, signed: Corn. Gallæus sculpsit.

An ATTESTATION of many learned . . . divines. 1613. *See* JACOB, Henry; Independent Minister

A168 AU

AV ROY DV SOING QVE SA MAIESTE DOIT AVOIR DE LA conseruation de sa vie. A AMSTREDAM, 1603. 8° pp.87

8050.aa.15(1).

Warning Henry IV against the Jesuits and other orders. The imprint is probably false. Printed in France?

A169 AU

AV ROY DV SOING QVE SA MAIESTE DOIT AVOIR . . . A AMSTREDAM, 1603. 8° pp.84

1058.a.18.

Another edition of the preceding, with an errata slip pasted on to p.84. These errors are not corrected in the preceding. Also printed in France?

AUBÉRY DU MAURIER, Benjamin

For documents composed by Benjamin Aubéry du Maurier as French ambassador at The Hague, *see* FRANCE [1.5.1619] and [13.5.1619]

A170 AUGUSTINE; Saint, Bishop

[Confessions.] [Divi Aurelii Augustini . . . Libri tredecim Confessionum, ad tria manuscripta exemplaria emendati. Operâ ac studio R.P. Henrici Sommalij . . . Duaci, Typis Balthazaris Belleri, 1607.] 24° pp.410

945.f.5.

Imperfect; wanting the titlepage and preliminary matter. The title has been reconstructed from *Sommervogel* and *Labarre*. The date of this edition is doubtful: it may in fact be 1608 or 1628, assuming that the date of the approbation, i.e. 1607, has been retained in those of later date. The earlier dating has been tentatively retained here as given in the General Catalogue.

A171 AUGUSTINE; Saint, Bishop
[Confessions.] THE CONFESSIONS OF . . . S. AVGUSTINE, Translated into English. TOGEATHER With a large Preface . . . M.DC.XX. 8° pp.108, 800
3627.aa.7.
Translated by Sir Tobias Matthew. Without imprint; published by the English College press at St. Omer.

A172 AUGUSTINE; Saint, Bishop
[Confessions.] De Boecken der Belijdenissen van S. Augustijn . . . nu eerst wtet Latijn int Duyts ouergheset . . . T'EMMERICK by Jacob van Eckeren. M.DC.III. 8° ff.204
1568/5998.
Translated by Johannes Semnius. The first four leaves and the last four leaves are slightly mutilated.

A173 AUGUSTINE; Saint, Bishop
[Supposititious works. Two or more works] DIVI AVRELII AVGVSTINI . . . MEDITATIONES, SOLILOQVIA, ET MANVALE. MEDITATIONES. B. ANSELMI cùm tractatu de humani generis redemptione. D. BERNARDI. IDIOTÆ, viri docti, de amore Diuino. Omnia ad ms. exemplaria emendata, & in meliorem ordinem distributa, opera ac studio R.P. HENRICI SOMMALII . . . DVACI, Ex officina Typographica BALTAZARIS BELLERI . . . M.D.C.VIII. 32° pp.513; port.
1606/1611.
With an additional engraved titlepage, reading: Fasciculus divini amoris atque devotionis ex S.S. Patrum opusculis confectus opera, ac studio R.P. Henrici Summalii . . . Duaci. Typis Baltazaris Belleri . . . 1608.

A174 AUGUSTINE; Saint, Bishop
[Supposititious works. Manuale.] THE MANVEL OF S. AVGVSTIN . . . Otherwise tearmed a little booke treating of the contemplation of CHRIST . . . Printed at Doway, By LAVRENCE KELLAM . . . M.DC.XXI. 24° pp.110
C.65.a.3.
Translated by Anthony Batt as pt.3 of 'St. Augustine, A heavenly treasure of confortable meditations and prayers'.

A175 AUGUSTINE; Saint, Bishop
[Supposititious works. Soliloquia animae ad Deum.] THE BOOKE OF S. AVGVSTIN . . . Commonly called his Soliloquies, that is the secret discourses . . . of his soule with God. Printed at Doway, By LAVRENCE KELLAM . . . M.DC.XXI. 24° pp.121[221]
C.65.a.4.
Translated by Anthony Batt as pt.2 of 'St. Augustine, A heavenly treasure of confortable meditations and prayers'.

AUGUSTINE; Saint, Bishop. [Extracts] A shorte relation of divers miracles. 1608. *See* GREGORY I; the Great, Saint, Pope. The dialogues.

AUGUSTINUS, Antonius. *See* AGUSTÍN, Antonio

A176 AUSONIUS, Decius Magnus
[Works] D. MAGNI AVSONII . . . OPERA, Ex recognitione IOSEPHI SCALIGERI . . . EX OFFICINA PLANTINIANA RAPHELENGII. M.D.V. long 16° pp.238
1069.a.2.
Published at Leiden.

A177 AUSONIUS, Decius Magnus
[Works] D. MAGNI AVSONII . . . Opera . . . EX OFFICINA PLANTINIANA RAPHELENGII. M.DC.XII. long 16° pp.238
1002.a.4.
A reissue of the edition of 1605, also published at Leiden.

A178 AUSONIUS, Decius Magnus
[Works] D. MAGNI AVSONII . . . Opera. Amstelredami Apud Guiljel: Iansso. A°. M DC XXI. long 16° pp.237
C.65.a.18.
The text in the edition by J. J. Scaliger. The titlepage is engraved. With the arms of Jean Jacques de Thou on the binding.

A179 AUSTRIA. Lower Austria. Landtag
[1620] SVPPLICATIE der Neder-Oostenrijcksche Lant-Stenden aen sijne Keyserlijcke Majesteyt. Over het grousaem . . . tyranniseren des Keyserlijck Krijchsvolck insonderheydt de Cosacken ende Waloenen, teghen zijne Keyserlijcke Majesteyts eyghen Onderdanen . . . Ghedruckt nae't Hoochduytsche Exemplaer . . . 1620. 4° 2 unsigned leaves.
T.2423(38).
Printed by Hillebrant Jacobsz van Wouw at The Hague?

A180 AUSTRIA. Lower Austria. Landtag
[1.1621] Articulen eñ Conditien besloten op den Neder-Oostenrijckschen Landtdach/ende wat elcke sal op brengen ende betalen. Overghesedt wt de Hooch-Duytsche sprake in onse Nederlantsche Tale. Ghedruckt den 3. Meert. 1621. T'Hantwerpen/By Abraham Verhoeven/[etc.] 4° pp.8; sig.A^4; illus.
P.P.3444.af(196).
Headed: Martius 1621. 28. The titlepage woodcut shows five men seated in an assembly. The text is a summary of the decisions, originally reached in January 1621, with other news.

A181 AVENTROOT, Johannes Bartholomeus
CARTA DE IOAN AVENTROTE AL . . . REY DE ESPANIA. EN LA QVAL BREVEMENTE se declara el mysterio de la Guerra sobre las XVII Provincias del Pays Baxo. Reuista, y emendada con vna Exhortaçion para los grandes. EN AMSTREDAME, En casa de Pablo de Ravesteyne. 1614. 8° sig.A-C^8D^2; illus.
1055.a.4.
The illustrations, in woodcut, are apocalyptic.

A182 AVENTROOT, Johannes Bartholomeus
[Carta . . . al Rey de Espania.] Ein Sendbrief Johan Aventroots Ahn den Groosmächtigē [*sic*] könig von Spanien/Darinn kurtzlich vermeldet wird das geheimnisz von dem kriege auf die 17. provintzen des Niderlands/In Hochteutsche sprache übersetzet aus dem Niderlandischen/so gedruckt in Amsterdam. Im jahre MDCXV. 8° pp.72
3908.de.6.
Probably printed in the Netherlands. Without the illustrations of the Spanish edition, but with spaces containing explanatory text in their place. The date given in the imprint may refer to the 1615 Dutch edition, printed by Paulus van Ravesteyn, as quoted; this edition could be of the same year or shortly thereafter.

A183 AVENTROOT, Johannes Bartholomeus
[Carta . . . al Rey de Espania.] EPISTOLA JOHANNIS AVENTROTII, AD . . . regem Hispaniarum; In qua breviter mysterium belli, super XVII Belgii provinciis gesti, exponitur: In Latinam linguam nunc conversa de exemplari Belgico, excuso AMSTERODAMI. ANNO MDCXV. 8° pp.80
8079.b.15(1).

Probably printed in the Netherlands. Without the illustrations of the Spanish edition, but with explanatory text in their place. From the same press as the German edition above. The date may refer to the 1615 Dutch edition, printed by Paulus van Ravesteyn, as quoted; this edition could be of the same year or shortly thereafter. In a binding stamped: J. Gomez de la Cortina et amicorum. With the exlibris of H. S. Ashbee.

A184 AVENTROOT, Johannes Bartholomeus

[Carta . . . al Rey de Espania.] EPISTOLA Johannis Aventroti, Ad . . . regem Hispaniæ, IN QVA BREVITER DECLARATur mysterium belli XVII. provinciarum Belgicarum, Recognita & aucta, Cum admonitione ad proceres: Vt fuit Belgice excusa AMSTERODAMI Apud Paulum Ravesteinium, anno 1615. 8° pp.85; illus.
281.a.22.

The preface describes the date of this edition as five years since the Spanish original (1612), three years since the first Dutch edition (1613). It is therefore of 1616 or 1617. The illustrations are those of the Spanish edition of 1614 and this edition may also have been printed by Paulus van Ravesteyn at Amsterdam.

A185 AVIANUS, Flavius

AVIANI ÆSOPICARVM FABVLARVM LIBER. A THEOD. PVLMANNO CRANEBVRGIO EX MEMBRANIS . . . EDITVS. ANTVERPIÆ, EX OFFICINA PLANTINIANA, Apud Ioannem Moretum. M.D.CII. 16° pp.29
12305.a.14.

A186 AVILA, Juan de; called the Apostle of Andalusía

[Libro espiritual sobre el verso, Audi, filia, et vide.] THE AVDI FILIA, OR A RICH CABINET FVLL OF SPRITVALL IEVVELLS. Composed by the Reuerend Father, DOCTOVR AVILA, Translated out of Spanish . . . M.DC.XX. 4° pp.584
1225.d.11.

The translator's dedication signed: L.T., i.e. Sir Tobias Matthew. Without imprint; published by the English College press at St. Omer.

A187 AVITY, Pierre d'

(tp.1) LES EMPIRES, ROYAVMES, ESTATS, SEIGNEVRIES, DVCHEZ, ET PRINCIPAVTEZ DV MONDE . . . AVEC L'ORIGINE DE TOVTES LES RELIGIONS QVI ONT ESTE iusques à present au Monde . . . ENSEMBLE LES ORIGINES DE TOVS LES CHEVALIERS & Ordres Militaires . . . Par le Sieur D.V.T.Y. Gentilhomme ordinaire de la Chambre du Roy. TOME I. A S. Omer. De l'Imprimerie de Charles Boscard . . . M.DC.XIIII. [etc.]
(tp.2=p.585bis) LES EMPIRES, ROYAVMES, ESTATS, SEIGNEVRIES, DVCHEZ, ET PRINCIPAVTEZ DV MONDE . . . Par le Sieur D.V.T.Y. Gentilhomme ordinaire de la Chambre du Roy. TOME II. A S. OMER. De l'Imprimerie de Charles Boscard . . . M.DC.XIIII.[etc.] (col.) A S. OMER. De l'Imprimerie de Charles Boscard . . . M.DC.XIIII. 4° pp.1104,59
10004.ccc.11.
Anonymous.

A188 AVONT-PRAETJEN

Avont-praetjen/Tusschen drye Personagien/waer van de 1. heet Iverich hert, de 2. Gaern-onderricht, ende de 3. Onnoosel-slecht. Die in't corte handelen van't ghene datter by de ghemeene Man in Hollandt al om gaet . . . Ghedruckt . . . 1612. 4° pp.21
T.2242(29).
On the Vorstius affair.

AYNSWORTH, Henry. *See* AINSWORTH, Henry

AYNSWORTH, John. *See* AINSWORTH, John

B

B1 BAERLE, Caspar van

Clachte ende Bede Der Remonstranten hier te Lande/AEN DEN . . . PRINCE VAN ORAENGIEN . . . Ghedruckt . . . By een Liefhebber des alghemeynen Vaderlandts. M.VI^{C}.XVIII. 4° pp.14

T.2248(27).

Anonymous. The civilité type in the 'imprint' was used by Nicolaes Biestkens of Amsterdam who sometimes printed Remonstrant books, but there is no proof that he is this 'lover of our country'.

B2 BAERLE, Caspar van

CASPARIS BARLAEI DISSERTATIVNCVLA. IN QVA Aliquot patriæ nostræ Theologorum ac Ecclesiastarum malesana consilia, & studia justâ orationis libertate reprehenduntur. LVGDVNI BATAVORVM, Ex Officinâ GODEFRIDI BASSON . . . 1616. 4° pp.43

700.h.7(2).

B3 BAERLE, Caspar van

[Dissertatiuncula.] DISCOVRS Oft Vertoogh van Caspar Barleus . . . Waer in . . . bestraft worden de ondeugende raedtslaghen . . . van sommige Theologanten ende Predikanten onses Vaderlandts. Wt den Latyne verduytscht/na de Copie Gedruckt tot Leyden by Govaert Basson . . . 1616. 4° sig.A-C^{4}D^{6}

T.2246(7).

The date given in the imprint refers to that of the Latin original. Probably also published in 1616.

B4 BAERLE, Caspar van

EPISTOLA ECCLESIASTARVM, Quos in Belgio Remonstrantes vocant, Ad EXTERARVM ECCLESIARVM REFORMATOS DOCTORES, PASTORES, THEOLOGOS: Qua Sententiam suam de PRÆDESTINATIONE & annexis ei capitibus exponunt, & enati aliquot abhinc annis ob hæc ipsa in Ecclesijs Belgicis, ac indies magis magisque gliscentis dissidij fontes causasque aperiunt, Oppositæ Epistolæ Delegatorum Classis Walachrianæ ad eosdem Doctores singulatim directæ. LVGDVNI BATAVORVM, Excudit Ioannes Patius . . . 1617. 4° pp.133

1560/3597.

Anonymous. With the text of the 'Epistola Delegatorum classis Walachrianæ'.

B5 BAERLE, Caspar van

Kort bewijs VAN DEN VERKEERDEN AERDT Caluminien/nieuwe/ongerijmde seditieuse en grouwelijcke opinien VAN PETER DV MOLIN GHETOGHEN Vyt sijn lest uytghegheuen boeck, ghenaemt ANATOME ARMINIANISMI Dat is Ontledinghe der Arminiaensche leeringhe. 1620. 4° pp.23

T.2250(19).

Anonymous.

B6 BAERLE, Caspar van

CASPARIS BARLÆI ORATIO DE ENTE RATIONIS. Habita in auditorio Theologico cum Logicam auspicaretur, iv.Non.Febr. Anno 1618. LVGDVNI BATAVORVM, Ex Officinâ GODEFRIDI BASSON . . . M.D.C.XVIII. 4° pp.27

525.d.13(42).

B7 BAERLE, Caspar van

THESES LOGICÆ ΠΡΟΘΕΩΡΙΑΝ CATEGORIARVM COMPLECTENTES: QVAS . . . SVB PRÆSIDIO D.CASPARI BARLÆI . . . Exercitii gratia defendere sustinebit IACOBVS RIDDERVS . . . LVGDVNI BATAVORVM Excudit Ioannes Patius . . . 1614. 8° sig. A^{6}

534.c.36(40).

B8 BAERLE, Caspar van

VALE Houdende verclaringe/In wat voeghen de SINODVS NATIONAEL TOT DORDRECHT, Den Remonstranten afscheyt heeft ghegheven. 'tIaer CHRISTI, 1619.
4° pp.36
1509/3683.

Anonymous. Translated without the author's knowledge from a submission in Latin to the Synod which was not separately issued.

BAERLE, Caspar van. Verroogh [*sic*] ende supplicatie. 1619. [Sometimes attributed to Caspar van Baerle.] *See* VERTOOGH.

B9 BAERLE, Caspar van

Vertroostinghe/Aen de Remonstrantsche Kercken hier te Lande ghesonden. Over het onrechtveerdigh BANNISSEMENT Van hare . . . Gheleerde ende ghetrouwe Predicanten/op het Nationael Synode gheciteert. Ghedruckt . . . M.DC.XIX.
4° pp.6[14]
T.2249(31).

Anonymous. The pagination runs [1]-11,4-6; the last leaf of sig.B is blank.

B10 BAHẎA IBN YUSUF; called Ibn Bākūdā

LIBRO INTITVLADO OBLIGACION DE LOS CORACONES COMPVESTO POR . . . Moseh de AEgipto. TRADVZIDO, AGORA DE NVEVO DE Hæbraico en lengua Española por Dauid Pardo . . . Emprimero de Nisan de 5370 . . . Por despesa del Señor Dauid Senior.
4° pp.261
Or.1963.b.50.

The attribution to Moses de Aegypto, i.e. Maimonides, is erroneous. First translated into Judaeo-Spanish by Tsaddik ben Joseph Formon and transcribed into roman characters by David Pardo. Printed at Amsterdam. Published in 1610.

BAILE, Guillaume. Schat-boeck der Roomscher dwalinghen. 1617. For this book, to a large extent quoting Baile's 'Catéchisme et abbregé des controverses de nostre temps' in a Dutch translation, but in fact consisting of the Dutch translation of André Rivet's confutation of it, *see* RIVET, André. Sommaire et abbregé des controverses de nostre temps.

BALADE. Op en teghen den partialen Domp-hoorn. 1603. *See* YSELVEER, Willem Jansz

BALANCE pour peser . . . la harangue du . . . seigneur Dudley Carleton. 1618. *See* TAURINUS, Jacobus. Weegh-schael.

B11 BALDERICUS; Chantre de Térouane

CHRONICON CAMERACENSE ET ATREBATENSE, SIVE HISTORIA VTRIVSQVE ECCLESIÆ, III. LIBRIS . . . conscripta A BALDERICO NOVIOMENSI ET TORNACENSI EPISCOPO. Nunc primùm in lucem edita, & Notis illustrata Per GEORGIVM COLVENERIVM . . . DVACI, Ex officina IOANNIS BOGARDI. M.DC.XV. 8° pp.607: plates; illus.
482.a.33.

The description in the title of the author as Bishop of Noyon and Tournai is due to a confusion between him and his namesake known as Chantre de Térouane.

B12 BALIN, Jean

DE BELLO BELGICO, AVSPICIIS . . . AMBROSII SPINOLÆ . . . Et . . . Archiducis Alberti ab Austria . . . Cum expositione causarum & rationis confectæ Pacis, seu Induciarum, additis Articulis, & litteris Principum ad ipsas inducias spectantibus. AVCTORE Ioan. Balino . . . BRVXELLÆ, Ex Officina Rutgeri Velpij . . . 1609. [etc.]
8° pp.174
157.a.7.

With 'Ioannis Balini poema elegiacum de pace Belgica', 'Ianus bifrons Belgicus' and other poems.

B13 BALINGHEM, Antoine de

APRESDINEES ET PROPOS DE TABLE CONTRE L'EXCES AV BOIRE, ET AV MANGER POVR VIVRE LONGVEMENT SAINEMENT ET SAINCTEMENT. DIALOGISEZ ENTRE VN PRINCE & sept scauants personnages . . . Par . . . ANTHOINE DE BALINGHEM . . . A LILLE, De l'Imprimerie de Pierre de Rache . . . 1615. [etc.] 8° pp.588
G.16487.

B14 BALINGHEM, Antoine de

ΖΩΟΠΑΙΔΕ'ΙΑ, SEV MORVM A BRVTIS PETITA INSTITVTIO ordine alphabetico TVM VIRTVTVM, TVM VITIORVM. AVTHORE. R.P. ANTONIO DE BALINGHEM . . . ANTVERPIAE, Apud MARTINVM NVTIVM, & Fratres . . . M.DC.XXI. 8° pp.637
847.d.17.

B15 BARAENUS, Justus

EPISTOLA JUSTI BARÆNI ANTWERPIANI AD AD [*sic*] THEOLOGUM REGIUM . . . ABRAHAMUM SCULTETUM . . . In qua DISSENSUS ILLE SUI CAUSAS . . . EXPONIT ET ROGAT, UT REGIÆ MAIESTATI Fides Lutheranorum candidè commendetur. ANTWERPIÆ . . . M.DC.XX. 4° pp.19
3907.aa.23(3).
The imprint appears false; probably printed in Germany.

BARBATUS, Josephus. *See* ABUDACNUS, Josephus

B16 BARCLAY, John

(tp.1) EVPHORMIONIS LVSININI SATYRICON. Multò quam ante emendatius. LEYDAE Ex officina IACOBI MARCI, MD CXIX.
(tp.2=p.139) EVPHORMIONIS LVSININI SATYRICON. PARS II. LEYDAE Ex officina IACOBI MARCI. MD CXIX.
(tp.3=p.265) EVPHORMIONIS SATYRICI APOLOGIA PRO SE. PARS III. LEYDAE Ex officina IACOBI MARCI, M D C XIX.
(tp.4=p.309) EVPHORMIONIS SATYRICI ICON ANIMORVM. PARS IV. LEYDAE Ex officina IACOBI MARCI, M D C XIX. 12° pp.478
1080.b.4.
Pseudonymous. A key identifying the characters has been added at the end in manuscript.

BARDINUS, Joannes. Positiones philosophicae. 1606. *See* JACCHAEUS, Gilbertus

BARLAAM; Saint. For editions of the legend of Barlaam and Josaphat wrongly attributed to St. John of Damascus *see* JOHN of Damascus; Saint

BARLAEUS, Caspar. *See* BAERLE, Caspar van

B17 BARLANDUS, Adrianus

[Rerum gestarum a Brabantiae ducibus historia.] CHRONIICKE VAN DE HERTOGHEN VAN BRABANT . . . verciert met de figuren nae t'leuen. Vergadert vvt diueersche Historien ende schrijuers, ende ouergheset door Laurens van Haecht Goidtsenhoven. T'HANDTVVERPEN, BY IAN BAPTISTA VRIENTS . . . M.DC.VI. (col.) TYPIS HIERONYMI VERDVSSEN. fol. pp.116; illus., map, ports.
10759.l.1.
In fact a translation of the work by Barlandus, with additional matter taken from various other listed sources, including an extended geographical section. The chapters on the dukes originally omitted by Barlandus are incorporated in their correct chronological sequence. Ending with events of 1606 and an account of the miracles of the Virgin of Scherpenheuvel. The portraits of the dukes after designs by Antonius de Succa, engraved by Philips Galle or his studio. The additional plate showing Albert and Isabella signed: Otho Vaenius inuent. Ioan. Woutneel excudit. Ioan. Collaert sculp. Interleaved with maps, portraits and historical prints of the sixteenth and seventeenth centuries.

B18 BARLANDUS, Adrianus

[Rerum gestarum a Brabantiae ducibus historia.] CHRONIICK VANDE HERTOGHEN VAN BRABANT: Verciert met hunne figuren nae t'leuen . . . Vergadert . . . ende ouergheset door Laurens van Haecht Goidtsenhouen. T'ANTWERPEN, Is te koope inden PLANTIINSCHEN WINCKEL By de Weduwe ende de Sonen van Ian Moerentorf. M.DC.XII. (col.) TYPIS HIERONYMI VERDVSSEN. fol. pp.116; illus.

155.a.17.

A reissue of the preceding, with a new titlepage and a reprint of the list of dukes and of sources on its conjugate leaf. Without the map of Brabant.

B19 BARLANDUS, Adrianus

[Rerum gestarum a Brabantiae ducibus historia.] CHRONIQUES DES DVCS DE BRABANT, Composees par ADRIAN DE BARLANDE . . . Nouuellement enrichies de leurs figures & pourtraicts. A ANVERS, Se vendent en la BOVTIQVE PLANTINIENNE, chez la Vefue & les fils de Iean Moretus. M.DC.XII. fol. pp.192; illus., ports.

591.f.18.

Translated from the Latin edition, Antwerp, 1600, arranged and with the additional chapters by Andreas Schottus, with those on the dukes originally omitted by Barlandus added at the end following the chapter on Albert and Isabella and ending with events of 1599. The portraits are the same as in the two preceding entries. The whole a reissue of an edition originally printed by Hieronymus Verdussen and published by Vrients who has signed the editor's preface and the introduction to the additional chapters on the dukes omitted by Barlandus, with a new titlepage. Without the map.

B20 BARLEMENT, Noel van

[Vocabulare.] COLLOQVIA ET DICTIONARIOLVM OCTO LINGVARVM, LATINÆ, GALLICÆ, BELGICÆ, TEVTONICÆ, HISPANICÆ, ITALICÆ, ET PORTVGALLICÆ . . . Colloques ou Dialogues . . . Colloquien oft t'samen sprekinghen . . . HAGÆ-COMITIS, Ex officinâ Hillebrandi Iacobi . . . 1613. obl.8° sig.A-Ee^8

Voyn.57.

Anonymous. Enlarged edition of the work by Noel van Barlement, edited by Jacob and Assuerus Boon. The poem 'Liber ad emtores' signed: L.B.I.B.F., i.e. Ludimagister [Assuerus] Boon Jacobi Boon Filius? Ownership inscription: Monast. B.M. Albomantellorum ord. S. Bened. Cong. S. Maurj Ex dono DD. Des Gouges. 1716.

B21 BARLOW, William; Bishop

[The summe and substance of the conference.] De Summe ende Substantie vande Conferentie de welcke syne Konincklicke Majesteyt van Groot Britannien belieft heeft te houden met de Heeren/Bisschoppen ende andere van sijn Clergie . . . opt' Hoff tot Hampton den 14. Januarij 1603. Tsamen ghestelt door Willem Barlow . . . Overgheset uyt de Engelsche Copie/ghedruckt tot London by Ian Windet . . . 1604. TOT LEYDEN, Gedruckt by Govert Basson . . . 1612. 4° pp.56[46]

T.2242(10).

B22 BARNAUD, Nicolas

DE OCCVLTA PHILOSOPHIA, Epistola cuiusdam Patris ad Filium, A NICOLAO BARNAVDO . . . Nunc primum in lucem edita . . . NIHIL SINE NVMINE. LVGDVNI BATAVORVM, Ex Officinâ Thomæ Basson . . . 1601. 8° sig.AB^8

1033.e.30(1); 234.a.24(1).

B23 BARNAUD, Nicolas

TRACTATVLVS CHEMICVS, THEOSOPHIAE PALMARIVM dictus, Anonymi cuiusdam Philosophi antiqui A NICOLAO BARNAVDO . . . nunc primum editus, & AVRIGA Ad quadrigam auriferam, quam superiore anno emisit, ducendam factus . . . NIHIL SINE NVMINE. LVGDVNI BATAVORVM, Ex Officinâ Thomæ Basson . . . 1601.
8° sig. A-C^8D^2
1033.e.30(2); 234.a.24(2).

B24 BARNES, Robert; Chaplain

[Vitae Romanorum Pontificum.] SCRIPTORES DVO ANGLICI, Coætanei ac Conterranei; DE VITIS PONTIFICVM ROMANORVM. VIDELICET: ROBERTVS BARNS, & IOHANNES BALEVS Quos A tenebris vindicavit, veterum testimonijs . . . confirmavit, & vsque ad PAVLVM QVINTVM hodie regnantem continuavit IOHANNES MARTINI LYDIVS . . . LVGDVNI BATAVORVM, Excudebat Georgius Abrahami A Marsse, 1615. Sumptibus Henrici Laurentij Biblipolæ Amstelodamensis. [etc.]
8° pp. 264, 587, 358
484.a.21; G.19554.

Consisting of 'Vitae Romanorum Pontificum' by Barnes, 'Acta Romanorum Pontificum' by Bale and additional chapters by Lydius.

B25 BARONIUS, Caesar; Cardinal

(general tp.) ANNALES ECCLESIASTICI, AVCTORE CÆSARE BARONIO . . . Tomis duodecim distincti. Nouissima Editio, postremùm ab Auctore aucta et recognita. ANTVERPIÆ EX OFFICINA PLANTINIANA Apud Viduam et Filios Io. Moreti. M.DC.XII.
(tp. 1) ANNALES ECCLESIASTICI, AVCTORE CÆSARE BARONIO . . . Tomus Primus. Nouissima Editio . . . ANTVERPIÆ Ex officina Plantiniana, M.DC.X. (col. 1) ANTVERPIÆ, EX OFFICINA PLANTINIANA, APVD IOANNEM MORETVM. M.DC.X.
(tp. 2) ANNALES ECCLESIASTICI, AVCTORE CÆSARE BARONIO . . . Tomus Secundus. Editio nouissima. ANTVERPIAE Ex officina Plantiniana, M.D.XCVII. (col. 2) ANTVERPIAE EX OFFICINA PLANTINIANA APVD IOANNEM MORETVM . . . M.D.XCVII.
(tp. 3) ANNALES ECCLESIASTICI, AVCTORE CÆSARE BARONIO . . . Tomus Tertius. Editio nouissima. ANTVERPIAE Ex officina Plantiniana, M.D.XCVIII. (col. 3) ANTVERPIAE EX OFFICINA PLANTINIANA, APVD IOANNEM MORETVM . . . M.D.XCVIII.
(tp. 4) ANNALES ECCLESIASTICI, AVCTORE CÆSARE BARONIO . . . Tomus Quartus. Editio nouissima. ANTVERPIAE Ex officina Plantiniana, M.D.CI.
(tp. 5) ANNALES ECCLESIASTICI AVCTORE CÆSARE BARONIO . . . Tomus Quintus. Editio nouissima. ANTVERPIAE Ex officina Plantiniana, M.D.CI.
(tp. 6) ANNALES ECCLESIASTICI, AVCTORE CÆSARE BARONIO . . . Tomus Sextus. Editio nouissima. ANTVERPIAE Ex officina Plantiniana, M.D.CIII. (col. 6) ANTVERPIAE, EX OFFICINA PLANTINIANA, APVD IOANNEM MORETVM . . . M.D C II.
(tp. 7) ANNALES ECCLESIASTICI, AVCTORE CÆSARE BARONIO . . . Tomus Septimus. Editio nouissima. ANTVERPIAE Ex officina Plantiniana, M.D.CIII. (col. 7) ANTVERPIAE, EX OFFICINA PLANTINIANA, APVD VIDVAM ET FILIOS IOANNIS MORETI. M.DC.XI.
(tp. 8) ANNALES ECCLESIASTICI, AVCTORE CÆSARE BARONIO. Tomus Octauus. ANTVERPIAE Ex officina Plantiniana, M.D.C.
(tp. 9) ANNALES ECCLESIASTICI, AVCTORE CÆSARE BARONIO. Tomus Nonus. ANTVERPIAE Ex officina Plantiniana, M.D.C.I. (col. 9) ANTVERPIAE, EX OFFICINA PLANTINIANA, APVD IOANNEM MORETVM . . . M.DCI.
(tp. 10) ANNALES ECCLESIASTICI, AVCTORE CÆSARE BARONIO. Tomus Decimus. ANTVERPIAE Ex officina Plantiniana, M.DC.III. (col. 10) ANTVERPIAE, EX OFFICINA PLANTINIANA, APVD IOANNEM MORETVM . . . M.DC.III.
(tp. 11) ANNALES ECCLESIASTICI, AVCTORE CÆSARE BARONIO. Tomus Vndecimus. ANTVERPIÆ Ex officina Plantiniana, M.DC.VIII. (col. 11) ANTVERPIAE, EX OFFICINA PLANTINIANA, APVD VIDVAM ET FILIOS IOANNIS MORETI. M.DC.XII.

(tp.12) ANNALES ECCLESIASTICI, AVCTORE CÆSARE BARONIO. Tomus Duodecimus. ANTVERPIAE Ex officina Plantiniana, M.DC.IX. (col.12) ANTVERPIÆ, EX OFFICINA PLANTINIANA, APVD IOANNEM MORETVM. M.DC.IX.
fol. 12 tom.: pp.747; 819; 785; 746; 696; 696; 731; 708; 908; 972; 747; 943; illus., port.
486.g.1–12.
All the titlepages are engraved. tom.4,5,8 have no colophon. tom.8–12 no longer described as 'latest edition'. In a hitherto unidentified armorial binding.

B26 BARRA, Jacobus
DISPVTATIO INAVGVRALIS DE CALCVLO RENVM, Quam . . . Pro supremo in Medicina gradu, privilegijsque Doctoratus obtinendis, publicè Disputandam proponit IACOBVS BARRA . . . ad diem 15. Iulij. 1610 . . . LVGDVNI BATAVORVM, Ex officina THOMÆ BASSON. 4° sig.A^4
1185.g.1(38); 7306.f.6(21*).

B27 BARRADAS, Sebastianus
SEBASTIANI BARRADAS . . . ITINERARIVM FILIORVM ISRAEL EX ÆGYPTO IN TERRA REPROMISSIONIS. Opus varium . . . PRODIT NVNC PRIMVM. Quatuor indicibus insignitum . . . ANTVERPIÆ, Apud Hieronymum Verdussium. M.DC.XXI. [etc.]
fol. pp.890
690.h.12.

BARREIROS, Gaspar. Commentarius de Ophyra regione. 1616. *See* NOVUS orbis.

B28 BARTHOLAMEU dos Martyres; Dominican, Archbishop
[Compendium spiritualis doctrinae.] ABBREGE' DE LA DOCTRINE SPRITIVELLE, Recueilly la plus part de diuerses sentences des saincts Peres par . . . BARTHOLOMY DES MARTIRS . . . Mis en lumiere à l'instance du Sainct Personnage F. LOVYS DE GRENADE . . . Et traduit de Latin en François par IAN DE LA RIVIERE Cheualier Sr. de VVarnes. A DOVAY, De l'Imprimerie de BALTAZAR BELLERE . . . 1620. 12° pp.498
1650/1.
With an ornament containing the initials L.K., i.e. the printer Laurence Kellam the Younger at Douai.

B29 BASE, P. vanden
Ontdeckinghe Vande valsche Munte/Die Samuel Beyer aende Post-bode van HENRICVS SLATIVS tot een Loon heeft willen gheven. Op de Toetse ghestelt/Door P, V, BASE . . . Ghedruckt by Matthijs Bastiaensz , 1617. 4° sig.A B^4C^2
T.2247(8).
Signed: P. vanden Base. Printed at Rotterdam.

B30 BASE, P. vanden
Sekere Vraghen aen D. BALTHAZAR LYDIUS, Predicant tot Dordrecht/om daer over met hem in nader Conferentie te treden . . . Ghedruct tot Rotterdam, 1618. fol. a single sheet
T.2248(38).
Signed and dated: P. vanden Base. Rotterdam, 5 May 1618. Printed by Matthijs Bastiaensz?

B31 BASELIUS, Jacobus; the Younger
IACOBI BASELII, FIL. DE OBSIDIONE BERGOPZOMI, AD EIVS VRBIS SENATVM COMMENTARIVS. BERGOPZOMII. Ex officinâ Jacobi Canini . . . M.DCIII. 4° pp.55
1055.g.37(3).
A Dutch edition was published the same year, but the Latin version apparently is the original.

B32 BASELIUS, Jacobus; the Younger

Historisch-verhael inhoudende sekere notable explooten van Oorloge in de Nederlanden, sedert het oprechten van de Companien der Heerē Gouverneurs eñ Ritmeesteren vā PAVLUS ende MARCELIS BAX . . . beschrevē do[or] IACOBUM BASELIUM. TOT BREDA, By Isaac Schilders, 1615. 4° pp.149; ports.
1197.e.29.

The titlepage is engraved and contains the equestrian portraits of P. and M. Bax. The editors' preface signed: De kinderen Iacobi Baselij. The titlepage is slightly mutilated.

B33 BASIL; Saint, Bishop

BASILII SELEVCIÆ IN ISAVRIA EPISCOPI De Vita ac Miraculis D. THECLAE Virginis Martyris Iconiensis LIBRI DVO. SIMEONIS METAPHRASTÆ LOGOTHETÆ de eadem MARTYRE Tractatus singularis. PETRVS PANTINVS TILETANVS . . . è tenebris nunc primùm eruit, Latinè vertit, notisque illustrauit. ANTVERPIÆ, EX OFFICINA PLANTINIANA, Apud Ioannem Moretum. M.DC.VIII. (col.) ANTVERPIÆ, EX OFFICINA PLANTINIANA, Apud Ioannem Moretum. M.DC.VIII. 4° pp.291; illus.
487.h.21.

The titlepage engraving shows the arms of Philip III, the other illustration consists of a centrepiece showing St. Thecla and the lion, surrounded by scenes from her life, the whole engraved.

B34 BASSON, Fredericus

THESES MEDICÆ DE APOPLEXIA, quas . . . PRO GRADV DOCTORATVS in MEDICINA consequendo discutiendas proponit FREDERICVS BASSON . . . LVGDVNI BATAVORVM, Excudebat THOMAS BASSON, 1611. 4° sig.A^4
7306.f.6(1).

BASUYNE der waerheyt. 1617. *See* DRIELENBURCH, Vincent van

BASUYNE. Dienende om . . . slapende zielen yverich . . . te maken. 1620. *See* ENGELRAEVE, Petrus

B35 BATAVUS

DE MACVLIS IN SOLE ANIMADVERSIS, &, tanquam ab APELLE, in tabulâ spectandum in publicâ luce expositis, BATAVI DISSERTATIVNCVLA: AD . . . CORNELIVM VANDER-MILIVM . . . EX OFFICINA PLANTINIANA RAPHELENGII, M.D.C.XII. 4° pp.18
531.l.44(7).

Published at Leiden.

BATTAEFSCHE vrienden-spieghel. 1615. *See* KOLM, Jan Siewertsz

B36 BATTUS, Johannes

THESES MEDICÆ DE EPILEPSIA, Quas . . . Pro insignibus Doctoralibus in arte Medica consequendis, tueri conabitur . . . IOHANNES BATTVS . . . LUGDUNI BATAVORUM, Ex Officinâ Ioannis Patii . . . M.D.CIII. 4° sig.A^5
7306.f.6(2).

B37 BAUCE, Jean

COPIE D'VNE LETTRE contenant la description de l'entrée triomphale de Don Pedro de Tholedo faicte à Fontainebleau, le dixneufiesme de Iuillet, 1608. Ensemble un Sonet & quelques petits Discours sur la mort de Bartholomæo Borghese, executé à Paris, le vingtiesme de Novembre, l'an 1608. A VENISE, Par Corneille le Caillier . . . 1609. 4° sig.A^4
T.2420(23).

Signed: Jean Bauce. The imprint is false; probably printed in the Netherlands.

B38 BAUDAERT, Willem

AF-BEELDINGE Der Coninghinne Elyzabeth: des Conincks Iacobi.VI. De Coninginne Annæ syner Vrouwe: ende Henrici Frederici des Princen van Wallia. Met een corte beschrijvinghe haerer Stammen, als oock haerer aencomste, tot de Croone van Engelandt . . . Wt verscheyden Historien vergadert/ende . . . wtghegheven/Door W.B. Lief-hebber der Historien. T'AMSTELREDAM, By Willem Ianszoon, de Veen Boeckdrucker, [etc.] 4° pp.32

10806.bb.4.

Anonymous. Issued without portraits. Published 1603 or 1604. The standard form of the publisher's name is Willem Jansz van Campen.

B39 BAUDAERT, Willem

AF-BEELDINGE Der Coninghinne Elyzabeth . . . wtghegheven/Door W.B. Lief-hebber der Historien. T'AERNHEM, By Ian Ianszoon, [etc.]
(add. tp., engraved) REGIAE ANGLICAE Maiestatis pictura, et Historica declaratio. COLONIAE apud Crispianum Passæum . . . 1604. 4° pp.32; plates.

G.6182.

Another issue of the preceding, with the addition of six plates by Crispin van de Passe the Elder, bearing Latin captions, some signed: Matth. Quad. ludebat. The plates were also published separately at Cologne in 1604.

B40 BAUDAERT, Willem

[Afbeeldinghe ende beschrijvinghe van alle de veldslagen.] (tp.1) LES GVERRES DE NASSAV. Descriptes par Guillaume Baudart . . . A Amsterdam, Chez Michel Colin . . . 1616. On les vend a Paris chez Melchior Tavernier au Pont Marchands.
(add. tp., engraved) Pourtraits en taille douce, Et Descriptions des Sieges, Batailles . . . & autres choses advenues durant les Guerres des Pays bas . . . A Amsterdam, Chez Michel Colin . . . 1616. [etc.]
(tp.2) SECOND TOME DV LIVRE INTITVLE LES GVERRES DE NASSAV . . . Par Guillaume Baudart . . . A AMSTERDAM, Chez Michel Colin de Thovoyon . . . 1616. [etc.] obl.4° 2 tom.: pp.466; 493; illus., map

591.b.6.

The illustrations are based on those of Frans Hogenberg in 'Nederlandsche geschiedenissen', engraved by Simon Frisius. The portraits are by various artists. All engravings have Latin captions or verses. The engraved map is of the XVII Provinces. This copy agrees on the whole with the description of other copies in the *Bibliotheca Belgica* no. B113, but illustrations 53 and 239 are correctly printed in this copy, while illustration 5 has been pasted over one originally wrongly printed in this place.

B41 BAUDAERT, Willem

[Afbeeldinghe ende beschrijvinghe van alle de veldslagen.] (tp.1) Viva delineatio, ac Descriptio omnium præliorum, obsidionum, aliarumque rerum memoratu dignarum, quæ, durante bello adversus Hispaniarum Regem in Belgij provincijs, sub ductu ac moderamine Guilelmi & Mauritij . . . Principum auspicijs Potentissimorum Ordinum Generalium, gestæ sunt. Amstelodami, Apud Michaelem Colinum . . . 1622. [etc.]
(tp.2) POLEMOGRAPHIAE NASSOVICÆ PARS SECUNDA . . . Authore GVILHELMO BAVDARTIO . . . AMSTELODAMI, apud Michaëlem Colinum . . . 1621. obl. 4° 2 pt.: pp.454; 382; illus.

1486.gg.16.

Tp.1 is engraved, followed by a half-title reading: Polemographia Auraico-Belgica, scriptore Wilhelmo Baudartio Deinsiano Flandro. The plates, as in the preceding, engraved by Simon Frisius. The edition corresponds to the one described in the *Bibliotheca Belgica* no. B114 as for some copies with illustrations 108–109 and 146–147 transposed.

B42 BAUDAERT, Willem

IAER-CLACHTE Over den schreckelijcken Moort begaen aen HENRICVM IIII. Coninck van Vranckrijck ende Nauarre/ den XIV. dach May . . . 1610. Mitsgaeders een cort verhael der geboorte/kindtsche jaeren/ende treffelijcke daeden deses Conincks. Verrijckt met vele . . . Historyen? [*sic*] T'saemen ghestelt ende beschreuen Door WILHELMVM BAVDARTIVM. T'AERNHEM Ghedruckt by Jan Janszen . . . 1611. 4° pp.94
114.k.12.

B43 BAUDAERT, Willem

Morghen-wecker der vrye Nederlantsche Provintien: ofte, Een cort verhael van de bloedighe vervolghinghen ende wreetheden door de Spanjaerden ende haere Adherenten inde Nederlanden, gheduerende deese veertich-jarighe Troublen ende Oorloghen, begaen . . . Tot Dansvvick, by Crijn Vermeulen de Jonge, op de leege zijde van Schotlandt . . . 1610. 4° sig. *A-L^4
106.d.32.

The dedication signed: G.W.B.F.V.D., i.e. Guilielmus Wilhelmi Baudartii Filius van Deynze. The imprint is false. The edition is that described in the *Bibliotheca Belgica* no. B99.

B44 BAUDAERT, Willem

Morghen-wecker der vrye Nederlantsche Provintien. Ofte, Een cort verhael van de bloedighe vervolginghen ende wreetheden door de Spaenjaerden ende hare Adherenten inde Nederlanden, gheduerende dese veertich-jarighe Troublen ende Oorloghen begaen . . . Tot Danswick, bij Crijn Vermeulen de Jonge, op de leege zijde van Schotlandt . . . 1610. 4° sig.(.˙.)A-L^4
T.1713(29).

The dedication signed: G.W.B.F.V.D., i.e. Guilielmus Wilhelmi Baudartii Filius van Deynze. The imprint is false. In this edition leaf L2 is wrongly signed Kij. The edition corresponds to the one described in the *Bibliotheca Belgica* no. B103.

B45 BAUDAERT, Willem

[Morghen-wecker.] De Spaensche Tiranije. Dienende tot een Morghen-wecker Der Vrye Nederlantsche Provintien [etc.] (col.) Na de Copye tot Danswijck, by Crijn Vermeulen de Jonghe, op de leeghe zijde van Schotlant. 4° ff.36; illus.
8079.d.8.

Another edition of Baudaert's 'Morghen-wecker'. Published ca.1620. The edition is that described in the *Bibliotheca Belgica* no. B106. The engraved titlepage border shows eight scenes of events.

BAUDAERT, Willem. Viva delineatio, ac descriptio omnium prœliorum. 1622,21. *See* supra: Afbeeldinghe ende beschrijvinghe van alle de veldslagen.

B46 BAUDIUS, Dominicus

[Collections] DOMINICI BAVDII ORATIONES Quatuor, I. Ad Studiosos Leidenses, II. In obitum Iosephi Scaligeri, III. Ad Elizabetham Angliæ Reginam, IV. Ad Iacobum VI. Magnæ Britanniæ Regem, Nunc primum coniunctim editæ. LVGDVNI BATAVORVM, Apud Iacobum Marci, M D C XVII. (col.) Lugduni Batavorum, Excudebat Georgius Abrahami a Marsse, 1617. 8° pp.138
1090.f.4.

B47 BAUDIUS, Dominicus

[Collections] DOMINICI BAVDI ORATIONES QVÆ EXSTANT, Quarum maior pars nunc primum prodit Ex Bibliotheca IANI RVTGERSI, Edente Matthiâ Byvortio. LVGDVNI BATAVORVM. Typis IACOBI MARCI. M D CXIX. (col.) LVGDVNI BATAVORVM. M D C XIX. 8° pp.415
1090.h.4(2).

B48 BAUDIUS, Dominicus
[Letters] (tp.1) DOMINICI BAUDII EPISTOLARVM Centuriæ duæ. Accedunt Epistolæ Clarorum Virorum AD D. BAVDIVM, ET Prolixa DAN. HEINSII inter Baudianas reperta, in qua agitur: An, & qualis literato viro uxor sit ducenda. Item ejusdem D. BAVDII Commentariolus DE FOENORE. LVGDVNI BATAVORVM Apud GODEFRIDUM BASSON. M.D.C.XV.
(tp.2) DOMINICI BAVDII . . . DE FOENERE Commentariolus. LVGDVNI BATAVORVM, Apud GODEFRIDVM BASSON. M.DC.XV. 8° pp.599; 25
1084.h.11.

B49 BAUDIUS, Dominicus
[Letters] DOMINICI BAVDII . . . EPISTOLARVM Centuriæ tres. Quarum TERTIA nunc in lucem emissa. LVGDVNI BATAVORVM. Apud Godefridum Basson. M D CXX. 8° pp.732; illus., port.
1084.h.12.
With a biographical sketch, a list of his works and a commemorative poem by Janus Gruterus. The portrait of Baudius is engraved. From the library of John Morris.

BAUDIUS, Dominicus. De foenore commentariolus. 1615. *See* supra: Letters

B50 BAUDIUS, Dominicus
LIBRI TRES DE INDVCIIS BELLI BELGICI AVTHORE DOMINICO BAVDIO . . . LVGDVNI BATAVORVM, Apud LVDOVICVM ELZEVIRIVM . . . M.D C XIII. 4° pp.318
C.74.c.15.
With laudatory poems in Greek by Daniel Heinsius and in French by Richard Iean de Nerée.

B51 BAUDIUS, Dominicus
LIBRI TRES DE INDVCIIS BELLI BELGICI. AVCTORE DOMINICO BAVDIO . . . SECVNDA EDITIO. LVGDVNI BATAVORVM, Apud Ludovicum Elzevirium . . . M. DC XVII. (col.) LVGDVNI BATAVORVM. Excudebat ISAACVS ELZEVIRIVS . . . M D CXVII. 8° pp.343
1055.a.3(2); 156.b.16.
With the laudatory poems in Greek by Daniel Heinsius.

B52 BAUDIUS, Dominicus
[De induciis belli Belgici.] VAN'T BESTANT DES Nederlantschen Oorloghs/Drie Boecken: BESCHREVEN DOOR DOMINICVM BAVDIVM . . . Vertaelt door P. Iacobi Austro-Sylvium. 't AMSTERDAM, By Dirck Pietersz . . . 1616. 4° pp.240: plates
T.2419(1).
The translator's full name is Pieter Jacobsz Semmes van Suyderwoude. The plates sometimes said to be by or after Simon Frisius.

B53 BAUDIUS, Dominicus
DISSERTATIVNCVLA SVPER INDVCIIS BELLI BELGICI. Auctore LATINO PACATO . . . M.D.C.IX. 4° pp.20
1508/42.
Pseudonymous and without imprint. Probably printed by Thomas Basson at Leiden.

B54 BAUDIUS, Dominicus
DOMINICI BAVDII EPICEDIVM DICTVM honori & felici memoriæ . . . IACOBI ARMINII . . . ACCEDVNT HVGONIS GROTII . . . Epicedia in eundem. LVGDVNI-BATAVORVM, Apud Andream Cloucquium . . . M.D.C.IX. Typis H. ab Haestens. 4° sig. A-D^4; illus., port.
835.g.14(2).
The portrait of Arminius is engraved.

BAUDIUS, Dominicus. Gnomæ. 1607. *See* infra: Poemata. Selections

B55 BAUDIUS, Dominicus

MONVMENTVM consecratum honori & memoriæ . . . BRITANNIARVM PRINCIPIS HENRICI FREDERICI Authore DOMINICO BAVDIO . . . LVGDVNI BATAVORVM, Ex officina Ulrici Cornelij & Georgij Abrahami. Impensis Iohannis Ganne . . . M D CXII. 4° sig.A-C[4]
1070.l.6(3).

B56 BAUDIUS, Dominicus

DOM. BAVDII . . . ORATIO Ad Studiosos Leidenses ob cædem commilitonis tumultuantes, EDENTE IANO RVTGERSIO. LVGDVNI-BATAVORVM, Excudebat Henricus ab Haestens, M.D.C.IX. 8° pp.142
1055.a.3(1).

With 'Eadem oratio versibus expressa auctore Dominico Baudio' and with a laudatory poem in French by Richard Jean de Nerée.

B57 BAUDIUS, Dominicus

DOMINICI BAVDII I.C. ORATIO DICTA IN ILLUSTRI BATAVORUM ACADEMIA XVII IUNII M.D.CIII. Cum auspicaretur C. PLINII PANEGYRICUM AD TRAJANUM AUG. LUGDUNI BATAVORUM, Ex Officinâ Ioannis Patii . . . M.D.CIII. 4° sig.A[4]B[6]
837.h.13(19).

Author's presentation copy to Isaac Casaubon.

B58 BAUDIUS, Dominicus

ORATIO FVNEBRIS Dicta honori & memoriæ . . . IOSEPHI IVSTI SCALIGERI. Auctore D. BAVDIO . . . LVGDVNI BATAVORVM. Prostant apud Ludov. Elzevirium, & Andream Cloucquium . . . 1609. 4° pp.23
610.k.17(2); 133.c.19(2).

With 'Sonnet acrostique sur le mesme' by Richard Jean de Nerée. Printed by Jan Paets Jacobszoon at Leiden?

B59 BAUDIUS, Dominicus

DOMINICI BAVDII POEMATVM NOVA EDITIO . . . LVGDVNI BATAVORVM, Ex officina Thomæ Basson, M D CVII. 8° pp.601
1213.h.11.

The poems are in Latin or Greek.

B60 BAUDIUS, Dominicus

DOMINICI BAVDII POEMATVM NOVA EDITIO, tertiâ parte nunc locupletata, & in concinniorem ordinem redacta. Accedit Autoris Vita, & Epitaphia. LVGDVNI BATAVORVM, Ex Officina GODEFRIDI BASSON, M D C XVI. 8° pp.614, 216
1213.h.12.

From the library of John Morris.

B61 BAUDIUS, Dominicus

DOMINICI BAVDII POEMATVM NOVA EDITIO . . . LVGDVNI BATAVORVM, Ex Officina GODERFRIDI BASSON, M D C XVI. 8° pp.614, 216
1578/7197.

Another issue of the preceding, with a cancel titlepage lacking the printer's dedication to the States General on the verso. Ownership inscription: James Hilton, 1888.

B62 BAUDIUS, Dominicus

[Poemata. Selections] DOMINICI BAVDEI GNOMÆ COMMENTARIO ILLVSTRATÆ. LVGODVNI [*sic*] BATAVORVM Ex Officina Thomæ Basson. M D CVII. 8° pp.88
1120.a.1(1).

Compiled and edited by Carolus Scribani as part of the polemics between him and Baudius. The imprint is false; in fact, printed at Antwerp, possibly by Joachim Trognaesius.

BAUDIUS, Dominicus. Van't bestant des Nederlantschen oorloghs. 1616. *See* supra: De induciis belli Belgici.

B63 BAUHUSIUS, Bernardus

BERNARDI BAVHVSII . . . EPIGRAMMATVM SELECTORVM LIBRI V. ANTVERPIÆ, EX OFFICINA PLANTINIANA, Apud Viduam & Filios Io. Moreti. M.DC.XVI. 12° pp.116
11409.a.8.

Printed throughout in italics. With the author's (?) dedication to Petrus Scriverius on the titlepage.

B64 BAUHUSIUS, Bernardus

BERNARDI BAVHVSII . . . EPIGRAMMATVM LIBRI V. Editio altera, auctior. ANTVERPIÆ, EX OFFICINA PLANTINIANA, Apud Balthasarem Moretum, & Viduam Ioannis Moreti, & Io. Meursium. M.DC.XX. (col.) ANTVERPIAE, Ex OFFICINA PLANTINIANA BALTHASARIS MORETI. M.DC.XX. 12° pp.135
11403.a.41(1).

B65 BAXIUS, Nicasius

H.P.F.NICASI BAXI . . . POEMATA . . . ANTVERPIÆ, Ex Officina Hieronymi VerdussI . . . MDC.XIV. [etc.] 8° pp.211
1213.h.17.

Partly in both Latin and Greek. Ownership inscriptions: M. B. Collegij Soct[is] Jesv Loua; J. Fazakerley 1799.

B67 BAY, Jacobus de

DE VENERABILI EVCHARISTIÆ SACRAMENTO ET SACRIFICIO LIBRI III. Quorum PRIMVS CONTRA SACRAMENTARIOS . . . SECVNDVS CONTRA LVTHERANOS . . . TERTIVS DE SACRIFICIO . . . Vnà cum totius missæ ac sacrarum vestium expositione, canonisq̃ue Paraphrasi. Auctore IACOBO BAYO . . . LOVANII, Ex officina GERARDI RIVII . . . M.DCV. 8° pp.406[418]
4324.f.14.

B68 BAYNES, Roger

THE BAYNES OF AQVISGRANE, The I. Part, & I. Volume, INTITVLED VARIETY. Contayning Three Bookes . . . vnder the Titles . . . PROFIT, PLEASVRE, HONOVR . . . Related by ROG. BAYNE S . . . Printed at Augusta in Germany. M.DC.XVII. 4° pp.112; illus.
C.107.b.33.

The part entitled 'Profit' only; no more published. The imprint is false; in fact, printed by the English College press at St. Omer. The illustration consists of a heraldic woodcut.

B69 BEATI

BEATI GOSVINI VITA CELEBERRIMI AQUICINCTENSIS MONASTERII ABBATIS SEPTIMI, A DVOBVS DIVERSIS eiusdem cœnobij Monachis separatim exarata, E VETERIBVS MS. NVNC PRIMVM EDITA. Cura . . . RICHARDI GIBBONI . . . DVACI, Ex Officinâ MARCI WYON . . . M.DC.XX. 8° pp.274
1126.a.3.

BECA, Johannes de. *See* BEKA, Johannes de

B70 BECANUS, Martinus

[De iudice controversiarum.] A TREATISE OF THE IVDGE OF CONTROVERSIES. WRITTEN In Latin, by . . . Martinus Becanus . . . AND Englished by W. W. Gent . . . M.DC.XIX. 8° pp.170
C.26.k.10.

The translator is William Wright, S. J. Without imprint; published by the English College press at St. Omer.

B71 BECANUS, Martinus

[Dissidium Anglicarum de primatu regis.] THE ENGLISH IARRE. OR DISAGREEMENT AMONGST the Ministers of great Brittaine, CONCERNING the KINGES Supremacy. VVritten in Latin by . . . F. MARTINVS BECANVS . . . And translated into English by I.W.P. . . . M.DC.XII. 4° pp.62

3936.bbb.33.

The translator is John Wilson, Priest. Without imprint; published by the English College press at St. Omer.

B72 BECLACH

Beclach gedaen vanden Praechschen Hoff-Kock, vande Wintermaent des Jaers/ ouer den verdreuen Coninck van Bohemen. 'THantwerpen [*sic*]/By Abraham Verhoeuen/[etc.] (col.) Ghedruckt int Iaer 1621. 4° pp.7; sig.A^4; illus.

P.P.3444.af.(169).

A satirical poem. The titlepage woodcut shows the cook in his kitchen.

B73 BEDENCKEN

BEDENCKEN, Op de Aggreatie des Conincx van Spangien/gestelt in forma van stamen-spreeckinghe [*sic*] tusschen Swaar-hooft ende Truert-niet. Noch zijn hier-bij gevoeght, De Articulen gesloten bij den Hertoghe Alba, ende zijnen nieuwen Raadt van XII. Getranslateert uyt d'Originale Spaansche Articulen . . . Item, Een Extract . . . uyt een Boecxken Gedruckt in-den Jare 1576. geintituleert/ Vertoogh ende Openinge, om een goede ende zalige Vrede te maken in deze Neder-Landen. In welcke de dobbelheyt ende Bloedt-dorstichheyt der Spaangiaarden . . . ontdeckt werdt. Door eenen Patriot voor eenige weken t'samen gestelt, ende nu . . . in't licht ghebracht . . . Ghedruckt in den jare onzes HEEREN . . . M.D.C.VIII. 4° sig. AB^4

106.d.11(1).

Ending: HEERE! behoedt u Volck voor schandt: End' beschermt ons lieve Vader-Landt.

B74 BEDENCKEN

BEDENCKEN Opde Aggreatie des Conincx van Spangien/gestelt in forma van tsamensprekinge tusschen Svvaer-hooft ende Truert-niet. Noch zijn hier by ghevoeght De Articulen ghesloten by den Hartoghe van Alba ende synen nieuwen Raedt van XIJ. Ghetranslateert wt d'originale Spaensche Articulen . . . Item, Een Extract . . . wt een Boecxken ghedruct inden jare 1576. gheintituleert Vertooch ende openinghe, om een goede . . . Vrede te maken . . . Door eenen Patriot voor eenighe vveken tsamen ghestelt, ende nu . . . in het licht ghebracht . . . Buyten EMBDEN, By Johan van Oldersum. Anno M.D.C.VJJJ. 4° sig.AB^4

1607/4226.

Ending: Heere! behoedt u Volck voor schandt/ End' beschermt ons lieve Vader-landt. The imprint is false. This edition and the preceding are based one upon the other, but it is difficult to decide which is the original one. The choice made here supposes that the misprint 'stamen-spreeckinghe' precedes the correct form 'tsamensprekinge'.

BEDENCKINGEN, over de beroepinghe D.D. Conradi Vorstii. 1611. *See* HOLLAND. Staten [29.4.1611]

BEDENCKINGHEN over den staet vande vereenichde Nederlanden. 1608. *See* USSELINCX, Willem

BEELDENAER ofte figuer-boeck. Various dates. *See* HOLLAND. Staten, or NETHERLANDS. United Provinces. Staten Generaal, then according to the date of the decree fixing the value of money to which the particular edition relates.

B75 BEKA, Johannes de

(tp.1) HISTORIA VETERVM EPISCOPORVM VLTRAIECTINÆ SEDIS, & COMITVM

*[Illustration of **B76** overleaf]*

De Ominoso Sereniss.ᵗ Principis ALBERTI Archid. Austriæ, Maximiliani II. Inuictiß.ᵢ Romann. Imp. Filij, vnà cum Sereniss.ᵃ ISABELLA CLARA EVGENIA, Potētiß.ᵢ Monar. PHILIPPI II. Hispp. Indd. Q. Regis filia eius vxore, Belgicæ Dominorum, in eandem Belgicā aduētu. Aᵒ. Do. 1599.

Alba daret Belgis quondam cecinere Sybillæ,
Albo qui Princeps aduehezetur equo.
ALBERTVM VXOREMQVE simul Cognomine vtrosque
AVSTRIADES, Albis Belgica vidit equis.
Bruxellam Hispanis grati vt vectantur ab oris
Belgarum Domini Rege iubente Patre.
ALBA igitur, bello ALBERTE atque ISABELLA fugato,
Nunc date Belgiacis, Belgica vosque Beet.

HOLLANDIÆ, EXPLICATA Chronico Iohannis de Beca . . . ab anno nativitatis Christi usque ad annum 1345. ET Historia Guilhelmi Hedæ . . . completa Appendice usque ad annum Christi 1574. AVCTORE SVFFRIDO PETRI . . . BERNARDO FURMERIO . . . recensente, & notis illustrante. FRANEQVERÆ, Excudebat ROMBERTVS DOYEMA. M.D.CXII.
(tp.2) HISTORIA EPIScoporum Trajectensium, AUCTORE VVILHELMO HEDA . . . FRANEQVERÆ, Excudebat ROMBERTVS DOYEMA. M.D.CXII. 4° pp.426
4661.e.19.
The second titlepage, together with a leaf bearing a dedication, has been inserted between pp.192, 193. With manuscript notes.

BELGIAE pacificatorum vera delineatio. 1608. *See* HONDIUS, Henrik; the Elder.

BELIJDENISSE ofte verklaringhe van't ghevoelen der leeraren. 1621. *See* EPISCOPIUS, Simon

BELLARMINO, Roberto; Cardinal. *See* ROBERT Bellarmino; Saint

BELLEROPHON, of lust tot wysheyd. 1614. *See* PERS, Dirck Pietersz

B76 BELLEVILLE, Philippe de
THEATRE D'HISTOIRE. OV̀, AVEC LES GRĀD'S PROÜESSES ET Auentures êtranges, du Noble et Vertueux Cheualier, POLIMANTES, PRINCE D'ARFINE, se representent au vrâi, plusieurs occurences . . . tant de paix, que de guerre; arriuées de son temps, es plus celebres & renommés Päis, Roiaumes, et Prouinces du monde. OÊVRE, NON MOINS PLAISANT' ET agreable, qu'vtile, et propre à tous Princes, Cheualiers, Seigneurs, Dames et Demòiselles, et autres Amateurs de Vertu, du siecle present . . . À BRVXELLES. Chés Rutger Velpius & Hubert Ant. . . . 1613. 4° pp.588; illus.
86.g.20.
The dedication signed: Philippe de Belleville. The titlepage is engraved, as are the illustrations showing the entry of Albert and Isabella in Brussels and a text in memory of Philip II.

B77 BELLI
BELLI BOHEMICI Origo, PROGRESSVS, & finis . . . ANTVERPIÆ, Apud Abrahamum Verhœuium, M.DC.XX. [etc.] 4° pp.8; sig. B^4; illus.
P.P.3444.af(149).
The titlepage illustration shows a castle and bears the woodcut inscription: CAƧTEE VAN PRAGE, with a letterpress caption, ARX PRAGENSIS, above.

BELONIUS, Hieronymus. Theses philosophicae de primis naturalium principiis, 1602. *See* MURDISONIUS, Joannes

B78 BENEDETTI, Pietro
IL MAGICO LEGATO Tragicomedia Pastorale di Pietro Benedetti . . . 1607 . . . IN ANVERSA Apresso Giouanni Keerbergio. 12° ff.118
1071.l.11(1).
The titlepage is engraved. Imperfect; wanting all between the titlepage and f.17[=sig.B5]. Cropped.

B79 [BENEDICT; Saint, Abbot of Monte Cassino
REGVLA SANCTISSIMI PATRIS nostri Benedicti omnium Monachorum Patriarchæ. DVACI. Apud LAVRENTIVM KELLAM. M.DC.X. 32° pp.166,16
1606/1350.]
This book is missing from the shelf, perhaps given a new shelfmark which has not been recorded. The title has been reconstructed from the entry in the General Catalogue, and from *Albareda* no.153. Copies are recorded at Maredsous, Compostela, San Payo. Perhaps the British Library's copy will be found again.

B80 BENZONI, Girolamo

[La Historia del mondo nuouo.] De Historie/van De nieuwe weerelt/te weten/de Beschrijvinghe van West-Indien . . . Door Ieronimus Benzonius van Milanen. Wt het Italiaens Overgheset in Nederduyts/door Carel vander Mander Schilder. Tot Haerlem/by Paeschier van Wesbus . . . 1610. 8° pp.404; illus., port.

1061.a.6.

The portrait, on the titlepage, is of Benzoni.

B81 BERGEN, Paulus von

DEO TRINVNO AVSPICE ET PRAESIDE DISPUTATIONEM INAUGURALEM DE APOPLEXIA Auctoritate . . . D. REINERI BONTII Publicè proponit PAVLVS BERGIVS . . . LVGDVNI BATAVORVM, Ex officina IACOBI MARCI . . . M.D.CXX. 4° sig.A[4]

1185.g.2(1).

BERGEN, Paulus von. Disputationum anatomicarum quarta . . . de ossibus . . . quam . . . propugnandum suscipiet Paulus Bergius. 1618. *See* WINSEMIUS, Menelaus

BERGEN, Paulus von. Disputationum anatomicarum decimam, de carnibus . . . proponit Paulus Bergius. 1619. *See* WINSEMIUS, Menelaus

BERGEN, Paulus von. Disputationum anatomicarum decimam-sextam, de organis sanguificationis . . . proponit Paulus von Bergen. 1619. *See* WINSEMIUS, Menelaus

B82 BERGH, Adriaen van den

A. vanden BERGHS IERONIMO, Verthoond op de Kamer VVT-RECHTE LIEFD, Der Stad Vtrecht, Den 6. May 1621. 't VTRECHT, Bẏ IAN AMELISZ . . . 1621. (col.) 't VTRECHT, By IAN AMELISZ . . . 1621. 4° sig.A-G[4]; illus.

11755.bb.72(1).

Based on Thomas Kyd's 'The Spanish tragedy'. With the engraved device of the Chamber, signed: Joannes Ameliss exc. Anno 1621', on the titlepage and his own woodcut device in the colophon, reading 'Raison defaut ou gist impatience'.

BERGIUS, Paulus. *See* BERGEN, Paulus von

B83 BERICHT

Bericht Was die Evangelische/nach Gottes Wort Reformierte Kirchen halten/I. Vom Fegfewr: II. Von Anrůffung der Heyligen: III. Von Bildern: IV. Vom Ablass: vnd darbey auch vom Beichten/Fasten/Wallfahrten/Jubeljahren vnd dergleichen. Sampt Bescheidēlicher . . . Ableynung der Grůnden dess Gegentheyls . . . Zu Ambsterdam. M.DC.XIV. 8° pp.322

3559.aa.2(1).

The imprint is false; in fact printed by Johann Francke at Magdeburg.

B84 BERNARD; Saint, Abbot of Clairvaux

[Works] SANCTI BERNARDI . . . OPERA OMNIA. Tam quæ verè germana . . . quàm quæ spuria & supposititia . . . nunc primùm recognita, aucta ac emendata, & in ordinem concinniorem disposita. Accessere huic postremæ editioni aliquot Opuscula S. BERNARDI è Bibliotheca RR. PP. Carthus. Erfordiensium: necnon de Passione Domini fragmenta ex Epistolis ac Tractatibus per R.P. HENRICVM SOMMALIVM . . . collecta . . . Cum Indice duplici . . . COLONIÆ AGRIPPINÆ, Sumptibus Antonij Hierati . . . M.DC.XX. (col.) ANTVERPIÆ, Ex Typographiâ Henrici Ærtsij. MDC.XX. fol. coll.2402

1505/67.

The editor's preface signed: Joannes Gillotius.

B85 BERNARDI, Stefano

(tp.1) MISSAE QVINQVE . . . STEPHANI BERNARDI ET ALIORVM QVATVOR VOCVM, Cum BASSO CONTINVO ad Organum. TENOR. ANTVERPIÆ PETRVM PHALESIVM . . . M.D.CXIX.

(tp.2) MISSAE QVINQVE . . . STEPHANI BERNARDI . . . BASSVS. ANTVERPIÆ APVD PETRVM PHALESIVM . . . M.D.CXIX.

(tp.3) MISSAE QVINQVE . . . STEPHANI BERNARDI . . . BASSVS AD ORGANVM. ANTVERPIÆ APVD PETRVM PHALESIVM . . . M.D.CXIX. 4° 3 pt.: pp.32; 29; 31

Music C.169a.

With works by Giovanni Rambelli, Giovanni Biseghini and Michael Serre.

B86 [*BERNARDINO di Balbano; Capuchin

[Il mistero della flagellazione di N.S. Gesù Cristo.] THEYLICH MYSTERIE Van die Gheeselinghe ons Heeren IESV CHRISTI. Ghestelt in seuen Meditatien/voor elcken dach vander weke. Door den Eerw. Vadere P. Bernardin de Balbano . . . Ouerghestelt vvtet Franchois in Nederduytsch door Philips Numan . . . Tot Louen, by Jan Maes/1607. 8° ff.67; illus.

3395.d.8(2).]

*Destroyed. Described from the General Catalogue and from the copy at the Royal Library Albert I, Brussels (II.25886.no.7). The illustrations are woodcuts.

B87 BERNEVELLISTE

[Le Bernevelliste repenti.] Den BEROVDEN BERNEVELLIST, Sijn Leetwesen ende bekentenisse. Ghedaen door eenen die gheweest is van des Advocaets Factie. IN S'GRAVEN-HAGHE. By Aert Meuris . . . 1620. 4° sig.AB^4

T.2250(1); T.2422(32).

Both the French and Dutch editions were published in 1620. The French version is presumed to be the original one, according to the order adopted in the Dutch pamphlet catalogues.

B88 BEROALDUS, Philippus; the Elder

PHILIPPI BEROALDI LVDVS ORATORIVS DE PHILOSOPHI, MEDICI, ET ORATORIS PRÆSTANTIA: ITEM SCORTATORIS ALEATORIS ET EBRIOSI FOEDITATE. Editio castigatissima. LOVANII, Typis IO. CHRISTOPH. FLAVI. ANNO M.DC.XII. [etc.] 8° pp.96

T.2287(1).

With 'De scriptis Philippi Beroaldi, & locis, ubi docuit: ex eius vitâ à Pino Tolosano editâ'. The editor's dedication signed: E. Puteanus.

Den BEROVDEN Bernevellist. 1620. *See* BERNEVELLISTE

B89 BERTIUS, Petrus

PETRI BERTII AEN-SPRAECK, aen D. FR. GOMARVM, op zijne Bedenckinghe over de Lijck-oratie, ghedaen na de Begraefenisse van D. IACOBVS ARMINIVS . . . TOT LEYDEN, By IAN PAEDTS IACOPSZOON . . . 1610. 4° sig.$A\text{-}E^4$

T.2240(2).

B90 BERTIUS, Petrus

P. BERTII COMMENTARIORVM RERVM GERMANICARVM Libri Tres . . . Amstelodami apud Joannem Janssonium . . . 1616. obl.4° pp.732; illus., maps.

L.R.110.b.20.

The titlepage and illustrations are engraved. Some of the inscriptions on the views are in German.

B91 BERTIUS, Petrus

[Hymenaeus desertor, sive de sanctorum apostasia.] HYMENÆVS DESERTOR. Ofte: Twee Vraegh-stucken/Van den Afval der Heylighen . . . Beschreven in Latijnscher sprake: DOOR . . . Petrus Bertius . . . Ende nu . . . overgheset in onse Nederduytsche tale . . . Ghedruckt . . . 1613. 4° pp.143

T.2243(13).

The suggestion in the General Catalogue that this was printed at Schiedam seems most unlikely. Perhaps published at Leiden by J. J. Paets who published the Latin edition in or after 1610, or by Louis Elzevier at Leiden who republished it in 1615.

B92 BERTIUS, Petrus

Illustrium & clarorum Virorum EPISTOLAE SELECTIORES, Superiore sæculo scriptæ vel à Belgis, vel ad Belgas . . . LVGDVNI BATAVORVM, Apud LVDOVICVM ELZEVIRIVM . . . MDCXVII. (col.) Lugduni Batavorum, Typis ISAACI ELZEVIRI . . . M D C XVII. 8° pp.988

1084.g.18.

A collection of letters belonging to Cornelius vander Myle. The editor's preface signed: P. Bertius. With a dedicatory letter by Daniel Heinsius.

B93 BERTIUS, Petrus

PETRI BERTII LOGICAE PERIPATETICAE LIBRI SEX. LVGDVNI BATAVORVM, Ex Officina Iohannis Patii . . . 1604. 8° pp.332

527.b.8.

B94 BERTIUS, Petrus

P. BERTII ORATIO De vita & obitu . . . D. IANI DOVSÆ . . . HABITA LVGDVNI BATAVORVM post exsequias ejusdem. LVGDVNI BATAVORVM, Ex Officinâ Ioannis Patii . . . M.D.CIV. 4° sig.A-D^4

835.g.13(1).

With a list of Dousa's works and with poems by various authors. Author's presentation copy to Cornelius Swanenburch.

B95 BERTIUS, Petrus

PETRI BERTII ORATIO In obitum . . . D. IACOBI ARMINII . . . Habita post exsequias . . . LVGDVNI BATAVORVM Excudebat Ioannes Patius . . . M D CIX. 4° pp.60

835.g.14(1).

With poems by Janus Dousa, Hugo Grotius, Simon Episcopius and others.

B96 BERTIUS, Petrus

[Oratio in obitum . . . Iacobi Arminii.] PETRI BERTII LIICK-ORATIE over de doot vanden . . . Heere IACOBVS ARMINIVS . . . Ghedaen inde latijnsche tale . . . Ende . . . door een liefhebber verduyst. TOT LEYDEN BY IAN PAEDTS IACOBSZOON . . . 1609. 4° sig.A-D^4E^2

T.2239(16).

Translated by Joannes Arnoldi Corvinus. With additional poems signed: A.M.P.

B97 BERTIUS, Petrus

P. BERTII ORATIO, QVA RATIONEM REDDIT, CVR relictâ Leydâ Parisios commigrarit, & hæresi repudiata Romano-Catholicam fidem amplexus sit. Habita Lutetiæ Parisiorum . . . ACCEDIT Replicatio . . . Cardinalis Perronij ad . . . Iacobum Regem Angliç, de collatione Ecclesiç Catholicç veteris cum Romana. ANTVERPIAE, Ex Officina IOANNIS CNOBBARI . . . M.DC.XXI. 8° pp.60

867.d.23.

With accompanying poems by various authors. Cropped. With manuscript notes.

B98 BERTIUS, Petrus

P. BERTII Quum librum L. ANNÆI SENECÆ DE BREVITATE VITÆ publicè explicare adgrederetur, ORATIO, Habita Lugduni Batavorum, vii. Eid. Quinctileis, Anno M DC XIX. LVGDVNI BATAVORVM Ex Officina Iacobi Marci. M DC XIX. 4° pp.38
835.c.28(5).

B99 BERTIUS, Petrus

P Bertij TABVLARVM GEOGRAPHICARVM CONTRACTARVM Libri septem In quibus Tabulæ . . . supra priores editiones politiora Auctioraqȝ . . . . ad . . . LVDOVICVM XIII. Amsterodami Sumptibus et typis æneis Iudoci Hondij . . . 1616. obl. 8° pp.892[829]; illus., maps
Maps C.39.a.8.

The titlepage is engraved. The privilege states that Judocus Hondius edited the maps. Ownership inscriptions: Ja: Jenkins 1698; Ex dono Thomæ Fairfax . . . Richard Pype (Pipe).

B100 BERTIUS, Petrus

P Bertij TABVLARVM GEOGRAPHICARVM CONTRACTARVM Libri septem . . . Amsterodami Sumptibus et typis æneis Iudoci Hondij . . . 1618. obl. 8° pp.829; illus., maps
Maps C.39.a.9.

The titlepage is engraved. Judocus Hondius named as editor of the maps. With two additional preliminary leaves bearing manuscript poems and prose tributes in Latin or French dated: La Haye, 10 December 1642. Ownership inscription: Michel Barrilles (?), ex dono amicissimi mei H. Pelate.

B101 BERTIUS, Petrus

(tp. 1) THEATRI GEOGRAPHIAE VETERIS Tomus prior in quo CL. PTOL. ALEXANDRINI Geographiæ libri VIII Græcé et Latiné Græca ad codices Palatinos collata aucta et emendata sunt Latina infinitis locis correcta opera P. BERTII [etc.]
(tp. 2) THEATRI GEOGRAPHIAE VETERIS TOMVS POSTERIOR in quo ITINERARIVM ANTONINI IMPERATORIS . . . PROVINCIARVM ROMANARVM Libellus CIVITATES PROVINCIARVM GALLICARVM TABVLA PEVTINGERIANA cum notis Marci Velseri ad Tabulæ eius partem PARERGI ORTELIANI Tabulæ aliquot, edente P. BERTIO . . . AMSTELODAMI Ex officina Iudoci Hondij . . . 1619. (col.) LVGDVNI BATAVORVM, Excudebat typis suis ISAACVS ELZEVIRIVS, Sumptibus IVDOCI HONDII . . . M D C XVIII. fol. 2 tom.: pp.253; 28, 46, 16: plates; illus.
684.l.5; 210.h.4; G.8179.

Both titlepages are engraved. The copy at 210.h.4 has coloured plates. The illustrations are partly woodcuts, partly engravings. With an engraved portrait of Mercator on the verso of tp. 2, preceding Mercator's maps as derived from Ptolemy. The titlepage of tom. 1 of the copy at G.8179 has had the imprint: Amstelodami Ex officina Iudoci Hondij 1618 added and this copy contains the portrait of Bertius not found in the other two copies.

B102 BERTIUS, Petrus

THESES PHILOSPHICÆ DE POLITIARVM PRINCIPIIS. QVAS . . . SVB PRÆSIDIO . . . D.M. PETRI BERTII . . . defendere conabor PETRVS COVRTEN . . . LVGDVNI BATAVORVM, Typis ISAACI ELZEVIRI . . . M D CXVII. 4° sig. A^6
523.g.14(2).

B103 BERTIUS, Petrus

TVVEE DISPVTATIEN: de eene D. PETRI BERTII, Van de Ketterije Pelagij ende Cælestij. de andere D. IACOBI ARMINII, Van des Menschen vrije-vvillekeur en hare crachten. VVt den Latijne overgheset. IN S'GRAVEN-HAGHE, By Hillebrant Iacobsz . . . 1609. 4° sig. $A\text{-}E^4$
T.2239(6).

An alleged Latin edition of the same year is mentioned in *Petit Lijst* p.147 no.9, but no copy has been located.

BESCHRIJVINGHE. *See* also BESCHRYVINGE, BESCHRYVINGHE

BESCHRIJVINGHE van Out Batavien. 1612. *See* SCRIVERIUS, Petrus

B104 BESCHRIJVINGHE

Beschrijvinghe vant belegh ende Verraedt van de stadt weenen/in Oosten-rijck/ hoe dat sommighe van binnen meynden de stadt te leveren aen de Boheemsche . . . Ende hoe dat ons volck . . . Noch twee steden hebben inghenomen met ghewelt als Frons-berch/ende Rosenberch/ met noch de stadt gheplundert van Rodolfstadt . . . Eerst Ghedruckt int Hoochduytsche/ende nv Ouerghesedt in onse Nederlantsche sprake/ende Ghedruckt t'Hantwerpen den xij. Julij 1619. T'Hantwerpen/By Abraham Verhoeuen . . . 1619. 4° pp.7; sig.A^4; illus.

1480.aa.15(1); P.P.3444.af(11).

The titlepage illustration shows armies by a river, with a city in an inset. The titlepage is considerably wider than the rest of the book and has been mutilated in the copy at P.P.3444.af(11) and wholly cut back to the size of the other pages in that at 1480.aa.15(1) with loss of some of the text.

BESCHRYVINGE. *See* also BESCHRIJVINGHE; BESCHRYVINGHE.

BESCHRYVINGE ende historisch verhael, vant gout koninckrijck van Gunea. 1602. *See* MAREES, Pieter de

BESCHRYVINGE vande begraefnisse van . . . Walraven, Heere tot Brederode. 1615. *See* HONDIUS, Henrik; the Elder

BESCHRYVINGHE. *See* also BESCHRIJVINGHE; BESCHRYVINGE

BESCHRYVINGHE vande voyagie om den geheelen werelt cloot. 1602. *See* NOORT, Olivier van

BESCHRYVINGHE vander Samoyeden landt. 1612. *See* GERRITSZ, Hessel

B105 BESONDER

Een besonder Tractaet/Van de voornaemste Leer-stucken/over welcken ten huydigen dage 'tverschil is: wesende d'oprechte Copijen/eerst van het Wederleg-schrift der . . . Predicanten der Stadt Dordrecht . . . tegens een Remonstrantie/ uytgegheven by Adolphus Tectander Venator . . . Ende daer nae . . . Tectanders Apologie tot Refutatie des . . . Wederleg-schrifts ende verdedingh [*sic*] zijner Belijdenissen . . . In den Druck ghebracht door een Lidtmaet van de suyvere . . . Ghereformeerde Kercke . . . Ghedruckt . . . 1612. 4° pp.182

T.2242(32).

The editor's preface signed: C.D.V.L.

B106 BEUCKELAER

BEVCKELAER Tegens de scherpe pijlen geschoten op de Vrede-soeckende Predicanten/Inhoudende haere REMONSTRANTIE Aende . . . Staten van Hollandt ende VVest-vrieslandt overgegeven in Iulio . . . 1610 . . . met Een ANATOMIE, ofte clare ende naeckte ontledinge der vijf Articulen die de Remonstranten verclaert hebben niet te konnen toestaen . . . 1611. 4° pp.67

T.2241(22).

BEUCKELIUS, Johannes. *See* BUECKELIUS, Johannes

B107 BEYER, Samuel

Antwoordt Op een zeker Faem-roovend' LASTER-SCHRIFT. door HENRICVS SLATIVS uytghegheven/ende den 14 ende 15 Mey . . . tot Bleyswijck aengheslaghen/ Teghens de Schuer-Predicanten/Oft de Ware Leeraers der ghereformeerde

Kercken . . . Door SAMVEL BEYER . . . TOT ROTTERDAM, By David Jacobsz van Hakendover . . . 1617. 4° sig.★-★★★[4]
T.2247(5).
With manuscript notes.

B108 BEYER, Samuel
t'LOON, Twelck SAMVEL BEYER kende schuldich te zijn aenden POST-BODE, Die den opgheblasen ende hoochmoedighen HENRICVS SLATIVS aen de Schuer-Predicanten . . . heeft ghesonden/Door SAMVEL BEYER . . . TOT ROTTERDAM, By David Jacobsz van Hakendover . . . 1617. 4° sig.(★)[4]
T.2247(6).

B109 BEYERLINCK, Laurentius
LAVRENTII BEYERLINCK . . . APOPHTHEGMATA CHRISTIANORVM. ANTVERPIÆ, EX OFFICINA PLANTINIANA, Apud Ioannem Moretum. M.DC.VIII. 8° pp.584
1020.g.8.

B110 BEYERLINCK, Laurentius
LAVDATIO FVNEBRIS D. PHILIPPI III. HISPANIARVM ET INDIARVM REGIS, Dicta in Exequiis eiusdem . . . celebratis in Ecclesia Cathedrali Antuerpiensi . . . a LAVRENTIO BEYERLINCK . . . ANTVERPIÆ, EX OFFICINA PLANTINIANA, M.DC.XXI. (col.) ANTVERPIÆ, EX OFFICINA PLANTINIANA BALTHASARIS MORETI. M.DC.XXI. 4° pp.30
1199.f.3(7).
With 'Philippi III . . . Epitaphium'.

B111 BEYERLINCK, Laurentius
LAVRENTIVS BEYERLINCK . . . PROFECTIONIS MARCI ANTONII DE DOMINIS quondam Archiepiscopi Spalatensis CONSILIVM EXAMINAT. ANTVERPIÆ, EX OFFICINA PLANTINIANA, Apud Balthasarem & Ioannem Moretos. M.DC.XVII. 8° pp.84
1020.e.5(4).

B112 BEYERLINCK, Laurentius
LAVRENTII BEYERLINCK . . . ORATIO IN FVNERE . . . D. MATTHIAE HOVII III. ARCHIEPISCOPI MECHLINIENSIS, Habita in Exequiis eiusdem . . . ANTVERPIÆ, EX OFFICINA PLANTINIANA. M.DC.XX. (col.) ANTVERPIÆ, EX OFFICINA PLANTINIANA BALTHASARIS MORETI. M.DC.XX. 4° pp.44
1199.f.3(6).

B113 [★BEYERLINCK, Laurentius
Seminarij Antuerpiensis parentalia in fvnere reverendissimi domini Ioannis Miræi Antverpiensivm episcopi svique institvtoris; perorante Lavrentio Beyerlinck eiusdem seminarij præside, vii.Kal. April. M.DC.XI. 8° pp.36
4423.bb.20(3).]
★Destroyed. The title has been reconstructed from the entry in the General Catalogue and *NUC*. Probably printed at Antwerp. A copy is recorded at the Andover-Harvard Theological Library, Harvard University.

B114 BEYERLINCK, Laurentius
SERENISS. PRINCIPIS ALBERTI AVSTRIÆ ARCHIDVCIS . . . LAVDATIO FVNEBRIS: DICTA A LAVRENTIO BEYERLINCK . . . In exsequiis eiusdem . . . ANTVERPIÆ, EX OFFICINA PLANTINIANA. M.DC.XXI. (col.) ANTVERPIÆ, EX OFFICINA PLANTINIANA BALTHASARIS MORETI. M.DC.XXI. 4° pp.52
1199.f.3(3).
Issued together with Aubert Le Mire's 'De vita Alberti', dated 1622.

B115 BEYERLINCK, Laurentius

TRACTATVS SYNODICVS AD SYNODVM DORDRACENAM In quo de Synodorum siue Conciliorum Institutione, Usu, Causis, Firmitate, Authoritate, & Prærogatura. AVTHORE LAVRENTIO BEYERLINCK . . . ANTVERPIÆ. Apud GVLIELMVM A TONGRIS . . . M.D.C.XIX. [etc.] 8° pp.154
862.c.12(1).

BIBLE

Arrangement:

Complete Bibles
- Polyglot
- Latin
- English
- Dutch
- Spanish

Selections. Dutch

Old Testament
- Polyglot
- Minor Prophets. Latin
- Hagiographa. Hebrew
  - Latin
- Job. English
- Psalms. Polyglot
  - Latin
  - English
  - Dutch
  - French
  - Selections. Dutch
- Proverbs. Latin

Old Testament (Cont.)
- Song of Solomon. Greek
  - Latin
- Lamentations. English
- Hosea. Polyglot
- O. T. Apocrypha. Polyglot

New Testament
- Greek
- Polyglot
- Latin
- English
- Dutch
- Gospels. Polyglot
  - Harmonies. Latin
- Liturgical Epistles and Gospels. Latin
- Luke. Latin
- Revelation. Latin
  - French

Concordances. Latin

B116 BIBLE. Polyglot

(tp.1) BIBLIA HEBRAICA, cum interlineari interpretatione Latinâ XANTIS PAGNINI . . . Quæ quidem interpretatio, cùm ab Hebraicarum dictionum proprietate discedit . . . in margine libri est collocata; atque alia BEN. ARIÆ MONTANI . . . aliorumqȝ collato studio è verbo reddita, ac . . . in eius locum est substituta. Accessit Bibliorum pars quæ Hebraicè non reperitur, item Testamentum Nouum Græcè, cum vulgatâ interpretatione Latinâ . . . EX OFFICINA PLANTINIANA RAPHELENGII, 1613.

(tp.2) LIBRI IEHOSVAH, IVDICVM, SAMVELIS, ET REGVM, Hebraicè: Cum interlineari versione XANTIS PAGNINI: BEN. ARIÆ MONTANI & aliorum collato studio ad Hebraicam dictionem diligentissimè expensa. EX OFFICINA PLANTINIANA RAPHELENGII, M.D.CXI.

(tp.3) ISAIAS, IEREMIAS, EZECHIEL: Osee . . . Malachias; Hebraïcè; Cum interlineari versione XANTIS PAGNINI; BEN. ARIÆ MONTANI & aliorum collato studio, ad Hebraicam dictionem diligentissimè expensa. EX OFFICINA PLANTINIANA RAPHELENGII, 1610.

(tp.4) PSALMI DAVIDIS Hebraici, Cum interlineari versione XANTIS PAGNINI; BEN. ARIÆ MONTANI, & aliorum collato studio ad Hebraicam dictionem . . . expensa. EX OFFICIN'A [*sic*] PLANTINIANA RAPHELENGIJ, 1615.

(tp.5) BIBLIORVM PARS GRÆCA QVÆ HEBRAICE NON INVENITVR; Cum interlineari interpretatione LATINA, ex Biblijs Complutensibus deprompta. EX OFFICINA PLANTINIANA RAPHELENGII, 1612.

(tp.6) NOVVM TESTAMENTVM GRÆCE, Cum vulgata Interpretatione Latina, Græci contextus lineis inserta. Quæ quidem interpretatio, cùm à Græcarum dictionum proprietate discedit, sensum, videlicet, magis quàm verba exprimens, in margine libri est collocata; atque alia BEN. ARIÆ MONTANI . . . operâ è verbo reddita, ac diuerso characterum genere distincta, in eius est substituta locum. EX OFFICINA PLANTINIANA RAPHELENGII, 1613. 8° 6 vol.: pp.657; 763; 527; 548; 344; 681
217.g.8–13.
Published at Leiden. Another, separate, copy of vol.6 is entered below under BIBLE. New Testament. Polyglot.

B117 BIBLE. Latin
BIBLIA SACRA Vulgatæ Editionis SIXTI V. . . . IVSSV recognita atque edita. ANTVERPIÆ EX OFFICINA PLANTINIANA Apud Ioannem Moretum. M.DC.III. (col.) ANTVERPIÆ, EX OFFICINA PLANTINIANA, APVD IOANNEM MORETVM. M.DC.III. fol. pp.956,24
L.12.f.3.
The titlepage is engraved and has been mounted.

B118 BIBLE. Latin
BIBLIA SACRA Vulgatæ Editionis SIXTI V. . . . IVSSV recognita atque edita. ANTVERPIÆ EX OFFICINA PLANTINIANA Apud Ioannem Moretum. M.DC.V. (col.) ANTVERPIÆ, EX OFFICINA PLANTINIANA, Apud Ioannem Moretum. M.DC.V. 4° pp.995,30
1408.l.15.

B119 BIBLE. Latin
(tp.3) NOVVM IESV CHRISTI TESTAMENTVM Complectens præter Vulgatam, Guidonis Fabricij è Syriaco, & Benedicti Ariæ Montani Translationes, Insuper Des. Erasmi . . . versionem permissam. ANTVERPIÆ, Apud Ioannem Keerbergium. M.DC.XVI [etc.] fol. vol.3: pp.651,46
464.d.7.
Edited and with prefatory matter by Laurentius Beyerlinck. Imperfect; wanting the two volumes containing the Old Testament.

B120 BIBLE. Latin
BIBLIA SACRA CVM GLOSSA ORDINARIA Primum quidem a STRABO FVLDENSI . . . Nunc verò nouis . . . Explicationibus locupletata, ET POSTILLA NICOLAI LYRANI . . . nec non additionibus PAVLI BVRGENSIS Episcopi, et MATTHIÆ THORINGI replicis, opera et studio Theologor. DVACENSIVM . . . emendatis. TOMIS SEX COMPREHENSA . . . DVACI Excudebat BALTAZAR BELLERVS suis et IOANNIS KEERBERGII Antuerpiensis sumptibus . . . M.DC.XVII. [etc.]
(tp.2–6) BIBLIA SACRA . . . ANTVERPIÆ, Apud Ioannem Keerbergium . . . M.DC.XVII. [etc.] fol. 6 tom.: coll.1740; 1704; 2283; 2490; 1330; 1734; illus.
L.16.f.1.
The engraved titlepage of vol.1 and vignettes on other titlepages signed: Pet.Paul Rubenius inuent.,Ioan.Collaert sculpsit. One illustration in vol.6 signed: Mart.bas.f. The engraving on coll.41–42 in tom.5 has been covered over with a diagram. tom.1 has both cancellands and cancels in sigg.Ii, Kk, with irregular numbering of the columns.

B121 BIBLE. Latin
(tp.1) BIBLIA SACRA Vulgatæ Editionis . . . ANTVERPIÆ EX OFFICINA PLANTINIANA Apud Balthasarem et Ioannem Moretos fratres. M.DC.XVIII.
(tp.2) ROMANÆ CORRECTIONIS, IN LATINIS BIBLIIS EDITIONIS VVLGATÆ . . . LOCA INSIGNIORA: Obseruata & denuò aucta à FRANCISCO LVCA Brugensi . . . Accessit

libellus alter, continens alias lectionum varietates . . . collectas . . . eodem obseruatore & collectore. ANTVERPIÆ, EX OFFICINA PLANTINIANA, Apud Balthasarem & Ioannem Moretos. M.DC.XVIII. (col.) ANTVERPIÆ, EX OFFICINA PLANTINIANA, APVD BALTHASAREM ET IOANNEM MORETOS FRATRES. M.DC.XVIII. 4° 2 pt.: pp.1055,30; 85
3023.b.6.

Tp.1 is engraved. The 'Libellus alter' in pt.2 occupies pp.69–85.

B122 BIBLE. English

(tp.1) THE HOLIE BIBLE FAITHFVLLY TRANSLATED INTO ENGLISH . . . Diligently conferred with the Hebrew, Greeke, and other Editions in diuers languages. With ARGVMENTS . . . ANNOTATIONS . . . BY THE ENGLISH COLLEGE OF DOWAY . . . Printed at Doway by LAVRENCE KELLAM . . . M.DC.IX.
(tp.2) THE SECOND TOME OF THE HOLIE BIBLE . . . Printed at Doway by LAVRENCE KELLAM . . . M.DC.X. 4° 2 tom.: pp.1115; 1124
C.110.d.3; 465.a.6.

The Old Testament only. A portrait of Cardinal Allen has been inserted in tom.1 of the copy at C.110.d.3. The copy at 465.a.6. is imperfect; wanting tom.1.

B123 BIBLE. Dutch

BIBLIA: Dat is, De gantsche heylighe Schrift, grondelick ende trouvvelick verduytschet. Met verclaringhe duysterer woorden/redenen ende spreucken . . . Met noch rijcke aenwijsinghen, der ghelijck ofte onghelijcstemmenden plaetsen . . . TOT LEYDEN, By Jan Paedts Jacobszoon/ende Jan Bouwenszoon . . . M.DC.VIII. 8° ff.531, XXxiiiir-DDddiiiir,pp.34; music
3041.aaa.20.

'Deux aes' Bible, with 'De Psalmen . . . overgheset door Petrum Dathenum' and 'Catechismus'. Ownership inscriptions: Arnoldus Geesteranus; Petrus van Ede; Wilh: Greve.

B124 BIBLE. Dutch

BIBLIA: Dat is, De gantsche heylighe Schrift, grondelick ende trouvvelick verduytschet. Met verclaringhe duysterer woorden/redenen ende spreucken . . . Met noch rijcke aenwijsinghen . . . TOT LEYDEN, By Ian Paedts Iacobszoon/ende Ian Bouwenszoon . . . M.DC.XI. 8° ff.531, XXx4r–DDdd4r; pp.34: music
C.65.l.5.

With the Psalms and Catechism. In a silk embroidered velvet binding.

B125 BIBLE. Dutch

(tp.1) BIBLIA: Dat is, De gantsche heylige Schrift/grondelijck ende trouwelijck verduytschet. Met verclaringhe duysterer woorden, redenen, ende spreucken . . . Met noch rijcke aenvvijsinghen . . . TOT DELF, By Bruyn Harmansz. Schinckel . . . 1612.
(tp.2=f.235) De Prophecien Der PROPHETEN . . . TOT DELF, By Bruyn Hermanszoon Schinckel . . . 1611.
(tp.3) De Boecken ghenoemt APOCRYPHI . . . TOT DELF, By Bruyn Hermanszoon Schinckel . . . 1611.
(tp.4) HET NIEVVE TESTAMENT . . . TOT DELF, By Bruyn Hermanszoon Schinckel . . . 1611. 4° 3pt.: ff.325[326?]; 84; 109
3041.d.8.

The last leaf of pt.1 is mutilated; wanting pagination?

B126 BIBLE. Dutch

(tp.1) BIBLIA. Dat is: De gantsche Heylighe Schriftuere/grondelijck ende trouwelijck verduytschet. Met . . . Annotatien nae den Geneefschen exemplaer uyt de Fransoysche tale . . . overgeset, nu ten vierdemale oversien ende

verbetert . . . ende . . . vermeerdert. Met eene noch byghevoechde Cronijcke ofte Tijt-rekeninghe over de gheheele Bibel/tot op het tweentseventichste Jaer der geboorten Christi . . . te samen ghevoecht/Door P. H. Dienaer des Goddelijcken Woorts. TOT DORDRECHT, Gedruckt by Fransoys Bosselaer . . . 1613.
(tp.2) HET NIEVWE TESTAMENT . . . Tot Dordrecht, Gedruckt by Isaac Iansz. Canin . . . 1612. 4° 3 pt.: ff.454; 130; sig.Riiij–Z^8Aa^1; music
3040.eee.7.

Compiled by Petrus Hackius. With the Psalms and Catechism.

B127 BIBLE. Dutch

(tp.1) Biblia: Dat is/De gantsche Heylighe Schriftuere/grondelijck ende trouwelijck verduytschet/Met verclaringhe duysterer woorden . . . Alles tsamen gevoeght Door P.H.Dienaer des Goddelicken Woorts. T'AMSTERDAM By Ian Evertsz. Cloppenburch . . . 1613.
(tp.2) HET NIEVWE TESTAMENT . . . In Nederduytsche, na der Griecxscher vvaerheyt, overgheset . . . Gedruct . . . 1613. fol. 2 pt.: ff.372; 96
3036.g.12.

Compiled by Petrus Hackius. Printed on yellow paper. With a printer's device sometimes used by Nicolaes Biestkens at Amsterdam.

B128 BIBLE. Dutch

(tp.1) BIBLIA SACRA Des Oudē ende Nieuwē Testamēts ofte DE GANTSCHE HEYLIGHE SCHRIFT. . . Met verclaringen ende Annotatien, van Emanuel Tremellius, Franciscus Junius, Theodorus Beza ende Joannes Piscator. Ende nu jn onse Nederlantsche Tale overgeset, door ABRAHAMUM À DORESLAER . . . t'ARNHEM BY IAN IANSZEN . . . 1614.
(tp.2) Het vervolgh Der Bybelsche Schriften des Ouden Testaments: Vervatende alle de Boecken ende Prophecien der . . . Propheten . . . Nu op nieus verrijckt met corte Verclaringhen ende Annotatien, in de Latijnsche tale . . . Ghestelt door Emanuelem Tremellium ende Franciscum Iunium. Ende nu . . . overgheset/ende ghepast op onse ghewoonlijcke Bybelsche Translatie; Door Abraham van Doreslaar . . . TOT ARNHEM, By Ian Ianssoon . . . 1614.
(tp.3) De boecken ghenaemt APOCRYPHI. Ofte Een aen-hangsel des Ouden Testaments . . . Verrijckt met corte aenteeckeninghen . . . in de Latijnsche tale . . . ghestelt Door Franciscum Iunium: Ende nu . . . over-gheset . . . door Abraham van Doreslaer. TOT ARNHEM, By Ian Iansz . . . 1614.
(tp.4) HET NIEVVVE TESTAMENT . . . Met Verclaringhen ende Annotatien van Theodorus Beza, Emanuel Tremellius, Franciscus Iunius, ende Ioannes Piscator . . . overgheset, Door Abrahamum à Doreslaer . . . Tot Arnhem, By Ian Iansz . . . 1614. [etc.] (col.) Ghedruckt tot Amsterdam/by Nicolaes Biestkens . . . 1614. fol. 4 pt.: ff.274; 120; 81; 143; illus.
469.f.4.

The titlepage of pt.1 is engraved. The woodcut illustration occurs on the titlepage of pt.3.

B129 BIBLE. Dutch

BIBLIA Dat is De gantsche heylighe Schrift grond:elick [*sic*] ende trouwelick verduytschet. Met verclaringhe duysterer woor:den [*sic*], redenen end Spreucken . . . MEN VINTSE TE COOP BY Cornelis Lodewijcksz vander Plasse . . . T'Amstelredam. (col.) 'TAMSTERDAM, Ghedruckt by Paulus van Ravesteyn . . . 1614. 8° ff.542; sig.A–G7; music
3042.a.9.

With the Psalms and Catechism. The titlepage is engraved, signed: Michel le Blon fecit. Imperfect; wanting all after sig.G7 of the Psalms and Catechism. The titlepage is mutilated and partly pasted on to the next leaf.

B130 BIBLE. Dutch

BIBLIA: Dat is/De gantsche heylige Schriftuere/grondelick ende trouwelick verduytschet: Met Verclaringe duysterer Woorden/Redenen/Spreucken . . . Met Previlegie van de Heeren Staten Generael voor 4. jaren. TOT AMSTELREDAM. Voor Jacob Ysbrantsz Bos . . . 1614. 8° ff.535; sig.A1-O4; pp.1-[26]; music

3050.aaa.12.

With the Psalms and Catechism. The privilege is made out to Jacob Canin, Dordrecht, in 1613. The last leaf is mutilated, wanting the pagination.

B131 BIBLE. Dutch

BIBLIA: Dat is, De gantsche Heylighe Schriftuere/grondelick ende trouwelick verduytschet/Met verclaringhe duysterer vvoorden . . . Met noch rijcke aenvvijsinghen . . . TOT LEYDEN, By Jan Paedts Jacobszoon/ende Jan Bouwenszoon . . . M.DCXIIII. fol. ff.534

L.11.g.6.

B132 BIBLE. Dutch

(tp.1) BIBLIA: Dat is De gantsche Heylige Schriftuere . . . Met verclaringe duysterer woorden . . . Met noch rijcke aenwijsingen . . . Met eene noch by-gevoechde Cronijcke . . . Alles te samen ghevoecht. Door P. H. Dienaer des Godlicken woorts. TOT DORDRECHT, By Isaack Abrahamsz. Canin . . . 1615

(tp.2) HET NIEVWE TESTAMENT . . . Ghedruckt . . . 1615. fol. 2 pt.: ff.372; 96.

3040.f.6.

'Deux aes' Bible. Compiled by Petrus Hackius. Tp.1 and the last leaf have been mounted. Without either of the booksellers' names recorded elsewhere, e.g. *Briels* p.227, for this edition.

B133 BIBLE. Dutch

BIBLIA Dat is De Gansche heylige Schrift . . . Met verclaringhe . . . Gedruckt tot Leyden By Vldrich Corneliss 1615 Voor Jan Everss Cloppenburch eñ Isack Ianss Canin . . . 1615. 12° ff.438; pp.35; music

3040.a.17.

The titlepage is engraved, signed: Blon fecit. With the Psalms and Catechism. The booksellers' addresses are Amsterdam and Dordrecht respectively.

B134 BIBLE. Dutch

Biblia: Dat is/De gantsche Heylige Schrift . . . Met verclaringhe . . . Met noch rijcke aenwijsinghen . . . Tot Dordrecht, Gedruckt by Isaack Jansz. Caen/ende Thomas Willemsz van Orten . . . M.D.CXVIJ [*sic*]. (col.) Tot Dordrecht, Ghedruckt by Isaack Jansz. Caen . . . M.D.XVIJ [*sic*]. 8° ff.608; 18; music

C.127.g.25.

With the Psalms and Catechism. The dates on the titlepage and in the colophon are misprints. In fact, printed in 1597.

B135 BIBLE. Dutch

(tp.1) BIBLIA Dat is DE GANTSCHE Heylighe Schriftuere voortijts uyt gegeven tot Geneven, Getrouwelijck overgeset in onse Nederduytsche spraeke ende voor de vierde reijse oversien, gecorrigeert, eñ verbetert Door P. H. Dienaer des Goddelijcken Woorts. MET RIICKE AENWIISINghen . . . t'Amsterdam voor Jan Marcus . . . 1621.

(tp.2) DE PROPHECIEN DER PROPHETEN . . . Ghedruckt 1615.

(tp.3) HET NIEVVE TESTAMENT . . . Met de Annotatien Augustin. Marlorati . . . overgheset wt de Fransoysche in Nederduytsche sprake . . . Ghedruckt . . . 1614. fol. 3 pt.: ff.240; 177; 118: plates; maps.

3037.ee.1.

Compiled by Petrus Hackius. The first titlepage is engraved, signed: JMatham fecit. The second and third titlepages bear the device of Isaac Jansz Canin, Dordrecht.

B136 BIBLE. Dutch

BIBLIA: Dat is: De gantsche heylighe Schrift, grondelijck ende trouwelijck verduytschet. Met rijcke aenwijhsinghen . . . T'AMSTELREDAM, By Hendrick Laurensz . . . 1621. (col.) Ghedruckt ter Goude/by Jaspar Tournay. 12° ff.582, sig.a–F8r^{8}, pp.37; music

3049.bb.15.

Another edition of that printed at Leiden in 1615. With the Psalms and the Catechism. The gatherings are in eights.

B137 BIBLE. Spanish

LA BIBLIA. Que es, LOS SACROS LIBROS DEL VIEIO Y NVEVO TESTAMENTO. Segunda Edicion. Revista y conferida con los textos Hebreos Griegos y con diversas translaciones. Por CYPRIANO de VALERA . . . En Amsterdam, En casa de Lorenço Iacobi. M.DC.II. (col.) . . . esta Biblia se acabô en Septiembre. Año M.DC.II. fol. ff.268,67,88

1.b.4.

Another edition of that of 1569. With a printer's device sometimes used by Nicolaes Biestkens at Amsterdam. With a facsimile made in 1858 of the dedication found in a copy belonging to Luis de Usoz i Rio.

B138 BIBLE. Selections. Dutch

SOMMIGHE GHEBEDEN, Dienende tot slissinge/afkeer ende verbiddinge vande perijckelen ende oproeringhen des Nederlants/vuyt de woorden der H. Schrifturen in diuersche passagien by een vergadert: Ende . . . vuyt den Latijne int Nederduytsch ouerghesedt. MET EEN VOORREDEN . . . waer inne verhaelt wort de oorsaecke, het eynde, ende de crachte van dese Ghebeden. TOT LOVEN, By Jan Maes . . . M.CCCCCC.II. 8° sig.ab^{4}; illus.

4407.bb.11(5).

The titlepage woodcut shows Christ bearing the cross. With another woodcut on sig.a4v.

B139 BIBLE. Old Testament. Polyglot.

(tp.1) BIBLIA HEBRAICA. EORVNDEM LATINA INTERPRETATIO XANTIS PAGNINI . . . BENEDICTI ARIÆ MONTANI . . . & quorundam aliorum collato studio . . . Accesserunt libri Græcè scripti, quos Ecclesia orthodoxa . . . inter Apocryphos recenset; cum interlineari interpretatione Latina ex Bibliis Complutensibus petita. EX OFFICINA PLANTINIANA RAPHELENGIJ, 1613.

(tp.2) LIBRI IEHOSVAH, IVDICVM, SAMVELIS, ET REGVM, Hebraicè: Cum interlineari versione XANTIS PAGNINI: BEN.ARIAE MONTANI, & aliorum collato studio ad Hebraicam dictionem diligentissimè expensa. EX OFFICINA PLANTINIANA RAPHELENGII, M.D.CXI.

(tp.3) PSALMI DAVIDIS Hebraici . . . EX OFFICINA PLANTINIANA RAPHELENGII. 1608.

(tp.4) ISAIAS, IEREMIAS, EZECHIEL: Osee . . . Malachias; Hebraïcè . . . EX OFFICINA PLANTINIANA RAPHELENGII, 1610.

(tp.5) DANIEL, HEZRA, & NECHEMIAH, Hebraicè . . . EX OFFICINA PLANTINIANA RAPHELENGII, 1611. 8° vol.1–5: pp.659; 581; 412; 527; 763

675.d.4–8.

Published at Leiden. Imperfect; wanting the Apocrypha. A separate copy of these in this edition, dated 1612, is entered below under BIBLE. Old Testament Apocrypha. Polyglot.

B140 BIBLE. Minor Prophets. Latin

R.P. FRANCISCI RIBERÆ . . . IN LIBRVM DVODECIM PROPHETARVM COMMENTARII. SENSVM . . . Historicum & Moralem . . . complectentes. HAC . . . POSTREMA

EDITIONE AB INFInitis mendis Typographicis expurgati, & . . . elucidati, Opera R. P. RICHARDI GIBBONI . . . CVM QVATVOR . . . INDICIBVS . . . DVACI, Ex Officina Typographica BALTAZARIS BELLERI . . . 1612. [etc.] fol. pp.602
4.d.13.
With the text. With an ornament containing the initials of the Douai printer Laurence Kellam. In a vellum binding, the covers stamped in gold with the arms of George III.

B141 BIBLE. Hagiographa. Hebrew
[Hebrew] . . . Prouerbia Salomonis, Iob, Canticum Canticorum, Ruth, Lamentationes Ieremiæ, Ecclesiastes, Esther. EX OFFICINA PLANTINIANA RAPHELENGII, 1608. 16° sig.a-t^{8}u^2
G.19956.

B142 BIBLE. Hagiographa. Latin
CORNELII IANSENII EPISCOPI GANDAVENSIS PARAPHRASIS IN OMNES PSALMOS DAVIDICOS CUM ARGVMENTIS ET ANNOTATIONIBVS: Itemq́ʒ in Prouerbia, & Ecclesiasticum Commentaria, veterisq́ʒ Testamenti Ecclesiæ Cantica, ac in Sapientiam Notæ. In quibus omnibus hoc agitur, vt sublatis mendis . . . genuina lectio retineatur . . . ANTVERPIÆ, EX TYPOGRAPHIA GISLENI IANSENII . . . M.DC.XIV. [etc.] fol. pp.583; illus.
690.h.3.
With an engraved portrait of Cornelius Jansenius on the titlepage.

B143 BIBLE. Job. English
(tp.1) IOB. TO THE KING. A Colon-Agrippina studie of one moneth, for the metricall translation: But Of many yeres, for Ebrew difficulties. By HVGH BROVGHTON . . . 1610.
(tp.2=p.102) IOB. BROVGHT ON TO FAMILIAR DIALOGUE AND PARAPHRASE . . . BY HVGH BROVGHTON. 4° pp.144
1003.b.9(9).
Printed by Giles Thorp at Amsterdam.

BIBLE. Psalms. Editions of the Psalms considered as musical compositions rather than as editions of the text are entered under the names of their composers.

B144 BIBLE. Psalms. Polyglot
SOVTER LIEDEKENS, gemaeckt ter eeren Gods/op alle die Psalmen van David . . . Eerst t'Hantwerpen by Symon Kock. Ende nu wederom herdruct t'Vtrecht/by Herman van Borculo . . . M.DC.XIII. 8° sig.A-Z^8; music
Music K.8.a.9; Music K.a.10.
In Dutch and Latin. Translated by Willem van Zuylen van Nyevelt. The Latin text is printed in the margin. The copy at Music K.8.a.10 with the ownership inscription: Ex Bibliotheca Wachendorffiana.

B145 BIBLE. Psalms. Latin
(tp.1) IOANNIS BOCHII . . . PSALMORVM DAVIDIS PARODIA HEROICA. Eiusdem variæ in PSALMOS Obseruationes, Physicæ, Ethicæ, Politicæ, & Historicæ. ANTVERPIÆ, EX OFFICINA PLANTINIANA, Apud Ioannem Moretum. M.DC.VIII.
(tp.2) IOANNIS BOCHII . . . IN PSALMOS DAVIDIS Variæ OBSERVATIONES . . . Item PROPHETÆ REGII Vita, & alia nonnulla, ad PSALMORVM lvcem. ANTVERPIÆ, EX OFFICINA PLANTINIANA, Apud Ioannem Moretum. M.DC.VIII. (col.) ANTVERPIÆ, EX OFFICINA PLANTINIANA, APVD IOANNEM MORETVM. M.DC.IX. 8° 2 pt.: pp.229; 817
3089.d.23.

B146 BIBLE. Psalms. Latin
PARAPHRASIS PSALMORVM DAVIDIS POETICA, Auctore GEORGIO BVCHANANO . . . EX OFFICINA PLANTINIANA RAPHELENGII, M.D.CIX. long 16° pp.286
C.20.f.56.
With Buchanan's 'Baptistes'. Published at Leiden. From the travelling library of Sir Julius Caesar.

B147 [*BIBLE. Psalms. Latin
Psalmi et Hymni Ecclesiastici cum Officio Defunctorum. Ad Romani Breuiarii nuperime correcti quod cantu in ecclesiis peragitur officii vsum accommodati, Bruxellæ apud I. Mommartium, 1618. 4°
3366.e.8.]
*Destroyed. The titlepage is engraved. The title is that of the General Catalogue.

B148 BIBLE. Psalms. English. Prose and Metrical Versions
THE BOOK OF PSALMES: Englished both in Prose and Metre. With Annotations . . . By H.A. . . . Imprinted at Amsterdam, By GILES THORP . . . 1612. 4° pp.348; music
C.36.e.23.
The preface signed: Henry Ainsworth.

B149 BIBLE. Psalms. English. Prose Versions
ANNOTATIONS Upon the Book of PSALMES. Wherein the Hebrew words and sentences are . . . explained . . . By Henry Ainsworth . . . The second edition: in the yere 1617. 4° sig.A-O^4
3155.dd.7(2).
An edition of the text. Previous edition 1612. Issued as pt.6 of the same author's 'Annotations upon the first book of Moses [etc.]', but actually part of a two volume edition of the Psalms in a prose and metrical version. Printed by Giles Thorp at Amsterdam.

B150 BIBLE. Psalms. English. Metrical Versions
THE PSALMES OF DAVID IN METRE, WITH DIVERS NOTES, and Tunes augmented to them . . . MIDDELBVRGH, Imprinted by Richard Schilders . . . 1602. 8° pp.441; music
G.20001.

BIBLE. Psalms. Dutch. Metrical Versions. Petrus Dathenus. For editions joined to editions of the Bible *see* BIBLE. Dutch

B151 BIBLE. Psalms. Dutch. Metrical Versions. Petrus Dathenus
[–] (col.) TOT DORDRECHT, By Fransoys Bosselaer. 1612. 16° sig.A-Nn^8
C.108.cc.20.
With the Catechism and 'Ghebeden'. Imperfect; wanting the titlepage.

B152 BIBLE. Psalms. Dutch. Metrical Versions. Petrus Dathenus
DE CL. Psalmen Davids/uyt den Fransoyschen/in Nederlandtschen dichte overgheset/Door Petrum Dathenum. Midtsgaders den Christelicken Catechismo/ ende Bekentenisse des gheloofs der Nederlandtscher Kercken/etc. Item, hier is by ghevoecht . . . den Duytschen Text, overgeset uyt den Hebreeuschen door Philips van Marnix, ghenaemt van S. Aldegonde. TOT MIDDELBVRCH, By Adriaen vande Vivere . . . M.DC.XVII. 8° sig.A-T^8V^3, pp.1–94, sig.Cc3-Dd10; music
3089.bb.1.
Printed by Richard Schilders at Middelburg?

B153 BIBLE. Psalms. French. Metrical Versions. Clément Marot and Théodore de Bèze

LES PSEAVMES MIS EN RIME Françoise. Par Clement Marot & Theodore de Beze. Mis en Musique à quatre parties par CLAVDE GOVDIMEL. A DELF, Par Bruyn H. Schinckel . . . 1602. 16° sig.A-Qq^{8}Rr^{12}; music

Music K.8.i.11; Music R.M.15.a.8.

With 'La forme des prieres ecclesiastiques', 'Le catechisme' and 'Confession de foy'.

B154 BIBLE. Psalms. Selections. Dutch

Godt de wraeck. Ofte: TROOST DER SCHRIFTVRE IN TEGHENHEYT. Begrepen In een korte uytlegginghe eenigher Psalmen Davids op Nederduytsche rijmen ghestelt: Mitsgaders andere ghedichten . . . 1620. 4° pp.31[23]

11555.e.24(2).

Translations from the Psalms by Dirck Camphuysen, interspersed with original poems by the same author. Printed by Pieter Arentsz at Norden?

B155 BIBLE. Proverbs. Latin

COMMENTARII Succincti & Dilucidi IN PROVERBIA SALOMONIS AVTHORE THOMA CARTVVRIGHTO . . . Quibus adhibita est Præfatio . . . IOHANNIS POLYANDRI . . . LVGDVNI BATAVORVM. Apud Guiljelmum Brevvsterum . . . 1617. 4° coll.1514.

3165.c.28.

With the text. Ownership inscription: Ex libris Caroli Niceæ Daviesii 1818.

B156 BIBLE. Song of Solomon. Greek

EVSEBII, POLYCHRONII, PSELLI, IN CANTICVM CANTICORVM Expositiones Græcè. IOANNES MEVRSIVS Primus nunc è tenebris eruit, & publicavit. LVGDVNI BATAVORVM, Ex Officinâ ELZEVIRIANA. Typis GODEFRIDI BASSON . . . M.D.C.XVII. 4° pp.186

3166.c.34.

With the text. Ownership inscriptions: R. M. van Goens; Pinelli Sale. April 7, 1789. 5285.

B157 BIBLE. Song of Solomon. Latin

MICHAELIS GHISLERI . . . COMMENTARIA IN CANTICVM CANTICORVM Salomonis, iuxta Lectiones, Vulgatam, Hebræam, & Græcas, tum LXX. tum aliorum veterum Interpretum, AB AVCTORE RECOGNITA ET AVCTA duplici Elencho . . . CVM DVPLICI . . . INDICE . . . ANTVERPIÆ, APVD IOANNEM KEERBERGIVM . . . M.DC.XIX. (col.) ANTVERPIÆ, TYPIS IOANNIS KEERBERGII . . . M.DC.XIX. fol. pp.962

L.16.e.11.

Ownership inscriptions: Ex Catalogo librorum Ioannis Woniecky. Oretur pro eo; Pro Conventu Posnaniensi Fratrum Minorum Reformatorum ac Sanctum Casimirū.

B158 BIBLE. Lamentations. English

THE LAMENTATIONS OF IEREMY, TRANSLATED VVITH GREAT CARE OF HIS HEBREW ELEGANCIE . . . VVITH EXPLICATIONS from other Scriptures touching his story & phrases. BY HVGH BROVGHTON 1608. 4° sig.A-E^{4}F^2

1003.b.9(8); T.812(3).

Printed by Jan Theunisz at Amsterdam?

B159 BIBLE. Hosea. Polyglot

HOSEAS PROPHETA, Ebraice & Chaldaice. Cum duplici versione Latina: ET Commentarijs Ebraïcis trium Doctissimorum Judeorum; Masorâ item parvâ, ejusque, & Commentariorum Latinâ quoque interpretatione. Accedunt in fine succinctæ sed necessariæ annotationes GVLJELMI GODDAEI . . . Lugduni Batavorum, Typis RAPHELEGIANIS. Prostant apud IOHANNEM MAIRE . . . M.DC.XXI. 4° pp.255

Or.01901.c.6.

The authors of the commentaries named in the preliminaries as: Salomon Iarhi, Abraham Aben Ezra and David Kimhi.

B160 BIBLE. Old Testament Apocrypha. Polyglot
BIBLIORVM PARS GRÆCA QVÆ HEBRAICE NON INVENITUR: Cum interlineari interpretatione LATINA, ex Biblijs Complutensibus deprompta. EX OFFICINA PLANTINIANA RAPHELENGII, 1612. 8° pp.344
1408.h.11.
Published at Leiden. Intended as part of an edition entitled 'Biblia Hebraica'. A copy of a set of the other volumes belonging to this is entered above under BIBLE. Old Testament. Polyglot.

B161 BIBLE. New Testament. Greek
ΤΗΣ ΚΑΙΝΗΣ ΔΙΑΘΗΚΗΣ ΑΠΑΝΤΑ. Nouum Iesu Christi D.N. Testamentum. Ex Officina Plantiniana APVD CHRISTOPHORVM RAPHELENGIVM . . . M.D.CI. 24° pp.767
C.19.a.33.
Published at Leiden.

B162 BIBLE. New Testament. Greek
ΤΗΣ ΚΑΙΝΗΣ ΔΙΑΘΗΚΗΣ ΑΠΑΝΤΑ. Nouum Iesu Christi D.N. Testamentum. EX OFFICINA PLANTINIANA RAPHELENGII M.D.CXII. 16° pp.670
3015.aa.16.
Published at Leiden. In the device the word 'Labore' is facing backwards and other letters have been printed upside down. Imperfect; wanting pp.25–28. Ownership inscriptions: Ex libris M. de Bönninghausen; R: V: Canniford 1820; C. W. Meadows Right e Coll. Univ. Oxon.

B163 BIBLE. New Testament. Polyglot
LE NOVVEAV TESTAMENT . . . Het nieuwe Testament . . . V [*sic*] LEYDEN, Chez Antoine Maire. M.DCII. 16° pp.1104
3049.aa.12.
In French and Dutch.

B164 BIBLE. New Testament. Polyglot
NOVVM TESTAMENTVM GRÆCE, Cum vulgata Interpretatione Latina . . . Quæ quidem interpretatio, cùm à Græcarum dictionum proprietate discedit . . . in margine libri est collocata: atque alia BEN. ARIÆ MONTANI . . . operâ è verbo reddita . . . in eius est substituta locum. EX OFFICINA PLANTINIANA RAPHELENGII, 1613. 8° pp.681
1408.h.15.
Published at Leiden. Ownership inscription: ex Conuentu S. Joseph paris. Carmel. Discal. Another copy of one included in an edition of the Bible which is entered above under BIBLE. Polyglot.

BIBLE. New Testament Latin. Nouum Iesu Christi Testamentum. Antuerpiæ, 1616. *See* supra: BIBLE. Latin

B165 BIBLE. New Testament. English
THE NEW TESTAMENT OF OVR LORD IESVS CHRIST, TRANSLATED out of the Greeke by THEOD. BEZA. And Englished by L.T. . . . AT DORT Printed, by Isaac Canin, 1601. At the expensis of the aires of Henrie Charteris, and Andrew Hart, in Edinburgh [etc.] (col.) AT DORT Printed, by Isaac Canin. 1601. 32° sig.A-K^{8}xx^4
C.38.b.39.
The translator is Laurence Tomson.

B166 BIBLE. New Testament. English

THE NEVV TESTAMENT OF IESVS CHRIST FAITHFVLLY TRANSLATED INTO ENGLISH . . . VVITH ANNOTATIONS, AND OTHER HELPES, for the better vnderstanding of the text and specially for the discouerie of corruptions in diuers late translations . . . IN THE ENGLISH COLLEGE OF RHEMES. PRINTED AT ANTVVERP. By Iames Seldenslach. 1621. 12° 2 pt.: pp.285; 349
1006.a.17; C.69.bb.24.

The second edition. The copy at C.69.bb.24 is imperfect, consisting of the Annotations only.

B167 BIBLE. New Testament. Dutch

Het Nieuvve Testament/ons Heeren Jesu Christi. Van nieuș . . . ouersien, eñ naer den lesten Roomschen text verbetert door sommige Doctoren . . . inde vermaerde Vniuersiteyt van Louen. Na de Copie gheprent T'HANTWERPEN, By Jan van Keerberghen . . . 1601. (col.) Typis Henrici Swingenij. 8° pp.748; illus.
3040.bb.4.

The approbations, dated 1598, apply to the whole Bible. The illustrations are in woodcut. Ownership inscription: J.F. van Audenrode Pastor in Sterrebeke 1788.

B168 BIBLE. New Testament. Dutch

Dat Nieuwe Testament ons liefs Heeren Jesu Christi . . . GEDRVCT. Naer het oude Exemplaer van Nicolaes Biestkens. Voor PASCHIER VAN WESBVSCH . . . TOT HAERLEM. 1602. (col.) Ghedruckt tot Alckmaer, by Iacob de Meester . . . 1602. 4° ff.274
3041.ccc.6.

The titlepage is engraved; signed: KMandre Inue.; JMaetham sculp.

B169 BIBLE. New Testament. Dutch

HET NIEV TESTAMENT ONSES HEEREN IESV CHRISTI Met korte uytlegghingen DOOR FRANCISCVM COSTERVM . . . T'ANTWERPEN BY IOACHIM TROGNÆSIVS M.DCXIV. [etc.] (col.) T'ANTWERPEN BY IOACHIM TROGNÆSIVS M.DCXIV. fol. pp.962[952]
1605/16.

The titlepage is engraved. The pagination is faulty throughout.

B170 BIBLE. New Testament. Dutch

Het nieuwe TESTAMENT onses Heeren Iesu Christi. Wt den Grieckschen overgheset. Neerstelick nu oversien . . . ende . . . ghesuyvert . . . midtsgaders annotatien . . . Door H.F. TOT MIDDELBVRCH, By Adriaen vande Vivere . . . M.DC.XVJJ. [etc.] 8° sig.(***)^{4}A-Eee^8
3040.b.25.

The preface signed: Hermannus Faukelius. With 'Geloofs-forme ende bekentenisse' on the last leaf. Ownership inscription: Henry Stevens of Vermont 1882.

B171 BIBLE. Gospels. Polyglot

(tp.1) IN SACROSANCTA QVATVOR IESV CHRISTI EVANGELIA FRANCISCI LVCÆ BRVGENSIS . . . COMMENTARIVS. Alia eiusdem Auctoris ad S. SCRIPTVRÆ lucem opuscula. ANTVERPIAE. EX OFFICINA PLANTINIANA Apud Ioannem Moretum M.DC.VI.

(tp.2 = between pp.571, 572) IN SACROSANCTA QVATVOR IESV CHRISTI EVANGELIA FRANCISCI LVCAE BRVGENSIS . . . COMMENTARIORVM Tomus posterior. ANTVERPIÆ, EX OFFICINA PLANTINIANA, Apud Ioannem Moretum. M.DC.VI.

(tp.3) . . . COMMENTARIORVM Tomus tertius. ANTVERPIÆ, EX OFFICINA PLANTINIANA, Apud Viduam & Filios Ioannis Moreti. M.DC.XII.

(tp.4) . . . COMMENTARIORVM Tomus Quartus & Vltimus continens Complementum Euangelij secundùm Iohannem. ANTVERPIÆ, EX OFFICINA

PLANTINIANA, Apud Viduam & Filios Ioannis Moreti. MDC.XVI. (col., tom.2 only) ANTVERPIÆ, EX OFFICINA PLANTINIANA, APVD IOANNEM MORETVM. M.DC.VI. fol. 4 tom.: pp.1124; 317; 192
689.h.3.
The titlepage is engraved.

B172 BIBLE. Gospels. Harmonies. Latin
TRIVMPHVS UERITATIS ORDINATI EVANGELII QVADRIGA INVECTÆ, SANCTORVM PATRVM EXERCITV STIPATÆ, AVTHORE R.P. IOANNE DE LA HAYE . . . DVACI, Ex Typographia BALTHAZARIS BELLERI, Suis, & IOANNIS KEERBERGII Bibliopolæ Antuerpiensis sumptibus . . . 1609. fol. 2 tom.: pp.808; 165[567]
3205.h.6.
The engraved titlepage of tom.1 signed: Martinus Bas Sculp. Duaci. Ownership inscription: Monasterij S. Crucis Donawerdæ.

B173 BIBLE. Liturgical Epistles and Gospels. Latin
ADNOTATIONES ET MEDITATIONES IN EVANGELIA QVÆ IN SACROSANCTO MISSÆ SACRIFICIO TOTO ANNO LEGVNTVR: Cum eorundem EVANGELIORVM Concordantia. Auctore HIERONYMO NATAL . . . EDITIO VLTIMA: In qua Sacer Textus ad emendationem Bibliorum SIXTI V. et CLEMENTIS VIII. restitutus. ANTVERPIÆ, EX OFFICINA PLANTINIANA, Apud Ioannem Moretum. M.DC.VII. (col.) ANTVERPIAE, EX OFFICINA PLANTINIANA, Apud Ioannem Moretum. M.DC.VII. fol. pp.636: pl.153
689.i.9.
The editor's dedication signed: Jacobus Ximenes. The plates are by the brothers Wierix and others, the engraved titlepage is dated 1596.

B174 BIBLE. Luke. Latin
(tp.1) R^DI PATRIS FRATRIS DIDACI STELLÆ . . . in sacrosanctum Iesu Christi . . . Euangelium secundum Lucam enarrationum TOMVS PRIMVS. Nunc tandem ab infinitis erroribus, ad sanctæ Inquisitionis Hispaniæ decreta prosus elimati, & . . . repurgati . . . ANTVERPIÆ, Sumptibus Viduæ & Hæredum Petri Belleri . . . M.D.C.VIII. [etc.] (col.1) ANTVERPIÆ, Excudebat Andreas Bacx. 1606.
(tp.2) R^DI PATRIS . . . DIDACI STELLÆ . . . in . . . Euangelium secundum Lucam enarrationum TOMVS SECVNDVS. Editio vltima ab authore recognita. ANTVERPIÆ, Sumptibus Viduæ & Hæredum Petri Belleri . . . M.D.C.VIII. [etc.] fol. 2 tom.: pp.282; 319
3205.f.21.
With the text. With a laudatory poem signed: Emanuel Correa Lusitanus, Typographiæ Corrector.

B175 BIBLE. Revelation. Latin
REV. PATRIS LVDOVICI AB ALCASAR . . . VESTIGATIO ARCANI SENSVS IN APOCALYPSI. Cum opusculo de sacris Ponderibus ac Mensuris. ANTVERPIÆ, Apud Ioannem Keerbergium. M.DC.XIV. [etc.] (col.) ANTVERPIAE Typis GERARDI WOLSCHATI, & HENRICI AERTSI. M.DC.XIV. fol. pp.1025,80; illus.
L.7.c.4.
With the text. The illustrations signed: Don Iuan de Iauregi inuentor.

B176 BIBLE. Revelation. French
CLAIRE EXPOSITION DE L'APOCALYPSE OV REVELATION DE S. IAN. Avec deduction de l'histoire, & chronologies. PAR IAN TAFFIN. A FLESSINGVE. Imprimé par Martin Abrahams vander Nolijck . . . M DC IX. 8° pp.254,762
219.c.2.
With the text.

B177 BIBLE. Concordances. Latin

CONCORDANTIAE BIBLIORVM SANCTORVM VVLGATAE EDITIONIS AD RECOGNITIONEM IVSSV SIXTI V. . . . BIBLIIS ADHIBITAM RECENSITÆ ATQVE EMENDATÆ Operâ & studio FRANCISCI LVCÆ BRVGENSIS . . . Accessit Correctorum Plantinianorum industria; qui . . . innumeros . . . errores sustulere . . . ANTVERPIÆ, EX OFFICINA PLANTINIANA, Apud Balthasarem & Ioannem Moretos. M.DC.XVII. [etc.] (col.) ANTVERPIÆ, EX OFFICINA PLANTINIANA, APVD BALTHASAREM ET IOANNEM MORETOS FRATRES. M.DC.XVII. fol. sig. $\star^4$A-Rrr^{6}Sss^4
689.i.4.

B178 BIDERMANUS, Jacobus

IACOBI BIDERMANI . . . EPIGRAMMATVM LIBRI TRES . . . ANTVERPIÆ, Apud Heredes Martini Nutij . . . M.DC.XX. 12° pp.216
1213.c.9.

B179 BIE, Jacques de

IMPERATORVM ROMANORVM NVMISMATA AVREA A Julio Caesare ad Heraclium continua serie collecta et ex archetypis expressa. Industria et manu Iacobi de Bie. Accedit breuis et Historica eorundem explicatio. ANTVERPIÆ, Typis Gerardi Wolschatij et Henrici Aertsij . . . M.DC.XV. 4° sig.a-c^4: pl.64: pp.233
C.83.c.10.

The titlepage is engraved, after a design by Rubens. In a binding bearing the arms and initials of Charles I as Prince of Wales, dated 1621.

B180 BIE, Jacques de

LIVRE. CONTENANT. LA. GENEALOGIE. ET. DESCENTE. DE. CEUX. DE. LA. MAISON. DE. CROY . . . IACOBVS. DE. BYE . . . SCALPTOR. FEC. fol.
607.m.9.

Engraved throughout. Sixty leaves, made up from first, second and third issues, the first printed at Antwerp circa 1612, the second and third at Amsterdam in the 18th century. Wanting ten plates of the first issue. Paper and manuscript inscriptions not always as described in the *Bibliotheca Belgica* no. B4.

B181 BIESIUS, Nicolaus

NICOLAI BIESII . . . DE NATVRA, LIB. V. . . . ANTVERPIÆ, Apud Gislenum Ianssenium. M.D.CXIII. 8° ff.180
1135.d.11.

B182 BIESTKENS, Nicolaes; the Younger

(tp.1) Het eerste deel Van Claas Kloet. Ghespeelt op de Duytsche Academie. T'AMSTERDAM, Voor Jan Marcusz . . . 1619.
(tp.2=sig.B4r) Het tvveede deel Van Claas Kloet . . . T'AMSTERDAM, Voor Jan Marcusz . . . 1619.
(tp.3=sig.E2r) Het derde deel Van Claas Kloet . . . T'AMSTERDAM, Voor Jan Marcusz . . . 1619. (col.) By Nicolaas Biestkens/Boeckdrucker . . . 1619. 4° sig.A-G^4
11555.bb.4.

Signed: C. Biestkens. With Nicolaes Biestkens's printer's device on leaves B3r and G4r.

B183 BIGA

BIGA MINISTRORVM SEV DVPLEX REGVLA MORVM. IVXTA ITER ERRORVM sine lege REFORMATORVM. LVDVS LEONIVS . . . BREDÆ Apud Henricum Capricornum ad insigne Sybillæ. 1615. 4° sig.A^{4}B^2
11408.e.67(4).

Satirical verses, mainly in Latin, but with two lines in Dutch, against Hendrik Boxhorn and Gerard Lievens. The imprint is false; printed at Antwerp?

B184 BILSON, Thomas; Bishop
[A sermon preached at Westminster.] Een Sermoon: Ghepredickt tot VVestminster/voor des Konings ende der Koninginnen Majesteyten/op hare Crooninghe . . . den 25. Julius/Anno M.VJ.C.JJJ. Door den . . . Bisschop van VVinchester. Ende uyt de Engelsche inde Nederlandtsche Tale . . . overgheset door VINCENTIVM MEVSEVOET. TOT AMSTELREDAM. By Ian Evertsz. Cloppenburgh . . . 1604. 4° sig.AB^4
T.2417(8).

Den BINCKHORST. 1613. *See* BORSSELEN, Philibert van

B185 BIONDI, Giuseppe
[Relazione della prigionia e morte del Signor Troilo Sauelli.] A RELATION OF THE DEATH, OF . . . Sig.^{r} Troilo Sauelli, a Baron of Rome; Who was there beheaded . . . on the 18. of Aprill, 1592 . . . M.DC.XX. 8° pp.255
C.26.h.8; G.14681.
Anonymous. The Italian original circulated in manuscript only and was first printed in French, with the title of 'Discours pitoyable de la mort du seigneur Troïle Savelle'. The English version translated and with an introduction by Sir Tobie Matthew. Without imprint; published by the English College press at St. Omer. The copy at G.14681 has manuscript notes in French, including the name 'Toby Matthews Knight' at the end of the preface.

B186 BLAEU, Willem Jansz
[Het licht der zeevaert.] (tp.1) THE LIGHT OF NAVIGATION VVHERIN ARE DECLARED AND LIVELY POVRtrayed, all the Coasts and Havens, of the VVest, North and East Seas. COLLECTED PARTLY OVT OF THE BOOKS OF the principall Authors, (as Lucas Iohnson VVaghenaer and divers others) partly also out of manie other expert Seafaring Mens writings and verball declarations: corrected from manie faults . . . Divided into tvvo Books. HEERVNTO ARE ADDED (BESIDE AN INSTITVTION in the Art of Navigation) nevve Tables of the Declination of the Sonne, according to Tycho Brahes Observations . . . BY WILLIAM IOHNSON. AT AMSTERDAM Printed by William Iohnson . . . 1612. [etc.]
(tp.2) THE FIRST BOOKE OF THE LIGHT OF NAVIGATION . . . AT AMSTERDAM Printed by William Iohnson . . . 1612.
(tp.3) THE SECOND BOOK OF THE LIGHT OF NAVIGATION . . . AT AMSTERDAM PRINTED BY WILLIAM IOHNSON . . . 1612. obl.4° 3 pt.: sig.$A\text{-}D^4E^8F^2$; pp.114; 118: pl.41; illus., maps, volvelles
Maps C.8.a.1.
The English text on the first, engraved, titlepage is printed on a label pasted over the original engraved Dutch text which has been removed although traces remain. Titles of maps in Dutch and French, some dated 1607, as in the original edition of 1608. The movable parts of the volvelle on C3r are missing.

B187 BLAEU, Willem Jansz
[Het licht der zeevaert.] (tp.1) LE FLAMBEAV DE LA NAVIGATION, MONSTRANT LA description & delineation de toutes les Costes & Havres de la Mer Occidentale, Septentrionale, & Orientale . . . A quoy est adjoustée une Instruction de l'Art de Marine, avec Tables de la Declination du Soleil suivant les Observations de Tycho Brahe . . . Par GVILLAVME IANSZOON.· A AMSTERDAM, Chez Guillaume Ieansz. . . . 1619. [etc.]
(tp.2) LE PREMIER LIVRE DV PHALOT DE LA MER . . . A AMSTERDAM, Imprimé par Guillame Ianson . . . 161 [*sic*].

(tp.3) DEVXIESME LIVRE DV PHALOT DE MER . . . Nouvellement traduict de Flameng en François. A AMSTERDAM, Chez VVillem Iansz. . . . MDCXIX. obl.4° 3 pt.: sig. A-F^4G^2; pp.119; 122: pl.41; illus., maps, volvelles
Maps C.8.a.17.

The French title on the first, engraved, titlepage has been printed on a label pasted over the original Dutch title. The space for a volvelle on D2v is empty.

B188 BLAEU, Willem Jansz

[Het licht der zeevaert.] (tp.1) LE FLAMBEAV DE LA NAVIGATION . . . Par GVILLAVME IANSZOON. A AMSTERDAM. Chez Iean Ieansson . . . 1620.

(tp.2) LE PREMIER LIVRE DV PHALOT DE LA MER . . . A AMSTERDAM, Chez Ian Iansson . . . 1620.

(tp.3) DEVXIESME LIVRE DV PHALOT DE MER . . . Nouvellement traduict de Flameng en François. A AMSTERDAM. Chez Ian Iansson . . . 1620. obl.4° 3 pt.: sig. A-F^4G^2; pp.119; 127: pl.41; illus., maps, volvelles
Maps C.8.a.2.

An imitation of the Blaeu edition. The French text on the first, engraved, titlepage printed on a label pasted over the engraved Dutch title. Only part of the volvelle on D2v still in place.

B189 BLEFKEN, Dithmar

DITHMARI BLEFKENII ISLANDIA, SIVE Populorum & mirabilium quæ in ea Insula reperiuntur ACCVRATIOR DESCRIPTIO: Cui de GRONLANDIA sub finem adjecta. LVGDVNI BATAVORVM, Ex Typographeio Henrici ab Haestens, M D CVII. 8° pp.71
794.d.5; 153.a.40.

B190 BLEFKEN, Dithmar

[Islandia.] EEN Corte ende warachtige beschrijvinge der twee Eylanden/Ijslandt ende Groen-lant. In drucke wtghegheven door Dithmarum Blefkenium . . . Wt de Latijnsche tale ouergheset in de Nederduytsche. TOT GORINCHEM, Voor Adriaen Helmichsz . . . 1608. 8° pp.48
572.a.28.

With use of civilité on the titlepage.

B191 BLOEMHOF

DEN Bloem-Hof Van de Nederlantsche Ieught. beplant. met uytgelesene Elegien, Sonnetten, Epithalamien, ē gesangen . . . t'Amstelredam. By Dirck Pieterss . . . 1608. (col.) t'AMSTELREDAM, By Dirck Pietersz. [etc.] obl.4° pp.102: illus.
11557.df.16.

By various authors. Compiled by D. P. Pers? The engraved titlepage signed F.B. fecit, i.e. Floris Balthasarsz van Berckenrode. Some of the engravings signed: CJV, i.e. Claes Jansz Visscher. The pagination is irregular. Printed largely in civilité.

B192 BLUM, Hans; of Lohr am Main

Grundtlicher bericht Von den fünff Sülen/vnnd deren eigentliche contrafeyung/ nach Symmetrischer vszteilung der Architectur. Durch . . . M. Hans Blumen von Lor am Mayn . . . Getruckt zu Amsterdam bey Wilhelm Janssz. Jm M.DC.XII. Jar. fol. sig.★,A-H^2; illus.
1811.b.12(2).

Except for the dedication on sig.★2, woodcuts with accompanying text printed on one side of the leaf only.

Die BLYDE incompste den hertochdomme van Brabant. 1607. *See* BRABANT. Customs and Privileges

B193 BLY-LIEDEN

BLY-LIEDEN Op de vvtcomste van de Predicanten, die om de vercondinghe des Euangeliums ghevanghen vvaeren . . . ONDER t'CRUYS, Gedruckt . . . 1621. 4° sig.A^2

T.2251(8).
Printed by Pieter Arents at Norden?

BLYVENBURCH, Henricus Gregorius a (=BLYVENBURGIUS, Henricus Gregorius) *See* GREGORIUS, Henricus

B194 BOCCACCIO, Giovanni

[Decamerone. Dutch] (tp.1) Vijftich Lustighe Historien oft Nieuwicheden Joannis Boccatij/Van nieus overgheset in onse Nederduytsche sprake deur Dirick Coornhert . . . Tot Amstelredam. Voor Cornelis Claesz . . . 1607.
(tp.2) De Tweede 50. Lustige Historien ofte Nieuwicheden IOHANNIS BOCCATII. Nu Nieuwelijcks vertaelt . . . t'AMSTELREDAM. Ghedruckt by Hendrick Barentsz. . . . 1605. 4° 2 pt.: ff.135; pp.104; illus., port.
12470.c.3.
The translator's preface to pt.2 signed: G.H.V.B., i.e. Gerrit Hendricksz van Breughel.

B195 BOCHIUS, Joannes

HISTORICA NARRATIO PROFECTIONIS ET INAVGVRATIONIS SERENISSIMORVM BELGII PRINCIPVM ALBERTI ET ISABELLÆ . . . Et eorum optatissimi in Belgium Aduentus, Rerumq́ue gestarum et memorabilium . . . hactenus editorum accurata Descriptio. AVCTORE IOANNE BOCHIO . . . ANTVERPIÆ EX OFFICINA PLANTINIANA. APVD IOANNEM MORETVM. M.DC II. (col.) ANTVERPIAE, EX OFFICINA PLANTINIANA, APVD IOANNEM MORETVM . . . M.DCII. fol. pp.500; illus., music, ports.
L.23.dd.10; Hirsch I.76; 808.m.2(1).
Including 'Descriptio pompæ et gratulationis publicæ . . . a Senatu Populoq. Gandavensi . . . decretæ. Maximo Æmyliano Vrientio . . . auctore' and 'Descriptio triumphi et spectaculorum . . . Principibus Alberto et Isabellae . . . in . . . Comitatum ac ciuitatem Valentianam ingredientibus editorum . . . Auctore Henrico d'Oultremanno'. The plates are by Josse de Momper and Pieter van der Borcht. The copy at L.23.dd.10 has a label on the titlepage reading: BRVXELLIS, Apud SIMONEM T'SERSTEVENS. The copy at 808.m.2(1) is imperfect; wanting pp.185–188, 195/196, 203–206, 409/410, 451–454.

BOCHIUS, Joannes. Ioannis Bochii . . . Psalmorum . . . parodia heroica. 1608. *See* BIBLE. Psalms. Latin

B196 BOCKENBERCH, Jacob Dircxs

Een Pelgerimsche Reyse nae de H. Stadt Ierusalem, Die gedaen heeft den E. Iacob Dircx Bockenberch van der Goude in Hollant. Die al t'voornaemste/so op den wech/als oock int H. Landt . . . beschreven eñ fijguyrlick . . . afghebeeldet . . . Noch een Pelgerimsche reyse die ghedaen heeft den E. Heer Ieronimus Scheydt van Erffort int Iaer 1615 van Ierusalem nae de Iordaen, eñ voorts nae Sodoma ende Gomorra, ende vvederom door Egypten nae Ierusalem. Gedruckt tot Coelen, Voor Henrick van Witten . . . 1620. 8° pp.122, sig.H6–O8; illus.
10077.aa.31.
The imprint is false; in fact printed by Henrick van Haestens at Leiden. The illustrations are woodcuts.

B197 BOCKENBERG, Petrus Cornelisz

P. CORNELISSONII BOCKENBERGII AD NONNVLLA IANI Dousæ V.N. aspera scripta, extemporalis responsio . . . DELPHIS. Ex officina Brunonis H. Schinckelij . . . 1601. 8° pp.48
1568/5522.
With quotations from Dousa's works in Latin or Dutch.

BOECK. Het tweede boeck, journael oft dagh-register. 1601. *See* NECK, Jacob van

B198 BOEREN-LITANIE

BOEREN-LITANIE Ofte CLACHTE DER KEMPENSCHE LAND-LIEDEN over de ellenden van

dese lanck-durighe Nederlandsche Oorloghe. Met De Antvvoorde der Chrijgslieden op de selve Boeren-clachte. Noch Eenighe Gedichten van Bestand ende Vrede. Noch Sommighe Graf-schriften van den Admirael Iacob Heemskerck. M.D.C.VII. 4° 8 unsigned leaves
106.d.9.

In verse. An enlarged version of one originally printed the same year by Dirck Cornelisz Troost at Amsterdam.

B199 BOEREN-LITANIE

BOEREN-LITANIE Ofte Klachte der Kempensche Landt-lieden/over de ellenden van deze lanck-duerighe Nederlandtsche Oorloghe. Ghedruckt bij Dirck Cornelisz. Troost . . . M.D.C.VJII. 4° 4 unsigned leaves; illus.
T.1713(26).

In verse. With reference to the death of Jacob van Heemskerck. Published at Amsterdam, first published by Troost in 1607.

B200 BOEREN-SLACH

Den Boeren-Slach Gheslaghen/Door dese Personagien. Remmet Coeje-clauwer, Dirck Slodder, Heyndrick Goesmoes, en Adriaen Modder. Ghedruckt . . . 1618. 4° sig. A^4
11555.e.41(4).

In verse, with reference to events at Hoorn. Signed: Elck wacht hem.

B201 BOERTIGHE

Een Boertighe Clucht, Ofte Een Tafel-spel van twee Personagien/te weten/een Quacksalver met zijn Knecht: de Quacksalver is ghenaemt Meester Canjart, ende de Knecht is genaemt Hansje quaet Cruyt. t'AMSTERDAM, By Cornelis Lodewijcksz. vander Plasse . . . 1615. 4° sig. A^4(+ title-leaf)
11556.cc.26.

The publisher's preface states 'Dese Cluyt . . . by die van de Hollandsche Kamer ghespeelt'.

The first and second BOOKE of discipline. 1621. *See* SCOTLAND. Church of Scotland

B202 BOETHIUS, Anicius Manlius Torquatus Severinus

[De consolatione philosophiae. Latin] ANICI MANLI SEVERINI BOETI DE CONSOLATIONE PHILOSOPHIÆ LIBRI QVINQVE. IOH. BERNARTIVS recensuit, & Commentario illustrauit. ANTVERPIÆ, EX OFFICINA PLANTINIANA, Apud Ioannem Moretum. M.DC.VII. (col. 1. p. 142) ANTVERPIÆ, EX OFFICINA PLANTINIANA, APVD IOANNEM MORETVM. M.DC.IV. (col. 2) ANTVERPIÆ, EX OFFICINA PLANTINIANA, Apud Ioannem Moretum. M.DC.VII. 8° pp. 394
524.d.24; 677.b.6; 683.b.10.

The approbation is dated 1601. The copy at 683.b.10 has manuscript notes by Richard Bentley.

B203 BOETHIUS, Anicius Manlius Torquatus Severinus

[De consolatione philosophiae. Dutch] Boëthius vande Vertróósting der wíjsheíjd: uyt't Latyn op nieus vertaalt. Door D. V. Coornhert. t'Amsterdam, Voor Pieter Jacobsz. Paets . . . 1616. (col.) 't AMSTERDAM, Ghedruckt by Paulus van Ravesteyn . . . 1616. 8° pp. 212; music, port.
1578/1.

The frame surrounding the woodcut portrait of Coornhert on the titlepage signed: CVS, i.e. Christoffel van Sichem.

BOGERMAN, Johannes. Spieghel der Iesuyten. 1608. *See* PASQUIER, Étienne

B204 BOHEMIA

[5.7.1609] TRANSLAET Van des Keysers Octroy-brief/ende 't Accoort verleent den Evangelischen drie Stenden des Coninckrijcks van Bohemien . . . den 5^{en}.

Julij . . . 1609. Daer by denselven Stenden de vrye openbare Oeffeninghe van haerlieder Religie toeghestaen wordt. IN 'SGRAVEN-HAGHE, By Hillebrandt Jacobsz . . . 1609. 4° sig. A^4
T.2421(11).

B205 BOHEMIA
[7.11.1619] A DECLARATION ON THE CAVSES, FOR THE WHICH, WEE FREDERICK . . . KING OF BOHEMIA . . . haue ACCEPTED OF THE CROWNE OF BOHEMIA, AND OF THE COVNTRYES THEREVNTO annexed. MIDDLEBVRG. Printed by Abraham Schilders. M.D.C.XX. 4° pp.23
1315.c.2(1).
Dated 7.11.1619. Written by Ludovicus Camerarius as 'Friderici . . . Regis . . . Declaratio Publica', 'Unsser Friderichs . . . Offen Aussschreiben'. The imprint is false; printed by William Jones or William Stansby at London?

B206 BOHEMIA
[28.11.1619] PVBLIIQVE VYTSCHRIIVINGHE Van ons Frederick . . . Coninck in Bohemen . . . Waeromme wy de Croone van Bohemen . . . aenghenomen hebben. IN 'SGRAVEN-HAGE. By Aert Meuris . . . 1619. 4° sig. AB^4
T.2249(54); T.2423(27).
Dated 28.11.1619. In fact, a Dutch version of the preceding.

B207 BOHEMIA
[15.1.1620] ARTYCKELEN Van het Eeuwich Verbondt/ghemaect tusschen Frederick/ Koninck van BOHEMEN . . . Met GABRIEL, Prince van Hungarien ende Transsylvanien . . . t'samentlijck de Stenden des voor-ghemelten Rijcks. 't AMSTERDAM, By Ian Evertsz. Kloppenburgh . . . 1620. 4° sig. AB^4
T.2250(22).
Dated 15.1.1620.

B208 BOHEMIA
[15.1.1620] ARTICVLEN Vande Confederatie der Hongarische/Bohemische ende gheincorporeerde Provintien. IN 'SGRAVEN-HAGHE, By Hillebrant Iacobssz . . . 1620. 4° sig. AB^4
T.2250(21); T.2423(34).
Concluded 15.1.1620. A different translation from the preceding.

B209 BOHEMIA
[24.3.1620] COPIE Vanden Brief des Conings van Bohemen/aenden . . . Coningh van Vranckrijck ende van Navarre. IN S'GRAVEN-HAGHE, By Hillebrant Iacobssz . . . 1620. 4° sig. A^4
T.2250(27); T.2423(35).
Dated 24.3.1620.

*B209** BOHEMIA
[12.1620–1.1621] COPIA Vande Brieven gheschreven van Frederick Pfaltzgraeff aen de Standen van Slesien. Met noch eenen anderen gheschreven aen den ouden Grave van Thouren. Overghesedt vvt de hooch-Duytsche sprake in onse Nederlantsche Tale. Eerst ghedruckt den 10. Meert/1621. T'hantwerpen/By Abraham Verhoeuen/[etc.] 4° pp.8; sig.(–); illus.
P.P.3444.af(198).
Headed: Martius.1621.32. Containing only one letter to the Silesian States and one to the Count of Thuringia. With other news. The titlepage woodcut shows a queen with a child.

B210 BOHEMIA
[23.5.1621] Copye/Van den Brieff van KONINCK FREDERICK Met de Commissie aenden MARG-GRAVE VAN IAGERSDORP Ghegeven . . . den 23 May, 1621. (col.) Ghedruckt t'Amstelredam by Ioris Veseler . . . 1621. fol. a single sheet
T.2424(19).

B211 BOHEMIA. States

[25.5.1618] APOLOGIA Ordinum inclyti Regni Behemię, sub Vtraque, cur defendendi Regis, & sui causâ militem legere statuerint . . . PRAGAE primum edita: Nunc verò Latinè excusa. HAGÆ Comitum Hollandiæ. Apud Arnoldum Meuris . . . M.IC.C.XIX. [*sic*] Mense Ianuario. 4° pp.26

8072.d.15.

A translation of the so-called 'first' Apology, compiled by Peter Milner von Milhausen, issued by the States of Bohemia on 25 May 1618 under the title 'Apologia, oder Entschuldigungs Schrifft'.

B212 BOHEMIA. States

[25.5.1618] APOLOGIA Ofte Volcomen verantwoordinghe/Waeromme die drie Standen des . . . Coninckrijcx Bohemen . . . haer hebben moeten defenderen/ Insonderheyt teghen die schadelicke Secte der Jesuyten. Overgheset uyt den Hoochduytsche in onse Nederlantsche spraecke. Gedruckt in d'oude Stadt Praagh, by Samuel Adamsz van VVeleslavvin 1618 Ende nu Tot Amsterdam. 4° sig.AB^4

T.2423(10).

A translation of the document compiled by Peter Milner von Milhausen, entitled 'Apologia, oder Entschuldigungs Schrifft' and issued by the States of Bohemia on 25 May 1618. The Dutch edition also published in 1618? Cropped.

B213 BOHEMIA. States

[25.5.1618] PLACCAET, Ende waerachtige beschrijvinghe/vande groote verraderye die de bloet-dorstighe Jesuwyten binnen Prage (tegens de . . . Ghereformeerde Religie) hebben ghepractiseert . . . voor den dach . . . gecomen op den 18. May/1618. Ende hoe de Heere-standen mette andere Heeren vant Rijck/hier in teghen den . . . verraders hen hebben ghedragen: ende mede vanden grooten op loop die . . . binnen Praeg op den 23. May is gheweest . . . Gedruct tot VVtrecht, Voor Melis Jansz/1618. 4° sig.A^2

T.2423(9).

Dated 28 May 1618, but in fact an abridged version of Peter Milner von Milhausen's 'Apologia', issued by the States of Bohemia on the 25th.

B214 BOHEMIA. States

[June/July 1618] Cort Bericht ende wederlegginge/der beswaernissen eñ betichtinghen/dewelcke den Evangelischen Stenden/in't Coninckrijcke van Bohemen/tot derselver ongelimp ende naedeel/te laste willen geleyt werden. Ghedruckt nae de Copie tot Prage. IN 'SGRAVEN-HAGE. By Aert Meuris . . . 1618. 4° pp.18

T.2248(32); T.2423(12).

A translation of 'Kurtzer Bericht und Ableinung der Beschwerungen', issued by the States of Bohemia in June or July 1618.

B215 BOHEMIA. States

[December 1618] APOLOGIE OV Declaration des raisons pour lesquelles les trois Estats du Royaume de Boheme Sub vtraque ont esté contraints de prendre les armes pour leur defence & conseruation. ITEM, VN EXTRAIT D'vn liure publié à Pauie par Gaspard Scioppius . . . soubs ce tiltre CLASSICUM BELLI SACRI . . . Le tout traduit en François par S.W. l'An 1619. 4° pp.245[244]

1056.i.10.

The first piece is a translation of 'Druha apologie' or 'Die andere Apologie', issued by the States of Bohemia in December 1618. Dedicated to the States General and Prince Maurice. The translator is S. Weis. Published in the Netherlands; the General Catalogue suggests printed at Deventer.

B216 BOHEMIA. States

[9.9.1619] ANTWOORDT Op den Brieff van den Princc van Transylvanien GABRIEL BETHLEMI. Ghesonden Vande Heeren Directeurs ende Raetsluyden des Rijcks Bohemen/uyt Prage. IN 'SGRAVEN-HAGE. By Aert Meuris . . . 1619. 4° sig.A^3

T.2423(19).

Gabriel Bethlen's letter was dated 18 August 1619, the reply of the States of Bohemia 9 August 1619.

B217 BOHEMIA. States

[1–7.11.1619] THE REASONS which compelled the States of Bohemia to reiect the Archiduke Ferdinand &c. & inforced them to elect a new King. Togeather VVITH THE PROPOSition which was made vppon the first motion of the chocie [*sic*] of th' Elector Palatine to be King of Bohemia, by the States of that Kingdome . . . Translated out of the french copies. at.Dort. Printet by. George Waters. 4° pp.30

1315.c.2(2).

A translation of the document issued by the States of Bohemia between 1 and 7 November 1619 as 'Brevis causarum coniectio'. The address to the reader signed: Iohn Harrison. Published in 1619?

B218 BOHEMIA. States

[1–7.11.1619] DE REDENEN die De Staten van Bohemen beweecht hebben den Erts-hertoch Ferdinandus te verworpen/etc. Ende haer gedrongen hebben/eenen nieuwen Coninck te kiesen. Als oock De propositie . . . om te kiesen den . . . Palts graef tot Coninck van Bohemen, door de Staten van dat Conincrijcke . . . op den 16^{en}. Augustij . . . Overgeset uyt de france Copie. Tot Dordrecht, By Niclaes Vincentz . . . 1619. 4° pp.40

T.2423(26).

A translation of the 'Brevis causarum coniectio', issued by the States of Bohemia between 1 and 7 November 1619.

B219 BOHEMIA. States

[3?1620] Extract ende Conditien, vvt de Propositien van den Generalen Landt-dagh/de welcke de Rebellen van Bohemien/binnen . . . Prage met hare Gheconfedereerde ghesloten hebben. Overgheset uyt de Hooch-duytsche sprake, in onse Nederlandtsche Tale. Nu eerst Ghedruckt/den 4. Mey 1620. t'Hantwerpen/By Abraham Verhoeuen . . . 1620. 4° pp.7; sig.L^4; illus.

P.P.3444.af(46).

A variant of an earlier issue dated 28 April 1620. The titlepage woodcut shows portraits of two Turks.

B220 BOHEMIA. States

[1620] ARTICVLEN Die op den al ghemeenen Generalen Lant-dach/in presentie van . . . FREDERICK . . . Coninck in Bohemen . . . Begonst op Donderdach na Oculi, Anno M.DC.XX. op 'tSlot tot Praga/ende gheeyndicht op Maendach na Iubilate desselvighen Jaers/inghewillight ende besloten zijn . . . IN S'GRAVEN-HAGHE. By Aert Meuris . . . 1620. 4° sig.A-I^4

T.2250(20); T.2423(36).

B221 BOHEMIA. States

[1620] TVVO LETTERS OR EMBASSIES. The one Sent by the States of Bohemia, to the Elector of Saxony: The other from the Popes Holines to the Emperour, concerning the Troubles of Germany. Printet, at Amsterdam. 1620. 4° sig.A^2B-F^4

G.15499(1).

The editor's preface signed: William Barlow. The second piece sent to Barlow at Amsterdam by Thomas Fodringham. The imprint is false; printed by William Jones or William Stansby at London?

BOLLEVILLE, le Prieur de. *See* SIMON, Richard

B222 BOM, Jacobus
THESES MEDICÆ DE TRIPLICI HYDROPE, Quas . . . Pro GRADV DOCTORATVS in Medicina consequendo, publicè tuebitur IACOBVS BOM van CRANENBVRCH . . . LVGDVNI BATAVORVM, Ex Officinâ Ioannis Patii . . . M.D.C.V. 4° sig.A⁴
1185.g.1(23).

B223 BOMBAST VON HOHENHEIM, Philipp Aureol Theophrast; called Paracelsus
[Selections] Dat Secreet der Philosophien/inhoudende hoemen alle aertsche dingen/gelijck als Alluyn/Solfer/Coperroot . . . bereyden sal ende gebruycken . . . Altesamen getogen wt die Boecken Paracelsi, Door . . . Philippus Hermanni . . . TOT LEYDEN, By Vldrick Cornelissz. ende Joris Abramsz. . . . 1612. (col.) Ghedruckt tot Leyden/voor Danneel Roels . . . 1612. 8° ff.xxvii; illus.
1400.a.44.
The illustrations are woodcuts. Cropped.

B224 BOMBAST VON HOHENHEIM, Philipp Aureol Theophrast; called Paracelsus
[Supposititious works] FASCICVLVS. Oft Lust-Hof der Chimescher Medecijnen/uyt allen Boecken ende Schriften Doctoris Theophrasti Paracelsi van Hogenheym vergadert . . . Mitzgaders eenen Dictionarium dienende tot vertalingh aller onduytsche woorden die Paracelsus in sijne Schriften is ghebruyckende . . . Nn [*sic*] eerst uyt de Latijnsche in onse Nederduytsche Tale vertaelt/door M. LAVRENS GYSBERTSZ. van Nyendal . . . TOT VTRECHT, By Ian Amelissz . . . 1614. 8° pp.276
1032.b.3.
The date on the titlepage has been altered in manuscript to 1616. With manuscript notes. Ownership inscription: Abraham van Herke [?] 10 aprill anno 1620 pris 1^{β} 8.

B225 BOMBINO, Pietro Paolo
VITA ET MARTYRIVM EDMVNDI CAMPIANI MARTYRIS ANGLI è Societate IESV. Auctore R.P. PAVLO BOMBINO . . . ANTVERPIAE Apud Heredes Martini Nutij, & Ioannem Meursium. M.DC.XVIII. 12° pp.360
859.a.9; G.14378.

BONA fides Sibrandi Lubberti. 1614. *See* GROOT, Hugo de

BONARSCIUS, Clarus; pseudonym of Carolus Scribani. *See* SCRIBANI, Carolus

B226 BONAVENTURA; Saint, Bishop
[Collections. Latin] SANCTI BONAVENTVRÆ . . . SOLILOQVIVM De quatuor Exercitijs, quod dicitur IMAGO VITAE: & DIALOGVS. FASCICVLVS MYRRHÆ De Passione Christi. EXERCITIA XIII. SPIRITVALIA. ANTVERPIAE Apud Gasparem Bellerum. M.DC.XVI. 16° pp.280
C.20.f.21.
From the travelling library of Sir Julius Caesar.

B227 BONAVENTURA; Saint, Bishop
[Legenda S. Francisci.] THE LIFE OF THE HOLIE FATHER S. FRANCIS WRITTEN BY SAINT BONAuenture, and as it is related by the Reuerend Father Aloysius Lipomanus . . . Printed at DOVAY by LAVRENCE KELLAM. 1610. 8° pp.233
1231.a.44.
The editor's dedication signed: E.H., i.e. Edward Hughes. Translated by Anthony Browne, Viscount Montagu. Ownership inscriptions: Haddington; R. J. Grieve.

B228 BONAVENTURA; Saint, Bishop
[Doubtful or supposititious works. Meditationes Vitae Christi.] THE MIROVRE OF THE BLESSED LIFE OF OVR LORDE AND SAVIOVRE IESVS CHRISTE. WRITTEN. In latin by . . . Saint Bonauenture. NEWLIE. Set forth in Englishe for the profitte and consolacion of all deuoute persons. with Licence. 12° pp.646; illus.
C.53.gg.17.
Translated by Nicholas Love. Without imprint; published by Charles Boscard at Douai ca.1609. Illustrated with woodcuts.

BONIFACIUS, Nicolaus; pseudonym of Jan Wtenbogaert. *See* WTENBOGAERT, Jan

B229 BONNE, François de; Duke de Lesdiguières
Antwoorde vandē Hertoghe Desdiguieres, Op de klachten aen hem ghesonden by die vande verghaderinghe van ROCHELLE. Ouerghesedt vvt het Fransoys in onse Neder-Lantsche Tale. Eerst Ghedruckt den 19. Meert 1621. T'hantwerpen/By Abraham Verhoeuen/[etc.] 4° pp.8; sig.$+^4$; illus.
P.P.3444.af(207).
Headed: Martius 1621.42. The letter dated 1 February 1621. The titlepage woodcut shows the portrait of Louis XIII.

BONTEBAL, Jacobus. Disputationum physicarum octava de elementis. 1608. *See* JACCHAEUS, Gilbertus

B230 BONTIUS, Jacobus
DISPVTATIO INAVGVRALIS DE COLICO QVAM . . . Pro Gradu Doctoratus in MEDICINA consequendo, Publicè defendet IACOBVS BONTIVS . . . Excudebat GODEFRIDUS BASSON, M.D.C.XIII. 4° sig.A^4
1185.g.1(53).
Published at Leiden.

BOOGAERT, Cornelis. Andere vraech-al. 1618. [Sometimes attributed to Cornelis Boogaert.] *See* VRAECH-AL

B231 BOOMIUS, Theodorus Willem
POST-BODE, VERHALENDE DE PROCEDVREN, AENGAENDE HET AEN-nemen van de Godvruchtige ende Gheleerde Dienaeren des H. Euangelii respective tot BUREN ende YSELSTEYN: Teghens het snaeteren van eenighe onrustighe Menschen . . . Ghestelt door THEODORVS BOOMIVS . . . Ghedruckt . . . 1617. 4° pp.49
T.2247(3).

B232 BOR, Pieter
Den oorspronck, begin ende aenvanck der Nederlandtscher Oorlogen, geduyrende de Regeringe vande Hertoginne van Parma, de Hertoge van Alba, ende eensdeels vanden groot Commandeur. Beschreven deur PIETER BOR CHRISTIAENSOON . . . ende nu deur den selven in Liedekens vervaet. Tot Leyden, By GOVERT BASSON, 1617. 4° pp.96; illus., ports.
11556.dd.11.
The illustrations are engravings.

B233 BOR, Pieter
[Oorspronck, begin ende aenvang der Nederlandscher oorlogen.] (tp.1) NEDERLANTSCHE OORLOGHEN, beroerten ende Borgerlijcke oneenicheyden, Beginnende Mette Opdrachte der selver Landen/gaedaen by Keyser Karel de V. aen zijnen zoon Koninck Philippus van Spangien/tot de droevige doot van . . . Willem Prince van Orangien . . . BESCHREVEN Door PIETER BOR Christiaensz. 1621. TOT Leyden by GOVERT BASSON Amsterdā. by MICHIEL COLYN.

(tp.2) Vervolgh der Nederlandtscher OORLOGHEN . . . TWEEDE DEEL . . . BESCHREVEN Door PIETER BOR Christiaensz. 1621. TOT Leyden by GOVERT BASSON Amsterdã by MICHIEL COLYN.
(tp.3=dl.3.pt.1) VERVOLCH VANDE NEERLANDSCHE OORLOGHEN . . . door PIETER BOR CHRISTIAENZOON. Gedruckt tot Leyden by Govaert Basson . . . Amsterdam bij Michiel Colijn [etc.]
(tp.4) Derden-deels tweede stuck VANT VERVOLCH DER NEDERLANTSCHE Oorloghen . . . Beschreven door Pieter Bor Christiaenszoon. By Govert Basson . . . tot Leyden. By Michiel Colijn . . . tot Amsterdam . . . 1626.
(tp.5) VERVOLCH VANDE NEDERLANTSCHE OORLOGHEN . . . warachtich en onpartijdelick beschreven door PIETER BOR CHRISTIAENSZOON. Gedruckt tot Leyden by Govaert Basson . . . Amsterdam by Michiel Colijn [etc.]
(tp.6) VERVOLCH VANDE NEDERLANDSCHE OORLOGHEN . . . Beschreven door PIETER BOR CHRISTIAENSZOON. Gedruckt tot Amsterdam, By Michiel Colijn [etc.] fol. 5 dl.(=6 vol.): ff.350, 192; 193–318, 230, 60; 73, 91, 120,102; 103, 118, 63, 63, 33; 56, 48, 78, 90, 126; 100, 83, 69, 66,69; illus., port.
803.l.15.

The dedication of dl.4(=vol.5) is dated 28 March 1630; dl.5(=vol. 6) was published in 1634. The titlepages and illustrations are engraved; tp.3 signed: T. Matham fe. 1621. The portrait of Bor in dl.5 (=vol.6) signed: F. Hals pinxit, A. Matham schulpsit.

B234 BOR, Pieter

Tvvee TRAGI-COMEDIEN In prosa/D'eene van Appollonius Prince van Tyro. Ende d'ander Van den zelven/ende van Tarsia syn Dochter . . . Door P.B.C. IN 'SGRAVEN-HAGHE, By Aert Meuris . . . 1617. 4° pp.82
11755.bbb.42.

The dedication signed in full: P. Bor Christiaensz. The poem on the titlepage verso printed in civilité. The text is interspersed with poems.

BORGIA, Francisco; Duke de Gandia, Saint. *See* FRANCIS de Borja; Saint

B235 BORS, Jan Jansen

COPYE Des Briefs van den ouden ende grysen IAN IANSEN BORS . . . gewesene Kercken-dienaer in t'Remonstrants ghevoelen tot Leyder-dorp . . . ende nu . . . af-ghesettet/ende in Ballinckschap buyten s'Lants sich onthoudende. Gheschreven Aen de . . . Staten des Lants Hollant ende West-vrieslant. TOT Weder-roupinghe zijner Onder-teyckeninghe op den 24. October/1619. GHEDRVCKT . . . 1619. 4° sig.A^4
T.2249(48*).

B236 BORSSELEN, Philibert van

DEN BINCKHORST, OFTE HET LOF DES GELVCSALIGHEN ENDE GHERVSTmoedighen Land-levens. AEN . . . Jacob SNOVCKAERT, Heere van den BINCKHORST . . . AMSTELREDAM, Dirck Pietersz . . . M D CXIII. 4° pp.36; illus.
11556.cc.64(3).

Anonymous, but with the poet's anagram 'Sober, bli *van geest,* simpel van hert' in the prefatory poem. The titlepage illustration shows an emblem of mortality. With Latin mottoes in the margins. The illustrations are engravings.

B237 BORSSELEN, Philibert van

STRANDE, OFT GHEDICHTE VAN DE SCHELPEN, KINCKHORNEN, ENDE ANDERE VVONDERlicke Zee-schepselen, TOT LOF Van den Schepper aller Dinghen . . . Door P.V.B. TOT AMSTELREDAM, By Dirck Pietersz . . . 1614. 4° pp.55
11556.cc.64(2).

Anonymous. The poet's anagram, pointed out by a marginal note, occurs on p.50: '*Sober, simpel, bli van* leven, *hert,* gemoed'. With the device 'Templum Dei estis vos' used by Joris Abrahamsz van der Marsce at Leiden on the titlepage.

't BOSCH der eremyten ende eremytinnen. 1619. *See* VITAE patrum.

B238 BOSIO, Antonio

LA CHASTETÉ VICTORIEVSE EN L'ADMIRABLE CONVERSION de S. Valerian espoux de Saincte Cecile, de Tiburce, Maximus & autres. ENSEMBLE L'histoire de la Constance & Martyre de ceste Saincte Vierge . . . LE TOVT Fidellement . . . recherché es archiues & Bibliothecques de la ville de Rome . . . par . . . Antoine Bozius A. De la Traduction de C.D.C.S^r. de Welles. A ARRAS, De l'Imprimerie de Robert Maudhuy . . . M.DC.XVII. [etc.] (col.) A ARRAS, DE L'IMPRIMERIE DE ROBERT MAVDHVY AV NOM DE IESVS. 8° pp.332; illus.

860.h.8(2).

There is one woodcut on p.303.

B239 BOSIO, Giacomo

[La trionfante Cruce.] CRVX TRIVMPHANS ET GLORIOSA, A IACOBO BOSIO descripta LIBRIS SEX . . . ANTVERPIAE, EX OFFICINA PLANTINIANA, Apud Balthasarem et Ioannem Moretos. M.DC.XVII. (col.) ANTVERPIÆ, EX OFFICINA PLANTINIANA, APVD BALTHASAREM ET IOANNEM MORETOS FRATRES. M.DC.XVII. fol. pp.689; illus.

471.g.2.

Translated by the author. The titlepage is engraved, signed: Pet. Paul. Rubenius inuenit; Corn. Galleus sculpsit. Apart from one other engraving on sig.*8r the illustrations are in woodcut.

BOSKHIERUS, Philippus. *See* BOSQUIER, Philippe

B240 BOSQUIER, Philippe

ORATOR TERRÆ SANCTÆ, ET HVNGARIÆ: SEV SACRARVM PHILIPPICARVM, IN TVRCARVM BARBARIEM, ET IMPORTVNAS CHRISTIANORVM DISCORDIAS, NOTÆ. Autore . . . PHILIPPO BOSKHIERO . . . DVACI CATVACORVM Apud PETRVM BORREMANS . . . 1606. (col.) Ex Typographia LAVRENTII KELLAM . . . Sumptibus PETRI BORREMANS . . . 1605. 8° pp.422; illus.

696.a.3.

The engravings signed on sig.*8v: J. Waldor fecit.

BOUCHEREAU, Samuel. Disputationum theologicarum tertia de essentia Dei. 1602. *See* DU JON, François; the Elder

B241 BOURICIUS, Hector

ORATIO ANNIVERSARIA DICTA HONORI LITERARVM PRINCIPIS ISAACI CASAVBONI. LEOVARDIÆ, Ex Officina IOANNIS STARTERI . . . M.DC.XV. 4° sig.A-C^4

835.b.16(1).

The dedication and one poem signed: H. Bouritius, a laudatory poem by Pierius Winsemius addressed to the author, Hector Bouricius.

BOURITIUS, Hector. *See* BOURICIUS, Hector

BOZIUS, Antonius. *See* BOSIO, Antonio

B242 BRA, Henricus a

CATALOGUS MEDICAMENTORUM simplicium & facilè parabilium adversus EPILEPSIAM, Et quomodo iis utendum sit brevis INSTITVTIO, AVTORE HENRICO à BRA . . . ARNHEMI, Apud Iohannem Iohannis. M.D.CV. 8° pp.115

1168.e.11(3); 1190.d.16.

B243 BRA, Henricus a

DE CURANDIS VENENIS, PER MEDICAMENTA SIMPLICIA & facilè parabilia, LIBRI DUO, AUthore HENRICO à BRA . . . ARNHEMI, APUD IOHANNEM IOHANNIS. 1603. 8° pp.360

778.a.5.

B244 BRABANT. Customs and Privileges

DIE BLYDE INcomste den Hertochdomme van Brabant/in voortijden by haren Landtsheeren verleent/ende van Keyser Carolo den v. gheconfirmeert ende by Philippus zijnen Sone den II. Coninck van Spaengnien . . . gesworen. ANNO M.D.XLIX. Ghedruckt tot Ceulen. 1607. 4° sig.A-C^4

T.1723(6).

With the arms of Antwerp used as a device. Printed in the Northern Netherlands? The imprint appears to be no more than a repetition of that of earlier editions published at Cologne.

B245 BRABANT. Customs and Privileges

INAVGRATIO Philippi II. Regis Hispaniarum, qua se Iuramento Ducatus Brabantiæ & ab eo dependentibus Provincijs obligavit, cum Substitutione Ducissæ Mariæ Gubernatricis. Adjuncta sunt quædam alia huc spectantia, unitis Provincijs utilissima. Authore HENRICO AGYLÆO . . . qui Articulos Inaugurationis, Commentarijs illustravit. VLTRAIECTI. Ex Officina Abrahami ab Herwijck . . . 1620. 8° pp.188

1492.n.31.

Edited by Joannes Agylaeus. With the bookplate of Bishop Gilbert Burnet.

B246 BRABANT

[3.1.1601] ORDONNANTIE ENDE INSTRUCTIE DAER OP MEN VAN WEGEN DIE DRY Staeten des lants, ende Hertochdoms van Brabandt collecteren, verpachten ende Innen sal respectiue de middelen gheaccordeert . . . in betalinghe ende tot onderstande vande ordinarise Guarnisoenen in Brabant, ende anderen volcke van Oorloghe. TOT BRVESSEL, By Rutgeert Velpius . . . M.D.C.I. [etc.] 4° sig.A-C^{4}D^2

107.g.26(15).

Dated 3 January 1601. The arms of Brabant on the titlepage are supported by the allegorical figures of Justice and Peace. The verso of the last leaf bears the privilege, dated 11 January 1601, given to Rutgeert Velpius for the printing of this order.

B247 BRABANT

[3.1.1601] ORDONNANTIE ENDE INSTRUCTIE DAER OP-MEN VAN WEGHEN DIE DRY Staeten des Landts ende Hertochdoms van Brabandt collecteren, verpachten ende innen sal respective de middelen . . . gheaccordeert . . . in betalinghe . . . van de ordinarise Garnisoenen in Brabandt . . . TOT BRVSSEL, By Rutgeert Velpius . . . 1601. 4° sig.A-C^{4}D^2

107.g.26(14).

Another edition of the preceding. The arms, without supporters, are of a much cruder design. The statement 'Met privilegie' at the end is not followed by the text of the privilege. The typographical appearance of the text, especially the initial 'O', and its position in the volume next to an 'amplification' of the same law dated 1643 make it probable that this is a later reprint, perhaps also of 1643 and by Huybrecht Anthoon Velpius at Brussels. Occurrences of the same initial 'O', including its use in a reprint of the 'amplification' of the same law of 1683, show it damaged in a way not apparent in this edition. The suspicion about the true date of this edition is shared by Mevrouw Geneviève Glorieux of the Nationaal Centrum voor de Archeologie en de Geschiedenis van het Boek at the Royal Library, Brussels, to whom I express my thanks.

B248 BRABANT

[10.10.1608] ORDONNANTIE ENDE REGLEMENT, Waer naer haere Hoocheden ordineren eenen yegelyck hem sal hebben te reguleren int inne-brenghen vande Peerden, van Hollandt ende Zeelandt, opden bodem van Brabant. TOT BRVESSEL, By Rutgeert Velpius . . . 1608. [etc.] 4° sig.A^4

107.g.26(5).

Dated 10 October 1608.

B249 BRABANT

[11.8.1609] AMPLIATIE VAN ZEKER ORDINANTIE van haere Hoocheden in date den x. October, anno 1608. ghepubliceert in dese landen ende Hertochdomme van Brabant, op het lichten van het recht vande licenten op de Peerden . . . TOT BRVESSEL, By Rutgeert Velpius . . . 1609. 4° sig. A^4

107.g.26(1).

Dated 11 August 1609.

B250 BRABANT

[31.1.1614] ORDINANCIE ENDE PLACCAET VANDE EERTSHERTOGEN . . . Verbiedende de dracht van alle soorten Vierstocken/ende namentlyck van Roerkens oft Pistoletten . . . TOT BRVESSEL, By Rutgeert Velpius/ende Huybrecht Anthoni . . . 1614. [etc.] 4° sig. A^4

107.g.26(6).

Dated 31 January 1614.

B251 BRADSHAW, William; Puritan

A SHORTE TREATISE, OF the crosse in Baptisme contracted into this syllogisme . . . Amsterdam Printed by I.H. 1604. 8° pp.25

698.b.15(1); 116.a.4.

Anonymous. The imprint, suggesting Jodocus Hondius, is false; in fact secretly printed by William Jones in London. The copy at 116.a.4. is imperfect; wanting the last leaf.

B252 BRADSHAW, William; Puritan

A Treatise OF DIVINE WORSHIP, TENDING to prove that the Ceremonies imposed vpon the Ministers of the Gospell in England, in present controversie, are in their vse vnlawfull. 1604. 8° pp.47

697.a.18; 698.b.15(2); 116.a.18.

Anonymous and without imprint. Printed by Richard Schilders at Middelburg.

B253 BRADSHAW, William; Puritan

Twelve generall Arguments, Proving that the Ceremonies imposed upon the Ministers of the Gospell in England, by our Prelates, are unlawfull; And therefore that the Ministers of the Gospell, for the bare and sole omission of them in Church Service, for conscience sake, are most unjustlie charged of disloyaltie to his Maiestie . . . 1605. 8° sig. $A\text{-}C^8DE^6F^4$

701.c.24(1); 116.a.19.

Anonymous and without imprint. Printed by Richard Schilders at Middelburg. The titlepages of both copies are mutilated.

B254 BRADSHAW, William; Puritan

(tp.1) THE VNREASONABLENESSE of the separation. Made apparent, by an examination of M[r]. Iohnsons pretended reasons, published an. 1608 . . . AT DORT, Printed by George Waters. 1614.

(tp.2=sig.P4r) A MANVDICTION FOR M[r]. ROBINSON, AND such as consent with him in privat communion, to lead them on to publick. BREIFLY COMPRIZED IN A letter written to M[r]. R.W. AT DORT, Printed by George Waters . . . 1614. 4° sig. $A^3B\text{-}Q^4$

T.2108(3,4).

Anonymous. 'A Manudiction' continues the signatures of 'The Unreasonablenesse'. The additional leaf signed A3, bearing the address to the reader, has been inserted between the titlepage and leaf A2.

B255 BRANCACCIO, Lelio

I CARICHI MILITARI DI FRA' LELIO BRANCACCIO . . . IN ANVERSA, A presso Ioachimo Trognesio. M.DC.X. 4° pp.272: pl.V

534.i.9.

Printed throughout in italics. The titlepage and last leaf are mutilated. Imperfect; wanting sig.*2,4.

B256 [*BRANDENBURG

[24.2.1614] PLACCAET Vanden Doorluchtichsten Heere Churfurst tot Brandenburch/Hertoghe in Prussen [*sic*]/Gulich/Cleve etc. Teghen de Predicanten: Die gewoon zijn op den Predickstoel hare bittere galle wt te gieten teghen hare parthyen . . . Overgheset wt het Hooch-duytsch. In 'sGraven-Haghe/By Hillebrant Jacobssz. . . . 1614. 4° sig. A^4

5686.a.23(15).]

*Destroyed. Described from the General Catalogue, corrected from the copy in the Royal Library, The Hague, *Knuttel* no. 2105. Translated from 'Edict an alle der Chur Brandenburg Kirchendiener', issued 24 February 1614.

B257 BRANDENBURG

[24.2.1614] PLACCAET . . . Teghen de Predicanten: Die gewoon zijn op den Predickstoel hare bittere galle wt te gieten tegen hare partijen . . . TOT VTRECHT, By Jan Amelissz. . . . 1615. 4° sig. L2-4

T.2245(14).

Dated 24 February 1614. This edition forms part of 'Eenvoudich ende ernstich bericht' by Thomas von Knesebeck, at T.2245(9).

BRANDT, Sebastiaen. *See* BRANT, Sebastian

B258 BRANT, Sebastian

[Narrenschiff. Dutch] Aff-ghebeelde Narren Speel-schuyt/verciert met meer als hondert schoone figueren . . . Beschreven int Latijn ende Hooch-Duytsch/ door . . . D. SEBASTIAEN BRANDT. Getrouwelick overgheset . . . door A.B. Ghedruckt tot LEYDEN, By Henrick Lodewicxsz. van Haestens . . . 1610. 4° ff. 109; illus., port.

11511.a.7.

Apart from the titlepage engraving the illustrations are in woodcut.

B259 BRAUWER, Marijn de

T'werck van M. de Brouwer, ghenaemt Eenvuldighe waerschouwinghe aen de Gevluchte Vreemdelinghen/Haer radende hunne Magistraten (die haer ontfangen ende beschermt hebben) te gehoorsamen . . . Anno 1618. 4° sig. A^2

700.h.25(12*); 11555.e.41(3).

In verse.

B260 BREDA, Cornelius

CORNELI BREDÆ ERRORES. LIBER PHILOLOGVS. Ad eosdem BREVES NOTÆ. LOVANII, Typis IO. CHRISTOPH. FLAVI. M.DC.XII. [etc.] 4° pp. 115

837.g.21(3).

B261 BREDERO, Gerbrand Adriaensz

APOLLO OF Ghesangh der Musen/wiens lieflijcke stemmen merendeels in vrolijcke en eerlijcke gheselschappen werden ghesonghen. t'Amsterdam, by Dirck Pietersz. . . . 1615. obl. 4° pp. 120; illus.

11556.bbb.67(2).

Anonymous. The compiler's prefatory poem signed: G. A. Bredero, but his responsibility for the volume remains doubtful. The pagination is irregular.

B262 BREDERO, Gerbrand Adriaensz

G. A. BREDEROOS Treur-spel Van RODD'RICK ende ALPHONSVS. Eerst ghespeelt op de Amsterdamsche Kamer/in't Jaar 1611. Ende daar na vervat 1616 . . . t'Amsterdam. Voor Cornelis Lodewijcksz. vander Plasse . . . 1616. 4° sig. A^6B-J^4

11755.bb.68(2).

BREEDER verhael ende klare beschrijvinge van tghene den Admirael Cornelis Matelief de Jonge . . . wedervaren is. 1608. *See* L'HERMITE, Jacques

BREF recueil des antiquitez de Valentienne. 1619. *See* LE BOUCQ, Simon

B263 BRERELY, John; sometimes believed to be the pseudonym of Lawrence Anderton

[The apologie of the Romane church.] THE PROTESTANTS APOLOGIE FOR THE ROMAN CHVRCH. Deuided into three seuerall Tracts. VVHEROF, THE FIRST Concerneth the Antiquity & Cōtinuāce of the Romā Church & Religiō . . . By Iohn Brerely Priest . . . M.DC VIII. 4° pp.751

Cup.403.i.1.

Without imprint; published by the English College press at St. Omer.

B264 BRERELY, John; sometimes believed to be the pseudonym of Lawrence Anderton

[The apologie of the Romane Church.] THE PROTESTANTS APOLOGIE . . . VVHEROF THE FIRT [*sic*] Concerneth the Antiquity & Continuance of the Roman Church & Religion . . . By Iohn Brerely Priest . . . M.DC.VIII. 4° pp.751

858.c.4.

Another issue of the preceding, with a reset titlepage and additional preliminary pages bearing the signature q. Equally without imprint, published by the English College press at St. Omer.

B265 BREUGHEL, Gerrit Hendricksz van

Een arge verward Miaensch[e en]de quaet Gespin der Iesu-vvijt, Als een rechte afbeeldinghe o[p den] tegenwoordighen tijt/ fol. a single sheet

1871.e.1(65).

Signed: G. H. Breugel. In verse. Without imprint or date. Referring to Cleve, Juliers and Berge and to Henry IV. Printed ca.1610? Mutilated.

B266 BREUGHEL, Gerrit Hendricksz van

CUPIDO'S LUSTHOF ENDE Der Amoureuse Boogaert Beplant ende Verciert Meet [*sic*] 22 Schoone Copere figuiren ende vele nieuwe Amoureuse Liedekēs Baladen ende Sonnetten . . . gecomponeert door een wt levender Jonst. Tot Amsterdam by Jan Evertsz Cloppenburch [etc.] obl.4° pp.157; illus.

11555.aaa.60(1).

The author's verse dedication signed: G.H. van B., i.e. Gerrit Hendricksz. van Breughel. The printer's verse dedication signed: W.I.Stam and dated 1 January 1613. The engravings are by Nicolaes van Geilkercken. The engraved titlepage is mutilated.

BREVICULUS duorum nuper in publicis Comitijs Anglicanis actorum. 1606. *See* ENGLAND [1606]

BREVIS explicatio privilegiorum iuris . . . circa sacramentum . . . Eucharistiae. 1609. *See* WHITE, Richard; of Basingstoke

BREVIS explicatio martyrii sanctae Ursulae. 1610. *See* WHITE, Richard; of Basingstoke

BRIEF. *See also* BRIEFE; BRIEFF

BRIEF aen de verdruckte ghemeynte Jesu Christi binnen . . . Utrecht. 1619. *See* RYCKEWAERT, Carel

BRIEF aende . . . Staten Generael. Over de sententie Ioh. Grevii. 1620. *See* WTENBOGAERT, Jan

A BRIEF and cleere confutation. 1603. *See* WALPOLE, Richard

B267 BRIEF

BRIEF ET VERITABLE DISCOVRS, DE LA MORT D'AVCVNS VAILLANTS ET GLORIEVX MARtyrs, lesquelz on à faict mourir en Angleterre, pour la Foy & Religion Catholicque, l'An passé de 1600. Et semblablement aussi ceste presente Année de M.D.CI. Ensemble vne Responce à la fin, sur quelques Liurets calomnieux & imprimeries publiées par les Geux, contre . . . l'Archiduc Albert, touchant vne Anabaptiste, n'agueres iusticiée à Bruxelles. A ANVERS, Chez Hyerosme Verdussen . . . M.D.CI. 8° sig.A-D^{8}E^4
G.19973(1).

BRIEF gheschreven van eenen backer tot Bolongien. 1609. *See* BRIEF van eenen backer.

BRIEF tot afrading van't Pausdom. 1621. *See* CAMPHUYSEN, Dirck Raphaëlsz

B268 BRIEF

BRIEF Van eenen Backer tot Bolongien aen den Paus/ghetrouwelick over gheset nae de Copye ghedruckt tot Florence. 4° 2 unsigned leaves
107.g.1(25).
Anonymous and without imprint or date. Possibly written or translated by Jacobus Migoen and also published by him at Gouda in 1607 or 1608.

B269 BRIEF

[Brief van eenen backer.] BRIEF Gheschreven van eenen Backer tot Bolongien aen den Paus. Ghetrouwelijck overgheset na de Copye ghedruckt tot Florence. Ghedruckt buyten Rome. Zonder Privilegie van syne Heylicheyt. Anno 1609. 4° 2 unsigned leaves
T.2420(44).
Another edition of the preceding. Also published by Jacobus Migoen at Gouda?

A BRIEFE admonition to all English Catholikes. 1610. *See* WALPOLE, Michael

A BRIEFE and cleare declaration. 1611. *See* HOSKINS, Anthony

A BRIEFE description of the reasons that make the declaration of the ban against the King of Bohemia . . . of no value. 1621. *See* DEDUCTIO nullitatum.

A BRIEFE discourse containing certaine reasons. 1601. *See* PERSONS, Robert

A BRIEFE refutation of John Traskes . . . fancyes. 1618. *See* FALCONER, John

A BRIEFE relation of the persecution made against the Catholike Christians, in . . . Japonia. 1619. *See* MOREJON, Pedro

Den BRIEFF ghesonden aen de Standen . . . des Coninckrijckx Bohemien. 1620. *See* GERMANY. Electors [21.3.1620]

B270 BRIELLE

[16.2.1618] PRESENTATIE BY BAILLIV/BVRGHEMEESTEREN, OVDT ENDE NIEVWE Gherechte der Stede vanden Briele, ghedaen aende afghesonderde Broederen der selver Stede. Ghepubliceert den sesthienden Februarij, sesthien-hondert achthien. IN S'GRAVEN-HAGHE, By Hillebrant Iacobssen . . . 1618. 4° sig.A^4
T.2248(9).

B271 BRIELLE

[7.3.1618] COPIE. Op't versoek van de Ghecommitteerde van de dolerende Broeders binnen der stede van den Briele [etc.] 4° a single sheet
T.2248(30).
Issued by the city authorities of Brielle, 7 March 1618. Cropped.

B272 BRIGHTMAN, Thomas

A REVELATION of the Reuelation that is THE REVELATION of S. John opened clearely with a logicall Resolution and Exposition . . . By Thomas Brightman . . . imprinted at Amsterdam. 1615. 4° pp.921

3187.aaaa.8.

Printed by Giles Thorp or Jodocus Hondius? The titlepage is engraved.

B273 BRIGHTMAN, Thomas

[A revelation of the Revelation.] THE REVELATION of S. Iohn illustrated with an Analysis & scholions. Wherein the sence is opened by the scripture, & the euent of things fore-told, shewed by Histories. The third Edition Corrected & amended. With supply of many things formerly left out. By THOMAS BRIGHTMAN. Imprinted at Leyden by John Class. A° 1616. (col.) Imprinted at Leiden, by Iohn Claesson van Dorpe . . . 1616. 8° pp.1143

3185.bb.50.

Another edition of the preceding. The engraved titlepage is an inferior copy of the earlier one.

B274 BRISTOW, Richard

RICHARDI BRISTOÏ . . . MOTIVA, OMNIBVS CATHOLICÆ DOCTRINÆ Orthodoxis Cultoribus pernecessaria; vt quæ singulas . . . hæreses funditùs extirpet: Romanæ autem Ecclesiæ auctoritatem fidemq; . . . stabiliat . . . ATREBATI, Ex Officinâ Typographicâ ROBERTI MAVDHVY . . . M.D.C.VIII. 4° 2 tom.: pp.332,321

3936.h.7.

Ownership inscriptions: Bibl. S. Sepul: Cameraci; Bibl. C^ale^, Cambrai.

B275 BROECK, Hubrecht wten

PYLKOKER Der dwaesheyt/Op Het Mandaet des Paus Adams Hart-wech . . . TOT ROTTERDAM, By Philips Philipssz. . . . 1612. 4° sig. A, A-D^4E^2; illus.

T.2242(17).

Signed: Hubrecht wten Broeck. The titlepage illustration has been separately engraved and pasted over a typographical ornament.

B276 BROECKER, Frederik

F. BROECKERI . . . ANTIDOTVM ERRORVM PRÆCIPVORVM: Comprehensorum, In Tractatu de Deo, sive de natura, & attributis Dei; & Apologetica Exegesi, D. CONRADI VORSTII, CVM RESPONSIONE PLACIDA ad Argumenta, errores confirmantia. AMSTELREDAMI Ex Officina Petri Petræi . . . M D XII [*sic*]. 4° ff.102

1255.cc.6.

The date at the end of the dedication is also misprinted as 1512 in place of 1612.

B277 BROERSZ, Jan

Vriendelijcke ende Christelijcke t'samensprekinghe/over 't verschil tusschen die vande openbare Ghereformeerde Kercke, ende d'Afghesonderde Vergaderinghe in de Ramen. EERSTE DEEL. Waer-inne . . . ghehandelt werdt van de Conditie, waer op soo die van de Kercke, als oock die vande Ramen den Menschen de saligheyt . . . toeseggen. Ghestelt tot onderwijsinghe der Ghereformeerde Christenen, door I.B. . . . TOT HOORN, Ghedruckt by Willem Andriessz. . . . 1617. 4° pp.47

T.2247(16).

The preface signed: IAN BROERSZ. No more published.

B278 BROUAERT, Joannes

DISPVTATIO INAVGVRALIS DE ΥΔΡΟΦΟΒΙΑ SANABILI, Quam . . . Pro DOCTORATV in Medicina consequendo, adserere conabitur IOANNES BROVAERT . . . LVGDVNI BATAVORVM, Ex Officinâ THOMÆ BASSON. M.D.C.X. 4° sig.AB^4

1185.g.1(41); 7306.f.6(23*).

The spelling of the author's name as Brouaert rather than Brovaert follows that of the 'Album studiosorum' of Leiden University.

B279 BROUGHTON, Hugh

AN ADVERTISEMENT OF CORRVPTION IN OVR HANDLING OF RELIGION. To the Kings Majestie. By HVGH BROVGHTON. 1604. 4° sig.A-O^4

1490.d.61

Without imprint; printed by Richard Schilders at Middelburg.

B280 BROUGHTON, Hugh

AN ADVERTISEMENT OF CORRVPTION IN OVR HANDLING OF RELIGION. To the Kinges Maiesty. BY HVGH BROVGHTON. 1605. 4° pp.111

T.812(8).

Without imprint; printed by Jan Theunisz or Jodocus Hondius at Amsterdam?

B281 BROUGHTON, Hugh

A Censure of the late translation for our Churches: [etc.] 4° 4 unsigned leaves

1003.ff.7.

Anonymous and without imprint; printed by Richard Schilders at Middelburg in 1611?

B282 BROUGHTON, Hugh

CERTAYNE QVESTIONS Concerning 1. Silk, or vvool . . . 2. Idol temples . . . 3. The forme of Prayer, commonly called the Lords prayer. 4. Excommunication, &c. Handled betvveen Mr Hugh Broughton . . . And Mr Henry Ainsvvorth . . . 1605. 4° pp.39

4103.c.7.

The editor's preface signed: F.B., i.e. Francis Blackwell. Without imprint; printed by Giles Thorp at Amsterdam?

B283 BROUGHTON, Hugh

A COMMENT VPON COHELETH OR ECCLESIASTES: Framed for the instruction of PRINCF [*sic*] HENRI Our hope. BY HVG [*sic*] BROVGHTON . . . 1605. 4° pp.79

3166.c.7.

The titlepage is engraved. This and the Hebrew type are by Jodocus Hondius. Without imprint; printed by Jan Theunisz or Jodocus Hondius at Amsterdam? Cropped.

B284 BROUGHTON, Hugh

Declaration of generall corruption of Religion, Scripture and all learning; wrought by D. Bilson. While he breedeth a new opinion, that our Lord went from Paradise to Gehenna. To . . . IOHN WH. By HVGH BROVGHTON. 1603. 4° 4 unsigned leaves

T.812(12).

Without imprint; printed by Richard Schilders at Middelburg.

B285 BROUGHTON, Hugh

Declaration of generall corruption . . . To . . . IOHN W.H. . . . By HVGH BROVGHTON. 1604. 4° 4 unsigned leaves

1016.h.21.

A different setting from the preceding. Without imprint; printed by Richard Schilders at Middelburg.

B286 BROUGHTON, Hugh
A Defence of the Booke entitled A Cōcent of Scripture, for amendment of former Athean . . . and Iudaique errours, which our translations and notes had: Against the libel . . . that the Iewes Epistle . . . was a forged worke . . . By HVGH BROVGHTON. 1609. 4° sig. A-D^4
1003.b.9(4).
Two additional, conjugate, leaves have been inserted between leaves A1 and A2. Without imprint; printed by Richard Schilders at Middelburg.

B287 BROUGHTON, Hugh
ANEXPLICATION [*sic*] OF THE ARTICLE Κατῆλθεν ἐις ᾅδω, of our Lordes soules going from his body to Paradise . . . vvith a defense of the Q. of Englands religion . . . Sundry Epistles are prefixed & affixed. by H. Br. The second edition . . . 1605. 4° pp. 50
4225.b.9.
Signed: Hugh Broughton. Without imprint; printed by Jan Theunisz or Jodocus Hondius at Amsterdam?

B288 BROUGHTON, Hugh
AN EXPOSITION VPON THE LORDS Prayer, compared with the Decalogue, as it was preached in a Sermon, At Oatelands AUG. 13. Anno 1603. VVith a postscript . . . Also, the Creed is annexed . . . BY HUGH BROUGHTON. 4° pp. 34
T.812(6).
Without imprint; probably printed at Amsterdam, by Giles Thorp or Jan Theunisz, in or after 1603.

B289 BROUGHTON, Hugh
[Hebrew] . . . FAMILIA DAVIDIS, QVA-tenus regnum spectat: cum Chronographia sacra ad redemtionem usque continuata, Ad . . . principem Henricum . . . Impressit Amsteldami . . . Zacharias Heinsius. 1605. 8° sig. AB^4
Or.1939.b.62.
The 'Epilogus ad . . . Principem Henricum' signed: Hugo Broughton. Printed for Heyns by Jan Theunisz or Jodocus Hondius both at Amsterdam. A suggestion that this book was printed by the Officina Plantiniana at Leiden is not borne out by the Hebrew type used which is that of Hondius.

B290 BROUGHTON, Hugh
[Hebrew] . . . THE FAMILIE OF DAVID, FOR THE SONNES OF THE KINGDOME, VVITH A CHROnicle vnto the redemtion . . . Printed at Amstelredam . . . By Zacharias Heyns. 1605. 8° sig. [A]B^4
873.i.23(2).
Signed: Hugh Broughton. Printed for Heyns by Jan Theunisz or Jodocus Hondius at Amsterdam. A suggestion in *Moes Burger* vol.4 p.255 that this book was printed by the Officina Plantiniana at Leiden is not borne out by the Hebrew type used which is that of Hondius.

B291 BROUGHTON, Hugh
OVR LORDE[S] FAMILE AND MANY OTHER POINCTES DEPENDING VPON IT: opened against a Iew, Rabbi David Farar . . . With a Greke Epistle to the Geneveans. By H. Broughton. Printed at Amsterdam . . . 16[08]. 4° 4 unsigned leaves, (∴) A-I^{4}K^{2}L^3
482.b.3(1).
Printed by Jan Theunisz or Jodocus Hondius? The titlepage is mutilated.

B292 BROUGHTON, Hugh

A PETITION TO THE KING. FOR AVTHORITY AND ALLOWANCE to expound the Apocalyps in Hebrew and Greek, To shew Iewes and Gentiles: that Rome in Cęsars and Pope, is therein still damned. And for translaters to set over all into other large-vsed tongues. 4° pp.6

10921.cc.32.

The dedication signed: H. Broughton. The dedication only is of the original edition, with the text in photographic reproduction. Without imprint; printed in 1611, by Jan Theunisz or Giles Thorp at Amsterdam? A Middelburg printing has also been suggested, originally in the first edition of *STC,* from there taken over via *Hirschel* by H. F. Wijnman in his article on Broughton in *NNBW* vol.9. col.109.

B293 BROUGHTON, Hugh

A PETITION TO THE KING TO HASTEN ALLOWance for Ebrew INSTITVTION of Ebrevves. 4° 3 unsigned leaves

1003.b.9(3).

Signed: Hugh Broughton. Without imprint; printed by Jan Theunisz or Giles Thorp at Amsterdam, 1610?

B294 BROUGHTON, Hugh

A REPLIE VPON THE R. R. F. TH. VVINTON FOR HEADS OF HIS DIVINITY IN HIS SERMON AND SVRVEY: Hovv he taught à perfect truth, that our Lord vvent hēce to Paradise: But adding that he vvent thence to Hades, & striving to prove that, he injurieth all learning & Christianitie . . . 1605. 8° pp.48

873.i.23(1).

Signed: Hugh Broughton. Without imprint; printed by Jan Theunisz or Jodocus Hondius at Amsterdam?

B295 BROUGHTON, Hugh

A REQVIRE OF AGREEMENT To the groundes of Divinitie studie: wherin great Scholers falling, & being caught of Iewes disgrace the Gospel: & trap them to destruction. By H.B. 1611. 4° pp.92

T.812(7); 1019.e.7(2); 1016.h.20.

The dedication signed: Hugh Broughton. Without imprint; printed by Richard Schilders at Middelburg. The copy at 1016.h.20 is another issue, with an additional leaf at the end, containing errata.

B296 BROUGHTON, Hugh

RESPONSVM AD EPISTOLAM IVdæi . . . Expetentis cognitionem fidei Christianorum: cum versione Latinâ, Auctore vtriusque Hugone Broughtono. Amsteldamj. 1606. 4° sig.A-D[4]

T.812(9).

Printed by Jan Theunisz or Jodocus Hondius?

B297 BROUGHTON, Hugh

[Responsum ad Epistolam Iudaei.] (tp.1) TRALATIO EPISTOLAE HEBRAEAE, QVA BYZANTIACO IVdæo respondetur de religione, cum versione vocum Hebræarum quæ attinent Iconas adnexas Hebræo Opusculo . . . INTERPRETE IPSO AVCTORE QVOD IDEM Græcanice & Britannicè præstat. Impressum Amsteldami . . . 1606. (tp.2) ΜΕΤΑΦΡΑΣΙΣ ΠΟΝΗΜΑΤΙΟΥ, ΕΚΔΟΘΕΝΤΟΣ ΕΒΡΑΙΣΤΙ . . . ἑλληνιζομένη διὰ τοῦ συγγραφέως τῶν Συριακῶν ἀυτου. Ετυπώθη ἐν Αμστελδάμῳ, δια Ιωδώχου του Ονδίου . . . α, χς. 4° sig.AB[4]C[2]; A-C[4]: plates

1003.b.9(2); 482.b.20.

The Greek text signed: Υγων ὁ Βροχθωνός. Without English or Hebrew versions. The plates are engraved by Jodocus Hondius. The copy at 482.b.20 has an additional gathering F[E]^4 with a letter in Greek to James I, but lacks the plates. Printed by Jan Theunisz or Jodocus Hondius?

B298 BROUGHTON, Hugh

A REVELATION OF THE HOLY APOCALYPS. BY HVGH BROVGHTON. Printed . . . 1610. 4° pp.36

3186.a.24.

Corresponding to the copy described in *STC* no.3883. Printed by Giles Thorp or Jan Theunisz at Amsterdam? An edition described by H. F. Wijnman in *NNBW* vol.9 (1933) col.108 as reading 'revalation' has been assigned there to Middelburg (?), perhaps in error for this edition or the one described in *STC* no.3884.

B299 BROUGHTON, Hugh

TVVO EPISTLES VNTO GREAT MEN OF BRITANIE, IN THE YEARE 1599. Requesting them to put their neckes vnto the work of theyr Lord: To break the bread of the soule unto the hungry Iewes . . . Printed now the second time . . . 1606. Translated by the Auctour [etc.] 4° sig.AB^{4}C^2

1077.e.42.

The dedication signed: Hugh Broughton. Without imprint; printed by Giles Thorp at Amsterdam? Cropped.

B300 BROUGHTON, Hugh

Two little workes defensiue of our Redemption, That our Lord went . . . into Heaven . . . Which iourney a Talmudist . . . would terme, a going vp to Paradise: But Heathen Greek, a going down to Hades, and Latin, Descendere ad inferos. Wherein the vnlearned . . . anger God and man . . . By HVGH BROVGHTON . . . 1604. 4° four unsigned leaves

T.812(11).

A copy of the edition in which line 6 of the titlepage ends: Hea-. without imprint; printed by Richard Schilders at Middelburg.

B301 BROUGHTON, Hugh

Two little workes defensiue of our Redemption . . . By HVGH BROVGHTON . . . 1604. 4° four unsigned leaves

1016.h.19(2).

Another issue of the preceding in which line 6 of the titlepage ends: heathen. Without imprint; printed by Richard Schilders at Middelburg.

B302 BROUGHTON, Richard

An Apologicall Epistle: Directed to the right honorable Lords, and others of her Maiesties priuie Counsell. Seruing aswell for a Præface to a Booke entituled, A Resolution of Religion: as also, containing the Authors most lawfull Defence . . . for publishing the same . . . Printed at Antwerp with licence, the fiue and twenty day of March, 1601. Stilo novo. (col.) At Antuerpe Printed by Arnold Coninx 1601. 8° pp.132

699.a.39; 3935.a.27(1).

Signed: R.B., i.e. Richard Broughton. The imprint is false; in fact, printed secretly in England.

B303 BROUGHTON, Richard

ENGLISH PROTESTANTS PLEA AND PETITION, FOR ENGLISH PREISTS AND PAPISTS, TO THE present Court of Parlament . . . 1621. 8° pp.109

3939.aa.43.

Anonymous and without imprint; published by Charles Boscard at St. Omer. Pt.1 only, wanting the last leaf, blank.

B304 BROUGHTON, Richard

THE FIRST PART OF THE RESOLVTION OF RELIGION, DIVIDED INTO TWO BOOKES, CONTEYNING A DEMONSTRATION OF THE NECESSITIE OF A DIVINE AND SVPERNATVRALL WORSHIPPE . . . NEVVLY PRINTED AND AMENDED. PRINTED AT ANTWERPE BY RICHARD VESTEGAN [*sic*]. M.DI.III [*sic*]. 4° pp.104
113.f.31.

The preface signed: R.B., i.e. Richard Broughton. The imprint is false; in fact, printed secretly in England. No more published.

B305 BROUWER, Jacobus de

CLAVIS APOSTOLICA, SEV THEOLOGICA DEMONSTRATIO, QVA . . . CONCLVDITVR DIVINA FIDE CREDENDVM, PAVLVM V. ESSE SVMMVM MAXIMVMQVE PONTIFICEM. AVCTORE . . . IACOBO DE BROVWER . . . DVACI, Ex Officina Typographica BALTAZARIS BELLERI . . . 1621. 8° pp.85
1020.kk.11(3).

With the printer's ornament signed: L.K., i.e. Laurence Kellam the Younger at Douai.

BROUWER, Marijn de. *See* BRAUWER, Marijn de

B306 BROUWERUS, Christophorus

FVLDENSIVM ANTIQVITATVM LIBRI IIII. AVCTORE R. P. CHRISTOPHORO BROVVERO . . . ANTVERPIÆ EX OFFICINA PLANTINIANA, Apud Viduam & Filios Ioannis Moreti. M.DC.XII. [etc.] 4° pp.374; illus.
206.a.4; 487.h.18.

The decication signed: Christophorus Brouuerus. Most of the illustrations are engravings. The copy at 487.h.18 is imperfect; wanting the illustration on leaf ★2.

BRUIN, Nicolaus de. *See* BRUYN, Nicolaes de

B307 BRUITSMA, Regnerus

Regneri Bruitsma . . . IATRICVM VOTVM IN Publicæ Salutis, & Medicinæ Sanctioris TVTELAM, AD ILL. AC AMPLISSIMOS VV. S.P.Q.M. MECHLINIÆ, Apud HENRICVM IAEY, M.DC.XVII. 4° pp.91
1179.d.1(6).

Partly in Greek.

B308 BRUNO, Georgius

THESES INAVGVRALES MEDICÆ, DE CALCVLO RENVM ET VESICÆ, QVAS . . . PRO Gradu Docturæ in Medicina consequendo Publico examini subijcit [*sic*], GEORGIVS BRVNO . . . LVGDVNI BATAVORVM. Ex Officina IACOBI PATII . . . 1616. 4° sig.A^4
1185.g.1(62).

B309 BRUNO, Joannes

THESES INAVGVRALES MEDICÆ DE EPILEPSIA Quas . . . PRO GRADV DOCTORATVS in Arte Medicâ consequendo examinandas proponit M. IOANN. BRVNO . . . LUGDUNI BATAVORUM, Excudebat GODEFRIDUS BASSON, 1612. 4° sig.A^4
7306.f.6(3).

B310 BRUNO, Vincenzo

[Meditationi sopra i principali mysteri della vita . . . di Christo.] AN ABRIDGMENT OF MEDITATIONS of the Life, Passion, Death, & Resurrection of . . . IESVS CHRIST. Written in Italian by . . . Vincentius Bruno . . . And translated into English by R. G. . . . VVhereunto is premised a briefe Methode for Instruction & Practice of Meditation . . . 1614. 12° pp.244
C.26.k.20.

Translated by Richard Gibbons. The dedication signed: I. W. P., i.e. John Wilson Priest. The 'Methode' is by Edward Dawson. Without imprint; published by the English College press at St. Omer.

B311 BRUSSELS

[1.9.1603] ORDINANTIE OM TE VERHVEDEN ENDE BELETTEN den voortganck vande contagieuse sieckte. TOT BRVESSEL, By Rutgeert Velpius . . . M.D.C.III. [etc.] 4° sig. AB^4
107.g.4(13).
Issued by the city of Brussels on 1 September 1603.

BRUYDEGOMS mantelken. 1607. *See* VERVOORT, Frans

B312 BRUYN, Nicolaes de

ANIMALIVM QVADRVPEDVM varij generis effigies in tyronum, præcipuè tamen aurifabrorum gratiam, tabellis æneis incisa per Nicolaum de Bruin. tot Amsterdam Gedruckt by Claes Janss Visscher, 1621. Allerley vierfuessiger thier eigentliche abbildung, den goltschmiden dienlich. obl.4° pl.12
C.175.m.32(5).
Without text apart from the title in Latin and German on the titlepage which is engraved. Some of the plates dated 1594.

B313 BUCER, Martin

[Epistola . . . nuncupatoria . . . de servanda unitate Ecclesiae.] GVLDEN BRIEF, Des . . . MARTINI BVCERI, Daer inne gheleert vvordt, vvat Ketterye is:vvie Ketters zijn: ende hoe verre men met de Verschillende, Christelicke ghemeynschap behoort te houden . . . uyt het Latijn . . . over-gheset ende uyt-ghegheven/Door J. UUTENBOGAERT . . . S'GRAVEN-HAGHE, By Hillebrant Jacobsz . . . 1616. 4° pp.30
T.2246(23).
A translation of the dedicatory letter only.

B314 BUECKELIUS, Johannes

[Historien ende mirakelen gheschiet tot Aerlen bij Helmont door het aenroepen van Ons L. Vrou.] (half-title) DAT EERSTE DEEL VAN DIE HISTORIEN ENDE MIRACVLEN VAN AERLEN. 8° dl.1:ff.127
1606/277(4).
Imperfect; wanting the titlepage. The dedication signed: Joh. Beuckelius. The 'Vermaninghe tot den Leser' on f.[128] calls the book 'dit eerste deel' and expresses the hope 'cortelingh noch dat ander deel wt te laten comē', but no second part is recorded. Published by Anthoni Scheffer at 's-Hertogenbosch in 1614.

B315 BULLE

BVLLE Oft Mandaet des Paus van Roomen/aende Gheestelicheyt al om bevolen/om haer advijs te vernemen opt stuck van de Vrede-handel met de Hollantsche ketters . . . Sonder Costeri visitatie/Sonder zijn Heylicheyts aprobatie . . . Ghedruckt buyten Roomen/Voor den tijdt voorleden en noch te comen. (col.) Gheteeckent, gheseghelt, sonder Visschers Ringh„ Dach en Iaer als den Paus Stadthouderschap ontfingh. Si Peu Que Rien. 4° sig. A^4; illus.
106.b.8.
A copy of the edition without prose prologue on the verso of the titlepage. The titlepage woodcut shows the 'MANDATA' with six seals. Published in 1608.

B316 BULLINGER, Heinrich

[Sermonum decades.] HET ACHSTE SERMOEN HENRICI BULLINGERI. Ghenomen uyt het Huys-boeck uyt de tweede Decades . . . IN 'SGRAVEN-HAGE. By Aert Meuris . . . 1619. 4° sig. $A\text{-}D^4$
T.2249(43).

B317 BURCHIUS, Lambertus van der

GVIDONIS FLANDRIAE COMITIS VITA, VARII SVCCESSVS, ET TRISTIS TANDEM EXITVS. Authore LAMBERTO VANDER BVRCHIO . . . VLTRAIECTI, Ex Officina HERMANNI BORCVLOI . . . 1615. 8° ff.56
C.77.a.10(1).
Ff.21–29 mutilated by worms with loss of text.

B318 BURDON, Galfridus

VISIO [S]CIPIONIS CHRISTIANI: sive TRACTATVS DE SOLE, LVMINARI MAIORE: IN QVO DISTINCTA QVAtuor dierum opera, vsque ad creationem eius, memorabilibus tabulis exprimuntur. Opus inchoatum: GALFRIDO BVRDONE Auctore. Epistolicæ item aliquot Meditationes: præcipuè de aliquibus verbis Leonis Magni . . . eodem auctore. LVGDVNI BATAVORVM, Apud Ioannem Maire. 1616. 8° pp.83; illus.
702.a.52.
Dedicated to James I and to Charles, Prince of Wales. With letters to Isaac Casaubon, Robert Abbot and others. The illustrations are woodcuts. The titlepage is mutilated.

B319 BURGERSDIJCK, Franco

PROBLEMA VTRVM, QVOD VERVM EST IN THEOLOGIA, POSSIT ESSE FALSVM IN PHILOSOPHIA, AUT VICE VERSA: Cujus partem negativam . . . SVB PRÆSIDIO . . . D. M. FRANCONIS BVRGERSDICI . . . publicè . . . tueri annitar PETRVS I. F. DOORNYCK . . . LVGDVNI BATAVORVM, Ex officina IACOBI MARCI . . . M.D.CXX. 4° sig.A^6
534.c.36(56).

B320 BURGESUS, Joannes

DISPVTATIO INAVGVRALIS DE CHOLERA VERA, Quam . . . Pro Gradu Doctoratus in Medicina obtinendo discutiendam proponit IOANNES BVRGESVS . . . Lugduni Batavorum, Excudebat THOMAS BASSON, 1611. 4° sig.A^4
1185.g.1(45).
With the oath sworn by Burgesus.

B321 BURGGRAV, Johann Ernst

IOAN. ERNESTI BURGGRAVI . . . ACHILLES ΠΑΝΟΠΛΟΣ Redivivus, Seu Panoplia Physico-Vulcania [quâ] in prælio φίλοπλος in Hostem educitur Sacer et inviolabilis. Cui præmissa est MARCELLI VRANCKHEIM . . . ἐπικρισις στοχαστικὴ ad Achillem πανυπεροπόμαχον. Amsterodami apud Hendricum Laurentium. 8° pp.130; illus.
621.b.24(1).
The word 'quâ' has been added to the title in manuscript. The titlepage is engraved. The dedication dated 1612 and presumably published that year. With the arms of Simon, Count of Lippe, engraved on the verso of the titlepage. From the library of John Morris.

B322 BURGGRAV, Johann Ernst

BIOLYCHNIVM seu LVCERNA, Cum vita ejus, cui accensa est Mysticè, vivens jugiter; cum morte ejusdem expirans . . . Huic accessit Cura Morborum Magnetica ex Theophr. Parac MVMIA: itémq; omnium venenorum Alexipharmacum. Auctiora & emendatiora omnia curis secundis IOAN. ERNESTI BURGGRAVI . . . FRANEKERAE Ex officinâ Vlderici Dominici Balck 1611. 8° pp.176
1033.e.8.
With laudatory poems by Marcellus Vranckheim.

B323 BURGOS, Pedro Alfonso de

[Libro de la historia y milagros hechos a inuocacion de nuestra Señora de Montserrat.] L'HISTOIRE DES MIRACLES FAICTS PAR L'INTERCESSION DE NOSTRE DAME DE MONT-SERRAT, DEPUIS L'AN 888. iusques à l'an 1599 . . . Traduicte d'Espagnol en

François . . . A DOVAY De l'Imprimerie de BALTAZAR BELLERE . . . 1601. 8° pp.602
1367.a.16.
Anonymous, as is the translator. The attribution to Gonzalo de Sojo as author and Antoine Jurge as translator, found in the catalogue of the Bibliothèque Nationale, Paris, and elsewhere, is due to a misinterpretation of the title of the enlarged edition of 1627.

B324 BURGUNDIUS, Nicolaus
NICOLAI BVRGVNDII . . . POËMATA . . . ANTVERPIAE, Apud Guilielmum Lesteenum . . . 1621. 12° pp.189
11409.a.20.
Author's presentation copy to — Vandeburcht [?].

B325 BUSAEUS, Joannes
ENCHIRIDION PIARVM MEDITATIONVM IN OMNES DOMINICAS, SANCTORVM Festa, Christi passionem, & cætera . . . Opera & studio IOANNIS BVSÆI . . . concinnatum . . . DVACI, Typis BALTAZARIS BELLERI . . . 1616. 16° pp.653
C.20.f.17.
From the travelling library of Sir Julius Caesar.

B326 BUSCHIUS, Joannes
(tp.1) CHRONICON CANONICORVM REGVLARIVM ORDINIS S. AVGVSTINI CAPITVLI WINDESHEMENSIS Auctore IOANNE BVSCHIO . . . Accedit CHRONICON MONTIS S. AGNETIS Auctore THOMA à KEMPIS . . . nunc primùm in lucem edita Vnà cum VINDICIIS KEMPENSIBVS HERIBERTI ROS-WEYDI . . . pro libro de Imitatione Christi. ANTVERPIAE, Apud Petrum & Ioannem Belleros . . . M D C XXI.
(tp.2) CHRONICON CANONICORVM REGVLARIVM MONTIS S. AGNETIS. AVCTORE THOMA à KEMPIS . . . ANTVERPIAE, Apud HIERONYMVM VERDVSSIVM . . . M D XXI [*sic*].
(tp.3) HERIBERTI ROS-VVEYDI . . . VINDICIAE KEMPENSES PRO LIBELLO THOMAE à KEMPIS DE IMITATIONE CHRISTI, ADVERSVS CONSTANTINVM CAIETANVM . . . ANTVERPIÆ, Apud Petrum & Ioannem Belleros. MDC.XXI. 8° 3 pt.: pp.636; 183; 127
4660.a.1.
Compiled and edited by H. Rosweyde; the dedication signed: H.R. Ownership inscription: W. Turner.

B327 BUSIUS, Paulus
[Pauli Busii IC. Commentarii brevis in pandectas Dni. Iustiniani . . . tomus primus (etc.)] (half-title 1=p.259) PARS II P. BVSII . . . COMMENTARII IN PANDECTAS DNI IVSTINIANI . . . cum differentijs IVRIS CANONICI, ET CONSVETVDINVM AD VSVM huius seculi compositi [etc.]
(half-title 2=p.465) P. BVSII . . . COMMENTARII IN PANDECTAS . . . Pars III [etc.] 4° pt.1: pp.263–712
497.d.3.
Imperfect; wanting pt.1 of vol.1 and all of vol.2. The dedication of pt.2 of vol.1 dated: 1608. Comparison kindly carried out by Mr. R. Breugelmans at Leiden University Library with the copy available at that library of the edition published at Zwolle by Zacharias Heyns in 1608 proved the British Library copy here described to be part of that edition.

B328 BUYRPRAETJEN
Buyr-praetjen: Ofte Tsamensprekinge ende Discours/op den Brieff vanden Agent Aerssens uyt Vranckrijck/aende . . . Staten Generael geschreven. Dienende tot ontdeckinge van der Spaengiaerden ende hare adherenten listicheyt/ trouweloosheyt/ende . . . wraeckgiericheydt. 4° sig.AB^4
T.2422(16).
On the negotiations for a peace or truce. The letter of Frans van Aerssen was read at a meeting in July 1608. Published in 1608.

De BYEN-CORF, der H. Roomscher Kercke. 1611. *See* MARNIX, Philips van

C

For headings beginning with the possible alternative spelling K, see also K.

C1 CABILLIAVUS, Balduinus

BALDVINI CABILLAVI . . . EPIGRAMMATA SELECTA. ANTVERPIÆ, EX OFFICINA PLANTINIANA, Apud Balthasarem Moretum, & viduam Ioannis Moreti, & Io. Meursium. M.DC.XX. (COL.) ANTVERPIÆ, EX OFFICINA PLANTINIANA BALTHASARIS MORETI. M.DC.XX. 12° pp.78

11403.a.41(2).

C2 CABILLIAVUS, Balduinus

LEMMATA NOVO-ANTIQVA PANCARPIA, Ex Natura, Historia, Moribus, In gratiam studiosæ Iuuentutis tetrastichis illigata . . . IPRIS FLANDRORVM, Apud FRANCISCVM BELLETTVM, M.DC.XIV. 12° pp.352

11409.b.7.

Anonymous. Imperfect; wanting pp.7, 8; 17, 18. Ownership inscription: Conventus Carmel. descal. Brugis.

C3 CAERT-THRESOOR

Hand-boeck; Of Cort Begrijp der Caerten Ende Beschryvinghen van alle Landen des Werelds. Van nieuvvs oversien ende vermeerdert. 't Amstelredam by Cornelis Claesz. . . . 1609. obl. 8° pp.761; illus., maps

Maps C.39.a.5.

The preface states that this work was 'over eenighe jaren van eenen Iongh-man (ons onbekent) in Druck ghegheven', referring to the earlier edition entitled 'Caert-thresoor', published by Barent Langenes, to whom authorship has sometimes wrongly been ascribed. The editor's dedication signed: Iacobus Viverius. Of the maps and views some are signed: I., or Iodocus, Hondius cælavit; Pe. Kærius fecit; P.K. cælavit, and one map is by Benjamin Wright. The text is interspersed with verses.

C4 CAESAR, Caius Julius

[Works. Latin] C. IVLII CÆSARIS QVÆ EXSTANT: Ex noua & accuratissima viri docti recognitione. EX OFFICINA PLANTINIANA RAPHELENGII, M.D.CVI. 8° pp.480: plates; illus., maps, port.

586.c.8.

Edited by J. J. Scaliger. With the commentaries of Aulus Hirtius and others. Printed in italics. Published at Leiden. Ownership inscription: Tho. Caister.

C5 CAESAR, Caius Julius

[Works. Latin] C. IVLII CÆSARIS QVÆ EXSTANT. EX OFFICINA PLANTINIANA RAPHELENGII, M.D.CXIV. 16° pp.550

C.20.f.28.

Edited by J. J. Scaliger. With the commentaries of Aulus Hirtius. Published at Leiden. From the travelling library of Sir Julius Caesar.

C6 CAESAR, Caius Julius

[Works. Dutch] (tp.1) Wyt beroemde COMMENTARIEN ofte Corte historische aenteyckeningen van . . . Cajus Iulius Cæsar . . . Het eerste Deel. Van sijn Fransche ende Nederlantsche oorlogen Vervatet in acht boecken. Waer van . . . zeven door hem selven . . . Ende het achste door Aulus Hirtius Pansa. Verduijtscht . . . door Iohannes Fenacolius. Tot Delft. By Adriaen Geritsen . . . 1614.

(tp.2=f.185) De wijdt-beroemde COMMENTARIEN . . . vanden . . . Prince Cajus Julius Cæsar . . . Het tweede deel. Van de Burgherlicke oorloghe . . . vervatet in zes Boecken/waer van de drye eerste met syn eyghen . . . handt beschreven zijn: ende de andere drye . . . door AVLVS HIRTIVS PANSA. Alles . . . overghezet . . . door Ioannes Fenacolius Lenaertz . . . TOT DELF, By Adriaen Gerritsz . . . 1614. (tp.3=f.417) Verklaringhe Van zommighe oude Romeynsche krijchswoorden ende Oorlochs-wercken . . . Insghelijcx een Register van alle de oude namen van Volckeren/Landen/Steden . . . Door IOHANNES FENACOLIVS LENAERTZ . . . TOT DELF, By Adriaen Gerritsz . . . 1614. 8° ff.443: plate; illus., map
1568/5109.

The titlepage is engraved. The foliation is at times irregular. The illustrations and the map are in woodcut.

C7 CAESARIUS, Henricus

DANCK SERMOON Over het teghenwoordighe ghemaeckte bestant van twaelf Jaeren . . . Ghepredickt . . . den vj[en]. May nieuwe stijl . . . ende daer nae beschreven DOOR HENRICVS CÆSARIVS . . . TOT VTRECHT Gedruckt by my Jan a Meliszoon . . . M.DC.IX. [etc.] 4° pp.71
T.2421(9).

On conditions at Zaltbommel.

C8 CALDERWOOD, David

DE REGIMINE ECCLESIÆ SCOTICANÆ BREVIS RELATIO. Jmpressus . . . 1618. 8° pp.29
C.53.aa.14.

Anonymous and without imprint; printed by William Brewster at Leiden. Ownership inscription: Wil. Douglas.

C9 CALDERWOOD, David

PERTH ASSEMBLY. CONTAINING 1 The Proceedings thereof. 2 The Proofe of the Nullitie thereof . . . MDCXIX. 4° pp.101
110.a.2; 4175.a.77.

Anonymous and without imprint; printed by William Brewster at Leiden. The copy at 4175.a.77 is imperfect; wanting the last leaf, the text of which has been supplied in manuscript.

C10 CALDERWOOD, David

[Perth Assembly.] PARASYNAGMA [*sic*] PERTHENSE ET IVRAMENTVM ECCLESIÆ SCOTICANÆ ET A. M. ANTITAMICAMICATEGORIA . . . M.DC.XX. 4° pp.47
4175.c.72.

Anonymous. An abridged translation of David Calderwood's 'Perth Assembly'. The running title of the additional poem is 'A Meluini Antitamicamicategoria'. Without imprint; printed in Holland? by Giles Thorp at Amsterdam?

C11 CALDERWOOD, David

A SOLVTION OF DOCTOR RESOLVTVS, His Resolutions for kneeling . . . M.DC.XIX. 4° pp.55
4323.bb.17.

Anonymous. Directed against Bishop David Lindsay. Without imprint; printed by Joris Veseler at Amsterdam.

C12 CALDERWOOD, David

THE SPEACH OF THE KIRK OF SCOTLAND TO HER BELOVED CHILDREN . . . Imprinted . . . 1620. 8° pp.125
873.b.31.

Anonymous. The attribution to Calderwood follows *Johnson* p.229. Without imprint; printed by Giles Thorp at Amsterdam.

CALENDIER ofte almanach, waer inne men . . . sien kan de apocalyptische beeste. 1617. *See* DRIELENBURCH, Vincent van

C13 CALVIJNSCHEN

De Calvijnschen VVTROEPER. Waer door het ghevoelen der Calvinisten van de Prędestinatie met den aencleve van dien/naecktelijck ende cortelijck wt ghedruckt wordt. Hier is noch een Dialogus by ghevoecht. Gedruckt onder't + int jaer . . . 1621. 4° sig. A^2

T.2251(8*).

Without imprint; printed by Pieter Arents at Norden?

C14 CALVIN, Jean

[Institutio Christianae religionis.] (tp.1) INSTITVTIE, OFTE ONDERVIISINGE INDE CRISTELICKE RELIGIE . . . DOOR Ioannem Calvinum: Wt de Latijnsche ende Fransoysche sprake . . . verduytschet . . . Daer is oock achter aen ghevoecht een schoone Tafel Augustini Marlorati . . . Noch van nieus hier achter aen gevoecht een schoon stucxken van de Reformatie der Christelicker Kercke in het Pausdom/ gemaect int Latijn door den selven Autheur: Eñ nu . . . overgeset . . . Door Car-Agric. . . . TOT AMSTELREDAM, By Jan Evertsz Cloopenborch [*sic*] . . . 1617. (tp.2) EEN SVPPLICATIE, VANDE NOODIGHE REFORMATIE DER CHRISTELICKER KERCKE IN HET PAVSDOM, Over ghegheven van . . . Iohanne Calvino, aen KEYSER KAREL DE VIIFDE . . . Wt het Latijn . . . over gheset, door CAR. AGRIC. . . . TOT DORDRECHT, Ghedruckt by Jacob Canin . . . 1617. fol. 2 pt.: ff.375; 27; illus., port.

1565/72.

The whole translated by Carolus Agricola. The portrait of Calvin engraved on the titlepage.

CALVIN, Jean. [Supplex exhortatio.] Een supplicatie, vande noodighe Reformatie der Christelicker Kercke in het Pausdom. 1617. *See* supra: [Institutio Christianae religionis.] Institutie. pt.2.

C15 CALVINISCHE

Die CALVINISCHE Predestinatie, Tusschen eenen GOMMARIST ende ARMINIAEN. 4° pp.3–7. sig. $A2–4^4$

P.P.3444.af(7).

In verse. Imperfect; wanting the titlepage. The title is taken from p.3. Published by Abraham Verhoeven at Antwerp in February 1621, numbered 22.

C16 CALVINISCHER

Caluinischer Vortantz/Welcher in Ober Oesterreich geschmidtet/ zu Praag in Boͤheim angefangen/vnd wider die Papisten allenthalben gehalten worden ist . . . Durch Vincentz Rupffenbart/Caluinischen Schulmaister zu Purla in Laussnitz/ gemehrt vnd gebessert. Getruckt zu Genff in Hollandt/bey Niclasen Gumperle . . . 1621. 8° sig. AB^4

11515.a.57(4).

The imprint is fictitious. Printed in Germany?

C17 CAMDEN, William

GVILIELMI CAMDENI . . . BRITANNIA- SIVE . . . Regnorum Angliæ, Scotiæ, Hiberniæ, & Insularum adjacentium ex intima antiquitate descriptio. IN EPITOMEN CONTRACTA à Regnero Vitellio . . . & Tabulis Chorographicis illustrata. AMSTELREDAMI, Ex Officina Guilielmi Ianssonij, M.DC.XVII. 8° pp.714: plates; illus., maps

796.a.2; 577.a.2.

The copy at 577.a.2 has a comma in place of the hyphen after the word 'Britannia' on the titlepage, sig.–5 is mutilated and the folding maps have been cut out and mounted with loss of binder's instructions. A portrait of Camden with the address of Geo. Humble, London, has been inserted.

CAMPANELLA, Franciscus. *See* CAMPANELLA, Tommaso

C18 CAMPANELLA, Tommaso

[Discursus de Belgio . . . redigendo.] Discours FR. CAMPANELLÆ Van Het Nederlant te brengen onder de macht des Conincx van Spagnien. Wt Latijn in Nederduyts overgheset/tot dienst vande goede Ingesetenen van het vereenichde Nederlant. Hier by Is herdruckt seeckeren brief geschreven vande Heeren van Antwerpen aen de Heeren van Gendt . . . VVtgegeven ten beveele der Heeren Staten van Frieslant. Ghedruckt tot Franeker/By Ian Lamrinck . . . 1618. 4° pp.23

700.h.25(14).

Without the 'seeckeren brief' which has been separated from this work, placed at 700.h.25(9). For a description *see* ANTWERP [1584]

C19 CAMPANELLA, Tommaso

[Discursus de Belgio . . . redigendo.] Discours van Franciscus Campanella, Hoe de Nederlanden onder des Coninghs van Hispaengien ghehoorsaemheyt weder te brenghen zijn. Dienende tot opmerckinge aller getrouwe Voester-Heeren onses lieven Vaderlants. Gedruckt by een Liefhebber des Vaderlants. 1618. 4° sig. A^4B^2; illus.

T.2422(5).

The titlepage woodcut is a presumed portrait of Campanella.

C20 CAMPHUYSEN, Dirck Raphaëlsz

BRIEF Tot AFRADING van't Paus-dom. Gheschreven van seker uytghebannen Predikant aen eenen zijnen Vriendt . . . Ghedruckt onder 't † Anno 1621. 4° pp.21

T.2251(5).

Anonymous. Printed by Pieter Arentsz at Norden.

CAMPHUYSEN, Dirck Raphaëlsz. Godt de wraeck. 1620. *See* BIBLE. Psalms. Selections. Dutch

C21 CAMPHUYSEN, Dirck Raphaëlsz

HET SCHILT Der Verdructer Ghemoederen. Dat is: Een Voorschrift/Hoe sich een yder Mensche in teghenspoet/draghen sal . . . Ghedruckt . . . 1619. 4° pp.8

11555.e.41(5); T.2249(40).

In verse. Anonymous and without imprint. The 'printer's', or rather, editor's, preface to the reader signed: R.T., i.e. Reinier Telle, and with other additional matter by him. Completed after Telle's death and edited, perhaps by Henricus Slatius at Antwerp. Camphuysen's own title, when he published it later, was 'Ghewillighe patientie ofte Lydens remedie'.

C22 CAMPHUYSEN, Dirck Raphaëlsz

VICTORIA VICTIS. Dat is, Den waren zeghen Gods/Ofte Lydens nutticheyt. Dienende tot een vol-komen Lydens remedie. Int Jaer 1620. 4° sig. AB^4

11555.e.24(1).

In verse. Anonymous and without imprint; printed by Pieter Arentsz at Norden?

C23 CANNENBURGH, P.

Een Cleyn Vensterken/waer door Gekeëcken werdt hoe die groote Meesters haer tot de poorten der hellen wentelen/soo met Haer gevangen zielen te vermoorden/ alsoo/naer dat hy ghesouten waer/zijn inghewandt in een Dieff-put begraven werdt. in dicht gestelt. Door een cloeck moedich Seuw. 4° sig. A^4

T.2250(28); T.2424(34).

Anonymous. Published in 1618.

C24 CANONIERO, Pietro Andrea

DELLE CAVSE DELL' INFELICITA E DISGRAZIE DE GLI HVOMINI LETTERATI E GVERRIERI LIBRI OTTO DI PIETRO ANDREA CANONHIERO . . . All'Jllustrissimo Signor Don ALFONZO D'AVALOS. IN ANVERSA Appresso IOACH. TROGNESIO. M.DC.XII. 8° pp.531
616.a.2.
Printed in italics.

C25 CANONIERO, Pietro Andrea

FLORES ILLVSTRIVM EPITAPHIORVM EX PRÆCLARISSIMARVM TOTIVS EVROPÆ CIVITATVM Et præstantissimorum poëtarum monumentis excerpti PER PETRVM ANDREAM CANONHERIVM. AD . . . LEONARDVM BONTEMPVM . . . ANTVERPIÆ APVD IOACH. TROGNÆSIVM. M.DCXIII. 8° pp.544
11409.b.41.
Ownership inscription: ex libris suis Justiniani foppei Augustiniane familie.

CAP-COVEL om op t'hooft te setten van Drielenburgh. 1617. *See* PAGIUS, H.

CARBASIUS, Thomas. Theses medicae de febri hectica. 1608. *See* VORSTIUS, Aelius Everardus

C26 CARDINAEL, Sybrand Hansz

[Hondert geometrische questien.] TRACTATVS GEOMETRICVS, Darinnen hundert schöne/ausserlesene/liebliche Kunst Quæstiones, Durch welche allerley Longi: Plani: vnd Solidi metrische Messung . . . zu thun vnd zu verrichten seind/mit beygefuegten aufflösungen . . . Von . . . Sybrand Hansz . . . Niederlandisch beschrieben. Jetzt aber . . . mit beygesetztem vnterricht der Surdischen vnd Binomischen zaln: auss gemelter Niederländischen sprach in Hochteutsch Transferieret, Durch Sebastianum Curtium . . . Gedruckt zu Ambsterdam bey Wilhelm Jansz . . . 1617. 4° pp.126; illus.
1570/778.

C27 CARELSZ, Pieter

(tp.1) Instrucktie ende generale Methodus der vrijer Conste van de Medicijne ende Chirurgie/ghecopuleert . . . door Meester Pieter Carelsz. . . . Tot Dordrecht/By Abraham Canin/1605. [etc.]
(tp.2=sig.k5r) Een generale Methodus om te cureren die Contagieuse Sieckte der Pestilentiale Cortse . . . gecopuleert door Pieter Carelsz. [etc.] 4° pp.144; sig.k5-8,L^8
549.e.6(1).
The 'Register' on L7 indicates 'Het Peste boeck' for p.146: it should be 147. tp.2, without imprint, bears the Canin device on the titlepage.

C28 CARIER, Benjamin

A TREATISE VVRITTEN by M[r]. Doctour Carier, vvherein he layeth dovvne sundry learned and pithy considerations, by vvhich he vvas moued, to forsake the protestant Congregation, and to betake hym self to the Catholicke Apostolicke Roman church: [etc.] 4° pp.52
3902.bbb.28.
In the form of a letter, dated: Liege Decemb. 12. A°. 1613. Without imprint; printed by Jan Mommaert at Brussels in 1614.

C29 CARLETON, Dudley; Viscount Dorchester

[The speech of Sir Dudley Carlton . . . made in the Assembly of the . . . Estates Generall of the united Provinces of the Low Countries.] ORATIE Ghedaen door . . . Dudley Carleton . . . Aende . . . Staten Generael vande Vereenichde Provintien. Tot wechneminghe vande . . . oneenicheden/inde Kercke ende Policie ontstaan

uyt ende door de Leere Arminij . . . Ghedruct . . . M.DC.XVII. 4° sig. A[4]
T.2247(23**).
With manuscript notes.

C30 CARMINA

CARMINA DVO SÆCVLARIA; DE ADMIRABILI DEPRAVATÆ RELIGIONIS Restitutione in Integrum. Condita Cal. Novemb. ANNO XVII. SÆCVLI CVRRENTIS . . . Decimi Septimi. [etc.] 4° pp. 13
1054.h.9(5*).
The text refers to 'we' as subject to the Pope and the King of Spain, rejecting both in favour of the Emperor Matthias. Printed in the Netherlands?

C31 CARNINUS, Claudius

TRACTATVS DE VI ET POTESTATE LEGVM HVMANARVM . . . Authore CLAVDIO CARNINO . . . DVACI CATVACORVM, Apud LAVRENTIVM KELLAM . . . M.D.C.VIII. [etc.] 4° pp. 144
C.73.b.13.

C32 CARON, Noel de

NIEVS uyt Engelandt gheschreven door . . . NOEL DE CARON. aende . . . Staten Generael der Vereenichde Nederlanden . . . 1621. 4° sig. A[4]
1325.e.4.

C33 CARPENTER, John

QVÆSTIO DE PRECIBVS ET leiturgijs, ab hominibus præscriptis: Vtrùm in cultu divino licitum sit, eiusmodi leiturgijs vti . . . an non: Duabus epistolis tractata: Quarum altera scripta erat, Per Iohannem Carpenterum . . . Altera, Per Franciscum Iohnsonum . . . Prostat apud viduam Levini Hulsij: Francofurti . . . 1610. 4° pp. 42
1476.bb.42.
According to *Johnson* p. 226 printed at Amsterdam by Giles Thorp. With some Hebrew characters: printed there by Jan Theunisz?

CARTE ou liste contenant le pris de chascun marq. 1621. *See* NETHERLANDS. Southern Provinces [1.1621]

C34 CARTHENAY, Jean de

[Le voyage du chevalier errant.] VANDER REYSE DES DOOLENDEN RIDDERS HET EERSTE DEEL. 4° pp. 1–72
11557.e.63(2).
A fragment, wanting the titlepage, preliminaries if any, and all after p. 72. A different translation is known, published at Ghent in smaller formats, but this translation by then apparently forgotten and not recorded since. Could it have appeared ca. 1620, perhaps at Antwerp? The author and original title kindly identified for me by Dr. Bert van Selm. From the library of C. P. Serrure.

CARTWRIGHT, Thomas. Commentarii succincti & dilucidi in Proverbia Salomonis. 1617. *See* BIBLE. Proverbs. Latin

C35 CARTWRIGHT, Thomas

A CONFVTATION OF THE RHEMISTS TRANSLATION, GLOSSES AND ANNOTATIONS ON THE NEVV TESTAMENT . . . By . . . THOMAS CARTWRIGHT . . . Printed . . . 1618. fol. pp. 761
689.g.10; 3205.c.16; 1475.c.12; 1602/471.
Without imprint; the attribution to the press of William Brewster at Leiden made in *Harris & Jones (1)* no. 16 is questioned in *Harris & Jones (2)* p. 160. The copy at 3205.c.16 inscribed on the titlepage: H. Wotton; the copy at 1475.c.12 inscribed at the end: I allowe this booke wth such corrections as I shall adde therevnto for ye presse. Daniel Featley, Anthony Gilmyre. Lambeth Jan 2°1625.

C36 CARVALHO, Valentino

IAPPONIENSIS IMPERII ADMIRABILIS COMMVTATIO EXPOSITA LITTERIS AD . . . Claudium Aquauiua . . . quas ex Italis latinas fecit IO. HAYVS . . . ANTVERPIÆ Sumptibus Viduæ & Heredum IO: BELLERI . . . M.DC.IV. 8° pp.92

867.e.21; 295.g.32.

Letters from the Jesuit mission to Japan, signed: Valentinus Carvaglio.

CASANDRA Hertoginne van Borgonie. 1617. *See* RODENBURGH, Theodore

C37 CASAS, Bartolomé de las; Bishop

[Brevissima relación de la destruycion de las Indias.] Spieghel der Spaenscher tyrannye/in West-Indien. Waer inne verhaelt wordt de moordadighe . . . feyten/ die de selve Spaenjaerden ghebruyckt hebben . . . Mitsgaders de beschryvinghe vander ghelegentheyt/zeden ende aert van deselfde Landen ende Volcken. In Spaenscher Talen beschreven, door . . . Bartholome de las Casas . . . t'Amstelredam, By Cornelis Claesz . . . 1607. 4° sig.A-L^4; map

T.1713(22).

Reprinted from the prose-edition published by Nicolaes Biestkens de Jonghe at Amsterdam in 1596.

C38 CASAS, Bartolomé de las; Bishop

[Brevissima relación de la destruycion de las Indias.] Den SPIEGEL der Spaensche tierannije-geschiet in Westindien . . . In Spans beschreven door . . . bartholome de las Casas . . . Gedruckt tot AMSTERDAM by Cornelis Lodewijcksz. vander Plasse . . . 1620. 4° sig.A-N^4; illus.

9180.cc.2.

The titlepage and illustrations are engraved. The latter are accompanied by verses derived from the 1611 edition, *Knuttel* no. 1837, where they are said to be by Nicasius vander Clyte. The plates are those previously used for an edition of 1609, for which *see* below: Abridgment.

C39 CASAS, Bartolomé de las; Bishop

[Brevissima relación de la destruycion de las Indias.] Den Vermeerderden SPIEGHEL der Spaensche tierannije-geschiet in Westindien waerin te sien is de onmenschelijke wreede feijten der Spanjærden . . . allen Vaderlant lieuende . . . ten exempel voorgestelt. In Spans beschreeven door bartholome de las Casas . . . Gedruckt tot AMSTERDAM by Cornelis Lodwijcksz. vander Plasse . . . 1621. 4° sig.A,a,B-M^4; illus.

1055.g.8(2).

The titlepage is engraved. Most of the engraved illustrations, accompanied by the verses of Nicasius vander Clyte, are the same as in the preceding, with one plate substituted by another, showing Columbus discovering America. With some additional text.

C40 CASAS, Bartolomé de las; Bishop

[Brevissima relación de la destruycion de las Indias.] LE MIROIR De la Tyrannie Espagnole Perpetree aux Indes Occidentales . . . Mise en lumiere par . . . Bartholome de las Casas . . . Nouvellement refaicte, avec les Figures en cuyvre. tot AMSTERDAM Ghedruckt by Ian Evertss, [*sic*] Cloppenburg . . . 1620. 4° pp.68; illus.

278.f.28; G.7102(1).

Published as companion piece to Joannes Gysius's 'Le miroir de la . . . tyrannie espagnole . . . au Pays Bas'. The engraved scenes surrounding the title on the titlepage, including portraits of Philip II, 'Don Ian' and 'Duc Dalve', signed: DvB [i.e. David Vinckboons? or Daniel van den Bremden?] in., I.D.C.fe. The copy at G.7102(1) has this work wrongly bound in before the Gysius which is preceded by a combined preface for both works. A map showing 'THE NEWE WORLDE' beside one of Western Europe and North Africa has been inserted in the same copy. The copy at 278.f.28 has been completely separated from the Gysius.

C41 CASAS, Bartolomé de las; Bishop
[Brevissima relación de la destruycion de las Indias. Abridgment] DEN SPIEGHEL Vande Spaensche Tyrannie beeldelijcken afgemaelt/leest breederen in-hout door het schrijven van . . . Bartholome de las Casas . . . aen . . . Philips de tweede. Ghedruckt tot Amstelredam by Cornelis Claesz. 1609. 4° pl.XVII
9551.b.9.
The prose text accompanying the plates is abridged from the edition of 1607 to which the reader is referred at the end. pl.VIII is repeated on the titlepage. The running title is 'Af-beeldinghe vande Spaensche Tyrannije'.

C42 CASAUBON, Isaac
[Isaaci Casauboni Ad epistolam . . . Cardinalis Perronii, responsio.] Antwoort/ ISAACI CASAVBONI Op den Brief vanden . . . Cardinael Perronius . . . Wt de Latijnsche Tale in onse Nederlantsche Over-gheset, ende met een kleyne Voor-reden . . . ver-rijckt. Nae de Copije Ghedruckt tot Londen by Ioannes Norton . . . M.DC.XII. 4° sig.(∴)A-D^{4}E^5; illus.
701.g.22.
The titlepage woodcut shows the English royal arms.

C43 CASAUBON, Isaac
ISAACI CASAVBONI AD FRONTONEM DVCÆVM . . . Epistola; Jn qua de Apologia disseritur communi Iesuitarum nomine ante aliquot menses Lutetiæ Parisiorum edita. Iuxta exemplar LONDINI, Excusam per IOANNEM NORTON . . . M DC XI. 8° pp.140
1120.h.1.
Printed in the Netherlands? Ownership inscriptions: C. Burney; Baignoux.

CASAUBON, Isaac. Misoponeri satyricon. 1617. Sometimes wrongly ascribed to Isaac Casaubon. *See* MISOPONERUS

C44 CASAUBON, Isaac
[Doubtful or supposititious works.] IS. CASAVBONI CORONA REGIA. Id est PANEGYRICVS . . . Quem Iacobo I. Magnæ Britanniæ . . . Regi . . . delinearat, FRAGMENTA, Ab EVPHORMIONE . . . inuenta, collecta, & in lucem edita. M.DC.XV. Pro Officina Regia IO. BILL. LONDINI. 12° pp.127
1389.a.49(2).
Sometimes wrongly attributed to Caspar Schoppe. The imprint is false; in fact, printed by J. C. Flavius at Louvain.

C45 CASSEL in Flanders
[Customs and Privileges.] COSTVMEN ENDE VSANTIEN VANDEN STEDEN ENDE CASSELRIE VAN CASSELE . . . TOT GHENDT Bij Jan vañ Steene . . . 1613. 4° pp.263
C.31.b.24.
The titlepage is engraved, showing the Court of Cassel surrounded by coats of arms of 'Cassele', 'Hazebrouck', 'Waetene' and 'Stegers'. P.[268] bears the statement: Met Gratie ende Preuilegie, followed by the manuscript words 'Vanden Coninck'. There is also a printed privilege. Printed on vellum.

C46 CASTELEYN, Matthijs de
[Collections.] (tp.1) De Konst van RHETORIKEN . . . Item de Baladen van Doornijcke/ende de Historie van Pyramus ende Thisbe: alles in dichte ghestelt by . . . Matthijs de Casteleyn . . . Hier achter zijn noch ghevoecht alle de Liedekens/by den zelven Autheur op Noten ghestelt. TOT ROTTERDAM, By Jan van Waesberghe de Jonghe . . . 1616.
(tp.2=sig.N3r) Baladen van Doornijcke/ghemaeckt door H. Matthijs de Casteleyn [etc.]

(tp.3) HISTORIE van Pyramus ende Thisbe, Speel-wijse ghestelt by . . . MATHYS DE CASTELEYN . . . TOT ROTTERDAM, By Jan van Waesberghe/de Jonghe . . . 1616. (tp.4) Diversche LIEDEKENS Ghecomponeert by . . . Mathys de Casteleyn . . TOT ROTTERDAM, By Jan van Waesberghe/de Jonghe . . . 1616. 8° 3 pt.: pp.196, sig.N3-P4; sig.A-D^8E^4; sig.A-D^8; plate; illus., music, port.
11555.b.5.

The illustrations in pt.1 consist of a large woodcut of 'Rhetorica' at the end of the preliminaries, a portrait of Charles V on tp.2 and a map of various cities in the Southern Netherlands around 'Doornyke'; pt.2 contains numerous woodcuts; pt.3 has the portrait of Casteleyn on tp.4. The plate, or rather table, is referred to in the text as the 'schaeckbert', i.e. 'chessboard', misbound in pt.3 instead of between pp.178–179. Its solution is given in *Bibliotheca Belgica* I p.459, no.C154.

CASTELIUS, Joannes. Historie Van B. Cornelis Adriaensen van Dordrecht. 1607. [By Joannes Castelius?] *See* CHRISTIANUS NEUTER

C47 CASTELLANUS, Petrus; Professor of Greek at Louvain

VITÆ ILLVSTRIVM MEDICORVM Qui toto orbe, ad hæc tempora floruerunt, Authore PETRO CASTELLANO . . . ANTVERPIÆ, Apud Guilielmum à Tongris . . . M.DC.XVII. 8° pp.255
551.a.3.

The date on the titlepage has been altered in manuscript to M.DC.XVIII.

CASTELLIO, Sebastianus. *See* CHÂTEILLON, Sébastien

C48 CASTILE

DN. ANTONII GOMEZII . . . AD LEGES TAVRI. COMMENTARIVS. Cui accesserunt Doctoris Diegi Gomezij . . . Annotationes vtilissimæ, & pernecessariæ . . . ANTVERPIAE Apud PETRVM & IOANNEM Belleros. M.DC.XVII. [etc.] (col.) Antuerpiæ. Excudebat Andreas Bacx, sumptibus Petri & Ioannis Belleri. M.DC.XVII. fol. pp.590
1480.c.9.

The text, in Latin and Spanish, with manuscript notes in both languages. With the ownership inscription and a manuscript poem of Manuel Carpintero Heraso.

CASTRO, Benedictus a. Disputatio medica de apoplexia. 1621. *See* VORSTIUS, Aelius Everardus

C49 CATALOGE

CATALOGE vande Coningen/Princē/Graven ende andere Vorsten/met den Keyser FERDINANDVS II. opentlijck houdende teghen de Vnie der Calvinisten ende alle Adherente Protestanten. Nv eerst ghedruckt den 5. December. T'Hantwerpen/By Abraham Verhoeuen/[etc.] 4° pp.7; illus.
P.P.3444.af(155); 1480.aa.15(52).

With 'Naemen vande Protestante . . . Princen van Duytslandt'. The titlepage woodcut shows the Imperial Eagle.

A CATALOGUE of divers visible professors of the Catholike faith. 1614. *See* PIERCY, John

C50 CATALOGUS

CATALOGVS INSIGNIVM LIBRORVM Ex Bibliotheca . . . D. LVCAE TRELCATII . . . Quorum Auctio fiet LEYDÆ, die xii Decembris & sequentibus: Apud IOANNEM MAIRE Bibliopolam. LVGDVNI BATAVORVM, Excudebat Ioannes a Dorp, 1607. 4° sig.A-C^4D^2
821.e.2(2).

HISTORIE
van
Pyramus ende Thisbe,
Speel-wijse ghestelt by wijlent
HEER MATHYS DE CASTELEYN,
Priester ende excellent Poët.

TOT ROTTERDAM,
By Jan van Waesberghe / de Jonghe / op't Steygher / aen de Koren-merct, ANNO 1616.

C46 (tp.3)

C51 CATALOGUS

CATALOGVS LIBRORVM . . . D.D. IACOBI ARMINII . . . Quorum Auctio habebitur in ædibus viduæ . . . xix. May, & seqq. LVGDVNI BATAVORVM, Ex Officina THOMÆ BASSON. M.D.C.X. 4° pp.50

11901.e.27.

The auction date has been altered in manuscript to 26 May.

C52 CATALOGUS

CATALOGVS PLVRIMORVM INSIGNIVM LIBRORVM Ex Bibliotheca . . . D. ANTONII BIESII . . . Quorum Auctio fiet LEYDÆ, die xv Decembris & sequentibus: Apud IOANNEM MAIRE Bibliopolam. LVGDVNI BATAVORVM, Excudebat Ioannes a Dorp, 1607. 4° sig.a–d^{4}e^2

821.e.2(1).

LE CATECHISME du Palatin. 1621. *See* POSTILLIOEN. Postillion

C53 CATECHISMUS

CATECHISMUS CALVINISTICUS FIDE perquam optima concinnatus. EXCVDEBAT PLANCIVS VANDEN BOGAERD . . . 1609. 8° pp.20

11409.ee.26(4).

In part in both Latin and Dutch. Sometimes wrongly ascribed to Carolus Scribani. The imprint is fictitious; in fact printed at Antwerp, perhaps by Joachim Trognaesius.

C54 CATECHISMUS

CATECHISMVS ROMANVS, EX DECRETO CONCILII TRIDENTINI . . . EDITUS: Postea . . . quæstionibus . . . distinctus, breuibusq́ȝ annotatiunculis elucidatus, studio & industria ANDREÆ FABRICII LEODII . . . Accessit postrema hac editione Index . . . quo Euangelia per annum ad Catechismi huius capita referuntur & explicantur. ANTVERPIÆ, EX OFFICINA PLANTINIANA, Apud Ioannem Moretum. M.DC.VI. 8° pp.470

1018.h.2.

C55 CATECHISMUS

CATECHISMVS Voor de Catholiike Kinderen van het Bisdom van Brugghe. van vveghen den . . . Heere CAROLVS PH, A RHODOAN, Bisschop van Brugghe . . . Tot Brugghe, By Guiliaem de Neeue [etc.] 8° sig.A–D^8; illus.

3504.de.24(1).

Published ca.1615. The illustrations are woodcuts.

CATERINUS Senensis. The life of . . . Sainct Catharine of Siena. 1609. *See* VINEIS, Raymundus de; de Capua.

C56 CATHECISME

[Cathecisme de la paix pretenduez.] DIALOGVS oft Tzamensprekinge/gemaect op den Vredehandel. Ghestelt by Vraghe ende Antwoordt. Overghezet wt de Fransoysche in onse Nederduytsche tale . . . 1608. 4° sig.(⁎⁎⁎)^4

106.d.13.

A translation of 'Cathecisme de la paix pretenduez', probably from manuscript.

Der CATHOLIJCKEN supplicatie. 1603. *See* PETITION

C57 CATO, Marcus Porcius

[Works] (tp.1) M. PORCI CATONIS DE RE RVSTICA Liber. FRAGMENTA, quæ supersunt. AVSONIVS POPMA . . . iterum recensuit, & NOTAS addidit. Accesserunt IOANNIS MEVRSI ad librum De re rustica, NOTÆ, AVSONI POPMÆ De instrumento fundi Liber. Pro Bibliopolio Commeliniano. Sumptibus I. Commelini Viduæ. FRANEKERÆ, Excudebat Ioannes Lamrinck . . . 1620.

(tp.2) AVSONI POPMAE FRISI DE INSTRVMENTO FVNDI LIBER QVI APPENDIX ad Rei rusticæ scriptores Latinos veteres. FRANEKERAE, Excudebat Ioannes Lamrinck . . . 1620. (col.) FRANEKERAE, Apud Ioannem Lamrinck . . . 1620. 8° 2 pt: pp.311; 51
246.c.9(2,3); 1607/5991.

The widow of Joannes Commelinus lived at Amsterdam. The Bibliopolium Commelinianum began at Heidelberg, but extended also to Leiden and Amsterdam. The copy at 1607/5991 is imperfect, wanting sig.★.

C58 CATS, Jacob

AENMERCKINGHE OP DE TEGENWOORDIGE STEERT-STERRE, Ende den loop deser tijden so hier als in ander Landen, Met aenwijsinge vande rechte wetenschap om alle teykenen des hemels . . . uyt to leggen, alles tot een Nieuwe-Iaer gifte alle rechtsinnige Verstanden toe-geeygent. [etc.] 4° sig.AB^4C^2; illus.
8562.c.22; T.2423(1).

Anonymous. Partly in verse. The titlepage illustration is engraved, after Adriaen van de Venne? The titlepage verso gives the date of publication as 1619. Printed at Middelburg?

C59 CATS, Jacob

MAECHDEN-PLICHT OFTE AMPT DER IONCK-VROVVVEN, IN EERBAER LIEFDE, AENGHEWESEN DOOR SINNE-BEELDEN. OFFICIVM Puellarum . . . Emblemate expressum. TOT MIDDELBURGH, Ghedruckt by Hans vander Hellen . . . M.DC.XVIII. [etc.] 4° pp.92; illus.
1485.r.19(1).

The dedicatory poem signed: J. C. The author's full name given in laudatory poems. In Dutch and Latin, with mottoes in French. Without the 'Hardersclachte' found in other editions, but with an additional laudatory poem by J.A.F. The engravings by Jan Sweelinck after Adriaen vande Venne. Is this a later reprint or pirated edition? With the exlibris of Mountague Garrard Drake, 1708.

C60 CATS, Jacob

(tp.1) SELF-STRYT, DAT IS Crachtighe bevveginghe van Vlees en Gheest, poëtischer wijse verthoont in den persoon . . . van Joseph, ten tijde hy by Potiphars huys-vrouwe wiert versocht tot overspel. MITSGADERS Schriftmatighe beschrijvinghe van de heymenisse . . . des Christelijcken Self-strijts . . . Door J. CATS. TOT MIDDELBVRGH, Ghedruckt by Hans vander Hellen, voor Jan Pietersz van de Venne . . . 1620. [etc.]
(tp.2=p.107) SINNE-BEELT, De heymenisse . . . des Christelijcken SELF-STRYTS . . . aen-wijsende . . . TOT MIDDELBVRGH, Ghedruckt by Hans vander Hellen, voor Jan Pietersen van de Venne . . . 1620. 4° pp.119; illus.
11556.g.8.

The letterpress titlepage illustrated with a woodcut showing Joseph and Potiphar's wife. With an additional titlepage, engraved, signed: AV. Venne inven., F. Schillemans scult. The engraving on p.50 signed: AV. Venne f., P.S: i.e. Philips Serwouter, scalpsit; the engraving on p.64 signed: A.V. inv., P. D. Jode sc.; the engraving on p.111 unsigned, but also after Adriaen vande Venne.

C61 CATS, Jacob

(tp.1) SELF-STRYT, DAT IS Crachtighe bevveginghe van Vlees en Gheest . . . verthoont in Ioseph . . . MITSGADERS Schriftmatighe beschrijvinghe van de heymensisse . . . des Christelijcken Self-strijts . . . Door J. CATS. TOT MIDDELBVRGH, Gedruckt by Hans van der Hellen, voor Jan Pietersz van de Venne . . . 1620. [etc.]

(tp.2=p.107) SINNE-BEELT, De heymenisse . . . des Christelijcken SELF-STRYTS . . . AEN-WIJSENDE . . . Na de Copye TOT MIDDEL-BVRGH, Ghedruckt . . . 1620. 4° pp.119; illus.
11556.g.32(3).
With an additional titlepage, engraved, unsigned, as are the other engravings which are in reverse. The text is differently set and printed with different type. tp.2 admits to this part being a copy: the whole a later reprint or a pirated edition?

C62 CATS, Jacob
(tp.1) J. CATS SELF-STRYD . . . TWEEDE DRVCK. Op een nieuw verciert met Copere Platen; over-sien, verbetert, ende vermeerdert, by den Auteur, met by-vouginghe van de aff-beeldinghe des Velt-teyckens eenes Christelicken IongheIincx . . . TOT MIDDELBVRGH, Gedruckt by Hans vander Hellen, voor Ian Pieters van de Venne . . . 1621. [etc.]
(tp.2=p.107) SINNE-BEELD . . . des Christelicken SELF-STRYTS . . . TOT MIDDELBURGH. Ghedruckt by Hans vander Hellen, voor Jan Pietersen van de Venne . . . 1621. 4° pp.119; illus.
11556.g.9.
With the additional titlepage, engraved, signed, as are the other engravings, as in the genuine 1620 edition. A new bifolium, signed ★★★★3,4, has been inserted in the preliminaries, containing the 'Veld-teycken', a poem with an engraving, signed: I.G., i.e. Johann Gelle, and dated 1621. This is the genuine second edition, with a reprint of the 1620 privilege on the verso of the titlepage and a preface by the publisher on the verso of the engraved titlepage.

C63 CATS, Jacob
(tp.1) J. CATS SELF-STRYD . . . TVVEEDE DRVCK . . . TOT MIDDELBVRGH, Gedruckt by Hans vander Hellen, voor Ian Pietersz. vande Venne . . . 1621. [etc.]
(tp.2=p.107) SINNE-BEELD . . . des Christelijcken SELF-STRYTS . . . TOT MIDDELBVRGH. Ghedruckt by Hans van der Hellen, voor Ian Pietersen van de Venne . . . 1624. 4° pp.119; illus.
11556.h.28(1).
The main body of the book corresponds to the doubtful edition of 1620. New material added in the preliminaries is copied from the genuine second edition, the engraving misdated 1651 and unsigned. tp.2 dated 1624: the whole printed that year? The verso of the engraved titlepage bears the preface, that of the letterpress titlepage is blank.

C64 CATS, Jacob
(tp.1) SILENUS ALCIBIADIS, SIVE PROTEVS, Vitæ humanæ ideam, Emblemate trifariàm variato, oculis subijciens . . . MIDDELBVRGI, Ex Officina Typographica Iohannis Hellenij, M.DC.XVIII. [etc.]
(tp.1a) Sinn-en-Minne-Beelden. EMBLEMATA Amores Moresque spectantia. EMBLEMES Touchants Les Amours et Les Moeúrs. Lúsús Jngeny Júvenilis Lib. I.
(tp.2a) Sinne-Beelden, eertijts Minne-beeldē, nù gebrúyckt tot Leere der Seden. EMBLEMATA . . . EMBLEMES, [etc.]
(tp.2) SILENI ALCIBIADIS . . . PARS SECVNDA. MIDDELBVRGI . . . M.DC.XVIII. [etc.]
(tp.3) SILENI ALCIBIADIS . . . PARS TERTIA. MIDDELBVRGI . . . M.DC.XVIII. [etc.]
(tp.3a) Sinne-Beelden, eertyts Minne-beelden, nu ghetoghen tot Stichtelijcke bedinckingen . . . EMBLEMATA . . . EMBLEMES; [etc.] 4° 3 pt.: pp.120; 111; 107; illus.
831.i.17.
The author's preface signed: J. Cats. In Dutch, Latin and French. tp.1a, 2a, 3a are additional, engraved, those of pt.1,3 signed: AV. Venne Inventor; Fran. Schillemans sculp. The same 51 circular emblems in each part engraved by Jan Swelinck?

C65 CATS, Jacob

[Silenus Alcibiadis. Editio altera.] 4° pp.119

1485.r.19(2).

Probably part of what is known as the third edition, printed by Willem Jansz Blaeu in Amsterdam in 1619. Imperfect; wanting the titlepage, most of the preliminary pages and all of pts.2 and 3. The only preliminaries present, sig.★2,3, containing part of the poem 'Aen de Zeeusche ionck-vrouwen', differ in their setting from the corresponding pages, ★★★★1–3, of the copy at 831.i.17. p.119 ends with 'Finis', lacking the additional poems found on this page and p.120 in that copy.

C66 CATULLIUS, Andreas

(tp.1) ANDREÆ CATVLLI . . . SEPTVPLEX TRIVMPHVS, SIVE DEIPARÆ VIRGINIS SEPTEM GAVDIA. TORNACI, Ex officinâ CAROLI MARTINI, M.DC.XIV.

(tp.2) ANDREÆ CATULLI . . . SEPTVPLEX GLADIVS: SIVE DEIPARÆ VIRGINIS SEPTEM DOLORES. TORNACI, Ex officinâ CAROLI MARTINI. M.DC.XIV.

(tp.3) ANDREÆ CATVLLI . . . LACHRYMÆ SIVE AMORES CASTI. TORNACI, Ex officinâ CAROLI MARTINI. M.DC.XIV. 8° 3 pt.: pp.48; 45; 19

11408.aaa.12.

The running title of pt.1,2 is 'ANDREÆ CATVLLI ELEGIÆ'. The single approbation refers to all three parts. pt.1 contains the 'Elegia de Natali Domini' with changes and additions by the author on pp.11–25. Ownership inscription: Bibliotheca Monrij S[ti] Martini Tornac., 1620.

C67 CATULLUS, Caius Valerius

[Works. Latin] CATVLLVS, TIBVLLVS, PROPERTIVS: Seriò castigati. EX OFFICINA PLANTINIANA RAPHELENGII. M.D.CIII. 16° pp.213

835.a.23; C.66.a.8.

With the 'Pervigilium Veneris'. Published at Leiden. Ownership inscription in the copy at C.66.a.8: Ex dono Ben: Rudyard Armig. Jun.

C68 CATULLUS, Caius Valerius

[Works. Latin] CATVLLVS, TIBVLLVS, PROPERTIVS: Seriò castigati. EX OFFICINA PLANTINIANA RAPHELENGII M.D.CXIII. 16° pp.213

C.20.f.47.

A reissue of the preceding. This copy has been rubricated. From the travelling library of Sir Julius Caesar.

C69 CAUMONT, Jean de; Champenois

[Du firmament des Catholiques.] THE FIRME FOVNDATION OF CATHOLIKE RELIGION AGAINST THE BOTTOMLLES [*sic*] pitt of heresies, wherein is shewed that onlye Catholikes shalbe saued, and that all heretikes . . . are excluded frō the knigdome [*sic*] of heauen. Compyled by Iohn Caumont of Champanye, and translated out of Frenche into Englishe by Iohn. Paunchfoot the elder [etc.] 8° pp.120[119]

C.110.a.28.

Without imprint or date. The approbation dated Antwerp, 1590. In fact, printed by Charles Boscard at Douai, probably in 1605.

CAVELLUS, Hugo. *See* MAC CAGHWELL, Hugh

C70 CEBES

ΚΕΒΗΤΟΣ ΘΗΒΑΙΟΥ ΠΙΝΑΞ. CEBETIS THEBANI TABVLA. Cum versione & NOTIS . . . IOANNIS CASELII . . . Ex Bibliotheca GEVERHARTI ELMENHORSTI nunc primum edita. LVGDVNI BATAVORVM, Apud IACOBVM MARCI . . . M.D.CXVIII. (col.) LVGDVNI BATAVORVM, Typis GODEFRIDI BASSON. M.D.C.XVIII. 4° pp.126

C.74.b.6.

From the library of King George II.

C71 CECIL, Robert; Earl of Salisbury

[An answere to certaine scandalous papers.] ANTWOORDT van Robert Cecil Graeve van Salisbury . . . op Seeckere scandaleuse Schriften over al (tegens hem) ghestroyt . . . Gedruct in Engels tot Londen by Robert Barker . . . Ende nu in Nederduyts tot Leyden by Thomas Basson . . . 1606. 4° pp.16

1568/8635.

Translated by Thomas Basson.

CELESTINA. 1616. *See* ROJAS, Fernando de

CENSURA Sacræ Facultatis Theologiæ Parisiensis. 1618. *See* PARIS. Université de Paris

The CENSURE of the Sacred Facultie of Divinitie of Paris. 1618. *See* PARIS. Université de Paris

C72 CEPARI, Virgilio

[Vita del Beato Luigi Gonzaga.] HET LEVEN Vanden Salighen LODEWYCK GONZAGA . . . Vyt dry Italiaensche Boecken door P. VIRGILIVS CEPARIVS beschreven, ende verduytscht door P. LEONARDVS DE FRAYE . . . T'ANTWERPEN, By GEERAERDT van WOLSSHATEN [*sic*], ende HENDRICK AERTSSEN. M.D.C.XV. [etc.] 8° pp.538; illus., port.

1481.de.21; 4827.df.5.

The portrait signed: Io. Collaert. The copy at 4827.df.5 is cropped.

C73 CEPARI, Virgilio

[Vita del Beato Luigi Gonzaga.] VITA B. ALOYSII GONZAGÆ . . . A R.P. VIRGILIO CEPARIO . . . TRIBVS LIBRIS comprehensa. Hac secunda editione accuratiùs in capita & paragraphos distincta. ANTVERPIÆ, Apud Ioannem Keerbergium . . . M.DC.IX. 8° pp.452

862.g.6(1).

Translated by Joannes Horrion. Imperfect; wanting the half-title bearing the portrait of St. Aloysius by J. Collaert. Ownership inscriptions: Ex liberali dona'e Caroli Boccabella Gandavensis Canonicj; Societatis Jesu Crucenacj.

C74 CEPARI, Virgilio

[Vita del Beato Luigi Gonzaga.] VITA B. ALOYSII GONZAGÆ . . . VALENCENIS, Apud Ioannem Vervliet . . . M.DC.IX. 8° pp.452

4825.a.9.

Another issue of the Antwerp edition, with the same privilege. With the half-title bearing the portrait. Ownership inscription: Ludovicus de Carnin 1798.

C75 CERTAINE

CERTAINE CONSIDERATIONS drawne from the Canons of the last Sinod, and other the Kings Ecclesiasticall and statute law, ad informandum animum Domini Episcopi Wigornensis, seu alterius cuiusvis iudicis ecclesiastici, ne temere & inconsulto prosiliant ad depriuationem Ministrorum Ecclesiæ: for not subscription, for the not exact vse of the order and forme of the booke of common prayer . . . within the Diocesse of Worcester . . . 1605. 4° pp.52

1608/1116; T.499(3); 108.b.9.

Without imprint; printed by Richard Schilders at Middelburg.

C76 CERTAINE

CERTAINE DEMANDES WITH their grounds, drawne out of holy writ, and propounded in foro conscientiæ by some religious Geñtl. vnto the reverend Fathers, Richard Archbishop of Canterbury, Richard Bishop of London, William Bishop of Lincolne, Garvase Bishop of Worcester, William Bishop of Exeter, &

Thomas Bishop of Peterborough, wherevnto the said Gentl. require that it would please their Lordships to make a true . . . aunswere . . . 1605. 4° pp.68
T.499(4); 108.b.10.

Without imprint; printed by Richard Schilders at Middelburg.

C77 CERTAINE
[Certaine questions and answeres touching the doctrine of predestination.] SEKER VRAGHEN ende Antwoorden: belanghende de leere vande Predestinatie, van het gebruyck van Godes vvoort ende van de Sacramenten. Inhoudende het gevoelen vande Gereformeerde Kercken van Groot Britanien . . . Waerinne een yeder mach claerlick sien, Dat de Kercken van Groot Britanien in de leere, de Predestinatie aengaende, met dese onse Kercken van Neder-lant over een comen . . . Overgheset van een Lief-hebber der waerheyt . . . ende genomen wt den Enghelschen Bijbel in quarto gedruckt tot London by Robert Barker . . . 1606. Ende ghestelt tusschen het Oude ende Nieuwe Testament. TOT DORDRECHT. By Joris Waters. M.D.C.XJ. 4° sig.A^4
T.2241(12).

The translator, 'Lover of truth', has sometimes been identified as Henry Hexham.

C78 CERTAINE
[Certaine questions and answers touching the doctrine of predestination.] Seker Vragen ende Antwoorden/belanghende de leere vande Predestinatie/van het gebruyck van Godes woort . . . TOT DORDRECHT. By Joris Waters. M.D.CXJ. 4° sig.A^4
1484.cc.11.

Another issue of the preceding, with the titlepage printed in Gothic throughout, except for the words 'Tot Dordrecht', and with some slight changes in spelling.

C79 CERVANTES SAAVEDRA, Miguel de
[Don Quixote. Pt.1. Spanish] EL INGENIOSO HIDALGO DON QVIXOTE DE LA MANCHA. COMPVESTO POR Miguel de Ceruantes Saauedra . . . EN BRVSSELAS, Por ROGER VELPIVS . . . 1607. 8° pp.592
G.10144.

C80 CERVANTES SAAVEDRA, Miguel de
[Don Quixote. Pt.1. Spanish] EL INGENIOSO HIDALGO DON QVIXOTE DE LA MANCHA. COMPVESTO POR Miguel de Ceruantes Saauedra . . . EN BRVCELAS, Por Roger Velpivs y Huberto Antonio . . . 1611. 8° pp.583
C.59.b.18; G.10146.

The copy at C.59.b.18 with the ownership inscriptions: Jq. Roostee; Bibliothecæ Fratrum mino: Bruxellæ.

C81 CERVANTES SAAVEDRA, Miguel de
[Don Quixote. Pt.1. Spanish] PRIMERA PARTE DEL INGENIOSO HIDALGO DON QVIXOTE DE LA MANCHA. COMPVESTO POR Miguel de Ceruantes Saauedra . . . EN BRVCELAS, Por Huberto Antonio . . . 1617. 8° pp.583
C.58.bb.13.

C82 CERVANTES SAAVEDRA, Miguel de
[Don Quixote. Pt.2. Spanish] SEGVNDA PARTE DEL INGENIOSO CAVALLERO DON QVIXOTE DE LA MANCHA. Por Miguel de Ceruantes Saauedra . . . EN BRVSELAS, Por Huberto Antonio . . . 1616. 8° pp.687
Cerv.24; C.63.f.6.

C83 CERVANTES SAAVEDRA, Miguel de
[Novelas ejemplares. Spanish] NOVELAS EXEMPLARES DE MIGVEL DE Ceruantes Saauedra . . . EN BRVSSELAS. Por ROGER VELPIO, y HVBERTO ANTONIO . . . 1614. 8° pp.616
1074.d.11.
Ownership inscriptions: Fournier; de Bernapré(?).

C84 CERVANTES SAAVEDRA, Miguel de
[Los trabajos de Persiles y Sigismunda. Spanish] LOS TRABAIOS DE PERSILES Y SIGISMVNDA, HISTORIA SETENTRIONAL. POR MIGVEL DE CERVANtes Saauedra . . . EN BRVCELAS, Por Huberto Antonio . . . 1618. 8° pp.604
12490.d.18.

C85 CEULEN, Ludolf van
DE Arithmetische en Geometrische fondamenten, VAN M^r. LVDOLF VAN CEVLEN . . . TOT LEYDEN, By IOOST van COLSTER, ende IACOB MARCVS . . . M.D.CXV. (col.) GHEDRUCKT TOT LEYDEN, By Vlderick Cornelisz. ende Joris Abramsz. . . . M.D.CXV. fol. pp.271; illus., port.
8504.h.8.
The portrait is engraved on the titlepage. With manuscript notes.

C86 CEULEN, Ludolf van
[De arithmetische en geometrische fondamenten.] FVNDAMENTA ARITHMETICA ET GEOMETRICA cum eorundem usu . . . AVTHORE LVDOLPHO A CEVLEN . . . E vernaculo in Latinum translata A WIL. SN. R.F. LVGDVNI BATAVORVM, Apud IVSTVM A COLSTER Bibliopolam . . . M D CXV. 4° pp.269; illus.
530.k.7.
The translator is Willebrordus Snellius. Printed by Joris Abramsz van der Marsce.

C87 CEULEN, Ludolf van
[Van den circkel.] LVDOLPHI À CEVLEN De CIRCVLO & ADSCRIPTIS LIBER . . . Omnia é vernaculo Latina fecit, & annotationibus illustravit Willebrordus Snellius . . . LVGD. BATAV. Apud IODOCVM À COLSTER . . . 1619. (col.) LVGD. BATAV. Excudebat Georgius Abrahami à Marsce . . . 1619. 4° pp.220,56; illus., port.
530.e.1.
The portrait of the author aged 56 engraved on the titlepage, signed: I. Gheijn fe. The pagination between pp.79 and 89 is erratic.

C88 CHAMBERS, Sabine
THE GARDEN OF OVR B. LADY. OR A deuout manner, how to serue her in her Rosary. Written by S.C. of the Society of IESVS . . . M.DC.XIX. 8° pp.272
C.26.gg.1.
Anonymous and without imprint; printed by the English College press at St. Omer.

C89 CHAMPNEY, Anthony
MR PILKINGTON HIS PARALLELA DISPARALLED. AND The Catholicke Roman faith maintained against Protestantisme. By ANT. CHAMPNEY . . . AT S.OMERS, For IOHN HEIGHAM . . . 1620. 8° pp.220
3935.aa.22.
Printed by Charles Boscard at St. Omer for John Heigham at Douai.

C90 CHAMPNEY, Anthony

A TREATISE OF THE VOCATION OF BISHOPS, AND OTHER ECCLESIASTICALL MINISTERS. PROVING THE MINISTERS OF THE PRETENDED REFORMED CHVRCHES IN GENERALL, TO HAVE NO CALLING: AGAINST Monsieur du Plessis, and M.r Docteur Feild: And in particular the pretended Bishops in England, to be no true Bishops. Against M.r Mason. BY ANTH. CHAMP. . . . AT DOVAY, By IOHN HEIGHAM . . . 1616. 4° pp.326
3935.bbb.8.

The dedication signed: A. Champney. Printed by Pierre Auroi at Douai, who had difficulties with 'w's and 'k's, especially in the preliminary pages where these letters are supplied in manuscript. In the main text the 'w' comes from a different fount.

C91 CHANCAEUS, Mauritius

[Historia aliquot nostri saeculi martyrum.] (tp.1) COMMENTARIOLVS DE VITAE RATIONE ET MARTYRIO OCTODECIM CARTVSIANORVM QVI IN ANglia sub Rege Hērico VIII . . . crudeliter trucidati sunt. EDITVS Primum à . . . Mauritio Chancæo . . . nunc verò recenter recognitus, & paulùlum illustratus melioriq; stilo digestus. Vna cum noua Historica relatione duodecim Martyrum Cartusianorum Ruræmundensium qui Anno M.D.CXXII [*sic*]. Angonem [*sic*] suum compleuerunt. Auctore V. P. Arnoldo Hauensio . . . GANDAVI. Apud Gualterum Manilium . . . 1608. [etc.]
(tp.2) HISTORICA RELATIO DVODECIM MARTYRVM CARTVSIANORVM, QVI RVRAEMVNDAE . . . Anno M.D.LXXII. Agonem suum fœliciter compleuerunt. AUCTORE . . . ARNOLDO HAVENSIO . . . ACCESSIT EIVSDEM EXHORTATIO ad Cartusianos, de obseruantia disciplinæ Regularis vitæque Solitariæ commendatione . . . 1608. 8° 2 pt.: pp. 111; 77: plate; illus.
699.c.4(1); G.19975.

Printed by Bernhard Walter at Cologne and issued there with the title 'Innocentia et constantia victrix'. The part of the edition sent to Ghent has had a different titlepage and preliminary leaves signed ⋆1–4 substituted for the originals and a new plate added, pasted onto leaf ††2r, taking the place of the dedication and verses found in the Cologne issue. The engravings signed: Johannes Leopoldus, or Leopoltus, fec. The copy at 699.c.4(1) with the ownership inscription of 'Shene'. The copy at G.19975 imperfect; wanting the plate.

C92 CHANLER, Georg; the Elder

Nieuwe Keysers Chronica Ofte Gheschicht-boeck van alle de Roomsche . . . Keyseren . . . Van Cajus Iulius Cæsar . . . af/tot op den tegenwoordigen Keyser Mathias toe . . . Ghetoghen vvt de gheloofvveerdichste Originele Munten, Antiquiteyten ende Autheuren te samen vergaert: door . . . Georgius Chanler . . . Ende nu Wt den Hoochduytschen in Nederlandtsche sprake doen oversetten/ende in den Druck bekosticht ende verveerdicht/door Georgius Chanler, des Autheurs Soons Sone, Interprete Iacobo VVestfrisio . . . t'AMSTELREDAM, By Nicolaes Biestkens . . . 1617. fol. pp.317; illus.
9042.i.3.

Translated from manuscript. The illustrations are woodcuts.

CHANSONS. Livre . . . des chansons vulgaires de diverses autheurs. 1601; 1608; 1609; 1613; 1615. *See* PHALÈSE, Pierre

C93 CHAPEAVILLUS, Joannes

(tp.1) HISTORIA ADMIRANDARVM CVRATIONVM, QVÆ DIVINITVS OPE DEPRECATIONEQVE DIVI PERPETVI LEODIENSIS EPISCOPI ET CONFESSORIS, AD EIVS SACRAS reliquias Dionanti, Anno 1599. & aliquot Superioribus, contigerunt. ADIECTA EST, VITA D. PERPETVI, CVM DESCRIPTIONE OPPIDI Dionantensis, & quibusdam alijs, Historiam illustrantibus. LEODII, Ex Officina HENRICI HOVII. M.DCI. [etc.]

(tp.2=sig.D3) VITA B. PERPETVI . . . EX OFFICIALIBVS ECCLESIAE DIONANTENSIS LIBRIS COLLECTA . . . LEODII, Ex Officina HENRICI HOVII. M.DCI. [etc.] 4° sig. A–I[4]; illus. 4828.aa.7.

The author named in the preface, as is the compiler of the material: Petrus Frerart. The illustrations consist of the woodcut arms of Ernest Elector, Archbishop of Cologne and Prince Bishop of Liège, and an engraved imaginary portrait of St. Perpetuus.

C94 CHAPEAVILLUS, Joannes

(tp.1) Qui GESTA PONTIFICVM TVNGRENSIVM, TRAIECTENSIVM, ET LEODIENSIVM SCRIPSERVNT, AVCTORES PRÆCIPVI. Ad seriem rerum & temporum collocati, ac in tomos distincti, Nunc primùm studio & industriâ R. D. Ioannis Chapeavilli . . . typis excusi, & annotationibus illustrati . . . Accessit . . . Ægidij Bucherij . . . de primis Tungrorum seu Leodiensium Episcopis historica disputatio, itemq́ue chronologia posteriorum. TOMVS I. LEODII, Typis Christiani Ouvverx iunioris . . . 1612. Venundantur apud Lambertum Costerum [etc.]

(½ title) DISPVTATIO HISTORICA DE PRIMIS TVNGRORVM, SEV LEODIENSIVM EPISCOPIS . . . STVDIO ET OPERA ÆGIDII BUCHERII, [etc.]

(tp.2) Qui GESTA PONTIFICVM LEODIENSIVM SCRIPSERVNT AVCTORES PRÆCIPVI. Ad seriem rerum & temporum collocati, ac in tomos distincti. Nunc primùm studio & industria R. D. Ioannis Chapeauilli . . . typis excusi, & annotationibus illustrati. TOMVS II. . . . LEODII, Typis Christiani Ouvverx iunioris . . . 1613.

(tp.3) Qui GESTA PONTIFICVM LEODIENSIVM SCRIPSERVNT AVCTORES PRÆCIPVI . . . studio & industria R. D. Ioannis Chapeauilli . . . typis excusi, & annotationibus illustrati. TOMVS III. ET VLTIMVS. LEODII, Typis Christiani Ouvverx iunioris . . . 1616. 4° 3 tom.: pp.434, 52; 658; 680
484.b.7–9.

The last page of tom. 1 signed: ÆGIDIVS BOVCHIER. Bouchier supplied also the chronology for tom. 2, but could not do so for tom. 3.

The CHARACTER of the beast. 1609. *See* SMYTH, John; the Se-Baptist

CHARACTEREN oft scherpsinnighe beschrijvinge. 1619. *See* VERSTEGAN, Richard

C95 CHÂTEILLON, Sébastien

[Collections. Latin] (tp.1) SEBASTIANI CASTELLIONIS Dialogi IV. De Prædestinatione. Electione. Libero Arbitrio. Fide. Ejusdem Opuscula quædam . . . GOVDÆ, Typis Caspari Tournæi . . . 1613. Prostant apud Andream Burier.

(tp.2) ANNOTATIONES SEBASTIANI CASTELLIONIS in caput nonum ad Rom. . . . 1613.

(tp.3) Quinque IMPEDIMENTORVM, QVÆ MENtes hominum & oculos à veri in divinis cognitione abducunt . . . ENVMERATIO . . . Auctore Seb. Castellione.

(tp.4) Tractatus DE IVSTIFICATIONE . . . 1613. 8° 4 pt.: pp.443; 30; 30; 89; illus. 847.h.14.

Tp.2 bears Jasper Tournay's device 'Spero Fortunæ regressum'. tp.3 has neither imprint nor date, tp.4 has the date only.

C96 CHÂTEILLON, Sébastien

[Collections. Dutch] (tp.1) OPERA Sebastiani Castellionis . . . Waer in crachtelijck bewesen wordt dat niemant den anderen om de verscheydenheyt in Religie benijden noch gewelt aen doen/ofte vervolgen en sal. Met noch een . . . uytlegginge der Predestinatie . . . Ende een verclaringhe van den Vryen wille des Menschen. Nu alder eerst uyt den Latyne in Nederduytsche sprake tsamen gestelt . . . TOT HAERLEM, Gedruct by Vincent Casteleyn, ende David VVachtendonck, Voor Pieter Arentsz.

(tp.2) Van het Rechtveerdigh-worden/EEN Schriftuerlijck ende heylsaem BERICHT . . . Eerst gheschreven in Latijn, door . . . SEBASTIAEN CASTELLIO . . . TOT HAERLEM, Voor Pieter Arentz. . . . 1613.

(tp.3) VANDE GHEHOORSAEMHEYT GESCHREVEN INT LATYN DOOR SEBASTIAEN CASTELLIO, Ende vertaelt in Nederlantsch, door D. V. COORNHERT . . . TOT HAERLEM. Voor Pieter Arentz. . . . 1613.
(tp.4) Tsamen-spreucken Vande Predestinatie . . . Eerst ghemaeckt in latijn door . . . Sebastiaen Castellion, Ende nu . . . overgheset . . . door DIRCK ADRIAENSEN KEMP, Ende . . . D. V. COORNHERT . . . TOT HAERLEM. Voor Pieter Arentsz . . . 1613.
(tp.5) RAET AEN DAT VERVVOESTE VRANCRYC . . . DOOR SEBASTIANVM CASTALIO . . . TOT HAERLEM. Voor Pieter Arentsz. . . . 1613. 4° 5 pt.: pp.190; 70; 22; 156; 64; illus.
T.2243(4–8).

The translators of several parts named in them as Honoricus Macherius, A.B.C., i.e. Adriaen Bogaert or Boomgaert Cornelisz., Dirck Adriaensen Kemp and D. V. Coornhert. The titlepage illustration is an emblematic woodcut on the Dutch Revolt.

C97 CHÂTEILLON, Sébastien
Contra Libellum Calvini in quo ostendere conatur Hæreticos jure gladij coercendos esse . . . M.D.LC.XII. 8° sig. (⋆⋆⋆)A–P8
C.134.a.24.

The author is named in the preface as S. Castellio. The preface makes it clear that the book was printed in the United Provinces. It was probably printed by Jasper Tournay at Gouda. The date is intentionally composed of the date of the original and until then unpublished manuscript, i.e. 1562, and the date of publication, i.e. 1612.

C98 CHÂTEILLON, Sébastien
[Contra libellum Calvini.] DISSERTATIO, QVA disputatur, quo jure, quove fructu Hæretici sunt Coercendi gladio vel igne. [etc.] 8° sig. (⋆⋆⋆) A–P8
C.124.dd.35; 1020.d.8(7).

Another issue of 'Contra libellum Calvini', with a different titlepage and its conjugate leaf, (⋆⋆⋆) 6. The copy at 1020.d.8 is imperfect; wanting the titlepage, but is identifiable by this leaf in the preliminaries as belonging to this issue, which is undated. Printed also by Jasper Tournay at Gouda in 1612?

CHICHESTER, Bischop van. 1610. *See* ANDREWES, Lancelot

C99 CHIFFLET, Jean Jacques
LACRYMAE . . . FVSÆ IN EXSEQVIIS . . . ARCHIDVCIS ALBERTI PII, BELGICÆ SEQVANICIQ. PRINCIPIS Per Io. Iac. CHIFFLETVM, [etc.] 4° pp.23; illus.
1199.f.3(4).

The approbation for this work is included in that for L. Beyerlinck's 'Sereniss. Principis Alberti . . . Laudatio funebris', made out to the Officina Plantiniana at Antwerp and dated 1621. Issued with A. Le Mire's 'De vita Alberti' of 1622? The engravings include one of a collection of tear bottles.

C100 CHOKIER DE SURLET, Jean de
TRACTATVS DE RE NVMMARIA PRISCI ÆVI, QVAE COLLATA AD æstimationem monetæ præsentis. AD Historiæ . . . intelligentiam non parum vtilis. Auctore. IOANNE A CHOKIER . . . LEODII, Typis Christiani Ouvverx iun. . . . M.DC.XIX. 8° pp.72
609.a.2(2); 278.b.39.

The date on the titlepage of the copy at 278.b.39 has been altered to M.DC.XX.

C101 CHOQUETIUS, Franciscus Hyacinthus
SANCTI BELGI ORDINIS PRÆDICATORVM. Collegit & recensuit . . . F. HYACINTHVS CHOQVETIVS . . . DVACI . . . 1618. Typis B. BELLERI. [etc.] 8° pp.277; illus.
862.d.4.

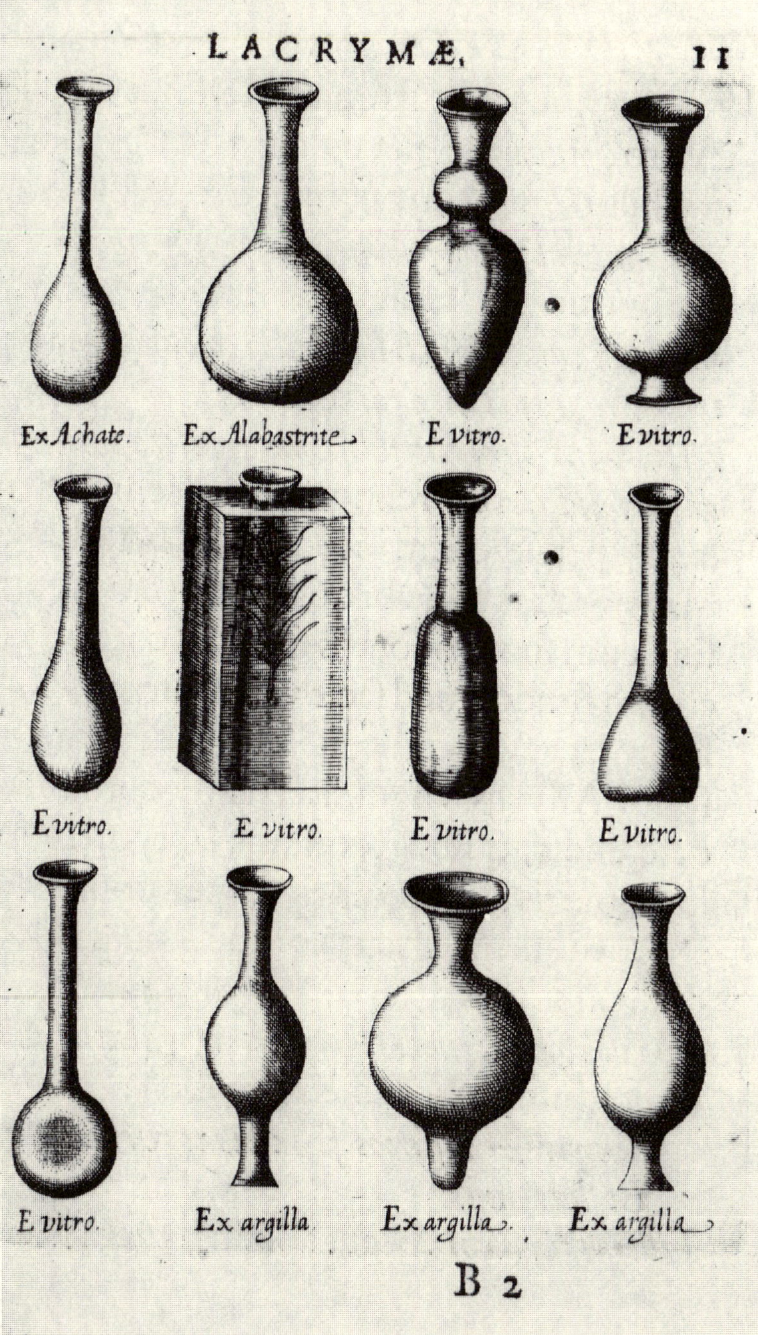
LACRYMÆ.
11
Ex Achate.
Ex Alabastrite
E vitro.
E vitro.
E vitro.
E vitro.
E vitro.
E vitro.
E vitro.
Ex argilla
Ex argilla.
Ex argilla
B 2

C99 (p. 11)

The dedication is signed: F. Franciscus Choquetius. The titlepage, engraved, is signed: M. Bass. f.i.e. Martin Baes. Other engravings signed: M.B.f. or M. Bas f. With the ornament bearing the printer's initials: L. K., i.e. Laurence Kellam of Douai.

C102 CHRIJSTELICK
EEN Chrijstelick vermaen voor alle menschen/het sy Rijcke ofte Armen/int stuck van desen Stilstant ofte Treves/hoe wy behooren te bidden/ende oock nae te laten onse verkeerde oordeelen . . . 1609. 4° 4 unsigned leaves
T.2420(36).

CHRISTALIJNEN bril. 1613. *See* DWINGLO, Bernardus

CHRISTALIJNEN spiegel. 1619. *See* SLATIUS, Henricus

CHRISTELICKE ende ernstighe vermaninghe tot vrede aen R. Donteclock. 1609. *See* CORVINUS, Joannes Arnoldi

CHRISTELICKE gedichten ghemaeckt tot lof van 't bestandt. 1609. *See* NIEROP, Adriaen van

CHRISTELIJCKE aenspraeck. 1618. *See* LIVIUS, Gerardus

CHRISTELIJCKE ende wettelijcke beroepinge der dienaren Jesu Christi. 1620. *See* ACRONIUS, Ruardus

Een CHRISTELIJCKE tragedia. 1613. *See* KIRCHMAYER, Thomas

C103 CHRISTELIJCKE
Christelijcke vermaen Brief aende Catholijcke Ghereformeerde Ghemeente binnen der Stadt Utrecht. Over de Troublen aldaer onlanghs gevallen/ghesonden door eenen Liefhebber der selver Ghemeenten/ende der oprechter waerheyt . . . TOT AMSTELREDAM. By Barent Adriaenssz. . . . 1611. 4° ff.25
T.2241(7).
Tentatively attributed in *Rogge Taurinus* p.168 to Joannes Matthisius.

C104 CHRISTELYCK
CHRISTELYCK ende ZEDICH VERTOOGH met Een seer ernstige ende ootmoedige bede aen den Provincialen Synodum van Frieslandt, den xxx. May, Anno 1621. Ghehouden binnen Sneeck. Ghedaen Van een deel Ledematen der Ghereformeerde Kercke te Doccum . . . Ghedruckt onder't + Anno 1621. 4° pp.18
T.2251(4).
Printed by Pieter Arents at Norden.

CHRISTELYCKE ende nootwendighe verclaringhe. 1615. *See* TRIGLAND, Jacobus; the Elder

A CHRISTIAN and modest offer of a most indifferent conference. 1606. *See* JACOB, Henry

The CHRISTIAN directory. 1607. *See* PERSONS, Robert

C105 CHRISTIAN II.; Elector of Saxony.
[Letters. 6.10.1608] COPYE Eenes Briefs gheschreven van den Cuervorst Christianus van Sassen/aen den Eertz-Hertoch Mathias van Oostenrijck. Ghetrouwelijck overgheset uyt den Hoochduytschen in onse Nederlantsche tale. Nae de Copye van Dreesden. Anno/1609. 4° sig.A[4]
T.2420(35).
Translated from 'Ein tapffers und wolgegrůndtes Schreiben', dated 6 October 1608.

C106 CHRISTIANS

THE CHRISTIANS MANNA. OR A TREATISE Of the most Blessed and Reuerend Sacrament of the EVCHARIST . . . Written by a Catholike Deuine, through occasion of Monsieur Casaubon his Epistle to Cardinal Peron . . . 1613. 4° pp.244

4324.cc.20.

The dedication signed: R.N. Without imprint; printed by the English College press at St. Omer.

C107 CHRISTIANUS NEUTER

HISTORIE Van B. Cornelis Adriaensen van Dordrecht . . . Inde welcke waerachtelick verhaelt wert/de Discipline ē̄n secrete Penitentie . . . die hy gebruycte met zijn Devotarigē/de welcke veroorsaect hebben seer veel wonderlicke sermoonen/die hy te Brugge gepredict heeft . . . Amstelredam by Cornelis Claesz. 1607. 8° ff.218[230]; illus.

1372.a.34.

A satire. The alleged editor's, or rather, author's preface signed: Christianus Neuter, variously identified as Hubertus Goltzius and/or Joannes Castelius and most probably the latter.

CHRISTIANUS-MERCURIUS. Christianus Mercurius ghesangh. 1615. *See* DRIELENBURGH, Vincent van

CHRISTOPHERSON, Michael; Priest. A briefe admonition. 1610. *See* WALPOLE, Michael

The CHRONICLE and institution of the Order of . . . S. Francis. 1618. *See* SILVA, Marcos da

CHRONICON Hollandiae. 1617. *See* GROOT, Hugo de [De antiquitate reipublicae Batavicae.]

CHRONIICK vande Hertoghen van Brabant. 1612. *See* BARLANDUS, Adrianus

CHRONIICKE van de Hertogen van Brabant. 1606. *See* BARLANDUS, Adrianus

C108 CICERO, Marcus Tullius

[Two or more works] M.TVLLII CICERONIS DE OFFICIIS LIBRI TRES: Cum eiusdem opusculis addi solitis. EX Officina Plantiniana RAPHELENGII, M. bcx [*sic*]. 64° pp.1–272

C.121.ee.1.

Published at Leiden. Imperfect; wanting the other works.

C109 CICERO, Marcus Tullius

[Two or more works] M.T.CICERONIS DE OFFICIIS LIBRI TRES. Cato Maior . . . Lælius . . . Paradoxa . . . Somnium Scipionis . . . Cum annotationibus Pauli Manutij . . . ANTVERPIAE, Apud PETRVM & IOANNEM Belleros. M.DC.XVIII. 16° pp.297

1568/6162.

Inscribed: John Thurloe (Jonathan Perry not his book! [*sic*])

C110 CICERO, Marcus Tullius

[Two or more works] M. TVLLII CICERONIS DE OFFICIIS, LIBRI TRES. Omnia ex postrema doctissimorum virorum recognitione quàm emendatissima. LVGD. BAT. Apud IOANNEM MAIRE, M.D.C.XIX. 32° pp.393

C.20.f.27.

With 'Cato maior', 'Laelius', 'Paradoxa' and 'Somnium Scipionis'. From the travelling library of Sir Julius Caesar.

C111 CICERO, Marcus Tullius

[Letters. Ad familiares. Latin] M. TVLLII CICERONIS EPISTOLAE FAMILIARES: Cum PAVLI MANVTII Annotationibus . . . Additis in fine SCHOLIIS eiusdem PAVLI MANVTII, & DIONYSII LAMBINI, AC GVLIELMI CANTERI Emendationibus . . . EX OFFICINA PLANTINIANA, RAPHELENGII. M.D.CV. 8° pp.480
1082.d.4.
Published at Leiden.

C112 CICERO, Marcus Tullius

[Orations. Latin] ORATIONVM M. TVLLII CICERONIS VOLVMEN I . . . à IOANNE MICHAELE BRVTO emendatvm. CAELII SECVNDI CVRIONIS scholijs . . . illustratum . . . DVACI, Ex officina IOANNIS BOGARDI, M.DC.XVII. 12° pp.568
11397.a.5.
Imperfect; wanting vol.2,3, but the leaf following the titlepage and bearing the index also has a list of authors of emendations 'quae hoc tertio volumine comprehenduntur'.

C113 CICERO, Marcus Tullius

[Selections. Latin] ELOGIA CICERONIANA ROMANORVM DOMI MILITIÆQ. ILLVSTRIVM . . . SELECTA à IOANNE BRANTIO . . . ANTVERPIÆ, Ex Typographeio Hieronymi Verdussen. M DCXII. 4° pp.57[257]
588.d.25.

CLAAS Kloet. 1619. *See* BIESTKENS, Nicolaes; the Younger

C114 CLACH-DICHT

CLACH-DICHT Over de doot des ghetrouwen Dienaers Jesu Christi EGBERTI AEMILII. Dienaer des Goddelijcken Woorts, binnen . . . LEYDEN. [etc.] 4° sig.A^4
11555.e.44(7).
Egbertus Aemylius died in 1610. Published at Leiden, in 1610? Cropped.

C115 CLACHTE

CLACHTE DER GHEMEYNTE TOT OVDEWATER, Der ghener die houden by de oude Religie. Aen de . . . Staten van Hollandt ende West-Frieslandt/dienende tot weder-legginghe van de valscheden/die haer naghegeven worden in't boeck uytghegeven onder den name Ontdeckinghe van den oproerighen gheest der Contra-Remonstranten tot Oudewater. Uyt-ghegheven by een Lief-hebber der VVaerheyt . . . Ghedruckt . . . 1618. 4° pp.43[40]
T.2248(12).

CLACHTE ende bede der Remonstranten. 1618. *See* BAERLE, Caspar van

C116 CLAECH-LIEDT

CLAECH-LIEDT Der Remonstranten/Over het beroven van hare Privilegien/ende datmen haer alle hare Rechten ende Vryheden met ghewelt soeckt te benemen . . . Noch is hier by-ghevoecht een Duyn-meyers Praetgen/ghestelt in maniere van 'tsamen-sprekinge tusschen Jaep en Kees . . . M.D.C.XX. [*etc.*] 4° 4 unsigned leaves
11555.e.40(2).

CLAEGH-GHEDICHT op het overlyden vanden wysen . . . Warnerus Helmichius. 1608. *See* VIVERIUS, Jacobus

Een CLAER ende doorluchtich vertooch van d'Alckmaersche . . . gheschillen. 1611. *See* VENATOR, Adolf Tectander

CLAGHE ende troost, over de doot vanden vromen . . . Iohannis Bogaert. 1615. *See* GERWEN, Jonas van

C117 CLAGHTE

Claghte Vanden Cloecken Soldaet/ende vanden Poltron: als oock een Disput vanden Soldaet ende Boer. Wt het Fransche in Nederlandsche ghetranslateert . . . Int Iaer ons Heeren/1609. 4° sig. A^6
T.2420(29).

In verse. Sig. A4 has been mis-signed Av.

C118 CLAPHAM, Henoch

HENOCH CLAPHAM His Demaundes and Answeres touching the Pestilence. Methodically handled, as his time and meanes could permit . . . 1604. 4° pp.32
C.31.e.4.

The editor's preface and verse epilogue signed: P.R. Without imprint; printed by Richard Schilders at Middelburg.

C119 CLAUDIANUS, Claudius

[Works. Latin] (tp.1) CL. CLAVDIANVS, THEOD. PVLMANNI . . . Diligentia . . . è vetustis codicibus restitutus. Vnà cum M. Ant. Del-rio Notis. ANTVERPIÆ. EX OFFICINA PLANTINIANA, Apud Ioannem Moretum. M.D.CII.
(tp.2) AD CL. CLAVDIANI . . . OPERA MARTINI ANTONII DEL-RIO NOTAE. ANTVERPIÆ, EX OFFICINA PLANTINIANA, Apud Ioannem Moretum. M.D.CII. 8° 2 pt.: pp.349; 90
1067.a.3.

C120 CLAUDIANUS, Claudius

[Works. Latin] CL. CLAVDIANI quæ exstant: Ex emendatione virorum doctorum. EX OFFICINA PLANTINIANA RAPHELENGII. M.D.CVII. 32° pp.263
C.20.f.53.

Published at Leiden. From the travelling library of Sir Julius Caesar.

C121 CLAVIUS, Christophorus

L'ALGEBRE DE CHRISTOPHLE CLAVIUS . . . Sommairement recueillie, & traduicte du Latin PAR GILLE GVILLION . . . Enrichie d'vn Auant-propos, traictant de tout ce qui est requis és nombres . . . Outre plus, d'vne amplification de l'Algebre . . . A LIEGE, Chez Leonard Streel . . . M.DC.XII. 4° pp.282
C.106.cc.23.

The 'Au lecteur', printed in civilité, signed: Tempora, tempore tempera. With poems by Guillion in Latin to his friends printed at the end. There is a space for a portrait of the author, left blank. Ownership inscriptions: Collegij Soc.[s] Jesu Leodij; Moenen 1795; J. L. Massau, fils. Verviers.

A CLEARE demonstration that Ferdinand is . . . fallen. 1619. *See* LUCULENTA demonstratio

C122 CLEMANGIIS, Nicolaus de

NICOLAI DE CLEMANGIIS . . . OPERA OMNIA qua' partim ex antiquissimis Editionibus, partim ex MS. . . . Theodori Canteri, descripsit, Coniecturis Notisque ornavit, & edidit IOHANNES MARTINI LYDIVS . . . Accessit ejusdem. GLOSSARIVM LATINOBARBARVM . . . LVGDVNI BATAVORVM. Apud Iohannem Balduinum. impensis Lud. Elzeuirij & Henr. Laurencij . . . M D C XIII [etc.] 4° 3 pt.: pp.191, 359, 86
697.i.11.

The titlepage is engraved, showing 'Religio' and 'Pax', the symbols of the four Evangelists, and the inscription: Vivant aeternum . . . Ordines Belgiæ . . . Belloque magnus Mauritius a Nassov. pt.3. pp.31–34: Gualtheri Dysse De Schismate Ecclesiae, in verse. Hendrick Laurence was at Amsterdam.

C123 CLEMENT of Alexandria

[Works. Greek and Latin] ΚΛΗΜΕΝΤΟΣ ΑΛΕΞΑΝΔΡΕΩΣ ΤΑ ΕΥΡΙΣΚΟΜΕΝΑ. CLEMENTIS ALEXANDRINI OPERA GRAECE ET LATINE QVÆ EXTANT. DANIEL HEINSIVS TEXTVM GRÆCVM RECENSVIT, INTERPRETATIONEM VETEREM . . . meliorem reddidit: breues . . . Emendationes adiecit. Accedunt diuersæ lectiones & emendationes . . . à FRIDERICO SYLBVRGIO collectæ . . . LVGDVNI BATAVORVM Excudit Ioannes Patius . . . 1616. Pro Bibliopolio Commeliniano. fol. pp.580, 50, 67

L.19.g.1(1).

C124 CLERICUS, Ubertus; Insulensis

SACRA POESIS VBERTI CLERICI SACERDOTIS INSVLENSIS PSALMORVM ALIQVOT PARAPHRASIS, HYMNI, Epigrammata, Panegyrica. ELEGIÆ, EPITAPHIA. TORNACI, Apud NICOLAVM LAVRENTIVM . . . M.DC.X. [etc.] 8° pp.122

11405.b.6.

With a list of 'Belgici poetæ sacri'.

CLIFTON, Richard. *See* CLYFTON, Richard

Een CLEYN vensterken. 1618. *See* CANNENBURGH, P.

CLIGNETUS, Petrus. Disputationum theologicarum decima-septima, de legis & Euangelii . . . comparatione. 1603. *See* GOMARUS, Franciscus

C125 CLOCK, Leendert

(tp.1) Het groote Liedeboeck van L.C. Inhoudende veelderhande Schriftuerlijcke Liedekens, Vermaningen, Leeringen, Gebeden ende Lofsangen . . . Mitsgaders het tweede Liedeboecxken/van gelycken propooste/ghenaemt: Een hell Cymbaelken des Juychens/als oock mede: die Forma eenigher Christelijcker Ghebeden . . . Gedruckt tot Haerlem/by Gillis Rooman . . . 1604.

(½tp.=Ee6v) FORMA Eenigher/Christelijcker Ghebeden . . . Volherdende verwintmen. L.C. 16° sig. A–Ff^8Gg^4

3437.aaa.1.

The prefaces signed: L.C. Volherdende verwintmen, the last song signed: Volherdende verwintmen, motto of Leendert Clock.

C126 CLUCHTICH

EEN Cluchtich Verhael/van eenen Gepredestineerden Cappuyn. Midts-ghaeders eenighe Vonnissen in dicht/die daer over zijn ghegheven. T'hantwerpen/By Abraham Verhoeven . . . 1619. 4° pp.12; sig. A^4B^2; illus.

P.P.3444.af(8).

Signed: N.D. Sometimes attributed to Richard Verstegan. The titlepage illustration shows a cook chasing a dog who has stolen the chicken.

CLUSIUS, Carolus. *See* L'ÉCLUSE, Charles

C127 CLUVERIUS, Philippus

PHILIPPI CLUVERI COMMENTARIVS DE TRIBVS RHENI ALVEIS, ET OSTIIS; ITEM, DE QVINQVE POPVLIS QVONDAM ACCOLIS: SCILICET DE TOXANDRIS, BATAVIS, CANINEFATIBVS, FRISIIS, AC MARSACIS . . . Adjectæ sunt tres tabulæ geographicæ. LVGDVNI BATAVORVM, Apud IOANNEM BALDVINVM; impensis LVDOVICI ELZEVIRI . . . M.DC.XI. 4° pp.232: plates; maps

794.e.15.

Without the device described in *Willems* no.64.

C128 CLUVERIUS, Philippus

PHILIPPI CLÜVERI GERMANIÆ ANTIQVÆ Libri tres . . . Adjectæ sunt VINDELICIA et NORICUM ejusdem auctoris. LUGDUNI BATAVORUM Apud Ludovicum Elzevirium . . . M DC XVI. fol. pp.400, 203, 230, 36: plates; maps
568.k.4; M.L.f.13.

The titlepage is engraved. It and the plates in the copy at 568.k.4. have been coloured. Printed by Henrick Lodewijcxsoon van Haestens at Leiden.

C129 CLUVERIUS, Philippus

PHILIPPI CLVVERI SICILIA ANTIQVA, cum minoribus insulis, ei adjacentibus. ITEM, SARDINIA et CORSICA . . . LVGDVNI BATAVORVM; EX Officinâ ELSEVIRIANA . . . M DC XIX. fol. pp.510: pl.V; illus., maps
178.g.6; C.74.g.1; G.4606.

Printed by Isaac Elzevier at Leiden. The maps signed: Nicolaus Geilker(c)k caelavit. In the copies at C.74.g.1 and G.4606 maps II and V are of the second state.

C130 CLYFTON, Richard

THE PLEA FOR INFANTS AND ELDER PEOPLE, concerning their Baptisme. OR A PROCESSE OF THE PASSAGES between M. Iohn Smyth and Richard Clyfton: Wherein . . . is proved, That the baptising of Infants of beleevers, is an ordinance of God . . . Printed at Amsterdam by Gyles Thorp . . . 1610. 4° pp.226
4323.b.19.

The preface signed: Richard Clifton, the 'Answer to Mr. Smythes Epistle' signed: Richard Clyfton.

C131 COBBAULT, Arnoldus

DEN PYL DER LIEFDEN. T'AMSTELREDAM, By Wilhem Iansen . . . 1609. (col.) TOT ZWOLLÆ, By Thomas Henrickz, Boeckdrucker. 8° sig.$[A]^4B\text{-}E^8$
11755.a.95(2).

Laudatory verses address the author as Arnoldus Caubbault; some of the author's own poems signed: Arnoldus Cobbault or Cobautius. With the device of Zacharias Heyns, then at Zwolle, on the titlepage.

C132 COBERGHER, Wenceslaus

MONS PIETATIS . . . Albertj et Isabellæ SS. Principū auspicijs feliciter erectus . . . BRVXELLÆ In Officina Hub. Antonij . . . 1619. 4° pp.17
8282.bbb.3.

The preface signed: Wenceslaus Cobergher. Consisting of 'Copie des lettres patentes de commission de Wenceslaus Cobergher' and 'Discours, sommaire de l'erection, ordre et conduite des monts de pieté es Pays de pardeça soubs la surintendance . . . de Wenceslaus Cobergher'. The titlepage, engraved, signed: St . .fe., i.e. Robert Staes?

COCCIUS, Bero. Disputationum physicarum decima-quarta, de anima vegetante. 1608. *See* JACCHAEUS, Gilbertus

C133 COCHELET, Anastase

CALVINI INFERNVS aduersus IOANNEM POLYANDRVM . . . AVCTORE F. ANASTASIO COCHELETIO . . . ANTVERPIÆ, EX OFFICINA PLANTINIANA Apud Ioannem Moretum. M.DC.VIII. (col.) ANTVERPIÆ, EX OFFICINA PLANTINIANA, APVD IOANNEM MORETVM. M.DC.VIII. 8° pp.192
3910.a.59; 3910.a.58.

The copy at 3910.a.58 is imperfect; wanting sig.N, containing the poem by Bochius, errata, approbation, privilege and colophon.

C134 COCHELET, Anastase

RESPONCE A L'ABIVRATION DE LA VRAIE FOY QVE FONT LES CALVINISTES . . . fausement appellée, par eux, Declaration Chrestienne. A ESTIENNE LE BRVN. Par F. ANASTASE COCHELET . . . A ANVERS, Chez Hierosme Verdussen . . . M.DC.IIII. 8° ff.179

3901.c.10.

Imperfect; wanting f.1. With a printed label pasted onto the titlepage reading: Iste liber est Conuent. Torn. FF. Præd.

C135 CODDAEUS, Gulielmus

ORATIO FVNEBRIS IN Obitum . . . D. RVDOLPHI SNELLII . . . recitata. Ipso exequiarum die, 6. Martij Anni M.DCXIII . . . A GVLIELMO CODDÆO . . . LVGDVNI BATAVORVM, Ex Officina Ioannis Patij . . . 1613. 4° pp.27; illus., port.

835.g.14(3).

Including a poem by Daniel Heinsius.

COELI & siderum in eo errantium observationes Hassiacae. 1618. *See* SNELLIUS, Willebrordus

C136 COFFIN, Edward

A REFVTATION OF M. IOSEPH HALL HIS APOLOGETICALL DISCOVRSE, FOR THE Marriage of Ecclesiasticall Persons, directed vnto M. Iohn VVhiting. IN WHICH Is demonstrated the Marriages of Bishops, Priests &c to want all warrant of Scriptures or Antiquity . . . Written at the request of an English Protestant By C.E. a Catholike Priest . . . M.DC.XIX. 8° pp.376

3939.b.3.

Anonymous and without imprint; published by the English College press at St. Omer.

C137 COLEVELDT, Jacobus Janszoon

LVST-HOOFIEN, Ofte de Vermaeck'lyckheyt der MAECHDEN. By eenghevoecht door een Liefhebber der Nederduytsche Academie. I.I.Coleveldt. T'Amsterdam, Ghedruckt by Paulus van Ravesteyn. 1619. obl.4° sig.$A\text{-}D^4$

11556.b.12.

Printed mainly in civilité. Followed by a manuscript collection of Dutch poems in various hands. The printed poems signed: I.I. Coleveldt. Een in 't hart, or other mottoes.

C138 COLIJN, Michiel

(tp.1) Oost-Indische ende Vvest-Indische voyagien/Namelijck/De waerachtighe beschrijvinge vande drie seylagien/drie Jaren achter malkanderen deur de Hollandtsche ende Zeelandtsche Schepen/by noorden . . . nae . . . Catthay ende China ghedaen . . . TOT AMSTERDAM, By Michiel Colijn . . . 1619. (col.1) GHEDRVCKT TOT ENCHUYSEN, By Jacob Lenaertsz. Meyn . . . 1617.

(tp.2) 'TEERSTE BOECK. Historie van Indien . . . Door G.M.A.W.L. Tot Amstelredam, By Michiel Colijn . . . 1617.

(tp.3) Historiale Beschrijvinghe, Inhoudende een waerachtich verhael vande reyse gedaen met acht Schepen van Amsterdam/onder't beleydt van . . . Iacob Cornelisz. Neck, ende VVybrant van VVarvvijck . . . t'Amsterdam, By Michiel Colijn . . . 1619.

(tp.4) Historiael Journael/van tghene ghepasseert is van wegen drie Schepen/ghenaemt den Ram, Schaep ende het Lam, ghevaren uyt Zeelandt . . . naer d'Oost-Indien/onder t'beleyt van Ioris van Speilberghen . . . t'Amsterdam, By Michiel Colijn. . . . 1617.

(tp.5) Beschrijvinghe ende Historische verhael/vant Gout Koninckrijck van Guinea . . . door: P.D.M. Tot Amstelredam, by Michiel Colijn . . . 1617.

(tp.6) Beschryvinge vande overtreffelijcke . . . Zee-vaerdt vanden Edelen Heer . . . Thomas Candish . . . Beschreven door M. Francois Prettie van Eye in Suffolck . . . Hier noch by ghevoecht de Voyagie van Siere Françoys Draeck, en Siere Ian Haukens . . . naer West-Indien . . . Beschreven door eenen die daer mede inde Vlote gheweest is. Van nieus Gecorrigeert ende verbeetert. Tot Amsterdam by Michiel Colijn . . . 1617.
(tp.7) VVarachtighe ende grondige beschryvinghe van . . . Guiana . . . ontdekt ende beschreven inden Jare 1595. ende 1596. Door . . . Walter Ralegh . . . ende . . . Laurens Keymis. Tot Amsterdam/By Michiel Colijn . . . 1617.
(tp.8) VVaerachtighe ende grondighe beschryvinghe vande tweede Zeevaert der Engelschē nae Guiana . . . beschreven inden Iare 1596. Door . . . Laurentium Keymis. t'Amstelredam by Michiel Colijn . . . 1617.
(tp.9) IOVRNAEL Oft Daghelijcx-register van de Voyagie na Rio de Plata/ghedaen met het Schip ghenoemt de Silveren Werelt . . . onder 'tAdmiraelschap van Laurens Bicker/ende het bevel van Cornelis van Heems-kerck . . . beschreven Door . . . Hendrick Ottsen . . . Tot Amstelredam by Michiel Colijn . . . 1617. (col.9) Tot Amstelredam by Michiel Colijn . . . 1617.
(tp.10) HISTORISCH Ende VVijdtloopigh verhael/van 't ghene de vijf Schepen (die int Jaer 1698 [*sic*]. tot Rotterdam toegherust zijn/om door de Straet Magellana haren handel te dryven) wedervaren is/tot den 7. September 1599 . . . Meest beschreven door M. Barent Iansz. Chirurgijn. Tot Amstelredam by Michiel Colijn . . . 1617. (col.10) Tot Amstelredam/by Michiel Colijn . . . 1617.
(tp.11) Beschrijvinge vande Voyagie om den geheelen Werelt-Kloot/ghedaen door Olivier van Noordt . . . t'AMSTERDAM, By Michiel Colijn . . . 1618.
obl.4° 11 pt.: ff.80; 83; 64; 41; 104; 39; 28[31]; 49; pp.53; 73; 131[132]: plates; illus., maps.
983.ff.6.

The compiler's dedication to the Admiralty at Amsterdam signed: Michiel Colijn. Other issues are known, dedicated to other bodies and signed instead: Marten Heubeldinck who has therefore sometimes been considered to be the actual compiler. With an additional titlepage in pt.1, engraved, reading: IOVRNALEN VANDE REYSEN OP OOSTINDIE. Separate editions are entered under their authors: LODEWIJKSZ, Willem; NECK, Jacob Cornelisz; SPILBERGEN, Joris van; MAREES, Pieter de; RALEIGH, Sir Walter; NOORT, Olivier van

C139 COLIUS, Jacobus

SYNTAGMA HERBARVM ENCOMIASTICVM, Earum vtilitatem & dignitatem declarans . . . Editio secunda. EX OFFICINA PLANTINIANA RAPHELENGII, 1614.
4° pp.61
968.k.6(2); B.161(1); 235.k.35.

The dedication signed: Iacobus Colius Ortelianus. The running title is 'Encomium herbarum'. Published at Leiden.

C140 COLLAERT, Adriaen

ANIMALIVM QVADRVPEDVM OMNIS GENERIS VERAE ET ARTIFICIOSISSIMAE DELINEATIONES IN AES INCISAE ET EDITAE AB ADRIANO COLLARDO. obl.4° pl.19
436.b.24(4).

Published at Antwerp, ca.1612? Each plate signed: Adrian. Collaert fecit et excud. Imperfect; wanting pl.7.

C141 COLLAERT, Adriaen

AVIVM VIVAE ICONES, in æs incisæ & editæ ab Adriano Collardo. obl.4° 16 unsigned leaves
436.b.24(1).

Published at Antwerp, ca.1610? Each plate signed: Adrian Collaert fecit et excud. The titlepage is mounted and has a manuscript note: Octauius Pisani recensuit.

C142 COLLAERT, Adriaen

AVIVM ICONVM EDITIO SECVNDA. obl.4° pl.16

436.b.24(2).

The plates are new and in much better condition than those of the preceding. Each plate signed: Adr. Collaert fecit et excud. Published at Antwerp, ca.1620?

C143 COLLAERT, Adriaen

PISCIVM VIVÆ ICONES In æs incisæ et editæ ab Adriano Collardo. obl.4° pl.24

436.b.24(3).

Each plate signed: Adr. Collaert fecit et excud. Published at Antwerp, ca.1610? Imperfect; wanting pl.5,7.

C144 COLLAERT, Adriaen

[Piscium vivae icones.] obl.4° pl.25

1257.i.7.

Each plate signed: Adr. Collaert fecit. Theod. Galle excud. Without a titlepage. The numeration of the original plate no.15 has been altered to 25 and another plate numbered 15 been inserted in its place. Published at Antwerp, ca.1615?

COLLATIO scripto habita Hagae Comitis anno . . . 1611. 1615. *See* SCHRIFTELICKE conferentie. [The Hague 1611.]

COLLATIO scripto inter sex ecclesiastas Delphis Batavorum . . . 1613 . . . habita. 1615. *See* SCHRIFTELICKE conferentie. [The Hague 1611. pt.2]

COLLOQUIA et dictionariolum octo linguarum. 1613. *See* BARLEMENT, Noel van

C145 COLLOQUIUM

[Colloquium trium principum.] T'SAMEN-SPREKINGHE TVSSCHEN DRY PRINCEN, Gehouden tot worms. Vanden tegenvvoordigen staet des Landts. Ouerghesedt vvt den Latyne in onse Nederlantsche sprake. Eerst ghedruckt in Februarius. 1621. T'Hantwerpen/By Abraham Verhoeuen/[etc.] 4° pp.8; without signatures; illus.

P.P.3444.af(185); 1193.f.29.

A translation, in verse, of 'Colloquium trium principum' which was published in Germany (B.L. copy at 1347.a.16(15)). The titlepage headed: Februarius 1621. 16. The titlepage woodcut shows a scene at the emperor's court, of three persons.

COLM, Jan Sievertsen. *See* KOLM, Jan Siewertsz

C146 COLONIUS, Daniel

THESES THEOLOGICAE Ex 13. priorib. vers. cap. 2. epist. Iacobi Analytice collectæ QVAS PRAESIDE . . . D. DANIELE COLONIO . . . tueri annitar . . . DAVID DE LA HAYE . . . Ad 6. diem Decemb. anno 1617. LVGDVNI-BATAVORVM, Ex Officina Henrici Ludovici ab Haestens. 4° sig.A^4

T.2188(1).

Published in 1617.

C147 COLSON, William

Liure, ou Instruction de L'ART DE L'ARITHMETIQVE ES NOMBRES ENTIERS SELON les cinq Especes, auec vne table contenante sommairement toutes les Reigles dudit art . . . y ioinct l'Art, ou l'ordre Militaire . . . Imprimé à Liege par Leonard Streel . . . 1603. [etc.] 8° 20 unsigned leaves, pp.44, sig.A-F^4: plate

8503.aaa.25.

Mainly in verse. The dedicatory verses in French and English signed: William Colson, laudatory verses in French and Latin. The plate bearing the colophon: A LIEGE, Par Leonard Streel . . . 160[4], the last figure of the date having been entered in ink.

C148 COMALADA, Miguel

[Spill dela vida religiosa.] EMANUEL [Irish . . .] DESIDERIUS [Irish . . . domo] S. FROASIAS [*sic*] F. C. . . . [Lovain] 1616. 8° pp.344

C.69.d.8; G.4771; G.4332.

Translated and edited by Florence Conroy from the anonymous Catalan work by Miguel Comalada. The approbation gives the title as 'Speculum vitæ: vel Desiderius'. Printed by the Irish Franciscans at Louvain. The copy at C.69.d.8 in a contemporary olive morocco binding with the inscriptions 'Francisco Nugent'. 'Robertus Kearney D.D.' tooled respectively on the covers. The copy at G.4771 has an added leaf bearing a printed dedication by Robertus Kearney to Richard Boyle, Viscount Dungarvan, inserted before the titlepage and is in a contemporary red morocco binding with the inscription 'Richard Dungarvan' tooled on the covers. The copy at G.4332 is imperfect, wanting the titlepage and three preliminary leaves.

C149 COMMENTARIUS

COMMENTARIVS DE BESTIA APOCALYPTICA. DELPHIS . . . M DC.XXI. fol. pp.164

3166.g.6.

Imperfect; wanting pp.87–100, which have been replaced with another set of pp.83, 84 and 93, 94.

The COMMUNION of Saincts. 1607; 1615. *See* AINSWORTH, Henry

COMOEDIA vetus. 1612. *See* MEERMAN, Willem

C150 COMPAIGNON

DEN COMPAIGNON Vanden verre-sienden WAERSCHOVWER, Thoonende met veele redenen waerom tot bevestinghe vanden Staet van dese Landen den OORLOGH veel dienstiger is dan den TREVES . . . IN 'SGRAVEN-HAGHE, By Aert Meuris . . . 1621. [etc.] 4° sig.A^4B^2

1490.s.5; T.2251(24).

Sometimes wrongly attributed to Thomas Scott.

C151 COMPAIGNON

[Den compaignon vanden verre-sienden waerschouwer.] A Relation OF SOME speciall points concerning the State of Holland. OR THE PROVIDENT Counsellours Companion . . . shewing, why for the good and security of the Netherland vnited Prouinces Warre is much better then peace . . . Printed at the Hage by Aert Muris [*sic*] . . . 1621. 4° pp.19

8081.a.16.

Sometimes wrongly attributed to Thomas Scott. A translation of 'Den compaignon vanden verre-sienden waerschouwer'. The imprint is false, being that of the original Dutch edition; in fact, printed by Edward Allde at London.

CONFESSIO fidei Anglorum. 1607. *See* CONFESSION. The confession of faith

A CONFESSION and protestation of the faith of certaine Christians in England. 1616. *See* JACOB, Henry

C152 CONFESSION

THE CONFESSION of faith of certayn English people, living in exile, in the Low countreyes . . . Reprinted in the yeare 1607. 8° pp.72

3506.a.31.

Sometimes said to have been drawn up by Francis Johnson. Printed by Giles Thorp at Amsterdam.

C153 CONFESSION

[The confession of faith.] (tp.1) CONFESSIO FIDEI ANGLORUM QUOrundam in nonnullis rebus ab Ecclesia Anglicana dissidentium. [etc.]

(tp.2) CONFESSIO Fidei Anglorum quorundam in Inferiori Germania exulantium. Vnâ cum annotatione brevi præcipuarum rerum in quibus differimus ab Ecclesia Angliæ . . . 1607. 8° pp.55
4136.a.35.
The Latin version of the preceding. Drawn up by Francis Johnson? Printed by Giles Thorp at Amsterdam. The second titlepage is a cancel and was at one time pasted over the first, original, titlepage.

C154 CONINCK FEEST
CONINCK FEEST Vanden Palatin/Anno 1621. Eerst Ghedruckt den 18. Januarius 1621 . . . T'Hantwerpen/By Abraham Verhoeuen/[etc.] 4° pp.8; sig.A^4; illus., port.
P.P.3444.af.(177); P.P.3444.af.(177*).
Headed: Ianuarius 1621. 8. A play without action, in verse. The titlepage woodcut shows the Winter King losing his crown.

C155 CONSIDERATIEN
Consideratien vande Vrede in Nederlandt gheconcipieert/Anno 1608. 4° sig.A^2
107.g.18(35).
Published in 1608.

CONSPECTUS Scholae Publicae, in civitate Alcmariana. 1615. *See* ALKMAAR. Schola Publica

C156 CONSTANTINE VII; Emperor of the East, called Porphyrogenitus
[Works.] CONSTANTINI Porphyrogennetæ Imperatoris OPERA. In Quibus TACTICA Nunc primùm prodeunt. IOANNES MEVRSIVS Collegit, coniunxit, edidit. LVGDVNI BATAVORVM, Ex Officinâ ELZEVIRIANA . . . M D CXVII. (col.) LVGDVNI BATAVORVM, TYPIS ISAACI ELZEVIRII . . . M D C XVII. 8° pp.230, 45; 56; 307
8007.aa.11.
In Greek and Latin. Contents: De administrando imperio (reissue of the edition of 1611 printed by Jan Bouwensz); Tactica; Thematum lib.i. Bonaventura Vulcanius edidit; Thematum lib.II. Federicus Morellus edidit; Novellae constitutiones XIII, Joannes Leunclavius edidit; Novellae IV, Carolus Labbæus edidit. With Meursius's dedication to Johan van Oldenbarnevelt.

C157 CONSTANTINE VII; Emperor of the East, called Porphyrogenitus
CONSTANTINI IMPERATORIS PORPHYROGENITI DE ADMINISTRANDO IMPERIO, AD ROMANVM F. Liber nunquàm antehac editus. IOANNES MEVRSIVS primus vulgavit, LATINAM interpretationem, ac NOTAS adjecit. LVGDVNI BATAVORVM, Ex officinâ IOANNIS BALDUINI, impensis . . . LUDOVICI ELZEVIRI. M.DC.XI. (col.) LUGDUNI BATAVORUM, Typis Iohannis Balduini: impensis . . . Ludovici Elzevirij . . . M.C.XI [*sic*]. 8° pp.230, 45
1053.a.10.
In Greek and Latin.

CONSTITUTIONES et decreta Synodi dioecesanae Iprensis. 1610. *See* YPRES. Diocese

C158 CONST-RIJCK
CONST-RIICK BEROEP Ofte Antwoort/op de Kaerte uyt-gesonden by de Hollantsche camer binnen Leyden, onder t'woort LIEFD' ES t'FONDAMENT, aen alle nabuerighe Reden-rijcke vrye cameren in Nederlant/tegens den 6. Octob. Anno 1613. Op de Vraghe ende Regels als volght . . . TOT LEYDEN. By Jacob Janszoon Paets . . . 1614. 4° sig. $(\star\star\star)^4$ $(\star\star\star)$ $(\star\star\star)^4$ $(\star\star\star)$ $(\star\star\star)^2$A–Q^4
1509/2107; 1490.s.16(1).
In the copy at 1509/2107 the catchword at the end of the preface is misprinted: CHAETRƎ; this has been corrected to: CHAERTE in the copy at 1490.S.16(1) which contains the exlibris of H. E. Kern.

CONST-THOONENDE Juweel. 1607. *See* HEYNS, Zacharias

C159 CONSULTATION

Consultation vnd vnderredung dess Ehrwürdigen Hochweisen Raets von wegen der Hispanischen Cron/vber gegenwertige Niderlendtsche Pacification . . . 1608. obl.fol. a single illustrated sheet

1750.c.1(16).

In verse. A warning against making peace with Spain. The engraving entitled 'Iberæ Næniæ', with verses in Latin. Very probably published in the Netherlands.

CONTINUATIE vande tollerantie . . . vanden cours van alle . . . penninghen. 1609. *See* NETHERLANDS. United Provinces. Staten Generaal [27.8.1609]

CONTRA libellum Calvini. 1612. *See* CHÂTEILLON, Sébastien

CONTRADISCOURS kerckelic ende politijck. 1621. *See* WTENBOGAERT, Jan

Der CONTRAREMONSTRANTEN kerf-stock. 1617. *See* TELLE, Reinier

C160 COOLHAES, Caspar

Een cort vvarachtich verhael Van tsorgelicke vyer/der hatelicker/ende van God vervloecter oneenicheyt/in Religions saken/ontsteecken zijnde in Hollandt Anno 1574 . . . Geschreven van CASPARVS COOLHAES . . . TOT LEYDEN, By Ian Bouwenszoon . . . 1610. 4° pp.205[209]

1568/9167.

COORNHERT, Dirck Volckertsz. Of Godt . . . siet op des menschen doen. 1611. *See* infra: Vande predestinatie.

COORNHERT, Dirck Volkertsz. Recht ghebruyck ende misbruyck van tydlicke have. 1620. *See* FURMERIUS, Bernardus

COORNHERT, Dirck Volckertsz. Van Godes verkiesinghe. 1611. *See* infra: Vande predestinatie.

C161 COORNHERT, Dirck Volckertsz

[Vande Leydtsche disputatie.] Vande Vreemde {Sonde Schulde Straffe} nasporinghe. Waer inne . . . werdt ontdeckt de . . . oorsake vande schadelijcke dolingen gheslopen inde Leeringhen vande Vrije-wille . . . in druck ghegheven door D. V. Coornhert . . . Ghedruckt ter Goude, By Jasper Tournay/voor Andries Burier . . . 1616. 4° pp.164

T.2246(24).

A new edition of 'Vande Leydtsche disputatie warachtich verhael' of 1583.

C162 COORNHERT, Dirck Volckertsz

[Vande predestinatie.] Of Godt in sijn Predestineren, Verkiesen ende Verwerpen siet op des Menschen doen/dan niet. Ghesprake Tusschen Ghereformeerde Calvinist, ende D. Demostenes . . . Ghedruckt . . . 1611. 4° pp.31

T.2241(9).

Anonymous and without imprint. Originally published as the third 'Ghesprake' in 'Vande predestinatie'. Printed by Jasper Tournay at Gouda.

C163 COORNHERT, Dirck Volckertsz

[Vande predestinatie.] Van Godes Verkiesinghe. Of Godt door sijn eyghen werck alleen/sonder eenighe medewerckinghe der Menschen/eenighe der selver saligh

maackt. Waar over de Conferentien . . . in s'Graven-Haghe ghehouden zijn . . . Tweede Ghesprake Tusschen Ghereformeerde Calvinist, ende D. Demostenes . . . Ghedruckt . . . 1611. 4° pp.27
T.2241(10).
Anonymous and without imprint. Originally published as the fourth 'Ghesprake' in 'Vande predestinatie'. Printed by Jasper Tournay at Gouda.

C164 COORNHERT, Dirck Volckertsz
[Vande predestinatie.] Vande Verworpelinghen. Of Godes Predestinatie door sijn Verlatinghe ende Noodtdrang/ende nyet door der Menschen Zonden/oorsake is van yemants eeuwighe Verdoemenisse. Derde Ghesprake Tusschen Ghereformeerde Calvinist, ende D. Demostenes . . . Ghedruckt . . . 1611. 4° pp.31
T.2241(11).
Anonymous and without imprint. originally published as the fifth 'Ghesprake' in 'Vande predestinatie'. Printed by Jasper Tournay at Gouda.

COORNHERT, Dirck Volckertsz. Vande vreemde . . . nasporinghe. 1616. *See* supra: Vande Leydtsche disputatie.

C165 COORNHERT, Dirck Volckertsz
VRE-REDEN of Onderwijs tot Eendracht, Vrede ende Liefde, in dese tijden hoochnoodich. Aenwijsende Dat een Christen tot sijn Gheloof ende leven de Vrede ende Liefde hebben moet om salich te werden. Eerste Deel. Gheschreven over veel jaren van een Godsvruchtich Christen . . . Ghedruckt ter Goude, By Jasper Tournay . . . 1612. 4° pp.24
T.2242(19).
Anonymous.

C166 COORNHERT, Dirck Volckertsz
[Vre-reden.] Verclaringhe Vande uyterlijcke ende innerlijcke Religie. Ende hoe dat alle de Ceremonien/t'zy van God of de menschen/inghestelt/den mensche sonder de Liefde nyet salich maken en konnen. Tweede Deel. Gheschreven over veel jaren van een Godsvruchtich Christen . . . Ghedruckt ter Goude, By Jasper Tournay . . . 1612. 4° pp.24
T.2242(19*).
Anonymous. The second part of 'Vre-reden'.

C167 COPERNICUS, Nicolaus
[De revolutionibus orbium coelestium.] NICOLAI COPERNICI . . . ASTRONOMIA INSTAVRATA . . . Nunc demum . . . integritati suæ restituta, Notisque illustrata, opera & studio D. NICOLAI MVLERII . . . AMSTELRODAMI, Excudebat VVilhelmus Iansonius . . . M.DC.XVII. 4° pp.487; illus.
8560.f.14.
With an address by the printer explaining the choice of format.

COPIA des briefs vãde Keur-Vorsten ende Vorsten tot Mulhausen vergadert. 1620. *See* GERMANY. Electors [21.3.1620]

COPIE d'une lettre contenant la description de l'entrée triomphale de Don Pedro de Tholedo faicte à Fontainebleau. 1609. *See* BAUCE, Jean

The COPIE of a letter sent from Paris. 1611. *See* OWEN, Thomas

COPIE van de synodale sententie over . . . Haerlem. 1618? *See* ENKHUIZEN. Synod of 1618

C168 COPIE

COPIE Van de t'Samen-sprekinghe DES Paus ende Coninghs van Spangjen/over henlieder ghenaemde Nederlandtsche Rebellen. Gheschiedt in haren Droom . . . Wt het Italiaens ende Spaens getranslateert DOOR ALEETHEIA. GHEDRVCKT Ende herwaerts over gesonden uyt den Roomschen ende Spaenschen Dormter . . . 1618. 4° pp.16; illus.
700.h.25(17).
The titlepage woodcut shows the King and the Pope.

COPIE van het schrijven aen Chur Phalts ghedaen, door de Chur: ende Vorsten. 1620. *See* GERMANY. Electors [21.3.1620]

COPIE van sekere brieven de welcke twee persoonen aen malcanderen hebben gheschreven. 1612. *See* HARTWECH, Adam

C169 COPIE

COPIE Van sekeren Brief/geschreven inden Legher voor de Stadt Gulick/ende van't groot ongheluck datter in't op-trecken nae de selve Stadt ghebeurt is/door't springhen van xxiiij. Waghenen met Buspoeder. Daer by ghevoeght Verscheyden Nieuvvicheden, soo uyt het Keyserlijcke Hof tot Prague als oock uyt de Stadt Ceulen geschreven . . . TOT DELF. Ghedruckt by Ian Andriessz. . . . 1610. 4° 4 unsigned leaves
T.1729(5); T.2421(18).
Signed: N.N.

COPIE vande belijdenisse ende sententie capitael van Cornelis de Hoogh. 1608. *See* HOLLAND. Hof [29.3.1583]

COPIEN vande sententien ofte vonnissen binnen Utrecht gewesen. 1611. *See* NETHERLANDS. United Provinces [9.5.1611]

COPIJE vande brieff door den Marck-Grave van Jaghersdorp gheschreven aende vorsten ende standen in Slesien. 1621. *See* JOHN GEORGE, Margrave of Jägerndorf

C170 COPINGER, John

THE THEATRE OF CATHOLIQVE AND PROTESTANT RELIGION . . . WRITTEN By I.C. Student in diuinitie . . . 1620. 8° pp.632
3936.aa.42.
Anonymous. Sometimes wrongly attributed to John Colleton. Without imprint; printed by Charles Boscard at St. Omer.

C171 COPPIES

[Cop]PIES [de di]VERSES LETTRES, [les o]RIGINAVX DESQVELS [peuven]t estre representés, pour faire voir quelle [est] la forme ordinaire des procés, en la Cour Imperiale, & quelle a esté . . . la procedure tenuë par l'Empereur au fait du Ban, dont il s'agit á present . . . touchant le different de Boheme. A LA HAYE, Chez Hillebrant Iacobssz. . . . 1621. 4° pp.27
1054.c.25(5).
Letters by Ferdinand II to various princes and their replies and other letters. Mutilated throughout; the passages between brackets supplied from the description of a copy at Leiden in *Petit* no.1286.

C172 COPY

COPY Van een seecker Boecxken dat onlanckx is vvt ghegaen, Trackterende van een Miraeckel oft Spectakel/dat te Amsterdam gheschiet is van eenen groenen Linden boom/die ghestaen heeft voor het Huys . . . van Reyner Paeu . . . En den seluen boom is in vier-en-twintich uren dor gheworden . . . Ghestelt in Rijm . . .

Eerst ghedruckt buyten Heydelberch/en daer naer ouergesedt in onse Nederlantsche spraeck buyten Amsterdam tot Gras-rijck . . . Men vintse te coop daerse veyl sijn. 4° pp.7; sig.G; illus.
1480.aa.15(60); P.P.3444.af(125).

The imprint is fictitious; printed by Abraham Verhoeven at Antwerp in October 1620. The titlepage woodcut shows a dead tree.

COPYE des Sendtbriefs van . . . Borghermeesteren ende Schepenen der Stadt Antwerpen . . . M.D.LXXXIIII. 1618. *See* ANTWERP [1584]

C173 COPYE

Copye van een Discours tusschen een Hollander ende een Zeeuw. 4° sig.★[4]
T.1713(17).

Published in 1608. Corresponding to the copy described in *Knuttel* no.1454.

C174 COPYE

Copye van een Discours tusschen een Hollander ende een Zeeuw. 4° sig.A[4]
106.d.15.

Published in 1608. Another edition of the preceding, corresponding to the copy described in *Knuttel* no.1455.

COPYE van seker vertooch. 1617. *See* WTENBOGAERT, Jan

COPYE van sekeren brief. 1616. *See* TAURINUS, Jacobus

COPYE vande belijdenisse ende sententie capitael van Cornelis de Hooghe. 1608. *See* HOLLAND. Hof [29.3.1583]

C175 COPYE

COPYE Vande Namen der Coninclicke/ende andere Potentaten Ghesanten/van weghen de . . . Staten Generael versocht/Omme mede te staen over de Vredehandelinghe tusschen de vereenichde Nederlandtsche Provintien . . . ter eender/ende den Coninc van Spaegnien ende . . . de Eerts hertoghen ter ander zijden. Oock mede de Namen ende Qualiteyten vande Ghecommitteerde soo van den Coninck van Spaegnien/ende de Eerts hertoghen als vande vereenichde Nederlanden . . . M.VI^c. ende VIII. 4° 2 unsigned leaves
107.g.14(33).

Texts in Dutch, French or Spanish. Without imprint; printed by Hillebrant Jacobsz van Wouw at The Hague?

COPYE vande procuratien. 1609. *See* NETHERLANDS. Southern Provinces [9.4.1609]

CORANTE. *See* also CORRANT; COURANT; COURANTE

C176 CORANTE

CORANTE, OR, NEVVES FROM Italy and Germanie. (col.) Printed in Amstelredam by Broer Ionson . . . The 6. of Iune 1621. fol. a single sheet
Harl.Ms.389(87).

Begin: From Rome 15. of May 1621. Mutilated. *STC* no. 18507.20, which erroneously supplies the pressmark Harl.Ms.389/82, suggests this could have been printed at London for Thomas Archer, with a false imprint.

C177 CORANTE

CORANTE, OR, NEVVES FROM Italy and Germanie. (col.) Printed in Amsterdam by Ioris Veselde the 20. of Iune 1621. fol. a single sheet
Harl.Ms.389(106).

Begin: From Rome the 26 of May 1621.

C178 CORANTE

CORANTE, OR, NEVVES FROM Italy, Germanie, Hungarie, and Spaine. 1621. (col.) Printed at Amstelredam by Broer Ionson . . . the 25. of Iune. 1621. fol. a single sheet

Harl.Ms.389(82).

Begin: From Rome the 30. of May 1621. The pressmark supplied in *STC* 18507.21 as Harl. Ms.389/83 is erroneous.

C179 CORANTE

CORANTE, OR, NEVVES FROM Italy, Germanie, Hungarie, Poland, Bohemia and France. 1621. (col.) Printed at Amstelredam by Broer Ionson . . . the 20. of Iuly. fol. a single sheet

C.55.l.2(11); Harl.Ms.389(104).

Begin: From Venice the 1. of Iuly 1621. *STC* no. 18507.24 suggests this could have been printed at London for Thomas Archer, with a false imprint.

C180 CORANTE

CORANTE, OR, NEVVES FROM Italy, Germanie, Hungarie, Spaine and France. 1621. (col.) Printed at Amstelredam by Broer Ionson . . . the 3. of Iuly. 1621. fol. a single sheet

Harl.Ms.389(83).

Begin: From Rome the 3. of Iune 1621.

C181 CORANTE

CORANTE, OR, NEVVES FROM Italy, Germanie, Hungarie, Spaine and France. 1621. (col.) Printed at Amstelredam by Broer Ionson . . . the 9. of Iuly. 1621. fol. a single sheet

C.55.l.2(9); Harl.Ms.389(84).

Begin: From Lyons the 6 of Iune 1621.

C182 CORANTE

CORANTE, OR, NEVVES FROM Italy, Germany, Hungaria, Bohemia, Spaine and Dutchland. 1621. (col.) Imprinted by Broyer Iohnson . . . the 2. of August. 1621. fol. a single sheet

C.55.l.2(13).

Begin: From Rome the 2 of Iuly 1621. Printed at Amsterdam. *STC* no. 18507.25 suggests this could have been printed at London for Thomas Archer, with a false imprint.

C183 CORANTE

CORANTE, OR, NEVVES FROM Italy, Germany, Hungaria, Polonia, France, and Dutchland. 1621. (col.) Imprinted at the Hage by Adrian Clarke, the 10. of August. 1621. fol. a single sheet

C.55.l.2(14).

Begin: From Rome the 8. of Iuly 1621. The imprint is false; printed at London. No printer of this name is known at either place.

CORRANT. *See also* CORANTE; COURANT; COURANTE

C184 CORRANT

Corrant out of Italy, Germany, &c. (col.) Imprinted at Amsterdam by George Veseler, A°. 1620. The 23 of December. And are to be soulde by Petrus Keerius, [etc.] fol. a single sheet

C.55.l.2(2).

Begin: From Venice 27. of November, 1620.

C185 CORRANT
Corrant out of Italy, Germany, &c. (col.) Imprinted at Amsterdam by George Veseler, Ao. 1621. The 4 of Nanuari [*sic*]. And are to be soulde by Petrus Keerius, [etc.] fol. a single sheet
C.55.l.2(3).
Begin: From Rome the 5. of December.

C186 CORRANT
Corrant out of Italy, Germany, &c. (col.) Imprinted at Amsterdam by George Veseler, Ao. 1621. The 21 of Ianuari. And are to be soulde by Petrus Keerius, [etc.] fol. a single sheet
C.55.l.2(4).
Begin: From Roome the 19. of December.

CORT begrijp van acht oeffeninghen. 1602. *See* MAKEBLYDE, Ludovicus

CORT bericht ende wederlegginge der beswaernissen. 1618. *See* BOHEMIA. States [June/July 1618]

CORT bericht van de redenen. 1612. *See* ROTTERDAM

CORT en waerachtich verhael wt de mont van eenighe . . . borgers van Goch. 1615. *See* VISIOEN

CORT en warachtich verhael wt de mont van eenighe . . . borgers van Goch. 1615. *See* VISIOEN

CORT ende klaer contra-discours. 1617. *See* DRIELENBURCH, Vincent van

C187 CORT
Cort ende waerachtich verhael van eenige exorbitante Proceduiren/door het beleyt van weynich personen sedert seven ofte acht jaren herwaerts/jegens die vande ware Gereformeerde Religie by der handt ghenomen ende int werck ghestelt. GHEDRVCKT By't rechte voorstant van Orangien Tot teghenstandt van Spangien . . . 1618. 4° sig. A^4
T.2248(14).
The imprint 'D. Verhaghen', i.e. Peeter Verhaghen at Dordrecht?, has been added in a modern handwriting.

C188 CORT
EEN Cort ende warachtich verhael van de ghedenckweerdige gheschiedenisse in Barbaryen, ende vanden grooten slagh ontrent Maroques, gheschiet den 25 Aprilis/1607 . . . Nae de Copye In s'Graven-haghe, By Hillebrant Jacobsz. . . . M.DC.VII. 4° 2 unsigned leaves
T.1729(15).

CORT examen ende sententie Johannis Vtenbogaerts. 1615. *See* DRIELENBURCH, Vincent van

C189 CORT
Cort verhael hoe dat sijn Excellentie den Marquis Spinola met den Legher in Pfaltz-Graven Landt ghetrocken is. Nv éerst Ghedruckt den xviij. September . . . 1620. T'hantwerpen/By Abraham verhoeuen . . . 1620. [etc.] 4° pp.7; sig. N. vj^4; illus.
P.P.3444.af(100).
The titlepage woodcut shows a battle below a castle.

C190 CORT

Cort verhael hoe dat sijn Excellentie den Marquis Spinola met den Legher in Pfaltz-Graven Landt ghetrocken is. Nv eerst Ghedruckt den xxiiij. September . . . 1620. T'hantwerpen By Abraham verhoeuen . . . 1620. [etc.] 4° pp.7; sig.N.vj^4; illus.

P.P.3444.af(104).

A variant of the preceding, with a different date of publication.

Een CORT verhael, hoe ende in wat maniere die Gommarissen van Hollant, Hemel en eerde willē innemen. 1619. *See* LIEFF-HEBBER

C191 CORT

CORT VERHAEL Hoe subtyl en vvonderlyck M^R. HVGO GROTIVS . . . Met een Koffer wt zijne Ghevanckenisse te Loevensteyn in Hollant/ghedraghen/ende voorder ontkomen is. Nieuw ghedruckt den 1. April. 1621. T'Hantwerpen/By Abraham Verhoeuen . . . 1621. 4° pp.7; sig.A^4; illus.

P.P.3444.af(216).

The titlepage headed: Appril 1621. 52. Sometimes attributed to Aubert le Mire. The titlepage woodcut shows the open trunk.

C192 CORT

Cort verhael uyt seeckere tydinghe gecomen uyt Engelant/waer in verhaelt wert de tryumphante Krooninghe van Coningh Jacobus/met de Coninginne Anna . . . gheschiet inde Kercke te West-Munster den xxv. Julius . . . Item noch de tryumphante verthooninghe vanden Coninck ende Coninghinne op de Riviere van Londen. TOT DELF, Ghedruckt by Jacob Cornelissz Vennecool . . . 1603. 4° sig.A^2

1568/8640.

C193 CORT

Cort verhael Van al tghene binnen Utrecht gepasseert is/zeder dat de . . . Staten Generael met den . . . Prince van Orangien daer gekomen zyn/soo in't afdancken der Waert-ghelders/als in't verstellen van nieuwe Vroetschappen/Publicatie/ t'Inruymen vande Buer-kercke/voor de oude Ghereformeerde (die-men Contra-Remonstranten noemt) als mede de eerste . . . Predicatie die daer . . . ghedaen is . . . Amsterdam, by Broer Jansz. . . . 1618. 4° 2 unsigned leaves; illus.

1314.e.24(4).

With the text of the proclamation of 27 July 1618. The titlepage woodcuts show the portrait and arms of Prince Maurice.

C194 CORT

Een cort verhael van die Principaelste puncten/die in Hollandt tot Dort/in die Synode ghetrackteert worden/ghestelt in Rijme. Tot confusie van die selue Synode . . . Gemaect door een Liefhebber der C.A.R.R. Gheprint t'hantwerpen/by Abraham Verhoeuen . . . M.DC.XIX. 4° pp.8; sig.A^4; illus.

P.P.3444.af(2).

The woodcut on p.3 showing a devil on horseback holding a book refers to the beginning which is: Balade. Den Duyvel is te post zijn vrienden gaen besoecken.

Een CORT verhael van eenen nieuwen draeck. 1621. *See* LIEFHEBBER

C195 CORT

Cort Verhael Van t'gene nu passeert binnen Praghe. Overghesedt wt de Hooch-Duytsche sprake in onse Nederlantsche Tale. Eerst Ghedruckt den 8. Januarius 1621. T'Hantwerpen/By Abraham Verhoeuen/[etc.] 4° pp.8; unsigned; illus.

P.P.3444.af(171).

The titlepage headed: Ianuarius 1621.2. The titlepage woodcut shows the siege of Prague.

C196 CORT

Cort Verhael vande Heerlijcke Incompste van dē Keyser Ferdinandus/binnen de stadt van Auspurg. Nv eerst Ghedruckt den xxv. October. T'Hantwerpen/By Abraham Verhoeven/[etc.] 4° pp.8; sig.A[4]; illus.

P.P.3444.af(24).

Published in 1619. The titlepage woodcut shows the portrait of Ferdinand II, on p.4 illustration of a coin.

C197 CORT

CORT VERHAEL, Vande Ontschutteringe/gedaen aen eenige vrome ende gequalificeerde Borgers/binnen de Stadt Leyden/eñ vande Proceduren aen sommighe vande Ontschutterde aenghestelt . . . met de Autentijcke stukken bevesticht. Dienende tot Iustificatie vande selve schutters . . . VVaer by oock is ghevoecht een kleyn verhael van sommighe insolentien, by de Waertgelders aldaer ghepleeght. GHEDRVCKT By 'trechte voorstant van Oragnien/Tot teghenstant van Spangnien. A°. 1618. 4° pp.35

T.2248(7).

The titlepage bears a device of a lion with the motto 'Den leeu los synde wil geen halsbant dragen', first used with an emblem in a 1598 pamphlet.

C198 CORT

Cort Verhael Vande Oorloghe in Duyt-slandt [*sic*]/Met t'ghene nv onlanckx gepasseert is/ende hoe dat ons volck in Marheren Landt ghevallen is. Overghesedt Wt den Hooch-duyts/ende nv eerst Gheprint den xxx. Augusti 1619. T'hantwerpen/By Abraham Verhoeven/[etc.] 4° pp.8; sig.A[4]; illus.

P.P.3444.af(16).

The titlepage woodcut shows a cavalry battle.

C199 CORT

Cort Verhael Vande Oorloghe in Duyt-slandt . . . T'hantwerpen/By Abraham Verhoeven/[etc.] 4° pp.8; sig.A[4]; illus.

P.P.3444.af(17).

A variant of the preceding, the titlepage woodcut showing the imperial arms.

C200 CORT

Cort verhael vanden gheweldigen Slach tegen dē Turck gheschiedt/ende hoe dat den Primo Visier/Capiteyn Generael . . . is ghecomen met 200000. mannen int Conick-rijck vā Persien/tot by de stadt Taurus/alwaer den Coninck van Persien hem heeft verwacht by Ardevil met 100000. mannen/ende dē Perssiaen heeft den Turck geslagen . . . T'Hantwerpen, By Abraham Verhoeuen . . . 1619. 4° pp.7; sig.A[4]; illus.

P.P.3444.af(5).

The titlepage woodcut shows a cavalry battle.

C201 CORT, Cornelis

[The story of Noah.] M. Heemskerck invent. CJVISSCHER excudebat. Cor. Cort. Fcit [*sic*]. obl.fol. pl.6

L.R.110.c.10(2).

A late reprint, at Amsterdam, datable 1620? of an earlier set of copperplates. Cort's name may be a supposititious addition.

C202 CORTE

CORTE ANTVVOORD', Op sekere Balade/ghemaeckt by eenen Quidam der Pauscher zijde/welcken sijnen Naeme begrijpt in . . . de Letteren/I.H. . . . TOT DELF, Ghedruct by Ian Andriesz. [etc.] 4° sig.A[4]

1560/4443.

In verse, with the original poem, 'Ghedicht/ter eeren den vromen Ridder ende Krijghs-helt Marquis Spignola' preceding the 'Antvvoort'. Published in 1607.

C203 CORTE

Corte beschrijvinghe ende Affbeeldinghe des seer grooten ende Schrickelijcken Comeets, de vvelcke den 27. November . . . 1618. ons verschenen is. Mitsgaders veel schoone Exempelen van verscheyden Cometen. Tot Leyden/by Jacob Marcus . . . wt ghegeven tot een nieuwen Jaer 1619. 4° sig.A^4; illus.
T.2248(64); T.2423(3).

With a titlepage engraving.

C204 CORTE

Corte ende Christelijcke Aenmerckinghen/Op den schandeleusen Loffsangh BERNARDI BVSSCHOF Nu Predicant tot Wtrecht: wiens beginsel is/Ghelooft sy Godt die my heeft uytvercoren. Neffens zyne uytlegginghe/vande doodelijcke sonden: ende daer op volgende Censure . . . Waer in zijne/ende zijner medestanders (der Contraremonstranten) . . . dolinghen . . . ontdeckt ende wederleydt worden . . . Ghedruckt . . . MDCXX. Met Privilegie vanden Autheur. 4° pp.28
T.2250(7).

With the text of the poem.

C205 CORTE

Een Corte ende eenvoudige antwoorde op vier poincten. By Doctor Iacob Arminius in syn leven tegen ghesproken/als te syn ontschrift-matich [*sic*] . . . Aengaende de Predestinatie Godts. Met een kordt ondersoek/van vier poincten by Doctor Iacob Arminius hier tegen ghestelt . . . Maer hier teghens wert bewesen dat de oprechte Leere vande . . . Predestinatie Godts/zulcx is: Die altydts inde Ghereformeerde Kercke hier te landen ghe-leert is . . . TOT SCHIEDAM. Voor Jan Wolfferssz. . . . M.N.J.X.J. [*sic*]. 4° sig.A-E^4
T.2241(8).

The date of publication is meant to read 1611.

C206 CORTE

Corte ende naeckte ONTDECKINGHE Vande Bedrieghelijckheydt des DORTSCHEN SYNODI, In't smeden van seeckere Artijckelen van Moderatie en onderlinghe Verdraegsaemheyt/tusschen den Remonstranten ende Contra-Remonstranten . . Ghedruckt . . . M.DC.XIX. 4° pp.23
T.2249(9).

With a manuscript attribution to Simon Episcopius on the titlepage.

CORTE ende naecte ondeckinghe van den luegen-geest. 1617. *See* TAURINUS, Jacobus

C207 CORTE

Corte ende seeckere tydinghe van het veroveren ende innemen der stercke Stadt ende weerachtighe Casteel Gulick. Geschiet op . . . den 30. Augustus . . . Ghedruckt alhier/by den voorgaenden Courantier. 4° 2 unsigned leaves
T.1729(1).

Printed by Broer Jansz or by Gerrit van Breughel, both at Amsterdam? Published in 1610.

CORTE ende warachtige beschrijvinge. 1619. *See* PROCESSUS

CORTE historische beschryvinghe der Nederlandscher oorlogen. 1612. *See* DUYM, Jacob

C208 CORTE

Corte Verclaringhe Ende bewijs/met wat ghestaltenisse ende Ceremonien . . . Ferdinandus Coninck van Hungharijen . . . tot Roomschen Keyser den xxviij. Augusti deses Jaers is ghekosen gheworden/binnen Franck-fort. Overghesedt wt

den Hooch-duytsche/in onse Nederlantsche Tale. T'hantwerpen/By Abraham Verhoeven/[etc.] 4° pp.8; sig.A^4; illus.
P.P.3444.af(15).
The titlepage woodcut shows the portrait of Ferdinand II. Published in 1619.

C209 CORTE
CORTE Verclaringhe/Vande VYF ARTYCKELEN, Daer over Tusschen de Remonstranten/ENDE Contra-Remonstranten/Ghedisputeert wort. GHEDRVCKT . . . 1619. Met onversochte Privilegie. 4° pp.30
T.2249(30).

C210 CORVINUS, Joannes Arnoldi
CHRISTELICKE Ende ernstighe vermaninghe tot vrede aen R. Donteclock/over sijne t'samensprekinge vande vertaelde Theses ofte disputatie D. Francisci Gomari ende D. Iacobi Arminij, aengaende de Goddelijcke Predestinatie . . . De tvveede Editie. IN S'GRAVEN-HAGHE. By Hillebrant Jacobsz . . . 1609. 4° sig.★A-H^4 I^2
T.2239(8).
Anonymous.

C211 CORVINUS, Joannes Arnoldi
DEFENSIO SENTENTIAE D. IACOBI ARMINII, DE PRÆDESTINATIONE, GRATIA DEI, LIBERO HOMINIS ARBITRIO, &c. Adversus eiusdem, A . . . D. DANIELE TILENO editam considerationem, AVTHORE IOANNE ARNOLDO CORVINO . . . LVGDVNI BATAVORVM. Ex Officina Ioannis Patij . . . 1613. 8° pp.533
4255.aa.21.

C212 CORVINUS, Joannes Arnoldi
(tp.1) RESPONSIO AD JOANNIS BOGERMANNI . . . ANNOTATIONES, Quibus vindicatam à . . . D. HVGONE GROTIO . . . Pietatem Illustrium Ordinum Hollandiæ & Westfrisiæ denuo impugnavit . . . PARS PRIMA. AVTHORE IOANNE ARNOLDO CORVINO . . . LVGDVNI BATAVORVM Excudit Ioannes Patius . . . 1614.
(tp.2) RESPONSIONIS . . . PARS ALTERA . . . A IOANNE ARNOLDO CORVINO . . . LVGDVNI BATAVORVM Excudit Ioannes Patius . . . 1616. 4° 2 pt.: pp.114; 590
4255.cc.13.
With the bookplate of University College, Oxford, 'ex Testamento Jo. Hudson . . . 1719'.

C213 CORVINUS, Joannes Arnoldi
SCHOVVVE, Over D. FRANCISCI GOMARI PROEVE, Van D.M, P. BERTII AENSPRAECK, By een van sijn Discipulen, tot nodige protestatie voor de eere sijns meesters, ende voorbode van de Wederlegginghe van D. Gomari Waerschouwinghe uytgegheven . . . By Ian Paedts Iacopszoon . . . 1610. 4° sig.AB^{4}C^2
T.2240(4).
Anonymous. Published at Leiden.

C214 CORVINUS, Joannes Arnoldi
TEGHEN-BERICHT jeghens D. FRANCISCI GOMARI WAERSCHOVWINGE OVER DE VERMANINGHE TOT VREDE DIE ONlanghs, aen D.R. Donteclock Christelijck ende ernstelijck ghedaen is . . . Vyt ghegeven door I.B.R. bedienaer des H. Euangelij . . . By Jan Paedts Iacopszoon . . . 1610. 4° pp.56,60
T.2240(1).
Anonymous. With 'Antwoort op't Proef-stuck vande leere D. Iacobi Arminij'. Published at Leiden. Imperfect; wanting sig.A=pp.9–16 in the first part.

C215 CORVINUS, Joannes Arnoldi

Verantwoordinge Tegens de hevige Predicatie FESTI HOMMII, gedaen in de S[te] Pieters Kerke tot Leyden den xvj. Octobris . . . 1616. Daerinne claerlijck bewesen wordt/hoe deselve Festus hem gheenfsins [*sic*] en heeft gesuyvert . . . van de . . . dolingen/hem aengewesen in't Munster van de Leere der Amsterdamsche Predicanten . . . Ghedruckt ter Goude, By Jasper Tournay/voor Andries Burier . . . 1616. 4° pp.39

T.2246(16).

Anonymous. The title on p.1 is 'Naemscherminge [etc.]'. The work referred to is 'Monster vande leere [etc.]' by Bernardus Dwinglo.

C216 COSTER, Samuel

Duytsche ACADEMI, Tot Amsterdam ghespeelt, Op den eersten dach van Oegstmaant . . . 1619. S.A.C. T'AMSTERDAM, Voor Cornelis Lodovviicksz. vander plassen . . . 1619. 4° sig. AB^4C^2

11754.bbb.14.

The initials stand for Samuel Adriaenszoon Coster. The last page inscribed: Finis coronat opus.

C217 COSTER, Samuel

Ghezelschap der Goden vergaert Op de ghewenste Bruyloft van APOLLO . . . Met De eenighe en eerste Nederduytsche ACADEMIE . . . T'AMSTERDAM, By NICOLAES BIESTKENS . . . 1618. (col.) T'AMSTERDAM, By Nicolaes Biestkens . . . M.DC.XVIII. 4° sig. $A\text{-}C^4$

11556.cc.16.

Anonymous. Sometimes wrongly attributed to Suffridus Sixtinus.

C218 COSTER, Samuel

SAMVEL COSTERS IPHIGENIA Treur-Spel . . . T'AMSTERDAM, By Nicolaas Biestkens . . . 1617. fol. pp.63; illus.

11755.k.6.

C219 COSTER, Samuel

SAMVEL COSTERS IPHIGENIA . . . Na de Copy, t'AMSTERDAM, By Nicolaas Biestkens . . . 1617. 4° sig. $A\text{-}F^4$

11755.e.56(1).

An (unauthorised?) reprint, published 1619?

C220 COSTER, Samuel

Samuel Costers ITHYS Treur-spel . . . Tvveede Druck. T'AMSTERDAM, Voor Cornelis vander Plassen . . . 1619. 4° sig. $A\text{-}F^4$

11755.b.14.

A reprint by Nicolaas Biestkens at Amsterdam of the second edition originally published by him in 1618. sig. E2 misprinted T2.

C221 COSTER, Samuel

Begin. Op s'Oegst-maents eerste dagh ('tis nu een jaer geleên) . . . Anno 1618 DVB in CJV fe. obl. fol. a single sheet, engraved

Maps C.9.d.6(25).

An engraving by Claes Jansz Visscher, Amsterdam, in honour of the first anniversary of Coster's Nederduytsche Academie, showing a scene from his 'Ghezelschap der Goden'. The verses signed: Tecum habita, a Latin form of Coster's motto. The designer is David Vinckboons.

C222 COSTER, Samuel
S. COSTERS POLYXENA Treur-spel . . . T'AMSTERDAM, Voor VVillem Iansz. Cloppenburch . . . 1619. (col.) T'AMSTERDAM, By Nicolaas Biestkens . . . 1619. 4° pp.85[77]
11755.e.56(2).
The pagination is misprinted after p.72.

C223 COSTER, Samuel
SPEL van TIISKEN VANDER SCHILDEN . . . TOT DELF, By Ian Andriesz. . . . M.VI^{C}.XV. 4° sig.A-F^{4}
11755.b.60.
Anonymous.

C224 COSTER, Samuel
Spel vande Rijcke-Man/Ghespeelt op de Lotery van't Oude Mannen ende Vrouwen Gast-huys/binnen Amsterdam. 1615. Op Kermisse . . . t'Amsterdam, By Cornelis Lodewijcksz. vander Plassen . . . 1615. 4° sig.A-F^{4}
11754.bbb.59.
Anonymous. With 'De clucht van Meyster Berendt' which is probably not by Coster.

C225 COSTERUS, Abraham
Vreemde ende onghehoorde TYDINGHE: Comende uyt Roomsch-Babel. Vanden Esel aen den VVijnstock ghebonden: ende het tarwen Coecxken/boven alle Bergen verheven. Voortgebracht Door Pater Maximiliaen, Iesu-wijt tot Antwerpen. Ende ter proeve ghestelt aen den Toetsteen der Waerheydt. Door Abrahamum Costerum . . . IN 'SGRAVEN-HAGE. By Aert Meuris . . . 1620. 4° pp.31
T.2250(23).
With the letter of Maximiliaen van Habbeke.

C226 COSTERUS, Franciscus
[Het cabinet der ghebeden.] LE CABINET DE PRIERES ET ORAISONS PAR P. FRANCOYS COSTERE . . . EN ANVERS Chez Ioachim Trognese. M.DCXV. [etc.] 12° pp.489; illus.
1018.c.36.
With the engraved Jesuit device on the titlepage and woodcuts in the text.

C227 COSTERUS, Franciscus
[De universa historia Dominicae Passionis meditationes.] IHS. MEDITATIONS of the whole Historie of the Passion of CHRIST. Written by Franciscus Costerus . . . Translated . . . into English by R. W. Esquire . . . Printed at Doway. 1616. 12° pp.629
C.26.k.19.
Translated by Laurence Worthington, possibly begun by Richard Worthington. The imprint is false; printed secretly in England.

C228 COSTERUS, Franciscus
Libellus Sodalitatis: HOC EST, Christianorum Institutionum Libri quinque, In gratiam Sodalitatis B. Virginis Mariæ: Auctore R.P. FRANCISCO COSTERO. ANTVERPIÆ, EX OFFICINA PLANTINIANA, Apud Ioannem Moretum. M.D.CI. 16° pp.470; illus.
3558.a.26.

C229 COSTERUS, Franciscus

[Libellus sodalitatis.] Het Boecsken Der Broederschap; Dat is; Vijf Boecken der Christelijcker leeringhen/Voor de Broederschap der H. Maghet Maria: Eerst int Latijn gheschreuen deur . . . FRANCISCVS COSTERVS . . . ende nv ouer-gheset in onse Neder-duytsche taele/deur M. Godeuaert vanden Berge . . . T'ANTVVERPEN, Inde Plantijnsche Druckerije/By Jan Moerentorf. M.DC.IIII. [etc.] (col.) T'ANTVVERPEN, Inde Plantijnsche Druckerije/By Ian Moerentorf. M.DC.IV. 8° pp.488; illus.
1578/1248.

The titlepage woodcut shows the adoration of the Virgin Mary.

C230 COTON, Pierre

INTERIEVRE OCCVPATION D'VNE AME DEVOTE. Par le R.P. PIERRE COTON . . . A DOVAY, De l'Imprimerie de BALTAZAR BELLERE . . . 1609. [etc.] 12° pp.217; illus.
C.183.d.10.

The illustrations consist of small devotional engravings.

C231 COTON, Pierre

[Intérieure occupation d'une âme dévote.] THE INTERIOVR OCCVPATION OF THE SOVLE . . . Composed in French . . . by . . . Pater Cotton . . . and translated into English by C.A. . . . Whereunto Is prefixed a Preface by the Translator . . . Printed at Doway. 1618. 12° sig.⋆,ĵ,ĵ§,A-K[12]
C.53.gg.6.

The imprint is false; printed secretly in England.

C232 COTON, Pierre

[Lettre declaratoire de la doctrine des Peres Jesuites.] (tp.1) BRIEF, Dienende tot verclaringe vande leere der Vaderen Jesuijten/ghelijckformich den besluyten van t'Concilium van Constans: Ghestelt AENDE CONINGINNE, MOEDER des Conincx, Regente in Vranckrijck. DOOR Pater P Cotton . . . Metten ANTI-COTTON DAER TEGHEN GHESTELT.
(tp.2=p.11) ANTI-COTON Dat is TEGEN-COTTON . . . IN S'GRAVEN-HAGHE. By Hillebrant Iacobsz . . . 1610. 4° pp.54
T.2421(23,24).

The preface to the 'Anti-Coton' signed: P.D.C., i.e. César de Plaix, though sometimes attributed to Pierre du Moulin the Elder.

C233 COTOVICUS, Joannes

ITINERARIVM HIEROSOLYMITANVM ET SYRIACVM, IN QVO VARIARVM GENTIVM MORES ET INSTITVTA: Insularum, Regionum, Vrbium situs, vnà ex prisci recentiorisq́ȝ sæculi vsu; vnà cum Euentis, quæ Auctori . . . acciderunt . . . recensentur. Accessit Synopsis Reipublicæ Venetę. AVCTORE IOANNE COTOVICO . . . ANTVERPIÆ, Apud Hieronymum Verdussium. M.DC.XIX. 4° pp.518: plates; illus., charts, maps
983.a.15.

Presumably the first issue, with the printer's device on the titlepage, several engravings only loosely inserted, some rather careless printing and a blank space on p.515. The titlepage, sig.†1, has 'Elenchus' on the verso. The charts belonging to the final chapter have been bound in at the beginning.

C234 COTOVICUS, Joannes

ITINERARIVM HIEROSOLYMITANVM ET SYRIACVM, IN QVO VARIARVM GENTIVM MORES ET INSTITVTA; . . . AVCTORE IOANNE COTOVICO . . . ANTVERPIÆ, Apud Hieronymum Verdussium . . . M.DC.XIX. 4° pp.518: plates; illus., charts, maps
149.c.7.

Probably the second issue, with a copy of the illustration from p.285 on the titlepage in place of the device. The titlepage, signed ā1, has a laudatory poem by Gerardus Sandelin on the verso. sig.ā2–4 followed by sig. ē1–4; followed by an unsigned leaf with a blank recto, bearing the 'Elenchus' on its verso, and by sig.†2 etc. The two small engravings on p.282 are as badly aligned as in the preceding. An illustration has been printed into the space on p.515. The illustration opposite fol.227 has been imposed twice. Author's presentation copy, dated 1621. Another inscription: Stukely 1730.

C235 COTOVICUS, Joannes
(tp.1) ITINERARIVM HIEROSOLYMITANVM ET SYRIACVM; IN QVO VARIARVM GENTIVM MORES ET INSTITVTA; . . . Accessit Synopsis Reipublicæ Venetę . . . AVCTORE IOANNE COTOVICO . . . ANTVERPIÆ, Apud Hieronymum Verdussium . . . M.DC.XIX.
(tp.2=sig.†1) ITINERARIVM HIEROSOLYMITANVM ET SYRIACVM, IN QVO VARIARVM GENTIVM MORES ET INSTITVTA: . . . Accessit Synopsis Reipublicæ Venetę AVCTORE IOANNE COTOVICO . . . ANTVERPIÆ, Apud Hieronymum Verdussium. M.DC.XIX.
4° pp.518: plates; illus., charts, maps
G.6781.
Probably the third issue. tp.1 is that of the preceding, tp.2, which follows sigg. ā and ē, has the text of the presumed first issue, with a copy of the illustration of p.149 in place of the device and with the 'Elenchus' on the verso. It is followed by sig.†1 bearing the text of †2 of the other issues, with †3 following immediately after. The engravings on pp.227, 282 are printed correctly. Ownership inscription: Admodum R^do viro Dnō D. Wilgero à Moerendal . . . Traiectensis Decano Joēs Cotovicus D.D. The dedication must precede 30 June 1619, date of Van Moerendal's death.

C236 COTOVICUS, Joannes
[Itinerarium Hierosolymitanum.] DE LOFFLYCKE REYSE VAN IERVSALEM ENDE SYRIEN . . . in het Latijn beschreuen by H^r. IAN VAN COTVVYCK . . . Ende nu vertaelt by M. ADRIAEN van MEERBEECK . . . T'ANTVVERPEN By Hieronymus Verdussen . . . 1620. 4° pp.575; illus., maps
566.e.5.
Some of the plates cropped.

C237 COTOVICVS, Joannes
[Itinerarium Hierosolymitanum.] SYNOPSIS REIPVBLICAE VENETAE. fol.
L.R.270.a.50.
Extracted from, or a separate issue of the charts contained in, the 'Itinerarium Hierosolymitanum' of Joannes Cotovicus, here mounted to form one continuous sheet. This material based on Gaspare Contarini's 'De magistratibus, & republica Venetorum'.

COTTON, Pierre. *See* COTON, Pierre

COTWYCK, Jan van. *See* COTOVICUS, Joannes

COUNTERPOYSON. 1608. *See* AINSWORTH, Henry

COURANT. *See* also CORANTE; CORRANT; COURANTE

C238 COURANT
Courant Newes out of Italy, Germany, Bohemia, Poland, &c. (col.) Printed at Amsterdam, By GEORGE VESELER. The 25 of May. fol. a single sheet
Harl.Ms.389(79).
Begin: From Breslaw the 28. of April. 1621. *STC* no.18507.7 assigns the sale of this item to Petrus Keerius.

C239 COURANT
Courant Newes out of Italy, Germany, Bohemia, Poland, &c. (col.) Printed at Amsterdam, By GEORGE VESELER. The 5. of IULY. fol. a single sheet
C.55.l.2(7).
Begin: From Roome the 5. of Iunij, 1621. *STC* no.18507.10 assigns the sale of this item to Petrus Keerius.

C240 COURANT
Courant Newes out of Italy, Germany, Bohemia, Poland, &c. (col.) Printed at Amsterdam, By GEORGE VESELER. The 9. of IULY. fol. a single sheet
C.55.l.2(8).
Begin: From Roome the 12. of Iunij, 1621. *STC* no.18507.11 assigns the sale of this item to Petrus Keerius.

C241 COURANT
Courant Newes out of Italy, Germany, Bohemia, Poland, &c. (col.) Printed at Amsterdam, By GEORGE VESELER. The 15. of IULY. fol. a single sheet
C.55.l.2(10).
Begin: From Venize the 25. of Iune, 1621. *STC* no.18507.12 assigns the sale of this item to Petrus Keerius.

C242 COURANT
Courant out of Italy and Germany, &c. (col.) AT AMSTERDAM Printed by George Veseler. The 6. of Septembre. 1621. fol. a single sheet
C.55.l.2(16).
Begin: From Venise, the 10. of August. *STC* no.18507.14 assigns the sale of this item to Petrus Keerius.

C243 COURANT
The Courant out of Italy and Germany, &c. (col.) AT AMSTERDAM Printed by George Veseler. The 12. of Septembre. 1621. fol. a single sheet
C.55.l.2(17).
Begin: From Rome, the 7. August. We have from Palerma [*sic*]/that there was at [etc.] *End:* should have beseidge the city of Riga/in Lyfland. *STC* no.18507.15 assigns the sale of this item to Petrus Keerius.

C244 COURANT
The Courant out of Italy and Germany, &c. (col.) AT AMSTERDAM Printed by George Veseler. The 12. of Septembre. 1621. fol. a single sheet
C.55.l.2(18).
Begin: From Roome, the 7 August, 1621. Vvehere [*sic*] from Palermo that there is in [etc.] *End:* The Prince hath also given good order for the riviers. *STC* no.18507.16 assigns the sale of this item to Petrus Keerius.

C245 COURANT
The Courant out of Italy and Germany, &c. (col.) AT AMSTERDAM Printed by George Veseler. The 18 of Septembre. 1621. fol. a single sheet
C.55.l.2(19).
Begin: From Roome the 14. of August, 1621. *STC* no.18507.17 assigns the sale of this item to Petrus Keerius.

C246 COURANT
Courant out of Italy and Germany, &c. (col.) Imprinted at Amsterdam by George Veseler, A^{o}.1621. The 31 of March. And are to be soulde by Petrus Keerius, [etc.] fol. a single sheet
C.55.l.2(5).
Begin: From Venize the 8. of Martij, 1621.

C247 COURANT
Courant out of Italy, Germany, &c. (col.) Imprinted at Amsterdam by George Veseler, A°, 1621. The 9 of April. And are to be soulde by Petrus Keerius, [etc.] fol. a single sheet
C.55.l.2(6).
Begin: From Roome the 6. of March, 1621.

C248 COURANTE
Courante der Stadt LEYDEN Also vande Publicatie ende verkiesinghe des Raets aldaer gheschiet. Met het gheen dat dese daghen aldaer ghepasseert is. Ghedruckt voor N. Gel-kerck. 4° 2 unsigned leaves; illus.
1314.e.24(3).
With the text of the official proclamation dated 23 October 1618 and a list of the new officers and council members. The titlepage woodcut shows the arms of Prince Maurice. Published at Leiden in 1618.

C249 COURANTE
COVRANTE, Or, Newes from Italy and Germany. (col.) Translated out of the Dutch Copie, and Printed at Amsterdam the 9. of Aprill, 1621. fol. a single sheet
Harl.Ms.389(56).
Begin: From Rome the 6. of March 1621. *STC* no.18507. 18 lists this item under the printer Broer Jansz, but also suggests that it could have been printed at London for Thomas Archer, with a false imprint.

C250 COURANTE
COVRANTE, Or, Newes from Italy and Germany, &c. (col.) Translated and taken out of the Letters come from these places aforesaid, and augmented with some newes from hence. Printed at Amsterdam this 22. of April. 1621. fol. a single sheet
Harl.Ms.389(68).
Begin: From Rome the 23. of March 1621. *STC* no.18507.19 lists this item under the printer Broer Jansz, but also suggests that it could have been printed at London for Thomas Archer, with a false imprint.

C251 COURANTE
Courante uyt Italien, Duytslandt, &c. (col.) Gedruct 't Amsterdam by Ioris VESELER . . . A°. M DC XIX. Den 25. November. fol. a single sheet
T.2423(24).
Begin: VVt Venetien, den 8 November, 1619. Cropped.

C252 COURANTE
Courante uyt Italien, Duytslandt, &c. (col.) 'tAmsterdam by IORIS VESELER, A° 1621. Den 12. Februarius. Voor Caspar van Hilten, [etc.] fol. a single sheet
T.2424(5).
Begin: VVt Roomen den 16. Ianuarij, 1621. Cropped.

COURTEN, Sir Peter; Bart. Theses philosophicae de politiarum principiis. 1617. *See* BERTIUS, Petrus

C253 COURTILZ DE SANDRAS, Gatien de

MEMOIRES DE M[R]. L.C.D.R. Contenant ce qui s'est passé de plus particulier sous le ministere du CARDINAL DE RICHELIEU, ET DU CARDINAL MAZARIN . . . DERNIERE EDITION. Revûë, corrigée, & augmentée d'une Table des Matieres . . . A LEYDE, Chez THEODORE HAAK . . . M.DC.XII. [etc.] 8° pp.456; illus.
10661.aaa.17.

Anonymous. The date is an obvious misprint for 1712.

C254 COUSIN, Jean; Chanoine

(tp.1) HISTOIRE DE TOVRNAY OV QVATRE LIVRES DES CHRONIQVES, ANNALES, OV DEMONSTRATIONS DV CHRISTIANISME DE L'EVESCHE' DE TOVRNAY. PAR M[re]. IEAN COVSIN . . . A DOVAY, De l'Imprimerie de MARC WYON . . . M.DC.XIX. [etc.] (tp.2–4) HISTOIRE DE TOVRNAY OV LE SECOND(-QVATRIE'ME) LIVRE DES CHRONIQVES . . . Par M. IEAN COVSIN . . . A DOVAY. De l'Imprimerie de MARC WYON . . . M.DC.XX. [etc.] 4° 4 pt.: pp.340; 258; 311; 371: plates; illus.
596.g.15.

The engraving on p.145 of bk.1 signed: M. bas f.

C255 COUTEREELS, Johan

QVESTIONNAIRE, CONTENANT LE FONDEMENT D'ARITHMETIque & ses Regles principales . . . Ensemble LA VRAYE METHODE DE DISCONTER . . . PAR IEAN COVTEREELS . . . A MIDDELBOVRG. PAR SYMON MOVLERT. M.DC.X. 8° sig.A–P[8]
1607/155(1).

CRAS credo hodie nihil. 1621. *See* HEINSIUS, Daniel

C256 CRASSO, Niccolò

NESCIMVS QVID VESPER SERVS VEHAT, SATYRA MENIPPÆA VINCENTII LIBERII HOLLANDI. MDCXIX. 4° pp.35
1081.m.23(2).

Pseudonymous. A satire on Lorenzo Mottirro, an opponent of Paolo Sarpi, with a prefatory letter, dated from Amsterdam, addressed to Franciscus de Ingenuis, pseudonym of Paolo Sarpi. Without imprint; possibly printed in the Netherlands, perhaps at Leiden.

C257 CRASSO, Niccolò

NESCIMVS QVID VESPER SERVS VEHAT SATYRA MENIPPAEA LIBERI VINCENTI Hollandi . . . M.DC.XX. 4° pp.46
1081.m.23(3).

Pseudonymous. Another edition of the preceding. Without imprint; possibly printed in the Netherlands, perhaps at Leiden. Ownership inscription: Andr. Melvil.

C258 CRASSO, Niccolò

NESCIMVS QVID VESPER SERVS VEHAT SATYRA MENIPPAEA LIBERI VINCENTI Hollandi . . . M.DC.XX. 4° pp.46
90.i.17.

Another issue of the preceding, with an errata list on leaf F4 which is wanting in the preceding and was probably blank.

C259 CRESPIN, Jean

(tp.1) L'ESTAT DE L'EGLISE, AVEC LE DISCOVRS DES TEMPS DEPVIS LES APOStres iusques au present. Augmenté & reueu tellement en ceste derniere edition que ce qui conçerne le siege Romain, & autres Royaumes depuis l'Eglise primitive . . . y est en brieues Annales proposé. PAR IEAN TAFFIN . . . Jtem vn traité de la religion & republiqȝ des Iuifs . . . A BERGVES SVR LE ZOOM. Par Jaques Canin . . . M.D.C.V. (tp.2) L'ESTAT DE LA RELIGION ET REPVBLIQVE DV PEVPLE IVDAIQVE, Depuis le retour de l'exil de Babylone iusques au dernier saccagement de Jerusalem. PAR PAVL

EBER . . . EN BERGVES SVR LE ZOOM, Par Iaques Canin . . . 1604. 4° 2 pt.: pp.779; 150
1125.d.22; 1492.p.4.
The author of pt.1 is named in the prefaces. In the copy at 1492.p.4 the order of the parts is reversed.

C260 CROCE, Flaminio della
THEATRO MILITARE DEL CAPITANO FLAMINIO DELLA CROCE . . . La Seconda volta dato all' Impressione con l'aggiunta di molte figure, molti Capitoli nuoui, & gli altri tutti ampliati . . . IN ANVERSA, Appresso HENRICO AERTSSIO. M.DC.XVII. [etc.] (col.) ANTVERPIÆ, Ex Typographiâ Henrici Aertsij. M.DC.XVII. 4° pp.343; illus.
C.65.gg.15; C.175.dd.29.
The copy at C.175.dd.29 bound in vellum with the initials W.L., i.e. Willem Lodewijk van Nassau (?) and the arms of the house of Nassau Dillenburg on the covers. Presentation copy signed: Henricus Nassoviorum. The engravings are unsigned.

C261 CROCE, Giovanni
(tp.1) DI GIOVANNI CROCE . . . MADRIGALI A SEI VOCI, Nouamente Ristampati. CANTO, IN ANVERSA Appresso Petro Phalesio . . . M.D.CXVIII.
(tp.2) DI GIOVANNI CROCE . . . MADRIGALI A SEI VOCI . . . ALTO. IN ANVERSA Appresso Petro Phalesio . . . M.D.CXVIII.
(tp.3) DI GIOVANNI CROCE . . . MADRIGALI A SEI VOCI . . . TENORE. IN ANVERSA Appresso Petro Phalesio . . . M.D.CXVIII.
(tp.4) DI GIOVANNI CROCE . . . MADRIGALI A SEI VOCI . . . BASSO. IN ANVERSA Appresso Petro Phalesio . . . M.D.CXVIII.
(tp.5) DI GIOVANNI CROCE . . . MADRIGALI A SEI VOCI . . . QVINTO. IN ANVERSA Appresso Petro Phalesio . . . M.D.CXVIII.
(tp.6) DI GIOVANNI CROCE . . . MADRIGALI A SEI VOCI . . . SESTO. IN ANVERSA Appresso Petro Phalesio . . . M.D.CXVIII. obl.4° 6 pt.: pp.21; 21; 21; 21; 21; 21
Music A.200.
The titlepage of the 'Tenore' part slightly mutilated. With the bookplate of Thomas Bever LLD, 'Coll: Omn.[9] Anim.[9] Socius' 1777.

C262 CROCHE, A.
S'GHEESTS LVST-HOF. Inhoudende veel schoone Spreucken/notabele Sententien ende Ghedichten . . . Wt verscheyde plaetsen by een vergadert . . . Per A. CROCHE . . . TOT VTRECHT. By Herman van Borculo . . . 1603. 8° ff.118
11565.a.14.

C263 CULENS, Henricus
IVBILEI VETERIS HEBRÆORVM ET NOVI CHRISTIANORVM COLLATIO . . . Auctore HENRICO CVLENS . . . ANTVERPIÆ, EX OFFICINA PLANTINIANA, Apud Balthasarem & Ioannem Moretos. M.DC.XVII. 8° pp.63
4376.aa.33(2).

CUMINGIUS, Thomas. Theses theologicæ. 1604. *See* THYSIUS, Antonius; the Elder.

C264 CUNAEUS, Petrus
PETRI CVNÆI ANIMADVERSIONVM LIBER IN NONNI DIONYSIACA . . . DANIELIS HEINSII DISSERTATIO De Nonni Dionysiacis, & ejusdem Paraphrasi. IOSEPHI SCALIGERI CONIECTANEA. Ad editionem Plantini & Wecheli. LVGDVNI BATAVORVM, Ex officina Ludovici Elzeviri. M.D.CX. 8° pp.216
832.d.29.
For an issue added to an edition of the text *see* NONNUS of Panoplis, Δυονυσιακα. 1610.

C265 CUNAEUS, Petrus

EXERCITATIONVM ORATORIARVM quæ autoritate publica in Academia Leydensi institutæ sunt, INAVGUVRATIO . . . A PETRO CVNÆO . . . 10. Novembris. 1620. LVGDVNI BATAVORVM, Ex Officinâ ISAACI ELSEVIRI . . . M.D.CXXI. 4° pp.30
835.f.17(4).

C266 CUNAEUS, Petrus

(tp.1) SARDI VENALES. SATYRA MENIPPEA Jn huius seculi homines plerosque ineptè eruditos. PETRVS CVNÆVS SCRIPSIT . . . addita est ex eiusdem interpretatione D. IVLIANI IMPERATORIS SATYRA IN PRINCIPES ROMANOS. EX OFFICINA PLANTINIANA RAPHELENGII, M.D.CXII.
(tp.2) D. IVLIANI IMPERATORIS CÆSARES, siue SATYRA IN ROMANOS IMPERATORES: interprete PETRO CVNÆO . . . EX OFFICINA PLANTINIANA RAPHELENGII, M.D.CXII. 12° 2 pt.: pp.144; 154; illus.
1079.d.6.

Pt.2 in Latin and Greek. Published at Leiden. With a woodcut portrait of Julian reproduced from a coin.

CUPIDO'S lusthof. 1613. *See* BREUGHEL, Gerrit Hendricksz van

C267 CUPUS, Petrus

Aenwysinghe VANDE ONBEHOORLICKE WYSE VAN DOEN, DIE M. ADRIANVS SMOVTIVS Ghepleecht heeft in syn Boeck . . . ghenaemt . . . EENDRACHT &c. . . . Door P. CVPVM . . . TOT ROTTERDAM, By Matthijs Bastiaensz . . M.D.C.X. 4° pp.82
T.2240(9).

The preface signed: C.S.a G., i.e. Nicolaas Grevinchoven.

C268 CUPUS, Petrus

PETRI CUPI ONDERSOECK over D'onschult ende Afwijsinghe ADRIANI SMOVTII. Waer in bewesen wordt/dat D. Smoutius sick niet alleen . . . niet onschuldicht/maer oock P. Cupo nieuwe oorsaeck heeft gegeven/om hem meer ende meer sijne onbehoorlijcke wijse van doen . . . aen te wijsen . . . TER GOVDE, By Jasper Tournay . . . 1610. 4° pp.53[63]
T.2421(22).

C269 CURIANDER, Abel

VITÆ, OPERVMQVE IOH. DRVSII EDITORVM ET NONDVM EDITORVM, DELINEATIO, ET TITVLI. PER ABELVM CVRIANDRVM. FRANEKERÆ, Excudebat FREDERICUS HEYNSIUS . . . 1616. 4° pp.185–192, 9–52
1017.f.10(3).

With 'Varia variorum doctorum virorum epicedia in obitum & laudem Domini Drusii'. In this issue the gathering paginated 185–192 bears the signature Aa and the running title 'Iohannis Drusii Vita et Opera' divided over every two facing pages after 'Drusii', while sig.B-F, paginated 9–52, have it as 'Vita et Opera Iohannis Drusii'.

C270 CURIANDER, Abel

VITÆ, OPERVMQVE IOH. DRVSII . . . DELINEATIO . . . PER ABELVM CVRIANDRVM. FRANEKERÆ, Excudebat FREDERICUS HEYNSIUS . . . 1616. 4° pp.52.
489.a.6(1).

Another issue of part of the preceding, with sig.A paginated 1–8 and its running title transposed.

C271 CURTIUS RUFUS, Quintus

QVINTI CVRTII RVFI DE REBVS GESTIS ALEXANDRI MAGNI LIBRI QVI EXSTANT. EX OFFICINA PLANTINIANA RAPHELENGII. M.D.CXIII. 32° pp.312
C.20.f.34.

Published at Leiden. From the travelling library of Sir Julius Caesar.

C272 CUYCKIUS, Henricus; Bishop

HENRICI CVYCKII . . . AD MAVRITIVM COMITEM NASSAVIVM PARÆNETICA EPISTOLA. LOVANII, APVD IOANNEM MASIVM, M.D.CI. 8° sig.a–c8
3925.b.2.

C273 CYRIL; Saint, Patriarch of Alexandria

[Two or more works.] CYRILLI ARCHIEPISCOPI ALEXANDRINI Adversus Anthropomorphitas, Liber unus Græcè & Latinè. Ejusdem, DE INCARNATIONE VNIGENITI, Et, QVOD VNVS SIT CHRISTVS AC DOMINVS secundum Scripturas, ad Hermiam Dialogi duo . . . Interprete BONAVENTVRA VULCANIO, Cum NOTIS eiusdem, Quibus Epistolæ aliquot Isidori Pelusiotæ & Ioannis Zonaræ, idem . . . argumentum tractantes . . . sunt inserta. LVGDVNI BATAVORVM, Typographia Ioannis Patii . . . M.DC.V. 4° pp.205
860.l.2.

With manuscript notes.

C274 CYRIL; Saint, Patriarch of Alexandria

[Commentaria in Pentateuchum.] SANCTI PATRIS NOSTRI CYRILLI ΓΛΑΦΥΡΑ ΕΙΣ ΠΕVΤΑΤΕΥΧΟV. SCITA & elegantia COMMENTARIA IN QVINQVE PRIORES MOYSIS LIBROS . . . Nunc primum Græcè & Latinè . . . edita studio R. P. ANDREÆ SCHOTTI . . . ANTVERPIÆ Apud Heredes MARTINI NVTII, ET IOANNEM MEVRSIVM . . . M.DC.XVIII. fol. pp.360
689.i.5(1).

C275 CYRIL; Saint, Patriarch of Alexandria

[Sermones Paschales.] SANCTI PATRIS NOSTRI CYRILLI . . . ΕΟΡΤΑΣΤΙΚΟΙ ΛΟΓΟΙ Λ'. SERMONES PASCHALES TRIGINTA: Ex interpretatione ANTONII SALMATIÆ . . . GRÆCE nunc primum & LATINE typis editi . . . ANTVERPIÆ Apud Heredes MARTINI NVTII, ET IOANNEM MEVRSIVM . . . M.DC.XVIII. [etc.] fol. pp.304
689.i.5(2).

D

D. RVARDI TAPPART . . . apotheosis. 1615. *See* GELDORPIUS, Henricus

D1 DAMIUS, Mathias

ANTIDOTVM OFTE Hertsterckinghe tegens het schadelijck recept van Iohannes Wtenboogaert, Moderatie ghenaemt. DOOR GALENVM PHILALETHIVM. t'AMSTERDAM, By Marten Jansz Brandt . . . 1616. 4° pp.47
T.2246(22).

With 'Advys Hoemen die schadelijcke Oneenigheyt ende Scheuringen der Kercken in Hollandt sal remedieren. Ghegheven by eenen IRENIO ENBVLO'. The main part by Mathias Damius under the pseudonym Galenus Philalethius. The second part by Jacobus Trigland? under the pseudonym of Irenius Enbulus.

D2 DAMIUS, Mathias

ANTIPROCVRATIE, Ofte REPLIICKE, Op de verdediginge vande Resolutie. Eerste deel, door LVCIVM VERVM. TOT AMSTERDAM, Voor Louris Hemling . . . 1617. 4° pp.74
T.2247(10).

Pseudonymous. Directed against Jan Wtenbogaert.

D3 DAMIUS, Mathias

ANTIPROCVRATIE, Ofte REPLIICKE, Op de verdediginge vande Resolutie . . . Door LVCIVM VERVM. TOT AMSTERDAM, Voor M.I.B. . . . 1617. 4° pp.74
T.2247(50).

Pseudonymous. Another issue of the preceding, published by Marten Jansz Brandt.

D4 DAMIUS, Mathias

Nootwendigh TEGEN-VERTOOGH, VVaer in D'onnooselheyt vanden Vromen ouden KERCKEN-RAEDT, Tegens de . . . lasteringhen van den Haerlemschen Vertooger op haer nytgeworpen [*sic*] verdedicht wert . . . Door D.M.D.I.D.F.P.H.P. 'TAMSTELREDAM, By Jan Evertsz van Heerden . . . 1617. 4° pp.74

T.2247(43).

Anonymous. Directed against Dionysius Spranckhuisen's 'Justificatie' and Isaac Junius's 'Nootwendich vertooch'. In this copy sig. F has been bound in twice.

D5 DAMMAN, Sebastiaan

MISPRYSINGHE ALLER NIEVVICHEDEN, DIE TEGHENS DE OVDE LEERE ENde de ordre der Kercken . . . van sommighe vvorden in-ghevoert. Dat is/Verantwoordinghe Sebastianus [*sic*] Damman/teghens die ghene/welcke hem 'tonrecht bedencken ende beschuldighen/als oft hy met die eens waer/welcke de huydendaechsche moeyten in Hollandt aenrechten . . . Nae de Copye, Ghedruckt tot Zutphen by Andries Jansz. Ende nu tot Amsterdam by Jan Evertsz. Cloppenburch . . . 1611. 4° sig.$[A]^2B^4D^3$

T.2241(28).

Wanting leaf D4; blank?

D6 DAMMAN, Sebastiaan

Van de Volhardinghe der Heylighen/Tegens M. Petri Bertij twee Vraech-stucken/ Van den Afval der Heylighen. Beschreven ende . . . uytghegheven door Sebastianum Damman . . . Ghedruct tot Enchuysen, By Jacob Lenaertsz Meyn . . . 1615. 4° pp.200

T.2245(5).

D7 DAMMAN, Sebastiaan

Vande Eenicheyt Die de Remonstranten houden met De Gereformeerde Kercken . . . aengaende het stuck der Leere begrepen in de vijf articulen. Beschreven . . . door SEBASTIANUM DAMMAN . . . TOT ZUTPHEN, By Andries Janssen van Aelst . . . 1616. 4° pp.122

T.2246(6).

DAMMIUS, Theodorus. Theses theologicae de Deo. 1613. *See* LINDEN, Henricus Antonides van der

D8 DANCKAERT, Jan

BESCHRYVINGE Van Moscovien ofte Ruslant . . . Beschreven door I. DANCKAERT. TOT AMSTERDAM, By Broer Iansz . . . 1615. 4° pp.75

1427.f.18.

The title is enclosed by a woodcut border used earlier by the Officina Reusneriana at Rostock and other German printers, showing allegorical figures of Faith, Hope and Charity and the monogram M within a circle.

D9 DANCKAERTS, Sebastiaen

HISTORISCH Ende Grondich Verhael/Vanden Standt des Christendoms int quartier van Amboina . . . ghestelt door Sebastiaen Danckaerts . . . IN 'SGRAVEN-HAGHE, By Aert Meuris . . . 1621. [etc.] 4° pp.30

4765.a.34.

The dedication signed: H. ende I. Danckaerts, brothers of Sebastiaen.

D10 DANEAU, Lambert

Antvvoort LAMBERTI DANEI . . . op drie voorghestelde Vragen/nopende het Ampt der Overheydt inde regeeringhe der Kercken . . . Mitsgaders/Een cort ende claer Bewijs/dat de Verkiesinghe/ende Afsettinghe der Dienaren des Goddelicken

Woorts/der Ouderlingen/ende Diaconen niet en staet by de Borgherlicke Magistraet/maer by de kercke. item/Sekere Artijckelen/van het Seggen/ende de Macht der Overheyt inde bedieninghe der Kercke Christi in Hollandt . . . Door Arnoldum Cornelij . . . TOT DELF, Ghedruckt by Ian Andriesz. . . . 1613. 4° pp.16
T.2243(17).
The editor's dedication signed: Sebastianus Damman.

D11 DANEAU, Lambert
POLITICORVM APHORISMORVM SILVA, Ex optimis quibusque tum Græcis, tum Latinis scriptoribus . . . collecta, PER LAMBERTVM DANAEVM . . . EX OFFICINA PLANTINIANA RAPHELENGII, M.D.CXII. 32° pp.482
C.20.f.41.
Published at Leiden. From the travelling library of Sir Julius Caesar.

D12 DANEAU, Lambert
POLITICORVM APHORISMORVM SILVA, Ex optimis . . . scriptoribus . . . collecta, PER LAMBERTVM DANAEVM . . . LVGDVNI BATAVORVM, Apud IOANNEM MAIRE. M.D.C.XX. 32° pp.645[467]
1094.a.2.
The pagination on pp.43, 215, 400, 466, 467 is misprinted 34, 213, 440, 644, 645.

D13 DANS, Adolphus van
(tp.1) ELIZA. Sive de Laudibus . . . Principis ELIZABETHÆ, Angliæ, Franciæ, & Hiberniæ Reginæ. Auctore ADOLPHO VAN DANS. LVGD. BATAV. Ex Officina Iacobi Marci, M DCXIX.
(tp.2=sig.D5) VITA . . . Principis ELIZABETHÆ Anglorum Reginæ. AVCTORE Adolpho van Dans. LVGDVNI BATAV. Apud Bartolomeum vander Bild, [etc.] (col.) LVGDVN. BATAV. Excudebat Georgius Abrahami a Marsce . . . 1619. 8° pp.54; sig.D5–G4
1213.g.15(2,3).
The signatures are continuous. Pt.1 dedicated to Sir Dudley Carleton, pt.2 to Jacob van Dyck, both dedications signed: Bartholomaeus van Bilt. With 'Hymnus ad Divam Elizabetham', dedicated to John Davenant by A. van Dans.

D14 DANS, Adolphus van
(tp.1) ELIZA. Sive de Laudibus . . . ELIZABETHÆ . . . Reginæ. Auctore ADOLPHO VAN DANS. LVGD. BATAV. Apud Bartholomæum vander Bild [etc.]
(tp.2=sig.D5) VITA . . . ELIZABETHÆ . . . Reginæ. AVCTORE Adolpho van Dans. LVGDVNI BATAV. Apud Bartolomeum vander Bild, [etc.] (col.) LVGDVN. BATAV. Excudebat Georgius Abrahami a Marsce . . . 1619. 8° pp.54; sig.D5–G4
G.1508.
Another issue of the preceding, with Bartholomaeus vander Bild's imprint on the titlepage of pt.1 and with the misprint 'Ad Posteritaten' on p.51 corrected. Leaves F7,8 are misbound to follow the first dedication, preceding sig.A.

D15 DANTZIG, Hans van
Een Tafereelken/ofte Een Aenwijsingh[e] van eenighe Schriften der Belofte Gods/de welcke een Vader by een ghevoeght heeft . . . daer mede dat hy zijne kinderen vereert . . . Noch is hier achter by ghevoeght een Cort Bewijs/welcke dat rechte Wijf/met oock de rechte Slanghe/ende haer beyder zaedt is . . . Door H.V.D.. . . . Voor Passchier van Westbusch [*sic*] . . . tot Haerlem . . . 1609. 8° pp.[112]
1658/2779.
The anonymous author's name is sometimes spelled: Hans van Dantzich. The first three leaves and the last leaf are mutilated, with loss of pagination.

D16 DARES Phrygius

[Supposititious Works.] DARETIS PHRYGII . . . DE BELLO TROIANO LIBRI SEX A CORNELIO NEPOTE Latino carmine donati. ANTVERPIAE APVD IOACH. TROGNÆSIVM. M D CIIX [etc.] 8° pp.256

802.d.14.

Ownership inscriptions: 'Praesentia opuscula Henrico Hennino famulantur ab anno 1676'; 'Iscanius'.

DAT s'Pals-graven dwaesheydt niet en is te verschoonen. 1621. *See* LIEF-HEBBER

D17 DAVID, Jan; Jesuit

(tp.1) CHRISTELIICKEN WAERSEGGHER . . . Met een ROLLE DER DEVGTSAEMHEYT daer op dienende. Ende een Schildt-Wacht teghen de valsche Waersegghers . . . DEVR . . . P. IOANNES DAVID . . . T'ANTWERPEN Inde Plantijnsche Druckerije, BY IAN MOERENTORF. M.D.CIII.

(½ title=p.351) ROLLE DER DEVGDSAEMHEYDT: Tot naer-volginghe Christi op den Christelijcken Waerseggher dienende.

(tp.2=p.i) SCHILD-WACHT TOT SEKER VVAERSCHOVVINGHE Teghen de valsche Waersegghers . . . Deur P. IOANNES DAVID . . . T'ANTVVERPEN, Inde Plantijnsche Druckerije/By Jan Moerentorf. M.D.CII. (col.) T'ANTVVERPEN, Inde Plantijnsche Druckerije/By Jan Moerentorf. M.D.CII. 4° 2 pt.: pp.372: pl.100[102]; pp.xxvij

3560.bb.12.

The engraved titlepage is an adaptation of that seen in the Latin version, 'Veridicus Christianus'. Pl.1 signed: Ioan Galle excudit Antuerpie: but Ioannes Galle was only born in 1600 and it, like the other plates, must be the work of his father Theodoor Galle. The engraving on the half-title, showing Christ among the painters, was formerly attributed to one of the Wierix brothers. The additional plate at the end, 'Soeckt ende sult vinden' in a flower border, allows a volvelle bearing the monogram of the Virgin Mary to be pointed at various proverbs. This plate is here mounted, but is part of sig.Aa. Imperfect; wanting sig.E4 of pt.2, bearing the device.

D18 DAVID, Jan; Jesuit

[Christelijcken waerseggher.] (tp.) VERIDICVS CHRISTIANVS: Auctore P. IOANNE DAVID . . . ANTVERPIÆ Ex officina Plantiniana, M.DCI.

(½ title 1=p.351) ORBITA PROBITATIS AD CHRISTI IMITATIONEM VERIDICO CHRISTIANO SVBSERVIENS.

(½ title 2, neither paginated nor signed) Concentus Musicus VERSIBVS VERIDICI CHRISTIANI coaptatus. (col.) ANTVERPIÆ, EX OFFICINA PLANTINIANA, APVD IOANNEM MORETVM, M.DCI. 4° pp.374: pl.100 [102]; 4 unsigned leaves music

C.27.k.9.

The translation was published before the original version. The plates are by Theodoor Galle, the one on the 'Orbita' half-title again the pseudo-Wierix. The additional plate is entitled 'Quaerite et invenietis' and its volvelle is fastened with labels bearing the monograms of Christ and the Virgin Mary. All the plates except the 'Orbita' plate have ornamental borders.

D19 DAVID, Jan; Jesuit

[Christelijcken waerseggher.] VERIDICVS CHRISTIANVS: Auctore P. IOANNE DAVID . . . EDITIO ALTERA, AVCTIOR. ANTVERPIÆ Ex officina Plantiniana, M. DCVI. (col.) ANTVERPIÆ, EX OFFICINA PLANTINIANA, APVD IOANNEM MORETVM, M.DC.VI. 4° pp.374: pl.100 [101]

849.l.6.

The plates are by Theodoor Galle, with the 'Wierix' plate of Christ among the painters preceding the 'Orbita probitatis' part. Captions on the plates are in Latin, Dutch and French. The titlepage is engraved.

D20 DAVID, Jan; Jesuit
[Christelijcken waerseggher.] SCHILD-WACHT TOT SEKER VVAERSCHOVVINGHE Teghen de valsche Waerseggher/Toooueraers . . . Deur . . . P. IOANNES DAVID . . . T'ANTVVERPEN, Inde Plantijnsche Druckerije/By Jan Moerentorf. M.D.C.II. (col.) T'ANTVVERPEN, Inde Plantijnsche Druckerije/By Jan Moerentorf. M.D.CII. 4° pp.xxxvij
4373.g.17.
A separate issue, without additional leaves beyond E4, of pt.2 of 'Christelijcken waerseggher' of the 1602 edition, later reissued in 1603, but according to the preface always intended to accompany that work.

D21 DAVID, Jan; Jesuit
DOMPE-TROMPE OP HET NIEVW REGISTER VAN S'HERTOGENBOSCH, VAN OSTENDE, ENDE VAN VRIES-LANDT GESTELT, ETC. Tot verquicken van de svvaermoedige gheesten: onse Princen ter eeren, ende Gode tot danckbaerheyt . . . Tot Louende-ghem. By Roose-mondt Goe-maere/inden Voghelen-sanck . . . M.D.CVJ. [etc.] 4° sig.A–E^4; illus.
106.d.8.
Anonymous and with a fictitious imprint. A verse on the titlepage and both the verse and prose prefaces signed: W. B. The text signed: Fecit, V. Qui sssss. Psal.46.

D22 DAVID, Jan; Jesuit
DOMP-HOOREN DER HOLLANSCHER FACKEL, Tot blusschinghe des Brandt briefs ende Missiue die onlancks met de volle Mane vut S'Grauen haghe gheschoten vvierden . . . Tot Landt-vit/By Colophon van Bacharach . . . Int Jaer XVJ. hondert/twee. 4° sig.A-C^4D^2; illus.
1508/61.
In verse. Anonymous and with a fictitious imprint. Directed against a letter from the States of Holland of 7 June 1602 inviting the Southern Netherlands to rebel. The titlepage woodcut shows a drummer and a trumpeter with a devil. The *Bibliotheca Belgica* no.D137 suggests Rutgeert Velpius at Brussels as printer, a modern manuscript note suggests Jan Maes at Louvain.

D23 DAVID, Jan; Jesuit
DVODECIM SPECVLA DEVM ALIQVANDO VIDERE DESIDERANTI concinnata. Auctore P. IOANNE DAVID . . . ANTVERPIÆ, EX OFFICINA PLANTINIANA, Apud Ioannem Moretum. M.DC.X. (col.) ANTVERPIÆ, EX OFFICINA PLANTINIANA, APVD IOANNEM MORETVM. M.DC.X. 8° pp.184; illus.
700.e.34.
The titlepage is engraved, signed: Theodor. Galle fecit. The illustrations are also engravings.

D24 DAVID, Jan; Jesuit
HISTORIE VAN DE KETTERSCHE KERCKE GHENAEMT DE VVYLE BRVYDT Beschreuen tot schrick ende schroom der seluer. TOT VRANOPOLI In't huys der Waerheydt . . . M.DC.XI. 8° pp.112; illus.
1578/1805.
Anonymous and with a fictitious imprint; printed by Joachim Trognaesius at Antwerp? With special reference to and quoting part of the text of 'Helschen raedt, of grouwelijcke practijcken, die de Iesuiten gebruycken'. The titlepage engraving shows Luther, Calvin and Menno Simons with their followers being led with the 'dirty bride' to hell.

D25 DAVID, Jan; Jesuit

LOT VAN VVIISHEYD ende GOED GELVCK: Op drije hondert ghemeyne Sprekvvoorden [*sic*]: in rijme gestelt, deur DONAES IDINAV . . . T'ANTVVERPEN, Inde Plantijnsche Druckerye/By Jan Moerentorf. M.DC.VI. (col.) T'HANTVVERPEN, Inde Plantijnsche Druckerije/By Jan Moerentorf, M.DC.VI. obl.16° pp.307

11556.a.23.

The pseudonym Donaes Idinau is an anagram of Ioannes Dauid.

D26 DAVID, Jan; Jesuit

OCCASIO ARREPTA, NEGLECTA. HVIVS COMMODA: ILLIVS INCOMMODA. Auctore R.P. IOANNE DAVID . . . ANTVERPIÆ, Ex officina Plantiniana, apud Ioannem Moretum. M.DC.V.

(tp.2=p.271) OCCASIO. DRAMA, P. IOANNIS DAVID . . . ANTVERPIÆ, EX OFFICINA PLANTINIANA, Apud Ioannem Moretum M.DC.V. (col.) ANTVERPIÆ, EX OFFICINA PLANTINIANA, APVD IOANNEM MORETVM. M.DC.V. 4° pp.307; illus.

12305.g.8.

With the engravings by Theodoor Galle originally published anonymously as 'Typus occasionis', 1603, for which *see* below.

D27 DAVID, Jan; Jesuit

(tp.1) PARADISVS SPONSI ET SPONSÆ: IN QVO MESSIS MYRRHÆ ET AROMATVM, ex instrumentis ac mysterijs Passionis Christi colligenda, vt ei commemoriamur. ET PANCARPIVM MARIANVM . . . Auctore P. IOANNE DAVID . . . ANTVERPIÆ, EX OFFICINA PLANTINIANA, Apud Ioannem Moretum. M.DC.VII.

(tp.2) PANCARPIVM MARIANVM . . . Auctore P. IOANNE DAVID . . . ANTVERPIÆ, EX OFFICINA PLANTINIANA, Apud Ioannem Moretum. M.DC.VII. (col.) ANTVERPIÆ, EX OFFICINA PLANTINIANA, APVD IOANNEM MORETVM. M.DC.VII. 8° 2 pt.: pp.212: pl.50; pp.213: pl.50

854.e.3,4.

The titlepages are engraved. The two unnumbered plates respectively preceding pl.1 of each part signed: Theodor. Galle fecit et excud. The engraved captions are in Latin, Dutch and French.

DAVID, Jan; Jesuit. Schild-wacht. 1602. *See* supra: Christelijcken waerseggher.

D28 DAVID, Jan; Jesuit

TYPVS OCCASIONIS. IN QVO RECEPTAE COMMODA, NEGLECTAE VERÒ INCOMMODA, PERSONATO SCHEMATE PROPONVNTVR. ANTVERPIAE delineabat et incidebat Theodorus Gallæus. M.D.CIII. 4° pl.12

12305.d.8.

Engraved throughout. The captions in the form of spoken words are by Jan David. This work is also incorporated in his 'Occasio arrepta', for which *see* above.

DAVID, Jan; Jesuit. Veridicus Christianus. 1601; 1606. *See* supra: Christelijcken waerseggher.

D29 DAVY DU PERRON, Jacques; Cardinal, Archbishop

A LETTER VVRITTEN FROM PARIS, BY THE Lord Cardinall of Peron, TO MONS[r]. CASAVBON in England. Translated out of the French corrected Copie, into English . . . M.DC.XII. 8° pp.51

C.26.k.6(2).

Translated anonymously by Thomas Owen. Without imprint; printed by the English College press at St. Omer. Ownership inscription for the volume on the titlepage of (1): Dom[9] Prof. Rom. S.I., Bibl. comm. P. Laurence Anderton S.J.

D30 DAVY DU PERRON, Jacques; Cardinal, Archbishop

AN ORATION MADE ON THE PART OF THE LORDES SPIRITVALL, In the Chamber of the Third Estate . . . of France, vpon the Oath . . . exhibited in the late Generall Assembly of the three Estates of that Kingdome: By the Lord Cardinall of PERON . . . Translated into English . . . Whereunto is adioyned a Preface, by the Translator . . . M.DC.XVI. 4° pp.128
1059.e.26.

Translated anonymously, by Thomas Owen? Without imprint; published by the English College press at St. Omer.

D31 DE

DE REBVS ab AMBROSIO SPINOLA GESTIS in Palatinatu, Mense Septembri 1620. Et de præsenti rerum statu in Germania, vicinisque prouincijs, EPISTOLA Coloniæ data 30. Sept. 1620. ANTVERPIÆ, Apud Abrahamum Verhoeuen . . . 1620. [etc.] 4° pp.7; sig.A^4
P.P.3444.af(109).

A Dutch version entitled 'Seyndt-brief vant' ghene den Marquis Spinola . . . vvtgerecht heeft', dated 28 September 1620, may be derived from the same German original, perhaps a manuscript. That version has the signature Nom.X. It is described below under SEYNDT-BRIEF.

DE regimine Ecclesiæ Scoticanæ brevis relatio. 1618. *See* CALDERWOOD, David

D32 DE

DE TRIBVS IVRIS PRÆCEPTIS. ORATIO PRIMA. HAGÆ-COMITIS, Ex Officina Hillebrandi Iacobi. M.D.CII. 4° sig.AB^4
707.a.16(5).

Attributed tentatively in the General Catalogue to Regnerus Antverpianus, the name inscribed in contemporary handwriting in the normal author's position on the titlepage. The title preceded by the phrase: Quod Deus benè vertat.

DECISIONES et declarationes . . . cardinalium Concilii Tridentini interpretum. 1615. *See* TRENT. Council of Trent

DECLARATIE der Ghereformeerde Kercken van Vrancrijc. 1621. *See* MANIFESTE ou declaration des eglises reformees de France.

DECLARATIE vanden Coninck van Vranckrijck. [27.5.1621.] 1621. *See* FRANCE [27.5.1621]

DECLARATION des eglises reformees de France & de Souveraineté de Bearn. 1621. *See* MANIFESTE ou declaration des eglises reformees de France.

DECLARATION du Roy contre les Ducs de Vendosme, de Mayenne [etc.] [13.2.1617.] 1617. *See* FRANCE [13.2.1617]

D33 DECLARATION

[Declaration et protestation des princes . . . contre la coniuration . . . du Mareschal d'Ancre.] Erklärung Vnd Protestation der Fürsten/Hertzogen/ Geschlechter/Fürnembsten im Königreich Franckreich Officier . . . welche sich . . . in eine . . . verbündnuss begeben. Wider dess marschalcks von Ancre vnd seiner Gesellen . . . zusammenrottierung vnd Tyranney. 1617. 4° pp.35
8050.bbb.51.

Without imprint; probably printed in the Northern Netherlands. A French edition published by Aert Meurs at The Hague and a Dutch edition published by Adriaen Cornelisz van Delf at Schiedam are in the Royal Library, The Hague, and are described in *Knuttel* no.2326a, 2327.

D34 DECLARATION

[A declaration of the demeanor and cariage of sir Walter Raleigh.] Verclaringe ende verhael hoe de Heere Wouter Raleighe . . . hem ghedreghen [*sic*] heeft/soo wel in sijnen Voyaghe/als in ende sedert sijne wedercomste. Ende vande ware motiveu [*sic*] ende redenen/die sijne Majesteyt bewoghen hebben/teghens hem te procederen by forme van Justitie . . . Naer de Copye tot London, by Bonham Norton. IN S'GRAVEN-HAGE. By Aert Meuris . . . 1619. [etc.] 4° pp.40
T.1718(9).
Sometimes attributed to James I.

DECRETA et statuta synodi dioecesanae Gandavensis. 1614. *See* GHENT. Diocese

DECRETA Synodi Dioecesanae Antverpiensis. 1610. *See* ANTWERP. Diocese. Synod

D35 DECULEO, Justus Judocus

IVSTI IVDOCI DECVLEONIS CORTRACENSIS ORATIONES EPISTOLAE ET CARMINA. ANTVERPIÆ Ex Officina Hieronymi VerdussI. M.DC.XIII. 12° pp.345
1090.b.4(1).

DEDUCTIE ofte beleydt. 1621. *See* DEDUCTIO nullitatum.

D36 DEDUCTIO

[Deductio nullitatum.] A Briefe Description of the reasons that make the Declaration of the Ban made against the King of Bohemia, as being Elector Palatine, Dated 22. of Ianuarie last past, of no value nor worth, and therefore not to be respected. PRINTED At the Hayf [*sic*] by Arnold Meuris . . . 1621. 4° pp.13
1054.b.31; Burney 2a(7).
The imprint is false; printed by Edward Allde for Thomas Archer at London? The copy at 1054.b.31 cropped, with loss of catchwords. The Burney copy with ownership inscription: Jo. Robinson.

D37 DEDUCTIO

[Deductio nullitatum.] DEDVCTIE OFTE BELEYDT, Daer inde Nulliteyten/van de Acht teghen den Ceur Forst Pals-Graven . . . nul ende . . . crachteloos . . . werden aengewesen. Vertaelt uyt het Latijnsche exemplaer, in s'Graven Hage, by Hillebrant Iocobsz [*sic*] . . . gedruckt . . . TOT ARNHEM, By IAN IANSSEN . . . 1621. 4° pp.28
T.2424(9).

A DEFENCE of the Catholyke cause. 1602. *See* FITZ-HERBERT, Thomas

A DEFENCE of the ministers reasons, for refusall of subscription to the Booke of Common prayer. 1608. *See* HIERON, Samuel

D38 DELICIAE

DELICIÆ BATAVICÆ, quibus adjunctæ sunt diversæ elegantes picturæ & effigies, quæ ad album studiosorum cõficiendum deservire possunt. LVGDVNI BATAVORVM. apud Jacobum Marci. obl.8° sig.·.·^{2}: 30 unnumbered plates
685.a.31.
Imperfect; wanting the plate showing the Anatomy Theatre at Leiden and perhaps others. The plates are bound out of order. Shorter as well as longer compilations are known published between 1610 and 1616; this issue published ca.1614?

D39 DELINEACION

Delineacion del sitio adonde su Altesa la Ser.^{ma} Infanta a deriuado el papagayo, con laballesta [*sic*] de la Confradria de los bourgeses. a los 15 de Mayo. Año 1615. Afbeeldinghe der plaetse daer hare Hoochheyt den papegay heeft afgeschoten . . . Delineation de la place [etc.] obl. fol. a single sheet

Dept. of Mss. Kings 179(39–40).

An engraving, tentatively ascribed in *Atlas Van Stolk* no. 1315 to Esaias vande Velde. With Latin verses on a scroll 'Nunc orbis volitat [etc.]' and their equivalents in Spanish, Dutch and French and a key in Dutch on a pasted-on label in the right-hand top corner. Published in 1615? at Antwerp?

D40 DELMANHORSTIUS, Henricus Salamonis

THESES MEDICÆ DE DIABETE, Quas . . . PRO DOCTORATV in MEDICINA obtinendo publicè tueri adnitar H.S. DELMANHORSTIVS . . . LVGDVNI BATAVORVM, Ex Officina Thomæ Basson, 1607. 4° sig. A^4

1185.g.1(30).

D41 [*DEL-RIO, Joannes

ORATIO IN FVNERE REVERENDISSIMI DOMINI IOANNIS MIRÆI IV. ANTVERPIENSIVM EPISCOPI: Habita XVI. Ianuarij M.D C.XI. . . . à R.D. IOANNE DEL-RIO . . . ANTVERPIÆ, EX OFFICINA PLANTINIANA, Apud Viduam & Filios Io. Moreti M.DC.XI. 8° pp.20; illus.

4423.bb.20(2).[

*Destroyed. Described from the General Catalogue and the copy in the Royal Library Albert I, Brussels (VB 5933(1)). The titlepage engraving shows the arms of the Bishop.

D42 DELRIO, Martinus Antonius

PENICVLVS FORIARVM ELENCHI SCALIGERIANI PRO Societate IESV, Maldonato, Delrio. Auctore Liberio Sanga Verino Cantabro Ad CLARVM BONARSCIVM BELGAM. METELLOBVRGI MATTIACROVM Apud Hæredes Matthianos. M.DC.IX. 12° pp.103[203]

860.f.12.

Pseudonymous and with a fictitious imprint. Published at Antwerp.

D43 DELRIO, Martinus Antonius

VINDICIÆ AREOPAGITICÆ MARTINI DELRIO . . . CONTRA IOSEPHVM SCALIGERVM . . . ANTVERPIÆ, EX OFFICINA PLANTINIANA, Apud Ioannem Moretum. M.DC.VII. 8° pp.134

1120.a.1(2).

DEMETRE, André. *See* MEESTER, Andries de

DEMETRIUS, Andreas. *See* MEESTER, Andries de

D44 DENCKWAERDICH

Een denckwaerdich Modell, Of MONSTERSTVCK. Claerlijck ontdeckende des Keysers partijsche/onwettighe/jae gheweltdadighe proceduren over sijne voorhebbende gantsch nulle Achts-verclaringhe ende Executie/betreffent de saecke VAN Bohemien. Soo dit alles t'oordeelen is/uyt die hier naer gedruckte des Keysers/en der sijnen . . . schriften . . . Met d'Annotatien van dien/nu . . . uyt den Hoochduytschen ghetranslateert. IN S'GRAVEN-HAGE By Aert Meuris . . . 1620. 4° sig. A-D^4E^2

T.2250(24); T.2423(46).

D45 DERING, Richard

(tp.1) CANTICA SACRA AD MELODIAM MADRIGALIVM ELABORATA SENIS VOCIBVS, Cum Basso Continuo ad Organum, AVCTORE RICHARDO DIRINGO . . . CANTVS. ANTVERPIÆ Apud Petrum Phalesium M.D.CXVIII.
(tp.2) CANTICA SACRA . . . AVCTORE RICHARDO DIRINGO . . . ALTVS. ANTVERPIÆ Apud Petrum Phalesium M.D.CXVIII.
(tp.3) CANTICA SACRA . . . AVCTORE RICHARDO DIRINGO . . . TENOR. ANTVERPIÆ Apud Petrum Phalesium M.D.CXVIII.
(tp.4) CANTICA SACRA . . . AVCTORE RICHARDO DIRINGO . . . BASSVS. ANTVERPIÆ Apud Petrum Phalesium M.D.CXVIII.
(tp.5) CANTICA SACRA . . . AVCTORE RICHARDO DIRINGO . . . QVINTVS. ANTVERPIÆ Apud Petrum Phalesium M.D.CXVIII.
(tp.6) CANTICA SACRA . . . AVCTORE RICHARDO DIRINGO . . . SEXTVS. ANTVERPIÆ Apud Petrum Phalesium M.D.CXVIII.
(tp.7) CANTICA SACRA . . . AVCTORE RICHARDO DIRINGO . . . BASSO CONTINVO. ANTVERPIÆ Apud Petrum Phalesium M.D.CXVIII. 4° 7 pt.: pp.21; 21; 21; 21; 21; 21; 22
Music K.7.a.4; Music R.M.15.f.1(8).

D46 DERING, Richard

(tp.1) CANZONETTE A QVATTRO VOCI, CON IL BASSO CONTINVO. DI Sr RICHARDO DIRINGO . . . Nuouamente Composte & date in luce. CANTO. IN ANVERSA Appresso PETRO PHALESIO . . . M.DC.XX.
(tp.2) CANZONETTE . . . DI Sr RICHARDO DIRINGO . . . CANTO II. IN ANVERSA Appresso PETRO PHALESIO . . . M.DC.XX.
(tp.3) CANZONETTE . . . DI Sr RICHARDO DIRINGO . . . ALTO. IN ANVERSA Appresso PETRO PHALESIO . . . M.DC.XX.
(tp.4) CANZONETTE . . . DI Sr RICHARDO DIRINGO . . . BASSO. IN ANVERSA Appresso PETRO PHALESIO . . . M.DC.XX.
(tp.5) CANZONETTE . . . DI Sr RICHARDO DIRINGO . . . BASSO CONTINVO. IN ANVERSA Appresso PETRO PHALESIO . . . M.DC.XX. obl.4° 5 pt.: pp.25; 25; 25; 25; 25
Music K.7.b.3.

DES habits moeurs, ceremonies. 1601. *See* GLEN, Jean Baptiste de

D47 DESCHAMPS, Joannes

(tp.1) [Novae missae novem quinis, senis, octonis accommodatae vocibus: praestantissimorum auctorum operâ concinnatae ad numeros variarum cantionum avctore R.D. Ioanne Deschamps . . . Altus. Antverpiae ex officina typographica Petri Phalesii . . . M.DCXV.]
(tp.2) NOVÆ MISSAE NOVEM QVINIS, SENIS, OCTONIS ACCOMMODATÆ VOCIBVS: Præstantissimorum Auctorum operâ concinnatæ ad numeros variarum Cantionum AVCTORE R.D. IOANNE DESCHAMPS . . . TENOR. ANTVERPIÆ Ex Officina Typographica Petri Phalesij . . . M.DCXV.
(tp.3) NOVÆ MISSAE . . . concinnatæ ad numeros variarum Cantionum AVCTORE R.D. IOANNE DESCHAMPS . . . BASSVS. ANTVERPIÆ Ex Officina Typographica Petri Phalesij . . . M.DCXV.
(tp.4) NOVÆ MISSAE . . . concinnatæ ad numeros variarum Cantionum AVCTORE R.D. IOANNE DESCHAMPS . . . SEXTVS. ANTVERPIÆ Ex Officina Typographica Petri Phalesij . . . M.DCXV. 4° 4 pt.: pp.3–72; 72; 65; 72
Music C.288.
The Altus part lacks all of sig.A. The title is adapted from the text of the other titlepages.

DESCRIPTIO ac delineatio geographica detectionis freti sive transitus ad occasum. 1612; 1613. *See* GERRITSZ, Hessel

D48 DESCRIPTION

DESCRIPTION DE L'ASSIETTE, MAISON ET MARQVISAT D'HAVRÉ. Redigée en vers Francoys. A MONS De l'Imprimerie de Charles Michel. M.DC.VI. 8° sig.A-D^{8}; illus.
8052.aaa.17(8).
The dedication signed: A.A.D. The titlepage engraving shows the arms of the house of Croy.

DESCRIPTION du penible voyage fait entour de l'univers. 1610. *See* NOORT, Olivier van

DESCRIPTION et recit historial du . . . royaume d'or de Gunea. 1605. *See* MAREES, Pieter de

DESCRIPTION et representation de toutes les victoires. 1612. *See* ORLERS, Jan

La DESCRIPTION de la ville d'Ath. 1610. *See* ZUALLART, Jean

DESDIGUIERES, François; Duke. *See* BONNE, François de, Duke de Lesdiguières

DESE seltsame figure. 1621. *See* JOHN of Capistrano; Saint

DES FREUX, André. *See* FRUSIUS, Andreas

DESIDERIUS, Emanuel. 1616. *See* COMALADA, Miguel

DEUTECHUM, Baptista van. *See* DOETECHUM, Baptista van

D49 DEVEREUX, Robert; Earl of Essex

[An apologie of the Earle of Essex.] Apologie oft verantwoordinge Vanden Grave van Essex, teghen de ghene die hem jalourselick ende ten onrechten schelden als beletter des vredes ende ruste zijnes Vaderlandts . . . uyt het Engelsche exemplaer (Ghedruct tot London by Richard Bradocks 1603) Overgheset by C.C. TOT MIDDELBVRGH, Voor Bernaert Langhenesse . . . 1603. 4° pp.39; plate; port.
T.1713(6); 101.l.2; E.1940/4.
The translator is Caspar Coolhaes. The portrait of the Earl of Essex, with inscriptions in Latin and Dutch, signed: N.de Clerck exc. The copy at E.1940/4 lacks the plate.

DIALOGUES rustiques. 1615. *See* MONCY, Jean de

D50 DIALOGUS

DIALOGVS OF TE [*sic*] TVVE-SPRAEC IN RYM GHESTELT Tusschen twee Personagien ghenaemt Ghereformeert Patriot ende Roomsch Catholijck. Vervatende in 't corte den handel vande Tvvaelf-jarighen Treves . . . Fabricatus, in Cijclopes Academi Per Vlisses, in Caverna Poliphemi. INCARNATIE. Anno reDeMtorIs IhesV ChrIstI. 4° sig.AB^{4}
T.2421(10); 161.n.65.
According to the colophon the author's name is hidden in his verses. The chronogram in the imprint is 1609.

DIALOGUS oft tzamensprekinge gemaect op den vredehandel. 1608. *See* CATHECISME

D51 DICKENSONUS, Joannes

MISCELLANEA EX HISTORIIS ANGLICANIS CONCINNATA, Autore I.D. LVGDVNI BATAVORVM, ex Officina Thomæ Basson, Sumpt. LOD. ELSEVIRII. 1606. 4° pp.70
G.4666; 1070.l.5(4).
In verse. The author's name given in full in the preface and in the text. The copy at 1070.l.5(4) is imperfect; wanting the titleleaf.

D52 DICKENSONUS, Joannes

SPECVLVM TRAGICVM. REGVM, PRINCIPVM, & Magnatum superioris sœculi [*sic*] celebriorum ruinas exitusque calamitosos breviter complectens: In quo & iudicia divina & imbecillitas humana insignibus exemplis declarantur, Auctore I.D. DELPHIS BATAVORVM, Excudebat Iacobus Fœnicolius . . . 1601. 8° pp.126
1448.a.4.

The dedication and preface signed with the author's full name.

D53 DICKENSONUS, Joannes

SPECVLVM TRAGICVM . . . Auctore I.D. Editio secunda, auctior & castigatior. Ex Officina Ludouici Elzeverij [*sic*] . . . 1602. (col.) DELPHIS BATAVORVM, Excudebat Iacobus Fenicolius . . . M.DC.II. 8° pp.136
1197.b.4.

The dedication and preface signed with the author's full name. Without catchword on p.K2r and a short list of errata on p.K2v. Published at Leiden. From the library of John Morris.

D54 DICKENSONUS, Ioannes

SPECVLVM TRAGICVM . . . Auctore I.D. Editio secunda, auctior & castigatior. DELPHIS BATAVORVM, Excudebat Iacobus Fenicolius . . . 1602. (col.) DELPHIS BATAVORVM, Excudebat Iacobus Fenicolius . . . M.DC.II. 8° pp.136
1080.f.31(1).

Another issue of the preceding. With the catchword 'Admonitio' on p.K2r and a printer's address to the reader and a longer list of errata covering both editions on p.K2v.

D55 DICKENSONUS, Joannes

SPECVLVM TRAGICVM . . . Tertiò editum, & adauctum. Accessit etiam Bironij exitus, & alia Auctore I.D. LVGDVNI BATAVORVM, Ex officina Ludovici Elzevirij. M.D.C.III. 8° pp.148
10604.aa.12(1); G.15651.

The preface signed with the author's full name. The copy at 10604.aa.12(1) has the arms of Stuart de Rothesay stamped in gold on the covers. In the copy at G.15651 leaf L6 is slightly mutilated.

D56 DICKENSONUS, Joannes

SPECVLVM TRAGICVM . . . Editio quarta, cùm aliàs, tum & Baronis Montinij historiolâ suo loco insertâ, auctior. Accessit etiam, memorabilium humilioris fortunæ, intra Speculi tempus, calamitatum Decas; & Parallela tragica. AVCTORE I.D. LVGDVNI BATAVORVM, Ex officina Ludovici Elzevirij. M.D.C.V. 8° pp.262
1313.a.15; 1448.a.5.

The dedication and preface signed with the author's full name.

DIRINGUS, Richardus. *See* DERING, Richard

D57 DISCOURS

DISCOVRS by Forme van Remonstrantie: Vervatende DE NOODSAECKELICKHEYD VANDE OOS-INDISCHE [*sic*] NAVIGATIE, BY MIDDEL vande vvelcke, de vrye Nederlandsche Provintien, apparent zijn te gheraecken totte hooghste Prosperiteyt . . . GHEDRVCKT ANNO 1608. 4° sig.AB^4
8022.a.9; T.1731(3).

Sometimes wrongly attributed to Willem Usselincx.

D58 DISCOURS

DISCOVRS by Forme van Remonstrantye: Vervatende DE NOOTSAECKELICKHEYDT VANDE OOST-INDISCHE NAVIGATIE . . . GHEDRVCKT ANNO 1608, [*sic*] 4° sig.AB^4
106.d.14.

Another edition of the preceding, with many corrections.

D59 DISCOURS

DISCOVRS ET TRAICTE' VERITABLE DV MARTIRE ENDVRE' A LONDRES EN ANGLETERRE. PAR LE R. PERE IEAN DE MERVINIA, AVTREMENT DIT ROBERTS, Religieux . . . de l'Ordre de S. Benoist . . . executé le 10. de Decembre . . . 1610. A DOVAY, De l'Imprimerie de LAVRENT KELLAM . . . M.DC.XI. 8° pp.31; illus.
Huth 129.

D60 DISCOURS

[Discours oft t'saemen spreken, aengaende Christianus Hertoch van Bruyns-vvijck, Halberstadt, &c. Tusschen Ian de Vraegher, ende Andries den Antvvoorder . . . T'Hantwerpen, By Abraham Verhoeuen, etc.] 4° pp.1–14; sig: A–E[4] F[3]
P.P.3444.af(333).

Headed: Junius 1622. 83. Imperfect; wanting the titleleaf and all after p.14. Title, numeration and date inferred from p.3 and from the gap left for this issue and its signatures in the list of issues in the *Bibliotheca Belgica* no. V198 p.545.

D61 DISCOURS

Discours op den swermenden Treves. TOT MIDDELBVRCH, By Symon Janszoon . . . M.D.C.IX. 4° sig.AB[4]; illus.
T.1713(28); T.2420(37).

The titlepage woodcut shows an astrologer and his equipment. A border taken from elsewhere has been cut into strips and pasted onto the titlepage.

D62 DISCOURS

[Discours op het leuen ende miserable doodt vanden Marquis ende de Marquise van Ancre in Vranck-rijck. Jtem van Don Rodrigo Calderon in Spagnien. Ende van Barnevelt in Hollandt, ende andere Favoriten elders. Eerst ghedruckt den 15. December 1621. T'Hantwerpen, By Abraham Verhoeuen etc.] 4° pp.14; sig.H, Hh[4]; [illus.]
P.P.3444.af(329); 1471.aa.7.

Headed: December 1621. 184. Both copies imperfect; wanting the titleleaf bearing the illustration, and the last leaf, bearing the Spanish arms. The title transcribed from the description in the *Bibliotheca Belgica* no. V197 p.529.

D63 DISCOURS

DISCOVRS van Pieter en Pauwels/op de Handelinghe vanden Vreede . . . 1608. 4° sig.A[2]
T.1713(16); 107.g.18(36).

DISSERTATIO, qua disputatur, quo jure . . . haeretici sunt coercendi. 1612? *See* CHÂTEILLON, Sébastien. Contra libellum Calvini.

D64 DIVAEUS, Petrus

RERVM BRABANTICARVM LIBRI XIX, AVCTORE PETRO DIVÆO . . . Studio AVBERTI MIRÆI . . . primùm nunc editi, & illustrati. ANTVERPIÆ, Ex Officina HIERONYMI VERDVSSI. M.DC.X. [etc.] 4° pp.148
1197.i.4(2); C.83.d.19; 153.e.15.

The copy at C.83.d.19, once the property of Charles II, inscribed: 'From George Stevens, bought by him at the British Museum sale of duplicates, 1769'; date of return not stamped. The copy at 153.e.15 with the cypher of George III on the covers.

D65 DIVERSCHE

Diuersche Tijdinghen wt weenen in Oostenrijck/ende andere omligghende Quartieren. Overghesedt wt de Hooch-Duytsche sprake in onse Nederlantsche Tale. Eerst Ghedruckt den 8. Januarius 1621. T'Hantwerpen/By Abraham Verhoeuen [etc.] 4° pp.8; without signature; illus.

P.P.3444.af(170).

Headed: Ianuarius 1621. 1. The titlepage woodcut shows a cavalry engagement near a mill.

D66 DOD, John

[The bright star which leadeth wise men to our lord Jesus Christ.] A PLAINE AND FAMILIAR EXPOSITION OF THE TENNE COMMANDEMENTS. WITH A METHODICALL short Catechisme, containing briefly all the principall grounds of Christian RELIGION. According to the last corrected and inlarged Copie by . . . M^r. IOHN DOD . . . Printed . . . 1617. 4° pp.279

3506.ee.15.

The dedicatory letter signed: John Dod, Robert Cleaver. Without imprint; printed by William Brewster at Leiden.

D67 DODOENS, Rembert

REMBERTI DODONÆI . . . STIRPIVM HISTORIÆ PEMPTADES SEX SIVE LIBRI XXX. Varié ab AVCTORE, paullò ante mortem, aucti & emendati. ANTVERPIÆ EX OFFICINA PLANTINIANA Apud Balthasarem et Ioannem Moretos. M.DC.XVI. (col.) ANTVERPIÆ, EX OFFICINA PLANTINIANA, APVD BALTHASAREM ET IOANNEM MORETOS FRATRES. M.DC.XVI. fol. pp.872; illus.

442.i.7; 450.k.3.

The titlepage is engraved. With a polyglot glossary.

D68 DODOENS, Rembert

[Stirpium historia.] Cruydt-Boeck van REMBERTVS DODONÆVS, volgens sijne laetste verbeteringe: Met BIIVOEGSELS achter elck Capittel, vvt verscheyden Cruydtbeschrijvers: Item in't laetste een Beschrijvinge vande Indiaensche Gewassen, meest getrocken wt de schriften van CAROLVS CLVSIVS. TOT LEYDEN, Inde Plantijnsche Druckerije van Françoys van Ravelingen. 1608. fol. pp.1580; illus., ports.

450.k.4.

The engraved titlepage border signed: W. Swan. Fecit, 1608, i.e. Willem Swanenburgh. The preface is printed in civilité.

D69 DODOENS, Rembert

[Stirpium historia.] Cruydt-Boeck van REMBERTVS DODONÆVS, volgens sijne laetste verbeteringe: Met BIIVOEGSELS . . . vvt verscheyden Cruydtbeschrijvers: Item . . . een Beschrijvinge vande Indiaensche Gewassen, meest getrocken wt de schriften van CAROLVS CLVSIVS. TOT LEYDEN, Inde Plantijnsche Druckerije van Françoys van Ravelingen. 1618. fol. pp.1495; illus., ports.

450.k.5.

The preface, printed in civilité, signed: Joost van Ravelingen. With a polyglot glossary. The engraved titlepage border signed: W. Swan. Fecit. 1608, i.e. Willem Swanenburgh. Imperfect; wanting pp.603–646.

DODONAEUS, Rembertus. *See* DODOENS, Rembert

D70 DOETECHUM, Baptista van

Afconterfeytinghe der stercke Stadt Grave/met alle hare bollewercken/Wallen/en graften/oock alle de voornaemste plaetsen/straten/en stegen/met hare namen

aengeteeckent: Insgelijcks die belegeringhe der selver stadt . . . onder het beleyt van . . . Graf Mauritius van Nassouwen . . . belegert. (col.) t'Amsterdam by Baptista van Duytecom. fol. 2 leaves
inserted between ff.17, 18 of 10759.l.1.
An engraved map, inscribed: Ghedruckt eñ ghemaeckt tot Amsterdam by Baptista van Deutechum. The separate letterpress text, originally in three columns to be attached to the map, has been cut and mounted back to back to form two pages. The date given in the text as in the current month of July, 1602. A variant bearing the imprint of Cornelis Claesz at Amsterdam is described in *Muller* no.1183.

D71 DOETECHUM, Baptista van
[Afconterfeytinghe der . . . stadt Grave.] VRAY POVRTRAICT DE LA TREFFORTE INVADIBLE VILLE DE GRAVE, ASSIEGEE PAR . . . LE CONTE MAVRICE DE NASSOV, DEPVIS LE 18. IVILLET. 1602. fol. a single sheet
1750.c.1(10).
The same map as the preceding, with the same inscription in Dutch: Ghedruckt eñ ghemaeckt tot Amsterdam by Baptista van Deutechum. With letterpress title and key in French on a strip attached to the map. Published in 1602. Corresponding to the copy described in *Muller* no.1183Ab.

The DOLEFULL knell. 1607. *See* WOODWARD, Philip

D72 DOMINIS, Marco Antonio de; Archbishop
[Predica fatta . . . la prima domenica dell' Avvento . . . 1617. in Londra.] Concio Habita A REVERENDO PATRE MARCO ANTONIO De Dominis . . . primo die dominico Adventus Anno 1617. Londini in Mercatorum Capella, coram Italis ibi commorantibus . . . LEOVARDIÆ, Apud IOANNEM STARTERVM . . . 1618. 4° sig. (∴) A-D^{4}E^1
477.a.26(7).

D73 DOMINIS, Marco Antonio de; Archbishop
MARCVS ANTONIVS DE DOMINIS . . . SVÆ PROFECTIONIS CONSILIVM EXPONIT. (col.) Denuo impressum Hagæ-Comitis, in Officina Hillebrandi Iacobi, Die 23. Novembris, 1616. 4° pp.20
477.a.26(2).

D74 DOMINIS, Marco Antonio de; Archbishop
[Suae profectionis consilium.] REVERENDISSIMI . . . PATRIS MARCI ANTONII DE DOMINIS CONSILIVM. Caussas discessus sui ex Italia, & è Psychotyrannide Pontificis Romani exponit longè gravissimas . . . Iam denuò . . . recusum 12. Januarij . . . 1617. 4° pp.20
477.a.26(3).
Without imprint; the General Catalogue suggests Leiden as place of publication.

D75 DOMINIS, Marco Antonio de; Archbishop
[Suae profectionis consilium.] VERCLARINGHE, Van de Motiven ende Oorsaecken/ Daer door . . . MARCVS ANTONIVS DE DOMINIS . . . bewogen is geweest 'tPausdom te verlaten, ende sich herwaerts over te begheven. Wt het Latijn . . . over-gheset. IN S'GRAVEN-HAGHE, By Hillebrant Jacobsz . . . 1616. 4° pp.11
T.2246(1).
Translated anonymously by Jan Wtenbogaert.

DOMPE-TROMPE. 1606. *See* DAVID, Jan; Jesuit

DOMP-HOOREN der Hollanscher fackel. 1602. *See* DAVID, Jan; Jesuit

D76 DONTECLOCK, Reginaldus

ANTVVOORDE Op een seker Schrift/eens Onbekenden/'tonrechte geintituleert/ Christelicke ende ernstighe Vermaninghe tot vrede, aen R. Donteclock, over sijne 'tSamensprekinghe . . . Door R. Donteclock . . . TOT DELF. Ghedruckt by Ian Andriesz . . . 1609. 4° sig.A-O^{4}P^1
T.2239(9).

A reply to the anonymous work by Joannes Arnoldi Corvinus.

D77 DONTECLOCK, Reginaldus

Bedenckinghe Op de verantwoordinge D. Vorstij/ghedaen ende uytghegeven/ over de Propositie der . . . Curateuren/van de Universiteyt/ende Burghemeesteren der Stadt Leyden: aengaende syn beroepinge tot de profeffie [*sic*] der H. Theologie . . . Tot vvaerschouvvinghe . . . gestelt, door R. Donteclock . . . TOT DELF. gedruckt by Ian Andriessz . . . 1611. 4° pp.50
T.2241(24).

D78 DONTECLOCK, Reginaldus

EEN Grondich onderrecht wt Godts Heylighe Woort: Vande PREDESTINATIE . . . Onpartijdelic Over langhe beschreven: Door Reginal: Donteclock . . . ende nu in Druc wtghegheven . . . Na de Kopie, ghedruckt tot Leyden/By Heynderick L. van Haestens/Voor Jacob Marcus . . . 1611. 4° pp.76
T.2241(13).

D79 DONTECLOCK, Reginaldus

Overlegginghe Vande Oorsaecken der schadelicker Twist in de Kercken van Hollant ende West-vriestlant op-geresen. Ende eerst van de Kerckelicke Ordinantie ofte Regieringhe int ghemeyn . . . Ghestelt ende uyt-ghegheven: door R. Donteclock . . . TOT DELF. Ghedruckt by Ian Andriessz . . . 1612. 4° pp.27,33
T.2242(12).

D80 DONTECLOCK, Reginaldus

PROEVE Des Gouschen Catechismy/ofte Korte Onderwijsinge inde Christelijcke Religie/tot waerschouwinge van andere Steden/ende haere Ghereformeerde Kercken/voor alle onnoodighe ende schadelijcke Nieuwicheden/in saecken/de Leere ende Religie aengaende. Geschreven door Reginald Donteclock . . . Den tweeden Druck . . . TOT DELF. Ghedruckt by Ian Andriesz . . . M.VI^c.VIII. 8° pp.73
3505.bbb.25.

Directed against 'Korte onderwijsinge der kinderen in de Christelijke religie', Gouda, 1607, believed to be by Hendrik Herberts.

D81 DONTECLOCK, Reginaldus

t'Samen-spreeckinghe VANDE VERTAELDE THESES, OFTE Disputatien de eene Doct. Francisci Gomari, de andere Doct. Iacobi Arminij, aenghaende de Goddelicke Predestinatie . . . Tot behulp vanden Leser/ghestelt ende uyt-ghegheven door Reginald. Donteclock . . . TOT DELF. By Jan Andriesz . . . 1609. 4° sig.A-E^4
T.2239(7).

DOORNYCK, Petrus. Problema. 1620. *See* BURGERSDIJCK, Franco

D82 DORDRECHT. Synod

ACTA SYNODI NATIONALIS, In nomine Domini nostri IESV CHRISTI, Autoritate . . . ORDINVM GENERALIVM FOEDERATI BELGII PROVINCIARVM, DORDRECHTI HABITÆ ANNO M D CXVIII ET M D CXIX. Accedunt Plenissima, de Quinque Articulis, Theologorum Judicia. LVGDVNI BATAVORVM, Typis ISAACI ELZEVIRI . . . Societatis DORDRECHTANÆ sumptibus. M.D.CXX. [etc.] (col.) LVGDVNI BATAVORVM, Typis ISAACI ELSEVIRI . . . Societatis DORDRECHTANÆ sumptibus. M D C XX. fol. pp.360,252,292
C.24.d.5.

Edited by Festus Hommius. This copy, printed on large paper, brought by Hommius to King James I. In a red velvet binding with the arms of James I embroidered in gold, silver and blue on the covers.

D83 DORDRECHT. Synod
(tp.) ACTA SYNODI NATIONALIS . . . DORDRECHTI HABITÆ ANNO M D CXVIII ET M D CXIX. Accedunt Plenissima, de Quinque Articulis, Theologorum Iudicia. DORDRECHTI, Typis ISAACI IOANNIDIS CANINI & Sociorum, M.D.CXX. [etc.]
(½ title) IVDICIA THEOLOGORVM PROVINCIALIVM, De quinque Controversis Remonstrantium Articulis, SYNODO DORDRECHTANÆ Exhibita. Anno MDCXIX. fol. 2 pt.: pp.352; 323
1605/604.
Edited by Festus Hommius.

D84 DORDRECHT. Synod
ACTA SYNODI NATIONALIS . . . DORDRECHTI HABITÆ ANNO M D CXVIII ET M D CXIX. Accedunt Plenissima, de Quinque Articulis, Theologorum Iudicia. DORDRECHTI, Typis ISAACI IOANNIDIS CANINI, & Sociorum ejusdem Urbis Typographorum. 1620. [etc.] 4° pp.411; illus.
491.d.15.
Edited by Festus Hommius. With a woodcut showing the Synod. Imperfect; wanting the 'Judicia'. Ownership inscription: Joseph Dunstan.

D85 DORDRECHT. Synod
[Canones.] (tp.) SYNODVS[.] DORDRECHTI, Apud Ioannem Berewout, & Franciscum Bosselaer, Socios Caninij 1619.
(½ title) IVDICIVM SYNODI NATIONALIS, REFORMATARVM ECCLESIARVM BELGICARVM, habitæ DORDRECHTI, Anno 1618. & 1619 . . . DE QUINQUE DOCTRINAE Capitibus in Ecclesiis Belgicis Controversis. Promulgatum VI. May, M.DC.XIX. [etc.] 4° pp.128; illus.
1124.g.11.
Edited by Festus Hommius. The titlepage woodcut showing the Synod.

D86 DORDRECHT. Synod
[Canones.] Oordeel des SYNODI NATIONALIS Der Gereformeerde Kercken van de Vereenichde Nederlanden: ghehouden binnen DORDRECHT . . . 1618. ende 1619 . . . OVER De bekende Vijf Hooft-stucken der Leere/daer van . . . verschil is gevallen. uytghesproken op den 6. May. 1619. uyt het Latijn . . . overgheset. [etc.] (col.) Tot Dordrecht, Gedruckt by Pieter Verhagen/Isaac Jansz. Canin/Joris Waters/Jan Leendertsz Berewout/Francoys Bosselaer/Niclaes Vincenten/ Zacharias Jochemsz. Francoys Boels. 1619. 4° pp.114
T.2249(10).
With an additional titlepage reading: SYNODVS TOT DORDRECHT By Isaac Ianssen Canin . . . 1619, showing a woodcut of the Synod, here coloured and with a vertical crack. Edited by Festus Hommius.

D87 DORDRECHT. Synod
[Canones.] Oordeel des SYNODI NATIONALIS Der Gereformeerde Kercken [etc.] (col.) Tot Dordrecht, Gedruckt by Pieter Verhagen/Isaac Jansz. Canin/Joris Waters/Jan Leendertsz Berewout/Francoys Bosselaer/Niclaes Vincenten/ Zacharias Jochemsz. Francoys Boels. 1619. 4° pp.114
1608/882.
Another edition of the preceding, with the same crack in the woodcut on the additional titlepage, but with a differently set preface, including a different decorative initial and differently positioned signatures as well as different spelling, e.g. 'Dē' instead of 'De' on p.6, 'weghen' instead of 'wegen' on p.81, p.99 is correctly numbered where it is misprinted 69 in the preceding, while other misprinted pagination is uncorrected.

D88 DORDRECHT. Synod
[Canones.] OORDEEL DES NATIONALEN SYNODI VAN Dordrecht, over de Theologie ofte Leere Conradi Vorstij . . . Mitsgaders De Resolutie van de . . . Staten van Hollandt ende West-Vrielandt daer op ghevolght. IN S'GRAVEN-HAGHE, By Hillebrant Iacobssz . . . 1619. [etc.] 4° sig. A^4
T.2249(6).
Edited by Festus Hommius.

D89 DORDRECHT. Synod
Kercken-Ordeninghe, Ghestelt In den Nationalen Synode der Ghereformeerde Kercken . . . Binnen Dordrecht, inde Jaren 1618. ende 1619. Ende (naer veranderinghe van eenighe weynighe poincten) goedt-ghevonden ende ghearresteert by de . . . Staten des Furstendoms GHELRE vnd Graefschaps ZVTPHEN. TOT ARNHEM, By Jan Jansz. . . . 1620. 4° pp.27
1230.a.32.

D90 DORDRECHT. Synod. Remonstrants
ACTA ET SCRIPTA SYNODALIA DORDRACENA MINISTRORVM REMONSTRANTIVM IN FOEDERATO BELGIO . . . HERDER-VVICII EX OFFICINA TYPOGRAPHI SYNODALIS . . . M.DC.XX. 4° pp.211
1124.g.32.
Compiled and edited with an introduction by Jan Wtenbogaert. Imperfect; wanting all after pt.1 'Scripta historica'. The imprint, suggesting Harderwijk, is doubtful. It has been suggested that the work was published at Antwerp, perhaps printed there by Abraham Verhoeven.

D91 DORDRECHT. Synod. Remonstrants
ACTA ET SCRIPTA SYNODALIA DORDRACENA MINISTRORVM REMONSTRANTIVM IN FOEDERATO BELGIO . . . HARDER-VVICII EX OFFICINA TYPOGRAPHI SYNODALIS . . . M.DC.XX. 4° 2 pt.: pp.211; 370,349
1570/5667.
Pt.1 is a later variant of the preceding, containing an added errata list at the end of the preliminary pages. Some of the mistakes described as 'in quibusdam exemplaribus . . . commissa' have been corrected while they are present in the preceding. Ownership inscriptions: Ex libris Wilhelmi Henrici; Ex libris Jac. Hort (or: Hart); Ex libris Guilielmi Livingstone 1859.

D92 DORDRECHT. Synod. Remonstrants
Request Aende . . . Staten Generael der Vereenichde Proviutien [*sic*]. Van weghen De Remonstranten, gheciteerde ende gedeputeerde tot den Synodum Nationael binnen Dordrecht. Ghedruckt . . . 1619. 4° sig. A^4
T.2249(50).
Dated 18 June 1619. Printed with some civilité.

DOULYE, George; pseudonym of William Warford. *See* WARFORD, William

D93 DOUSA, Janus; the Elder
NOBILISSIMI VIRI IANI DOVSAE . . . AD Amplissimum virum IOANNEM GROTIVM ELEGIA DE OPPIDIS HOLLANDIÆ EORVMQVE PRÆCIPVIS INGENIIS. Nunc primum edita Ex Musæo IOACHIMI MORSII[.] LVGDVNI BATAVORVM Excudebat Georgius Abrahami à Marsce, M.DC.XIX. 4° sig. A^2
1870.d.1(190*).

D94 DOUSA, Janus; the Elder
IANI DOVSÆ . . . Echo, sive LVSVS IMAGINIS IOCOSÆ quibus Titulus HALCEDONIA.

Alia quædam . . . Omnia recèns nunc primùm publicata. HAGÆ-COMITIS, Ex Officinâ Bucoldi Nieulandii . . . M.DC.III. 4° ff.124
77.f.5.
Author's presentation copy to Johan van Oldenbarnevelt to whom the work is dedicated.

D95 DOUSA, Janus; the Elder
IANI DOVZÆ . . . POEMATA PLERAQVE SELECTA. PETRVS SCRIVERIVS Ex Auctoris schedis & liturarijs magnam partem descripsit, sparsa collegit, ac . . . edidit. Accedunt IOSEPHI SCALIGERI, IVSTI LIPSII, aliorumq; ad DOVZAM Carmina. LVGDVNI BATAVORVM, Ex officina THOMÆ BASSON, M.D.C.IX. 8° pp.677
1213.b.41; G.17461(1).
The copy at G.17461(1) is on large paper.

D96 DOUSA, Janus; the Younger
BATAVIÆ HOLLANDIÆQ. ANNALES: à IANO DOVSA FILIO Concepti atque inchoati iam olim; Nunc verò à PATRE recogniti, suppleti, nouaque octo librorum accessione ad . . . Decadis finem perducti & continuati . . . Ex Officina Plantiniana, APVD CHRISTOPHORVM RAPHELENGIVM . . . M.D.CI. 4° pp.501
C.74.c.1; 153.e.18.
Published at Leiden. Reissued in 1617 in Hugo de Groot's 'Chronicon Hollandiæ'.

D97 DOUSA, Janus; the Younger
IANI DOVSÆ FILII POEMATA olim à patre collecta; nunc ab amicis edita. LVGDVNI BAT. Apud Andream Cloucquium, M.D.CVII. 8° pp.227; illus.
1213.c.6(1).
In Latin, Greek or Dutch. The illustrations consist of two astronomical woodcuts on p.27. From the library of John Morris.

D98 DOUSA, Theodorus
ECHO, SIVE LVSVS Nobilium Poetarum, studio THEODORI DOVZÆ . . . conquisiti. Hic additum est Præsagium quoddam Iani Douzæ in Hispanicam Pacem iam olim conceptum editumque. LVGDVNI BATAVORVM, Ex officina THOMÆ BASSON. M.D.C.IX. 8° pp.15
G.17461(2).

DRACHT-THONEEL. 1601. *See* HEYNS, Zacharias

D99 DREBBEL, Cornelis Jacobszoon
EEN KORT TRACTAET VAN DE NATVERE DER ELEMENTEN, ENDE HOE SY VEROORSAECKEN, DEN WINT, REGHEN, BLIXEM, DONDER, ende waeromme dienstich zijn. Gedaen door CORNELIS DREBBEL. TOT HAERLEM, Ghedruckt By Vincent Casteleyn . . . 1621. 8° pp.64; illus.; port.
1136.c.3(1).
The woodcut portrait of Drebbel on the titlepage signed: C.V.S., i.e. Christoffel van Sichem. With a letter concerning Drebbel by Gherrit Pieter van Schagen to Adriaen Thonisz Metius, the so-called dedication to James I and a laudatory poem.

D100 DREBBEL, Cornelis Jacobszoon
[Een kort tractaet.] Ein kurtzer Tractat von der Natur Der Elementen Vnd wie sie den Windt/Regen/Blitz vnd Donner vervrsachen/vnd vvar zu sie nutzen. Durch Cornelium Drebbel in Niederlandisch geschrieben/vnnd . . . ins Hochteutsch . . . vber gesetzt. Gedruckt zu Leyden . . . Bey Henrichen von Haestens . . . 1608.
8° sig.AB[8]; illus., port.
1033.c.34.
The illustrations, including the portrait, here on the titlepage verso, are engraved; unsigned.

DREMMIUS, Gosardus. Disputationum physicarum septima de coelo. 1607. *See* JACCHAEUS, Gilbertus

DREMMIUS, Gosardus. Disputationum physicarum decima-septima . . . de anima rationali. 1608. *See* JACCHAEUS, Gilbertus

D101 DRESDANI

DRESDANI Prædicantis EPISOLA [*sic*], AD N. FRANCOFVRTENSEM, De Caluinistis bello persequendo. Scripta Dresdæ in Saxonia, Die 20. Nouembris. Anno 1260 [*sic*]. 4° pp. 8; sig. Pp
P.P.3444.af(148).

Published by Abraham Verhoeven at Antwerp in 1620.

DRIE artijckelen aengaende een moderatie. 1609. *See* ENGLAND [25.8.1604]

D102 DRIE-ERLEY

Drie-erley VOORSTELLINGHEN Ofte Vraghen Aen alle de gene die de getrouwe Dienaren ende Gemeynte Godes ende Christi in dese 7. vereenichde vrye Nederlandtsche Provincien/bespot . . . hebben . . . Doch voornamelyck aen die ghene, die door haer eyghen versierde ONDERLINGE VERDRAECHSAEMHEYDT het . . . ghescheurde Christendom willen vereenigen heylen ende heyligen. fol. a single sheet; illus.
1889.d.3(306).

The illustrations in woodcut consist of two circular emblems and a rectangular scene of Armageddon. Directed against Jacobus Taurinus. Printed by Paulus van Ravesteyn at Amsterdam and possibly published by Marten Jansz Brandt also at Amsterdam, ca. 1616.

D103 DRIELENBURCH, Vincent van

Basuyne der Vvaerheyt teghen Vrouw Leughen. Mitsgaders een korte ende klare aenwysinghe ende presentatie van't warachtich ende rechtvaerdich bewijs/waer mede nae waerheyt ende gerechticheyt bewesen wert . . . 'tgene by Vincent van Drielenburch in zyne schriften/Barnevelt, Ledenbergh ende Vtenbogaert te laste gheleyt is. [etc.] 4° sig. AB^4; illus.
700.h.25(2).

Anonymous. In verse. Printed by Nicolaes Biestkens at Amsterdam in 1617. The titlepage woodcut of Truth blowing her trumpet is typical for the author.

D104 DRIELENBURCH, Vincent van

(tp. 1) Calendier Ofte Almanach/Waer inne men . . . sien kan de Apocalyptische BEESTE, ende de Babylonsche Hoere daer op sittende„ Mitsgaders die ghene die d'selve Figuerlijcker wyse in de seven vrye Nederlandtsche Provincien . . . representeren. Ghepractiseert door seeckeren Sterckijcker. Met een wonderlijcke nieuwe Practica/en noch wat wonders wat nieuws . . . Beschreven door de Penne des Schryvers.
(tp. 2=p. 15) Vvat vvonders vvat nieuvvs Van de Kercke Godes ende Christi/ende van hare Bescherm-Heeren/etc. . . . Beschreven door den Sterckijcker. 1617. 4° pp. 21; illus.
1578/1232; T.2247(49).

Signed: Door Vincent van Drielenburch. Directed against Oldenbarnevelt and his supporters. The titlepage illustration shows an astrologer, that of tp. 2 is of Truth blowing her trumpet. Printed by Nicolaes Biestkens at Amsterdam. The copy at T.2247(49) is imperfect, consisting of 'Wat wonders wat nieuws' only.

D105 DRIELENBURCH, Vincent van

[Christianus-Mercurius t'samensprekinghe.] Christianus-Mercurius Ghesangh

van VVaerschouwinghe aen allen Trouwen/Rechtsinnighen ende Rechtghematichden Herderen ende Schapen Jesu Christi/tegen het woeden . . . eens . . . Stiers . . . Buyten Vtrecht. t'Amsterdam, By Marten Jansz. Brandt . . . 1615. 4° 2 leaves; illus.
T.2245(7).
A fragment or possibly a separate issue of the last two leaves published by Brandt as substitute for the corresponding leaves at the end of Drielenburch's attack on Jacobus Taurinus entitled 'Christianus-Mercurius t'samensprekinghe' which was printed by Nicolaes Biestkens at Amsterdam. Signed with Vincent van Drielenburch's monogram. The titlepage woodcut shows the arms of Amsterdam, the woodcut at the end is emblematic.

D106 DRIELENBURCH, Vincent van
Cort ende klaer Contra-Discours, Over den Nederlantschen TREVES, Ofte VOORLOOPER: Waer mede voor d'ooghen ghebeeldet werdet wat den Coningh van Spangien ende de Eertshertoghen vande Overheerde Provincien/voor ghehadt hebben met het maecken vanden Treves. tVVelck te sien is uyt het Discours Eryci Puteani . . . in desen jare 1617 uytghegheven, als oock uyt Lypsii Brief. Beschreven door een Sterckijcker. 4° pp.9; illus.
T.2422(3).
Pseudonymous. The titlepage illustration of an astrologer is the same as that in the author's signed 'Calendier', described above. Printed also by Nicolaes Biestkens at Amsterdam, published in 1617.

D107 DRIELENBURCH, Vincent van
Cort Examen ende Sententie Johannis Vtenbogaerts over seker Tractaet/welckes tytel is: Verdediging van de Resolutie der . . . Staten van Hollandt . . . Totten Vrede der Kercken . . . Over seker Antwoort op drie Vraghen/dienende tot advijs inde huydendaechsche swaricheden: by . . . Wtenbogaert lasterlijck een Libel ghenaemt . . . t'Amste[r]dam, By Marten Jansz. Brandt . . . 1615. 4° sig. A^6B-K^4L^2; illus.
T.2245(1).
Signed: Door Vincent van Drielenburch. With emblematic woodcuts on the titlepage and at the end, where there is also a chronogram. Printed by Nicolaes Biestkens at Amsterdam. The 'r' in 'Amsterdam' in the imprint has failed to print.

D108 DRIELENBURCH, Vincent van
Ernstighe Teghen-spraeck Aen de Maeght van Hollandt/over seker Aenspraeck by eenen MOPSUS ghedaen . . . Met een uytlegginge van Mopsus droom. Ghedruckt M.DC.XVII. 4° sig. AB^4; illus.
11555.e.41(1).
Anonymous. In verse. The titlepage woodcut is of Truth blowing her trumpet, typical for Van Drielenburch. Printed by Nicolaes Biestkens at Amsterdam.

D109 DRIELENBURCH, Vincent van
Figuerlijcke Verthooninghe Van't Groote Vasten-Avont-spel des grooten duysteren Nachts van de Blinde Werelt/de groote Babylon/uytgebeeldet door verscheyden Figueren/ende voornamentlijck in een Stieren-Jacht . . . Ghedruckt buyten Vtrecht/voor de Rechtsinnighe Spekulateurs . . . 1616. 4° 4 unsigned leaves; illus.
700.h.25(1).
Anonymous. In verse. With a large woodcut. Directed against Jacobus Taurinus. Printed by Nicolaes Biestkens at Amsterdam.

D110 DRIELENBURCH, Vincent van
Gheestelijcke Klock-luyinghe/Ende Klocke-gheslach Over TVVEEDERLEYE VOORSTELLINGEN ghedaen/Voornamelijck Aen Iohan WTENBOGAERT ende zyne ... mede-Stryders„ ende aen ... alle die, welcke GODS KERCKE teghen zyn ... Ghedruckt Auro Dammani Aurei, sive ISAACI GOUTII. [etc.] 4° pp.20
T.2247(2).
Anonymous and with a fictitious imprint; probably printed by Paulus van Ravesteyn and published by Marten Jansz Brandt, both at Amsterdam, in 1616.

D111 DRIELENBURCH, Vincent van
GHESANGH Over Den CAP-ende COVELMAECKER der Remonstranten, die de Kinderen Gods voor Sotten ende Dwasen uytroept/ende op haar Hooft (welcke Christus alleenelijck is) syne BEESTIGE, PAEPSCHE ende ANTICHRISTISCHE CAP-COVEL setten wil ... Ghedruckt in de Druckerye vande Almanacken. 1617. 4° sig.A^4; illus.
700.h.25(7).
Anonymous. In verse. The titlepage woodcut is of Truth blowing her trumpet, typical of Van Drielenburch. The pseudonymous imprint is that of Nicolaes Biestkens at Amsterdam.

D112 DRIELENBURCH, Vincent van
Grove Lasteren ende Beschuldiginghen Johannis Utenbogaerts/ghetoghen uyt zijn Tractaet/Gheintituleert Verdedigingh vande Resolutie der Mo. Staten van Hollandt ende West-Frieslandt: Waer mede hy den ... Dienaren des H. Euangeliums/ende de Ghemeynte Jesu Christi ... belasteret ... t'Amsterdam, By Marten Jansz Brandt ... 1616. 4° sig.A^4
T.2246(9).
Anonymous. A separate issue of part of 'Cort examen ende Sententie Johannis Vtenbogaerts', 1615, described above. Printed by Nicolaes Biestkens at Amsterdam.

D113 DRIELENBURCH, Vincent van
PROEFKEN OFT STAELKEN van Iohannis Vtenbogaerts ende Iacobi Taurini Onderlinghe Verdraeghsaemheyt. Dat is: Een Register van verscheyden vinnighe bittere ... laster-redenen ... Ghenomen uyt haer schriften ... Het eene/ Verdedingh [*sic*] vande Resol. &c. Het ander Onderlinghe Verdraeghsaemheyt ... t'AMSTERDAM, By Marten Jansz. Brandt ... 1616. 4° pp.40
T.2246(20).
Anonymous. Drielenburch's authorship is considered probable in *Knuttel* no.2268 and accepted as certain by *De Bie & Loosjes,* dl.2.p.594. Sometimes wrongly ascribed to Jacobus Trigland.

D114 DRIELENBURCH, Vincent van
VISIOEN, Ofte Vertreckinghe der zinnen ende des Gheestes. Anders gheseyt/Een Dach-ghesichte, Belanghende den doot-crancken staet van de Oprechticheyt. Ghesien binnen corte Jaren/ter plaetsen van wijlen Het Woudt sonder Ghenaden. In Alexandrijnsche Rijm-verskens ghestelt/Door eenen Lief-hebber der Poësie. Tot Franeker, Voor Jelis Claesz Verhal ... 1616. 4° sig.A-C^4
11557.e.2.
Pseudonymous. The imprint is doubtful. With the exlibris of 'J.M. Grypt als't rypt'; H.C. (or: C.H.) Quæro.

D115 DRIELENBURCH, Vincent van
VVTKOMSTE ende Verthooninghe Van den Vtrechtschen Martelaer IOHANNES VVTENBOGAERT: De welcke zijn eyghen Examen ende ... Sententie ... voorghesteldt zijnde ... voortgecomen is met ... een opschrift van zijn verkeerde noodighe ontschuldiginghe, over zyne Grove Lasteringhen ende

GHESANGH
Over
Den CAP. ende COVELMAECKER
der Remonstranten, die de Kinderen Gods voor Sotten ende Dwasen uytroept/ende op haer Hooft (welck Christus alleenelijck is) syne BEESTIGE, PAEPSCHE ende ANTICHRISTISCHE CAP-COVEL setten wil.

1. Corinth. 1 :27/25.
Het dwase der Werelt heeft Godt uytverkozen/ om de Wyse te beschamen: Ende het krancke des Wereldts heeft God uytverkozen/om het stercke te beschamen.
Dedwaesheyt Gods is wyser dan de Menschen [zijn:] ende de kranckheyt Gods/is stercker dan de Menschen[zijn.]

Ghedruckt inde Druckerye vande Almanacken. 1617.

7.

D111

Beschuldiginghen . . . Door Vincent van Drielenburch . . . t'Amsterdam, By Marten Jansz. Brandt . . . 1616. 4° pp.97
T.2246(11*,13).
Printed by Nicolaes Biestkens at Amsterdam. The preliminaries of this work, sig.∴, have been bound before the tract preceding it in this volume.

DROGENHAM, Hermannus Pet. Disputatio theologica de coena Domini. 1613. *See* LINDEN, Henricus Antonides van der

D116 DROOM-GESICHT
DROOM-GESICHT Eenes metter Herten tot GODT op-getrockenen Mensches: In hem veroorzaeckt (zoo't schijnt) door . . . over-denckinge van GODES Goetheyt (bijzonder nu/door d'aenmerckinghe der goeder hope tot den lang gewenschten Vrede vernieut zijnde) . . . BLY-EYND-SPELS-WYZE in Druck uyt-ghegeven . . . Gedruckt . . . M.CCCCCC VII. 4° sig.A^2B-I^4; illus.
1485.tt.54.
With several poems. The titlepage woodcut shows King David, an allusion to the Dutch version of Psalm 103 included in the text.

D117 DRURAEUS, Gulielmus
ALVREDVS SIVE ALFREDVS TRAGICOMOEDIA TER EXHIBITA, In Seminario Anglorum Duaceno ab eiusdem Collegii Iuuentute . . . M DCXIX. AVTHORE GVILIELMO DRVREO . . . DVACI, Ex officina Ioannis Bogardi. M DC XX. 16° pp.158
840.a.4; G.17412.
The copy at 840.a.4 from the library of John Morris. The copy at G.17412 has a slightly mutilated titlepage.

D118 DRUSIUS, Johannes; the Elder
[Collections] (tp.1) IOH. DRVSII OPVSCVLA, quæ ad Grammaticam spectant, OMNIA, in unum volumen compacta . . . FRANEKERÆ, EXCVDEBAT AEGIDIUS RADAEUS . . . 1609.
(tp.2) I. DRVSII DE LITTERIS MOSCHE VECHALEB LIBRI DVO. Editio tertia . . . auctior multo & emendatior. FRANEKERÆ, EXCVDEBAT AEGIDIUS RADAEUS . . . 1608.
(tp.3) ALPHABETVM EBRAICVM VETVS . . . Omnia recens edita, & notis illustrata, per I. DRVSIVM . . . Editio altera melior & auctior. FRANEKERAE Excudebat Ægidius Radæus . . . 1609. 4° 3 pt.: pp.152; 55; 63
1017.f.10(5–7); 63.m.28(1–3); 621.d.18.
All three parts are listed on the verso of tp.1 as included in this edition. The copy at 63.m.28 is imperfect; wanting pt.3 while containing 'Grammatica linguae sanctae' within pt.1. The copy at 621.d.18 is imperfect; wanting pt.3.

D119 DRUSIUS, Johannes; the Elder
[Collections] IOH. DRVSII DE SECTIS IVDAICIS COMMENTARII Trihæresio & Minervali NIC. SERARII . . . oppositi, atque antehac seorsim editi. Accessit denuo IOSEPHI SCALIGERI . . . Elenchus Trihæresii eiusdem. SIXTINVS AMAMA Omnia . . . redegit atque secundam hanc editionem varijs additamentis locupletiorem accuravit, nec non Græca . . . Latiné vertit . . . ARNHEMIÆ, Apud IOANNEM IANSONIVM. Typis Frederici Heynsii Typograph. In Acad. Franekeranâ, 1619. 4° pp.460
1017.f.10(1); 219.e.17.
With other works.

D120 DRUSIUS, Johannes; the Elder
[Ad fratres Belgas epistola.] Brief Van IANVS DRVSIVS . . . Aen de Nederlandtsche Broeders. Waer in vvederleyt vvordt de valsche lasteringhe van't gheschapen vvoordt onlanx tegen den Autheur gestroyt by SIBRANDVS LVBBERTVS . . . Wt den Latyne verduytscht . . . M.DC.XV. 4° pp.7
T.2245(8).
The translator's sonnet signed: R.T., i.e. Reinier Telle. With manuscript notes.

D121 DRUSIUS, Johannes; the Elder

CL. V. IOH. DRVSII AD LOCA DIFFICILIORA IOSVÆ, IVDICVM, & SAMVELEM COMMENTARIVS . . . Additus est SIXTINI AMAMA Commentariolus de decimis Mosaïcis. FRANEKERÆ FRISIORVM, Excudebat FREDERICUS HEYNSIUS . . . 1618. Sumptibus Iohannis Iohannis Bibliopolæ Arnhemiensis. 4° pp.572

1017.f.4; 219.e.12.

D122 DRUSIUS, Johannes; the Elder

CL. V. IOH. DRVSII AD LOCA DIFFICILIORA PENTATEVCHI . . . COMMENTARIVS . . . Opus Posthumum. FRANEKERÆ FRISIORVM, Excudebat FREDERICUS HEYNSIUS . . . 1617. Sumptibus Iohannis Iohannis Bibliopolæ Arnhemiensis. 4° pp.619

1017.f.3(1); 219.e.11.

The editor's preface and index signed: Sixtinus ab Amama. Ownership inscription in the copy at 1017.f.3: C.DAuuergne.

D123 DRUSIUS, Johannes; the Elder

I. DRVSII AD MINERVAL SERARII RESPONSIO . . . FRANEKERAE Ex officina AEGIDII RADAEI . . . M.D.CVI. 8° pp.115

689.a.7(3).

With two Hebrew poems by Joannes Drusius the Younger and with a publisher's advertisement.

D124 DRUSIUS, Johannes; the Elder

(tp.1) I. DRVSII AD VOCES EBRAICAS NOVI TESTAMENTI Commentarius duplex: Prior ordine Alphabetico conscriptus est, alter antehac editus fuit . . . In utroque autem variæ . . . Censuræ ITEM Ejusdem Annotationum in N. Testamentum PARS ALTERA. NEC NON Vitæ, Operumque I. DRVSII . . . delineatio & tituli, PER ABELVM CVRIANDRVM. FRANEKERÆ FRISIORVM, Excudebat FREDERICUS HEYNSIUS . . . 1616. Sumptibus Iohannis Iohannis F. Bibliopolæ Arnhemiensis.

(tp.2) VITÆ, OPERVMQVE IOH. DRVSII EDITORVM ET NONDVM EDITORVM, DELINEATIO, ET TITVLI. PER ABELVM CVRIANDRVM. FRANEKERÆ, Excudebat FREDERICUS HEYNSIUS . . . 1616. 4° pp.226,192; 9–52

219.e.10(2); 1017.f.9(2).

Pp. 1–8 of the 'Vitae . . . delineatio' have been absorbed into the preceding part. The copy at 219.e.10(2) has the last gathering misbound; the copy at 1017.f.9(2) is imperfect, wanting the contribution by Curiander.

D125 DRUSIUS, Johannes; the Elder

I. DRVSII ANNOTATIONVM in totum JESU CHRISTI TESTAMENTVM, sive PRÆTERITORVM libri decem . . . Sumptib. Iohannis Iohannis Bibliopolæ Arnhemiensis. FRANEKERÆ, Excudebat AEGIDIVS RADAEVS . . . 1612. 4° pp.454

1017.f.9(1); 219.e.10(1).

With a biographical sketch of Joannes Drusius the Younger in the preface. Ownership inscription in the copy at 1017.f.9(1): C. D'Auuergne.

D126 DRUSIUS, Johannes; the Elder

APOPHTHEGMATA EBRAEORVM AC ARABVM, Ex Avoth R. Nathan, Aristea, Libro selectarum margaritarum, & aliis auctoribus collecta, Latinéque reddita, cum brevibus Scholiis, Per I. DRVSIVM . . . Editio altera melior & auctior. FRANEKERAE, Excudebat Ægidius Radæus . . . M.DC.XII. 4° pp.92

621.g.4(3); C.75.b.12(1).

D127 DRUSIUS, Johannes; the Elder

I. DRUSII DE HASIDAEIS, quorum mentio IN LIBRIS MACHABAEORUM LIBELLUS AD IOHAN. VTENBOGARDUM. FRANEKERAE, Ex Officina Typographica AEGIDII RADAEI . . . 1603. 8° pp.64

C.119.dd.24(2).

In Latin, Hebrew and Latin, or Greek. With special reference to the 'Historia Ebraica' of Gorionides.

D128 DRUSIUS, Johannes; the Elder
I. DRUSII ELOHIM SIVE de nomine Dei . . . Additę sunt ejusdem notæ, in quibus epistola Hieronymi 136. ad Marcellam explicatur, emendatur . . . FRANEKERAE Ex officina AEGIDII RADAEI . . . 1603. 8° pp.62
C.119.dd.24(1).
With an epitaph for Claudius Puteanus in Hebrew by Joannes Drusius the Younger. With the author's manuscript dedication of the volume containing this and two other works to Jacques Auguste de Thou whose arms are stamped in gold on the covers.

D129 DRUSIUS, Johannes; the Elder
(tp.1) I. DRUSII ELOHIM . . . FRANEKERAE Ex officina AEGIDII RADAEI . . . 1604.
(tp.2) I. DRUSII RESPONSIO AD QVAESTIONES Anonymi Theologi è Germania. Jungi debet Libello de nomine ELOHIM. FRANEKERAE, Apud AEGIDIVM RADAEVM . . . M D CVI. 8° 2 pt.: pp.62; 32
689.a.7(4,5).

D130 DRUSIUS, Johannes; the Elder
GRAMMATICA CHALDAICA, descripta EX TABULIS MERCERI ad usum juventutis; sed inter describendum ita mutata . . . ut nova planè Grammatica dici meritò queat. FRANEKERAE, APUD AEGIDIUM RADAEUM . . . M.D.CII. 8° pp.110
1568/2861(1).
The dedication signed: I. Drusius.

D131 DRUSIUS, Johannes; the Elder
GRAMMATICA LINGVAE SANCTAE NOVA. In usum Academiæ quæ est apud Frisios occidentales . . . FRANEKERAE. Excudebat Ægidius Radæus . . . M.DC.XII. 4° pp.124
63.l.6; 63.m.28(2).
The author referred to in the Hebrew 'Epistola filii Iohannis'. The copy at 63.m.28(2) has been inserted in pt.1 of the 'Opuscula', but is not listed as belonging to that collection on the titlepage verso of that work.

D132 DRUSIUS, Johannes; the Elder
I. DRVSII HENOCH. SIVE De patriarcha Henoch . . . FRANEKERÆ, Excudebat FREDERICUS HEYNSIUS . . . 1615. 4° pp.36
1017.f.10(2).

DRUSIUS, Johannes; the Elder. I. Drusii Responsio ad quaestiones anonymi theologi è Germania. 1606. *See* supra: Elohim. 1604.

D133 DRUSIUS, Johannes; the Elder
(tp.1=pt.1. sig. acorn 1r) I. DRVSII RESPONSIO AD SERARIVM De Tribus Sectis Judæorum. Accessit IOSEPHI SCALIGERI Elenchus Trihæresii NICOLAI SERARII etc. FRANEQVERÆ, Ex Officina AEGIDII RADAEI . . . M.D.CV.
(tp.2=pt.1. sig.★1r) I. DRVSII DE TRIBVS SECTIS Iudæorum, LIBRI QVATVOR, Qui Apologiam continent libelli de Hasidæis. EIUSDEM Spicilegium Trihæresii NICOLAI SERARII. FRANEKERAE, APVD AEGIDIVM RADAEVM . . . M.D.CV.
(tp.3=pt.2. sig.A1r) IOSEPHI SCALIGERI . . . Elenchus Trihæresii NICOLAI SERARII. Ejus in ipsum Scaligerum animadversiones confutatæ . . . FRANEKERAE, Excudebat AEGIDIVS RADAEVS . . . M.DC.V. 8° 2 pt.: pp.287, 272
C.79.a.4.
With a Hebrew poem by Johannes Drusius the Younger. From the library of Isaac Casaubon.

D134 DRUSIUS, Johannes; the Elder

(tp.1) I. DRUSII Tetragrammaton, SIVE DE Nomine Dei proprio, quod TETRAGRAMMATON vocant. Accesserunt additamenta epistolarum aliquot & NOTAE. ITEM, Pauli Burgensis Episcopi, de nomine Tetragrammato, quæstiones duodecim: ET I. DRUSII in easdem Scholia, FRANEKERAE, Excudebat AEGIDIUS RADAEVS . . . M D CIIII.
(tp.2=p.115) PAULI de sancta Maria BVRGENSIS EPISCOPI . . . DE Nomine divino Quæstiones duodecim . . . 1604. 8° pp.143
C.119.dd.24(3).

D135 DRUSIUS, Johannes; the Younger

LACHRYMAE IOHANNIS DRVSII IUNIORIS, tribus carminum generibus expressæ, IN OBITVM . . . IOSEPHI SCALIGERI . . . adjuncta sunt alia duo epitaphia diu ante conscripta; unum, quo dux . . . cognominatus de Moy, à famulo suo interfectus scribitur: alterum, de obitu . . . D. Theodori Bezæ . . . FRANEKERÆ, EXCVDEBAT AEGIDIUS RADAEUS . . . 1609. 4° sig. AB^4
1124.h.16(8); 1017.f.10(4); 63.m.28(4).
In Hebrew, Latin or Greek. The copy at 1124.h.16(8) is the author's presentation copy to Jacques Auguste de Thou. The other two copies are imperfect; wanting all after the first four, unsigned, leaves, consisting of the titlepage and Hebrew text.

DRY artyckelen aengaende de moderatie. 1609. *See* ENGLAND [25.8.1604]

DRYDERLEY refereynen. 1614. *See* SPELEN van sinne . . . Rotterdam . . . 1561.

DU BARTAS, Guillaume de Saluste. *See* SALUSTE DU BARTAS, Guillaume de

D136 DUERER, Albrecht

[Elementa geometrica.] ALBERTI DVRERI INSTITVTIONVM GEOMETRICARVM LIBRI QVATVOR . . . versi olim è Germanicâ in linguam Latinam, & nunc iteratô editi . . . ARNHEMIÆ IN DVCATV GELDRIÆ Ex Officina Iohannis Iansonii . . . 1606. fol. pp.185; illus.
530.m.9(1).
A leaf with an extraneous illustration has been inserted in this copy. The pagination is irregular.

D137 DUERER, Albrecht

[Vier Bücher von menschlicher Proportion.] LES QVATRE LIVRES D'ALBERT DVRER . . . de la proportion des parties & pourtraicts des corps humains. TRADVICTS PAR LOYS MEIGRET . . . de langue Latine en Françoise. A ARNHEM, Chez Iean Ieansz. 1613. fol. ff.124; illus.
786.l.44.

D138 DU JARRIC, Pierre

L'HISTOIRE DES CHOSES PLVS MEMORABLES ADVEnuës tant ès Indes Orientales, qu'autres pays de la descouuerte des Portugais. EN L'ESTABLISSEMENT ET progrez de la foy Chrestienne & Catholique. ET principalement de ce que les Religieux de la Compagnie de IESVS y ont faict, & enduré pour la mesme fin. Depuis qu'ils y sont entrez iusques à l'an 1600. Par le P. PIERRE DV IARRIC . . . A ARRAS, Chez GILLES BAVDVIN . . . M.DC.XI. (col.) A ARRAS, DE L'IMPRIMERIE DE GVILLAVME DE LA RIVIERE . . . M.D.C.XI. 8° pp.977
G.14962.
Ownership inscription: Guyon de Sardiere.

D139 DU JON, François; the Elder

[Letters] Certayne letters/translated into English/being first written in Latine.

Two, by . . . Mr. Francis Iunius . . . The other, by the exiled English Church, abiding . . . at Amsterdam in Holland. Together with the Confession of faith prefixed . . . Printed . . . 1602. 4° pp. 57
4135.b.28.
With a further letter letter of F. Du Jon. The translator's preface signed: R. G. Printed at Amsterdam.

D140 DU JON, François; the Elder
DISPVTATIONVM THEOLOGICARVM TERTIA DE ESSENTIA DEI, ET ATTRIBVTIS ILLIVS, Quam . . . Præside . . . D. FRANCISCO IUNIO . . . pro virili sustinebo SAMVEL BOVCHEREAV . . . LVGDVNI BATAVORVM, Ex Officinâ Ioannis Patii . . . D.M.CII. 4° sig. C^6
4376.de.16(73).
Leaf C4 is wrongly signed A4.

D141 DU JON, François; the Elder
DISPVTATIONVM THEOLOGICARVM QVARTA, DE ATTRIBVTIS DEI, Quam . . . Sub Præsidio . . . D. FRANCISCI IUNII . . . tueri conabitur DANIEL PLANCIUS . . . LVGDVNI BATAVORVM, Ex Officinâ Ioannis Patii . . . M.D.CI. 4° sig. D^4
4376.de.16(74).

D142 DU JON, François; the Elder
DISPVTATIONVM THEOLOGICARVM DECIMA-TERTIA, DE Statu duplici Christi Θεανθρώπου, HVMILIATIONIS ET EXALTATIONIS: Cujus defensionem . . . Sub auspiciis . . . D. FRANCISCI IUNII . . . aggrediar HENRICVS NOLTHENIVS . . . LVGDVNI BATAVORVM, Ex Officinâ Ioannis Patii . . . M.D.CI. 4° sig. N^4
4376.de.16(6).

D143 DU JON, François; the Elder
Disputationum Theologicarum repetitarum Sexagesima-prima, DE MISSA, Quam . . . Præside D. FRANCISCO IUNIO . . . sustinebo PETRUS HONDIUS . . . Ad . . . Reipub. Flissing. SENATUM. LVGDVNI BATAVORVM, Ex Officinâ Ioannis Patii . . . M.D.CI. 4° sig. Qqq^4
4376.de.16(54).

D144 DU JON, François; the Elder
[Ecclesiastici sive De natura et administrationibus ecclesiae Dei, libri tres.] VERCLARINGHE Van twee vraghen/door D. Franciscus Junius . . . DE EERSTE, Van de over-een-cominghe ende het onderscheyt der Politijcke ende Kerckelijcke bedieninghe. DE TWEEDE, Van het Recht des Magistraets in de sichtbare Kercke. Vertaelt ende ghestelt teghens het . . . Tractaet van Iohannes VVten Bogaerdt . . . AMSTERDAM. By Jan Eversz. Cloppenburch . . . 1610. 4° sig. $A–D^4$
T.2240(17); T.2421(15).

D145 DU JON, François; the Elder
FRANCISCI IVNII ORATIO FVNEBRIS, IN obitum . . . D. LVCÆ TRELCATII . . . Habita in auditorio publico Academiæ Lugdunensis in Batavis, A.D. XXX. Kal. Augusti . . . M.D.C.II. LVGDVNI BATAVORVM, Ex Typographeîo Christophori Guyotij, Impensis IOANNIS ORLERS. M.D.C.II. 4° pp. 14
834.g.35(1).
With a poem by Daniel Heinsius.

D146 DU JON, François; the Elder
THESES THEOLOGICÆ, DE Fœderibus, & Testamentis divinis, Quas . . . Sub Præsidio . . . D. FRANCISCI IUNII . . . tueri adnitar GVILIELMVS RIVETVS . . . LUGDUNI BATAVORUM, Ex Officinâ Ioannis Patii . . . M.D.CII. 4° sig. AB^4
4376.de.16(28).

D147 DU JON, François; the Elder

THESES THEOLOGICÆ DE VETERI ET NOVO DEI FOEDERE, Quas . . . Sub Præsidio . . . D. FRANCISCI IUNII, publicè defendet SAMVEL MEJENREIS . . . LUGDUNI BATAVORUM, Ex Officinâ Ioannis Patii . . . D.D.CII [*sic*]. 4° sig. A[4]
4376.de.16(29).
Cropped.

D148 DU JON, Johan Kazimir

WEDERLEGGINGE VAN DE WEEGSCHAAL Onlangs uytgegeven tegens d'Oratie des Ed. Heere DUDLEY CARLETONS . . . dienende tot verantwoording van de voorss. Oratie, ende om te sien, hoe valsch . . . die voorñ. Weegschaal is, gemaeckt deur . . . H.C. du ION . . . Gedruckt . . . 1618. 4° pp.438
T.2248(1).

DU MAURIER, Benjamin Aubery. *See* AUBÉRY DU MAURIER, Benjamin

DU MAURIER, I. *See* AUBÉRY DU MAURIER, Benjamin

D149 DU MOULIN, Pierre; the Elder

[De la juste providence de Dieu.] TRACTAETGEN VANDE Rechtveerdighe Voorsienigheyt GODS: Daer in ondersocht wort een . . . geschrift van Heer Arnoux Iesuyt, met het welcke hy soeckt te bewijsen/dat Calvinus Godt een Autheur vande Sonde maeckt. Tot Verdedigingh Calvini . . . ende der Ghereformeerde Kercken . . . Door P.D.M. Wt de Fransche . . . Tale overgheset/ende met een Voor-reden verrijckt/inde welcke vande lasteringhen der Remonstranten een weynich ghehandelt wordt. 'TAMSTELREDAM, By Marten Jansz. Brant . . . 1617. 4° pp.24
T.2247(47).
The author's full name given in the preface.

DU MOULIN, Pierre; the Elder. Dialogues rustiques. 1615. [Sometimes attributed to Pierre du Moulin.] *See* MONCY, Jean de

DUNCKER, Hermannus. Disputatio theologica de libertate Christiana. 1602. *See* LINDEN, Henricus Antonides van der

D150 DUNS Scotus, Joannes

(tp.1) F. IOANNIS DVNS SCOTI . . . IN PRIMVM ET SECVNDVM SENTENTIARVM QVÆSTIONES SVBTILISSIMÆ. Nunc nouiter recognitæ, & . . . ab innumeris mendis & vitiis . . . castigatæ; annotationibus marginalibus, doctorumque . . . citationibus exornatæ; scholiis . . . insertis, indicibus . . . illustratæ. Per P.F. HVGONEM CAVELLVM . . . Accesserunt per eundem, Vita Scoti, Apologia pro ipso contra P. Abrahamum Bzouium . . . ANTVERPIÆ, Apud IOANNEM KEERBERGIVM. M.DC.XX. [etc.]
(tp.2) F. IOANNIS DVNS SCOTI . . . IN TERTIVM ET QVARTVM SENTENTIARVM QVÆSTIONES SVBTILISSIMÆ . . . ANTVERPIÆ, Apud IOANNEM KEERBERGIVM. M.DC.XX. [etc.] (col.) ANTVERPIÆ, EX TYPOGRAPHIA IOANNIS KEERBERGII . . . M.DC.XX. fol. 2 vol.: pp.456,343; 266, 564; illus.
3835.f.4.
The illustrations consist of two astronomical woodcuts on p.194 of vol.1. pt.2.

DU PERRON, Jacques. *See* DAVY DU PERRON, Jacques

D151 DU PRÉAU, Gabriel

NARRATIO HISTORICA CONCILIORVM OMNIVM ECCLESIÆ CHRISTIANÆ Gabrielis Prateoli, Cui addidit Castigationes suas & alia nonnulla IOHANNES LYDIVS . . .

LVGDVNI-BATAVORVM, Ex Typographio Henrici ab Haestens . . . M.D.C.X. Impensis Auctoris. 8° pp.189
1607/1039.

D152 DURANDUS, Gulielmus; the Elder, Bishop
RATIONALE DIVINORVM OFFICIORVM, A R.D. GVLIELMO DVRANDO . . . concinnatum: atque nunc recens . . . Annotationibus illustratum. Adiectum fuit . . . aliud Diuinorum officiorum Rationale ab Ioanne Beletho . . . conscriptum, ac nunc . . . in lucem editum . . . Hæc editio . . . diligenter correcta . . . ANTVERPIAE, Apud Viduam & hæredes PETRI BELLERI . . . M.DC.XIV. 8° 2 tom.: ff.568
3478.aa.29.
The editor's dedication signed: Nicolaus Doard. The 'Rationale divinorum officiorum' of Joannes Beleth edited by Cornelius Laurimanus.

DUTIFULL and respective considerations. 1609. *See* LEECH, Humfrey

D153 DUVAL, André; Professor
LA VIE ADMIRABLE DE SOEVR MARIE DE L'INCARNATION, RELIGIEUSE CONVERSE EN l'ordre de notre Dame du mont Carmel, appellée au monde la DAMOISELLE ACARIE . . . Par M. ANDRE' DV VAL . . . A DOVAY, Chez BALTAZAR BELLERE . . . 1621, [etc.] 12° pp.660
862.f.23.

D154 DUYCKIUS, Franco
Amplissimi Viri FRANCONIS DVYCKII Comparatio elegans VENATORIS ET AMATORIS. Edita ex Museo IOACHIMI MORSI. Adiungitur Epigrammation in Cupidinem Arantem, & Elogium eiusdem à Nobilissimo DN: IANO DOVSA conscriptum. LVGDVNI BATAVORVM Excudebat IACOBVS MARCI M D C XIX. 4° pp.8
1213.m.7(6).
A wedding gift from Morsius to Henricus Rumpius of Hamburg.

D155 DUYM, Jacob
(tp.1) EEN GHEDENCK-BOECK, Het welck ons Leert aen al het quaet en den grooten moetwil van de Spaingnaerden . . . ons aen-ghedaen te ghedencken. ENDE de groote liefde ende trou vande Princen uyt den huyse van Nassau, aen ons betoont . . . te onthouden. Speel-wijs in dicht ghestelt door IACOB DVYM. GHEDRVCKT TOT LEYDEN, By Henrick Lodowijcxszoon van Haestens . . . 1606.
(tp.2) EEN NASSAVSHCE [*sic*] PERSEVS, verlosser van Andromeda, OFTE de Nederlantsche Maeght . . . Door IACOB DVYM. Reden Verwindt.
(tp.3) HET MOORDADICH STVCK VAN Balthasar Gerards . . . door IACOB DVYM. GHEDRVCKT TOT LEYDEN, By Henrick Lodowixsoon van Haestens . . . 1606.
(tp.4) BENOVDE BELEGHERINGE der stad Leyden . . . Ende het vvonderbaerlijck ontset daer op . . . ghevolght . . . door IACOB DVYM. GHEDRVCKT TOT LEYDEN, By Henrick Lodowixsson van Haestens . . . 1606.
(tp.5) Belegheringhe der Stadt ANTWERPEN, By den Prince van Parma . . . door IACOB DUYM. GHEDRVCKT TOT LEYDEN, By Henrick Lodowixsoon van Haestens . . . 1606.
(tp.6) DE CLOECK-MOEDIGHE ENDE Stoute daet, van het innemen des Casteels van Breda . . . door IACOB DVYM. GHEDRVCKT TOT LEYDEN, By Henrick Lodowixsoon van Haestens . . . 1606.
(tp.7) EEN BEWYS DAT BETER IS eenen goeden Crijgh, dan eenen gheveynsden Peys . . . door IACOB DVYM. GHEDRVCKT TOT LEYDEN, By Henrick Lodowixsoon

van Haestens . . . 1606. 4° 7 pt.: sig.x-xxx^4; A-G^4; A-F^4; a-i^4; A-G^4; A-G^4; A-F^{4}G^5; illus., port.

11754.bb.31(1).

The first part contains the preliminaries. The parts are misbound in the order: 2,5,3,4,6,1,7, The portrait of the author, signed: IDGheyn, is a late impression of the plate used for Duym's 'Spiegelboeck', 1600, bound after the 'Ghedenck-boeck'. The vignettes include portraits of William and Maurice of Orange, views of Leiden, Antwerp, Breda, and emblems.

D156 DUYM, Jacob

[Historie der gouverneurs.] CORTE HISTORISCHE BESCHRYVINGHE DER NEDERLANDSCHER Oorlogen/Vanden beginne ende aenvangh aff der Beroerten tot het twaelff-jaerich Bestandt toe . . . Met d'Articulen van't Bestandt ende Verclaringhe van dien. D.I.I.D. TOT ARNHEM, By Jan Janssoon . . . 1612. 8° pp.213; illus.

1436.c.24(2).

Anonymous. The device on the titlepage is one used by the printer Henrick Lodewijckszoon van Haestens. The illustrations are woodcut portraits with 5-line Dutch verses.

DUYTSCHE Academi. 1619. *See* COSTER, Samuel

D157 DWINGLO, Bernardus

Christalijnen Bril, Tot versterckinge van t'schemerende ghesicht der Een-Voudighen die inde huydens-daechsche verschillen der Religie met onverstant yveren; VVaer door sy claerlick aenschouwen moghen het weder-schriftelijcke . . . ghevoelen ADRIANI SMOVTII, van datmen de Voor-standers en Drijvers der vijf articulen . . . behoort . . . met de doot te straffen . . . Ghedruckt . . . 1613. (col.) Ter Goude by Iasper Tournay . . . 1613. 4° sig.A-P^{4}Q^6

T.2243(16).

Anonymous.

D158 DWINGLO, Bernardus

MONSTER Vande leere der Amsterdamsche Predicanten over de voornaemste Poincten die huydendaechs ghedisputeert werden tusschen de . . . Remonstranten, ende ende [*sic*] de . . . Contra-Remonstranten . . . ghetrocken wt hare, ende bysonder wt Iacobi Triglandij Schriften teghen . . . Ioannem Wtenbogaert . . . Waer by noch sijn gevoecht eenige andere nieuwicheden FESTI HOMMII ende IOANNIS POLYANDRI Mede ghetrocken uyt hare Schriften Ten dienste van Maerten Jansz. Brandt . . . om by hem behandicht te werdē aenden Autheur vaude [*sic*] . . . Staet der voor-naemste Quæstien onlangs voor hem ghedruckt. GEDRVCKT Voor Ian Paedts Iacobsz. . . . TOT LEYDEN . . . 1616. 4° sig.):(^{6}A-E^4

T.2246(8).

Anonymous. The 'autheur vande . . . Staet der voor-naemste quaestien' is Johannes Polyander.

D159 DWINGLO, Bernardus

Noodighe ende getrouwe waerschouwinghe aen de Remonstrantsche Predicanten/voor de valsche ende bedrieghelijcke handelinghe van Iaques van Hecke, ende andere verspieders tot haer ghesonden . . . 1620. 4° sig.A-D^4

T.2250(8).

Anonymous.

D160 DWINGLO, Bernardus

Nulliteyten, Mishandelinghen/ende onbillijcke Proceduren des Nationalen Synodi/ghehouden binnen Dordrecht . . . 1618.61119 [*sic*] . . . Ghedruckt in de Druckerye van N.N. 1619. 4° sig.AB^{4}C^1

T.2249(22).

Anonymous.

D161 DWINGLO, Bernardus
PROTEST Des Autheurs vanden Christalijnen Bril, tegens den gepretendeerden Polijst-steen . . . TOT ROTTERDAM. Voor Matys Bastiaensen . . . 1614. 4° sig. AB^4C^5
T.2244(2).
Anonymous.

D162 DWINGLO, Bernardus
VOORBODE Vande Antwoort op seker boecxken gheintituleert Ontrouwe des valschen VVaerschouwers &c . . . TOT LEYDEN By Ian Paedts Iacobsz. . . . 1616. 4° sig. A^6
T.2246(25).
Anonymous. Directed against Jacobus Trigland.

D163 DYEMENUS, Gulielmus
GVILIELMI DYEMENI . . . AD REGVLAS IVRIS ROMANORVM ANTIQVI NOTÆ: Ab ARN. DYEMENO . . . in lucem editæ . . . LVGDVNI BATAVORVM, Ex Officina Ludovici Elzevirij . . . M.DC.XVI. 8° pp. 551
1608/1174.

E

EBER, Paul. L'estat de la religion . . . du peuple iudaique. 1604. *See* CRESPIN, L'estat de l'église. 1605.

D'EDICTALE cassatie . . . van . . . Ferdinandus II. 1620. *See* GERMANY [29.1.1620]

E1 EEMBD, Govert vander
G. vander Eembd Haerlemse Belegeringhs TREVR-BLY-EYNDE-SPEL . . . IN 'sGRAVEN-HAGE. By Aert Meuris . . . M.DC.XIX. 4° sig. ⋆, ⋆⋆/⋆⋆⋆⋆⋆, $A–E^4F^3$; illus.
11755.b.20.
The woodcut shows the emblem of 'Liefd' boven al', motto of the Haarlem chamber of rhetoric 'De Wijngaertrancke'.

E2 EEMBD, Govert vander
Mr. G. vander Eembd. Treur-spel SOPHONISBA . . . IN s'GRAVEN-HAGHE. By Aert Meuris . . . 1621. [etc.] 4° sig. ⋆, $A–E^4F^2$
11754.bb.9.

E3 EENENTWINTIGH
Eenentwintigh Artijckelen/waervan de zeventien toucheren de trafijcken/ende de vier de liberteyt der conscientie/overghegheven door de generale Kooplieden van Enghelandt/aen de Ghecommitterde [*sic*] van syne Majesteyt/tracterende met den Ambassadeur van Spaengien . . . Overghezet vvt d'Enghelsche . . . in Nederduytsche tale. TOT ROTTERDAM, By Jan van Waesberghe . . . XVI^{c}. IIII. 4°
4 unsigned leaves
597.e.28.

Den EENIGEN ende rechten waerom. 1619. *See* WTENBOGAERT, Jan

EENVOUDICH ende ernstich bericht. 1615. *See* KNESEBECK, Thomas von

EFFIGIES D. Johannis Bogermanni. 1620. *See* FEDDES, Pieter

E4 EFFIGIES

[Effigies et insignia omnium Brabantiæ Ducum.] (col.) 1613. Impressæ Amstelodami in ædibus Nicolai Ioannis Visscheri. fol. 22 plates

551.e.23(1).

Wanting a titlepage. The title has been taken from a manuscript titlepage provided for the copy at the Royal Library, The Hague (at 317.G.10), in which the plate bearing the image of the herald and carrying the imprint and date is wanting and the portraits have been cut into separate leaves whereas in the British Library copy they are printed two to a page, numbered: 1–42, the last being a double portrait of Albert and Isabella. The portrait numbered 35 is signed: WH, i.e. Willem Hondius? All the portraits are reduced and simplified copies of those found in the editions of Adrianus Barlandus.

EGIDIO; de Lieja. *See* AEGIDIUS; of Liège

EGLENTIERS nieuwe-jaers-gift . . . op't iaer M.DC.XIX. 1619. *See* RODENBURGH, Theodore

E5 EGLISHAM, George

HYPOCRISIS APOLOGETICÆ ORATIONIS VORSTIANÆ. Cum secunda provocatione ad D. CONRADVM VORSTIVM missa. Autore, D. GEORGIO EGLISEMMIO . . . DELPHIS Ex Officina Iohannis Andreæ . . . 1612. 4° pp.62

1010.a.7(4); 12301.bbb.33(1).

E6 EIGENTLICHE

Eigentliche Erzehlung/welcher gestalt . . . Ambrosius Spinola . . . von Graff Moritzen van Nassaw . . . Bey . . . Ryswick . . . empfangen worden . . . VERA NARRATIO. QVOMODO . . . AMBROSIVS Spinola . . . ab illustriss. Comite Mauritio à Nassau, ad pagum Risouicum . . . exceptus sit . . . LES PROPOS DE SON Excellence à l'embrassement du Marquis Spinola, auec la Response, le 10. iour de Feburier, l'an 1608. pres de Risvvick, [etc.] fol. a single sheet; illus.

1750.c.1(15).

Probably printed in the Netherlands. The French text is of the speeches only. Further news is promised in the German and Latin texts. Published in 1608. The attached engraving has been attributed in *Muller* no.1249 to Simon Frisius. Its inscribed title is 'Eigentliche Abbildung, welcher gestalt Marquis Spinola von Graf Moritzen bey dem Hage in Holland den 7. Febr. 1608. empfangen worden'.

EIRENEPHILUS, Eubulus; pseudonym of Jacobus Trigland. *See* TRIGLAND, Jacobus

E7 EISONIUS, Theodorus

DECLAMATIO SCHOLASTICA DE LAVDIBVS ELOQVENTIAE Quam publicè in maximo SCHOLÆ GRONINGANÆ AVDITORIO Habuit THEODORVS EISONIVS . . . GRONINGAE. Excudebat IOHANNES SASSIVS . . . 1621. 4° sig.A–D^4E^2

836.f.18(4).

E8 ELBOGEN

[1621] Puncten eñ Articulen/Wat die van de Stadt Ellenboghen vanden Heer Generael vanden Beyerschen Leger hebben begheert/ende wat Puncten men hun heeft gheaccordeert/daer op sy hen hebben ouer ghegheuen. Overghesedt wt het Hooch-Duyts in onse Nederlantsche sprake. Eerst Ghedruckt den 4. Junij. 1621. T'Hantwerpen/By Abraham Verhoeuen/[etc.] 4° pp.7; sig.B^4; illus.

P.P.3444.af(240).

Headed: Iunij. 1621. 84. The titlepage woodcut shows a fortified town with troops moving in and out.

ELIGII, Gerardus. *See* ÈLOI, Gérard

E9 ELOGIUM

ELOGIUM HISTORICUM HENRICI IV. FRANCIÆ ET NAVARREÆ REGIS. ANTVERPIÆ, EX OFFICINA PLANTINIANA, Apud Ioannem Moretum. M.DC.X. 8° pp.15; illus; port.
9200.aaa.35.
The titlepage bears the engraved portraits of Henry IV and Maria de' Medici. Another issue, attached to Petrus Roverius, *Henrico IIII . . . Panegyricus,* 1610, is described under ROVERIUS, Petrus.

E10 ÉLOI, Gérard

VIRGÆ LVDOVICO SCHLAAFFIO BAVDEI GNOMIS FACEM PRÆLVCENTI A GERARDO ELIGII Rhetoricæ Studioso transmissæ. PALÆOPOLI ADVATICORVM Ex officina Alexandri Verheyden. MDCVIII. 8° pp.59
11409.ee.26(4).
An attack on Schlaaffius's defence of Baudius who had attacked Scribani. The imprint stands for Antwerp. Printed by Joachim Trognaesius?

EMANUEL. 1616. *See* COMALADA, Miguel

EMBLEMATA amatoria. 1611; 1618. *See* HOOFT, Pieter Corneliszoon

EMBLEMATA amatoria iam dudum emendata. 1608; 1612. *See* HEINSIUS, Daniel

EMBLEMATA moralia. 1609. *See* FURMERIUS, Bernardus. De rerum usu et abusu.

E11 EMBLESMES

EMBLESMES SVS LES ACTIONS PERFECTIONS ET MOEVRS DV SEGNOR Espagnol. Traduit de Castillien. A MILDELBOVRG, Par Simon Molard. 1608. 8° pp.32; illus.
554.a.19.
Engravings accompanied by verses. The original cannot possibly have been in Spanish; a Dutch original or Dutch translation from the French is implied in the English prose translation, *A pageant of Spanish humours,* of 1599. The imprint, phrased to suggest Symon Moulert at Middelburg, probably hides a place of publication in France, possibly Rouen. The catchword at the foot of p.32, suggesting another leaf to follow, has been covered by a label.

E12 EMDEN

[21.12.1607] Ehe-Ordnungh Wo idt mit dem Hilligen Ehestandt/vnd allem wat dem anbehörich . . . in der Stadt Embden soll geholden werden. Gedruckt tho Groningen, By Hans Sasz . . . Voor Jan vanden Rade . . . 1608. 4° sig.AB[4]
5176.bb.8.
The law as issued at Emden, dated 21 December 1607.

E13 EMMIUS, Ubbo

[Collections] (Tp.1) RERVM FRISICARVM HISTORIA, Autore VBBONE EMMIO . . . Accedunt præterea DE FRISIA, ET REPVBL. FRISIORVM, INTER FLEVVM ET VISVRGIM FLVMINA, LIBRI ALIQVOT, Ab eodem AVTORE conscripti. LVGDVNI BATAVORVM, APVD LVDOVICVM ELZEVIRIVM. M DC XVI. [etc.] (col.=p.962) Typis, HENRICI AB HAESTENS, 1616.
(tp.2) DE FRISIA, ET FRISIORVM REPVBLICA, DEQVE CIVITATIBVS, FORIS, ET VICIS inter Flevum & Visurgim flumina, LIBRI ALIQVOT, Auctore VBBONE EMMIO . . . LVGDVNI BATAVORVM, APVD LVDOVICVM ELZEVIRIVM, M D C XVI. [etc.] fol. 2 pt.: pp.963; 71, 92, 62, 60: plates; maps
155.e.9.
Printed at Leiden. The plans of Groningen and Emden by Nicolaes Geelkerck. This copy is part of the second impression, with plates.

E14 EMMIUS, Ubbo

DE ORIGINE ATQVE ANTIQVITATIB. FRISIORVM, contra SVFFRIDVM PETRI & BERNARDVM FVRMERIVM . . . perspicua & solida veritatis assertio, AB UBBONE EMMIO . . . scripta . . . GRONINGÆ, Imprimebat GERHARDVS KETELIVS . . . M VIC.III. 8° pp.160
9327.a.18.

Ownership inscriptions: Stephanus Baluzius Tutelensis; Philip Nalle 1854.

E15 EMMIUS, Ubbo

GVILHELMVS LVDOVICVS COMES NASSOVIVS, ID EST, ΛΟΓΟΣ ΕΠΙΤΑΦΙΟΣ, quo genus, vita, res gestæ, & mors hujusce Comitis . . . succinctè exposita sunt AB VBBONE EMMIO . . . Accessit in calce . . . domus Nassoviæ schema genealogicum . . . GRONINGÆ Excudebat IOHANNES SASSIVS . . . M DC XXI. 8° pp.246; illus., port.
1090.k.6(1).

The portrait of Count William Louis of Nassau is engraved.

E16 EMMIUS, Ubbo

(tp.1) OPVS CHRONOLOGICVM NOVVM . . . elaboratum & concinnatum ab VBBONE EMMIO . . . GRONINGAE Excudebat IOANNES SASSIVS . . . Sumptibus ELSEVIRIORVM. M DC XIX. [etc.]
(tp.2) CHRONOLOGIA RERVM ROMANARVM . . . Eodem auctore VBBONE EMMIO . . . GRONINGAE Excudebat IOANNES SASSIVS . . . Sumptibus ELSEVIRIORVM. M DC XIX. [etc.] fol. 3 pt.: pp.252, 327; 95
Cup.402.i.12.

Published at Leiden. With 'Tempora Turcarum Othmenidarum seu Othomanorum' by Nicolaus Mulerius.

Les EMPIRES, royaumes, estats. 1614. *See* AVITY, Pierre d'

E17 ENGELRAEVE, Petrus

BASVYNE. Dienende om allerley traghe slapende Zielen yverich ende wacker te maken/mitsgaders verflaude en vertsaechde harten moedt te gheven tot continuatie hares Christelijcken beroeps . . . Alles cortelijck vervatet in drie Brieven . . . gheschreven . . . van eenen Remonstrantschen Predicant . . . 1620. 4° pp.64
T.2250(18).

Anonymous.

E18 ENGLAND

[9.2.1601] VVARACHTICH VERHAEL VAN TGENE DATTER ghebeurt is in Ingelant binnen Londen/nopende den aenslach vande Grauen vā Essex/Rutland ende Southamton . . . tegen de Coninginne: Ende hoe zy gheuanghen syn gheweest/ ende gheleyt inden Toren oft geuangenhuys van Londen, By maniere van Placcaet. TOT BRVESSEL/By Rutgeert Velpius . . . 1601. 8° 4 unsigned leaves
8133.a.8.

The proclamation dated 9 February 1601.

E19 ENGLAND

[9.2.1601] TRANSLAT DE CERTAIN PLACCART PVBLIE A LONDRES le 9. de Feburier 1601. Et selō la calculation des Anglois, 1600. Touchant l'inuasion & interprinse des Cōtes de Essex, Rutland & Southampton, auec leurs adherens. A BRVXELLES, Par Ruger [*sic*] Velpius . . . M.DC.I. [etc.] 8° sig.A^4
G.19973(2).

E20 ENGLAND

[15.11.1602] By de Coninghinne Proclamatie/waermede belast wort het procederen teghen Iesuiten en weireltsche Priesters/Midtsgaders tegen de gene die de selue Herberghen . . . Gepubliceert den xv^{en}. November 1602. stilo nouo.

[Illustrations of ***E22*** and ***E23*** overleaf]

VERCLARINGHE,

Ghedaen by den Raedt ende principale Heeren ende Edelen van Engelant/ op de successie vanden machtigen Coninc Iacobus, Coninck van Schotlant/ totte Rijcken van Engelandt/ Vranckrijck ende Yrlandt/ by de doodt vande laetst-overledene souveraine Coninginne Elizabeth.

VVt het Engelsch Exemplaer in Nederduytsch overghesett.

Na de Copie
Ghedrukt tot Londen/ by Robert Bercker/ Drucker der leste souveraine Coninginne van Engelandt/ den 24 Martij 1602.
IN S'GRAVEN-HAGHE,
By Aelbrecht Heyndricxsz. Drucker ordinaris der Heeren Staten Generael. ANNO 1603.
Met privilegie ende consent der voorsz. Heeren.

VERCLARINGHE

Ghedaen by den Raedt

ende principalen Adel van Enghelandt/ op de successie vanden machtighen Coninck Iacobus van Schotlandt / als nu Coninck van Enghelandt inde plaetse vande lest-overleden souveraine Coninginne Elizabeth.

VVt het Engelsch Exemplaer int Nederduytsch overgeset.

Na de Copye gedruckt tot Londen/ by Robert Berker / Drucker der leste souveraine Coninginne van Enghelandt den 24 Martij 1602.

In s'Graven Haghe by Aelbrecht Heyndricxsz, Drucker ordinaris der Heeren Staten Generael 1603.

Met privilegie ende consent der voorsz Heeren.

Ouerghesedt wt den Enghelschen in onse Nederlantsche sprake. MIDDELBVRGH, Ghedruct by Richard Schilders . . . 1602. 4° sig. A^4B^2
596.e.30.

E21 ENGLAND
[24.3.1603] Proclamatie Waermede IACOBVS den sesten, Coninck in Scotlandt, verclaert wort Coninck van Englandt, Vranckrijck ende Yrelant: Gedaen tot Londen den xxiiij^{en}. Meert Anno 1602. Stijl van Englandt. Wt den Enghelschen ouergheset. MIDDELBVRGH, By Richard Schilders . . . 1603. Na de Copye Gedruct tot Londen by Robert Barker. 4° sig. A^4
1578/7921.

E22 ENGLAND
[24.3.1603] VERCLARINGHE, Ghedaen by den Raedt ende principale Heeren ende Edelen van Engelant/op de successie vanden machtigen Coninc Iacobus, Coninck van Schotlant/totte Rijcken van Engelandt/Vranckrijck ende Yrlandt/by de doodt vande laetst-overledene souveraine Coninginne Elizabeth. VVt het Engelsch Exemplaer in Nederduytsch overgheset. Na de Copie Ghedruckt tot Londen/by Robert Bercker . . . den 24 Martij 1602. IN S'GRAVEN-HAGHE, By Aelbrecht Heyndricxsz . . . 1603. [etc.] 4° 2 unsigned leaves
597.e.32.

E23 ENGLAND
[24.3.1603] VERCLARINGHE Ghedaen by den Raedt ende principalen Adel van Enghelandt/op de successie vanden . . . Coninck Iacobus van Schotlandt/als nu Coninck van Enghelandt inde plaetse vande lest-overleden souveraine Coninginne Elizabeth. VVt het Engelsch Exemplaer int Nederduytsch overgeset. Na de copie gedruckt tot Londen/by Robert Berker . . . den 24 Martij 1602. In s'Graven Haghe by Aelbrecht Heyndricxsz . . . 1603. [etc.] 4° 2 unsigned leaves
597.e.31.
A different edition from the preceding.

E24 ENGLAND
[23.6.1603] Proclamatie, Ofte ordonantie van de Coninlijcke [*sic*] Maiesteyt van Engelant/waer in verclaert wert dat de Goederen die genomen zijn vande Ondersaten des Conincx van Spaengiē sedert den 24. Aprilis lestleden: sullen werden gerestitueert aende eygenaers/ende die te vooren genomē sijn/werden verclaert goeden buyt/met verbot van nu voortaen te beschadigen eenighe die in Confederatie ende Vrientschap zijn met zijn Maijesteyt. VVt d'enghelsch . . . ouergheset in onse Nederduytsche spraecke. T'HANTVVERPEN, By Gheleyn Janssens/nae de Copie ghedruckt tot Londen door Robert Barcker . . . 1603. 8° sig. A^4
8027.a.11.
Originally issued 23 June 1603. The approbation, signed by G.L. Boxtellius, is dated 23 July 1603.

E25 ENGLAND
[23.6.1603] Proclamatie, Ofte wille van de Coninlicke [*sic*] Maijesteyt van Engelandt/waer in verclaert wert dat de Goederen ghenomen vande Ondersaten des Conincx van Spaengien sedert den 24. Aprilis lestleden sullen werden gerestitueert . . . met verbot van nu voortaen te beschadigeu [*sic*] eenighe die in Confederatie ende Vrientschap zijn met syn Mayesteyt. Wt Engelsche spraecke . . . vertaelt in onse Nederduytsche spraecke. Ghedruckt nae de Copie van Robert Barcke [*sic*] . . . 1603. 8° sig. A^4
8050.aa.15(11).
A different edition from the preceding, without approbation.

E26 ENGLAND

[23.6.1603] PVBLICATIE ENDE VERBODT GHEDAEN By Iacobus den sesten Coninck van Schotlant, teghenvvoordich Coninck van Ingelant, Vranckryck ende Yrlandt. Doort welck alle Inghelschen ende Yrlandoisen zyn wederom innegheroepen/met verbot van eenighe oorloghe aen te doen den ondersaten vanden Coninck van Spaignien/ende inghesetenen vande Neder-landen/op pene van ghehouden te worden voor Piraten ende Zee-roouers/ende ouer sulx worden Ghestraft . . . Ghepubliceert tot Londen den 23. dach Iunii . . . 1603. TOT BRVESSEL, By Rutgeert Velpius . . . M.D.C.III. Nae de Copye gedruckt tot Londen, by Robert Barcker. [etc.] 4° 4 unsigned leaves

C.33.b.24(15); 106.a.46.

E27 ENGLAND

[6.7.1603] By den Coninck. Verkondinghe/bewijsende des Conincklijcke Majesteyts goedt welbehaghen aengaende de versamelinge van allen Volcken komende op de Crooninge. In s'Graven-Haghe. By Hillebrandt Jacobszoon . . . 1603. 8° sig.A^4

573.b.34.

Issued 6 July 1603.

E28 ENGLAND

[22.2.1604] PLACCAET Des Conincx van Engelandt/nopende het banissement der Jesuiten/Priesters/ende alle Pausche Gheestelijcke personen/uyt het Coninckrijcke van Enghelandt. Overgheset . . . in onse Nederlantsche tale. Nae de Copye Ghedruckt tot Londen by Robert Barker . . . 1604. 4° sig.A^2

T.2417(10).

The proclamation issued 22 February 1604.

E29 ENGLAND

[25.8.1604] Drie ARTIICKELEN aengaende Een Moderatie te hebben in de proceduyren van de Inquisitie tegens de Con. Maijesteyt van Engelants onderdanen; in Spanien . . . een extract . . . in Engels/ende t'selve . . . overghestelt in duytsch/ghetrocken uyt de copije ghedruckt by Robert Barker . . . 1606. TOT LEYDEN, By Thomas Basson/1609. 4° 2 unsigned leaves

1608/1585; T.1724(8); 107.g.1(24).

Part of treaty negotiations with Spain, dated 25 August 1604. Translated by Thomas Basson.

E30 ENGLAND

[25.8.1604] Dry ARTYCKELEN aengaende De Moderatie in de procedueren van de Inquisitie teghens de Kon. Majesteyt van Enghelants Onderdanen; in Spagnien . . . een extract . . . in Engels/ende tselve . . . overghestelt in Duytsch/ghetrocken wt de copije ghedruct by Robert Barker . . . 1606. Na de Copye ghedruct TOT LEYDEN, By Thomas Basson. 1609. 4° 2 unsigned leaves

1607/1820; 107.g.1(23).

A reprint of the preceding, also published in 1609.

E31 ENGLAND

[28.8.1604] ARTICVLI PACIS ET CONFEDERATIONIS PERPETVO DVRATVRÆ INTER . . . REGEM HISPANIARVM &C. ET ARCHIDVCES AVSTRIÆ &C. EX VNA. ET . . . REGEM ANGLIÆ &C. EX ALTERA PARTIBVS, EORVMQVE hæredes & successores . . . 1604. BRVXELLÆ. Ex Officina Rutgeri Velpij . . . 1604. [etc.] 4° sig.A-C^4

101.l.37; [*6915.aa.9].

Dated 28 August 1604. Parts of the text printed in Spanish and French. *The copy at 6915.aa.9 has been destroyed.

E32 ENGLAND

[28.8.1604] Articulen van het Contract ende Accoort ghemaeckt tusschen Jacobus

den eersten . . . Coninck van Enghelandt . . . Ende Philips den derden . . . Coninck van Spaengnien: midtsgaders de Eerts-hertoghen Albertus ende Isabella Clara Eugenia. Gemaect ende geconcludeert den xviij[en]. der Maent Augusti duysent ses-hondert en viere/naer den ouden stijl. VVt het Engels in het Neder-duytsch overgheset. Nae de Copie. Ghedruckt tot Londen/by Robert Barker. [etc.] 4° sig. AB^4
T.1713(8); 595.f.21(1).
Published in 1604.

E33 ENGLAND
[17.11.1605] Tweede Placcaet der Konincklijcker Majesteyt van Engelant . . . ghepubliceert tot Londen . . . den xvij. November lest-leden . . . teghens de persoonen van Thomas Percy ende sijne Complicen . . . Vertaelt vvt d'Enghelsche in onse Nederlandtsche sprake. TOT ROTTERDAM. By Jan van Waesberghe. 1605. 4° sig. A^4; illus.
T.2417(11).
The titlepage woodcut shows the portrait of James I.

E34 ENGLAND
[1606] BREVICVLVS DVORVM nuper in publicis Comitijs Anglicanis ACTORVM, Anno Christi M.DC.VI. IACOBI Angliæ Regis tertio. LONDINI, [*sic*] 8° sig. A^8B^4
809.c.12.
Extracts from the statutes against the Recusants, with a commentary. B2 erroneously signed E2. The imprint is false; printed by Pierre Auroi at Douai. Published in 1606. Cropped?

E35 ENGLAND
[10.6.1606] By de Koninck. (col.) Ghedruckt tot Londen by Robert Backer [*sic*] . . . 1606. ende nu tot Leyden by Thomas Basson. 4° sig. A^2
1568/8636.
A proclamation dated 10 June 1606 on the expulsion of Catholic priests. Translated by Thomas Basson. Published in 1606.

E36 ENGLAND
[2.6.1610] A PROCLAMATION PVBLISHED VNDER THE NAME OF IAMES King of Great Britanny. With a briefe & moderate Answere therunto. WHERETO Are added the penall Statutes, made . . . against Catholikes. TOGEATHER With a Letter which sheweth the said Catholikes piety . . . Translated out of Latin into English . . . M.D.XI [*sic*]. 4° pp.178
3932.cc.3; C.26.k.1(1).
The proclamation dated 2 June 1610. The editor's preface signed: B.D. de Clerimond, pseudonym of Joseph Creswell. Without imprint, published by the English College press at St. Omer. The copy at C.26.k.1(1) with the ownership inscription: Dom. Prof. Rom. S.J. Bibl. Com.

E37 ENGLAND
[2.6.1610] BY DEN CONINCK Een Proclamatie omme de behoorlijcke executie van alle voorgaende Wetten tegen de Paepse Refusanten . . . Ende mede/dat alle Papen ende Jesuyten uyten Lande . . . sullen vertrecken/om niet meer . . . weder te comen; ende omme het voorhouden van Eedt van Ghetrouwicheydt volghende de Wet. t'AMSTELREDAM, Gedruckt by Paulus Aertsz. van Ravensteyn/nae de Copye Ghedruckt TOT LONDEN, By Robert Barker . . . 1610. 4° sig. A^4
3935.cc.28.
The proclamation dated 2 June 1610. Published in 1610. Two extraneous portraits of James I have been added to this copy, one of them signed: N. de Clerck excu. and belonging to his *Tooneel der Keyseren* of 1615.

E38 ENGLAND

[24.12.1620] Nieuwe Tijdingen wt Engelãt Met het PLACCAET Vanden Coninck van Enghelant door den welcken hy Verbiedende is/dat zijn Ondersaten niet en souden spreecken van matterie van Staet. Ghedruckt den 10. Meert. 1621. T'Hantwerpen/By Abraham Verhoeuen/[etc.] 4° pp.8; sig. ¶[4]
P.P.3444.af(200).

Headed: Martius 1621. 34. Other news from England is also included.

E39 ENGLAND

[24/28.12.1620] TVVEE PLACATEN des Conings van Groot-Britannien. t'Eene belanghende het uyt-stel des Parlaments. t'Andere, teghen het verachtelick ende onghebonden spreecken van Materie van State . . . Gedruct tot Delf, by Ian Andriesz. [etc.] 4° sig.A^4
T.2424(14).

Proclamations dated, the first, 28 December 1620, the second, 24 December 1620. Published in 1621.

E40 ENGLAND

[4.6.1621] VERCLARINGE GHEDAEN BY de Ghemeynte in Engelandt, vergadert in't Parlement tot Westmunster den 4. Iunij 1621. Ouden Stijl. IN 'SGRAVEN-HAGHE, By Aert Meuris . . . 1621. 4° 2 unsigned leaves
T.2424(20).

E41 ENGLAND

[3.11.1621] BY DEN CONINCK. Proclamatie, aengaende het beroepen van 't Parlement. (col.) By Aert Meuris nae de Copye tot Londen, by Bonham Norton ende Iohn Bill . . . 1621. fol. a single sheet
T.2424(23).

The proclamation dated 3 November 1621. Published in 1621.

The ENGLISH martyrologe. 1608. *See* WILSON, John; Priest

ENGLISH Protestants plea. 1621. *See* BROUGHTON, Richard

E42 ENKHUIZEN. Synod of 1618

COPIE Van de Synodale Sententie Over de Kercken-zaecke tot Haerlem. Besloten . . . inden Synode TOT ENCHVYSEN. Op den 2. Novemb. 1618. 4° sig.A^2
700.h.25(16).

Possibly part of a larger work. Published in 1618?

E43 ENNODIUS; Saint, Bishop

BEATI ENNODII . . . OPERA Quæ reperiri potuerunt, omnia . . . Partim edita nunc primum, partim emendata, NOTISQ. illustrata, opera AND. SCHOTTI . . . TORNACI, Apud NICOLAVM LAVRENTIVM. M.DC.XI. [etc.] 8° pp.557,79
630.b.5.

With 'Ennodii . . . poemata sacra'.

EPHEMERIDES ecclesiasticae. 1601. *See* OUDAERT, Nicolaus

E44 EPHRAIM; the Syrian, Saint

[Collections] SANCTI PATRIS EPHRAEM SYRI . . . OPERA OMNIA . . . Nunc recens Latinitate donata, Scholiisque illustrata, Interprete & Scholiaste . . . GERARDO VOSSIO . . . ANTVERPIÆ, Apud IOANNEM KEERBERGIVM . . . M.DC.XIX. (col.) ANTVERPIÆ, TYPIS IOANNIS KEERBERGII . . . M.DC.XIX. fol. pp.619
1575/65.

E45 EPICEDIA

EPICEDIA IN OBITVM . . . IVSTI LIPSII . . . LVGDVNI BATAVORVM, APVD IOHANNEM MAIRE, M.D.CVII. 4° pp.38; illus.

631.k.4(10).

The authors include J. Scaliger, D. Baudius, B. Vulcanius, P. Scriverius and many more. The titlepage woodcut shows the phoenix arising from the flames.

EPICITHARISMA. 1609. *See* VRANCKEN, Godefridus

E46 EPICTETUS

EPICTETI ENCHIRIDION, ET CEBETIS TABVLA, Græcè & Latinè. Ex Officina Plantiniana RAPHELENGII, M.D.CXVI. 64° pp.247

C.20.f.26.

Published at Leiden. From the travelling library of Sir Julius Caesar.

E47 EPICTETUS

[Enchiridion. Dutch] EPICTETVS Handt-boexken/ENDE CEBES TAFEREEL . . . NOCH Cebes tafereels kort begrip, in rijm ghestelt door H.L. Spiegel. T'Amsterdam gedruckt by Cornelis Fransz. Voor Cornelis Dirxzoon Kool . . . 1615. 8° sig. A-D^4E^1

11555.c.37(2).

The translator of both works named as Marc. Ant. Gillis.

E48 EPINICIUM

EPINICIVM AD DVCES CÆSARIANOS FORtissimos recuperata PRAGA. ANTVERPIÆ, Apud Abrahamum Verhœuium. M.DC.XX. [etc.] 4° pp.6; sig. A^{1-3}

P.P.3444.af(150).

In verse. Wanting the last leaf, blank.

E49 EPISCOPIUS, Simon

[Letters] BRIEF van SIMON EPISCOPIVS Met eenighe Aenteyckeninghen ofte Commentarien breeder verclaert. Daer in verscheyden raetslagen ende mysterien der Arminianen ondeckt worden. Waer by noch gevoecht is een Kerckelyck ende Polityck Discours, om te bethoonen dat de Arminianen geen Reden en hebben/ dese . . . scheuringe te voeden/ende afgesonderde Vergaderingen te houden . . . T'AMSTELREDAM, Voor Marten Iansz. Brandt . . . 1620. [etc.] 4° pp.40

T.2250(10).

A letter written to Paulus Stochius. The anonymous editor is Jacobus Trigland. Printed by Paulus van Ravesteyn at Amsterdam.

E50 EPISCOPIUS, Simon

[Letters] SIMONIS EPISCOPII BRIEF. In de welcke de gront van de Remonstranten, aengaende hare Belijdenis ende eenstemminge in het geloove, naecktelick ontdeckt wort. MET Een Voor-reden aende . . . Staten Generael der Vereenighde Nederlanden. IN S'GRAVEN-HAGHE, By Hillebrant Iacobssz . . . 1620. 4° pp.26[18]

T.2250(9).

The same letter as in the preceding entry, addressed to Paulus Stochius, in another hostile edition. The anonymous preface is by Daniel Heinsius, a portrait of whom has been inserted in this copy. The pagination jumps from p.8 to p.17, but the signatures are continuous.

E51 EPISCOPIUS, Simon

ANTIDOTVM, ENDE Naerder Openinghe Van het eyghene ghevoelen des Nationalen Synodi/ghehouden binnen Dordrecht/ANNIS, 1618. en 1619. Tot onderrechtinge . . . der ghener, die de CANONES van het selfde Synode souden moghen komen te lesen . . . Ghedruckt . . . 1619. 4° pp.124

T.2246(15).

Anonymous and without imprint; printed by Nicolaes Biestkens at Amsterdam.

E52 EPISCOPIUS, Simon

ANTIDOTVM CONTINENS PRESSIOREM DECLARATIONEM PROPRIÆ ET GENUINÆ SENTENTIÆ QVÆ IN SYNODO NATIONALI DORDRACENA ASSERTA EST ET STABILITA. Belgicè primum in lucem editum, nunc vero non parum auctum & Latinitate donatum. Accessit duplex Index . . . HERDER-VVICI EX OFFICINA TYPOGRAPHI SYNODALIS . . . M.DC.XX. 4° pp.143

1482.b.17.

Anonymous. The imprint is doubtful. It has been suggested that it stands for Antwerp and perhaps Abraham Verhoeven. This copy with contemporary manuscript notes.

E53 EPISCOPIUS, Simon

COLLEGIVM DISPVTATIONVM THEOLOGICARVM In Academiâ LEYDENSI privatim institutarum à M. SIMONE EPISCOPIO . . . Addita est præfatio, in quâ demonstratur, in citandis hisce Thesibus aliisq; scriptis, OPTIMA FIDES FESTI HOMMII. DORDRECHTI, Ex officina Ioannis Berevvout, 1618. 4° pp.100

3504.bb.30(1).

Ownership inscription: Joseph Mayna[rd], Coll. Exon. A separate edition of the preface is entered under OPTIMA.

E54 EPISCOPIUS, Simon

[Confessio.] Belijdenisse ofte VERKLARINGHE Van't ghevoelen der Leeraren/die in de Gheunieerde Neder-landen Remonstranten worden Ghenaemt/over de voornaemste Articulen der Christelijcke Religie. Ghedruckt . . . 1621. 4° pp.139

T.2251(17).

Anonymous. Translated by Jan Wtenbogaert.

E55 EPISCOPIUS, Simon

Noodige Verantwoordinge der REMONSTRANTEN Nopende Soo wel het stellen van een eyghene en bysondere Confessie, verclaeringe haers Gevoelens, vereeninge met de Lutersche: als mede/over haere Leere/van den Doop, Avontmael, ende Rechtvaerdich-makinge uyt den gheloove/etc. MITSGAEDERS, Van de vruchten der Contra-Remonstranten gheloove. Dienende tot . . . wederlegginge van de notoire valscheden/die DANIEL HEYNSIUS . . . onlangs gepleecht heeft in syne voor-rede/over seeckerē brief SIMONIS EPISCOPII . . . Hier uyt kan oock werden ghespeurt de ydelheyt van de Amsterdamsche Aenteykeningen op den selffden Brief EPISCOPII . . . 1620. 4° sig.A-G^4H^2

T.2250(12).

Anonymous.

EPISCOPIUS, Simon. Optima fides Festi Hommii. 1618. [By Episcopius or one of his pupils.] *See* above: Collegium disputationum theologicarum.

E56 EPISCOPIUS, Simon

ORATIE Van . . . SYMON EPISCOPIVS . . . By hem inde Synode Nationael tot Dordrecht, soo voor hem selfs/als van weghen de xij. andere Remonstrantsche hem byghevoechde Kercken-Dienaren . . . gedaen/den 7. December . . . 1618. Ghedruct . . . 1619. 4° pp.29

T.2248(24).

The original Latin text was not published separately. A portrait of Episcopius, dated 1643, has been inserted in this copy.

E57 EPISCOPIUS, Simon

[Synodi Dordr. . . . crudelis iniquitas.] Onbillijcke wreetheyt DER DORTSCHE SYNODE . . . TEGHEN DE REMONSTRANTEN IN DE NEDERLANDTSCHE GHE-VNIEERDE PROVINCIEN . . . Ghedruckt . . . 1619. 4° pp.27

T.2249(21).

Anonymous.

An EPISTLE of comfort, to the reverend priests. 1616. *See* SOUTHWELL, Robert

An EPISTLE sent unto two daughters of Warwick. 1608. *See* NICLAES, Hendrik

EPISTOLA ecclesiastarum, quos in Belgio Remonstrantes vocant. 1617. *See* BAERLE, Caspar van

E58 EPITAPHIEN

EPITAPHIEN ofte GRAF-SCHRIFTEN gemaeckt op het afsterven van CAREL VAN MANDER . . . overleden zijnde op den 11 September 1606 . . . GHEDRUCKT TOT LEYDEN, By Marten vanden Vijver/Voor Passchier van Wesbusch . . . tot Haerlem . . . 1609. 8° pp.61

11557.a.42.

Verses in Dutch, Latin or Greek.

E59 EPITAPHIUM

EPITAPHIVM ENDE KLACHDICHT Over Den doot vande Rechtveerdige/Wel-geleerde ende Wijdt-vermaerde Nederlandtsche Oorloghe. Met eenighe Graf-schriften op syn Graff. Ghedruckt . . . 1609. 4° sig.A^4

T.2420(21); T.2421(8); 161.k.59.

Sometimes attributed to Adriaen van Nierop on the strength of the initials 'ALVN' under the sonnet on the titlepage verso.

E60 ERASMUS, Desiderius

[Collections. Dutch] (tp.1) OPVSCVLA DESIDERII ERASMI ROTERODAMI. Eenighe Tractaetkens vanden Eerweerdighen . . . Desiderio Erasmo van Rotterdam. Wt het Latijn overghezet int Nederduytsch. TOT LEYDEN, Voor Mathijs Bastiaensz/ Boec-vercooper tot Rotterdam . . . 1616.

(tp.2) Bereydinghe totter Doot: Een costelick ende devoot Boecxken ghemaeckt van . . . Erasmo van Rotterdam . . . int Latijn eerst wtghegheven/ende nu . . . int Nederduytsch overgheset . . . TOT ROTTERDAM. By Mathijs Bastiaensz. . . . 1616.

(tp.3) Een Schoon Tractaet Vande Eendrachtighheydt der Kercken/tot nederlegghinghe vande Tweedracht der Opinien. Beschreven door D. Erasmus van Rotterdam. Wt het Latijn overghezet in't Nederduytsch. TOT ROTTERDAM, By Mathijs Bastiaensz. . . . 1616.

(tp.4) Van de Versmaetheydt der werelt/eenen Brief/ghemaeckt van . . . ERASMVS van ROTTERDAM . . . Noch een Boecxken/van . . . ERASMVS VAN ROTTERDAM, van de ghelijckenisse van eender Maget, ende eenen Martelaer. Hier is noch by geset . . . Eeen Sermoon van S. IAN CHRISOSTOMVS, Welck hy gepredickt heeft opten dach vander Passien vanden Heyligen Machabeen. TOT ROTTERDAM, By Mathijs Bastiaensz. . . . M.D.C.XVI. (col.1) Gedruct tot LEYDEN, By Jan Claesz. van Dorp . . . 1616.

(tp.5) Vande suyverheyt Des Tabernakels oft der Christelijcker Kercken: Beschreven door D. Erasmum van Rotterdam. TOT ROTTERDAM. By Mathijs Bastiaensz. . . . 1616.

(tp.6) SYMBOLVM APOSTOLORVM, Oft: Een clare wtlegginghe des Apostelschen Geloofs/ende der thien Gheboden Gods: Door . . . ERASMVM van Rotterdam, ghemaeckt . . . wt de Latijnsche spraecke in onser Duytscher tale overgheset. TOT ROTTERDAM, By Mathijs Bastiaensz. . . . M.D.C.XVI. (col.2) Gedruct tot LEYDEN, By Jan Claesz. van Dorp . . . 1616.

(tp.7) Den Kerstelicken Ridder˙. . . Eerst int Latijn gheschreven door . . . Erasmus van Rotterdam. TOT ROTTERDAM. By Matthijs Bastiaensz. . . . 1616.

(tp.8) Vermaninghe door welcke betoont wordt dat alle menschen . . . behooren den heylighen Euangelie te Lesen. Beschreven door D. Erasmum van Rotterdam. TOT ROTTERDAM. By Mathijs Bastiaensz. . . . 1616.

(tp.9) DE MANIERE Om Godt te bidden. Ghestelt int Latijn, Door . . . Des: Erasmus van Rotterdam ende nu in onse Nederduytsche Tale overgheset. TOT ROTTERDAM. By Mattijs Bastiaensz. . . . 1616.

(tp.10) MORIÆ ENCOMION, Dat is: Eenen Lof der Sotheyt . . . Speelwijs beschreven door . . . ERASMVM van ROTTERDAM. TOT ROTTERDAM, By Mathijs Bastiaensz. . . . 1616.

(tp.11) EEN Christelycke nootsakelycke Claghe des Vredes . . . Eerst door Erasmum Roterodamum inden Latijne beschreven, ende nu . . . in de Nederduytsche Tale overgheset . . . TOT ROTTERDAM By Mathijs Bastiaensz . . . M.D.C.xvj. 4° 10 pt.: pp.48; 64; 92; 43 [33]; 128; 98; 18; sig. $A^8BC^6D^4$; pp.97; sig. $A^4BC^8D^2$
629.h.25.

The general titlepage (tp.1) and preliminaries are followed by twelve tracts, eleven of which are numbered, no.3–5 all belonging to the part described under tp.4. The unnumbered tract is the last part. The translator's address in 'Moriae encomion' signed: J.G. The titlepage engraving shows the arms of Rotterdam. Ownership inscription: G.D.J. Schotel 1837.

E61 ERASMUS, Desiderius

ENCOMIVM MORIÆ DES. ERAS. ROTEROD. sive Declamatio In laudem STVLTITIÆ. Accedunt aliorum CL. virorum Satyræ . . . Editio Secunda priori auctior & emendatior. LEYDÆ ex officina IACOBI MARCI, M D CXVIII. 12° pp.361, 128
12330.a.45; C.79.a.15.

With 'Iusti Lipsii Satyra Menippea, Somnium' and 'P. Cunæi Sardi venales'. The copy at C.79.a.15 is imperfect; wanting the part containing 'Sardi venales'.

E62 ERASMUS, Desiderius

[Vidua Christiana. Dutch] De Kersten Weduwe Eerst door . . . D. Erasmus van Rotterdam/aende . . . Princesse/Vrouwe Maria/wijlen Coninginne van Hungarien ende Bemen/int Latijn Gheschreven/ende nu in onse ghemeene tale overgheset. Hier is noch byghevoecht een Oratie ofte Sermoen ter eeren het Kint Jesus/byden selfden Autheur int Latijn wtghegheven. TOT AMSTERDAM. By Jan Gerritsz . . . M.DC.VII. 8° sig. $A–H^8$
1019.e.33.

The 'Oratie' is a translation of 'Concio de puero Jesu'.

E63 ERASMUS, Desiderius

VITA DES. ER ASMI [*sic*] ROTERODAMI. ex ipsius manu . . . repræsentata; comitantibus, quæ ad eandem, alijs. Additi sunt EPISTOLARVM, quæ nondum lucem aspexerunt, Libri duo: QVAS conquisivit, edidit . . . PAVLLVS G.F.P.N. MERVLA. LVGDVNI BATAVORVM, In officina typographica Thomæ Basson. M. DCVII. 4° pp.214 [216]; illus., port.
489.g.18(1); 613.k.48.

The woodcuts show the portrait and 'Terminus' emblem of Erasmus.

E64 ERASMUS, Desiderius

MAGNI DES. ERASMI Roterodami VITA; partim ab ipsomet Erasmo, partim ab amicis æqualibus . . . descripta. Accedunt EPISTOLÆ ILLVSTRES plus quam septuaginta, quas ætate provectiore scripsit . . . P. SCRIVERII, & fautorum auspicijs. LVGDVNI BATAVORVM Ex Officina Godefridi Basson M DCXV. 12° pp.286; illus., port.
10759.a.7.

Ownership inscription: Patrick Fraser Tytler.

E65 ERCILLA Y ZUÑIGA, Alonso de

[La Araucana.] HISTORIALE Beschrijvinghe der Goudtrijcke Landen in Chili ende Arauco, ende andere Provincien in Chili gheleghen/mitsgaders d'oorloghen die d'Inwoonders aldaer ghehadt hebben teghens de Spagniaerden. In Spaens

ghemaect by Don Alonso de Ercilla, ende Cuñiga . . . Overgheset wt de Spaensche in de Nederlantsche tale, door ISAAC IANSZ. BYL van Rotterdam. TOT ROTTERDAM, By Jan van Waesberghe . . . 1619. 4° pp. 59; illus.
C. 32. d. 33(3).
The titlepage woodcut shows American Indian natives.

Den ERENTFESTEN, achtbaren . . . heeren, Balieu, Borgemeesteren ende Schepenen der stede van Rotterdam. 1610. *See* SWEERTIUS, Robertus

ERKLAERUNG und Protestation der Fuersten . . . im Koenigreich Frankreich. 1617. *See* DECLARATION et protestation des princes.

E66 ERNEST I; Margrave of Brandenburg
Inhoudt des Briefs/gheschreven vanden Marckgrave Ernst van Brandenburgh . . . eñ Wolfgangh Wilhelm Pfaltsgrave/aen syne . . . Majesteyt: waer inne sy alle ghelegentheyt vanden handel int Lant van Cleve/Gulick ende Bergh sijne M. weten laten. Mitsgaders wat wt desen handel soude moghen volghen . . . Overgheset wt den Hooghduytschen brief . . . in onse Nederlantsche Tale. Nae de Copye van Dusseldorp. 4° sig. A^4
T. 2420(27).
The letters dated 27 June and 7 July 1609. Published in 1609.

ERNSTIGE teghen-spraeck aen de Maeght van Hollandt. 1617. *See* DRIELENBURCH, Vincent van

ERNSTIGHE aen-spraeck aen de Maeghdt van Hollandt. 1617. *See* TAURINUS, Jacobus

E67 ERPENIUS, Thomas
GRAMMATICA ARABICA, quinque libris methodicè explicata. A THOMA ERPENIO . . . LEIDÆ, In Officina Raphelengiana, 1613. 4° pp. 192
622. h. 5(2); G. 17796(2).
The copy at 622. h. 5(2) is the author's presentation copy to Isaac Casaubon, printed on heavier paper than the copy at G. 17796(2).

E68 ERPENIUS, Thomas
THOMAE ERPENI GRAMMATICA ARABICA. LEIDÆ, In Officina Raphelengiana, 1613. 4° pp. 124
1560/1710.
Interleaved, with manuscript notes.

E69 ERPENIUS, Thomas
THOMAE ERPENII GRAMMATICA EBRÆA generalis. Lugduni Batavorum. Typis Raphelengianis. Prostant apud IOHANNEM MAIRE . . . M.DC.XXI. 8° pp. 317
1568/3025.
P. 315 is misprinted 301.

E70 ERPENIUS, Thomas
THOMÆ ERPENII ORATIONES TRES, DE Linguarum EBREÆ, atque ARABICAE Dignitate. LEIDAE, Ex Typographia AVCTORIS . . . 1621. 12° pp. 132
1090. b. 7.

E71 ERPENIUS, Thomas
THOMÆ ERPENII RVDIMENTA LINGVAE ARABICAE. Accedunt ejusdem Praxis Grammatica; & Consilium de studio ARABICO feliciter instituendo. LEIDAE, Ex Typographia AVCTORIS . . . 1620. 8° pp. 184
1568/3062(2).
With 'Catalogus librorum arabicorum'.

E72 ESLAVA, Antonio de

PARTE PRIMERA DEL LIBRO INTITVLADO Noches de Inuierno. Compuesto por Antonio de Eslaua . . . EN BRVSSELAS, Por Roger Velpio, y Huberto Antonio . . . 1610. [etc.] 12° pp.494
C.135.e.24.

Ownership inscription: Geraldo de Waldenburgh . . . Brusselas 30.7.1614. With the exlibris of Jean Peeters Fontainas.

E73 ESTIUS, Guilielmus

HISTORIÆ MARTYRVM GORCOMIENSIVM . . . QVI PRO FIDE Catholica à perduellibus interfecti sunt anno Domini M.D.LXXII, LIBRI QVATVOR, AVTHORE GVILIELMO ESTIO . . . DVACI, Ex officina BALTAZARIS BELLERI . . . 1603. 8° pp.288
4685.a.30.

Including stories of other martyrs. Printed by Laurence Kellam at Douai? Ownership inscription: Bibliotheca Monasterij S. Martini Tornacensis.

E74 ESTIUS, Guilielmus

HISTOIRE VERITABLE DES MARTYRS DE GORCOM EN HOLLANDE . . . Le tout composée par . . . GVILLAVME ESTIVS . . . Et depuis translatée de Latin en François par M.M.D.L.B. A DOVAY, De l'Imprimerie de BALTAZAR BELLERE . . . 1606. 8° pp.471
4886.aaa.36.

The translation sometimes attributed to Benoît de la Grange. Printed by Laurence Kellam at Douai?

E75 ESTIUS, Guilielmus

HISTOIRE VERITABLE DES BIEN-HEVREVX MARTYRS DE GORCOM EN HOLLANDE . . . Le tout composé par . . . GVILLAVME ESTIVS . . . Et . . . translaté . . . par M.M.D.L.B. Et . . . nouuellement r'Imprimé à l'instance . . . du V. Pere Frere ANTOINE GAMBIER . . . A DOVAY. De l'Imprimerie de MARC VVYON . . . 1618. 8° pp.471
861.g.17.

The translation sometimes attributed to Benoît de la Grange. The dedicatory epistle signed: A. Gambier.

E76 ESTIUS, Guilielmus

GVILIELMI ESTII . . . ORATIONES THEOLOGICÆ. DVACI, Typis Viduæ LAVRENTII KELLAMI . . . 1614. 8° pp.328; illus., port.
4378.a.17.

The editor's dedicatory letter signed: Bartholomæus Petrus. The portrait signed: Mart. bas. f.

E77 EUCHERIUS; Saint, Bishop

D. EVCHERII . . . DE CONTEMPTV MVNDI Epistola parænetica ad Valerianum cognatum. ACCEDIT VITA D. PAVLINI NOLANI . . . ANTVERPIAE, EX OFFICINA PLANTINIANA Apud Balthasarem Moretum, & Viduam Ioannis Moreti, & Io. Meursium. M.DC.XXI. (col.) ANTVERPIAE, EX OFFICINA PLANTINIANA BALTHASARIS MORETI. M.DC.XXI. 12° pp.188
4399.a.19(1).

The editor's dedication signed: Heribertus Ros-vveydus.

E78 EUCHERIUS; Saint, Bishop

D. EVCHERII . . . DE LAVDE EREMI Ad Hilarium Lerinensem monachum LIBELLVS. ANTVERPIAE, EX OFFICINA PLANTINIANA, Apud Balthasarem Moretum, & Viduam Ioannis Moreti, & Io. Meursium. M.DC.XXI. (col.) ANTVERPIAE, EX OFFICINA BALTHASARIS MORETI. M.DC.XXI. 12° pp.52
4399.a.19(2).

The editor's dedication signed: Heribertus Ros-vveydus.

E79 EUCLID

[Elementa. bk.1–6] C. DIBVADII IN GEOMETRIAM EVCLIDIS prioribus sex Elementorum libris comprehensam Demonstratio linealis . . . LVGDVNI BATAVORVM, Ex Typographeîo Christophori Guyotij. Impensis Ioannis Ioannidis Bibliopolæ Arnemensis. M.D.C.III. 4° pp.100; illus.
C.19.c.14(1).

Text and commentary. In a seventeenth-century pierced vellum over silk binding.

E80 EUCLID

[Elementa. bk.1–6] C. DIBVADII IN GEOMETRIAM EVCLIDIS prioribus sex Elementorum libris comprehensam Demonstratio Numeralis . . . LVGDVNI BATAVORVM, Ex Typographeîo Christophori Guyotii. Impensis Ioannis Ioannidis Bibliopolæ Arnemensis. M.D.C.III. 4° pp.72; illus.
C.19.c.14(2).

Text and commentary. For the binding see preceding entry.

E81 EUCLID

[Elementa. bk.1–6] (tp.1) EVCLIDIS ELEMENTORVM LIBRI SEX PRIORES. Quorum demōstrationes . . . ad faciliorem captum accommodauit CAROLVS MALAPERTIVS . . . DVACI, Typis BALTAZARIS BELLERI . . . 1620.
(tp.2) CAROLI MALAPERTII . . . ORATIO Habita Duaci dum lectionem Mathematicam auspicaretur: IN QVA De nouis Belgicis Telescopij phænomenis non iniucunda quædam Academice disputantur. DVACI, Typis BALTAZARIS BELLERI, [etc.] 8° 2 pt.: pp.142; 42; illus.
C.115.d.11.

The approbation on A3v lists both titles as parts of the same book. Printed by Laurence Kellam at Douai.

E82 EUCLID

[Elementa. bk.7–9] C. DIBVADII IN ARITHMETICAM RATIONALIVM EVCLIDIS Septimo, Octavo & Nono Elementorum libris comprehensam Demonstratio . . . ARNHEMII GELDRIÆ, Apud IOHANNEM IANSONIVM . . . M.D.C.V. 4° pp.80
C.19.c.14(3).

Text and commentary. For the binding see C.19.c.14(1) above. Printed by Christoffel Guyot at Leiden before 1605?

E83 EUCLID

[Elementa. bk.10] C. DIBVADII IN ARITHMETICAM IRRATIONALIVM EVCLIDIS Decimo Elementorum libro comprehensam Demonstratio Linealis & Numeralis . . . ARNHEMII GELDRIÆ, Apud IOHANNEM IANSONIVM . . . M.D.C.V. 4° pp.200: plate; illus.
C.19.c.13.

Text and commentary. Printed by Christoffel Guyot at Leiden before 1605? In a seventeenth-century pierced vellum over silk binding.

E84 EUFRENIUS, Albertus

Poëmata ALBERTI EVFRENI . . . LVGDVNI BATAVORVM, Ex officinâ CHRISTOPHORI GVYOTI . . . M.D.C.I. Ineunte Mense Principe. 8° pp.128
11409.aa.31.

Interleaved, with manuscript translations of some of the poems. The last interleaved page inscribed: Br. Johannes Houwaert . . . 1686.

EUPHORMIONIS Lusinini Satyricon. 1619. *See* BARCLAY, John

EUSEBIUS Pamphili; Bishop. Eusebii, Polychronii, Pselli, in Canticum Canticorum expositiones Græcè. 1617. *See* BIBLE. Song of Solomon. Greek

E85 EUSEBIUS Pamphili; Bishop

THESAVRVS TEMPORVM. EVSEBII PAMPHILI . . . Chronicorum Canonum omnimodæ historiæ libri duo, interprete HIERONYMO, ex fide vetustissimorum Codicum castigati . . . EIVSDEM EVSEBII Vtriusque partis Chronicorum Canonum reliquiæ Græcæ . . . Opera ac studio IOSEPHI IVSTI SCALIGERI . . . LVGDVNI BATAVORVM Excudebat THOMAS BASSON Sumptibus COMMELINORVM. M.D.C.VI. [etc.] (col., at the end of the fourth pagination) LVGDVNI BATAVORVM, Ex Typographia THOMAE BASSON . . . M D CVI. fol. pp.197,70,403,192[292],342
582.k.2.

EXEMPLAR libelli supplicis. 1612. *See* GERRITSZ, Hessel

E86 EXEMPLAR

EXEMPLAR LITERARVM A QVODAM SACERDOTE COLLEGII ANGLORVM DVACENII QVONDAM ALVMNO EX ANGLIA AD IDEM COLLEGIVM TRANSMISSARVM. DE MARTYRIIS QVATVOR EIVSDEM COLLEGII ALVMNORVM OB SACERDOTIVM HOC ANNO 1616. IN ANGLIA MORTE DAMNATORVM . . . DVACI, Typis PETRI AVROI . . . M.DC.XVII. 8° pp.56
1126.a.2(1).
Compiled under the supervision of Matthew Kellison. With 'Catalogus martyrum Collegii Anglorum Duaceni'.

EXERCITIUM hebdomadarium. 1621. *See* LITURGIES. Latin Rite. Various Offices

E87 EXPLOICTEN

De Exploicten vā Oorloghe ghedaen door den Hertoch van Espernon int Landt van Bearn, stellende des Conincx Ordonnantien ter Executien. Ouergesedt vvt het Fransoys in onse Nederlantsche sprake, ende vvas eerst gedruct tot Parijs . . . Nv Eerst Ghedruckt den 2. Iunij 1621. T'Hantwerpen/By Abraham Verhoeuen/[etc.] 4^{6} pp.8; sig.A^{4}; illus.
P.P.3444.af(238).
Headed: Iunij, 1621. 82. The titlepage woodcut shows a portrait of Louis XIII.

E88 EXTRACT

Extract eens briefs gheschreven uyt den Leger voor Kingsael in Yrlandt/van den Secretaris van Milord Montjoy/aen Milord Buckhorst . . . Inhoudende warachtighe verclaringhe van een heerlicke Victorie die Godt de Here de Enghelschen verleent heeft teghen de Rebellen ende Spangiaerden. Ende van de veroveringe van de stadt Kingsael/den 7 Januarij 1602. Voor Henrick Moody/ op den Dam inde nieuwe huysen. 4° 2 unsigned leaves; illus.
573.f.33.
Published at Amsterdam in 1602. The titlepage woodcut shows the portrait of a gentleman. The name of Lord Montjoy's secretary is not known.

EXTRACT ende conditien, wt de Propositien van den Generalen Landt-dagh . . . binnen . . . Prage. 1620. *See* BOHEMIA. States

EXTRACT wt de Annotatien ende verclaringhen van de Acten des vredehandels te Colen . . . 1597. 1618. *See* NETHERLANDS. United Provinces. Staten Generaal

E89 EXTRACT

Extract wt de laetste Courante der ghelooffwaerdichster gheschiedenissen inde belegheringe voor de Stadt ende Casteel van Gulick/tsedert den sevenentwintichsten Augusti tot den teghenwoordighen dach . . . Met verbodt . . . van tegen de stadt ende Sticht van Ceulen yet te misdoen . . . t'Amstelredam/by Gerrit van Breugel [etc.] 4° 2 unsigned leaves; illus.
T.1729(4).

Published in 1610, according to a date quoted in the text. The titlepage woodcut shows men on horseback arriving before a castle.

E90 EXTRACT

EXTRACT wt sekere Missiue geschreuen wt Constantinopolē. Daer wt te sien is/hoe ende in wat manieren die Gherebelleerde Hongheren . . . trachten . . . Den Turck te persuaderen den krijch t'aenveerden tegēs haere keyserlijcke Majesteyt ende de gheheele Christenheydt . . . Overghesedt wt den Hoochduytsche/in onse Nederlantsche sprake. t'Hantwerpen/By Abraham Verhoeuen/[etc.] 4° pp.8; sig. W^4; illus.

P.P.3444.af(27).

The titlepage illustration shows a Turkish commander holding a flag. Published in 1619?

E91 EYNATTEN, Maximilianus ab

MANVALE EXORCISMORVM: Continens INSTRVCTIONES, & EXORCISMOS ad eiiciendos è corporibus obsessis spiritus malignos, & ad quæuis maleficia depellenda, & ad quascunque infestationes dæmonum reprimendas: R.D. MAXIMILIANI AB EYNATTEN . . . industria collectum: Reuerendiss. aliquot BELGII ANTISTITVM aliorumq́ue doctorum virorum iudicio recensitum & probatum. ANTVERPIÆ, EX OFFICINA PLANTINIANA, Apud Balthasarem Moretum, & Viduam Ioannis Moreti, & Io. Meursium. M.DC.XIX. (col.) ANTVERPIÆ, EX OFFICINA PLANTINIANA BALTHASARIS MORETI. M.DC.XIX. 8° pp.314

719.d.13.

E92 EYNDIUS, Jacobus

IACOBI EYNDII AB HAEMSTEDE . . . Poëmata . . . LVGDVNI BATAVORVM, Ex Typographio Henrici ab Haestens. M DC XI. 4° pp.1–29, 72, 33–192; illus.

11408.f.24.

With the engraved arms of Jacobus Eyndius on the titlepage, signed: WS, i.e. Willem Swanenburgh.

F

FABER, Joannes. In imagines illustrium ex Fulvii Ursini bibliotheca . . . commentarius. 1606. *See* GALLE, Theodoor. Illustrium imagines.

F1 FABER, Petrus

PETRI FABRI IN LIBROS ACADEMICOS CICERONIS EDITIONIS PRIMÆ COMMENTARIUS. Eiusdem P. Fabri in orationem pro Cæcina alius Commentarius. LUGDUNI BATAVORUM, Apud Andream Cloucquium . . . M.D.CI. 8° pp.147

835.c.24(3).

F2 FABER, Timaeus

(tp.1) Disputationes ANNIVERSARIAE, AD QVATVOR LIBROS INSTITVTIONVM IMPERIAL. PROPOSITÆ In Academia Franequerana A TIMÆO FABRO . . . Editio Tertia: Cui accessit DIATYPOSIS ANNOTATIONVM Selectarum ad varia iuris civilis loca explicanda vel illustranda. LUGDUNI BATAVORUM, APVD LVDOVICVM ELZEVIRIVM . . . 1615.
(tp.2) QVÆSTIONVM ILLVSTR. sive ANNOTATIONVM SELECTARVM, Quibus varia juris civ. loca illustrantur aut emendantur, DIATYPOSIS AVTHORE TIMÆO FABRO IC. LVGD. BATAV. Apud LVDOV. ELZEvirium . . . 1615. 4° 2 pt: sig.★★, $★★^2$, a–z, aa–hh, A–S; $A\text{–}F^4G^2$

5206.c.11.

The 'Disputationes', defended by different students and printed by various printers, none named.

F3 [*FABRIS, Salvator

[Sienza e pratica d'arme.] Des Kunstreichen vnd weitberümeten Fechtmeisters SALVATORIS FABRI Italiänische FECHTKVNST . . . in vnsere algemeyne Hochteutsche sprache vertolmetschet . . . LEIDEN, Bey ISACK ELZEVIER . . . M D C XIX. fol. pp. 196; illus.
7905.k.12.]

*Destroyed. The title has been transcribed from the General Catalogue, supplemented by the descriptions in *Willems* no. 157 quoting the title from the second original titlepage 'De lo schermo, overo scienza d'arme' and *Bruckner* no. 27 referring to a copy at Göttingen University Library.

F4 FALCONER, John

A BRIEFE REFVTATION OF IOHN TRASKES IVDAICAL AND NOVEL FANCYES . . . By B. D. Catholike Deuine . . . Imprinted . . . M.DC.XVIII. 4° pp. 102
C.26.k.3(1).

Anonymous and without imprint. Published by the English College press at St. Omer.

F5 FAMA

FAMA POSTVMA PRAESVLVM ANTVERPIENSIVM, Vulgata à Rhetoribus Collegij SOC. IESV eiusdem Ciuitatis. ANTVERPIÆ, EX OFFICINA PLANTINIANA, Apud Viduam & Filios Io. Moreti. M.DC.XI. (col.) ANTVERPIÆ, EX OFFICINA PLANTINIANA, APVD VIDVAM ET FILIOS IOANNIS MORETI. M.DC.XI. 8° pp. 113
1474.aaa.23(3); 4423.bb.20(1).

Verses, by the pupils of Hermannus Hugo. The second copy not available during compilation, perhaps destroyed.

F6 FEDDES, Pieter

EFFIGIES D. IOHANNIS BOGERMANNI PRAESIDIS SYNODI DORDRACENÆ HABITÆ ANNO 1618 ET 1619 . . . Petrus Harlingensis ad vivum Pinxit, Sculp. & Excud: 1620. fol. a single sheet, engraved
Maps C.9.d.4(8).

With a small picture of the Synod of Dort in the top right-hand corner and with verses in Latin and Dutch, signed: Maertinus geratus. Published at Leeuwarden? Part of the Beudeker collection.

F7 FEDDES, Pieter

UYTVAERT VAN WILLEM LUDWIGH GRAVE TOT NASSAU [etc.] (col.) Gedruckt t'Amsterdam, by Claes Jansz Visscher. fol. pl. 4; ff. [15]; port.
604.i.27.

Engravings, signed: PHarlingensis inventor et sc. et cum C.J. Visschero excudit. They are preceded by the title printed on a strip intended for cutting and mounting and followed by Jan Starter's 'Lyck-klachte' and descriptive text on mounted leaves numbered 2–15, cropped in such a way that the foliation on leaves 3–15 is lost. Published in 1620.

FELIX, Joannes. Disputationum theologicarum vigesima-octava. 1604. *See* TRELCATIUS, Lucas

F8 FENNER, Dudley

AN ANTIQVODLIBET, OR AN ADVERTISEMENT TO BEWARE OF SECular priests . . . MIDDELBVRGH, By Richard Schilders . . . 1602. 8° pp. 164
1360.a.2(2).

Anonymous.

F9 FENNOR, William

DE OPSTANDINGHE VAN MARS, Den Godt der Oorloghen/binnen den Landen van Gulick/Cleve ende Berghs-Landt . . . Ghecomponeert/door Wilhelmus Vener

Enghels-man. TOT ROTTERDAM, By Jan Van Ghelen . . . M.DC.X. 4° sig. a^4; illus.
T.2421(12).
In verse, with unrelated woodcuts. The author's name is in the Dutch spelling.

F10 FENNOR, William
Vvat nieus boven nieus/by Wilm Vener Enghelsman/tot . . . Prins . . . Mauritius van Nassou . . . Item hier is noch by ghevoecht een liedeken van het Bestandt. Anno. M. D.C.IX. 4° four unsigned leaves; illus.
1568/8637.
In verse. The author's name is in the Dutch spelling. Without imprint. Published by Jan van Ghelen at Rotterdam.

FERDINAND II; Emperor. For decrees and official messages issued by Ferdinand II *see* GERMANY

FERNANDEZ DE QUEIROS, Pedro. Verhael van seker memoriael. 1612. *See* GERRITSZ, Hessel. Beschryvinghe.

F11 FERNANDEZ DE VELASCO, Juan; Duke, Constable of Castile
[Dos discursos en que se defiende la venida del Apostol Santiago in España.] HISPANIARVM VINDICIAE TVTELARES, IN II. LIBROS DIVISÆ: Venisse in hæc Regna IACOBVM APOSTOLVM, Fideíque lumen intulisse, Adversùs Cardinalis BARONII, Aliorúmque Opinionem. E. Bibliothecâ IO. FER. VELASCI . . . depromptæ, Ab ERYCIO PVTEANO Latinitate donatæ. LOVENI, In Officinâ typographicâ GERARDI RIVI. M.DC.VIII. 4° pp.66
1124.h.16(9); 700.d.7(1).
The copy at 1124.h.16(9) in a binding bearing the arms of Jacques Auguste de Thou.

F12 FERNANDEZ DE VELASCO, Juan; Duke, Constable of Castile
RELACION DE LA IORNADA DEL EXC^MO^ CONDESTABLE DE CASTILLA, A LAS PAZES ENTRE HESPAÑA Y INGLATERRA, QVE SE CONCLVYERON . . . EN LONDRES, por el mes de Agosto . . . M.DC.IIII. EN ANVERES, EN LA EMPRENTA PLANTINIANA, POR IVAN MORETO. M.DC.IIII. 4° pp.53
C.66.c.4.
Anonymous. Generally attributed to Fernandez de Velasco himself.

FIDELIS ANNOSUS; Veremontanus Druinus, pseudonym of John Floyd. *See* FLOYD, John

F13 FIELD, John
AN ADMONITION TO THE PARLIAMENT HOLDEN IN THE 13. YEARE OF THE REIGNE OF QVEENE ELIZABETH . . . Begun Anno 1570. and ended 1571 . . . Imprinted Anno 1617. 4° pp.62[68]
3932.cc.8.
Anonymous and without imprint. Compiled from John Field and Thomas Wilcox's *Admonition* and Thomas Cartwright's *Second admonition.* Printed by William Brewster at Leiden.

F14 FIENUS, Thomas
THOMÆ FIENI . . . DE CAVTERIIS LIBRI QVINQVE . . . LOVANII, Apud Ioan. Baptistam Zangrium . . . M.D.CI. [etc.] 8° ff.258: plates
783.c.5.
The engravings show surgical instruments and equipment.

F15 FIENUS, Thomas

DE COMETA ANNI M.DC.XVIII. DISSERTATIONES THOMÆ FIENI . . . ET LIBERTI FROMONDI . . . In quibus tum istius motus, tum aliorum omnium essentia, effectus, & præsagiendi facultas declarantur. Eiusdem THOMÆ FIENI Epistolica quæstio. An verum sit, Cœlum moueri, & Terram quiescere. ANTVERPIÆ, Apud GVLIELMVM à TONGRIS . . . M.DC.XIX. 8° pp.153
531.e.5(2).

F16 FIENUS, Thomas

DE FORMATRICE FOETVS LIBER In quo ostenditur animam rationalem infundi tertia die. AVTHORE THOMA FIENO . . . ANTVERPIÆ, Apud Gulielmum à Tongris . . . M.DC.XX. [etc.] 8° pp.283
1173.f.3.

F17 FIENUS, Thomas

DE VIRIBVS IMAGINATIONIS TRACTATVS, AVTHORE THOMA FIENO . . . LOVANII, In Officinâ Typographicâ GERARDI RIVII . . . M.DC.VIII. [etc.] 8° pp.200
784.c.9.

FIGUERLIJCKE verthooninge van't groote vasten-avont-spel. 1616. *See* DRIELENBURCH, Vincent van

FIGUEROA, Francisco. [Memorial presentado a su Magestad acerca del martyrio de nueve religiosos.] Histoire du massacre de plusieurs religieux [and other reports]. 1620. *See* VERVLIET, Jean

F18 FINETTI, Giacomo

(tp.1) IACOBI FINETTI . . . CONCERTI ECCLESIASTICI II. III. ET IIII. VOCIBVS. Cum Basso Generali ad Organum. Iam de nouo, multis sublatis erroribus, in lucem editi. TENOR. ANTVERPIÆ APVD PETRVM PHALESIVM . . . M.D.C.XXI.

(tp.2) IACOBI FINETTI . . . CONCERTI . . . BASSVS. ANTVERPIÆ APVD PETRVM PHALESIVM . . . M.D.C.XXI.

(tp.3) BASSVS GENERALIS. IACOBI FINETTI . . . CONCERTI . . . editi. ANTVERPIÆ APVD PETRVM PHALESIVM . . . M.D.C.XXI. 4° 3 pt.: A-L^4; aa-ee^4; aaa-lll^4
Music C.209.

F19 FITZ-HERBERT, Thomas

AN ADIOYNDER TO THE SVPPLEMENT OF FATHER ROBERT PERSONS HIS DISCVSSION of M. Doctor Barlowes Ansvvere &c. CONTAYNING A Discouery, and Confutation of . . . many . . . Absurdities, Falsities, and Lyes in M. Andrewes his Latin Booke intituled, Responsio ad Apologiam Cardinalis Bellarmini . . . WRITTEN By F.T. Author of the Supplement . . . ALSO. An Appendix touching a Register alleaged by M. Franc. Mason for the Ordayning of Protestant Bishops in Q. Elizabeths Raigne . . . M.DC.XIII. 4° pp.495
3939.cc.6.
Anonymous and without imprint. Published by the English College press at St. Omer.

F20 FITZ-HERBERT, Thomas

(tp.1) A DEFENCE OF THE CATHOLYKE CAVSE, CONTAYNING A TREATISE IN CONFVTATION OF SVNDRY VNTRVTHES AND slanders . . . against all english Catholyks in general, & some in particular . . . VVritten by T.F. WITH AN APOLOGY, OR DEFENCE, OF HIS INNOCENCY IN A FAYNED CONSPIRACY AGAINST HER Maiesties person . . . in the yeare 1598 . . . Written by him the yeare folowing, and not published vntil now . . . Imprinted . . . 1602.

(tp.2) AN APOLOGY OF T.F. IN DEFENCE OF HIM-SELF AND OTHER CATHOLYKS . . . 1602. 4° 2 pt.: ff.71; 51
3936.bb.49; 1019.i.33.

Anonymous and without imprint. Published by Arnout Coninx at Antwerp. In the copy at 1019.i.33 the *Apology* has been bound first.

F21 FITZ-HERBERT, Thomas

THE OBMUTESCE OF F.T. TO THE EPPHATA OF D. COLLINS, OR The Reply of F.T. to D. Collins his defence of my Lord of VVinchesters Answere to Cardinal Bellarmines Apology . . . WRITTEN By Thomas Fitzherbert . . . in defence of his Adioynder . . . M.DC.XXI. 8° pp.LXXX, 548, 4
860.f.21.

The last set of pages contain passages in Aramaic. Without imprint. Published by the English College press at St. Omer.

F22 FITZ-HERBERT, Thomas

A SVPPLEMENT TO THE DISCVSSION OF M.D. BARLOWES ANSVVERE To the Iudgment of a Catholike Englishman &c. interrupted by the death of the Author F. ROBERT PERSONS. WHEREIN Many . . . Absurdities . . . are discouered in M.D. Barlow. AND By the way is briefly censured M. Iohn Dunnes Booke, intituled PSEUDO-MARTYR. ALSO An Adioynder . . . By F.T. . . . M.DC.XIII. 4° pp.400
3939.cc.3.

Anonymous and without imprint. Published by the English College press at St. Omer.

F23 FITZ-HERBERT, Thomas

[A treatise concerning policy.] THE FIRST PART OF A TREATISE CONCER NING [*sic*] POLICY, AND RELIGION . . . Written by THOMAS FITZHERBERT . . . Printed at Doway by LAVRENCE KELLAM . . . M.DC.VI. 4° pp.461
484.a.29.

The titlepage is a cancel. Ownership inscriptions: Wenceslaus Hollar, 1660 Londini; Johannes Burgis 1699.

F24 FITZ-HERBERT, Thomas

(tp.1) THE FIRST PART OF A TREATISE CONCERNING POLICY, AND RELIGION . . . Written by THOMAS FITZHERBERT . . . The second Edition, newly set foorth, corrected, and . . . augmented by the Author . . . Printed . . . 1615.
(tp.2) THE SECOND PART OF A TREATISE CONCERNING POLICY, AND RELIGION . . . Written by THOMAS FITZHERBERT . . . Printed . . . 1610. 4° 2 pt.: pp.373; 697
697.e.18(1,2).

Without imprint. Printed by Pierre Auroi at Douai.

FITZIMON, Henry. *See* FITZ-SIMON, Henry

F25 FITZ-SIMON, Henry

(tp.1) A CATHOLIKE CONFVTATION OF M. IOHN RIDERS CLAYME OF ANTIQVITIE AND A CAVLMING COMFORT AGAINST HIS CAVEAT . . . And . . . a replye to M. RIDERS Rescript . . . By HENRY FITZIMON . . . Printed at ROAN . . . 1608.
(tp.2) A REPLIE TO M. RIDERS RESCRIPT. AND A DISCOVERIE OF PVRITAN PARTIALITIE IN HIS BEHALFE . . . At Roan . . . 1608. 4° 2 pt.: pp.394; 118
3936.bbb.32.

The imprint is false; pt.1 printed by Pierre Auroi, pt.2 by Charles Boscard, both at Douai.

F26 FITZ-SIMON, Henry

(tp.1) THE IVSTIFICATION AND EXPOSITION OF THE DIVINE SACRIFICE OF THE MASSE, AND OF AL RITES AND CEREMONIES therto belonging deuided into two bookes . . . By Henry Fitz Simon . . . 1611.
(tp.2=p.[181 bis]=sig.Z4r) THE SECOND BOOKE. VVHERIN THE FIRST MASSE IN THE MISSAL Is iustified . . . By Henry Fitz Simon . . . 1611. 4° 2 pt.: pp.417
C.26.h.1.

Without imprint. Printed by Laurence Kellam at Douai.

F27 FITZ-SIMON, Henry

BRITANNOMACHIA MINISTRORVM, IN PLERISQVE ET FIDEI FVNDAMENTIS, ET FIDEI ARTICVLIS DISSIDENTIVM. Authore P. HENRICO FITZ SIMON . . . DVACI, Ex Officina BALTAZARIS BELLERI . . . 1614. [etc.] 4° pp.355
4092.f.34(1); 697.f.20; G.5590(1).

FITZ-SIMON, Henry. Hiberniae . . . vindiciae. 1621. [Sometimes wrongly attributed to Henry Fitz-Simon.] *See* FLEMING, Richard

F28 FLANDERS

[29.1.1610] *Begin.* De President ende raedslieden vande Eertz-Hertoghen van Oostenrijcke . . . Gheordonneert in Vlaendren. (col.) Te Ghendt, By Jan vanden Steene . . . Anno M. zeshondert ende thiene. [etc.] 4° sig. A^3
106.a.6(8).

Issued 29 January 1610. Prohibiting the importation of heretical books. Without titlepage and wanting the last leaf, blank?

F29 FLANDERS

[29.1.1610] De President ende Raedtslieden vande Eerts-Hertoghen van Oostenrijcke . . . Gheordonneert in Vlaenderen. Nae de Copye. Gedruckt tot Ghend/by Gaultier Manilius . . . 1610. [etc.] 4° sig. A^2
T.1717(45); 1568/381.

Another edition of the preceding.

F30 FLANDERS

[29.1.1610] De President ende Raetslieden van de Eerdts-hertoghen . . . Geordonneert in Vlaenderen. Op't uyt-gheven . . . van Diversche Boecxkens . . . Na de Copye, Ghedruckt tot Ghend/by Gaultier Manilius . . . 1610. [etc.] 4° sig. A^2
T.2421(13).

Another edition of the preceding. An engraved figure of 'FLANDRIA' holding a shield and an olive branch has been cut from elsewhere and pasted onto the titlepage of this copy.

F31 FLANDERS

[29.1.1610] De President ende Kaetslieden [*sic*] vande Eerdts-hertogen van Oostenrijcke . . . Gheordonneert in Vlaenderen. Op't uyt-gheven ende stroyen van diversche Boecxkens, Tractaten, Refereynen, ende Liedekens. Nae de Copye, Ghedruckt tot Ghend/by Gaultier Manilius . . . 1610. [etc.] 4° sig. A^2
T.1727(12).

Another edition of the preceding. The titlepage bears an armorial shield divided into two halves showing the Austrian Eagle on the left and the Flemish Lion on the right, with the initials 'B H' in a rectangle below.

F32 FLANDERS

[29.4.1616] *Begin.* SVR ce que les President & gens du Conseil Prouincial de Flandres, ont par leurs letres du dixneufiesme de ce mois escrit aux Chef President & gens du Conseil Priué des Ser^{mes}. ARCHIDVCQZ . . . Qu'aiant . . . este examiné le proces . . . d'entre Adrien Alart . . . & les heritieres de Iehan de Scheppere . . . Leurs Al^{zes} ont . . . ordonné [etc.] (col.) A Gand, Chez Iean vanden Steene. 4° sig. A^3
106.a.52.

A decision dated 29 April 1616 concerning claims of inheritance under the laws of Oudenarde. Published 1616.

F33 FLEMING, Richard

HIBERNIÆ SIVE ANTIQVIORIS SCOTIÆ VINDICIÆ aduersus IMMODESTAM PARECBASIM Thomæ Dempsteri . . . nuper Editam . . . His accessit Nomenclatura Scotorum

& Scotiæ, &c. Authore G.F. Veridico Hiberno. ANTVERPIÆ. Apud HERMANNVM COPMAN. M.DC.XXI. (col.) Leodij, Typis Ioannis Ouvverx . . . M.DC.XIX. 8° pp.121
C.24.e.13(1); G.5715.
Anonymous. Sometimes wrongly attributed to David Rothe who compiled the 'Nomenclatura' or to Henry Fitz-Simon who edited the anonymous 'Catalogus sanctorum', by Richard Fleming, included at the end, which was published, first at Douai in 1615, then at Liège in 1619, the colophon of that edition being literally reproduced in the 1621 edition. The imprint is false; in fact, printed by the Widow of Jerôme Blageart at Paris.

F34 FLINTON, George
(tp.1) A MANVAL OF PRAYERS Gathered out of many famous and Godly Authors: Augmented With diuers deuout pointes collected out of the Princes Manual . . . 1613.
(tp.2=p.507) CERTAINE DEVOVT AND GODLY PETITIONS COMMONLY CALLED IESVS PSALTER . . . CVM PRIVILEGIO. (col.) By IOHN HEIGHAM, at Doway, [etc.] 12° pp.576; illus.
1121.b.8.
Anonymous. Compiled by George Flinton, based on the *Precationes liturgicae* and *Precationum piarum enchiridion* by Simon Verepaeus and other works. Revised and enlarged by John Heigham. Printed by Pierre Auroi at Douai. The titlepage and illustrations are engraved.

F35 FLODOARDUS Remensis
HISTORIÆ REMENSIS ECCLESIÆ LIBRI IIII. AVCTORE FLODOARDO PRESBYTERO ET CANONICO EIVSDEM ECclesiæ . . . conscripti. NVNC PRIMVM CVM SCHOLIIS IN LVCEM EDITI OPERA ET STVDIO GEORGII COLVENERII . . . ADDITA EST APPENDIX, ET CATAlogus omnium Archiepiscoporum Remensium. DVACI, In officina IOANNIS BOGARDI, M.DC.XVII. 8° pp.739, 185
861.e.9; 296.k.3.
The copy at 861.e.9 from the library of John Morris.

F36 FLORENTIUS, Henricus
DISPVTATIO MEDICA DE PESTE ad quam . . . Pro gradu & Docturæ privilegijs in Medicina consequendis Publicè sine præside respondebit HENRICUS FLORENTIUS . . . LUGDUNI BATAVORUM, Excudebat GODEFRIDUS BASSON, 1612. 4° sig.A^4
1185.g.1(52).

F37 FLORES, Juan de
[Historia de Grisel y Mirabella.] HISTOIRE DE AVRELIO, ET ISABELLE, FILLE DV Roy d'Escoce, nouuellement traduict en quatre langues, Italien, Espaignol, François, & Anglois . . . A BRUXELLE, Chez IEAN MOMMART . . . 1608 [etc.] 8° sig.$A^2A\text{-}O^8 P^6$
1075.e.21.
Anonymous. Originally written in Spanish. The French translation by Gilles Corrozet, the Italian by Lelio Aletifilo.

FLORILEGIUM sacrarum cantionum. 1613. *See* PHALÈSE, Pierre

F38 FLORIO, Michel Angelo
HISTORIA DE LA VITA E DE LA morte de l'Illustriss. Signora GIOVANNA GRAIA, gia Regina eletta e publicata d'Inghilterra: e de le cose accadute in quel Regno dopo la morte del Re Edoardo VI . . . L'argumento . . . si dichiara ne L'Auuertimento seguente, e nel Proemio de l'Authore M. Michelangelo Florio . . . Stampato appresso Richardo Pittore . . . 1607. 8° pp.378
292.a.5(1); G.968.
The printer is Richard Schilders at Middelburg.

F39 FLOYD, John

HYPOCRISIS MARCI ANTONII DE DOMINIS DETECTA, SEV CENSVRA IN EIVS LIBROS DE REPVBLICA ECCLESIASTICA, præambula pleniori responsioni. Auctore Fideli Annoso Verementano Theologo. ANTVERPIÆ, EX OFFICINA PLANTINIANA, Apud Balthasarem Moretum, & Viduam Joannis Moreti, & Io. Meursium. M.DC.XX. (col.) ANTVERPIÆ, EX OFFICINA PLANTINIANA BALTHASARIS MORETI. M.DC.XX. 8° pp.181

477.a.26(8).

Pseudonymous.

F40 FLOYD, John

THE OVERTHROVV OF THE PROTESTANTS PVLPIT-BABELS, CONVINCING their preachers of LYING & RAYLING . . . PARTICVLARLY confuting VV. Crashawes Sermon at the Crosse . . . VVITH a Preface to the Gentlemen of the Innes of Court . . . TOGEATHER with a discouery of M. Crashawes spirit . . . By I.R. Student in Diuinity . . . M.DC.XII. 4° pp.328

C.108.bb.2.

Anonymous and without imprint. Published by the English College press at St. Omer.

F41 FLOYD, John

PVRGATORIES TRIVMPH OVER HELL, Maugre The barking of Cerberus in Syr Edvvard Hobyes Counter-snarle. DESCRIBED In a Letter to the sayd Knight, from I.R. Author of the Answere vnto the Protestants Pulpit-Babels . . . M.DC.XIII. 4° pp.199

3935.c.22.

Anonymous and without imprint. Published by the English College press at St. Omer.

F42 FLOYD, John

SYNOPSIS APOSTASIÆ MARCI ANTONII DE DOMINIS, OLIM ARCHIEPISCOPI SPALATENSIS, NVNC APOSTATÆ, EX IPSIVSMET LIBRO DELINEATA, Auctore Fideli Annoso Verimentano Theologo. ANTVERPIÆ Apud Heredes Martini Nutij & Joannem Meursium. M.DC.XVII. 8° pp.137

477.a.26(4).

Pseudonymous.

F43 FLOYD, John

[Synopsis apostasiae Marci Antonii de Dominis.] A SVRVEY OF THE APOSTASY OF MARCVS ANTONIVS DE DOMINIS . . . Drawne out of his owne Booke, and written in Latin, by Fidelis Annosus, Verementanus Druinus, Deuine: AND Translated into English by A.M. . . . M.DC.XVII. 4° pp.146

C.132.h.26.

Pseudonymous and without imprint. Published by the English College press at St. Omer. Translated by Henry Hawkins.

FLUCTIBUS, R. de. *See* FLUDD, Robert

F44 FLUDD, Robert

APOLOGIA Compendiaria, Fraternitatem de ROSEA CRUCE suspicionis & infamiæ maculis asspersam [*sic*], Veritatis quasi Fluctibus abluens & Abstergens: Auctore R. de FLVCTIBVS . . . LEYDÆ, Apud Godefridum Basson. 1616. 8° pp.23

C.112.aa.16(1).

F45 FLUDD, Robert

TRACTATVS APOLOGETICVS Integritatem Societatis DE ROSEA CRVCE defendens. In qua probatur contra D. Libavij & aliorum . . . calumnias, quod admirabilia præstigijs . . . præstari possint. Authore R.DE FLVCTIBVS . . . LVGDVNI BATAVORVM, Apud GODEFRIDVM BASSON . . . 1617. 8° pp.196

C.112.aa.16(2).

F46 FOLLINUS, Hermannus

(tp. 1) AMVLETVM ANTONIANVM seu Luis pestiferæ fuga, In duos libros distributa . . . cui accessit vtilis libellus DE CAVTERIIS. Auctore HERMANNO FOLLINO . . . ANTVERPIÆ, Apud Hieronymum Verdussium M.DC.XVIII. [etc.] (tp. 2) DE CAVTERIIS LIBELLVS PERVTILIS, AVCTORE M. HERMANNO FOLLINO . . . ANTVERPIÆ, Apud Hieronymum Verdussium. M.DC.XVIII. 8° pp. 310; illus., port.
1167.c.13(2).

The portrait is engraved on the titlepage verso.

F47 FOLLINUS, Hermannus

Den Nederlandtsche SLEVTEL Van t'Secreet der Philosophie, in welck . . . bewesen wert/d'aert . . . aller Metallen . . . En die gheheele Alchijmie . . . Door HERMANNVS FOLLINVS . . . Ghedruckt t'Haerlem, by Adriaen Rooman, Voor Daniel de Keyser . . . 1613. 8° ff. 76; illus.
7410.dg.24(2).

F48 FOLLINUS, Hermannus

(tp. 1) PHYSIOGNOMIA, Ofte MENSCHEN-Kenner. Midtsgaders SIMONIDES, Ofte die MEMORI-CONST. Crachtelijck . . . uyt Aristoteles . . . bewesē. DOOR HERMANNUS IANSZ. FOLLINVS . . . Ghedruckt t'Haerlem, by Adriaen Rooman, Voor Daniel de Keyser . . . 1613.
(tp. 2) SIMONIDES, Ofte die MEMORI-CONST . . . DOOR HERMANNUS IANSZ. FOLLINVS . . . Ghedruckt t'Haerlem, by Adriaen Rooman. Voor Daniel de Keyser . . . 1612. 8° 2 pt.: ff. 52; 57
7410.dg.24(1).

The 'Tafel' referred to at the end as bound in at the beginning has been omitted from this copy.

F49 FONTANUS, Saxus

Bediedenisse vande NIEVWE COMETE Ofte Sterre metten Steerte/die in't laetste vande maendt November/sich eerst aenden Hemel geopenbaert heeft . . . Deur D. Saxum Fontanum. [etc.] (col.) In 'sGraven-Hage. By Aert Meuris . . . 1619. 4° pp. 11; illus.
T.2423(4).

The titlepage woodcut shows the portrait of an astronomer.

F50 FONTANUS, Saxus

Die groote Practica Ofte Prognosticatie op het Jaer . . . 1619. waer in voorseyt werden . . . veele seltsame . . . geschiedenissen . . . Insonderheyt oock de dappere nederlaghe die den Coninck van Spaengien hebben sal in d'Oost ende West-Indien. Ghepractiseert door D. Saxum Fontanum . . . Gedruckt tot Amsterdam by Broer Jansz. 1619. 4° 4 unsigned leaves; illus.
T.2423(6).

The titlepage woodcut shows the portrait of an astronomer, with an insert showing a comet, signed: L.H.

F51 FORBES, John

A LETTER First written and sent by IO. FORBES . . . vnto certen of the companie of Marchands Adventurers at STOADE . . . for resolving this Question: How a Christian man may discerne the testimonie of Gods spirit . . . And now againe renewed and enlarged by the Authour . . . and published by those of his flocke, to whom he did dedicate it . . . AT MIDDELBVRGH, Printed by Richard Schilders, 1616. 8° pp. 93
4257.f.1.

Edited by John Turner and Edward Kay.

F52 FORBES, John

A TREATISE TENDING TO CLEARE THE DOCTRINE OF IVSTIFICATION. Written by IO. FORBES . . . AT MIDDELBVRGH, Printed by Richard Schilders, 1616. 4° pp.189
4255.b.33.

F53 FORBES, Patrick; Bishop

A DEFENCE OF THE LAWFVL CALLING OF THE MINISTERS OF REFORMED CHVRCHES, AGAINST THE CAVILLATIONS OF ROMANISTS. Whereto is subjoined, AN EPISTLE TO A RECVSANT . . . WITH A SHORT DISCOVERY OF THE ADVERSARIE his dottage . . . By PATRIK FORBES . . . Printed at Middelburgh, by Richard Schilders . . . 1614. 4° pp.66,30,21[25]
1490.s.24.

F54 FORBES, Patrick; Bishop

(tp.1) AN LEARNED COMMENTARIE VPON THE REVELATION OF SAINT IOHN . . . By PATRIK FORBES . . . WHEREVNTO IS ADDED AN PROFITABLE Treatise of the Author, in defence of the lawfull calling of the Ministers of reformed Churches . . . And an Epistle to a Recusant . . . Printed at Middelburg, by Richard Schilders . . . 1614. (tp.2) A DEFENCE OF THE LAWFVL CALLING OF THE MINISTERS OF REFORMED CHVRCHES . . . By PATRIK FORBES . . . Printed at Middelburgh, by Richard Schilders . . . 1614. 4° 2 pt.: pp.256; 66,30,25
690.b.8.

Pt.2 is another issue of the preceding in which the misprinted pagination has been corrected. Ownership inscription: Dedit Mr Guliel: Terrie.

FORCKENBECK, Bernhardus. Disputationum theologicarum duodecima. 1609. *See* LUBBERTUS, Sibrandus

F55 FOREESTIUS, Joannes

ΙΩΑΝΝΟΥ ΤΟΥ ΦΟΡΕΣΤΙΟΥ ΕΙΔΥΛΛΙΑ Η ΗΡΩΕΣ, ΚΑΙ ALLA ΠΟΙΗΜΑΤΙΑ ΤΙΝΑ. IOANNIS FOREESTII IDYLLIA siue HEROES, ET ALIA POEMATIA QVAEDAM. EX OFFICINA PLANTINIANA RAPHELENGII. M.D.CV. 4° pp.78[87]
837.h.8(5); 837.i.29.

Published at Leiden. The copy at 837.h.8(5) the author's presentation copy to Cornelius Hillenius, that at 837.i.29 with the ownership inscription of William Tomline and manuscript additions by him.

La FOREST des hermites et hermitesses. 1619. *See* VITAE patrum.

F56 FOURMENNOIS, Gabriel

L'HISTOIRE DE TOBIT REPRESENTEE . . . EN FORME DE TRAGICOMEDIE . . . NOVVELLEMENT COMPOSE PAR Gabriel Fourmennois . . . A VTRECHT, Par Salomon de Roy . . . 1601. 4° pp.80
839.d.21(9).

In verse.

F57 FRANCE

[1603–1610] THE APOLOGIES OF THE MOST CHRISTIAN KINGES OF FRANCE AND NAVAR, HENRY IIII. AND LEVVIS XIII. As also of the . . . Bishop of Paris, for the Fathers of the Society of IESVS. Translated out of Latin into English . . . M.DC.XI. 4° pp.28
8050.c.12; C.26.k.1(2).

Documents dated September 1603 to July 1610, translated and edited by Anthony Hoskins. Without imprint. Published by the English College press at St. Omer.

F58 FRANCE

[13.2.1617] DECLARATION DV ROY CONTRE LES DVCS de Vendosme, de Mayenne,

Mareschal de Buillon, Marquis de Cœuvre, le President le Iay, & tous ceux qui les assistent. Verifiée en Parlement, le 13. Fevrier, 1617. La Declaration du Roy sur le subiect des nouveaux remuemens de son Royaume. A LA HAYE, Chez Hillebrant Iacobssz . . . 1617. [etc.] 4° pp.15
1195.c.4(5).
From the library of John Morris.

F59 FRANCE
[1.5.1619] PROPOSITIE, Ghedaen aende Heeren Staten Generael der Vereenichde NEDERLANDEN, Door den Heere MAVRIER . . . Den 1. May/A°. 1619. Ende by gheschrifte overghelevert/des anderen daeghs . . . 1619. 4° pp.11
T.2249(13).
A plea for clemency on behalf of the King of France for Johan van Oldenbarnevelt and other prisoners. Signed: I [*sic*]. du Maurier.

F60 FRANCE
[13.5.1619] Brief des Ambassadeurs van Vranckrijck aen de Heeren Staten Generael den 13 Mey 1619. Eenen Brief des Ambassadeurs van Vrancrijck/aen de Heeren van Braquel ende Dorth . . . 1619. 4° sig.A,A3,4
T.2249(12).
A plea made by Du Maurier on behalf of the King of France not to go through with the execution that day of Johan van Oldenbarnevelt. The second letter asks for transmission of the first. Without imprint and without a leaf A2.

F61 FRANCE
[27.5.1621] Declaratie vanden Coninck van Vranckrijck, daer by alle de Inwoonders ende andere Persoonen . . . inde Steden van Rochelle ende S.Jan d'Angely . . . zijn Ghedeclareert te wesen Criminels van læse Majesteyt . . . Ouerghesedt vvt het Fransoys, in onse Nederlandtsche sprake, ende was Ghedruct tot Parijs . . . Nv eerst Ghedruckt den 25. Iunij. 1621. T'Hantwerpen, By Abraham Verhoeuen, [etc.] 4° pp.6[14]; illus.
P.P.3444.af(250).
Headed: Iunij, 1621. 94. With a woodcut of the arms of Louis XIII on the titlepage. The original decree issued 27 May 1621.

F62 FRANCE
[7.6.1621] Opene BRIEVEN Vande Verklaringhe des KONINCKS, Nopende die vande vermeynde Ghereformeerde RELIGIE. Afghekondicht tot Rouaën in't Parlament den 7. Iunij, Ao. 1621. Na de Copy Tot ROUAEN, By Marten de Mesgissier . . . 1621. 4° sig.A^4
T.2251(21).

F63 FRANCIS de Borja; Saint, Duke
[Collections] (tp.1) THE PRACTISE OF Christian Workes. Written in Spanish by . . . FRANCIS BORGIA sometymes Duke of Gandia, and the third Generall of the Society of IESVS. Togeather with a short Rule, How to liue well. Englished by a Father of the same Society. VVhereunto are adioyned certaine pious Meditations vpon the Beades: translated also out of the Spanish . . . M.DC.XX.
(tp.2=p.193) PIOVS MEDITATIONS VPON THE BEADES . . . Translated out of Spanish. M.DC.XX. 12° pp.163[363]
C.26.k.16.
The first and second works translated by Thomas Everard from 'Espejo de las obras del Christiano' and 'Espejo de bien vivir'. The 'Pious meditations' are by Joseph Creswell, translator unknown. Without imprint. Published by the English College press at St. Omer.

F64 FRANCIS de Sales; Saint, Bishop

[Introduction à la vie devote.] AN INTRODUCTION TO A DEVOVTE LIFE COMPOSED IN FRENCHE By . . . Francis Sales . . . AND TRANSLATED INTO ENGLISG [*sic*], By I.Y. The 2. Edition. By IOHN HEIGHAM . . . 1617. (col.) At Douay by Iohn Heigham . . . 1617. 12° pp.532

C.175.d.13.

Translated by John Yakesley. Printed by Pierre Auroi at Douai. The titlepage is engraved.

F65 FRANCIS de Sales; Saint, Bishop

[Introduction à la vie devote.] [An introduction to a deuote life . . . Translated into Englisg [*sic*] by I.Y. the 2. edition. Iohn Heigham. 1617.] 12° pp.695

1477.cc.45.

Another edition of the preceding, printed by Charles Boscard at St. Omer. Imperfect, wanting the titlepage which was that of the edition of 1617, with the date altered in ink to 1622.

FRANCK, Franciscus. *See* VRANCK, Franchois

F66 FRANCUS, Germanus

REPRÆSENTATIO PACIS GENERALIS inter Orbis Christiani REGES, PRINCIPES ET STATVS PONTIFICVM, ET SEDIS ROManæ sollicitudine, ab exordio superioris seculi ad hæc vsque tempora procuratæ. In qua eorundem in illa scopus, & dolosæ artes ad veterum Romanorum consilia comparata . . . exhibentur . . . Nunc secundùm . . . reuisa, & . . . adaucta. Auctore GERMANO FRANCO. AMSTERODAMI, Sumtibus Bonauenturæ Elzeuirii. MDCIX. 8° pp.196

4789.h.12(2).

An issue for sale at Amsterdam of the work believed to have been originally printed and published at Geneva. The identity of the author using the pseudonym Germanus Francus has not been established.

F67 FRANEAU, Jean

IARDIN D'HYVER OV CABINET DE FLEVRS CONTENANT EN XXVI ELEGIES Les plus rares et signalez Fleurons des plus fleurissans parterres. Illustré d'excellentes Figures representantes au naturel les plus belles Fleurs des Jardins domestiques. Par IEAN FRANEAV . . . A DOVAY, De l'Imprimerie de PIERRE BORREMANS 1616 [etc.] 4° pp.198,22; illus.

C.106.b.14.

The titlepage is engraved. The engravings signed: Antoine Serrurier f. The second set of pagination contains the twenty-sixth elegy.

F68 FRANKFURT ON THE MAIN

[21.8.1620] TRANSLAET vanden Brief gheschreuen by de Heeren/Borgher-meesteren/ende Raedt der Stadt van Franckfort AENDE HEEREN Borgher-meesteren, ende Schepenen deser Stadt van Antvverpen. T'Hantwerpen/By Abraham Verhoeuen . . . 1620. 4° sig.Nomb VJ^2

P.P.3444.af(94).

A document dated 21 August 1620 declaring that neither army will interfere with the coming autumn fair.

F69 FRASER, John; Prior

A LERNED EPISTLE OF M. IOHN FRASER . . . TO THE MINISTERS OF GREAT BRITANIE. Wherin he sheweth that no man ought to subscribe to their confession of faith. And that their presumed authorite to excommunicate anie man, especially Catholiques, is vaine and foolish . . . 1605. 8° pp.98

3936.aaa.17.

Without imprint. Printed by Laurence Kellam at Douai.

Ane. double de lauende 15
Ane. de Poutrain 16
Berrurier fe.

F67 (p. 51)

F70 FRASER, John; Prior

AN OFFER MADE TO A GENTLEMAN OF QVAlitie by M. Iohn Fraser, to subscribe and embrace the Ministers of Scotlands religion, if they can sufficiently proue, that they haue the true kirk and lawful calling . . . Nevvlie corrected and set forth . . . M.DC.V. 12° pp.106
3935.a.19.
Without imprint. Printed by Laurence Kellam at Douai.

FREDERICK I; King of Bohemia. Documents issued by Frederick I, King of Bohemia, in that capacity are entered in chronological order under BOHEMIA.

F71 FREILINGIUS, Georgius

Korte t'zamensprekinghe/tusschen twee Persoonen: In forme van Vraghen ende Antwoorden/Ghestelt/Ter eeren der . . . Magistraten en Regeerders des Volcks: Ten tweedden/van den Onderzaten/ende haren schuldighen plicht tot de Overheden . . . door Georgium Freilingium . . . TOT ROTTERDAM, By Jan van Waesberghe . . . 1612. 4° sig.AB[4]
T.2242(6).

FRIDEMBURG, Herimano Chunrrado; Baron. *See* FRIEDENBERG, Hermann Conrad von

F72 FRIEDENBERG, Hermann Conrad von; Baron

AVISOS, Y EXORTACIONES A LOS REYES, Y PRINCipes tocantes al pesso, y conseruaçion de su autoridad. Y las causas que producen las Guerras en Europa. Compuestas en Latin por HERIMANO CHVNRRADO Varon de Fridemburg . . . Traducidas de Frances, en Español . . . Por Pedro Pardo Riuadeneyra . . . EN BRVSELAS, En casa de IVAN MOMARTE . . . M.DC.XX. 8° pp.61
8026.aa.9.
The French and German versions, entitled respectively 'Deux discours' and 'Ein kurtze vermahnung', neither of which bears an imprint and of which the German version has been attributed in the General Catalogue to '[Amsterdam]', do not appear to have been produced in any part of the Netherlands.

F73 FRIESLAND.

[Collection of laws] STATVTEN, ORDONNANTIEN, ende Costumen van Frieslandt . . . Nieuwelijcx by een vergadert/ghaugmenteert/verbetert ende . . . uytghegheven . . . 1602. Tot Franeker/by Gillis vanden Rade/[etc.] 4° pp.309
1609/1566.
The compilers named in the preface as Sicke Dekema and others. Partly printed in civilité.

F74 FRIESLAND

[12.9.1616] PLACCAET . . . omme egeene persoonen . . . tot den Kercken-Dienst toe te laten/dan die bereydt zijn de Nederlantsche Confessie ende den Heydelbergschen Catechismum t'onderteyckenen/[etc.] fol. a single sheet
T.2246(26).
Issued by the States of Friesland, 12 September 1616. Printed by Rombertus Doyema or his widow at Franeker?

F75 FRIESLAND

[1616] IESVITICA PER Vnitas Belgij Provincias NEGOCIATIO bono publico in lucem edita; jussu DD. Deputatorum ORDINVM FRISIÆ. FRANEKERÆ APVD VIDVAM ROMBERTI DOYEMA, ORDINVM FRISIÆ, priusquam vivere desiit [*sic*], Typographi. Anno 1616. 4° sig.★A-M[4]N[3]
860.d.2(3).

F76 FRIESLAND
[1616] [Iesuitica . . . negociatio.] Der IESUITEN Negotiatie Ofte Coop-handel/inde Vereenichde Nederlanden tot ghemeenen beste. [*sic*] In druck uytghegeven door last vande E.M. Heeren Ghedeputeerde Staten van Vrieslandt. Ghedruct na de Copye van Leeuwarden, By Abraham vanden Rade . . . M.DC.XVI. 4° pp.67
T.2246(27).

FRISON, Jean (or: Ioan) Vredeman. *See* VRIES, Jan Vredeman de

F77 FROMONDUS, Libertus
Serenissimi BELGARVM PRINCIPIS ALBERTI PII Laudatio Funebris. A LIBERTO FROMONDO . . . Habita . . . LOVANII, Typis HENRICI HASTENII. M.DC.XXI. [etc.] 8° pp.50
1193.l.6(2).
Mainly in prose, with a poem at the end.

Les FRUICTS de la paix. 1609. *See* LE PETIT, Jean François

F78 FRUSIUS, Andreas
EPIGRAMMATA IN HÆRETICOS. Authore ANDREA FRVSIO . . . DVACI Ex officina Ioannis Bogardi. M.DC.VI. 12° ff.46
11403.a.12.
Ownership inscription: Ex libris Dominici Sartoris.

A FULL and plaine declaration of ecclesiastical discipline. 1617. *See* TRAVERS, Walter

F79 FUNGERUS, JOANNES
SYLVA CARMINVM . . . Auctore IOANNE FUNGERO . . . FRANEKERÆ Apud AEGIDIVM RADAEVM . . . M.D.CVII. 8° pp.206
1213.h.1(2).

F80 FURMERIUS, Bernardus
(tp.1) ANNALIVM PHRISICORVM LIBRI TRES . . . Auctore BERNARDO FVRMERIO . . . FRANECARÆ, EXCVDEBAT AEGIDIVS RADAEUS . . . 1609.
(tp.2) ANNALIVM PHRISICORVM TRIAS ALTERA . . . Auctore BERNARDO RVRMERIO . . . 1612. LEOVARDIÆ, EXCVDEBAT ABRAHAMVS RADAEVS, [etc.]
(tp.3) ANNALIVM FRISICORVM TRIAS TERTIA . . .AUCTORE BERNARDO FVRMERIO . . . LEOVARDIÆ, EXCVDEBAT ABRAHAMVS RADAEVS . . . 1617. 4° 3 vol.: pp.244; 255; 187
590.c.23(1) & 590.c.24(1); 154.e.9; C.74.c.17(2).
Vol.3 edited by Pierius Winsemius. The copy at C.74.c.17(2) consists of vol.1 only.

F81 FURMERIUS, Bernardus
[De rerum usu et abusu.] EMBLEMATA MORALIA, ET OECONOMICA, DE RERVM VSV ET ABVSV, OLIM INVENTA ET BELGICIS RITHmis explicata à Theodoro Cornhertio . . . nunc verò varijs carminum generibus recens illustrata à Richardo Lubbæo . . . ARNHEMI. Apud Ioannem Iansonium . . . sumptibus Theodori Petri Bibliopolæ Amstelrodamiensis, 1609. 4° ff.24
C.76.b.4(2).
Anonymous. A half-title preceding the titlepage reads: DE RERVM. VSV ET ABVSV above the original title engraving of the Plantin edition of 1575. Twenty-four numbered engraved emblems follow, succeeded by one further engraving, the plate numbered 2 signed with the monogram IH.W, i.e. Johannes Wierix. Above and below the engravings the original Biblical quotations and Latin verses by Bernardus Furmerius, accompanied on the opposite page by new Latin versions of the poems translated from Furmerius by Coornhert. For the removal of the initials IH.W. from the original plates and the attribution of the work to Coornhert *see Mauquoy-Hendrickx* III pt.1. no.2289–2314.

F82 FURMERIUS, Bernardus
[De rerum usu et abusu.] (tp.1) Recht Ghebruyck ende Misbruyck Van tydlicke Have. Welckers sin-rijcke af-beeldingen van D.V. Coornhert zyn bedacht/ oock . . . in't koper gesneden. Hier by is gevoeght 't bedrogh des Werldts/of het luije en leckere leven door Pandulphus Collenutius, mede den Lof-zang van 'tGoud/oock Gedichten op den A.B.C. . . . T'AMSTELREDAM, Voor Dirck Pietersz. [etc.]
(tp.2=p.[31]) 't Bedroch des vverelts . . . eertyts . . . in Latynschen dicht beschreven . . . van PANDVLPHVS COLLENVCIVS . . . van D.V.C. beneffens den Lofzangh van't Goudt, in Duytschen dicht gestelt . . . met aenwysingen verryckt . . . t'AMSTELDAM, voor Dirck Pietersz. [etc.] (col.) T'AMSTELDAM, Ghedruckt by Paulus van Ravesteyn . . . 1620. 4° ff.25, pp.26–67; port.
12304.ee.54; 11556.dd.18.
Anonymous. The engravings as in the preceding, but without the original titlepage and with an engraved portrait of Coornhert on the titlepage. The original Latin poems by Furmerius translated by Coornhert, with additional poems forming an alphabet. Pt.2 beginning: ODE HORATII II. LIB. EPOD. BEATVS ILLE, &c. Vertaalt. The 'Hymnus of Lofzang van't Goudt' (pp.58–60) followed by 'Lof van de Gevangenisse', both by Coornhert. Printed partly in civilité.

G

G1 GABRIEL Bethlen; Prince of Transylvania
[Letters] COPYE Vanden Brieff des Princes van Transylvanien. Ghenoemt GABRIEL BETHLEMI. IN 'SGRAVEN-HAGE. By Aert Meuris . . . 1619. 4° sig.A^3
T.2423(18).
Dated 18 September 1619.

G2 GABRIEL Bethlen; Prince of Transylvania
[Letters] BRIEF Van Gabriel Bethlemi Prince van Transylvanien Ghesonden Aen den Heere Grave van Toren in Moravia. IN 'SGRAVEN-HAGE. By Aert Meuris . . . 1619. 4° sig.A^3
T.2423(20).
Dated 18 September 1619. Leaf A3 signed: Oiij.

G3 GABRIEL Bethlen; Prince of Transylvania
[Letters] COPYEN Van eenighe Brieven/Van . . . GABRIEL KONINGH van HONGARIEN, &c. Aen . . . FREDERICII, KONINGH van BOHEMEN . . . Geschreven inde Maent van October . . . 1620 . . . T'AMSTELREDAM, Voor Marten Iansz. Brandt . . . 1620. [etc.] 4° sig.A^4B^2
T.2250(26*); T.2423(45).
Dated 9–12 October 1620. Printed by Paulus van Ravesteyn.

G4 GABRIEL Bethlen; Prince of Transylvania
[Letters] Gheschreuen brieff van GABRIEL BETHLEN, Prince van Transiluanien, Ghesonden aen Galga Zulthan, Prince der Tartaren, Anno 1621. Overghesedt wt zijn eyghen Handtschrifft/die vā ons volck is ghenomen/ende . . . gesonden aen den Keyser Ferdinandus. Eerst Ghedruckt den 25. Junij. 1621. T'Hantwerpen/By Abraham Verhoeuen/ [etc.] 4° pp.8; sig.A^4; illus., port.
P.P.3444.af(249).
The letter dated 1 April 1621. Headed: Iunij, 1621. 93. The titlepage woodcut shows a portrait of Gabriel Bethlen.

G5 GABRIEL Bethlen; Prince of Transylvania

[Letters] COPIA Van een zekere Missieve/DIE Gabriel Koninck van Hungarien/aen den Marck-Grave van Jagerensdorp/nu Konincklijcke Majesteyts van Bohemen Velt-Overste/geschreven. Waer in hy . . . verhaelt/de wonderbaerlijcke Victorie . . . van Nieuheusel . . . Wt het Latijn . . . overgheset. Ghedruckt in het Iaer . . . 1621. 4° sig. A^4

T.2424(22).

Dated 21 July 1621. Printed by Jan Jansz at Arnhem?

GABRIEL Bethlen; Prince of Transylvania. Verhael van de puncten ende articulē de welcke . . . Bethlin Gabor versocht heeft aen den nieuwen Boheemschen Coninck. 1619. *See* VERHAEL

GAL-BRAECKE. 1617. *See* TELLE, Reinier

G6 GALLE, Philips

DAMVS TIBI, BENIGNE LECTOR, VNO LIBELLO, TANQVAM IN SPECVLO EXHIBITAS, MEMORABILIORES JVDÆÆ GENTIS CLADES . . . MARTINVS. HEEMSKERCK. INVENTOR. PHILIPPVS. GALLE. FECIT. Car. Collaert ex̄. obl. fol. pl.22; port.

L.R.110.c.10(1).

A late reprint, ca.1620?, of earlier plates, with added titles in the upper parts. The plates have engraved frames of flowers, birds or geometrical patterns. The portrait is that of Maarten van Veen, known as Heemskerck.

G7 GALLE, Philips

Samsonis virorum fortissimi conceptio, ortus, robur, matrimonium, gesta, detonsio, excæcatio, et morientis . . . vindicta. M. Heemskerck inuentor. Ioan Galle excudit. obl. fol. pl.6

L.R.110.c.10(10).

Pl.2–6 signed: Philippus Galle fesit [or: fecit], Theodor. Galle excu. Circular plates, originally published by Hieronymus Cock, reprinted ca.1620?

G8 GALLE, Theodoor

(tp.1) ILLVSTRIVM IMAGINES, Ex antiquis marmoribus, nomismatibus, et gemmis expressæ: Quæ exstant Romæ, maior pars apud FVLVIVM VRSINVM. EDITIO ALTERA, aliquot Imaginibus, et I. FABRI ad singulas Commentario, auctior atque illustrior. Theodorus Gallæus delineabat Romæ ex Archetypis incidebat Antuerpiæ M.D.XCIIX. ANTVERPIÆ, EX OFFICINA PLANTINIANA M.DC.VI.

(tp.2) IOANNIS FABRI Bambergensis . . . IN IMAGINES ILLVSTRIVM EX FVLVII VRSINI Bibliotheca, Antuerpiæ à Theodoro Gallæo expressas, COMMENTARIVS . . . ANTVERPIÆ, EX OFFICINA PLANTINIANA, Apud Ioannem Moretum. M.DC.VI. 4° 2 pt.: pp.8: pl.151, A–R; pp.88

564.c.28; 602.e.20+C.74.c.7(2); 836.f.22(2).

The copy at 564.c.28 is complete; that at 602.e.20 contains the first part, i.e. the plates, only; those at 836.f.22(2) and C.74.c.7(2) contain only the commentary.

G9 GARASSE, François

LE RABELAIS REFORMÉ PAR LES MINISTRES, ET NOMMÉMENT PAR PIERRE DV MOVLIN MINISTRE de Charenton, pour response aux bouffonneries inserees en son liure de la Vocation des Pasteurs . . . A BRVXELLE, Par CHRISTOFLE GIRARD . . . M.DC.XIX. 8° pp.248

849.e.15.

Anonymous.

The GARDEN of Our B. Lady. 1619. *See* CHAMBERS, Sabine

G10 GASTOLDI, Giovanni Giacomo

BALLETTI A CINQVE VOCI Con li suoi Versi per cantare, sonare, & ballare, con vna Mascherata di cacciatori a Sei voci, & vn concerto de Pastori a Otto. DI GIO.

GIACOMO GASTOLDI . . . CANTO. IN ANVERSA. Appresso Pietro Phalesio. M.D.CI. obl. 4° pp.21
Music B.317.g.

G11 GASTOLDI, Giovanni Giacomo
(tp.1) BALLETTI A CINQVE VOCI . . . con vn [*sic*] Mascherata de Cacciatori à sei voci, & vn Concerto de Pastori à otto DI GIO. GIACOMO GASTOLDI . . . TENORE. IN ANVERSA Appresso Pietro Phalesio. M.DCV.
(tp.2) BALLETTI A CINQVE VOCI . . . DI GIO. GIACOMO GASTOLDI . . . BASSO . . . IN ANVERSA Appresso Pietro Phalesio. M.DCV. obl.4° 2 pt.: pp.21; 20
Music B.317.d.
A third part, 'Quintus', has been added in manuscript.

G12 GASTOLDI, Giovanni Giacomo
(tp.1) BALLETTI A CINQVE VOCI . . . con vn Mascherata . . . & vn Concerto de Pastori . . . DI GIO. GIACOMO GASTOLDI . . . CANTO. IN ANVERSA Appresso Pietro Phalesio . . . M.D.CXVII.
(tp.2) BALLETTI A CINQVE VOCI . . . DI GIO. GIACOMO GASTOLDI . . . BASSO. IN ANVERSA Appresso Pietro Phalesio . . . M.D.CXVII.
(tp.3) BALLETTI A CINQVE VOCI . . . DI GIO. GIACOMO GASTOLDI . . . ALTO. IN ANVERSA Appresso Pietro Phalesio . . . M.D.CXVII.
(tp.4) BALLETTI A CINQVE VOCI . . . DI GIO. GIACOMO GASTOLDI . . . TENORE. IN ANVERSA Appresso Pietro Phalesio . . . M.D.CXVII. obl.4° 4 pt.: pp.21; 20; 21; 21
Music b.317.c.

G13 GASTOLDI, Giovanni Giacomo
(tp.1) BALLETTI A TRE VOCI Con li suoi Versi per cantare, sonare & ballare DI GIO. GIACOMO GASTOLDI . . . Nuouamente Ristampati. Basso. IN ANVERSA Appresso Petro [*sic*] Phalesio . . . M.D.CXVII.
(tp.2) BALLETTI A TRE VOCI . . . DI GIO. GIACOMO GASTOLDI . . . Nuouamente Ristampati. Canto II. IN ANVERSA Appresso Petro Phalesio . . . M.D.CXVII.
(tp.3) BALLETTI A TRE VOCI . . . DI GIO. GIACOMO GASTOLDI . . . Nuouamente Ristampati. Canto. IN ANVERSA Appresso Petro Phalesio . . . M.D.CXVII. obl.4° 3 pt.: pp.16; 16; 16
Music K.1.d.23(3).
The signatures of these parts are E^4F^5; C^4D^6; A^4B^6, showing they have been wrongly assembled.

GAURICUS, Pomponius. Pomp. Gaurici de sculptura liber. 1609. *See* MARTINI, Matthias

G14 GAZET, Guillaume
L'HISTOIRE ECCLESIASTIQVE DV PAYS-BAS. CONTENANT L'ORDRE ET SVITE DE TOVS LES EVESQVES ET ARCHEVESQVES DE CHACVN Diocese . . . Ensemble vn Catalogue des Saincts, qui y sont specialement honnorez. LES FONDATIONS DES EGLISES, ABBAYES . . . & autres lieux pieux . . . PLVS LA SVCCESSION DES COMTES D'ARTHOIS . . . Par feu . . . M. GVILLAVME GAZET . . . A VALENCIENNES Chez IEAN VERVLIET . . . M.D.C.XIIII. (col.) A ARRAS, DE L'IMPRIMERIE DE GVILLAVME DE LA RIVIERE . . . M.DC.XIII. 4° pp.581
491.g.15.
The editor's dedicatory letter signed: Guillaume Moncarré.

G15 GAZET, Guillaume
(tp.1) TABLEAVX SACREZ DE LA GAVLE BELGIQVE POVRTRAITS AV MODELE du Pontifical Romain, Selon l'Ordre & Suite des Papes, & de tous les Euesques des Pays-bas. Auec les Saincts qui sont honnores en tous leurs Dioceses. ET LA BIBLIOTHEQVE DES DOCTEVRS Theologiens, Canonistes, Scholastiques, & autres escriuains celebres,

Anciens, & modernes de ces Pays. Par M. GVILLAVME GAZET . . . A ARRAS De l'Imprimerie de Guillaume de la Riuiere . . . 1610. [etc.]
(tp.2=p.97) LA BIBLIOTHEQVE SACREE DV PAYS-BAS. Contenant les noms des Autheurs Theologiens . . . AVEC Le Catalogue des œuures & escrits qu'ils ont laissé à la Posterité. Par M. GVILLAVME GAZET . . . A ARRAS, De l'Imprimerie de Guillaume de la Riuiere . . . M.DC.X. 8° pp.122
4662.aa.6.

G16 GAZETTE
De tweede GAZETTE des Maendts Iuny Anno 1621. Van Verscheyden Gheschiedenisse in Hongheren/Bemen/Engelandt/Vranckrijck/Nederlandt/Italie/Spanie/&c. Nv eerst Ghedruckt den 17. Iunij. 1621. T'Hantwerpen/By Abraham Verhoeuen/[etc.] 4° pp.8; sig.A^4; illus.
P.P.3444.af(248).

Headed: Iunij, 1621. 92. The titlepage woodcut shows a battle near a windmill.

G17 GAZETTE
DE TWEEDE GAZETTE des maents Augusti, 1621. Waer in verhaelt wordt de groote Victorie van de Polacken/teghen den Turck/ende den Staet van Hollandt/&c. Eerst Ghedruckt den 27. Augusti 1621. T'hantwerpen, By Abraham Verhoeuen, [etc.] 4° pp.8; sig.Ii; illus.
P.P.3444.af(275).

Headed: Augustus. 1621. 120. The news includes reports from Spain, England, Italy and elsewhere, that from Holland announces the publication of 'Nootwendighe ende vrypostige vermaeninghe'. The titlepage woodcut is of two armies in battle.

G18 GAZETTE
GAZETTE des Maents Iulij. 1621. Met Tijdinghe vvt Vranck-rijck, Duytslant, Hongharijen ende Polen. Nv eerst Ghedruckt den 10. Julij. T'Hantwerpen/By Abraham Verhoeuen/[etc.] 4° pp.8; sig.Hh; illus.
P.P.3444.af(257).

Headed: Julius 1621. 101. The titlepage woodcut shows a besieged town. The *Bibliotheca Belgica* describes no.101 of 1621 with a different title, the signature H and the date 9 July.

G19 GAZETTE
GAZETTE Des Maents Mey/Anno 1621. Verhalende verscheyden Tijdinghen wt Palslandt/Oostenrijck/Spanien/Hollant/ende andere Landen. Eerst Ghedruckt den 7. Mey 1621. T'Hantwerpen/By Abraham Verhoeuen/[etc.] 4° pp.7; sig.A^4
P.P.3444.af(228).

Headed: Mey 1621. 71. The titlepage bears an ornament instead of an illustration.

G20 GAZETTE
GAZETTE Vniuersele des maents Augusti, Vanden staedt der Oorloghe in Nederlandt/Palslandt/Bemen/Hongherijen, Vranck-rijck/Polen/ende andere Landen. Eerst ghedruckt den 18 Augusti. T'Hantwerpen/By Abraham Verhoeuen/[etc.] 4° pp.8; sig.Bb; illus.
P.P.3444.af(272).

Headed: Augustus, 1621.115. The news includes a report from London on Anglo-Dutch relations. The titlepage woodcut shows a portrait of Ferdinand II and one of a Turk with crown and sceptre.

G21 GAZETTE
DE TWEEDE GAZETTE Vniuersele Des maents Ianuarij, anno 1621. Hoe dat Morauia is ghereconcilieert met den Keyser/ende den Grave van Bucquoy is ghetrocken naer Hongheren. Eerst ghedruckt in Januarius. 1621. T'Hantwerpen/By Abraham Verhoeven/[etc.] 4° pp.8; sig.A^4; illus.
P.P.3444.af(183).

Headed: Ianuarius 1621. 14. The titlepage woodcut shows the portrait of 'L'Empereur Ferdinandu' [*sic*]. On p.8 there is an advertisement for Verhoeven's large print of the Heidelberg tun, i.e. 'Claere afbeeldinghe', which is stated to have come from the press on 27 January.

G22 GAZETTE

GAZETTE Vniuersele Des Maents Januarij Anno 1621. Met de doot vāde Pals-Gravinne/ende innemen der Stadt Hanau/Fridburg/ende Zweybrugghen in PfaltsLant door den Marquis Spinola. Eerst Ghedruckt den 15. Januarius 1621. T'Hantwerpen/By Abraham Verhoeuen/[etc.] 4° pp.8; 4 unsigned leaves; illus.
P.P.3444.af(174).

Headed: Ianuarius 1621. 5. The titlepage woodcut purports to show Princess Elizabeth on her deathbed. The news includes a report from London.

G23 GAZETTE

GAZETTE Uniuersele des Maēts October/anno 1620. Waer inne verhaelt wort dē gheluckighen voortganck der Keyserlijcke Leghers in Duytslandt. Getrocken wt . . . Brieven, ghesonden wt oostenrijck, Hongheryen, Bemerlandt . . . ende andere Quartieren van Duydtslandt. Eerst Ghedruckt den xvj. October 1620. T'Hantwerpen/By Abraham Verhoeuē . . . 1620. [etc.] 4° pp.7; sig. A^4
1480.aa.15(38); P.P.3444.af(120).

G24 GAZETTE

De tvveede GAZETTE van Blyschap Des Maents April 1621. Met vremde [*sic*] Tijdingen vvt diuersche quartierē. Eerst Ghedruckt den 27. Appril 1621. T'Hantwerpen by Abraham Verhoeven/[etc.] 4° pp.8; sig. A^4; illus.
P.P.3444.af(225).

Headed: Appril 1621. 66. The news includes a report on Spinola's triumphal entry into Brussels, a mocking description of events in Holland, etc. The titlepage woodcuts, one small and one large, both show Arion riding the dolphin.

G25 GAZETTE

GAZETTE Van Blijschap/des Maents Aprilis/Anno 1621. Van het ouergheuen van Hungherijen/Slesien/Pfaltz-Landt/Pilsen/ende andere plaetsen. Eerst ghedruckt den 19. April/1621. T'Hantwerpen by Abraham Verhoeven/[etc.] 4° pp.8; sig. A^4
P.P.3444.af(220).

Headed: April 1621. 59. The ornament on the titlepage consists of musical instruments.

G26 GAZETTE

Die tweede GAZETTE van Blyschap des Maents Mey, Over verscheyden Victorien der Catholijcken in Hungharijen/ Vranckrijck/ende andere Landen. Nv eerst Ghedruckt den 29. Mey 1621. T'Hantwerpen/By Abraham Verhoeuen/[etc.] 4° pp.6; sig. A^4; illus.
P.P.3444.af(237).

Headed: Mey 1621. 81. The titlepage woodcut shows Arion riding the dolphin in the larger of Verhoeven's two versions of this subject. The last leaf has a blank recto and bears the privilege on the verso.

GEESSEL om uyt te dryven. 1618. *See* TRIGLAND, Jacobus

GEISTERANUS, Cornelius. Disputationum physicarum quarta de caussis extrinsecis. 1607. *See* JACCHAEUS, Gilbertus

G27 GAZETTE

GAZETTE Van Blyschap, Ouer het ouercomen van den Graue van Mansfelt/met alle zijn Volck. Item ouer een groote Victorie by Franckendael &c. Eerst ghedruckt den 2. Nouember 1621. T'Hantwerpen/By Abraham Verhoeuen/[etc.] 4° pp.8; sig.Dddd; illus.

P.P.3444.af(305).

Headed: Nouember 1621. 158. The titlepage woodcut shows the double portrait of Maximilian of Bavaria and another general.

G28 GAZETTE

GAZETTE Van Blyschap wt Prage, Brussel, Parijs, ende andere plaetsen. Eerst ghedruckt den xxviij. Nouember. 1620. T'Hantwerpen/By Abraham Verhoeuen/ [etc.] 4° pp.8; sig.Bb; illus.

1480.aa.15(48); P.P.3444.af(145).

The titlepage illustration is a full page woodcut with architectural and heraldic images. The text ends with the promise of a further report on the occupation of Prague in the issue of 1 December, i.e. the 'Particulier relaes'.

G29 GELASIUS de Valle Umbrosa; pseudonym of Johannes de Laet?

Hoc volumine continentur, Ante omnia, ende voor al, Een nieu Liedeken/ ghemaeckt ter eeren Doctoris usꝗ ad miraculum mirifici, & charitate igniti CAR. BONARSII [*sic*], Poëtæ larvati, & Gardiani der Sociorum Almanack in Bilsteyn prope Antvverpiam. Modificatū & rhytmizatum per unum Scholarem de Leyda. Necnon, Iesuitographia. Item/Officina Sociorum. Noch Eenen Modus Exorcizandi. Et alia . . . Notabili diligentia compilata . . . per reverendmm [*sic*] admodum fratrem GELASIVM de valle umbrosa Ordinis Prędicatorum. Excudebatur inde Duyster steegh/apud Medemiam Vtis Viduam in officina Ioh. sine nomine asque [*sic*] ubi ofte quando. 8° sig.A-C^8; illus.

11408.b.9.

Poems, in mixed Latin and Dutch, Latin, Greek, or Latin and Greek mixed. The 'approbation' signed: Euseb. Philalethius. One of the pamphlets exchanged between the Antwerp Jesuit College and members of Leiden University. Bonarsius stands for Scribani whose real name is used as addressee of the dedicatory letter and in some of the items, including one allegedly taken from Scribani's 'Amphitheatrum' connected with the illustration of a spiritual signpost. The 'Leiden scholar' has been tentatively identified as Janus Rutgers. The attribution of the editorship of the whole in *Weller Lexicon* p.223 and of one of the Greek poems, signed: Cl. Sa., to Claude Saumaise has been proved to be erroneous. The first poem is described internally as 'nieu-jaer Liedeken'; this and evidence from 'Vae Victis' by Godefridus Vrancken dates publication December 1608. All Dutch words are printed in Gothic type. An ornament on B3v is typical of the press of Henrick van Haestens at Leiden.

G30 GELASIUS de Valle Umbrosa; pseudonym of Johannes de Laet?

Hoc volumine continentur, Ante omnia, ende voor al, Een nieu Mey-Liedeken . . . ter eeren . . . CAR. BONARSII . . . compilata . . . per . . . GELASIVM de Valle umbrosa Ordinis Prædicatorum. Excudebatur inde Duyster steegh, apud Medemiam Vtis Viduam in officina Ioh. sine nomine absque ubi ofte quando. 8° sig.A-C^8; illus.

860.b.15(2).

Another edition of the preceding. Dutch words are printed in italics. The description of the first peom as 'Mey-Liedeken' suggests publication in the spring of 1609, certainly again at Leiden, probably also by Henrick van Haestens. Ownership inscription: Ioh. Mauritius; with manuscript notes, i.e. by John Morris?

G31 GELDERLAND

[12.5.1604] REFORMATIE DER LANTRECHTEN, GEBRUYCKEN UND GEWOONTHEYDEN

DER GRAEFSCHAP ZUTPHEN . . . Ghedruckt tot Arnhem, By JAN JANSSEN . . . M.DC.IV. 4° sig.A-H⁴
1509/3790.

Issued on 12 May 1604 by the Ridderschap and Steden of Gelderland and Zutphen.

G32 GELDERLAND
[5.2.1617] Afgescheyt Van weghen de . . . Staten van Gelrelant den Kerckendienaren der selver Lantschap ghegheven. TOT ARNHEM, By Jan Janssen . . . 1617. 4° sig.A⁴
T.2247(30).

Issued 5 February 1617. With 'Artijckelen vanden Gelderschen Synode' of 1612.

G33 GELDERLAND
[6.2.1617] Sententie: Ende Condemnatie vanden Hove van Ghelder-Landt/over seecker Tafereel/nopende de huydendagehsche [*sic*] questieuse poincten/by de Remonstranten hatelijck ghestelt ende van Leyden derwaerts over-ghesonden. TOT DELF, Ghedruckt by Ian Andriessz. . . . 1617. 4° sig.A²
T.2247(29*).

The verdict, dated 6 February 1617, on the work of Reinier Telle.

G34 GELDERLAND
[15.9.1618] PLACCAET. VVt-ghegheven. Van weghen de Heeren Staten des Furstendoms Gelre ende Graeffschaps Zutphen/Teghen de ghestroyde lasteringhen ende Calumnien/van de Evangelische Ghereformeerde Christelijcke Religie. TOT ARNHEM, By Jan Janssen . . . 1618. 4° sig.A⁴
700.h.25(18).

Dated 15 September 1618. With 'Extract vvt de acten van den Synode van Gelderlandt, in Iulio 1618. tot Arnhem ghehouden'. With Janssen's device 'Peccata frangunt Dei tabulas' on the titlepage.

G35 GELDERLAND
[15.9.1618] PLACCAET. VVyt-ghegheven Van weghen de . . . Staten des Furstendombs Ghelre ende Graefschaps Sutphen/Teghen De ghestroyde lasteringhen ende calumnien/van de Evangelische Ghereformeerde Christelijcke Religie. TOT ARNHEM, Eerst ghedruckt by Jan Janssen . . . 1618. 4° sig.A⁴
T.2248(29*).

Another edition of the preceding. With a woodcut of the arms of Gelderland on the titlepage.

GELDERLAND. [5.1620] For the 'Kercken-ordeninghe', issued by the Staten of Gelderland in May 1620, *see* DORDRECHT. Synod

G36 GELDORPIUS, Henricus; the Elder
D. RVARDI TAPPART ENCHVSANI, Hæreticæ Pravitatis primi & postremi per Belgicum inquisitoris, Cancellarii Academiæ Lovaniensis, Apotheosis. Jtem, Facetum aliquod Euangelium Pasquilli olim Romani jam peregrini dictum. PRÆTEREA, De omnium statuum Mundi & seculi hujus corruptione, CARMINA ALIQVOT. Ab auctoritatibus celeberrimis, jam defunctis, quondam edita. FRANECARÆ, Ex officinâ Typographicâ, 1615. 12° pp.24; sig.A-E¹²
1020.a.10.

Anonymous reprint of the work first published in 1559 under the pseudonym Gratianus Verus. Anonymously printed by Ulderick Balck.

G37 GÉNÉBRARD, Gilbert; Archbishop
DE SACRARVM ELECTIONVM IVRE ET NECESSITATE. Ad Ecclesiæ Gallicanæ redintegrationem. Auctore G. Genebrardo . . . LEODII, Apud Arnoldum de Coersvvaremia . . . 1601. [etc.] 8° pp.142
1607/1077.

G38 GENERALE

Generale beschrijvinghe van alle de Steden/ende plaetsen die den Coninc heeft gewonnen/vande Huguenotten oft vā de Ghepretendeerde Ghereformeerde Religie. Ende dat met gheweldt van Wapenen/t'sedert den 28. April lestleden tot nv toe 1621. Alvvaer zijne Majesteydt byvvesende in Persoone. Eerst Ghedruckt den 10. September. T'Hantwerpen, Abraham Verhoeuen, [etc.] 8° pp.16; sig.QqRr^4; illus.
P.P.3444.af(281).

Headed: September, 1621. 126. The titlepage woodcut shows a portrait of Louis XIII. The Word 'by' has been accidentally omitted from the imprint.

G39 GENERALE

Generale Vermaninghe Aenden Switseren. Streckende tot harer behoudenisse ende besten/tegen de beroerten ende peryckelen deses jeghenwoordighen tijts. Wt den Francoisschen in Nederduyts (tot dienst ende waerschouwinge allen liefhebberen des Vaderlants) overgheset. Concordia res parvæ crescunt. Middelburgh, Voor Adriaen vanden Vivre, 1608. 4° sig.AB^{4}C^2; illus.
T.1713(32); T.2420(19).

The titlepage woodcut is of the head of a cow with a ribbon bearing coats of arms wound around the horns.

G40 GENEVA. Church of Geneva

[Les ordonnances ecclésiastiques.] KERCKELIICHE Ordonnantie der Gemeente van Geneven . . . Overgheset in Nederduytsch uyt de Fransche Copie . . . t'Amsterdam, Gedruckt by Broer Jansz . . . 1617. 4° pp.53[35]
T.2247(14).

G41 GENINGES, John

THE LIFE AND DEATH OF M^r. Edmund Geninges PRIEST, Crowned with Martyrdome at London, the 10. day of Nouember . . . M.D.XC I . . . At S. OMERS by Charles Boscard . . . 1614. 4° pp.110; illus.
G.1301; C.26.h.25.

Anonymous. With an appendix on the life and death of Swithune Welles. The engraved titlepage is signed: Mart. bas f. Duaci, other engravings, all with Latin inscriptions, signed: Mart. bas f., or: M.b.f. The copy at C.26.h.25 is imperfect, wanting pp.5,6,95,96.

DEN GEPREDESTINEERDEN dief. 1619. *See* SLATIUS, Hendrik

GERATUS, Maertinus. Ne magnam tenui mentem metire tabellâ. 1620. *See* FEDDES, Pieter. Effigies D. Johannis Bogermanni.

G42 GERMANY

[1.1.1607] Verhael vande ARTICVLEN ende conditien vanden Peyse/eñ verbont/ gesloten tusschen onsen . . . Keyser vā Roomen Rudolphus/ende den Turck/ende het Coninckrijck van Hongherijen. Ouerghesedt wt den Hoochduytsche in onse Nederlantsche tale. T'HANTVVERPEN, By Abraham Verhoeuen [etc.] 8° pp.14
1193.a.30(2).

Originally issued in January 1607, with a contemporary manuscript note on the titlepage giving the precise date. Published in 1607. Cropped.

G43 GERMANY

[9.10.1607] BRIEF Des Keyserlijcke Majest. van Duytslandt/aende . . . Heeren Staten vande Gheunieerde Provintien gheschreven. Op't stuck vande

[Illustrations of **G41** *overleaf]*

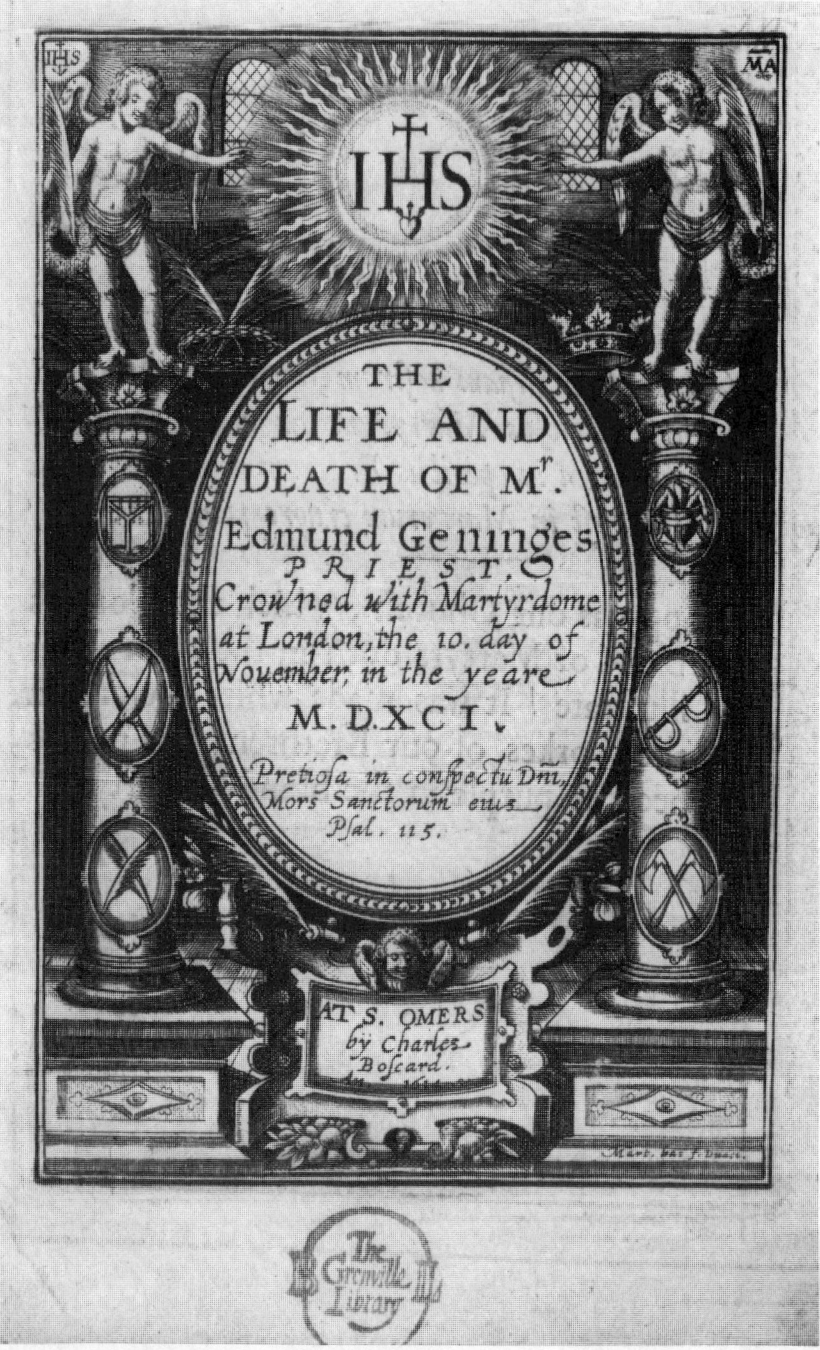
IHS
MA
THE
LIFE AND
DEATH OF Mr.
Edmund Geninges
PRIEST.
Crowned with Martyrdome
at London, the 10. day of
Nouember, in the yeare
M.D.XCI.
Pretiosa in conspectu Dni,
Mors Sanctorum eius
Psal. 115.
AT S. OMERS
by Charles
Boscard.
The Grenville Library

G41

Mittitur ad patrios ſocio comitante Penates;
Ad Thameſim cautùs ſeparat ambo timor.

G41 (p.46)

Nederlantsche Vredehandeling Midtsgaders d'Antwoort vande voornoemde Heeren Staten . . . Ghedruckt 1608. 4° sig. A4: plate; port.
T.1713(19); 106.d.4(1).
The Emperor's letter dated 9 October 1607. The copy at 106.d.4(1) without the portrait, signed: Henr. Hondius exc., which may not belong to the edition as it has French text and is not mentioned in the description given in *Knuttel* no.1513.

G44 GERMANY
[9.10.1607] BRIEF Des Keyserlijcke Mayest. van Duytslandt . . . Op't stuck vande Nederlandtsche Vredehandelingh . . . Ghedruckt Anno 1608. 4° sig. A4
106.d.4(2).
A different edition from the preceding, e.g. the Emperor's name spelt 'Rudolff' in place of 'Rodolf' in the preceding.

G45 GERMANY
[11.1619] Voordraginghe/Hoe de Roomsche Keyserlijcke MAIESTEYT, Door haren Ghesanten den Heeren Graven van Hoogen-Zolleren/op den Correspondenten dach tot Norrenbergh dien aldaer vergaderden Euangelischen Chur Vorsten ende andere Stenden ende hare Gesanten . . . mondelic gedaen/ende daer na schriftelijck overgegeven. Mitsgaders der Coninclijcker Majesteyt VAN BOHEMEN Ende andere . . . Euangelische Stenden . . . Antvvoort . . . 'TAMSTELREDAM, By Jan Marcusz . . . 1620. 4° sig. AB4C2
T.2423(31).
The speech dated November 1619, the reply 28 November 1619.

G46 GERMANY
[29.1.1620] d'Edictale Cassatie ende Annullatie, mette Aengehechte Protestatie, van . . . FERDINANDVS den II. teghens de Pretense nieuwe nulle verkiesinge oft Electie, ende Crooninge in Bohemen/etc. Eerst Ghedruct tot weenen in Oostenrijck, Nv ouerghesedt wt de Hooch-Duytsche sprake in onse Nederlantsche Tale. 1620. t'Hantwerpen/By Abraham Verhoeuen . . . 1620. [etc.] 4° pp.16; sig. AB4; illus.
P.P.3444.af(39).
Dated 29 January 1620. The titlepage woodcut shows the arms of Ferdinand II.

G47 GERMANY
[30.4.1620] De Rom. Keys. Majesteyt FERDINANDI II. Monotorial Mandaten, Aen de Cheur Pfaltz/Nopende de quitteringhe eñ Ruyminghe vant' Coninck-rijck Bohemen . . . Van ghelijcken oock Aen alle Rijckx-Steden, die hun met de Boheemsche Rebellen, deelachtich ghemaeckt hebben . . . T'Hantwerpen/By Abraham Verhoeven . . . 1620. [etc.] 4° pp.7; sig. Z4; illus.
P.P.3444.af(54).
Dated 30 April 1620. The titlepage woodcut shows a portrait inscribed 'LEMPEREVR FERDINANDVS'.

G48 GERMANY
[30.4.1620] Nieuwe Placcaten vande Keyserlijcke Majesteyt/Ferdinandus den tweeden/Aen alle Rijckxsteden/die hun met de Boheemsche Rebellen deelachtich ghemaeckt hebben/etc. T'Hantwerpen/By Abraham Verhoeuen . . . 1620. [etc.] 4° pp.7; sig. Ff4; illus.
P.P.3444.af(60).
Issued 30 April 1620. The titlepage woodcut shows the imperial arms.

G49 GERMANY
[30.6.1620] COPYA Van diuersche schriftelijcke Commissien ende Placcaten by de Roomsche Keyserlijcke Majesteyt aen . . . den Hertoge van Beyeren . . . ouer gesonden/raeckēde de gerebelleerde Bohemen . . . Nv eerst Ghedruckt den ix. October. T'Hantwerpen/By Abraham Verhoeven . . . 1620. [etc.] 4° pp.8; sig.Sss^4
1480.aa.15(33); P.P.3444.af(115).
Of the three letters listed on the titlepage, this issue contains only the first, dated 30 June 1620. The others, printed on signatures Ttt and Vvv respectively, are entered under MAXIMILIAN I; Duke.

G50 GERMANY
[3.9.1620] Waerachtighe COPPYEN van sommighe Placcaten eñ Brieven by de Roomsche Keyserlijcke Majesteyt als oock by . . . den MARQVIS SPINOLA gepubliceert ende geschreven aen die Staten van dē Rijnstroom ende Wetteravischen Cierckels/raeckende de verseeckeringhe vande Sauuegarde/etc. Gheduerende desen Neder-Bourgontschen Krijchs-leger. T'Hantwerpen/By Abraham Verhoeuen . . . 1620. 4° pp.7; sig.M^4; illus.
1480.aa.15(21); P.P.3444.af(95).
Dated 3 September 1620. The titlepage woodcut shows Spinola holding keys.

G51 GERMANY
[3.9.1620] B. Copia. Keyserlijck schrijven aē . . . MARQVIS SPINOLA, Pro Bescherminghe ende Sauvegarde/voor de Ridderschap aenden Rijnstroom . . . Overghesedt wt den Hooch-Duytsche/in onse Nederlantsche Tale. T'Hantwerpen/By Abraham Verhoeven . . . 1620. [etc.] 4° pp.6; sig.N^4; illus.
1193.f.19; 1480.aa.15(22); P.P.3444.af(96).
Issued separately from, but part of the preceding. The titlepage woodcut shows a messenger with letters.

G52 GERMANY
[3.9.1620] Onse ende des Rijckx Lieve/Ghetrouwe N. HOOFT-LIEDEN, RADEN, COMMISSARISSEN, der Ghevreyde Ridderschap aenden Rijnstroom/wetterou . . . Ferdinandus de 2. . . . T'Hantwerpen/By Abraham Verhoeuen . . . 1620. 4° pp.6; sig. O^4; illus.
1480.aa.15(23); P.P.3444.af(97); 1193.i.29.
Issued separately from, but part of the preceding two entries. The titlepage woodcut shows a portrait of Spinola. The copy at 1193.i.29 is imperfect; wanting the titlepage.

G53 GERMANY
[19.10.1620] Keyserlijck Decreet/oft Vonnis van CASSATIE teghens eeuighe [*sic*] Agenten . . . Overghesedt wt de Hooch-Duytsche sprake in onse Nederlantsche Tale. Eerst ghedruckt den 11. December. 1620. T'Hantwerpen/By Abraham Verhoeuen/[etc.] 4° pp.7; sig.Nn^4; illus.
P.P.3444.af(159); 1480.aa.15(56).
Dated 19 October 1620. The titlepage woodcut shows a shield with a Gorgon's head. The copy at P.P.3444.af(159) corresponds to that described in the *Bibliotheca Belgica* (V 196, 11.12.1620). The copy at 1480.aa.15(56) is a variant, possessing neither the text from 'Ad mandatum' to 'Bucher' on p.7 nor the approbation.

G54 GERMANY
[10.12.1620] Der H. Keyserlycker Ende . . . KONINCKLIICKER MAIESTEYT Edictale

Cassatie Vande Onwettelijcke/Pretensie/ende in Recht nulle verkiesinghe GABRIEL BETHLENS in't Coninck-Rijck van Hungharijen: ende Annullatie van alle Acten/ ende Conclusien inde Landtdaghen van Presborgh ende Nieuvven-zol. Ouerghesedt Wt het Latijn in onse Nederlantsche sprake. 1621. Ghedruckt den 17. Meert. t'hantwerpen/By Abraham Verhoeuen/[etc.] 4° pp.24; sig.A, ++B, +++C^4; illus.

P.P.3444.af(204).

Dated 29 January and issued 10 December 1620. Headed: Martius 1621. 38. The titlepage woodcut shows a portrait of Gabriel. Though numbered 38 and advertised in no.37, printed apparently after no.39 and 40.

G55 GERMANY

[29.1.1621] COPIA Vanden Keyserlycken, BAN, Acht, oft Banissement, Ghedeclareert teghens Hans Georgen dē Ouden/Marck-Grave van Brandenborch, met Christiaen Vorst van Anhalt, Ende George Frederick Graue van Hohenloe, &c. Overghesedt vvt de hooch-Duytsche sprake in onse Nederlandtsche Tale. Eerst ghedruckt den 16. Meert/1621. T'Hantwerpen/by Abraham Verhoeven/ [etc.] 4° pp.16; sig.(⁂) ☞ (⁂)^4; illus.

P.P.3444.af(205).

Dated 22 January 1621, proclaimed 29 January 1621. With a description of the reading of the ban. Headed: Martius 1621. 39. Advertised in no.37. The titlepage woodcut shows the arms of Ferdinand II in typographical borders.

G56 GERMANY

[29.1.1621] COPIA Vande Achts Verclaringhe, ofte Keyserlijcken Ban/gedaen Teghen Fredericus Pfaltz-Graue Ceur-Vorst, Als hooft vande Boheemsche Rebellen, Ghepubliceert binnen Weenen in Oostenrijck/ende andere Steden in Duytslandt. Nv eerst Ghedruct den 16. Meert, 1621. t'Hantwerpen/By Abraham Verhoueuen/[etc.] 4° pp.8[24]; sig.A-C^4; illus.

P.P.3444.af(206).

Headed: Martius 1621.40. Advertised in no.37. Published separately from, but apparently part of the preceding. Dated 22 January, proclaimed 29 January 1621. The titlepage woodcut shows the imperial eagle in a laurel wreath.

G57 GERMANY

[29.1.1621] COPIA Vande Keyserlijcke Achtsverclaringe/tegen Pals-Graef Frederick . . . Ende te ghelijck, de Copia, Vande keyserlijcke Achts-verklaringhe/ Tegen Hans Iorriaen, den Ouden Marck-Grave/van Brandenburgh. Christiaen. Vorste van Anholdt. Ende Iorriaen Frederick, Grave tot Hohenlo. NA de Copie, Ghedruckt int Iaer . . . 1621. 4° sig.AB^{4}C^2

T.2424(8).

The documents dated 22 January, proclaimed 29 January 1621. Without imprint; printed by Jan Jansz at Arnhem? Published in 1621.

G58 GERMANY

[5.4.1621] Accoordt gemaeckt/uyt den name ende van weghen hare Keyserlijcke ende Conincklijcke Majesteydt van Bohemien . . . Tusschen . . . Ambrosio Spinola . . . ter eendre. Ende oock . . . Mauritius/Lant Graue van Hessen . . . ter andere zyden/ende dat inde . . . Stadt Binghen Overghesedt wt de Hooch-Duytsche sprake. Eerst Ghedruckt den 21. Mey. 1621. T'Hantwerpen/By Abraham Verhoeuen/[etc.] 4° pp.8; sig.A^4

P.P.3444.af(231).

Dated 5 April 1621. Headed: Mey 1621. 75.

G59 GERMANY

[12.4.1621] Artijculen vā t'verdrach die deur tusschen spreken vande Heeren . . . Princen, Electeurs van Mentz, ende Loduick Lant-graue van Hessen, tusschen dē . . . Marquis Spinola . . . ter eenre/ende Heeren . . . Ioachim Ernest Marquis vā Brandenborch . . . ende Iean Fredericq Hertoghe van Wirtenberch soo in sijnen eyghen/als in name vande vereenichde Princen/ende Staten gehandelt ende ghesloten zijn, Eerst ghedruckt den 23. Appril. 1621. T'Hantwerpen/By Abraham Verhoeuen . . . 1621. 4° pp.7; sig.¶[4]

P.P.3444.af(221).

The peace made by Spinola as commander of the imperial troops with the representatives of the Union of Halle, dated 12 April 1621. Headed: April 1621. 62. Verhoeven also printed a Latin edition, entitled 'Articuli conventionis, qui . . . inter Marchionem Spinola . . . et . . . Ioachimum Ernestum Marchionem Brandenburgensem . . . tractati sunt et conclusi', from which a German edition published at Mainz is translated. The *Bibliotheca Belgica* claims that the Dutch edition preceded the Latin, which seems strange.

G60 GERMANY. League of Würzburg, 1610

[Newe Zeitung, von dem Verbindnusse.] TRANSLAET uyt den Hoochduytsche Van de Ligue ofte Verbintenisse/die de Catholijcke Vorsten van Duytslandt onder den anderen voor den tijdt van Negen Jaren ghemaeckt . . . hebben/int eynde vanden Jare 1609. Dienende Tot verklaringhe van haer Intentie. In 's Graven-Haghe Gedruckt by Hillebrandt Jacobsz. . . . 1610. 4° sig.A[2]

T.2421(17).

G61 GERMANY. League of Würzburg, 1610

[Accord. 23.6.1620] ACCOORDT ende Conditien ghesloten int ouergheuen der H. Rijckx-Stadt Vlm/in Julij lestleden/1620. Tusschen . . . den Hertoghe van Beyeren/van weghen de vereenichde Catholijcke Cheur-Vorsten/ende . . . den Marck-Grave Joachim Ernestus van Brandenborch/etc. Eerst Ghedruckt den v. Augusti 1620. T'Hantwerpen/by Abraham Verhoeuen/[etc.] 4° pp.7; sig.Yy[4]; illus.

P.P.3444.af(75).

Translated from the German 'Accord' of 23 June 1620, dated 3 July n.s. The titlepage woodcut shows a city under siege. For another edition, naming the Protestant side first, *see* below: GERMANY. Union of Halle, 1610

G62 GERMANY. Union of Halle, 1610

[19–29.12.1619] PROPOSITIE, Ghedaen by de Gesanten van de Corresponderende/Geunieerde/ende tot Nurenberg vergadert gewesene Ceurfursten/Stenden ende Heeren:aen . . . MAXIMILAEN, Paltzgrave aen den Rijn . . . Mitsgaders Derselven Doorluchticheden antwoorde/op deselve Propositie. Ende voorts/de Replijcke daerop by de voorschreven Ghesanten ghedaen. IN S'GRAVEN-HAGHE. By Aert Meuris . . . 1620. 4° sig.A-C[4]D[1]

T.2250(25); T.2423(33).

The documents dated 19 to 29 December 1619.

G63 GERMANY. Union of Halle, 1610

[3.7.1620] VREDE-PVNCTEN Tusschen den Euangelische ende Catholijcke Gheunieerde Standen tot Ulm besloten/den IIJ. Julij . . . M.DC.XX. Over-gheset uyt den Hoochduytschen in onse Nederlandtsche Tale. Ghedruckt . . . 1620. 4° 2 unsigned leaves

T.2423(40).

Dated 3 July 1620. Without imprint; printed by Hillebrand Jacobsz van Wouw at The Hague? Translated from the German 'Accord' of 23 June 1620, dated 3 July n.s. For another edition, naming the Catholic side first, *see* above: GERMANY. League of Würzburg, 1610.

G64 GERMANY. Electors

[21.3.1620] COPIE Van het Schrijven aen Chur Phalts ghedaen/door de Chur: ende Vorsten/dewelcke tot Mulhuysen vergadert zijn gheweest. Midtsgaders D'antwoorde by hare Conincklijcke Majesteyt van Bohemen Frederick de tweede daer op ghevolght. Ghedruckt nae het over-ghesette Hoochduytsche Exemplaer . . . 1620. 4° sig. A^4B^2

T.2423(30).

Dated 21 March 1620. Without imprint; printed by Hillebrant Jacobsz van Wouw at The Hague?

G65 GERMANY. Electors

[21.3.1620] COPIA Des Briefs vāde Keur-Vorsten/ende Vorsten tot Mulhausen/ vergadert aenden Cheur-Vorst Pfaltz-Grave. II. Aende Staten des Coninckrijckx Bohemiē . . . Schlesien/Moravien . . . III. Aende Staten vande Ausburchsche Confessie inden Rijck. IIII. Aende vrije Ridderschap des Rijckx inde Wetterauw . . . Francken en Swavenlandt. V. Aende Staten van Hungarien. T'Hantwerpen/By Abraham Verhoeuen . . . 1620. 4° pp.8; sig. Kk^4

P.P.3444.af(37).

Dated 21 March 1620. Containing only the letter to Frederick, signed: Johan Schweicthard [*sic*], and others.

G66 GERMANY. Electors

[21.3.1620] Den Brieff ghesonden aen de Standen oft Staten des Coninckrijcx Bohemien/ende Gheincorporeerde Landen. Overghesedt wt de Hooch-Duytsche sprake in onse Nederlantsche Tale. Eerst Ghedruckt den iij. Julij. T'Hantwerpen/ By Abraham Verhoeven . . . 1620. [etc.] 4° pp.7; sig. Ll^4

P.P.3444.af(63).

Dated: Mulhuysen den 21. Martij 1620. Published separately from, but as pt.II of the preceding.

G67 GERONIMO GRACIAN de la Madre de Dios

IOSEPHINA. SVMMARIO DE LAS EXCELENCIAS DEL GLORIOSO .S. IOSEPH. Esposo de la Virgen MARIA. Recopilado . . . por GERONIMO GRACIAN . . . EN BRVSELAS En casa de IVAN MOMARTE . . . 1609. 4° ff.132; illus.

C.120.b.9.

The titlepage borders and the illustrations are in woodcut.

G68 GERONIMO GRACIAN de la Madre de Dios

LEVIATHAN ENGAÑOSO. SVMA DE ALGVNOS ENGAÑOS En que se trata De los pecados ocultos: y agenos: de las malas costumbres: y vanidades . . . con que pretende el demonio destruyr astutamēte la gracia, y perfeccion de las almas. Recopilada por Fr. Geronymo Gracian de la Madre de Dios . . . EN BRVSSELAS, Por Roger Velpio, y Huberto Antonio . . . 1614. [etc.] 8° pp.136; illus.

4401.c.20.

With the author's personal device in woodcut on the titlepage verso.

G69 GERRITSZ, Hessel

Beschryvinghe Vander Samoyeden Landt in Tartarien. Nieulijcks onder 't ghebiedt der Moscoviten gebracht. Wt de Russche tale overgheset, Anno 1609. Met een verhael Vande opsoeckingh ende ontdeckinge vande nieuwe deurgang ofte straet int Noordwesten na de Rijcken van China ende Cathay. Ende Een Memoriael gepresenteert aenden Coningh van Spaengien/belanghende de ontdeckinghe ende gheleghentheyt van 't Land ghenaemt Australia Incognita. t'Amsterdam/by Hessel Gerritsz. . . . 1612. 4° sig. A, A-E^4: plates; illus., maps

C.32.d.31; C.114.b.6(2,3).

The editor's preface signed: Hessel Gerritsz van Assum, Liefhebber der Geographie. The first piece translated by Isaac Massa. The copy at C.114.b.6(2,3) is fragmentary.

G70 GERRITSZ, Hessel

[Beschryvinghe vander Samoyeden landt.] Descriptio ac delineatio Geographica DETECTIONIS FRETI, sive, TRANSITVS ad Occasum, suprà terras Americanas, in Chinam atq; Iaponem ducturi, Recens investigati ab M. Henrico Hudsono Anglo. Item, Narratio SER.[MO] REGI HISPANIÆ facta, super tractu, in quinta Orbis terrarum parte, cui AVSTRALIÆ INCOGNITÆ nomen est, recens detecto, Per Capitaneum Petrum Ferdinandez de Quir. Vnà cum descriptione Terræ SAMOIEDARVM & TINGOESIORVM, in Tartaria ad Ortum Freti VVaygats sitæ, nuperq; Imperio Moscovitarum subactæ. AMSTERODAMI Ex officina Hesselij Gerardi . . . 1612. 4° sig. A^6B-E^4F^1: plates; illus., maps

C.114.b.6(1); G.7163.

The editor's preface signed: Hesselius Gerardus Assumensis Philogeographus. The translation is by Reinier Telle, that of the last part originally translated from Russian into Dutch by Isaac Massa. The copy at G.7163 is imperfect; wanting the world maps, and misbound.

G71 GERRITSZ, Hessel

[Beschryvinghe vander Samoyeden landt.] Exemplar Libelli supplicis, Potentissimo Hispaniarum Regi exhibiti, à Capitaneo Petro Fernandez de Quir: Super Detectione quintæ Orbis terrarum partis, cui AVTRALIÆ [*sic*] INCOGNITÆ nomen est. Item, Relatio super Freto per m.Hudsonum Anglum quæsito, ac in parte detecto suprà Provincias Terræ Novæ . . . Chinam & Cathaiam versus ducturo: VNA Cum Freti ipsius, quatenus detectum est, TABVLA NAVTICA. Nec non Isaaci Massæ Harlemensis Samoiediæ atque Tingoëssæ . . . descriptio, ET Tractus eiusdem Tabula Russica. Latiné versa ab R. Vitellio. AMSTERODAMI Ex officina Hesselij Gerardi . . . 1612. 4° sig. A-F^4; plates; illus., maps

G.7165(2,3).

The second Latin edition. Leaf F2 is the titlepage of the first.

G72 GERRITSZ, Hessel

[Beschryvinghe vander Samoyeden landt.] Descriptio ac delineatio Geographica DETECTIONIS FRETI. Sive Transitus ad Occasum . . . recens investigati ab M. Henrico Hudsono . . . AMSTERODAMI Ex Officina Hesselij Gerardi . . . 1613. 4° sig. A-F^4: plates; illus., maps

C.114.b.6(4); 500.b.25(10).

Without the editor's name, edited by Hessel Gerritsz. The third Latin edition of Reinier Telle's translation, in part from the translation by Isaac Massa. Both copies are imperfect; that at C.114.b.6(4) wanting one of the maps, that at 500.b.25(10) wanting sig. E4 and the maps.

G73 GERRITSZ, Hessel

[Beschryvinghe vander Samoyeden landt.] Descriptio ac delineatio Geographica DETECTIONIS FRETI . . . recens investigati ab M. Henrico Hudsono . . . AMSTERODAMI Ex Officina Hesselij Gerardi . . . 1613. 4° sig. A-F^4G^2: plates; illus., maps

G.7164.

Another issue of the preceding, with an appendix by Hessel Gerritsz on the last two leaves.

G74 GERRITSZ, Hessel

HISTOIRE Du Pays nomme SPITSBERGHE. Monstrant comment qu'il est trouvée, son naturel & ses animauls, avecques. [*sic*] La triste racompte des maux, que noz Pecheurs, tant Basques que Flamens, ont eu a souffrir des Anglois, en l'esté passée. l'An de grace, 1613. Escrit par H.G.A. Et en apres une Protestation contre les Angloys, & annullation de touts leurs frivoles argumens, parquoy ils pensent avoir droict, pour se faire Maistre tout seul, dudict Pays. En Amsterdam, a l'ensiegne [*sic*] du Carte nautiq;. M.DC.XIII. 4° pp.30: plates; illus., maps

C.142.b.6; G.2937.

The initials stand for Hessel Gerritsz of Assum who is also the publisher 'at the sign of the nautical chart'. The copy at G.2937 has additional maps.

G75 GERRITSZ, Hessel

HISTOIRE du Pays nommé SPITSBERGHE. Comme il a esté descouvert, sa situation & de ses Animauls. Avec le Discours des empeschemens que les Navires esquippes pour la peche des Baleines tant Basques, Hollandois, que Flamens ont soufferts de la part des Anglois, Année presente 1613. Escript par H.G.A. Et une Protestation contre les Anglois, & annullation de tous leurs frivolz argumens, par lesquelz ils pensent avoir droit de se faire seuls Maistres dudit Pays. A AMSTERDAM, Chez Hessel Gerard A. a l'ensiegne [*sic*]de la Carte Nautiq̃3. M.D.C.XIII. 4° pp.30: plates; illus., maps

Cup. 403.h.44.

By Hessel Gerritsz. A reissue of the preceding, with a new titlepage bearing errata on the verso.

G76 GERSDORFF, Hans von; called Schylhans

[Feldtbuch der Wundtartzney.] CHIRVRGIA, Ofte Velt-boeck van den Beroemden M. Scheel-Hans. Ghetrouwelijck Overgheset uyt den Hoochduytsche in onse Nederlantsche tale/door Ian Pauwelszoon Phrisius. Ghedruckt t'Amsterdam/by Cornelis Claesz. . . . 1605. 4° pp.175; illus.

549.g.1(2).

The illustrations are woodcuts.

G77 GERWEN, Jonas van

CLAGHE Ende TROOST, Over de Doot Vanden Vromen . . . D. IOHANNIS BOGAERT, In sijn leven ghetrouwe Dienaer Jesu Christi/binnen Haerlem: de welcke . . . ontslapen is den 14 December/ANNO 1614, [*sic*] TOT HAERLEM, Gedruckt by Vincent Casteleyn . . . 1615. 4° sig.AB^4

11555.e.44(4).

Two poems, the first signed: In rouw saen gena, anagram of Jonas van Gerwen; the second signed: D.V.H. Ick houde van beraden, initials and anagram of David van Horenbeeck.

G78 GESELIUS, Cornelius

CORTE Vvaerachtighe Onderrichtinge ofte Beschrijvinghe/van de Proceduren ende Handelinghen der Heeren Burghemeesteren ende Vroetschappen der Stadt Rotterdam/ende der Predicanten/ met sommighe Ouderlinghen van de Duytsche Kercke aldaer. Teghens CORNELIVM GESELIVM, Dienaer der Ghemeente Christi eertijdts tot Rotterdam, nu tot Edam. Door den selven . . . te samen ghestelt. Ghedruckt . . . 1614. 4° sig.$A\text{-}R^4S^3$

T.2244(8).

Wanting the last leaf, blank.

GEYN, Jacob de. *See* GHEYN, Jacob de

t'GHEBESOIGNEERDE dat is t'ghene . . . binnen Rotterdam . . . is verhandelt gheworden. 1619. *See* GREVINCHOVEN, Nicolaas

GHEBODEN ende uyt-gheroepen [or:wt-gheroepen] [etc.] Official publications of the city of Antwerp beginning with this phrase are entered in chronological order under ANTWERP.

GHEDICHT, ter eeren den vromen ridder ende krijghs-helt Marquis Spignola. 1607. *See* CORTE antvoord' [etc.]

GHEESTELIJCKE klock-luyinghe. 1616. *See* DRIELENBURCH, Vincent van

Een GHEESTLIJCK spel van sinnen . . . hoe Christus sit onder die leeraers. 1606. *See* JANSZ, Louris

G79 GHENT. Diocese

DECRETA ET STATVTA SYNODI DIOECESANÆ GANDAVENSIS: Die decimâ Septembris Anni Millesimi sexcentesimi decimi-tertij inchoatæ, & die vndecimâ eiusdem mensis & anni absolutæ, Præsidente . . . D. HENRICO FRANCISCO VANDER BVRCH Episcopo Gandauensi. GANDAVI, Ex Officinâ Gualtéri Manilij . . . 1614. 8° pp.119
1607/1575(1).

Den GHEPREDESTINEERDEN dief. 1619. *See* SLATIUS, Hendrik

GHESANGH over den cap- ende covelmaecker. 1617. *See* DRIELENBURCH, Vincent van

G80 GHESPRAECKE

GHESPRAECKE VAN LIEFHEBBERS DES GHEMEYNEN NVTS. Die gesocht werden inde steden Opinio ende Sapientia Humana: maer ghevonden werden in het veracht Dorpken Veritas. Ghemaeckt inden Jare 1577. Ende Ghedruckt in't laetste van December, Anno 1608. 4° sig.A-C⁴D¹
T.1713(24); 106.d.17.

The editor's preface signed: P. Bor.

G81 GHETROUWEN

Ghetrouwen Raedt ende goede Waerschouwinghe eens ouden ervaren Schippers aen alle vrome Maetroosen ende trouwe Liefhebbers der vereenichde Provintien. Een oudt Schipper van Monickendam . . . Sprac, als volcht, naer Scheeps costuymen. ANNO 1608. 4° sig.⁂⁴
T.2420(6).

Other editions, entitled 'Een oud schipper van Monickendam', are entered under OUD.

GHEWISSEN doodt-steeck. 1620. *See* VORSTIUS, Conradus

G82 GHEYN, Jacob de; second of the name

ARATAEA, SIVE SIGNA COELESTIA: IN QVIBVS ASTRONOMICAE SPECVLATIONES VETERVM AD ARCHETYPA VETVSTISSIMI ARATÆORUM CAESARIS GERMANICI CODICIS 44. AEREIS FORMIS EXPRESSÆ, ARTIFICIOSE OB OCULOS PONUNTUR: A IACOBO DE GEYN . . . AMSTELODAMI, Apud IOANNEM IANSSONIUM . . . 1621. fol. pl.43
8562.f.11.

The titlepage is in letterpress. Imperfect; wanting an engraved titlepage or frontispiece? Ownership inscription: Bibliotecæ Colbertinæ.

G83 GHEYN, Jacob de; second of the name

[Wapenhandelinghe.] THE EXERCISE OF ARMES FOR CALIVRES, MVSKETTES, AND PIKES After the ordre of . . . Maurits Prince of Orange . . . Sett forthe in figures. by Jacob de Gheyn. With written Instructions for the service of all Captaines and Comaundours. For to shewe hereout the better vnto their jong or vntrayned Souldiers the playne and perfett maner to handle these Armes. 1607. Printed at the Hage. [etc.] fol. 3 pt.: pl.42; 43; 32
61.h.18.

The titlepage is engraved, leaving two blank spaces. In this copy the upper blank space has a label bearing the arms of Henry, Prince of Wales, put over it, the lower another label with the engraved imprint. A leaf bearing a dedication to Prince Henry has been inserted in this copy between the titlepage and the first of three leaves bearing the text for the drill with 'calivres'. Other text pages precede the other two sections. This text is based on the drill developed by Count John of Nassau. Some of the plates bear the artist's signature in what appears to be manuscript and some of the plate numbers are supplied in manuscript.

G84 GHEYN, Jacob de; second of the name

[Wapenhandelinghe.] [Waabenhandling. Om Rør, Musketter, oc Spedser . . . Figurlig Affbildit aff. Jacob de Geyn . . . Prentet Greffuenhagen y Hollandt.]

WAFFENHANDLVNG . . . FIGVRLICHEN ABGEBILDET, DVRCH Jacob de Geyn . . . 1608 . . . Gedruckt ins Grauen hagen . . . Ambsterdam bei Hendrick Laurenss . . . zu finden. fol. 3 pt.: pl.42; 43[44]; 32
1605/205.
An edition in Danish, with a titlepage from a German edition substituted for one in Danish, the wording of which has been supplied by the Royal Library at Copenhagen. The substitute German titlepage has no blank spaces left, but is all in one piece. The date 1608 is an emendation from 1607, made on the original plate. An additional plate, signed: Raphael de Mey fecit, Iohan Bussmecher excudit, and bearing German verses, has been inserted at the beginning of pt.2, with traces of offset from the opposite page. A portrait of Prince Maurice with Latin text has also been added. Both Raphael de Mey and Johann Bussemacher were active at Cologne around 1600.

G85 GHEYN, Jacob de; second of the name
[Wapenhandelinghe.] MANIEMENT D'ARMES D'ARQVEBVSES, MOUSQVETZ, ET PIQVES . . . REPRESENTÉ PAR FIGVRES, PAR Jacques de Gheijn. Ensemble les enseignemẽs par escrit . . . Imprimé a Amsterdam chez Robert de Baudous . . . 1608 . . . On les vend ausi a Amsterdam chez Henrij Laurens. fol. 3 pt.: pl.42; 43; 32
L.R.416.e.7.
The titlepage and all the plates in this copy have been handcoloured and mounted on large paper. The engraved labels on the titlepage contain, the one at the top, the arms of Prince Maurice of Orange, the one at the foot, a dedication to him. The date on the titlepage is from the emended plate. The text has been supplied in manuscript. The copy, formerly in the Patent Office Library, is inscribed: Presenté au Roy Louis XVe . . . par Courteille' and dated: 11 November 1715.

G86 GHEYN, Jacob de; second of the name
[Wapenhandelinghe.] MANIEMENT D'ARMES D'ARQVEBVSES, MOUSQVETZ, ET PIQVES . . . REPRESENTÉ PAR FIGVRES, PAR Jacques de Gheijn. Ensemble les enseignemens par escrit . . . Imprimé a la Haye en Hollande . . . 1608. [etc.] fol. 3 pt.: pl.42; 43; 32
61.h.19.
The top blank space on the titlepage has been left bare, the one at the foot contains an engraved Latin dedication to Prince Maurice of Orange. The title has also been engraved on a label. The date is the emendation. Most of the plates are numbered in manuscript.

G87 GHEYN, Jacob de; second of the name
[Wapenhandelinghe.] [Maniement d'armes, etc.] fol. 3 pt.: pl.42; 43; 32
785.m.2.
Imperfect; wanting the titlepage for which a manuscript copy of the English titlepage has been substituted. Plates 26–32 of pt.3 have been cut out and mounted. The printed text differs in arrangement and spelling from that in the preceding copies and may be part of an edition produced at Amsterdam or The Hague. Presented to the British Museum by Lady Banks.

G88 GHEYN, Jacob de; second of the name
[Wapenhandelinghe.] WAFFENHANDLVNG VON DEN RÖREN. MVSQVETTEN. VNDT SPIESSEN . . . FIGVRLICHEN ABGEBILDET, DVRCH Jacob de Geijn. Mitt beygefugten Schrifftlichen Vndterrichtungen . . . 1608. Gedruckt ins Grauen hagen . . . Ambsterdam bei Robbert de Baudous kupferstecher zu finden. fol. 3 pt.: pl.42; 43; 32
C.107.k.4.
No spaces left blank on the engraved titlepage. The arms at the top are German. The date is emended. The titlepage and all the plates have been handcoloured.

G89   GHEYN, Jacob de; second of the name

[Wapenhandelinghe.] MANIEMENT D'ARMES . . . Representé par figures de IAQVES de GEYN. WAPEN-HANDELINGHE . . . THE EXERCISE OF ARMES . . . WAFFEN HANDLUNG Von den Röhren . . . Figurlich abgebilt durch Iacob de Geyn. (col.) A ZVTPHEN Chez ANDRE IANSSEN d'Aelst. 4° 3 pt.: ff.42; 43; 32; illus.

C.107.df.30.

A polyglot edition in which the original plates have been copied in woodcut, arranged with facing text in French, German, Dutch and English. The titlepage is engraved. The publisher's preface dated 20 August 1619.

GHEZELSCHAP der Goden vergaert op de . . . bruyloft van Apollo. 1618. *See* COSTER, Samuel

GHIRLANDA di madrigali. 1601. *See* PHALÈSE, Pierre

GHISLERIUS, Michael. Commentaria in Canticum Canticorum. 1619. *See* BIBLE. Song of Solomon. Latin

G90   GHY

Ghy Patriotten thans„ kijck uut, kijck uut, kijck uut, Siet vvat een vreemden Dans„ om de Hollandtsche Bruut. (col.) Ghedruct buyten Antvverpen, In de Druckerije van een Lief-hebber des Vaderlants/Anno 1615. 4° pp.11: plate

11555.e.44(3).

In prose and verse. The engraved plate is badly cropped.

GHY patriotten [etc.] [printed in England] 1615. *See* VISIOEN

GIJS, Daniel Andreas. Disputationum physicarum tertia de natura. 1607. *See* JACCHAEUS, Gilbertus

GIJS, Daniel Andreas. Disputationum physicarum decima de alteratione et augmentatione. 1608. *See* JACCHAEUS, Gilbertus

G91   GIL POLO, Gaspar

LOS CINCO LIBROS DE LA DIANA ENAMORADA. COMPVESTOS POR GASPAR GIL POLO . . . EN BRVSSELAS. Por Roger Velpio, y Huberto Antonio . . . 1613. [etc.] 12° ff.172

245.a.27.

G92   GISBICE, Paulus a

PAVLLI A GISBICE . . . SCHEDIASMATVM FARRAGO NOVA. Nuper in itinere Belgico pleraque ut sub manu nata, ita foràs quasi gustu data . . . LVGDVNI BATAVORVM, Excudebat Christophorus Guyotius. ANNO DoMInICo. 8° pp.103

C.122.b.3.

The date is a chronogram for 1602, with the numerals printed in black and the other letters in red.

G93   GIUSTINIANO, Pompeo

DELLE GVERRE DI FIANDRA LIBRI VI. DI POMPEO GIUSTINIANO . . . Posti in luce da GIOSEPPE GAMVRINI . . . IN ANVERSA, Appresso Ioachimo Trognesio. M.DC.IX. 4° pp.329: pl.29; maps

591.e.13; 158.i.6; C.77.d.2.

G94   GLEN, Jean Baptiste de

DES HABITS MOEVRS, CER[E]MONIES, FACONS DE FAIRE ANCiennes & modernes du Monde, traicté . . . vtile . . . AVEC LES POVRTRAICTS DES HAbits taillés par Iean de Glen liegeois, diuisé en deux parties. PARTIE PREMIERE. Des principales Nations, Prouinces, Regions, & Villes de l'Europe. A LIEGE, Chez Iean de Glen . . . 1601. 8° ff.218[168]; illus.

G.16390.

Anonymous. The pagination is faulty. No more published. Printed by Leonard Streel at Liège. The illustrations are woodcuts. The titlepage is slightly mutilated.

La GLORIEUSE mort de neuf Chrestiens japponois. 1612. *See* RODRIGUES GIRAÕ, Joaõ

G95 GODDARD, William

[A] SATIRYCALL DIALOGVE OR A SHARPlye-invectiue conference, betweene Allexander the great, and . . . Diogynes. Imprinted in the Lowcountries [etc.] 4° sig. A-F^4
C.57.b.18.

The introductory poem signed: Willyam Goddard. Printed by Joris Waters at Dordrecht? Published 1616? Cropped.

GODETUS, Joannes. Theses theologicæ de iugi Christianorum sacrificio contra Missam papalem. 1603. *See* TRELCATIUS, Lucas

GODT de wraeck. 1620. *See* BIBLE. Psalms. Selections. Dutch

GODT ter eeren, en den Marquis Spinola vaillant. 1621. *See* LIEF-HEBBER

G96 GOETEERIS, Anthonis

IOURNAEL Der Legatie ghedaen inde Iaren 1615. ende 1616. by . . . Reynhout van Brederode . . . Dirck Bas . . . ende Aelbrecht Ioachimi . . . Te samen by de . . . Staten Generael . . . afghesonden aende . . . Coninghen van Sweden ende Denemercken; mitsgaders aenden Groot-Vorst van Moscovien, Keyser van Ruschlandt. Ende namentlick op den Vreden-handel tusschen den . . . Coninck van Sweden . . . ende den Groot-Vorst van Moscovien . . . Inhoudende cort ende waerachtich verhael, vande . . . ghesteltenisse des landts van Ruschlandt, ende de seer moeyelicke . . . Reyse aldaer gevallen. Verciert met . . . Copere Figueren . . . Door ANTHONIS GOETEERIS . . . IN S'GRAVEN-HAGE. By Aert Meuris . . . M.DC.XIX. [etc.] obl.4° pp.157: pl.4; illus.
L.R.110.b.22.

According to the preface, the engravings were made after the author's own drawings.

G97 GOLDMANNUS, Petrus

THESES MEDICÆ DE MELANCHOLIA, Quas . . . Pro Doctoratus gradu in Medicina consequendo, publicè Defendere conabitur PETRVS GOLDMANNVS . . . LVGDVNI BATAVORVM, Ex officina Typographica THOMÆ BASSON . . . M.D.C.X. 4° sig. A^4
1185.g.1(40).

G98 GOLTZIUS, Hubertus

(tp.1) FASTI MAGISTRATVVM ET TRIVMPHORVM AB VRBE CONDITA AD AVGVSTI OBITVM EX ANTIQVIS TAM NVMISMATVM QVAM MARMORVM MONVMENTIS: THESAVRVS ITEM REI ANTIQVARIAE HVBERRIMVS HVBERTI GOLTZI . . . FASTIQ. SICVLI DENVO RESTITVTI A P. AND. SCHOTTO . . . ANTVERPIAE APVD IACOBVM BIAEVM . . . M.DC.XVII.
(tp.2) THESAVRVS REI ANTQVARIAE HVBERRIMVS . . . conquisitus ac descriptus . . . PER HVBERTVM GOLTZIVM . . . ANTVERPIAE Ex Officina Gerardi WolsschatI. Sumptibus Iacobi Biæi. M.DC.XVIIJ. [etc.] fol. 2 pt.: pp.288; illus.; 314
1482.h.12.

The titlepage of pt.1 is engraved.

GOLTZIUS, Hubertus. Historie van B. Cornelis Adriaensen van Dordrecht. 1607. [Sometimes attributed to Hubertus Goltzius.] *See* CHRISTIANUS NEUTER

G99 GOMARUS, Franciscus

[Conciliatio doctrinae orthodoxae de providentia Dei.] Accoort VANDE Rechtsinnige Leere der Voorsienicheyt Gods. In't Latijn Beschreven, door . . . Franciscus Gomarus . . . Ende . . . inde Nederduytsche tale overgheset . . . TOT DELF, Ghedruckt by Ian Andriesz. . . . 1613. 4° pp.77
T.2243(12).

G100 GOMARUS, Franciscus
[. . . de] LIBERO ARBITRIO, Quam . . . Præside . . . D. FRANCISCO GOMARO . . . publicè examinandam proponit M. GILBERTVS IACCHAEVS . . . LUGDUNI BATAVORUM, Ex Officinâ Ioannis Patii . . . M.D.CIII. 4° sig. A^4
4376.de.16(61).
Cropped, with loss of the first line which must have included the word 'Disputatio' or 'Disputationum' followed by an ordinal number, to judge from the signature used, probably 'prima'.

G101 GOMARUS, Franciscus
DISPVTATIONVM THEOLOGICARVM QVARTA DE Trinitate Personarum in una Dei essentia, Quam . . . Sub Præsidio . . . D. FRANCISCI GOMARI . . . tueri adnitar NATHANAEL LAUNAEUS . . . LVGDVNI BATAVORVM, Ex Officinâ Ioannis Patii . . . D.M.CII. 4° sig. D^6
4376.de.16(17).

G102 GOMARUS, Franciscus
DISPVTATIONVM THEOLOGICARVM SEXTA DE PERSONA SPIRITVS SANCTI, Quam . . . Sub Præsidio . . . D. FRANCISCI GOMARI . . . suscepturus sum IOANNES NARSIVS . . . LVGDVNI BATAVORVM, Ex Officinâ Ioannis Patii . . . M.D.CII. 4° sig. F^6
4376.de.16(76).

G103 GOMARUS, Franciscus
DISPVTATIONVM THEOLOGICARVM NONA, DE LAPSV HOMINIS, EIVSQUE EFFECTO PRIMARIO PECCATO ORIGINALI, Quam . . . Sub Præsidio . . . D. FRANCISCI GOMARI . . . sustinere conabor IOANNES NARSIUS . . . LVGDVNI BATAVORVM, Ex Officinâ Ioannis Patii . . . M.D.CI. 4° sig. I^4
4376.de.16(79).

G104 GOMARUS, Franciscus
DISPVTATIONVM THEOLOGICARVM DVODECIMA, DE OFFICIIS FILII DEI INCARNATI seu, CHRISTI Θεανθρώπου, Quam . . . Præside . . . D. FRANCISCO GOMARO . . . publicè tuebitur IOHANNES TEXTOR . . . LVGDVNI BATAVORVM, Ex Officinâ Ioannis Patii . . . M.D.CI. 4° sig. M^4
4376.de.16(9).

G105 GOMARUS, Franciscus
[Disputationum theologicarum] DECIMA-TERTIA DE PECCATIS IN VNIVERSVM, Quam . . . Sub Præsidio . . . D. FRANCISCI GOMARI . . . suscepturus sum WINANDUS SCHUYLLIUS . . . LUGDUNI BATAVORVM, Ex Officinâ Ioannis Patii . . . M.D.CIII. 4° sig. N^4
4376.de.16(77).
Cropped.

G106 GOMARUS, Franciscus
[Disputationum theologicarum] DECIMA-QVARTA, DE LIBERO ARBITRIO, Quam . . . Sub Præsidio . . . D. FRANCISCI GOMARI . . . tueri ædnitar [*sic*] SAMUEL GRUTERUS . . . LUGDUNI BATAVORVM, Ex Officinâ Ioannis Patii . . . M.D.CIII. 4° sig. O^4
4376.de.16(62).
Cropped.

G107 GOMARUS, Franciscus
DISPVTATIONVM THEOLOGICARVM DECIMA-QVINTA, DE LEGE DEI, Quam . . . Sub Præsidio . . . D. FRANCISCI GOMARI . . . tueri adnitar ABRAHAMUS APPARTIUS . . . LVGDVNI BATAVORVM, Ex Officinâ Ioannis Patii . . . M.D.CIII. 4° sig. P^4
4376.de.16(34).

G108 GOMARUS, Franciscus
DISPVTATIONVM THEOLOGICARVM DECIMA-SEXTA, DE EVANGELIO, Quam . . . Sub Præsidio . . . D. FRANCISCI GOMARI . . . tueri adnitar IOANNES TEXTOR . . . LVGDVNI BATAVORVM, Ex Officinâ Ioannis Patii . . . M.D.CIII. 4° sig.Q^4
4376.de.16(36).

G109 GOMARUS, Franciscus
DISPVTATIONVM THEOLOGICARVM DECIMA-SEPTIMA, DE Legis & Euangelii, hujusque diversorum statuum comparatione, Quam . . . Sub Præsidio . . . D. FRANCISCI GOMARI . . . publicè examinandam proponit PETRUS CLIGNETUS . . . LVGDVNI BATAVORVM, Ex Officinâ Ioannis Patii . . . M.D.CIII. 4° sig.R^4
4376.de.16(30).

G110 GOMARUS, Franciscus
DISPVTATIONVM THEOLOGICARVM DECIMA-NONA, DE OFFICIO CHRISTI, Quam . . . Præside . . . D. FRANCISCO GOMARO . . . publicè examinandam proponit RENATVS TEXTOR . . . LUGDUNI BATAVORUM, Ex Officinâ Ioannis Patii . . . M.D.CIII. 4° sig.T^4
4376.de.16(7).

G111 GOMARUS, Franciscus
DISPVTATIONVM THEOLOGICARVM VIGESIMA, DE PERPESSIONIBVS CHRISTI, Quam . . . Præside . . . D. FRANCISCO GOMARO . . . publicè examinandam proponit CAROLUS LIEBAERT . . . LUGDUNI BATAVORUM, Ex Officinâ Ioannis Patii . . . M.D.CIII. 4° sig.V^4
4376.de.16(12).

G112 GOMARUS, Franciscus
DISPVTATIONVM THEOLOGICARVM VIGESIMA-PRIMA, DE EXALTATIONE CHRISTI, Quam . . . Præside . . . D. FRANCISCO GOMARO . . . publicè examinandam proponit ABRAHAMUS VLIET . . . LUGDUNI BATAVORUM, Ex Officinâ Ioannis Patii . . . M.D.CIII. 4° sig.X^4
4376.de.16(15).

G113 GOMARUS, Franciscus
DISPVTATIONVM THEOLOGICARVM VIGESIMA-SECVNDA, DE Merito Christi & beneficiis illius erga nos, Quam . . . Præside . . . D. FRANCISCO GOMARO . . . publicè examinandam proponit RICHARDVS IANVS NEREVS . . . LUGDUNI BATAVORVM, Ex Officinâ Ioannis Patii . . . 1603. 4° sig.Y^4
4376.de.16(17).

G114 GOMARUS, Franciscus
DISPVTATIONVM THEOLOGICARVM TRIGESIMA-SECVNDA, DE RESVRRECTIONE CARNIS ET VITA ÆTERNA, Quam . . . Præside . . . D. FRANCISCO GOMARO . . . defensurus est pro modulo suo CAROLVS C. F. RYCKEWARDVS . . . LUGDUNI BATAVORVM, Ex Officinâ Ioannis Patii . . . M.D.CIV. 4° sig.Ii^6
4376.de.16(21).

G115 GOMARUS, Franciscus
DISPVTATIONVM THEOLOGICARVM TERTIO-REPETITARVM QVADRAGESIMA-QVARTA DE MISSA, Quam . . . Sub Præsidio . . . D. FRANCISCI GOMARI . . . publicè discutiendam proponit IONAS VOLMAER . . . LVGDVNI BATAVORVM, Ex Officinâ Ioannis Patii . . . M.D.CIV. 4° sig.Xx^6
4376.de.16(56); 4376.de.16(58*).
The copy at 4376.de.16(58*) is imperfect; wanting leaf Xx2.

G116 GOMARUS, Franciscus

FRANCISCI GOMARI ORATIO FVNEBRIS, IN Obitum . . . D. FRANCISCI IUNII . . . Habita à funere, in auditorio publico Academiæ Leydensis, die VII. Kal. Novembris . . . M.D.C.II . . . LUGDUNI BATAVORUM, Ex Typographeîo Christophori Guyotij, M.D.C.II. 4° pp.36
834.g.35(2).

With 'Lacrymæ Academiæ Leydensis, in obitum D. Francisci Iunii', consisting of poems in Latin or French, signed: P. Merula, J. Scaliger, B. Vulcanius, P. Bertius, D. Heinsius, H. Grotius, P. S., i.e. Petrus Scriverius, J. Meursius, P. à Gisbice, P. Du-Pin, R. I. de Nerée, de Coignet.

G117 GOMARUS, Franciscus

FRANCISCI GOMARI PROEVE VAN M. P. BERTII AENSPRAECK. Ter eeren der Waerheydt . . . uytgegeven . . . De tweede Druck. TOT LEYDEN, Voor Jan Jansz. Orlers . . . 1610. 4° pp.35
T.2240(3).

GOMARUS, Franciscus. Schermutselinghen van sommighe licht-gewapende cryghsknechten. 1613. [Sometimes attributed to Gomarus.] *See* SCHERMUTSELINGHEN

G118 GOMARUS, Franciscus

TWEE DISPVTATIEN VANDE GODDELIICKE PREDESTINATIE: d'eene by DOCT. FRANCISCVS GOMARVS, d'ander by DOCT. IACOBVS ARMINIVS . . . Vertaelt uyt het Latijn. Tot Leyden, BY IAN PAETS IACOBSZOON . . . 1609. 4° sig.A-C^4
T.2239(11).

G119 GOMARUS, Franciscus

FRANCISCI GOMARI Vvaerschouwinghe/Over de Vermaninghe aen R. Donteclock . . . Hier is noch by ghevoecht F. Gomari 1. Verclaringhe der Hooft-puncten, ghehandelt in de laetste Conferentie, met D. Arminio: 2. Bedencken over de Lijck-Oratie M. P. Bertij: 3. Vertooch voor de . . . Staten gedaen over de leere ende beleydt D. Arminij . . . TOT LEYDEN, Voor Jan Jansz. Orlers . . . 1609. 4° pp.51, 56
T.2239(17).

Printed by Henrick Lodewijcxsz van Haestens at Leiden.

G120 GOMES, Manoel

EMMANVELIS GOMMESI . . . DE PESTILENTIÆ CVRATIONE METHODICA TRACTATIO . . . ANTVERPIÆ EX OFFICINA IOACH. TROGNÆSII. M.DCIII. 4° pp.39
1167.f.17(1).

GOMEZ, Antonio; Catedrático de la Universidad de Salamanca. Dn. Antonii Gomezii . . . Ad leges tauri commentarius. 1617. *See* CASTILE [Laws]

GOMMESIUS, Emmanuel. *See* GOMES, Manoel

G121 GORCUM, Jan van

DE GHEESTELYCKE BRVYLOFT TVSSCHEN GODT ENDE ONSE NATVRE, Verclarende hoe seer dat ons van noode is het cieraet der liefden/eñ alle deuchden/om tot de Bruyloft in te gaen. Door Heer IAN VAN GORICVM . . . T'SHERTOGENBOSSCHE, By Jan Scheffer . . . M.DC.XI. 8° pp.348
1568/9186.

In a contemporary blind-tooled brown calf binding.

G122 GORDON, James; of Huntley

[Controversiarum Christinae fidei . . . epitome.] A SVMMARY OF CONTROVERSIES. WHEREIN Are . . . treated . . . the cheefe Questions of Diuinity, now a dayes in

dispute betweene Catholikes & Protestants . . . WRITTEN IN LATIN By Iames Gordon Huntley . . . of the Society of IESVS. And translated into English by I.L. of the same SOCIETY. The I. Tome . . . THE SECOND EDITION . . . M.DC.XVIII. 8° pp.367
3935.a.24.

The translator is William Wright. Published by the English College press at St. Omer. No more published. Ownership inscription: Ric: Walmesley.

G123 GORDON, James; of Huntley
[Controversiarum Christianae fidei . . . epitome.] A TREATISE CONCERNING THE CHVRCH. WHERIN It is shewed . . . that the Church of Rome . . . is the only true Church of CHRIST. VVRITTEN In Latin, by . . . Iames Gordon Huntley . . . of the Society of IESVS. And translated into English, by I.L. of the same Society. The third part of the second Controuersy . . . M.DC.XIV. 8° pp.116
1020.h.10(2).

The translator is William Wright. Published by the English College press at St. Omer.

G124 GORDON, Patrick; Gentleman
[THE FAMOUS HISTORIE OF the Renouned and Valiant Prince ROBERT surnamed the BRVCE King of SCOTLAND e&. & of Sundrie Other valiant knights both Scots and English. Enlarged with an addition of the Scottishe Kinges . . . from him to Charles now Prince . . . A Historye . . . set forthe and done in heroik verse by PATRICK GORDON . . . At Dort by George Waters. 1615.] 4° sig.A-Aa^4
11623.c.17.

In verse. Imperfect; wanting the titlepage, for which a facsimile has been supplied in manuscript, and leaves A4, E4, F1-3, Z2-4, all supplied in manuscript. Ownership inscription: Joseph Philips.

G125 GORDON, Patrick; Gentleman
THE First booke of the famous Historye of PENARDO and LAISSA other ways called the warres of LOVE and AMBITIONE . . . Doone in Heroik verse, by Patrik Gordon. Printed at Dort By George waters. 1615. 8° sig.$\star^8$,$\star^2$A-Q^{8}R^2
C.34.e.38.

GORICUM, Jan van. *See* GORCUM, Jan van

G126 GORLAEUS, Abrahamus; the Elder
ABRAHAMI GORLÆI . . . DACTYLIOTHECA Seu Annulorum sigillarium quorum apud Priscos tam Græcos quam Romanos usus. E Ferro Aere Argento & Auro PROMPTVARIVM. Accesserunt variarum GEMMARVM . . . SCALPTVRÆ. [etc.] 4° pp.16: plates; port.
7706.b.15.

The plates bear 196 engraved figures of rings and 148 of gems. The titlepage is engraved. The portrait signed: I.D. Gheyn fe., and dated 1601. The dedication is also signed 1601. The preface by Everardus Vorstius is dated 1599. Published by the Officina Plantiniana at Leiden? Probably published in 1601.

G127 GORLAEUS, Abrahamus; the Elder
ABRAHAMI GORLÆI . . . THESAVRVS NVMISMATVM ROMANORVM. SIVE Numi Aurei, Argentei, Ærei, ad FAMILIAS ROMANAS spectantes usque ad obitum Augusti. ACCESSERVNT TYPI EORVNDEM NVMORVM quos FVLVIVS ORSINVS omisit, aut aliter edidit. AMSTELREODAMI, Ex Officina Cornelij Nicolai . . . M.DC.VIII. fol. pp.96: pl.45
602.i.20.

The titlepage is smaller than the remainder of the book and has been mounted. With contemporary manuscript notes.

G128 GORLAEUS, Abrahamus; the Elder

ABRAHAMI GORLÆI . . . THESAVRVS NVMISMATVM ROMANORVM AVREORVM ARGENTEORVM AEREORVM AD FAMILIAS EIVS VRBIS SPECTANTIVM VSQVE AD OBITVM AVGVSTI ACCESSERE EIVSDEM PARALIPOMENA SEV TYPI NVMORVM ROMANORVM QVOS A FVLVIO VRSINO PARTIM NON EDITOS OMNINO PARTIM NON ITA EDITOS POSSIDET . . . M.DC.V . fol. pp.96: pl.45

1572/875.

The titlepage, engraved in the style of Jacob de Gheyn, appears unfinished, the date is off centre and obviously incomplete. The plates are printed from the same copperplates as were used for the preceding edition or reissued sheets printed for Cornelis Claesz. With manuscript additions. The dedication mentions the death of the author and is signed: Abraham Gorlaeus, i.e. the Younger, and dated 1 March 1609. The 'Paralipomena' are annotations to the descriptions, not a separate work. Printed by Jan Paets at Leiden? Published in 1609?

G129 GORLAEUS, David

DAVIDIS GORLÆI . . . Exercitationes Philosophicæ quibus vniversa fere discutitur Philosophia Theoretica ET Plurima . . . Peripateticorum dogmata evertuntur . . . LVGD-BATAVORVM. Impensis Iohannis Ganne & Harmanni à Westerhuysen. 1620. 8° pp.352

8405.de.18.

GORRANUS, Nicolaus. *See* NICOLAUS Gorranus

G130 GORUS, Joannes; de S. Geminiano

SVMMA DE EXEMPLIS ET RERVM SIMILITVDINIBVS LOCVPLETISSIMA . . . F. Ioanne à S. Geminiano . . . Auctore. Nunc demum post omnes alias editiones, diligenti cura à Magistro ÆGIDIO GRAVATIO . . . ab innumeris pene erroribus castigata & aucta. Adiectus est primùm Index certissimus . . . ANTVERPIÆ, Sumptibus Petri & Ioannis Belleri. M.DC.XV. [etc.] (col.) ANTVERPIAE, Excudebat Andreas Bacx, sumptibus Petri & Ioannis Belleri. M.DC.XV. 8° ff.516

1568/2614.

G131 GOSWINIUS, Thomas

Oprecht ende Claer Bericht Waer in Cortelijck teghens een ander ghestelt is I. Wat die Predicanten van Campen . . . Overt' stuck van die Prædestinatie . . . voor die oude Suyvere Waerheijt nae Godes woort gevoelen. II. Wat die selvige oock daer tegens Als Onwaerheijden . . . verwerpen . . . Tot CAMPEN, Ghedruckt by VVillem Berendtss . . . 1617. 4° sig.AB^4C^2

T.2247(18).

Signed: Thomas Goswinius, and others.

G132 GOSWINIUS, Thomas

[Oprecht ende claer bericht.] VYTTOCH Van t'Ghevoelen der Predicanten tot Campen Hier-onder-benoemt/Over t'stuck van de Predestinatie . . . ghenomen uyt het Oprecht ende Claer Bericht . . . Tot CAMPEN, Ghedruckt By VVillem Berendtsz . . . 1618. fol. a single sheet

T.2248(36).

Signed: Thomas Goswinius, and others.

G133 GOUDA, Jan van

ANDWOORDE IOANNIS DE GOVDA . . . OP DE MEDESPRAKE aengaende de Transsubstantiatie MET FRANCISCO ENDE SAMVELE LANSBERGEN . . . T'HANTWERPEN By Hieronymus Verdussen, M.DC.IX. [etc.] 8° pp.269

1578/571.

With 'Andwoorde Ioannis de Gouda . . . op de Bedenckinghen Francisci Lansbergii' and the texts of the 'Ghespreck' and the 'XXII. bedenckinghen'.

G134 GOUDA, Jan van

Predicatie van P[r]. IOANNES DE GOVDA . . . t'Antwerpen op Alderheylighen dach ghedaen/ende over-ghezonden aen HENRICVM BOXHORNIVM . . . Die daer over PATREM GOVDAM metten Pastoor inden Haghe by Breda beroept tot Conferentie. Met eenighe marginale aenmerckinghen/op de zelve Predicatie . . . Tot Rotterdam, By Felix van Sambix . . . 1610. 4° pp.11

T.2240(20).

Edited, with an introduction and notes, by Henricus Boxhornius.

G135 GOULART, Simon; the Younger

Simon Goulart van Geneven, Bedienaer des Godtlijcken woorts/in de Walsche Kercke tot Amsterdam . . . heeft in September deses Jaers 1615. ghepredickt als volght; waer-over hy dadelijck by den Kercken-Raedt is geschorst/van de bedieninghe des Woorts/ende mede van de nuttinghe des H. Avontmaels . . . By Govert Basson. 4° pp.8

T.2245(15).

On predestination. Printed at Leiden and published in 1615.

G136 GOUTHOEVEN, Wouter van

D'oude Chronijcke ende Historien van HOLLAND (met West-Vriesland) van Zeeland ende van Wtrecht. Van nieus oversien, vermeerdert, verbetert ende verciert met eenighe Gheslacht-registeren . . . mitsgaders Steden, Dorpen, Heeren-Huysen, ende andere beschrijvinghen van Hollandt . . . Door W. van Gouthoeven . . . Tot Dordrecht, Ghedruckt by Peeter Verhaghen. 1620. fol. pp.629; illus.

155.b.9.

With additions by Petrus Scriverius. The illustrations are woodcuts.

G137 GOUVEA, Antonio; Bishop

[Iornada do Arcebispo Dom Frey Aleixo de Menezes.] (tp.1) HISTOIRE ORIENTALE, DES GRANS PROGRES DE l'Eglise Cathol. Apost. & Rom. en la reduction des anciens Chrestiens, dits de S. Thomas, de plusieurs autres Schismatiques & Heretiques a l'vnion de la vraye Eglise. Conuersion des Mahometains, Mores & Payens. Par les bons deuoirs du R.[me] . . . Don Alexis de Meneses . . . Composée en langue Portugaise par . . . Antoine Gouea . . . & tournée en François par F. Iean Baptiste de Glen . . . A BRVXELLES, Par Rutger Velpius . . . 1609. [etc.]

(tp.2) LA MESSE DES ANCIENS CHRESTIENS dicts de S. Thomas . . . repurgée des erreurs . . . du Nestoriasme, par . . . Don Alexis de Meneses . . . traduite . . . du Syriaque . . . en langue Latine. Y premise vne Remonstrance Catholique aux peuples du Pays-bas, des fruicts & vtilité de la precedente Histoire, & de la Messe subsequente: par F. Iean Baptiste de Glen . . . A BRVXELLES, Par Rutger Velpius . . . 1609. 8° pp.748, 123

4767.aaa.8.

The signatures are continuous throughout. The privilege extends to both Rutger Velpius and Hieronymus Verdussen.

G138 GOUVEA, Antonio; Bishop

[Iornada do Arcebispo Dom Frey Aleixo de Menezes.] (tp.1) HISTOIRE ORIENTALE . . . Composée . . . par . . . Antoine Gouea . . . & tournée en François par F. Iean Baptiste de Glen . . . EN ANVERS, Par Hierosme Verdussen . . . 1609. [etc.]

(tp.2) LA MESSE DES ANCIENS CHRESTIENS . . . y premise vne Remonstrance Catholique . . . par F. Iean Baptiste de Glen . . . EN ANVERS, Par Hierosme Verdussen . . . 1609. 8° pp.748, 123

867.f.3(1,2).

Another issue of the preceding.

GRACIAN, Geronymo, de la Madre de Dios. *See* GERONIMO GRACIAN de la Madre de Dios

G139 GRAMAYE, Joannes Baptista

(tp.1) I. B. GRAMAYE. ANTIQVITATES ILLVSTRISSIMI DVCATVS BRABANTIÆ . . . BRVXELLÆ. Ex Officina IOANNIS MOMARTII [*sic*] . . . 1610. [etc.]
(tp.2) BRVXELLA CVM SVO COMITATV. I. B. GRAMAYE . . . BRVXELLAE. Ex Officina IOANNIS MOMMARTII . . . 1606. [etc.]
(tp.3) ARSCOTVM DVCATVS CVM SVIS BARONATIBVS. I. B. GRAMAYE . . . BRVXELLÆ. Ex Officina IOANNIS MOMMARTII . . . 1606. [etc.]
(tp.4) THENÆ ET BRABANTIA VLTRA VELPAM . . . I. B. GRAMAYE . . . BRVXELLÆ. Ex Officina IOANNIS MOMMARTII . . . 1606. [etc.]
(tp.5) GALLO-BRABANTIA IOANNIS B. GRAMAYE . . . BRVXELLAE Apud Ioannem Mommartium . . . 1606. [etc.]
(tp.6) GALLO-BRABANTIA AD LIMITEM NAMVRCÆVM, I. B. GRAMAYE . . . BRVXELLAE. Ex Officina IOANNIS MOMMARTII . . . 1606. [etc.]
(tp.7) GALLO-BRABANTIA AD LIMITEM HANNONICVM, I. B. GRAMAYE . . . BRVXELLAE. Ex Officina IOANNIS MOMMARTII . . . 1606. [etc.]
(tp.8) GALLO-BRABANTIA AD LIMITEM EBVRONICVM, I. B. GRAMAYE . . . BRVXELLAE. Ex Officina IOANNIS MOMMARTII . . . 1606. [etc.] 4° 8 pt.: pp.182; 80, 47; 82; 39; 24; 40; 40; 36: plates
572.c.1(1–8); 153.k.1(1).

Pt.1 describes Louvain and surroundings. Imperfect sets; wanting 'Antverpiae antiquitates', 'Taxandria' and many of the plates, but no perfect sets are known. Pt.2 has the same text sheets as the separate copy, for which see below, but different plates. tp.1, 5 differ from the others by having no woodcut borders and tp.5 has no device. The arrangement in the copy at 153.k.1(1) is pt.1, 4, 3, 2, 5, 6, 8, 7, with the preliminary pages for pt.8 bound at the end of pt.7.

G140 GRAMAYE, Joannes Baptista

I. B. GRAMMAY. ANTVERPIAE ANTIQVITATES. ET OPIDORVM, MVNICIPORVM [*sic*], PAGORVM, DOMINIORVM, QVAE SVB EA. BRVXELLAE. Ex Officina IOANNIS MOMMARTII . . . 1610. [etc.] 4° pp.181: plates
572.c.15(1); 153.k.1(2).

G141 GRAMAYE, Joannes Baptista

ASIA, SIVE HISTORIA VNIVERSALIS ASIATICARVM GENTIVM ET RERVM DOMI FORISQVE GESTARVM . . . AVCTORE IO. BAPTISTA GRAMAYE . . . ANTVERPIÆ, Sumptibus Viduæ & Heredum IO. BELLERI . . . M.DC.IIII. 4° pp.722
C.74.c.9; C.108.dd.11.

The copy at C.108.dd.11 is bound in calf, bearing the crest inscribed 'Quid retribuam domino Henrisono' and the letters MTH, and has the exlibris of William, Marquis of Lothian.

G142 GRAMAYE, Joannes Baptista

BRVXELLA CVM SVO COMITATV, I. B. GRAMAYE . . . BRVXELLAE. Ex Officina IOANNIS MOMMARTII . . . 1606. [etc.] 4° pp.80, 47: plates
10271.bbb.7.

Some of the plates are mounted, others, described for this work in the *Bibliotheca Belgica* no. G 100d are not present. Ownership inscription: 'Fonthill copy'.

G143 GRAMAYE, Joannes Baptista

HISTORIA BRABANTICA I. B. GRAMAYE . . . LOVANII, Apud Ioannem Masium . . . 1607. [etc.] 4° ff.42
9150.d.2(2).

With a list of manuscripts consulted by the author.

G144 GRAMAYE, Joannes Baptista
(tp.1) I. B. GRAMAYE PRIMITIÆ ANTIQVITATVM GANDENSIVM. AVTVERPIÆ [*sic*], Ex Typographeio HIERONYMI VERDVSSI M D C XIII [etc.]
(tp.2) I. B. GRAMAYE ANTIQVITATVM GANDENSIVM VOLVMEN ALTERVM. In quo illustrata opida subsidiaria Gandæ, imprimísque CORTVRIACVM. ANTVERPIÆ, Ex Typographeio HIERONYMI VERDVSSI M D C XI: [*sic*] 4° 2 pt.: pp.68; 34
572.c.15(3).
On tp. 1 the date has been altered in manuscript to 1611 and a full stop, not originally printed, been added.

G145 GRAMAYE, Joannes Baptista
I. B. Gramaye TAXANDRIA, IN QVA Antiquitates & decora . . . ex archiuis singulorum locorum . . . collectæ . . . BRVXELLÆ, Ex Officina RVTGERI VELPII . . . M.D.C.X. [etc.] 4° pp.148
572.c.15(2).

GRAMMATICA linguae sanctae nova. 1612. *See* DRUSIUS, Joannes; the Elder

G146 GRAPALDI, Franciscus Marius
FRANCISCI MARII GRAPALDI . . . ONOMASTICON . . . DVRDRECHTI, Ex officinâ Ioannis Berewout. M.D.C.XVIII. 8° pp.314 [384]
1043.f.17.

G147 GRATIANUS, Thomas
ANASTASIS AVGVSTINIANA IN QVA SCRIPTORES Ordinis Eremitarum S. AVGVSTINI qui abhinc sæculis aliquot vixerunt, vnà cum neotericis, in seriem digesti sunt. Operà ac studio . . . THOMAE GRATIANI . . . ANTVERPIÆ Typis HIERONYMI VERDVSSI. M.DC.XIII. 8° pp.178; illus.
861.f.1(1).
The titlepage woodcut shows a portrait of St. Augustine.

G148 GRAVAMINA
GRAVAMINA ORTHODOXORVM CONTRA NOVATORES, IN QVINQVAGINTA DIGESTA ARTICVLOS, ET . . . in Comitiis RATISBONAE . . . proposita . . . M.DC.XIII. LEODII, Apud Guilielmum Houium . . . 1614. [etc.] 8° pp.30
C.48.c.14(2).
With the arms of Jacques Auguste de Thou on the covers.

G149 GREENE, Robert
[A quip for an upstart courtier.] Een Seer vermakelick Proces Tusschen Fluweele-Broeck ende Laken-Broeck . . . Gheschreven int Engelsch door Robert Greene, ende int Neder-landtsch overgheset. Wederom oversien. TOT LEYDEN By Thomas Basson. M.D.CI. 4° pp.32; illus.
C.30.e.22(1).
Translated by Thomas Basson. The preface signed: Kent u selven. The titlepage woodcut, showing the two characters of the play, is an imitation of that on the English original. The earlier edition of the translation was entitled 'Nieuws uyt Engeland'.

GREGORIUS, Henricus. Disputationum physicarum sexta de tempore. 1607. *See* JACCHAEUS, Gilbertus

GREGORIUS, Henricus. Disputationum physicarum decima-tertia, de anima in genere. 1608. *See* JACCHAEUS, Gilbertus

G150 GREGORY I; Saint, Pope, the Great
[Works] (tp.1) SANCTI GREGORII MAGNI PAPÆ PRIMI OPERA . . . emendata, aucta, & in Tomos sex distributa . . . ANTVERPIÆ, Apud Ioannem Keerbergium. M.DC.XV.

(tp.2) SANCTI GREGORII MAGNI . . . OPERVM Tomus II . . . ANTVERPIÆ, Apud Ioannem Keerbergium. M.DC.XV.
(tp.3) SANCTI GREGORII MAGNI . . . OPERVM Tomus III . . . ANTVERPIÆ, Apud Ioannem Keerbergium. M.DC.XV. fol. pt.1–3: coll.510; 1222; 602
L.19.k.6.
Edited by Petrus Rodolphius, Bishop of Venosa. With Pope Zachary's translation of the Dialogi into Greek. Imperfect; wanting tom.3–6. tp.1 is mutilated.

G151 GREGORY I; Saint, Pope, the Great
(tp.1) THE DIALOGUES OF S. GREGORIE, SVRNAMED THE GREATE . . . DEVIDED INTO fower Bookes . . . WITH A shorte treatise of sundry miracles . . . taken out of S. Augustin. Together with a notable miracle wrought by S. Bernarde, in confirmation of diuers articles of religion. Translated into our English tongue by P. W. . . . Printed at Paris. 1608.
(tp.2) A SHORTE RELATION OF DIVERS MIRACLES, WROVGHTE AT THE MEMORIES OR SHRINES OF CERTAINE MARTIRS . . . Written by . . . S. Augustin: and translated into our English tongue by P.VV. . . . Printed at Paris. 1608. 12° 2 pt.: pp.514; 48; illus.
699.a.24; 846.b.22; G.19947, 48.
Translated by Philip Woodward. The imprint is false; in fact, printed by Charles Boscard at Douai. The illustration consists of the arms of Queen Anne accompanied by four lines of verse engraved on the verso of the first titlepage.

GREUWEL der vornahmsten Haupt-ketzeren. 1608. *See* SICHEM, Christoffel van

G152 GREVINCHOVEN, Nicolaas
T'GHEBESOIGNEERDE Dat is T'Ghene/in sekere heymelijcke vergaderinghe binnen Rotterdam/by eenighe Remonstrantsche Predicanten/Ouderlinghen/ende Diaconen/is verhandelt gheworden in Martio deses Jaers. 1619. Met Een . . . voorreden . . . waer in verthoont wort met wat recht eenighe Remonstrantsche Predicanten . . . by den Hove van Hollandt worden . . . ghebannen. [etc.] 4° sig.$AB^4C^2\star^4\star\star^2$
T.2249(47).
Anonymous.

G153 GREVINCHOVEN, Nicolaas
Korte ende grondighe Refutatie/Oft wederlegginghe/van een zeker boecxken onlancx in Druc uytghegheven/door eenen onghenoemden Liefhebber der waerheyt/op den name van Adam Hertwech van Rotterdam/als den Auteur der zelver/int welcke hy . . . wil bewijsen/dat gheloovighe . . . sullen salich wesen . . . TOT ROTTERDAM. By Matthijs Bastiaensz . . . 1612. 4° sig.$A\text{-}I^4$
T.2242(18).
Anonymous.

G154 GREVINCHOVEN, Nicolaas
DER REMONSTRANTEN KERCK-GANGH: DAT IS, Verscheydene redenen/waerom de Remonstrans-ghesinde hare afghesonderde vergaderingen niet en behooren na te laten . . . Ghedruckt . . . 1619. 4° pp.134
T.2249(53).
Anonymous.

G155 GREVINCHOVEN, Nicolaas
THIEN Contra-Remonstransche POSITIEN, Voor Grouwelijc eñ Afgrijselijc verklaert in de laetste Geldersche Synode tot Arnhem ghehouden; ende in Druc uytghegheven tot opweckinge der Remonstranten, om vande Synoden noch wat

goedts te hopen . . . TOT ROTTERDAM, By Matthijs Bastiaensz. . . . 1618. 4° pp.28
T.2248(19).
Anonymously compiled and edited by Nicolaas Grevinchoven. A different compilation based on the same original theses is entered under GROUWEL.

G156 GREVINCHOVEN, Nicolaas
VERTOOGH Van verscheyden NIEUWIGHEDEN, nopende principalijc D'ABSOLUTE PRÆDESTINATIE metten aenkleven van dien/die by de Leeraers van de-zelve Predestinatie ghedreven worden: ENDE Om dewelcke de CONTRA-REMONSTRANSche Scheurmakers haer-zelven van eenighe openbare Kercken af-scheyden . . . TOT ROTTERDAM, By Matthijs Bastiaensz. . . . 1617. 4° ff.15
T.2247(27).
Anonymous.

G157 GREVINCHOVIUS, Casparus
Vande vryheydt der Secten/Hoe schadelijck dezelve zij . . . Door Casparum Grevinchovium . . . Tot Dordrecht. By Adriaen Jansz. Bot . . . 1611. 4° pp.83
T.2242(11).

GRIMERIUS, Gerardus. Vertaelde theses. 1611. *See* VORSTIUS, Conradus

G158 GRISONS
[Grawpündtnerische Handlungen.] Over-Rhetische ofte Grysonsche Acten ende Proceduren. Des Jaers M.DC.XVJJJ. Daer inne . . . verhaelt werden/de . . . oorsaken/der Vergaderinghe . . . ende wettelicke Procedurē . . . tot Tussis . . . Alles door die . . . Overheyden/Raeden/ende Gemeenten van Vry-Rethien der drie Liguen . . . ghepubliceert . . . Overgheset uyt den Hoochduytschen. IN 'SGRAVEN-HAGE. By Aert Meuris . . . 1619. 4° pp.41
T.2423(14).
Compiled anonymously. Sometimes attributed to Johann a Porta.

G159 GRISONS
[1620] COPYE Van een Brieff ghescreven by die drie Liguen ofte bontghenoten vande Grijsons/aen den Coninck van Vranckrijck ende Navarre. Ghetranslateert uyt de Franchoysche Copye/ghedruckt by Hillebrant Jacobsz. . . . 1620. 4° sig.A^4
T.2423(32).
Printed by Aert Meuris at The Hague?

G160 GRISONSCHE
Grisonsche HISTORIE des Iaers 1620. Vvaer inne claerlijcken . . . verhaelt worden de . . . oorsaken/eñ . . . Redenen/die de Inwoonders van Valtellina hebben bedwonghen die Waepenen aen te nemen teghen die Calvinische Grisons/ende den voortganck der Waepenen aldaer. Ghetrocken vvt twee Italiaensche Boecxkens, tot Pauien ende Genua ghedruckt, ende in onse Nederlantsche Taele Ouerghesedt . . . Ghedruckt int Jaer . . . 1620. 4° pp.8; sig.D^4
P.P.3444.af(91); 1480.aa.15(12).
One of the two books mentioned as sources can be identified as 'Vera relatione della vittoria', published at Pavia, 1620. Without imprint, but clearly one of the news reports published by Abraham Verhoeven at Antwerp. This piece is advertised in an earlier issue and itself advertises the following, separate, 'Manifesto'.

GROENESCHEI, Ulricus a. Disputatio medica de febribus putridis. 1619. *See* VORSTIUS, Aelius Everardus

G161 GROETENISSE

Groetenisse tot den zeer salighen Joseph . . . Tot Schiedam, Ghedruct by Adriaen Cornelisz. . . . 1609. 4° 2 unsigned leaves; illus.
T.2420(41).

A parody, in Dutch, Latin and Spanish, of 'Ave Joseph', published by Luys Sanchez at Madrid in 1608. The woodcut, showing only Joseph holding the child Jesus, is inscribed 'Iesus. Maria. Ioseph'.

GRONDICH discours over desen aen-staenden vrede-handel. 1608. *See* USSELINCX, Willem. Bedenckinghen.

G162 GROOT, Hugo de

[Poems] (tp.1) HVGONIS GROTII SACRA IN QVIBVS ADAMVS EXVL TRAGOEDIA ALIORVMQVE EIVSDEM GENERIS CARMINVM CVMVLVS . . . Ex Typographio Alberti Henrici, Hagæ Comitatensi . . . M D CI. 4° 2 pt.: pp.76; 55
C.28.f.10.

Author's presentation copy to Paul Choart de Buzanval.

G163 GROOT, Hugo de

[Poems] HUGONIS Grotij POEMATA, Collecta & magnam partem nunc primùm edita à fratre GVILIELMO GROTIO. LUGDUN. BATAV. Apud Andr. Clouquium . . . 1617. 8° pp.548
1213.h.19.

Poems in Latin or Greek, including poems addressed to Hugo de Groot. Some copies available already in 1616 (*Eyffinger* pp.215, 216). The titlepage is engraved. Ownership inscription: Ioh. Mauritius.

G164 GROOT, Hugo de

[Single poems] HVGONIS GROTII ALLOQVIVM ad Arcam, quâ e Carcere elatus est. fol. a single sheet
C.161.f.3(3).

With 'Nae-bootsinghe van HVG. GROTII Latijnsche Aenspraeck aen de kist/inde welcke sijns E. uyt de Ghevanckenisse is ghedraghen', the translation sometimes attributed to Hugo de Groot himself. Published in 1621?

G165 GROOT, Hugo de

[Single poems. Alloquium ad arcam.] Latijnsche Aen-spraeck van M$^{r.}$ HVGO DE GROOT aen De Kist in de welcke sijne E. uyt de Ghevanckenisse is ghedraghen den 27. Martij. 1621. In Neder-landtsch Rijm nae-ghebootst. Met Noch een Liedeken van de Hollandtsche Thuyn, en 't Calf, van een ander. Ghedruckt . . . 1621. 4° sig.A^4
11555.e.40(3).

The translation is sometimes attributed to Hugo de Groot himself. The other poem is by Reinier Telle.

G166 GROOT, Hugo de

[Single poems. Vraghe en antvvoordt: over den doop.] T'samensprake OVER DEN DOOP. Tusschen HVGO DE GROOT, Ende sijn Dochter CORNELIA DE GROOT. Door Vraghen ende Antwoorden. IN 'SGRAVEN-HAGE. By Aert Meuris . . . 1619. 4° pp.12
T.2249(24).

G167 GROOT, Hugo de

[Single poems] WTLEGGINGHE van het Gebedt ons Heeren IESV CHRISTI, ghenaemt het VADER-ONS, Ghemaeckt door M$^{r.}$ HVGO DE GROOT . . . TOT DELF, By Bruyn Harmanssz Schinckel . . . 1619. 4° pp.7
C.136.b.23.

With the text of the Lord's Prayer in the margin.

G168 GROOT, Hugo de

BONA FIDES SIBRANDI LVBBERTI DEMONSTRATA EX LIBRO QVEM INSCRIPSIT, Responsionem ad Pietatem Hugonis Grotij. LVGDVNI BATAVORVM Excudit Ioannes Patius . . . 1614. 4° pp.20

11.a.6(3).

Anonymous.

G169 GROOT, Hugo de

[De antiquitate reipublicae Batavicæ.] LIBER DE ANTQVITATE REIPVBLICÆ BATAVICÆ: auctore HVGONE GROTIO . . . LVGDVNI BATAVORVM EX OFFICINA PLANTINIANA RAPHELENGIJ, M.DC.X. 4° pp.LX

C.74.c.18(2).

G170 GROOT, Hugo de

[De antiquitate reipublicae Batavicae.] LIBER DE ANTQVITATE REIPVBLICÆ BATAVICAE: auctore HVGONE GROTIO . . . EX OFFICINA PLANTINIANA RAPHELENGIJ, 1610. 4° pp.LX

157.i.2.

Another issue of the preceding, differing only in omitting the place of publication in the imprint and in the use of Arabic numerals for the date.

G171 GROOT, Hugo de

[De antiquitate reipublicae Batavicae.] Chronicon Hollandiæ. DE HOLLANDORVM REPVB. & REBVS GESTIS Commentarii HVGONIS GROTII, IANI DOVSÆ PATRIS, IANI DOVSÆ FILII. LVGDVNI BATAVORVM Apud Ioannem Maire. 1617. 4° pp.LX, 501

9405.dd.3.

A reissue of the 1610 edition of 'De antiquitate reipublicae Batavicae' by Hugo de Groot and of 'Bataviae Hollandiaeque annales' by Janus Dousa the Younger of 1601, with new preliminary matter.

G172 GROOT, Hugo de

DEFENSIO FIDEI CATHOLICÆ DE SATISFACTIONE CHRISTI Adversus FAVSTVM SOCINVM . . . Scripta ab HVGONE GROTIO. SECVNDA EDITIO. LVGDVNI BATAVORVM Excudit Ioannes Patius . . . 1617. 4° pp.183

4226.e.20; 4224.dd.1(1).

Edited by Gerardus Vossius. The copy at 4224.d.1(1) is interleaved, with copious manuscript notes.

G173 GROOT, Hugo de

IVSTIFICATIE vande RESOLVTIE Der . . . Staten van Hollandt ende West-Vrieslandt ghenomen den 4. Augusti 1617 . . . Met by voeginghe van verscheyden VERIFICATIEN daer toe dienende. Ghedruckt . . . 1618. 4° pp.104

T.2248(51).

Documents, anonymously compiled, edited and in part drafted by Hugo de Groot. Pp.3–6 have accidentally been bound with the preceding item in the volume, p.3 is mutilated. Cropped.

G174 GROOT, Hugo de

MARE LIBERVM SIVE DE IVRE QVOD BATAVIS COMPETIT AD INDICANA COMMERCIA DISSERTATIO. LUGDUNI BATAUORUM, Ex officinâ Ludovici Elzevirij . . . M.DI.IX [*sic*]. 8° pp.42[66]

230.g.34; 1374.c.18.

Anonymous. Edited by Daniel Heinsius. The copy at 1374.c.18 is imperfect, wanting the last, unpaginated, leaf bearing the letters of King Philip III of Spain. Ownership inscription in that copy: Bibliothecae Conuentus PP. Carmelit. Discalceat. Patauij.

G175 GROOT, Hugo de

HVGONIS GROTI MARE LIBERVM SIVE De iure quod Batavis competit ad Indicana commercia DISSERTATIO. Vltima Editio. LVGDVNI BATAVORVM, Ex Officinâ ELZEVIRIANA . . . M.D.C.XVIII. 8° pp.108
1127.a.13(2); 1127.b.20.

G176 GROOT, Hugo de

ORDINVM HOLLANDIAE AC VVESTFRISIÆ PIETAS AB Jmprobissimis . . . calumnijs, præsertim verò à nuperâ SIBRANDI LVBBERTI Epistolâ quam ad . . . Archiepiscopum Cantuariensem scripsit vindicata: Per HVGONEM GROTIVM . . . Excudit LVGDVNI BATAVORVM Ioannes Patius . . . 1613. 4° pp.126
591.e.4; 11.a.6(1).

Both copies on large paper; the copy at 591.e.4 inscribed: Pour Monsr Casaubon, with manuscript notes.

G177 GROOT, Hugo de

ORDINVM HOLLANDIAE AC VVESTFRISIAE PIETAS . . . PER HVGONEM GROTIVM . . . Excudit LVGDVNI BATAVORVM Iohannes Patius . . . 1613. 4° pp.100[82]
3925.c.91.

G178 GROOT, Hugo de

[Ordinum Hollandiae . . . pietas.] Der Heeren Staten van Hollandt ende West-Vrieslandt GODTS-DIENSTICHEYT. Tegen veler schandelicke Calomnien/ende bysonder tegen den Brief onlangs by Sibrandum Lubberti geschreven aenden . . . Aerts-Bisschop van Cantelberch. Verdedicht door HVGO DE GROOT . . . Overgheset wt de Latijnsche spraecke . . . IN S'GRAVEN-HAGHE, By Hillebrant Iacobssen . . . 1613. 4° pp.128
T.2243(3).

Translated by Jan Wtenbogaert.

G179 GROOT, Hugo de

[Réfutation surtout de deux calomnies.] Stuytinge van een Tastelijcke Loghen al heymelyck gesonden uyt Vranckrijck/tot nadeel van . . . HVGO DE GROOT. Door een simpel verhael vande . . . vvaerheydt, by syne E. ghestelt, ende in't Latijn en Fransch uytghegheven. Nu verduytscht . . . 1621. 4° pp.6
1608/3910.

Against rumours spread by Gideon van den Boetzelaer van Langerak.

G180 GROOT, Hugo de

[Verhael van de heeren . . . Adriaen van Mathenes, etc.] ORATIO, A . . . HVGONE GROTIO . . . vernacula habita, In Senatu Amstelredamensi, nono Cal. Mai. 1616. Cum ab ILLVSTRIBVS AC POTENTIB. DD. Hollandiæ West-Frisiæque Ordinibus delegatus esset, unà cum . . . Adriano à Mathenes . . . Hugone Musio ab Holy . . . Gerardo ab Eyck . . . & Gulielmo Hases: ad informandum Consules & Senatum antedictum de sincera DD. Ordinum mente in conservanda vera Christiana reformata Religione . . . E Belgico in Latinum sermonem conversa . . . M.DC.XVI. 4° sig.A-H[4]
700.h.7(1).

Translated by Theodorus Schrevelius. Printed by Jan Everdsen van Doorn at Utrecht. The original Dutch text was issued by the States of Holland on 29 June 1616.

Het GROOTE liedeboeck. 1604. *See* CLOCK, Leendert

G181 GROTE

d'Grote seeff. fol. a single sheet
1750.b.29(99).

An engraving on the fall of Johan van Oldenbarnevelt. The engraved legends are in Dutch, but a sheet bearing German text has been pasted to the foot of the engraving where the remains of Dutch text are discernible. The German text is a translation from the original Dutch. Printed at Amsterdam in 1618.

GROTIUS, Hugo. *See* GROOT, Hugo de

G182 GROUWEL

GROVWEL, van de Contra-remonstrantsch-ghesinden/in den Synodo Provinciael van Gelderlandt/A°. 1618. in Julio ghehouden/verfoeyt ende ghedetesteert: vervaet in sekere Thien Poincten . . . onlanghs van weghen de . . . Staten des Furstendoms Gelre . . . uytghegheven . . . Ghedruckt . . . 1618. 4° pp.26
T.2248(44).

A different compilation based on the same original theses, entitled 'Thien Contra-Remonstransche positien', is entered under GREVINCHOVEN, Nicolaas.

GROUWELEN der voornaemste hooft-ketteren. 1607. *See* SICHEM, Christoffel van

GROVE lasteren ende beschuldiginghen Johannis Ùtenbogaerts. 1616. *See* DRIELENBURCH, Vincent van

G183 GRUDIUS, Nicolaus

NICOLAI GRVDII . . . Et HADRIANI MARII . . . POEMATA . . . Excusa apud Ioannem Patium . . . M.DC.IX. 8° pp.191,96
11408.bb.18.

Published at Leiden.

G184 GRUTERUS, Petrus

PETRI GRVTERI EPISTOLARVM CENTVRIA, CVM APOLOGIA EIVSDEM, IN QVA Instituti ratio redditur. LVGDVNI BATAVORVM, Ex Officinâ Ioannis Patii . . . M.D.C.IX. 8° pp.108
1492.ff.85.

GRUTERUS, Samuel. [Disputatio] decima-quarta, de libero arbitrio. 1603. *See* GOMARUS, Franciscus

G185 GRYNAEUS, Simon

(tp.1) NOVUS ORBIS. id est, NAVIGATIONES PRIMÆ IN AMERICAM: quibus adjunximus GASPARIS VARRERII DISCVRSVM super OPHYRA Regione . . . ROTERODAMI, Apud Iohannem Leonardi Berewout . . . M.D.CXVI.
(tp.2) CASPARIS VARRERII . . . Commentarius DE OPHYRA REGIONE . . . ROTERODAMI, Apud Ioannem Leonardi Berevvout . . . 1616. 8° 2 pt.: pp.570; sig.):(,)(,⋆,⋆⋆^{8},⋆⋆⋆^{10}
1060.a.23; G.6901.

Anonymous. Edited by Balthasar Lydius.

G186 GUALTHERUS, Marcus

DIALOGI DE SCHOLA LIBRI DVO . . . addita . . . conjectanea quædam philologa. FRANICAE, Excudebat Vlricus Dominici Balck, 1613. 4° pp.172,22
715.d.37.

Author's presentation copy to Willem Baudaert, dated 9 August 1613.

G187 GUARINI, Giovanni Battista

[Il pastor fido.] ANNA RODENBVRGHS Trouwen Batavier Treur-bly-eynde-spel. T'AMSTELREDAM, Voor Dirck Pietersz. Vos-cuyl/[etc.] (col.) 't AMSTERDAM, Ghedruckt by Paulus van Ravesteyn . . . 1617. 4° sig.⋆A-N^{4}; illus.
11755.bb.81(6).

A translation of Guarini's 'Pastor fido' by Theodore Rodenburgh, with his 'Nobilitas' emblem on the titlepage and his motto 'Chi sara sara' used as signature of the preface which mentions his and his wife's stay in England.

G188 GUARINI, Giovanni Battista
[Il pastor fido.] Treur-bly-eynde-spel/Vande Trouwe Liefd VAN CYPRIAEN EN ORIANA. Eerst en tweede deel. T'AMSTELREDAM, Voor Dirck Pietersz. Voscuyl . . . 1618. 4°
11755.bb.81(5*).
The titlepage only of Theodore Rodenburgh's version of Guarini's 'Pastor fido'. Printed by Paulus van Ravesteyn at Amsterdam.

G189 GUEVARA, Antonio de; Bishop
[Aviso de privados.] DESPERTADOR DE CORTESANOS, Compuesto por . . . Don ANTONIO DE GVEVARA . . . EN LA IMPRIMERIA PLANTINIANA. 1605. 8° pp.303
1606/1801.
Published at Leiden.

G190 GUICCIARDINI, Lodovico
[Descrittione di tutti i Paesi Bassi.] DESCRIPTION DE TOVTS LES PAYS-BAS . . . PAR . . . LOYS GVICCIARDIN . . . Derechef illustrée de plusieurs histoires & narrations remarquables. [etc.] (col.) A AMSTERDAM, Chez Cornille Nicolas . . . M DC IX. fol. pp.483: plates; maps
C.83.h.9.
The titlepage is engraved. An edition by Petrus Montanus of the translation by François de Belleforest. With maps and plates by Joannes van Doetechum, Jan Saenredam and Pieter van de Keere. Wanting the plates for p.184,217,456,467; that for p.217 probably never issued. With the arms of Prince Henry on the binding.

G191 GUICCIARDINI, Lodovico
[Descrittione di tutti i Paesi Bassi.] DESCRIPTION DE TOVS LES PAYS-BAS . . . PAR . . . LOYS GVICCIARDIN . . . Avec toutes les Cartes Geographiques desdicts Pays, & plusieurs pourtraicts de villes & autres bastimens . . . tirez par M. PIERRE KEERE. Derechef illustrée de plusieurs Additions remarquables, par PIERRE du MONT . . . A ARNHEM, Chez Iean Ieansz. 1613. obl.4° pp.606; plates; maps
1486.dd.10.
With an additional Titlepage, engraved, bearing the imprint: Arnhemi apud Joannem Janssoni et Petrum Kærium Amsterodamum. Ownership inscription: Ex libris Laurentij de Nyelvitz.

G192 GUICCIARDINI, Lodovico
[Descrittione di tutti i Paesi Bassi.] OMNIVM BELGII, sive INFERIORIS GERMANIAE REGIONVM DESCRIPTIO: LVDOVICO GVICCIARDINO . . . AVCTORE. Recèns ex idiomate Italico . . . in Latinum sermonem conversa. Regnero Vitellio . . . interprete. Insertis . . . tabulis Geographicis. Adjectisque . . . nonnullis additamentis. AMSTELRODAMI, Excudebat Guiljelmus Ianssonius . . . M DC XIII. fol. pp.315: plates; maps
576.l.23.
With commentary by Reinier Telle and with new plates, including views of Amsterdam by Claes Jansz Visscher. The date as printed actually reads 1614 but is generally presumed to be 1613. A map entitled 'Les Provinces Unies des Baïs [*sic*] Bas . . . Par N. de Fer, Paris, 1701', has been inserted in this copy.

G193 GUICCIARDINI, Lodovico
[Detti e fatti piacevoli.] LES HEVRES DE RECREATION ET APRES-DISNEES DE Louys Guicciardin . . . Traduit d'Italien en François, par François de Belle-Forest . . . EN ANVERS, Ches Guislain Ianssens . . . 1605. [etc.] 12° pp.257
12314.de.19.

The GUIDE of faith. 1621. *See* NORRIS, Sylvester

G194 GULDE

GVLDE COMPAS, Vvaer in kort eñ levendich af-ghepeylt wort het groot verschil der Remonstranten ter eener/ende de Ware Ghereformeerde ter ander zijden: Dienende allen eenvoudighen Christenen/tot bezeylinghe vande rechte Haven der zalicheyt. Door A.P.C. ghedruckt . . . 1618. 4° sig. AB^4
700.h.25(13).

G195 GULDEN

GVLDEN LEGENDE Van den Nieuwen S^t, Jan, Dat is: Cort verhael van den Edeldom/deuchden/ende handelingen van Meester Jan van Barnevelt . . . Ghedruckt Anno 1618. 4° pp.35; illus., port.
T.2422(22).
Sometimes attributed to François van Aerssen.

Den GULDEN winckel der konstlievende Nederlanders. 1613. *See* VONDEL, Joost van den [Other works]

GWALTERUS, Rodolphus. *See* WALTHER, Rudolf

G196 GYSIUS, Joannes

Oorsprong en Voortgang Der Neder-Landtscher Beroerten ende Ellendicheden . . . 1616. 4° pp.411: pl.2; illus.
9405.aaa.48.
Anonymous. Based mainly on Willem Baudaert's 'Morghenwecker'. Without imprint; printed by Henrick van Haestens at Leiden. Among the engravings the portrait of Margareta van Parma has been imposed upside down.

G197 GYSIUS, Joannes

[Oorsprong en voortgang der Nederlandtscher beroerten.] (tp.1) LE MIROIR de la Cruelle, & horrible Tyrannie Espagnole perpetree au pays Bas, par le Tyran Duc de ALBE, & aultres Cōmandeurs de par le Roy PHILIPPE le deuxiesme. On a adjoinct la deuxiesme partie de les Tyranni[es] commises aux Indes Occidentales par les Espagnols . . . tot AMSTERDAM Ghedruckt by Ian Evertss. Cloppenburg . . . 1620. (tp.2) LE MIROIR De la Tyrannie Espagnole Perpetree aux Indes Occidentales . . . Mise en lumiere par . . . Bartholome de las Casas . . . Nouvellement refaicte . . . tot AMSTERDAM Ghedruckt by Ian Evertss Cloppenburg . . . 1620. 4° 2 pt.: ff.87; 68; illus.
591.b.5 & 278.f.28; G.7102(1,2).
The titlepages are engraved, with letterpress wording. Pt.1 is a shortened version of 'Oorsprong en voortgang der Nederlandtscher beroerten' by Joannes Gysius, based on Willem Baudaert's 'Morghen-wecker'. The titlepage signed: DvB in et fet, i.e. David Vinckboons? or Daniel van den Bremden? An English map of 'The Newe Worlde' has been inserted in the copy at G.7102. A separate copy of pt.2 is entered under CASAS, Bartolomé de las; Bishop.

G198 GYSIUS, Joannes

[Oorsprong en voortgang der Nederlandtscher beroerten.] (tp.1) ORIGO & HISTORIA BELGICORVM TVMVLTVVM . . . Accedit Historia de furoribus Gallicis. Auctore ERNESTO EREMVNDO FRISIO. LVGDVNI BATAV. Apud Bartholomeum vander Bild . . . M.D.C.XIX.

(tp.2) APPENDIX sive HISTORIA TRAGICA de Furoribus Gallicis & cæde Admirallij NARRATIO. LVGDVNI BATAVORVM, Apud Batholomęum à Bilt . . . M.D.CXIX. 8° 2 pt.: pp.288; 46: plates; illus.
156.c.4; G.15275.

Both parts are anonymous; pt.1 is by Joannes Gysius, pt.2 by François Hotman. The titlepage of pt.1 has the same engraving as that of the preceding Dutch edition and only one plate has been added to those in the Dutch edition. Printed by Henrick Lodewijckxsoon van Haestens at Leiden.

H

H1 HAARLEM

[29.4.1617] Handelinghe tusschen de Magistraet der Stadt Haerlem ende dien van den Kerckenraet/by Interventie van de Classe van dien quartier/op d'Electie van Kerckelijcke persoonen ende t'beroep van den predicanten binnen . . . Haerlem/ ghevallen inden Jare 1616. Ghedruckt t'Haerlem/by Adriaen Rooman . . . By expresse Ordonnantie van de Heeren Burgermeesteren, ende Regeerders der Stadt Haerlem . . . 1617. 4° 4 unsigned leaves
T.2247(44).

Dated 29 April 1617. Badly cropped.

H2 HAARLEM

[27.1.1618] VERKLARINGHE vande . . . MAGISTRATEN ENDE REGEERDERS DER STADT HAERLEM, DOOR HAREN GHEDEPUTEERDEN ghedaen, inde Vergaderinghe DER . . . STATEN VAN HOLLANDT ENDE WEST-VRIESLANDT, ende BY DE . . . EDELEN ENDE MEESTE LEDEN VANDE ZELVE Vergaderinghe gheapprobeert. Ghedruct . . . By een LIEFHEBBER des alghemeynen Christelijcken Vredes, 1618. 4° pp.12
T.2248(28).

Compiled chiefly by Hugo de Groot. Dated 27 January 1618.

H3 HAARLEM

[19.4.1618] IVSTIFICATIE Van De Procedueren/by Schout/Burghermeesteren ende Regeerders der Stadt Haerlem, gehouden inden Jare xvj^{c}. ende zeven-thien/ teghens eenighe overhoorighe ende onrustighe Persoonen/binnen de zelve hare Stadt. Midtsgaders Eenighe Copien ende Extracten, dienende tot naerder verklaringhe ende verificatie vanden in-houden der zelver IVSTIFICATIE. TOT HAERLEM. Ghedruckt by Adriaen Rooman . . . 1618. 4° pp.91
T.2248(52).

Dated 19 April 1618. A copy of the edition corresponding to the one described in *Knuttel* no.2553.

H4 HAARLEM

[19.4.1618] IVSTIFICATIE Van De Procedueren . . . teghens eenighe . . . Persoonen . . . Midtsgaders Eenighe Copien ende Extracten, dienende tot . . . verklaringhe ende verificatie vanden i-nhouden [*sic*] der zelver IVSTIFICATIE. TOT HAERLEM. Ghedruckt by Adriaen Rooman . . . 1618. 4° pp.48
700.h.25(20).

Another edition of the preceding corresponding to the copy described in *Knuttel* no.2554.

H5 HAARLEM

[19.4.1618] IVSTIFICATIE Van De Procedueren . . . teghens eenighe . . . Persoonen/binnen de zelve Stadt . . . TOT HAERLEM. Ghedruckt by Adriaen Rooman . . . 1618. 4° pp.24
106.d.44.

Another edition of the two preceding entries corresponding to the copy described in *Knuttel* no.2555.

H6 HAARLEM

[25.10.1618] Publicatie. Ende verkiesinghe des Raets tot Haerlem. Met de namen Der Raets Persoonen alsoo nieu als out. Met den Eet der Schutterij. Ghedruct tot HAERLEM, By Adriaen Rooman, voor Niclaes van Geelkerck. 4° sig. A^2
1314.e.24(2).

The proclamation dated 25 October 1618. Containing names of new councillors only. Published at Leiden in 1618.

HACHTINGIUS, Johannes. Josephus praesul. 1617. *See* RAVENSPERGER, Hermann

H7 HAECHT GOIDTSENHOVEN, Laurens van

Μικροκόσμος. PARVVS MVNDVS. (col.) ARNHEMI. Apud Ioannem Iansonium . . . sumptibus Theodori Petri bibliopolæ Amstelrodamiensis. 4° sig. A-T^4V^1; illus.
C.76.b.4(1).

The author is named in the preface. The plates engraved by Gerard de Jode. The titlepage is engraved. Published ca. 1610. For an edition of the same engravings with Dutch text, dated 1608, *see* MOERMAN, Jan

HAEMMERLEIN, Thomas. *See* THOMAS a Kempis

H8 HAER, Floris vander

ANTIQVITATVM LITVRGICARVM ARCANA . . . Omnia ex diuersis authoribus tribus tomis comprehensa. DVACI. Ex Typographia BALTASARIS BELLERI . . . 1605. 8°
3 tom.: pp. 392; 965; 928
3478.b.24.

The author's name is revealed in a pun at the end of the preface. The titlepage of tom. 1 is engraved. Printed by Laurence Kellam at Douai. Ownership inscription: M[o]n[aste]rii Roth 1733. With a bookplate bearing the initials: H.A.Z.R.

H9 HAER, Floris vander

LES CHASTELAINS DE LILLE. LEVR ANCIEN ESTAT, OFFICE & Famille . . . Auec une particuliere description de l'ancien Estat de la ville de Lille . . . Par FLORIS VANDER HAER . . . A LILLE, De l'Imprimerie de CHRISTOFLE BEYS . . . M.DCXI. [etc.]
4° pp. 299: plates; illus., genealogical tables
154.m.13.

Part of the rarer of two known issues as described in *Houdoy* p.76 no.7.

HAERLEMS juweel. 1608. *See* HEYNS, Zacharias

H10 HAERLEMSCHEN

DEN HAERLEMSCHEN Harminiaen, Dat is: Verhael van de vreetheydt der Heeren van Haerlem, een Jaer oft drye herwaerdts ghepleeght aen verscheyden goede Patriotten: dienende tot meerder openbaringe van hare Iustificatie. GHEDRVCKT . . . 1618. 4° pp. 30
T.2248(34).

H11 HAESTENS, Henrick Lodewijksz van

De Bloedige ende strenge Belegeringhe Der Stadt Oostende/in Vlaenderen . . . Hier wort noch verhaelt alle het geene datter gepasseert is/soo te Water als te Lande/geduyrende dese Belegeringe. Met voordracht opgesocht ende beschreven, door HENRICK van HAESTENS. Tot Leyden, by Henrick van Haestens. 1613.
4° pp. 174: pl. 14; illus.
154.e.6.

With coloured engravings. A laudatory poem signed: D.H., i.e. Daniel Heinsius.

H12 HAESTENS, Henrick Lodewijksz van

[De bloedige ende strenge belegeringhe.] Beschrijvinghe, Des machtigen Heyrtochts uyt Hollandt nac Vlanderen/gedaen by de . . . STATEN GENERAEL der vereenichde Nederlanden. Van ghelijcken De Bloedige ende strenge Belegeringe Der Stadt OOSTENDE . . . Oock mede Figuerlijck affgebeeldet/hoe de Stadt bestormt/tot drye reysen vercleent eñ affgesneden is geweest. De tweede Editie met vlijt oversien, vergroot ende verbetert, door H. L. van Haestens. TOT LEYDEN, By Henrick Haestens/1614. 4° pp.160; illus.

RB.23.a.299.

Pp.17–72 have been misnumbered 21–76. Imperfect; wanting the preliminary leaf bearing the engraved arms of Prince Maurice and letterpress Latin verses by Daniel Heinsius preceding the titlepage, the leaf bearing pp.111, 112 and also all the plates.

H13 HAESTENS, Henrick Lodewijksz van

[De bloedige ende strenge belegeringhe.] LA NOUVELLE TROYE ou Memorable histoire du Siege D'OSTENDE . . . Recœuillie des plus asseurés memoires Par HENRY HAESTENS. A LEYDE, Chez LOYS ELZEVIER . . . M D C XV. 4° pp.293: pl.14; illus.

1055.h.19; 150.d.16.

Translated by Jean de la Haye. The poem by D.H. here signed: D. Heynsius. With poems by Richard Jean de Nerée, a portrait and arms of Prince Maurice not in the Dutch edition and with some different plates, their captions in Latin or Italian, but some of the explanatory text in Dutch. Printed by H. L. van Haestens at Leiden. Ownership inscription in the copy at 1055.h.19: Iean Maurice.

H14 HAGIUS, Joannes

Den Lust-hof der Medecijnen . . . Beschreven ende nagelaten by den welgeleerden Medecijn D. Ioannes Hagius, ende nu eerst int licht ghebracht door zijnen sone Matthijs Haghens . . . Tot Dordrecht. Ghedruckt by Peeter Verhagen . . . 1616. [etc.] fol. pp.617; illus., port.

773.m.6.

Another issue bearing the imprint: Ghedruckt by Isaack Jansz. Canin and with Canin's device on the titlepage in place of Verhagen's, has been described in 1982 in B.M. Israel's catalogue no. 96. Possibly Canin, the only printer and publisher named in the privilege, printed all copies. Imperfect; wanting sig. Gg=pp.467–482.

H15 HAINAULT

[12.1603] INSTRVCTION SERVANTE A LA LEVEE DES IMPOSITIONS MISES SVS PAR LES ESTATZ DV PAYS DE Haynnau, tant sur le Fer, Houblon, que Bestiaux, tant a la consũption, que sortie du Pays, en l'assemblée des Estatz tenu au commencement du Mois de Decembre xvj.^{C} & trois, pour le terme d'vng an . . . A MONS. De l'Imprimerie de Charles Michel. M.V.C.IIII [*sic*]. 4° sig.A^{4}

106.d.7.

H16 HALLOIX, Petrus

TRIVMPHVS SACER SS. TERENTIANI ET SOCII MARTYRVM, SIVE SACRORVM VTRIVSQVE CORPORVM Atrebato Duacum gloriosa translatio. ET DVACI IN EADEM TRANSLATIONE publica & solemnis SVPPLICATIO . . . Auctore R.P. PETRO HALLOIX . . . DVACI, Typis NATALIS WARDAVOIR . . . M.D.CXV. 8° pp.236; illus.

860.b.20.

Partly in verse. The illustrations are woodcuts. Ownership inscription: Eribertus Roswej[dus].

H17 HAMCONIUS, Martinus

CERTAMEN CATHOLICORVM CVM CALVINISTIS, CONTINVO CHARACTERE C. CONSCRIPTVM . . . ADIECTA SVNT Anagrammata, Chronologica Acrostichides &

quædam alia . . . MARTINO HAMCONIO . . . Authore. RECOGNITVM ET AVCTVM. LOVANII, Typis PHILIPPI DORMALII. M.DC.XII. [etc.] 4° pp.99
486.g.25.

Ownership inscription: ex libris Aduocati Columbani. A modern description of the book in manuscript has been pasted in at the end.

H18 HAMCONIUS, Martinus

MARTINI HAMCONII FRISIA SEV DE VIRIS REBVSQVE FRISIÆ ILLVSTRIBVS LIBRI DVO. Opus ab Authore recognitum, auctum, & Imaginibus Regum, Potestatum, ac Principum exornatum. ADIECTI SVNT PONTIFICES FRISIORVM . . . FRANEKERÆ, Excudebat IOANNES LAMRINCK . . . suis ET IOANNIS STARTERI . . . sumptibus . . . MDC.XX. (col.) FRANEKERÆ, Excudebat Ioannes Lamrinck . . . 1620. 4° ff.127[131]; illus., port.
1055.g.6; G.1648.

In verse. The editor's dedication signed: Pierius Winsemius. The illustrations engraved or woodcut; the portrait signed: P. Harling[S], i.e. Pieter Feddes, fecit et. dedit. The second publisher known to have been at Leeuwarden.

HAND-BOECK; of cort begrijp der caerten . . . van alle landen. 1609. *See* CAERT-THRESOOR

H19 HANDELINGE

Handelinge van de Prædestinatie, Perseverantie, ende Vrye Wille des menschen, Met eenighe circumstantien van dien. Tegens de Calumnien M. P. Bertij, Cupij, ende haren ghevolge. Tot dienste van die van Alckmaer ende andere vromen . . . Door een Liefhebber der waerheyt/genoemt I.C. . . . TOT DELFT, Voor Jan Andriesz. . . . 1610. 4° pp.23
T.2240(21).

HANDELINGHE tusschen de Magistraet der stadt Haerlem ende dien van den Kerckenraet. 1617. *See* HAARLEM [29.4.1617]

HANSZ, Sybrand. *See* CARDINAEL, Sybrand Hansz

H20 HARDUIJN, Justus de

(tp.1) GODDELICKE LOF-SANGHEN TOT VERMAEKINGHE van alle gheestighe Liefhebbers, Door IUSTUS DE HARDUYN P[r]. TE GHENDT, By Jan vanden Kerchove . . . 1620. [etc.]
(tp.2) DEN VAL ENDE OP-STAND Van den CONINCK ende PROPHETE DAVID Met By-voegh van de SEVEN LEED-TUYGENDE PSALMEN. DOOR IUSTUS DE HARDUYN, TE GHENDT, By Ian vanden Kerchove . . . 1620. [etc.] obl.4° 2 pt.: pp.180[188]; 47; music
Music K.7.c.10(1,2).

Published as a single work, with combined dedication, preface, privilege and approbation.

H21 HAREN, Jan

[La repentance de Jean Haren.] De Bekeeringhe van IAN HAREN, ende Syn weder-komen tot de Ghemeynte Godts: Door hem openbaerlijc wtghesproken inde Walsche Kercke tot Wezel . . . den 7 dach Martij 1610 . . . Wt het Fransoys int Nederduytsch overghezet door I. de la Haye . . . In 'sGraven-Haghe, Voor Lowijs Elsevier . . . 1610. [etc.] 4° sig.A-C^4D^6
T.2240(8); T.2421(20).

HARLINGENSIS, Petrus. *See* FEDDES, Pieter

HARMONIE dat is overeenstemminge. 1618. *See* RUYTINCK, Simon. Harmonia synodarum Belgicarum.

H22 HARRISON, John

THE MESSIAH ALREADY COME. OR PROFES OF CHRISTIANITIE, BOTH OVT of the Scriptures, and auncient Rabbins, to convince the Iewes, of their . . . blindnesse . . . Written in Barbarie, in the yeare 1610 . . . AMSTERDAM, Imprinted by Giles Thorp . . . M.DC,XIX [*sic*]. 4° pp.68
482.b.3(2).
The dedication to Frederick, King of Bohemia, signed: Iohn Harrison.

H23 HARRISON, John

A SHORT RELATION OF The departure of . . . Prince Frederick King Elect of Bohemia: with his royall . . . Ladie Elizabeth; and the . . . young Prince Henrie, from Heydelberg towards Prague, to receiue the Crowne of that Kingdome. Whearvnto is annexed the Solempnitie . . . of the Coronation. Translated out of dutch . . . At Dort, Prinred [*sic*] by George Waters. 1619. 4° sig.AB^4
605.b.39(2); 1054.h.28.
The address to the reader signed: John Harrison. With Latin verses, anagrams, etc. The description of the coronation originally published in Dutch as 'Levendich ende warachtich verhael aller omstandicheden'.

HARTUNGH, Bruno. Disputatio theologica de Deo. 1613. *See* LINDEN, Henricus Antonides van der

H24 HARTWECH, Adam

COPIE VAN SEKERE brieven/de welcke twee persoonen aen malcanderen hebben gheschreven/handelende vande perseverantie ofte volherdinghe der Heylighen. Hier is noch achter by ghevoecht eene antwoorde op de vraghe vande hedendaechsche gheschillen/de salicheyt betreffende . . . Wtghegheven door een Liefhebber der Waerheyt. Ghedruckt tot Dordrecht/by Niclaes Vincenten . . . 1612. 4° sig.A-C^{4}D^3
T.2242(16).
The first letter signed: Adam hart wech; the second: Caerle bluffier. The whole edited by Adam Hartwech.

H25 HARVENGIUS, Philippus

REVERENDI IN CHRISTO PATRIS AC D. PHILIPPI DE HARVENG . . . OPERA OMNIA . . . DVACI, Typis Viduæ LAVRENTII KELLAMI . . . M.DC.XX. [etc.] fol. pp.805
3705.ee.3.
Edited by Nicolaus Chamart. Editor's presentation copy to the Capuchins at Dinant.

H26 HASE, Willem de

VRIENDELICKE Ende corte verantwoordinghe teghens de groote lasteringhen/die daghelijcx soo buyten als binnen de Stadt werden uytghestrooyt/tot verachtinghe van WILHELM DE HASE . . . van hem . . . tsamen gestelt . . . Ghedruckt by Adriaen Rooman . . . Boeck-drucker/der Stadt Haerlem . . . 1615. 4° sig.A^4
T.2245(6).

H27 HASELIUS, Christianus

INAVGVRALIS DISPVTATIO DE CAUSO EXQVISITO Quam . . . Pro Doctoratu in Medicina obtinendo publicè asseret CHRISTIANVS HASELIVS . . . LVGDVNI BATAVORVM, Ex Officina THOMÆ BASSON, M.D.C.IX. 4° sig.A^6
1185.g.1(36); 1185.g.1(35).
The copy at 1185.g.1(35) is cropped.

H28 HATTRON, Carolus Philippus

AVLA, OTIVM, SCENA VITÆ ET CONSILIA. SERIES QVÆSTIONVM, ET RERVM QVÆ

HABENTVR, SEQVENTI INDICE PRÆSCRIPTA. BRVXELLÆ, In Officina HVBERTI ANTONII . . . M.DC.XIX. 8° pp.371
1030.c.17.
The author's preface signed: Car. P. Hattron. With an additional titlepage, engraved, signed with a crowned monogram of the initials I.O.

H29 HAVENSIUS, Arnoldus
HISTORICA RELATIO DUODECIM MARTYRUM CARTUSIANORUM QUI RURÆMUNDÆ . . . Anno M.D.LXXII. Agonem suum feliciter compleverunt. AUCTORE . . . ARNOLDO HAVENSIO . . . ACCESSIT EJUSDEM EXHORTATIO ad Carthusianos, de Observantia Disciplinæ Regularis Vitæque Solitariæ commendatione . . . 1608. 4° pp.viii,77
4825.c.23.
With a biographical sketch of the author preceding the text, giving the date of his death in 1620 and quoting another work by him from a 1643 catalogue. The dedication to Arnoldus de Backer, Prior of the Carthusian House at Brussels, names the printer P.F., i.e. Petrus Foppens?, at Brussels. The date 1608 is therefore a repetition of the original date of this work, the present edition datable 1753.

H30 HAY, John
DE REBVS IAPONICIS, INDICIS, ET PERVANIS EPISTOLÆ RECENTIORES. A Ioanne Hayo . . . in librum vnum coaceruatæ. ANTVERPIÆ, Ex Officina Martini Nutij . . . M.DC.V. 8° pp.968
4767.d.7; 295.g.14; G.8692.
Translations by various named and unnamed authors.

HAYMANNUS, Petrus. Disputatio medica de pleuritide vera. 1614. *See* PAAUW, Petrus

H31 HECKIUS, Joannes
DISPVTATIO VNICA DOCTORIS IOANNIS HECKII EQVITIS LYNCAEI DAVENTRIENSIS. DE PESTE ET QVARE PRAECIPVE GRASSETVR TOT AB HINC Annis in Belgio . . . CVM DESCRIPTIONE ELECTVARII Lyncæi . . . & de huius Antidoti præcipuis operationibus. DAVENTRIAE, Excudebat Ioannes Cloppenburch . . . M.D.C.V. 4° sig.A-D^4
1185.i.14(3).
The editor's and publisher's preface signed: Wilhelmus Heckius.

H32 HEER, Henri de
SPADACRENE. Hoc est, FONS SPADANVS: EIVS SINGVLARIA, BIBENDI modus, medicamina bibentibus necessaria. Henricus ab Heer . . . recensui. LEODII. Apud Arnoldum de Corsvvaremia . . . 1614. 8° sig.A-F^8G^3
1171.f.28(3); 1568/1662.

H33 HEER, Henri de
[Spadacrene.] LES FONTAINES DE SPA, DECRITES PREMIEREMENT EN LATIN . . . traduict en frãçois auec additions par Henry de Heer . . . A LIEGE, Chez Ardt de Coersvvarem . . . 1616. 8° sig.A-I^8K^2
1171.b.4(1).

H34 HEIGHAM, John
A DEVOVT EXPOSITION OF THE HOLIE MASSE . . . Composed BY IOHN HEIGHAM . . . AT DOVAY . . . 1614. 12° pp.431; illus.
3477.a.46.
Printed by Pierre Auroi at Douai. The titlepage is engraved. With a woodcut on p.264. Ownership inscription: Ste. Malthus & amicorum.

Eene HEILIGE tragi-comedie ge-intituleert Den Salighen Ignatius de Loyola. 1610. *See* TRAGICOMEDIE sacrée intitulée Le bien-heureux Ignace de Loyola.

H35 HEINSIUS, Daniel

[Collections] (tp.1) DANIELIS HEINSI . . . ELEGIARVM LIB. III. MONOBIBLOS, SYLVÆ . . . LVGDVNI BATAVORVM Apud Iohannem Maire . . . 1603.
(tp.2=p.149) DAN. HEINSII SYLVÆ. In quibus varia. LVGDVNI BATAVORVM Apud Iohannem Maire . . . 1603. (col.) Typis THOMÆ BASSON. 12° pp.312
11408.a.34.

Printed at Leiden.

H36 HEINSIUS, Daniel

[Collections] DAN: HEINSII Nederduytsche POEMATA: By een vergadert en uytgegeven Door P.S. Tot Amsterdam Gedruct By Willem Janssen a°. 1616. [etc.] 4° pp.92,65; illus.
11555.e.30(1).

With 'Emblemata amatoria'. The editor's dedicatory epistle signed: Petrus Scriverius. The engravings partly attributed to Crispijn de Passe II, others signed: Simon Pass, Michel le Blon. Corresponding to the description in *Sellin* (no.40) of the true first edition except for corrected signatures in 'Lofsanck van Bacchus': printed actually in 1615?

H37 HEINSIUS, Daniel

[Collections] DAN: HEINSII Nederduytsche POEMATA: By een vergadert en uytgegeven door P.S. Tot Amsterdam gedruct By Willem Janssen a°. 1618. [etc.] 4° pp.20,132,29*–67; illus.
C.108.gg.20(1).

Edited by Petrus Scriverius. The titlepage is engraved. A reissue of the second edition of 1616 of which there is no copy in the British Library. Corresponding to *Sellin* no.42. Described by *Landwehr* (no.197) as beginning with a p.27 for the third part, but there does not seem to be a leaf wanting at that place in this copy.

H38 HEINSIUS, Daniel

[Collections] DAN: HEINSII Nederduytsche POEMATA: By een vergadert en uytgegeven Door P.S. Tot Amsterdam Gedruct By Willem Janssen a.° 1618 [etc.] 4° pp.143; illus.
C.131.g.14(4).

Edited by Petrus Sciverius. The titlepage is engraved. Without the privilege and including the poem 'Ter eeren van de Moffeschans', written in 1621 in honour of the poem by Iodocus Hondius in 1619. Including 'Spiegel van de doorluchtige vrouwen'. Corresponding to *Landwehr* no.198, *Sellin* no.44. Published 1621? Ownership inscriptions: Johan Broekhuisen; B. Huydekoper; Ploos van Amstel.

H39 HEINSIUS, Daniel

[Collections] DAN: HEINSII Nederduytsche POEMATA; By een Vergadert en uytgegeven Door P.S. Tot Leyden By Hermen van Westerhuisen A° 1621. obl.24° pp.195,ff.48,pp.58; illus.
11557.a.63(1).

Edited by Petrus Scriverius. The titlepage is engraved. With a second set of pp.179–184=sig.(***)1–3, containing the 'Voor-reden aende Doorluchtige Vrouwen', bound between sig.M2 and M3.

H40 HEINSIUS, Daniel

[Collections] DANIELIS HEINSII ORATIONES: Nunc primum omnes simul, nonnullæ etiam nunc primum editæ. LVGD. BATAVORVM, Apud Ludovicum Elzeuirium . . . M.DC XII. (col.) EX OFFICINA HENRICI AB HAESTENS . . . M.D.CXII. 12° pp.407
1090.c.10.

Pp.5,6,29,30,53,54 are mutilated, with the missing text on pp.5,6,53,54 supplied in manuscript on labels. Printed at Leiden.

H41 HEINSIUS, Daniel
[Collections] DANIELIS HEINSII ORATIONES: Editio noua; altera parte auctior. LVGD. BATAVORVM, Apud Ludouicum Elzeuirium . . . M DC XV. Typis Henrici ab Haestens. 8° pp.551
12355.b.20.

H42 HEINSIUS, Daniel
[Collections] DANIELIS HEINSII ORATIONES: EDITIO NOVA: magna parte auctior. LVGD. BATAVORVM, EX officinâ ELZEVIRIANA . . . M DC XX. 8° pp.556
1090.c.11.

H43 HEINSIUS, Daniel
[Collections] DANIELIS HEINSII POEMATA emendata locis infinitis & aucta . . . Editio quarta LUGD. BATAVORŨ Apud Ioh. Orlers et Iohā. Maire. (col.) LVGDVNI BATAVORVM, Apud Iohannem Orlers, & Iohannem Maire. M.D CXIII. 8° pp.621
1213.h.14.
With a group of poems by other authors, mainly addressed to Heinsius and including some in French. The titlepage is engraved.

H44 HEINSIUS, Daniel
[Collections] DANIELIS HEINSII POEMATA . . . EDITIO SEXTA. LVGD. BATAVORVM Apud IOHANNEM MAIRE . . . M DC XVII. 8° pp.647
1213.h.15.
From the library of John Morris.

H45 HEINSIUS, Daniel
[Collections] (tp.1) DANIELIS HEINSII POEMATVM EDITIO NOVA. Accedunt . . . Libri, DE CONTEMPTV MORTIS . . . LVGDVNI BATAVORVM, Sumptibus ELZEVIRIORVM, Et IOHANNIS MAIRII. M D CXXI.
(tp.2) DANIELIS HEINSII DE CONTEMPTV MORTIS LIB. IV . . . LVGD. BATAVORVM, Ex Officinâ ELZEVIRIANA. M D CXXI. (col.) LVGDVNI BATAVORVM. Typis ISAACI ELZEVIRI . . . M D C XXI. 8° pp.474; 167
1070.c.21.
The 'D' in the date on tp.2 is printed upside down. Ownership inscription: Gabriell Quarles.

H46 HEINSIUS, Daniel
IANI PHILODVSI Ad Calumnias IACOBI BRASSICÆ PRO IANO DOVSA, ET SE, Responsio placida. LVGDVNI BATAVORVM, Ex Typographeîo Christophori Guyotij, M.D.C.III. 4° pp.16
837.h.13(18).
Pseudonymous.

H47 HEINSIUS, Daniel
DANIELIS HEINSII AVRIACVS, Siue LIBERTAS SAVCIA. Accedunt eiusdem IAMBI Partim morales, partim ad amicos, partim amicorum causâ scripti. LVGDVNI BATAVORVM, Apud Andream Cloucquium . . . M.D.CII. 4° pp.143
837.h.13(13).
With prose and verse pieces in Greek by Heinsius and others. Printed by Jan Paets at Leiden?

H48 HEINSIUS, Daniel
CRAS CREDO HODIE NIHIL. Siue, Modus tandem sit ineptiarum. SATYRA MENIPPÆA. LVGD. BATAVORVM, Ex Officinâ ELZEVIRIANA. M D CXXI. (col.) LVGD. BATAVORVM. Typis ISAACI ELZEVIRI . . . M D CXXI. 12° pp.101
1506/55.
Anonymous.

H49 HEINSIUS, Daniel

DANIELIS HEINSII DE CONTEMPTV MORTIS LIBRI IV . . . LVGDVNI BATAVORVM, Ex Officinâ ELZEVIRIANA. M D CXXI. (col.) LVGDVNI BATAVORVM, Typis ISAACI ELZEVIRI . . . M D CXXI. 4° pp.196
847.f.16.

H50 HEINSIUS, Daniel

DAN. HEINSII DISSERTATIO Epistolica, An viro literato ducenda sit vxor, & qualis. ITEM Ejusdem alia amœniora opuscula; pleraque hactenus non edita. Quibus additæ sunt incerti auctoris ORATIONES FVNEBRES in obitus aliquot animalium. LVGDVNI BATAVORVM, Apud GODEFRIDVM BASSON . . . 1616.
(½ title=p.73) APPENDIX ORATIONVM FVNEBRIVM in obitus aliquot animalium Incerto quodam Italo auctore, interprete GVLIELMO CANTERO, Vltrajectino. 12° pp.92
1080.d.42(1).

H51 HEINSIUS, Daniel

DAN. HEINSII DISSERTATIO Epistolica, An viro literato ducenda sit uxor, & qualis? ITEM Ejusdem alia AMOENIORA opuscula. Quibus hac novâ Editione nunc primùm accessere . . . IACOBI EYNDII ab Hæmstede LOCI FVNEBRES in Obitus aliquot Animalium. LVGDVNI BATAVORVM, Apud Godefridum Basson, M.D.CXVIII. 12° pp.140
1080.a.3.

The 'Loci funebres' consist largely of versifications of some of the 'Orationes funebres' in the preceding.

HEINSIUS, Daniel. Emblemata (aliquot) amatoria. 1608; 1612; 1620. *See* below: Quaeris quid sit amor.

H52 HEINSIUS, Daniel

HERCULES TVAM FIDEM, SIVE MVNSTERVS HYPOBOLIMÆVS. id est, SATIRA MENIPPEA, De vita, origine, & moribus GASPERIS SCIOPPII . . . Editio secunda, altera parte auctior, & emendata. Acccssit huic accurata FABVLAE BVRDONIAE CONFVTATIO. LVGDVNI BATAVORVM, Ex Officina Ioannis Patii . . . M D C VIII. 16° pp.411; illus.
1079.c.14.

Anonymous. The author of the 'Confutatio', described on the half-title as I. R. Batavus, i.e. Joannes Rutgers, is in fact Scaliger himself. The engraved titlepage illustration shows Hercules.

H53 HEINSIUS, Daniel

HERCVLES TVAM FIDEM . . . LVGDVNI BATAVORVM, Ex Officina Ioannis Patii . . . M.D.C.VIII. 16° pp.455
12316.ee.47.

Anonymous. A made-up copy consisting of sig. A-C of the 1608 edition of 'Hercules tuam fidem', followed by sig. D-Ee apparently of the 1609 edition under the title of 'Satirae duae', also published by Jan Paets.

H54 HEINSIUS, Daniel

[Hercules tuam fidem.] SATIRÆ DVÆ HERCVLES TVAM FIDEM SIVE MVNSTERVS HYPOBOLIMÆVS. ET VIRGVLA DIVINA . . . Accessit his accurata BVRDONVM FABVLÆ CONFVTATIO quibus alia nonnulla hac editione accedunt. Lugduni Batavorum, Apud LVDOVICVM ELZEVIRIVM . . . M D C XVII. (col.) Lugduni Batavorum, Typis ISAACI ELZEVIRI . . . M D C XVII. 12° pp.619
1080.d.5; 245.b.17.

Anonymous. With letters by Isaac Casaubon and others. The pagination jumps from p.510 to p.601, but the signatures are continuous.

H55 HEINSIUS, Daniel

DAN. HEINSI HOMILIA In locum Iohannis Cap. XVII vers. IX. in qua de Electione, & quæ ab ea pendet quinque Articulorum doctrina, deque eius quæ in Ecclesiis recepta est, vsu ac ædificatione, agitur. LVGD. BAT. Typis ISAACI ELZEVIRI, M D CXIX. [etc.] 12° pp.90

854.a.9.

H56 HEINSIUS, Daniel

ΔΑΝΙΗΛΟΣ ΤΟΥ Ε'ΙΝΣΙ'ΟΥ ΥΜΝΟΣ ΕΙΣ ΠΑΝΔΩΡΑΝ ΗΣΙΟΔΟΥ. DANIELIS HEINSII HYMNUS Jn Pandoram Hesiodi . . . EX OFFICINA PLANTINIANA RAPHELENGIJ. M.D.CIII. 4° sig.α^4

837.h.13(16).

In Greek only. Published at Leiden. Author's presentation copy to Isaac Casaubon.

H57 HEINSIUS, Daniel

DAN. HEINSII IN CRVENTVM CHRISTI SACRIFICIVM, Siue Domini Passionem, HOMILIA. LVGDVNI BATAVORVM, Apud Ludouicum Elzevirium . . . M.DC.XIII. 4° pp.36

610.g.34(2).

Printed by Jan Paets at Leiden?

H58 HEINSIUS, Daniel

DANIELIS HEINSII in obitum V. ILLVSTR. IOSEPHI SCALIGERI . . . ORATIONES DVAE. Accedunt EPICEDIA eiusdem & aliorum: effigies item ac monumentum Scaligeri . . . æri incisa. EX OFFICINA PLANTINIANA RAPHELENGIJ. M.D.C.IX. Lugd. Bat. prostant apud Lud. Elzeuirium & Andream Cloucquium. 4° pp.100: plates; illus., port.

133.c.19(1); 610.k.17(1).

With a poem by Janus Dousa. Printed at Leiden. The copy at 610.k.17(1) lacks the leaf bearing the half-title 'Danielis Heinsii Manes Scaligeri'.

H59 HEINSIUS, Daniel

DAN. HEINSII IN THEOPHANIA, Siue Domini Natalem, HOMILIA. LVGDVNI BATAVORVM, Apud Ludovicum Elzevirium . . . M.DC.XIII. 4° pp.35[36]

610.g.34(1).

HEINSIUS, Daniel. Inclyta Lugdunum. 1608. *See* SWANENBURCH, Willem. Ianus Hautenus.

H60 HEINSIUS, Daniel

[Dan. Heinsii Lof-sanck van Iesus Christus . . . Met noodelicke uytleggingen . . . uytgegeven door P.S. Tot Amstelredam, By Willem Jansz . . . 1616.] 4° pp.74

11555.e.30(2).

Edited by Petrus Scriverius. Imperfect; wanting the titlepage. Originally issued with the second edition of 'Nederduytsche poemata', 1616. The above title has been supplied from *UBA CNL* no.287.

H61 HEINSIUS, Daniel

DAN. HEINSII LOF-SANCK VAN IESVS CHRISTVS, den eenigen ende eeuvvigen SONE GODES: Met noodelicke Vytleggingen . . . Met een Voor-reden van den AVTEVR. TOT AMSTERDAM, BY VVILLEM IANSZ. . . . 1618. [etc.] 4° pp.92; illus.

C.108.gg.20(2).

Edited by Petrus Scriverius. The titlepage engraving shows the Adoration of the Shepherds.

H62 HEINSIUS, Daniel

DAN. HEINSII LOF-SANCK VAN IESVS CHRISTVS . . . t'AMSTERDAM, BY WILLEM BLAEV, [etc.] 4° pp.76; illus.

C.131.g.14(3).

Edited by Petrus Scriverius. With the titlepage illustration of the Adoration of the Shepherds. Issued jointly with the 1618 [1621] edition of 'Nederduytsche poemata'.

H63 HEINSIUS, Daniel

DAN. HEINSII LOF-SANCK VAN IESVS CHRISTVS . . . TOT LEYDEN, HERMAN WESTERHVYSEN. AN. 1621. obl. 24° pp. 226

11557.a.63(2).

Edited by Petrus Scriverius.

H64 HEINSIUS, Daniel

ODE IN LAVDEM Clarissimi adolescentis M. IOHANNIS CASIMIRI GERNANDI, Cùm anno ætatis XIII IN MATHESI ET PHILOSOPHIA MAGISTER BASILEÆ crearetur. 4° sig. A^4

837.h.13(15).

Signed: Daniel Heinsius. J. C. Gernandus received his degree at the University of Basel on 15 July 1602, the 'Ode' probably published the same year, printed by the Officina Plantiniana Raphelengii at Leiden.

H65 HEINSIUS, Daniel

DANIELIS HEINSII ORATIO AD MILITES FLANDROS, Qui in expeditione Flandrica . . . duce . . . Principe Mauritio Nassouio, militabant. LVGDVNI BATAVORVM. Ex Officinâ Thomæ Basson, 1605. 4° pp. 8

835.f.16(12).

H66 HEINSIUS, Daniel

DANIELIS HEINSII ORATIO, AD Nobilissimos, Amplissimos, Clarissimosq; CVRATORES, PROFESSORES, & reliqua illustris LUGDUNO-BATAVÆ Academiæ membra: Lectionibus publicis in Horatium præmissa IX. Septembris M.D.CII. EX OFFICINA PLANTINIANA RAPHELENGII. M.D.CII. 4° pp. 20

837.h.13(14).

Published at Leiden.

H67 HEINSIUS, Daniel

DANIELIS HEINSII ORATIO, DE CONIVNGENDIS GRÆCORVM LINGVA ET DISCIPLINIS . . . LVGDVNI BATAVORVM Apud Ioh. Orlers, And. Cloucq, & Ioh. Maire. M.d.C.XI [*sic*]. 4° sig. AB^4C^2

624.f.2(3).

Misbound; C1 following B3, C2 following B1. Printed by Henrick van Haestens?

H68 HEINSIUS, Daniel

DANIELIS HEINSI[I] ORATIO De prima Romanorum ætate, & prima eius pop. virtute. Habita, cum in L. Annæo Floro, ad primum bellum Punicum peruenisset. LVGDVNI BATAVORVM, Apud LVDOVICVM ELZEVIRIUM . . . M D CXIV. 4° pp. 27

589.d.19(1).

Printed in italics. The titlepage is slightly mutilated, the date in the imprint is badly printed. Printed by Henrick van Haestens?

H69 HEINSIUS, Daniel

DANIEL. HEINSII. ORATIO, HABITA Cum THEOCRITVM auspicaretur In Auditorio Philosophico. LVGDVNI BATAVORVM, Apud Iohannem Maire, M.D.CIII. 4° pp. 16

837.h.13(17).

With the printer's device of Thomas Basson. With manuscript notes.

H70 HEINSIUS, Daniel

DAN. HEINSII PANEGYRICI DVO, Illustri Viro IOSEPHO SCALIGERO DICTI. EX OFFICINA PLANTINIANA RAPHELENGIJ. M.D.CVIII. 4° pp. 32

610.k.17(3).

The second panegyric is in verse. Published at Leiden.

H71 HEINSIUS, Daniel

DANIELIS HEINSII PEPLVS GRÆCORVM EPIGRAMMATVM: In quo omnes celebriores

Græciæ Philosophi, encomia eorum, vita, & opiniones recensentur, aut exponuntur. LVGDVNI BATAVORVM, Ex officina Ioannis Patij . . . M D CXIII. Prostant apud LVDOVICVM ELZEVIRIVM. 4° pp.32
610.k.17(4); 832.i.21.

In Greek, with an introduction in Latin. The copy at 832.i.21 with translations into English added in manuscript [by Edward Ward?] and the price: 6d, dated: 1710.

H72 HEINSIUS, Daniel
[Quaeris quid sit amor.] [Emblemata amatoria: iam demum emendata.] (col.) T'AMSTELREDAM. By Dirck Pietersz . . . 1608. obl.4° sig.A-H^4; illus.
11555.aaa.60(2).

Poems in Dutch, mottoes in Latin, French or Italian. The dedicatory poem 'Aende ioncvrouwen van Hollandt' signed: Theocritus a Ganda, the pseudonym used for the first edition, entitled 'Quaeris quid sit amor'. Printed in civilité. The engravings are by Jacques de Gheyn. Imperfect; wanting the titlepage for which a manuscript title reading 'Flora's lusthof', has been substituted. The above title has been transcribed from a copy at Amsterdam University Library. This copy corresponds to the edition described in *Breugelmans* no.I5.

H73 HEINSIUS, Daniel
[Quaeris quid sit amor.] EMBLEMATA Amatoria: Iam demum emendata. (col.) T'AMSTELREDAM. By Dirck Pietersz. . . . 1612. obl.4° sig.A-H^4; illus.
11556.ccc.14.

The poem 'Aende ioncvrouwen van Hollandt' signed: Theocritus à Gauda [*sic*]', pseudonym of Daniel Heinsius. The correct form 'Theocritus a Ganda' and the author's real name have been inserted in the lower panels of the titlepage which is engraved. The engravings are by Jacques de Gheyn. This copy corresponds to the edition described in *Breugelmans* no.I7.

H74 HEINSIUS, Daniel
[Quaeris quid sit amor.] EMBLEMATA ALIQVOT AMATORI[A] D. Danielis Heinsii cum additamento aliorū nunc primum in lucem edito. obl.4° sig.A,ff.9–66[67]; illus.
C.125.cc.8.

A selection from 'Quaeris quid sit amor' with additional poems by Heinsius and others. The circular engravings here in square frames and with mottoes in Latin. Two coats of arms have been printed on the endpapers. The final 'A' of 'AMATORIA' in the title is hidden by an engraved figure. Published ca.1620. Corresponding to the copy described in *Breugelmans* no.III.

HEINSIUS, Daniel. Satirae duae. 1608; 1617. *See* above: Hercules.

H75 HEINSIUS, Daniel
DANIELIS HEINSII SOCRATES: Siue, De moribus & vita Socratis Oratio. Habita cum Vitam illius philosophi a Diogene Laertio descriptam, inchoaturus esset. LVGDVNI BATAVORVM, Excudebat Henricus Ludovici ab Haestens . . . M.DC.XII. 4° sig.$\star^2$A-C^4
520.c.20(4).

H76 HEINSIUS, Daniel
SPIEGEL VANDE Doorluchtige, eerlicke, Cloucke, Deuchtsame ende verstandege [*sic*] vrouwen: Genomen wt diveersche Griexsche eñ Latijnsche war-historyschryvers . . . Met . . . constige coperen Platen verciert eñ rijmswyse Beschreven door Theocritū à Ganda. Jodocus Hondius exc. Amsterdami 1606. obl.4° pp.(4),ff.8; illus.
11557.de.62.

Pseudonymous. The text is in verse. The titlepage engraved by Jodocus Hondius, the illustrations by Jacques de Gheyn.p. [(5)] = f.1r consists of a half-title dated 1607.

H77 HELDER

Een HELDER LICHT, Daer in klaerlick ghesien wort/dat d'Arminianen niet alleen de oorsaecke zijn van de hedendaechsche twisten der Kercken ende Landen/etc. Maer datse oock arbeyden . . . om de oude ware Gereformeerde Religie . . . uyt te roeyen . . . Alles vervatet . . . in tvve brieven, Den eenen uyt Bruyssel/door Iob Eenvout, Den anderen door Vrederijck Goemaer uyt AMSTERDAM [etc.] (col.) Inden Jare 1617. 4° pp.64
T.2247(48).

The names of the two correspondents are as fictitious as the letter form itself. With manuscript notes.

H78 HELMICH, Warner

Grondich Bericht van de wettelijcke beroepinghe der Predicanten . . . Mitdsgaders [*sic*] vande noodtwendicheydt des Kercken-raedts . . . Eertijdts beschreven door . . . VVERNERVM HELMICHIVM . . . Nu . . . wtghegheven door eenen die van herten wenscht ende bidt dat alles inden Huyse Godes met orden . . . mach toegaen. TOT DELF, By Jan Andriesz . . . M.D.C.XI. (col.) TOT SCHIEDAM. Ghedruct by Adriaen Cornelisz van Delf . . . M.D.C.XI. 4° sig.A-E[4]
T.2241(20).

H79 HELWYS, Thomas

AN ADvertisement or admonition, unto the Congregations, vvhich men call the New Fryelers, in the lowe Countries. wrirten [*sic*] in Dutche. Aud [*sic*] Publiched [*sic*] in Englis [*sic*]. VVherein is handled 4. Principall pointes of Religion . . . After these followes certen demandes concerning Gods decree of salvation and condemnation . . . 1611. 8° pp.93
702.c.32.

Addressed to the Mennonites. The preface signed: Thomas Helwys. Probably printed in the Netherlands.

H80 HELWYS, Thomas

OBIECTIONS: Answered by way of Dialogue, wherein is proved . . . That no man ought to be persecuted for his religion, so he testifie his allegeance by the Oath, appointed by Law . . . 1615. 8° pp.80
C.123.ff.4.

Anonymous. Also sometimes attributed to John Murton. The spelling 'Henry De 8.' in the introduction points to the Netherlands as place of printing. Leaf C6 is mutilated.

HEMELSCH. 'Themelsch synodus ende rechtmatigh oordeel. 1620. *See* NEOMAGUS, Arnoldus

H81 HEMMINGSEN, Niels

[Tractatus de gratia universali.] NICOLAI HEMMINGII, TRACTAET Vande Alghemeyne/ofte allen Menschen Salighe Ghenade. Wt de Latijnsche, in onse Nedereuytsche [*sic*] Sprake . . . overgheset, door B.H. . . . TOT ROTTERDAM, By Matthys Bastiaenssz . . . 1611. 4° sig.(∴)A-L[4]M[1]
T.2241(14).

H82 HENDLERUS, Andreas

DISPVTATIO MEDICA DE VTERI SVFFOCATIONE, Quam . . . pro indipiscendis, in MEDICINA, DOCTORATVS insignibus, & privilegijs . . . defendet ANDREAS HENDLERVS ZYLLENTIANVS, MARCHICVS . . . LVGDVNI BATAVORVM, Excudit Ioannes Patius . . . 1617. 4° sig.A[4]
1185.g.1(64).

With a laudatory poem in Greek. Entered in the General Catalogue under MARCHICUS.

H83 HENDRICKSZ, Lambert

Copye vanden Brieff gheschreven van Capiteyn Lambert/aende . . . ghecommitteerde Raden der Admiraliteyt binnen Rotterdam. Inhoudende Hoe de Hollantsche Armade/onder 'tbeleydt vanden Generael Heemskerck/heeft ghecombatteert/ende oock overwonnen/negen groote Gallioenen/mitsgaders noch sommige Oorlochschepen vanden Coninck van Spaignien/legghende inde Baye ende voor de Stadt Gibalter. TOT DELF Ghedruckt by Jan Andriesz. [etc.] 4° 2 unsigned leaves; illus.

1578/336.

Signed: Lambrecht Heyndricksz. The titlepage woodcut shows a man-of-war. Published in 1607.

H84 HENSBERGH, Vincentius

[Den geestelijcken rooselaer.] VIRIDARIVM MARIANVM Septemplici Rosario, varijs Exercitijs, Exemplis vt Plantationibus peramœnum . . . Auctore F. VINCENTIO HENSBERGIO . . . ANTVERPIÆ APVD GASPAREM BELLERVM. M.DC.XV. 12° pp.527; illus.

3456.c.57.

Largely a translation of 'Den geestelijcken rooselaer'. The titlepage is engraved. With partly emblematic engravings variously ascribed to Theodoor Galle or Adriaen Collaert.

HERCULANUS, Martinus. Theses medicæ de intestin. vermibus. 1605. *See* VORSTIUS, Aelius Everardus

HERCULES tuam fidem. 1608. *See* HEINSIUS, Daniel

H85 HEREMITA, Giulio

(tp.1) DI GIVLIO HEREMITA . . . IL PRIMO LIBRO DE MADRIGALI A SEI VOCI. NOVAMENTE POSITI IN LVCE. CANTO. IN ANVERSA. Appresso Pietro Phalesio. M.D.C.II.

(tp.2) DI GIVLIO HEREMITA . . . IL PRIMO LIBRO DE MADRIGALI A SEI VOCI . . . ALTO. IN ANVERSA. Appresso Pietro Phalesio. M.D.C.II.

(tp.3) DI GIVLIO HEREMITA . . . IL PRIMO LIBRO DE MADRIGALI A SEI VOCI . . . TENORE. IN ANVERSA. Appresso Pietro Phalesio. M.D.C.II.

(tp.4) DI GIVLIO HEREMITA . . . IL PRIMO LIBRO DE MADRIGALI A SEI VOCI . . . BASSO. IN ANVERSA. Appresso Pietro Phalesio. M.D.C.II. obl.4° 4 pt.: ff.12; 12; 12; 12

Music A.214.

H86 HERGUNDUS, Gangolphus

Kort verhael OFT Memorien/van den wonderlicken gheschiedenissen/aenslaghen/verandering/ende . . . Tyrannije/deur de IESVITEN aenghestift ende uytghericht in't Stift ende Stadt PADERBORN. In vier Boecken verdeylet deur GANGOLPHVS HERGVNDVS . . . Ghedruckt in't Jaer . . . 1605. 4° pp.62

4091.aaa.9.

Pseudonymous? Without imprint; printed by Hillebrant Jacobsz van Wouw at The Hague?

H87 HERLS, Cornelius

RESPONSIO AD APOLOGIAM IACOBI LANSBERGII, qua & parentis sui, & D. Davidis Vltralæi placita de Moscho tuetur. Authore CORNELIO HERLS . . . MIDDELBVRGI, Apud Symonem Moulert . . . 1613. 8° pp.39

1176.b.4(4).

H88 HERMANN, Gabriel

[Warhafftige History, von dem gerichtlichen Process.] Waerachtighe beschrijvinge: Des gherichtlicken Proces gehouden tot Sursee teghen Martijn van Voysin, Borger ende Passement-wercker tot Basel/om de belijdenisse des Evangelij/waer door hy veroordeelt is gheworden/om . . . onthooft eñ . . .

verbrant te worden: Midtsaders [*sic*] een verhael van sommighe omstandicheden . . . Ende dit alles den derden Octobris 1608 . . . Met noch een Christelick Sermoon vande eere Marie . . . Gedaen tot Basel den neghenden Octobris 1608. door Johannem Jacobum Grynaeum . . . Wt de Hoochduytsche sprake in onse Nederlantsche tale getrouwelick overgesedt. Door Iohannem Coitsium . . . Gedruckt tot Arnhem, By Ian Ianszen . . . M.VI^{C}.IX. 4° sig.AB^4
T.1716(16); T.2417(16); T.2420(28).
Signed: Gabriel Herman; better known as Hermann.

H89 HERPENER, Peter de
Een Factie oft Spel/openbaerlijc vanden Violieren binnen Antwerpen ghespeelt/ tot verheuginge der Ghemeynten/door de blijde tijdinge des Bestandts. Gheordinneert ende in dichte ghestelt door Peter de Herpener . . . gheprint t'Antwerpen by Gillis van Diest. 4° sig.AB^4
11556.cc.35; 108.a.24.
In verse. Published in 1609.

HERTOGINNE Celia. 1617. *See* RODENBURGH, Theodore

H90 HESIOD
[Works] (tp.1) ΗΣΙΟΔΟΥ . . . τὰ εὑρισκομενα. HESIODI . . . quæ extant, Cum Græcis SCHOLIIS, Procli, Moschopuli . . . Accessit liber singularis, in quo doctrina E''ργων καὶ Ἡμερων . . . ostenditur; ITEM Notæ, emendationes, obseruationes, & Index . . . Opera & studio DANIELIS HEINSII. EX OFFICINA PLANTINIANA RAPHELENGIJ. M.D.CIII.
(tp.2) DANIELIS HEINSI INTRODVCTIO in doctrinam, quæ libris Hesiodi E''ΡΓΩΝ ΚΑῚ Η'ΜΕΡΩ^Ν continetur . . . ITEM NOTÆ, EMENDATIONES, OBSERVATIONES . . . Accedit INDEX GRÆCVS . . . EX OFFICINA PLANTINIANA RAPHELENGIJ. M.D.CIII. 4° 2 pt.: pp.329; 159
C.83.d.7; 75.e.2.
Published at Leiden.

H91 HESIOD
[Works] ΗΣΙΟΔΟΥ . . . τὰ εὑρισκόμενα. HESIODI . . . quæ extant. DANIEL HEINSIVS Interpretationem . . . emendauit. Introductionem . . . item Notas, addidit. LVGDVNI BATAVORVM. Ex officina Ioannis Patij . . . M.D.CXIII. Prostant in Bibliopolio Commeliniano. 8° pp.312
997.b.13; G.17209.
The Commeliani's bookshop was also at Leiden. Ownership inscriptions, in the copy at 97.b.13: Thom. Otes; Ioh. Mauritius; in the copy at G.17209: Diodatus de Pontibus; Edmund Anderson and others; on the binding: Philippus Bourdonneau and the arms of Pierre Hurault, Count de Chiverny.

H92 HESYCHIUS of Miletus
[Works] HESYCHII . . . Opuscula, partim hactenus non edita. IOANNES MEVRSIVS Græcè ac Latinè simul primus vulgavit, cum NOTIS. His adjecta, BESSARIONIS Epistola Græcobarbara. LVGDVNI BATAVORVM Ex Officina GODEFRIDI BASSON. M.D.C.XIII. 8° pp.295
609.c.23.
With material by Hadrianus Junius and Henri Estienne. Dedicated to Johan van Oldenbarnevelt. From the library of John Morris.

H93 HEURNIUS, Joannes
[Works] (tp.1) IOANNIS HEVRNII . . . OPERA OMNIA. Edidit . . . OTTHO HEVRNIVS . . . EX OFFICINA PLANTINIANA RAPHELENGIJ, M.D.C.XI.

(tp.2=sig.°1) I. HEVRNII . . . INSTITVTIONES MEDICINÆ. Editio altera, priore emendatior, operâ . . . OTTHONIS HEVRNII . . . EX OFFICINA PLANTINIANA RAPHELENGIJ, M.D.C.XI.
(tp.3) IOANNIS HEVRNII . . . PRAXIS MEDICINÆ NOVA RATIO . . . Editio postrema, emendatior, operâ . . . OTTHONIS HEVRNII. EX OFFICINA PLANTINIANA RAPHELENGII, M.DC.IX. 4° pt.1, 2: pp.176; 376: pl.V; illus.
542.b.1.
Published at Leiden. Imperfect; wanting all after pt.2.

H94 HEURNIUS, Joannes
IOANNIS HEVRNII . . . DE GRAVISSIMIS MORBIS MVLIERVM LIBER, DE HVMANA FELICITATE LIBER, & DE MORBIS NOVIS ET MIRANDIS EPISTOLA. Edidit post mortem Auctoris . . . OTTHO HEVRNIVS . . . EX OFFICINA PLANTINIANA RAPHELENGIJ, M.D.CVII. 4° pp.101
1176.d.1(1).
The second work addressed to Petrus Forestus. Published at Leiden.

H95 HEURNIUS, Joannes
IOANNIS HEVRNII . . . DE MORBIS VENTRICVLI LIBER: RESPONSVM Ad . . . IOANNEM BANCHEMIVM . . . Nullum esse aquæ innatationem Lamiarum indicium: ORATIO De Medicinæ origine . . . Edidit post mortem auctoris . . . OTTHO HEVRNIVS . . . EX OFFICINA PLANTINIANA, RAPHELENGIJ, M.D.C.VIII. 4° pp.62
1176.d.1(2).
Published at Leiden.

H96 HEURNIUS, Justus
DE LEGATIONE EVANGELICA AD INDOS CAPESSENDA ADMONITIO IVSTI HEVRNII . . . LVGDVNI BATAVORVM, Ex Officinâ ELZEVIRIANA . . . M.D.C.XVIII. (col.) LVGDVNI BATAVORVM, Typis ISAACI ELZEVIRI . . . M.D.C.XVIII. 8° pp.299
867.d.9.
With a letter from Joannes Polyander.

H97 HEURNIUS, Otto
BABYLONICA, INDICA, ÆGYPTIA, &c. Philosophiæ primordia: Auctore OTTHONE HEVRNIO . . . Lugduni Batauorum Apud IOANNEM MAIRE M.D.C.XIX. 16° pp.314
524.a.24.
Author's presentation copy to Jacob Bernard Welstriens, dated 1622.

H98 HEURNIUS, Otto
DISPVTATIO MEDICA DE HYDROPE Quam . . . PRÆSIDE . . . D. OTTHONE HEVRNIO . . . publicè defendere conabitur IOHANNES LE PIPER . . . Lugduni Batavorum, Ex officinâ ZACHARIAE SMETII. M.D.C.XXI. 4° sig.H⁴
1185.g.2(11).

H99 HEURNIUS, Otto
DISPVTATIO MEDICA DE HYDROPE, Quam . . . SVB PRÆSIDIO . . . D. OTHONIS HEVRNII . . . Publicè . . . tueri conabitur CAROLVS LEONHARDVS . . . LVGDVNI BATAVORVM, Ex Officinâ THOMÆ BASSON, M.D.C.X. 4° sig.A-D⁴
1185.g.1(43).

H100 HEURNIUS, Otto
DISPVTATIO MEDICA DE PLEVRITIDE, QVAM . . . PRAESIDE . . . D. OTTHONE HEVRNIO . . . defendendam suscipiet Segerus Weierstrass . . . LVGDVNI-BATAVORVM, Excudebat Henricus Ludovicus ab Haesterns . . . 1610. 4° sig.A⁴B⁶
1185.g.1(39).
With the date of the examination added in manuscript.

H101 HEURNIUS, Otto

THESES MEDICÆ DE DYSENTERIA. Quas . . . PRÆSIDE . . . D. OTHONE HEVRNIO . . . Publicè examinandas proponit CLEMENS ROSÆVS . . . Lugduni Batavorum, Ex officina ZACHARIÆ SMETII, M.D.CXXI. 4° sig.F^4
1185.g.2(9).

H102 HEURNIUS, Otto

THESES MEDICÆ DE PHRENITIDE VERA QUAS . . . PRÆSIDE OTHONE . . . HEVRNIO . . . Publicè defendere annitetut [*sic*] GVILIELMVS NIVELLIVS . . . Lugduni Batavorum, Ex officinâ ZACHARIÆ SMETII, M.D.CXXI. 4° sig.B^4
1185.g.2(4).

H103 HEURNIUS, Otto

THESES MEDICÆ DE PLEVRITIDE QUAS . . . PRÆSIDE . . . D. D. OTHONE HEVRNIO . . . Publicæ censuræ subijcit [*sic*] GVILIELMVS LIBERGEN . . . Lugduni Batavorum, Ex officinâ ZACHARIÆ SMETII, M.D.CXXI. 4° sig.D^4
1185.g.2(6); 1185.g.2(8).

HEYNDRICKSZ, Lambrecht. *See* HENDRICKSZ, Lambert

H104 HEYNS, Zacharias

CONST-THOONENDE IVWEEL, By de loflijcke stadt Haerlem/ten versoecke van Trou moet blijcken, in't licht gebracht. Waer inne duydelick verclaert ende verthoont wordt alles wat den Mensch mach wecken om den Armen te troosten . . . In tvvaelf Spelen van Sinne/soo weel Intreden/Refereynen ende Liedekens ghestelt in Redenrijck naer de . . . voorgegevene Caerte van 't Speel-korenken. TOT ZWOL, By ZACHARIAS HEYNS, 1607. [etc.] 4° sig.A-Ss^4: plates; illus., music
C.175.ff.13(1); G.18275.

Compiled by Zacharias Heyns. Printed partly in civilité. The copy at C.175.ff.13(1) contains the folding plates as well as the 'Dancksegginghe' on the additional leaves Cc2,3. The copy at G.18275 is without the Latin dedication to the States General and the Dutch dedication to the city of Haarlem and has differences in the plates.

H105 HEYNS, Zacharias

DRACHT-THONEEL VVAER OP HET FATSOEN van meest alle de kleedren, Soo vvel der gener diemen nu ter tyt de gansche Weirelt door dragende is, als de oude afgeleyde eygentlyck afgebeelt synde, ten thoon gestelt ende . . . in rym beschreven wordt. TOT AMSTERDAM By Zacharias Heyns [etc.] 8° sig.A-H^8I^{10}
C.104.a.16.

Woodcuts. The author's as well as publisher's dedication to the Chamber 'Uyt Levender Ionsten' signed: Zacharias Heyns, and dated: 1 July 1601.

H106 HEYNS, Zacharias

Haerlems Juweel/Tot nut vande oude Arme uyt liefden ten thoon ghestelt nae de voorgegevene Caerte vant Speelcorentken. Tot Zwol/By Sacharias Heyns . . . 1608. 4° sig.A-C^4: plate; illus.
G.18275(2).

Anonymous. The illustration shows the engraved blazon of the Chamber 'Het wit Angierken van Haerlem'.

H107 HEYNS, Zacharias

HAERLEMS IVWEEL Tot nut vande oude Armen uyt liefde ten thoon ghestelt nae de voorghegevene Caerte van 'tSpeelcorentken. TOT ZWOL, By ZACHARIAS HEYNS . . . 1608. 4° sig.A-F^4: plates; illus., music
C.175.ff.13(2).

Anonymous. Printed partly in civilité. With two additional unsigned preliminary leaves.

H108 HEYNS, Zacharias

Jeucht SPIEGHEL door Z.G.H.P.H.S A° 1610. Allerhand Kurtzweilige Stücklein allen Studenten . . . zu lieb [etc.] obl.4° sig.A-D^4; illus.

555.a.32.

Anonymous. Dutch, with captions to the illustrations in German or German and Latin. One leaf printed in civilité. Leaf C3 erroneously given the same plate as leaf D1. Printed by Jan Jansz at Arnhem? The titlepage is engraved.

HEYNS, Zacharias. Vervolgh vande Weken van Bartas. 1628. *See* SALUSTE DU BARTAS, Guillaume de. Werken. 1621,28. vol.3.

HIBERNIAE sive antiquioris Scotiae vindiciae. 1621. *See* FLEMING, Richard

H109 HICHTUM, Johan van

Een tsamensprekinghe Van twee boersche persoonen/Wouter ende Tialle, Beschryvende den Bruyloft staet van den Edelen . . . MARCO à LYCKLEMA . . . ENDE Der Edele . . . Iuffrou, PERCK VAN GOSLINGA . . . Tot Leeuwarden, Voor Berent Arentsz . . . 1609. 4° sig.A^4

T.2420(33).

Anonymous. In a mixture of Dutch and Frisian, in verse.

H110 HIDALGO, Gaspar Lucas

DIALOGOS DE APACIBLE ENTRETENIMIENTO, Que contiene vnas Carnestolendas de Castilla . . . Compuesto por Gaspar Lucas Hidalgo . . . EN BRVSSELAS, Por Roger Velpius . . . 1610. [etc.] 12° ff.135

245.b.37.

H111 HIERON, Samuel

[A defence of the ministers reasons, for refusall of subscription to the Booke of Common prayer, and to Conformitie. 1607.] (tp.1=leaf★1) THE SECOND PARTE OF THE Defence of the Ministers Reasons For refusal of Subscription & Conformitie to the book of Common prayer. AGAINST THE SEVERAL ANSWERS OF Th. Hutton . . . in his two books against the Minist. of Dev. & Cornwel. William Covel . . . Th. Spark . . . Fran. Mason . . . Imprinted. 1608.

(tp.2=p.1) THE SECOND PARTE OF THE DEFENSE OF THE MINISTERS REASONS for refusal of subscription to the Booke of Comon praier, and of Conformity &c. Imprinted in the yere 1608. 4° pp.243

698.g.39; 109.a.16.

Anonymous. The second part tentatively assigned to the press of Jodocus Hondius at Amsterdam, part of it almost certainly from that press. Pt.1, of 1607, and a third part, entitled 'A dispute upon the question of kneeling . . . or A third parte of the Defence of the Ministers Reasons', of 1608, have been assigned to the secret press of William Jones in London, which may also have printed the first titlepage and the preliminary leaves of pt.2.

H112 HIGGONS, Theophilus

(tp.1) THE FIRST MOTIVE OF T. H. MAISTER OF ARTS, AND LATELY MINISTER, TO SVSPECT THE INTEGRITY OF HIS Religion: Which was DETECTION OF FALSEHOOD in D. Humfrey, D. Field, & other learned Protestants, touching the question of Purgatory, and Prayer for the dead. VVith his PARTICVLAR CONSIDERATIONS perswading him to embrace the Catholick doctrine . . . An Appendix intituled TRY BEFORE YOV TRVST. Wherein Some notable vntruths of D. Field, and D. Morton are discouered . . . 1609.

(tp.2) TRY BEFORE YOV TRVST . . . BY T.H. Maister of Arts, and lately Minister . . . 1609. 8° pp.172; 70

3935.a.40.

The preface signed: Theophilus Hyggons. Without imprint; printed by Pierre Auroi at Douai.

H113 HILLE, Cornelis van; the Younger

CORTE Ende Vvaerachtige Verantwoordinghe over de Proceduren ende Resolutien die de Vroedtschappen van Alckmar/gelijck teghen andere/als insonderheyt over ende teghen Cornelium Hillenium op den 17. Julij Anno 1610. hebben ghenomen. Ghestelt vveghen het meeste ende voornaemste deel der Ghemeynte Iesu Christi tot Alckmar . . . Ghedruct t'Enchuysen, By Jacob Lenaertsz. Meyn . . . 1610. 4° pp.144

T.2240(22).

The introduction signed: Cornelius Hillenius.

H114 HILLE, Cornelis van; the Younger

PROVISIONELE Ontdeckinge eeniger misslaghen, de welcke Adolphus Venator onder den naem der Burgh-meesteren, Vroetschappen ende Kerckenraedt van Alcmaer, tegen het (soo hy't . . . naemt) Lasterboeck Cornelij Hillenij . . . in sijn boeck, ghenaemt Nootvvendich Historisch verhael: heeft begaen . . . Tot Franeker/Ghedruckt by Vldericum Balck . . . 1611. 4° pp.120

T.2241(3).

The preface signed: Cornelius Hillenius.

H115 HINCHLOUS, Henricus

THESES INAVGVRALES DE SANGVINIS MISSIONE. Quas . . . Pro Doctorali Laurea in Medicina consequendo . . . Exagitandas proponit HENRICVS HINCHLOÜS . . . LVGDVNI BATAVORVM, Typis ISAACI ELZEVIRI . . . M DC.XVII. 4° sig.A^4

1185.c.2(17).

H116 HIPPOCRATES

[Aphorisms. Latin and Greek] HIPPOCRATIS COI APHORISMI Græcè, & Latinè. Breui Enarratione, fidaque Interpretatione . . . illustrati . . . Cum historiis, obseruationibus, cautionibus, & remediis selectis. A [*sic*] I. HEVRNIO . . . Ex Officina Plantiniana, APVD CHRISTOPHORVM RAPHELENGIVM . . . M.DC.I. 16° pp.512

774.a.12; 1506/816.

Published at Leiden.

H117 HIPPOCRATES

[Aphorisms. Latin] (tp.1) PETRI ANDREÆ CANONHERII . . . In septem Aphorismorum Hippocratis libros, Medicæ, Politicæ, Morales, ac Theologicæ Interpretationes. VOLVMEN PRIMVM. Materias politicas complectens . . . ANTVERPIÆ Apud PETRVM & IOANNEM Belleros M.DC.XVIII.

(tp.2) PETRI ANDREÆ CANONHERII . . . In septem Aphorismorum Hippocratis libros . . . Interpretationes. Volumen Secundum Materias morales ac Theologicas, & multas etiam Politicas complectens . . . ANTVERPIÆ Apud PETRVM & IOANNEM Belleros M.DC.XVIII.

(tp.3) PETRI ANDREÆ CANONHERII . . . In septem Aphorismorum Hippocratis libros . . . Interpretationes. Volumen Tertium Materias morales ac Theologicas, & multas etiam Politicas complectens . . . ANTVERPIÆ Apud PETRVM & IOANNEM Belleros M.DC.XVIII. 4° 3 pt.: pp.843; 725; 289

539.f.11,12.

The pagination of vol.1 is very irregular.

H118 HIPPOCRATES

[De capitis vulneribus. Greek and Latin] (tp.1) PETRI PAAW . . . SVCCENTVRIATVS ANATOMICVS. continens Commentaria in Hippocratem, de CAPITIS VVLNERIBVS. additæ In aliquot Capita libri VIII. C. Celsi Explicationes . . . LVGDVNI BATAVORVM, Apud IODOCVM COLSTER . . . M D CXVI.

(tp.2) A. CORNELII CELSI DE RE MEDICA liber octavus. Ejus priora quatuor Capita Commentarijs illustrata à PETRO PAAVV. LVGDVNI BATAVORVM, Apud IODOCVM à COLSTER . . . M D CXVI. 4° 2 pt.: pp.270; 128: plates; illus., port.
539.e.20; 541.a.6.
An edition of the text. The signatures of the two parts are continuous. The portrait is of P. Paauw. The plate of the anatomy lesson opposite pt.1.p.1 signed: I.D. Gheyn inu. Andr. Stoc. Scul. The copy at 541.a.6 is imperfect; wanting two of the plates.

H119 HISTOIRE
HISTOIRE ADMIRABLE Du Iuif errant. Où est prouué par le tesmoignage des Anciens Philosophes; comme l'homme peut prolonger sa vie, outre le commun cours de nature. Auec la description de la Sentence où arrest des Sanguinaires Iuifs, contre Iesus Christ le Sauueur du monde; Et comme ledit Iuif . . . est encores viuant-errant par le monde . . . A ANVERS, Par THOMAS ARNAVD D'ARMOSIN [etc.] 8° pp.16
12411.aa.12.
Published ca.1620?

HISTOIRE chronologique, de plusieurs grands capitaines. 1617. *See* MALINGRE, Claude

HISTOIRE de Aurelio, et Isabelle. 1608. *See* FLORES, Juan de

HISTOIRE des miracles advenuz n'agueres . . . au lieu dit Mont-aigu. 1604; 1605. *See* NUMAN, Philips

L'HISTOIRE des miracles faicts par l'intercession de nostre Dame de Mont-Serrat. 1601. *See* BURGOS, Pedro Alfonso de

HISTOIRE du massacre de plusieurs religieux. 1620. *See* FIGUEROA, Francisco

HISTOIRE du pays nommé Spitsberghe. 1613. *See* GERRITSZ, Hessel

HISTORIA admirandarum curationum. 1601. *See* CHAPEAVILLUS, Joannes

HISTORIA de los siete infantes de Lara. 1612. *See* VEEN, Otto van

HISTORIA septem infantium de Lara. 1612. *See* VEEN, Otto van

H120 HISTORIAE
HISTORIAE AVGVSTAE scriptores sex . . . ad postremas Cl. V. Is. CASAVB. I. GRVTERI, Cl. SALMASI editiones excusi. LVGDVNI BAT. Ex officina Iacobi Marci. M. ICCXXI [*sic*]. 12° pp.450
587.a.31.

H121 HISTORIAE
HISTORIÆ ROMANÆ Epitomæ LVCII IVLII FLORI, C. VEL. PATERCVLI, SEX. AVR. VICTORIS, SEXTI RVFI FESTI, MESSALÆ CORVINI, M. AVR. CASSIODORI, & EVTROPII. Ex officina Plantiniana RAPHELENGII 1615. 32° pp.1–544
C.20.f.36.
Published at Leiden. Imperfect; wanting pp.129–154, 225–528, and all after p.544. Pp.529–544 are misbound, preceding pp.155–224. From the travelling library of Sir Julius Caesar.

HISTORIE der warachtighe getuygen Jesu Christj. 1617. *See* OUTERMAN, Jacques

HISTORIE ende generale beschrijvinge van die heerlicke victorie die God verleent heeft . . . Iacob van Heemskercke. 1607. *See* SPILBERGEN, Joris van

HISTORIE van B. Cornelis Adriaensen van Dordrecht. 1607. *See* CHRISTIANUS NEUTER

HISTORIE van de kettersche kercke. 1611. *See* DAVID, Jan

H122 HISTORIE

Die historie Van Sandrijn ende Lantsloot . . . TOT ROTTERDAM 4° sig. A-C^{4}D^2; illus.

C.143.ff.34.

In verse. The titlepage is cropped, with the possible loss of the printer's name and date of publication. Printed by Jan van Ghelen, ca. 1610. The titlepage woodcut in black and red shows Sandrijn.

HISTORISCH verhael vande voorneemste swaricheden. 1618. *See* LYDIUS, Joannes

The HISTORY of our B. Lady of Loreto. 1608. *See* TORSELLINO, Orazio

H123 HOCK, Theobaldus

COMMONITORIUM: Sive amica ad amicum ADMONITIO: de ROBERTI BELLARMINI SCRIPTIS atque libris . . . LUGDUNI BATAVORUM apud Christophorum Pacificum. M DC VI. 4° sig. (:)^{2}A-Z, a^4

1116.c.31.

The author's dedication signed: Theobaldus Hock. The imprint is false; printed at Cologne.

H124 HOFF

t'Hoff vanden Paus. Dat is: Een Register van alle Collegien ende Vergaderinghen des Roomschen Levens. VVt den Italiaenschen . . . over-gheset. Ghedruckt int Jaer . . . M.VI^{C}.IX. 4° sig. AB^4

T.2421(1).

Dutch text, with chapter headings in Italian, but not a translation of Girolamo Lunadoro's 'Relazione della corte di Roma'. Without imprint; printed by Jasper de Craeyer at Middelburg?

HOGENHEYM, Theophrastus Paracelsus van. *See* BOMBAST VON HOHENHEIM, Philipp Aureol Theophrast, called Paracelsus

H125 HOGERBEETS, Pieter

PETRI HOGERBETII . . . Poëmatum Reliquiæ. Hornæ VVestfrisiorum Apud Gulielmum Andream . . . M.DC.VI. (col.) TOT HOORN Ghedruckt by Willem Andriessz. [etc.] 8° pp. 40, ff. [i]-[vii]

1213.h.10(1,1*).

The supplementary leaves contain 'Duytsche Gedichten/die behouden zijn/van Pieter Hogerbeets'. The editor's dedication signed: T.V.H., i.e. Theodorus Velius Hornanus.

H126 HOGHENDORP, Gijsbrecht van

TRVER-SPEL Van de Moordt/begaen aen WILHEM . . . Prince van Oraengien/etc. Ghedicht door G. van HOGHENDORP. t'AMSTERDAM, Voor Cornelis vander Plassen . . . 1617. (col.) t'AMSTERDAM, Ghedruckt by Paulus van Ravesteyn . . . 1617. 4° sig. ⋆^{6}A-G^{4}H^3; illus.

11754.bbb.31.

H127 HOLLAND. Hof van Holland

[29.3.1583] COPIE Vande Belijdenisse ende Sententie Capitael van Cornelis de Hoogh. Waer inne ghespeurt werden de aenslaghen ende middelen/welcke den Koninc van Spangien . . . ghebruyckt heeft/omme . . . dese Landen te brengen onder syn absoluyt ghewelt. Allen oprechten Lief-hebbers ende Yveraers der Nederlandtscher Vrijheyt tot vvaerschouvvinghe . . . M.D.C.VIII. 4° sig. A^4

T.2420(14).

The text of the sentence pronounced 29 March 1583, with a commentary.

H128 HOLLAND. Hof van Holland
[29.3.1583] COPYE Vande Belijdenisse ende Sententie Capitael van Cornelis de Hooghe . . . 1608. 4° sig. A^4
T.1713(25); T.1729(7).
Another edition of the preceding.

H129 HOLLAND. Hof van Holland
[19.7.1619] LIGVE Ofte verbintenisse by eenige Predicanten/meest van heuren dienst verlaten/op den vijfden Martij 1619. tot Rotterdam beraemt/ende aende Kercken gesondē/omme de Jngesetenen deser Landen in gestadige verdeeltheden . . . te houden. ENDE De Sententie ter saecke van dien by den Hove van Hollandt over eenige van hemluyden ghevvesen. Mitsgaders De Resolutie vande . . . Staten Generael daer op gevolght . . . in date den negenthiensten Julij 1619 . . . IN S'GRAVEN-HAGHE, By Hillebrant Iacobssz . . . 1619. 4° sig. AB^4
T.2249(46).

H130 HOLLAND. Staten
[1.4.1580] Ordonnantie van de Polityen/Binnen Hollant. IN S'GRAVEN-HAGHE, By Hillebrant Iacobssen . . . 1617. 4° pp. 22
106.a.62(6).
Laws affecting the family, first issued 1 April 1580.

H131 HOLLAND. Staten
[8.3.1591] Kercken-Ordeninghe van den Jare 1591. Door last van de . . . Staten van Hollandt ende West-Vrieslandt in ghestelt. Ende De Resolutie van de selve . . . Staten daer op ghevolght Anno 1612. Belanghende het poinct in't verkiesen van den Kercken-Dienaren . . . TOT DELF. Gedruckt by Ian Andriesz. . . . 1617. 4° pp. 26
T.2247(12).
First issued 8 March 1591.

H132 HOLLAND. Staten
[13.5.1594] Verklaringhe van de Heeren Staten van Hollandt ende West-Vrieslandt/op de Ordonnantie vande Successien. IN S'GRAVEN-HAGHE, By Hillebrant Iacobssen . . . 1617. 4° 2 unsigned leaves
106.c.62(13).
First issued 13 May 1594.

H133 HOLLAND. Staten
[18.12.1599] PLACCAET OP t'stuck vande Successien ab intestato. IN S'GRAVEN-HAGHE, By Hillebrant Iacobssz . . . 1618. 4° sig. A^4
106.c.62(8).
First issued 18 December 1599.

H134 HOLLAND. Staten
[19.12.1601] Verbodt/Van weghen de Heeren Staten van Hollant ende West-Vrieslandt/vande kleyne Munte buyten de zelve Provintien gheslagen: Midtsgaders vanden ghecontrefeyten Philips Daelder tot Campen/ende silverē Gout-gulden in Vrieslant gheslagen . . . IN S'GRAVEN-HAGHE By Aelbrecht Heyndricksz. . . . 1601. [etc.] 4° sig. A^4; illus.
T.1712(14).
Issued 19 December 1601.

H135 [*HOLLAND. Staten
[25.10.1602] PLACCAET PROVISIONEEL Opte tollerantie zekerer Penninghen by de andere Provincien gheslagen/waer op d'selve by provisie inden Lan de [*sic*] van Hollandt ende West-Vrieslandt cours zullen hebben. IN S'GRAVEN-HAGHE, By Aelbrecht Heyndricksz . . . 1602. [etc.] 4° sig. A^3
5686.a.30(6).]

*Destroyed. Described from the General Catalogue and the copy in the Royal Library, The Hague (Plakkaat Q 365(3)). The titlepage verso bears the privilege printed in civilité. Issued 25 October 1602.

H136 HOLLAND. Staten
[19.12.1603] PLACCAET Ende Ordonnantie van de . . . Staten van Hollant ende West-Vrieslant/zo opten cours vanden Gelde/als op de Politie ende Discipline betreffende d'exercitie vander Munte ende Munt-slach/Gout ende Silver-smeeden/Juweliers/ende alle andere. IN S'GRAVEN-HAGHE, By Aelbrecht Heyndricksz . . . 1603. [etc.] 4° sig. AB^4C^6
T.1712(15).

Issued 19 December 1603. Signed in manuscript: S. (or: F.?) De Hondt.

H137 [*HOLLAND. Staten
[19.12.1603] BEELDENAER, Ofte figuer-boeck/dienende op de nieuwe Ordonnantie vander Munte/ghearresteert ende wt-ghegheven by de . . . Staten van Hollandt ende West-Vrieslandt op den XIX^en^ Decembris Anno 1603 . . . IN S'GRAVEN-HAGHE, By Aelbrecht Heyndricsz . . . 1604. [etc.] 4° sig. $A\text{-}F^4G^6$; illus.
5686.a.30(7).]

*Destroyed. Described from the General Catalogue and the copy in the Royal Library, The Hague (523 F 21(2)).

H138 HOLLAND. Staten
[11.3.1610] Sekere Missive geschreven wt den Raet vande . . . Staten/aende Classis van Rotterdam/ghedateert . . . den 11. Martij 1610, daer wt men sien can/het wit ende voornemen D. Arminio . . . Ghedruckt . . . sesthien hondert ende twaelff. 4° 2 unsigned leaves
T.2242(1).

An extract from the letter proclaiming the Hague Conference and forbidding all controversial publications.

H139 HOLLAND. Staten
[29.4.1611] BEDENCKINGEN, Over de Beroepinghe D.D. CONRADI VORSTII, tot de Professie der H. Theologie in de Vniversiteyt tot Leyden, By eenighe Dienaren des Godlicken Woorts Opt begeeren/ende uyt last van de . . . Staten/van Hollandt/ ende West-Frieslandt/voorghestelt/ende . . . overghelevert op den 29. Aprilis . . . 1611 . . . 1611. 4° sig. $A\text{-}D^4$
T.2241(23).

Signed: Ruardus Acronius, and others.

H140 HOLLAND. Staten
[15.7.1614] DECRETVM . . . ORDINVM HOLLANDIÆ ET WESTFRISIÆ PRO PACE ECCLESIARVM, MVNITVM Sacræ Scripturæ auctoritate, & Conciliorum, Antiquorum Patrum, Confessionum publicarum, & recentiorum Doctorum testimonijs. LVGDVNI BATAVORVM Excudit Ioannes Patius . . . M D CXIV. [etc.] 4° pp. 134
3925.k.17.

The Resolution of January 1614, edited by Hugo de Groot, Jan Wtenbogaert and Petrus Bertius. The privilege authorising publication dated 15 July 1614. Ownership inscription: A. Alberthoma(?). With manuscript notes.

H141 HOLLAND. Staten
[15.7.1614] DECRETVM . . . ORDINVM HOLLANDIÆ ET WEST-FRISIÆ PRO PACE ECCLESIARVM . . . Vltraiecti Ex Officina Salomon Rodius [*sic*]. 1614. 4° pp.101
3925.c.44.
Another edition of the preceding, without privilege.

H142 HOLLAND. Staten
[28.7.1614] RESOLVTIE Vande . . . Staten van Hollandt ende West-Vrieslandt. TOT DEN VREDE DER KERCKEN. Versterckt Met d'Authoriteyt der Heyligher Schrift/der Concilien/Oudt-Vaderen . . . Mitsgaders met de ghetuygenissen van sommige Leeraren deses tijdts. Dit leste overgheset uyt het Latijn int Nederduytsch. IN S'GRAVEN-HAGHE, By Hillebrant Iacobsz . . . 1614. [etc.] 4° pp.148
T.2244(5).
Edited by Hugo de Groot, Jan Wtenbogaert and Petrus Bertius. Issued 28 July 1614.

H143 HOLLAND. Staten
[28.7.1614] RESOLVTIE DER . . . Staten van Hollandt ende VVest-vrieslant. Totten Vrede der Kercken Midtsgaders Christelijcke ende nootwendige verclaringhe over dese Resolutie. Met eenighe Vraegh-stucken . . . Ghedruckt int Jaer Ses-thien-hondert ende sesthiene. 4° sig.A^4B^3
T.2246(11).
The Dutch text of the Resolution of 28 July 1614, with a commentary, the 'Christelijcke . . . verclaringhe' written by Jacobus Trigland; the whole edited by him?

H144 HOLLAND. Staten
[17.10.1614] DECRETVM . . . ORDINVM HOLLANDIÆ ET WESTFRISIÆ contra libellum SIBRANDI LVBBERTI inscriptum, RESPONSIO AD PIETATEM HVGONIS GROTII. LVGDVNI BATAVORVM, Excudit Ioannes Patius . . . 1614. 4° sig.A^2
11.a.6(2).
Issued 17 October 1614.

H145 HOLLAND. Staten
[29.6.1616] VERHAEL VANDE HEEREN IONCKER ADRIAN VAN Mathenes . . . Hugo Muys van Holy . . . Gerrit Ianssz vander Eyck . . . Meester Hugo de Groot . . . ende VVillem Pieterssz Hases . . . by de . . . Staten van Hollandt eñ VVest-Vrieslandt . . . gedeputeert, om de . . . Burgemeesteren ende Raden der Stadt Amsterdam te onderrichten van de oprechte intentie van haer Mog. Ed. tot conservatie vãde ware Christelicke Gereformeerde Religie . . . IN S'GRAVEN-HAGHE, By Hillebrant Iacobssz . . . 1616. 4° pp.103
106.d.39.
Consisting chiefly of the speech of Hugo de Groot on 23 April 1616. The privilege allowing publication dated 29 June 1616.

H146 HOLLAND. Staten
[5.8.1617] VERCLARINGHE VANDE . . . STATEN VAN HOLLANDT ENDE VVEST-Vrieslandt, waer by hare Mo. Ed. int kort verthoonen, die oprechte goede meeninghe die sy . . . hebben, omme . . . die ware Christelijcke Ghereformeerde Religie in suyverheydt te behouden; ende waeromme hare Mo. Ed. . . . toe-kompt, Kerckelijcke Wetten te maecken . . . ende om wat redenen sy goet gevonden hebben . . . te ordonneren, Dat die Kercken-dienaers . . . die vande Predestinatie . . . niet anders en konnen leeren, als conform die vijf poincten verhandelt tusschen twaelf Predicanten . . . inden Iare sesthien-hondert elf, mede inde gereformeerde Kercken behooren ghetolereert te worden, soo wel als die anders daer van gevoelen zijn. IN S'GRAVEN-HAGHE, By Hillebrant Iacobssen . . . 1617. [etc.] 4° pp.20
T.2247(11).
Issued 5 August 1617.

H147 HOLLAND. Staten

[14.5.1618] PROCVRATIE By eenighe Steden van Hollant gegeven aen heure gecommitteerden/ter Dach-vaert van de Heeren Staten van Hollant vanden 14 Mey/1618. Stilo Novo. Mitsgaders De Procuratie dien volgende by de Heeren Staten van Vtrecht gegeven aen heure Ghecommitterden [*sic*] ter vergaderinghe van de . . . Staten Generael vanden 3. Junij/1618/Stilo veteri. Met De Verclaringe ende Limitatie . . . op de selve procuratie ghedaen . . . den 10. Junij/1618 . . . IN S'GRAVEN-HAGE, By Hillebrant Jacobsz . . . 1619. 4° sig.A^5
700.h.25(32).

H148 HOLLAND. Staten

[22.6.1618] PLACCAET Omme alomme ghepubliceert ende gheaffigeert te worden . . . IN S'GRAVEN-HAGHE By Hillebrandt Iacobssz . . . 1618. 4° a single sheet
T.2422(10).

Issued 22 June 1618, declaring the 'Provisionele openinghe' to be libellous and offering a reward for the discovery of author and printer.

H149 [*HOLLAND. Staten

[2.12.1620] PLACCAET Provisioneel, Vande . . . Staten van Hollandt ende West-Vrieslandt/opt ontfangen ende uytgeven van alle de Schellinghen eenen Arent voerende/t'zy of deselve inde Geunieerde provintienof [*sic*] dae r [*sic*] gheslaghen zijn. IN S'GRAVEN-HAGHE, By Hillebrant Iacobssz . . . 1620. [etc.] 4° sig.A^4
5686.a.30(11).]

*Destroyed. Described from the General Catalogue and from the copy at Leiden University Library, recorded in *Petit* no.1272. Issued 2 December 1620.

H150 HOLLAND. Staten

[22.4.1621] PLACCAET Op den cours vanden Gelde: Gheemaneert by de . . . Staten van Hollandt ende West-Vrieslandt. IN S'GRAVEN-HAGHE, By Hillebrant Iacobssz . . . 1621. [etc.] 4° sig.AB^4
T.1712(25).

Issued 22 April 1621.

H151 HOLLAND. Staten

[23.4.1621] PLACCAET By de . . . Staten van Hollandt ende West-Vrieslandt/ gheemaneert teghen den uyt-voer vande Materialen op Munten buyten d'selve Landen ghelegen/ende 'topwisselen van alle specien: Mitsgaders tegen t'innebrengen van alle ongevalueerde/vervalschte . . . eñ verboden specien van gelde/van Gout, Silver ofte Koper. IN S'GRAVEN-HAGHE, By Hillebrant Iacobssz . . . 1621. [etc.] 4° sig.A^3
T.1712(26).

Issued 23 April 1621.

H152 HOLLAND, Henry; Bookseller

HERωOLOGIA ANGLICA HOC EST CLARISSIMORVM ET DOCTISSIMORVM, ALIQOUT [*sic*] ANGLORVM, QVI FLORVERVNT AB ANNO CRISTI [*sic*] M.D. VSQ[3] AD PRESENTEM ANNVM M.D.CXX Viuæ Effigies Vitæ et elogia Duobus tomis Authore H. H. Anglo Britanno: Impensis Crispini Passæi Calcographus [*sic*] et Jansonij Bibliopolæ Arnhemiensis. fol. pp.240: plates; illus.
491.i.6(2); 134.c.5; C.38.h.2; G.1453.

The author's name is given in full in several of the laudatory poems. Some of the engraved verses on the portraits are signed: AB, i.e. Arnoldus Buchelius. The two volumes run on, but have each a dedication of its own. The titlepage is engraved. Many of the portraits bear

[Illustrations of ***H152*** *overleaf]*

Pro Christo et Patria dulce periculum est in de Vit…ta.
Angliæ breuis descriptio
Audiui vocem de cœlo dicentem mihi, scribe, Beati mortui qui in Domino moriuntur A modo iam dicit Spūs ut requiescant a laboribus
HERWOLOGIA
ANGLICA
HOC EST
CLARISSIMORVM
ET DOCTISSIMORVM,
ALIQOVT ANGLORVM,
QVI FLORVERVNT AB ANNO
CRISTI .M.D. VSQ' AD
PRESENTEM ANNVM
M.D.C.XX.
Viuæ Effigies Vitæ et elogia
Duobus tomis
Authore H.H. Anglo Britanno:
Impensis Crispini Passæi Calcographi et Jansonij Bibliopolæ
Arnhemensis
LONDON

Ope eruditi Hollandi (quem divitis
Large beavit ingenii
Natura fructibus) priora secula
quos celebrarunt splendido
Viri decore, pectoris facundiam
Ob eruditi, et inclytam
Olim et partam in praelijs victoriam
Cruentis: quos oblivij
in infernis Tenebrae ingratae texerant
Diu latebris abditos.
Ora hi Resumunt, sensus pallidi
Patres, senescebant et qui
Dudum quasi apparatu prodeunt novo,
ex Tenebris eruti.
Te queis Minerva laudibus, Te quo queat
Decore Mavors prosequi!
Eorum alumnos qui perennas laudibus:
Eosque nobis exhibes
Nitore claros pristino, ne praemio
Orbata virtus lugeat.
In aevum Fata longum te superstitent
(Mi docte Hollandi) sospitem.
Et eruditionis sera secula
Tibi rependant praemia,
Nomen nec inclytum tuum senescere
Sinant: tenebris eruis
qui Tenebris Heroës, et splendido
Suo nitori vindicas.

T. Y.

H152 (t.p. verso)

initials of different engravers. Crispijn de Passe was at Utrecht. All the copies differ from each other in the mistakes in pagination especially pp.25, 36, 42 and 49.
The copy at 491.i.6(2) has had the text of the titlepage corrected in manuscript. A manuscript poem on the verso of the titlepage is signed: T.Y., probably Thomas Young, to whom the copy was given by Gulielmus Angellus.
The copy at 134.c.5 is imperfect; wanting leaf E4. An additional leaf bearing a poem by I. Gruterus has been inserted in the preliminaries. An additional index giving the locations of the original paintings from which the engravings are derived, made from manuscript notes found in a copy once owned by P. Mariette and printed in London in 1809 has been prefixed to this copy. The copy at C.38.h.2 is said in a manuscript note on the fly-leaf to have been made up from several copies 'at great expense'. With a manuscript list of the locations of the original portraits said to have been copied from notes allegedly made in another copy soon after publication 'in 1618'.
The copy at G.1453 contains the leaf bearing the poem by Gruterus. The index of portraits belonging to this volume has been bound at the beginning. Various slips bearing additional printed information relating to the portraits have been pasted onto several pages or inserted between them, including the epitaph on Sir Philip Sidney written by James I which has been inserted between pp.74, 75. An extra leaf bearing the engraved motto 'Mysteria mea mihi' and allegorical shields held by an angel, with verses in English on Henry Holland, signed: J. D. Cambro-Britannus, has been inserted at the end. This copy is a presentation copy by the author to Sir Thomas Holland, Knight.

H153 HOLLANDSCHE

Hollandsche Nieuwe Tijdinghen . . . Hoemen in Hollandt de strenghe Placcaten/ die teghen de Arminianen ghemaeckt zijn/soeckt in't werck te stellen . . . met hun het Prediken te beletten eñ de Predicanten te vanghen. Nv eerst Ghedruckt den xxi. Mey 1620. T'Hantwerpen/By Abraham Verhoeuen . . . 1620. [etc.] 4° pp.8; sig.T^4; illus.
P.P.3444.af(52); 1480.aa.15(8).
The titlepage woodcut shows a scene of persecution. The *Bibliotheca Belgica* no.V196 records an issue of 19 May.

HOLLANDTSCHE rijm-kronijk. 1620. *See* STOKE, Melis

HOLLANDUS, Joannes Isaacus. *See* JOANNES ISAACUS; called Hollandus.

H154 HOLLINGERUS, Henricus

REQVESTE Verduytscht uyt de Latijnsche Tale/Aen de . . . Heeren, de Gecommitteerde vande . . . Staten Generael; op den Synode Nationnael, binnen . . . Dordrecht vergadert. Ghedruckt . . . M.DC.XJX. 4° pp.8
T.2249(5).
Signed: H. Hollingerus, expanded within the text to: Henricus.

H155 HOMER

[Iliad. Greek. Book 1] ΤΗΣ ΟΜΗΡΟΥ ΙΛΙΑΔΟΣ ἡ ἄλφα ῥαψῳδία. HOMERI ILIADOS LIBER I. Lugduni Batavorum, Typis, ISAACI ELZEVIRI. Sumptibus, HENRICI LAVRENTII, M DCXIX. 4° pp.31
G.8765(1).
Published at Amsterdam.

H156 HOMER

[Iliad. Greek. Book 2] ΤΗΣ ΟΜΗΡΟΥ ΙΛΙΑΔΟΣ ἡ βῆτα ῥαψῳδία. HOMERI ILIADOS LIBER II. Lugduni Batavorum, Typis, ISAACI ELZEVIRI. Sumptibus, HENRICI LAVRENTII, M DCXX. 4° pp.43
G.8765(2).
Published at Amsterdam.

H157 HOMER

[Iliad. Dutch. Book 1-12] De eerste 12. Boecken VANDE ILYADAS Beschreven in't Griecks door Homerum . . . Wt Griecks in Franschen Dicht vertaeld door M^{r}. Huges Salel . . . Ende nu uyt Francoyschen in Nederduydschen Dicht vertaeld. Door KAREL VAN MANDER . . . Gedruckt t'Haerlem, by Adriaen Rooman, Voor Daniel de Keyzer . . . 1611. 8° pp.392; illus.
11315.b.11.
The woodcut illustrations have been attributed to Christoffel van Sichem.

H158 HOMER

[Iliad. Summaries. Latin and French] SPECVLVM HEROICVM, Principis omnium temporum Poëtarum. HOMERI, Id est argumenta xxiiij. librorum Iliados . . . LES XXIIII. LIVRES D'HOMERE. Reduict en tables demonstratives figurées, par Crespin de Passe . . . Chaque livre redigé en argument Poëticque. Par le Sieur I. Hillaire, Sr de la Riviere . . . Prostant in Officina CR. PASSAEI calcographi. TRAIECTI BATAVORVM, Et Arnhemiæ apud Ioannem Ianssonium . . . MDCXIII. 4° ff.24; port.
11315.c.10; G.8774.
Engravings, with poems in French or Dutch by Isaac Hillaire and the periochae of Ausonius. With an engraved imaginary portrait of Homer on the titlepage and one of Hillaire on sig.*4v.

H159 HOMER

[Odyssey. Dutch. Book 1–12] D'eerste xij. boecken Odysseæ: Dat is, DE DOLINGE VAN VLYSSE, Beschreven int Griecx, door . . . Homerum . . . nu eerstmael uyten Latijne in rijm verduytscht, door DIERICK COORNHERT. Tot Amstelredam. By Hendrick Barentsz. . . . 1607. 8° ff.84
11335.aaa.4.
Ownership inscription: R. F. Charles Priest Lov. 1808; Bought Mechlin Sept. 1818.

H160 HOMMIUS, Festus

Naerder advijs Over de Conferentie tot Delff gehouden/aengaende het Remedieren der yeghenwoordighe swaricheden in de kercken deser Landen opgheresen. T'samen gestelt Door drie Dienaren des Goddelijcken Woorts door last van de . . . Staten van Hollandt . . . ende overghelevert den ix$^{en.}$ November, 1613. Waerinne ghehandelt wort: In wat voegen . . . het verscheyden ghevoelen in de vijf poincten der Remonstranten soude mogen geleert ende getollereert worden. Tot ENCHVYSEN Nae de Copye Ghedruckt by Jacob Lenaertsz. Meyn . . . 1615. 4° pp.56
T.2245(3).
Anonymous. By Festus Hommius, Joannes Becius and Johannes Bogaert. Printed by Paulus van Ravesteyn at Amsterdam. The Enkhuizen imprint probably part of the copy imprint and not applicable to this edition. With manuscript notes.

H161 HOMMIUS, Festus

ORATIO FESTI HOMMII, Qua Discipulos compellavit, Cum à Nobilissimis . . . Academiæ Leydensis CVRATORIBVS, & Civitatis Leydensis CONSVLIBVS . . . Collegij Theologici Ill. Ordinum Hollandiæ & West-Frisiæ regimini . . . publice præficeretur . . . LVGDVNI BATAVORVM, Ex officina IACOBI MARCI . . . M.D.CXX. 4° sig.A-C^{4}
491.b.19(3).

H162 HOMMIUS, Festus

SPECIMEN CONTROVERSIARVM BELGICARVM, Seu CONFESSIO ECCLESIARVM REFORMATARVM IN BELGIO, Cujus singulis Articulis subjuncti sunt ARTICVLI DISCREPANTES, in quibus nonnulli Ecclesiarum Belgicarum doctores hodie à recepta Doctrinâ dissentire videntur. In usum futuræ Synodi Nationalis Latinè edidit, &

collegit, FESTVS HOMMIVS. Addita est in eundem usum HARMONIA SYNODORVM BELGICARVM. LVGDVNI BATAVORVM, Ex Officinâ ELZEVIRIANA . . . M.D.C.XVIII. 4° pp.162
697.c.15(3).
The 'Harmonia' is by Simeon Ruytinck.

H163 HOMMIUS, Festus
[Specimen controversiarum Belgicarum.] MONSTER Vande Nederlantsche Verschillē Ofte BELYDENISSE DER GHEREFORMEERDE KERCKEN IN NEDERLANT . . . Van FESTVS HOMMIVS . . . Alwaer . . . bygedaen is D'overeenstemminghe der Nederlantsche Synode. Alles . . . overgheset/DOOR IOHANNES à LODENSTEYN . . . TOT LEYDEN, By David Jansz. van Jlpendā . . . 1618. 4° pp.1-122
T.2249(11).
Imperfect; wanting all after p.122, including the 'Overeenstemminghe', by Simeon Ruytinck.

HOMMIUS, Festus. Trouhertighe vermaninghe aen alle swangere ende barende vroutgens. 1618. [Sometimes wrongly attributed to Festus Hommius.] *See* TROUHERTIGHE

H164 HONDIUS, Henrik; the Elder
BELGIÆ PACIFICATORUM VERA DELINEATIO. Pourtraicture vraye des Pacificateurs des Pays Bas. ware Afbeeldingen vande vredemakers der Nederlanden. HAGÆ COMITIS. EX OFFICINA HENRICI HONDII . . . 1608. fol. 31 unnumbered plates
C.125.dd.18.
Engraved throughout. The plates signed: Henr. Hondius delin. et excud. Imperfect? Knuttel mentions 33 portraits, but different copies may have been issued with further plates as they became available.

H165 HONDIUS, Henrik; the Elder
BESCHRYVINGE vande begraefnisse van . . . Heer Walraven, Heere tot Brederoede, Vry-Heere van Vianen . . . Gedaen binnen der stede van Vianen den XXIX Januari. An°. 1615. Hh. excud. obl. fol. pl.12; port.
557*.b.21.
The monogram is that of Henrik Hondius, at The Hague. Engraved throughout. The portrait is part of the titlepage.

H166 HONDIUS, Henrik; the Elder
LES CINQ RANGS DE L'ARCHITECTVRE . . . AVEC L'INSTRVCTION FONDAMENTALE, FAICTE PAR HENRY HONDIVS. Avec . . . quelques belles ordonnances d'Architecture, mises en perspective, Inventees par Iean Vredeman Frison, & son fils, & taillees par . . . H. Hondius, de nouveau reveues & corrigees . . . A AMSTERDAM Chez Iean Ianson . . . 1617. (col.) Imprime a Amsterdam l'An 1617. fol. sig. [A]B-Z, A-OO; illus.
560*.d.4.
Mainly engraved, with text in Latin. Some engravings signed: P. V. Vriese invent. Hondius formis. The titlepage woodcut shows Architecture. Imperfect; wanting some of the plates.

H167 HONDIUS, Henrik; the Elder
PICTORUM ALIQUOT CELEBRIUM PRÆCIPUÉ GERMANIÆ INFERIORIS, EFFIGIES . . . HAGÆ-COMITIS. EX OFFICINA HENRICI HONDII. [etc.] fol. 79 unnumbered plates
555.d.22; 747.f.13; C.74.d.6(2).
Engraved throughout, the plates signed: Hh, i.e. Henrik Hondius, except for a prefatory poem printed in letterpress, signed: Henr. Hondius. Published ca.1610. The plates are in part copied from those compiled by Hieronymus Cock, with text by Dominicus Lampsonius, published at Antwerp ca.1572. The copy at 747.f.13 is bound in a wrong sequence.

H168 HONDIUS, Petrus

PETRI HONDII Dapes inemptæ, Of de Moufe-schans/dat is, De soeticheydt DES BVYTEN-LEVENS, Vergheselschapt met de Boucken . . . Nieuwe editie. Nu eerst by den Autheur uyt laeten gaen. T'samen met zijn Hof-wetten. TOT LEYDEN, Voor Daniel Roels . . . 1621. (col.) TOT LEYDEN, By Joris Abrahamsz. vander Marsce . . . 1621. 8° pp.534

11555.b.18.

In verse. With the printer's device formerly used by Christoffel Guyot at Leiden.

HONDIUS, Petrus. Disputationum theologicarum repetitarum sexagesima-prima, de Missa. 1601. *See* DU JON, François; the Elder

HONERDIUS, Rochus. *See* HONERT, Rochus van den

H169 HONERT, Rochus van den

ROCHI HONERDI . . . THAMARA TRAGOEDIA. LVGDVNI BATAVORVM. Ex Officina Ioannis Patij . . . 1611. 8° pp.56

636.c.45.

Sig.⁂ is misbound. A slip bearing a new errata list has been pasted over the original errata at the end.

H170 HONORI

HONORI INAVGVRATIONIS . . . VVILTETI MATHIAE . . . CVM In Illustri BATAVORVM Athenæo I.V.D. renunciaretur, A . . . GERARDO TVNINGIO . . . POPVLARES & AMICI Congratulantes P. LVGDVNI IN BATAVIS, Ex Officina THOMÆ BASSON. M.D.C.IV. 4° sig.A^4

11409.f.31(5).

H171 HOOFT, Pieter Corneliszoon

P.C. HOOFTS, ACHILLIS en POLYXENAS Treur-spel. Met AYAX en VLISSES Reden-strijdt. TOT ROTTERDAM, Voor David Iacobsz van Hakendover . . . 1614. (col.) Ghedruct by Harman Huyghensz Monincx. 4° sig.A-F^4G^2

11754.g.29.

With an additional leaf A^2 bearing the preface. Printed at Rotterdam.

H172 HOOFT, Pieter Corneliszoon

P.C. HOOFTS Brief/Van Menelaus aen Helena. Anno 1615. 4° sig.AB^4

11556.cc.64(4).

Printed by Nicolaes Biestkens at Amsterdam?

H173 HOOFT, Pieter Corneliszoon

EMBLEMATA AMATORIA. AFBEELDINGHEN VAN MINNE. EMBLEMES D'AMOVR. Ghedruckt t'Amsterdam by Willem Ianszoon . . . 1611. obl.4° pp.144; illus.

11556.bbb.32.

Anonymous. With 'Sommighe nieuwe ghesangen, liedekens en sonnetten' following the thirty emblems. P. 11 is blank. The engraved titlepage is by Pieter Serwouters, the engraved emblems are attributed to Cri le Blon. The Latin versions are by Cornelis Plemp, those in French by Richard Jean de Nérée.

H174 HOOFT, Pieter Corneliszoon

EMBLEMATA AMATORIA. AFBEELDINGHEN VAN MINNE. EMBLEMES D'AMOVR. Ghedruckt t'Amsterdam by Willem Ianszoon . . . 1618. obl.4° pp.171; illus.

11556.bbb.67(1).

Anonymous. With 'P.C. Hoofts Brief van Menelaus aen Helena'. The part containing the emblems has the same plates as the preceding, but different typesetting for the text. An engraving, by a different artist?, has been mounted on p.11.

H175 HOOFT, Pieter Corneliszoon

P.C. HOOFTS GEERAERDT van VELSEN Treurspel. TOT AMSTERDAM, By Willem Iansz . . . M DC X$^{III.}$ 4° sig. A-G^{4}H^3
11754.g.28.

H176 HOOFT, Pieter Corneliszoon

P.C. HOOFTS GRANIDA SPEL. TOT AMSTERDAM, By Willem Iansz. . . . M D XX [*sic*]. 4° sig. A-H^4
11754.g.30.
Cropped. The date on the titlepage has been corrected in ink to M DCXX.

H177 HOOFT, Pieter Corneliszoon

HET SPEL van THESEVS ende ARIADNE P.C. Hoofts. TOT AMSTELREDAM, By Jan Gerritsz. . . . 1614. 4° sig. A-E^{4}F^2
11754.b.27.
Part of the issue with the reading 'nuw' in line 10 on sig. E1r.

H178 HOOGHEN

Den hooghen Godt ter eeren//En d'Hoogh' Moghende Heeren . . . VIVE Den PrInce Van OraIgnen. 1618. [etc.] fol. a single sheet; illus.
1889.d.3(298).
The woodcut illustration shows the arms of Prince Maurice.

H179 HORATIUS FLACCUS, Quintus

[Works. Latin] (tp.1) QVINTI HORATII FLACCI . . . POEMATA OMNIA. LVGDVNI BATAVORVM, EX OFFICINA PLANTINIANA, Apud Franciscum Raphelengium. M.D.XCIIII.
(tp.2) Q. HORATII FLACCI OPERA OMNIA: Cum Notis DANIELIS HEINSII. Accedit Horatij ad Pisones epistola, Aristotelis de poetica libellus, ordini suo nunc demum ab eodem restituta. EX OFFICINA PLANTINIANA RAPHELENGII. M.D.CX. 8° 2 pt.: pp.278; 158
1578/7237.
The whole published at Leiden in 1610; pt.1 is a reissue of the edition of 1594.

H180 HORATIUS FLACCUS, Quintus

[Works. Latin] Q. HORATIVS FLACCVS, Cum erudito LAEVINI TORRENTII Commentario, nunc primùm in lucem edito. ITEM PETRI NANNI . . . in Artem Poëticam. ANTVERPIÆ, EX OFFICINA PLANTINIANA, Apud Ioannem Moretum. M.DC.VIII. (col.) ANTVERPIÆ, EX OFFICINA PLANTINIANA, Apud Ioannem Moretum. M.DC.VIII. 4° pp.839; illus., ports.
C.19.d.20; 56.c.3; G.9515.
The illustrations are engravings. The copy at C.19.d.20 in a binding bearing the arms of Jacques Auguste de Thou.

H181 HORATIUS FLACCUS, Quintus

[Works. Latin] Q. HORATIVS FLACCVS: CVM COMMENTARIIS & Enarrationibus COMMENTATORIS VETERIS, ET IACOBI CRVQVII . . . Accedunt, IANI DOVSÆ . . . in eundem Commentariolus . . . ITEM AVCTARIVM Commentatoris veteris à Cruquio editi. EX OFFICINA PLANTINIANA RAPHELENGII, M.D.CXI. 4° pp.695
655.b.8.
Published at Leiden. Ownership inscriptions: Wm. Walsh; Willm Bromley; Thos Tyrwhitt 1786.

H182 HORATIUS FLACCUS, Quintus

[Works. Latin] Q. HORATI FLACCI OPERA. Cum Animaduersionibus & Notis DANIELIS HEINSI: longe auctioribus. Idem librum DE SATYRA præfixit . . . LVGDVNI BATAVORVM, Apud Ludouicum Elzeuirium . . . M.DC.XII. 8° pp.317,174,120
683.d.6; 1068.f.4.

The copy at 683.d.6 has the ownership inscription: C. Cole, and manuscript notes; the copy at 1068.f.4 is imperfect, its last leaves mutilated.

H183 HORATIUS FLACCUS, Quintus

[Works. Latin] QVINCTVS HORATIVS FLACCVS, AB OMNI OBSCOENITATE ROMÆ EXPVRGATVS. LVXEMBVRGI, TYPIS HVBERTI REVLANT . . . M.DC.XX. 12° pp.236
11386.a.3.

With the exlibris: Biblioth. Grundig.

H184 HORATIUS FLACCUS, Quintus

[Selections. Latin] Q. HORATI EMBLEMATA. Imaginibus in æs incisis, Notisq́ȝ illustrata, Studio OTHONIS VÆNI . . . ANTVERPIÆ, Ex Officina Hieronymi Verdussen, Auctoris ære & cura. M.DC.VII. (col.) Typis Hieronymi Verdussen. 4° pp.213; illus., port.
C.76.d.6; 86.g.1.

A portrait of Horace illustrates the titlepage. The copy at 86.g.1 has had Hugo de Groot's epigram on this work, copied in manuscript, pasted on the fly-leaf.

H185 HORATIUS FLACCUS, Quintus

[Selections. Latin] QVINTI HORATII FLACCI EMBLEMATA. Imaginibus in æs incisis, Notisq́ȝ illustrata Studio OTHONIS VÆNI . . . ANTVERPIÆ, Prostant apud Philippum Lisaęrt. Auctoris ære & cura. M.DC.XII. (col.) Typis Dauidis Martinij. 4° pp.212; illus., port.
637.k.8.

With versions in Spanish, by Diego de Barreda, French, by Leo de Meyere and Claude de Cordemoy, Italian, by Pietro Benedetti, and Dutch, by Otto van Veen himself under the motto 'dominatim', all named in the preface.

HORST, Walraven van. *See* WITTENHORST, Walraven van

H186 HORTENSIUS, Lambertus

[Tumultuum Anabaptistarum liber unus.] HET Boeck D. LAMBERTI HORTENSII van MONTFOORT . . . Van den Oproer der Weder-dooperen. EERST Int Latijn beschreven . . . ENDE Nu in Nederlandts overgheset. Mitsgaders Een Voor-reden van den selven Autheur aen de . . . Burghemeesteren Schepenen ende Raedt der Stadt Amsterdam. Ghedruct tot Enchuysen. By Jacob Lenaertsz Meyn . . . 1614. fol. ff.26; illus.
4661.f.21.

The dedication signed: I.M.P. One of the engravings signed: M. Pieter Colijn. F.5 has the same engraving printed on it as f.3; a copy of the correct one has been pasted over this.

H187 HOSKINS, Anthony

A BRIEFE AND CLEARE DECLARATION OF SVNDRY POINTES Absolutely dislyked in the lately enacted Oath of ALLEGIANCE, proposed to the Catholikes of England. TOGEATHER With a Recapitulation of the whole worke newly written by a learned Deuine, concerning the same Subiect. By H.I. . . . M.DC.XI. 4° pp.56
702.h.34; C.26.k.3(2).

Anonymous. Against George Blackwell. Without imprint; published by the English College press at St. Omer.

HOUDEMIUS, Joannes. *See* JOHN of Hoveden

H188 HOUT, Jan van

DER STADT LEYDEN DIENST-BOVC, Innehoudende verclaringe van tvvezen ende ghelegentheyt vande zelve Stadt, gelijck die van outs gheweest, ende verdeelt is: vande vermeerderinghen ende vergrootinghen van dien: Mitsgaders vande gestiften tot geestlicken ofte godsvruchtighen zaecken, aldaer . . . T'samen geboucht ende by een getrocken door IAN VAN HOVT . . . Ende Gedruct opt Raedthuys der voorschreven Stede, in den Iare zestien-hondert ende tvvee. fol. pp.58

C.115.s.24.

Printed at Jan van Hout's press, largely in civilité. With some poems by Jan van Hout. A portrait of the author by Willem Swanenburch, dated 1608, with verses by Daniel Heinsius, has been inserted in this copy. In an 18th-century Hague gold-tooled binding of stained calf.

H189 HOUTMAN, Cornelis de

[Iournael vande reyse der Hollandtsche schepen ghedaen in Oost Indien.] APPENDIX Oft By-voechsel achter tJournael vande Reyse der Hollantsche Schepen op Iava . . . Midtsgaders oock seker Vocabulaer der Maleysche woorden/in druck ghebracht door Cornelis Gerritsz van Zuydt-lant . . . men vintse te coop by Barent Langenes . . . tot Middelburgh . . . M.D.CXVIII. obl.4° sig.[Aa]Bb^{2}Cc^{6}; illus., maps

440.i.1(4); 1256.kk.32.

The leader of the expedition and compiler of the Journal was Cornelis de Houtman. Part of the issue in which the date is a misprint for 1598.

H190 HOUTMAN, Frederick de

Spraeck ende woord-boeck, Inde Maleysche ende Madagaskarsche Talen/met vele Arabische ende Turcsche woorden . . . Noch zijn hier byghevoecht de Declinatien van vele vaste Sterren/staende ontrent den Zuyd-pool . . . Alles ghesteldt, gheobserveert, ende beschreven door Frederick de Houtman . . . T'AMSTELREDAM, By Jan Evertsz. Cloppenburch . . . M.VJC.ende III. [etc.] obl.8° pp.222

C.71.a.32.

The preface signed in manuscript: F.v.Houtman. The text of the dictionary largely derived from Noel de Barlement's 'Colloquia'.

H191 HOUWAERT, Johan Baptista

DEN GENERALEN LOOP DER VVERELT . . . Beschreven door Iehan Baptista Houwaert . . . t'AMSTELREDAM. Gedruckt by Barent Otsz. Voor Willem Jansz. Stam . . . 1612. 4° sig.$\star^{4}$A–R^{8}S^{6}: plate; port.

11557.e.3.

In verse. The preface signed: A.D.C., i.e. Abraham de Coninck; the epilogue signed: ITP. The additional, engraved, titlepage signed: FMH, i.e. Hendrick Micker. The portrait engraved after Christoffel van Sichem. Largely printed in civilité.

H192 HOUWAERT, Johan Baptista

(tp.1) DEN handel der Amoureusheyt Inhoudende Vier Poetische Spelen, 1. Van Æneas ende Dido. 2. Narcissus ende Echo. 3. Mars ende Venus. 4. Leander ende Hero. Poetelijck geinventeert eñ Rethorijckelijck ghecomponeert, Door . . . Johan Baptista Houwaert. Tot Rotterdam By Jan van Waesberghe de Jonge . . . 1621.

(tp.2=sig.A1r) HET EERSTE BOECK, vanden Handel der Amoureusheyt . . . van Æneas ende Dido . . . door . . . Johan Baptista Houwaert. TOT ROTTERDAM, By Ian van Waesberghe de Ionghe . . . 1621.

(tp.3=sig.F4r) HET TWEEDE BOECK . . . van Narcissus ende Echo, &c. . . . door . . . Iohan Baptista Houwaert. TOT ROTTERDAM, By Ian van Waesberghe de Ionghe . . . 1621.

(tp.4=sig.Q1r) HET DERDE BOECK . . . van Mars ende Venus, &c. . . . door . . . Iohan Baptista Houwaert. TOT ROTTERDAM, By Ian van Waesberghe de Ionghe . . . 1621.
(tp.5=sig.Z2r) HET VIERDE BOECK . . . van Leander ende Hero . . . door . . . Iohan Baptista Houwaert. TOT ROTTERDAM, By Ian van Waesberghe de Ionghe . . . 1621.
8° sig.A-Ff[8]Gg[4]; illus.
011755.e.16.

The collective titlepage, =tp.1, is engraved and the illustration consists of one full-page engraving. Bk.2–4 contain more plays than the one mentioned on the titlepages.

H193 HOUWAERT, Johan Baptista
Parænesis Politica HOUWARDI J.B. Houwarts Politycke Onderwijsinghe Tot dienste van alle Menschen, om te gebruijcken Maticheijt in voorspoet, en Stantvasticheijt in Teghenspoet . . . Poëtelijck gevrocht . . . van Johan Babtista Houwart . . . Voor Jan Lamrinck van Bolswart. En Berent Arents van Leeuwarden . . . 1614. Tot Leeuwarden, by Abraham vanden Rade . . . 1614. (col.) Ghedruckt Tot Leeuwarden, By Abraham vanden Rade . . . M DC XIV. Voor Jan Lamrinck van Bolswaert/ende Barent Arents van Leeuwarden Boeckvercoopers. 4° pp.452; illus., port.
11555.cc.13.

The engraved titlepage signed: PH'arling. [=Pieter Feddes van Harlingen] Invent., Hendrick Micker Fri. sculp. The imprint is in letterpress. The portrait is a copy of that by Christoffel van Sichem after one of the Wierix brothers.

H194 HOUWAERT, Johan Baptista
(tp.1) PEGASIDES PLEYN, Ende DEN LVST-HOF DER MAEGHDEN . . . Poëtelijck Gheinventeert, ende Rhetorijckelijck ghecomponeert, by IEHAN BAPTISTA HOVWAERT . . . TOT LEYDEN, By Ian Paedts Iacobsz. . . . 1611.
(tp.2=p.107) T'CHIERAET VAN DIE DEVGHDELYCKE MAEGHDEN. Het tvveede Boeck. Poëtelijck Gheinventeert, ende Rettorijckelijck ghecomponeert, by Iehan Baptista Houvvaert . . . TOT LEYDEN, By Ian Paedts Iacobsz. . . . 1609.
(tp.3=p.195) DEN SPIEGHEL VAN DIE SCHOONE MAEGHDEN. Het derde Boeck . . . Gheinventeert . . . by Iehan Baptista Houvvaert . . . TOT LEYDEN, By Ian Paedts Iacobsz. . . . 1609.
(tp.4=p.295) DEN TRESOOR VAN D'EERLICKE MAEGHDEN. Het vierde Boeck . . . Gheinventeert . . . by Iehan Baptista Houvvaert . . . TOT LEYDEN, By Ian Paedts Iacobsz. . . . 1609.
(tp.5=p.391) DEN ONSCHAECK VAN DIE TRIVMPHANTE MAEGHDEN. Het vijfde Boeck . . . Gheinventeert . . . by Iehan Baptista Houvvaert . . . TOT LEYDEN, By Ian Paedts Iacobsz. . . . 1611.
(tp.6=p.513) DEN STRYT VAN DIE CLOECKE MAEGHDEN. Het seste Boeck . . . Gheinventeert . . . by Iehan Baptista Houvvaert . . . TOT LEYDEN, By Ian Paedts Iacobsz. . . . 1611.
(tp.7=p.615) DIE MANIEREN VAN DIE GRATIEVSE MAEGHDEN. Het sevenste Boeck . . . Gheinventeert . . . by Ian Baptista Houvvaert . . . TOT LEYDEN, By Ian Paedts Iacobsz. . . . 1611.
(tp.8=p.727) D'EXCELLENTIE VAN D'EDELE MAEGHDEN. Het achtste Boeck . . . Gheinventeert . . . by Ian Baptista Houvvaert . . . TOT LEYDEN, By Ian Paedts Iacobsz. . . . 1611. 8° pp.xxxix,1–845
C.129.f.20.

Printed in civilité. Imperfect; wanting bk.9–16.

H195 HOUWAERT, Johan Baptista
DE VIER VVTERSTE, VAN DE DOOT, VAN HET OORDEEL, VAN D'EEVVVICH LEVEN, VAN DE PYNE DER HELLEN . . . Schriftuerelijck gheinventeert, ende Rhethorijckelijck

ghecomponeert by Iehan Babtista Houvvaert . . . IN S'GRAVEN-HAGHE, By Hillebrandt Iacobsz. . . . 1613. 4° pp.224; illus., port.
11557.ee.16.

The titlepage woodcut contains the portrait, device and arms of the author.

H196 HOUWAERT, Johan Baptista

DE VIER WTERSTE . . . gheinventeert, ende . . . ghecomponeert, by Iehan Baptistâ Houvvaert . . . Ghedruckt Tot Leeuwarden, By Abraham vanden Rade . . . M.DC.XJV. (col.) Ghedruckt Tot Leeuwarden, By Abraham vanden Rade . . . M.DC.XJV. 4° pp.335; illus., port.
11557.ee.17.

The frontispiece full-page woodcut portrait, after Wierix, signed: CVS, i.e. Christoffel van Sichem. Printed in civilité.

H197 HOVE, Guilielmus vanden

DISPVTATIO INAVGVRALIS DE PHTHISI seu TABE. quam . . . Pro summo in Medicina DOCTORATVS gradu consequendo, tueri comabitur [*sic*] GVILIELMVS vanden HOVE . . . LUGDUNI BATAVORUM, Excudebat GODEFRIDUS BASSON, 1613. 4° sig.A⁴
1185.g.1(54).

H198 HOVE, Joachim vanden

DELITIÆ MVSICÆ SIVE Cantiones, e quamplurimis præstantissimorum nostri æui Musicorum Libris selectæ. Ad TESTVDINIS usum accommodatæ, OPERA atque industriâ IOACHIMI VANDEN HOVE . . . VLTRAIECTI, Apud Salomonem de Roy, & veneunt apud Ioannem de Rhenen . . . M.DC.XII. fol. ff.66; illus., music
Music K.1.i.20.

The titlepage engraving shows a group of people making music signed: L.L Inuentor, Ioãn. Barra Scalpsit.

H199 HOVIUS, Jacobus

IACOBI HOVII ORATIO SEV PARAENESIS PANEGYRICA AD Studium Eloquentiæ Habita publicè in auditorio Theologico ad Studiosam Iuuentutem Leydensem 20 die Iulij 1613 . . . LVGDVNI BATAVORVM, Excudebat Henricus Ludouici ab Haestens . . . M.D C XIII. 4° sig.∴A–E⁴F²
836.f.18(3).

Author's presentation copy to Cornelius Swanenburch.

H200 HOWARD, Charles; 1st Earl of Nottingham

ORATIE Vanden Enghelschen Ambassadeur/ghedaen in Hispaignien . . . Wt het Enghelsch ghetroulijck overgheset . . . 1606. 4° sig.A⁴
573.f.32.

Translated from the relevant passage in Robert Treswell's 'A relation'?

HOWLET, Jhon; pseudonym of Robert Persons. *See* PERSONS, Robert

H201 HOYUS, Andreas

ORATIO, DE NOVÆ APVD EUROPÆOS MONARCHIAE, PRO TEMPORE, ET AD INFRINgendam TURCICAE DOMINATIONIS impotentiam, & ad stabiliendum Christianae Statum, utilitate. Auctore ANDREA HOJO . . . Ante decennium Duaci apud Johannem Bogardum edita: nunc verò denuò recusa . . . M.DC.IX. 4° pp.44
698.f.41.

Originally published in 1598 in 'Ezechiel propheta paraphrasi poetica illustratus'. Published again at Douai?

H202 HUARTE, Juan

EXAMEN DE INGENIOS PARA LAS SCIENCIAS . . . Compuesto por . . . IVAN HVARTE . . . En la oficina PLANTINIANA. M.DC.III. 16° pp.464
536.a.39.

Published at Leiden.

H203 HUES, Robertus
TRACTATVS. DE GLOBIS COELESTI, ET TERRESTRI, AC EORVM VSV: Conscriptus à ROBERTO HVES. Denuo auctior & emendatior editus. AMSTELODAMI. Excudebat IVDOCVS HONDIVS . . . M DC XI. 8° pp.92
717.d.11.
The leaves have been laminated and mounted.

H204 HUES, Robertus
TRACTATVS DE GLOBIS . . . Primum conscriptus & editus à ROBERTO HVES . . . nunc elegantibus iconibus & figuris locupletatus: ac de novo recognitus multisque Observationibus . . . illustratus ac passim auctus operâ ac studio IOHANNIS ISACII PONTANI . . . AMSTELODAMI. Excudebat IUDOCUS HONDIUS . . . M DC XVII. (col.) AMSTELODAMI. Excudebat IUDOCUS HONDIUS . . . M DC XVII. 4° pp.130; illus.
3902.ee.18(2); 8562.eee.40.
The titlepage engraving of the globe has lettering in Dutch. The woodcuts are newly made for this edition. In the copy at 3902.ee.18(2) leaf A4 is cropped.

H205 HUES, Robertus
[Tractatus de globis.] TRACTAET Ofte Handelinge van het gebruijck der Hemelscher ende Aertscher Globe. Gheaccommodeert naer die Bollen, die eerst gesneden zijn . . . door IODOCVS HONDIVS . . . 1593. Ende nu gantsch door den selven vernieut . . . In't Latijn beschreven/door Robertum Hues . . . nu in Nederduytsch overgheset/ende . . . vermeerdert ende verciert. Door I. Hondium . . . Van nieus oversien ende verbetert. T'AMSTELREDAM, By Michiel Colijn . . . 1612. 4° pp.67; illus.
8563.aaa.22.
The titlepage engraving has inscriptions in Dutch; the woodcuts have inscriptions in Latin.

HUGO de Prato Florido. *See* VINAC, Hugo de; de Prato Florido

H206 HUGO, Hermannus
DE PRIMA SCRIBENDI ORIGINE ET VNIVERSA REI LITERARIÆ ANTIQVITATE, Ad . . . CAROLVM SCRIBANI . . . Scribebat HERMANNVS HVGO . . . ANTVERPIÆ, EX OFFICINA PLANTINIANA, Apud Balthasarem & Ioannem Moretos. M.DC.XVII. 8° pp.227; illus.
819.d.4; 1586/6285; 275.e.17; G.592.

H207 HUNINGA, Joannes
ORATIO FVNEBRIS IN HONOREM . . . EGGRICI EGGÆI PHEBENS Senatoris in rep. Groningana præstantissimi . . . defuncti Anno M.DC.XV. die XII. Novemb. Habita in auditorio Academiæ Theologico XXII. Novemb. A IOH. HVNINGA . . . Addita sunt programma D. Magnifici & amicorum in defuncti laudem Epigrammata & Epitaphium. GRONINGÆ Excudebat Ioannes Sassius . . . 1616. 4° sig.A-C^4D^2
296.k.11(2).
Author's presentation copy to Jacques Auguste de Thou.

HUNTLEY, James Gordon. *See* GORDON, James; of Huntly

HUSSUS, Daniel Andreas Gijs. *See* GIJS, Daniel Andreas

H208 HUTTON, Matthew; Archbishop of York
Brevis & dilucida expl[icatio, ve]ræ, certæ, & consolationis [plenæ] doctri[næ de] ELECTIONE, [PRAE]DESTINATIONE [AC RE]PROB[A]TIONE, Authore MAT[T]HÆO, EBORACEN[I ARCHIEPISCOPO] . . . Cui accesserunt . . . [D. ESTAEI,] SOMI, CHATERTONI, ET VV[ILLETI,] Eiusdem argumenti scripta . . . Hardrevici, Ex

*[Illustration of **I1** overleaf]*

EXERCITIA SPIRITVALIA B. P. IGNATII Loyolæ.

AVDOMAROPOLI,
In Collegio Anglicano Societatis IESV.

M. DC. X.

Typographéo Thomæ Henrici, Impensis HENRICI LAVRENTII Amsterodamensis Librarii . . . M.DC.XIII. 8° pp.256
1485.tt.20.
The title-leaf and leaf A2 are mutilated. The titlepage has been partially substituted with a photographic reproduction.

HUYSINGIUS, Henricus. Disquisitio theologica de angelis. 1614. *See* LINDEN, Henricus Antonides van der

HYGGONS, Theophilus. *See* HIGGONS, Theophilus

H209 HYMNI
HYMNI ofte LOFF-SANGEN op de Christelycke Feest-Dagen, ENDE Ander-sins . . . IN S'GRAVEN-HAGHE Bij Hillebrant Iacobsz . . . 1615. 8° ff.54; music
Music A.1231.cc.
Compiled by the ministers at Utrecht, for use there. The titlepage is engraved. Ownership inscription: manuscript note by the writer of an article in 'Kerkelijke raadvrager en raadgever' who bought this copy in 1830 from the estate of Thomas Hoog, having given his previous and only known copy to the University Library at Utrecht. This owner is identified in the copy now at Utrecht as Jodocus Heringa, Eliza'szoon.

I

Names of authors or first words of anonymous titles whose initial 'I' in fact represents the letter 'J' are entered under J.

ICONES ad vivum delineatae . . . virorum clariorum qui . . . Academiam Lugduno-Batavam illustrarunt. 1609. *See* MEURSIUS, Joannes; the Elder

ICONES, elogia ac vitae professorum Lugdunensium apud Batavos. 1617. *See* MEURSIUS, Joannes; the Elder

ICONICA et historica descriptio praecipuorum haeresiarcharum. 1609. *See* SICHEM, Christoffel van

IDINAU, Donaes; pseudonym of Jan David. *See* DAVID, Jan; Jesuit

I1 IGNATIUS of Loyola; Saint
EXERCITIA SPIRITVALIA B.P. IGNATII Loyolæ. AVDOMAROPOLI, In Collegio Anglicano Societatis IESV. M.DC.X. 24° pp.273
C.26.gg.11.
The only edition of this press to bear its imprint.

I2 IGNATIUS of Loyola; Saint
EXERCITI[A] SPIRITVALI[A] B.P. IGNATII DE LOYOLA . . . 1619. 32° pp.300
1506/420.
Published by the English College press at St. Omer. The titlepage is mutilated.

I3 IGNATIUS of Loyola; Saint
[Exercitia spiritualia. Abridgments] A MANVALL OF DEVOVT MEDITATIONS AND EXERCISES . . . Drawne for the most part, out of the spirituall Exercises of B.F. Ignatius . . . Written in Spanish by . . . Thomas de Villa-castin of the Society of IESVS, AND Translated into English by a Father of the same SOCIETY . . . 1618. 12° pp.558
3455.df.9.
Translated by Henry More. Edited by John Wilson. Published by the English College press at St. Omer.

ILLUSTRIS Academia Lugd-Batava. 1613. *See* MEURSIUS, Joannes; the Elder

ILLUSTRIUM & clarorum virorum epistolae selectiores. 1617. *See* BERTIUS, Petrus

ILLUSTRIUM Hollandiae & Westfrisiae Ordinum Alma Academia Leidensis. 1614. *See* MEURSIUS, Joannes; the Elder

ILLUSTRIUM quos Belgium habuit pictorum effigies. ca.1615. *See* LAMPSONIUS, Dominicus

IN liefde ghetrouw. 1602. *See* MANDER, Karel van

INAUGURATIO Philippi II . . . qua se . . . Brabantiae . . . obligavit. 1620. *See* BRABANT. Customs and Privileges

IN-HOUDT van eenighe brieven. 1617. *See* TAURINUS, Jacobus

INSTRUCTION servante à la levée des impositions mises sus par les Estatz du Pays de Haynnau. 1604. *See* HAINAULT [12.1603]

J

(including headings beginning with the letter 'I' where it represents 'J' and treated as such in the alphabetical sequence)

J1 JACCHAEUS, Gilbertus
DISPVTATIO INAVGVRALIS DE EPILEPSIA, Quam . . . Pro Docturæ gradu in Medicina consequendo . . . Publce [*sic*] examinandam proponit GILBERTVS IACCHÆVS . . . Lugduni Batavorum, Excudebat THOMAS BASSON. 1611. 4° sig.A[4]
1185.g.1(44).

J2 JACCHAEUS, Gilbertus
DISPVTATIONVM PHYSICARVM PRIMA DE CONSTITVTIONE PHYSICÆ, Quam . . . Præside . . . D.M. GILBERTO JACCHÆO . . . publicè excutiendam proponit EVERHARDVS HERMANNI F. SCHVYL LOOSLEVER . . . LUGDUNI BATAVORUM, Ex Officinâ Ioannis Patii . . . M.D.C.VII. 4° sig.A[4]
536.f.8(1).

J3 JACCHAEUS, Gilbertus
DISPVTATIONVM PHYSICARVM SECVNDA DE PRINCIPIIS PHYSICIS, Quam . . . Præside . . . D.M. GILBERTO IACCHÆO . . . discutiendam proponit publicè THEODORUS SCHALICHIUS . . . LUGDUNI BATAVORUM, Ex Officinâ Ioannis Patii . . . M.D.C.VII. 4° sig.B[4]
536.f.8(2).

J4 JACCHAEUS, Gilbertus
DISPVTATIONVM PHYSICARVM TERTIA DE NATVRA, Ad cujus examen . . . Præside . . . GILBERTO IACCHÆO . . . publicè respondebit D.A.G. Hussus . . . LUGDUNI BATAVORUM, Ex Officinâ Ioannis Patii . . . M.D.C.VII. 4° sig.C[4]
536.f.8(3); 7306.f.6(40*).
The respondent's full name appears on the verso of the titlepage: Daniel Andreas Gijs Hussus.

J5 JACCHAEUS, Gilbertus
DISPVTATIONVM PHYSICARVM QVARTA DE CAVSSIS EXTRINSECIS, Quam . . . Præside . . . D.M. GILBERTO IACCHÆO . . . publicè examinandam suspendit CORNELIVS GEISTERANVS . . . LUGDUNI BATAVORUM, Ex Officinâ Ioannis Patii . . . M.D.C.VII. 4° sig.D[4]
536.f.8(4).

J6 JACCHAEUS, Gilbertus
DISPVTATIONVM PHYSICARVM QVINTA DE MOTV, Quam . . . Præside . . . D.M. GILBERTO IACCHÆO . . . publicè examinandam proponit GISBERTUS VOETIUS . . . LUGDUNI BATAVORUM, Ex Officinâ Ioannis Patii . . . M.D.C.VII. 4° sig.E[4]
536.f.8(5).

J7 JACCHAEUS, Gilbertus
DISPVTATIONVM PHYSICARVM SEXTA DE TEMPORE, LOCO ET FINITO, Quam . . . Præside . . . D.M. GILBERTO IACCHÆO . . . publicè examinandam proponit HENR. GREGORIVS À BLYVENBVRCH . . . LUGDUNI BATAVORUM, Ex Officinâ Ioannis Patii . . . M.D.CVII. 4° sig.F[4]
536.f.8(6).

J8 JACCHAEUS, Gilbertus
DISPVTATIONVM PHYSICARVM SEPTIMA DE COELO, Quam . . . Præside . . . D.M. GILBERTO IACCHÆO . . . publicè examinandam proponit GOSARDUS DREMMIUS . . . LUGDUNI BATAVORUM, Ex Officinâ Ioannis Patii . . . M.D.C.VII. 4° sig.G[4]
536.f.8(7); 7306.f.6(1).
With a poem by Cornelius Geisteranus.

J9 JACCHAEUS, Gilbertus
DISPVTATIONVM PHYSICARVM OCTAVA DE ELEMENTIS, Quam . . . Præside . . . D.M. GILBERTO IACCHÆO . . . publicè examinandam proponit IACOBUS BONTEBAL . . . LUGDUNI BATAVORUM, Ex Officinâ Ioannis Patii . . . M.D.C.VIII. 4° sig.H[4]
536.f.8(8); 7306.f.6(39*).

J10 JACCHAEUS, Gilbertus
DISPVTATIONVM PHYSICARVM NONA DE Elementorum Qualitatibus, Quam . . . Præside . . . D.M. GILBERTO IACCHÆO . . . publicè examinandam proponit BERNARDUS PALUDANUS . . . LUGDUNI BATAVORUM, Ex Officinâ Ioannis Patii . . . M.D.C.VIII. 4° sig.I[4]
536.f.8(9); 7306.f.8(39**).

J11 JACCHAEUS, Gilbertus
DISPVTATIONVM PHYSICARVM DECIMA DE ALTERATIONE ET AVGMENTATIONE, Quam . . . Præside . . . D.M. GILBERTO IACCHÆO . . . publicè examinandam proponit DANIEL ANDREÆ GIIS . . . LUGDUNI BATAVORUM, Ex Officinâ Ioannis Patii . . . M.D.C.VIII. 4° sig.K[4]
536.f.8(10).
The same respondent as D.A.G. Hussus.

J12 JACCHAEUS, Gilbertus
DISPVTATIONVM PHYSICARVM VNDECIMA, CVM DE GENERATIONE ET CORRVPTIONE, TVM DE MIXTIONE, Quam . . . Præside . . . D.M. GILBERTO IACCHÆO . . . publicè examinandam proponit GERHARDVS DE NEVFVILLE . . . LUGDUNI BATAVORUM, Ex Officinâ Ioannis Patii . . . M.D.C.VIII. 4° sig.L[6]
536.f.8(11).
Misbound; the titlepage follows L5 and L6 is bound after M3 which is part of the following tract. Leaf L6 bears a poem by D. Massis addressed to G. de Neufville.

J13 JACCHAEUS, Gilbertus
DISPVTATIONVM PHYSICARVM DVODECIMA, DE METEORIS, Quam . . . Præside . . . D.M. GILBERTO IACCHÆO . . . publicè examinandam proponit . . . EVERHARDVS HERMANNI F. SCHVYL LOOSLEVER . . . LUGDUNI BATAVORUM, Ex Officinâ Ioannis Patii . . . M.D.C.VIII. 4° sig.M[4]
536.f.8(12).
Misbound; the titlepage follows after M3 and L6, the latter being part of the preceding tract, and M4 follows N3 which is part of the following tract.

J14 JACCHAEUS, Gilbertus

DISPVTATIONVM PHYSICARVM DECIMA-TERTIA, DE ANIMA in genere, Quam . . . Præside D.M. GILBERTO IACCHÆO . . . publicè examinandam proponit . . . HENR. GREGORIVS Blijvenburgius . . . LUGDUNI BATAVORUM, Ex Officinâ Ioannis Patii . . . M.D.C.VIII. 4° sig. N^4

536.f.8(13); 7306.f.6(41*).

The copy at 536.f.8(13) is misbound; the titlepage follows N3 and M4, the latter being part of the preceding tract, N4 follows O3 which is part of the following tract.

J15 JACCHAEUS, Gilbertus

DISPVTATIONVM PHYSICARVM DECIMA-QVARTA, DE ANIMA VEGETANTE, Quam . . . Præside . . . D.M. GILBERTO IACCHÆO . . . publicè examinandam proponit BERO COCCIUS . . . LUGDUNI BATAVORUM, Ex Officinâ Ioannis Patii . . . M.D.C.VIII. 4° sig. O^4

536.f.8(14).

Misbound; the titlepage follows O3 and N4, the latter being part of the preceding tract, and O4 follows P4 which is part of the following tract.

J16 JACCHAEUS, Gilbertus

DISPVTATIONVM PHYSICARVM DECIMA-QVINTA, DE SENSIBVS EXTERNIS, Quam . . . Præside . . . D.M. GILBERTO IACCHÆO . . . publicè examinandam proponit . . . EVERHARDVS H. SCHVYL LOOSLEVER . . . LUGDUNI BATAVORUM, Ex Officinâ Ioannis Patii . . . M.D.C.VIII. 4° sig. P^6

536.f.8(15).

Misbound; leaf O4 of the preceding tract is bound after P4. P6 bears a poem by Victor Rickelsma.

J17 JACCHAEUS, Gilbertus

DISPVTATIONVM PHYSICARVM DECIMA-SEXTA, DE SENSIBVS INTERNIS ET APPETITO SENSITIVO, Quam . . . Præside . . . D.M. GILBERTO IACCHÆO . . . publicè examinandam proponit GERHARDVS DE NEVFVILLE . . . LUGDUNI BATAVORUM, Ex Officinâ Ioannis Patii . . . M.D.C.VIII. 4° sig. Q^4

536.f.8(16).

J18 JACCHAEUS, Gilbertus

DISPVTATIONVM PHYSICARVM DECIMA-SEPTIMA ET VLT. DE ANIMA RATIONALI, Quam . . . Præside . . . D.M. GILBERTO IACCHÆO . . . publicè examinandam proponit . . . GOSARDVS DREMMIUS . . . LUGDUNI BATAVORUM, Ex Officinâ Ioannis Patii . . . M.D.C.VIII. 4° sig. R^4

536.f.8(49*).

JACCHAEUS, Gilbertus. [Disputationum theologicarum prima (?) de] libero arbitrio. 1603. *See* GOMARUS, Franciscus

J19 JACCHAEUS, Gilbertus

POSITIONES PHILOSOPHICÆ Ex Logica DE DEFINITIONE. Ex Physica DE MOTV ET QVIETE. Quarum veritatem . . . PRÆSIDE . . . D. GILBERTO IACCHÆO . . . publice tueri conabitur MELCHISEDEC SANDRA . . . LVGDVNI-BATAVORVM, Ex Officina Henrici Lodovici ab Haestens . . . 1608. 4° sig. A^4B^2

7306.f.6(47).

J20 JACCHAEUS, Gilbertus

POSITIONES PHILOSOPHICÆ, Quas . . . præside . . . D. GILBERTO IACHÆO [*sic*] . . . asserendas propugnandas appendit IOANNES BARDINUS . . . LVGDVNI BATAVORVM, Ex Officinâ Ioannis Patii . . . M.D.C.VI. 4° sig. AB^4C^2

7306.f.6(49).

J21 JACCHAEUS, Gilbertus
PRIMÆ PHILOSOPHIÆ INSTITVTIONES. AVTHORE GILBERTO IACCHÆO. LVGDVNI BATAVORVM, Ex Typographia IACOBI PATII . . . M.DC.XVI. 8° pp.353
8463.aaa.5.

J22 JACCHAEUS, Gilbertus
THESES PHILOSOPHICÆ DE MATERIA PRIMA, Quas . . . Præside . . . D. GILBERTO IACCHÆO . . . Exercitii gratia examinandas proponit DANIEL HOCHEDÆUS A VINEA . . . LVGDVNI BATAVORVM, Ex Officinâ Ioannis Patii . . . M.D.C.VI. 4° sig.A^4
7306.f.6(45).

J23 JACCHAEUS, Gilbertus
THESES PHYSICÆ. DE Anima Rationali, Quarum veritatem . . . PRÆSIDE . . . D.M. GILBERTO IACCHÆO . . . Publicè . . . tuebitur, IACOBVS LAVRENTIVS . . . LVGDVNI BATAVORVM, Ex officina Thomæ Basson, 1606. 4° sig.$\star^6$
7306.f.6(43).

J24 JACCHAEUS, Gilbertus
THESES PHYSICÆ DE ANIMA VEGETATIVA, Quas . . . Præside D. GILBERTO IACCHÆO . . . Publicè ventilandas exhibet ISAACVS VANDER-VOORT . . . LVGDVNI BATAVORVM, Ex Officinâ Ioannis Patii . . . M.D.CIV. 4° sig.A^6
7306.f.6(42).
With laudatory poems by Daniel Heinsius and I. Foreestius.

J25 JACCHAEUS, Gilbertus
TRACTATIO THETICA DE ANIMA SEPARATA Quam . . . Sub Præsidio . . . D.M. GILBERTI IACHÆI [*sic*] . . . publice ventilandam exhibet IACOBVS REEFSENVS . . . LVGDVNI BATAVORVM, Ex Officina Thomæ Basson, 1607. 4° sig.A1–3
7306.f.6(44).
Imperfect; wanting all after A3.

J26 JACOB, Henry; Independent Minister
Anno Domini 1616. A CONFESSION AND PROTESTATION OF THE FAITH OF CERTAINE CHRISTIANS in England, holding it necessary to observe, & keepe all Christes true . . . Ordinances . . . though the same doe differ from the common order of the Land. Published for the clearing of the said Christians from the slaunder of Schisme . . . Also an humble Petition to the K. Majestie for toleration therein. [etc.] 8° sig.A-D^8E^4
4103.a.19; C.37.d.58.
Anonymous and without imprint. Printed by Giles Thorp at Amsterdam.

J27 JACOB, Henry; Independent Minister
An Attestation of many Learned, Godly, and famous Divines . . . iustifying this doctrine, viz. That the Church-government ought to bee alwayes with the peoples free consent . . . In the discourse whereof . . . Doctor Downames & also D. Bilsons chiefe matters . . . are answered . . . 1613. 8° pp.323
698.a.35(1).
The preface signed: Henry Jacob. Without imprint; printed by Richard Schilders at Middelburg.

J28 JACOB, Henry; Independent Minister
THE Divine Beginning and Institution of Christs true Visible or Ministeriall Church. ALSO The Vnchangeablenes of the same by men . . . Written by HENRY IACOB. IMPRINTED At Leyden by Henry Hastings. 1610. 8° sig.$\star$A-F^8G^4
4103.b.34.

J29 JACOB, Henry; Independent Minister

A plaine and cleere Exposition of the Second Commandement. By HENRY IACOB . . . 1610. 8° sig.$\star\star^{2}$A-E^{8}F^{2}

4347.a.30.

Without imprint, but with a device bearing the motto 'Lilium inter spinas'; printed by Henrick van Haestens for Jacob Marcusz at Leiden?

J30 JACOB, Henry; Independent Minister

REASONS TAKEN OF GODS WORD AND THE BEST HVMANE TESTIMONIES PROVING A NECESSITIE OF REFORMING OVR CHVRCHES IN ENGLAND . . . 1604. 4° pp.83

4135.a.43; 109.a.13.

The preface and the text signed: Henry Iacob. Without imprint; printed by Richard Schilders at Middelburg.

J31 JACOB, Henry; Independent Minister

To the right High and mightie Prince, IAMES . . . King of great Britannie . . . An humble Supplication for Tolerations and libertie to enioy and observe the ordinances of Christ IESVS in th'administration of his Churches in lieu of humane constitutions . . . 1609. 4° pp.48

4135.a.44.

Anonymous and without imprint; printed by Richard Schilders at Middelburg.

J32 JACOBI, Johann; of Wallhausen

[Kriegskunst zu Fuss.] KRYCHS-KONST TE VOET . . . Ghepractiseert ende in Hooch-duytsche tale beschreven, door Iohanni Iacobi van VValhuysen . . . Ende nu . . . in Nederduytsche vertaelt. TOT LEEUVVAERDEN, By Jan Jansz. Starter . . . 1617. fol. pp.313: plates

533.k.17(1).

Consisting of part I of the original work only which contained a second part, entitled 'Kriegskunst zu Pferdt'. The titlepage is engraved, with letterpress text, containing a portrait of Prince Maurice. One of the plates, showing infantry drill, based on Jacques de Gheyn's 'Wapenhandelinghe'.

JAGHERSDORP, Marck-Grave van. *See* JOHN GEORGE; Margrave of Jägerndorf

IALOERSE studenten. 1617. *See* RODENBURGH, Theodore. Jalourse studentin.

JALOURSE studentin. 1617. *See* RODENBURGH, Theodore

J33 IAMERTIENS

IAMERTIENS Oft aventuersche berouw Clacht gedaen/aen den Ouwe trouwe Geus van de Cort Rijcke Heeren tot een Nieu-Jaer. Ghedruckt . . . 1619. 4° sig.A^{4}; illus.

T.2422(24).

Signed: V.E.G.B., and:Elck heeft zijn tijt. Verses on the death of Johan van Oldenbarnevelt. The titlepage, partly engraved, is larger than the text pages and is folded.

J34 JAMES I; King

[Speeches and Letters, in chronological order] [His Maiesties speach in this last session of Parliament.] Het Relaes van syne Majesteyt in dese leste sessie van t'Parlamente/soo nae syne eyghen woorden als die conden vergadert worden teghenwoordelick. Tsamen met een discours van het ontdecken van dit leste voorghenomen Verraet: Met de Examinatie van veele vande ghevanghenen. Nae de Copie ghedruckt tot Londen by Robert Barker . . . Eñ men vintse te coop tot Amstelredam by Cornelis Claesz . . . Ende by Desiderius de la Tombe . . . 1606. 4° pp.39; illus; port.

524.e.35.

The engraved portrait on the titlepage inscribed: Tomas Persi.

J35 JAMES I; King
[Speeches and Letters] Translaet Vanden Brief des Conincks van groot Britaegnien . . . aende . . . Staten Generael vande Vereenichde Nederlanden. Aengaende de beroepinghe Conradi Vorstij, tot de professie der H. Theologie inde Vniversiteyt tot Leyden . . . M.DC.XJ. 4° sig.A^3
T.2242(21); T.2241(26).
The copy at T.2241(26) is imperfect; wanting the titlepage.

J36 JAMES I; King
[Speeches and Letters] VERKLARINGHE Van den . . . Koning van groot Britannien/ over de handelingen met de Staten Generael van de vereenichde Neder-landen/ nopende het feyt van Conradus Vorstius . . . TOT AMSTERDAM, Ghedruct ende over-ghezet na de Fransche Copye . . . 1612. 4° sig.A-F^4(∴)^2
T.2242(20).
With the first speech of Ralph Winwood. Printed largely in civilité, not traceable to a particular printer.

J37 JAMES I; King
[Speeches and letters] COPIE D'une lettre escrite de sa Majesté de la Grande-Bretaigne Iacques I. aux . . . Estats des Provinces Vnies des Pays-bas, contenant declaration de ses lettres precedentes touchant les differents Ecclesiastiques és dits pays„ avec l'advis pour les assopir . . . 1617. 4° sig.A^2
8026.bbb.58(1).
Dated 20 March 1617. Printed in the Netherlands?

J38 JAMES I; King
[Speeches and letters] COPIE Van een Brief geschreven vande Coninckliјcke Majesteyt van groot Brittannien Iacobus de I. aende . . . Staten vande Geunieerde Provincien/Inhoudende verklaringhe van sijn voorighe brieven aengaende de kerckelijcke verschillen in de selfde Landen . . . Overgheset uyt de Françoysche tale . . . 1617. 4° sig.A^2
T.2247(23*).
Dated 20 March 1617. A translation of the preceding.

J39 JAMES I; King
[Speeches and letters] Copie Van den Brief des CONINCKS Van Groot Brittannien/ aen mijn Heer den Marquis Ioachim Ernest van Brandeburch en Anspach. TOT LEYDEN, Voor Niclaes Geelkercke . . . 1621. 4° sig.A^2
T.2424(3).
Dated 10 December 1620.

J40 JAMES I; King
[Speeches and letters] [The King's speech to the Parliament.] ORATIE, VVelcke DE CONINCK van GROOT BRITANNIEN ghedaen heeft, op de by een-comste, des Parlements, binnen Londen, den 23. Ianuarij, Anno 1621. Wt d'Enghelsche/in Neder-duytsche sprake over-gheset. TOT ARNHEM, Ghedruckt by Jan Jansz. . . . 1621. 4° sig.A^4
T.2424(15).

J41 JAMES I; King
[Speeches and letters] [The Kings speech to the Lords.] TVVEEDE ORATIE Van den KONINCK VAN Groot-Brittaignien: Inden Boven-huyse des Parlements/als het uytghestelt was tot Paesschen/Ghehouden op Maendach den 26 Meert/1621. Nae de Copye, Ghedruckt te Londen, by Bonham Norton, ende Iohan Bill, [etc.] 4° pp.8
T.2424(16).
Published in 1621. This edition does not correspond to any of those described in *Knuttel* no.3162–3164.

J42 JAMES I; King

[Triplici nodo triplex cuneus.] (tp.1) APOLOGIA PRO IVRAMENTO FIDELITATIS: Primùm quidem ΑΝΩΝΥΜΟΣ: Nunc vero ab Ipso AVCTORE . . . IACOBO . . . MAGNÆ BRITANNIÆ . . . Rege . . . denuò edita. Cui præmissa est PRÆFATIO MONITORIA . . . Cæsari RODOLPHO II . . . inscripta, eodem AVCTORE . . . AMSTELRODAMI, MDCIX.
(tp.2) Triplici nodo triplex cuneus. SIVE APOLOGIA PRO IVRAMENTO Fidelitatis . . . Editio altera. AMSTELRODAMI. M DC IX. 8° 2 pt.: pp.164; 139
3935.a.25.
Ownership inscription: Carmes de Fornes(?)

J43 JAMES I; King

[Triplici nodo triplex cuneus.] (tp.1) APOLOGIA PRO IVRAMENTO Fidelitatis. PRIMVM QVIDEM ΑΝΩΝΥΜΟΣ: NVNC VERO AB IPSO AVCTORE . . . IACOBO . . . MAGNÆ BRITANNIÆ . . . Rege . . . denuò edita. CVI PRÆMISSA EST PRÆFATIO MONITORIA . . . Cæsarí RODOLPHO II. . . . inscripta, eodem Auctore . . . Nunc de nouo Ad exemplar, Londini apud Iohannem Norton impressum, edita. HAGÆ-COMITIS. Excudebat Hillebrandus Iacobi . . . 1609.
(tp.2) Triplici nodo triplex cuneus. SIVE APOLOGIA PRO IVRAMENTO Fidelitatis . . . Nunc de nouo . . . edita. HAGÆ-COMITIS. Excudebat Hillebrandus Iacobi . . . 1609. 8° 2 pt.: pp.114; 97
3935.aaa.1.

J44 JAMES I; King

Triplici nodo, triplex cuneus. OV APOLOGIE POVR LE SERMENT DE FIDELITÉ. Contre les deux Brefs du Pape Paul cinquiesme, & la lettre du Cardinal Bellarmin . . . a G. Blackvvell . . . A LEYDEN, Par Iean le Feure. 1608. 12° pp.168
860.f.11.
Anonymous and with a false imprint. Probably printed in France. A different version from the one 'Traduict . . . par P.P. Aduocat au Parlement de Paris', placed at 3932.b.49.

J45 JAMES I; King

[Triplici nodo triplex cuneus. Extracts] Den Eedt Dic Jacobus de IIII[de] Coninck in groot Britanien zijne Onderdanen voor-stelt ende heeft doen zweeren. Ghetrocken uyt zijn boeck gheintituleert Apologia pro Iuramento fidelitatis. Ghedruckt tot Londen by Jan Norton . . . 1609. Over gheset uyt Latyn in Nederduyts . . . 1609. (col.) Ghedruckt tot Londen by Robert Backer [*sic*] . . . 1605 [*sic*]. ende nu tot Leyden by Thomas Basson. 4° 2 unsigned leaves, sig.A^2
T.2417(9).
The Latin edition bearing the title 'Apologia [etc.]' was printed by John Norton in London in 1609; the English edition, entitled 'An apologie for the oath of allegiance' was printed by Robert Barker in London in 1609.

J46 IAMMER-LIEDEKENS

IAMMER-LIEDEKENS ENDE RIIMEN, Voor desen in Hollant gestroyt ende gesongen: DOCH Nu voor de Lief-hebbers by een ghestelt/ende door den Druck uytghegheven . . . 1620. 4° sig.A^4
11555.e.27(1).
Poems directed against Prince Maurice and lamenting the fate of Johan van Oldenbarnevelt and other Remonstrants. Sometimes said to have been compiled by Hendrik Slatius. Probably printed by Abraham Verhoeven at Antwerp.

IAN Josepsens droom. 1619. *See* VERSTEGAN, Richard

JANSEN, Cornelius; Bishop of Ghent. Paraphrasis in omnes Psalmos. 1614. *See* BIBLE. Hagiographa. Latin

JANSEN, Nicolaes. *See* JANSSENS, Nicolaes

IANSON, Guilla[u]me. *See* BLAEU, Willem Jansz

J47 JANSSENS, Nicolaes

Een nieu Devoot Geestelijck Liedt-Boeck. Ghemaeckt door NICOLAES IANSEN van Rosendael . . . Desen lesten druck is van nieus oversien ende . . . vermeerdert. T'HANTWERPEN. By Gheleyn Jansz. [etc.] 8° pp.206; illus.

11555.aaa.25.

The titlepage woodcut shows a Nativity scene. The 1605 edition is recorded as having 157 pages and the 1612 edition as having a second approbation added, therefore probably published ca.1610.

J48 JANSSONIUS, Jacobus

LITVRGICA SIVE DE SACRIFICIIS MATERIATI ALTARIS LIBRI QVATVOR. Adiunctâ in Coronidem . . . SACRI CANONIS quo Romana Ecclesia vtitur expositione. AVTHORE IACOBO IANSSONIO . . . LOVANII, Apud Ioannem Masium . . . 1604. [etc.] 8° pp.388

3475.aa.58.

J49 JANSZ, Louris

[Een spel van zinnen van Jesus onder die leeraers.] Een Gheestlijck Spel van Sinnen seer leerlijck: Hoe Christus sit onder die Leeraers . . . Ghedruckt int Iaer 1606. obl.8° ff.84

11556.aa.16.

Anonymous. Adapted from a text by Louris Jansz surviving in manuscript and known to have been performed at Haarlem. Printed at Haarlem?

IANSZ, Willem. *See* BLAEU, Willem Jansz

IANSZOON, Guillaume. *See* BLAEU, Willem Jansz

IAPONICA, Sinensia, Morgana. 1601. *See* JESUITS [Letters 1598,99]

JAPPONIENSIS imperii admirabilis commutatio. 1604. *See* CARVALHO, Valentino

IEANSZ, Guillaume. *See* BLAEU, Willem Jansz

IEPHTHAS ende zijn eenighe dochters treur-spel. 1615. *See* KONING, Abraham de

J50 JEROME; Saint

[Letters] BEATI HIERONYMI . . . EPISTOLARVM SELECTARVM. LIBRI III . . . TORNACI, Apud NICOLAVM LAVRENTIVM . . . M DC XI. [etc.] 12° pp.619

846.a.6.

Edited by Andreas Schottus. Without the additional works listed on the verso of the titlepage.

J51 JEROME; Saint

[Vitae patrum.] VIES ET MIRACLES DES SAINCTS PERES HERMITES D'EGYPTE . . . DESCRITES EN PARTIE, traduites du Grec & recueillies . . . par sainct Ierosme . . . Nouuellement mises en François Corrigees & enrichies des marges, Par I.G. Parisien. A ARRAS, De l'Imprimerie de Robert Maudhuy . . . M.D.C.X. 8° pp.596,316

1371.b.3.

Editions not naming St. Jerome as the author are entered under VITAE.

JESUIJTEN. *See* JESUYTEN.

IESUITICA per Unitas Belgii Provincias negociatio. 1616. *See* FRIESLAND [1616]

Der IESUITEN negotiatie. 1616. *See* FRIESLAND [1616]

J52 JESUITS
[Rules] INSTRVCTIONES ET ORDINATIONES AD PROVINCIALES ET SVPERIORES SOCIETATIS, In Sexta CONGREGATIONE GENERALI partim . . . approbatæ: partim ad PRÆPOSITVM GENERALEM delatæ . . . M.DC.IX. 8° pp.43
4785.d.9(2).
The approbation signed: Franciscus Flerontinus, eiusdem Societatis per Belgium Præpositus Prouincialis, i.e. published at Antwerp?

J53 JESUITS
[Rules] REGLES DE LA COMPAGNIE DE IESVS . . . M.DC.X. 16° pp.184,15
4785.a.17.
With 'Regles des coadiuteurs temporels: que . . . Claude Aquaviva . . . a envoyé à toutes les Prouinces'. Printed by Laurence Kellam at Douai?

JESUITS [Letters from missions. Collections only: letters written by one or no more than two authors, named or identifiable, are entered under the single author or the first of the two authors.]

J54 JESUITS
[Letters 1598,99] IAPONICA, SINENSIA, MOGORANA. Hoc est, De rebus apud eas Gentes à Patribus Societatis IESV, Ann. 1598. & 99. gestis. A P. Ioanne Orano . . . in Latinam linguam versa . . . LEODII, Apud Arnoldum de Coersvvaremia . . . 1601. 8° sig.$A\text{-}F^8G^7$
867.e.20(1); G.6690.
The letters signed: Franciscus Pasius; Nicolaus Longobardus; Hieronymus Xavier.

J55 JESUITS
[Letters 1600] LITTERÆ ANNVÆ SOCIETATIS IESV ANNI MDC. ANTVERPIÆ Apud Heredes MARTINI NVTII, & IOANNEM MEVRSIVM . . . M.DC.XVIII. 8° pp.586
4785.c.12(1).

J56 JESUITS
[Letters 1601] LITTERÆ ANNVÆ SOCIETATIS IESV ANNI MDCI. ANTVERPIÆ Apud Heredes MARTINI NVTII, & IOANNEM MEVRSIVM . . . M.DC.XVIII. 8° pp.789
4785.c.12(2).

J57 JESUITS
[Letters 1602] LITTERÆ ANNVÆ SOCIETATIS IESV, ANNI M.DC.II. ANTVERPIÆ Apud Heredes Martini Nutij . . . M.DC.XVIII. 8° pp.775
4785.c.13.
Ownership inscription: Societatis Jesu, Nouesij, á 1625.

J58 JESUITS
[Letters 1603] ANNVÆ LITTERÆ SOCIETATIS IESV. Anni M.DC.III . . . DVACI, Ex Officina Viduæ LAVRENTII KELLAMI, & Thomæ filij eius . . . M.DC.XVIII. 8° pp.706
4785.c.15.
Ownership inscription: Collegij Soctis Jesv Nouesij 1624.

J59 JESUITS
[Letters 1604] ANNVÆ LITTERÆ SOCIETATIS IESV. Anni M.DC.IV . . . DVACI, Ex Officina Viduæ LAVRENTII KELLAMI, & Thomæ filij eius . . . M.DC.XVIII. 8° pp.758
4785.c.16.
Ownership inscription: Collegij Soctis Jesv Nouesij 1624.

J60 JESUITS

[Letters 1605] ANNVÆ LITTERÆ SOCIETATIS IESV. Anni M.D.C.V. . . . DVACI, Ex Officina Viduæ LAVRENTII KELLAMI, & Thomæ filij eius . . . M.DC.XVIII. 8° pp.978

4785.c.17.

Ownership inscription: Collegij Soctis Jesv Nouesij 1624. This date has been corrected to 1620 on the titlepage and the inscription repeated with the latter date only in the colophon.

J61 JESUYTEN

Der Jesuijten SPIEGHEL. Waerin elck een/bysonder de Princen en Furstelijcke persoonen/claerlijck ende grondelijck te sien heeft. Het leven/wandel ende Practijcken derselven . . . Eerst in de Italiaensche spraecke/te Rome selfs ghedruckt Anno 1618 . . . by Antonio Brugiotti . . . ende nu . . . in de Nederduytsche ghetranslateert ingaende het Jaer 1620. IN 'SGRAVEN-HAGHE. By Aer [*sic*] Meuris . . . 1620. 4° sig.AB^4C^1

T.2250(26).

No printer of the name Antonio Brugiotti seems to be known at Rome at that time.

J62 IESUYTEN

Der Iesuyten Pas-poort . . . Ghedruckt nae die Copij van Pragh, voor Samuel VV . . . 1619. fol. a single sheet; illus.

T.2423(17).

The engraving at the top of the sheet showing the Jesuits leaving Prague for Amsterdam where they enter the 'Rasphuis', i.e. prison, is related to one in one of two editions of 'Relatio nuper itineris [etc.]' published at Prague in 1619, but the text is not a translation of the 'Relatio'. The original publisher's name implied is Samuel Weleslawin.

JEUCHT spieghel. 1610. *See* HEYNS, Zacharias

J63 JEWS

[Service books. Daily prayers] ORDEN DE ORACIONES DE MES ARREO SIN BOLTAR de vna à otra parte. Y LA ORDEN DE HANVcah, Purim, y Pascuas de Pesah, Sebuoth, y Sucoth; con mucha diligentia emendada. Y las Bakassot al principio en ladino con la pronunçiaçion Hebrayca escrita en Hespannol. Impresso a despeza de la Santa Hebra de Talmud Torah, del Kahal Kados Bet Yaahkob en Amstradama . . . 5378. 8° ff.251

Or. C.049.a.7.

There is no Hebrew lettering in this book, although some Hebrew has been transcribed. A description of apparently the same title quoted in *Palau* no.202331 adds: Traducido por el Dr. Yshac, hijo de D. Semtob Caballero, por industria de A. Netto en Amsterdam, 5378. The year of publication is 1617/18.

JOANNES a S. Geminiano. *See* GORUS, Joannes

IOANNES Calvinus vreedt, bitter, vals. 1619. *See* SLATIUS, Henricus

J64 JOANNES ISAACUS; called Hollandus

D. MAGISTRI IOANNIS ISAACI HOLLANDI . . . OPERA MINERALIA, ET VEGETABILIA, SIVE de lapide Philosophico, quæ reperire potuimus, omnia . . . ex optimis manuscriptis Teutonicis exemplaribus . . . in Latinum sermonem conuersa. ARNHEMII, Apud IOANNEM IANSONIVM . . . M.DC.XVI. 8° pp.431; illus.

1033.d.6.

The illustrations are woodcuts.

J65 IOANNIS, Adrianus

SPIEGHEL Ende sonderlinghe Exempel Van Christelijcke verdraechzaemheydt/ tusschen . . . IOHAN CALVIN. ende . . . PHILIP. MELANTH. onverbrekelijck onderhouden . . . hoe wel zy over de hedendaechsche verschil poincten/van contrarie ghevoelen gheweest zijn . . . TOT ROTTERDAM, By Matthijs Bastiaensz. . . . 1618. 4° pp.53

T.2248(41).

The dedication signed: A. Joannis.

J66 JODE, Pieter de; the Elder

NOBILIVM IN BELGIO VTRIVSQVE SEXVS ORNATVS. Sebastian. Vrancx inuent. Pet. de Iode sculp. et excud. 4° & obl.4°

146.i.10(fol.121).

Two single sheet engravings, the first of a couple in a landscape with the above title and engraved Latin verses beginning 'Belgica nobilitas animis generosa, nec armis'; the second inscribed 'Wie sick een Monsiur a la mode kleeden sal', with four figures and explanatory text in German and French. Published at Antwerp, ca.1620?

J67 JOHANN Lichtenberger

Prognostique, Voorsegginghe van IOANNES LIECHTENBERGER, De welcke hy geschrevē heeft nu over de hondert ende ses en dertich Jaren/op die groote versaminghe van Saturnus ende Jupiter/die gheweest is int Jaer . . . 1484. Daerenboven oock op den Eclipsis in de Sonne/ghesien int . . . Jaer 1485. Gedruckt eerst te Ceulen int Jaer . . . 1526 by Peeter Quentel/ende nu herdruckt anno 1620. 4° pp.8; sig.C^4

P.P.3444.af(32); 1607/724.

Printed by Abraham Verhoeven at Antwerp.

J68 JOHANN JUSTUS Landsberger

[Alloquia Jesu Christi ad quamvis animam fidelem.] AN EPISTLE OR EXHORTATION OF IESVS CHRIST to the soule, that is deuoutly affected towards him . . . VVritten in latin by . . . Ioannes Landspergius . . . And translated . . . by the Lord Philip late Earle of Arundell . . . M.DC.X. 8° pp.288

G.20019.

The dedication to the Revd. Mother and Sisters of the Order of St. Clare at Graveling[en] signed: I.W. Priest, i.e. John Wilson. Translated with the assistance of John Gerard. Without imprint; published by the English College press at St. Omer.

J69 JOHN of Capistrano; Saint

Begin. Dese seltsame Figure is twee hondert Jaer voor Carolus gheboorte . . . by Venetien . . . ghevonden/[etc.] (col.) 't AMSTELREDAM, By Willem Jansz Cloppenburgh . . . 1621. fol. a single sheet; illus.

T.2423(47).

An allegorical woodcut with explanatory text, ascribed in the text to Capistranus.

J70 JOHN of Capistrano; Saint

PROPHETIE Dewelcke is tot Saumeurs in Vranckrijck/in't Jaer . . . 1620. PROPHETIE Trouvé à Saumur en France . . . 1620. Ghedruckt in't Jaer . . . 1620. 4° 2 unsigned leaves

T.2423(39).

The alleged author named in the text as Capistranus. Published by Hillebrand Jacobsz van Wouw at The Hague?

J71 JOHN of Damascus; Saint

VITÆ ET RES GESTÆ SS. BARLAAM EREMITÆ, ET IOSAPHAT INDIÆ REGIS, S. IO.

Dese seltsame Figure is twee hondert Jaer voor Carolus gheboorte/ aldus gheschildert of afghemaeldt by Venetien in een Steenrotse ghevonden/ dan heel sonder eenighe beduydinghe/ al-

[illegible]

Ick Capistranus een Dienaer Godts/ hebbe ghesien door de openbaringhe des Alderhooghsten de beduydinghe [illegible] ... In dese dry Jaren sullen sy CAROLUM met alle syne heerschappije erven/ ende [illegible]

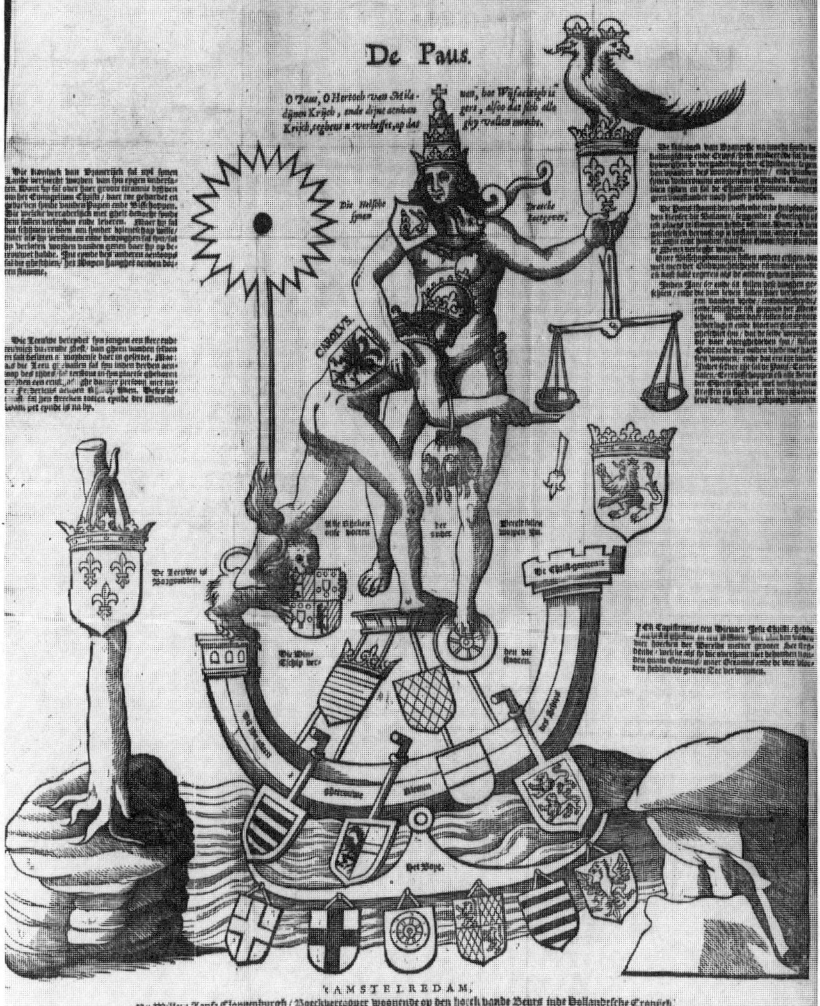

t'AMSTELREDAM,
By Willem Jansz Cloppenburgh / Boeckvercooper woonende op den hoeck vande Beurs inde Hollandtsche Cronijck,
ANNO 1621.

DAMASCENO AVCTORE, Iac. Billio Prunæo interprete. ANTVERPIÆ, Sumptibus Viduæ & hæredum Ioannis Belleri. 1602. 12° pp.435
859.a.7.
The attribution to St. John of Damascus is erroneous.

J72 JOHN of Hoveden
R.P. IOANNIS HOVDENI . . . CHRistiados Rhytmicæ Libri sex. EX V.P.F. PHILIPPI Boskhieri . . . recensione. EDITIO TERTIA. Luxemburgi, Apud Matt: Birthon . . . 1603. [etc.] 8° sig.†[8])([4]A-M[8]
11403.a.15.
With a recommendation by Henricus Sedulius. Ownership inscription: John ffrithe.

J73 JOHN Ogilvie; Saint
RELATIO INCARCERATIONIS, ET MARTYRII P. IOANNIS OGILBEI . . . EX Autographo ipsius Martyris, in carcere exarato . . . octiduo ante mortem: continuata verò deinceps per eiusdem concaptiuos . . . DVACI, Typis Viduæ LAVRENTII KELLAMI . . . 1615. 8° pp.51
1370.c.17.

J74 JOHN CHRYSOSTOM; Saint, Patriarch of Constantinople
[Works. Latin] (tp.1) DIVI IOANNIS CHRYSOSTOMI . . . OPERA OMNIA. Ad collationem vtriusque linguæ Exemplarium hactenus editorum, integritati primæve restituta, à mendis repurgata, nouoque Auctuario seu TOMO SEXTO, Et ea quæ per FRONTONEM DVCAEVM . . . recognita sunt, accessione locupletatus . . . TOMVS PRIMVS. ANTVERPIAE, Apud Ioannem Keerbergium . . . M.DC.XIV.
(tp.2–6) DIVI IOANNIS CHRYSOSTOMI . . . OPERVM TOMVS SECVNDVS (TERTIVS; QVARTVS; QVINTVS; SEXTVS . . . QVO CONTINENTVR EA, QVAE . . . nondum fuerunt aggregata) . . . ANTVERPIAE, Apud Ioannem Keerbergium. M.DC.XIV. fol. 6 tom.: pp.627: plate; port.; pp.620; 392; 803; 927; col.2322
1483.dd.10.
With the life of St. John Chrysostom by Georgius Merula Alexandrinus, translated by Godefridus Tilmannus. With the exlibris of the R. Hon. Washington Sewallis Earl Ferrers.

J75 JOHN GEORGE; Elector of Saxony
Copye vande Antwoorde geschreuen byden Keurvorst van Saxen/AENDEN Pfaltz-Graeff Jan/Stadt-houder tot Heydelberch. Eerst Ghedruckt den xxv. September 1620. T'Hantwerpen/By Abraham Verhoeven . . . 1620. [etc.] 4° pp.8; sig.Mm; illus., port.
P.P.3444.af(106).
The letter dated 9 August 1620. The titlepage woodcut shows the portrait of John George.

J76 JOHN GEORGE; Margrave of Jägerndorf
Copije vande Brieff door den Marck-Grave van Jaghersdorp gheschreven aende Vorsten ende Standen in Slesien. fol. a single sheet
T.2424(21).
The letter dated 1621. Apparently part of a news sheet, cropped. Published in 1621, at Amsterdam?

J77 JOHNSON, Francis; Brownist
CERTAYNE REASONS and Arguments Proving that it is not lawfull to heare or have any spirituall communion with the present Ministerie of the Church of England . . . Printed . . . 1608. 4° pp.112
4135.b.44.
The preface signed: Francis Iohnson. Without imprint; printed by Giles Thorp at Amsterdam.

J78 JOHNSON, Francis; Brownist

A CHRISTIAN PLEA Conteyning three Treatises. The first, touching the Anabaptists . . . The second, touching such Christians, as now are here, commonly called Remonstrants or Arminians . . . The third, touching the Reformed Churches, with vvhom my self agree . . . Made by FRANCIS IOHNSON . . . PRINTED, In the yeere of our Lord 1617. 4° pp.324
707.a.34(1).

Without imprint. The attribution to the press of William Brewster at Leiden doubted in *Harris & Jones (1)* no.7, rejected in *Harris & Jones (2)*; printed by Giles Thorp at Amsterdam? Cropped.

J79 JOHNSON, Francis; Brownist

A short Treatise Concerning the exposition of those words of Christ, Telle the Church, &c. Mat. 18. 17. Written by Francis Iohnson . . . PRINTED . . . 1611. 4° sig.A-D^4
698.g.41.

Printed at Amsterdam?

JOHNSON, William. *See* BLAEU, Willem Jansz

JONES, John. *See* LEANDER de Sancto Martino; name in religion of John Jones

J79a JONGE, Boudewijn de. *See* Addendum p.719

J80 JONSTONUS, Johannes; Abredonensis

CONSOLATIO CHRISTIANA SVB CRVCE Ex vivifico Dei verbo. Per IOHAN. IONSTONVM . . . EIVSDEM IAMBI de Felicitate Hominis DEO reconciliati, & alia Poematia. LVGDVNI BATAVORVM, Apud Ludovicum Elzevirium . . . M.DC.IX. 8° pp.110
4400.i.8.

In verse. With an additional, unsigned oblong leaf also paginated "11", bearing the text of a passage from Cor.II in Greek with two different Latin translations. Printed by Henrick van Haestens at Leiden? Ownership inscription: D. Laing.

J81 JONSTONUS, Johannes; Abredonensis

HEROES EX OMNI HISTORIA SCOTICA lectissimi. AVCTORE IOHAN. IONSTONO . . . LVGDVNI BATAVORVM, Excudebat Christophorus Guyotius, sumtibus ANDREÆ HARTII Bibliopolæ Edinburgensis. M.D.CIII. 4° pp.56
600.g.19(2).

J82 JONSTONUS, Johannes; Abredonensis

ICONES Regum Iudæ & Israelis Carmine expressæ PER IOHANNEM IONSTONVM . . . Accessit PRINCIPIS Institutio Prophetica, Illustrata Metaphrasi poeticâ ejusdem Jonstoni AD . . . HENRICVM Principem Britanniarum. LVGDVNI BATAVORVM, Ex Officina Vlrici Cornelij, & Georgij Abrahami . . . M D CXII. 4° sig.A-E^4F^2
1015.d.8.

With a printer's device used by Henrick van Haestens at Leiden.

J83 JONSTONUS, Johannes; Abredonensis

INSCRIPTIONES HISTORICÆ REGVM SCOTORVM . . . IOH. IONSTONO . . . Auctore. Præfixus est GATHELVS, sive de Gentis origine Fragmentum An. Melvini. Additæ sunt icones omnium regum nobilis Familiæ Stuartorum in ære sculptæ. AMSTELDAMI, Excudebat Cornelius Claessonius Andreæ Hartio bibliopolæ Edemburgensi . . . 1602. 4° pp.60; illus.
600.g.19(1); G.5381.

In verse. There are six preliminary leaves, including the titlepage, and ten portraits printed on one side of the leaf only. The portrait of James VI shows him in civilian dress and wearing a high hat; that of Queen Anne shows her in a highnecked dress and is framed in a border of roses.

J84 JONSTONUS, Johannes; Abredonensis

INSCRIPTIONES HISTORICÆ REGVM SCOTORVM . . . IOH. IONSTONO . . . Auctore . . . AMSTELDAMI, Excudebat Cornelius Claessonius Andreæ Hartio bibliopolæ Edemburgensi . . . 1602. 4° pp.60; illus.
288.e.2.

Another issue of the preceding, perhaps published in 1603. There are eight leaves of preliminaries, including the titlepage and one further leaf bearing a dedication to the King as James VI consisting of poems by Joseph Justus Scaliger, Janus Dousa and Daniel Heinsius. The portrait of James VI shows him in armour and hatless; Queen Anne is shown wearing a low-cut dress, with a jewel in her hair, and the portrait is framed in trailing foliage with small flowers. Ownership inscription: ex lib Ro Gray colleg med Edinburg et Londin socii.

J85 JONSTONUS, Johannes; Abredonensis

INSCRIPTIONES HISTORICÆ REGVM SCOTORVM . . . IOH. JONSTONO . . . Auctore . . . AMSTELDAMI, Excudebat Cornelius Claessonius Andreæ Hartio bibliopolæ Edemburgensi . . . 1602. 4° pp.60; illus.
C.24.b.27.

A reissue of the preceding, with eight preliminary leaves bearing additional texts congratulating James I on his accession to the English throne and a chronogram reading MDCIII, signed respectively: I.I. and I, Ionstonus. The original leaf ★2 has been omitted. The date on the titlepage has been altered in manuscript to 1603.

J86 JONSTONUS, Johannes; Abredonensis

[Inscriptiones historicæ regum Scotorum.] [A TREVVE DESCRIPTION OF the nobill race of the Stevvards . . . vvith their lyvvelie portraturs, [etc.]] (col.) Printed in Amsterdam, Ad the expensis of Andro Hart . . . in Edinburgh . . . 1603. [etc.] fol. 10 unsigned leaves; illus.
600.k.4(3).

Anonymous. Each leaf contains a portrait with the prose translation of the text of the 'Inscriptiones'. The portraits of James VI and Anne are as those in the issue described above at no.J84. Printed by Cornelis Claesz? Imperfect; wanting the titlepage which has been supplied by a photograph from an unnamed copy.

J87 JOSEPHI, Joannes

Een schoone heerlicke Ende WARACHTIGE AENWYSINGE, Waer in by malcander Als in een schoon Tafereel claerlick gesien can worden/in hoe menige . . . plaetsen de Remonstranten . . . teghen haer selven ghesproken hebben. Mitsgaders: Dat sy ooc oorsake zijn van desen . . . twist/in de Gereformeerde Kercke. Hier is oock by malcanderen . . . ghestelt/alle de Artijckelen die in de Conferentie verhandelt zijn gheweest . . . Alles by een ghestelt door I.F.I. Liefhebber vande heylighe waerheydt Gods. Anno 1614. 4° pp.56
T.2242(35).

The second edition, entitled 'Een gouden tafereel', giving the compiler's full name as: Joannes Filius Josephi, is entered below.

J88 JOSEPHI, Joannes

[Een schoone . . . aenwysinge.] Een Gouden TAFEREEL, Ofte een . . . REGISTER, Getrocken so uyt de Haechsche ende Delfsche Schriftelijcke Conferentien, Als oock uyt andere Schriften van de Voorstaenders van Arminius. Waer in ghesien can worden/in hoe menighe . . . plaetsen de Remonstranten teghen haer selven ghesproken hebben . . . Alles by een ghestelt Door Ioannes Filius Iosephi . . . Met groote neersticheyt oversien/vermeerdert ende verbetert. Ende voor de tweede mael Gedruckt Naer de Copie. Anno 1614. 4° pp.59
T.2244(4).

Another edition of the preceding. A variant of the copy described in *Knuttel* no.2129 which has the imprint: Gedruckt Naer de Copie t'Amsterdam. 1614.

J89 IOURNAEL

IOVRNAEL, Ende corte Beschrijuinghe/wat in den Bloedigen slach/teghen den Erf Christen Vyant/den Turck/met de Polacken/van dach tot dach ghepasseert is . . . Eerst Ghedruct den 23. Nouember. T'Hantwerpen/By Abraham Verhoeuen/ [etc.] 4° pp.16; sig. RrrrSsss⁴; illus.
P.P.3444.af(316).

Headed: Nouember, 1621. 171. The titlepage has been printed oblong, the woodcuts on it in two strips showing soldiers driving camels through a village in the upper and a battle in the lower strip. The text ends with mockery of false news being spread in Holland.

JOURNAEL van de reyse der Hollandtsche schepen ghedaen in Oost Indien. 1598. Appendix. 1618 [or rather, 1598]. *See* HOUTMAN, Cornelis de

The IUDGE wherein is shewed, how Christ . . . is to iudge the world. 1621. *See* ARIAS, Francisco

The JUDGMENT of a Catholicke English-man. 1608. *See* PERSONS, Robert

J90 JÜLICH

[2.9.1610] ARTICULEN, Die gheaccordeert zijn aenden Gouverneur/Capiteynen/ Officieren/Magistraten/Burgeren/Inwoonderen/ende Soldaten van Gulick/op't overgeven der selver Plaetse/ende van Bredenbent. IN S'GRAVEN-HAGHE. By Hillebrant Iacobsz . . . 1610. [etc.] 4° sig.A²; illus.
T.1729(2).

The engraving shows the city under siege. It is described separately in *Knuttel* no.1743 whereas the 'Articulen' corresponds to *Knuttel* no.1745.

J91 JÜLICH, KLEVE AND BERGE

[12.3–24.5.1612] Vryheden ende Privilegien Van des Keurvorsts van Brandenburgh/Hertoghs in Pruyssen/van Gulick/Cleve/Berge/&c. En Vrou Anne, Paltzgravinne byden Rijn . . . verleent den ghenen die haer onder de protectie ende bescherminghe van henne V.V.GG. tot Mullem huyslijcken begeeren neder te setten/Burgherlijcke Vryheyt . . . Wt den Hoogduytschen . . . overgheset. Eerst ghedruckt tot Dusseldorp by Bernard Buysz . . . Anno 1612. Ende nu gedruckt t'Amsterdam/by Pieter Pietersz. [etc.] 4° sig.A-C⁴
T.2242(31).

The proclamation of 12 March 1612 as part of the administration of Jülich, Kleve and Berge, with related documents. Published in 1612.

J92 JUNIUS, Adrianus

NOMENCLATOR, OMNIVM RERVM PROPRIA NOMINA SEPTEM . . . LINGVIS EXPLICATA INDICANS; AVCTORE HADRIANO IVNIO . . . FRANCOFVRTI, Excudebat NICOLAVS HOFFMANNVS, Sumptibus Ionæ Rosæ. M.DC.XI. 8° pp.545
625.g.11.

Including Dutch translations.

J93 JUNIUS, Adrianus

NOMENCLATOR OCTILINGVIS, OMNIVM RERVM propria nomina continens. AB ADRIANO IVNIO antehac collectus. Nunc verò renouatus, auctus . . . Accessit huic postremæ editioni alter NOMENCLATOR è duobus veteribus GLOSSARIIS. HERMANNI GERMBERGII Opera & studio . . . EX TYPOGRAPHIA IACOBI STOER. M.DCXIX. 8° pp.713
627.b.1.

Including Dutch translations. Printed at Geneva. Ownership inscription: Johannes Hill.

J94 JUNIUS, Adrianus

PHALLI, Ex fungorum genere in HOLLANDIÆ sabuletis passim crescentis descriptio &

ad viuum expressa pictura, HADRIANO IVNIO . . . auctore . . . LVGDVNI BATAVORVM, Ex Typographeîo Christophori Guyotij, Impensis Ioannis Orlers . . . M.D.C.I. 4° sig.AB^4; illus.
968.k.1(4); B.178(6).
With a poem on the same subject by the author.

JUNIUS, Balduinus. *See* JONGE, Boudewijn de

JUNIUS, Franciscus. *See* DU JON, François

J95 JUNIUS, Isaac
NOOTVVENDICH VERTOOCH Vande Onnoselheyt ende oprechticheyt des E. Kercken Raets van Haerlem ende de . . . abuysen/van sekere uyt de Gemeente/die den dienst van den voorsz Kercken Raedt in twijffel trecken . . . Tsamenghestelt/ Tot . . . Wederlegginghe van een seecker Boecxken met desen Titel/Requeste vande dolerende Kercke tot Haerlem . . . TOT HAERLEM, Gedruckt by Adriaen Rooman . . . 1617. Voor Francoys Beyts [etc.] 4° pp.48
T.2247(42).
Anonymous.

J96 JUNIUS, Lodewijk
Tsamen-sprekinghe van PHILEMON EN ONESIMVS Over Het vertooch vande onnoselheyt- des E. Kerckenraets tot Haerlem/ende het Teghenvertooch/ uytghegheven . . . Door. Ludovicum Iunium . . . Ghedruckt tot HAERLEM. By Adriaen Rooman . . . Voor Françoys Beyts . . . 1618. 4° pp.67
T.2248(33).
The authors of the 'Nootwendich vertooch' and the 'Tegen-vertooch' are Isaac Junius and Mathias Damius respectively.

IUS belli Sabaudici. 1601. *See* ARNAULD, Antoine; Avocat-général

JUSTI Lipsii defensio postuma. 1608. *See* SCRIBANI, Carolus

IUSTI Lipsii sapientiae et litterarum antistitis fama postuma. 1607. *See* MORETUS, Balthasar

JUSTIFICATIE van de Procedueren by Schout, Burghermeesteren ende Regeerders der Stadt Haerlem. 1618. *See* HAARLEM [19.4.1618]

J97 IUSTIFICATIE
IVSTIFICATIE Vande COVRS Die ghehouden wort by de Steden/Dordrecht, Amstelredam, Schiedam, Enchuysen, Edam ende Purmereynde, als leden vande Vergaderinge vande . . . Staten van Hollant ende West-Vrieslant/tot bewaringe vande Wettige regieringe der Landen/hanthoudinghe vande suyvere Leere/ende goede ordre vande . . . ware Ghereformeerde Christelijcke Religie . . . Den tweeden Druck. t'AMSTELREDAM, By Marten Jansz. Brant . . . 1618. 4° pp.136
T.2248(4).
A collection of documents.

IVSTIFICATIE vande resolutie der . . . Staten van Hollandt . . . den 4. Augusti 1617. 1618. *See* GROOT, Hugo de

J98 JUSTIFICATION
[La justification du Prince d'Orange.] De verantvvoordinghe Des Princen van Orangien/teghen de valsche leughenen/daer mede zijn Wedersprekers hem soecken t'onrechte te beschuldighen . . . t'Amsterdam/voor Michiel Colijn . . . 1610. 4° pp.84; illus.
T.2419(2).
Sometimes attributed to Hubert Languet. With the arms of William I of Orange on the titlepage.

J99 JUVENALIS, Decimus Junius

D. IVNII IVVENALIS SATYRARVM LIBRI V. A. PERSII FLACCI SATYRARVM LIBER VNVS. EX OFFICINA PLANTINIANA RAPHELENGII, M.D.CIX. 16° pp.111

C.20.f.49.

Published at Leiden. With Christophe Plantin's original dedication to Carolus Tisnakus. From the travelling library of Sir Julius Caesar.

K

For names of authors or anonymous headings spelt alternatively with initial K or C and not found under K: *see* also C

K1 KEERE, Pieter van de

(tp.1) Den standt van Jerusalem Voor CHRISTI komste. (col.1) t'Amstelredam/ ghedruckt by Peeter vande Keere Plaetsnijder . . . 1610.
(tp.2) Den standt van Jerusalem naer CHRISTI komste. (col.2) t'Amstelredan [*sic*] ghedruckt by David Meyne/Caert ende Cunst-vercooper . . . 1610.

10759.l.1. (insertion between ff.45, 46.)

Two leaves with cut out texts mounted on them, perhaps originally intended for columns to be pasted below the map now bound between them. The map, with inscriptions in Dutch, is neither signed nor dated. From the colophons it appears that Pieter van de Keere may have engraved the map and printed the text and both he and David Meyne sold the whole. Apparently unrecorded in bibliographies of the Holy Land.

K2 KELLISON, Matthew

EXAMEN REFORMATIONIS NOVÆ PRÆSERTIM CALVINIANÆ IN QVO SYNAGOGA ET DOCTRINA CALVINI . . . REFVTATVR. AVTHORE MATTHÆO KELLISONO . . . DVACI, Typis PETRO AVROI . . . M.DC.XVI. [etc.] 8° pp.774

3935.aa.29.

Author's presentation copy to his friend Damanetto. With the exlibris of the Bibliotheca Venerabilis Capituli Remensis, Ex dono . . . Petri Frizon.

K3 KELLISON, Matthew

THE RIGHT AND IVRISDICTION OF THE PRELATE, and the PRINCE. OR, A TREATISE OF ECCLESIASTICALL, and REGALL authoritie. COMPYLED BY I. E. STVDENT IN DIVINITIE . . . Imprinted . . . 1617. 8° pp.317

1607/1264.

Anonymous and without imprint; printed by Pierre Auroi at Douai. Ownership inscription: E libris Joh: Applebee.

K4 KELLISON, Matthew

THE RIGHT AND IVRISDICTION OF THE PRELATE . . . COMPYLED BY I. E. STVDENT IN DIVINITIE . . . Imprinted with licence of Superionrs [*sic*] . . . 1621. 8° pp.412

1607/1270.

Anonymous and without imprint; printed by Pierre Auroi at Douai.

K5 KELLISON, Matthew

A SVRVEY OF THE NEW RELIGION, DETECTING MANIE GROSSE ABSVRDITIES . . . Set forth by Matthevv Kellison . . . Printed at Dovvay, by LAVRENCE KELLAM . . . 1603. 8° pp.733

3936.b.38.

In fact, printed by Simon de Foigny at Rheims with a new titlepage and leaf a8 only printed at Douai. Ownership inscription: Robert Gordone.

K6 KELLISON, Matthew

A SVRVEY OF THE NEW RELIGION, DETECTING MANY GROSSE ABSVRDITIES . . . Set forth by Matthevv Kellison . . . Nevvly augmented by the Author . . . Printed at Doway by LAVRENCE KELLAM . . . M.DC.V. 4° pp.404
1413.e.6; C.26.l.2.

KERCKEN-ORDENINGHE, ghestelt in den Nationalen Synode . . . binnen Dordrecht . . . ende . . . goedt-ghevonden . . . by de . . . Staten des Furstendoms Ghelre. 1620. *See* DORDRECHT. Synod

KERCKEN-ORDENINGHE van den Jare 1591. 1617. *See* HOLLAND. Staten [8.3.1591]

K7 KERCKEN-ORDENINGHEN

De Kercken-Ordeninghen Der ghereformeerder Nederlandtscher Kercken/in de vier Nationale Synoden ghemaeckt ende ghearresteert. MITSGADERS Eenige anderen in de Provinciale Synoden van Hollandt ende Zeelandt gheconcipieert ende besloten . . . De tvveede Editie. TOT DELF Ghedruckt by Ian Andriesz . . . 1617. 4° pp.128
T.2247(13).
Believed to have been edited by Reginaldus Donteclock. Reprinted from an edition of 1612.

KHPYKEION. 1618. *See* MARSELAER, Fredericus de

KESSELER, Frans. *See* KESSLER, Franz

K8 KESSLER, Franz

[Unterschiedliche . . . Secreta.] CONST-BOECXKEN. Daer in ghevonden worden, Vier onderscheidelijcke secreten oft Konst-stucken . . . 1. Om een Instrument te maken/daer door men elckanderen zijn meeninghe oft secreten kan doen verstaen/over't Water oft Landt ende zoo wijt als men malkanderen kan zien. 2. oock om te maken een Water Harnas/daer mede men onbeschadicht sommighe uren onder 't Water kan zyn . . . 3. Noch om een Lochtbroeck te maken . . . 4. Met noch eenen Swemriem te maken . . . Beschreven ende in de Hoochduytsche sprake aen den dach ghegeven door FRANS KESSELER . . . Ende nu . . . overgheset . . . door M. C. H. TOT ARNHEM, By Ian Iansz . . . 1619. 4° pp.28
1481.b.27.
Without the plates mentioned in the preface.

KEYSER Otto den derden. 1616. *See* RODENBURGH, Theodore

K9 KEYSERLYCKE

KEYSERLYCKE GHENADE. Dat is Kort Sommier ende verhael vande wreede eñ tyrannelijcke Execntie [*sic*]/ghedaen door last ende bevel van . . . Keyser Ferdinand de II. . . . binnen der Stadt Prage . . . op den 21. der Maent van Junij/aen vier-en-veertich Adelijcke . . . Persoonen . . . Dienende tot . . . waerschouwinghe allen den ghenen/die sich teghens den Roomschen Antichrist ende Keyser . . . hebben ghestelt . . . IN 'SGRAVEN-HAGHE, By Aert Meuris . . . 1621. [etc.] 4° pp.7
T.2424(24).

K10 KIEL, Cornelis van

[Dictionarium teutonico-latinum.] ETYMOLOGICVM TEVTONICÆ LINGVÆ: SIVE DICTIONARIVM TEVTONICO-LATINVM, PRÆCIPVAS TEVTONICÆ LINGVÆ DICTIONES ET PHRASES Latinè interpretatas . . . complectens: Studio & Opera CORNELII KILIANI . . . Quartæ editioni Auctarium est additum, continens propriorum nominum Germanicæ originis Etyma & significationes . . . & Nomenclaturas

animalium . . . Opera D. LVDOLPHI POTTERI . . . ALCMARIÆ, Ex Typographeïo Iacobi Meesteri. Et Prostant Amsteldami, apud Cornelium Nicolai . . . M.VI^C.V. 8° pp.789; illus.
628.g.14.
The titlepage engravings show 'Retorica' with books and caduceus, a dramatic poet seeking advice from a scholar and the scene of a stage through a window.

K11 KIEL, Cornelis van
ETYMOLOGICVM TEVTONICÆ LINGVÆ . . . Studio & Opera CORNELII KILIANI . . . Quartæ editioni Auctarium est additum . . . Opera D. LVDOLPHI POTTERI . . . ALCMARIÆ, Ex Typographeïo Iacobi Meesteri. Et Prostant Amsteldami, apud Henricum Laurentij . . . M.VI^C.XIII. 8° pp.789; illus.
628.g.15.
The titlepage shows the same illustrations as that of the 1605 edition, but this is not a reissue of the preceding.

K12 KIEL, Cornelis van
ETYMOLOGICVM TEVTONICÆ LINGVÆ . . . Studio & Opera CORNELII KILIANI . . . Quartæ editioni Auctarium est additum . . . Opera D. LVDOLPHI POTTERI . . . ALCMARIÆ, Ex Typographeïo Iacobi Meesteri. Et Prostant Amsteldami, apud Theodorum Petri . . . M.VI^C.XIII. 8° pp.789; illus.
68.a.23.
Another issue of the preceding. Ownership inscriptions: Cornelis Boom; G. P. Hooft.

K13 KIEL, Cornelis van
ETYMOLOGICVM TEVTONICAE LINGVAE . . . Studio & Opera CORNELII KILIANI . . . Quartæ editioni Auctarium est additum . . . Opera D. LVDOLPHI POTTERI . . . AMSTELRODAMI, Ex Officina HENRICI LAVRENTII, M.D.VIC.XX [*sic*]. 8° pp.789; illus.
1568/3670.
Not a reissue of the preceding editions. With the same titlepage illustrations as in the earlier editions. Ownership inscription: Simonds D'Ewes, presented by Albertus Joachimi.

KILIANUS, Cornelius. *See* KIEL, Cornelis van

K14 KIRCHMEYER, Thomas
[Tragoedia alia nova Mercator.] Een Christelijcke TRAGEDIA. Die Coopman ofte dat Oordeel geheeten. Daerinne die Hoovet-stucken ofte Gront-leeringhen van twee Religien/die Romische Papistische/ende die Gereformeerde Euangelische . . . teghens een ander worden voor Ooghen ghestelt. Met eene . . . Sluyt-Reden . . . Aen de Provinciale Stadt Groeningen ende Ommelanden. Voormaels in exilio ghestellet, ende al nu van nieus vveder revideret door eenen vvtghevveken liefhebber des Vader-Landes. Tot Groeningen, Gedruckt by Hans Sas . . . 1613. 8° sig.A-Z^8
11754.e.28.
Anonymous. The translator's preface signed: D.V.A., i.e. Doede van Amsweer, thus named in a manuscript note on the titlepage by the owner Henr. Carolinus van Bijler.

K15 KITĀB
[Kitāb al-amthal.] [Arabic] SEV PROVERBIORVM ARABICORVM Centuriæ duæ, ab Anonymo quodam Arabe collectæ & explicatæ: cum interpretatione Latina & Scholiis IOSEPHI SCALIGERI . . . ET THOMÆ ERPENII. LEIDÆ, In Officina Raphelengiana, 1614. 4° pp.126
1363.b.6(1); 622.h.5(1); G.17796(1).
Edited by Thomas Erpenius.

Dono mihi dedit hoc Lexicon Vir Amplissimus Albertus Joachimi mihi amicissimus, eques auratus, Dominus Legatus a Serenis. DD[is] Ordinum Generalium Foederatorum Regi Magnae Britanniae Carolo.

Simonds D'Ewes.

ETYMOLOGICVM TEVTONICAE LINGVAE: SIVE

DICTIONARIVM TEVTONICO-LATINVM,

PRAECIPVAS TEVTONICAE LINGVÆ DICTIONES ET PHRASES Latinè interpretatas, & cum aliis nonnullis linguis obiter collatas, complectens.

Studio & Opera Kiel (C. van)

CORNELII KILIANI DVFFLÆI

Opus Germanis tam superioribus quàm inferioribus, Gallis, Anglis siue Anglosaxonibus, Italis, Hispanis, & aliis lectu perutile.

Quid hic præstitum sit, Præfatio ad Lectorem docebit.

Quartæ editioni Auctarium est additum, continens propriorum nominum Germanicæ originis Etyma & significationes vtriusque sexus, & Nomenclaturas animalium quadrupedum volatilium, ac piscium, in vsum tam docentium quàm discentium ex variis Autoribus collectum:

Opera D. LVDOLPHI POTTERI Groeningensis.

AMSTELRODAMI,

Ex Officina HENRICI LAURENTII,

M. D. VIC. XX.

K13

K16 KLAER
Klaer ende grondich Teghen-vertoogh/van eenighe Kercken-Dienaren van Hollandt ende West-Vrieslandt/gestelt tegen seker VERTOOGH DER REMONSTRANTEN, den . . . Staten . . . in Aprili voorleden over gegeven, ende daer na door den Druck ghemeen ghemaeckt . . . t'AMSTERDAM, Voor Marten Jansz. Brandt . . . 1617. (col.) t'AMSTERDAM, Ghedruckt by Paulus van Ravesteyn, ANNO 1617. 4° pp.120
T.2247(39).
Sometimes attributed to Jacobus Trigland. Written against Jan Wtenbogaert's 'Copye van seker vertooch'.

KLAER vertoogh van de onwettige successie des Keysers Ferdinandi II. 1620. *See* LUCULENTA demonstratio

K17 KNESEBECK, Thomas von
[Einfältiger Bericht.] Eenvoudich ende ernstich bericht/HOE SICH EEN YEGELYCK CHRISTEN IN DESEN TYDEN, Maer voornamelijck/D'ONDERDANEN TEGEN HARE OVERICHEDEN, DIE VAN VERanderinge . . . der Religie eenichsins beschuldicht worden, houden zullen. In ses t'samen sprekinghen vervaet/Door een liefhebber van vrede ende waerheyt: eerst ghedruckt tot Berlijn . . . daer nae . . . overgeset uyt het Hoochduytsch. Hier is noch by ghevoecht een PLACCAET VANDEN CHVRFVRST TOT BRANDENburch, teghen die Predicanten, Die ghewoon zijn op den Predickstoel hare bittere gulle [*sic*] uyt te gieten teghen hare partijen. t'Vtrecht/By my Jan Amelissz . . . 1615.
(tp.2=sig.L2r) PLACCAET Vanden . . . Churfurst tot Brandenburch . . . Teghen de Predicanten: Die gewoon zijn op den Predikstoel hare bittere galle wt te gieten tegen hare partijen . . . Overgheset uyt het Hooch-duytsch. TOT VTRECHT, By Jan Amelissz. . . . 1615. 4° pp.86
T.2245(9 &14).
Pseudonymous. The 'Placcaet' consists of sig.L2-4. It is dated 24 February 1614.

K18 KOLM, Jan Siewertsz
BATTAEFSCHE: Vrienden-Spieghel: WT LEVENDER IONSTE. t'Amsteldam By Gerrit H. van Breugel 1615. 4° sig.A^6B-K^4; illus.
11755.c.39(1).
Signed: Ian Sievertsen Colm. The titlepage woodcut shows the emblem of the Amsterdam Chamber of Rhetoric. Woodcuts on sig.E4r show 'Mercurius' and 'Venus'.

K19 KOLM, Jan Siewertsz
I. S. KOMLS [*sic*] Nederlants Treur-spel. Inhoudende Den Oorspronck der Nederlandsche beroerten . . . Speel-wijs vertoont By de Brabandtsche Camer UYT LEVENDER IONST. Binnen AMSTELREDAM. 't AMSTERDAM, Ghedruckt by Paulus van Ravesteyn, Voor Abraham Huybrechtsz. . . . 1616. (col.) t'AMSTERDAM, Ghedruckt by Paulus van Ravesteyn . . . 1616. 4° sig.$\star^6$A-I^4
11754.bb.7.

K20 KONING, Abraham de
ACHABS TREVR-SPEL . . . TOT ROTTERD'AM, By Jan van Waesberghe de jonghe . . . 1618. 4° sig.-, A-G^4H^2; illus.
11755.bb.68(1).
The dedication signed: Abraham de Koning. The titlepage engraving shows a scene from the play.

K21 KONING, Abraham de

IEPHTHAHS Ende zijn Eeenighe Dochters TREVR-SPEL 'TAMSTERDAM Voor Abraham de Koning . . . 1615. (col.) 'TAMSTERDAM, Ghedruckt by Paulus van Ravesteyn . . . 1615. 4° sig.★A-R^4; illus.

11754.bb.14.

The dedication signed: A. de Koning. The titlepage engraving shows a scene from the play.

K22 KONING, Abraham de

SIMSONS Treur-spel . . . t'AMSTERDAM. Voor Cornelis Lodewijksz. vander Plasse . . . 1618. (col.) 'TAMSTELREDAM, Ghedruckt by Paulus van Ravesteyn . . . 1618. 4° sig.A-H^4

11754.bbb.36.

The dedication signed: Abraham de Koning.

K23 KONING, Abraham de

't Spel van Sinne/Vertoont op de Tweede Lotery van d'Arme Oude Mannen ende Vrouwen Gast-Huys. Tot Lof, Eere en Leere der Wijt-Beroemder COOPSTADT AMSTELREDAM . . . t'AMSTERDAM, Ghedruckt, by Paulus van Ravesteyn. Voor Abraham de Koningh . . . 1616. 4° sig.A-E^4

11755.e.34.

The dedication signed: A. de Koning. Printed by Paulus van Ravesteyn.

K24 KORAN

[Selections. Arabic and Latin] [Arabic.] HISTORIA IOSEPHI Patriarchæ, Ex Alcorano, Arabicè. Cum triplici versione Latina, & scholijs THOMAE ERPENII, cuius & ALPHABETVM ARABICVM præmittitur. LEIDAE, Ex Typographia ERPENIANA Linguarum Orientalium. 1617. 4° sig.A-S^4

483.a.18; 222.g.19.

The titlepage has an architectural border in woodcut.

KORT bewijs van den verkeerden aerdt. 1620. *See* BAERLE, Caspar van

K25 KORT

Een kort Monickendammer Discours/Ende Hoorns Liedt/Gheestigh bediedt: Teghens 't Levendich Discours van Amsterdam. Ende achter aen-hangende Een levendige Af-beeldinge der oproerige Prædestinateuren: Door Een Lief-hebber der Neder-Landtsche Vrijheyt In Dicht ghestelt//aber nicht ghemelt. Ghedruckt in Hollandt, Teghens Leughens voorstandt, By Monnick Knods ind' handt; Remedie voor't onverstandt . . . 1618. 4° pp.12

11555.e.36.

Sometimes tentatively attributed to Jacobus Taurinus. Written against 'Noodtwendigh ende levendigh discours', sometimes attributed to François van Aerssen.

KORTE ende grondighe refutatie . . . van een zeker boecxken. 1612. *See* GREVINCHOVEN, Nicolaas

K26 KORTE

Korte ende klare Verantwoordinghe/Der REMONSTRANTEN: Teghens Verscheyden onvvaere ende ongefundeerde blaemen, die hun over hun handel inde Synode Nationael . . . nagestroyt ende te laste gheleyt vverden. Ghedruckt . . . M.DC.XIX. 4° pp.13

T.2249(7).

K27 KRACHTELOOSE

Krachteloose DONDER van den Helschen Hondt, Tegē de naecte VVaerheyt en t'eendrachtich verbondt. VVaer in Vertoont wort al het principaelste dat in tsestich

Jaren herwaerts ghepasseert is in desen teghenwoordighen Staet . . . Ghedruckt int Jaer ons Heeren. 4° sig. A⁴: plate; illus.
T.1718(2*).
Variously dated in different catalogues as published in 1614, 1615 or 1617, and if the 'sixty years' of the war are taken literally, it would be in 1628 which is however too late as the main event referred to is Spinola's conquest of Wesel in 1614. The titlepage woodcut shows St. Michael slaying the Devil. The plate consists of an allegorical engraving satirising the Roman Catholic Church.

K28 KRACHTIGHE
Krachtighe redenen, Waerom De goede Ghemeynte tot HAERLEM haer onghenoeghen toont. Over het invoeren vanden eersten Artijckel Der KERCKEN-ORDENINGHE Vanden Iare 1591 aengaende de beroepinghe der KERCKEN-DIENAREN. GHEDRVCKT . . . 1618. 4° pp.62
700.h.25(19).
Printed at Haarlem?

K29 KRIJNSZ, Willem
ANNOTATIEN Op de Voor-reden van CORNELIS BOOGAERTS Aendachtighe Ghebeden ende Meditatien over den 51^en Psalm Davids. Gheannoteert door een Lidtmaet der Ghereformeerde Kercke tot Delf . . . TOT SCHIEDAM, By Adriaen Cornelisz van Delf . . . 1618. 4° pp.31
T.2248(42).
Anonymous. The preface signed: SVH. IZ.

K30 KUCHLINUS, Joannes; M.D.
DISPVTATIO MEDICA DE COLICO DOLORE, Ad quam . . . Pro GRADV DOCTORATVS in MEDICINA consequendo, Respondebo . . . IOANNES KUCHLINUS . . . LUGDUNI BATAVORUM, Ex Officinâ Ioannis Patii . . . M.D.CIV. 4° sig. A³
7306.f.6(20).

K31 KUCHLINUS, Joannes; Theologian
THESES THEOLOGICÆ DE REMISSIONE DEBITORVM: Quas . . . Sub Præsidio . . . D. IOHANNIS KUCHLINI . . . tueri adnitar IOANNES ARNOLDUS . . . LVGDVNI BATAVORVM, Ex Officinâ Ioannis Patii . . . M.D.CI. 4° sig. A⁴
4376.de.16(65).

L

L1 LA BASSECOURT, Fabrice de; the Elder
APOLOGIE DE FABRICE DE LA BASSECOVRT, A l'encontre de deux libelles diffamatoires, l'un intitulé le Tableau, l'autre. [*sic*] La Verification, faits par vn Quidam sans nom. Avec une demande aux Remonstrans, touchant leur sentiment en la doctrine du franc arbitre . . . A AMSTREDAM, Imprimé par PAUL de RAVESTEYN. Pour PIERRE MOSTARDE . . . 1618. 4° pp.64
3900.bb.46.
Directed against Charles de Nielle.

L2 LA BASSECOURT, Fabrice de; the Elder
[Réponse à quelques demandes.] Antwoorde Op dry Vraghen/dienende tot advijs inde huydendaechse swaricheden. Ghetrouwelijck uyt de Fransoyse Tale . . . overgeset . . . 1615. 4° pp.48
T.2245(12).
Anonymous. Translated by Jacobus Trigland. Without imprint; with the device of Marten Jansz. Brandt on the titlepage.

L3 LACHRYMAE

Lachrymæ Lachrymarum. dat is/Traenen der traenen/ghestort over de doot des Edele Heer IOHAN van OLDENBARNEVELT . . . Ende oock over den Om-keer van Batavia. MITSGADERS, Een nieu Liedeken/ghedicht ter eeren vant Dortsche Synode. Ghedruckt . . . 1620. 4° sig.A[4]
T.2422(38).

LACRYMAE in obitum Hispaniarum Reginae Margaretae. 1612. *See* ANDRIES, Jodocus

L4 LAEN, Gerrit van der

Copye Van den Lasterlijken Brief Van VERLAEN, In den Haerlemschen Harminiaen ghementioneert/met korte Annotatien gheillustreert. Ghelijck mede van den Brieff aen de H. Burghemeesteren, van den selfden ter selfder tijdt gheschreven . . . 1618. 4° pp.37
700.h.25(21).
The letters dated 7 and 11 August 1615 respectively.

LAET, Johannes de; sometimes believed to have used the pseudonym Gelasius de Valle Umbrosa. *See* GELASIUS de Valle Umbrosa

L5 LAET, Johannes de

IOANNIS LATII . . . DE PELAGIANIS, ET SEMIPELAGIANIS, COMMENTARIORVM Ex veterum Patrum scriptis Libri duo . . . Accesserunt Vadiani & Cassandri quædam de eodem argumento. HARDERVICI, Ex officinâ Thomæ Henrici, Impensis IOANNIS IANSONII Arnemiensis Librarij . . . M.D.C.XVII. 4° pp.203
4534.aa.13.
The editor named in a laudatory poem as Antonius Thysius.

LA FITE, Petrus. Disputationum theologicarum quarto repetitarum quinta de persona Patris, et Filii. 1605. *See* ARMINIUS, Jacobus

LA FONTAYNE,– de; French Protestant. *See* LE MAÇON, Robert

LA HAYE, David de. Theses theologicae. 1617. *See* COLONIUS, Daniel

LA HAYE, Joannes de; Jesuit. Triumphus veritatis. 1609. *See* BIBLE. Gospels. Harmonies. Latin

L6 LA MARCHE, Olivier de

LES MEMOIRES DE MESSIRE OLIVIER DE LA MARCHE, TROISIESME EDITION. A BVXELLES [*sic*], Chez Hubert Anthoine . . . 1616. [etc.] 4° pp.655
1482.b.15.

L7 LA MARCHE, Olivier de

LES MEMOIRES DE MESSIRE OLIVIER DE LA MARCHE, TROISIESME EDITION, Reuë, & augmenté d'vn Estat particulier de la maison du Duc Charles le Hardy, composé du mesme Auteur, & non imprimé cy-deuant. A BRVXELLES, Chez Hubert Antoine . . . 1616. [etc.] (col.) Acheué d'imprimer en l'Imprimerie de Hubert Antoine . . . le vingtseptiesme d'Aougst . . . 1615. 4° pp.715
1197.g.1; 154.g.5.
Sig.⋆,⋆⋆ and pp.1–655 are a reissue of the preceding. The titlepage and preface are cancels. Ownership inscriptions in the copy at 1197.g.1: J. de Laet 1662; Thos Tyrwhitt 1786.

LAMBERT, Capiteyn. *See* HENDRICKSZ, Lambert

L8 LAMBRECHT, Mathias

HISTORIA ECCLESIASTICA. OFT KERCKELICKE HISTORIE . . . ghenomen ende by een int corte vergadert wt verscheyden . . . Legenden/Historien, ende oude Schrijuers. DOOR . . . MATHIAS LAMBRECHT . . . Ouersien ende vermeerdert door . . . Aubertus Le Mire . . . T'HANTWERPEN bij Hieronymus Verdussen . . . 1609. fol. pp.161
1572/173(2).
The titlepage is engraved, with letterpress title.

L9 LAMENTATIE

Lamentatie des Pfaltz Graeff ouer syn Gepretendeer-Croon van Bohemen/ Gheschreuen inde stadt Praeghe den lesten November 1620. Overghesedt Wt de Hooch-Duytsche sprake in onse Nederlantsche Tale. Eerst Ghedruckt in December 1620. T'Hantwerpen/By Abraham Verhoeuen/[etc.] 4° pp.8; sig. Ss^4; illus.
P.P.3444.af(146).
In verse, followed by one Latin and one Dutch chronogram on 8 November 1620. The titlepage woodcut shows a crown and three rings.

L10 LAMENTATIE

Lamentatie des Pfaltz Graeff ouer syn Gepretendeer-deCroon van Bohemen . . . Eerst Ghedruckt in December 1620. T'Hantwerpen/By Abraham Verhoeuen/ [etc.] 4° pp.8; sig. Ss^4; illus.
P.P.3444.af(165).
Another issue of the preceding, with attempted correction in the title.

L11 LAMPSONIUS, Dominicus

[Pictorum aliquot celebrium Germaniae Inferioris effigies.] ILLVSTRIVM QVOS BELGIVM HABVIT PICTORVM EFFIGIES, AD VIVVM . . . DELINEATÆ, Nec non, quo quisque tempore et vixerit, et obierit. ANTVERPIÆ, Apud Theodorum Gallæum [etc.] fol. pl.24
564.f.1(2).
A new edition of 'Pictorum . . . effigies', compiled by Dominicus Lampsonius and with some of the engraved verses on the plates signed by him. With a different portrait of Lucas van Leyden from that in the original [1572?] edition and with the portrait of Joannes Stradanus in place of that of Hieronymus Cock on pl.23 as well as the additional portrait of Philips Galle who died in 1612. A made-up copy, with the engraved titlepage described in the *Bibliotheca Belgica* no. L 693 and with the plates, except for pl.10,24, of ibidem no. L694. The plates are by various artists. Published ca.1615?

L12 LANARIO Y ARAGÓN, Francisco; Duke

LE GVERRE DI FIANDRA Breuemente Narrate Da DON FRANCESCO LANARIO. In Anuersa appresso Geronimo Verdussen. (col.) ANTVERPIÆ, APVD HIERONYMVM VERDVSSIVM. M. DC.XV. 4° pp.208; illus.
9405.cc.6.
The titlepage is engraved, showing a trophy. A woodcut below the colophon consists of the date 1615 and what appears to be the author's personal cypher: SMFLD under a crown. *Jöcher* and *Adelung* record a Spanish title, 'Las guerras de Flandes', under this author, the latter describing the edition as Madrid 1592. The preface of the British Library copy however states that the book was written in Italian and the historical account includes events up to the declaration of the Truce in April 1609. *Palau* no.130884 describes this edition as the first and a Spanish translation as published in Madrid in 1623 under no.130886, of which the British Library has two copies.

L13 LANCEL, Antoine

COMMEDIE. EN LAQVELLE SE REPRESENTE LES QVATRE ESTATS DV monde. Leurs disputes & leur fin en outre le triomphe de la Charité & de la Iustice. Nouvellement mise en lumiere. Par. ANTOINE LANCEL . . . A LA HAYE. Chez Hillebrand Iaques . . . 1605. 8° sig.A-C^8D^3
11737.aa.10.
In verse.

L14 LANCILOTTUS, Cornelius

S. AVRELII AVGVSTINI . . . VITA . . . Auctore R.P.F. CORNELIO LANCILOTTO . . . ANTVERPIÆ, EX OFFICINA PLANTINIANA, Apud Viduam & Filios Io. Moreti. M.DC.XVI. (col.) ANTVERPIÆ, EX OFFICINA PLANTINIANA, APVD VIDVAM ET FILIOS IOANNIS MORETI. M.DC.XVI. 8° pp.428; illus.; port.
4825.a.25.
Ownership inscription: Oratorij Louan. dono R.P. Andreæ vande Sande.

L15 LANCILOTTUS, Henricus

HÆRETICVM QVARE PER CATHOLICVM QVIA Auctore . . . HENRICO LANCILOTTO . . . Editio tertia, correctior . . . ANTVERPIÆ, Apud Guilielmum à Tongris . . . M.DC.XIX. 8° pp.503; illus.
1607/1333(1).
The titlepage engraving shows four church fathers stamping on heretics.

L16 LANCILOTTUS, Henricus

Paralleli LXXIII. AVGVSTINI CATHOLICI ET Augustinomastigis HÆRETICI, Quibus Orthodoxæ D. Augustini & Nouellæ Sectatorum, fidei atque doctrinæ, oppositio diametralis, clarè indigitatur. Auctore . . . HENRICO LANCILOTTO . . . ANTVERPIÆ, Apud Guilielmum à Tongris . . . M.DC.XIX. [etc.] 8° pp.60
1607/1333(2).
Using quotations from St. Augustine to confute Luther and Calvin.

LANGENES, Barent. Hand-boeck; of cort begrijp der caerten. 1609. Sometimes wrongly attributed to Barent Langenes. *See* CAERT-THRESOOR.

L17 LANGIUS, Johannes

Redenen ende oorsaken/Waerom de DIENAREN DES GODDELIICKEN VVOORTS, Gehoorende onder het Classis van Vollenhoo ende Steenwijck, Niet en konnen de Resolutie van Ridderschap ende Steden/ghenomen tot Campen den . . . Lantdach op den 11. Martij Ao. 1616. Onderteeckenen . . . M.DC.XVJ. 4° sig.A^4B^2
T.2246(4).
The address to the reader signed: Johannes Langius and others.

LANNOY, Matthieu de. *See* LAUNOY, Matthieu de

L18 LA NOÜE, François de; called Bras-de-fer

[Discours politiques et militaires.] Den Ghematichden Christen/Of Vande Maticheyt diemen ghebruycken moet in Religions verschillen/tot ghemeene ruste der Kercke/eenicheyt der Christenen/ende s'Landts welvaren . . . Ghetrocken meestendeel uyt het Boeck/van . . . mijn Heere De la Nove, gheintituleert/ Discours Politiques & Militaires, ende by een ghestelt: Door I. De la Haye . . . IN S'GRAVEN-HAGHE, By Hillebrandt Jacobssz. . . . 1613. 4° pp.25
T.2243(14).
Part of the edition with the misprint 'yaten' in place of 'haten' in the first of the omitted passages on the titlepage, corresponding to the copy described in *Knuttel* no.2074.

L19 LANSBERGEN, Philips

PHILIPPI LANSBERGII CYCLOMETRIÆ NOVÆ LIBRI DVO . . . MIDDELBVRGI Ex officina RICHARDI SCHILDERS M IC CXVI [*sic*]. 4° pp.62; illus.
1608/323; C.66.e.12(1).

The textual illustrations printed in red. The copy at C.66.e.12(1) in a binding bearing the arms of Jacques Auguste de Thou.

L20 LANSBERGEN, Philips

Disputatio Epistolaris . . . Philippi Lansbergij. Cum . . . medicinæ Doctoribus Mittelburgensibus eorumque nomine . . . Carolo Franco . . . de Moscho. Cum Apologia D. Iacobi Lansbergij . . . pro Parente . . . Aduersus Cornelium Herrels Chyrurgum. Medicorum Mittelburgensium placita, contra . . . Davidem Vltralæum tuentem. MIDDELBVRGI, Excudebat Isaacus Schilders, 1613. 8° sig. A-E^8
1176.b.4(3).

L21 LANSBERGEN, Philips

PHILIPPI LANSBERGII PROGYMNASMATVM ASTRONOMIÆ RESTITVTÆ LIBER I. DE MOTV SOLIS . . . MIDDELBVRGI, Ex officina RICHARDI SCHILDERS M D CXIX. Prostant GOESÆ apud Yemannum Ioannis Nachtegael Bibliopolam. 4° pp.116; illus.
531.k.12(2).

L22 LANSBERGIUS, Franciscus; Predikant te Gend

GHESPRECK, OVER DE LEERE, vande TRANSVBSTANTIATIE: ONLANCKS GHEHOVDEN BINNEN ANTWERPEN, TVSSCHEN FRANCISCVM LANSBERGIVM . . . ende PATREM GAVDA . . . Wt-ghegheven door Samuelem Lansbergium . . . Ende by hem met sekere Annotatien . . . verrijkt . . . TOT ROTTERDAM, By Matthijs Bastiaensz. . . . 1609. 4° pp.40
T.2417(14).

L23 LANSBERGIUS, Franciscus; Predikant te Gend

Kort ende Christelijck EXAMEN, Over de Leer-poincten/Die ten huydighen daghe in gheschil ghetrocken werden/ofse het fondament der saligheyt raken ofte niet? Hoe weynich datse importeren/ende hoe men dezelfde . . . kan vereenighen/ofte ten minsten verdraghen. Te zamen ghestelt: Door FRANCISCVM LANSBERGIVM . . . TOT ROTTERDAM, By Matthijs Bastiaensz . . . 1612. 4° sig.A-H^4J^2
T.2242(36).

L24 LANSBERGIUS, Franciscus; Predikant te Gend

XXII. Bedenckinghen Francisci Lansbergij, Over de Leere vande Transubstantiatie/Vraegh-wijs/R. D. Patri Gaudæ . . . voor-ghestelt. 4° pp.23
T.2417(15).

Issued together with the author's 'Ghespreck' and published by Matthijs Bastiaensz at Rotterdam in 1609, without a separate titlepage.

L25 LANSBERGIUS, Franciscus; Predikant te Gend

Verantwoordinghe/FRANCISCI LANSBERGII . . . Teghens ROBERTVM SWEERTIVM . . . TOT ROTTERDAM, By Matthijs Bastiaensz . . . 1610. 4° pp.64
T.2240(19).

A reply to Sweertius's letter addressed to the city of Rotterdam on Lansbergius's 'Ghespreck'.

LANSBERGIUS, Franciscus; Predikant te Gend. Een verklaringhe van den 133. Psalm. 1611. [Sometimes attributed to Franciscus Lansbergius.] *See* VERKLARINGHE

LANSBERGIUS, Franciscus; the Younger. Disputatio medica, de angina vera. 1615. *See* VORSTIUS, Aelius Everardus

LANSBERGIUS, Philippus. *See* LANSBERGEN, Philips

LANSPERGIUS, Joannes. *See* JOHANN JUSTUS Landsberger

L26 L'APOSTRE, George

LA COMETE Qui est apparuë le 25. de Septe[mbre,] 1607. Par G. L'APOSTRE. A S. OMER, Chez François Bellet. [etc.] 8° sig. A^8
531.e.8(2).
Published in 1607. Badly mutilated.

L27 LA ROCHE-GUILHEM, –; Mademoiselle

JACQUELINE DE BAVIERE, Comtesse de Hainaut. Nouvelle Historique. Par Mademoiselle la Roche Guilhen [*sic*]. A AMSTERDAM, Chez PAUL MARRET . . . M.DCVII. 12° pp.161
012550.de.49.
The date is a misprint for 1707.

L28 LATE

THE LATE GOOD SVCCESSE AND VICTORY, which it pleased God to giue to some of the King of BOHEMIA's forces, vnder the conduct of the Prince of ANHALT . . . Against . . . BVCQVOY and DAMPIERE, atchieued neare Horne in Austria . . . Vnto which is added the Articles of agreement, made betweene the said King of Bohemia and Bethlem Gaber, Prince of Hungaria and Transiluania. MIDDLEBVRG, Printed by Abraham Schilders. M.D.C.XX. 4° sig. AB^4C^2
C.55.c.24.
Wanting the 'Articles'. The imprint is probably false; printed in London?

LATIUS, Joannes. *See* LAET, Johannes de

LAUNAEUS, Nathanael. Disputationum theologicarum quarta de trinitate. 1602. *See* GOMARUS, Franciscus

L29 LAUNOY, Matthieu de

REMONTRANCE CHRETIENNE ET MODESTE, POVR LA Iustification des Chrêtiens Enfans fideles de la S. Eglise Chrêtienne, Apost. Cathol. & Rom. Cõtre les blâmes, impostures, & calomnies des Huguenotz & autres . . . Heretiques . . . Par Matthieu de Lannoy [*sic*] . . . A Bruxelles, Ches Rutger Velpius . . . M.D.C.I. [*etc.*] 8° pp.500
3901.c.27.
Ownership inscriptions: R. Kieldoncq; J. F. Vandevelde.

L30 LAUNOY, Matthieu de

REMONTRANCE CHRETIENNE ET MODESTE, POVR LA Iustification des Chrêtiens Enfans fideles de la S. Eglise Chrêtienne, Apost. Cathol. & Rom. Cõtre les blâmes, impostures & calomnies des Huguenotz & auctres . . . Heretiques . . . Par [Matthieu de Lannoy] . . . IMPRIME EN L'AN M.D.C.I. 8° pp.500
3835.a.1.
Another issue of the preceding, without the imprint. The author's name, doubtless also misprinted 'Lannoy', has been erased.

L31 LAUREMBERGIUS, Gulielmus; the Elder

PHILOSOPHI ET MEDICI CLARISSIMI, GVLIELMI LAUREMBERGII, EPISTOLICA DISSERTATIO continens curationem calculi vesicæ. Edita Ex Bibliotheca IOACHIMI MORSII. LVGDVNI BATAVORVM, Apud Bartholomeum à Bild. M.DC.XIX. 8° pp.45
1172.b.20; 1189.a.9.
The dedication signed: L. [or rather, I.] M.D.D.D. editor, i.e. Ioachimus Morsius. With poems by Morsius in Latin and Greek.

L32 LAUREMBERGIUS, Petrus
ΑΝΩΝΥΜΟΥ ΕΙΣΑΓΩΓΗ ΑΝΑΤΟΜΙΚΗ. Cum interpretatione . . . PETRI LAVREMBERGI. Nunc primum . . . edita Auspicijs ac sumptibus IOACHIMI MORSI. LVGDVNI-BATAVORVM, M.DC.XVIII. 4° pp.87
780.d.1; C.112.b.19(2).
The copy at 780.d.1 is the editor's presentation copy to Martinus Ruarus.

L33 LAUREMBERGIUS, Petrus
PETRI LAVREMBERGI LAVRVS DELPHICA, SEV Consilium, quo describitur Methodus perfacilis ad Medicinam. Lugduni Batavorum, Apud IOHANNEM MAIRE . . . MDCXXI. (col.) Lugduni Batavorum, Typis PETRI MOLINÆI . . . MDCXXI. 12° pp.56
544.a.10(1).
The editor's dedication signed: Gulielm. Laurembergius.

L34 LAUREMBERGIUS, Petrus
(tp.1) PETRI LAVREMBERGI LAVRVS DELPHICA, SEV Consilium, quo describitur Methodus perfacilis ad Medicinam. Cui adjecta VNIVERSÆ MEDICINÆ METHODVS H. THRIVERI. Lugduni Batavorum, Apud IOHANNEM MAIRE . . . MDCXXI.
(tp.2) VNIVERSÆ MEDICINÆ BREVISSIMA . . . METHODVS, AVCTORE HIEREMIA THRIVERO . . . LVGDVNI BATAVORVM, EX OFFICINA PLANTINIANA, Apud Franciscum Raphelengium. M.D.XCII. 8° pp.32; 131
544.c.8(2,1).
The work by Jeremias Triverius, edited by Dionysius Triverius, is a reissue. It has here been bound before the work by Laurembergius to which it is intended to be an addition.

L35 LAURENTIUS, Jacobus
IACOBI LAVRENTII APOLOGETICVS ALTER Adversus MAXIMILIANVM SANDÆVM . . . SIVE Examen CASTIGATIONIS Sandæanæ de PRODIGA IESVITARVM LIBERALITATE in Vocibus Vniversalibus, Omnis, Nullus, Semper, Nunquam . . . quæ est liber Tertius in sua quam nuper edidit, HYPERBOLE. AMSTELREDAMI, Ex Officina Iacobi [*sic*] Laurentij, 1619. 8° pp.147
4092.c.16(3).
Should the name in the imprint read: Henrici Laurentii?

L36 LAURENTIUS, Jacobus
DISSERTATIO THEOLOGICA, De Libris Gentilium, Judæorum, Turcarum, Veterum Patrum, & Pontificiorum permittendis ac tolerandis: PROTESTANTIVM vero prohibendis, abolendis ac comburendis, OPPOSITA Disputationi IACOBI GRETZERI . . . in Tractatu ejus de jure & more prohibendi . . . libros hæreticos & noxios. AD MAXIMILIANVM SANDÆVM . . . Iesuitam HYPERBOLICVM. Operâ & studio IACOBI LAVRENTII . . . AMSTELREDAMI, Ex Officina Henrici Laurentij, 1619. 8° pp.110
1020.d.13; 4092.c.16(2).

L37 LAURENTIUS, Jacobus
Prodiga IESUITARUM LIBERALITAS in vocibus universalibus, OMNIS, NVLLVS, SEMPER, NVNQVAM, VBIQVE, NVSQVAM, TOTVM, NIHIL. Tum veritate tum proprio testimonio refutata. Sive APPENDIX Ad CAVTERIATAM IESVITARVM CONSCIENTIAM, Jam ante ab authore editam . . . Operâ & studio IACOBI LAVRENTII . . . AMSTELREDAMI Ex Officina Henrici Laurentij 1618. 8° pp.202
862.e.19(2).

LAURENTIUS, Jacobus. Theses physicæ. De anima rationali. 1606. *See* JACCHAEUS, Gilbertus

L38 LAURENTIUS, Jacobus

VVLPINA IESVITICA, hoc est Censura ADMONITIONIS Sandeanæ de CAVTERIATA IESVITARVM CONSCIENTIA, In quá ostenditur Tum ADMONITIONIS Nullitas, tum ADMONITORIS multiplex Mendacium . . . Operâ & studio IACOBI LAVRENTII . . . AMSTELREDAMI, Ex Officina Henrici Laurentij, 1620. 8° pp.82

4092.c.16(1).

With the bookplate of University College, Oxford.

L39 LAZARILLO de Tormes

LA VIDA DE LAZARILLO DE TORMES, y de sus fortunas y aduersidades. EN LA OFICINA PLANTINIANA. M.D.CII. 16° pp.120

12490.a.11.

Part 1 and the chapter 'de los tudescos'. Published at Leiden. With the bookplate of Herbert Charles Marsh.

L40 LEANDER de Sancto Martino; name in religion of John Jones

(tp.1) OTIVM THEOLOGICVM TRIPARTITVM: SIVE AMÆNISSIMÆ DISPVTATIONES DE DEO, INTELLIGENTIIS, ANIMABVS SEPARATIS, EARVMQVE VARIIS REceptaculis, trium . . . Authorum. BARTHOLOMÆI SIBYLLÆ, IOANNIS TRITHEMII, ALPHONSI TOSTATI . . . DVACI, Ex Typographia BALTHAZARIS BELLERI, M.DC.XXI.

(tp.2) Curiositas Regia. OCTO QVÆSTIONES IVCVNDISSIMÆ . . . A MAXIMILIANO I. CÆSARE Ioanni Trithemio . . . propositæ, & ab eodem . . . solutæ . . . DVACI, Ex Typographia BALTAZARIS BELLERI.

(tp.3) ÆNIGMATVM SACRORVM PENTAS, ALPHONSI TOSTATI . . . PARADOXA. DE CHRISTI, MATRISQVE EIVS MISTERIIS, ANIMARVM RECEPTACVLIS POSTHVMIS, IVCVNDISSImæ disputationes. In epitomen . . . contraxit . . . LEANDER de S. MARTINO . . . DVACI, Ex Typographia BALTHAZARIS BELLERI . . . M. C XXI. 8° 3 pt.: pp.429; 72; 392

1018.d.26.

According to the approbation 'totum opus collegit . . . Leander à S. Martino'. The work by Bartholomaeus Sybilla is entitled: 'Speculum peregrinarum quaestionum, de Deo, intelligentiis, animabus separatis, earumque receptaculis post mortem'. Printed by Laurence Kellam the younger at Douai.

L41 LE BOUCQ, Simon

BREF RECVEIL DES ANTIQVITEZ DE VALENTIENNE. Où est representé ce qui s'est passé de remarquable en ladicte Ville & Seigneurie, depuis sa fondation iusques à l'an 1619. Par S.L.B. A VALENTIENNE, De l'Imprimerie de Iean Vervliet . . . M.DC.XIX. (col.) A VALENTIENNE, DE L'IMPRIMERIE DE IEAN VERVLIET, M.DC.XIX. 8° pp.42

576.b.21(1).

The dedication signed: Simon Le Boucq.

L42 LE CANU, Robbert Robbertsen

Nieuwe Jaars Claach-Liedt/over de Doodt van D.D. Iacobus Arminius . . . Op de wijse vanden tweeden Psalm . . . Ghedruckt int Jaer/1610. 4° 2 unsigned leaves

T.2240(23); T.2421(21).

Signed: Een O int Cijfer, i.e. Robbert Le Canu. Published by the author at Amsterdam.

L43 LE CANU, Robbert Robbertsen

De Noortsche Rommel-pot/[etc.] fol. a single sheet

L.23.c.11(59).

In verse. With a quotation, printed in civilité. Signed: Een o int Cyffer, i.e. Robbert Le Canu. Published by the author at Amsterdam in 1608. Imperfect; wanting the second leaf containing 'Liedeken'.

L44 LE CANU, Robbert Robbertsen
Onder verbeteringh. Een Mey-praetjen/tusschen Vader ende Sone/over 'tgheschil der Professoren/der Heylighe Theologie in-de hooghe Schole tot Leyden/in Hollandt . . . Ghedruct . . . duysent, ses hondert ende thien. 4° sig. A-C^4
T.2421(16).
The preface signed: Een o in't Cyfer, i.e. Robbert Le Canu. Without the 'Nieuwe Jaars Claech-Liedt' found added in a later edition, according to *Rogge* dl. 1 p.276. Published by Robbert Le Canu at Amsterdam.

L45 LE CANU, Robbert Robbertsen
(tp. 1) Onder Verbeteringh. Sommighe Buer-praetgens/van de Resolutie der . . . Staten van Hollandt ende West-vrieslandt/ende de Magistraten der stadt Hoorn . . . Door Robert Robertsz. Le Canu . . . TOT HOORN, Ghedruct by Willem Andriessz. . . . 1614.
(tp. 2=sig. D4r) Onder Verbeteringh. Het derde Buer-praetgen/van de Religions vrijheyt/teghen een Boeck/t'samen gheset uyt meer dan duysent Boecken/soo Pieter Jansz. in Twisch seyt . . . TOT HOORN . . . 1614. 4° sig. A-F^4; illus.
T.2244(9).
Partly in verse. The titlepage woodcut shows the Golden Calf, another on sig. D1r the emblem of Hoorn.

L46 LE CANU, Robbert Robbertsen
Ratelwachts Roeprecht/tegent Boeck vanden schijndeuchtsamen Engel/ofte Geest Cornelis van Hil . . . Ghedruckt . . . 1611. 4° 4 unsigned leaves
T.2241(4).
Anonymous and without imprint. Published by the author at Amsterdam.

L47 L'ÉCLUSE, Charles de
[Collections] (tp. 1) CAROLI CLVSI . . . RARIORVM PLANTARVM HISTORIA . . . ANTVERPIÆ Ex officina Plantiniana Apud Ioannem Moretum. M D CI.
(tp. 2=p. CCCXXI) PLANTÆ seu SIMPLICIA . . . QVAE IN BALDO MONTE, ET IN VIA AB VERONA AD BALDVM REPERIVNTVR . . . nunc à IOANNE PONA . . . repertæ, descriptæ, & editæ. ANTVERPIÆ, EX OFFICINA PLANTINIANA, Apud Ioannem Moretum. M.DCI.
(col.) ANTVERPIAE, EX OFFICINA PLANTINIANA, APVD IOANNEM MORETVM . . . M.DCI.
fol. pp. 364, cccxlviij: plate; illus., port.
35.g.8.
Considered as part 1 of the collected works. With letters by Honorius Bellus and Thobias Roelsius and with Clusius's 'Commentariolum de fungis'. The titlepage engraving showing Adam, Solomon, Theophrastus and Dioscorides, by Jacques de Gheyn? The portrait by J. de Gheyn follows the preliminary pages, the last of which bears the poem by Joannes ab Hoghelande only.

L48 L'ÉCLUSE, Charles de
[Collections] CAROLI CLUSI . . . RARIORVM PLANTARVM HISTORIA . . . ANTVERPIÆ, EX OFFICINA PLANTINIANA, Apud Ioannem Moretum. M.DCI. fol. pp. 364, cccxlviij: plate; illus., port.
441.i.8(1); 449.k.5(1).
Another issue of the preceding. The last page of the preliminaries has been reset to bear the two poems, 'In effigiem Caroli Clusii' by Bonaventura Vulcanius and 'In eandem' by Joannes ab Hoghelande. The copy at 441.i.8(1) with manuscript notes and the ownership inscription: Ex libris Jacobi Clusij . . . ex dono Auct. Patricij sui Carolj Clusij an. MDCXV. Lutetiæ Parisiorum. The copy at 449.k.5(1) has had the 'Altera Appendix' with 'Appendicis alterius auctarium' from the 'Exoticorum libri decem' of 1605 added and is from the library of Sir Joseph Banks. Imperfect; wanting the portrait.

L49 L'ÉCLUSE, Charles de

[Collections] (tp.1) CAROLI CLVSII EXOTICORVM LIBRI DECEM: Quibus Animalium, Plantarum, Aromatum, aliorumque peregrinorum Fructuum historiæ describantur: ITEM PETRI BELLONI OBSERVATIONES, eodem Carolo Clusio interprete . . . Ex Officinâ Plantinianâ RAPHELENGII, 1605.

(tp.2) PETRI BELLONII . . . Plurimarum . . . rerum in Græcia, Asia, Ægypto, Iudæa, Arabia, aliisque exteris Provinciis . . . conspectarum OBSERVATIONES tribus libris expressæ. CAROLVS CLVSIVS . . . è Gallicis Latinas faciebat, & denuò recensebat. Altera editio . . . EX OFFICINA PLANTINIANA RAPHELENGII. M.D.CV. fol. 2 pt.: pp.378,52; 242; illus.

C.83.i.6; 35.g.9(1); 449.k.6.

Considered as part 2 of the collected works. Containing Clusius's translations of works by Garcia ab Orto, Christophorus a Costa, Nicolaus Monardus and the 'Altera Appendix ad historiam Rariorum Plantarum'. The titlepage engraving shows Nature, Atlas, Isis, birds, animals, fishes and Pallas, with the Plantinian device on the plinth. Published at Leiden. The copy at 449.k.6 lacks the 'Altera Appendix'.

L50 L'ÉCLUSE, Charles de

[Collections] (tp.1) CAROLI CLVSII . . . CVRÆ POSTERIORES . . . ACCESSIT SEORSIM EVERARDI VORSTII . . . de eiusdem CAROLI CLVSII Vita & Obitu ORATIO, aliorumque de eisdem EPICEDIA. Ex officina Plantiniana Raphelengij, 1611.

(tp.2) EVERARDI VORSTII . . . Oratio funebris IN OBITVM . . . CAROLI CLVSII . . . Accesserunt VARIORVM EPICEDIA. IN OFFICINA PLANTINIANA RAPHELENGIJ. 1611. fol. 2 pt.: pp.71; 24; illus.

441.i.8(2); 449.k.5(2); 35.g.9(2).

Considered as part 3 of the collected works. Edited by Matthaeus Caccini. The titlepage engraving is the same as the one on the 'Rariorum plantarum historia'. Published at Leiden.

L51 L'ÉCLUSE, Charles de

(tp.1) CAROLI CLVSII . . . CVRAE POSTERIORES, SEV Plurimarum non antè cognitarum, aut descriptarum stirpium, peregrinorumque aliquot animalium NOVÆ DESCRIPTIONES . . . ACCESSIT SEORSIM EVERARDI VORSTII . . . de eiusdem CAROLI CLVSII Vita & Obitu ORATIO, aliorumque EPICEDIA. IN OFFICINA PLANTINIANA RAPHELENGII, 1611.

(tp.2) EVERARDI VORSTII . . . Oratio funebris IN OBITVM . . . CAROLI CLVSII . . . Accesserunt VARIORVM EPICEDIA. IN OFFICINA PLANTINIANA RAPHELENGII, 1611. 4° 2 pt.: pp.134; 39; illus.

454.a.23; 446.c.23(1).

Published at Leiden. The copy at 454.a.23 from the library of Sir Joseph Banks. The copy at 446.c.23(1) imperfect; wanting pt.2.

L52 L'ÉCLUSE, Charles de

SVMMI BOTANICI CAROLI CLVSI GALLIAE BELGICAE COROGRAPHICA DESCRIPTIO POSTHVMA Edita ex Museo IOACHIMI MORSI. LVGD. BATAV. Typis Iacobi Marci, M D C XIX. 8° pp.64

1050.b.4.

With obituary poems on Charles de l'Écluse.

L53 LEECH, Humfrey

DVTIFVLL AND RESPECTIVE CONSIDERATIONS VPON FOVRE SEVERALL HEADS OF PROOFE AND TRIALL IN MATTERS OF RELIGION. PROPOSED BY . . . IAMES King of Great Britayne . . . By a late Minister & Preacher in England . . . M.DC.IX. 4° pp.243

860.k.2.

Anonymous and without imprint. Edited by Robert Persons. Published by the English College press at St. Omer.

L54 LEECH, Humfrey

A TRIVMPH OF TRVTH. OR Declaration of the doctrine concerning EVANGELICALL COVNSAYLES: lately deliuered in OXFORD by HVMFREY LEECH . . . WITH Relation of sondry occurrents, and particularly of D. KING, the Vicechancellor, his exorbitant proceedings against the said H.L. vpon his constant propugnation thereof. ALSO The peculiar MOTIVES, ensuing therevpon, which perswaded him to renounce the faction of hereticall Congregations, & to embrace the vnity of the CATHOLIQVE Church . . . M.D.C.IX. 8° pp.135
3936.aa.20.

Without imprint; printed by Laurence Kellam at Douai. Ownership inscription: John Egan.

LEEW, Gerhardus de. Disputationum anatomicarum primam . . . de anatome . . . propugnabit Gerhardus de Leew. 1618. *See* WINSEMIUS, Menelaus

LEEW, Gerhardus de. Disputationum anatomicarum septima . . . de cartilaginibus . . . quam . . . ventilandam exhibet Gerhardus de Leew. 1618. *See* WINSEMIUS, Menelaus

LEEW, Gerhardus de. Disputationum anatomicarum decimam-tertiam, de organis chylificationi inservientibus . . . proponit Gerhardus de Leew. 1619. *See* WINSEMIUS, Menelaus

LEEW, Gerhardus de. Disputationum anatomicarum decima-octava, de organis generationis . . . ad quam . . . respondebit Gerardus de Leew. 1619. *See* WINSEMIUS, Menelaus

LEGENDE doree ou sommaire de l'histiore [*sic*] des freres mendians. 1608. *See* VIGNIER, Nicolas; the Younger

L55 LEGENDE

[Legende veritable de Iean le blanc.] (tp.1) VVaerachtighe LEGENDE van Ian de VVitte. In Françoysche Tale ghenaemt Iean le Blancq. Waerinne . . . vervatet wordt de afkoemste/het op-wassen/den voort-ganc/de kracht . . . staet/ende . . . gheleghentheyt vander Papisten Broot-God/overghezet wt de fransoysche rijme/ door IAN FRVYTIERS. Hier is noch by-ghevoeght der Papen Apen-spel/midtsgaders noch eenighe Refereynen ende Liedekens . . . In s'Graven-Haghe, Voor Aert Meuris . . . M.D.C.IX.
(tp.2=sig.C1r) Papen Apen-spel, Misbruyck ende Misgheloove der zelver . . . Door een Lief-hebber der oprechte Apostolike ende Catholike Kercke. Ghedruct . . . 1609. 4° sig.A-D[4]; illus.
11555.d.23; T.2421(4).

In verse. Pt.1 is a new edition of a work originally published in 1575. Pt.2 sometimes attributed to Jan Fruytiers. Extracts of the original French text are printed in the margin of pt.1. The copy at T.2421(4) is imperfect; wanting sig.C,D. The woodcut on tp.2 shows an astrologer(?) and the motto: Nosce teipsum.

L56 LEIDEN

[8.4.1604] ORDONNANTIE ghemaect by die van de Gherechte dezer stadt Leyden, opt stuck van de nacht-wachten. Ten bevele van die vande Gerechte der voorschreven Stede, Gedruct opt Raedthuys aldaer . . . 1604. 4° sig.A[4]B[6]
C.136.b.13.

Dated 7 April 1604; issued 8 April 1604. Printed by Jan van Hout, in civilité.

L57 LEIDEN

[5.4.1618] Aflesinghe opten vijfdē Aprilis sestien-hondert ende achthien/van t'Raethuys der stadt Leyden voor den volcke ghedaen. GEDRUCT Naer t'autentijcque Extract daer . . . uytgegeven. 4° sig.A4
T.2248(5).
Published at Leiden in 1618?

L58 LEIGHTON, Alexander

DISPVTATIO INAVGVRALIS de Melanch. Hypochond. Quam . . . pro supremis in Medicina titulis consequendis . . . Examinandam proponit. ALEXANDER LICHTONIVS . . . LVGDVNI BATAVORVM, Ex officina IACOBI PATII . . . MDCXVII. 4° sig.A4
1185.g.1(65).

L59 LEIUS, Matthias

REGINAE PECVNIAE LIBRI V. MATTHIÆ LEII . . . AMSTELODAMI, Ex Typographia RAVESTENIANA . . . M.DC.XVIII. 4° pp.40
1213.l.11(3).
In verse.

L60 LE MAÇON, Robert; calling himself De la Fontaine

Eene Oratie Vande Francoysche ende Duytsche Ghemeynten/versamelt in Engelandt, uytghesproken . . . by Mr. de la Fontayne, aen den . . . Coninck IACOB den eersten/Coninc van Engelant . . . Eerst, TOT MIDDELBVRCH, Ghedruct by Richard Schilders . . . 1603. 8° sig.A4
8050.aa.15(9).
With a summary of the King's reply.

LE MIRE, Aubert. Cort verhael hoe subtyl en wonderlyck Mr. Hugo Grotius . . . wt zijne ghevanckenisse . . . ontkomen is. 1621. [By Aubert Le Mire?] *See* CORT

L61 LE MIRE, Aubert

CORT VERHAEL VAN HET LEVEN VANDEN H. VVILLIBRORDVS . . . Met een cort verhael van het leuen van sijne mede-ghesellen. By een vergadert door den . . . Heer AVBERTVS LE MIRE . . . T'ANTWERPEN, Inde Plantijnsche Druckerije M.DC.XIII. 12° pp.36
4827.de.10.
Ownership inscriptions: H. Schouten 1685; J. F. Vandevelde Lovanii.

L62 LE MIRE, Aubert

ELOGIA ILLVSTRIVM BELGII SCRIPTORVM, Qui vel Ecclesiam Dei propugnarunt, vel disciplinas illustrarunt. CENTVRIA Decadibus distincta. Ex Bibliotheca AVBERTI MIRÆI . . . ANTVERPIÆ SVMPTIBVS VIDVÆ ET HEREDVM IOANNIS BELLERI . . . 1602. (col.) ANTVERPIÆ EX OFFICINA TYPOGRAPHICA DANIELIS VERVLIET . . . 1602. 8° pp.205
10759.a.9.
Partly in verse.

L63 LE MIRE, Aubert

[Elogia illustrium Belgii scriptorum.] ILLVSTRIVM GALLIÆ BELGICÆ SCRIPTORVM ICONES ET ELOGIA. Ex museio Auberti Miræi . . . ANTVERPIA E [*sic*] Apud Theodorum Gallæum M.DCVIII. fol. pl.51
564.f.1(1).
Engraved throughout, with additional plates numbered 6b, 7b, 12b, 30b, 35b and three unnumbered ones, i.e. two portraits of Lipsius and one of Plantin by Philips Galle and others, all with engraved verses by different authors.

L64 LE MIRE, Aubert
[Elogia illustrium Belgii scriptorum.] ELOGIA BELGICA SIVE ILLVSTRIVM BELGI SCRIPTORVM, Qui nostrâ patrumq́ue memoriâ, vel Ecclesiam Dei propugnarunt, vel disciplinas illustrarunt, VITÆ BREVITER COMMEMORATAE. Studio AVBERTI MIRÆI . . . ANTVERPIAE. APVD DAVIDEM MARTINIVM. M.DCIX. 4° pp.210
1197.i.4(1).
Ownership inscription: Sum Aemily Rosendaly.

L65 LE MIRE, Aubert
EQVITVM REDEMTORIS IESV CHRISTI ORDO. A . . . VINCENTIO GONZAGA . . . M.DCVIII. institutus. AVB. MIRÆVS . . . publicabat. ANTVERPIÆ. Apud Hieronymum Verdussium. M.DCVIII. 4° sig.$+^4$
487.f.8(3); 4785.f.24(3).

LE MIRE, Aubert. Illustrium . . . scriptorum icones et elogia. 1608. *See* above: Elogia illustrium . . . scriptorum.

L66 LE MIRE, Aubert
[Notitia episcopatuum orbis universi.] NOTITIA EPISCOPATVVM ORBIS CHRISTIANI: In quâ CHRISTIANAE RELIGIONIS amplitudo elucet. LIBRI V. AVBERTVS MIRÆVS . . . publicabat. ANTVERPIÆ, EX OFFICINA PLANTINIANA, Apud Viduam & Filios Io. Moreti. M.DC.XIII. (col.) ANTVERPIÆ, EX OFFICINA PLANTINIANA, APVD VIDVAM ET FILIOS IOANNIS MORETI. M.DC.XIII. 8° pp.418: plates; maps
857.d.5.
The maps signed: Fran. Haraeus. With manuscript notes.

LE MIRE, Aubert. Ordinis B. Mariae Annuntiatarum virginum origo. 1608. *See* below: Originum monasticarum origo.

L67 LE MIRE, Aubert
ORIGINES EQVESTRIVM SIVE MILITARIVM ORDINVM. LIBRI DVO. AVBERTVS MIRÆVS . . . scrutando publicabat. ANTVERPIAE. APVD DAVIDEM MARTINIVM. M.DC.IX. 4° pp.46
487.f.8(4); 4785.f.24(2).

L68 LE MIRE, Aubert
[Origines equestrium . . . ordinum.] ORIGINE DES CHEVALIERS ET ORDRES MILITAIRES, Recueillie Par AVBERT LE MIRE . . . A Anuers, Chez Dauid Martens. M.DC.IX. 8° pp.63
608.e.4.

L69 LE MIRE, Aubert
[Originum monasticarum libri IV.] ORDINIS B. MARIÆ ANNVNTIATARVM VIRGINVM ORIGO. Accessit ordinis Carmelitani, virginum præsertim TERESANARVM, origo. AVBERTVS MIRÆVS . . . ex suis Originum monasticarum libris exscribebat. ANTVERPIÆ. APVD DAVIDEM MARTINIVM . . . M.DCVIII. 4° sig.A-G^4H^2: plate
4785.f.24(1).
The plate, showing the portrait of St. Theresa, signed: Adr. Collaert excud. The complete work not published until 1626.

L70 LE MIRE, Aubert
(tp.1) RERVM TOTO ORBE GESTARVM CHRONICA A Christo nato vsque ad nostra tempora. AVCTORIBVS EVSEBIO . . . B. HIERONYMO . . . SIGEBERTO . . . ANSELMO . . . AVBERTO MIRÆO . . . ALIISQ. Omnia ad antiquos codices mss. partim comparata, partim nunc primùm in lucem edita. Operâ ac studio eiusdem AVBERTI MIRÆI . . . ANTVERPIÆ. APVD HIERONYMVM VERDVSSIVM . . . M.DC.VIII.

(tp.2=sig.†1r) CHRONICON SIGEBERTI GEMBLACENSIS MONACHI . . . ACCESSIT ANSELMI Gemblacensis Abbatis Chronicon, cum Auctarijs GEMBLACENSI, AFFLIGEMENSI, VALCELLENSI & AQVICINCTINO, primùm typis nunc editum. STVDIO AVBERTI MIRÆI . . . ANTVERPIÆ, Apud Hieronymum Verdussen . . . M.DC.VIII.
(tp.3=p.182) ANSELMI GEMBLACENSIS . . . CHRONICON . . . primùm nunc erutum Studio AVBERTI MIRÆI . . . ANTVERPIÆ, Apud Hieronymum Verdussen.
(tp.4=p.265) RERVM TOTO ORBE GESTARVM CHRONICON . . . AVBERTVS MIRÆVS . . . ex vetustis scriptoribus concinnauit. ANTVERPIÆ, Apud Hieronymum Verdussen . . . M.DC.VIII. 4° sig.xx, x-xx, *A-H*^{4}; †^{4}, pp.1-399; 390; 101-120[420]
C.74.d.8.

After p.399 the pagination is irregular, running 390 [=400], 101-120[401-420].

L71 LE MIRE, Aubert

VITA IVSTI LIPSI SAPIENTIAE ET LITTERARVM ANTISTITIS. AVBERTVS MIRÆVS . . . ex scriptis illius potissimùm concinnabat. Editio altera auctior & emendatior. ANTVERPIÆ. Apud Dauidem Martinium. M.DC.IX. 8° pp.78
10707.a.1(2); 612.a.1(2).

The copy at 612.a.1(2) is imperfect; wanting all after p.76.

LEMMATA novo-antiqua pancarpia. 1614. *See* CABILLIAVUS, Balduinus

L72 LE MONNIER, Pierre

ANTIQVITEZ, Memoires, & OBSERVATIONS REMARQVABLES, D'EPITAPHES, TOMBEAVX, COLOSSES, OBELISQVES, HISTOIRES, ARCS Triomphaux . . . & Inscriptions, tant antiques, que modernes, veües & annotées en plusieurs villes & endroits, tant du Royaume de France . . . Bourgogne, Sauoye, Piedmont, que d'Italie & d'Allemagne. Par M[e]. PIERRE LE MONNIER . . . Auec vne briefue description des lieux . . . qui peut seruir de guide . . . à tous voyageurs . . . A LILLE, De l'Imprimerie de Christofle Beys . . . 1614. Aux despens de l'Autheur, chez lequel sont les exemplaires. 8° pp.275
574.b.19.

L73 LEO VI; Emperor of Constantinople

[Greek and Latin] LEONIS IMP. TACTICA: SIVE De Re Militari LIBER. IOANNES MEVRSIVS Græce primus vulgauit, & NOTAS adiecit. LVGDVNI BATAVORVM, Apud IOANNEM BALDVINVM: Impensis Ludouici Elzeuirij . . . M.DC.XII. (col.) EXCUDEBAT IOANNES BALDVINI, IMPENSIS LVDOVICI ELZEVIRI. LVGDVNI BATAVORVM XII. MART. Anno M.DC.XII. 4° pp.447,7
C.76.c.5(1); 63.c.1.

With 'Modesti libellus de vocabulis rei militaris'. A 1613 reissue published in a combined edition of this text with that of Aelianus Tacticus is entered under AELIANUS Tacticus.

L74 LEONARDUS Nervius; Capuchin

(tp.1) R.P. LEONARDI NERVII . . . MISSAE DECEM QVATVOR, QVINQVE, SEX ET SEPTEM VOCVM, Cum BASSO pro ORGANO. CANTVS. ANTVERPIÆ, APVD PETRVM PHALESIVM . . . M.D.CXVIII.
(tp.2) R.P. LEONARDI NERVII . . . MISSAE DECEM . . . ALTVS. ANTVERPIÆ, APVD PETRVM PHALESIVM . . . M.D.CXVIII.
(tp.3) R.P. LEONARDI NERVII . . . MISSAE DECEM . . . TENOR. ANTVERPIÆ, APVD PETRVM PHALESIVM . . . M.D.CXVIII.
(tp.4) R.P. LEONARDI NERVII . . . MISSAE DECEM . . . SEXTVS. ANTVERPIÆ, APVD PETRVM PHALESIVM . . . M.D.CXVIII. 4° 4 pt.: pp.77; 70; 68; 67
Music C.89.

All titlepages except that of the Cantus inscribed: Sum Winandi Hanssen Cauo Cliuensis.

LEONHARDUS, Carolus. Disputatio medica de hydrope. 1610. *See* HEURNIUS, Otto

L75 LEONINUS, Elbertus

ELBERTI LEONINI . . . EMENDATIONVM SIVE OBSERVATIONVM LIBRI SEPTEM. IN QVIBVS PRÆTER INNVMEROS IVRIS LOCOS CVM EMENDATOS TVM ILLVstratos, pleræque vtilissimæ & in praxi vsitatissimæ materiæ . . . pertractantur . . . ARNHEMI GELRORVM, Ex officinâ typographicâ Ioannis Iansonij . . . M.DC.X. 4° pp.415

1570/1047.

The editor's dedication and preface signed: Elbertus Zosius.

L76 LE PETIT, Jean François

LES FRVICTS DE LA PAIX, SOVBS le nom de TREFVES, entre . . . Philippe troisieme . . . Roy des Espagnes, les Archiducs Albert, & Isabelle d'Austrice . . . Et les . . . Estats Generaulx de la Republique des Provinces vnies du Pays-Bas, Concluë en Anvers le neufiesme du moi d'Apuril [*sic*] 1609 . . . A VTRECHT, Par Salomon de Roy . . . 1609. 4° sig.A^2BC^4

T.2421(5).

The dedication signed: Iean François le Petit.

L77 LE PETIT, Jean François

(tp.1) LA GRANDE CHRONIQVE ANCIENNE ET MODERNE, de Hollande, Zelande, VVest-Frise, Vtrecht, Frise, Overyssel & Groeningen, jusques à la fin de l'An 1600. Receüillee . . . Par IEAN FRANÇOIS LE PETIT . . . A DORDRECHT, De l'impression de Iacob Canin, pour l'Auteur . . . 1601.

(tp.2) LA GRANDE CHRONIQVE . . . DE Hollande, Zelande, VVest-Frise, Vtrecht, Overyssel & Groeninghen iusques a la fin de lan, 1600. Recuilliee [*sic*] . . . par IEAN FRANÇOIS LE PETIT . . . A DORDRECHT, De l'impression de Guillaume Guillemot . . . 1601. (col.) A DORDRECHT. CHEZ GVILLAVME GVILLEMOT, M.VI.C.I. fol. 2 tom.: pp.650, 240; 779; illus., port.

591.i.4,5; 155.b.11,12.

The titlepages are engraved, that of tom.1 with text in letterpress. The engravings signed: Christoffel von (or: van) Sichem; one woodcut, unsigned.

L78 LE PETIT, Jean François

NEDERLANTSCHE REPVBLYCKE, Bestaende inde Staten so generale/als particuliere . . . int breede beschreven/met alle hare Steden/Forteressen, Vestingen . . . Geconfereert . . . met die van de Swytsersche Cantoenen/ Inhoudende d'oorsaecken ende redenen diese beyde beweecht hebben het Jock van t'Huys van Oostenrijck te verwerpen . . . Door IAN-FRANCOIS LE PETIT . . . TOT ARNHEM, By Ian Ianszen . . . M.DC.XV. obl. 4° pp.470; illus., maps

C.107.l.74.

With an additional, engraved, titlepage, reading: Eygentlycke Beschryuinge der Vrye Nederlantsche Provintien.

LE PIPER, Joannes. Disputatio medica de hydrope. 1621. *See* HEURNIUS, Otto

LE PIPER, Joannes. Disputationum anatomicarum quinta . . . de ossibus . . . quam . . . defendere conabitur Iohannes le Piper. 1618. *See* WINSEMIUS, Menelaus

LE PIPER, Joannes. Disputationum anatomicarum undeciman, de musculis . . . proponit Iohannes le Piper. 1619. *See* WINSEMIUS, Menelaus

LE PIPER, Joannes. Theses medicae de melancholia. 1621. *See* VORSTIUS, Aelius Everardus

L79 LERNUTIUS, Janus

IANI LERNVTII INITIA, BASIA, OCELLI, & alia Poëmata . . . Ab ipso auctore publicata. LVGDVNI BATAVORVM, Apud Ludovicum Elzevirium. M D C XIIII. 8° pp.301[401]
1070.c.20.

Printed in italics, by Henrick van Haestens at Leiden.

L80 L'ESPAGNOL, Jean

[Histoire de la vie et miracles de Saincte Vaubourg.] HISTOIRE NOTABLE DE LA CONVERSION DES ANGLOIS, DES SAINCTS DV PAYS, DES MONASTERES, EGLISES ET ABBAYES . . . RAPPORTEE SOVBS LA VIE MIRACVLEVSE DE SAINCTE VAVBOURG . . . Illustree d'amples annotations . . . par IEAN L'ESPAGNOL . . . A DOVAY, Chez BALTAZAR BELLERE . . . 1614. [etc.] 8° pp.792
488.a.11; 4705.a.1; G.11682.

A reissue, with a new titlepage and leaf a2, of the 'Histoire de la vie et miracles de Saincte Vaubourg', originally published by Simon de Foigny at Rheims in 1612.

LESSIUS, Leonardus. A consultation what faith and religion is best to be imbraced. 1618; 1621. *See* below: Quae fides et religio sit capessenda.

L81 LESSIUS, Leonardus

DE ANTICHRISTO ET EIVS PRÆCVRSORIBVS Disputatio Apologetica gemina: Qua refutatur PRÆFATIO MONITORIA, falsò, vt creditur, adscripta Magnæ BRITANNIÆ REGI. Auctore LEONARDO LESSIO . . . ANTVERPIÆ, EX OFFICINA PLANTINIANA, Apud Viduam & Filios Io. Moreti. M.DC.XI. (col.) ANTVERPIÆ, EX OFFICINA PLANTINIANA, Apud Viduam & Filios Io. Moreti. M.DC.XI. 8° pp.297
1650/4.

A refutation of the preface to James I's 'Triplici nodo, triplex cuneus'.

L82 LESSIUS, Leonardus

[De bono statu eorum qui vovent et colunt castitatem.] (tp.1) THE TREASVRE OF VOWED CHASTITY in secular Persons. Also the WIDDOWES GLASSE. VVritten by . . . Leonard Lessius, and Fuluius Androtius . . . Translated into English by I.W.P. . . . 1621.
(tp.2=p.217) THE WIDDOWES GLASSE. ABRIDGED Out of . . . Fuluius Androtius M.DC.XXI. 18° pp.348
C.26.gg.12.

Originally published under the name of Leo Hubertinus. Translated by John Wilson. Without imprint; published by the English College press at St. Omer.

L83 LESSIUS, Leonardus

DE PERFECTIONIBVS MORIBVSQVE DIVINIS LIBRI XIV . . . Auctore LEONARDO LESSIO . . . ANTVERPIÆ, EX OFFICINA PLANTINIANA, Apud Balthasarem Moretum, & Viduam Ioannis Moreti, & Io. Meursium. M.DC.XX. (col.) ANTVERPIÆ, EX OFFICINA PLANTINIANA BALTHASARIS MORETI. M.DC.XX. 4° pp.592
C.82.d.4.

L84 LESSIUS, Leonardus

DE PROVIDENTIA NVMINIS ET ANIMI IMMORTALITATE LIBRI DVO aduersus Atheos & Politicos: AVCTORE LEONARDO LESSIO . . . ANTVERPIÆ, EX OFFICINA PLANTINIANA, Apud Viduam & Filios Io. Moreti. M.DC.XIII. (col.) ANTVERPIÆ, EX OFFICINA PLANTINIANA, APVD VIDVAM ET FILIOS IOANNIS MORETI. M.DC.XIII. 8° pp.351
697.c.14(1).

L85 LESSIUS, Leonardus

DE PROVIDENTIA NVMINIS ET ANIMI IMMORTALITATE LIBRI DVO . . . AVCTORE LEONARDO LESSIO . . . Editio secunda. ANTVERPIÆ, EX OFFICINA PLANTINIANA, Apud Balthasarem & Ioannem Moretos. M.DC.XVII. (col.) ANTVERPIÆ, EX OFFICINA PLANTINIANA, Apud Balthasarem & Ioannem Moretos. M.DC.XVII. 8° pp.351
1489.r.13.

L86 LESSIUS, Leonardus

DE SVMMO BONO ET ÆTERNA BEATITVDINE HOMINIS LIBRI QVATVOR: Auctore LEONARDO LESSIO . . . ANTVERPIÆ, EX OFFICINA PLANTINIANA, Apud Balthasarem & Ioannem Moretos. M.DC.XVI. 8° pp.603
1568/8383.

L87 LESSIUS, Leonardus

DISPVTATIO DE STATV VITÆ DELIGENDO ET RELIGIONIS INGRESSV, Quæstionibus XII. comprehensa: AVCTORE LEONARDO LESSIO . . . ANTVERPIÆ, EX OFFICINA PLANTINIANA, Apud Viduam & Filios Io. Moreti. M.DC.XIII. (col.) ANTVERPIÆ, EX OFFICINA PLANTINIANA, APVD VIDVAM ET FILIOS IOANNIS MORETI. M.DC.XIII. 8° pp.210
697.c.14(2).

L88 LESSIUS, Leonardus

HYGIASTICON SEV VERA RATIO VALETVDINIS BONÆ ET VITÆ vnà cum SENSVVM, IVD[I]CII, & MEMORIÆ integritate ad extremam senectutem cōseruandæ: Auctore LEONARDO LESSIO . . . Subiungitur Tractatus LVDOVICI CORNARI . . . eọdem pertinens, ex Italico in Latinum sermonem ab ipso LESSIO translatus. ANTVERPIÆ, EX OFFICINA PLANTINIANA, Apud Viduam & Filios Io. Moreti. M.DC.XIII. (col.) ANTVERPIÆ, EX OFFICINA PLANTINIANA, APVD VIDVAM ET FILIOS IOANNIS MORETI. M.DC.XIII. 8° pp.108
697.c.14(3).

The work by Cornaro is entitled: Tractatus de vitæ sobriæ commodis. The titlepage is slightly mutilated.

L89 LESSIUS, Leonardus

HYGIASTICON SEV VERA RATIO VALETVDINIS BONÆ ET VITÆ vnà cum SENSVVM, IVDICII, & MEMORIÆ integritate . . . Auctore LEONARDO LESSIO . . . Subiungitur Tractatus LVDOVICI CORNARI . . . Editio secunda. ANTVERPIÆ, EX OFFICINA PLANTINIANA, Apud Viduam & Filios Io. Moreti. M.DC.XIV. 8° pp.127
1169.d.8(3); 1039.e.4(2).

The copy at 1039.e.4(2) is cropped.

L90 LESSIUS, Leonardus

QVAE FIDES ET RELIGIO SIT CAPESSENDA, Consultatio: Auctore LEONARDO LESSIO . . . ANTVERPIÆ, EX OFFICINA PLANTINIANA, Apud Ioannem Moretum. M.DC.IX. (col.) ANTVERPIÆ, EX OFFICINA PLANTINIANA, APVD IOANNEM MORETVM. M.DC.IX. 8° pp.145
3925.aaa.9.

L91 LESSIUS, Leonardus

QVAE FIDES ET RELIGIO SIT CAPESSENDA, Consultatio: Auctore LEONARDO LESSIO . . . Editio secunda. ANTVERPIÆ, EX OFFICINA PLANTINIANA, Apud Ioannem Moretum. M.DC.X. (col.) ANTVERPIÆ, EX OFFICINA PLANTINIANA, APVD IOANNEM MORETVM. M.DC.X. 8° pp.153
1607/5209(2).

L92 LESSIUS, Leonardus

[Quae fides et religio sit capessenda.] (tp.1) A CONSVLTATION WHAT FAITH AND RELIGION is best to be imbraced. WRITTEN IN LATIN By . . . Leonard Lessius . . . AND Translated into English by W.I. . . . M.DC.XVIII.
(tp.2=p.215) AN APPENDIX TO THE FORMER CONSVLTATION. WHETHER Euery One may be saued in his owne Fayth and Religion. WRITTEN By . . . Leonard Lessius . . . M.DC.XVIII. 8° pp.256
3935.a.7.

The translator is William Wright. Without imprint; published by the English College press at St. Omer. Ownership inscription: Ric: Walmesley.

L93 LESSIUS, Leonardus

[Quae fides et religio sit capessenda.] (tp.1) A CONSVLTATION WHAT FAITH AND RELIGION is best to be imbraced WRITTEN IN LATIN By . . . Leonard Lessius . . . AND Translated into English by W. I. Whereunto is also annexed a little Treatise VVhether the Church of Rome hath fallen in Fayth, or no? THE SECOND EDITION . . . M.DC.XXI.
(tp.2=p.215) AN APPENDIX TO THE FORMER CONSVLTATION. WHETHER Euery One may be saued in his owne Fayth and Religion. WRITTEN By . . . Leonard Lessius . . . M.DC.XXI.
(tp.3=p.257) A DEFENCE OF THE ROMAN CHVRCH. WHERIN Is treated, VVhether the sayd Church hath fallen in fayth, or no? Written in Latin by . . . Martin Becanus . . . AND Translated into English, by W.W. . . . M.DC.XXI. 8° pp.304
C.26.k.11 & C.26.k.14(1).
Translated by William Wright. The 'Defence of the Roman Church' by Becanus is placed at C.26.k.14(1) and has the ownership inscription: Dom. Prof. Rom. S. J. Bibl. Com. Without imprint; published by the English College press at St. Omer.

LESSIUS, Leonardus. The treasure of vowed chastity. 1621. *See* above: De bono statu eorum qui vovent et colunt castitatem.

A LETTER of a Catholike man. 1610. *See* OWEN, Thomas

L94 LETTER

A LETTER WRITTEN BY A FRENCH GENT: of the King of BOHEMIA his Army: Concerning the Emperour FERDINAND his Embassage into FRANCE. Translated out of the French Coppie. Printed at Flushing. 1620. 4° pp.13
8026.b.19.
The imprint is false; published at London.

LETTERS patentes graunted by the States of the United Netherland Provinces, to the West Indian Company of Merchants. 1621. *See* NETHERLANDS. United Provinces, States General [9.6.1621]

LETTRE mistique responce, replique. 1603. *See* below: LETTRE mystique touchant la conspiration

L95 LETTRE

LETTRE MYSTIQVE TOVCHANT LA CONSPIRATION derniere, AVEC L'OVVERTVRE DE LA CAballe Mysterielle des Iesuites, reuelee par songe, à vn Gentilhomme des Trouppes du Conte MAVRICE, escrite à Frère Iean Boucher. Cum examine Indicis Expurgatorij. Le tout dedié à l'Excellence du Conte MAVRICE. Par M.D.L.F. . . . A LEIDEN, Par Piere Caillou. 1603. 12° pp.168
1192.b.15(1).
The imprint is very probably false.

L96 LETTRE

[Lettre mystique touchant la conspiration.] LETTRE MISTIQVE RESPONCE, REPLIQVE . . . Louuerture de la Cabale amplifiee, L'index d'Espagne examiné, le desespoir de l'ombre acheué. Le tout dedié à l'excellence du Conte Maurice, Par M.D.L.F. . . . A LEIDEN. M. DCIII. 8° pp.103, 165
1059.a.16(1).
Another edition of the preceding. The imprint 'Leiden' is very doubtful.

LEUGEN-STRICK. 1619. *See* SAPMA, Dominicus

L97 LEVEN
Het Leuen ende Steruen van PHILIPPVS den III. Hooch-loffelijcker ghedachten, Catholijck Coninck van Hispanien, beyde de Indien, &c. T'Hantwerpen/By Abraham Verhoeuen/[etc.] 4° sig. (⁎⁎⁎)^3; illus.
1193.f.33; PP.3444.af(219).
Headed: Appril 1621. 58. The titlepage woodcut shows a family portrait of Philip III. Wanting the last leaf; blank?

L98 LEVEN
HET LEVEN, HISTORIE ENDE MIRAKELEN van die Heylighe maget ende martelersse CRISTI S. ALENA . . . Nv onlancx vuyter Latijnsche sprake in Duytsche ouerghesedt . . . TOT BRVESSELE By Rutgeert Velpius ende Huybrecht Antoon . . . 1614. 8° sig. A-C^{8}D^4: plate
4823.a.8.
The plate has a Latin caption, is smaller than the pages and is loosely inserted.

L99 LEVENDIGE
[Leuendige vertooninge van den tegenwoordigen staet der landen Gulich, Cleue [etc.]] Naijfue description des regrets de la Paix, et de la cholere de Mars. 4° sig. AB^{4}C^2
1560/4446.
A verse translation of 'Leuendige vertooninge van den tegenwoordigen staet der landen van Gulich, Cleue, ende andere bijliggende plaetsen', with an additional sonnet 'A l'auteur', signed: Anthoine Lancel, i.e. the translator? The engraved titlepage signed: Blon. Printed at Amsterdam? in 1615?

LEX Frisionum. 1617. *See* SICCAMA, Sibrandus

L100 L'HERMITE, Jacques
Breeder verhael ende klare beschrijvinge van tghene den Admirael Cornelis Matelief de Jonge inde Oost-Indien voor de Stadt Malacca, ende int belegh der zelver wedervaren is . . . Overgheschreven by eenen der Commisen inde Vlote. Tot Rotterdam, By Jan Janssz. . . . 1608. 4° sig. AB^4; illus.
1295.b.21.
Anonymous. The titlepage woodcut showing ships full of soldiers landing near a city, one ship bearing the initial A, is one found in editions of Amadis de Gaule published by Jan van Waesberghe at Rotterdam. Is Jan Janssz the same as Jan II van Waesberghe?

LIBERGEN, Guilielmus. Disputatio de lue venerea. 1621. *See* VORSTIUS, Aelius Everardus

LIBERGEN, Guilielmus. Theses medicae de pleuritide. 1621. *See* HEURNIUS, Otto

LICHTONIUS, Alexander. *See* LEIGHTON, Alexander

LIEBAERT, Carolus. Disputationum theologicarum vigesima, de perpessionibus Christi. 1603. *See* GOMARUS, Franciscus

LIECHTENBERGER, Joannes. *See* JOHANN Lichtenberger

L101 LIEDEKENS
LIEDEKENS, Nopende de eeuwighe ghevanckenisse der Remonstrantsche Predicanten, ende den Moort tot Rotterdam begaen int apprehenderen van Simon Luce: den 24. Augustus . . . 1621. 4° sig. A^4
T.2251(8⁎⁎).
Published in 1621.

L102 LIEFF-HEBBER

Een cort verhael/hoe ende in wat maniere die Gommarissen [*sic*] van Hollant/ Hemel en eerde willē innemen met eene slach/Nac dic Leere . . . van Plancius . . . En nae die Leere van Calvinus die nv in die Synode beuesticht wort . . . Ghesteldt in Rijme, ende Ghemaeckt door een Lieff-hebber. T'Hantwerpen/By Abraham Verhoeuen . . . 1619. 4° pp.7; illus.

P.P.3444.af(4).

The titlepage woodcut shows a preacher, named as Peter Plancius, before his congregation, inspired by the devil. Without signatures.

L103 LIEFHEBBER

Een cort verhael van eenen nieuwen Draeck ende Afgoden van Hollant/mits hoe de selve de H. Schriftuere misbruycken/willende ende begheerende dat den Marquis Spinola haerlieden aen bidden sal . . . Ende oock van die groote . . . Victorie in den slach van Bohemen by die Stadt van Praegh . . . Ghestelt in Rijme seer ghenuechlijck om lesen. Ghemaeckt door eenen Lief hebber. Eerst ghedruckt den 15. Ianuarius 1621 . . . T'Hantwerpen/by Abraham Verhoeven/[etc.] 4° pp.13; sig.[A]^{4}B^3; illus.

P.P.3444.af(173); P.P.3444.af(173*).

A reply to Johannes Thuryn's 'Den uyttoght van Spinola'. Headed: Ianuarius 1621. 4., followed by a Latin distich. The titlepage woodcut shows the 'dragon'. Both copies wanting the last leaf, blank. The copy at P.P.3444.af.(173*) wanting also the last but one leaf, for which another leaf bearing the text of p.13 and that of the privilege in manuscript has been substituted.

L104 LIEF-HEBBER

Dat s'Pals-grauen dvvaesheydt niet en is te verschoonen. Sullen vvy den vromē Leser int cort gaen verthoonen. Ghemaeckt door eenen Lief-hebber Godt wil hem verblijen, Hy soeckt de bekeering' van die gheen Die de waerheyt bestrijen. Eerst ghedruckt in Februarius/1621. T'Hantwerpen/by Abraham Verhoeven/[etc.] 4° pp.8; sig,A^4; illus.

P.P.3444.af(188).

In verse. Another poem in praise of the Emperor is added. Headed: Februarius 1621. 19. The titlepage woodcut shows two dogs chasing another.

L105 LIEF-HEBBER

Godt ter eeren, en den Marquis Spinola vaillant . . . Ghemaect door eenen Lief-hebber Godt wil hem verblijen, Hy soect de bekeering' van die gheen Die de waerheyt bestrijen. Eerst Ghedruckt in Februarius 1621. T'Hantwerpen/By Abraham Verhoeven/[etc.] 4° pp.7; sig.A^4; illus.

P.P.3444.af(189); 1471.aa.8.

In verse. Headed: Februarius 1621. 20. The titlepage woodcut shows a portrait of Spinola, wearing armour. The titlepage of the copy at 1471.aa.8 is badly mutilated.

L106 LIEF-HEBBER

Een nieu Liedeken vande wilde vogelen strijt, Die sy onder een hebben, maer singhen Godt lof altijt, Het gaet op de voys, willet wel onthouwen, Van der Kettren voorstaender, VVilhelmus van Nassouwen. Ghemaect door eenen Lief-hebber Godt wil hem verblijen, Hy soect de bekeering' van die gheen Die de waerheyt bestrijen. Eerst ghedruckt in Februarius. 1621. T'Hantwerpen/By Abraham Verhoeuen/[etc.] 4° pp.8; sig.A^4; illus.

P.P.3444.af(190).

In verse. Headed: Februarius 1621. 21. The titlepage woodcut shows a stork, or crane, with a stone in one foot in a marshy landscape.

Een nieu Liedeken vande wilde vogelen strijt,
Die sy onder een hebben, maer singhen Godt
lof altijt,
Het gaet op de voys, willet wel onthouwen,
Van der Kettren voorstaender, VVilhelmus
van Nassouwen.

Ghemaeckt door eenen Lief-hebber
Godt wil hem verblijen,
Hy soeckt de bekeering' van die gheen
Die de waerheyt bestrijen.

Eerst ghedruckt in Februarius, 1621.

T'Hantwerpen/ By Abraham Verhoeuen / op de
Lombaerde Veste/inde gulde Sonne.

L107 LIÈGE

[28.5.1616] ORDINANTIE ENDE PLACCAET VANDEN HEERE FERDINAND HERTOCH van Beyeren, Eertsbisschop eñ Cuervorst tot Ceulen, Bisschop eñ Prince van Luyck, &c. Op het stuck vanden loop ende permissie vande goude ende siluere munten, t'onderhouden binnen zijn Stadt ende Steden, van zijn Bis: ende Vorstendōme Luyck. TOT LUYCK, By Christiaen Ouwercx . . . M.DC.XVI. 4° sig. $A\text{-}C^4D^2$
106.c.56(2).

Issued 28 May 1616. With the arms of the Prince-Bishop on the titlepage.

L108 LIÈGE. Synod

DECRETA SYNODI DIOECESANAE LEODIENSIS, IN Ecclesia Cathedrali Leodij Anno Dñi 1618. celebratæ. Præsidente . . . FERDINANDO, Archiepiscopo, & Electore Coloniēsi, Episcopo, ac Principe Leodiensi . . . LEODII, Ex Officina CHRISTIANI OVWERX . . . 1618. [etc.] 4° pp.68
1609/938.

With the arms of the Prince-Bishop on the titlepage.

L109 LIENS, Cornelis

CORNELII LIENS . . . cum adversarijs D.P. Lansbergij amica consertatio Epistolica. Huius causæ ex præscripto fidei narratio, approbatio. ZIRIZEÆ, Excudebat Iohannes vander Hellen . . . 1614. 8° pp.75[82]
1170.c.8(1).

Ownership inscription: Joseph Fenton.

L110 LIENS, Cornelis

CORNELII LIENS . . . Mittelburgensium Medicorum responsi postliminij & Epistolæ Apologeticæ ex superabundanti cautela refutatio pro D.P. Lansbergio. ZIRIZEÆ, Excudebat Iohannes vander Hellen . . . 1614. 8° pp.181
1170.c.8(2).

LIEVENS, Gerard. *See* LIVIUS, Gerardus

The LIFE and death of Mr. Edmund Geninges. 1614. *See* GENINGES, John

The LIFE and gate of Christianitie. 1614. *See* ALMOND, Oliver

L111 LILLE

COVSTVMES ET VSAGES GENERAVX DE LA SALLE, BAILLAGE ET CHASTELLENIE DE LILLE . . . Auec les Coustumes localles & particulieres des lieux gisans en ladite Chastellenie, ressortissans à la Gouuernance de Lille. Augmentees des Coustumes localles de la Viscomté de Haubourdin & Amerin . . . A LILLE, De l'Imprimerie de CHRISTOFLE BEYS . . . 1621. [etc.] 4° pp.134
5423.bbb.26.

Ownership inscription: Jean Wettes 14 May 1622.

L112 LINDANUS, David

DAVIDIS LINDANI . . . DE TENERAEMONDA LIBRI TRES . . . ANTVERPIÆ, Ex Typographeio HIERONYMI VERDVSSI. M.DC.XII. 4° pp.246
1502/586.

LINDANUS, Wilhelmus; Bishop. *See* LINDT, Willem van der

L113 LINDEN, Henricus Antonides van der

DISPUTATIO THEOLOGICA DE COENA DOMINI QUAM . . . SUB PRAESIDIO . . . D. HENRICI ANTONIDIS . . . Publice defendere conabitur IOHANNES PETRI . . . FRANEKERÆ, EXCVDEBAT AEGIDIUS RADAEUS . . . 1604. 4° sig. A^4
4374.l.22(42).

L114 LINDEN, Henricus Antonides van der
DISPVTATIO THEOLOGICA, DE COENA DOMINI, QVAM . . . Sub tutela ac præsidio . . . D. HENRICI ANTONIDIS . . . publicè defendendam suscipit HERMANNVS PET. DROGENHAM . . . FRANEKERAE, Ex Officinâ Vlderici Dominici Balck . . . 1613. 4° sig. A⁴
4374.l.22(43).

L115 LINDEN, Henricus Antonides van der
AVSPICE CHRISTO DISPVTATIO THEOLOGICA, DE CREATIONE, QUAM . . . SUB TUTELA . . . D. HENRICI ANTONIDIS . . . Publicè . . . defendere conabitur, PHOCÆVS TEIONIS . . . FRANICÆ, Ex officinâ Vlderici Balck . . . M.DC.XIII. 4° sig. A⁴
4374.l.22(20).

L116 LINDEN, Henricus Antonides van der
Disputatio THEOLOGICA, DE DEO VNO ET TRINO, Quam . . . SUB PRÆSIDIO . . . D. HENRICI ANTONIDIS . . . Ventilandam exhibet BRUNO HARTUNGH . . . FRANEQUERÆ, Excudebat Rombertus Doyma 1613. 4° sig. A⁴
4374.l.22(17).

L117 LINDEN, Henricus Antonides van der
DISPUTATIO THEOLOGICA DE LIBERTATE CHRISTIANA, QUAM . . . SUB PRAESIDIO . . . D. HENRICI ANTONIDIS . . . defendere tentabit HERMANNUS DUNCKER . . . FRANEKERÆ Excudebat Ægidius Radæus . . . 1602. 4° sig. A⁴
4374.l.22(33).

L118 LINDEN, Henricus Antonides van der
DISPVTATIONVM THEOLOGICARVM VICESIMA OCTAVA, DE LIBERO ARBITRIO, QVAM . . . SUB ALIS . . . D. HENRICI ANTONIDIS . . . defendere conabitur: GUILIELMUS VVALRAVEN . . . FRANEKERÆ, EXCUDEBAT AEGIDIUS RADAEUS . . . 1605. 4° sig. A⁴
4374.l.22(27).

L119 LINDEN, Henricus Antonides van der
DISQVISITIO THEOLOGICA, DE ANGELIS, QVAM . . . PRÆSIDE . . . D. HENRICO ANTONIDE . . . Publicè . . . defendet HENRICVS HVYSINGIVS . . . FRANEQVERÆ, Excudebat AEGIDIVS RADAEVS . . . Anno VIVentes DIsCIte MorI. 4° sig. A⁴
4374.l.22(22).
The chronogram reads: 1614.

L120 LINDEN, Henricus Antonides van der
HENRICI ANTONII NERDENI, INITIA ACADEMIAE, Franequerensis, Ejusdem, TEMPLI & GVBERNATIONIS. Tempus institutæ Academ. Dedicatoria Autoris, Consilium, eam proximè sequens Oratio D. Ab. Frankena exponit. FRANEKERAE. Excudebat Ægidius Radæus . . . M.DC.XIII. 4° pp. 72, 91
731.e.2(15).

L121 LINDEN, Henricus Antonides van der
THESES THEOLOGICÆ DE Æterna DEITATE Domini Nostri Iesu Christi, AD QVAS . . . PRAESIDE . . . D. HENRICO ANTONIDE . . . respondebit ADRIANVS RADÆVS . . . FRANEKERÆ, EXCVDEBAT AEGIDIVS RADAEVS . . . 1612. 4° sig. A⁶
4374.l.22(18).

L122 LINDEN, Henricus Antonides van der
Theses Theologicæ DE DEO, Quarum veritatem . . . Sub præsidio . . . D. HENRICI ANTONIDIS . . . Pro tenuitate ingenij defendere conabitur THEODORVS DAMMIVS . . . FRANEQUERÆ, Excudebat ROMBERTVS DOYEMA, M.D.XIII [*sic*]. 4° sig. A⁴
4374.l.22(16).

L123 LINDEN, Henricus Antonides van der
THESES THEOLOGICÆ DE INVOCATIONE SANCTORVM, QVAS . . . PRÆSIDE . . . D. HENRICO ANTONIDE . . . Publice discutiendas propono HERMANNVS TIMANNI . . . FRANECAE, Apud Vlricum Balck . . . 1614. 4° sig. A^4
4374.l.22(35).

L124 LINDEN, Henricus Antonides van der
Theses Theologicæ, DE LIBERO HOMINIS ARBITRIO, Quas . . . Sub tutela . . . D. HENRICI ANTONIDIS . . . Publicè excutiendas proponit HENRICUS ALUTARIUS. FRANEKERÆ FRISIORUM, Ex Officina Romberti Doyma. 1610. 4° sig. A^4
4374.l.22(28).

L125 LINDEN, Henricus Antonides van der
Theses Theologicæ DE PECCATO ORIGINALI, Quas . . . Sub præsidio . . . D. HENRICI ANTONIDIS . . . Publicè defendere conabitur FRANCISCVS WERNERIVS . . . FRANEQUERÆ, Excudebat ROMBERTVS DOYEMA, M.D.XIII [*sic*]. 4° sig. A^4
4374.l.22(25).

L126 LINDSAY, David; Bishop
[De potestate principis aphorismi.] Seeckere Articulen Van de MACHT EENS PRINCEN, Ofte Des Magistraets: Ghestelt by David Lindesay in't Latijn . . . Ende nu . . . in onse Duytsche Tale over-gheset . . . 1617. 4° pp. 8
700.h.25(5); 8142.bbb.4.

L127 LINDT, Willem van der; Bishop
GLAPHYRA IN CHRISTI DOMINI APOCALYPTICAS ad Episcopos Epistolas . . . Authore WILHELMO LINDANO. QVIBVS EPILOGI LOCO ACCESSIT ECCLESIÆ PROSOPOPEIA AD EOSDEM. LOVANII, Apud Iohannem Masium . . . M.D.CII. [etc.] 8° ff. 84
3185.a.65.
The editor's dedication signed: Joannes Malderus.

L128 LINSCHOTEN, Jan Huygen van
(tp. 1) ITINERARIO, Voyage ofte Schipvaert/van Jan Huygen van Linschoten naer Oost ofte Portugaels Indien . . . Alles beschreven ende by een vergadert, door den selfden . . . t'AMSTELREDAM, By Cornelis Claesz. [etc.]
(tp. 2) Beschrijvinghe van de gantsche Custe van Guinea/Manicongo/Angola . . . Midtsgaders de . . . beschrijvinge op de Caerte van Madagascar . . . met de ontdeckinge aller droochten, clippen . . . Eylanden . . . int boeck van Ian Huyghen van Linschoten . . . int licht ghebracht . . . 't Amstelredam/By Cornelis Claesz . . . Anno xvj^{C}.v.
(tp. 3) REYS-GHESCHRIFT Van de Navigatien der Portugaloysers in Orienten . . . Alles . . . by een vergadert, ende uyt die Portugaloysche ende Spaensche in onse . . . Nederlandsche Tale . . . overgheset. Door IAN HVYGHEN van LINSCHOTEN. t'AMSTELREDAM, By Cornelis Claesz. . . . 1604. fol. 3 pt.: pp. 160; 160; sig. ★★★–★★★★★★^{6} ★★★★★★^{3}: plates; maps; illus., port.
10025.f.15.
With annotations and additions by Bernardus Paludanus. Some leaves from another book have been inserted.

L129 LINSCHOTEN, Jan Huygen van
(tp. 1) ITINERARIVM, Ofte Schipvaert naer Oost ofte Portugaels Indien . . . Alles beschreven door Ian Huygen van Linschoten. Op't nieuw gecorrigeert eñ verbetert. TOT AMSTERDAM, By Jan Evertsz. Cloppenburch . . . 1614. [etc.]
(tp. 2) REYS-GHESCHRIFT Van de Navigatien der Portugaloysers . . . Alles by een vergadert, ende . . . overgheset . . . door Ian Huyghen van Linschoten. TOT AMSTERDAM, By Jan Evertsz. Cloppenburch . . . 1614. [etc.]

(tp.3) Beschrijvinghe van de gantsche Custe van Guinea . . . TOT AMSTERDAM, By Jan Evertsz Cloppenburch . . . 1614. fol. 3 pt.: pp.160; 147; sig.a–h[4]: plates; maps; illus., port.
1298.m.13.

The titlepage is engraved with letterpress text.

L130 LINSCHOTEN, Jan Huygen van
[Itinerario.] HISTOIRE DE LA NAVIGATION DE IEAN HVGVES DE LINSCOT . . . ET DE SON voyage es Indes Orientales . . . AVEC ANNOTATIONS DE BERNARD PALVdanus . . . A QVOY SONT ADIOVSTEES QVELQVES AVtres descriptions . . . LE TOVT RECVEILLI ET DESCRIT PAR LE MESME de Linscot en bas Alleman, & nouuellement traduict en François. A AMSTELREDAM, De l'Imprimerie de Henry Laurent. M.DC.X. fol. pp.275: plates; illus., maps
L.R.408.e.7.

The engravings are those used in the De Bry edition of 'Petits voyages' 2–4.

L131 LINSCHOTEN, Jan Huygen van
[Itinerario.] HISTOIRE DE LA NAVIGATION DE IEAN HVGVES DE LINSCOT . . . A AMSTELREDAM, De l'Imprimerie de Theodore Pierre. M.DC.X. fol. pp.275: plates; illus., maps
G.7009.

Another issue of the preceding, with a cancel titlepage. The Dutch plates have been added to this copy. Wanting the de Bry maps of Sumatra and Java and of Goa.

L132 LINSCHOTEN, Jan Huygen van
[Itinerario.] (tp.1) HISTOIRE DE LA NAVIGATION DE IEAN HVGVES de Linschot . . . Avec annotations de B. PALVDANVS . . . Deuxiesme edition augmentee. A AMSTERDAM, Chez Iean Evertsz Cloppenburch . . . 1619.
(tp.2) LE GRAND ROVTIER DE MER, De IEAN HVGVES de Linschot . . . Le tout fidelement recueilli des memoires & observations des Pilotes Espagnols & Portugais. Et nouvellement traduit de Flameng en François. A AMSTERDAM, Chez Iean Evertsz Cloppenburch . . . 1619.
(tp.3) DESCRIPTION DE L'AMERIQVE & des parties d'icelle . . . A AMSTERDAM, Chez Iean Evertsz Cloppenburch . . . 1619. fol. 3 pt.: pp.205; 181; 86: plates; maps, port.
10498.d.9.

The titlepages of pt.1,2 are engraved, with letterpress text. With the plates of the Dutch editions.

L133 LINSCHOTEN, Jan Huygen van
VOYAGIE, OFTE SCHIP-VAERT, VAN IAN HVYGHEN VAN LINSCHOTEN, van by Noorden om langes Noorvvegen de Noortcap, Laplant, Vinlant, Ruslandt, de VVitte Zee . . . door de Strate . . . van Nassau tot voorby de Revier Oby . . . Ghedruct tot Franeker, By GERARD KETEL. (col.) Ghedruct tot Franeker, By GERARD KETEL, Voor Jan Huyghen van Linschoten resideerende binnen Enchuysen . . . 1601. fol. ff.38: plates; maps
10025.f.12.

The titlepage is engraved, with letterpress text. The engraved part signed: Ioannes á Doetechum, Baptista á Doetec. fecerunt.

L134 LIPSIUS, Justus
[Collections] IVSTI LIPSI OPERA OMNIA QVÆ AD CRITICAM PROPRIE SPECTANT: Postremùm ab ipso aucta, correcta, digesta . . . ANTVERPIÆ, EX OFFICINA PLANTINIANA, Apud Viduam & Filios Ioannis Moreti. M.DC.XI. [etc.] (col.)

ANTVERPIÆ, EX OFFICINA PLANTINIANA, APVD VIDVAM ET FILIOS IOANNIS MORETI. M.DC.XI. 4° pp.645
836.k.21(1).
Contents: Variarum lectionum libri tres; Antiquarum lectionum libri quinque; Epistolicarum quaestionum libri quinque; Electorum libri duo; In Valer. Maximum notae; Animadversiones in Senecae tragoedias; Iudicium De consolatione Ciceronis; Satyra Menippaea Somnium.

L135 LIPSIUS, Justus
[Collected letters.] (tp.1) IVSTI LIPSI EPISTOLARVM SELECTARVM CENTVRIA QVARTA MISCELLANEA POSTVMA. ANTVERPIÆ, EX OFFICINA PLANTINIANA, Apud Ioannem Moretum. M.DC.VII. [etc.]
(tp.2) IVSTI LIPSI EPISTOLARVM SELECTARVM CENTVRIA QVINTA . . . ANTVERPIÆ, EX OFFICINA PLANTINIANA, Apud Ioannem Moretum, M.DC.VII. [etc.] (col.) ANTVERPIÆ, EX OFFICINA PLANTINIANA, Apud Ioannem Moretum. M.DC.VII. 4° 2 pt.: pp.83;112
1562/322(2,3).
The editor's dedication signed: Ioannes Woverius. The signatures of pt.2 are Aa–Pp, i.e. the two parts form a continuous whole.

L136 LIPSIUS, Justus
IVSTI LIPSI ADMIRANDA, siue, DE MAGNITVDINE ROMANA LIBRI QVATTVOR. Tertia editio correctior, auctiórque. ANTVERPIÆ, EX OFFICINA PLANTINIANA, Apud Ioannem Moretum. M.DC.V. [etc.] (col.) ANTVERPIÆ, EX OFFICINA PLANTINIANA, APVD IOANNEM MORETVM. M.DC.V. 4° pp.223
800.k.23(1).
Imperfect; wanting the last leaf, bearing a device.

L137 LIPSIUS, Justus
IVSTI LIPSI ADMIRANDA . . . Editio vltima. ANTVERPIÆ, EX OFFICINA PLANTINIANA, Apud Balthasarem & Ioannem Moretos. M.DC.XVII. [etc.] (col.) ANTVERPIÆ, EX OFFICINA PLANTINIANA, APVD BALTHASAREM ET IOANNEM MORETOS FRATRES. M.DC.XVII. 4° pp.223
1601/513(2).
With an exlibris reading: Pertinet ad bibliothecā B. Woodcroft. From the old Patent Office Library.

L138 LIPSIUS, Justus
(tp.1) IVSTI LIPSI DE AMPHITHEATRO LIBER . . . Cum æneis figuris. OMNIA AVCTIORA VEL MELIORA. ANTVERPIÆ, EX OFFICINA PLANTINIANA, Apud Ioannem Moretum. M.DC.IV. [etc.]
(tp.2=p.57) IVSTI LIPSI DE AMPHITHEATRIS QVÆ EXTRA ROMAM LIBELLVS. Jn quo Formæ eorum aliquot & typi. ANTVERPIÆ, EX OFFICINA PLANTINIANA, Apud Ioannem Moretum. M.DC.IV. [etc.] (col.) ANTVERPIÆ, EX OFFICINA PLANTINIANA, APVD IOANNEM MORETVM. M.DC.IV. 4° pp.77: plates; illus.
785.i.4.

L139 LIPSIUS, Justus
IVSTI LIPSI DE AMPHITHEATRO LIBER . . . EDITIO VLTIMA. ANTVERPIÆ, EX OFFICINA PLANTINIANA, Apud Balthasarem Moretum, & Viduam Ioannis Moreti, & Io. Meursium. M.DC.XXI. [etc.] (col.) ANTVERPIÆ, EX OFFICINA PLANTINIANA BALTHASARIS MORETI. M.DC.XXI. 4° pp.77: plates; illus.
812.k.19(2); 1601/513(4).
For the provenance of the copy at 1601/513(4) *see* above: Admiranda.

L140 LIPSIVS, Justus

IVSTI LIPSI DE BIBLIOTHECIS SYNTAGMA. ANTVERPIÆ, EX OFFICINA PLANTINIANA, Apud Ioannem Moretum. M.DCII. [etc.] 4° pp.34

631.k.4(1); 124.k.16.

The titlepage of the copy at 631.k.4(1) is slightly mutilated.

L141 LIPSIUS, Justus

IVSTI LIPSI DE BIBLIOTHECIS SYNTAGMA. Editio tertia, & ab vltimâ Auctoris manu. ANTVERPIÆ, EX OFFICINA PLANTINIANA, Apud Balthasarem Moretum, & Viduam Ioannis Moreti, & Io. Meursium. M.DC.XIX. [etc.] 4° pp.35

1601/513(6).

For the provenance of this copy *see* above: Admiranda.

L142 LIPSIUS, Justus

IVSTI LIPSI DE CONSTANTIA LIBRI DVO . . . Ex Officina Plantiniana RAPHELENGII. M.D.CXIII. 32° pp.219

527.a.7; C.20.f.25.

Published at Leiden. The copy at C.20.f.25 from the travelling library of Sir Julius Caesar.

L143 LIPSIUS, Justus

IVSTI LIPSI DE CONSTANTIA LIBRI DVO . . . Vltima editio. ANTVERPIÆ, EX OFFICINA PLANTINIANA, Apud Viduam & Filios Io. Moreti. M.DC.XV. [etc.] 4° pp.86

812.k.19(5).

L144 LIPSIUS, Justus

IVSTI LIPSI DE MILITIA ROMANA LIBRI QVINQVE, COMMENTARIVS AD POLYBIVM. Editio vltima. ANTVERPIÆ, EX OFFICINA PLANTINIANA, Apud Viduam & Filios Ioannis Moreti. M.DC.XIV. [etc.] 4° pp.397; illus.

1398.i.27(1).

The illustrations are either woodcuts or engravings. The latter are by Theodoor Galle after Pieter vander Borcht.

L145 LIPSIUS, Justus

I. LIPSI DE RECTA PRONVNTIATIONE LATINÆ LINGVÆ DIALOGVS. Editio vltima. ANTVERPIAE, EX OFFICINA PLANTINIANA, Apud Ioannem Moretum. M.DC.IX. [etc.] (col.) ANTVERPIÆ, EX OFFICINA PLANTINIANA, APVD IOANNEM MORETVM. M.DC.IX. 4° pp.66

836.k.21(2).

With the original dedication to Sir Philip Sidney.

L146 LIPSIUS, Justus

IVSTI LIPSI DE VESTA ET VESTALIBVS SYNTAGMA. ANTVERPIÆ, EX OFFICINA PLANTINIANA, Apud Ioannem Moretum. M.DCIII. [etc.] (col.) ANTVERPIÆ, EX OFFICINA PLANTINIANA, APVD IOANNEM MORETVM. M.DCIII. 4° pp.50

631.k.4(3).

L147 LIPSIUS, Justus

IVSTI LIPSI DE VESTA ET VESTALIBVS SYNTAGMA. Tertia editio, atque ab vltimâ Auctoris manu, Notis auctior, & Figuris illustrior. ANTVERPIÆ, EX OFFICINA PLANTINIANA, Apud Balthasarem Moretum, & Viduam Ioannis Moreti, & Io. Meursium. M.DC.XXI. [etc.] 4° pp.59; illus.

812.k.19(3); 1601/513(5).

The illustrations are engravings. For the provenance of the copy at 1601/513(5) *see* above: Admiranda.

L148 LIPSIUS, Justus

IVSTI LIPSI DISPVNCTIO NOTARVM MIRANDVLANI CODICIS AD COR. TACITVM. ANTVERPIÆ, EX OFFICINA PLANTINIANA, Apud Ioannem Moretum. M.DCII. [etc.] 4° pp.40

631.k.4(2).

A defence against Pompeo Lampugnano's 'Justi Lipsii in Corn. Tacitum notae'.

L149 LIPSIUS, Justus

IVSTI LIPSI DIVA SICHEMIENSIS siue ASPRICOLLIS: Noua eius BENEFICIA & ADMIRANDA. ANTVERPIÆ, EX OFFICINA PLANTINIANA, Apud Ioannem Moretum. M.DC.V. [etc.] (col.) ANTVERPIÆ, EX OFFICINA PLANTINIANA, APVD IOANNEM MORETVM. M.DC.V. 4° pp.69; illus.

631.k.4(6); 1560/4441(2).

The titlepage illustration shows the image of the Virgin of Scherpenheuvel.

L150 LIPSIUS, Justus

I. LIPSI DIVA VIRGO HALLENSIS. BENEFICIA eius & MIRACVLA . . . ANTVERPIÆ, EX OFFICINA PLANTINIANA, Apud Ioannem Moretum. M.DC.IIII. [etc.] (col.) ANTVERPIÆ, EX OFFICINA PLANTINIANA, APVD IOANNEM MORETVM. M.DC.IIII. 4° pp.86: plates; illus., port.

631.k.4(5).

According to documents quoted in the *Bibliotheca Belgica* no.L306 there should be a plate showing the chapel between pp.14 and 15, by Cornelius Galle. This copy has a different plate, i.e. a portrait of Lipsius, signed: Io. Baptista Zangrius 1601, following the titlepage and not mentioned in the *Bibliotheca Belgica*. The titlepage engraving shows the image of the Virgin, the other plate the siege of Halle in 1489 and 1580, by Adriaen Collaert.

L151 LIPSIUS, Justus

[Diva Virgo Hallensis.] I. LIPSII HEYLIGE MAGHET VAN HALLE . . . VVt de Latijnsche in onse Nederlantsche tale ouergheset deur eenen Lief-hebber der eere sijns eenigen Salichmakers; tot bespottinghe der Pauselicke Roomsche afgoderije. Tot welcken eynde cleyne Annotatiē . . . op de kant gestelt zijn . . . ende een Appendix . . . achter aen. Tot Delff, by Bruyn Harmansz. Schinckel . . . 1605. 4° pp.90,24; illus.

3925.c.76.

The translator/editor's preface signed: Æ.V.O., i.e. Aelbrecht van Oosterwijck? The titlepage engraving is copied from the Latin edition. At the end: Vanden Spinnekop ende t'Bieken. A separate edition of this is entered under VANDEN.

L152 LIPSIUS, Justus

IVSTI LIPSII EPISTOLA, quâ respondet cuidam viro Principi deliberanti BELLVMne an PAX an potius INDVCIAE expediant Regi Hispaniarum cum Gallo, Angla, Batavo. Scripta III. Januarij, M.D.XCV. Nunc primùm edita . . . M D C VIII. 4° sig.A^4

591.b.11(2).

The titlepage ornament in this edition incorporates a cherub and measures 60 × 82 mm. Corresponding to the copies described in the *Bibliotheca Belgica* no.L259 and in *Knuttel* no.1493.

L153 LIPSIUS, Justus

IVSTI LIPSII EPISTOLA, quâ respondet cuidam viro Principi deliberanti BELLVMne an PAX an potius INDVCIÆ expediant Regi Hispaniarum cum Gallo, Angla, Batavo. Scripta III Ianuarij, M.D.XCV. Nunc primùm edita . . . M D C VIII. 4° sig.A^4

106.d.21(1).

Another edition of the preceding. The titlepage ornament in this edition is that of a smiling face, measuring 36 × 46 mm. Corresponding to the copies described in the *Bibliotheca Belgica* no.L260 and in *Knuttel* no.1494.

L154 LIPSIUS, Justus

[Epistola qua respondet cuidam principi.] IVSTI LIPSII SENT-BRIEF, In welcke Hy antwoorde gheeft aen een seker groot Heer op de vraghe/welck van dryen den Coninck van Hispaengien best gheraden ware/Oorloghe oft Pays oft liever Bestant met den Fransman/Engelsche ende Hollander . . . Gheschreven den derden Ianuarij M.D.XCV. Ghetrouvvelijck uyt den Latijn in Nederduytsche tale over-gheset . . . Ghedruckt, tot Duysseldorp, By Werner vander Horst . . . M.D.C.VIII. 4° sig. A^4

T.1721(15).

The imprint is false.

L155 LIPSIUS, Justus

[Epistola qua respondet cuidam principi.] IVSTI LIPSII SENDTBRIEF/IN VVELCKE Hy Antwoorde gheeft/aen een seker groot Heere/op de Vraghe: VVelc van drien den Coninc van Hispaengien best gheraden vvare, oorloghe oft Peys, ofte liever Bestant met den Frans-man, Enghelsche ende Hollander. Gheschreven den derden Ianuarij M.D.XCV. Ghetrouwelijck uyt den Latijn in Neder-duytsche tale over-gheset . . . Na de Copye, Ghedruckt tot Duysseldorp, By VVerner vander Horst . . . M.VI^{C}.VIII. 4° sig. A^4

106.d.21(2).

Corresponding to the copies described in the *Bibliotheca Belgica* no.L269 and in *Knuttel* no.1498.

L156 LIPSIUS, Justus

[Epistola qua respondet cuidam principi.] Iusti Lipsij Send-brief/in welcke hy antwoorde gheeft aen een seker groot Heer/op de vraghe/welck van dryen den Coninck van Hispaengien best gheraden ware/Oorloge oft Peys/oft lieuer Bestant met den den [*sic*] Fransman/Engelsche ende Hollander . . . Ghetrouwelick wt den Latijn in Nederduytsche tale ouergeset . . . Na de Copije gedruct tot Disseldorp, By Wernar vander Horst . . . 1608. 4° sig. A^4

T.2420(16).

Corresponding to the copies described in the *Bibliotheca Belgica* no.L270 and in *Knuttel* no.1499.

L157 LIPSIUS, Justus

[Epistola qua respondet cuidam principi.] Justi Lipsij Sendt-brieff/In welcke hy antwoorde gheeft aen een seker groot Heer/op de vrage/welck van dryen den Coningh van Hispaengien best gheraden ware/Oorloghe oft Peys/oft liever Bestant met den Frans-man/Enghelsche ende Hollander. Ghetrouvvelijck uyt den Latijn in Nederduytsche tale overgheset. 4° sig. A^4: illus., port.

573.f.26.

Corresponding to the copies described in the *Bibliotheca Belgica* no.L.271 and in *Tiele* no.308. The order assigned here to the various Dutch editions follows that given them in the *Bibliotheca Belgica*, but this one, which does not claim to be copied from the one purporting to be printed by Werner vander Horst at Düsseldorf, could as easily be the earliest as the latest. *Tiele* describes it under the year 1595, i.e. the date the letter was originally composed, and assigns the edition to Aelbrecht Hendricksz at The Hague. However, Hendricksz ceased publishing in 1605 while this publication cannot be earlier than 1608 and would therefore be more likely to have been printed by Hendricksz's successor, Hillebrant Jacobsz van Wouw. Published in 1608?

L158 LIPSIUS, Justus

IVSTI LIPSI EPISTOLICA INSTITVTIO, Excepta è dictantis eius ore . . . Adiunctum est

Demetrij Phalerei eiusdem argumenti scriptum. EDITIO VLTIMA. ANTVERPIÆ, EX OFFICINA PLANTINIANA, Apud Ioannem Moretum. M.D CI. [etc.] 8° pp.31
T.909(5).
Partly in Latin only, partly in both Latin and Greek.

L159 LIPSIUS, Justus
LEGES REGIAE ET LEGES X.VIRALES, I. LIPSI operâ . . . collectae. Editio vltima. ANTVERPIAE, EX OFFICINA PLANTINIANA, Apud Viduam & Filios Ioannis Moreti. M.DC.XIII. [etc.] 4° pp.8
1480.bb.25(3).
The titlepage bears one of the Plantin devices in woodcut, but including the initial G, not visible in the reproduction in the *Bibliotheca Belgica* no.L355.

L160 LIPSIUS, Justus
IVSTI LIPSI LOVANIVM: siue OPIDI ET ACADEMIÆ EIVS DESCRIPTIO. LIBRI TRES. ANTVERPIÆ, EX OFFICINA PLANTINIANA, Apud Ioannem Moretum. M.DC.V. [etc.] (col.) ANTVERPIÆ, EX OFFICINA PLANTINIANA, APVD IOANNEM MORETVM. M.DC.V. 4° pp.119: plates; illus.
800.k.23(2); C.83.d.10(1).
The engraved plates and illustrations are by Theodoor Galle. The copy at 800.k.23(2) is imperfect; wanting the last leaf, bearing the device.

L161 LIPSIUS, Justus
(tp.1) IVSTI LIPSI MANVDVCTIONIS AD STOICAM PHILOSOPHIAM LIBRI TRES: L. ANNAEO SENECAE, aliísque scriptoribus illustrandis. ANTVERPIÆ, EX OFFICINA PLANTINIANA, Apud Ioannem Moretum. M.DC.IV. [etc.]
(tp.2) IVSTI LIPSI PHYSIOLOGIÆ STOICORVM LIBRI TRES: L. ANNAEO SENECAE, aliísque scriptoribus illustrandis. ANTVERPIÆ, EX OFFICINA PLANTINIANA, Apud Ioannem Moretum. M.DC.IV. [etc.] (col.) ANTVERPIÆ, EX OFFICINA PLANTINIANA, APVD IOANNEM MORETVM. M.DC.IIII. 4° pp.212; 188
527.l.2(1,2).
The two books were published together.

L162 LIPSIUS, Justus
IVSTI LIPSI MONITA ET EXEMPLA POLITICA. LIBRI DVO, Qui VIRTVTES ET VITIA Principum spectant. ANTVERPIÆ, EX OFFICINA PLANTINIANA, Apud Ioannem Moretum. M.DC.V. [etc.] (col.) ANTVERPIÆ, EX OFFICINA PLANTINIANA, APVD IOANNEM MORETVM. M.DC.V. 4° pp.213
522.k.5.

L163 LIPSIUS, Justus
IVSTI LIPSI MONITA ET EXEMPLA POLITICA . . . ANTVERPIÆ, EX OFFICINA PLANTINIANA, Apud Ioannem Moretum. M.DC.VI. [etc.] (col.) ANTVERPIÆ, EX OFFICINA PLANTINIANA, APVD IOANNEM MORETVM. M.DC.VI. 4° pp.213
1560/4440(2).

L164 LIPSIUS, Justus
CLARISS. VIRI IVSTI LIPSI MVSAE ERRANTES. Ex Auctoris schedis partim descripsit, sparsas collegit, ac iunctim . . . edidit FRANCISCVS SWEERTIVS F. . . . ANTVERPIÆ, Apud Ioannem Keerbergium. M.DC.X. 4° pp.103
837.g.45; C.83.d.8(1).
Both copies belong to the issue with poems to Lernutius and Divaeus only on pp.12–14, corresponding to the copy described in the *Bibliotheca Belgica* no.L399, note beginning "Dans l'exemplaire . . . ". The copy at 837.g.45 is the editor's presentation copy to Andreas Schottus.

LIPSIUS, Justus. Physiologiae Stoicorum libri tres. 1604. *See* above: Manuductionis ad Stoicam philosophiam libri tres.

L165 LIPSIUS, Justus
IVSTI LIPSI POLIORCETICΩN SIVE DE MACHINIS. TORMENTIS. TELIS. LIBRI QVINQVE . . . Editio tertia, correcta & aucta. ANTVERPIÆ, EX OFFICINA PLANTINIANA, Apud Ioannem Moretum. M.DC.V. [etc.] (col.) ANTVERPIÆ, EX OFFICINA PLANTINIANA, APVD IOANNEM MORETVM. M.DC.VI. 4° pp.219; illus.
1398.i.27(2); 1601/513(1).
The illustrations are either woodcuts or engravings. For the provenance of the copy at 1601/513(1) *see* above: Admiranda.

L166 LIPSIUS, Justus
IVSTI LIPSI POLITICORVM SIVE CIVILIS DOCTRINÆ LIBRI SEX . . . Additæ NOTÆ auctiores, tum & DE VNA RELIGIONE liber. Omnia postremò Auctor recensuit. Ex officina PLANTINIANA. 1605. 24° pp.654
527.a.6.
Published at Leiden.

L167 LIPSIUS, Justus
IVSTI LIPSI POLITICORVM SIVE CIVILIS DOCTRINÆ LIBRI SEX . . . Ex officina PLANTINIANA, 1615. 32° pp.605
C.20.f.39.
Published at Leiden. From the travelling library of Sir Julius Caesar.

L168 LIPSIUS, Justus
IVSTI LIPSI SATVRNALIVM SERMONVM LIBRI DVO, QVI DE GLADIATORIBVS. Editio vltima, & castigatissima . . . ANTVERPIÆ, EX OFFICINA PLANTINIANA, Apud Ioannem Moretum. M.DC.IV. [etc.] 4° pp.136: plates; illus.
1476.c.26.
Some of the engravings signed by Theodoor Galle.

L169 LIPSIUS, Justus
IVSTI LIPSI SATVRNALIVM SERMONVM LIBRI DVO . . . Editio vltima, & castigatissima . . . ANTVERPIÆ, EX OFFICINA PLANTINIANA, Apud Balthasarem & Ioannem Moretos. M.DC.XVII. [etc.] 4° pp.136: plates; illus.
1601/513(3).
For the provenance of this copy *see* above: Admiranda.

LIPSIUS, Justus. Sen(d)tbrief, in welcke hy antwoorde gheeft aen een seker groot heere. 1608. *See* above: Epistola qua respondet cuidam principi.

L170 LIPSIUS, Justus
[Selections] CL. V. IVSTI LIPSI FLORES, Ex eius operibus decerpti, per locos communes digesti. Accessêre eiusdem TESTIMONIA ET SYMBOLA òperâ FRANC. SVVEERTI. Editio auctior & melior. ANTVERPIAE Apud Gasparem Bellerum M.DC.XVI. 32° pp.387
C.20.f.40.
With 'Cl. v. Iusti LipsI vita in compendium redacta, per Franc. Svveertium ex Elogio . . . Auberti Miraei'. From the travelling library of Sir Julius Caesar.

L171 LIPTITZ, Johann von
[Judicium apocalypticum.] Apocalijptische oordeel/IOANNIS a LIPTITZ . . . over den Boheemschen Oorloch. Item eene tijdinghe uyt Chur-Paltz/ van het teghenwoordighe verloop aldaer. IN 'SGRAVEN-HAGE By Aert Meuris . . . 1621. 4° sig.A^4B^1
T.2251(22); T.2424(4).

L172 LISCA, Alessandro

AD PAVLVM V. PONTIficem Maximum EPISTOLÆ IIII. CLARISSIMORVM ITALIÆ IVRIS CONsultorum parænetícæ quibus iusticia causæ Venetæ, Pontificiæ Censuræ nullitas, ac belli incommoda proponuntur. PHINOPOLI, Anno M.DCVI. 8° sig.AB[8]
175.f.18(2).

Anonymous spoof. The third and fourth letters purporting to be by Cardinals Cesare Baronio and Ascanio Colonna respectively. Printed by Jan Jansz at Arnhem. Another edition, at 8073.aaa.1(6), of pp.21 and sig.A[8]B[4], seems to be of French origin.

LISTE van alle de nieuwe capiteynen ghemaeckt door Albertus. 1621. *See* NETHERLANDS. Southern Provinces. Army

LITTERAE annuae Societatis Iesu. 1618. *See* JESUITS [Letters 1600; 1601; 1602; 1603; 1604; 1605]

LITTERAE Japonicae a R.P. Provinciali transmissae. 1612. *See* RODRIGUES GIRAÕ, Joaõ

LITTERAE Japonicae annorum M.DC.IX. et X. 1615. *See* RODRIGUES GIRAÕ, Joaõ

LITTERAE Societatis Iesu e regno Sinarum annorum 1610 & 1611. 1615. *See* TRIGAULT, Nicolas

LITURGIES

Arrangement:

Latin Rite. Antiphoners
- Breviaries. Orders
- Hours
- Litanies
- Martyrologies
- Missals
- Missals. Extracts
- Missals. Local
- Processionals
- Processionals. Orders
- Rituals. Local
- Various Offices

Church of Scotland. Book of Common Order

Calvinistic Churches. Local

L173 LITURGIES. Latin Rite. Antiphoners

PARS ÆSTIVALIS ANTIPHONARII ROMANI SECVNDVM NOVVM BREVIARIVM RECOGNITI. ANTVERPIÆ APVD IOACH. TROGNÆSIVM M.D C XI. (col.) ANTVERPIÆ, APVD IOACHIMVM TROGNÆSIVM M.DC.XI. fol. pp.984, cclxxxiiij; illus.
1481.e.24.

With: Commune sanctorum. The titlepage is engraved. The illustration is an engraved portrait of Archbishop Matthias Hovius. With additional music in manuscript. The titlepage and portrait are slightly mutilated.

L174 [*LITURGIES. Latin Rite. Antiphoners

Antiphonarium, selectum ex integro Romano Antiphonario, ad cantum in Ecclesijs ruralibus ac alijs similibus pro officijs per totum annum accommodatum. Tornaci Nerviorum ex officina Caroli Martini 1615. fol. pp.288, cclxvi
3366.h.11.]

*Destroyed. Described from the General Catalogue which relied on the privilege as the titlepage was wanting and from *BCNI* no.6344 which records an edition of 1617 from the catalogue of the Haarlem Bisschoppelijk Museum, possibly now at the Rijksmuseum Het Catharijneconvent, Utrecht.

L175 [*LITURGIES. Latin Rite. Breviaries. Benedictines
Diurnale secundum usum reuerendorum patrum ordinis diui Benedicti de obseruantia per Germaniam. Louanii ex officina Gerardi Riuii 1604. 24°
3366.c.6(1).]
*Destroyed. Described from the General Catalogue.

L176 LITURGIES. Latin Rite. Breviaries. Brigittines
BREVIARIVM SORORVM AC SANCTIMONIALIVM SACRI ORDINIS DIVÆ BRIGITTÆ . . . OPVS PIVM . . . A mendis . . . expurgatum. ATREBATI, Excudebat ROBERTVS MAVDHVY . . . M.D.C.X. (col.) ATREBATI, TYPIS ROBERTI MAVDHVY [etc.] 4° pp.384; illus.
Legg 65.
The rubric is in French. The woodcut showing the Crucifixion signed: IL. Cropped.

L177 LITURGIES. Latin Rite. Hours
THE PRIMER, OR OFFICE OF THE BLESSED VIRGIN MARIE, in Latin and English: According to the reformed Latin: AND vvith lyke graces Priuileged. PRINTED At Antwerp by Arnold Conings . . . M.DC.IIII. 12° ff.292; pp.106; illus.
C.136.b.16.
The translator's preface signed: R.V., i.e. Richard Verstegan. With: The hymnes through the whole year. The illustrations consist of pairs of medallions, engravings on the recto, woodcuts on the preceding verso like lids of lockets, some of the woodcuts in red and black. By Philips Galle?

L178 [*Liturgies. Latin Rite. Hours
The Primer, or Office of the Blessed Virgin Marie, in English. According to the last Edition of the Romane Breviarie. Printed at Mackline by Henrie Iaey . . . 1615. 18° pp.495,181
3366.c.1.]
*Destroyed. Translated by Richard Verstegan. With 'The hymnes'. Described from the General Catalogue, *Rogers* no.4 and *Blom* no.I/4. A perfect copy is in the possession of Mr. Rogers, an imperfect one at the London Oratory. A reprint has been published in 1978 by the Scolar Press, Ilkley as vol.390 in the series 'English recusant literature'.

L179 [*LITURGIES. Latin Rite. Litanies
Verscheyden Litanien, geordineert op die seven daghen vande VVeecke. Loven, Françoys Fabri, 1604. 8°
3395.d.8(1).]
*Destroyed. The description is that of the General Catalogue.

L180 LITURGIES. Latin Rite. Martyrologies
MARTYROLOGIVM ROMANVM Ad nouam Kalendarij rationem . . . restitutum, Gregorij XIII. Pont. Max. iussu editum. ANTVERPIÆ, EX OFFICINA PLANTINIANA, Apud Ioannem Moretum. M.DC.VIII. 8° pp.430; illus., music
4824.cc.43.
The titlepage engraving 'Mirabilis Deus in sanctis suis'. Ownership inscriptions: Sum Bleysz 1626; H. Hub à Lutzendael 1627; Liber Monrii sti Trudonis.

L181 LITURGIES. Latin Rite. Martyrologies
MARTYROLOGIVM ROMANVM ad nouam Kalendarij rationem . . . restitutum, GREGORII XIII. PONT. MAX. IVSSV EDITVM, CÆSARIS BARONII . . . NOTATIONIBVS illustratum. Nouissimæ & correctissimæ huic editioni seorsim accedit VETVS ROMANVM MARTYROLOGIVM . . . vnà cum MARTYROLOGIO ADONIS, ad MSS. exemplaria recensito, opera & studio HERIBERTI ROSWEYDI . . . ANTVERPIAE, EX

OFFICINA PLANTINIANA, Apud Viduam & Filios Ioannis Moreti. M.DC.XIII. fol. pp.XXXVI,550,228; illus., music
4824.l.5.
The frontispiece is engraved.

L182 LITURGIES. Latin Rite. Missals
MISSALE ROMANVM . . . ANTVERPIÆ, EX OFFICINA PLANTINIANA, Apud Ioannem Moretum. M.DC.V. 8° pp.672,cxxvj; illus., music
1484.cc.4.
The illustrations are engraved scenes from the life of Christ.

L183 LITURGIES. Latin Rite. Missals
MISSALE ROMANVM . . . In quo Missæ propriæ de SANCTIS omnes ad longum recèns positæ sunt . . . ANTVERPIÆ, EX OFFICINA PLANTINIANA, Apud Balthasarem & Ioannem Moretos. M.DC.XVIII. fol. pp.608, ciiij; illus., music
L.1.g.7(1).
The illustrations are full page and smaller engravings and borders. Grangerised with numerous later plates from various sources.

L184 LITURGIES. Latin Rite. Missals. Extracts
LES CAVTELES CANON ET CEREMONIES DE LA MESSE. Ensemble la Messe intitulee, DV CORPS DE IESVS CHRIST. Le tout en Latin & en François: le Latin extraict du MESSEL à l'vsage de Rome, imprimé a Lyon par Iean de Cambray, l'an mil cinq cens vingt . . . Auec certaines annotations . . . A LEYDEN, Iouxte la copie imprimee à Lyon par Claude Rauot. 1605. 16° pp.355
1412.a.4.
The commentary, and perhaps the translation, by Pierre Viret. The imprint may be false.

L185 LITURGIES. Latin Rite. Missals. England
MISSAE ALIQVOT PRO SACERDOTIBVS itinerantibus in Anglia. EX Missali Romano Reformato . . . M.DC.XV. 4° pp.152
C.26.h.23.
Without imprint; published at St. Omer? Ownership inscription: J.B.

L186 [*LITURGIES. Latin Rite. Missals. Poland
Missæ propriæ Patronorum et Festorum Regni Poloniæ . . . Antuerpiæ Ex officina Plantiniana, apud Viduam & Filios Ioannis Moreti. 1611. fol. pp.33
3366.dd.4(3).]
*Destroyed. The description is that of the General Catalogue. *BCNI* no.15414 describes an edition of 1695, a copy of which is preserved at the Plantin Moretus Museum at Antwerp.

L187 LITURGIES. Latin Rite. Processionals
PROCESSIONALE, RITIBVS ROMANAE ECCLESIAE ACCOMMODATVM: Antiphonas & Responsoria . . . complectens: iussu . . . D. MATTHIAE HOVI . . . concinnatum ac editum. ANTVERPIÆ, EX OFFICINA PLANTINIANA, Apud Ioannem Moretum. M.DCII. 4° pp.422; illus., music
C.110.d.11.
The titlepage engraving shows a procession.

L188 LITURGIES. Latin Rite. Processionals. Franciscans
PROCESSIONALE AD NORMAM MISSALIS AC RITVALIS NVPER A SEDE APOSTOLICA REFORMATORVM CONCINNATVM In vsum Fratrum Minorum Regularis Obseruantiæ De Mandato R.P. HENRICI SEDVLII eiusdem Ordinis Prouinciæ Germaniæ Inferioris Ministri editum. ANTVERPIÆ, APVD GERARDVM WOLSSCHATIVM. M.DC.XIX. obl.8° pp.125; music
C.110.a.21.
With additional music in manuscript. Ownership inscription: Voor de Annuntiaten tot Thienen.

L189 LITURGIES. Latin Rite. Rituals. St. Omer

PASTORALE ECCLESIAE AVDOMARENSIS Desumptum ex Sacerdotali Romano. Adiectis variis instructionibus . . . Editum à . . . D. IACOBO BLASAEO Episcopo Audomarensi in Synodo diæcesana, an. 1606 . . . AVDOMAROPOLI, Excudebat FRANCISCVS BELLET . . . M.DC.VI. [etc.] 4° pp.128,82,77; illus., music
Legg 270.

The illustration is an engraving of the Bishop's arms. Ownership inscriptions: Fran. Desmarquais pastoris in Kraiwic [?]; Pieter Desmarquais coster van Gorinchem 1636.

L190 LITURGIES. Latin Rite. Rituals. Salisbury

SACRA INSTITVTIO BAPTIZANDI : MATRIMONIVM CELEBRANDI : INFIRMOS VNGENDI : MORTVOS SEPELIENDI : AC ALII NONNVLLI RITVS ECCLESIASTICI : iuxta vsum . . . Ecclesiæ Sarisburgiensis . . . DVACI, Excudebat LAVRENTIVS KELLAM . . . M.DC.IIII [etc.] 4° pp.168, [18?=16?]
C.26.i.1; C.26.h.24.

The copy at C.26.i.1 has the 'Annotationes', but the last three leaves of this part are mutilated with loss of pagination which is faulty to begin with; the copy at C.26.h.24 is imperfect; wanting the 'Annotationes'.

L191 LITURGIES. Latin Rite. Rituals. Salisbury

MANVALE SACERDOTVM HOC EST. RITVS ADMINISTRANDI SACRAMENTA BAPTISMI, MATRIMONII, ET EXTREMÆ VNCTIONIS. ITEM PVRIFICANDI MVLIEREM POST PARTVM: VISITANDI INFIRMOS: SEPELIENDI MORTVOS . . . IVXTA VSVM INSIGNIS ECCLESIÆ SARISBVRIENSIS . . . DVACI, Excudebat LAVRENTIVS KELLAM . . . 1610. 8° pp.298
C.35.c.25.

L192 LITURGIES. Latin Rite. Various Offices

EXERCITIVM HEBDOMADARIVM, COLLECTORE IOANNE WILSONO . . . ANTVERPIAE, EX OFFICINA PLANTINIANA, Apud Balthasarem Moretum, & Viduam Ioannis Moreti, & Io. Meursium. M.DC.XXI. (col.) ANTVERPIAE, EX OFFICINA PLANTINIANA BALTHASARIS MORETI. M.DC.XXI. 12° pp.127; illus.
C.183.g.31(1).

With engravings. In an Italian morocco armorial binding, the arms unidentified. With the exlibris of Augustus Frederick, Duke of Sussex.

L193 LITURGIES. Latin Rite. Various Offices

OFFICIVM PASSIONIS IESV CHRISTI, ex oraculis Prophetarum desumptum. ANTVERPIÆ EX OFFICINA PLANTINIANA M.DC.XXI. (col.) ANTVERPIAE, EX OFFICINA BALTHASARIS MORETI. M.DC.XXI. 12° pp.57; illus.
C.183.g.31(2).

Illustrations, binding and provenance as for preceding.

L194 LITURGIES. Church of Scotland. Book of Common Order

(tp.1) THE CL. PSALMES OF DAVID IN METER, WITH THE PROSE. For the vse of the Kirk of SCOTLAND . . . MIDDELBVRGH, Imprinted by Richard Schilders . . . 1602.
(tp.2) THE PSALMES OF DAVID IN METRE, WITH DIVERS NOTES, and Tunes augmented to them. Also with the prose on the margen . . . MIDDELBVRGH, Imprinted by Richard Schilders . . . 1602.
(tp.3) THE CATECHISME OR MANER TO TEACH CHILDREN THE CHRISTIAN RELIGION . . . made by . . . IOHN CALVIN . . . MIDDELBVRGH, Imprinted by Richard Schilders . . . 1602. 8° 3 pt.: pp.225; 466; 128; music
C.25.c.11.

L195 LITURGIES. Calvinistic Churches. England
A Booke OF THE FORME of common prayers, administration of the Sacraments, &c. agreeable to . . . the vse of the reformed Churches. To this fourth editiō is added the maner of ordination and admission of a Pastor to his charge . . . MIDDELBVRGH, Imprinted by Richard Schilders . . . 1602. [etc.] 8° sig. A-E^8F^7
C.25.d.23.

L196 LIVIUS, Gerardus
Christelijcke AEN-SPRAECK Der Predicanten van NIMMEGEN, Aen eenighe Lidtmaten der Ghemeynte/die sich t'onrecht bedroeft ende beswaert noemen; Tot VVeeringe vande Blaem, daer mede de voornoemde Predicanten . . . beschuldicht worden . . . Ghedruckt . . . 1618. 4° pp. 44
T.2248(13).
Signed: Gerardus Livius, Henricus Leflerus, Joannes Coitsius. Ownership inscription: Libellus Henrici Brimani.

L197 LIVIUS, Gerardus
Sendt-brief Gerardus Livius Predicant tot Nymeghen/gheschreven aen Henricum Brimanij Predicant tot Arnhem/Aengaende 'tghene daer ghepasseert is. Daer achter aen ghevoeght is een Tuyltgen van sommighe Bloemen uyt den Sendt-brief gheplucht. Met een Liedeken. Ghedruckt na de Copie van den Brief uyt Nymeghen gheschreven. Anno 1618. 4° sig. AB^4
700.h.25(22).
The editor's preface signed: Aerd Adams, who is also the author of the commentary and additional matter.

L198 LIVIUS, Titus
DE ROMEYNSCHE Historien ende Gheschiedenissen door TITVM LIVIVM . . . Met schoone Figuren verciert: ende met nieuwe byvoegingen vermeerdert . . . TOT AMSTELREDAM, By Hendrick Laurentsz. . . . 1614. fol. ff. 368: plate; illus., maps
9039.i.18.
With the epitome of the lost books by Lucius Florus and a description of Rome by Paulus Merula. The maps are engraved, the other illustrations are woodcuts.

LIVRE . . . des chansons vulgaires. 1601; 1609; 1613; 1615. *See* PHALÈSE, Pierre

L199 LOARTE, Gaspare
[Esercitio de la vita christiana.] THE EXERCISE OF A CHRISTIAN LIFE. Written in Italian by . . . Gaspar Loartes . . . And translated into English by S.B. Newly perused, & set forth in a more perfect method . . . With certaine . . . Exercises & Praiers added therunto . . . M.DC.X. 8° pp. 440
C.26.gg.2.
Translated by Stephen Brinkley. Without imprint; published by the English College press at St. Omer. Ownership inscription: Joseph Avarn[?]

LOCMANNUS. *See* LUḲMĀN

L200 LOCRE, Ferry de
FERREOLI LOCRII . . . CHRONICON BELGICVM. Ab Anno CCLVIII. ad Annum vsque M.DC. . . . perductum. TOMI TRES. ATREBATI, Ex Officinâ GVILIELMI RIVERII . . . M.D.C.XVI. [etc.] (col.) ATREBATI, EX OFFICINA TYPOGRAPHICA GVILIELMI RIVERII, M.D.C.XVI. 4° pp. 696
C.77.c.2; 153.e.19.

L201 LOCRE, Ferry de

DISCOVRS DE LA NOBLESSE AV QVEL PAR VNE CONFERENCE DES FAMILLES DE CASTILLE, FRANCE ET AVSTRICE, AVEC L'EGLISE CATHOLIQVE, EST DESCOVVERTE L'INFAMIE DE L'HERETIQVE. PAR M. FERRY DE LOCRE . . . A ARRAS, De l'Imprimerie de GVILLAVME DE LA RIVIERE . . . M.DC.V. (col.) A ARRAS, DE L'IMPRIMERIE DE GVILLAVME DE LA RIVIERE . . . M.D.C.V. 8° pp.104; illus.

596.a.10(3).

The engraving on the verso of the titlepage shows the arms of the dedicatee. From the library of John Morris.

L202 LOCRE, Ferry de

(tp.1) MARIA AVGVSTA VIRGO DEIPARA IN SEPTEM LIBROS TRIBVTA: Chronico & Notis . . . illustrata. AVCTORE FERREOLO LOCRIO . . . ATREBATI, EX OFFICINA R. MAVDHVY . . . M.DC.IIX. [etc.]
(tp.2=p.81) MARIÆ AVGVSTÆ VIRGINIS DEIPARÆ REGNA, PROVINCIÆ, OPIDA. LIBER SECVNDVS. AVCTORE FERREOLO LOCRIO . . . ATREBATI, EX OFFICINA R. MAVDHVY . . . M.DC.IIX. [etc.]
(tp.3=p.177) MARIÆ . . . ORDINES, MONASTERIA, XENODOCHIA. LIBER TERTIVS. AVCTORE FERREOLO LOCRIO . . . ATREBATI, EX OFFICINA R. MAVDHVY . . . M.DC.IIX. [etc.]
(tp.4=p.329) MARIÆ TEMPLA. LIBER QVARTVS. AVCTORE FERREOLO LOCRIO . . . ATREBATI, EX OFFICINA R. MAVDHVY . . . M.DC.IIX. [etc.]
(tp.5=p.477) MARIÆ . . . ICONES ET RELIQVIÆ. LIBER QVINTVS. AVCTORE FERREOLO LOCRIO . . . ATREBATI, EX OFFICINA R. MAVDHVY . . . M.DC.IIX. [etc.]
(tp.6=p.573) MARIÆ . . . FESTA ET SODALITATES. LIBER SEXTVS. AVCTORE FERREOLO LOCRIO . . . ATREBATI, EX OFFICINA R. MAVDHVY . . . M.DC.IIX. [etc.]
(tp.7=p.685) MARIÆ . . . OFFICIVM SVIS AVCTORIBVS ILLVSTRATVM. AVCTORE FERREOLO LOCRIO . . . ATREBATI, EX OFFICINA R. MAVDHVY . . . M.DC.IIX. [etc.]
4° pp.722,70; illus.

4807.eee.4.

The titlepage engraving of the Virgin signed: L. Gaultier sculp. 1608. The other titlepages each bear a woodcut pietà. With a stamp: Soc. Reg. Lond. ex dono Henr. Howard Norfolciensis.

L203 LODEWIJCKSZ, Willem

[Historie van Indien.] PREMIER LIVRE DE L'HISTOIRE DE LA NAVIGATION AVX INDES ORIENTALES, PAR LES HOLLANDOIS; ET DES CHOSES A EVX ADVENVES . . . Par G.M.A.W.L. Imprimé á Amsterdam, chez Cornille Nicolas . . . 1609. fol. ff.53: plate; illus., maps

C.73.g.2(1); G.6620(1).

Anonymous. Describing the voyage of Cornelis de Houtman in 1595–97. Wanting the plate showing the market at Bantam which is said to be missing from most copies.

Het LOF van de stadt Haerlem. 1621. *See* AMPSING, Samuel

Den LOF van Haerlem. 1616. *See* AMPSING, Samuel

LOF-GHEDICHT ter eeren . . . Vorst Maurits. 1620. *See* VOCHT, N.

t'LOFF vande mutse. 1612. *See* VISSCHER, Roemer

L204 LOON

HET LOON van den Brouwer/voor zijn werck t'onrecht ghenaemt/Eenvuldighe waerschouwinge, aen de ghevluchte Vreemdelingen: Daer in hy zijn eygen Lants-luyden . . . voor oproerigen is scheldende [etc.] 4° pp.12

700.h.25(12,12*).

Signed: I.D.V.D.N.L. With 'T' werck van M. de Brouwer, ghenaemt Eenvuldighe waerschouwinghe . . . 1618', consisting of sig. A^2, printed in the same type and intended to accompany the refutation. Published in 1618.

L205 LOUVAIN
[2.5.1621] Nieuwe Ordinancie opde Wachte der Stadt van Louene . . . TOT LOVEN, By Geerardt Rivius . . . M.D.C.XXI. 4° sig. AB^4
106.d.56.
Dated: 2 May 1621.

LOOSLEVER, Everhardus Hermanni F. Schuyl. *See* SCHUYL LOOSLEVER, Everhardus Hermanni F.

L206 [*LOYAERTS, Samuel
ENODATIONES EVANGELIORVM DOMINICIS ET FESTIS diebus / occurrentium, A Dominica SS. TRINITATIS vsque ad decimam post Pentecosten . . . AVCTORE SAMVELE LOYAERTS . . . LOVANII, Ex Officina GERARDI RIVII . . . 1612. [etc.] 8°
3356.aa.19.]
*Destroyed. Described from the General Catalogue and information received from Limburg University Library, copy at W 137 B 39. One of the volumes in the author's 'Sacrae conciones ad populum'.

L207 LOYS, Jean
LES OEVVRES POETIQVES DE IEAN LOYS . . . Diuisées en IIII. Liures . . . A DOVAY, De l'Imprimerie de PIERRE AVROY . . . M.DC.XII. [etc.] 8° pp.243
11475.a.28.
The half-title reads 'Les œures poetiques de Iean et Iacques Loys Pere, et Fils', but the book contains poems by Jean only. The editor's dedication signed: Nicolas Philippe Loys.

LUBBAEUS, Richard. Emblemata moralia. 1609. *See* FURMERIUS, Bernardus. De rerum usu et abusu.

LUBBERTUS, Sibrandus. Antwoort . . . op de Gods-diensticheyt van Hugo de Groot. 1614. *See* below: Responsio ad Pietatem Hugonis Grotii.

L208 LUBBERTUS, Sibrandus
SIBRANDI LVBBERTI COMMENTARII, AD Nonaginta novem Errores CONRADI VORSTII. FRANEKERÆ FRISIORVM, Ex officina Vlrici Dominici Balck. M.D.C.XIII. 8° pp.46,841
1020.i.13.

L209 LUBBERTUS, Sibrandus
[Commentarii ad nonaginta novem errores Conradi Vorstii.] Brief D. SIBRANDI LVBBERTI . . . gheschreven aenden . . . Aertsbisschop van Cantelberch . . . ghestelt voor seecker syn Boeck tegen D. Conradum Vorstium. Met seeckere Extracten uyt andere Sibrandi Boecken ghetogen . . . ende aenwijsinge vande plaetsen/daer op . . . Hugo de Groot . . . in sijn Boeck ghenaemt Der Heeren Staten &c. Godts-diensticheyt gheantwoort heeft. VVt het Latyn int Duytsch . . . overgheset. TOT DELF. By Bruyn Harmanssz Schinckel . . . 1613. 4° pp.26
T.2243(2).
Translated and edited by Jan Wtenbogaert.

L210 LUBBERTUS, Sibrandus
SIBRANDI LUBBERTI DE IESU CHRISTO SERVATORE, hoc est, Cur, & qua ratione JESUS CHRISTUS noster Servator sit, Libri quatuor. Contra FAUSTUM SOCINUM. In Academia Franekerana Excudebat Ægidius Radæus . . . M.DC.XI. 4° pp.632
1492.a.61.

L211 LUBBERTUS, Sibrandus

SIBRANDI LUBBERTI DE PAPA ROMANO REPLICATIO AD Defensionem tertiæ controversiæ ROBERTI BELLARMINI Scriptam à IACOBO GRETZERO. FRANEKERÆ Apud AEGIDIVM RADAEVM . . . M.D.CIX. 8° pp.274
860.c.1.

L212 LUBBERTUS, Sibrandus

DECLARATIO RESPONSIONIS D. Conradi Vorstij. Scripta à SIBRANDO LUBBERTO ad . . . ORDINES GENERALES fœderatarum provinciarum Belgicæ. FRANEKERÆ, Excudebat AEGIDIVS RADAEVS . . . M.D.C.XI. 8° pp.151
1054.a.9(3).

L213 LUBBERTUS, Sibrandus

DISPVTATIONVM THEOLOGICARVM DVODECIMA, DE ECCLESIA, QVAM . . . SUB PRÆSIDIO . . . D. SIBRANDI LVBBERTI . . . Publicè excutiendam proponit BERNHARDUS FORCKENBECK . . . FRANEKERÆ Apud AEGIDIVM RADAEVM . . . 1609. 4° sig.A^4
491.b.37.

L214 LUBBERTUS, Sibrandus

EPIS^T^OLICA [*sic*] DISCEPTATIO DE FIDE IVSTIFICANTE. DEque nostra coram Deo justificatione, HABITA Inter . . . D. SIBRANDVM LVBBERTI . . . ET PETRVM BERTIVM . . . DELPHIS Batauorum. Apud Ioannem Andreæ . . . 1612. 4° pp.164
4376.dd.6(3).
The missing letter 'T' in 'EPISOLICA' has been added by means of a stamp.

L215 LUBBERTUS, Sibrandus

[Responsio ad Pietatem Hugonis Grotii.] Antwoort Van SIBRANDVS LVBBERTVS. Op de Gods-diensticheyt Van HVGO DE GROOT. Overgheset uyt het Latijns Exemplaer. Ghedruckt tot Franicker. By Rombertus Doyema. 1614. 4° pp.158
T.2244(7).

L216 LUCANUS, Marcus Annaeus

[Pharsalia. Latin] M. ANNÆI LVCANI, DE BELLO CIVILI . . . LIBRI X. Eiusdem Ad Calpurnium Pisonem Poëmation. EX OFFICINA PLANTINIANA RAPHELENGII. M.D.CV. 16° pp.199
1069.a.7.
Published at Leiden.

L217 LUCANUS, Marcus Annaeus

[Pharsalia. Latin] M. ANNÆI LVCANI DE BELLO CIVILI . . . LIBRI X. Eiusdem Ad Calpurnium Pisonem Poëmation. EX OFFICINA PLANTINIANA RAPHELENGII. M.D.CXII. 16° pp.199
1069.a.8(2); C.20.f.46.
Published at Leiden. The copy at C.20.f.46 from the travelling library of Sir Julius Caesar.

L218 LUCANUS, Marcus Annaeus

[Pharsalia. Latin] M. ANNÆI LVCANI PHARSALIA . . . Ex emendatione V.C. HVGONIS GROTII, cum eiusdem . . . NOTIS. Accesserunt VARIARVM LECTIONVM Libellus; & . . . INDEX . . . operâ THEODORI PVLMANNI & aliorum concinnati. EX OFFICINA PLANTINIANA RAPHELENGII. M.D.C.XIV. 8° pp.432
684.b.9; 684.b.10; 684.b.11; 1068.i.4.
Published at Leiden. The variant readings compiled by Pulmannus and Gregorius Bersmannus. All copies with manuscript notes, those at 684.b.9–11 with notes by Richard Bentley.

L219 LUCANUS, Marcus Annaeus

[Pharsalia. Latin] M. ANNÆI LVCANI PHARSALIA . . . Ex emendatione V.C. HVG: GROTII. Amsterodami, Apud Guiljelm. Janssonium . . . 1619. 32° pp.201
1471.a.12(2).

With 'M. Annæi Lucani ad Calpurnium Pisonem Poemation' and 'Petronii Arbitri specimen Belli Civilis' and other matter. The titlepage is engraved.

L220 LUCANUS, Marcus Annaeus

[Pharsalia. Dutch] DE EERSTE SES BOVCKEN vanden voortreffelycken . . . Poeet MARCVS ANNEVS LVCANVS, van't BORGER OORLOG DER ROMEYNEN . . . Overgheset in Nederlandsche rym door D. Henrick Storm. T'AMSTERDAM, By Michiel Colÿn [etc.] 4° ff.120
11556.i.15.

The titlepage is engraved. The dedication dated: 11 July 1617.

L221 LVCAS, Franciscus; Brugensis

Romanæ Correctionis in LATINIS BIBLIIS EDITIONIS VVLGATÆ . . . Loca insigniora; Obseruata à FRANCISCO LVCA Brugensi . . . ANTVERPIAE, EX OFFICINA PLANTINIANA, Apud Ioannem Moretum. M.DC.III. (col.) ANTVERPIÆ, EX OFFICINA PLANTINIANA APVD IOANNEM MORETVM. M.DC.III. 12° pp.367
1017.e.17.

L222 LUCAS, Franciscus; Brugensis

ROMANÆ CORRECTIONIS, IN LATINIS BIBLIIS . . . LOCA INSIGNIORIA: Obseruata à FRANCISCO LVCA Brugensi . . . ANTVERPIAE, EX OFFICINA PLANTINIANA, Apud Ioannem Moretum. M.DC.VIII. 4° pp.67
3104.d.3.

L223 LUCAS, Franciscus; Brugensis

Romanæ Correctionis IN LATINIS BIBLIIS . . . Loca insigniora; Obseruata à FRANCISCO LVCA Brugensi . . . ANTVERPIAE, EX OFFICINA PLANTINIANA, Apud Ioannem Moretum. M.DC.VIII. (col.) ANTVERPIAE, EX OFFICINA PLANTINIANA, Apud Ioannem Moretum. M.DC.VIII. 8° pp.125
1012.d.11.

L224 LUCAS, Franciscus; Brugensis

ROMANÆ CORRECTIONIS, IN LATINIS BIBLIIS . . . LOCA INSIGNIORIA: Obseruata & denuò aucta à FRANCISCO LVCA Brugensi . . . Accessit Libellus alter, continens alias lectionum varietates, in eisdem Bibliis Latinis, ex vetustis manuscriptis exemplaribus collectas . . . eodem obseruatore & collectore. ANTVERPIÆ, EX OFFICINA PLANTINIANA, Apud Balthasarem & Ioannem Moretos. M.DC.XVIII. (col.) ANTVERPIÆ, EX OFFICINA PLANTINIANA, APVD BALTHASAREM ET IOANNEM MORETOS FRATRES. M.DC.XVIII. 4° pp.85
3015.b.9.

L225 LUCIANE SECUNDE

VAN DEN OS, OP DEN ESEL. fol. a single sheet; illus.
T.2422(35).

In verse. Signed: LVCIANE SECVNDE. The mention of Oldenbarnevelt's imprisonment would date this 1618 or 1619. The woodcut shows a group of soldiers. Another edition, described in *Knuttel* no.2685, contains the statement: Actum t'Amsterdam Sept: 8. Anno 1618.

L226 LUCRETIUS CARUS, Titus

[De rerum natura. Latin] T. LVCRETII CARI DE RERVM NATVRA. LIBRI SEX. EX OFFICINA PLANTINIANA RAPHELENGII. M.D.CXI. 16° pp.176
1069.a.8(1).

With 'Carmen Varronis Atacini' and a glossary. Published at Leiden.

L227 LUCRETIUS CARUS, Titus

[De rerum natura. Latin] TITVS LVCRETIVS CARVS De rerum natura. Amsterodami Apud Guilj: Janssonium . . . M DC XX. 32° pp. 168

1471.a.12(1).

The titlepage is engraved. Ownership inscription: St. John's College Oxford ex legato N. Crynes 1745.

L228 LUCULENTA

[Luculenta demonstratio, Ferdinandum suo ipsius merito Regno Bohemiae excidisse.] A cleare Demonstration that FERDINAND is by his owne demerits fallen from the Kingdome of BOHEMIA, and the incorporate Prouinces. Written by a Noble-man of POLONIA. And translated out of the second Edition enlarged. at. Dort. Printed by. George Waters. 4° pp. 25

1054.h.26; C.55.d.15(1).

Published in 1619.

L229 LUCULENTA

[Luculenta demonstratio, Ferdinandum suo ipsius merito Regno Bohemiae excidisse.] A PLAINE DEMONSTRATION OF THE VNLAWFVL SVCCESSION OF THE NOW EMPEROVR Ferdinand the Second . . . Translated out of the Latine printed Copie. Printed at the Hage. M.D.C.XX. 4° sig. ¶[4]

8073.ccc.1.

The imprint is false; in fact, printed by William Stansby for Nathaniel Butter at London.

L230 LUCULENTA

[Luculenta demonstratio, Ferdinandum suo ipsius merito Regno Bohemiae excidisse.] Klaer vertoogh Van de Onwettige Successie des KEYSERS FERDINANDI II. Van weghen het Bloedt-schandigh Houwelijck van zijn Ouders. VVtgegeven tot vvaerschouvvinghe van Duytschlandt, ende Hungarijen. Ende . . . Uyt den Latynschen over-geset/ende vermeerdert. Ghedruckt . . . 1620. 4° sig. A[4]

T.2423(41).

L231 LUIS de Granada; Dominican [Luís Sarría]

[Libro de oracion y meditacion.] OF PRAYER, AND MEDITATION WHEREIN ARE CONTEINED FOVVERTIEN DEVOVTE Meditations for the seuen daies of the Weeke . . . Written firste in the Spanishe tongue by . . . F. LEWIS de GRANADA . . . AT DOVAY. By John Heigham . . . 1612. 8° ff. 345; illus.

1507/167.

Translated by Richard Hopkins. The titlepage and the illustrations are engraved. Printed for Heigham by Pierre Auroi at Douai.

L232 LUIS de Granada; Dominican [Luís Sarría]

[Selections. Paradisus precum.] HET CLEYN LVST-HOFKEN Der Ghebeden. Vergadert wt de boecken vanden Eerw. Pater B. Lodouicus van Granaden . . . ende wt andere Auteurs. VVt den grooteren Lust-hof der selue gecompendieert door P. Guiliam Somers . . . T'SHERTOGEN-BOSSCHE. By Antonius Scheffer . . . 1621. [etc.] 12° pp. 487; illus.

C.66.a.27.

In a gold-tooled binding with a Crucifixion medallion. The illustrations are small woodcuts. Ownership inscription: C.P. Serrure.

L233 LUJAN DE SAYAVEDRA, Mateo; pseudonym, of Juan Marti?

SEGVNDA PARTE DE LA VIDA DEL PICARO GVZMAN DE ALFARACHE. COMPVESTO POR

MATHEO Luxan de Sayauedra . . . EN BRVCELLAS, Por Roger Velpius . . . 1604. [etc.] 8° pp.382
12489.a.47; 12490.c.9; 12490.c.10.
The copy at 12489.a.47 has an inscription saying it was bequeathed to the 'Fuliensi Monasterio SS. Angelorum Custodum' by Franciscus Clausse de Marchaumont, Paris, 18 December 1641.

L234 LUḲMĀN, called Al-Ḥakīm
[Arabic] LOCMANI SAPIENTIS FABVLÆ ET SELECTA QVÆDAM ARABVM ADAGIA. Cum interpretatione Latina & Notis THOMAE ERPENII. LEIDAE, In Typographia ERPENIANA Linguarum Orientalium. 1615. (col.) LEIDAE, In Typographia Linguarum Orientalium ERPENIANA. 1615. 8° pp.78
637.cc.44(1); 1568/3062(1); Or.14579.b.7.

L235 LUMMENAEUS A MARCA, Jacobus Cornelius
[Works] IACOBI CORNELII A MARCA OPERA OMNIA, QVA POETICA, QVA ORATORIA, QVA HISTORICA. LOVANII Typis Phil. Dormalij. M.DC.XIII. [etc.] 8° pp.382,163
11409.ccc.9.
The titlepage is engraved. Ownership inscription: Stephanus Baluzius Tutelensis.

L236 LUMMENAEUS A MARCA, Jacobus Cornelius
AMNON TRAGOEDIA SACRA. Autore . . . D. IACOBO CORNELIO LVMMENÆO à MARCA. GANDAVI Apud Cornelium Marium . . . M.DC.XVII. 8° pp.40
11707.aa.22.

L237 LUTHER, Martin
[De servo arbitrio. Dutch] Servum Arbitrium, Dat is, Een uytnemend Tractaet van de Knechtelijcke wille. Verclarende/dat de Vrije-wille niet en is: Gheschreven teghen Erasmus van Rotterdam. DOOR Martinus Luther. Ende uyt het Latijn . . . vertaelt. Tot Deventer/by Jan Christianus . . . 1610. 4° ff.137; illus., port.
C.127.bb.8.
The editor's preface signed: Iacobus Kim̃edoncius. With a woodcut portrait of Luther on the titlepage. The imprint may be false.

L238 LYCKLAMA A NYEHOLT, Marcus
MARCI A LYCLAMA IN NYEHOLT . . . BENEDICTORVM LIBRI IV. Aduersus Male-dicta & Errores, cum Pragmaticorum, tum aliorum variorum, circa actiones, ex delicto merè pœnales, mixtas, merè rei persecutorias, perpetuas, annales, ad, & aduersus heredes quatenus transitorias, vel non transitorias, aliaque varia, opus varium & novum. LVGDVNI BATAVORVM, Ex officinâ ELZEVIRIANA . . . 1617. 8° pp.720
1509/4381.
Printed by Henrick van Haestens at Leiden.

L239 LYCKLAMA A NYEHOLT, Marcus
ORATIO FVNEBRIS QVAM MEMORIÆ D. RAPHAELIS CLINGBYL . . . dixit MAR. LYCKLAMA à Nyeholt IC. FRANEKERÆ, EXCVDEBAT AEGIDIUS RADAEUS . . . 1608. 4° sig.AB^4C^2
1185.k.2(3).

L240 LYDIUS, Balthasar
(tp.1 preceding preface) WALDENSIA id est, CONSERVATIO VERAE ECCLESIAE, Demonstrata Ex confessionibus, cùm TABORITARVM . . . tum BOHEMORVM . . . Studio & operâ BALTHASARIS LYDII . . . ROTERODAMI Apud Ioannem Leonardi Berewout . . . 1616.
(tp.2=sig.A1r) CONFESSIO FIDEI AC RELIGIONIS, BARONVM AC NOBILIVM REGNI BOHEMIÆ . . . Ferdinando . . . Regi . . . Sub anno Domini 1535 oblata. DORDRACI, Sumptibus Ioannis Leonardi Berevvout . . . M D CXVII.

(tp.3) WALDENSIVM Tomus II, CVM Schediasmatibus BALTHASARIS LYDII . . . In quibus . . . inanis strepitus IESVITARVM . . . refutatur . . . DORDRACI, Apud Iohannem Leonardum Berewout . . . 1617. 8° 2 tom.: pp.261,367; 415,358
692.a.14,15.

Tp.2, in spite of its different imprint and date, follows the preface of tom.1 preceded by tp.1. Each tom. is in two parts. The largest part of tom.1 pt.2 is 'Apologia veræ doctrinæ, eorum qui . . . appellantur Waldenses . . . Ex Bohemico exemplari translata . . . per Burigenam Doctorem de Kornis'. tom.2 pt.1 consists of 'Iohannis Lukawitz . . . Confessio Taboritarum' and 'Æneæ Silvii Historia Bohemica', with the annotations by Lydius in pt.2.

L241 LYDIUS, Joannes
DRY TRACTAETGENS Vande Ordre int beroepen ende beleydinge der jaerlijcsche Synoden. Het I, D. IACOBI ARMINII . . . II. Sommiger . . . Dienaren van Duytslant. III. D. Andreæ Hyperii . . . Alles by een gebracht ende uyt de Latijnsche tale overgheset/Door, IOANNEM LYDIVM . . . t'Amsterdam/voor Jan Evertsz. Cloppenburch . . . 1610. 4° pp.75
T.2240(15) & T.2242(9).

The division into two sequences of signatures, each running A-I^4K^2, may have been the reason for the separation of the parts.

L242 LYDIUS, Joannes
Historisch Verhael/Vande Voorneemste Swaricheden/verschillen en Procedeuren/so wel in Kerckelijcke als Politijcke saken/dry Jaren herwaerts voorghevallen binnen de Stadt OVDEVVATER. Wtghegheven By de Kerckeraet aldaer/ende eenighe vande Magistraten. T'Amsterdam, By Jan Evertsz. Cloppenburgh . . . 1618. 4° sig.A^2B-L^4; illus.
T.2248(11).

Anonymous. The titlepage illustration shows the banished congregation building a hut.

L243 LYDIUS, Joannes
VELITATIO EPISTOLICA, IOANNIS LYDII . . . cum ANDREA PEVERNAGIO qui se dicit Societatis Iesu Sacerdotem Gandavi. LVGDVNI BATAVORVM, Apud Andræam [*sic*] Cloucquium. M.D.CX. 8° pp.109
1016.d.21.

LYSCA, Alexander. *See* LISCA, Alessandro

M

MAC AINGIL, Hugh. *See* MAC CAGHWELL, Hugh

M1 MAC CAGHWELL; Hugh; Archbishop
[Irish] . . . [a Louvain Emanuel Telaph] . . . 1618 12° pp.581
853.b.4; G.19711; 872.c.7.

The approbation reads: 'Vidimus . . . tractatū de pænitentia & indulgentiis quē nuper edidit . . . Hugo Cavellus [etc.]' Printed at Louvain. In the copy at G.19711 leaf (*2) is mutilated; the copy at 872.c.7 is imperfect; wanting the titlepage and all before p.72 and all after p.132.

MADRIGALI pastorali. 1604. *See* PHALÈSE, Pierre

M2 MAETROESJES
Maetroesjes OPWECKER. Op, op, Maetroosjen, op . . . Gedruct . . . 1618. 4° sig.aB^4
T.2248(57).

The titlepage ornament is geometrical, measuring 23×21mm. The initial I on page a2r measures 31×29mm.

M3 MAETROESJES

Maetroesjes OPWECKER . . . 1618. 4° sig.ab^4

106.d.45.

Another edition of the preceding. The titlepage ornament is in the shape of a cross measuring 28×38mm. The initial I on page a2r measures 34×33mm and the same page has a typographical border. This is another copy of *Knuttel* no.2655.

M4 MAFFEI, Giovanni Pietro

DE VITA ET MORIBVS B.P. IGNATII LOIOLÆ . . . LIBRI III. Auctore IOANNE PETRO MAFFEIO . . . DVACI, Typis IOANNIS BOGARDI. M.DCXXI. 12° pp.192; illus., port.

4824.b.34.

The engraved portrait of St. Ignatius on the verso of the titlepage bears French verses beginning 'La Plume, et le burin . . . '.

M5 MAFFEI, Giovanni Pietro

IOAN. PETRI MAFFEI . . . HISTORIARVM INDICARVM LIBRI XVI. SELECTARVM, ITEM, EX INDIA EPISTOLARVM LIBRI IV. Accessit liber recentiorvm Epistolarum, à Ioanne Hayo . . . nunc primùm excusus . . . DVOBVS TOMIS DISTRIBVTI. Omnia ab Auctore recognita & emendata . . . ANTVERPIÆ, Ex Officina Martini Nutij . . . M.DC.V. 8° 2 pt.: pp.478; 401

1489.i.7; 4765.aa.1.

The copy at 4765.aa.1 is imperfect; wanting pt.2.

MAGINI, Giovanni Antonio. Histoire universelle des Indes orientales. 1607, 11. *See* WYTFLIET, Cornelius. Histoire universelle des Indes Occidentales.

M6 MAGINI, Giovanni Antonio

Den Italiaenschen Vvaerseggher/dat is een PROGNOSTICATIE, Op het Jaer . . . 1621. Gepractiseert door Anthonio Magino . . . Met eenen Romeynschen Calendier . . . De tweede Edicie gecorrigeert ende verbetert. Ghedruckt naer de Copije van Bolognia voort Jaer Anno 1621. Stillo [*sic*] novo. 4° sig.AB^{4}C^2

T.2424(6).

Published in 1621.

MAGIRUS, Antonius; pseudonym of Peter Scholier. *See* SCHOLIER, Peter

M7 MAGNUM

MAGNVM SPECVLVM EXEMPLORVM EX PLVSQVAM SEXAGINTA AVTORIBVS . . . excerptum Ab Anonymo quodam, qui circiter annum . . . 1480. vixisse deprehenditur. Opus ab innumeris mendis . . . vindicatum, varijs notis, Autorumq; citationibus illustratum. PER QVENDAM PATREM E SOCIETATE IESV AC . . . PER EVNDEM NOVORVM Exemplorum appendice locupletatum. Cum Indice . . . DVACI, Ex officina BALTAZARIS BELLERI . . . M.DC.III. 4° pp.724, 75

486.g.2.

Sometimes attributed to Aegidius Aurifaber, Herman van Ludingakerke or Joannes Busch of Windesheim. Edited by Joannes Major. Printed by Laurentius Kellam at Douai?

M8 MAGNUM

MAGNVM SPECVLVM EXEMPLORVM . . . Secunda editio priore castigatior. Cum Indicibus . . . DVACI, Ex officina BALTAZARIS BELLERI . . . 1605. 4° 2 tom.: pp.348; 360, 75.

486.g.3.

For the authorship attributions see preceding entry. The preliminary poems addressed to the book and readers signed: P. Io. Maior. Printed by Laurence Kellam at Douai?

M9 MAGNUM

MAGNVM SPECVLVM EXEMPLORVM EX PLVSQVAM OCTOGINTA AVTORIBVS . . . excerptum . . . Opus varijs notis . . . illustratum, & . . . locupletatum . . . studio R. P. IOANNIS MAIORIS . . . Tertia editio omnium commodissima . . . cvm tribvs indicibvs . . . Antverpiæ, Apud IOANNEM KEERBERGIVM . . . 1607. [etc.] 4° pp.795
1489.a.63.

For the authorship attributions see the entry for the first edition. The leaf intended for pp.481, 482 is apparently a cancel with p.481 blank, but p.482 printed. Its cancelland is inserted after p.794 bearing the text of p.481 and a different text on p.482. Printed by Laurence Kellam at Douai. Ownership inscription: Jacobus Waltonus.

M10 MAIGRET, George

LES LARMES ET REGRETS DV TRES-CHRESTIEN HERACLIT. Recueillies et dediëes a son ALTEZE DE LIEGE. Par Fr. GEORGE MAIGRET . . . Chez Christian Ouwerx . . . 1613. 8° tom.1: pp.565; illus.
4413.aa.42.

Published at Liège. The titlepage is engraved. The illustrations are woodcuts, showing monsters. No more published.

M11 MAIGRET, George

LA VIE DV BIEN-HEVREVX S. IEAN DE SAHAGOVNE . . . Extraite . . . de l'Espagnol de diuers Autheurs . . . & composé plus ordõnément, Par F. GEORGE MAIGRET . . . A TOVRNAY, De l'Imprimerie Ioseph du Hamel [*sic*] & de Charles Martin . . . M.DC.X. [etc.] 12° pp.381
4824.a.30.

Although the book is dated 1610, it is known that the author presented two copies to the magistrates of Tournay on 10 November 1609.

M12 MAKEBLYDE, Ludovicus

CORT BEGRIIP van acht Oeffeninghen/alle Christen menschen seer dienende om wel te leuen/eñ deuchdelijck in Godts teghenwoordicheyt te verkeeren . . . TOT LOVEN, By Jan Maes . . . 1602. 8° sig.a–d^8; illus.
4407.bb.11(2).

Anonymous. The illustrations are woodcuts.

MALAPERTIUS, Carolus. Oratio habita Duaci. 1620. *See* EUCLID. Elementa. [bk. 1–6]

M13 MALAPERTIUS, Carolus

CAROLI MALAPERTII . . . POEMATA. ANTVERPIÆ, EX OFFICINA PLANTINIANA, Apud Viduam & Filios Io. Moreti. M.DC.XVI. (col.) ANTVERPIÆ, EX OFFICINA PLANTINIANA, Apud Viduam & Filios Io. Moreti. M.DC.XVI. 12° pp.135
11405.a.55(1).

With additional poems by Angelinus Gazaeus and Antonius des Lions. The signatures are AA-FF, suggesting that this book was produced as a second part to another work. The titlepage is mutilated. Ownership inscription: Monasterii Rothnacensis 1757.

M14 MALCOLM, John; Minister of Perth

COMMENTARIVS IN APOSTOLORVM ACTA M. IOANNIS MALCOLMI . . . PERSPICVVS, AC ANALYTICVS, NOTIS . . . illustratus . . . Nunc primum in lucem editus . . . MIDDELBVRGI, Excudebat RICHARDVS SCHILDERS . . . M.DC.XV. 4° pp.477
3225.c.28.

Ownership inscriptions: Jv: Sawyer; [John?] Tranberg; J. Chr King Londini 1716; ex dono ejus . . . Johanni Maydwell; A. W. Miller.

MALDERUS, Joannes; Bishop. Publications by Joannes Malderus in his capacity as Bishop of Antwerp are entered under ANTWERP. Diocese

M15 MALDERUS, Joannes; Bishop

IOANNIS MALDERI . . . ANTI-SYNODICA, SIVE ANIMADVERSIONES IN DECRETA CONVENTVS DORDRACENI, Quam vocant SYNODVM NATIONALEM, de quinque doctrinæ Capitibus, inter Remonstrantes & Contraremonstrantes controuersis. ANTVERPIÆ, EX OFFICINA PLANTINIANA, Apud Balthasarem Moretum, & Viduam Ioannis Moreti, & Io. Meursium. M.DC.XX. (col.) ANTVERPIÆ, EX OFFICINA PLANTINIANA BALTHASARIS MORETI. M.DC.XX. 8° pp.309

1018.d.30.

M16 MALINGRE, Claude; Sieur de Saint-Lazare

HISTOIRE CHRONOLOGIQVE, DE PLVSIEVRS GRANDS CAPITAINES, PRINCES, SEIGNEVRS . . . & autres hommes illustres qui ont paru en France depuis cent soixante & quinze ans iusques à present . . . Où se void par suite de discours les vieilles . . . Alliances entre la France & l'Escosse . . . A ARRAS, Chez FRANÇOIS BAVDVIN . . . M.DC.XVII. 8° pp.358

1059.a.21(2).

The dedication signed: C. Malingre. The privilege, made out to Adrian Tiffaine, Paris, is repeated from an earlier edition, also of 1617.

MALLEOLUS, Thomas. *See* THOMAS a Kempis

M17 MANASSES, Constantinus

CONSTANTINI MANASSIS ANNALES, Græcè ac Latinè. IOANNES MEVRSIVS . . . primus nunc vulgavit. LVGDVNI BATAVORVM, Ex Officinâ IOANNIS PATII . . . M.D.C.XVI. 4° pp.551

1476.c.19.

The translator named in the preface as Joannes Leunclavius. Ownership inscription: J. J. [or T.?] Akerman.

M18 MANDER, Karel van

IN LIEFDE GHETRAVW. HAERLEM CJVisscher Excudebat. An°. M.DI.II [*sic*]. fol. a single sheet

Maps C.9.d.4(13).

An engraving showing the emblem of the Chamber of Rhetoric 'Het wit Angierken' at Haarlem whose motto was 'In Liefde Ghetrouw', originally designed by Karel van Mander and engraved by Jacob Matham for publication in 1602, the present edition being a later copy without the artists' initials, published by C. J. Visscher at Amsterdam, ca. 1620?, and perhaps engraved by him. The Dutch verses above and below the emblem and the Latin prose dedication are supposedly by Karel van Mander. Part of the Beudeker collection.

M19 MANDER, Karel van

Den Nederduytschen HELICON . . . Daer vertoont worden . . . veelderley versamelde, ende aen een geschakelde soetluydende leersame Ghedichten/in suyver Nederduytsche sprake ghemaeckt/door verscheyden Dicht-Konst-oeffenaers . . . Ghedruckt tot Alckmaer, by Iacob de Meester, Voor Passchier van Westbusch . . . tot Haerlem. 1610. 8° pp.332

C.125.cc.21.

Anonymous. Compiled by Karel van Mander and edited by Jacques van der Schuere.

M20 MANDER, Karel van

Olijf-Bergh ofte Poëma van den laetsten Dagh. In Nederlandtschen dicht beschreven door Karel van Mander . . . Ghedruckt by Iasper Tournay. Voor Passchier van Westbusch/Boeckvercooper t'Haerlem . . . 1609. 8° pp.128

11556.b.27.

Printed at Gouda. Imperfect; wanting two preliminary leaves bearing laudatory verses.

M21 MANDER, Karel van

(tp.1) HET Schilder-boeck waer in Voor eerst . . . den grondt der Edel Vry SCHILDERCONST . . . Wort Voorghedraghen. Daer nae . . . t'leuen der vermaerde . . . Schilders des ouden, en nieuwen tyds Eyntlyck d'wtlegghinghe op den METAMORPHOSEON pub. Ouidij Nasonis . . . Door Carel van Mander . . . voor PASCHIER VAN WESBUSCH . . . Tot HAERLEM 1604. [etc.]
(tp.2=f.58) Het Leven der oude Antijcke . . . Schilders/soo wel Egyptenaren/ Griecken als Romeynen/uyt verscheyden Schrijvers by een ghebracht/en . . . uytgegheven . . . Door Carel van Mander . . . Mitsgaders . . . het Leven der moderne . . . Italiaensche Schilders. Desghelijcx oock der vermaerde Nederlanders ende Hooghduytschen. TOT ALCKMAER, Gedruckt by Jacob de Meester . . . voor Passchier van West-busch . . . tot Haerlem . . . 1603.
(tp.3=f.91) Het Leven der Moderne . . . Italiaensche Schilders . . . Door Karel van Mander . . . Het tweedde Boeck/van het Leven der Schilders. TOT ALCMAER, Ghedruckt by Jacob de Meester . . . voor Passchier van West-busch . . . tot Haerlem . . . 1603.
(tp.4=f.196) Het Leven der . . . Nederlandtsche/en Hooghduytsche Schilders . . . Door Carel van Mander . . . TOT ALCKMAER, Ghedruckt by Jacob de Meester/voor Passchier van West-busch . . . tot Haerlem . . . 1604.
(tp.5) WTLEGGHINGH Op den METAMORPHOSIS Pub. Ouidij Nasonis . . . by een ghebracht en gheraemt DOOR Carel van Mander . . . VOOR PASCHIER VAN WESTBVSCH . . . Tot HAERLEM . . . 1604. [etc.]
(tp.6=f.123)Vvtbeeldinge der Figueren: waer in te sien is/hoe d'Heydenen hun Goden uytghebeeldt . . . hebben . . . Alles seer nut den . . . Schilders/en oock Dichters . . . By een ghebracht en gheraemt/door C. van Mander . . . TOT ALCKMAER. Ghedruckt by Jacob de Meester/Voor Passchier van West-busch . . . tot Haerlem . . . 1604. 4° 2 pt.: ff.300; 135
564.a.5.

The first piece of pt.1, the 'Grondt der edel vry schilderconst', is in verse. The titlepages of the parts, i.e. tp.1 and tp.5, are engraved and signed: KMander inuentor, IMatham sculp. Imperfect; wanting the portrait. Ownership inscription: Ex Bibl. P. de Cardonnel MDCLXI.

M22 MANDER, Karel van

(tp.1) Het Schilder Boeck . . . DOOR Carel van Mander . . . Hier is op nieu bygevoecht het leven des Autheurs. T'Amsterdam by Jacob Pietersz Wachter . . . 1618.
(tp.2) Het leven Der OVDE ANTYCKE . . . SCHILDERS . . . Door CAREL van MANDER . . . t'AMSTERDAM, Voor Cornelis Lodewijcksz. vander Plasse . . . 1617.
(tp.3=f.26) Het Leven Der Moderne . . . Italiaensche Schilders . . . Door Karel van Mander . . . t'AMSTERDAM. Voor Cornelis Lodewijcksz. vander Plasse . . . 1616.
(tp.4=f.120) Het Leven der . . . Nederlandtsche/en Hooghduytsche Schilders . . . door CAREL van MANDER . . . t'AMSTERDAM, Voor Cornelis van der Plasse . . . 1617. (col.1=f.[216v]) T'AMSTERDAM, Ghedruckt by Paulus van Ravesteyn . . . 1616.
(tp.5) Vytleggingh Op den METAMORPHOSIS . . . Door CAREL VAN MANDER . . . t'AMSTERDAM, Voor Cornelis Lodewijcksz. vander Plasse . . . 1616.
(tp.6=f.109) Vytbeeldinghe der Figueren . . . door C. van MANDER . . . t'AMSTERDAM, Voor Cornelis Lodewycksz. van der Plasse . . . 1616. (col.2=f.[124v]) t'AMSTERDAM, Ghedruckt by Paulus van Ravesteyn . . . 1616. 4° 3 pt.: ff.22; 213; 122; illus., port.
1401.g.53.

With "tGeslacht/de geboort/plaets/tydt/leven ende wercken van Karel van Mander', formerly attributed to Gerbrand Adriaensz Bredero, more recently to Karel van Mander the Younger, on sig. R, S of pt. 3. The general titlepage, i.e. tp. 1, is engraved. It and the portrait signed: W. val inuē. N. Las., or: Nicola Lastman, sculp.

M23 MANGOTIUS, Adrianus

ADRIANI MANGOTII . . . MONITA MARIANA EX S. SCRIPTVRA & SS. PATRIBVS . . . COLLECTA, Sodalibus Deiparæ Virginis Antuerpi ædicta . . . Additur duplex declaratio Dominicæ Passionis . . . ANTVERPIAE, Apud Hieronymum Verdussen. M.DC.XIV. pp. 348; illus.

861.d.7.

The titlepage woodcut shows the Virgin and Child with angels. The leaf following p. 348 is mutilated.

M24 MANIFEST

HET MANIFEST OFT Oorsaecken van t'ghene lestmael bestaen is van de Valtellinoisen/teghen d'overtollighe handelinghe ende wreede Tyrannije van de Grisons ende omligghende Ketters/teghen hen. Overghesedt vvt de Italiaensche sprake in onse Nederlantsche Tale. Ghedruct int Iaer . . . 1620. 4° pp.[20]; sig. $I^4B^4C^2$

P.P. 3444.af.(93).

With 'Artyckelen des Verbondts, tusschen den . . . Bischop van Coire, ende de . . . dry Liguen . . . der Grisons, ende de Valtellinoisen' of 1513. Without imprint; published by Abraham Verhoeven at Antwerp as part of his series of newsletters, already advertised in an earlier issue. Cropped, with partial loss of the pagination on p. 19 and complete loss of pagination on p. 20.

A MANIFESTATION of great folly. 1602. *See* PERSONS, Robert

M25 MANIFESTE

[Manifeste ou declaration des eglises reformees de France.] DECLARATION DES EGLISES REFORMEES DE FRANCE & de Souveraineté de Bearn. De l'injuste persecution qui leur est faicte par les ennemis de l'Estat & de leur Religion. Et de leur legitime & necessaire defense. A LA ROCHELLE, Par Pierre Pié de Dieu. M.VI.C.XXI. 4° sig. A–D^4E^3

4535.bbb.17(2).

Without the last leaf. The imprint is false; printed in the Netherlands.

M26 MANIFESTE

[Manifeste ou declaration des eglises reformees de France.] DECLARATIE Der Ghereformeerde Kercken van Vrancrijc ende Souverainiteyt van Bearn. Vande onrechtveerdighe vervolginge die haer aengedaen wert vande Vyanden des Staets ende harer Religie: Ende van hare wettelijcke ende noodighe beschermінghe. Overghezet vvt het Fransche exemplaer, Ghedruct tot Rochelle. TOT ROTTERDAM, By Jan van Waesberghe . . . 1621. [etc.] 4° sig. A–D^4E^2

T.2251(20).

M27 MANSFELT, Carolus a

MANVDVCTIO AD VITAM CANONICAM Ratiocinante. CAROLO A MANSFELT . . . LVXEMBVRGI Typis Huberti Reulandt . . . M.DC.XX. 12° pp. 139

1121.b.13(1).

MANUAEL, ofte handtboeck, inhoudende die weerde vanden marck. 1606. *See* NETHERLANDS. United Provinces. Staten Generaal [21.3.1606]

A MANUAL of prayers. 1613. *See* FLINTON, George

A MANUDUCTION for Mr. Robinson. 1614. *See* BRADSHAW, William

M28 MARBAIS, Nicolas de
SVPPLICATION ET REQVETTE A L'EMPEREVR, Aux Roys, Princes, Estats, Republiques & Magistrats Chrestiens, Sur Les causes d'assembler un Concile general Contre Paul Cinquiesme. Dressée par NICOL. de MARBAIS . . . Sur le subiect d'une autre petite en Latin . . . A LEYDE, Chez LOYS ELZEVIER, 1613. 12° pp.293
1606/453
Treating the same subject matter as 'Supplicatio ad Imperatorem', published in London in 1613 and sometimes attributed to Marco Antonio de Dominis, but not a translation of it.

MARCA, Cornelius a. *See* LUMMENAEUS A MARCA, Jacobus Cornelius a

MARE liberum. 1609. *See* GROOT, Hugo de

M29 MAREES, Pieter de
Beschryvinge ende Historische verhael/vant Gout Koninckrijck van gunea . . . perfect ende neerstich ondersocht ende beschreven, door eenen persoon die daer tot verscheyden tyden gheweest heeft. P.D. M. Ghedruct tot Amstelredam, by Cornelis Claesz. . . . 1602. obl. 4° pp.129; sig.A–S⁴: pl.17; illus.
440.i.1(2); 566.k.15(2); 1858.a.1(6).
Anonymous. Pl.9 is in two parts. With a Dutch-Guinean dictionary. A later edition is entered under COLIJN, Michiel.

M30 MAREES, Pieter de
[Beschryvinge.] DESCRIPTION ET RECIT HISTORIAL DV RICHE ROYAVME D'OR DE GVNEA . . . descript par l'autheur qui par diverses fois y a esté. P.D.M. A AMSTERDAMME. Imprime chez Cornille Claesson . . . M.VIC.V. fol. pp.99; sig.A–O⁴; illus.
G.6620(5); G.6833.
Anonymous. The titlepage engraving is a repeat of illustration no.19.

M31 MAREES, Pieter de
[Beschryvinge.] DESCRIPTION . . . DV . . . ROYAVME D'OR DE GVNEA . . . descript par . . . P.D.M. A AMSTERDAMME. Imprimé chez Cornille Claesson . . . M.VIC.V.
566.k.15(7).
Another issue of the preceding. The accent has been added to 'Imprimé' and the titlepage engraving is a repeat of no.7. Mounted and cropped. The titlepage is slightly mutilated.

M32 MARENZIO, Luca
(tp.1) LVCÆ MARENTII CANTIONES SACRÆ PRO FESTIS TOTIVS ANNI ET COMMVNI SANCTORVM QVATERNIS VOCIBVS Nunc denuo in lucem editæ. CANTVS. ANTVERPIÆ Apud Petrum Phalesium. M.DCIII.
(tp.2) LVCÆ MARENTII CANTIONES SACRÆ . . . TENOR. ANTVERPIÆ Apud Petrum Phalesium. M.DCIII.
(tp.3) LVCÆ MARENTII CANTIONES SACRÆ . . . ALTVS. ANTVERPIÆ Apud Petrum Phalesium. M.DCIII.
(tp.4) LVCÆ MARENTII CANTIONES SACRÆ . . . BASSVS. ANTVERPIÆ Apud Petrum Phalesium. M.DCIII. 4° 4 pt.: pp.44; 44; 44; 44
Music K.7.a.6.
The signatures run on consecutively through the four parts from A–V.

M33 MARENZIO, Luca
(tp.1) MADRIGALI A QVATTRO VOCI DI LVCA MARENZIO. Nuouamente Ristampati. TENORE. IN ANVERSA Appresso Pietro Phalesio. M DC VII.
(tp.2) MADRIGALI A QVATTRO VOCI DI LVCA MARENZIO . . . BASSO. IN ANVERSA Appresso Pietro Phalesio. M DC VII. obl. 4° 2 pt.: pp.29; 29
Music B.270.g.
The Tenor part begins on the titlepage verso; in the bass part this is blank, with an Italian poem added in manuscript. Wanting the other voices.

M34 MARENZIO, Luca
(tp.1) DI LVCA MARENZIO . . . Il Primo, Secondo, Terzo, Quarto & Quinto Libro DE MADRIGALI A CINQVE VOCI Nuouamente Ristampati & in vn Corpo ridotti. CANTO. IN ANVERSA Appresso Pietro Phalesio . . . M DC IX.
(tp.2) DI LVCA MARENZIO . . . MADRIGALI A CINQVE VOCI . . . ALTO. IN ANVERSA Appresso Pietro Phalesio . . . M DC IX.
(tp.3) DI LVCA MARENZIO . . . MADRIGALI A CINQVE VOCI . . . TENORE. IN ANVERSA Appresso Pietro Phalesio . . . M DC IX.
(tp.4) DI LVCA MARENZIO . . . MADRIGALI A CINQVE VOCI . . . BASSO. IN ANVERSA Appresso Pietro Phalesio . . . M DC IX.
(tp.5) DI LVCA MARENZIO . . . MADRIGALI A CINQVE VOCI . . . QVINTO. IN ANVERSA Appresso Pietro Phalesio . . . M DC IX. obl. 4° 5 pt.: pp.56; 56; 56; 56; 56
Music B.270.e; Music B.270.f.
The copy at Music B.270.f consists of Tenor and Bass only.

M35 MARENZIO, Luca
(tp.1) DI LVCA MARENZIO . . . IL SESTO, SETTIMO, OTTAVO ET NONO Libro . . . DE MADRIGALI A CINQVE VOCI Nuouamente Stampati & in vn Corpo ridotti. TENORE. IN ANVERSA Appresso Pietro Phalesio . . . M DC IX.
(tp.2) DI LVCA MARENZIO . . . MADRIGALI A CINQVE VOCI . . . BASSO. IN ANVERSA Appresso Pietro Phalesio . . . M DC IX. obl. 4° 2 pt.: pp.18 [81]; 18 [81]
Music B.270.h.
Wanting the other parts.

M36 MARENZIO, Luca
(tp.1) DI LVCA MARENZIO . . . Il Primo, Secondo, Terzo, Quarto & Quinto Libro DE MADRIGALI A SEI VOCI Nouamente Ristampati & in vn Corpo ridotti. CANTO. IN ANVERSA Appresso Pietro Phalesio . . . M.DC X.
(tp.2) DI LVCA MARENZIO . . . MADRIGALI A SEI VOCI . . . ALTO. IN ANVERSA Appresso Pietro Phalesio M.DC X.
(tp.3) DI LVCA MARENZIO . . . MADRIGALI A SEI VOCI . . . TENORE. IN ANVERSA Appresso Pietro Phalesio . . . M.DC X.
(tp.4) DI LVCA MARENZIO . . . MADRIGALI A SEI VOCI . . . BASSO. IN ANVERSA Appresso Pietro Phalesio . . . M.DC X.
(tp.5) DI LVCA MARENZIO . . . MADRIGALI A SEI VOCI . . . QVINTO. A ANVERSA Appresso Pietro Phalesio . . . M.DC X.
(tp.6) DI LVCA MARENZIO . . . MADRIGALI A SEI VOCI . . . SESTO. IN ANVERSA Appresso Pietro Phalesio . . . M.DC X. obl. 4° 6 pt.: pp.106 [107]; 106; 106 [107]; 106; 106 [107]; 106 [107]
Music R. M.15.b.2.

M37 MARENZIO, Luca
(tp.1) DI LVCA MARENZIO . . . IL SESTO LIBRO DE MADRIGALI A SEI VOCI Nouamente stampati & dati in luce. CANTO. IN ANVERSA Appresso Pietro Phalesio . . . M.DC X.
(tp.2) DI LVCA MARENZIO . . . IL SESTO LIBRO DE MADRIGALI A SEI VOCI . . . ALTO. IN ANVERSA Appresso Pietro Phalesio . . . M.DC X.
(tp.3) DI LVCA MARENZIO . . . IL SESTO LIBRO DE MADRIGALI A SEI VOCI . . . TENORE. IN ANVERSA Appresso Pietro Phalesio . . . M.DC X.
(tp.4) DI LVCA MARENZIO . . . IL SESTO LIBRO DE MADRIGALI A SEI VOCI . . . BASSO. IN ANVERSA Appresso Pietro Phalesio . . . M.DC X.
(tp.5) DI LVCA MARENZIO . . . IL SESTO LIBRO DE MADRIGALI A SEI VOCI . . . QVINTO. IN ANVERSA Appresso Pietro Phalesio . . . M.DC X.
(tp.6) DI LVCA MARENZIO . . . IL SESTO LIBRO DE MADRIGALI A SEI VOCI . . . SESTO. IN ANVERSA Appresso Pietro Phalesio . . . M.DC X. obl. 4° 6 pt.: pp.21; 21; 21; 21; 17; 17
Music B.270.j.

M38 MARENZIO, Luca

(tp.1) DI LVCA MARENZIO . . . DE' MADRIGALI SPIRITVALI A CINQVE VOCI Nouamente stampati. TENORE. IN ANVERSA Appresso Pietro Phalesio . . . M.DC X.
(tp.2) DI LVCA MARENZIO . . . DE' MADRIGALI SPIRITVALI A CINQVE VOCI . . . BASSO. IN ANVERSA Appresso Pietro Phalesio . . . M.DC X. obl. 4° 2 pt.: pp.23; 23
Music B.270.i.

The titlepage of the Basso part is mutilated. Wanting the other parts.

M39 MARISSAL, Antonius

(tp.1) FLORES MELODICI, SIVE CANTIONES SACRÆ V. VI. VIII. ET PLVRIVM VOCVM, PRO FESTIS PRAECIPVIS TOTIVS ANNI, TAM VOCI VIVÆ QVAM OMNIBVS INSTRVMENTIS ACCOMMODATÆ. AVCTORE D. ANTONIO MARISSAL . . . SVPERIVS. DVACI, Typis IOANNIS BOGARDI. M.DCXI.
(tp.2) FLORES MELODICI . . . AVCTORE D. ANTONIO MARISSAL . . . TENOR. DVACI, Typis IOANNIS BOGARDI. M.DCXI.
(tp.3) FLORES MELODICI . . . AVCTORE D. ANTONIO MARISSAL . . . CONTRATENOR. DVACI, Typis IOANNIS BOGARDI. M.DCXI.
(tp.4) FLORES MELODICI . . . AVCTORE D. ANTONIO MARISSAL . . . BASSVS. DVACI, Typis IOANNIS BOGARDI. M.DCXI.
(tp.5) FLORES MELODICI . . . AVCTORE D. ANTONIO MARISSAL . . . SECVNDVS BASSVS. DVACI, Typis IOANNIS BOGARDI. M.DCXI.
(tp.6) FLORES MELODICI . . . AVCTORE D. ANTONIO MARISSAL . . . QVINTA VOX. DVACI, Typis IOANNIS BOGARDI. M.DCXI. obl. 4° 6 pt.: pp.40; 40; 39; 39; 23; 39
Music A.184.

M40 MARNIX van Sint Aldegonde, Philips van

(tp.1) DE BYEN-CORF, der H. Roomscher Kercke. Voorstellende een clare ende grondelicke uytlegginge des Sendt-briefs van Meester Gentianus Hervet, uytghegheven in Fransoys ende Duyts/aen den afgedwaelfden van het Christen Geloove. By den Autheur selve vergroot, ende verrijckt, nae den Fransoyschen Bijen-corf, ofte Tableau, &c. by hem int Licht Ghebracht, int Iaer 1599. TOT DELF, By Bruyn Harmansz. Schinckel [etc.]
(tp.2=f.263) De uytlegginge des Bijencorfs der H. Roomscher Kercken. Ghedruckt/Anno 1611. 8° ff.274; illus.
1607/4052.

The author is named in the preface. With the same woodcut on both titlepages.

M41 MARNIX van Sint Aldegonde, Philips van

PHILIPPI MARNIXII . . . DE INSTITVTIONE Principum, ac Nobilium Puerorum, LIBELLVS . . . Luci è Manuscripto jam recens datus A SIXTO ARCERIO . . . FRANECARÆ, EXCVDEBAT ROMBERTVS DOYEMA . . . 1615. 4° pp.48
523.g.15(7).

M42 MARNIX van Sint Aldegonde, Philips van

[Examen rationum quibus Rob. Bellarminus pontificatum Romanum adstruere nititur, auctore Phil. Marnixio, 1603.] 8° pp.164
1020.kk.15.

Imperfect; wanting the titlepage. A manuscript title reads: Philippi Marnix contra Bellar. de Pontifice Diatribe. The above title taken from the dropped head title, is that also found with author's name and this date in *Lacroix Meenen*, p.102, whereas *Van der Aa* gives it as 1607. The catalogue of the Bodleian Library Oxford says 1602. Printed in the Netherlands?

M43 MARNIX van Sint Aldegonde, Philips van

[Le tableau des differens de la religion.] TAFEREEL der Religions verschillen . . . door PHILIPS VAN MARNIX Heere van S. Aldegonde Overgeset uyt den Fransoyse in nederduytsche tale door B.N. T'AMSTELREDAM By Jan Evaertsz. Cloppenborch . . . 1601. (col.) Gedruct t'Amsterdam/by Herman de Buck/[etc.] 4° ff.36; illus., port.

C.135.d.10.

The translator identified by *Lacroix Meenen* (p.102) as Bodel Nijenhuis. The titlepage and the portrait are engraved. The colophon is printed in civilité.

M44 MARQUE

MARQVE DE PREDESTINATION. Auec vn moyen tres-puissant . . . pour se sauuer . . . Reueu & augmentée par l'Autheur. A LOVVAIN, Chez GERARD RIVIVS. M.D.C.XVIII. 12° pp.142; illus.

4257.e.6.

The illustrations are woodcuts. With the exlibris of Robert Craig.

M45 MARSELAER, Fredericus de

KHPYKEION, SIVE LEGATIONVM INSIGNE . . . M.DC.XVIII. ANTVERPIAE APVD GVIL. A TONGRIS. [etc.] 8° pp.251; illus.

8005.e.34.

The dedication signed: Fred. Marselaer. The titlepage is engraved. With an emblematic engraving featuring the 'ambassador' on the verso of the dedicatory leaf. Ownership inscription: Collegii Soctis Jesu Antverpiæ 1619.

M46 MARTIALIS, Marcus Valerius

M. VAL. MARTIALIS EPIGRAMMATON LIBRI XII. Xeniorum Liber I. Apophoretorum Liber I. EX OFFICINA PLANTINIANA RAPHELENGII, M.DC.VI. 32° pp.272

1490.c.51.

Published at Leiden. Ownership inscription: Findlay.

M47 MARTIALIS, Marcus Valerius

M. VAL. MARTIALIS EPIGRAMMATON LIBRI XII . . . EX OFFICINA PLANTINIANA RAPHELENGII, M.D.CXII. 32° pp.272

1069.a.42; C.20.f.51.

Published at Leiden. Not a reissue of the preceding. The copy at C.20.f.51 from the travelling library of Sir Julius Caesar.

M48 MARTIALIS, Marcus Valerius

(tp.1) M. VAL. MARTIALIS NOVA EDITIO. Ex Museo PETRI SCRIVERII. LVGDVNI BATAVORVM, Apud IOANNEM MAIRE, M.DC.XIX.

(tp.2) P. SCRIVERII ANIMADVERSIONES IN MARTIALEM . . . LVGDVNI BATAVORVM, APVD IOANNEM MAIRE . . . M.DC.XVIII.

(tp.3) CL. VV. IVSTI LIPSII, IANI RVTGERSII, I. ISAACI PONTANI, Notæ IN MARTIALEM. Ad Petrum Scriverium. Lugduni Batavorum, APVD IOANNEM MAIRE . . . M D CXIX. 32° 3 vol.: pp.8, 312; 285; 24, 280

238.l.12–14; G.9634; 1001.a.12.

With additional notes by Joannes Brodaeus and others. Vol.1, 2 with the device of the Officina Plantiniana Raphelengii, Leiden, who printed the edition. Vol.3 with the device of Joannes Maire. The copy at 1001.a.12 is imperfect; consisting of vol.3. pp.1–280 with the addition of the first set of pp.1–8 of vol.1 only, wanting the titlepage and the first set of pp.1–24. The copy at 238.l.12 has the ownership inscription: Ch [?] Farmer.

M49 MARTIALIS, Marcus Valerius

M. VAL. MARTIALIS, Ex Museo Petri Scriverii. Amstelredami, Apud Guiljel. Ianssonium M DC XXI. 32° pp.318

1068.a.17.

The titlepage is engraved.

M50 MARTIN, Corneille

GENEALOGIES DES FORESTIERS ET CONTES DE FLANDRES Auec brieue HISTOIRE de leurs vies: Recueillies . . . par Cornille Martin: Ornées des vrais pourtraicts et habits . . . par Pierre Balthasar. A ANVERS SE VENDENT EN LA BOVTIQVE PLANTINIENNE M.DC.XII. (col.) A ANVERS, IMPRIME PAR ROBERT BRVNEAV, POVR BAPTISTE VRIENT . . . M.DC.VIII. 4° pp.121; illus., map
9916.de.37.

A reissue of the edition of 1608 published by Jean Baptiste Vrients, with plates additional to the 1598 edition. The titlepage is engraved. The portrait of Albert and Isabella signed: Ottho Vaenius inuent., Ioan Collaert sculp.

MARTINI Antonii Del-Rio . . . vita. 1609. *See* SUSIUS, Nicolaus

M51 MARTINI, Matthias

POMP. GAVRICI . . . DE SCVLPTVRA LIBER. LVDO DEMONTIOSII De veterum Sculpturâ, Cælatura, Gemmarum Scalpturá, & Picturâ Libri duo. ABRAHAMI GORLÆI . . . DACTYLIOTHECA. Omnia accuratius edita . . . 1609. 4° pp.174
1043.f.44.

The compiler's dedicatory letter signed: Matthias Martini. The titlepage is engraved, matching that of the separate copy of the work by Gorlaeus (of the first edition of 1601?) which is entered under GORLAEUS, Abrahamus. Published at Leiden? Imperfect; wanting the part containing the work by Gorlaeus.

M52 MASQUERIER, Guilielmus

THESES INAVGVRALES DE MEDICINA IN GENERE. Quas . . . Pro Doctorali Laurea in Medicina consequendo, Publicè ventilandas proponit GVILIELMVS MASQVERIER . . . Lugduni Batavorum. Excudebat Georgius Abrahami a Marsse, 1617. 4° sig.A^4
1185.g.1(63).

M53 [*MASSOTTE, Thomas; the Elder

Speculationum Notarii Publici, libri quinque e præclaris multorum haud vulgarium Jureconsultorum vigiliis decerpti, atque collecti per Thomam Massotte. Leodii, apud Guilielmum Sapidum 1601. 8° pp.419
6006.a.50(1).]

*Destroyed. Described from the General Catalogue and *De Theux,* col.28.

M54 MATELIEF, Cornelis

HISTORIALE ende ware Beschrijvinge vande reyse des Admiraels Cornelis Matelief de Jonghe/naer de Oost-Indien/wtghetrocken in Mayo 1605. Mitsgaders de belegheringhe voor Malacca, als ooc den slach ter Zee teghen de Portugijssche armade/ende andere discourssen. Tot Rotterdam, By Jan Janssz. . . . 1608. 4° sig.$**^6$; illus.
T.1730(23).

Anonymous; probably by Cornelis Matelief. The titlepage woodcut resembles those used by Jan van Waesberghe the younger at Rotterdam who may be the publisher of this.

M55 MATOS, Gabriel de

[Lettera annua di Giappone.] LETTRE ANNVELLE DV IAPON DE L'AN MIL SIX CENS ET TROIS. Escrite par . . . GABRIEL DE MATOS . . . Auec vne Epistre de la Chine, & des Moluques. Translaté d'Italien en nostre langue vulgaire . . . A DOVAY, De l'Imprimerie de BALTAZAR BELLERE . . . 1606. [etc.] 12° pp.187
G.6691.

With additional letters by Luis Fernandez, Laurent Masonio and Diego Anthunes. The translation has been attributed to Antoine de Balinghem. Printed by Laurence Kellam at Douai?

MATTHAEUS; Eboraceni Archiepiscopus. *See* HUTTON, Matthew

*[Illustration of **M59** overleaf]*

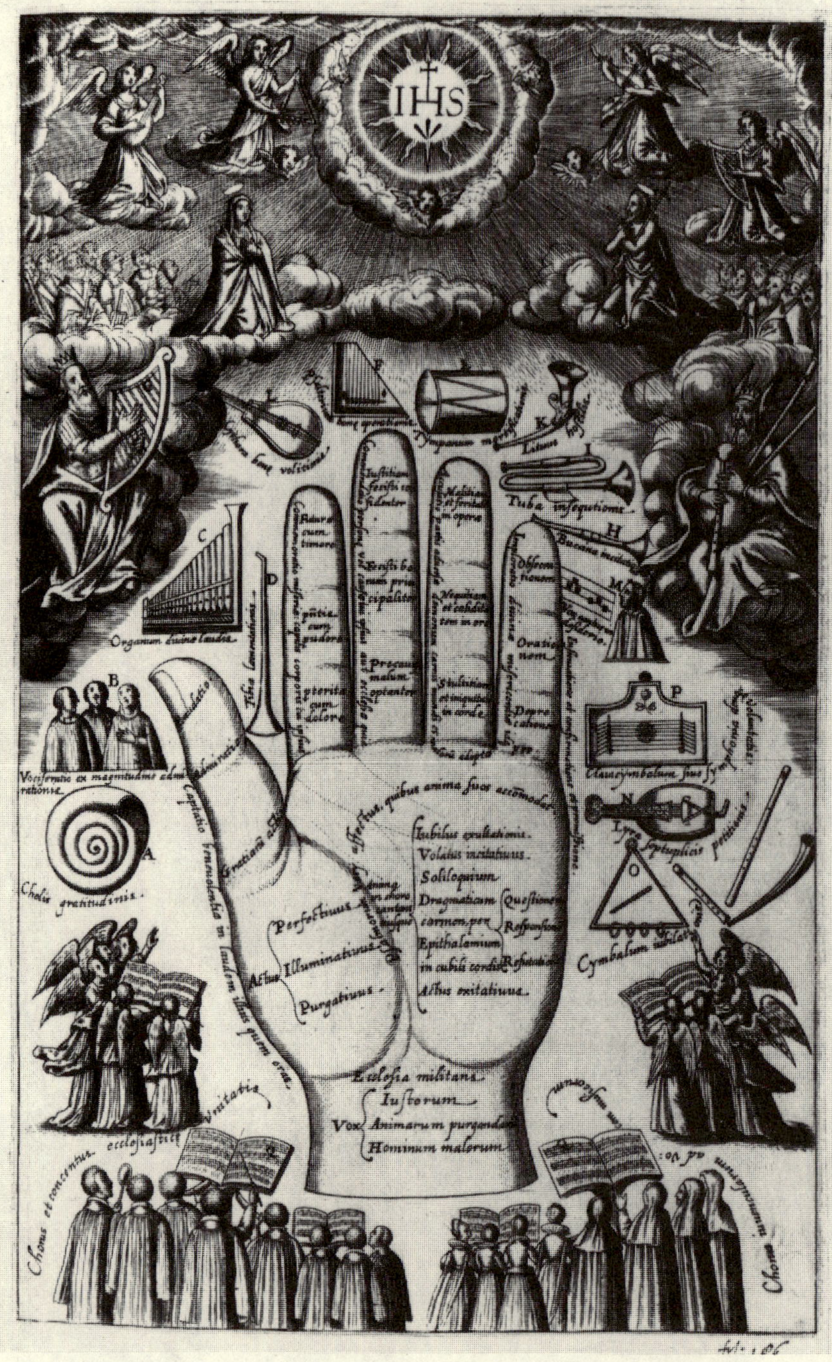

M59 (facing p. 185)

M56 MATTHIAE, Wiltetus
DISPVTATIO INAVGLARIS [*sic*] DE VSVCAPIONIBVS ET Præscriptionibus longi temporis, Quam . . . Pro Titulis & Privilegiis DOCTORATUS in Iure consequendis, publicè defendam WILTETVS MATTHIÆ . . . LUGDUNI BATAVORUM, Ex Officinâ Ioannis Patii . . . M.D.CIV. 4° sig.A^4
11409.f.31(11).

M57 MATTHIEU, Pierre
(tp.1) HISTOIRE DE FRANCE, & DES CHOSES MEMORABLES ADVENVES AVX PROVINCES estrangeres durant sept annees de Paix . . . A LEYDEN, Par Corneille Bonauenture. 1608.
(tp.2) HISTOIRE DE FRANCE . . . TOME SECOND . . . Pour MATT. BERJON. 1610. 8° 2 tom.: pp.692; 802
1200.a.6,7(1).
The imprint of tom.1 is false; both volumes published by Mathieu Berjon at Geneva. The work following 1200.a.7(1) is 'Suite de l'Histoire de France' with the imprint: A Montbelliard, Par Iaques Foîllet. MDCXII.

M58 MATTHIEU, Pierre
HISTOIRE DE LA MORT DEPLORABLE DE HENRY IIII. ROY DE FRANCE ET DE NAVARRE. Ensemble VN POEME, VN PANEgyrique, & vn Discours funebre . . . Par PIERRE MATTHIEV . . . A BRVXELLES, Chez RVTGER VELPIVS, & HVBERT ANTOINE . . . M.DC.XII. [etc.] 8° pp.425
610.c.29.

MATTHISIUS, Joannes. Christelijcke vermaen brief. 1611. [Sometimes attributed to Joannes Matthisius.] *See* CHRISTELIJCKE

M59 MAUBURNUS, Joannes
ROSETVM EXERCITIORVM SPIRITVALIVM, ET SACRARVM MEDITATIONVM, AVCTORE IOANNE MAVBVRNO . . . Opus dignissimum . . . Nunc recens vltrà omnes alias editiones, verius, emendatius, & distinctius edidit . . . LEANDER DE S. MARTINO . . . DVACI, Ex Typographia BALTAZARIS BELLERI . . . 1620. fol. pp.834: plates; illus.
471.e.5.
Some plates and woodcut illustrations are wrongly bound.

M60 MAURICE; Prince of Orange
[Letters] TWEE BRIEVEN Des . . . Vorsten/MAVRITII . . . Prince van Orangie . . . ghesonden tot waerschouwinge aende Steden van Hollandt ende West-Vrieslandt/ nopende het maecken van de Treves . . . IN 'SGRAVEN-HAGE, By Aert Meuris . . . 1621. 4° pp.15
1560/4444.
The letters dated 21 September and 21 October 1608. The date on the titlepage has been altered in manuscript to 1608.

MAURIER, Benjamin Aubery du. *See* AUBERY DU MAURIER, Benjamin

M61 MAXIMILIAN I; Elector of Bavaria
[Letters. 17.8.1620] DE RESOLVTIE Die . . . Hertoch Maximilianus van Beyeren . . . aende drije pollliticque Standen in Oostenrijck/ende d'Landt op der Ens/op haere ontschuldinghe ghegeuen heeft. Nv eerst Ghedruckt den jx. October. T'Hantwerpen/By Abraham Verhoeven . . . 1620. [etc.] 4° pp.8; sig.Ttt^4
1480.aa.15(34); P.P.3444.af(116).
A letter, dated 17 August 1620.

M62 MAXIMILIAN I; Elector of Bavaria

[Letters. 25.8.1620] Schriftelijcke INSINVATIE ghedaen by . . . Hertoch Maximiliaen van Beyeren/AENDEN Ceurvorst Pfaltz-Grave belanghende de Keyserlijcke Commissie/aende Staten van Bohemen. Ghedateert wt de Vrystadt den 25. Augusti 1620. Overghesedt wt de Hooch-Duytsche sprake in onse Nederlantsche Tale. T'Hantwerpen/By Abraham Verhoeven . . . 1620. [etc.] 4° pp.7; sig. Xxx

1480.aa.15(19); P.P.3444.af(84).

M63 MAXIMILIAN I; Elector of Bavaria

[Letters. 25.8.1620] Sekeren Brief geschreuen aende Staten/ende Ondersaten van Bohemen/by . . . hertoch Maximilianus van Beyeren/Waer beneffens de selue oock ouer ghesonden hebben/de Keyserlijcke Patente/in Origniael [*sic*] . . . Overghesedt wt den Hooch-Duytsche in onse Nederlantsche sprake. Eerst Ghedruckt den ix. October 1620. T'hantwerpen/By Abraham verhoeven . . . 1620. [etc.] 4° pp.7; sig. Vvv

1480.aa.15(35); P.P.3444.af(117).

The letter dated 25 August 1620.

M64 MAXIMUS Tyrius

(tp.1) V.C. MAXIMI TYRII . . . DISSERTATIONES XLI. Græce. Cum Interpretatione, Notis, & Emendationibus DANIELIS HEINSII. Accessit Alcinoi in Doctrinam Platonis Introductio ab eodem emendata . . . LVGDVNI BATAVORVM, Apud Ioannem Patium . . . M.D.C.VII.

(tp.2) MAXIMI TYRII . . . DISSERTATIONES XLI. Interprete DANIELE HEINSIO. LVGDVNI BATAVORVM, Apud Ioannem Patium . . . M.D.C.VII.

(tp.3) DANIELIS HEINSII NOTÆ ET EMENDATIONES AD MAXIMVM . . . LUGDUNI BATAVORUM, Ex Officina Ioannis Paetzij . . . M.D.C.VII. 8° 3 pt.: pp.408; 411; sig. a–k[8]

524.d.4; 160.b.1,2.

The copy at 160.b.1,2 is imperfect; wanting pt.3.

M65 MAXIMUS Tyrius

(tp.1) MAXIMI TYRII DISSERTATIONES PHILOSOPHICÆ, Cum Interpretatione & Notis DANIELIS HEINSII hac secunda editione emendatioribus. Accessit ALCINOI IN PLATONEM INTRODVCTIO. LVGDVNI BATAVORVM Apud Ioannem Patium . . . M.D.C.XIV.

(tp.2) DANIELIS HEINSII NOTÆ ET EMENDATIONES AD MAXIMVM Philosophum. LVGDVNI BATAVORVM Excudit Ioannes Patius . . . M.D.C.XIV. 8° 2 pt.: pp.534; 157

715.b.9.

The Greek and Latin texts are printed in parallel columns.

M66 MAZZOLINI, Silvestro; da Prierio

[Aurea rosa super Evangelia.] ENCHIRIDION CONCINIATORVM Ex Roseto aureo Rosæ aureæ R.P.F. SILVESTRI DE PRIERIO . . . Quasi rosulis concinnatum, ac elaboratum per R.P.F. GVILLELMVM OONSELIVM . . . In quo . . . sensus litteralis & doctrina moralis omnium Euangeliorum de tempore proponuntur . . . ANTVERPIÆ Apud Gerardum Wolschatium. M.DC.XXI. 8° pp.189, 136 [137]

4499.a.57.

M67 MECHELEN. Synod

DECRETA ET STATVTA SYNODI PROVINCIALIS MECHLINENSIS: Die vigesima sexta mensis Iunij anni millesimi sexcentesimi septimi . . . Præsidente in ea . . . D.

MATTHIA HOVIO . . . ANTVERPIÆ, EX OFFICINA PLANTINIANA, Apud Ioannem Moretum. M.DC.VIII. 8° pp.127
4372.b.36(4).
Pp.113–127: 'Placcaet ende ordinancie . . . waerby wordt ordre ghestelt, tot . . . onderhoudinghe van sekere poincten ende articulen . . . in het Synode Prouinciael van Mechelen [etc.]', dated 31 August 1608.

MEDICI Londinensis eximii epistola. 1619. *See* THORIUS, Raphael

M68 MEERBEECK, Adrianus van
CHRONIICKE VANDE GANSTCHE [*sic*] WERELT, ende sonderlinghe VANDE SEVENTHIEN NEDERLANDEN . . . vanden tijdt des Keysers Caroli V. af, M.D. tot M.DC.XX. Seer ghetrouwelijck . . . vergadert ende beschreven Door M. ADRIANVS VAN MEERBEECK . . . T'ANTWERPEN By Hieronymus Verdussen . . . M.DC.XX. fol.: 2 pt.: pp.1286: pl.19; port.
156.g.1,2.
With a second titlepage, mounted on an unsigned leaf between pp.648, 649, reading the same as the first and with the same elaborate engraved border signed: P. de Jode inuent., Guiliel. de Haan sculp. The portrait of the author not numbered. Pl.19, a portrait of Ambrosio Spinola, signed: Pet. de Jode excudit, and dated 1623. With one of the engraved devices of the Antwerp printing house of Nutius pasted on the inside of all covers. Ownership inscription: Fagel pt.2 no.6808.

M69 MEERMAN, Willem
COMOEDIA VETUS. [etc.] (col.) uytt' Hantwerpeñ inde Druckery vande Almanacken des Iaers 1612. 4° sig.A–D^4; illus.
T.1718(8); T.2418(2).
Anonymous. In Dutch, with some Latin. Partly in verse. The imprint is false; probably printed in the Northern Netherlands. A 'Druckerije vande almanacken' is known at Amsterdam in 1617, believed to be the press of Nicolaes Biestkens. Corresponding to the copy described in *Tiele* no.1050.

M70 MEESTER, Andries de
[Der Griecken opganck ende onderganck.] LES ACTES MEMORABLES DES GRECS. Contenant leurs haults & vaillans exploits . . . Depuis la guerre Persiēns, iusques a ce qu'ils perdirent leurs liberté soubs ALEXANDRE LE GRAND . . . Recueillis de divers Autheurs, en bas Alleman, par ANDRE DEMETRE. Et nouvellement traduits en François, par IEHAN POLYANDRE . . . A DORDRECHT, Pour André Demetre. 1602. 8° pp.746 [747]; plate; map
9026.b.29.
The publisher and printer named in the privilege as Isaac Canin and Guillaume Guillemot respectively, both at Dordrecht. The apparent device on the titlepage is a smaller woodcut reproduction of the engraving used for the original edition of 1599 in which the author's name is given as Andreas Demetrius. The map signed: Ioan: Doetechomius junior.

MEJENREIS, Samuel. Theses theologicæ de Veteri et Novo Dei Foedere. 1602. *See* DU JON, François; the Elder

M71 MELANCHTHON, Philipp
[De officio principum.] Van Het Offitie ofte Ampt der Princen ende Vorsten . . . Beschreven door . . . D. PHILIPPVS MELANCTHON. Inden Jare 1537 . . . IN 'SGRAVENHAGE. By Aert Meuris . . . 1619. 4° sig.A–E^{4}F^3
T.2249(43*).

MELIBÉA. 1618. *See* RODENBURGH, Theodore

M72 MELLEMA, Elcie Édouard Léon

(tp.1) DICTIONAIRE OV PROMPTVAIRE FRANCOIS-FLAMENG . . . Par ELCIE EDOVARD LEON MELLEMA. A ROTTERDAM, Chez Iean VVaesbergue . . . 1602.
(tp.2) DICTIONAIRE OV PROMPTVAIRE FLAMENG-FRANCOYS . . . PAR Elcie Edoüard Leon Mellema . . . A ROTTERDAM, Chez Iean VVaesbergue . . . 1602. 4° 2 pt.: sig. (.?.) A–Hh^{8}Ii^4; (·.·) A–Qq^8
1560/1815.

MELLINUS, Abramus. Disputatio philosophica de origine . . . animae. 1602. *See* MURDISONIUS, Joannes

M73 MELZO, Lodovico

REGOLE MILITARI DEL CAVALIER MELZO SOPRA IL GOVERNO E SERVITIO DELLA CAVALLERIA. IN ANVERSA Appresso Gioachino Trognæsio. M.DC.XI. (col.) ANTVERPIÆ APVD IOACHIMVM TROGNÆSIVM. M.DCXI. fol. pp.221:pl.16; illus.
717.l.45.
Printed in italics. The illustrations are engraved vignettes.

MEMOIRES de M^r. L.C.D.R. 1612 [1712]. *See* COURTILZ DE SANDRAS, Gatien de

M74 MEMORIE

Memorie vande ghevvichtighe redenen die de Heeren Staten generael behooren te bevveghen, om gheensins te wijcken vande handelinghe ende vaert van Indien. (col.) In dese tvveede Editie verbetert. 4° sig. A^4
106.b.33.
Without titlepage. Originally published as part of 'Waerschouwinghe van de . . . redenen' in 1608, of which the British Library has no copy. This extract also first published in 1608. In this edition the first line of the title ends with 'die de'; the catchword on A1r is 'te'.

M75 MEMORIE

Memorie vande . . . redenen die de Heeren Staten generael behooren te bevveghen, [etc.] (col.) In dese tvveede Editie verbetert. 4° sig. A^4
T.1731(11).
Another edition of the preceding, published probably also in 1608. The first line of the title ends with 'die de Hee-', the catchword on A1r is 'te wil-' and there are other differences in the setting of the text.

M76 MENNENS, Gulielmus

AVREI VELLERIS SIVE SACRÆ PHILOSOPHIÆ VATVM SELECTÆ AC VNICÆ MYSTERIORVMQVE DEI, NATVRÆ, & Artis admirabilium, Libri tres. AVCTORE AC COLLECTORE GVILIELMO MENNENS . . . ANTVERPIÆ, Sumptibus Viduæ & Heredum IO. BELLERI . . . M.DC.IV. [etc.] 4° pp.178
525.f.16(1).

M77 MENNHER, Valentin

LIVRE D'ARITHMETIQVE contenant plusieurs belles Questions & Demandes, bien propres & vtiles à tous Marchands. Par M. VALENTIN MENNHER de Kempten. A ROTTERDAM, Chez Iean VVaesbergue . . . 1609. 8° sig. A–G^{8}H^4
1607/155(2).

MERA deliratio Iesuitalis, eene h. tragi-comedie ge-intituleert Den Salighen Ignatius de Loyola. 1610. *See* TRAGICOMEDIE sacrée intitulée Le bien-heureux Ignace de Loyola.

M78 MERCATOR, Gerard

GERARDI MERCATORIS ATLAS SIVE COSMOGRAPHICÆ MEDITATIONES DE FABRICA MVNDI ET FABRICATI FIGVRA. Denuò auctus. EXCUSUM SUB CANE VIGILANTI EDITIO QVARTA

Sumptibus & typis æneis Iudoci Hondij, Amsterdami . . . 1619. fol. ff. 378: plates; illus., maps, ports.
Maps C.3.c.8.

In French. Revised by Judocus Hondius I and Petrus Montanus. The maps of Xaintonge, f. 145v, signed: Amstelodami. Excusum apud Iudocum et Henricum Hondium, that of Beauvais, ff. 157v–158r: Amstelodami, Judocus Hondius ex[dit]. The preface is by Judocus Hondius the Elder. The letterpress text printed by Joannes Janssonius at Amsterdam? All the engravings are coloured. This copy corresponds to the description in *Koeman* no. Me 26B. Ownership inscriptions: Wm Thaw 167⁷/₈; Edwin Lovegrove 1853.

MERULA, Gulielmus. Theses de peste. 1614. *See* VORSTIUS, Aelius Everardus

M79 MERULA, Paulus
Paulli . . . Merulæ COSMOGRAPHIÆ GENERALIS LIBRI TRES: Item GEOGRAPHIÆ PARTICVLARIS LIBRI QVATVOR: Quibus EVROPA in genere; speciatim HISPANIA, GALLIA, ITALIA, describuntur. Cum tabulis Geographicis æneis. EX OFFICINA PLANTINIANA RAPHELENGIJ. M.D.CV. Væneunt etiam Amsteldami apud CORNELIVM NICOLAI. 4° pp. 1358: plates; illus., maps
C.74.d.9.

The maps signed: I. Hondius, Joannes â Doetechum, Baptista a Doetechum, Petrus Kærius. With an engraved view of Madrid on p. 342. Published at Leiden.

M80 MERULA, Paulus
Paulli . . . Merulæ COSMOGRAPHIÆ GENERALIS LIBRI TRES . . . Cum tabulis Geographicis æneis multo . . . accuratioribus. AMSTERODAMI, Apud Iudocum Hondium. M DC XXI. (col.) LVGDVNI BATAVORVM, Typis ISAACI ELZEVIRI . . . M.D.CXX. Sumptibus IVDOCI HONDII. fol. pp. 1075; illus., maps
C.73.g.4.

The titlepage is engraved. The view of Madrid, on p. 262, is in woodcut.

M81 MERULA, Paulus
FIDELIS ET SVCCINCTA RERVM ADVERSVS ANGELVM MERVLAM TRAGICE ANTE XLVII. ANNOS, QVADRIENNIVM, ET QVOD EXCVRRIT, AB INQVISITORIBVS GESTARVM COMMEMORATIO, AVCTORE PAVLLO . . . MERVLA . . . Qui omnia . . . ex Autographis conlecta FIXIT . . . LVGDVNI BATAVORVM, Apud LVDOVICVM ELZEVIRIVM . . . TYPIS, Ioannis NicolaI F. DorpI. M DC IV. 4° pp. 109
491.c.24.

With a genealogy.

M82 MERULA, Paulus
V. CL. PAVLI MERVLÆ Oratio posthuma. DE NATVRA REIP. BATAVICÆ Ex auctoris schedis descripta. IOACHIMVS MORSIVS vulgavit. LVGDVNI BATAVORVM, Typis IACOBI MARCI. M.DC XVIII. 4° sig.):(^{3}AB^{4}C^6
835.c.28(4); 12301.bbb.34(3).

The preliminaries consist of the title-leaf and sig.):(3,4. The catchword on the titlepage verso is correctly taken up on the following page.

MERULA, Paulus. Placaten ende ordonnantien op 'tstuck vande wildernissen. 1605. *See* NETHERLANDS. Before 1581 [Collections]

M83 MERULA, Paulus
(tp. 1) Tijdt-Threzoor. Ofte kort ende bondich Verhael Van den STANDT DER KERCKEN, Ende de VVERELTLICKE REGIERINGE: Vervatende . . . De gedenckwaerdichste geschiedenissen over den Aertbodem/van Christi Geboorte af tot . . . 1614 . . . opgesocht ende by een gestelt, den tijdt ontrent van twaelf hondert Iaren; Door PAVLLVM MERVLAM . . . Voltrocken/ende vervolght . . . by . . . GVLIELMVM MERVLAM. GEDRVCT TOT LEYDEN, By Jan Claesz. van Dorp . . . 1614. [etc.]

(tp.2=p.793) VERVOLGH . . . Door GVLIELMVM MERVLAM . . . GEDRVCT TOT LEYDEN, By Jan Claesz. van Dorp . . . 1613. fol. pp.1016: plate; port.
1505/354.

With a biography of Paulus Merula by Bartholomaeus Clingius. The portrait dated 1602, signed: J. Mattham fecit, with Latin verses by Daniel Heinsius.

M84 MERWEN, Franciscus vander
THESES MEDICÆ DE ANGINA. QVAS . . . Pro Gradu in Medicina consequendo DEFENDET FRANCISCVS vander MERWEN . . . LVGDVNI BATAVORVM, Ex Officina THOMÆ BASSON . . . 1603. 4° sig. A^4
7306.f.6(8).

M85 METEREN, Emanuel van
[Belgische ofte Nederlantsche historie.] Commentarien Ofte Memorien Van-den Nederlandtschen Staet/Handel/Oorloghen ende Gheschiedenissen van onsen tyden . . . Beschreven door EMANVEL van METEREN. Ende By hem voor de tweede ende leste reyse over-sien/verbetert ende vermeerdert . . . Oock soo verre ghebrocht totten af-standt van Wapenen ende Vrede/in't Jaer 1608. Ghedruckt op Schotlandt/buyten Danswijck/by Hermes van Loven. Voor den Autheur. (col.) Tot Londen, Voor Emanuel van Meteren/1610. fol. ff.244, CXCIX, 167, 36; illus.; port.
9405.h.6.

With an appendix up to the conclusion of the Truce in 1609. The portrait of Van Meteren signed: R. D. Boud: sculp. The titlepage is partly engraved. Both imprint and colophon are false; printed at Amsterdam.

M86 METEREN, Emanuel van
[Belgische ofte Nederlantsche historie.] EMANVELS VAN METEREN Historie der Neder-landscher ende haerder Na-buren Oorlogen ende geschiedenissen, TOT DEN IARE M.VI.^{C}XII. Nu de laestemael bij hem . . . merckelijck verbetert en in, XXXII. boecken voltrocken. Is mede hier by gevoegt des Autheurs leven. Verrijckt beneffens de Land-Caerte met by na hondert correcte Conterfeytsels . . . gedruckt . . . M.DC.XIV. IN S'GRAVEN-HAGHE, By Hillebrant Iacobssz . . . 1614. [etc.] fol. ff.671: plate; illus., map, port.
9405.g.4.

The officially approved edition, sometimes said to have been edited by Gilles van Ledenberg and Hugo de Groot. The biography by Simeon Ruytinck. The partly engraved titlepage signed: W. Delff. sculp. Some of the engraved portraits with engraved Dutch captions signed: N. de Clerck exc.

M87 METEREN, Emanuel van
[Belgische ofte Nederlantsche historie.] L'HISTOIRE DES PAYS-BAS D'EMANUEL DE METEREN . . . Traduit du Flamend en Francoys par IDL Haÿe. Auec La Vie de lAutheur. EN LA HAYE. Chez Hillebrant Jacobz Wou . . . 1618. fol. ff.720: plate; illus., map, port.
591.i.8.

A translation of the 1614 Dutch edition. With the same map and portrait, but most of the illustrations are reverse copies, signed: H. Jacobsen, or: Jacopsen, exc., but with the original engraved Dutch captions. The map is mutilated.

M88 METEREN, Emanuel van
[Belgische ofte Nederlantsche historie.] (tp.1) HISTORIA, Oder Eigentliche vnd warhaffte Beschreibung aller fuͤrnehmen Kriegshaͤndel . . . so sich in Niderlandt . . . zugetragen haben . . . Alles . . . beschrieben/vnd in 19. Buͤcher

abgetheilt . . . Durch Emanuel Materanum, sampt einer General der Niderlanden Charten/vnd aller Gubernatorn Bildnussen . . . in Kupffer aussgestochen . . . Jetzo wider auffs new aussgangen/vnd . . . gebessert vnd vermehrt. Gedruckt zu Arnhem Bey Johan Jansen . . . M.DCJJJJ.
(tp.2) Niderländische Historia . . . von Anfang des Jahrs 99. biss in gegenwertiges . . . Jahr vñ Monat Septemb. 1604 . . . zu continuation vnd verföglicher ergäntzung der Historischen Beschreibung Emanuelis von Meteren/ zusamen getragen . . . Gedruckt zu Arnheim/Bey Johan Jansen . . . M.DCIIII. fol. 2 pt.: pp.878; 876 [238]; illus.
C.47.i.22.
The illustrations occur in pt.1 only and are reverse copies of the circular portraits found in the first Latin edition. Imperfect; wanting the map. Ownership inscription: Monasterij Zwifaltens.

M89 METIUS, Adriaan
(tp.1) VNIVERSAE ASTRONOMIÆ brevis . . . INSTITVTIO . . . Opus Tomis IV. distinctum: AVTORE ADRIANO ADRIANI METIO . . . FRANEKERÆ, Ex Officina AEGIDII RADAEI . . . M.D.CV.
(tp.2) INSTITVTIONIS ASTRONOMICÆ TOMVS SECVNDVS . . . FRANEKERÆ, Apud AEGIDIVM RADAEVM . . . M.D.CVI.
(tp.3) INSTITVTIONIS ASTRONOMICAE TOMVS TERTIVS . . . FRANEKERÆ, Apud AEGIDIVM RADAEVM . . . M.D.CV.
(tp.4) De Novis ab autore inventis INSTRVMENTIS ET Modo quo per eadem stellarum fixarum situs solisque motus annuus observantur. Tractatus brevis & utilis. 8° 4 pt.: pp.264; 235; 292; 135: plate; illus.
C.74.a.13; 531.e.43.
Pt. 4 includes records of observations made in September 1607 and was probably published in 1608. The copy at C.74.a.13 lacks the plate; that at 531.e.43 consists of pt.4 only, but has the plate. Ownership inscription in the copy at 531.e.43: H. Gellibr. 1620.

M90 MEURSIUS, Joannes; the Elder
IOANNIS MEURSI AESCHYLVS, SOPHOCLES, EVRIPIDES. Sive DE TRAGOEDIIS EORVM, Libri III. LVGDVNI BATAVORVM, Apud GODEFRIDVM BASSON . . . M.DC.XIX. 4° pp.127
999.d.2; G.8415.
The copy at G.8415 is the author's presentation copy to Rochus van Honert.

M91 MEURSIUS, Joannes; the Elder
(tp.1) IOANNIS MEVRSI DE FVNERE Liber Singularis. In quo Græci & Romani ritus. Additum est DE PVERPERIO Syntagma. HAGÆ-COMITIS, Ex Officinâ Hillebrandi Iacobi. M.D.C.IV.
(tp.2) IOANNIS MEVRSI DE PVERPERIO Syntagma . . . M.D.C.IV. 8° pp.233; 21
802.b.12.

M92 MEURSIUS, Joannes; the Elder
(tp.1) IOANNIS MEVRSI DE GLORIA LIBER VNVS. Cum AVCTARIO PHILOLOGICO. LVGDVNI BATAVORVM, Apud Andream Cloucquium . . . M.D.CI.
(tp.2=p.107) IOANNIS MEVRSI AVCTARIVM PHILOLOGICVM. LVGDVNI BATAVORVM, Apud Andream Cloucquium . . . M;D.CI. 8° pp.196
528.e.1.

M93 MEURSIUS, Joannes; the Elder
IOANNIS MEVRSI DE LVXV ROMANORVM Liber Singularis. Sive Commentarius Vberior in locum Senecæ Epist. CXIV. ITEM MANTISA. HAGÆ-COMITIS. Ex Officinâ Hillebrandi Iacobi . . . M.DC.V. 4° pp.88
590.d.3.

M94 MEURSIUS, Joannes; the Elder

IOANNIS MEVRSI De POPVLIS ATTICAE Liber singularis . . . LVGDVNI BATAVORVM, Ex Officinâ LVDOVICI ELZEVIRI. Typis GODEFRIDI BASSON . . . M.DC.XVI. 4° pp. 149
584.b.29.

Ownership inscriptions: J.v.Toup; Thos Tyrwhitt 1786.

M95 MEURSIUS, Joannes; the Elder

IOANNIS MEVRSI ELEVSINIA. SIVE, DE CERERIS Eleusinæ sacro, ac festo. Liber singularis. LVGDVNI BATAVORVM, Ex Officinâ ELZEVIRIANA . . . M D.C.XIX. 4° pp. 104
4505.b.28.

MEURSIUS, Joannes; the Elder. Ferdinandus Albanus. 1615. *See* below: Rerum Belgicarum libri quatuor.

M96 MEURSIUS, Joannes; the Elder

IOANNIS MEVRSI GLOSSARIVM Græcobarbarum . . . LVGDVNI BATAVORVM, Ex Officinâ THOMÆ BASSON. M D.C.X. (col.) Exemplaria etiam prostant apud Ludovicum Elzevirium. 4° pp. 808
C.79.b.8.

M97 MEURSIUS, Joannes; the Elder

IOANNIS MEVRSI GLOSSARIVM GRAECO-BARBARVM . . . EDITIO ALTERA Emendata, & . . . aucta. LVGDVNI BATAVORVM, Apud LVDOVICVM ELZEVIRIVM . . . M.D.C.XIV. 4° pp. 672; illus., port.
1560/1689; 66.b.3.

Printed by Henrick van Haestens at Leiden.

M98 MEURSIUS, Joannes; the Elder

IOANNIS MEVRSI GRÆCIA FERIATA. Siue, DE FESTIS Græcorum, Libri VI. LVGDVNI BATAVORVM, Ex Officinâ ELZEVIRIANA . . . M.D.C.XIX. (col.) Lugduni Batavorum, Typis ISAACI ELZEVIRI . . . M D CXIX. 4° pp. 341
585.c.21.

With the exlibris of Charles Burney.

M99 MEURSIUS, Joannes; the Elder

IOANNIS MEVRSI GVLIELMVS AVRIACVS. SIVE, De rebus toto Belgio tam ab eo, quam ejus tempore, gestis; ad excessum Ludouici Requesensij. Pars prima . . . LVGDVNI BATAVORVM, Excudebat ISAACVS ELZEVIRIVS . . . M D CXXI. (col.) LVGDVNI BATAVORVM, Excudebat ISAACVS ELZEVIRIVS . . . M D CXXI. 4° pp. 418; illus., port.
1055.g.7; 154.i.20.

No more published. Ownership inscriptions: 1055.g.7: Joannis Mauritii ex dono . . . Ioannis de Laet; 154.i.20: C. H. de Luttichau.

M100 MEURSIUS, Joannes; the Elder

ICONES Ad vivum delineatæ et expressæ, VIRORVM CLARIORVM qui præcipue scriptis Academiam LVGDVNO-BATAVAM illustrarunt. LVGD.-BAT. Apud ANDREAM CLOUCQUIUM M.D.CIX. fol. 36 unnumbered and unsigned leaves
C.74.d.6(1).

Compiled anonymously by Joannes Meursius. The proofs of the plates later used in 'Illustris Academia Lugd-Batava'. Engraved throughout except for the preface. The titlepage signed: G: Swan. fecit Anno 1609. In a binding bearing the English royal arms and the Prince of Wales's feathers.

MEURSIUS, Joannes; the Elder. Icones, elogia ac vitae professorum Lugdunensium apud Batavos. 1617. *See* infra: Illustris Academia Lugd-Batava.

M101 MEURSIUS, Joannes; the Elder

Illustris ACADEMIA LUGD-BATAVA: id est VIRORVM Clarissimorum ICONES, ELOGIA ac vitæ, qui eam scriptis suis illustrarunt. LUGD-BAT. Apud ANDREAM CLOUCQUIUM M.D.C.XIII. 4° sig. ★-★★★, A–X⁴Y¹; illus.

731.g.16(1).

Compiled anonymously by Joannes Meursius. The titlepage is engraved, signed: G: Swan. fecit. The illustrations include the engraved portraits published in 1609, entitled: 'Icones ad vivum delineatae'.

M102 MEURSIUS, Joannes; the Elder

[Illustris Academia Lugd-Batava.] Illustrium HOLLANDIAE & VVESTFRISIAE ORDINVM ALMA ACADEMIA LEIDENSIS . . . LVGDVNI BATAVORVM. Apud Iacobum Marci, & Iustum à Colster . . . M.DC.XIV. 4° sig.a-g⁴, pp.231, sig.★-★★★★★★★★⁴: plate; illus.

731.g.16(2); 8355.c.14.

The compilation by Joannes Meursius originally published as 'Illustris Academia Lugd-Batava', here published without naming him and with additional matter sometimes attributed to Jan Orlers. The portraits of the professors are smaller and less good than in the Clouck editions. The plate appears to be optional, not found in a large proportion of known copies of this edition. It represents the inaugural procession at the foundation of Leiden University in 1575 and is present in the copy at 731.g.16(2), but absent from that at 8355.c.14. Other additional engravings show the University, the library, the anatomy theatre and the botanic garden. The copy at 8355.c.14 has the ownership inscription of John Percival, Earl of Egmont, 1736, and is in a binding with the arms of Louis Henri, Comte de Loménie.

M103 MEURSIUS, Joannes; the Elder

[Illustris Academia Lugd-Batava.] 4° 2 leaves

Maps C.9.d.4(83).

The plate showing the inaugural procession of Leiden University in 1575, apparently published for inclusion in the 1614 edition by Jacob Marcusz and Joost van Colster of Joannes Meursius's 'Illustris Academia Lugd-Batava', but sometimes found separate and probably made between 1610 and 1614. Part of the Beudeker collection.

M104 MEURSIUS, Joannes, the Elder

[Illustris Academia Lugd-Batava.] ICONES, ELOGIA ac vitæ PROFESSORVM Lugdunensium apud Batavos: quibus addita sunt omnia Academiæ ORNAMENTA . . . æri incisa. LVG. BATAV. Apud ANDREAM CLOUQUIUM . . . 1617. 4° sig.★-★★★, A–X⁴Y¹, pp.38

132.b.15.

A reissue of the edition of 1613, entered above, still anonymous, with additional matter. The engraved titlepage has been cut to allow for insertion of the new letterpress title and imprint. Imperfect; wanting the plates described on pp.33–38; or was this copy issued before the plates were ready?

M105 MEURSIUS, Joannes; the Elder

IOANNIS MEVRSI ORCHESTRA. SIVE DE SALTATIONIBVS VETERVM, Liber Singularis. LVGDVNI BATAVORVM, Ex Officinâ GODEFRIDI BASSON . . . M.D.C.XVIII. 4° pp.111

802.b.13(1); 802.d.18(3).

M106 MEURSIUS, Joannes; the Elder

IOANNIS MEVRSI PANATHENÆA. SIVE, DE MINERVÆ Illo gemino festo, Liber Singularis. LVGDVNI BATAVORVM, Ex Officinâ ELZEVIRIANA . . . M D.C.XIX. 4° pp.48

4505.c.31.

M107 MEURSIUS, Joannes; the Elder

IOANNIS MEVRSI RERVM BELGICARVM Libri Quatuor. In Quibus FERDINANDI ALBANI Sexennium, belli Belgici principium. ADDITVR QVINTVS, seorsim anteà excusus, in quo INDVCIARVM Historia; & eiusdem belli finis. LVGDVNI BATAVORVM, Apud LVDOVICVM ELZEVIRIVM . . . M D C XIV. 4° pp.319

C.81.c.3; 154.n.1.

The original title of bk. 5 was 'Rerum Belgicarum liber unus', published in 1612. Printed by Henrick van Haestens at Leiden.

M108 MEURSIUS, Joannes; the Elder

[Rerum Belgicarum libri quatuor.] IOANNIS MEVRSI FERDINANDVS ALBANVS. Sive, De rebus eius in Belgio per Sexennium gestis, LIBRI IV. in quibus Belli Belgici Principium. ADDITVR DE INDVCIIS, Liber singularis . . . in quo eiusdem belli finis. LVGDVNI BATAVORVM, Apud LVDOVICVM ELZEVIRIVM . . . M DC XV. 4° pp.319

591.b.11(1).

A new edition of 'Rerum Belgicarum libri quatuor'. Printed by Henrick van Haestens at Leiden.

M109 MEXIA, Pedro

SILVA DE VARIA LECION, AGORA VLTIMAMENTE EMENDAda, y de la quarta parte añadida, Compuesta por . . . PEDRO MEXIA . . . EN ANVERES, En la casa de Martin Nucio . . . 1603. [etc.] 8° pp.898

8405.b.50.

Ownership inscription: Ex lib. Matthæi Procopij Niseni.

M110 MEYSIUS, Joannes

DISPVTATIO MEDICA DE Suffocatione Vterina, QVAM . . . tueri conabitur IOANNES MEYSIVS . . . LVGDVNI BATAVORVM, Apud Thomam Basson . . . 1605. 4° sig. A^4

7306.f.6(23).

MIDDELGEEST, Simon van. For books issued under the pseudonym Yemant Adams, sometimes used by Simon van Middelgeest, but not attributable to him with certainty, *see* ADAMS, Yemant. For publications under the pseudonym Yemand van Waer-mond, sometimes used by Simon van Middelgeest, but not attributable to him with certainty, *see* WAER-MOND, Yemand van

M111 MIGOEN, Jacobus Wilhelmi

Proeve Des nu onlangs uyt-ghegheven Drooms/off t'samen spraack tusschen den Coning van Hispanien ende den Paus van Roomen. Met noch eenen anderen Droom/contrarie den voorschreven. Mits gaders eene vermaninghe/Aan alle Vroome ende Ghetrouwe Vader-landers/hoe zij haar in dezer Tijdt te draghen hebben . . . Beschreven door een Lief-hebber aller Menschen/maar in sonderheydt den Godt-zoeckeñ ende Trou-Hertighen In-gheboorne dezer Vrijer Provincien. Door NISEMVOLBG 472HC58A22W. 4° sig. A^4

8079.c.50.

Pseudonymous. Sometimes wrongly attributed to Willem Usselincx. The book referred to is 'Eene treffelijcke tsamensprekinge tusschen den Paus ende Coninck van Spangien'. Published in 1607/8, probably by Jacobus Migoen himself at Gouda.

M112 MIJLE, Cornelis van der

NAERDER VERTOOCH AEN DE . . . STATEN GENERAEL, Over ghegheven By den Heere van der MYLE. ENDE Antwoort/aen de selve . . . STATEN GENERAEL. Overghegeven by d'Heer van SOMMELSDIICK. In Augusto In s'Graven-Haghe. 1618. 4° pp.14

T.2422(20).

A defence of François van Aerssen. Printed by Aert Meuris at The Hague? This copy corresponds to the one described in *Knuttel* no. 2648.

M113 MIJLE, Cornelis van der
NAERDER VERTOOCH . . . Overghegheven by d'Heer van SOMMELSDIICK. In Augusto In s'Graven-Haghe. 1618. 4° pp. 14
106.c.46(2).
A variant of the preceding, with some differences in the position of signatures and catchwords, a different number 9 in the pagination and different justification, e.g. the left-hand margin of the first paragraph on p. 14. Printed by Aert Meuris at The Hague?

M114 MIJLE, Cornelis van der
NAERDER VERTOOCH Aen de . . . Staten Generael/overgegheven by den Heere Van der Mijlen. waer inne deselve versocht worden . . . goet te vinden . . . dat sekere poincten int Cort Antwoort gheteeckent Francois van Aerssen/hare Hog. Mog. overgegeven/by den selven/mogen werden bewesen. Met corte Annotatien . . . verclaert ende vereert. GHEDRVCT Voor't goet bericht der Mijlen/Die verbreeckt sijn quade pijlen. 4° pp. 13
T.2422(21).
Published in 1618. A defence of François van Aerssen, subsequent to the preceding. Corresponding to the copy described in *Knuttel* no. 2649.

M115 MIJLE, Cornelis van der
NAERDER VERTOOCH Aen de . . . Staten Generael/overghegheven by den Heere Van der Mijlen. Waer inne deselve versocht worden . . . goet te vinden . . . dat sekere poincten int Cort Antwoordt gheteeckent Francois van Aerssen . . . mogen werden bewesen. Met corte Annotatien op de kant verklaert ende vereert. GHEDRVCT Voor't goet bericht der Mijlen/Die verbreeckt sijn quade pijlen. 4° pp. 13
106.d.46(1).
A different edition from the preceding. Published in 1618. Corresponding to the copy described in *Van der Wulp* no. 1574.

M116 MIJLE, Cornelis van der
ONTDECKINGE Vande valsche Spaensche Iesuijtische Practijcke: Ghebruyckt jegens eenige vande beste Patriotten, ende ghetrouste Dienaren van t'Landt, by de Autheurs van tvvee . . . Libellen: Het een gheintituleert/Noodtwendigh ende levendigh Discours &c. Het ander/Practijcke vanden Spaenschen Raedt &c. Inghestelt by een Liefhebber vande VVaerheydt, ende van het Vaderlandt. IN S'GRAVEN-HAGHE, By Hillebrant Jacobssen . . . 1618. 4° pp. 34
T.2422(8).
Pseudonymous. The 'Noodtwendigh . . . discours' sometimes attributed to François van Aerssen.

M117 MIJLE, Cornelis van der
VERTOOGH AENDE . . . Staten Generael der Vereenighde Nederlanden. By den Heere vander Mijle overghegheven. Teghen seecker Fameus Libel hare Ho. Mog. gepresenteert/onder den Naem van Remonstrantie, wesende onderteyckent François van Aerssen. IN S'GRAVEN-HAGHE, By Hillebrant Iacobsz . . . 1618. 4° pp. 37
T.2422(13).
Corresponding to the copy described in *Knuttel* no. 2642.

M118 MIJLE, Cornelis van der

VERTOOGH AENDE . . . Staten Generael . . . By den Heere vander Mijle overghegheven. Teghen seecker Fameus Libel . . . IN S'GRAVEN-HAGHE, By Hillebrant Iacobsz . . . 1618. 4° pp.48

106.d.47.

An enlarged edition of the preceding, containing 'Translaten van eenige Latijnsche ende Fransche proposten ende brieven'. Corresponding to the copy described in *Van der Wulp* no.1572.

MIKROKOSMOS. 1610. *See* HAECHT GOIDTSENHOVEN, Laurens van

MILIUS, Abrahamus. *See* MYL, Abraham vander

MIRACLES lately wrought by the intercession of the . . . Virgin Marie. 1606. *See* NUMAN, Philips. Histoire des miracles.

MIRAEUS, Aubertus. *See* LE MIRE, Aubert

MIRAEUS, Joannes; Bishop

For publications by Joannes Miraeus in his capacity as Bishop of Antwerp *see* ANTWERP. Diocese

Le MIROIR de la . . . tyrannie espagnole . . . au Pays-Bas. 1620. *See* GYSIUS, Joannes

M119 MISOCOSMUS

CONTEMTVS MVNDI Opusculum antiquum, hactenus non editum; Pio, & eleganti RHYTHMO Christiani hominis vitam ad Pietatis normam, & RHYTHMVM . . . componens: Authore MISOCOSMO. Ex vetustis Membranis nobilis Monasterij s. HVBERTI in Arduenna, descriptum, & vulgatum. LVXEMBVRGI, Excudebat Hubertus Reulandt . . . M.DC.XVIII. 8° pp.31

1213.k.20(1).

The editor's address to the reader signed: I.R.S.I., i.e. Joannes Roberti S. J.

M120 MISOPONERUS

MISOPONERI SATYRICON. Cum notis aliquot . . . LVGDVNI BATAVORVM, Apud SEBASTIANVM VVOLZIVM. M.DCXVII. 8° pp.143

90.i.31(1).

The attribution suggested in the introductory verses to Isaac Casaubon is intentionally misleading. The imprint is false.

M121 MISSA

MISSA ROMANA, Ofte Roomsche Misse. Al waer int corte . . . aengewesen wert/wat in der Pape Misse wert bedreven . . . Wt het gheschreven Hoochduytsch Exemplaer . . . in dese Nederlandtsche algemeene Tale . . . rijmens wijse/overgheset/gebetert ende vermeerdert. Ende . . . in openbaren Druck uytgegeven. Door (I.C.N.P.B.) eenen bysondere Lief-hebber der Christelicken Religie . . . Hier achter aen is mede by-gevoeght, een Echo Iesuitica. IN 'SGRAVEN-HAGE, By Aert Meuris . . . 1621. [etc.] 4° pp.11

3925.bbb.31.

The main part in Dutch with occasional quotations in Latin; the Echo Iesuitica in Latin only.

MISSAE quinque . . . quatuor vocum. 1619. *See* BERNARDI, Stefano

MISSAE V, VI, et VII vocum. 1602. *See* PEVERNAGE, Andreas

MISSAE sex IV, V et VI vocum. 1604. *See* RIMONTE, Pietro

MISSAE decem quatuor, quinque, sex et septem vocum. 1618. *See* LEONARDUS Nervius; Capuchin

MISSALS. *See* LITURGIES. Latin Rite

M122 MISSIVE

MISSIVE. Daer in Kortelijck ende grondigh werdt vertoont/hoe veel de Vereenighde Nederlanden gheleghen is aen de Oost ende WestIndische Navigatie . . . Gheschreven aen een seker Vriendt ende Lief-hebber van de Wel-standt des Vader-landts, eñ tot ghemeenen dienst der Inghesetene van dien. TOT ARNHEM, By Ian Iansz. . . . 1621. 4° sig. A-D^4E^2

1029.e.53.

A copy of the edition with the additional lines on the last page, corresponding to the copy described in *Knuttel* no. 3237.

M123 MOERBERGHEN, Wilhelmus a

THESES MEDICAE DE OBSTRVCTIONE HEPATIS, Quas . . . Pro gradu doctoratus in Medicina consequendo, Tueri conabitur WILHELMVS A MOERBERGEN . . . LVGDVNI BATAVORVM, Ex Officina Thomæ Basson, 1607. 4° sig. A^4

7306.f.g.(14).

The spelling 'Moerberghen' is used in the dedication.

M124 MOERMAN, Jan

DE CLEYN VVERELT: Daer in . . . door . . . Poêtische, Moralische en Historische exempelen betoont vvort, alles vvat den mensche . . . heeft te vlieden ende naer te volghen . . . Rethorijckelick uytgestelt door M[r]. Ian Moerman, ende met . . . Const-platen . . . verciert. T'AMSTELREDAM, By Dirck Pietersz. . . . 1608. (col.) T'AMSTELREDAM, By Dirck Pietersz. [etc.] 4° ff. 74; illus.

637.g.15.

The engravings are derived from those of Gerard de Jode in his Μικροκόσμος with text by Laurens van Haecht Goidtsenhoven. The additional titlepage, engraved and dated 1608, is signed by C. J. Visscher and reads 'De Cleyne Werreld'.

M125 MOLANUS, Joannes; Lovaniensis

D. IOANNIS MOLANI . . . De Historia SS. IMAGINVM ET PICTVRARVM PRO VERO EARVM VSV CONTRA ABVSVS. LIBRI IIII. DVACI, Apud GERARDVM PINCHON . . . 1617. (col.) DVACI, Ex Typographia PETRI AVROI . . . 1617. 8° pp. 456

1492.d.77.

Ownership inscription: In usum Collegii Hibernorum Antuerpiæ.

M126 MOLANUS, Joannes; Lovaniensis

NATALES SANCTORVM BELGII, & eorundem CHRONICA RECAPITVLATIO, AVCTORE IOANNE MOLANO . . . Recogniti, notis aucti & illustrati opera quorundam S. Theol. Doctorum & in vniversitate Duac. Professorum. DVACI, Typis Viduæ PETRI BORREMANS . . . M.DC.XVI. 8° ff. 200

1371.c.1.

An 'Auctarium' to this work was published in 1626.

M127 MOLINA, Antonio de; Carthusian Monk

[Exercicios espirituales.] A TREATISE OF MENTAL PRAYER . . . By Fr. Ant. de Molina . . . WHEREVNTO Is adioyned a . . . Treatise of Exhortation to Spirituall Profit. VVritten by F. Francis Arias . . . Togeather with a Dialogue of CONTRITION and ATTRITION. All translated out of Spanish into English by a Father of the Society of IESVS . . . M.DC.XVII. 12° pp. 365

4412.f.39.

The 'Dialogue' is by Richard Haller. The first piece translated by John Sweetnam, the other two by Thomas Everard. The editor's dedication signed: I. VV., i.e. John Wilson. Without imprint; published by the English College press at St. Omer. Ownership inscription: NL.

M128 MOLINA, Ludovicus; Jesuit

LIBERI ARBITRII CONCORDIA CVM GRATIAE DONIS DIVINA PRAESCIENTIA PROVIDENTIA PRAEDESTINATIONE ET REPROBATIONE AVCTORE LVDOVICO MOLINA . . . Tertia editio, auctior & emendatior. ANTVERPIÆ EX OFFICINA IOACH. TROGNÆSII. M.DCIX. [etc.] 4° pp.405
1568/5993.

Ownership inscriptions: Gabriel Wessels; S. Maria de Scala; Bibl. Carmelitanum Merkelbeek.

M129 MONARDES, Nicolas

[Primera y segunda y tercera parte de la Historia medicinal de las cosas que se traen de nuestras Indias.] Beschrijvinge van het heerlijcke ende vermaerde kruydt/ wassende in de West Indien aldaer ghenaemt Picielt, ende by den Spaenjaerden Tabaco, eñ van desselvē wonderlijcke operatien eñ krachten/gemaect by D. Monardes . . . eñ overgheset Door Nicolaes Iansz vander Woudt. TOT ROTTERDAM, By Jan van Waesberghe. 8° sig.AB^8; illus.
1038.a.54.

Translated from pt.2 of the 'Historia'. The translator has added an extract from Mathias de Lobel's 'Herbarium' and reports some medical experiments of his own. He mentions a Spanish sailor, wounded in 1588 and not healed until he used tobacco some eight or nine years later, suggesting a publication date about 1610. The titlepage woodcut shows the plant and its use.

M130 MONCAEIUS, Franciscus

AARON PVRGATVS SIVE DE VITVLO AVREO, LIBRI DVO. SIMVL CHERVBORVM MOSIS, VITVLORVM IEROBOAMI, THERAPHORVM MICHÆ, Formam, & historiam . . . explicantes. Auctore FRANCISCO MONCÆIO . . . ATREBATI, Ex Typographia Gulielmi Riuerij . . . M.D.C.VI. [etc.] 8° pp.393
481.a.23; 1019.f.15.

With an additional titlepage, engraved, signed: MB f., i.e. Martin Baes fecit. The copy at 1019.f.15 lacks the printed titlepage. It has two cancel leaves bearing pp.31, 32 and 133, 134 bound between sig. ***1, 2, but has the cancellands in their correct places, the first having been cut. The copy at 481.a.23 has had the cancels put in their correct places where the cancellands have been removed.

M131 MONCAEIUS, Franciscus

ECCLESIÆ CHRISTIANÆ VETERIS BRITANNICÆ INCVNABVLA REGIA. SIVE DE CLAVDIA RVFINA . . . syntagma. Autore FRAN. MONCÆIO . . . TORNACI, Typis CAROLI MARTINI. M.DC.XIV.
8° pp.35
1371.b.27.

M132 MONCY, Jean de

(tp.1) DIALOGUES RVSTIQVES D'VN PRESTRE DE Village, d'vn Berger, le Censier, & sa femme. TRES-UTILE PVR CEVX qui demeurent es pays où ils n`ont [*sic*] le moyen d'estre instruits par la predication de la Parole de Dieu. Seconde edition reueuë & corrigée. A LEYDEN, Chez LOYS ELZEVIER. M.D.C.XV.
(tp.2) PARTIE II. DES DIALOGVES RVSTIQVES . . . Par I.D.M. A FRANCKENTHAL. Par Jaques Flamand . . . 1615. 16° 2 pt.: pp.192; 267
855.a.7.

Anonymous. The preface to pt.1 signed: I.D.M., the poem at the end of pt.2 signed: J.D.M. Loué soit Dieu. The work has also been attributed to Pierre du Moulin. A copy described in *Willems* no.70 has a device which is not present in this copy. (Willems enquired at the British Museum, but was not told of this copy.) Both parts printed by Jaques Flamand at Frankenthal. Another, imperfect, edition of pt.1, placed at T.1590 (2), cannot be dated precisely and may be part of an earlier edition, printed at Geneva?

MONS pietatis. 1619. *See* CORBERGHER, Wenceslaus

MONSIGR. fate voi. 1617. *See* SWEET, John

MONSTER vande leere der Amsterdamsche predicanten. 1616. *See* DWINGLO, Bernardus

MONSTERKENS van de nieuwe Hollandsche inquisitie. 1620. *See* SLATIUS, Henricus

M133 MONTAIGNE, Michel de

LES ESSAIS DE MICHEL SEIGNEUR DE MONTAIGNE. EDITION NOVVELLE, PRISE SVR L'EXEMPLAIRE trouué apres le deces de l'Autheur, Reueu & augmenté d'vn tiers outre les precedentes impressions . . . A LEYDEN, PAR JEHAN DOREAV. M.DCII. 8° pp.1031

C.107.d.9.

The imprint is false; published at Geneva. With the exlibris of George Percival Best and ownership inscriptions: Edward Cane; Mortimer L. Schiff.

M134 MONTAIGNE, Michel de

LES ESSAIS DE MICHEL SEIGNEVR DE MONTAIGNE. EDITION NOVVELLE ENRICHIE DANOTATIONS en marge. Corrigée- & augmentée d'un tiers outre les precedentes Impressions Auec vne Table . . . Plus la vie de lAutheur Extraite de ses propres escrits . . . A ENVERS, CHEZ ABRAHAM MAIRE. 8° pp.1129: plate; port.

1478.aaa.41.

The titlepage is engraved. The imprint appears false: no other work known with it and no such printer or publisher known at Antwerp. A typed note in this copy mentions another issue with a colophon naming the printer Nicolas l'Oyselet at Rouen and the date 1617. The typography of this copy appears French. A copy at the Municipal Library at Antwerp bears an inscription by Frans Olthoff doubting the imprint and suggesting the date 1649. More recent suggestions that this pirated edition was published at Antwerp are not supported by any evidence. With the exlibris of George Percival Best and his references to similar copies with various publishers' addresses.

MONTANEA, Georgia. *See* MONTENAY, Georgette de

M135 MONTANUS, Eusebius

[Een clare beantwoordinghe.] Een claer bevvijs Dat een Christen het Ampt der Overheydt mach bedienen . . . Midtsgaders, Antwoort op dese Vraghe: Of de Christelijcke onder-Overheden hare hoogher-Overheydt . . . moghen teghenstaen . . . Door Eusebius Montanus . . . t'Amsterdam, By Marten Jansz. Brandt . . . 1616. 4° pp.31

T.2246(5).

A new edition of 'Een clare beantwoordinghe', 1588. The name Eusebius Montanus has sometimes been thought to be a pseudonym of Petrus Dathenus.

M136 MONTENAY, Georgette de

[Emblemes, et devises chrestiennes.] MONVMENTA EMBLEMATVM CHRISTIANORVM VIRTVTVM . . . chorum . . . adumbrantia. RHYTHMIS GALLICIS . . . primùm conscripta, Figuris æneis incisa, & ad instar ALBI AMICORVM exhibita, à GEORGIA MONTANEA . . . ET NVNC INTERPRETATIOne Metrica, Latina, Hispanica, Italica, Germanica, Anglica & Belgica, donata. Curâ & impensâ IOANNIS-CAROLI VNCKELII . . . Francofurt. ad Mœnum . . . MDCXIX. 8° pp.447; illus., port.

637.d.10.

Including a Dutch version. The emblems and portrait engraved by Pierre Woeriot. The engraved titlepage border signed: Peter Rollos fecit. Imperfect; wanting pp.5,6.

M137 MONTENAY, Georgette de

[Emblemes, et devises chrestiennes.] A Booke of armes, or remembrance, WHEREIN AR [*sic*] . . . GODLY EMBLEmata . . . First by . . . GEORGETTA de Montenay, invented and only in the Frenchtongve elabourated; Bot now, in severall Langvages, As; Latin, Spanish, Italian, Highdutch, Euglish [*sic*], and Lovedutch [*sic*], méetre or verse Wys . . . declared, and augmented. Printed by care, and charges, of Iohann-Carl Vnckels . . . in Franckfurtt am Mayn . . . MDCXIX. 8° pp.447; illus., port.

637.d.11.

Another issue of the preceding.

M138 MONTGOMMERY de Courbouzon, Louis de

[Le fléau d'Aristogiton.] Den Aristogitonschen Dorsch-vlegel/Oft Teghen den Lasteraer der Vaderen Jesuyten/onder den Titel van ANTI-COTON. Door Lovvys de Montgommery, Heere van Courbouzon. Met de dancseggingh der Botervercoopsters van Parijs/dienende tot de antwoorde opt voorgaende/alles wt de Fransche . . . tale overgheset. t'Amsterdam/voor Michiel Colijn . . . 1610. 4° sig.A⁴

T.2421(25).

Imperfect; wanting all after sig.A4, i.e. the text of 'De bedanckinghen der Botter vercoopsters van Parijs'.

M139 MONTMORENCY-WASTINES de Vendegies, Nicolaus de

SOLEMNE CONVIVIVM BIPARTITVM De præcipuis solemnitatibus D.N. IESV CHRISTI, B. MARIÆ ET SANCTORVM . . . AVTHORE . . . NICOLAO A MONTMORENCY . . . ANTVERPIAE APVD GASPAREM BELLERVM CIↃ.ICↃ.XVII [*sic*]. [etc.] 8° 2 pt.: pp.534; 708; illus.

1578/1507; 848.c.6.

The titlepage engraving shows the Crucifixion. The copy at 848.c.6 is imperfect, consisting of the dedication, preface and pt.2 only.

M140 MORAVIA

[6.5.1619.] EDICT Ofte PLACCAET. Van de Stenden des Marquisats van Moravien . . . Waer by de Secte der IESVYTEN . . . werden gheproschribeert ende ghebannen . . . vanden 6. May/1619. Mitsgaders Ghelijcke Edict der Evangelische Stenden des Coninckrijcks van Hungarien, jeghens de IESVYTEN: vanden 16. May/1619. IN 'SGRAVEN-HAGE. By Aert Meuris . . . 1619. [etc.] 4° sig.A⁴

T.2423(15).

M141 MOREJON, Pedro

[Relacion de la persecucion que huuo . . . contra la Iglesia de Iapon.] A BRIEFE RELATION OF THE PERSECVTION LATELY MADE Against the Catholike Christians, in the Kingdome of IAPONIA, Deuided into two Bookes. Taken out of the Annuall Letters of the Fathers of the Society of IESVS, and other Authenticall Informations. Written in Spanish . . . AND Newly translated into English by W. W. Gent. THE FIRST PART. M.DC.XIX. 8° pp.349

C.26.h.16.

Anonymous. The translator is William Wright. No more published in English. Without imprint; published by the English College press at St. Omer.

M142 MORETUS, Balthasar

IVSTI LIPSI SAPIENTIÆ ET LITTERARVM ANTISTITIS Fama postuma. ANTVERPIAE, EX OFFICINA PLANTINIANA Apud Ioannem Moretum. M.DC.VII. 4° pp.114; illus., port.

631.k.4(7); 1481.e.12.

Poems by various authors. Anonymously edited by Balthasar Moretus. The engraved portrait signed: Theodorus Galle. In the copy at 631.k.4(7) the leaves bearing the epitaphs and the portrait are laminated. The copy at 1481.e.12 is imperfect; wanting the portrait.

MORGEN-WECKER der vrye Nederlantsche Provintien. 1610. *See* BAUDAERT, Willem

M143 MORO, Giacomo

(tp.1) IACOBI MORI . . . CONCERTI ECCLESIASTICI I. II. III. ET IIII. VOCVM. Cum Basso Continuo ad Organum. EDITIO ALTERA. CANTVS II. ANTVERPIÆ APVD PETRVM PHALESIVM . . . M.D.C.XXI.
(tp.2) IACOBI MORI . . . CONCERTI ECCLESIASTICI . . . BASSVS. ANTVERPIÆ APVD PETRVM PHALESIVM . . . M.D.C.XXI.
(tp.3) IACOBI MORI . . . CONCERTI ECCLESIASTICI . . . BASSO CONTINVO . . . EDITIO ALTERA. ANTVERPIÆ APVD PETRVM PHALESIVM . . . M.D.C.XXI. 4° 3 pt.: pp.22; 12–23; 22
Music C.268.
The Bassus part lacks all between the titlepage and p.12.

M144 MORTON, Thomas; Bishop

[An exact discoverie of Romish doctrine.] EEN Volcomen ontdeckinghe van de Roomsche Leere/in saecken van Conspiratie ende Rebellye/opghesocht uyt bondighe aenmerckinghe: Vergadert . . . uyt clare ende uyt-ghedruckte hooftstucken ende regulen/vande Leere der Papistische Priesters ende Doctoren. Ghetrouwelijck over-gheset uyt het Enghelsche Exemplair/ghedruckt tot Londen by Felix Kyngston . . . 1605. Hier is noch by ghevoucht een naerder verclaringhe van sommighe stucken die in dit Boeccxken vervatet staen. Alles door F.V.B. Eerst gedruckt in s'Graven-Haghe, By Beuckel Cornelisszoon Nieulandt. Anno 1606. Ende nu Tot Amstelredam by Broer Jansz. [etc.] 4° pp.40
1490.s.3; T.1713(11).
Signed: T.M., i.e. Thomas Morton. The date of publication suggested in *Knuttel* no.1329 is 1609.

MOSES BEN MAIMUN. Libro intitulado obligacion de los coracones compuesto por . . . Moseh de Aegipto. 1610. For this supposititious attribution to Maimonides *see* BAḤYA IBN YUSUF, called Bākūdā

M145 MOST

A Most true Relation of the late Proceedings in Bohemia, Germany, and Hungaria. Dated the 1. and 10. and 13. of Iuly, this present yeere 1620. As also of the happie Arriuall of Sir Andrevv Gray into Lusatia. Together with the Articles of Peace betweene the Catholikes, and the Princes of the Reformed Religion, in the Citie of Vlme, the third of Iuly last . . . Faithfully translated out of the high Dutch. DORT, M.D.C.XX. 4° pp.14
9315.bb.10.
Printed by Joris Waters? Or printed in England with a false imprint?

The first MOTIVE of T.H. . . . to suspect the integrity of his religion. 1609. *See* HIGGONS, Theophilus

M146 MUETER, Lauwereys vander

CORTE GHEBEDEKENS TOT TROOST VAN DIE SIECKEN, Als zy liggen onder haer vonnis/oft ghelijck den H. Gheest dat leeren sal. Ghemaeckt by Broeder Lauvvereys vander Mueter . . . TOT BRVSSEL, By Jan Mommaert . . . 1616. 12° pp.45; illus.
4402.e.9(2).
Illustrated with woodcuts of scenes from the Passion on the titlepage and the last three pages.

M147 MUḤAMMAD IBN KHĀVAND SHĀH; called Mīr Khāvand

RELACIONES DE PEDRO TEIXEIRA D'EL ORIGEN DESCENDENCIA Y SUCCESSION de los Reyes de Persia, y de Harmuz, Y DE VN VIAGE HECHO POR EL MISMO AVTOR dende la India Oriental hasta Italia por tierra. EN AMBERES En casa de Hieronymo Verdussen. M.DC.X. [etc.] 8° pp.384,115[215]

9055.aa.7; 803.d.39; 280.f.23; G.2725.

The author of the chronicle of Persia named in the preface as 'Mirkond'. The chronicle of Hormuz is described as 'siguiendo la historia de Torunxa Rey del mismo Reyno'. Ownership inscriptions in the copy at 803.d.39: exl. Henrici Som: Coll. Regal. Cant. 1652; Tho. Bell 1663; Grente mesnil; in the copy at G.2725: FF. Praedicatorum parisiensium via S[i] Honorati; F. Jacobi Quétif Paris. O.P.

M148 MUḤAMMAD IBN MUḤAMMAD, Al-Ṣinhājī; called Ibn Ajurrūm

[Arabic] . . . GRAMMATICA ARABICA DICTA GJARVMIA, & Libellus CENTVM REGENTIVM Cum versione Latina & Commentariis THOMAE ERPENII. LEIDAE, Ex Typographia ERPENIANA Linguarum Orientalium. 1617. 4° pp.157

622.h.7.

M149 MULERIUS, Nicolaus

Hemelsche Trompet Morgenwecker/OFTE COMEET Met een Langebaert Erschenen ANNO 1618. in Novembri ende Decembri, ghestelt door NICOLAVM MVLERIVM . . . TOT GRONINGEN. Gedruct by Hans Sas . . . 1618. 4° sig.A–C^4; illus.

T.2423(2).

The titlepage woodcut shows the comet as a man's face with a long flowing beard across the night sky.

M150 MULERIUS, Nicolaus

TABVLÆ FRISICÆ Lunæ-Solares quadruplices; è fontibus Cl. Ptolemæi, Regis Alfonsi, Nic. Copernici, & Tychonis Brahe, recens constructæ Operâ et studio NICOLAI MVLERI . . . Quibus accessêre Solis tabulæ totidem; hypotheses Tychonis illustratæ: Kalendarium Rom. vetus, cum methodo Paschali emendatâ. ALCMARIÆ Excudebat Iacobus Meesterus . . . Veneunt Amstelrodami apud Wilhelmum Ianssonium . . . 1611. [etc.] 4° pp.464, 77; illus.

532.g.9.

The titlepage is engraved. Signed by the author. Ownership inscriptions: P. Nolle (?); Fr. Hildyard. The binding stamped in gold with a tree bearing a tablet reading: Noli altum sapere.

M151 MURDISONIUS, Joannes

DISPVTATIO PHILOSOPHICA DE ORIGINE, ESSENTIA, ET NATVRA ANIMÆ, Contra veterum de ea errores, Quam . . . Sub Præsidio . . . IOANNIS MURDISONI . . . sustinere conabor ABRAMVS MELLINVS . . . LUGDUNI BATAVORUM, Ex Officinâ Ioannis Patii . . . D.D.CII. [*sic*] 4° sig.A^4

7306.f.6(41).

M152 MURDISONIUS, Joannes

THESES PHILOSOPHICÆ DE PRIMIS NATVRALIVM PRINCIPIIS, Quas . . . Præside . . . IOHANNE MURDISONIO . . . tueri adnitar HIERONYMUS BELONIUS . . . LVGDVNI BATAVORVM, Ex Officinâ Ioannis Patii . . . D.M.CII. [*sic*]. 4° sig.A^6

7306.f.6(40).

M153 MURET, Marc Antoine

(tp.1) M. ANTONII MVRETI . . . ORATIONVM VOLVMINA DVO. EDITIO NOVA CASTIGATA, DVABVS Orationibus antea non editis aucta, & scholijs viri eruditi . . . illustrata. DVACI Apud Ioannem Bogardum . . . M.DC.III.

(tp.2) M. ANTONII MVRETI . . . ORATIONVM VOLVMEN SECVNDVM: A MENDIS . . .

VINDICATVM. DVACI, Apud Ioannem Bogardum . . . M.DC.III. 12° 2 vol.: pp.196; 312
1090.b.2.

MUYLWIJCK, Jacobus a. Disputatio medica de humoribus alimentariis. 1607. *See* VORSTIUS, Aelius Everardus

M154 MUYLWIJCK, Jacobus a
DISPVTATIO MEDICA DE MORBO REGIO SEV ICTERO FLAVO, Quam . . . Pro GRADV DOCTORATVS in Medicina consequendo, asserere conabitur IACOBVS à MVYLWIICK . . . LVGDVNI BATAVORVM, Ex Officinâ Ioannis Patii . . . 1608. 4° sig.A[4]
7306.f.6(13).

M155 MUYR, Hendrick vander
Vreeds-Triumph-gedicht, Gecomponeert eñ Rethorijckelijcken vertoont by de Camer, Vernieut wt Liefden tot Gorinchem, op den generalen Vreeds-Triumph dach/ghecelebreert den 5. Mey . . . 1609 . . . TOT GORINCHEM, Ghedruct voor Adriaen Helmich . . . 1609. 4° sig.A–D[4]
1578/341; 161.k.60; T.2420(32).
The author's dedication signed: Hendrick vander Muyr, the poem signed with his motto: K'verbey den tijt. The copy at T.2420(32) is imperfect; wanting all after sig.A4.

M156 MUYSENHOL, Gommarus
CONSPICILIA BATAVICA. Brillen, Brillen, PRO DOCTORIBVS VALLIS VMBROSAE PER GOMMARVM MVYSENHOL. Excudebat Arminius Bockhorinc sumptibus Iani Ruytgersij. 8° pp.32
11409.ee.26(3).
The author's, publisher's and printer's names, which suggest a Leiden origin, are fictitious, the text, a mixture of Latin and Dutch, sometimes wrongly attributed to Carolus Scribani, is a reply to 'Hoc volumine continentur' by 'Gelasius de Valle Umbrosa'. With a made-up device showing a pair of spectacles and the legend 'Brillen van alle ghesicht, Lunettes a toutte eäge'. Printed in 1609, by Joachim Trognaesius at Antwerp?

M157 MYL, Abraham vander
ABRAH. VANDER-MILII LINGVA BELGICA. Sive De Linguæ illius communitate . . . cum Latinâ, Græcâ, Persicâ . . . de Linguæ illius origine & . . . diffusione . . . LVGDVNI BATAVORVM, Pro Bibliopolio Commeliniano, Excudebant anno M D C XII. Vlricus Cornelij & G. Abrahami. 4° pp.259
C.77.a.1; 70.a.17.
The copy at 70.a.17 is the author's presentation copy to Balthazar Lydius.

N

NAARDER openinge. 1616. *See* TAURINUS, JACOBUS

N1 NAEDER-WAERSCHOUWINGHE
Naeder-Waerschouwinghe/over seeckere verantwoordingen D. D. VORSTII, Onlancx tot syner verschooninge uytghegeven. Gestelt by den Dienaren des Godtlijcken Woorts . . . tot Leeuvvarden . . . Gedruckt tot Leeuvvarden, By Abraham vanden Rade . . . 1611. Men vintse oock te coop by Jan Lamrinck . . . tot Bolswaert. 4° pp.88
T.2241(30).
Drawn up by Johannes Bogerman and others. The attribution by *Carter & Vervliet* (no.327) to A. Aysma, who has signed as witness to the authenticity of documents, is obviously erroneous. Printed partly in civilité.

N2 NAEMREGISTER

NAEMREGISTER Van alle de Ghecommitteerde/soo Politijcke als Kerckelijcke/opt NATIONAEL SYNODE van de Nederlantsche Gepretendeerde Ghereformeerde Kercken/d'welcke ghehouden wordt binnen der Stede van Dordrecht int Jaer 1618. Naer de Coppije tot Dordrecht Ghedruckt by Pieter Verhaghen . . . t'HANTWERPEN. By Abraham Verhoeuen . . . M.DC.XIX. 4° sig. A^4; illus.
P.P.3444.af(1).

According to *Knuttel* no.2832 the list corrects an error found in the Verhaghen edition where two names had accidentally been fused into one. When compared with the edition published by Jacob Marcusz at Leiden, entitled 'De namen der . . . ghecommitteerden', there is still a discrepancy in the name of the second person listed: here: Henricus van Essen, there: Johannes van Essen. The spelling of names also indicates that the two lists derive from different sources. The titlepage woodcut shows a fireball.

NAERDER advijs over de Conferentie tot Delff gehouden. 1615. *See* HOMMIUS, Festus

NAERDER bedenckingen, over de zee-vaerdt. 1608. *See* USSELINCX, Willem

N3 NAERDER

NAERDER OPENINGHE VAN EEN Hooch-wichtighe sake/Betreffende de wel-vaert van ons bedroeft Vader-landt. Dewelcke den Autheur aenvanght, met een Christelijcke betrachtinghe/onser vvonderlijcker verlossinghe, vande grauvvsame tyrannie der Spaengiaerden. ANNO 1618. 4° sig. A–C^4D^1
T.2422(17).

Sometimes tentatively attributed to François van Aerssen. Corresponding to the copy described in *Knuttel* no.2650.

N4 NAERDER

NAERDER OPENINGHE VAN EEN Hooch-wichtighe sake/betreffende De wel-vaert van ons bedroeft Vader-landt. De welcke den Autheur aenvanght/met een Christelijcke betrachtinghe/onser wonderlijcker verlossinghe/vande grauwsame tyrannie der Spaengiaerden . . . 1618. 4° sig. AB^4
106.d.48.

Another edition of the preceding. Corresponding to the copy described in *Knuttel* no.2651.

NAERDER-BERICHT ende openinge vande proceduren by den kerckendienaren Remonstranten ghehouden. 1612. *See* WTENBOGAERT, Jan

NAIJFUE description des regrets de la Paix. 1615. *See* LEUENDIGE vertooninge

N5 NAMEN

De Namen der Edelen ende H.M. Heeren STATEN GENERAEL GHECOMMITTEERDEN. Soo wel Vytheemsche, als in-Landtsche Theologanten, Van Coninghen/Princen/Republijcken/ende den Geunieerden Provintien/tot desen Nationael Synodus te houden gesonden binnen Dordrecht. Anno 1618. Tot Leyden/by Jacob Marcus . . . 1618. 4° sig. A^4
T.2248(65).

N6 NAMEN

NAMEN Der vier-en-twintig gedelegeerde RECHTERS VAN DEN ADVOKAAT JOHAN VAN OLDENBARNEVELT, By den Ambassadeur van Vrankryk BEULS genoemt [etc.] fol. a single sheet: illus., port.
T.2249(16).

The portrait dated 1617 and signed: I. Mirevelt pinxit. Published in 1619.

N7 NANNIUS, Petrus

D. PETRI NANNII . . . DE BELLO TVRCIS INFERENDO, DECLAMATIO . . . LOVANII, Apud Ioannem Masium . . . 1611. 4° sig. A–D[4]
804.b.44(16).

Edited by Simon Walravius. Ownership inscription: Adriaen Gardijn Penninck Mr. vanden Zijpe, ende Raedt der Stede Alcmaer.

NANSIUS, Adolphus. Theses medicae de apoplexia. 1605. *See* VORSTIUS, Aelius Everardus

N8 NARRATIO

NARRATIO FIDELIS ET SVCCINCTA DE NVPERA ILLA PRODITIONE LONGE IMMANISSIMA, A IESVITIS ET CONIVRATIS IN MAGNVM MAGNÆ BRITANNIÆ REGEM INTENTATA, Ex Commentarijs Anglicis . . . in unum Historiæ corpus congesta. LVGDVNI BATAVORVM, Prostant apud Ioannem Orlers . . . MDCVII. 4° pp. 38
1093.b.73.

NARSIUS, Joannes. Disputationum theologicarum sexta de persona Spiritus Sancti. 1602. *See* GOMARUS, Franciscus

NARSIUS, Joannes. Disputationum theologicarum nona, de lapsu hominis. 1601. *See* GOMARUS, Franciscus

N9 NA-SOECK

NA-SOECK ende Overlgginghe [*sic*] int korte/Hoe . . . vele . . . gheleerde . . . Autheuren, tzedert hondert Jaren herwaerts/hebben verstaen/dat d'oprechte Gods-dienst aenghestelt . . . ende vande twisten der Religie gheoordeelt moet werden/Als D. Erasmus . . . D. M. Lutherus ende D. P. Melanthon, midtsgaders D. Franciscus Iunius, D. I. Wtenbogaerdt . . . ende . . . andere . . . Daer mede de Remonstranten . . . hen zoecken te behelpen teghen de Contra-Remonstranten. Met Applicatie Discoursghewijse . . . Ghedruckt in Januario 1618. 4° pp. 26
T.2248(47).

NA-SPORINGH. 1617. *See* TAURINUS, Jacobus

N10 NAUWE

Nauwe Overlegging van de Noodtsaeckelijckheden/Op't aennemen der WAERTGELDERS. Gedruckt . . . 1618. 4° pp. 8
T.2248(68).

N11 NECK, Jacob Cornelisz van

Het tvvede Boeck, Journael oft Dagh-register/inhoudende een warachtich verhael ende Historische vertellinghe vande reyse/gedaen door de acht schepen van Amstelredamme/gheseylt in den Maent Martij 1598. onder tbeleydt vanden Admirael Iacob Cornelisz. Neck, ende Wybrant van VVarvvijck als Vice-Admirael. Van hare zeylagie . . . Oock Historisch verhael vande plaetsen die sy beseylt hebben inde Molucken . . . Ghedruckt tot Amstelredam by Cornelis Claesz. . . . 1601. obl. 4° ff. 50; sig. A–P[4]; illus., maps
1858.a.1(1.pt.2).

With a Dutch-Malay dictionary. The running title reads: Het tweede Boeck der Oost-Indische Navigatie. For bk. 1 *see* the *Dutch STC* s.v. L., G.M.A.W. Historie van Indien.

N12 NECK, Jacob Cornelisz van

[Journael ofte dagh-register.] (tp. 1) LE SECOND LIVRE, IOVRNAL OV COMPTOIR, CONTENANT LE VRAY DISCOVRS ET NARRATION HISTORIQVE, DV VOIAGE faict par les huict Navires d'Amsterdam, au mois de Mars l'An 1598. soubs la conduitte de l'Admiral Iaques Corneille Necq, & du Vice-Admiral VVibrant de VVarvvicq . . . Imprimé a Amsterdam chez Corneille Nicolas . . . Pour Bonaventure Davicelle Libraire a Calais . . . 1601.

(tp.2) APPENDICE, VOCABVLAIRE DES MOTS IAVANS ET MALAYTS . . . Imprimé chez Cornille Nicolas . . . 1601. fol. ff.21; sig. A–F^4G^6; illus., maps
455.b.10(2); 566.k.15(2); G.6617(2).

The running title reads: Le second livre de la navigation des Indes Orientales. The Javanese words in the dictionary are printed in civilité. For bk. 1 *see* the *Dutch STC* s.v. L., G.M.A.W. Premier livre de l'histoire de la navigation.

N13 NECK, Jacob Cornelisz van

[Journael ofte dagh-register.] (tp.1) LE SECOND LIVRE, IOVRNAL OV COMPTOIR, CONTENANT LE VRAY DISCOVRS . . . DV VOYAGE fait par les huit navires d'Amsterdam . . . sous la conduite de l'Admiral Iaques Cornille Nec, & du Vice-Admiral VVibrant de VVarvvic . . . Imprimé à Amsterdam, chez Cornille Nicolas . . . 1609.

(tp.2) APPENDICE, VOCABVLAIRE DES MOTS IAVANS ET MALAYTS . . . Imprimé à Amsterdam, chez Cornille Nicolas . . . 1609. fol. ff.22; sig. A–F^4G^6; illus., maps
566.k.15(3); C.73.g.2(1.pt.2); G.2851(2); G.6620(2).

Illus. no. 18 has been recut. The copy at G.2851(2) is in a binding bearing the arms of Le Clerc de Lesseville. For bk. 1 *see* LODEWIJCKSZ, Willem

NEDER-DUYTSCHE epigrammen op verscheide saecken. 1617. *See* VERSTEGAN, Richard

Den NEDERDUYTSCHEN Helicon. 1610. *See* MANDER, Karel van

Den NEDERLANDTSCHEN bye-korf. *See* USSELINCX, Willem

NEDERLANTSCHE antiquiteyten. 1613. *See* VERSTEGAN, Richard

N14 NEDERLANTSCHE

DIE NEDERLANTSCHE Traenen ouer die Doot vanden . . . Prince Albert . . . Met het Beclach ouer de Doot van zijn Hoocheyt soo wel die van Hollandt, Zeelandt, Vrieslant ende Steden Ouer-Yssel, &c. Eerst Ghedruckt den 18. Augusti 1621. T'Hantwerpen, By Abraham Verhoeuen/[etc.] 4° pp.15; sig. $CcDd^4$; illus.
P.P.3444.af(273).

Headed: Augustus, 1621. 116. In verse. The titlepage woodcut shows the Archduke lying in state.

N15 NEERDER-LANDEN

Der Neerder-Landen ende Kerken VRIHEIDT: van Spanjens ende Roomens Hoogher tirannijheidt. [etc.] (col.) IE MAIN-TIENDRAY. 1610. 4° pp.8
T.2421(19).

In verse.

N16 NEGENTHIEN

NEGENTHIEN Refereynen int Sot/Gheprononcieert om Prijs/na de beroepinghe van alle de vrye Cameren in Leyden, den 8. October, Anno 1613 . . . TOT LEYDEN. By Jacob Janszoon Paets . . . 1614. 4° sig. A–G^4; illus.
1490.s.16(2); 11755.bb.36.

With 'Elf baladen . . . Den 25. November, 1613'. The invitation signed: L.X.N. Tijt Piero, i.e. Pieter Cornelis van der Morsch, who may also be the editor. The repeated illustration shows a hooded figure, i.e. the jester, with the legend: Lust om weten, and the verses beginning 'Is yver blint'.

N17 NEGRONE, Giulio

IVLII NIGRONI . . . Orationes XXV. NVNC PRIMVM . . . IN BELGIO EDITÆ, & ab auctore recognitæ. DVACI, Typis IOANNIS BOGARDI. M.DC XIV. [etc.] 12° pp.762
1090.a.1.

Ownership inscription: Thomas Birch his Book.

N18 NEOMAGUS, Anton

EXPEDITIO MAVRITIANA FLANDRICA, Cum Exercitu . . . ORDINVM VNITARVM BELGIÆ PROVINCIARVM. ANNO 1600. 2. Iulij. Authore A. NEOMAGO. Lugduni Batavorum, Apud IOANNEM MAIRE . . . 1617. 4° pp.60
1193.k.6(2).

N19 NEOMAGUS, Arnoldus

'THEMELSCH SYNODVS ENDE RECHTMATIGH OORDEEL GEHOVDEN TOT ZION. Teghen 't Aerdsche Synodus Nationael Ende Onrechtueerdich Oordeel/Ghehouden binnen Dordrecht in de Dool-Cappelle. Anno 1618. ende 1619. Met Priuilegie des ALDERHOOGSTEN tot aen het eynde der vvereldt. 4° pp.96
T.2249(23).

Anonymous. Edited by Henricus Slatius. Published in 1620.

N20 NEOMAGUS, Arnoldus

(tp.1) OPENINGHE DER SYNODALE CANONES, Begrepen In het eerste Hooftstuck. Waer in . . . bewesen wort hoe onghefondeert de selve zijn . . . Br. Typ. Haest. AN. milles. sexcentes. viges. pr.
(tp.2) OPENINGHE DER SYNODALE CANONES Begrepen in het Tvveede Hooftstuck . . . Ghedruckt in't Iaer . . . 1621. 4° 2 pt. pp.:54; 36
T.2249(52).

Anonymous. The imprint on tp.1 suggests: Brussel Typis Haestenianis.

N21 NEOSTADIUS, Cornelius

DE FEVDI IVRIS SCRIPTI, HOLLANDICI, VVESTFRISICIQVE, SVCCESIONE. NEC NON OBSERVATIONVM FEVDISTICARVM DECAS PRIMA EX REBVS IVDICATIS Curiæ Feudalis Hollandiæ, Zelandiæ, Frisiæque Selecta. Auctore CORNELIO NEOSTADIO . . . LVGDVNI BATAVORVM, Ex Officinâ ELZEVIRIANA . . . M D C XX. 4° pp.44,20
5206.c.12(1).

N22 NEOSTADIUS, Cornelius

[De pactis antenuptialibus rerum judicatarum observationes. Auctore Cornelio Neostadio . . . Lugduni Batavorum, ex Officina Elzeviriana . . . M.D CXX.] 4° pp.64
5206.c.12(2).

Wanting the titlepage and second, preliminary, leaf. This copy is attached to the preceding and may have been issued jointly, without its own titlepage and preliminary leaf. The title has been transcribed from *Willems* no.173.

NERDENUS, Henricus Antonides. *See* LINDEN, Henricus Antonides van der

NERÉE, Richard Jean. Disputationum theologicarum quarto repetitarum vigesima tertia de fide. 1605. *See* ARMINIUS, Jacobus

NERÉE, Richard Jean. Disputationum theologicarum vigesima-secunda, de merito Christi. 1603. *See* GOMARUS, Franciscus

N23 NETHERLANDS. Before the division

[Collections of laws] (tp.1) PLACATEN ende Ordonnantien op 'tstuck vande Wildernissen; in ordre ghestelt deur PAVLLVM G.F.P.N. MERVLAM . . . IN S'GRAVENHAGE By Beuckel Corneliss. Nieulant . . . M̄ D̄C̄V̄.
(tp.2) TWEEDE BOECK INHOVDENDE ΚΥΝΗΓΕΤΙΚΑ of IACHT-BEDRYF . . . DAT IS, meest alle 'tghene de IAGHT aengaende, ghevonden werdt by verscheyden AVCTEVRS, GRIECKSCHE, LATYNSCHE, FRANCOISCHE, ende Andere: Vergadert, midsgaders in ordre ende Nederlandtsche sprake ghebraght deur PAVLLVM G.F.P.N. MERVLAM . . . IN 'SGRAVEN-HAGHE, By Beuckel Corneliszoon Nieulandt. M D CV.

(tp.3) DERDE BOECK VERVATENDE IΞEYTIKA of VLVGHT-BEDRYF, DAT IS, De voornaemste Aenmerckinghen, die op de VLVGHT by verscheyden AVCTEVRS ghevonden werden: Mit [*sic*] een ghetrouwe Inmenginghe van de PLACATEN ende ORDONNANTIEN, uytghegheven in dese Landen by de Hooghe Overigheyd op 'tstuck van de VOGELRIE: Alles opghesocht, ende in ordre ghestelt deur PAVLLVM G.F.P.N. MERVLAM . . . IN 'SGRAVEN-HAGHE, By Beuckel Cornelisz. Nieulandt: M D CV. fol. 3 pt.: pp.264; 124; 59: plates
501.g.9.

The first titlepage is engraved; the plates consist of woodcut views of castles. Ownership inscription: W. del Court tot Krimpen.

N24 NETHERLANDS. Before the division

[31.7.1571] PLACCAET Vanden Thienden ende twintichsten Penninck/op-gestelt by den Hertoge van Alva, op alle roerende ende onroerende goederen inde Nederlantsche Provintien . . . gepubliceert . . . inden Jaere M.D.LXXI . . . Daer nu Hier by ghevoeght is, (tot vreversinghe [*sic*] inde Memorie . . .) de groote alteratie ende beroerte die inde selve Nederlanden . . . ghevolght is. Oock mede Hoe de Stede vanden Briele . . . inghenomen werde . . . Ghedruckt M.VI^{C}.IX. 4° sig.A-C^4: plate
T.1723(1); 107.g.17(13).

The law is dated 31 July 1571. The plate is an engraved portrait of the Duke of Alva, signed: Ticianus Pinxit, P. de Iode excudit. It is not mentioned by *Knuttel* no.568 and is lacking in the copy at 107.g.17(13) and may therefore not be part of the pamphlet as published.

N25 NETHERLANDS. Southern Provinces

[16.1.1601] PLACCAET Van haere Hoocheden, Aengaende hoe de Coopluyden/ende alle andere . . . hen sullen moeten reguleren op de Boursse/ter Borsse tijdt. T'ANTWERPEN, Inde Plantijnsche Druckerije/By Jan Moerentorf. M. D CI. 4° sig.A^4
107.g.19(21).

Issued 16 January 1601.

N26 NETHERLANDS. Southern Provinces

[27.2.1601] ORDONNANTIE ende PLACCAET VANDE EERTZHERTOGHEN TEGENS die ghene die hunnen dienst van Oorloghe verlaeten, sonder oorlof van hunne Ouerste, ende teghen andere Ledichganghers. TOT BRVESSEL, By Rutgeert Velpius . . . 1601. [etc.] 4° 2 unsigned leaves
107.g.5(34).

Issued 27 February 1601.

N27 NETHERLANDS. Southern Provinces

[20.3.1601] ORDONNANTIE ENDE PLACCAET VANDE EERTZHERTOGHEN TEGHEN D'ABUYSEN DIER GEschieden in sommighe plaetsen, ende Landen van Herwertsouer, door den ommatighen [*sic*] dranck . . . vande brande-wynen . . . ende andere ghelycke distillatien. TOT BRVESSEL, By Rutgeert Velpius . . . 1601. [etc.] 4° 2 unsigned leaves
107.g.5(35).

Issued 20 March 1601.

N28 NETHERLANDS. Southern Provinces

[20.3.1601] ORDONNANTIE ende PLACCAET VANDE EERTZHERTOGHEN TEGHEN d'abuysen dier geschieden in sommighe plaetsen, ende Landen van hervvertsouer, deur dē ommatigen [*sic*] drāck ende slete vande Ghebrande-vvynen . . . ende ander gelycke distillatien. TOT BRVESSEL, By Rutgeert Velpius . . . 1601. [etc.] 4° 2 unsigned leaves
107.g.15(19).

Another edition of the preceding.

N29 NETHERLANDS. Southern Provinces

[13.4.1601] PLACCAERT ende ORDINANTIE VANDE EERTSHERTOGEN . . . vvaer mede . . . vvordt verboden alle het vervueren vvtte landen van heervveertsouere van Salpeterē ende Buspoeyeren . . . TOT BRVESSEL, By Rutgeert Velpius . . . 1601. [etc.] 4° 4 unsigned leaves

107.g.17(12).

Issued 13 April 1601.

N30 NETHERLANDS. Southern Provinces

[13.4.1601] PLACCAERT ET ORDONNANCE DES ARCHIDVCQZ . . . Par laquelle leurs Altezes deffendent le transport des Salpetres, & Poudres . . . hors des pays de pardeça . . . A BRVXELLES, Par Rutger Velpius . . . 1601. [etc.] 4° sig.a^4

107.g.5(38).

The French edition of the preceding.

N31 NETHERLANDS. Southern Provinces

[15.5.1601] PLACCAET ENDE ORDONNANTIE VANDE EERTZHERTOGHEN . . . opt stuck vande Spelen van Sinnen, oft Moraliteyt, Battementen, Rondeelkens, Refereynen, ende dierghelycke dichten. TOT BRVESSEL, By Rutgeert Velpius . . . 1601. [etc.] 4° 2 unsigned leaves

107.g.5(37).

Issued 15 May 1601.

N32 NETHERLANDS. Southern Provinces

[25.6.1601] OPENE BRIEVEN VAN ORDINANTIEN ENDE EVVVICH EDICT VAN HEVRE HOOCHEDEN. Verclarende tot wat prys/valeur ende estimatie van Gout ende Ziluer men sal moghen ontlasten/ende lossen de hooftpenningen van Renten/by brieuen gheconstitueert/scheydinghen ende deylinghen/beleeninghen/etc. TOT BRVESSEL, By Rutgeert Velpius . . . 1601. 4° sig.A^4

107.g.15(21).

Issued 25 June 1601.

N33 NETHERLANDS. Southern Provinces

[25.6.1601] LETTRES PATENTES D'ORDONNANCE ET EDICT PERPETVEL, Declairant à quel pris, valeur & estimation d'or & d'argent lon pourra descharger & rembourser les deniers capitaux de Rentes par lettres, partaiges, gaigieres . . . & semblables obligations & contracts anciens & nouueaux. A BRVXELLES, Par Rutger Velpius . . . 1601. 4° sig.A^4

107.g.5(36).

The French edition of the preceding.

N34 NETHERLANDS. Southern Provinces

[15.9.1602] TRANSLAET VAN DEN BAN ENDE PLACCAET, Vuytghegaen ende ghedecreteert by de Ertzhertoghen . . . Teghens die Ghemuytineerde van Tcastel van Hoochstraten. TOT BRVESSEL, By Rutgeert Velpius . . . M.D.C.JJ. [etc.] 4° 4 unsigned leaves

106.d.5; 106.d.6.

Issued 15 September 1602. In the copy at 106.d.6 the final signature of I. de Mancicidor has been erased.

N35 NETHERLANDS. Southern Provinces

[15.9.1602] TRANSLAET VAN DEN BAN ENDE PLACCAET Wtgheghaen ende ghedecreteert by de Ertzhertoghen . . . Teghens de Ghemuytineerde van t'Casteel van Hoochstraten. IN S'GRAVEN-HAGHE, By Aelbrecht Heyndricksz . . . Na de Copie ghedruct tot Brussel, By Rutgeert Velpius. 1602. [etc.] 4° sig.A^2

T.1717(34).

Reprinted from the preceding.

N36 NETHERLANDS. Southern Provinces

[15.9.1602] TRANSLAT DV BAN ET PLACCART DECRETE' PAR LES ARCHIDVCZ . . . contre les Amutinez du Chasteau de Hooch-Straeten. A BRVXELLES, Chez Rutger Velpius . . . M.D.C.II. [etc.] 4° sig. A^4

D.NLA.1.

The French edition of the preceding.

N37 NETHERLANDS. Southern Provinces

[5.4.1603] PLACCAET ENDE ORDINANCIE BELANGENDE DE OEPENINGE Ende restauratie vanden Traffyck ende Coopmans-handel van Spaignien/mette Landen van herwerts-ouere/hoewel zij gheweken zijn vande onderdaenicheyt vande . . . Eertz-hertogen . . . Oick mit [*sic*] alle andere Vassaelen ende ondersaeten van Princen ende Republycken/wesende hunne Vrienden oft Neutraelen. TOT BRVESSEL, By Rutgeert Velpius . . . M.D.C.III. [etc.] 4° sig. AB^4C^2

107.g.16(14).

Issued 5 April 1603.

N38 NETHERLANDS. Southern Provinces

[5.4.1603] PLACCAET ENDE ORDINANCIE BELANGhende de openinghe ende restauratie vanden Traffijck ende Coopmanshandel van Spangien, mette Landen van hervvaerts-over, hoevvel sy ghevveken zijn vande onderdanicheyt vande . . . Eertz-hertogen . . . TOT BRVESSEL, By Rutgeert Velpius . . . M.VJC. ende III. [etc.] 4° sig. A^4

T.1717(35).

Another edition of the preceding. With the arms of Brabant on the titlepage instead of those of the Archdukes. The last leaf is cropped and mutilated.

N39 NETHERLANDS. Southern Provinces

[8.4.1604] ORDINANTIE VANDE EERTSHERTOGEN . . . OP HET STVCK vande Pouderen ende Salpetren. TOT BRVESSEL, By Rutgeert Velpius . . . M.D.C.IIII. 4° sig. AB^4

107.g.5(39).

Issued 8 April 1604.

N40 NETHERLANDS. Southern Provinces

[12.3.1605] PLACCAET VANDE EERTSHERTOGHEN . . . SOO OP DE REVOcatie van seekere voorgaende Placcaet vanden vyfden Aprilis 1603. aengaende den Coopmanshandel van Spaignien, als nopende t'ghene sijne Majesteyt alsnv heeft geresolueert belanghende den seluen Coopmans-handel. TOT BRVESSEL, By Rutgeert Velpius . . . M.D.C.V. 4° sig. A^4

107.g.5(40).

Issued 12 March 1605. Leaf A3 is erroneously again signed A2.

N41 NETHERLANDS. Southern Provinces

[15.2.1606] PLACCAET ENDE ORDONNANTIE VAN HVNNE HOOCHEDEN, STELlende ordre ende reglement op de swaericheyden ende beletselen hier voormaels ghedaen inde Haeuenen vanden Conincryke van Spaignien/aengaende de Coopmanschappen ende Manufacturen gemaect inde ghehoorsaeme Prouincien . . . eñ die vā hunne Rebellē. TOT BRVESSEL, By Rutgeert Velpius . . . M.D.C.VJ. 4° sig. A^4

T.1717(37).

Issued 15 February 1606.

N42 NETHERLANDS. Southern Provinces

[19.9.1606] PLACCAET VANDE EERTSHERTOGEN . . . Verbiedende op een nieuw het

innebrenghen . . . vande Munten gheslaeghen byde gherebelleerde Prouincien . . . TOT BRVESSEL, By Rutgeert Velpius . . . M.D.C.VJ. [etc.] 4° sig. A[4]
107.g.19(7).
Issued 19 September 1606.

N43 NETHERLANDS. Southern Provinces
[19.9.1606] Placcaet eñ Ordonnantie vande Eertz-Hertoghē . . . op t'faict vande Munte/daerby verclaerst wordt dat alle voorgaende Placcaten eñ Edicten . . . zullen moeten onderhouden worden . . . By welckē Placcate alleenlick toeghelaten wordt den nieuwen gouden Penninck gheslaghē byden Coninck van groot Bretaignen/voor neghene Guldens thien Stuyuers . . . Ghegheuen te Bruessele dē XIX. dach van September. 1606. Te Ghendt, By Jan vandē Steene . . . Año Duysent Zeshondert Zesse. [etc.] (col.) Typis Gualtéri Manilij. 4° sig. A[4]B[2]
107.g.19(6).
The text is the same as in the preceding, endorsed and reissued by the Council of Flanders on 14 October 1606.

N44 NETHERLANDS. Southern Provinces
[27.9.1606] PLACCAET VANDE EERTSHERTOGHEN . . . Stellende ordre op de bedroghen ende abusen dyer gheschiedeu [*sic*] int feyt van het verwen vañ rouwe Syde ende anderssins. TOT BRVESSEL, By Rutgeert Velpius . . . M.D.C.VJ. [etc.] 4° sig. A[4]
107.g.4(12).
Issued 27 September 1606.

N45 NETHERLANDS. Southern Provinces
[3.11.1606] PLACCAET VANDE EERTZHERTOGHEN . . . om te verhueden allen abuysen/bedroch ende verswijgingen/van't recht d'welck ghelicht wort herwaerts ouere op die Alluynen . . . TOT BRVESSEL, By Rutgeert Velpius [etc.] 4° sig. A[4]
107.g.5(41).
Issued 3 November 1606.

N46 NETHERLANDS. Southern Provinces
[3.11.1606] PLACCART ET ORDONNANCE DES . . . ARCHIDVCQZ . . . pour obvier aux fraudes & recelemens du droit qui se leue sur les Alluns pardeça. A BRVXELLES, Par Rutger Velpius/[etc.] 4° 4 unsigned leaves
107.g.7(18).
The French edition of the preceding.

N47 NETHERLANDS. Southern Provinces
[3.2.1607] LES ARCHIDVCQZ . . . A Bruxelles, par Rutger Velpius, [etc.] fol. a single sheet
112.f.33(1).
Dated 3 February 1607. On the defection of troops to the enemy at Breda.

N48 NETHERLANDS. Southern Provinces
[14.2.1607] LES ARCHIDVCQZ . . . A Bruxelles, par Rutger Velpius, [etc.] fol. a single sheet
105.f.4(4).
Dated 14 February 1607. A warrant for the apprehension of the rebel known as Electo.

N49 NETHERLANDS. Southern Provinces

[19.2.1607] PLACCAET VANDE EERTZHERTOGHEN . . . Beuelende alle Wisselaers/ Muntmeesters/Goudtsmeden . . . niet te nemen oft ontvanghen/hoogheren prys van Goude ende Silueren stucken/als den ghenen die ghestelt is by Ordinancie van hunne Hoocheyden. TOT BRVESSEL. By Rutgeert Velpius . . . 1607. [etc.] 4° 2 unsigned leaves

107.g.7(17); 107.g.15(40).

Issued 19 February 1607.

N50 NETHERLANDS. Southern Provinces

[19.2.1607] PLACCAET VANDE EERTSHER TOGEN [*sic*] . . . Verbiedende eenenyeghelijcken te draeghen oft transporteren Goudt oft Ziluere wt de Landen van hunne ghehoorsaemheyt. TOT BRVESSEL. By Rutgeert Velpius . . . 1607. [etc.] 4° sig. A^3

107.g.5(43).

Issued 19 February 1607.

N51 NETHERLANDS. Southern Provinces

[13.3.1607] BRIEF van hare Hoocheden aende . . . Staten der Vereenichde Nederlantsche Provintien ghesonden . . . Mitsgaders seeckere antwoorde der . . . Staten . . . aen hare Hoocheden. Ghedruckt Anno 1607. 4° 2 unsigned leaves

T.1713(13); 107.g.18(35).

The original letter is dated 13 March 1607, the answer 12 April 1607. The titlepage device is that of the Dutch lion in his garden, indicating that it was printed in the North.

N52 NETHERLANDS. Southern Provinces

[29.4.1607] COPYE Vanden Brieff gheschreven van zijn Hoocheyt aen Graeff Herman vanden Bergh Gouverneur van't Hertochdom van Geldre. Inhoudende d'Ordre waer naer allen Gouverneuren/Capiteyen [*sic*] eñ Soldaten/wesende onder zijn gebiet/haer sullen hebben te reguleren/gheduyrende desen Stilstant van Wapenen. Ghedruckt/Anno 1607. 4° 2 unsigned leaves

107.g.18(38).

Signed: Albert; dated 29 April 1607. Printed in the North; *Knuttel* no.1367 suggests the press of Jan Andriesz Cloeting at Delft.

N53 NETHERLANDS. Southern Provinces

[30.6.1607] PLACCAET Ende ordinantie vande . . . Ertzhertoghen . . . opt stuck vande munten. Thantwerpen by Hieronymus Verdussen . . . 1607. [etc.] 8° sig. $A\text{-}D^8E^7$; illus.

603.a.11(1).

Issued 30 June 1607. With the value of coins taken out of circulation.

N54 NETHERLANDS. Southern Provinces

[18.9.1607] COPIE Vande Aggreatie des . . . Konincx van Spangien Philippus III. ghezonden aende . . . Staten generael der vereenichde Nederlanden. Mitsgaders De Antwoorde vande . . . Staten Generael/op de voorsz Aggreatie ghedaen . . . M.D.C.VIII. 4° sig. a^4

106.d.11(2).

The original document dated 18 September 1607, the answer 4 November 1607. Concerning peace negotiations.

N55 NETHERLANDS. Southern Provinces

[20.9.1607] Placcaet eñ Ordonnantie vande Eerts-Hertoghen . . . op het

onderhoudt vā Heylighe Zondaghen eñ Feestdaghen. Ghegheuen te Bruessel den twintichsten September duysent zeshondert Zeuene. Te Ghendt, By Jan vanden Steene. Anno Zestienhondert en Achte. [etc.] (col.) Typis Gualtéri Manilij. 4° sig. A4
107.g.5(42).
The text reissued by the Council of Flanders on 6 September 1608.

N56 NETHERLANDS. Southern Provinces
[4.12.1607] PROCLAMATIE Byde Eertzhertoghen van Oostenrijck ghedaen/teghens de Ghemutineerde van Diest . . . IN S'GRAVEN-HAGHE, By Hillebrant Jacobsz . . . 1607. 4° 2 unsigned leaves
T.1717(38).
Dated 4 December 1607.

N57 NETHERLANDS. Southern Provinces
[16.1.1608] INSTRUCTIE Gegeven by hare Hoocheden aenden Marquiz Ambrosio Spinola/den President Richardot/den Secretaris Mancicidor . . . eñ den Audiencier Verreycken/Ghedeputeerde . . . tot de handelinghe van Vrede/ tusschen den Koninc van Spangien ende hare . . . Hoocheden ter eenre/ende de Staten generael der vereenichde Neder-landen ter ander zijden. Wt het Fransoys . . . overghezet. Ghedruct . . . M.D.C.VIII. 4° sig. A4
T.1731(9).
Translated from 'Instruction donné par leurs Altesses, au Marquis Ambrosio Spinola', dated 16 January 1608.

N58 NETHERLANDS. Southern Provinces
[16.1.1608] Copye Vande Instructie by hare Hoocheden ghegheven aenden Marquis Ambrosio Spinola, Den President Richardot, Mancicidor Secretaris . . . ende den Audiencier Verreycken, als zijne Gedeputeerde . . . tot het Tractaet ofte handelinge van Peyse/tusschen den Coninck van Spagnien, ende hare Hoocheden ter eener/ende . . . de Staten generael der vereenichde Provintien ter ander sijde. Wt het Fransche vertaelt. M.D.C.VIII. 4° sig. A2
106.d.20.
Another edition of the document dated 16 January 1608. Printed by Jan van Ghelen at Rotterdam?

N59 NETHERLANDS. Southern Provinces
[31.8.1608] PLACCAET ENDE ORDINANCIE VANDE EERTZHERTOGHEN . . . Waerby wort ordre ghestelt/tot goede neerstighe onderhoudinghe van zekere poincten ende articulen/ghesloten ende ghearresteert in het Synode Provinciael van Mechelen/ghehouden inde maenden van Junius ende Julius/sesthien hondert seven. TOT BRVESSEL. By Rutgeert Velpius . . . 1608. [etc.] 4° sig. AB4
T.2420(13); T.1727(11).
Dated 31 August 1608.

N60 NETHERLANDS. Southern Provinces
[31.8.1608] PLACCAET ENDE ORDINANCIE . . . Waerby wort ordre ghestelt/tot goede ende neirstighe onderhoudinghe van zekere poincten ende articulen/ ghesloten . . . in het Synode Provinciael van Mechelen/gehouden in de maenden van Junius ende Julius/sesthien hondert seuen. Eerst TOT BRVESSEL, By Rutgeert Velpius . . . 1608. [etc.] 4° sig. A4
T.1717(42); T.1729(13).
Another edition of the preceding.

N61 NETHERLANDS. Southern Provinces

[20.10.1608] EDICT ENDE ORDINANCIE VANDE EERTZHERTOGEN . . . op't stuck ende exercicie van d'Ambacht vande Go[u]dt ende Siluer-smeden . . . inde Landen van herwaertsovere. TOT BRVESSEL, By Rutgeert Velpius . . . 1608. 4° sig. AB^4C^2

107.g.9(10).

Dated 20 October 1608. The titlepage is slightly mutilated.

N62 NETHERLANDS. Southern Provinces

[20.10.1608] EDICT ET ORDONNANCE DES ARCHIDVCQZ . . . sur le faict et exercice du Mestier des Orfebures . . . A BRVXELLES, Par Rutger Velpius . . . 1608. [etc.] 4° sig. $A\text{-}C^4D^2$

107.g.4(7).

The French edition of the preceding.

N63 NETHERLANDS. Southern Provinces

[9.4.1609] ARTICLES DE LA TREFVE CONCLVE ET ARRESTEE POVR DOVZE ans, entre la Ma^té du Roy d'Espaigne, &c. & les . . . Archiducqz noz Princes Souuerains d'vne part, Et les Estatz des Prouinces vnies du Pais bas d'autre. A BRVXELLES, Par Rutger Velpius . . . 1609. [etc.] 4° sig. $A\text{-}D^4$

106.a.49.

Dated 9 April 1609. With 'Teneur des procurations' partly in French and partly in Spanish. Corresponding to the copy described in *Knuttel* no.1587.

N64 NETHERLANDS. Southern Provinces

[9.4.1609] ARTICLES DV TRAICTE' DE TREFVE FAICT ET CONCLV EN LA VILLE ET CITE' d'Anvers, le neufiesme d'Auril 1609. entre les Commissaires des . . . Archiducz . . . Avec les Commissaires & deputez des . . . Estats Generaulx des Provinces Vnies des Pays bas: & ce avec l'intervention & par l'advis des . . . Ambassadeurs des Roys Tres-Chrestien, & de la grande Bretaigne. A LA HAYE, Par Hillebrant Iacobssz, [etc.] 4° sig. A^4

106.a.48.

Published in 1609. Corresponding to the copy described in *Knuttel* no.1586.

N65 NETHERLANDS. Southern Provinces

[9.4.1609] TRactaet van t'Bestant/ghemaeckt ende besloten binnen de Stadt eñ Cité van Antwerpen/den negensten Aprilis 1609. voor den tijt van twaelf Jarē/tusschen de Commissarisen van de . . . Eertshertoghen . . . soo wel in den naem vande Majesteyt Catholicke als dē haeren: met de Commissarisen ende Ghedeputeerde vande . . . Staten Generael vande vereenichde Provincien der Nederlanden: Ende dat door het tusschen-comen/ende met advijs vande . . . Ambassadeurs vande Coningē/den Alder-Christelicksten/ende van groot Bretaignien. IN S'GRAVENHAGHE, By Hillebrant Iacobsz. [etc.] 4° sig. A^6

106.d.27.

Corresponding to the copy described in *Knuttel* no.1589.

N66 NETHERLANDS. Southern Provinces

[9.4.1609] Tractaet van tBestandt/gemaect ende besloten binnen de Stadt ende Cité van Antwerpen/den negensten Aprilis 1609 voor den tijdt van twaelf Jaren/tusschen de Commissarisen vande . . . Eertshertoghen zoo wel in den naem vande Majesteyt Catholicke/als den haren. Met de Commissarisen ende Ghedeputeerde van de . . . Staten Generael vande vereenichde Provincien der Nederlanden: Ende dat door het tusschen-komen/ende met advijs vande . . . Ambassadeurs vande Koningen/den alder-Christelijcsten/ende van groot Bretaignien. TOT ROTTERDAM, By Jan van Waesberghe. 1609. Met consent vande

Heeren Burghermeesteren. 4° sig. A^6
T.2420(47).
Corresponding to the copy described in *Knuttel* no. 1591.

N67 NETHERLANDS. Southern Provinces
[9.4.1609] Tractaet van tBestandt/gemaect ende besloten binnen de Stadt ende Cité van Antwerpen/den negensten Aprilis 1609 . . . Ende dat door het tusschen komen . . . vande . . . Ambassadeurs . . . TOT ROTTERDAM, By Jan van Waesberghe/na de Copye ghedruct inden Haghe by Hillebrandt Jacobsz. Met consent vande Heeren Burgemeesteren. 4° sig. A^6
106.b.7.
Another issue of the preceding. Published in 1609. Corresponding to the copy mentioned in the footnote to *Knuttel* no. 1591.

N68 NETHERLANDS. Southern Provinces
[9.4.1609] ARTIICKELEN VAN HET BESTANT ghesloten ende gheconcludeert voor XII. iaren tusschen de MAIESTEYT DES KONINCKS VAN SPANIEN, &C. ENDE DE . . . EERTSHERTOGHEN . . . van d'eene sijde, ENDE DE STATEN van de vereenighde Prouincien der Nederlanden van d'andere sijde. T'ANTVVERPEN BY IOACHIM TROGNESIVS. [etc.] 4° pp. 31
106.d.25.
Issued 9 April 1609. With documents in French and Spanish. The privilege, in French, is dated 24 April 1609. Published in 1609. Corresponding to the copy described in *Knuttel* no. 1593.

N69 NETHERLANDS. Southern Provinces
[9.4.1609] ARTYCKELEN VAN HET BESTANDT ghesloten ende gheconcludeert voor xij jaren, tusschen de MAIESTEYT DES KONINCX VAN SPAGNIEN, &C. ENDE DE . . . EERTS-HERTOGHEN . . . van d'eene zijde, ENDE DE STATEN van de vereenichde Provincien der Nederlanden van d'andere zijde. Na de Copye ghedruct T'HANTVVERPEN, BY IOACHIM TROGNESIVS [etc.] 4° sig. AB^4C^2
T.1723(11); T.1731(7).
With documents in French and Spanish and with the same privilege granted to Joachim Trognaesius as in the preceding. Published in 1609. Corresponding to the copy described in *Knuttel* no. 1594.

N70 NETHERLANDS. Southern Provinces
[9.4.1609] COPYE VANDE PROCVRATIen ghegheven by de Majesteyt des Conings van Spagnien &c. ENDE DE Eerts-hertoghen . . . van d'eene zyde, ENDE DEN . . . STATEN GENERAEL VANDE Vereenichde Nederlantsche Provintien van d'ander zyde. Over t'bestandt van twaelff Jaeren. Ghetranslateert na de Copye Ghedruckt t'Antwerpen by Ioachim Trognesius. [etc.] 4° sig. $(?)^4$
T.1723(12); 106.d.29.
Translated from the documents originally printed in French and Spanish. Published in 1609. Corresponding to the copy described in *Knuttel* no. 1596.

N71 NETHERLANDS. Southern Provinces
[9.4.1609] Procuratie oft bevestinghe der Coninckljcke Ma^eyt^. van Spaignien/etc. Ende haer . . . Hoocheden/Souverayne Princen ter eenre/ende de . . . Staten der vereenichde Nederlantsche Provincien/ter andere zijden. Waer in het Bestant ofte Trefues van 12. Iaren besloten binnen . . . Antwerpen den 9. April 1609 . . . geconfirmeert ende bevesticht worden. Na de Copije: Tot Bruessel. By Rutgert Velpius . . . 1609. Men vintse te coop: Tot Dordrecht. By Philips Jansz [etc.] 4° sig. $(\therefore)A^6$
106.d.28.
The documents previously published together with the treaty of 9 April 1609. Corresponding to the copy described in *Knuttel* no. 1597.

N72 NETHERLANDS. Southern Provinces
[14.4.1609] Vercondinghe van het Bestandt/Tusschen zijne Majesteyt/ende hunne Doorluchtichste Hoocheden ter eenre ende de Staten Generael vande vereenichde Nederlanden ter ander sijden. Ghedaen voor den Stadt-huyse der stadt van Antvverpen, den 14. April, Anno 1609. T'HANTVVERPEN, By Abraham Verhoeven . . . 1609. 4° 2 unsigned leaves
107.g.14(34).
Corresponding to the copy described in *Knuttel* no.1600.

N73 NETHERLANDS. Southern Provinces
[14.4.1609] Vercondinge van het Bestandt/tusschen sijne Majesteyt . . . ende de StatenGenerael vande vereenichde Nederlanden . . . Ghedaen voor den Stadt-huyse der stadt van Antvverpen, den 4 [*sic*] April, Anno 1609. Na de Copye, ghedruct T'HANTVVERPEN, By Abraham Verhoeven . . . 1609. 4° 2 unsigned leaves
T.2420(42); 107.g.14(36); 107.g.18(34).
Corresponding to the copy described in *Knuttel* no.1599.

N74 NETHERLANDS. Southern Provinces
[1.6.1609] PLACCAET ENDE ORDONNANTIE . . . opt stuck vande Straet-schenders / Kneuelaers / Vrybuters / Moordenaers / Bosch-dieuen / ende andere ghelijcke Quaetdoenders ende Delinquanten. TOT BRVESSEL, By Rutgert Velpius . . . 1609. [etc.] 4° sig.AB^4
107.g.18(24).
Dated 1 June 1609.

N75 NETHERLANDS. Southern Provinces
[7.7.1609] Copie vande AGREATIE Ghesonden by de Mayesteyt des Conincx van Spagnien/etc, Aende . . . Staten generael vande vereenichde Nederlantsche Provintien. Op tBestant van twaelf Jaren. Gegeven tot Segovia/den vii^{en}. Julij 1609. 4° 2 unsigned leaves
T.2420(48).
Knuttel no.1628 suggests that this was printed by the Officina Plantiniana at Antwerp in 1609.

N76 NETHERLANDS. Southern Provinces
[7.7.1609] COPIE VANDE AGGREATIE Ghesonden by de Majesteyt des Conings van Spagnien &c. AENDE . . . Staten generael vande vereenighde Nederlantsche Provintien. Op t'Bestandt van twaelff Jaren. Ghegheven Tot Segovia den vij^{en} July 1609. 4° 2 unsigned leaves
107.g.14(34).
Another edition of the preceding, also published in 1609. Corresponding to the copy described in *Knuttel* no.1629.

N77 NETHERLANDS. Southern Provinces
[13.7.1609] ORDONNANTIE ENDE PLACCAET gemaeckt . . . by de Eertshertogen, teghen het disputeren ende debatteren ter saecke vande Religie. etc. Nae de Copye Tot Breussel [*sic*]/by Rutgeert Velpius . . . 1609. 4° 2 unsigned leaves
T.1717(43).
Dated 13 July 1609.

N78 NETHERLANDS. Southern Provinces
[12.12.1609] LES ARCHIDUCZ . . . A Bruxelles, par Rutger Velpius . . . 1609. fol. a single sheet
112.f.32(2).
On the maintenance of army discipline. Issued 12 December 1609.

N79 NETHERLANDS. Southern Provinces

[12.12.1609] PLACCAET. Van de Eerts-hertoghen over de ghemutineerde Soldaten. Ghepubliceert den 12 Decembris/1609. Nae de Copye, Ghedruckt tot Brussel by Rutger Velpius [etc.] 4° 2 unsigned leaves

T.2420(43).

The year 1610 is described in the text as the coming year: published in 1609.

N80 NETHERLANDS. Southern Provinces

[12.12.1609] PLACCAET. Van de Eerts-hertoghen over de ghemutineerde Soldaten. Ghepubliceert den 12 Decembris/1609. Ende ghebannen teghen den 15. Ianuarij 1610. Nae de Copye, Ghedruckt tot Brussel by Rutger Velpius . . . 1610. 4° 2 unsigned leaves

T.1729(19).

N81 NETHERLANDS. Southern Provinces

[31.12.1609] PLACCAET VANDE EERTZHERTOGHEN . . . verbiedende de scandaelen ende exercitien die eenige soo hunne ondersaten als andere/doen ende gebrucken [*sic*] tot verachtinge van onse Heylige Catholijcke . . . Religie. TOT BRVESSEL, By Rutgeert Velpius . . . 1610. 4° sig. A4

T.2420(46).

Issued 31 December 1609. The imprint is false. The typographical appearance of this pamphlet is unlike the normal work of the press of Rutger Velpius. The ornament on the titlepage is one more often used in the United Provinces and the initial on A2r is one normally found in the work coming from the press of Richard Schilders at Middelburg.

N82 NETHERLANDS. Southern Provinces

[31.12.1609] PLACCAET Van de Eertzhertoghen . . . verbiedende de schandalen ende exercitien die eenige soo hunne ondersaten als andere/doen ende gebruyckē tot verachtinge vā onse Heylige Catholijcke . . . Religie. TOT BRVESSEL. By Rutgeert Velpius . . . 1610. 4° sig. A4

T.2240(18).

Another edition of the preceding, also without the usual armorial device employed by Velpius for official documents.

N83 NETHERLANDS. Southern Provinces

[31.12.1609] PLACCAET Vande Eertzhertoghen . . . verbiedende de schandaelen eñ exercitien die eenige soo hunne ondersaten als andere/doen ende ghebruycken tot verachtinghe van onse Heylighe Catholijcke . . . Religie. Nae de Copye van Brussel/By Rutger Velpius . . . 1610. 4° 2 unsigned leaves

107.g.17(10).

Another edition of the two preceding entries, this time admitting to being a reprint.

N84 NETHERLANDS. Southern Provinces

[31.12.1609] PLACCAET VANDE Eertzhertoghen . . . verbiedende de schandalen ende exercitien die eenige soo hune ondersaten als andere/doen ende ghebruycken tot verachtinge van onse Heylige Catholijcke . . . Religie. Item PLACCAET Vande Eertzhertoghen over de ghemuyteneerde Soldaten. Ghepubliceert den 12. Decembris/1609. Item Ordonnantie ende Placcaet ghemaeckt . . . by de Eertzhertoghen/tegen het disputeren ende debatteren ter saecke vande Religie/etc. Nae de Copye Ghedruckt tot Bruyssel by Rutgeert Velpius [etc.] (col.) TOT DORDRECHT. By Philips Jansz. . . . 1610. 4° sig. A4

T.2420(26).

The first is the decree of 31 December 1609, the third that of 13 July 1609.

N85 NETHERLANDS. Southern Provinces

[7.1.1610] NAERDER VERCLARINGE Ende vermeerderinge vande Articlen des Bestants, mette interpretatien der seluer, GEACCORDEERT ENDE GHESLOTEN Tusschen de Gecommitteerde vande Ertshertoghen/ende die vande Staten Generael/vande vereenichde Prouincien/inden Haghe in Hollandt/den zeuensten Januarij 1610. TOT BRVESSEL, By Rutgeert Velpius ende Huybrecht Anthoon . . . 1610. 4° sig.AB^4

106.d.33.

Corresponding to the copy described in *Knuttel* no.1720.

N86 NETHERLANDS. Southern Provinces

[7.1.1610] VLTERIEVRE DECLARATION ET AVGMENTATION DES Articles de la Trefue, auec les Interpretations sur iceulx. ACCORDEE ET CONCLVE entre les Deputez des Archiducqz, & ceux des Estatz Generaulx des Prouinces vnies, a la Haye . . . le septiesme de Ianuier 1610. A BRVXELLES, Par Rutger Velpius, & Hubert Anthoon . . . 1610. 4° sig.AB^4

106.d.35.

The French edition of the preceding. With the text of the 'Procurations' in French and Dutch respectively. Corresponding to the copy described in *Knuttel* no.1719.

N87 NETHERLANDS. Southern Provinces

[7.1.1610] Verdrach gemaeckt . . . inden Haghe in Hollandt/den sevenden Januarij . . . sesthien-hondert eñ thien/tusschen den Ghecommitteerden van hare Hoocheden die EertzHertoghen van Oostenrijck/etc. Ende vande . . . Heeren die Staten Generael der Vereenichde Nederlanden/op eenighe swaricheden ende twijffelachticheyden . . . gheresulteert/uyt den Tractate vanden Trefue . . . IN S'GRAVEN-HAGHE. By Hillebrant Iacobsz. . . . 1610. [etc.] 4° sig.A^6

T.2420(49).

Corresponding to the copy described in *Knuttel* no.1714.

N88 NETHERLANDS. Southern Provinces

[7.1.1610] Verdrach gemaeckt . . . inden Hage . . . den sevenden Januarij inden Jare sesthien-hondert eñ thien/tusschen den Ghecommitteerden van . . . die EertzHertoghen . . . Ende vande . . . Staten Generael der Vereenichde Nederlanden/op eenighe swaricheden . . . gheresulteert/uyt den Tractaete vanden Trefue . . . IN S'GRAVEN-HAGHE, By Hillebrant Iacobsz, . . . 1610. 4° sig.A^5

106.d.34.

Another edition of the preceding. Probably imperfect, wanting the final leaf, A6, bearing the privilege. Otherwise corresponding to the copy described in *Knuttel* no.1717.

N89 NETHERLANDS. Southern Provinces

[31.1.1610] PLACCAET VAN DE EERTZHERTOGEN . . . Om te behouden de hantwercken/besondere van Laeckenen, Sayetten . . . midts-gaders de stoffen/daer toe noodich wesende. TOT BRVESSEL, By Rutgert Velpius . . . 1610. [etc.] 4° sig.A^4

106.g.7(15).

Issued 31 January 1610.

N90 NETHERLANDS. Southern Provinces

[19.2.1610] PLACCAET VAN ONSE . . . HEEREN . . . DIE EERTZHERTOGEN. Ghemaeckt opt collecteren van hunne Hoocheden Recht/d'welck zy lichten op die Waeren ende Coopmanschappen gaende/oft commende naer/oft van de Ghevnieerde Prouincien. TOT BRVESSEL By Rutgeert Velpius/ende Huybrecht Anthoon . . . 1610. 4° sig.A^4B^2

107.g.7(16).

Issued 19 February 1610.

N91 NETHERLANDS. Southern Provinces

[27.2.1610] PLACCAET VANDE EERTZHERTOGEN . . . teghen de beroepinghen tot Vechten by vorme van Duel. TOT BRVESSEL, By Rutgeert Velpius/ende Huybrecht Anthoon . . . 1610. 4° sig. A^4B^2

107.g.18(25).

Issued the last but one day of February 1610.

N92 NETHERLANDS. Southern Provinces

[27.2.1610] PLACCAERT DES ARCHIDVCQZ . . . Contre les Defiz & Duelz. A BRVXELLES, Par Rutger Velpius, & Hubert Anthoon . . . 1610. 4° sig. A^4B^2

107.g.15(20); 107.g.18(26).

The French edition of the preceding.

N93 NETHERLANDS. Southern Provinces

[1.4.1610] PLACCAET ET ORDONNANCE . . . Sur la confirmation & declaration des preuileges & exemptions, competans aux Chiefz, Capitaines, Lieutenants, Enseignes, Guydons, hommes d'Armes, & Archiers des Bendes & Compaignies d'Hommes d'armes es pays de pardeça. A BRVXELLES, Par Rutger Velpius, & Hubert Anthoon . . . 1610. 4° sig. A^4

1568/8816.

Dated 1 April 1610.

N94 NETHERLANDS. Southern Provinces

[22.3.1611] ORDINANTIE Ende Placcaet van de Ertz-hertoghen . . . op den loop ende permissie van de Munten. T'ANTWERPEN By Hieronymus Verdussen . . . 1611. [etc.] 4° sig. $A–E^4F^2$; illus.

107.g.4(16).

Dated 22 March 1611.

N95 NETHERLANDS. Southern Provinces

[12.7.1611] ORDONNANTIE ENDE EEWICH EDICT VANDE EERTZ-HERTOGHEN . . . Tot beter directie vande saeken van Justitie/in hunne Landen van herwerts-ouer. TOT BRVSSEL, By Rutgeert Velpius ende Huybrecht Anthoon . . . 1611. 4° sig. $A–C^4$

107.g.8(7).

Issued on 12 July 1611. The privilege printed on the titlepage verso is in French. The arms of the Archdukes on the titlepage are supported by blind Justice.

N96 NETHERLANDS. Southern Provinces

[12.7.1611] ORDONNANTIE ENDE EEWICH EDICT VANDE EERTZ-HERTOGHEN . . . Tot beter directie vande saken van Justicie in hunne Landen van herwertsouer. TOT BRVESSEL, By Rutgeert Velpius ende Huybrecht Anthoon/gezworen Boecuercoopers . . . 1611. 4° sig. $A–C^4$

107.g.4(8).

Another edition of the preceding. The privilege printed on the titlepage verso is in Dutch. The arms of the Archdukes are supported by blind Justice. Dated: 'ghegheuen te Mariemont den xij. dach van Julio/int jaer . . . duysent/ses hondert ende elffue'. End: 'Ende is de voors. Ordinancie gheseghelt metten Grooten Zeghel [etc.]'.

N97 NETHERLANDS. Southern Provinces

[12.7.1611] ORDONNANTIE ENDE EEWICH EDICT VANDE EERTZ-HERTOGHEN . . . Tot beter directie vande saken van Justicie/in hunne Landen van herwertsouer. TOT BRVESSEL, By Rutgeert Velpius ende Huybrecht Anthoon/ghezworen Boeckvercoopers . . . 1611. 4° sig. $A–C^4$

107.g.13(9).

Another edition of the two preceding entries. The privilege is in Dutch. The arms of the Archdukes on the titlepage are supported by blind Justice. Dated: 'Ghegheuen te Mariemont den xij. dach van Julio/int jaer . . . ses hondert ende elfue'. End: 'Ende is de voors. Ordinancie ghesegelt metten grooten Zeghel [etc.]'

N98 NETHERLANDS. Southern Provinces

[12.7.1611] ORDONNANCIE ENDE EEWICH EDICT VANDE EERTZ HERTOGHEN . . . Tot Beter directie vande saken van Justicie in hunne Landen van herwertsouer. TOT BRVESSEL, By Rutgeert Velpius ende Huybrecht Anthoon . . . 1611. 4° sig. A–C[4]

107.g.8(4).

Another edition of the three preceding entries. The privilege is in Dutch. The arms of the Archdukes on the titlepage are different from the above and are supported by sighted Justice. Leaf A2 is erroneously signed B2.

N99 NETHERLANDS. Southern Provinces

[12.7.1611] ORDONNANCE ET EDICT PERPETVEL DES ARCHIDVCQZ . . . Pour meilleure direction des affaires de la Iustice en leurs Pays de pardeça. A BRVXELLES, Par Rutger Velpius & Hubert Anthoine . . . 1611. [etc.] 4° sig. A–C[4]

107.g.9(9).

The French version of the preceding.

N100 NETHERLANDS. Southern Provinces

[28.11.1611] INTERPRETATIE ENDE VERCLARINGHE VAN ZEKERE TWYFELACHticheden ende zwaricheden die voorgeuallen zijn inde Ordinantie ende eeuwich Edict . . . vanden xij. Julij . . . 1611. Ghemaeckt tot beter directie van de saken van Justicie inde Landen van herwertsouer . . . TOT BRVESSEL, By Rutgeert Velpius/ende Huybrecht Anthoon . . . 1611. 4° sig. A[4]

107.g.4(9).

Dated 28 November 1611. The arms on the titlepage are those supported by blind Justice.

N101 NETHERLANDS. Southern Provinces

[28.11.1611] INTERPRETATIE ENDE VERCLARINGHE VAN ZEKERE TWYFELACHticheden ende zwaricheden die voorgeuallen zijn inde Ordinantie ende eeuwich Edict . . . vanden xij. Julij . . . 1611.Ghemaeckt tot beter directie van de saken van Justicie inde Landen van herwetsouer [*sic*]. TOT BRVESSEL, By Rutgeert Velpius/ende Huybrecht Anthoon . . . 1611. 4° sig. A[4]

107.g.8(5).

Another edition of the preceding. The arms on the titlepage are those supported by sighted Justice.

N102 NETHERLANDS. Southern Provinces

[28.11.1611] INTERPRETATIE ENDE VERCLARINGHE VAN ZEKERE TVVYFFELACHticheden ende zwaricheden die voorgeuallen syn inde Ordinantie ende eeuwich Edict vande Eertzhertoghen . . . vanden xij. Julij . . . 1611.Ghemaeckt tot beter directie vande saken van Justicie inde landen van herwaertsouer. TOT BRVESSEL, By Rutgeert Velpius/ende Huybrecht Anthoon . . . 1611. 4° sig. A[4]

107.g.8(6).

Another edition of the two preceding entries. The privilege printed on A4r is in French. The arms on the titlepage are those supported by blind Justice.

N103 NETHERLANDS. Southern Provinces

[28.11.1611] INTERPRETATIE ENDE VERCLARINGHE VAN ZEKERE TWYFFELACHticheden ende zwaricheden die voorgeuallen zijn inde Ordinantie ende eeuwich Edict . . . vanden xij. Julij . . . 1611. Ghemaeckt tot beter directie van de saken van Justicie inde Landen van herwertsouer. TOT BRVSSEL, By Rutgeert Velpius/ende Huybrecht Anthoon . . . 1611. 4° sig. A[4]

107.g.13(8).

Another edition of the three preceding items. The arms on the titlepage are those supported by blind Justice.

N104 NETHERLANDS. Southern Provinces

[28.11.1611] INTERPRETATION ET ESCLAIRCISSEMENT DE CERTAINES DOVBTES ET difficultez qui se sont rencontrées en l'Ordonnance & Edict perpetuel des Archiducqz . . . du xij. de Iuillet . . . 1611. decreté pour la meilleure direction des affaires de la iustice és Pays de pardeça. A BRVXELLES, Par Rutger Velpius & Hubert Anthoine . . . 1611. [etc.] 4° sig. A^4

107.g.9(8).

The French edition of the four preceding entries. The arms on the titlepage are those supported by sighted Justice.

N105 NETHERLANDS. Southern Provinces

[14.4.1612] ORDONNANCE & Placcart des Archiducqz . . . sur le fait du cours & permission des monnoyes & aultres choses en dependantes. EN ANVERS Chez Hierosme Verdussen . . . 1612. [etc.] 4° sig. AB^4C^2

107.g.15(41).

Issued 14 April 1612.

N106 NETHERLANDS. Southern Provinces

[14.4.1612] TRANSLAET VANDE AMPLIATIEN ENDE MODERATIEN PROVISIOnele ghedaen by de . . . Eeertzhertoghen [*sic*] . . . tot beter onderhoudenisse ende obseruatie van hun eeuwich Edict/ghedecreteert opt feyt ende exercitie van d'Ambacht vanden Goutsmeden den twintichsten . . . van October . . . 1608. TOT BRVESSEL, By Rutgeert Velpius ende Huybrecht Anthoon . . . 1612. 4° sig. AB^4

107.g.17(30).

Dated 14 April 1612.

N107 NETHERLANDS. Southern Provinces

[14.4.1612] TRANSLAET VANDE AMPLIATIEN ENDE MODERATIEN PROVISIONEle ghedaen byde . . . Eertzhertoghen . . . tot beter onderhoudenisse ende obseruatie van hun eeuwich Edict . . . opt feyt ende exercitie van d'ambacht vanden gous-meden [*sic*] den xx . . . van October . . . 1608. TOT BRVSSEL, By Huybrecht Anthoon [etc.] 4° sig. A^4B^3

107.g.18(27).

Another edition of the preceding. Published after 1613?

N108 NETHERLANDS. Southern Provinces

[1613] PLACCAET ENDE ORDONNANTIE . . . opt stuck vande Straet-schenders . . . Bosch-dieuen/Vagabonden/Ledichgangers . . . TOT BRVESSEL, By Rutgeert Velpius/ende Huybrecht Anthoon . . . 1613. [etc.] 4° sig. AB^4

107.g.18(28).

Renewal dated 1613 of the ordinance of 1 June 1609.

N109 NETHERLANDS. Southern Provinces

[4.2.1613] DIE EERTS-HERTOGHEN . . . Tot Bruessel/by Rutgeert Velpius/ende Huybrecht Anthoon . . . 1613. 4° a single sheet

105.f.4(6).

A proclamation concerning collection of taxes, dated 4 February 1613. Slightly mutilated.

N110 NETHERLANDS. Southern Provinces

[31.8.1613] EDICT ET ORDONNANCE DES ARCHIDUCQZ . . . Sur le fait de la Chasse. A BRVXELLES, Chez Rutger Velpius, & Hubert Anthoine . . . 1613. 4° sig. A-E^4

107.g.8(2).

Issued 31 August 1613.

N111 [*NETHERLANDS. Southern Provinces
[31.8.1613] TRANSLAET VAN HET EDICT Ende Ordonnantie van de Erts-Hertoghen . . . Op het stuck vande Jachte. TOT BRVSSEL, By Rutgeert Velpius/ende Huybrecht Anthoon . . . 1613. 4° sig. A-E⁴
5695.a.18.]
*Destroyed. Issued 31 August 1613. Translation of the preceding. Described from the General Catalogue and the copy in the Royal Library, The Hague (1703 B 14(15)).

N112 NETHERLANDS. Southern Provinces
[30.9.1613] PLACCAET ENDE ORDINANCIE VAN HAERE HOOCHEDEN Teghens de excessen vande Bruyloften, ende bancquetten op de Vuytvaerden. TOT BRVESSEL, By Rutgeert Velpius ende Huybrecht Anthoon . . . 1613. 4° sig. A⁴
107.g.17(31); 107.g.19(30).
Dated 30 September 1613.

N113 NETHERLANDS. Southern Provinces
[20.12.1613] PLACCAET ENDE ORDINANTIE GHEMAECKT ENDE GHESTATueert by . . . de Eerts-hertogen, tot conservatie ende betaelinge van hunne Heerlicke Rechten van hunne Domeynen des Lants van Mechelen. TOT MECHELEN, Ghedruckt by HENDRICK IAEY . . . 1617. 4° sig. A⁴
106.d.41(2).
Issued 20 December 1613.

N114 NETHERLANDS. Southern Provinces
[29.11.1614] ORDINANTIE Ende Placcaet van de Ertzhertoghen . . . waer by verboden wordē alle vrempde copere munten/oock de stuyuers ende halue stuyuers van siluer/gheslagen buyten de landen vande onderdanicheyt van heure Hoocheden. T'HANTWERPEN By Hieronymus Verdussen . . . 1614. [etc.] 4° sig. AB⁴
1560/4299.
Issued 29 November 1614.

N115 NETHERLANDS. Southern Provinces
[3.6.1615] ORDONNANTIE Vande Ertz-hertoghen . . . opt faict van sekere Munte van Luyck by de selue gepermitteert ende te prijse ghestelt: Ende van andere vremde verboden penninghen/met die figuren van dien ende declaratie van de weerde der seluer. T'ANTWERPEN, By Hieronymus Verdussen . . . 1615. [etc.] 4° sig. A-D⁴; illus.
1609/1590.
Issued 3 June 1615.

N116 NETHERLANDS. Southern Provinces
[15.10.1615] PLACCAET ENDE ORDONNANCIE GHEMAECT ENDE GHESTATueert by . . . de Eeertshertoghen [*sic*]/opt stuck vande Brant-stichters/Straet-schenders/Kneuelaers / Vry-buters / Moordenaars / Bosch-dieuen / Vagabonden / Ledichganghers/ende andere . . . Quaetdoenders ende Delinquanten. TOT BRVESSEL, By Huybrecht Anthoon . . . 1615. [etc.] 4° sig. AB⁴
107.g.17(32); 107.g.18(29).
Dated 1615, with a manuscript note '15 October' added in the copy at 107.g.17(32).

N117 NETHERLANDS. Southern Provinces
[28.4.1616] DIE EERTZHERTOGHEN . . . Tot Bruessel/by Huybrecht Anthoon . . . 1616. 4° a single sheet
112.f.33(9).
A proclamation on crime, dated 28 April 1616.

N118 NETHERLANDS. Southern Provinces
[28.4.1616] PLACCAET ENDE ORDONNANCIE GHEMAECT ENDE GHESTAtueert by . . . de Eeertshertoghen [*sic*]/opt stuck vande Brant-stichters/Straet-schenders/ Kneuelaers / Vry-buters / Moordenaers / Bosch-dieuen / Ledich-gangers ende vagabonden. TOT BRVESSEL, by Huybrecht Anthoon . . . 1616. [etc.] 4° sig. A-C^4
107.g.17(33); 107.g.18(30).
Dated 28 April 1616.

N119 NETHERLANDS. Southern Provinces
[14.12.1616] EDICT ENDE ORDINANTIE BY VORME VAN VERCLARINghe ende ampliatie/ ghemaeckt . . . by-de Eertz-hertoghen . . . nopende het draghen ende vueren van Wapenen/Tymbren/Titulen ende andere teeckenen van eeren ende van Edeldom. TOT BRVESSEL, By Huybrecht Anthoon . . . 1616. 4° sig. AB^4
107.g.18(23).
Issued 14 December 1616.

N120 NETHERLANDS. Southern Provinces
[14.12.1616] EDICT ET ORDONNANCE PAR FORME D'ESCLAIRCISSEment & ampliation, faicte & decretée par les Archiducz . . . touchant le port des Armoires, Tymbres, Tiltres, & autres marques d'honneur & de Noblesse. A BRVXELLES, Chez Hubert Antoine . . . 1616. 4° sig. AB^4
107.g.15(18).
The French edition of the preceding.

N121 NETHERLANDS. Southern Provinces
[21.4.1617] ORDONNANTIE Ende Placcaet van de Ertz-Hertoghen . . . inhoudende de specien vande goude ende siluere munten die voortaen . . . sullen moghen ganck ende loop hebben inde landen van hunne onderdanicheyt. T'ANTWERPEN, By Hieronymus Verdussen . . . 1617. [etc.] 4° sig. A-E^4; illus.
107.g.13(7).
Dated 1617 only, but with the full date supplied in manuscript, together with secretary Verreyken's initials W.V., as 21 April 1617.

N122 NETHERLANDS. Southern Provinces
[12.10.1617] PLACCAET ENDE ORDONNANCIE GHEMAECKT ENDE GHEStatueert by . . . de Eerts Hertoghen/opt stuck vande Roouers/Straetschenders/Vrybuyters/ Brandtstichters/ende andere . . . quaetdoenders ende delinquanten. TOT BRVESSEL, By Huybrecht Anthoon . . . 1617. 4° sig. A^4B^2
107.g.16(14); 107.g.17(34).
Dated 12 October 1617.

N123 NETHERLANDS. Southern Provinces
[15.1.1618] ORDO[NANTIE] VAN[DE] ERTSHERT[OGHEN] . . . Rakende het stuck vande Gulden [ende Borghe]lijcke Wachte der Stadt van A[ntwerpen.] T'ANTWERPEN, By Geerardt van Wolsschaten . . . M.DC.XVIII. [etc.] 4° pp.19
107.g.21(5).
Issued 15 January 1618. The titlepage is mutilated, with the missing text supplied in manuscript.

N124 NETHERLANDS. Southern Provinces
[16.1.1618] TRANSLAET VANDE ORDINANTIE VANDE EERTZ-HERTOGHEN . . . By de welcke hunne Hoocheden verbieden het vervueren vande salpetren ende buspoeyeren . . . TOT BRVESSEL, By Huybrecht Anthoon . . . 1618. 4° sig. AB^4
107.g.17(35).
Dated 16 January 1618.

N125 NETHERLANDS. Southern Provinces
[21.5.1618] ORDONNANTIE Ende Placcaet van de Ertz-Hertoghen . . . opt stuck vande Munte/inhoudende Specien/prijs ende ghewichte van de Goude/Silvere ende Copere munten/die voortaen alleenlijck sullen moghen ganck ende loop hebben inde Landen van hunne onderdanicheydt. T'ANTWERPEN, By Hieronymus Verdussen . . . 1618. 4° sig. A-$D^4E^6F^3$
107.g.4(17); 107.g.15(17).
Issued 21 May 1618.

N126 NETHERLANDS. Southern Provinces
[12.9.1619] ORDINANCIE vande Ertzhertoghen . . . op't feyt vande munte. TOT ANTVVERPEN, By Hieronymus Verdussen . . . 1619. [etc.] 4° sig. $A^4B^2C^3$
107.g.15(16).
Issued 12 September 1619.

N127 NETHERLANDS. Southern Provinces
[9.11.1619] DECLARATIE ENDE DECRET VAN HAERE . . . HOOCHEDEN, Op de Requeste van die vande Natien der Stadt van Bruessele. TOT BRVESSEL, By Huybrecht Anthoon . . . 1619. 4° sig. A^4
107.g.29(6).
Issued 9 November 1619. The privilege is in French.

N128 [*NETHERLANDS. Southern Provinces
[1.1621] Carte ou Liste contenant le pris de chascun Marcq, Once, Estrelin, & Aes poids de Troyes, de toutes les especes d'or & d'argent déffendues, legieres, ou trop usées, & moyennant ce declarées pour billon, comme les Maistres des monnoies & changeurs sermentez sont tenuz d'en payer pour iceulx, selon l'Ordonnance de leurs Altezes sereniss., faicte par les Maistres generaulx des Monnoies au mois de Janvier 1621. Avec les figures des mesmes monnoyes. Anvers . . . 1621. 4°
7755.aaa.31.]
*Destroyed. No other copy located. Transcribed from the General Catalogue. An edition in Dutch, published by Hieronymus Verdussen, is described in *Van der Wulp* no.1767, containing 158 pages.

N129 NETHERLANDS. Southern Provinces
[18.4.1621] L'ARCHIDVC . . . A ANVERS, EN L'IMPRIMERIE PLANTINIENNE, M.DC.XXI. 4° a single sheet
112.f.33(2).
Dated 18 April 1621. On the billeting of troops in villages.

N130 NETHERLANDS. Southern Provinces. Army
LISTE Van alle de nieuwe CAPITEYNEN Nv cordts ghemaeckt in de Maent van Februarius anno 1621. door zijn HOOCHEYT den Eertz-Hertoghe ALBERTVS. Eerst Ghedruckt den 5. Meert 1621. T'Hantwerpen/by Abraham Verhoeven/[etc.] 4° pp.7; sig. A^4; illus.
P.P.3444.af(197).
Headed: Martius 1621. 30. The titlepage woodcuts showing a double portrait of Albert and Isabella within a typographical border and the picture of an officer bearing a pike in a plain square frame.

N131 NETHERLANDS. Southern Provinces. Army
LISTE Van alle de nieuwe CAPITEYNEN . . . T'Hantwerpen/by Abraham Verhoeven/[etc.] 4° pp.7; sig. A^4; illus.
P.P.3444.af(197*).
A new edition of the preceding, with additional names replacing the statement 'De plaetse en is noch niet versien' of the previous edition and corrections elsewhere. Published in 1621.

With a manuscript inscription to the titlepage illustration of the officer: 'monssûr d vyant gaet naer den krijg medt die Hellebaert in de Handt'.

N132 NETHERLANDS. United Provinces. Constitutional documents
[29.1.1579] Verhandelinghe vande Unie/eewich verbont ende eendracht. Tusschen die Landen/Provincien/Steden ende Leden van dien hier nae benoempt/ binnen die Stadt Vtrecht ghesloten . . . den 29. Januarij/Anno M.D.LXXJX. Na de Copye ghedruct tVtrecht, by Coenraedt Henricksz. IN S'RAVEN-HAGHE [*sic*], By Hillebrandt Iacobsz . . . 1607. 4° sig. $A–C^4$
T.1723(10).
The text of the Union of Utrecht. Corresponding to the copy described in *Knuttel* no.412.

N133 NETHERLANDS. United Provinces. Constitutional documents
[29.1.1579] VERHANDELINGE Vande Vnie/eewich Verbondt ende Eendracht, Tusschen de Landen Provincien, Steden ende Leden van dien hier na benoemt, binnen de Stadt Vtrecht ghesloten . . . den XXIX. Ianuarij . . . M.D.L.XXIX. T'VTRECHT, By Salomõ de Roy . . . 1618. 4° sig. $A–C^4D^2$
T.2419(4).
Another edition of the preceding. Corresponding to the copy described in *Knuttel* no.413.

N134 NETHERLANDS. United Provinces. States General
[1580] EXTRACT Wt de Annotatien ende Verclaringhen van de Acten des Vredehandels te Colen gheschiet/A°. 1579 . . . Vervattende 't Recht der Volck'ren, de Macht der Ov'richeden, ende de justificatie van die van de Gereformeerde Religie inde Nederlandtsche Provincien . . . t'AMSTERDAM, By Marten Jansz. Brandt . . . 1618. 4° sig. A^4
T.2248(6); 106.d.43.
Originally part of the commentary added by the States General to the peace negotiations of Cologne and published at Leiden in 1580. Printed by Paulus van Ravesteyn at Amsterdam.

N135 NETHERLANDS. United Provinces. Staten Generaal
[20.9.1591] PLACCAET Van den Tarra opt stuc vande Enghelsche Laeckenen. Wtghegheven den twintighsten Septembris/Anno 1591. IN S'GRAVENHAGE. By Aelbrecht Heyndricksz. . . . 1591. Ende nu t'Amsterdam, By Broer Jansz. . . . 1616. 4° sig. A^4
573.f.35.
Reprinted from the original proclamation issued by the States General on 20 September 1591.

N136 NETHERLANDS. United Provinces. Staten Generaal
[7.6.1602] [A haults, illustres, reuerends, nobles, doctes, prudens & discrets Seigneurs, etc.] RESPONCE OV SOLVTION, Sur vne Lettre des Estatz de Hollande, le vij. de Iuin en cest an 1602. escripte aux Estatz des prouinces fideles du Pays bas. Par certain amateur de la Patrie . . . Imprimé, En l'an Mil six Cens & deux. 8° sig. $A–D^8E^4$
8079.b.11.
Containing the text of the original letter, 'A Haults, illustres, reuerends, nobles, doctes, prudens & discrets Seigneurs, etc.' with the reply. The original letter signed 'de V.E.R.S. & G. bons amys & voisins, les Estatz generaulx des Prouinces vnies'. Printed and published by Rutger Velpius at Brussels?

N137 NETHERLANDS. United Provinces. Staten Generaal
[18.2.1606] PLACCAET Ende Ordre Provisioneel waer nae alle goude ende silvere penninghen/voorts aen in de Vereenichde Nederlanden sullen werden ontfanghen ende uytghegeven. IN S'GRAVEN-HAGHE, By Hillebrandt Iacobsz. . . . 1606. [etc.] 4° sig. A^4
T.1712(16).
Dated 18 February 1606.

N138 [*NETHERLANDS. United Provinces. Staten Generaal
[21.3.1606] Placcaet ende Ordonnantie van . . . die Staten Generael . . . soo opten cours van't Gelt, als opte Politie ende discipline, betreffende d'exercitie vande Munte, ende Muntslach . . . In s'Graven-hage, by Hillebrant Jacobsz . . . 1606. 4° 38 pages
7757.aaa.32(3).]
*Destroyed. Issued 21 March 1606. Described from the General Catalogue and *Petit* no. 826.

N139 [*NETHERLANDS. United Provinces. Staten Generaal
[21.3.1606] MANUAEL, Ofte Handtboeck/Jnhoudende die Weerde vanden Marck/ Once/Engelsche ende Aes/van alle gevalueerde ende ongevalueerde Munte/ dienende den Wisselaers deser Vereenichde Nederlantsche Provintien voor Instructie op d'Ordonnantie vander Munte/vanden Jare 1606 . . . IN S'GRAVEN-HAGHE, By Hillebrandt Iacobsz. . . . 1606. [etc.] 4° sig. A–M⁴; illus.
7757.aaa.32(2).]
*Destroyed. Described from the General Catalogue and the copy in the Royal Library, The Hague (557 C 13) in which additional information and corrections printed in roman on loose labels are attached to the original letterpress which is partly printed in civilité.

N140 NETHERLANDS. United Provinces. Staten Generaal
[21.3.1606] BEELDENAER, Ofte Figuer-boeck/dienende op de nieuwe Ordonnantie vander Munte/gearresteert . . . by . . . de Staten Generael der Vereenichde Nederlanden/op den 21^en^ Marty . . . 1606. In welcke gerepresenteert zijn/alle de Figuren van Goude ende Silvere Munte/cours . . . hebbende in crachte der selver Ordonnantie . . . IN S'GRAVEN-HAGHE, By Hillebrandt Iacobsz. . . . 1606. [etc.] 4° sig. A–I⁴K¹; illus.
T.1712(17).
Another copy or edition of this publication once at 7757.aaa.32(4) has been destroyed. As its collation was not recorded it cannot be identified as another copy of the preceding or a later edition, published in 1608, consisting of sig. A–H⁴I⁶, recorded without date as a later edition in *Tiele* no. 569 and dated 1608 in *Petit* no. 827, of which a copy also exists at the Royal Library, The Hague, at 523 F 22(2).

N141 NETHERLANDS. United Provinces. Staten Generaal
[22.6.1607] COPYE Vande Brievẽ der Heeren Generale Staten vande Gheunieerde Provincien. Gheschreven aen den . . . Staten van Hollandt ende West-vrieslandt/ ofte haere E. Ghecommitteerde Raden. Inhoudende de Limiten hoe verre den Stil-standt van VVapenen te Water ende te Lande is streckende. TOT DELF, Ghedruckt by Jan Andriesz. [etc.] 4° 2 unsigned leaves
T.1713(14); C.30.e.22(2).
Dated 22 June 1607. Published in 1607. Corresponding to the copy described in *Knuttel* no. 1381.

N142 NETHERLANDS. United Provinces. Staten Generaal
[22.6.1607] COPYE Vande Brieven der Heeren Generale Staten vande Gheunieerde Provintien. Gheschreven Aen den . . . Staten van Hollandt ende West-vrieslandt/ Ofte haere E. Ghecommitteerde Raden. Inhoudende de Limiten hoe verre den Stilstandt van Wapenen te Water ende te Lande is streckende. TOT DELF, Ghedruckt by Jan Andriesz. [etc.] 4° 2 unsigned leaves
107.g.14(32).
A different edition of the preceding, also published in 1607. Corresponding to the copy described in *Knuttel* no. 1382.

N143 NETHERLANDS. United Provinces. Staten Generaal
[1608] Artijckelen Vanden Treffues oft bestant/voor ghestelt by de . . . Ambassadeurs vande Coninghen van Vranckrijck ende groot Britagnien, inde vergaderinghe vande Heeren Staten Generael. Anno M.VI^{C}.VIII. 4° sig. A^4
106.d.10.
No precise date given for the assembly of the States General. Printed by Richard Schilders at Middelburg. Corresponding to the copy described in *Knuttel* no.1543.

N144 NETHERLANDS. United Provinces. Staten Generaal
[25.8.1608] HET AF-SCHEIDT vande . . . Heeren Staten vande Gheunieerde Provintien/Gegeven aende Ghecommitteerde vanden Coninck van Spaegnien ende d'Eerts-herghen [*sic*]/inden Haghe vergadert op't stuck vande Vredehandelinge ANNO 1608. MIDDELBVRGH Voor Symon Iansz. [etc.] 4° sig. A^4
106.d.19.
Issued 25.8.1608. Published in 1608.

N145 [*NETHERLANDS. United Provinces. Staten Generaal
[6.10.1608] Beeldenaer ofte Figuer-boeck, dienende op de provisionele ordre vander Munte, uyt-ghegeven by de . . . Staten Generael . . . op den sesten Octobris, 1608. In welcke gerepresenteert zijn alle de Figueren van Goude ende Silvere Munte, cours . . . hebbende in crachte der selver Ordonnantie . . . s'Graven-Haghe . . . 1608. 4° illus.
7757.aaa.32(5).]
*Destroyed. No doubt printed by Hillebrant Jacobsz Wouw. Described from the General Catalogue.

N146 NETHERLANDS. United Provinces. Staten Generaal
[21.4.1609] Vercondinge van het Bestant, tusschen die Majesteyt vanden Coninck van Spaignien, &c., die . . . EertzHertoghen . . . ter eenre. Ende die . . . Staten Generael vande Vereenichde Nederlanden, ter anderer zijden. Ghedaen voor den Stadthuyse vanden Haghe, den een ende tvvintichsten Aprilis Anno 1609 . . . In s'Graven-Haghe, By Hillebrant Iacobsz. [etc.] fol. a single sheet
105.f.4(5).
Published in 1609.

N147 NETHERLANDS. United Provinces. Staten Generaal
[22.4.1609] Copye. Eersame/wijse/voorsienighe seer discreete Heeren. [etc.] fol. a single sheet; illus.
T.2420(45).
The text of a letter from the States General, dated 22 April 1609, to burgomasters and governors of various towns prescribing a general day of prayer on 6 May 1609. The woodcut illustration at the head of the letter entitled 'Het Hof van Hollandt'. Published in 1609.

N148 NETHERLANDS. United Provinces. Staten Generaal
[22.4.1609] Copye Des Briefs vāde . . . Heeren Staten der vereenichder Nederlanden/aengaende den Biddach/verordonneert te houden den 6. May 1609. tot dancksegginghe van't Bestant van xij. Jaren/Besloten binnen Antwerpen den 9. Aprilis . . . Met de drie secrete Artyckelen/vande welcke mentie gemaect wort int sevende Artyckel van t'Tractaet vandeñ Trevis oft Bestant. 1609. 4° 4 unsigned leaves
106.d.26.
The first item consists of the text of the preceding.

N149 NETHERLANDS. United Provinces. Staten Generaal
[20.8.1609] PLACCAET Vande . . . Staten Generael der Vereenichde Nederlanden/ Daer by hare Ho. Mo. E. (claerlijck bewesen hebbende/dat de Stadt Grave ende 'tLandt van Cuyck eene Heerlijckheyt is) Bevelen die Officiers/Justiciers/ende Ondersaten des Landts van Cuyck/niemants bevelen/in saecken de Hooghe Overicheyt der voorsz Landen aengaende/te ontfanghen nochte ghehoorsamen/ als die ghene van hare Hooge Mo. E. Opte penen daer by ghestatueert. IN S'GRAVEN-HAGHE, By Hillebrant Iacobsz . . . 1609. [etc.] 4° sig. A^2
107.g.16(13).
Issued 20 August 1609.

N150 [*NETHERLANDS. United Provinces. Staten Generaal
[27.8.1609] CONTINVATIE Vande Tollerantie ofte permissie vanden cours van alle Goude ende Silvere penninghen, inde Vereenichde Provintien/voor de Maenden van September/October/eñ November des Jaers sesthien-hondert ende negen . . . by ordre vande Staten Generael . . . IN S'GRAVEN-HAGHE, By Hillebrant Iacobsz . . . 1609. [etc.] 4° sig. A^4
7752.aaa.32(6).]
*Destroyed. Described from the General Catalogue and the copy in the Royal Library, The Hague (Plakkaat Q 358 no.11).

N151 NETHERLANDS. United Provinces. Staten Generaal
[30.3.1610] MISSIVE Vanden . . . Staten Generael der vereenichde Nederlandē/ aende . . . Staten vande particuliere Provintien/tot Justificatie vande dadelijcke proceduren die heurer Ho. Mo. ghenootdruckt zijn jeghens de Stadt Utrecht/tot maintenement vande wettelicke authoriteyt voor te nemen. IN S'GRAVEN-HAGHE. By Hillebrant Jacobsz. . . . 1610. [etc.] 4° sig. A^4
T.2240(24); 106.d.31.
Dated 30 March 1610.

N152 NETHERLANDS. United Provinces. Staten Generaal
[1.7.1610] PLACCAET Ende Ordonnantie van de . . . Staten Generael der Vereenichde Nederlanden/op den Cours vanden ghelde/zoo goude als silvere specien/Waer nae alle . . . Ingesetenen . . . sich voorts-aen sullen hebben te reguleren . . . IN S'GRAVEN-HAGHE. By Hillebrant Iacobsz . . . 1610. [etc.] 4° sig. A^6
T.1712(18).
Dated 1 July 1610.

N153 NETHERLANDS. United Provinces. Staten Generaal
[6.7.1610] PLACCAET Ende Ordonnantie vāde . . . Staten Generael der Vereenichde Nederlanden/Soo opten cours van t'Gelt/als opte Politie ende discipline/ betreffende d'exercitie vande Munte . . . IN S'GRAVEN-HAGHE. By Hillebrant Iacobsz . . . 1610. [etc.] 4° sig. A-D^4
T.1712(19).
Issued 6 July 1610.

N154 NETHERLANDS. United Provinces. Staten Generaal
[6.7.1610] BEELDENAER Ofte Figuer-boeck/dienende op de nieuwe Ordonnantie vander Munte/gearresteert . . . by de . . . Staten Generael der Vereenichde Nederlanden/op den sesten Julij 1610 . . . IN S'GRAVEN-HAGHE. By Hillebrant Iacobsz . . . 1610. [etc.] 4° sig. A-I^4; illus.
T.1712(20).
What appears to have been another copy, once at 7757.aaa.30, was destroyed.

N155 NETHERLANDS. United Provinces. Staten Generaal

[6.7.1610] BEELDE[N]A[ER] Ofte Figuer-boeck/dienende op de nieuwe Ordonnantie vander Munte/gearresteert . . . op den sesten Julij 1610 . . . IN S'GRAVEN-HAGHE, By Hillebrant Iacobssz . . . 1613. [etc.] 4° sig. A-H^4I^6

602.b.30.

A reprint of the preceding. The titlepage and many other leaves are mutilated.

N156 NETHERLANDS. United Provinces. Staten Generaal

[6.7.1610] MANVAEL OFTE Handtboeck/Inhoudende die Weerde vanden Marck/ Once/Engelsche/ eñ Aes/van alle ghevalueerde ende onghevalueerde Munte/ dienende den . . . Wissel-bancken ende Wisselaers deser Vereenichde Nederlantsche Provintien/voor Instructie op d'Ordonnantie vander Munte/ vanden Jare 1610 . . . IN S'GRAVEN-HAGHE. By Hillebrant Iacobsz . . . 1610. 4° sig. A-O^4; illus.

T.1712(21).

Issued to accompany the decree of 6 July 1610.

N157 NETHERLANDS. United Provinces. Staten Generaal

[9.5.1611] COPIEN Vande Sententien/ofte Vonnissen binnen Vtrecht gewesen/ teghens verscheyden Persoonen: Die ghecomplotteert ende voorgenomen hadden/omme den . . . Commandeur ende Krijghs-volck binnen de Stadt . . . te vermeesteren/ende de . . . Staten s'Lants van Vtrecht te overvallen/om te brenghen . . . Ende haer selven . . . met ghewelt inde Regieringhe . . . te stellen. Ghedruckt voor Jan Evertsen van Doorn . . . tot Wtrecht . . . M DC XI. 4° sig. A-D^4

T.2241(6); 106.d.36.

The sentences passed on 9 May 1611 on Jan Ruysch and others by a judicial body made up by the States General, the States of Utrecht and the court of the city of Utrecht. Dated 9 May 1611. The copy at T.2241(6) wanting the last leaf, blank. Corresponding to the copy described in *Tiele* no.913.

N158 NETHERLANDS. United Provinces. Staten Generaal

[27.3.1612] PLACCAET Vande . . . Staten Generael der Vereenichde Nederlanden: Inhoudende Ordre/waer naer de Jesuijten/Priesters/ende Monicken vande Pausselijcke ofte Roomsche Religie inde selve Landen komende/hen sullen dragen etc. Verboth aende Ingesetenen van hen . . . te verbinden tot voorstant vande macht des Paus van Roome . . . IN S'GRAVEN-HAGHE, By Hillebrant Iacobssz . . . 1612. [etc.] 4° sig. A^6

T.1727(15); 107.g.19(10).

Dated 27 March 1612.

N159 NETHERLANDS. United Provinces. Staten Generaal

[26.9.1615] PLACCAET Ende Ordonnantie vande . . . Staten Generael der Vereenighde Nederlanden/op den Cours vanden Ghelde/soo Goude als Silvere specien . . . IN S'GRAVEN-HAGHE, By Hillebrant Iacobssz . . . 1615. 4° sig. A^6

T.1712(22).

Dated 26 September 1615.

N160 NETHERLANDS. United Provinces. Staten Generaal

[26.9.1615] BEELDENAER OFTE Figuer-boeck/dienende op de nieuwe Ordonnantie vander Munte/gearresteert . . . by de . . . Staten Generael der Vereenighde Nederlanden/op den sessentwintichsten Septembris sesthien-hondert ende vijfthien . . . IN S'GRAVEN-HAGHE, By Hillebrant Iacobssz . . . 1615. [etc.] 4° sig. A-H^4I^6; illus.

T.1712(23).

N161 NETHERLANDS. United Provinces. Staten Generaal
[22.5.1617] PLACCAET OP de Commercien vande Coopluyden Adventuriers vande Engelsche Natie. IN S'GRAVEN-HAGHE, By Hillebrandt Iacobsz . . . 1617. 4° sig. A^4
107.g.14(7).
A reissue dated 22 May 1617 of the proclamation of 22 March 1599.

N162 NETHERLANDS. United Provinces. Staten Generaal
[8.12.1617] COPIE DIE Staten Generael der Vereenichde Nederlanden . . . Doen te vveten: Alzo . . . Dudley Carleton . . . vertoont heeft/dat . . . een Boucxken was uytghegaen . . . gheintituleert Weeghschaal . . . SOO IST/dat die . . . Staten Generael . . . gheordonneert hebben . . . de . . . Boucxkens . . . wederom in te trecken/Verbiedende de selve inde Vereenichde Provintien voortane [*sic*] meer te ontfanghen/verkoopen/oft . . . uyt te gheven . . . 1617. 4° a single sheet
T.2247(25).
Dated 8 December 1617.

N163 NETHERLANDS. United Provinces. Staten Generaal
[22.12.1618] PLACCAET Vande . . . Staten Generael der Vereenighde Nederlanden/ teghens het Inbrenghen/Drucken/Verkoopen ofte stroyen van alderhande argerlijcke eñ seditieuse Boucxkens/Liedekẽs etc. . . . S'GRAVEN-HAGHE, By Hillebrant Iacobssz . . . 1618. [etc.] 4° sig. A^4
1560/2937; 1608/3548.
Dated 22 December 1618.

N164 NETHERLANDS. United Provinces. Staten Generaal
[13.2.1619] PROVISIONEEL PLACCAET Ende Ordonnantie vande . . . Staten Generael der Vereenighde Nederlanden/op den Cours vanden Ghelde/soo Goude als Silvere specien . . . IN S'GRAVEN-HAGHE, By Hillebrant Iacobssz . . . 1619. [etc.] 4° sig. AB^4C^2
T.1712(24).
Dated 13 February 1619.

N165 NETHERLANDS. United Provinces. Staten Generaal
[13.2.1619] BEELDENAER OFTE Figuer-boeck/dienende op de Nieuwe Provisionele Ordonnantie vander Munte/gearresteert . . . by de . . . Staten Generael der Vereenighde Nederlanden/op den derthienden Februarij sesthien-hondert negenthien; In welcke gherepresenteert zijn/alle de Figueren vande Goude ende Silvere Munte/cours . . . hebbende in krachte der selver Ordonnantie/ende boven welcken gheene tot anderen prijse ontfangen ofte besteet sullen mogen werden. IN S'GRAVEN-HAGHE, By Hillebrant Iacobssz . . . 1619. [etc.] 4° sig. A-K^4; illus.
106.d.51.

N166 NETHERLANDS. United Provinces. Staten Generaal
[13.5.1619] SENTENTIE, uyt-ghesproocken ende ghepronuncieert over Iohan van Oldenbarnevelt . . . eñ geexecuteert den derthienden May Anno sesthienhondert negenthien . . . op't Binnen-Hof in 'sGraven-Haghe. IN S'GRAVEN-HAGHE, By Hillebrant Iacobssz . . . 1619. [etc.] 4° sig. AB^4
T.2422(28).
Corresponding to the copy described in *Knuttel* no.2884.

N167 NETHERLANDS. United Provinces. Staten Generaal
[13.5.1619] SENTENTIE, uyt-ghesproocken ende ghepronuncieert over Iohan van Oldenbarnevelt . . . eñ geexecuteert den derthienden May . . . sesthienhondert

negenthien . . . op't Binnen-Hof in 'sGraven-Haghe. IN S'GRAVEN-HAGHE, By Hillebrant Iacobssz . . . 1619. [etc.] 4° sig. AB^4
T.2249(15).

With an additional engraved portrait of Oldenbarnevelt, bearing an inscription in French, of which the signature has been erased. A plate showing the execution scene, signed: S. Fokke and dated 1754, published by Isaac Tirion, has been inserted in this copy which corresponds to that described in *Knuttel* no.2885.

N168 NETHERLANDS. United Provinces. Staten Generaal
[13.5.1619] SENTENTIA Lata & pronuntiata adversus Ioannem ab Oldenbarnevelt . . . & executioni mandata XIII Maij 1619 in area interiore Aulæ Hagæ Comitanæ. HAGÆ-COMITIS, Apud ARNOLDVM MEVRIS. [etc.] 4° sig. AB^4
517.g.18(3).

The Latin version of the preceding. Published in 1619.

N169 NETHERLANDS. United Provinces. Staten Generaal
[15.5.1619] SENTENTIE, uyt-ghesproocken ende ghepronuncieert over Gielis van Ledenberch . . . ende over desselfs Cadaver geexecuteert den vijfthienden May . . . sesthien hondert negenthien . . . IN S'GRAVEN-HAGHE, By Hillebrant Iacobssz . . . 1619. [etc.] 4° sig. A^6
T.2249(18).

N170 NETHERLANDS. United Provinces. Staten Generaal
[15.5.1619] SENTENTIA LATA ET PRONVNTIATA Adversus ÆGIDIVM LEDENBERGIVM . . . & in cadaver eius executioni mandata die decimo quinto Maii, anno millesimo sexcentesimo decimo & nono . . . HAGÆ-COMITIS, Apud ARNOLDVM MEVRIS. [etc.] 4° sig. A^4B^3
517.g.18(4).

The Latin version of the preceding. Published in 1619.

N171 NETHERLANDS. United Provinces. Staten Generaal
[17.5.1619] BRIEF Van de . . . STATEN GENERAEL vande Gheunieerde Provintien, Aen den . . . KONINCK Van Vrancrijck ende Navarre . . . 1619. 4° pp.7
T.2249(14).

Justifying the execution of Johan van Oldenbarnevelt. Dated 17 May 1619.

N172 NETHERLANDS. United Provinces. Staten Generaal
[18.5.1619] SENTENTIE, uyt-ghesproocken . . . over Hugo de Groot . . . den achthienden May . . . sesthien-hondert negenthien . . . IN S'GRAVEN-HAGHE, By Hillebrant Iacobssz . . . 1619. [etc.] 4° sig. AB^4
8079.d.20; T.2249(20).

The copy at T.2249(20) contains a portrait with engraved verses by Gerard Brandt and an additional engraved plate showing Hugo de Groot's escape from Loevestein, signed. S. Fokke and dated 1754, published by Isaac Tirion.

N173 NETHERLANDS. United Provinces. Staten Generaal
[18.5.1619] SENTENTIA Lata & pronuntiata adversus Hugonem Grotium . . . XVIII Maii . . . HAGÆ-COMITIS, Apud ARNOLDVM MEVRIS. [etc.] 4° sig. AB^4C^3
517.g.18(1).

The Latin version of the preceding. Published in 1619.

N174 NETHERLANDS. United Provinces. Staten Generaal
[18.5.1619] SENTENTIE, uyt-ghesproocken . . . over Rombout Hoogerbeetz . . . den achthienden May . . . sesthien-hondert negenthien . . . IN 'S-GRAVEN-HAGHE, By Hillebrant Iacobssz . . . 1619. [etc.] 4° sig. A^6; port.
T.2249(19).

The portrait, unsigned, has a Latin inscription.

N175 NETHERLANDS. United Provinces. Staten Generaal
[18.5.1619] SENTENTIA Lata & pronuntiata adversus Rumoldum Hogerbetium . . . XVIII Maii 1619 . . . HAGÆ-COMITIS, Apud ARNOLDVM MEVRIS. [etc.] 4° sig. AB^4
517.g.18(2).
The Latin version of the preceding. Published in 1619.

N176 NETHERLANDS. United Provinces. Staten Generaal
[19.5.1619] COPYE VANDEN BRIEF by de . . . Staten Generael, gheschreven aende respective Provintien. IN 'SGRAVEN-HAGHE, By Hillebrant Iacobssz . . . 1619. [etc.] 4° 2 unsigned leaves
T.2242(29); T.2249(17).
Dated 19 May 1619, justifying the execution of Johan van Oldenbarnevelt. Corresponding to the copy described in *Knuttel* no.2925.

N177 NETHERLANDS. United Provinces. Staten Generaal
[19.5.1619] EXEMPLAR EPISTOLÆ A . . . DD. Ordinibus Generalibus missæ AD Singulas fœderati Belgij Provincias. HAGÆ-COMITIS, Apud ARNOLDVM MEVRIS. 1619. [etc.] 4° sig. A^2
491.d.3.
The Latin version of the preceding.

N178 NETHERLANDS. United Provinces. Staten Generaal
[3.7.1619] PLACCAET Vande . . . Staten Generael der Vereenighde Nederlanden/ daer by alle Inghesetenen . . . verboden werdt te houden eenighe aparte vergaderinghen ofte Conventiculen/onder decksel van oeffeninghe vande Leere inde vijf bekende controverse Religions Poincten vervatet . . . IN S'GRAVEN-HAGHE, By Hillebrant Iacobssz . . . 1619. [etc.] 4° sig. A^6
T.2249(25); 107.g.19(11).
Dated 3 July 1619. The copy at T.2249(25) contains an engraved plate showing the scales on which the 'Institutio Calvini' is weighed against Arminius's ''tHeilig regt van elke stat', a version without text of the plate described in *Muller* no.1333. For the version with text, entitled 'Op de waeg-schael', 1618, *see* VONDEL, Joost van den [Other works].

N179 NETHERLANDS. United Provinces. Staten Generaal
[5.7.1619] RESOLVTIE By de . . . Staten Generael der Vereenighde Nederlanden/ ghenomen jeghens eenighe gheciteerde Remonstranten/ende met hun ghevouchden/op den vijfden Julij sesthienhondert negenthien. IN 'SGRAVEN-HAGHE, By Hillebrant Iacobssz . . . 1619. 4° 2 unsigned leaves
T.2249(26).
Cropped.

N180 NETHERLANDS. United Provinces. Staten Generaal
[1.2.1620] PLACCAET, Vande . . . Staten Generael der Vereenighde Nederlanden/ daer by 't Placcaet vanden derden Julij sesthienhondert ende negenthien/ gheconfirmeert/ende ordre ghestelt werdt teghen de uytghewesen ende afghesette Predicanten Mitsgaders Proponenten/ende andere Persoonen . . . die ongerusticheyt . . . onder dexel van Religie soucken aen te rechten. IN S'GRAVEN-HAGHE, By Hillebrant Iacobsz . . . 1620. [etc.] 8° sig. A^5
T.2250(2).
Dated 1 February 1620. The titlepage verso headed: PRIVILEGIE.

N181 NETHERLANDS. United Provinces. Staten Generaal
[1.2.1620] PLACCAET . . . daer by 't Placcaet vanden derden Julij sesthienhondert

ende negenthien/gheconfirmeert/ende ordre ghestelt werdt teghen de uytghewesen . . . Predicanten; Mitsgaders Proponenten . . . IN S'GRAVEN-HAGHE, By Hillebrant Iacobssz . . . 1620. [etc.] 4° sig. A^5
107.g.19(42).
Another edition of the preceding, with a different device on the titlepage and the titlepage verso headed: PREVILEGIE. Corresponding to the copy described in *Knuttel* no. 3061.

N182 NETHERLANDS. United Provinces. Staten Generaal
[16.5.1620] SENTENTIE IOHANNIS GREVII, Ghewesen Predicant tot Heusden. IN 'SGRAVEN-HAGHE, By Hillebrant Iacobssz . . . 1620. [etc.] 4° sig. A^4
T.2250(5).
Dated 16 May 1620.

N183 NETHERLANDS. United Provinces. Staten Generaal
[6.6.1620] VERKLARINGE VANDE SENTENTIEN GHEPROnuncieert jeghens Johan van Oldenbarnevelt ende sijne Complicen, by de Heeren Ghedelegeerde Rechteren, vande . . . Staten Generael inden Hage beschreven. Gedaen op den sesten Iunij 1620. IN S'GRAVEN-HAGHE, By Hillebrant Iacobssz . . . 1620. [etc.] 4° 2 unsigned leaves
T.2422(30).

N184 [*NETHERLANDS. United Provinces. Staten Generaal
[2.12.1620] Placcaet Provisioneel . . . opt ontfangen ende uytgeven van alle de Schellinghen eenen Arent voerende . . . 'sGraven-Haghe . . . Hillebrant Jacobssz. . . . 1620. 4° 4 leaves
5686.a.30(11).]
*Destroyed. Issued 2 December 1620. Described from the General Catalogue and *Petit* no. 1272.

N185 NETHERLANDS. United Provinces. Staten Generaal
[3.6.1621] ORDONNANTIEN ENDE ARTICVLEN Beraemt by de . . . Staten Generael/der Geunieerde Provintien/op het toe-rusten ende toe-stellen/van eene West-Indische Compagnie. Mitsgaders alle privilegien ende gherechticheden/de zelve ghegheven ende vergundt. Ghedruckt in het Iaer . . . 1621. 4° sig. AB^4
1029.e.1.
Issued 3 June 1621. Leaf B4 is mutilated. Corresponding to the copy described in *Tiele* no. 1863.

N186 NETHERLANDS. United Provinces. Staten Generaal
[5.6.1621] PROVISONEEL PLACCAET Ende Ordonnantie vande . . . Staten Generael der Vereenighde Nederlanden/op den Cours vanden Gelde/so Goude als Silvere specien . . . IN 'SGRAVEN-HAGHE, By Hillebrant Iacobssz . . . 1621. [etc.] 4° sig. AB^4
T.1712(27).
Dated 5 June 1621.

N187 NETHERLANDS. United Provinces. States General
[9.6.1621] PLACCAET By de . . . Staten Generael der Vereenighde Nederlanden/ghemaeckt op 'tbesluyt vande West-Indissche Compaignie. IN 'SGRAUEN-HAGHE, By Hillebrant Iacobssz . . . 1621. [etc.] 4° sig. A^4
T.2251(25); 107.g.19(12).
Issued 9 June 1621.

N188 NETHERLANDS. United Provinces. States General
[9.6.1621] Letters Patents graunted by the States of the vnited Netherland Prouinces, To the VVest Indian Company of Merchants, at this present resident in those Countries. fol. a single sheet
Harl. Ms.389(f.81).
The English version of the preceding. Printed by Broer Jansz at Amsterdam? Published in 1621.

N189 NETHERLANDS. United Provinces. States General
[15.7.1621] PLACCAET Vande . . . Staten Generael/op 'tstuck vant verkoopen ende transporteren van Actien inde Oost ende West Indische Compagnien . . . IN S'GRAVEN-HAGHE, By Hillebrant Iacobssz . . . 1621. [etc.] 4° sig.A^4
8179.aa.33.
Issued 15 July 1621. Corresponding to the copy described in *Tiele* no.1868.

N190 NETHERLANDS. United Provinces. Staatsraad
[1.6.1610] Publicatie by ende vā weghen de Heeren Radē van State der Gheunieerde Nederlanden. Ghedaen binnen Vtrecht opden xxij^{en} May. 1610. ouden stijl. t'Vtrecht, Ghedruckt by Salomon de Roy/voor Pieter Voet . . . 1610. 4° sig.A^3
T.1729(17).
Dealing with affairs at Utrecht. The date corresponds to 1 June new style. The last leaf, blank, has been cut off.

N191 NETHERLANDS. United Provinces. Staatsraad
[1.6.1610] Publicatie by ende van wegen de Heeren Raden van State der Gheunieerde Nederlanden. Gedaen binnen Vtrecht op den eersten Junij 1610. na den nieuwe stijl. t'Vtrecht/Na de Copye ghedruckt by Salomon de Roy/voor Pieter Voet . . . 1610. 4° 2 unsigned leaves
T.1729(16).
Another edition of the preceding. Published in 1610.

NEUFVILLE, Gerhardus de. Disputationum physicarum undecima . . . de . . . generatione. 1608. *See* JACCHAEUS, Gilbertus

NEUFVILLE, Gerhardus de. Disputationum physicarum decima-sexta, de sensibus internis. *See* JACCHAEUS, Gilbertus

NEUTER, Christianus. *See* CHRISTIANUS NEUTER

N192 NEW
Begin: The new tydings out of Italie are not yet com. Out of Weenen, the 6 November. (col.) Imprinted at Amsterdam by George Veseler, Ao 1620. The 2. of December. And are to be soulde by Petrus Keerius, [etc.] fol. a single sheet
C.55.1.2(1).
Without the usual title of similar news sheets, i.e. 'Corrant out of Italy and Germany, &c.'

N193 NEWES
NEVVES FROM THE LOVV COVNTRIES. (col.) Printed at Altmore by MH, Iuly 29. 1621. fol. a single sheet
C.55.l.2(12).
Begin: From Venice the 20 of Iune 1621. The imprint is false, made to suggest Alkmaar; printed at London.

N194 NEWES

Newes from the Low Countries, or a Courant out of Bohemia, Poland, Germanie, &c. (col.) Printed at Amsterdam by Ioris Veseler. August. 9. anno Dom. 1621. fol. a single sheet

C.55.l.2(15).

Begin: From Crakow in Poland. Iuly 4. The imprint may be false; printed in England?

N195 NICLAES, Henrik

AN EPISTLE SENT VNTO TVVO daughters of VVarwick from H.N. THE OLDEST father of the Familie of Love. VVith a refutation of the errors that are therin; by H.A. . . . Imprinted at Amsterdam by Giles Thorp. 1608. 4° pp.64

4106.b.74.

The author is named in the preface as Henry Nicholas. The editor's preface signed: Henry Ainsworth.

N196 NICOCLES CATHOLICUS

QVÆSTIO CATHOLICA, POLITICA, An à Rege Catholico, & Archiduce serenissimo, bellum hoc tempore in Belgio contra confœderatos Status sit resumendum? Sub fine induciarum tractata, & X. Propositionibus resoluta à NICOCLE CATHOLICO . . . M.DC.XXI. 4° pp.36

1103.e.31(1); 9325.b.51(8).

Probably printed at Antwerp.

N197 NICOLAI, Baulduinus

Verklaringhe Om yegelijcken te adverteren vande dreyghementen Godts/die wy aenmercken in't aenschouwen vanden Comeet/gesien in't Jaer . . . 1618 (na de konst der Astronomien) van oude Doctooren daer op gheschreven . . . Ghepractiseert door M[r]. Baulduinum Nicolai . . . Gedruckt tot Amsterdam, by Broer Iansz. [etc.] 4° 4 unsigned leaves; illus.

T.2423(7).

Published in 1618. The titlepage woodcut shows a scene of the comet, the astronomer seen in a bottom corner seated at his desk. Cropped.

N198 NICOLAI, Idzardus

[Grontlicke onderwijsinghe teghen allerleye dwalinghen der Wederdooperen.] Leere der Waerheyt/Van eenighe LEERSTVKKEN Die door de Drijvers der nieuwicheden berispt ende ghelastert worden. Beschreven door IDZARDVM NICOLAI F. . . . Tot Franeker/Ghedruckt by Vldericum Balck . . . 1611. 4° pp.79

T.2241(15).

Stated in the text to have been 'ghetrokken uyt het groot werck Idzardi Nicolai tegens de Wederdooperen'.

N199 NICOLAUS Gorranus

(tp.1) IN ACTA APOSTOLORVM, ET SINGVLAS APOSTOLORVM, Iacobi, Iohannis & Iudæ Canonicas Epistolas, & Apocalypsin Commentarij, AVTHORE R.P.F. NICOLAO GORRANO . . . QVIBVS ACCESSIT . . . Liber ille Sermonum Domenicalium eiusdem Authoris . . . ANTVERPIÆ . . . M.DC.XX.

(tp.2) OMNIVM ANNI SERMONVM FVNDAMENTVM AVREVM, AVTHORE . . . NICOLAO GORRANO . . . ANTVERPIÆ . . . M.DC.XX. fol. 2 pt.: pp.304; 215

692.f.5.

At the end of each part the author's name is given as Nicolaus de Gorrham. Without publisher's name; but with the device of Joannes van Keerberghen on the first titlepage.

N200 NIELLE, Charles de

VERIFICATION DE LA BONNE FOY DE M. FABRICE DE BASSECOVRT . . . Ou est . . . descouverte sa tresmauvaise conscience, & est monstré à lœil, que par sa response publiée . . . contre certain Tableau, il s'est . . . tacitemēt confessé coupable de divers mensonges . . . Mise en lumiere par un amateur de verité & de paix . . . 1618. 4° pp.36
3900.bb.47.

Anonymous. Published in the Netherlands.

N201 NIEROP, Adriaen van

CHRISTELICKE GEDICHTEN GHEMAECKT TOT LOF van t'Bestandt ende Vrede. MITSGADERS Een Echo ofte Weder-galm/op't Bestandt ende Vrede. ENDE NOCH Een Nederlandts VVellecom-dicht . . . Ghedruckt . . . M.VI^C.IX. 4° 4 unsigned leaves
T.2420(34); 161.k.62.

The author's name given in an acrostic on the verso of the titlepage. His motto 'Neempt den tijdt waer' is used as the signature under all the poems except the last.

N202 NIEROP, Adriaen van

ECHO ofte GALM, Dat is Vveder-klinckende Gedichte van de teghenwoordighe Vrede-handelinghe. DOOR Een Lief-hebber syns Vaderlandschen Vryheyds . . . M.D.C.VIII. 4° sig.A⁴
106.d.16.

Anonymous. The verses on the titlepage verso and the final 'Dystichon musico-chronicum' are in Latin. The words 'ofte' and 'Dat is' of the title are printed in gothic type.

N203 NIEROP, Adriaen van

ECHO Ofte GALM, Dat is: Vveder-klinckende Gedichte . . . Door Een Lief-hebber syns Vaderlandschen Vryheids . . . M.D.C.VIII. 4° sig.A⁴
T.2420(8).

Anonymous. Another edition of the preceding. The words 'Ofte' and 'Dat is' are printed in roman, the text pages are differently set and a 'Dystichon musicum' precedes the 'Dystichon musico-chronicum' at the end.

NIEROP, Adriaen van. Epitaphium ende klachdicht. 1609. [Sometimes attributed to Adriaen van Nierop.] *See* EPITAPHIUM

NIEROP, Adriaen van. Waerachtigh ende cort verhael vande groote ambitie des Conings van Hispaegnien. 1608. [By Adriaen van Nierop?] *See* WAERACHTIGH

NIEU. *See* also NIEUW

N204 NIEU

Een nieu Geusen Lieden-boecxken . . . Nieuwelijck vermeerdert, ende ghecorrigeert . . . 1601. 8° ff.105; illus.
11517.bb.34.

With the 'Viue le Gues' woodcut on the titlepage which is slightly mutilated.

N205 NIEU

Nieu Jaar Liedekens uyt ghegheven by de Retorijck kamer t'Amstelredam In lied [*sic*] Bloeyende Vanden Jare vijfthienhondert eenentachtentich tot den Jare 1608. t'AMSTELREDAM. Ghedruckt by my Harman Janszoon [etc.] 8° sig.A-C⁸D⁶; illus.
11556.bb.56(1).

The titlepage woodcut shows the emblem of the Chamber unframed, that on sig.A2v shows the same within a cartouche incorporating the arms of Amsterdam and the name of the Chamber IN LIEFD' BLOYENDE [*sic*]. Published in 1608.

[*Illustration of **N206** overleaf*]

Een Nieu Klaagh'-liedt: Vervatende de Eenighe ende de Rechte Oorsake, waarom dat de Remonstrantsche Leeraars ghebannen zijn. Op de wijze vanden 68. Psalm. Staat op Heer toont u onvertsaaght.

1.

HEer/ hoe treft ons verbolgens pijn:
Ons Leeraars nu gebannen * zijn
Verjaaght by ons Vyanden;
Geë rust/ nogh vreed'/ en vindẽ zy/
En onzen Gods-dienst mogen wy
niet oeff'nen/ in ders Landen.
't Is zeer verkeert/ by 'tvoortijdts was/
Doenm' in der Staten † schriften las/
Niemants ghemoet te dwinghen:
Maer/ waarom datmen nu verbiet/
Ons/ diemen Remonstranten hiet/
Zal u mijn klaagh-lied zinghen.

1. * Ziet hier van de Resolutien vande Staten vande 5. ende 19. Julij 1619. Ende de placcaten van dē 3. Julij 1619 Ende den 1. Februarius, Anno 1620. † Ziet hier van die meyninge der Staten An. 1590 Also sien is by Emanuel de Meteren, Lib. 16 fol. 306

2.

't IS/ midts wy leeren deze * Leer:
Dat door 'tbesluyt van God † de Heer
Door ‡ Christum zaligh werden/
Die door des Heyl'ghen † Gheests ghenaad'
in Christ' * ghelooven metter daad'/
En totten eynd' * volherden.
Waar teghens Godt verwerpt ghewis/
Den Mensch die † ongheloovigh is/
Ghelijk daar staat ghesch reven/
Wie inden Zoon † ghelooft/ die leeft;
Wie ongehoorzaam ‡ is/ die heeft
gheen deel aan't Eeuwigh' Leven.

2. * Ziet hier van die Verklaringe der Heeren Staten, uytgegeven An. 1617
* eerste punct
1 Tes. 1.13
2 Tim. 1.9.
† Eli 1.4.5.6
Joan 14. 6.
† Ephe. 1.17
† 1 Joh 1.23
Ebr. 13.39
* Ebr. 3.6.14
1 Joan 3.19
Mat. 16.16
‡ Joan 3.36
ende 6. 40.
Rom. 1.18
Habac. 2.4.

3.

DAt ook ons Zaligh-maker goet/
Voor * Allen heeft ghestort zijn Bloet:
Voor * Yder is ghestorven:
Soo dat hy door zijn bitt'ren doot/
Vergheving he der Sonden groot/
Voor † Allen heeft verworven.
Hoe wel dat niemant dogh gheniet
d' Vergheving he/ die hy aenbiet/
Dan die Gheloovigh † blijven.
Hy is d' Verzoeningh' ‡ voor ons Sond'/
En voor al 't Volk op 's Werelds * grond'/
Oft veel heel anders drijven.

3. tweede punct
* Hebr. 2.9.
Rom. 14.9.
* Esa. 53.6.7
2. Cor. 5.15.
† Rom. 5.6.
ende 18.
Collos. 2.13.
Joan. 1.16.
‡ Gal 3.22.
1. Tim. 4.10
1. Cor. 6.11.
‡ Col. 1.14.
ende 20.21.
1. Tim 2.6.
Ephe 2.16.
Hebr. 9. 15.
* 1. Joan. 2.2

4.

MAar ziet/ hoe grimt den Gomarist/
Ontsteken vol van Haat en Twist/
Hy tiert van d' Vryen * Wille:
Verstaat eerst recht/ eer ghy bekladt/
't Gunt ghy gheheel verkeerd'lijk vadt/
Hoogh-roemerd'/ of zwijgh 't stille.
Den Mensch heeft uyt zijn Vrye † kraght
zoo veel niet/ dat het in hem wraght
't Ghelooff/ † dat zaligh maket:
Den Heyl'ghen Gheest die moet hem voen/
Want sonder dien men niet * kan doen/
Voor hem 't verstant ontwaket.

4. * Ziet hier van t'Oordeel van t Synode, inde Verwerpinghen des 3. en 4. hooft stucx artijkel 3. ende 8. en im 1 hooft stuk artijkel 2
* derde punct
† Eph. 3 16.
‡ Phil. 1.29
Titum 3.5.
‡ 1. Cor. 12.3
Jacobi 1.17
Joan 15 5.
1. Cor. 1.31.

5.

WY leeren ook volkomen uyt/
Dat Gods * Ghenade is de spruyt/
Den voortgank/ en * 'tvolbrengen
van alles goedts: Die in het hert
van dien die † We'er-gheboren wert/
Zigh met den ‡ Wil moet menghen.
Maar/ dat die onwe'erstand'lijk werkt/
Wort gants niet in Schriftuyr bemerkt/
Dewijl daar wort ghesproken:
Dat veel/ die voortijdts zijn gheweest/
We'erstonden dezen Heyl'ghen * Gheest/
Hier leyt u Leer ghebroken.

5. vierde punct
* Ephe. 2.8.
Rom. 1.16.
Joan 6.44.
* Phil. 2.13.
Ephe. 2.10.
† 1. Tes. 1.23
1. Petri 1.2.
Mat. 19.28
Ephesen 1.8
‡ 2. Cor. 6.1
2. Pet. 3.17.
Hebr. 3.12.
* Mat 23.4.
* Ezech 15.8
Zepha. 3.5.
Luce. 7.30.
Actorum 5.9
ende 7.51.

6.

OOk/ dat die Christ' is in-ghelijft/
Zoo langh' * hy in dat stantzel blijft/
Heeft kraghten overvloedigh:
Om Sathan/ Zond'/ † en Werelt boos/
En ook zijn eyghen Vlees altoos/
Te overwinnen ‡ moedigh.
Maar/ dat wel door ‡ na-latigheyt/
Hy (vanden boozen gheest verleyt)
Christum we'er kan verliezen/
En de Ghenaad' * hem toe-ghebroght:
'tWelk uyt Schriftuyr is onderzoght/
Dus/ laat ons 'tbeste kiezen.

6. * vijfde punct
* Rom. 8.13
1 Joan 2.24
ende 3. 9.
2. Petri 1.5
6.7. ende 8.
† Eph. 6.11.
Hebr 12. 1.
1 Pet. 5.8.9
‡ 1. Joan 5.
4. ende 5.
2. Petri 2.
20.21.22.
Romeyn. 11
20.22.24.
Heb. 6.4.5.6
en 10 26.27
28. en 29.
* 2. Cor. 6.1.

7.

IS dit ghevoelen dan zoo quaat/
Datmen die 't leert niet blijven laet?
O Godt/ wat vreemder daghen:
O Dorts * Synode 'tis u schult/
Dogh/ ghy de † straf nogh draghen sult/
Ghy voelt alreedts de plaghen.
Maar Broeders vreest niet † wat ghy lijdt/
Wilt strijden eenen ‡ goeden strijdt/
Op dat ghy meugh 't ghewinnen
de kroon * des Levens: Die bereyt
is/ die hier niet ‡ stantvastigheyt/
Christum ghetrou beminnen.

7. * Ziet hier vande Sententie des Dortsche Synode folio 92.
1 2. Tes. 1.6
Jacob 2.13.
‡ Jaco 5.10.
Phil. 1.19.
Hebr. 10 36
‡ 1. Tim. 1.
18.19. 6.12.
* Apoc. 2 10.
2 Timo 4 8
Apoc. 3.5.21
‡ Mat. 13.13
1. Tim. 4.16
Mat. 10.22
ende 24. 13.

8.

ALmaghtig' * God/ Barmhertig' † Heer
Slaat u ghenadigh Oogh' eens neer/
Vergheeft ons onze ‡ Zonden:
Laat ons vervolgingh' houden op/
Weyrt die ‡ vervolghers van den kop/
't Gunt daat zy ons meed' wonden.
Wy zoecken 't Aardtsche * Cana'n niet/
Jeruzalem dat 't Nieuwe hiet/
Verwachten wy * alt'zamen:
De hope en verschijningh' † klaar/
Van Jesu Christi openbaar/
Ons Zaligh-maker/ Amen.

8. * Job 8.3.5
Jere. 32.17.
† Exod. 34.6
Deut. 4 31.
Hebr. 9.17.
Luce 1.50.
‡ Osea 14.3
Luce 11.4.
Psal. 9.13.
‡ Mat. 5.44
Luce 6.28.
Rom. 12.14
1. Petri 3.9.
* Hebr. 13.14
* Gal. 4.26.
Hebr. 11.10.
Phil. 3.20.
2. Pet. 3.13.
† Heb. 10.23
Titum 2.13

By my, die ik ben.

N206 NIEU

Een Nieu Klaagh'-liedt: Vervatende de Eenighe ende Rechte Oorsake/waarom dat de Remonstrantsche Leeraars ghebannen zijn. [etc.] fol. a single sheet
T.2249(29).

Signed: By my, die ik zy. Published in 1619?

N207 NIEU

NIEV REKEN-BOECK, Op den Arminiaensen Kerf-stock/Eertijts ghemaeckt tot spijt van de Gereformeerde Christenen/Met het advijs Van alle Steden ende Schanssen die den Prince Maurits ende de kerck des Christen gheloofs toegedaen zijn ende/getrouwicheyt ghesworen hebben . . . By een ghestelt door een Boer uyt de Veenen veel ghetrouwer voor't Lant/als den Balanse-maecker met al zijn verstandt. Ghedruckt na de Copye tot Dordrecht/by Pieter Verhaghe . . . 1618. 4° sig. A^4
11555.e.41(2).

N208 NIEU

[Nieu reken-boeck] Nieuwe Tijdinghe/Hoe de Arminianen teghen de Reformeerde Leeraers der Christelijcker Kercke hebben eenighe schimp ende Spot ghemaect op eenen kerf-stock . . . Waer op dit Reformeerde Reken-boeck weder is ghemaect . . . Hier zyn noch by ghevoecht Alle de Steden die de Prince Maurits . . . beminnen . . . Ende op dicht ghestelt door eenen ghetrouwen Liefhebber des Vaderlandts. Ghedruckt tot Franeker/by Jan Lammerinx . . . 1618. 4° sig. A^4
T.2248(48).

Another edition of the preceding.

N209 NIEU

[Nieu reken-boeck.] Nieuwe Tydinghe Hoe de Arminianen teghen de Reformeerde Leeraers der Christelijcker Kercke hebben eenighe schimp ende spot gemaect op eenen Kerf-stock/ende alsoo gestroyt tot spijt en achterdeel van onse Christelijcke Kercke/waer op dit Reformeerde Reken-boeck weder is ghemaeckt . . . Hier is noch by ghevoecht, alle de Steden die de Prince Maurits ende die Kercke des Christelijcken Gheloofs beminnen en bevesticht ende gesworen hebben/so wel Steden als Casteelen ende Schanssen/elc met sijnen naem genoemt/ende met schoone advijsen ghemaeckt. Ende op dicht ghestelt door eenen ghetrouwen Liefhebber des Vader-landts. Ghedruckt na de Copye tot Dordrecht/by Pieter Verhaghe . . . 1618. 4° sig. A^4
700.h.25(11).

Another edition of the preceding.

N210 NIEU

Nieu tijdinghe Gheschreven wt Vlm/ende hoe dat de Boeren rebelleren in Bohemen teghen haere Heeren oft Jonckers. Overghesedt wt de Hooch-Duytsche sprake in onse Nederlantsche Tale. Nv eerst Gedruckt den 24. Julij. 1620. T'Hantwerpen/by Abraham Verhoeuen . . . 1620. [etc.] 4° pp.7; sig. Tt^4; illus.
P.P.3444.af(71); 1480.aa.15(10).

The titlepage woodcut shows a portrait of Maximilian I, Duke of Bavaria.

N211 NIEU

Nieu tijdinghe vanden Graeff van Bucquoy/die wederom opghetrocken is met thien duysendt mannen/ende de Bemersche in Oostenrijck gheslaghen heeft ouer twee duysent 200. ghevangen . . . t'Hantwerpen/By Abraham Verhoeuen . . . 1620. Gheprint den 13. Meert 1620. [etc.] 4° pp.8; sig. E^4; illus.
P.P.3444.af(36).

With additional news from France. The titlepage woodcut shows an army outside a city, with a prominent view of the gallows and wheel.

De NIEUSGIERIGE hoop. 1618. *See* WARMINIAEN

NIEUW. *See* also NIEU

N212 NIEUW

Een nieuw Liedeken Ter Eeren SINT IAN. Op de VVijse vanden 5. Psalm, Verhoort ô Godt mijn vvoorden klachtigh. fol. a single sheet

T.2422(39).

On Johan van Oldenbarnevelt. Published in 1619.

N213 NIEUWE

Nieuwe const van Bossenschieten/principalick binnen scheeps boort noodich te weten . . . Noch vindy in dit Boecxken een remedie voor die ghene die met Buscruyt verbrant is . . . Door een Lief-hebber der selver const int licht ghebracht. Gedruckt tot Amstelredam by Cornelis Claesz . . . 1601. 4° sig. A-D^4; illus.

534.f.38(3).

The titlepage woodcut shows a cannon trained on a castle.

NIEUWE jaars claach-liedt. 1610. *See* LE CANU, Robbert

N214 NIEUWE

Nieuwe Tijdinge/geschreven wt Ausburch/hoe dat de Cosacken hebben bereet ghemaeckt 300. schepen . . . om te vreken het onghelijck dat hun vande Turcken aengedaen is. Overghesedt wt de Hooch-Duytsche sprake in onse Nederlantsche Tale. Eerst Ghedruckt den xxx. Julij. T'Hantwerpen/By Abraham Verhoeuen . . . 1620. 4° pp.7; sig. Ww^4; illus.

P.P.3444.af(73); 1480.aa.15(1).

News mainly of Bavarian events. The titlepage woodcut shows the Cossack leader 'Plachta'.

N215 NIEUWE

Nieuwe Tijdinge van Duytslant/Hongarijen/ende de stadt Presborch. Ende hoe datter drye Regimenten Volckx vãden Grave van Mansvelt/zijn aen den Hertoch van Beyeren ouergevallen. Ouerghesedt vvt het Hooch-duyts in onse Nederlantsche Taele. Eerst Ghedruckt den 28. September. T'Hantwerpen/By Abraham Verhoeuen/[etc.] 4° pp.8; sig. Ccc^4; illus.

P.P.3444.af(285).

Headed: September. 1621. 136. The titlepage woodcut shows a battle between Christian and Turkish forces.

N216 NIEUWE

Nieuwe Tijdinge van Hungharijen/Polen/ende Duytslandt/alwaer s'Keysers volck acht Steden in Hungarijen door den Omenaij voor den Keyser hebben in ghenomen. Ende hoe de Polackers . . . in der Slesien zijn ghevallen. t'Hantwerpen/By Abraham Verhoeuen . . . Gheprint den 17. Januarij . . . 1620. 4° pp.8; sig. A^4; illus.

P.P.3444.af(29).

The titlepage woodcut shows a battle scene with camels. This issue contains an advertisement for 'Den eyghen sin ende meyninghe vande oorloghen in Europa' by 'Heere-man Chunradus', i.e. Hermann Conrad von Friedenberg.

N217 NIEUWE

Nieuwe Tijdinge van tLeger in Duytslant. Met t'principaelste datter ghepasseert is/t'sedert de Crooninghe van . . . Ferdinandus . . . Nv eerst Ghedruckt den 14. October. T'Hantwerpen/by Abraham Verhoeuen/[etc.] 4° pp.8; sig. A^4; illus.

P.P.3444.af(21).

Published in 1619. The two titlepage woodcuts show (a) the Emperor Ferdinand holding a sword, and (b) a cavalry battle.

N218 NIEUWE

Nieuwe Tijdinge vãden Krijch nv onlanckx ghepasseert is/soo in Bohemen ende Moravien/hoe da[t] de nieuwe Italianen ende Walen/met xxv. Vendelen volcx wt Budweysz zijn ghevallen in Bohemen/onder t'beleydt van Don Balthasar . . . t'Hantwerpen/By Abraham Verhoeuen . . . Gheprint den 19. Februarij . . . 1621. 4° pp. 8; sig. A^4; illus.

1480.aa.15(7); P.P.3444.af(33).

The titlepage woodcut shows troops encamped by a river; an insert in the top right corner shows a fortress. The titlepage is cropped.

N219 NIEUWE

Nieuwe Tijdinge wt den Legher by Wesel/van . . . Marquis Spinola, met het innemen der Steden/ende Casteelen aldaer. Eerst Ghedruckt den 28. September, 1621. T'Hantwerpen, by Abraham Verhoeuen, [etc.] 4° pp. 8; sig. Ddd^4; illus.

P.P.3444.af(286).

Headed: September, 1621. 137. The titlepage woodcut shows an attack on a city.

N220 NIEUWE

Nieuvve Tijdinge vvt Duytslandt, vanden Legher vanden Hertoch vã Beyeren/ teghen Mansveldt. Met Tijdinge wt Vranck-rijck, ende het innemen der stadt Clerac, ende andere. Eerst Ghedruckt den 27. Augusti. 1621. T'hantvverpen, by Abraham Verhoeuen, [etc.] 4° pp. 8; sig. Kk^4; illus.

P.P.3444.af(276).

Headed: Augustus, 1621. 121. Containing also news from Scandinavia and Holland. The titlepage woodcut shows armies entering a town.

N221 NIEUWE

Nieuwe Tijdinge wt Engelant met noch het RELAES VANDE groote Victorie/die de Catholijcke Grisons hebben vercreghen teghen die Ketters, met het innemen van . . . Chiauenna, Item vande Valleye Engedina . . . Eerst Gedruckt den 10. December. 1621. T'Hantwerpen/By Abraham Verhoeuen/[etc.] 4° pp. 8; sig. F^4; illus.

P.P.3444.af(327).

Headed: December. 1621. 182. Containing also news from Spain and Germany. The titlepage woodcuts show (a) a king (James I?), and (b) a ship under full sail.

N222 NIEUWE

Nieuwe Tijdinge wt Roomen/Duytslandt/Hongharijen/ende Pfaltz-Graven Landt. Ouerghesedt wt de Hooch-Duytsche sprake in onse Nederlantsche Tale. Eerst Gedruckt den 11. Junij. 1621. T'Hantwerpen, By Abraham Verhoeuen, [etc.] 4° pp. 8; sig. D^4; illus.

P.P.3444.af(243).

Headed: Iunij 1621. 87. Containing also news from France. The titlepage woodcut shows a battle between Christian and Turkish forces outside a castle on a hill.

N223 NIEUWE

Nieuwe Tijdinge wt Spagniẽ van eenen sekeren Vriendt N.N. de welcke Gheschreuen heeft dese Nieuwicheden wt Madril, in Spagnien/zedert de doot vanden Coninck Philippus, den derden. Ouerghesedt vvt de Spaensche Taele, in onse Nederlantsche spraecke. Eerst Ghedruckt den 28. Mey 1621. T'Hantwerpen/ By Abraham Verhoeuen/[etc.] 4° pp. 8; sig. A^4; illus.

P.P.3444.af(235).

Headed: Mey 1621. 79. The letter is dated Madrid, 22 April 1621. The titlepage woodcut shows the portrait of Philip IV.

N224 NIEUWE
Nieuwe Tijdinge wt Vranckrijck/Ende hoe dat den Hertoch Monsieur Duc de Mayne, doot geschoten is/voor de stadt van Montalban, met t'gene in Vranckrijck gepasseert is. Ouerghesedt vvt het Fransoys, in onse Nederlandtsche sprake. Eerst Ghedruckt den 4. October 1621. T'Hantwerpen/By Abraham Verhoeuen/[etc.] 4° pp.7; sig.Jij^4; illus.
P.P.3444.af(291).

Headed: October. 1621. 142. The titlepage woodcut shows the arms of Louis XIII. At end a double-headed eagle on orb.

N225 NIEUWE
Nieuwe Tijdinge wt Vranckrijck/van t'ghene passeert tusschen de Catholijcken ende Hughenotten/met andere nieuwe Tijdinge wt Duytslant. Eerst Gedruckt den 16. Junij. 1621. T'Hantwerpen, By Abraham Verhoeuen, [etc.] 4° pp.8; sig. A^4; illus.
P.P.3444.af(245).

Headed: Iunij. 1621. 89. The titlepage woodcut shows the arms of France.

N226 NIEUWE
Nieuwe Tijdingen van eenighe Politijcke Saecken gepasseert in Hollandt. Eerst Ghedruckt den 8. October 1621. T'Hantwerpen/By Abraham Verhoeuen/[etc.] 4° sig.Mmm^4; illus.
P.P.3444.af(294).

Headed: October 1621. 145. The 'political matters' concern mainly the Remonstrants, escapes from prison, etc. The titlepage woodcut shows the arms of Amsterdam.

N227 NIEUWE
Nieuwe Tijdingē van t'ghene onlanghs tot Harlinghen/S'Graven-Haghe/Leyden/ Hoorn/Briel/en Campen is gheschiedt. Eerst Ghedruckt den IIJ. Junij 1620. T'Hantwerpen/By Abraham Verhoeuen . . . 1620. [etc.] 4° sig.Bb^4; illus.
P.P.3444.af(57).

The titlepage shows two clergymen in discussion.

NIEUWE tijdingen wt Engelāt met het placcaet vanden Coninck. 1621. *See* ENGLAND [24.12.1620]

N228 NIEUWE
Nieuwe Tijdinghe/hoe dat de Cosagghen d'weers door Hongherijen/ende Moravien geslagē zijn/ende de stadt Trenchin ingenomen hebben voor den Keyser . . . 1620. T'Hantwerpen/By Abraham Verhoeven . . . 1620. 4° pp.8; sig.Rr^4; illus.
P.P.3444.af(69).

With other news. The titlepage woodcut shows a picture of Gideon (Judges 7:5).

N229 NIEUWE
Nieuwe Tijdinghe hoe dat den Graef van Bucquoy heeft dry Steden in ghenomen Hooren/Rees/ende Egghenburgh . . . Eerst Ghedruckt den ix. October 1620. T'Hantwerpen/By Abraham verhoeven . . . 1620. [etc.] 4° pp.7; sig.Rrr^4; illus.
P.P.3444.af(114); 1480.aa.15(32).

The titlepage woodcut shows a city under siege.

N230 NIEUWE
Nieuwe tijdinghe Hoe dat zijn Forstelijcke Ghenade den Hertoch van Beyeren de Stadt Budna dapper heeft doen beschieten/ende daer na in Ghenade ontfanghen/ met het innemen der Stadt Bautzen. Overghesedt wt den Hoog-Duytsche/in onse Nederlantsche Tale. Eerst ghedruckt den xxiij. October. 1620. T'Hantwerpen/By Abraham Verhoeuen . . . 1620. [etc.] 4° pp.6; sig.H^4; illus.
P.P.3444.af(126); 1480.aa.15(42).

The titlepage woodcut shows cannons in action outside a townhall.

NIEUWE tijdinghe, hoe de Arminianen teghen de Reformeerde Leeraers der Christelijcke Kercke hebben eenighe schimp ende spot ghemaect. 1618. *See* NIEU reken-boeck

N231 NIEUWE
Nieuvve Tijdinghe van Bohemen met de Belegheringhe van Wittingauw/ghedaen door het volck van de Keyserlijcke Majesteyt. Met den Slach ende verlies van den Turck/gheschiedt in de Golfo van Venetien. Nv eerst Ghedruckt den xiiij. October. T'hantwerpen/By Abraham verhoeven . . . 1620. 4° pp.7; sig.Yyy^4; illus.
1480.aa.15(36); P.P.3444.af(118); 1193.f.22.
The titlepage woodcut shows the battle in the gulf of Venice; or rather, off Manfredonia? The copy at 1193.f.22 is imperfect; wanting the titlepage.

N232 NIEUWE
Nieuwe Tijdinghe Van de groote Victorie/ende Slach gheschiet teghen den Turck . . . ende hoe dat de Coninck van Polen 80000. Turcken heeft verslaghen/ ende grooten Buet becomen. Overgheset wt het Hoochduyts/in onse Nederlantsche sprake. Eerst Ghedruckt den 10. Nouember 1621. T'Hantwerpen/ By Abraham Verhoeuen/[etc.] 4° pp.8; sig.Hhhh^4; illus.
P.P.3444.af(309).
Headed: Nouember, 1621. 162. Containing also news from Italy and Holland. The titlepage woodcut shows a cavalry engagement between Christians and Turks.

N233 NIEUWE
Nieuwe Tijdinghe Van den Slach/hoe dat den Grave van Bucquoy 900. Hongheren heeft gheslaghen van den Bethlehem Gabor. Overghesedt wt de Hooch-Duytsche sprake in onse Nederlantsche Tale. Eerst Ghedruckt in Februarius 1621. T'Hantwerpen/By Abraham Verhoeven/[etc.] 4° pp.8; sig.A^4; illus.
P.P.3444.af(186).
Headed: Februarius 1621. 17. Containing also other news. The titlepage woodcut shows a cavalry skirmish.

N234 NIEUWE
Nieuvve Tijdinghe Van Duytslant gheschiet by Egenburgh/Met de slaghen/ende Scharmutselen die daer ghepasseert zijn. Eerst Ghedruckt den x. April 1620. T'Hantwerpen/by Abraham Verhoeuen . . . 1620. [etc.] 4° pp.8; sig.H^4; illus.
P.P.3444.af(41).
The titlepage woodcut shows a cavalry skirmish.

N235 NIEUWE
Nieuwe Tijdinghe van Duytslant met de namen der Steden die den Hertoch van Beyeren in den Ouer-Pfalts heeft in ghenomen. Overgheset wt het Hoochduyts/in onse Nederlantsche sprake. Eerst Ghedruckt den 15. October. 1621. T'Hantwerpen/By Abraham Verhoeuen/[etc.] 4° pp.8; sig.Sss^4; illus.
P.P.3444.af(296).
Headed: October, 1621. 149. Containing also news from Italy and elsewhere. The titlepage woodcuts show (a) a view of a city, and (b) a cavalry skirmish.

N236 NIEUWE
Nieuwe Tijdinghe/van een mirakel ende gheschiedenisse/het welc in Enghelant op de frontier van Schotlandt gheschiedt is/boven Nieukasteel ende Commerlant/het welck Godt almachtich heeft laten ghebeuren int Jaer duysent zes hondert ende vijf . . . Na de Copye ghedruct. TOT ALCMAER, By Jacques de Meester. 1605. 8° sig.A^4
1606/355.

N237 NIEUWE
Njeuwe [*sic*] Tijdinghe van Prage van het Verhael vant' Accoort ghedaen met den Grave van Mansveldt. Met noch Tijdinghe Wt Pfaltz-Grauen Landt met t'verhael van den Leger aldaer. Overgheset wt het Hoochduyts/in onse Nederlantsche sprake. Eerst Ghedruckt den 22. October 1621. T'Hantwerpen/By Abraham Verhoeuen/[etc.] 4° pp.8; sig. Zzz^4; illus.
P.P.3444.af(301).
Headed: October, 1621. 154. Containing also news from Switzerland and Turkey. The titlepage woodcuts show (a) a siege, and (b) the portrait of a general.

N238 NIEUWE
Nieuwe Tijdinghe Van s'Hertogenbos/hoe dat den Gouuerneur . . . Grobbendonck is wt ghetrocken naer Heusden/ende hoe dat den Gouuerneur van Heusden Kessel/is te ghemoet ghecomen mijn Heer van Grobbēdonc om te ouercomen datmen de dijcken niet deursteken en soude . . . Eerst Ghedruckt den 20. Januarius 1621. T'Hantwerpen/By Abraham Verhoeuen/[etc.] 4° pp.8; 4 unsigned leaves; illus.
P.P.3444.af(178).
Headed: Ianuarius 1621. 9. Containing also other war news. The titlepage woodcut shows a town under siege.

N239 NIEUWE
Nieuwe Tijdinghe van weenen in Oostenrijck Ende hoe dat den Grave van Bucquoy de stadt Thyrna in Hungarijen wilt belegheren. Overghesedt wt de Hooch-Duytsche sprake in onse Nederlantsche Tale. Eerst Ghedruckt den 5. Appril 1621. T'Hantwerpen/By Abraham Verhoeuen/[etc.] 4° pp.8; sig. (?)^4; illus.
P.P.3444.af(218).
Headed: Appril 1621. 54. Containing also other news. The titlepage woodcut shows the siege of a town.

N240 NIEUWE
Nieuwe Tijdinghe vande SPAENSCHE VLOTE, Met het Accoort/van de stadt Bautsen in Bohemen . . . Eerst Ghedruckt den 6. November 1620. T'Hantwerpen/By Abraham Verhoeuen . . . 1620. 4° pp.8; sig. R^4; illus.
1480.aa.15(43); P.P.3444.af(134).
The titlepage woodcut shows the embarcation of troops, with the King and Queen on the quayside.

N241 NIEUWE
Nieuwe Tijdinghe vanden Graeve van Mansfeldt/ende de Belegheringhe vande stadt Heydelbergh, Voor de Keyserlijcke Majesteydt. Eerst Ghedruckt den 26. Nouember. 1621 . . . T'Hantwerpen/By Abraham Verhoeuen/[etc.] 4° pp.8; sig. Vvvv^4; illus.
P.P.3444.af(318).
Headed: Nouember. 1621. 173. The titlepage woodcuts show (a) a portrait of Mansfeld, and (b) a fight in a ditch.

N242 NIEUWE
Nieuwe Tijdinghe Vanden grootē Slach gheschiedt inde Grysons/tegens de Calvinische Cantons/alwaer de Catholijckē de Victorie hebben behouden . . . Overghesedt wt het Italiaens in onse Nederlantsche sprake. Ghedruckt den xvj. October 1620. T'Hantwerpen/By Abraham Verhoeven/[etc.] 4° pp.8; sig. B^4; illus.
1480.aa.15(39); P.P.3444.af(121).
The titlepage woodcut shows a battle by a river.

N243 NIEUWE
Nieuwe Tijdinghe vanden Krijch ende Oorloge in Bohemē met het innemen der plaetsen/ende t ghene daer nv gepasseert is. Ghedruckt den xxvij. Meert 1620. T'Hantwerpen/by Abraham Verhoeuen . . . 1620. [etc.] 4° pp.8; sig.G⁴; illus.
P.P.3444.af(40).

The titlepage woodcuts show (a) a battle by a river, and (b) the storming of a city.

N244 NIEUWE
Nieuwe Tijdinghe wt de Stadt Praghe. Met Verhael van de Verraders de welcke daer ghevanghen zijn. Overghesedt vvt de hooch-Duytsche sprake in onse Nederlandtsche Tale. Eerst ghedruckt den 5. Appril/1621. t'Hantwerpen/By Abraham Verhoeuen/[etc.] 4° pp.8; sig.(??)⁴; illus.
P.P.3444.af(217).

Headed: April 1621. 53. The titlepage woodcut shows the castle at Prague.

N245 NIEUWE
Nieuwe Tijdinghe wt den Leger voor Montalbaē alwaer den Coninck van Vranckrijck seluer in persoone in de Batterije heeft gheweest/met t'ghene dat daer ghepasseert is. Overgheset wt het Fransoys/in onse Nederlantsche sprake. Eerst Ghedruckt den 16. Nouember 1621. T'Hantwerpen/By Abraham Verhoeuen/[etc.] 4° pp.8; sig.Mmmm⁴; illus.
P.P.3444.af(311).

Based on letters dated 15 October to 2 November 1621. Headed: Nouember, 1621. 166. The titlepage woodcut shows an artillery attack on a fortified city.

N246 NIEUWE
Nieuwe Tijdinghe wt dē Legher in Pfaltz-Grauen Lant met het in-nemen van de Steden ende Veroueringhe der Stadt Keysers Louter. Overgheset wt het Spaens/in onse Nederlantsche sprake. Eerst Ghedruckt den 20. October. 1621. T'Hantwerpen/By Abraham Verhoeuen/[etc.] 4° pp.8; sig.Xxx⁴; illus.
P.P.3444.af(299).

Headed: October, 1621. 152. Containing an advertisement for a map of Sluis for which *see* below no.N250. The titlepage woodcut shows a battle by a river.

N247 NIEUWE
Nieuwe Tijdinghe wt den Legher Van zijn EX. MARQVIS SPINOLA Ende hoe dat het Casteel Lans-berch int Pfaltz Grauen Lant ouergegeuen is. Eerst Ghedruckt den 13. November 1620. T'Hantwerpen/By Abraham Verhoeuen . . . 1620. [etc.] 4° pp.8; sig.S⁴; illus.
1193.l.28; P.P.3444.af(135).

The titlepage woodcuts show (a) a portrait of Spinola, and (b) an attack on a castle.

N248 NIEUWE
Nieuwe Tijdinghe wt den Legher Van zijn EX. MARQVIS SPINOLA . . . Eerst Ghedruckt den 19. November 1620. T'Hantwerpen/By Abraham Verhoeuen . . . 1620. [etc.] 4° pp.8; sig.S⁴; illus.
P.P.3444.af(136).

A reissue of the preceding.

N249 NIEUWE
Nieuwe Tijdinghe wt Den Legher/vanden Marquis Spinola. Noch hoe dat 20. van onse Ruyters, de vvelcke eenen Graue convoyeerden, hebben geslaghen teghen 43. Ruyters vanden Vyant by Meurs. Eerst Ghedruckt den 15. December 1621 . . . T'Hantwerpen/By Abraham Verhoeuen/[etc.] 4° pp.8; sig.K⁴; illus.
P.P.3444.af(331).

Headed: December, 1621. 186. With news also from France. The titlepage woodcut shows a portrait of Spinola.

N250 NIEUWE

Nieuwe Tijdinghe wt den Legher voor de Stadt Sluys in Vlaenderen/hoe dat die van Sluys eenen wt-val hebben ghedaen op ons Volck. Met noch Tijdinghe vvt Hollant, ende vvt den Legher voor Gulick. Eerst Ghedruckt den 19. Nouember 1621. T'Hantwerpen/By Abraham Verhoeuen/[etc.] 4° pp.8; sig.Qqqq^4; illus.
P.P.3444.af(315).

Headed: Nouember, 1621. 170. The titlepage woodcut shows a map of Sluis, lettered A-M, but without key.

N251 NIEUWE

Nieuwe Tijdinghe wt den Legher voor de Stadt van Gulick. Ende hoe dat die van Gulick eenen wt-val hebben ghedaen op onsen Legher/ende zijn wederom te rugghe ghedreuen. Ouerghesedt vvt het Hoochduyts in onse Nederlantsche Tale. Eerst Ghedruckt den 15. October 1621. T'Hantwerpen/By Abraham Verhoeuen/ [etc.] 4° pp.8; sig.Ttt^4; illus.
P.P.3444.af(297).

Headed: October. 1621. 150. Containing an advertisement for a map of Jülich. The titlepage woodcut shows an army besieging a fortified place. For this map *see* below no.N254.

N252 NIEUWE

Nieuwe Tijdinghe wt dē Legher voor Franckendael/hoe dat ons volck daer 3. halue Manen in hebben ghenomen/ende met het Gheschut onder de Vesten zijn/waer ouer den vyant de stadt heeft meynen comen t'ontsetten/maer zijn weder te rugge ghedreven. Eerst Ghedruckt den 29. October. 1621. T'Hantwerpen/By Abraham Verhoeuen/[etc.] 4° sig.Cccc^4; illus.
P.P.3444.af(304).

Headed: October, 1621. 157. The titlepage woodcut shows the siege of a fortified town with an island fortress.

N253 NIEUWE

Nieuwe Tijdinghe wt den Legher voor Gulick/Met Tijdinghe vanden Graue van Mansfeldt. Eerst Gedruckt den 15. December. 1621. T'Hantwerpen/By Abraham Verhoeuen/[etc.] 4° pp.7; sig.G^4; illus.
P.P.3444.af(328).

Headed: December. 1621. 183. Also containing news from Spain. The titlepage woodcuts show (a) the Emperor, (b) Spinola, (c) Mansfeld.

N254 NIEUWE

Nieuwe Tijdinghe wt den Marquis Spinola Legher/ende wt Pfalts-Grauen Landt/van de Maent Nouember. Ouergheset wt het Spaens in onse Nederlantsche sprake. Eerst Ghedruckt den 16. Nouember. 1621. T'Hantwerpen/By Abraham Verhoeuen/[etc.] 4° pp.7; sig.Nnnn^4; illus.
P.P.3444.af(312).

Headed: Nouember, 1621. 167. The titlepage woodcut shows a map of the siege of Jülich, lettered A-H, without key.

N255 NIEUWE

Nieuwe Tijdinghe wt des Coninckx van Vranckrijckx Legher/met de Steden die den Coninck ghewonnen heeft vande Hughenotten. Overghesedt wt het Fransoys in onse Nederlantsche sprake. Eerst Ghedruckt den 24. Julij. 1621. T'Hantwerpen/ by Abraham Verhoeuen/[etc.] 4° pp.8; sig.P^4; illus.
P.P.3444.af(263).

Headed: Iulius 1621. 106. The titlepage woodcut shows the defence of a town.

N256 NIEUWE

Nieuwe Tijdinghe wt des Conincx vā Vranckrijckx Legher/voor S. Ian d'Angely, met t'ghene daer ghepasseert is. Ouerghesedt vvt het Fransoys in onse

Nederlantsche sprake. Eerst Ghedruckt des 3. Julij 1621. T'Hantwerpen/by Abraham Verhoeuen/[etc.] 4° pp.8; sig.F[4]; illus.
P.P.3444.af(255).
Headed: Iulius 1621. 99. Also containing news from Germany and an advertisement for a print of the siege of St. Jean-d'Angely. The titlepage woodcut shows the Queen Regent and Louix XIII with the French arms.

N257 NIEUWE
Nieuwe Tijdinghe wt des Keysers Legher/Hoe de Boheemsche hebben meynen den leger op te slaen/ende met schaden hebben moeten wederom wt trecken met groot verlies van Volck. Overghesedt wt de Hooch-Duytsche sprake in onse Nederlantsche Tale. Eerst ghedruckt den x. Julij. T'Hantwerpen/By Abraham Verhoeven . . . 1620. [etc.] 4° pp.7; sig.Mm[4]; illus.
P.P.3444.af(64).
Containing much other news also. The titlepage woodcut shows a cavalry engagement between Christians and Turks. Another issue of the Tijdingen, also signed Mm, but dated 3 July and printing a letter from the Electors at Mühlhausen to the Protestant German States has been recorded in the *Bibliographia Belgica.* no.V196.

N258 NIEUWE
Nieuwe Tijdinghe wt Duytslandt/ende de Stadt Praghe. Overgheset wt het Hoochduyts/in onse Nederlantsche sprake. Eerst Ghedruckt den 10. Nouember 1621. T'Hantwerpen/By Abraham Verhoeuen/[etc.] 4° pp.8; sig. Iiii[4]; illus.
P.P.3444.af(310).
Headed: Nouember, 1621. 163. Containing also news from France. The titlepage woodcuts show (a) an assault on a castle, and (b) a cavalry skirmish.

N259 NIEUWE
Nieuwe Tijdinghe vvt Duytslandt, ende hoe dat vijftich Duyzent Cossagghen/ vande Polacken/zijn ouer den Donauw ghepasseeet [*sic*]/om te Rooven ende Branden voor Constantinopelen. Ouerghesedt vvt het Hoochduyts, in onse Nederlandtsche sprake. Eerst Gedruckt den 10. December. 1621. T'Hantwerpen/ By Abraham Verhoeuen/[etc.] 4° pp.8; sig.E[4]; illus.
P.P.3444.af(326).
Headed: December. 1621. 181. With news from Italy about the Spanish Marriage, the Grisons and shipping. The titlepage woodcut shows a cavalry engagement between Christians and Turks.

N260 NIEUWE
Nieuwe Tijdinghe wt Duytslandt/ende Polen/hoe dat den Oorloghe is begost/ tusschen den Coninck van Polen, ende den Turck, Ende hoe dat de Polacken . . . xij. Duysent Tarteren, hebben verslaghen/die tot secours quamen vanden Berhlehem [*sic*] Gabor. Nv Eerst ghedruckt den 30. Iulij. T'Hantvverpen, by Abraham Verhoeuen, [etc.] 4° pp.8; sig.R[4]; illus.
P.P.3444.af(265).
Headed: Iulius. 1621. 108. Containing also news from France. The titlepage woodcut shows a cavalry engagement between Christians and Turks.

N261 NIEUWE
Nieuwe Tijdinghe/wt Duytslandt/van Weenen in Oosten-rijck/ende Praghe, in Bohemen. Ouerghesedt vvt de Hoochduytsche sprake, in onse Nederlantsche Tale. Eerst Ghedruckt den 14. Mey 1621. T'Hantwerpen/By Abraham Verhoeuen/[etc.] 4° pp.8; sig.A[4]; illus.
P.P.3444.af(229).
Headed: Mey 1621. 73. The titlepage woodcut shows a large vase in a garden.

N262 NIEUWE
Nieuwe Tijdinghe wt Duytslandt/van Weenen in Oostenrijck. Noch hoe dat den Coninck van Vranck-rijckx Oorlochs-schepen, hebben neghen schepen genomen van die van Rochelle, waer onder vvas een Hollandts, Oorlochs schip gheladen met alderhande Ammonitie, dat na Rochelle voer. Eerst Ghedruckt den 19. Nouember 1621. T'Hantwerpen/By Abraham Verhoeuen/[etc.] 4° pp.7; sig.Xxxx^4; illus.
P.P.3444.af(319).
Headed: Nouember, 1621. 174. The titlepage woodcut shows a ship at sea.

N263 NIEUWE
Nieuwe Tijdinghe wt Duytslant/ende Bohemen h[oe] dat s'Keysers volck de stadt Praga-ditz heeft in ghenomen end[e] in Brandt ghesteken. Noch hoe dat den Marquis Spinola volck door den Gouvern[eur] van Creutzenach/de stadt Kirberch heeft in ghenomen in Pfa[ltz-]Grauen Landt/de Soldaten ghekleedt zijnde in Boeren kl[eeren.] Ghedruckt den xvij. October 1620. T'Hantwerpen/By Abraham Verhoeven/[etc.] 4° pp.8; sig.C^4; illus.
P.P.3444.af(122).
Containing also other news. The titlepage woodcut shows the siege of a city. The titlepage is mutilated, the text has been supplemented from the description in the *Bibliotheca Belgica*.

N264 NIEUWE
Nieuwe Tijdinghe wt Duytslant ende vrancrijck/van t'ghene daer ghepasseert is. Ghedruckt den 26. Februarius 1621. T'Hantwerpen/By Abraham Verhoeuen/[etc.] 4° pp.8; sig.A^4; illus.
P.P.3444.af(192).
Headed: Februarius 1621. 24. The titlepage woodcut shows the arms of Ferdinand II.

N265 NIEUWE
Nieuwe Tijdinghe wt Duytslant/vā weenen in Oostenrijck/ende noch wt den Legher voor Gulick. Ouerghesedt vvt het Hoochduyts in onse Nederlantsche Tale. Eerst Ghedruckt den 5. Nouember. 1621. T'Hantwerpen/By Abraham Verhoeuen/[etc.] 4° pp.8; sig.Ffff^4; illus.
P.P.3444.af(307).
Headed: Nouember, 1621. 160. Containing also news from Italy. The titlepage woodcut shows armies marching through a town.

N266 NIEUWE
NIeuwe Tijdinghe wt Hollant/den Haghe Dort/ende Amsterdam/van t'ghene daer nv corts ghepasseert is. Met vvat vrempts vvt Enghelandt. Nv eerst Ghedruckt den 30. Junij. T'Hantwerpen/By Abraham Verhoeuen/[etc.] 4° pp.8; sig.E^4; illus.
P.P.3444.af(254).
Headed: Iunij, 1621. 98. Containing also news from Germany. The titlepage woodcut shows a ship at sea.

N267 NIEUWE
Nieuwe Tijdinghe wt Hollandt/ende hoe dat de Soldaten van S'hertogen-Bossche in den Bommeleren-vveerdt met Sloepen hebben gheweest/ende veel Ghevanghenen ghehaelt. Met noch Tijdinghe vvt Zvvitserlandt. Eerst Gedruckt den 17. December. 1621. T'Hantwerpen/By Abraham Verhoeuen/[etc.] 4° pp.8; sig.J^4; illus.
P.P.3444.af(330).
Headed: December. 1621. 185. Containing also news from Germany. The titlepage woodcuts show (a) a fortress under assault, and (b) a ship in full sail.

N268 NIEUWE
Nieuwe Tijdinghe wt Hollant/van Amsterdam/ende weenen in Oosten-rijck. Eerst ghedruckt den 26. Februarius 1621. T'Hantwerpen/By Abraham Verhoeven/[etc.] 4° pp.8; sig.A⁴; illus.
P.P.3444.af(193).
Headed: Februarius 1621. 25. The titlepage woodcut shows the arms of Amsterdam.

N269 NIEUWE
Nieuwe Tijdinghe wt Hongharijen/hoe dat den Grave van Bucquoy de Stadt Nieuheusel belegert heeft/met s'Keysers Legher. Ouerghesedt vvt het Hoochduyts in onse Nederlantsche Sprake. Eerst Ghedruckt den 16. Julij. 1621. T'Hantvverpen, By Abraham Verhoeuen, [etc.] 4° pp.7; sig.N⁴; illus.
P.P.3444.af(261).
Headed: Iulius 1621. 104. Containing also news from Austria. The titlepage woodcut shows the siege of a city, with a fortified island in a river.

N270 NIEUWE
Nieuwe Tijdinghe wt Jtalien ende Roomen met de namen der Cardinalen die daer ghemaeckt zijn van . . . Paulus den vijfden. Noch van Venetien, Constantinopelen ende andere Plaetsen. Eerst ghedruckt den 26. Februarius/1621. T'hantwerpen/By Abraham Verhoeuen/[etc.] 4° pp.8; sig.A⁴; illus.
P.P.3444.af(191).
Headed: Februarius 1621. 23. The titlepage woodcut shows the emblems of the Pope.

N271 NIEUWE
Nieuwe: Tijdinghe wt Jtalien ende Spagnien. Eerst Ghedruckt den 1. October 1621. T'Hantwerpen/By Abraham Verhoeuen/[etc.] 4° pp.7; sig.Fff⁴; illus.
P.P.3444.af(288).
Headed: October. 1621. 139. Containing also news from Algiers, Constantinople and France. The titlepage woodcut shows a ship.

N272 NIEUWE
Nieuwe Tijdinghe wt Italien/ende Vranckrijck. Van t'ghene daer ghepasseert is/ende hoe datse de Hughenotten in Champagne ghedisarmeert hebben. Overghesedt vvt het Fransoys in onse Nederlantsche sprake. Eerst Ghedruckt den 6. Augusti 1621. T'Hantwerpen/By Abraham Verhoeuen/[etc.] 4° pp.7; sig.S⁴; illus.
P.P.3444.af(266).
Headed: Augustus. 1621. 109. The titlepage woodcut shows a naval engagement.

N273 NIEUWE
Nieuwe Tijdinghe wt Jtalien/ende weenẽ in Oosten-rijck/van t'ghene daer ghepasseert is. Overghesedt wt de Hooch-Duytsche sprake in onse Nederlantsche Tale. Eerst ghedruckt in Januarius/1621. T'Hantwerpen/by Abraham Verhoeven/[etc.] 4° pp.7; sig.A⁴; illus.
P.P.3444.af(181).
Headed: Ianuarius 1621. 12. The titlepage woodcut shows a sailing ship.

N274 NIEUWE
Nieuwe Tijdinghe wt Italien/Spagnien/ende Duytslandt. Eerst Ghedruckt den 26. Mey 1621. T'Hantvverpen, By Abraham Verhoeuen, [etc.] 4° pp.8; sig.A⁴; illus.
P.P.3444.af(234).
Headed: Mey 1621. 78. Containing an advertisement for a map showing the new route from Milan to Antwerp. The titlepage woodcut shows a seal featuring a gryphon.

N275 NIEUWE
Nieuwe Tijdinghe wt Legher van . . . Marquis Spinola. Hoe ende in wat manierē de stadt Bacharach . . . is inghenomen. Eerst Ghedruckt den xiiij. October 1620. T'Hantwerpen/By Abraham Verhoevē . . . 1620 [etc.] 4° pp.7; sig.Zzz^4; illus.
1193.l.30; 1480.aa.15(37); P.P.3444.af(119).
The titlepage woodcut shows a walled city by a river.

N276 NIEUWE
Nieuwe Tijdinghe wt Oostenrijck/Hongharijen/Bohemen/Palslandt/Grysons/ Italien/ende andere Landen. Nv eerst Ghedruckt den ij. October . . . 1620. T'hantwerpen/By Abraham verhoeven . . . 1620. [etc.] 4° pp.7; sig.Nnn^4; illus.
1193.f.23; 1480.aa.15(28); P.P.3444.af(110).
The titlepage woodcut shows the bird's-eye view of a fortress under siege.

N277 NIEUWE
Nieuwe Tijdinghe wt Polen/Duytslandt/Jtalien/ende Brussel in Brabant. Ouerghesedt vvt het Hoochduyts in onse Nederlantsche Tale. Eerst Ghedruckt den 22. October 1621. T'Hantwerpen/By Abraham Verhoeuen/[etc.] 4° pp.7; sig.Yyy^4; illus.
P.P.3444.af(300).
Headed: October. 1621. 153. The news from Brussels is of the beatification of Thomas de Villanova. Containing also news from Antwerp. The titlepage woodcut shows a cavalry engagement between Christians and Turks.

N278 NIEUWE
Nieuwe Tijdinghe wt Polen/ende Jtalien. Overgheset wt het Hoochduyts/in onse Nederlantsche sprake. Eerst Ghedruckt den 29. October 1621. T'Hantwerpen/By Abraham Verhoeuen/[etc.] 4° pp.8; sig.Bbbb^4; illus.
P.P.3444.af(303).
Headed: October, 1621. 156. Containing also news from Switzerland. The titlepage woodcuts show (a) Prague Castle taken by an army, and (b) a Turkish ruler.

N279 NIEUWE
Nieuwe Tijdinghe wt Prage in Bohemen/Ende van den Rhijnstroom. Overghesedt vvt de hooch-Duytsche sprake in onse Nederlandtsche Tale. Eerst ghedruckt den 26. Meert/1621. T'Hantwerpen/By Abraham Verhoeuen . . . 1621. 4° pp.8; sig.(??)^4; illus.
P.P.3444.af(212).
Headed: Martius 1621. 48. The titlepage woodcut shows a greyhound under a tree.

N280 NIEUWE
Nieuwe Tijdinghe wt Prage/Met allen de Naemen der ghevluchte Rebellen/de welcke Naemen aen de Galge zijn ghenagelt binnen Praghe. Ouerghesedt vvt de Hoochduytsche sprake, in onse Nederlandtsche Tale. Eerst Ghedruckt den 26. Mey 1621. T'Hantwerpen/By Abraham Verhoeuen/[etc.] 4° pp.6; sig.A^3; illus.
P.P.3444.af(233).
Headed: Mey 1621. 77. The titlepage woodcut shows a magistrate on horseback with attendants. Imperfect; wanting leaf A4.

N281 NIEUWE
Nieuwe Tijdinghe wt Roomen/Venetiē/Milanen/Spagnien/Ende andere Plaetsen. Overghesedt vvt de hooch-Duytsche sprake in onse Nederlandtsche Tale. Eerst ghedruckt den 19. Meert/1621. T'Hantwerpen/By Abraham Verhoeuen/[etc.] 4° pp.8; sig.(??)^4; illus.
P.P.3444.af(208).
Headed: Martius 1621. 43. The titlepage woodcut shows the portrait of an army commander.

N282 NIEUWE

Nieuwe Tijdinghe vvt s'Grauenhage, ende Amsterdam, Met de Naemen vande Hollantsche Schepen/ende Schippers die ghenomen ende ghebleuen zijn inden Slach te waeter teghen de Spagniaerden. Eerst Ghedruckt den 27. September. T'Hantwerpen/by Abraham Verhoeuen/[etc.] 4° pp.8; sig. Eee^4; illus.

P.P.3444.af(287).

Headed: September. 1621. 138. Describing the alarm and despondency in the Republic. The titlepage woodcut shows the portrait of Philip IV. On p.2 another woodcut of two ships, one with a broken mast.

N283 NIEUWE

Nieuwe Tijdinghe wt Spagnien/met het verhael/hoe dat de Hollantsche Schepen/ met de Zeerouers Schepen/gheslaghen zijn van de Spaensche Gallioenen/ende Galleyen/soo sy de stadt Mamorra hadden beleghert. Eerst Ghedruckt den 9. Julij 1621. T'Hantwerpen/by Abraham Verhoeuen/[etc.] 4° pp.8; sig. G^4; illus.

P.P.3444.af(256).

Headed: Julij, 1621. 100. Chiefly news of changes at court following the accession of Philip IV. The titlepage woodcut shows a naval battle, 'St. Helene' being the name of one of the ships rather than that of the island as suggested by the *Bibliographia Belgica* no. V197?

N284 NIEUWE

Nieuwe Tijdinghe wt Surich in zwitserlant/Ende Weenen in Oostenrijck/met de stadt Praghe/in Bohemen. Ouergesedt vvt de Hooch-Duytsche sprake, in onse Nederlantsche Tale. Nv Eerst Ghedruckt den 17. Iunij 1621. T'Hantwerpen/By Abraham Verhoeuen/[etc.] 4° pp.8; sig. A^4; illus.

P.P.3444.af(246).

Headed: Iunij, 1621. 90. The titlepage woodcut shows the portrait of Maximilian I, Duke of Bavaria.

N285 NIEUWE

Nieuwe Tijdinghe wt Switzerlandt ende Valtellina. Met Tijdinghe wt Hollandt ende andere Quartieren. Eerst ghedruckt den x. Meert. 1621. T'Hantwerpen/by Abraham Verhoeven/[etc.] 4° pp.8; sig. A^2; illus.

P.P.3444.af(201).

Headed: Martius 1621. 35. The titlepage woodcut shows a fortified town with a windmill.

N286 NIEUWE

Nieuwe Tijdinghe wt Venetien eñ Turckijen/hoe dat Emerido van Sorida, de Stadt Tripoli in heeft ghenomen/ende is gerebelleert teghen den Turck. Ouerghesedt wt het Jtaliaens in onse Nederlantsche sprake. Eerst Ghedruckt den 19. Nouember. 1621. T'Hantwerpen/By Abraham Verhoeuen/[etc.] 4° pp.7; sig. Pppp^4; illus.

P.P.3444.af(314).

Headed: Nouember. 1621. 169. Containing also news from Spain and Switzerland. The titlepage woodcut shows a Turkish prince on his throne, with a flag.

N287 NIEUWE

Nieuwe Tijdinghe wt Venetien/Prage/ende Weenen in Oostenrijck. Ouerghesedt vvt de Hooch-Duytsche sprake in onse Nederlantsche Tale. Eerst ghedruckt den 26. April/1621. t'Hantwerpen/By Abraham Verhoeuen/[etc.] 4° pp.7; sig. (??)^4; illus.

P.P.3444.af(223).

Headed: Appril 1621. 64. Containing various other news, including a report on the Algerian pirates. The titlepage woodcuts show (a) a turbaned figure seated on a plinth inscribed 'ISMAEL SOPHI' and (b) a small castle marked 'Answen'.

N288 NIEUWE

Nieuwe Tijdinghe wt Vranck rijc Parijs ende wt den Legher voor Montalbaen Ende hoe datter eenighe Rebellen in Normandien hun hadden op ghevvorpen. Overghesedt wt het Fransoys/in onse Nederlantsche sprake. Eerst Ghedruckt den 24. Nouember. 1621. T'Hantwerpen/By Abraham Verhoeuen/[etc.] 4° pp.8; sig.Tttt^4; illus.

P.P.3444.af(317).

Headed: Nouember. 1621. 172. The titlepage woodcuts show (a) a king with a sword, and (b) a cavalry skirmish.

N289 NIEUWE

Nieuwe Tijdinghe wt Vranckrijck/ende des Conincks Legher/met t'ghene daer ghepasseert is. Ouerghesedt vvt het Fransoys, in onse Nederlandtsche sprake. Eerst Gedruckt den 10. December. 1621. T'Hantwerpen/By Abraham Verhoeuen/[etc.] 4° pp.8; sig.C^4; illus.

P.P.3444.af(324).

Headed: December. 1621. 179. The news from France dated 25 November. The titlepage woodcut shows a cavalry skirmish.

N290 NIEUWE

Nieuwe Tijdinghe wt Vranckrijck/hoe dat Mōsieur le Connestable is ghetrocken naer Monsieur de Rohan dry mijlen van Montalbaen/om te sien oftmen tot eenich Accoert [*sic*] soude moghen comen/ende de Oorloghe slissen. Ouerghesedt vvt het Fransoys in onse Nederlantsche Tale. Eerst Ghedruckt den 29. October 1621. T'hantwerpen/by Abraham Verhoeuen/[etc.] 4° pp.8; sig.Aaaa^4; illus.

P.P.3444.af(302).

Headed: October, 1621. 155. Containing also other French news of various dates, the latest dated 14 October. The titlepage woodcut shows fighting in a burning city.

N291 NIEUWE

Nieuwe Tijdinghe wt Vrancrijck/van ettelijcke groote Heeren die ghebleuen zijn voor S. Ian d'Angely. Overghezedt wt het Fransoys in onse Nederlantsche sprake. Nv eerst Ghedruckt den 16. Julij. T'Hantwerpen/By Abraham Verhoeuen [etc.] 4° pp.8; sig.L^4; illus.

P.P.3444.af(103).

Headed: Iulius 1621 103. Containing also other French news. The titlepage woodcut consists of two parts of what was once a longer set of armorial shields.

N292 NIEUWE

Nieuwe Tijdinghe wt weenen/ende het legher van den Grave van Bucquoy. Overghesedt wt den Hooch-Duytsche in onse Nederlantsche sprake. Nv eerst Ghedruckt den xxiij. September . . . 1620. T'hantwerpen/By Abraham verhoeven . . . 1620.[etc.] 4° pp.7; sig.Kkk^4; illus.

1480.aa.15(26).

The titlepage woodcuts show two male portraits, one of them Bucquoy.

N293 NIEUWE

Nieuwe Tijdinghe wt weenen in Oostenrijck ende Polen/hoe dat de Polacken alreets ouer de 150. duysent mannen . . . ghereet hebben/ende zijn gheresolueert de Turcken met den eersten int Lant te vallen. Ouerghesedt vvt de Hooch-Duytsche sprake in onse Nederlantsche Tale. Eerst ghedruckt den 30. April/1621. t'Hantwerpen/By Abraham Verhoeuen/[etc.] 4° pp.8; sig.(.˙.)^4; illus.

P.P.3444.af (227).

Headed: Appril 1621. 68. Containing also other news. The titlepage woodcut shows three turbaned archers on horseback and a camel.

NIEUWE tydingen wt den Conseio. 1621. *See* SCOTT, Thomas. Vox populi.

NIEUWE tydinghe hoe de Arminianen teghen de Reformeerde Leeraers der Christelijcker Kercke hebben eenighe schimp ende spot gemaect. 1618. *See* NIEU reken-boek, op den Arminiaensen kerf-stock.

N294 NIEUWE
Nieuwe Tydinghe uyt Engelandt. Van het executeren van Acht van de voorneemste Verraders. Met veele zeer notabele Particulariteyten dit stuck aengaende. Gheschreuen uyt Londen den 2. Februarij ouden styl 1606. Nu Ghedruckt den 20. Februarij . . . 1606. 4° 2 unsigned leaves
1568/8638.
Without imprint; printed by Broer Jansz at Amsterdam?

N295 NIEUWE
Nieuwe tydinghe van het overgheven der Stadt Gulich/gheschiet Dinsdach den 31. Augustij . . . Midtsgaders het over gheven vant huys Bredenbent . . . t'Amstelredam/Ghedruckt by Broer Jansz. [etc.] 4° 2 unsigned leaves
T.1729(3).
Published in 1610.

N296 NIEUWE
(tp.1) NIEVVVE VVERELT, Anders ghenaempt VVEST-INDIEN. t'AMSTERDAM, By Michiel Colijn . . . 1622. [etc.]
(tp.2 =sig. (.˙.) 2) DESCRIPTIO INDIÆ OCCIDENTALIS per Antonium de Herrera [etc.]
(tp.3) Eyghentlijcke Beschryvinghe Van VVEST-INDIEN: Hoe die Landen en Provintien gheleghen zijn/op wat maniere datmen die door reysen sal: Ende wat Rijckdommen van gout en silver elcke plaetse begrijpt: Ghedaen Van Pedro Ordonnez, de Cevallos . . . TOT AMSTERDAM, By Michiel Colijn . . . 1621.
(tp.4) SPIEGHEL DER AVSTRALISCHE NAVIGATIE, Door . . . IACOB LE MAIRE . . . t'AMSTERDAM, By Michiel Colijn . . . 1622. fol. 3 pt.: pp.111; 29; 85: plates; illus., maps
10410.f.28.
Tp.2 is engraved. Tp.3, introducing pt.2, has a woodcut showing an animal which may be a polar bear. Printed with some civilité type.

NIEUWE-JAER vervattende stoffe tot goede en vreedsame bedenckinghen. 1621. *See* POPPIUS, Eduardus

N297 NIEUWELANDT, Willem van
CLAVDIVS DOMITIVS NERO TRAGOEDIE. DOOR GVIL. van NIEVVVELANDT . . . T'HANTWERPEN, By Guilliam van Tongheren . . . 1618. [etc.] 4° pp.55; illus.
C.129.i.11.
The titlepage engraving shows the death of Nero. One of an edition of 100 copies.

N298 NIEUWELANDT, Willem van
SAVL TRAGOEDIE, DOOR GVIL. van NIEVVVELANDT . . . T'HANTWERPEN, By Guilliam van Tongheren . . . 1617. [etc.] 4° sig.A-I[4]; illus.
11755.b.46.
The titlepage engraving shows a scene from the play.

N299 NIEUWEN

Nieuvven, Klarē Astrologen-Bril/tot verstercking van veel schemerende ooghen/ die niet wel en connen sien/die duystere Jesuyten Comeet-sterre: onlanghs verschenen inden noordtwesten. Nae de Roomsche Judictie/ghenaempt Lybertas . . . Ghestelt in forme van Dialogus . . . tusschen twee personagien/ d'eene ghenaemt/Meest elcken mensche, en d'ander zyn Ghebuyr. In dicht,,ghestelt . . . Door een Liefhebber der vvaerheyd, ende Vaderlandtsche vryheydt. [etc.] 8° sig. A-D^8

1578/338; 11556.bb.59(4).

Published in 1608.

Den NIEUWEN verbeterden lust-hof. 1607; 1608/10. *See* VLACQ, Michiel

N300 NIEUW-JAAR-LIEDEN

Nieuw-Jaar-Lieden: Wt-ghegheven by de Nederduytsche ACADEMI. Jnt Jaer/Ist nIet een Maegt DIe s'VVereLts VerLosser heeft ghebaert? Voor Cornelis Lodowijcksz. vander Plassen. 1618. (col.) 't Amsterdam, By Nicolaes Biestkens . . . 1618. 8° sig. A-C^8

11556.bb.56(2).

The device on the titlepage is the emblem of the Academie, that in the colophon is the printer's device of Nicolaes Biestkens.

NIGRONIUS, Julius. *See* NEGRONE, Giulio

N301 NIJMEGEN

[8.4.1618] AFSCHEYDT Den Predicanten van Nimmeghen ghegheven by den Raedt der-zelver Stede/waer aen men zien kan/wat uytkomste alle Remonstrantsche Predicanten te wachten hebben/als de Contra-Remonstranten de Magistraten tot hare Devotie zullen ghebraght hebben. 4° a single sheet

T.2248(25).

Dated 8 April 1618. Published in 1618.

N302 NIJMEGEN. Schola Publica

STATUS SCHOLAE IMPERIALIS REIPVBL. NOVIOMAGENS, SUB RECTORATU MICHAELIS A MANDEVVYLLE . . . ANNI 1601. FRANEKERÆ, ex Officina Typographica AEGIDII RADAEI . . . 1601. 4° sig. A-C^4

731.l.4(9).

With a dedicatory letter by Michael à Mandewylle.

N303 NILUS; Saint

ΝΕΙΛΟΥ ΕΠΙΣΚΟΡΟΥ ΠΑΡΑΙΝΕΣΕΙΣ. Nili Episcopi Admonitiones: In Latinam linguam traductæ: AC Testimoniis tum Sacris, tum profanis illustratæ: Operâ & labore STEPHANI SCHONING . . . FRANEKERÆ, Excudebat AEGIDIVS RADAEVS . . . M.D CVIII. 8° pp. 378

C.130.b.15.

In Greek and Latin. Containing also 'Expositio capitum paraeneticorum ex tempore edita ab Agapeto' and 'Αριστοτελους περι ἀρετων και κακιων'. With the arms of J. A. de Thou and his second wife stamped on the binding. Ownership inscription: Stephanus Baluzius.

NIVELLIUS, Guilielmus. Theses medicae de phrenetide vera. 1621. *See* HEURNIUS, Otto

NJEUW(E). *See* NIEUW(E)

NOLTHENIUS, Henricus. Disputationum theologicarum decima-tertia, de statu duplici Christi θεανθρώπου. 1601. *See* DU JON, François; the Elder

NONIUS, Ludovicus. *See* NONNIUS, Ludovicus

N304 NONNIUS, Ludovicus

LVDOVICI NONII . . . HISPANIA SIVE Populorum, Vrbium, Insularum, ac Fluminum in ea accuratior descriptio. ANTVERPIAE, Ex Officina Hieronymi VerdussI. M.DC.VII. 8° pp.330

574.e.1.

N305 NONNIUS, Ludovicus

LVDOVICI NONNI . . . ICHTYOPHAGIA SIVE DE PISCIVM ESV COMMENTARIVS. ANTVERPIÆ, Apud Petrum & Ioannem Belleros. M.DC XVI. 8° pp.176

1038.d.14(1).

N306 NONNUS of Panoplis

(tp.1) ΝΟΝΝΟΥ ΠΑΝΟΠΟΛΙΤΟΥ ΔΙΟΝΥΣΙΑΚΑ. NONNI PANOPOLITÆ DIONYSIACA. PETRI CVNÆI ANIMADVERSIONVM LIBER. DANIELIS HEINSII Dissertatio de Nonni Dionysiacis & ejusdē Paraphrasi. IOSEPHI SCALIGERI CONIECTANEA. Cum vulgata versione, & Gerarti Falkenburgi lectionibus. HANOVIÆ, Typis Wechelianis, apud Claudium Marnium & hæredes Ioannis Aubrii. M.D.CX.

(tp.2) PETRI CVNÆI ANIMADVERSIONVM LIBER IN NONNI DIONYSIACA . . . LVGDVNI BATAVORVM, Ex officina Ludovici Elzeviri M.D.CX. 8° 2 pt.: pp.1360; 216

160.k.9; G.8896.

The text in Greek and Latin. A reissue, with a new titlepage, of the 1605 Hanau edition which names the translator as Eilhardus Lubinus, to which the supplement has been added. *See* also CUNAEUS, Petrus. The copy at G.8896 lacks tp.2. The copy at 160.k.9 is divided into 2 volumes, with another copy of tp.1, mounted, as is the first, and inserted between pp.917 and 918 (misprinted 618). P.917 is taken from another copy, mounted and given a blank verso; p.918 has been given a blank recto.

NOODIGE verantwoordinge der Remonstranten. 1620. *See* EPISCOPIUS, Simon

NOODIGHE antwoordt. 1617,18. *See* WTENBOGAERT, Jan

NOODIGHE ende getrouwe waerschouwinghe aen de Remonstrantsche predicanten. 1620. *See* DWINGLO, Bernardus

NOODTWENDIGH. *See* also NOOTWENDICH, NOOTWENDIGH

N307 NOODTWENDIGH

NOODTWENDIGH ENDE levendigh Discours/Van eenige getrouwe Patriotten ende Liefhebbers onses Vaderlandts; over onsen droevigen . . . Staet . . . In't Licht ghebracht, Om tegen die veleyne boecxkens/VVeeghschael, Reuck-appel, Vraegh-al, &c. gelesen te worden. GHEDRVCKT, By 't recht Voorstant in Hollandt/Anno 1618. 4° pp.24

T.2248(55).

Sometimes attributed to François van Aerssen van Sommelsdijk.

N308 NOODTWENDIGH

[Noodtwendigh ende levendigh discours.] Oprechte TONGE, Waer door beproeft wort de WEEGH-SCHAEL REVCKAPPEL Ende VRAEGH-AL, Dienende tot waerschouwinge voor de getrouwe Patriotten onses Vaderlands . . . GHEDRVCKT, By 't recht voorstant in Hollandt/Anno 1618. 4° pp.24

106.d.38.

Another issue of the preceding.

N309 NOORT, Olivier van

Beschryvinghe vande Voyagie om den geheelen Werelt Cloot/ghedaen door Olivier van Noort . . . Te zeyl gegaen van Rotterdam/den tweeden July 1598. Ende den Generael met het Schip Mauritius is alleen weder ghekeert in Augusto/Anno 1601 . . . Tot Rotterdam. By Ian van Waesberghen, ende by Cornelis Claessz tot Amstelredam . . . 1602. obl.4° pp.92; illus., maps

1858.a.1(2).

The running title is 'Schipvaert ghedaen door de Strate Magellanes'. Some of the engravings signed: Bapt. a Deutechum fec., Bapt. a Doet. fec., B.W. [i.e. Benjamin Wright] Cæla., etc.

N310 NOORT, Olivier van

[Beschryvinghe vande voyagie.] DESCRIPTION DV PENIBLE VOYAGE FAICT ENTOVR DE L'VNIVERS OV GLOBE TERRESTRE, PAR ST. OLIVIER DV NORT . . . Le tout translaté du Flamand en Franchois . . . Imprimé a Amstelredame, Chez Cornille Claessz. . . . 1602. fol. pp.61; illus., maps

445.b.10(4); 566.k.15(4); G.7039; G.6617(4).

The engravings by Baptista van Doetecum, the maps by Benjamin Wright. The copy at G.6617(4) is imperfect; wanting the titlepage.

N311 NOORT, Olivier van

[Beschryvinghe vande voyagie.] DESCRIPTION DV PENIBLE VOYAGE FAIT ENTOVR DE L'VNIVERS OV GLOBE TERRESTRE, PAR S^{r}. OLIVIER DV NORT . . . Imprimé à Amsterdam, chez la Vefve de Cornille Nicolas . . . 1610. fol. pp.61; illus., maps

C.73.g.2(2); G.2851(1); G.6620(3).

With the engravings and maps as before. In the copy at G.2851(1) the pagination on p.61 is misprinted as 66. The same copy has the arms of the Le Clerc de Lesseville family on the binding.

NOOTWENDICH. *See* also NOODTWENDIGH, NOOTWENDIGH

N312 NOOTWENDICH

[Nootwendich vertoogh der alleen-suyverende springh-ader aller kinderen Gods.] Der Reden-rijcken Springh-Ader/Vervaet in verscheyden Andtwoorden/ op de uytgegeven Caerte der Wijngaertrancxkens, onder 'twoort Liefd'/boven al, Binnen . . . Haerlem . . . 1613 . . . op de Vraghe ende Reghel als volcht: Vraghe:Of Gods genade door Christi lijden en 'sgheests kracht Ons salicheyt maer ten deel,, of geheel,, heeft gevvracht? Reghel: VVant Reden leert deucht, oock sich selfs vervvinnen. TOT HAERLEM, Voor Daniel de Keyser . . . 1614. 4° sig.☞^{8} ☞☞^{6}A-Q^{8}R^{2}; illus.

11555.d.43.

The dedication signed: D. Wachtendonck, originally printed for David Wachtendonck's edition of this work under the same title, in fact a new edition of the work issued by the Chamber itself in 1613 under the title 'Nootwendich vertoogh, etc.' Wachtendonck's edition was printed by Vincent Casteleyn at Haarlem, as evident from his initials in the device on the titlepage. This edition was subsequently published by Daniel de Keyser, with a cancel titlepage. The three woodcuts show the same emblem of the Chamber. (For an account of the printing history of this work *see* Anna E.C. Simoni, 'Rhetorical conundrum, etc.' in: *Quaerendo* XIII, 1983, pp.38–49.) Ownership inscription: Sum Jani ab Hoogenhouck.

NOOTWENDICH vertooch vande onnoselheyt. 1617. *See* JUNIUS, Isaac

NOOTWENDIGH historisch verhael van allen swaricheyden . . . binnen der stadt Alckmaer voorghevallen. 1611. *See* VENATOR, Adolf Tectander

NOOTWENDIGH tegen-vertoogh. 1617. *See* DAMIUS, Mathias

N313 NOOTWENDIGHE
Nootwendighe ende vrypostighe Vermaninghe van eenighe oprechte Ghereformeerde Patriotten/AEN ALLE Vrome Lief hebbers der Vaderlantsche Vryheyt. Ghedruckt . . . 1621. 4° pp.16
T.2252(19).

N314 NORRIS, Sylvester
(tp.1) AN ANTIDOTE OR SOVERAIGNE REMEDIE AGAINST THE PESTIFEROVS WRITINGS OF ALL ENGLISH SECTARIES. AND In particuler against D. WHITAKER, D.FVLKE, D. BILSON, D. REYNOLDS, D. SPARKES, and D. FIELD . . . Deuided into three Partes . . . By S.N. Doctour of Diuinity. THE FIRST PART . . . M.DC.XV.
(tp.2) AN ANTIDOTE . . . AGAINST THE PESTIFEROVS WRITINGES . . . THE SECOND PART . . . M.DC.XIX. 4° 2 pt.: pp.322; 247
3935.c.32.
Anonymous and without imprint; published by the English College press at St. Omer. For pt.3 see the following entry.

N315 NORRIS, Sylvester
[An antidote.] The Guide of Faith. OR, A THIRD PART OF THE ANTIDOTE AGAINST THE PESTIFEROVS WRITINGS OF ALL ENGLISH SECTARIES . . . VVherein the Truth . . . of the Catholique Roman Church, is cleerly demonstrated. By S.N. Doctour of Diuinity . . . M.DC.XXI. 4° pp.229
3932.cc.5(1).
Anonymous and without imprint; published by the English College press at St. Omer.

N316 NORRIS, Sylvester
[An antidote.] AN APPENDIX TO THE ANTIDOTE. CONTEYNING A Catalogue of the . . . Succession of the Catholique Professours of the Roman Church . . . TOGEATHER WITH A Counter-Catalogue . . . of Hereticall Sectes . . . By S.N. Doctour of Diuinity . . . M.DC.XXI. 4° pp.107
3932.cc.5(2).
Anonymous and without imprint; published by the English College press at St. Omer.

A NOTABLE and wonderfull sea-fight. 1621. *See* A TRUE relation of a wonderfull sea fight.

NOTULEN, ofte aen-merckingen. 1618. *See* TAURINUS, Jacobus

N317 NOUVELLES
NOVVELLES D'ALLEMAGNE, OV, LA SVRPRISE DE PRAGVE PAR L'ARCHIDVC LEOPOLDE, ET CE QVI s'y est passé és mois de Feurier & Mars derniers. AVEC VN ABREGÉ DES CHOSES . . . aduenues depuis six mois, tant en France, Allemagne, Boheme, Transyluanie, qu'en Flandres, Espagne & Angleterre. A ARRAS. Iouxte la coppie imprimée à Paris, chez IEAN RICHER . . . M.DC.XI. [etc.] 8° pp.62
1054.a.28(4).

NOVI frutti musicali. 1610. *See* PHALÈSE, Pierre

NOVUS orbis. 1616. *See* GRYNAEUS, Simon

NULLITEYTEN, mishandelinghen, ende onbillijcke proceduren des Nationalen Synodi. 1619. *See* DWINGLO, Bernardus

N318 NUMAN, Philips
HISTORIE vande MIRAKELEN DIE ONLANCX IN grooten ghetale ghebeurt zyn/door die intercessie . . . van die H. Maget MARIA. Op een plaetse genoemt Scherpen heuuel . . . By een vergadert ende beschreuen door . . . PHILIPS NVMAN . . . Derde

Editie. Vermeerdert van verscheyden schoone Mirakelen naer den voorgaenden druck ghebeurt. TOT BRVESSEL, By Rugeert [*sic*] Velpius . . . 1606. 8° pp.257; illus.
1568/9275(1).
The titlepage engraving shows the image of the Virgin in glory against the oak where it was found, with pilgrims.

N319 NUMAN, Philips
[Historie vande mirakelen.] [Toevoechsels vande Mirakelen.] 8° pp.60
1568/9275(2).
Imperfect; wanting the titlepage and all before sig.A. The title is taken from the privilege issued to Rutgeert Velpius and Huybrecht Anthoon at Brussels. The verse preface signed: P. Numan. The prose preface describes this as 'Nieuwen druck vande tvveede partye oft Toevoechsel vā de Mirakelen van onse L. Vrouue op Scherpen-heuuel'. Published in 1610? By Rutgeert Velpius and Huybrecht Anthoon?

N320 NUMAN, Philips
[Historie vande mirakelen.] MIRAKELEN VAN ONSE LIEVE VROUWE, GHEBEVRT OP Scherpen-heuuel/zedert den lesten boeck daeraff vuytghegheuen/met eenighe andere die eerst onlancx tot kennisse zijn ghecomen. By een vergadert door Philips Numan . . . TOT BRVESSEL, By Rutgeert Velpius/ende Huybrecht Anthoni . . . 1614. [etc.] 8° sig.A-D^8E^2; illus.
1568/9275(3).
The titlepage woodcut shows the Virgin Mary.

N321 NUMAN, Philips
[Historie vande mirakelen.] TOE-VOECHSELE VANDEN MIRAKELEN GHESCHIEDT OP SCHERpen-heuuel . . . Vergadert . . . by M. Philips Numan . . . TOT BRVESSEL, By Huybrecht Anthoon . . . 1617. 8° pp.86; illus.
1568/9275(5).
The titlepage woodcut is the same as that used in the 1614 edition of the 'Mirakelen'.

N322 NUMAN, Philips
[Historie vande mirakelen.] ANDER MIRAKELEN VAN ONSE LIEVE VROUWE OP SCHERPEN-heuuel, gheschiet . . . zedert den lesten druck van . . . 1613. Vergadert door Philips Numan . . . TOT BRVESSEL, By Huybrecht Anthoon . . . 1617. 8° sig.A-C^8; illus.
1568/9275(6).
The titlepage woodcut is that of the 1614 edition of 'Mirakelen'.

N323 NUMAN, Philips
[Historie vande mirakelen.] MIRACLES LATELY VVROVGHT BY THE INTERCESSION OF THE GLORIOVS VIRgin Marie, at Mont-aigu, nere vnto Sichē in Brabant . . . Translated out of the French copie into English by M. Robert Chambers . . . PRINTED, At Antwarp, by Arnold Conings. 1606. [etc.] 8° pp.296
861.d.5; C.110.a.14; G.19689.
Anonymous.

N324 NUMAN, Philips
[Historie vande mirakelen.] HISTOIRE DES MIRACLES ADVENVZ N'AGVERES A L'INTERCESSION de la Glorieuse Vierge Marie, au lieu dit Mont-aigu, prez de Sichen, au Duché de Brabant. Mise en lumiere . . . Par authorité de Monseigneur l'Archeuecque de Malines. A BRVXELLES. Par Rutger Velpius . . . 1604. [etc.] (col.) A BRVXELLES, DE L'IMPRIMERIE DE RVTGER VELPIVS M.D.C.IIII. 8° pp.227; illus.
701.a.8.
Anonymous. With 'Chant a l'honneur de Nostre Dame au Mont-aigu par P.N.' and

'Sonnet', signed: P.N.B. [i.e. Philips Numan Bruxellois]. The full-page engraving on sig.*2v shows the image of the Virgin of Montaigu with pilgrims.

N325 NUMAN, Philips

[Historie vande mirakelen.] HISTOIRE DES MIRACLES . . . A LOVAIN, Chez Iehan Baptista Zangre . . . 1604. [etc.] (col.) A BRVXELLES, DE L'IMPRIMERIE DE RVTGER VELPIVS M.D.C.IIII. 8° pp.227; illus.

4807.aa.15.

Another issue of the preceding. Ownership inscription: Jehan du May.

N326 NUMAN, Philips

[Historie vande mirakelen.] HISTOIRE DES MIRACLES . . . Deuxieme edition augmentée de plusieurs beaux miracles. A LOVAIN, Chez Iehan Baptista Zangre . . . 1605. (col.) A BRVXELLES, DE L'IMPRIMERIE DE RVTGER VELPIVS M.D.C.V. 8° pp.263; illus.

4808.aa.15.

Anonymous. With the same additional poems as the preceding. The titlepage engraving shows the Virgin Mary.

N327 NUNNESIUS, Petrus Joannes

PET. IOAN. NVNNESI DE STVDIO PHILOSOPHICO, SEV De recte conficiendo curriculo Peripateticæ Philosophiæ, deque docentis ac discentis officio CONSILIVM . . . Subiungitur SEBAST. FOXI de ratione Studii Philosophici libellus. LVGDVNI BATAVORVM Apud IOANNEM DIEPHORST. M DC XXI. 8° pp.203, 172

526.f.4(3,4).

Partly in both Greek and Latin. With 'Vita Aristotelis auctore Ammonio siue Ioanne Philopono Græce & Latine'.

N328 NUTTELIJCKE

EEN Nuttelijcke ende seer stichtelijcke uyt-legginge in desen tijdt (voor alle menschen) vande Predestinatie of Verkiesinge Gods . . . Ghemaeckt door een Lief-hebber der waerheyt . . . TOT ROTTERDAM, By Matthijs Bastiaensz. . . . M.D.C.X. 4° sig.A-E^4

T.2240(7).

N329 NYS, Joannes

VITA ET MIRACVLA S.P. DOMINICI PRÆDICATORII ORDINIS PRIMI INSTITVTORIS. ANTVERPIÆ, Apud Theodorũ Gallæum, M.DC.XI. R.MO PATRI, F. AVGVSTINO GALAMINIO . . . MAGISTRO GENERALI TOTIVS ORD. PRÆD. FR. IOAN. NYS DOMINCANVS ANTVERP. D.D. (col.) F. Iões Nys inuenit. Pet. de Iode figurauit. Theodor. Galle sculp. et excud. 4° pp.8: pl.32; port.

4827.bbb.14.

The engraved titlepage shows St. Dominic with the portrait medallions of other saints and one of the Virgin Mary. sig.*2 contains the Latin preface, pp.1–8 contain the Dutch text relating to the plates. The plate containing the portrait of St. Dominic after the preface and all the plates bear engraved Latin verses. The colophon is engraved on pl.32.

O

OBIECTIONS: answered by way of dialogue. 1615. *See* HELWYS, Thomas

O1 OBSERVATIONS

OBSERVATIONS CONCERNING THE PRESENT AFFAIRES OF HOLLAND AND THE VNITED PROVINCES, Made by an English Gentleman there lately resident, & since written by himselfe from Paris, to his friend in ENGLAND . . . M.DC.XXI. 8° pp.131

9405.aa.27.

Without imprint; published by the English College press at St. Omer.

ODE in laudem . . . Johannis Casimiri Gernandi. 1602. *See* HEINSIUS, Daniel

ODES in imitation of the seaven penitential Psalmes. 1601. *See* VERSTEGAN, Richard

O2 OERTEL, Hieronymus
[Chronologia, oder Historische Beschreibung.] (tp.1) DE Chronycke van Hungariẽ ofte Warachtige Beschryvinghe, van alle de . . . oorlogen ende Veltslagen tusschen de Turckẽ ende Christen Princen. Mitsgaders De belegheringhe, ende inneminghe der Coninckrijcken, Vorstendommen, Steden ende forten, die van An° 1300 tot op desen tegenwoordigen tijt in Hongarien . . . Bohemen en Oostenrycke van Weder sijden sijn gheschiet. Seer aerdich verciert met copere figuren alsmede een Caerte van t lant van Hongarien beschreuen door Hieronimum Ortelium . . . ende vertaelt door PETRVM NEANDRVM. tAmsterdam, by Jan Evertsen Cloppenbvrch An°. 1619.
(tp.2=p.473) APPENDIX PARTIS QVARTÆ Chronologiæ Hungaricæ, Dat is: Vvaerachtighe . . . beschrijvinge: hoe ende op wat maniere dat den . . . Heere Matthijas, Ertz-Hertogh van Oosten-Rijcke &c. op den 19. Novembris/Anno 1608 . . . van sijn Keyserlicke Majesteyt Rudolpho . . . het Lant van Oosten-Rijcke is opgedraghen geworden/waer op dat sijn Vorstelicke Doorluchticheydt . . . Anno 1611 . . . tot Praag . . . Bohemisch Coninc/ ende . . . Anno 1612 . . . tot Franckfoort tot Roomsch Coninck gecoosen/ ende . . . aldaer . . . ghecroont/ende als Roomsch Keyser verclaert gheworden: . . . Met groote neersticheyt te samen vergadert ende beschreven. Door HIERONYMVM ORTELIVM . . . Ghedruckt in't Jaer 1618.
(tp.3=p.585) VVaerachtighe beschrijvinghe. Hoe . . . den . . . Heere MATTHIAS, gekoosẽ Rooms Keyser . . . in Anno 1612. inde . . . Stadt NORINBERCH sijn in ghereeden. Beschreven . . . Door HIERONYMVM ORTELIVM . . . Ghedruckt . . . 1618. fol. pp.595; illus.
1314.l.12.
Tp.1 is engraved and historiated. The illustrations consist of engraved portraits, that on p.92 signed: N. de Clerck. Imperfect; wanting the map.

OF Godt in sijn predestineren . . . siet op des menschen doen. 1611. *See* COORNHERT, Dirck Volckertsz. Vande predestinatie.

OF the author and substance of the Protestant Church and religion. 1621. *See* SMITH Richard; Bishop of Chalcedon

O3 OFFICINA PLANTINIANA
INDEX LIBRORVM QVI EX TYPOGRAPHIA PLANTINIANA PRODIERVNT. ANTVERPIÆ, EX OFFICINA PLANTINIANA, Apud Viduam & Filios Io. Moreti. M.DC.XV. 8° pp.92
618.b.31; 821.e.2(3); 269.b.28.

OFFICIUM Passionis Jesu Christi. 1621. *See* LITURGIES. Latin Rite. Various Offices

OGILBEI, John. *See* JOHN Ogilvie; Saint

O4 O'HUSSEY, Bonaventura; name in religion of Giolla Brighde O'Hussey
[Irish] 16° sig.a^8 b^7
C.53.h.37.
A collection of poems, including a metrical version of part of St. Bernard's 'De contemptu mundi'. Printed by the Irish Franciscans at Louvain, ca. 1615. Imperfect; wanting the titlepage?

O5 O'HUSSEY, Bonaventura; name in religion of Giolla Brighde O'Hussey
[Irish] . . . ANTVERPIÆ. Apud Iacobum Mesium . . . 1611. [etc.] 16° ff.136: plate
G.5485; C.36.a.34.

The titlepage is engraved. The plate is an engraved portrait of St. Patrick. With some texts in Latin, marginal notes in roman type and an approbation describing the work as 'Catechismus Hiberno idiomate conscriptus'. Printed by the Irish Franciscans at Louvain. The copy at C.36.a.34 is imperfect; wanting the plate and with the last leaf mutilated.

O6 O'HUSSEY, Bonaventura, name in religion of Giolla Brighde O'Hussey [Irish]. 16° ff.135
C.53.h.23.
Another edtion of the preceding, wholly in Irish type. The foliation is printed on the versos. Without imprint; printed by the Irish Franciscans at Louvain, ca. 1615.

O7 OLDENBARNEVELT, Johan van
BEKENTENISSE Van Joan vã Oldenbarnevelt ghewesen Ad. vocaet vanden Lande van Hollandt ende West-Vrieslandt. VVtghecomen den XV. Aprilis 1619. Stilo nouo, ende voorts op verscheyden tijden. IN S'GRAVEN-HAGHE, By Hillebrant Iacobssz, [etc.] 4° pp.7
T.2422(19).
Probably still published in 1619. Corresponding to the copy described in *Knuttel* no.2878.

O8 OLDENBARNEVELT, Johan van
REMONSTRANTIE Aende . . . Staten . . . van Hollandt ende West-Vrieslandt/van Heer Iohan van Oldenbarnevelt . . . IN S'GRAVEN-HAGHE, By Hillebrant Iacobssz . . . 1618. 4° pp.80
T.2422(7).
Corresponding to the copy described in *Knuttel* no.2624.

O9 OLDENBARNEVELT, Johan van
REMONSTRANTIE Aende . . . Staten . . . van Hollandt ende West-Vrieslandt/van Heer Iohan van Oldenbarnevelt . . . IN S'GRAVEN-HAGHE, By Hillebrandt Iacobssz . . . 1618. [etc.] 4° pp.1–48
106.d.49.
The words 'Met Privilegie' have been added to the title. Imperfect; wanting all after p.48. Corresponding to the copy described in *Tiele* no.1459?

O10 OLDENBARNEVELT, Johan van
WARACHTIGE HISTORIE Van de Ghevanckenisse/bekentenisse/leste woorden ende droevighe doot van wylen Heer Iohan van Olden-barnevelt . . . Te samen ghebracht meest uyt sijner Ed$^{t.}$ eyghene . . . Schriften . . . Mitsgaders uyt de verklaringe van . . . Iohan Francken . . . Ghedruckt . . . 1620. 4° pp.80
614.b.32; T.2422(36).
Without imprint; printed by Joris Veseler at Amsterdam. Corresponding to the copy described in *Knuttel* no.3069.

O11 OLDENDORPIUS, Cornelius Melchior
THESES MEDICÆ DE FEBRE ARDENTE EXQVISITA, Quas . . . asserere conabitur CORNEL. MELCH. OLDENDORPIVS . . . LVGDVNI BATAVORVM, Ex Officina Thomæ Basson, 1607. 4° sig.A^4
7306.f.6(28).

Den OMLOOP ofte afbeeldingen der plaetsen. 1621. *See* ABBILDUNG

O12 ONBEGRIJPELIJCKE
Onbegrijpelijcke Post Couranten. Met de Ceremonien Gehouden tot Roomen In het Verkiesen van zijn Heyligheyt. Met tydinghen vvt Duytslant. Ouerghesedt vvt de Hooch-Duytsche sprake in onse Nederlantsche Tale. Eerst ghedruckt den

24. Meert. 1621. T'Hantwerpen/by Abraham Verhoeven/[etc.] 4° pp.8; sig. (.˙.)[4]; illus.
P.P.3444.af(209).
Headed: Martius. 1621. 45. The newly elected Pope is Gregory XV. The titlepage woodcut shows an amphora with a broken handle.

ONBILLICKE wreetheyt der Dortsche Synode. 1619. *See* EPISCOPIUS, Simon. Synodi Dordr. . . . crudelis iniquitas.

ONDECKINGHE van verscheyden on-waerheyden. 1617. *See* WTENBOGAERT, Jan

ONDER verbeteringh. Een Mey-praetjen tussen vader ende sone. 1610. *See* LE CANU, Robbert

O13 ONPARTYDICH
ONPARTYDICH Discours opte handelinghe vande Indien. 4° sig.A[4]
T.1731(12); 106.b.16.
A translation of an unidentified French original, ascribed by *Asher* p.91 no.36 to Willem Usselincx. Published in 1608. The copy at T.1731(12) is cropped.

ONSE ende des Rijckx lieve/ghetrouwe N. Hooft-lieden. 1620. *See* FERDINAND II; Emperor

ONTDECKINGE vande valsche Spaensche Iesuijtische Practijcke. 1618. *See* MIJLE, Cornelis van der

ONTDECKINGHE van den oproerighen gheest der Contra-Remonstrants-ghesinde binnen . . . Oudewater. 1618. *See* OUDEWATER [1618]

O14 ONTDECKINGHE
Ontdeckinghe, Van eenighe secrete handelinghe der Jesuyten. Ghedruct . . . 1609. 4° pp.41 [14]
T.2417(22).

O15 ONTDECKINGHE
ONTDECKINGHE Van eenighe secrete handelinghe der Jesuyten. Int Licht ghebracht Door een van hun Nieuwelinghen/die't selfs meestendeel ghesien/ende van andere Jesuyten ghehoort heeft. Ghedruckt . . . 1609. 4° pp.13
T.2421(3).
Another edition of the preceding.

ONTMOETER. 1617. *See* TRIGLAND, Jacobus

ONTROUWE des valschen waerschouwers. 1616. *See* TRIGLAND, Jacobus

O16 OOGH-TEECKEN
OOGH-TEECKEN Der Inlantsche twisten ende beroerten/onder t'seghel van Henrick van Nassau/Soldaet onder de Guarde des . . . Heldts MAVRITII . . . Over-geset uyt het Latijnsche Exemplaer/ghedruckt in 'sGraven-Haghe/by Aert Meuris. 1620. 4° pp.38
T.2422(31).
The Latin original not traced.

O17 OORDEEL
Oordeel ende Censure Der Hooch gheleerder . . . Mannen Francisci Iunij, Luchę Trelcatij, ende Francisci Gomari . . . Midtsgaders D. Ieremie Bastingij, ende Iohannis VVtenbogaerts. Door bevel der . . . Staten van Hollant ende VVest-Vrieslant schriftelijck ghestelt/ende . . . overghegheven Anno 1595. over de doolinghen van Cornelis VViggersz . . . TOT DELF. Ghedruckt by Ian Andriesz. . . . 1612. 4° pp.28
T.2242(33).

[Illustration of ***O19*** *overleaf]*

IN D. CATHARINAM SENENSEM.

Cor sine corde mihi eſt, ſine vitâ viuere, vita:
Qui ſine vtroquè dedit viuere, vtrumq; tulit.
Nec tulit vt ſine vtroq; forem, ſed viuat vt in me
Cor ſine corde, nouum cor ſibi finxit amans.
Nunc neq; velle meum eſt, neq; nolle; at amantis vtrumq;
Qui mihi me rapuit, cor mihi cum rapuit.
Viue igitur, mea vita, meum cor: diſcet amare
Hinc, qui ſe nimium, dum ſibi viuit, amat.

OORDEEL ende uytsprake . . . van het Synode . . . tot Alez. 1621. *See* ALAIS. Synod

O18 OORLOGHEN

Oorloghen van BOHEEMEN Mitsgaders Alle Battalien/in nemen van Steden/ende Castelen . . . met de Kroninghen des Keysers als Koningen van begin tot op desen huydigen dage/seer vreemt om hooren. Ghedruckt tot Leyden, Nae de Copye van Praghe, voor Frans Franssz. 4° sig. AB^4C^2; illus.
T.2423(16).

Published in 1619. The titlepage engraving shows a historical map. The original printed by Daniel Carolides à Carlspergka.

OORSPRONG en voortgang der Neder-Landtscher beroerten. 1616. *See* GYSIUS, Joannes

OP de comeet oft ster met de staert. 1619. *See* RODENBURGH, Theodore. Eglentiers nieuwe-jaers gift . . . M.DC.XIX.

OP de waeg-schael. 1618. *See* VONDEL, Joost van den [Other works]

OP s'Oegst-maents eerste dagh. 1618. *See* COSTER, Samuel

OPENE brieven vande verklaringhe des Konincks. 1621. *See* FRANCE [7.6.1621]

OPENINGHE der synodale canones. 1621. *See* NEOMAGUS, Arnoldus

O19 OPHOVIUS, Michael

D. CATHARINÆ SENENSIS VIRGINIS SS.MÆ ORD. PRÆDICATORVM VITA AC MIRACVLA SELECTIORA FORMIS ÆNEIS EXPRESSA. Antuerpiæ Apud Philippum Gallæum. 1603. REVERENDO . . . PATRI P. ANDREÆ HEYNSIO . . . FRATER MICHAEL OPHOVIVS . . . DD. 4° pl. XXXII; illus.
4828.aa.34.

The illustration at the end of the preliminaries, captioned 'Vera effigies', and the final plate signed: Corn. Galle scp/fecit. Engraved throughout, except for the preliminaries which appear to have been printed by the Officina Plantiniana. With an eighteenth-century Dutch bookplate without a name and the ownership inscription: J. Lowe.

O20 OPMEER, Petrus ab; the Elder

(tp.1) OPVS CHRONOGRAPHICVM ORBIS VNIVERSI A MVNDI EXORDIO VSQVE AD ANNVM M.DC.XI. Continens HISTORIAM, ICONES, ET ELOGIA, SVMMORVM PONTIFICVM, IMPERATORVM, REGVM, AC VIRORVM ILLVSTRIVM: in duos Tomos diuisum. Prior Auctore PETRO OPMEERO . . . à condito Orbe ad suam vsqȝ ætatem . . . à PETRO FIL. euulgatus. Posterior Auctore LAVRENTIO BEYERLINCK . . . ANTVERPIÆ ex Typographeio HIERONYMI VERDVSSII M.D.CXI.
(tp.2) OPVS CHRONOGRAPHICVM . . . Ab anno M.D.LXXII. ad vsque M.DC.XI . . . Auctore LAVRENTIO BEYERLINCK . . . TOMVS II. ANTVERPIÆ, Ex Typographeio HIERONYMI VERDVSSI. M.DC.XI. fol. 2 tom.: pp. 516; 338: plate; illus. genealogical tables, port.
583.l.15.

With a biographical sketch of Petrus ab Opmeer the Elder. The engraved titlepage signed: P. de Iode inuent.; Guiliel. de Haen sculp. The author's portrait is engraved, other illustrations are woodcuts. With a large heraldic bookplate bearing the motto: jure non vi, signed: Jasp: Bouttats fecit.

O21 OPMEER, T. Petri ab

DISPUTATIO MEDICA INAUGURALIS DE PERIPNEVMONIA, Quam . . . Publicè instituit T. PETRI AB OPMEER . . . LVGDVNI BATAVORVM Ex officina IACOBI MARCI . . . M.D.C XXI. 4° sig. A^4
1185.g.2(2).

O22 OPPENHEIM

Articulen ende Conditien ghesloten int ouergheuen van de stadt van Oppenheym/ aen . . . den Marquis Spinola. Met noch den Nombre vant' graen ende Provisie dat in de stadt ghevonden is. Overghesedt wt den Hooch-Duytsche in onse Nederlantsche sprake. Nv eerst Ghedruckt den ij. October . . . 1620. T'hantwerpen/By Abraham verhoeven . . . 1620. [etc.] 4° pp.7; sig. Ooo^4; illus.
1193.f.28; 1480.aa.15(29); P.P.3444.af(111).
The titlepage woodcut shows Spinola's army on the Rhine.

OPRECHT ende claer bericht. 1617. *See* GOSWINIUS, Thomas

O23 OPRECHT

Oprecht verhael Van het geen den xxij. ende xxviij. Junij tusschen de Heeren van SOMMELSDYCK Ende Vander MYLE IS gepasseert. Ghedruckt in't Jaer . . . 1618. 4° sig. A^4
T.2422(15).

OPRECHTE tonge. 1618. *See* NOODTWENDIGH ende levendigh discours.

O24 OPTIMA

Optima Fides FESTI HOMMII, cuius specimen in citatione insignium locorum ex Thesibus privatis M. Simonis Episcopij . . . demonstratur ex libro quem inscripsit SPECIMEN CONTROVERSIARVM BELGICARVM. LVGDVNI BATAVORVM, Ex Officinâ GODEFRIDI BASSON . . . 1618. 4° sig. A^4
3504.bb.30(2).
The text differs from the preface to 'Collegium disputationum' by Simon Episcopius, but is probably by him or one of his pupils. Ownership inscription: Josephi Maynard.

O25 OPWECKER

DEN OPWECKER Der oude vermaerde wijt beroemde Bataviers/ghestelt ter eeren van Godt ende sijn H. Kercke/ende alle oprechte Christelijcke Bataviers herten . . . Ghedruckt . . . 1619. By E. N. No. 4° sig. AB, Bb^4
700.h.25(31).
Sig. Bb is entitled POST-BODE and dated 15 July 1616. It obviously belongs to another piece. It refers to 'Onderlinge Verdraagsaamheydt' and 'Naarder openinge' by Jacobus Taurinus. For a separate description of it *see* TAURINUS, Jacobus

O26 ORANGIEN-APPEL

DEN Orangien-Appel/dienende tot een ANTIDOTE, Om niet verghifticht te werden door den fenijnighen dampe daer mede den REVCK-APPEL . . . is besmet . . . Ghedruct . . . 1618. 4° pp.96
T.2248(3).

ORATIE, of uutspraecke van het recht der Nederland[t]sche oorloghe. 1608. *See* VERHEIDEN, Willem

ORATIE over het Synodi Nationael. 1619. *See* PAREUS, David

ORATIE vanden Enghelschen Ambassadeur, ghedaen in Hispaignien. 1606. *See* HOWARD, Charles; First Earl of Nottingham

ORATIO anniversaria dicta honori literarum principis Isaaci Casauboni. 1615. *See* BOURICIUS, Hector

ORDEN de oraciones. 1617. *See* JEWS. Service Books

ORDONNANTIE. Official publications of countries, towns or institutions beginning with this word are entered under their respective names and are arranged in chronological order.

ORDONNEZ DE CEBALLOS, Pedro. Eyghentlijcke beschryvinghe van West-Indien. 1621. *See* NIEUWE werelt. 1622, 21.

ORIGO et historia Belgicorum tumultuum. 1619. *See* GYSIUS, Joannes

O27 ORLANDINUS, Nicolaus

(tp.1) HISTORIÆ SOCIETATIS IESV PARS PRIMA SIVE IGNATIVS Auctore NICOLAO ORLANDINO . . . ANTVERPIÆ apud Filios Martini Nutij M.DC.XX. [etc.]
(tp.2) HISTORIÆ SOCIETATIS IESV PARS SECVNDA, SIVE LAINIVS, Auctore R. P. FRANCISCO SACCHINO . . . ANTVERPIÆ Ex officina Filiorum MARTINI NVTII . . . M.DC.XX. [etc.] fol. 2 pt.: pp.426; 340
C.76.h.3; 204.f.5.

Tp.1 is engraved, bearing the portraits of St. Ignatius and others. The work was continued in the eighteenth century in Rome. The copy at C.73.h.3 from the library of James I, that at 204.f.5 from that of the Jesuit College at Antwerp. The latter is imperfect; wanting pt.2.

O28 ORLERS, Jan

Beschrijvinge der Stad LEYDEN . . . Verçiert met verscheyden Caerten ende Figuren . . . uyt verscheyden Schriften ende Papieren by een vergadert/ende beschreven door I. I. ORLERS. TOT LEYDEN, By Henrick Haestens/Jan Orlers/ende Jan Maire . . . M.DC.XIIII. 4° pp.422: plates; illus., maps
794.e.25; 154.f.15.

One plate signed: Guilielm, hanius fecit; the plan of Leiden is signed: Ian [prs] Dou; the view of Leiden is said to be by Gaspar Bouttats. The arms of Leiden on the titlepage verso in a large cartouche signed: H.L., i.e. H. Liefrinck.

O29 ORLERS, Jan

LA GENEALOGIE des illustres Comtes de NASSAV Novellement imprimée: avec La description de toutes les VICTOIRES . . . Deuxsiesme EDITION, A LEYDEN, Chez IEAN ORLERS en l'An M DC XV. [etc.] (col.) A LEYDEN, Chez Iean Orlers, MDCXV. fol. pp.305: plates; illus., genealogical tables, ports.
608.l.8; 136.b.5.

The author's dedication of the 'Genealogie' signed: Iean Orlers. The 'Description' is by Jan Orlers and Henrick van Haestens. The titlepage is engraved, signed: ÞG, i.e. Jacques de Gheyn. The plates, including the map, are the same as in the edition entered below under 'Nassauschen laurencrans'. Only the second work is paginated. Printed by Henrick van Haestens at Leiden.

O30 ORLERS, Jan

[La genealogie des . . . Comtes de Nassau.] GENEALOGIA Illustrissimorum COMITVM NASSOVIAE. IN QVA Origo, incrementa, & res gestæ ab ijs, ab anno 682 ad præsentem hunc 1616. Cum effigiebus XVI præcipuorum inter eos heroum . . . Collecta ex varijs monumentis a I. O. LVGDVNI BATAVORVM, Apud IOANNEM ORLERS . . . M D C XVI. [etc.] (col.) Lugduni Batavorum, Excudebat GEORGIVS ABRAHAMI A MARSSE, M D C XVI. fol. pp.97: plates; illus., genealogical tables, map, ports.
608.l.9.

The dedication signed: Ioannes Orlers. The cartouche surrounding the 'Concordia invicta' device is signed: I. i.e. Jan Cornelis Woudanus or, less probably, Christoph Jeghers?

ORLERS, Jan. Illustrium Hollandiæ & Westfrisiæ Ordinum Alma Academia Leidensis. 1614. [Sometimes attributed to Jan Orlers.] *See* MEURSIUS, Joannes

O31 ORLERS, Jan

[Nassauschen laurencrans.] DESCRIPTION & representation de toutes les victoires . . . lesquelles Dieu a octroiees Aux . . . ESTATS des Provinces Vnies du Païs-bas, Souz la Conduite & Gouuernement de . . . MAVRICE de NASSAV. A LEYDEN, Par Iean Ieanszoon Orlers, & Henry de Haestens. en l'An M.D.C.XII. [etc.] fol. pp.282: plates; map, port.

814.m.13; C.107.f.26.

The authors' dedication signed: Iean Orlers, & Henry de Haestens. The titlepage has an engraved border around the letterpress title. With a half-title reading 'Les lauriers de Nassau'. The plates are by various artists, among them Jacques de Gheyn and Jacob Matham. Printed by Henrick van Haestens.

O32 ORTELIUS, Abraham

DEORVM DEARVMQVE CAPITA, Ex antiquis numismatibus ABRAHAMI ORTELII . . . Collecta, Et Historica narratione illustrata A FRANCISCO SWEERTIO F. . . . ANTVERPIÆ, Apud Ioannem Baptistam Vrintium . . . M.D.II. [etc.] (col.) TYPIS ROBERTI BRVNEAV. 4° sig.$_{\star}$A-Q^4; illus.

602.e.10(2); 682.b.27; C.134.c.3.

The titlepage is engraved with the addition of the imprint in letterpress. Compiled by Ortelius and previously published without the text, except for the preliminaries. The plates are by Philips Galle. The copy at 682.b.27 has the arms of Jacques Auguste de Thou and his second wife on the binding. The copy at C.134.c.3 is from the collection of Sir Robert Cotton.

O33 ORTELIUS, Abraham

(tp.1) THEATRVM ORBIS TERRARVM, ABRAHAMI ORTELI. Quod ante extremum vitæ suæ diem, postremùm recensuit, nouis Tabulis et Commentarijs auxit atque illustrauit. ANTVERPIÆ, EX OFFICINA PLANTINIANA Apud Ioannem Moretum . . . M.DCI.

(tp.2) NOMENCLATOR PTOLEMAICVS OMNIA LOCORVM VOCABVLA QVAE IN TOTA PTOLEMAEI GEOGRAPHIA occurrunt, continens . . . ANTVERPIÆ, EX OFFICINA PLANTINIANA, Apud Ioannem Moretum. M.DCI. fol. 2 pt.: pl.115, xxxvij; pp.30; illus., port.

Maps C.2.d.10.

The biographical sketch is by Franciscus Sweertius. The portrait is by Cornelis Galle. The plates bearing roman numerals are those of the 'Parergon', i.e. the atlas of the ancient world. The titlepage is engraved. All the engravings in this copy are coloured. For a full description *see Koeman* Ort 33.

O34 ORTELIUS, Abraham

THEATRVM ORBIS TERRARVM ABRAHAMI ORTELI . . . TABVLIS ALIQVOT NOVIS VITAQ. AVCTORIS ILLVSTRATVM. EDITIO VLTIMA. ANTVERPIÆ, APVD IOANNEM BAPT. VRINTIVM . . . M.D.CIII. fol. pl.80; illus., port.

9 Tab.13.

The titlepage is engraved. All engravings in this copy are coloured. Printed by Robert Bruneau. From the library of George III. Imperfect; wanting the 'Parergon' and 'Nomenclator'. *Koeman* Ort 36.

O35 ORTELIUS, Abraham

[Theatrum orbis terrarum.] (½ title) PARERGON, SIVE VETERIS GEOGRAPHIÆ ALIQVOT TABVLÆ [etc.]

(tp.2) NOMENCLATOR PTOLEMAICVS . . . ANTVERPIÆ, TYPIS ROBERTI BRVNEAV. M.DCIII. fol. 2 pt.: pl.XL; pp.30

Maps C.2.d.12.

Published by Joannes Baptista Vrients. Imperfect; wanting the 'Theatrum'. *Koeman* Ort.36.

O36 ORTELIUS, Abraham
(tp.1) THEATRVM ORBIS TERRARVM ABRAHAMI ORTELI . . . ANTVERPIÆ, EXTAT IN OFFICINA PLANTINIANA, M.DC.XII.
(tp.2) NOMENCLATOR PTOLEMAICVS . . . ANTVERPIÆ, TYPIS ROBERTI BRVNEAV . . . M.DC.IX. fol. 2 pt.: pl.128, XL; pp.30; illus., port.
Maps C.2.e.3.
With the contribution by Michael Coignet. Printed originally for Jan Baptist Vrients? *Koeman* Ort.41.

O37 ORTELIUS, Abraham
[Theatrum orbis terrarum.] (tp.1) THEATRO DEL MONDO DI ABRAHAMO ORTELIO: Da lui . . . riueduto, & di tauole nuoue, et commenti adorno, & arricchito, con la vita dell' Autore. Traslato in Lingua Toscana dal Sig.r Filippo Pigafetta. IN ANVERSA, APPRESSO GIOVANNI BAPTA. VRINTIO, M.DC.VIII.
(tp.2) NOMENCLATOR PTOLEMAICVS: OMNIVM LOCORVM VOCABVLA, QVAE IN TOTA PTOLEMAEI GEOGRAPHIA occurrunt, continens . . . ANTVERPIÆ, TYPIS ROBERTI BRVNEAV, M.DC.VII. fol. sig.A-D^6E^3; pl.127; sig.a^4: pl.XL; pp.30; illus., port.
Maps C.2.e.2.
The titlepage, engraved, signed: MB, i.e. Martin Baes. With the contributions by Franciscus Sweerts and Michael Coignet. *Koeman* Ort 38.

O38 ORTELIUS, Abraham
[Theatrum orbis terrarum.] (tp.1) THEATRO DEL MONDO DI ABRAHAMO ORTELIO: Da lui . . . riueduto, & di tauole nuoue, et commenti adorno, & arricchito, con la vita dell'Autore. Traslato in Lingua Toscana dal Sigr Filippo Pigafetta. IN ANVERSA, SI VENDE NELLA LIBRARIA PLANTINIANA, M.DC.XII.
(tp.2) NOMENCLATOR . . . ANTVERPIÆ, TYPIS ROBERTI BRVNEAV, M.DC.VII. fol. sig.A-D^6E^3; pl.127; sig.a^4: pl.XL; pp.30; illus., port.
Maps C.2.e.4.
A reissue of the preceding. With the portrait of Pope Clement VIII on the titlepage verso. *Koeman* Ort 42 does not describe the 'Nomenclator' with this edition.

O39 ORTELIUS, Abrahamus
[Theatrum orbis terrarum.] (tp.1) THEATRO D'EL ORBE DE LA TIERRA DE ABRAHAM ORTELIO. El qual . . . ha emendado, y con nueuas Tablas y Commentarios augmentado y esclarezido. EN ANVERES, SE VENDE EN LA LEBRERIA [*sic*] PLANTINIANA, M.DC.XII.
(tp.2) NOMENCLATOR PTOLEMAICVS . . . ANTVERPIÆ, TYPIS ROBERTI BRVNEAV . . . M.DC.IX. fol. 2 pt.: pl.128, XL; pp.30; illus., port.
9 Tab.11, 12.
With the contribution by Michael Coignet, but without that by Sweertius. From the library of George III. *Koeman* Ort 43.

O40 ORTELIUS, Abraham
[Theatrum orbis terrarum.] EPITOME THEATRI ORTELIANI, Præcipuarum Orbis Regionum delineationes, minoribus tabulis expressas, breuioribusque declarationibus illustratas, continens. Editio vltima, multis locis emendata, & nouis aliquot tabulis auctas. ANTVERPIÆ, APVD IOANNEM BAPT. VRIENTIVM . . . M.DCI. [etc.] (col.=f.[112]) Typis Henrici Swingenij. obl.8° ff.110, 13; illus.
Maps C.2.b.8.
With the 'Additamentum'. The plates are by Philips Galle. *Koeman* Ort 58.

O41 ORTELIUS, Abraham

[Theatrum orbis terrarum.] Epitome THEATRI ORBIS TERRARVM Abrahami Ortelij de nouo recognita, aucta et Geographica ratione restaurata, à Michaele Coigneto . . . ANTVERPIAE SVMPTIBVS IOANNIS KEERBERGII ANNO M.D.CI. obl.8° ff.110, 13; illus.
Maps C.2.b.7.

A different edition from the preceding. The maps are by Ambrosius and Ferdinand Arsenius. *Koeman* Ort 63.

O42 ORTELIUS, Abraham

[Theatrum orbis terrarum. Epitome.] ABREGE DV THEATRE D'ORTELIVS, Contenant la description des principales parties & regions du Monde, representees en petites Cartes, & illustrees de sommaires expositions. A ANVERS, CHEZ IEAN BAPTISTE VRIENTS . . . [1602] [etc.] obl.8° ff.118; illus.
Maps C.2.b.9.

The 'Addition d'aulcunes cartes' is not foliated. The date on the titlepage has been erased and altered in manuscript to 1702. *Koeman* Ort 60.

O43 ORTELIUS, Abraham

[Theatrum orbis terrarum. Epitome.] COMPENDIO DAL THEATRO DEL MONDO DI ABRAHAMO ORTELIO La postrema editione, corretta di nouo, & di alcune tauole aumentata. IN ANVERSA, Si vende nella LIBRARIA PLANTINIANA M.DC.XII. obl.8° ff.106; illus.
Maps C.2.b.12.

With the 'Additamento'. The translator named in the approbation as Giovanni Paulet. The title-leaf is a cancel and larger than the other leaves. It has taken the place of the original title-leaf reading 'Breve compendio, etc.', which was wrongly dated MD II. *Koeman* Ort 61.

ORTELIUS, Hieronymus. *See* OERTEL, Hieronymus

O44 OSSOLIŃSKI, Jerzy; Count

[The Latine oration.] ORATIE Vanden . . . HEERE, GEORGIVS OSSOLINSKY, Grave Palatijn . . . Camerlinck vande Konincklijcke Majesteyt van POLEN ende SWEDEN, Ende Ambassadeur aende Koninclijcke Majesteyt van GROOT-BRITTAIGNIEN. Voorghestelt aende voorsz syne Majesteyt tot Wit-hall . . . op Sondagh den 11. Martij, Ao. 1621. Overgheset uyt het Latijn in Duytsch. Na de Copy, Ghedruct te Londen by Bonham Norton ende Iohan Bill, [etc.] 4° pp.7
T.2424(17).

No copy of the original published by Norton and Bill is recorded although there are copies of an English edition printed by George Purslowe for William Lee.

OTIVM theologicum. 1621. *See* LEANDER de Sancto Martino

O45 OTTSEN, Hendrick

IOVRNAEL Oft Daghelijcx-register van de Voyagie na Rio de Plata/ghedaen met het Schip Ghenoemt de Silveren Werelt . . . onder 'tAdmiraelschap van Laurens Bicker/ende het bevel van Cornelis van Heems-kerck . . . Door den Schipper daer op gheweest zijnde Hendrick Ottsen . . . Gedruckt tot Amstelredam by Cornelis Claesz. . . . 1603. (col.) Ghedruckt tot Amstelredam by Cornelis Claesz . . . 1603. obl.4° pp.49: plates; chart
440.i.1(1); 1850.a.1(4).

The running title is: Beschrijvinghe van de Voyagie ghedaen na Rio de Plata.

O46 OUD

Een oud Schipper van Monickendam, [etc.] 4° sig.A^4
T.1713(30).

The titlepage is engraved. A copy of the edition in which the third line of verse on A2r has the reading 'Spaegniaerd' and the last word on A3v is 'dagen', corresponding to the copy described in *Knuttel* no.1468. Published in 1608.

O47 OUD
Een oud Schipper van Monickendam, [etc.] 4° sig.A⁴
T.1731(5); T.2420(24).
The titlepage is engraved. A copy of the edition in which the third line of verse on A2r has the reading 'Spaengiaert' and the last word on A3v is 'daghen'. The plate and type appear weaker than in the preceding. Corresponding to the copy described in *Knuttel* no.1466. Published in 1608.

O48 OUD
Een oud Schipper van Monickendam, [etc.] 4° sig.A⁴T.2248(54).
The titlepage is engraved. In this copy the third line of verse on A2r has the reading 'Spaengjaert', corresponding to none of the editions recorded in *Knuttel*. The last word on A3v is 'middel'. Published in 1608. Another edition of the three listed above, entitled 'Ghetrouwen raedt', is entered under GHETROUWEN.

O49 OUDAERT, Nicolaus
EPHEMERIDES ECCLESIASTICÆ, SEV Fastorum sacrorum Compendium. Adijciuntur . . . nonnulla ad COMPVTVM, quem vocant, ECCLESIASTICVM, & ad SPHÆRAM AC ASTRONOMIAM GEOMETRIAMQVE spectantia. AVCTORE NICOLAO OVDAERT . . . ANTVERPIÆ, EX OFFICINA PLANTINIANA, Apud Ioannem Moretum. M.D.CI. 24° pp.165
11409.e.43.
In verse.

O50 OUDEWATER
[1618] ONTDECKINGHE Van den oproerighen gheest der Contra-Remonstrants-ghesinde binnen der Stede van Oudewater. VERVATENDE Een cort ende waerachtigh verhael van't ghene binnen der Stede voorsz ghepasseert is/ voornementlijck binnen de tijdt van ontrent een Jaer herwaerts/inde vergaderinge vande . . . Staten van Hollandt ende Westvrieslandt . . . overgelevert op den xxij^en^ Januarij . . . 1618. Van verscheyden Vroedtschappen der voorsz Stede/daer toe . . . ontboden ende gelastet zijnde. Met Voor-reden ende Na-reden . . . daer by ghevoeght. Ghedruckt inden Jare M.DC.xviij. 4° pp.40
1608/4418.
Sometimes said to have been edited by Eduardus Poppius.

O51 OUDIN, Cesar
(tp.1) REFRANES O PROVERBIOS Españoles traduzidos en lengua Francesa. PROVERBES ESPAGNOLS TRADuits en François. Par Cesar Oudin . . . Con Cartas en Refranes de Blasco de Garay. A BRVXELLES, Chez Rutger Velpius . . . 1608.
(tp.2) CARTAS EN REFRANES DE BLASCO DE GARAY . . . EN BRVSSELAS, Por Roger Velpius . . . 1608. 12° 2 pt.: pp.269; 120
12305.ccc.51.
Pt.2. pp.99-120: 'Dialogo entre el amor y un Cauallero viejo, hecho por . . . Rodrigo Coto'. Ownership inscription: G. Christ.

O52 OUTERMAN, Jacques
[Historie der martelaren.] Historie der warachtighe getuygen Jesu Christj. Die De Evangelische waerheyt . . . betuycht ēn met haer bloet bevesticht hebben sint . . . 1524 tot desen tyt toe waerby ooc gevoecht syn hare bekentenissen disputatien,

ende schriften . . . Nu in desen laetsten Druck oversien ende verbetert, ende . . . vͤmeert Gedruckt tot Hoorn; voor Zacharias Cornelisz . . . 1617. (col.) Tot Hoorn, Ghedruckt by Jan Jochimsz. Byvanck . . . 1617. 4° pp.845
1229.e.12.

Anonymous. Compiled by Jacques Outerman and others. Known as the Hoorn martelaarsboek. The titlepage is engraved. Imperfect; wanting the preliminaries containing the 'Bekentenisse'.

The OVERTHROW of the Protestants pulpit-Babels. 1612. *See* FLOYD, John

O53 OVIDIUS NASO, Publius
[Heroides. Dutch] Heroïdum Epistolæ: oft der Griecscher Princessen ende Joncvrouwen klachtighe Zeynt brieven/beschreven int Latijn door . . . Ov[id]ius Naso. Overghezet in Duytsche Rhetorijcke door Cornelius van Ghistele. Met xij nieuwe antwoordende Epistelen daer op ghemaect . . . Anderwerf ghecorrigeert/ ende met twee nieuwe Epistelen door den zelven van Ghistele vermeerdert. TOT ROTTERDAM, By Jan van Waesberghe . . . 1615. 8° ff.128; illus., port.
11388.a.29.

The titlepage woodcut shows the presumed portrait of Ovid. The titlepage is multilated.

O54 OVIDIUS NASO, Publius
[Metamorphoses. Selections. Dutch] De vyerighe liefde vande Godinne Venus, tot den Jonghelingh ADONIS. Beschreven door . . . Ovidius Nason in het 10. Boeck/zijner herscheppinghe . . . In Neerduytsch Rijm ghestelt tot het eerste scheyden van Adonis, door een beminder der Reden-konst. Ende nu geeyndicht door I. W. vander Niss. IN 'SGRAVEN-HAGE, By Aert Meuris . . . 1621. [etc.] 4° sig.A-E^{4}
11555.bbb.28.

The completion by I. W. vander Niss of the earlier translation is printed on sig.D4v, with 'De iacht van't Swijn . . . door I. W. vander Niss' on sig.E.

O55 OVIDIUS NASO, Publius
[Metamorphoses. Illustrations] METAMORPHOSEON SIVE TRANSFORMATIONVM OVIDIANARVM LIBRI QVINDECIM, ÆNEIS FORMIS AB ANTONIO TEMPESTA . . . INCISI . . . NVNC PRIMVM . . . SVMPTIBVS A PETRO DE IODE ANTVERPIANO IN LVCEM EDITI. Petrus De Iode. excudit. A°. 1606. obl.8° pl.150
11355.a.12.

Engraved throughout, with captions only. A model book for artists.

O56 OWEN, Thomas; Jesuit
THE COPIE OF A LETTER SENT FROM PARIS TO THE REVEREND FATHERS of the Society of IESVS, who liue in England. CONTAYNING An Answere to the calumniations of the Anti-Coton against the same Society in generall, and Fa. COTON in particuler . . . M.DC.XI. 4° pp.93
860.c.26.

Signed: F.G. Without imprint; published by the English College press at St. Omer. Ownership inscription: Iohn Morris.

O57 OWEN, Thomas; Jesuit
A LETTER OF A CATHOLIKE MAN Beyond the seas, written to his friend in England: INCLVDING Another of Peter Coton Priest . . . to the Queene Regent of France. Translated out of French into English. TOVCHING The imputation of the death of Henry the IIII. late K. of France, to Priests, Iesuites, or Catholicke doctrine . . . M.DC.X. 8° pp.47
3935.aa.8.

Signed: T.A., i.e. Thomas Audoenus, i.e. Thomas Owen. The translation is also by Thomas Owen. Without imprint; published by the English College press at St. Omer.

P

P1 PAAUW, Petrus

DISPVTATIO DE CALCVLO RENALI, Quam . . . Præside . . . D. PETRO PAWIO . . . adserere studebo H. DELMANHORSTIUS . . . LUGDUNI BATAVORUM, Ex Officinâ Ioannis Patii . . . M.D.CIV. 4° sig. A^4

1185.g.1(4).

P2 PAAUW, Petrus

DISPVTATIO MEDICA DE ANGINA, QVAM . . . PRAESIDE . . . D. PETRO PAWIO . . . publicè defendendam suscipit ADRIANVS BOLLIVS . . . LVGDVNI-BATAVORVM, Excudebat Henricus Ludovici ab Haestens . . . 1610. 4° sig. A^6

1185.g.1(42).

The date of the examination has been completed in manuscript. With manuscript corrections and additions.

P3 PAAUW, Petrus

DISPVTATIO MEDICA DE ANGINA. Quam . . . PRÆSIDE . . . D. PETRO PAWIO . . . publicè defendet IACOBVS BORSELAER . . . LUGDUNI BATAVORUM, Excudebat GODEFRIDUS BASSON, 1614. 4° sig. AB^4

7306.f.6(9).

P4 PAAUW, Petrus

DISPVTATIO MEDICA DE ARTHRITIDE. quam . . . sub Præsidio . . . D. PETRI PAAW . . . Publice exagitandam proponit, NICOLAVS PETREIVS . . . LUGDUNI BATAVORUM, Excudebat GODEFRIDVS BASSON. 1614. 4° sig. A^4

7306.f.6(25).

P5 PAAUW, Petrus

DISPVTATIO MEDICA DE CALCVLO RENVM quam . . . sub Præsidio . . . D. PETRI PAAW . . . publicè adserere adnitar GULIELMUS STRATENUS . . . Lugduni Batavorum, Ex Officinâ THOMÆ BASSON. 1612. 4° sig. A^4

1185.g.1(50).

P6 PAAUW, Petrus

DISPVTATIO MEDICA DE COLICA PASSIONE Quam . . . PRÆSIDE D. D. PETRO PAWIO . . . Publicè exagitandam proponit, REYNERVS ROO-CLASIVS . . . LVGDVNI BATAVORVM, Excudebat Georgius Abrahami a Marsse, MDCXV. 4° sig. A^4

1185.g.1(61).

P7 PAAUW, Petrus

DISPVTATIO MEDICA DE CRISIBVS. quam . . . PRÆSIDE . . . D. D. PETRO PAWIO . . . Publicè defendere conabitur HVBERTVS BILIVS . . . LUGDUNI BATAVORUM, Excudebat GODEFRIDUS BASSON, 1614. 4° sig. A^4

1185.g.1(55); 7306.f.6(32).

P8 PAAUW, Petrus

DISPVTATIO MEDICA DE Hæmorrhoidibus. ad quam . . . PRÆSIDE . . . D. D. PETRO PAWIO . . . Publicè respondebit CORNELIVS SOETWATER . . . LUGDUNI BATAVORUM, Excudebat GODEFRIDUS BASSON, 1614. 4° sig. A^6

7306.f.6(22).

P9 PAAUW, Petrus

DISPVTATIO MEDICA DE MORBO COMITIALI, QVAM . . .PRÆSIDE . . . Dn. D. PETRO PAWIO . . . Publicè adserere conabitur IOANNES BROVAERT . . . LVGDVNI BATAVORVM. Ex officina THOMÆ BASSON. M.D.C.X. 4° sig.A^6
1185.g.1(37); 7306.f.6(4*).

P10 PAAUW, Petrus

DISPVTATIO MEDICA DE OBSTRVCTIONE HEPATIS, Quam . . . Præside . . . DD. PETRO PAW . . . Publicè defendet ADRIANUS BIMAN . . . LUGDUNI BATAVORUM, Ex Officinâ Ioannis Patii . . . M.D.C.V. 4° sig.A^4
1185.g.1(22).

P11 PAAUW, Petrus

DISPVTATIO MEDICA DE PARALYSI, Quam . . . PRÆSIDE . . . D. PETRO PAVW . . . defendendam suscipit publicè IOANNES VOORBVRCH . . . LVGDVNI BATAVORVM, Ex Officina THOMÆ BASSON, 1609. 4° sig.AB^4
1185.g.1(34).

P12 PAAUW, Petrus

DISPVTATIO MEDICA DE PESTE, Quam . . . Præside . . . D. D. PETRO PAAW . . . pro modulo suo tuebitur IOANNES KVCHLINVS . . . LUGDUNI BATAVORUM, Ex Officinâ Ioannis Patii . . . 1603. 4° sig.A^6
7306.f.6(26).

P13 PAAUW, Petrus

DISPVTATIO MEDICA DE PHLEBOTOMIA, QVAM . . . PRÆSIDE . . . D. PETRO PAWIO . . . Exercitii gratia sustinebo IOANNES PASSIVS . . . LVGDVNI BATAVORVM, Ex Officina Thomæ Basson, 1607. 4° sig.A^4
7306.f.6(34).

P14 PAAUW, Petrus

DISPVTATIO MEDICA DE PLEVRITIDE VERA. QVAM . . . PRÆSIDE . . . D. D. PETRO PAAVV . . . Publicè oppugnandam exhibet, PETRVS HAYMANNVS . . . LVGDVNI BATAVORVM, Excudebat Henricus ab Haestens. 1614. 4° sig.A^4
7306.f.6(12).

P15 PAAUW, Petrus

DISPVTATIO MEDICA DE PVRGATIONE. QVAM . . . Præside D. D. PETRO PAWIO . . . publicè defendere conabor IOANNES SWINNAS . . . LVGDVNI BATAVORVM Ex Officina GODEFRIDI BASSON, 1615. 4° sig.A^4
1185.g.1(59).

P16 PAAUW, Petrus

DISPVTATIO MEDICA DE SCORBVTO, QVAM . . . PRAESIDE . . . D. D. PETRO PAWIO . . . Publicè tueri adnitar TIMANNVS GESSELIVS . . . LVGDVNI BATAVORVM, Excudebat Henricus Ludouici ab Haestens . . . M.DC.XII. 4° sig.A^4
1185.g.1(49).

P17 PAAUW, Petrus

DISPVTATIO MEDICA DE VARIOLIS, & MORBILLIS. AD QVAM . . . SVB PRAESIDIO . . . D. D. PETRI PAAW . . . Publicè pro virili respondebit MENELAVS VINSHEMIVS . . . LVGDVNI BATAVORVM, Excudebat Henricus Ludouici ab Haestens . . . M.DC.XII. 4° sig.A^4
1185.g.1(47); 7306.f.6(24).
The date of the examination has been supplied in manuscript on the titlepage of both copies.

P18 PAAUW, Petrus

HORTVS PVBLICVS Academiæ LVGDVNO-BATAVÆ. EIVS Ichnographia, Descriptio,

Vsus . . . Operâ PETRI PAWI . . . Ex Officina Plantiniana, APVD CHRISTOPHORVM RAPHELENGIVM . . . M.DC.I. 8° pp.176: plate
988.e.10.
Published at Leiden. With manuscript notes listing plants.

P19 PAAUW, Petrus
HORTVS PVBLICVS Academiæ LVGDVNO-BATAVÆ . . . Operâ PETRI PAWI . . . Ex Officinâ IOANNIS PATII . . . M.D.CIII. 8° pp.176
968.b.2.
Published at Leiden. Not a reissue of the preceding and without the plate. With manuscript notes listing different plants from the preceding.

P20 PAAUW, Petrus
PETRI PAAW . . . Primitiæ Anatomicæ. DE Humani Corporis OSSIBVS. LVGDVNI BATAVORVM. Ex Officina IVSTI à COLSTER . . . M D CXV. 4° pp.188; illus.
548.c.7.
The titlepage is printed in red and black, with an engraving showing the dead rising up, with drums and trumpets. The other illustrations are also engraved. With manuscript notes.

P21 PAAUW, Petrus
Propositiones Medicæ-Chirurgicæ DE CAPITIS VVLNERIBVS AD QVAS . . . PRÆSIDE . . . D. D. PETRO PAWIO . . . Respondere conabitur M. LAVRENTIVS ERNONIVS . . . LVGDVNI BATAVORVM, Excudebat Henricus Ludovici ab Haestens. 1615. 4° sig.A^6
1185.g.1(58).

PAAUW, Petrus. Succenturiatus anatomicus. 1616. *See* HIPPOCRATES. De capitis vulneribus.

P22 PAAUW, Petrus
THESES MEDICÆ DE PLEVRITIDE, Quas . . . Præside . . . D. D. PETRO PAAW . . . publicè defendendas suscipiet WILHELMVS à MOERBERGHEN . . . LVGDVNI BATAVORVM, Ex Officinâ Ioannis Patii . . . M.D.C.VII. 4° sig.A^4
1185.g.1(29).

PACATUS, Latinus; pseudonym of Dominicus Baudius. *See* BAUDIUS, Dominicus

P23 PACENIUS, Bartholus
ΕΞΕΤΑΣΙΣ EPISTOLÆ, NOMINE REGIS MAGNÆ BRITANNIÆ, ad omnes Christianos Monarchas, Principes, & Ordines, scriptæ; quæ . . . ipsius Apologiæ pro iuramẽto fidelitatis, præfixa est. EISDEM MONARCHIS, PRINCIPIbus. & Ordinibus dedicata, à Bartholo Pacenio . . . MONTIBVS, Impressore Adamo Gallo . . . 1609. 4° sig.A-D^4E^5
3936.bb.52.
The writer using the pseudonym Bartholus Pacenius has sometimes been tentatively identified as Robert Abercromby. The imprint is false; published by Joannes Albinus, i.e. Hans Witte, at Mainz. The titlepage is mutilated.

PACTORUM de perpetua successione in regnis Hungariæ & Bohemiæ . . . instrumenta. 1617. *See* SPAIN [15.6.1617]

P24 PAGIUS, H.
CAP-COVEL Om Op t'Hooft te setten van DrIeLenbVrgh PaVs Van aLLe Sotten/Sterck-kijcker/ende Autheur vanden Nieuvven Calumnieusen ALMANACK, alias LEUGEN-SACK . . . Ghedruckt . . . 1617. 4° pp.8
T.2247(54).
Anonymous. In verse. The work by Vincent van Drielenburch referred to is entitled 'Calendrier'. The pages bearing sig. B following this work are part of the preceding tract, misbound.

P25 PAGIUS, H.

CAP-COVEL Om Op t'Hooft te setten van DrIeLenbuVrgh PaVs Van aLLe Sotten/Sterck-kijcker/ende Autheur vanden Nieuvven Calumnieusen ALMANACK, alias LEVGEN-SACK . . . Den tweeden Druck . . . 1617. 4° pp.8
700.h.25(3).
Anonymous.

P26 PAGIUS, H.

Clare Aenwijsinghe vande Gelegentheyt van Vincent van Drielenborgh, ende dat uyt sijne eyghene Schriften. Waer uyt men sien can/hoe waerachtigh het zy/dat hy met hooghe Hemelsche Inspiratien . . . van Godt begaeft/ende om t'ghetuyghenisse Iesu Christi ghebannen is. Door H. Pagium . . . Tot Leyden/By Govert Basson, 1616. 4° pp.35
T.2246(21).

P27 PAGNINUS, Sante

EPITOME THESAVRI LINGVÆ SANCTÆ, Auctore SANCTE PAGNINO . . . FR. RAPHELENGIVS . . . auxit, emendauit, & Appendicem dictionum Chaldaicorum addidit. Accessit hac editione Index Dictionum Latinarum, siue Lexicon Latino-Hebraicum. EX OFFICINA PLANTINIANA RAPHELENGIJ, M.D.CXVI. 8° pp.554
1568/2877.
Published at Leiden.

P28 PALEOTTI, Alfonso; Archbishop

[Esplicatione del lenzuolo.] (tp.1) HISTORIA ADMIRANDA DE IESV CHRISTI STIGMATIBVS SACRÆ SINDONI IMPRESSIS, AB ALPHONSO PALEOTO . . . explicata. Figuris æneis, Quæstionibus . . . & Meditationibus . . . illustrata. Cum vniuersa Passionis seriæ [*sic*] . . . AVCTORE R. P. F. DANIELE MAL[LONIO] . . . DVACI. M.D.C.VIII. EX TYPOGRAPHIA BALTAZARIS BEL[L]ERI.
(tp.2) IESV CHRISTI CRVCIFIXI STIGMATA SACRÆ SINDONI IMPRESSA. AB ALPHONSO PALEOTO . . . EXPLICATA. MELLIFLVIS ELVCIDATIONIBVS . . . [Nec]non ÆNE[I]S ICONIBVS . . . exornata . . . AVCTORE F. DANIELE MALLONIO . . . interprete. Adiectus est Index quintuplex, [etc.] 4° pp.429; illus.
1570/5639.
Tp.1 is engraved. It and the engraved illustrations are copied from the Latin edition published at Venice in 1606. Printed by Laurence Kellam at Douai. Both titlepages are mutilated. Imperfect; wanting vol.2.

P29 PALEOTTI, Alfonso; Archbishop

[Esplicatione del lenzuolo.] (tp.1) HISTORIA ADMIRANDA DE IESV CHRISTI STIGMATIBVS, AB ALPHONSO PALEOTO . . . EXRLICATA [*sic*]. FIGVRIS ÆNEIS, QVÆSTIONIBVS, CONTEMPLATIONIBVS, & Meditationibus . . . à . . . DANIELE MALLONIO illustrata . . . ACCESSIT TOMVS II. DE INCARNATI VERBI mysterijs, deque Jnstrumentis Dominicæ Passionis M. VIGERII . . . Adiectis plerisque per RICHARDVM GIBBONVM . . . ANTVERPIÆ, Apud IOANNEM KEERBERGIVM . . . M.DC.XVI.
(tp.2) HISTORIÆ ADMIRANDÆ Tomus alter, COMPLECTENS M. VIGERII . . . de præcipuis incarnati Verbi mysterijs DECACHORDVM CHRISTIANVM. EIVSDEM LVCVBRATIO DE INSTRVMENTIS DOMINICÆ PASSIONIS. Omnia ad vetera exemplaria castigata . . . indicibus adiectis per . . . RICHARDVM GIBBONVM. DVACI, Ex Officina BALTAZARIS BELLERI . . . 1616. [etc.]
(tp.3=tom.2. p.411) MARCI VIGERII . . . DE EXCELLENTIA INSTRVMENTORVM DOMINICÆ PASSIONIS LVCVBRATIO . . . DVACI, Ex Officina Typographica BALTAZARIS BELLERI . . . 1616. 4° 2 tom.: pp.429; 444; illus.
469.a.23.
Tom.1 has no engraved titlepage, but the same illustrations as in the 1608 edition. tpp.2, 3

bear small engraved vignettes. A reissue of the edition printed by Laurence Kellam at Douai, with the new titlepages printed by his widow as may be the additional work by Vigerius which seems not to have been part of the 1608 edition. Another issue is known, bearing the imprint of Balthasar Bellère on tp.1 also.

P30 PALET, Jean
(tp.1) DICCIONARIO MVY COPIOSO DE LA lengua Española y Françesa . . . Por . . . IOAN PALET . . . DICTIONAIRE TRES-AMPLE DE LA langue Espanole [*sic*] & Françoise. Par IEAN PALLET . . . A BRVXELLES Chez RVTGER VELPIVS . . . M.DC.VI.
(tp.2=sig.Cc8) DICTIONAIRE TRES-AMPLE DE LA LANGVE FRANCOISE & Espagnole. DICCIONARIO MVY COPIOSO DE LA LENGVA FRANCESA y Española. A BRVXELLES, Chez Rutger Velpius . . . 1607. [etc.] 8° 2 pt.: sig. A-Yy^8
827.b.43.

P31 PALLADIUS; Bishop
PALLADII EPISCOPI Historia Lausiaca. IOANNES MEVRSIVS Primus Græcè nunc vulgavit, & NOTAS adjecit. LUGDUNI BATAVORUM, Ex Officinâ LVDOVICI ELZEVIRI, Typis GODEFRIDI BASSON . . . M.D.C.XVI. 4° pp.208
486.g.8; 202.b.22.
The copy at 486.g.8 has the ownership inscription: Nicolas Stokes, that at 202.b.22 has the inscription: Lud. Bünemann.

P32 PALLAVICINO, Benedetto
[Madrigali a 5.] (tp.1) DI BENEDETTO PALLAVICINO MADRIGALI A CINQVE VOCI Di nouo Stampati & Corretti. TENORE. IN ANVERSA Appresso Pietro Phalesio. M.DCIV.
(tp.2) DI BENEDETTO PALLAVICINO MADRIGALI A CINQVE VOCI . . . BASSO. IN ANVERSA Appresso Pietro Phalesio. M.DCIV. obl.4° 2 pt.: pp.63; 51
Music A.305.a.

P33 PALLAVICINO, Benedetto
[Madrigali a 6.] TENORE. DI BENEDETTO PALLAVICINO . . . MADRIGALI A SEI VOCI NOVAMENTE STAMPATI. IN ANVERSA Appresso Pietro Phalesio. M.DCVI. obl.4° pp.21
Music A.305.b.
The word 'Tenore' has been inserted into the titlepage border

PALLET, Jean. *See* PALET, Jean

P34 PALMERIN de Oliva
[Palmerín d'Oliva.] Een seer schoone eñ genoechelicke Historie/vanden . . . Ridder/Palmerijn van Olijue . . . ende van de schoone Griane . . . Eerst ouerghesedt wt het Castiliaens in Fransoys ende nv getranslateert wt het Fransoys in onse ghemeyne Nederlantsche sprake. Gedruckt tot Arnhem/by Jan Janssz . . . 1602. (col.) Tot Arnhem. By Jan Janssz . . . 1603. 4° ff.241
12410.bb.3.
The woodcut titlepage border, made up of allegorical figures such as Peace and Justice, Faith, etc., is signed: I.M., or M.I., in a circle.

P35 PALMERIN de Oliva
[Palmerín d'Oliva.] Een seer schoone ende ghenoechelicke Historie/vanden . . . Ridder/Palmerijn van Olijve . . . ende de schoone Griane . . . Van nieuws oversien/ende met schoone figueren verciert. TOT ARNHEM By Ian Ianszen . . . M.DC.XIII. (col.) TOT AERNHEM, By Jan Janssz. . . . 1613. 4° ff.239; illus.
1162.i.40.
The illustrations are small woodcuts with typographical borders. The woodcut titlepage border is architectural, incorporating herms and fruit. Ownership inscription: Henry Weber (the gift of Walter Scott Esq.)

P36 PALMERIO, Giovanni Battista; Eremite Friar

[Lettera . . . alli fedeli sudditi del Dominio Venetiano.] BRIEF Vanden seer devoten Vader Broer Jan Battista Palmerio . . . Aende getrouwe onderdanen der Venetscher Heerlijckheyt. Waer inne . . . ghesien worden, de oorsaken der oneenicheyt tusschen de Venetianen ende den Paus . . . MDCVII. 4° 4 unsigned leaves

T.2417(24).

Cropped.

PALUDANUS, Bernardus. Disputationum physicarum prima, de physica. 1603. *See* VENO, Henricus de

PALUDANUS, Bernardus. Disputationum physicarum nona de elementorum qualitatibus. 1608. *See* JACCHAEUS, Gilbertus

PALUDANUS, Bernardus. Disputationum physicarum nona, de misti generatione. 1604. *See* VENO, Henricus de

P37 PALUDANUS, Bernardus

THESES MEDICÆ DE EPILEPSIA. Quas . . . pro Doctoratu in Medicina obtinendo Publicè defendere adnitar. BERNARDVS PALVDANVS . . . LVGDVNI BATAVORVM, Ex Officina Thomæ Basson, 1607. 4° sig.A^4

1185.g.1(31).

P38 PALUDANUS, Joannes

(tp.1) VINDICIÆ THEOLOGICÆ aduersus VERBI DEI CORRVPTELAS Authore IOANNE PALVDANO . . . ANTVERPIÆ apud Henricum Aertsium . . . M.DC.XX. [etc.] (col.1) ANTVERPIÆ, EX TYPOGRAPHIA HENRICI AERTSII. MDC.XX.

(tp.2) VINDICIÆ THEOLOGICÆ aduersus VERBI DEI CORRVPTELAS. Pars altera. Authore IOANNE PALVDANO . . . ANTVERPIÆ Apud Henricum Aertsium . . . M.DC.XXII. (col.2) ANTVERPIÆ, Ex Officinâ HENRICI AERTSII. M.DC.XXII. 8° 2 pt.: pp.347; 462

3125.de.12.

The titlepages are engraved.

PARACELSUS, Theophrast; von Hohenheim. *See* BOMBAST VON HOHENHEIM, Philipp Aureol Theophrast; called Paracelsus

P39 PARADIN, Claude

[Les deuises heroïques.] PRINCELIICKE Deuiisen van CLAVDE PARADIN, GABRIEL SIMEON, ende meer ander: Over ettelicke iaeren wtten Franschen . . . verduytscht: nu verbetert/ende met Wtlegginghen in Rijm/vermeerdert. Tot Leyden, Inde Plantijnsche Druckerije van Françoys van Ravelenghien. 1615. 12° pp.468; illus.

9917.a.12.

The editor's address to the reader signed: Joost van Ravelenghien; the postface signed: I.R.A., i.e. Justus Raphelengius Antverpiensis.

The PARADISE of delights. 1620. *See* SWEETNAM, John

PARASYNAGMA Perthense. 1620. *See* CALDERWOOD, David

P40 PAREUS, David

[Irenicum.] Vrede-schrift, TOT VEREENIGINGE DER EVANGELISCHER KERCKEN . . . Van D. DAVID PAREVS . . . over-gheset, Door IOHANNES à LODENSTEYN . . . TOT DELF, ghedruckt by Ian Andriesz . . . 1615. 4° pp.352

T.2245(13).

P41 PAREUS, David

[Oratio de synodo nationali Dordraci habita.] Oratie over het SYNODI Nationael,

gehouden binnen Dordrecht midtsgaders Des selven Oordeel/over de bekende vijf hooftstucken der Gereformeerde leere/deser vereenichde Nederlantsche Kercken/ door D. P. uyt den Latijn: in't Nederduyts overgeset. Ghedruckt tot LEYDEN, voor Isaac de Beer . . . 1619. 4° pp.32; illus.
T.2248(23).

Anonymous. With a list of the participants in the Synod. The illustration shows the Synod with the table of the Remonstrants in the centre.

P42 PARIS. Parlement

[2.5.1609] Arrest ende Sententie Op ende teghens eenen Guilaume Pingre Banckerottier: daer door allen persoonen . . . verboden werdt eenighe Banckerottiers te verberghen noch te verswijghen . . . overgeset uyt het Françoys, in onse Nederduytsche spraecke. TOT LEYDEN, By Henrick Lodewijcxs. van Haestens . . . 1609. Nae de Copie gedruct te Paris by Ian Millot. 4° sig. A[4]
T.2420(40).

P43 PARIS. Parlement

[14.1.1620] Sententie oft Arrest vā t'Hoff van t'Parlement den 14. Jan. 1620. tegens het Ghepretendeerde Reglement vande vergaderinghe te Lodun. Ouergesedt wt het Fransoys in onse Nederlantsche Tale/den xiij. Meert 1620. Naer de Coppije van Parijs, Par Fed. Morel, & Pierre Mettayer . . . Nv T'Hantwerpen/By Abraham Verhoeuen/1620. 4° pp.7; sig. D[4]; illus.
P.P.3444.af(35).

With news also of the French court. The titlepage woodcut shows the French royal arms in laurel branches.

P44 PARIS. Université de Paris

CENSVRA SACRÆ FACVLTATIS THEOLOGIÆ PARISIENSIS, IN QVATVOR PRIORES LIBROS de Republica Ecclesiastica, Auctore Marco Antonio de Dominis . . . LOVANII, Apud GERARDVM RIVIVM . . . M.DC.XVIII. 8° pp.24
874.f.1(4).

On the titlepage verso: 'De mandato Facultatis Sacræ Theologiæ Louanij impressit Gerardus Rivius dictæ Facultatis Bedellus & Notarius'. The signatures, in eights, are irregular. Cropped.

P45 PARIS. Université de Paris

[Censura . . . in . . . libros de Republica Ecclesiastica.] THE CENSVRE OF THE SACRED FACVLTIE OF DIVINITIE OF PARIS, AGAINST THE FOVRE BOOKES concerning the Ecclesiastical cōmonvvealth, COMPOSED BY MARCVS ANTONIVS DE DOMINIS . . . Translated by a Student in Diuinitie . . . Printed at Dovvay, By the Widdovve of L. Kellam, and Thomas his sonne. M.DC.XVIII. 8° pp.52
3901.a.54.

P46 PARKER, Robert

(tp.1) DE Politeia Ecclesiastica CHRISTI, ET HIERARCHICA OPPOSITA, Libri Tres . . . Authore ROBERTO PARKERO ANGLO . . . Prostant FRANCOFVRTI Apud GODEFRIDVM BASSON. M.D.C.XVI.

(tp.2) DE POLITEIA ECCLESIASTICA LIBRI TRES . . . A Roberto Parkero . . . conscripti . . . Anno Domini Nostri M D CXVI. 4° pp.368, 456
4106.c.43.

The introduction to the work is by William Ames. The 'Admonitio I.R. ad lectorem suo, suorumque nomine' is by John Robinson and in this copy, which has the introduction in the second setting, follows sigg.(:) 2-4 which follow tp.2. Probably printed by Govert Basson at Leiden, with tp.1 added before tp.2 for sale outside the United Provinces.

P47 PARKER, Robert

A SCHOLASTICALL DISCOVRSE AGAINST SYMBOLIZING WITH ANTICHRIST IN CEREMONIES: ESPECIALLY IN THE SIGNE OF THE CROSSE . . . 1607. fol. 2 pt.: pp.196; 144
689.f.23; 1226.f.23.

Anonymous and without imprint; printed by Richard Schilders at Middelburg.

P48 PARNASSUS

PARNASSVS dat is/Den blijdenbergh/der gheestelijcker vreught Ghemenght met deught Veur de ionghe ieught . . . T'ANTWERPEN, By Geeraerdt van Wolsschaten . . . M.DC.XIX. 8° pp.135
11557.df.45.

P49 PARTICULIER

PARTICVLIER RELAES Vande groote Victorie, ende het innemen der heele stadt van Praghe . . . T'Hantwerpen/By Abraham Verhoeven . . . 1620. [etc.] 4° pp.6; sig. Ee^4; illus.
P.P.3444.af(152); 1480.aa.15(49).

The titlepage woodcut shows the plan of a fortified city. This must be the issue of 1 December promised in that of 28 November, entitled 'Gazette van Blyschap'.

P50 PARTICULIER

Particulier verhael ende Ordre vāde Magnificentie gesch[iet] tot Weenen/op de Huldinghe des Keysers/ende vereeninghe met de Standen van Neder Oosten-Rijck. 1620. [T'Hantwerpen/By Abraham Verhoeuen . . . 1620.] 4° pp.7; sig. Aaa^4; illus.
P.P.3444.af(74); 1480.aa.15(9).

The titlepage woodcut shows a large battle scene. The copy at 1480.aa.15(9) has a mutilated titlepage, that at P.P.3444.af(74) is cropped all around, with loss of text. The title has been supplemented from the description in the *Bibliotheca Belgica* no.V196. p.483.

Het PASCHA ofte de verlossinge Israels wt Egypten. 1612. *See* VONDEL, Joost van den [Single plays]

P51 PASQUIER, Étienne

[Le catéchisme des Jesuites.] Spieghel der Iesuyten, OFTE Catechismus van der Jesuyten Secte ende leere . . . Eerst int Franchoys van een vermaert Papist beschreven/ende nu . . . in Nederduytsch vertaelt. Met een Vyttoch oft cort begrijp van een Poolsch Schrift . . . ghemaeckt van een treflijck Papist . . . Hier is byghevoeght een Na-bericht van den Paus, de Ordenen der Pauslicke Monicken . . . Daerin mede besonderlyck gheantwoordt wordt op de Schrifturen/die Bellarmijn heeft misbruyckt. DOOR IOHANNEM BOGERMANNVM . . . Tot Leeuwerdē/by Abraham vañ Rade . . . 1608. 4° pp.598
4092.f.21.

The unnamed author of the first piece is Étienne Pasquier; the second piece is a translation of the work known in Latin as 'Consilium datum amico de recuperanda et in posterum stabilienda pace Regni Poloniæ', ascribed to Felix Jan Herburt, no Polish edition of which has been identified.

P52 PASQUIL

Een PASQVIL genaempt Pater Arents lof, Tegen't viervoetig stof. Het ANTWOORDT. 4° sig. A^4; illus.
11555.e.35.

Partly in verse. The titlepage engravings show two allegorical scenes, corresponding respectively to the original threat from the Southern and the defence of the Northern Netherlands. Published in 1615.

P53 PASSE, Crispin van de; the Elder

(tp.1) COMPENDIVM OPERVM VIRGILIANORVM, Tàm oculis quàm auribus omnium expositum. ÆRE AC STVDIO CHRISPIANI PASSÆI CHALCOGRAPHI. MIROER [*sic*] Des œuures de le excellent Poete Virgile, taillez en rame . . . Anno 1612 . . . VLTRAIECTI BATAVORVM, Ex Officina typographica Hermanni Borculoi ET Prostant apud Ioannem Iansonium . . . Arnehemiæ.

(tp.2) SPECVLVM ÆNEIDIS VIRGILIANÆ. Brief recueil DES LIVRES DE L'ENEIDE . . . Ex Officina chalcographicâ CRISPINI PASSÆI . . . Prostant autem apud Ioannem Iansenium . . . Aernhemiæ. 4° 2 pt.: sig.A-C^4; A-F^4; illus.; port.

78.b.20.

The Latin verses in pt.1 signed: C.B., i.e. Christianus Bruningius; the French sonnets mainly by Louys de Masure who has signed the first in pt.2. All the leaves until pt.2 sig.D4 are printed on one side only; sig.E-F2 bear additional Latin poems, F3, 4 French poems, signed respectively: I.H.R. and T.D.L.

P54 PASSE, Crispin van de; the Younger

(tp.1) HORTUS FLORIDUS In quo rariorum & minus vulgarium florum Icones ad vivam veramqȝ formam accuratissime delineatæ. Et secundum quatuor anni tempora divisæ exhibentur . . . labore ac diligentia Crisp: Passæi junioris Delineatæ ac suum in ordinem redactæ A.° 1614. Extant Arnhemij. Apud Ioannem Ianssonium [etc.]

(tp.2) ÆSTAS HORTI FLORIDI, IN QVA PRAECIPVI AESTATIS FLORES EXCELLENTI, CR. PASSÆI STYLO ADVIVVM ADMODVM EXPRIMVNTVR. VLTRAIECTI. Ex Officina Hermanni Borculoi. ET Prostant apud Ioannem Iansonium Bibliopolam Arnemiensis [*sic*].

(tp.3) AVTVMNVS HORTI FLORIDI RARIORES AVTVMNI FLORES SVMMA INDVSTRIA ET LABORE. CRISP. PASSÆI FILII. In ære effictos, & in lucem recens datos continens. VLTRAIECTI. Ex Officina cælatoria CRISP. PASSÆI. ET Prostant apud Ioannem Iansonium Bibliopolam Arnhemiensem.

(tp.4) HORTVS FLORIDVS HYEMALIS CR. PASSÆI FIL. LABORE ET INDVSTRIA NVNC PRIMVM IN LVCEM EDITVS ANNO M.DC.XIIII. VLTRAIECTI. Ex Officina Calcograficâ CR. PASSÆI.

(tp.5) ALTERA PARS HORTI FLORIDI IN QVA PRÆTER FLORES, VARIA ETIAM COMPRÆHENDVNTVR ARBORVM FRVCTIFERARVM, FRVCTICVM, PLANTARRVM [*sic*] QVOQVE ET HERBARVM MEDICINALIVM GENERA. Per CRISP. PASSÆVM in lucem, edita. obl.4° 5 pt.: pl.41; 19; 25 [+2]; d12; [61]

453.a.10.

Tp.1 is engraved. pt.1-4 have a frontispiece showing a formal garden; pt.4 has an additional frontispiece, by Simon van de Passe, showing Flora and an epigram signed AB, i.e. Arnoldus Buchelius? pt.5 has a frontispiece signed: C. de Passe and J. Waldnelius, inscribed 'Cognoscite lilia'. pt.1 has one leaf bearing the preface and one leaf bearing laudatory poems on the recto and the index on the verso, plates, except pl.2, 6, 14, not showing insects, some not showing the earth; the plates are numbered in arabic numerals, the text leaves in roman numerals. In pt.2 the titlepage verso bears the index, cropped, and poems; plates and text are numbered in arabic; some of the plates do not show earth. pt.3 has a leaf bearing a preface printed in italics and a leaf with poems on the recto and the index on the verso; some of the plates show insects. pt.4 has the index on the titlepage verso. pt.5 has no text. The majority of the plates are said to be by Crispin van de Passe the Younger, with some contributions by the Elder, Simon and Willem van de Passe, some plates showing their signatures. A manuscript note on the titlepages reads: Octauius Pisani recensuit. From the library of Sir Joseph Banks.

P55 PASSE, Crispin van de; the Younger

HORTVS FLORIDVS . . . 1614. Extant Arnhemij. Apud Ioannem Ianssonium [etc.] obl.4° 5 pt.: pl.41; 18; 25 [+2]; d12; [61]

453.b.9.

Another edition of the preceding, with the following differences: pt.1: plates 12, 16-19, 21-28, 30, 33-41 are in a later state, with the addition of insects, bulbs, earth, landscape, or any combination of these features. All the plates showing plants lengthwise have had the text on the verso printed in such a way that they now face the other way, with the bottom of the plate towards the edge and no longer towards the gutter. pt.2: The text for pl.1 has been re-set and shows an ordinary initial instead of a decorated woodcut. pl.5 is in a later state; pl.18 is the last, without text on the verso, i.e. pl.19 has been intentionally omitted. pt.3: the dedication of pt.1 has been bound with it. pt.4: pl.1-10 are bound in back to front, probably in error. Imperfect; wanting the frontispiece to pt.1; pt.2 pl.3; the last plate of pt.4 and the 'Flora' frontispiece.

P56 PASSE, Crispin van de; the Younger

(tp.1) HORTVS FLORIDVS In quo rariorum . . . florum Icones . . . delineatæ . . . exhibentur . . . labore ac diligentia Crisp: Passæi junioris . . . A°. 1614. Extant Arnhemij. Apud Ioannem Ianssonium [etc.]
(tp.2) ÆSTAS HORTI FLORIDI IN QVA PRAECIPVI AESTATIS FLORES EXCELLENTI, CR. PASSÆI STYLO advivum admodum ingenios exprimuntur. ARNHEMI, Ex Officina Ioannis Ianszonij . . . 1617.
(tp.3) AVTVMNVS. HORTI FLORIDI RARIORES AVTVMNI FLORES SVMMA INDVSTRIA ET LABORE. CRISP. PASSÆI FILII. In ære effictos, & in lucem recens datos continens. ARNHEMII. Ex Officina, IOANNIS IANSONII. 1616.
(tp.4) [HORTVS FLORIDVS HYEMALIS CR. PASSÆI FIL. LABORE ET INDVSTRIA NVNC PRIMVM IN LVCEM EDITVS ANNO M.DC.XIIII. VLTRAIECTI. Ex Officina Calcographicâ CR. PASSÆI.]
(tp.5) ALTERA PARS HORTI FLORIDI IN-QVA PRÆTER FLORES, VARIA ETIAM REPERIVNTVR ARBORVM FRVCTIFERARVM, FRVCTICVM, PLANTARRVM [*sic*] QVOQVE ET HERBARVM MEDICINALIVM GENERA. Per CRISP. PASSÆVM in lucem, edita. obl.4° 5 pt.: pl.1-52; 20; 25 [+2]; d12; [61]
445.b.29.

Tp.1 is engraved. The text has been re-set throughout. pt.1 is without letterpress preliminaries. From pl.33-52 the accompanying texts have been printed in the wrong order, except for pl.42 which has the correct text facing it. The plates are in the later states. The last plate, numbered 52, has text numbered LIII on its verso, but lacks a plate corresponding to it. pt.3 has the 'Flora' frontispiece. pt.4 has no text printed on the titlepage, but bears a preface on the verso of this blank page and has the correct text for all the plates except for illustrations 54, 55 which have no text.

P57 PASSE, Crispin van de; the Younger

[Hortus floridus.] [Altera pars Horti floridi . . . Per Crisp: Passæum in lucem edita. (Arnhemii 1614 vel 1616.)] obl.4° pl.[61]
443.a.9.

Another copy(?) of pt.5 of the preceding, with coloured plates. Imperfect; wanting the titlepage which has been partly supplied in manuscript. Ownership inscription: Bibliothecæ Sloanianæ.

P58 PASSE, Crispin van de; the Younger

[Hortus floridus.] obl.4° pl.[25+2; 11,] d12
462.b.18(2).

A copy without titlepages, containing plates, in the early state, of pt.3, 4, with the first frontispiece, showing the garden, twice, and the 'Flora' frontispiece once, without any text. The plates are unnumbered except for pl.d12. Prepared for publication in 1614?

P59 PASSE, Crispin van de; the Younger

[Hortus floridus.] (tp.1) A GARDEN OF FLOVVERS, WHEREIN VERY LIVELY IS CONTAINED A TRVE AND PERFECT DISCRIPTION OF AL THE FLOVVERS CONTAINED IN THESE FOVRE FOLLOWINGE BOOKES. AS ALSO THE PERFECT TRVE MANNER OF COLOVRINGE THE SAME

VVITH THEIRE NATVRALL COLOVRES . . . ALL VVHICH TO THE GREAT CHARGES, and almost incredible laboure and paine, the diligent Authore . . . hath Laboriously compiled, and most excellently performed, both in theire perfect Lineaments in representing them in theire coper plates: as also after a most exquisite manner and methode in teachinge the practisioner te [*sic*] painte them even to the liffe. FAITHFVLLY AND TRVELY TRANSLATED OVT OF THE NETHERLANDish originall into English for the comon benifite of those that vnderstand no other languages, and also for the benifite of others nevvly printed both in the Latine and French tongues all at the Charges of the Author. Printed at Vtrecht, By Salomon de Roy, for Chrispian de Passe. 1615.
(tp. 2) ALTERA PARS HORTI FLORIDI . . . Per CRISP. PASSÆVM in lucem, edita. obl. 4° 2 pt.: sig. A-G^2: pl. 54, 20, 25, d12; [61]
C.66.e.1.
With the additional engraved Latin titlepage of 1614. The English text describing pl. 1-41 only precedes the plates which bear no text on their versos and which are divided into the seasons, but without separate titlepages. The 'Altera pars' has no text. An English acrostich added to the English titlepage, spelling out the name 'Crispian van de Passe iunior', is signed: Thomas Wood, another poem on sig. G2r is signed: T. W. On sig. G1v 'The translator to the readers, or practisioners' is signed: E. W. pt. 2 is preceded by the frontispiece of the garden in the state showing an architectural gate at the far end, bearing a sundial and the arms of Utrecht, and with the figures of a man and a woman. The two additional plates with the winter part are absent, as are the 'Flora' and 'Cognoscite lilia' plates. pl. 54 in the spring part is the true plate belonging to the text on pl. 53 verso, not a repeat of pl. 53, but pl. 42 is wanting. All the plates and the pages bearing the longer poems are coloured. A watercolour entitled 'Binguicula Gesnery. Butter wort' has been added at the end of pt. 2. Ownership inscriptions: E. Alexander; B.G.; Jos. Banks.

PATER Arents lof. 1615. *See* PASQUIL

P60 PATERSON, William; Conventual of Antwerp
THE PROTESTANTS THEOLOGIE, CONTAINING, The true solutions, and groundes of Religion, this day mainteyned, and intreated, betwixt the PROTESTANTS, AND CATHOLICKS. WRITEN, By . . . VVilliame Patersoune . . . THE I. PART . . . IMPRINTED . . . M.DC.XX. 4° pp. 309
3936.bb.13.
No more published. Without imprint; printed by Hendrik Jaey at Mechelen. Ownership inscription: William Talbot.

PATRIOT. Bedencken op de Aggreatie. 1608. *See* BEDENCKEN

P61 PATRIOTA, I.; pseudonym of François van Aerssen?
Advertissement Aen alle Goede In-woonderen en Liefhebbers van dese Nederlanden. Omme van een yeder gelesen . . . te worden. Ghedruckt uyt cracht der waerheyt-Beminners . . . 1618. 4° sig. A^4
T.2422(11).
Signed: I. Patriota.

PAWIUS, Petrus. *See* PAAUW, Petrus

P62 PECKIUS, Petrus; the Younger
PROPOSITIE Ghedaen vanden Ambassadeur PECKIVS, Inde Vergaderinghe vande . . . Staten Generael/Met het ANTVVOORDT Der Hooch-ghemelte Heeren/ opten vijf-en-twintichsten Meert/1621. IN S'GRAVEN-HAGHE. By Aert Meuris . . . 1621. 4° sig. A^4
1193.f.36.
With a manuscript addition taken from the original manuscript or from another edition.

P63 PECKIUS, Petrus; the Younger

PROPOSITIE VAN d'Heer Cancelier Peckius, AENDE . . . Staten Generael den XXIII. Martij XVI^C. ende XXI. in den Haghe ghedaen. Mitsgaders: De Antwoorde van de . . . Staten Generael den Heere Cancelier Peckio ghegheven. TOT MIDDELBVRGH, Gedruckt by Hans vander Hellen, voor Ian Pieterssen vande Venne . . . 1621. 4° 4 unsigned leaves

106.d.57.

P64 PEETERS, Bartholomaeus

APOSTOLICÆ SEDIS DEFINITIONES VETERES, DE GRATIA DEI. DVACI, Typis Viduę LAVRENTII KELLAMI . . . M.DC.XVI. 8° pp.64

4257.f.2.

The editor named in the approbation as Bartholomaeus Petrus Lintrensis.

P65 PEREIRA, Francisco; Bishop

[Relatione autentica.] RELATION AVTHENTIQVE, ENVOYEE PAR Les Prelats, Viceroys, grands Chanceliers & Secretaires de l'Estats des Indes. A LA MAIESTE CATHOLIQVE. De ce qui s'est passé auec les Mahometains Orientaux, qui . . . ont esté receus au S. Sacrement de Baptesme, l'an mil six cens & deux. Iuxte la copie imprimee à Rome par GVILLAVME FACCIOT, l'an 1606. EN ANVERS, Chez HIEROSME VERDVSSEN . . . 1607. [etc.] 4° sig.AB^4

4765.a.52.

The editor's dedication signed: F. François Pereyra. Printed in italics.

PEREYRA, François. *See* PEREIRA, Francisco

P66 PEREZ, Andres

LIBRO DE ENTRETENIMIENTO, DE LA PICARA IVSTINA, EN EL QVAL DEBAXO DE GRACIOSOS discursos, se encierran prouechosos auisos . . . Es juntamente ARTE POETICA que contiene cincuenta diferencias de versos . . . COMPVESTO POR . . . Francisco de Vbeda . . . EN BRVCELLAS, En casa de Oliuero Brunello . . . M.D.C.VIII. 8° pp.449: plate

1074.d.17.

Pseudonymous. The emblematic engraved frontispiece signed: Maximiliaen Derrere fe., and dated: 1608.

P67 PERKINS, William; Fellow of Christ's College, Cambridge

[De praedestinationis modo et origine.] Een Tractaet, Christelijck ende duydelijck verhandelende de Maniere ende het Vervolgh der PREDESTINATIE GODS, ende de Onbegrijpelijcke groote der Godtlijcker Ghenaden. Door M^r. Wilhelmus Perkinsus, ende Ghetrouwelijck uyt het Latijn in Neder-duyts over-gheset door Philippum Ruylium . . . Tot Amsterdam, By Jan Evertsz Cloppenburch . . . 1609. 8° pp.162

1568/6926(2).

P68 PERKINS, William; Fellow of Christ's College, Cambridge

[The foundation of Christian religion.] DE Catechismus ofte Somma van de gheheele Christelijcke Religie . . . t'samen ghestelt door D. Wilhelmum Perkinsum. Ende is uyt de Latijnsche in de Neder-duytsche tale overgheset. Item een Cort Begrijp van de Catechismus der Ghereformeerde Kercken Christi in Nederlant door F.D.V. t'Amsterdam/by Jan Evertsz. Cloppenburg . . . 1609. 8° pp.77

1568/6926(1).

Translated from the Latin edition entitled 'Catechesis', published at Hanau in 1608. The author of the second treatise and the translator and editor of the first is Frederik de Vry.

PERON, Cardinal of. *See* DAVY DU PERRON, Jacques

P69 PERPINIANUS, Petrus Joannes

PETRI IOANNIS PERPINIANI . . . ORATIONES duodeuiginti. EDITIO NOVA . . . DVACI, Apud Ioannem Bogardum. M DC VIII. 12° pp.552

12354.a.3.

The editor's dedication signed: Franciscus Bencius. Printed in italics.

P70 PERRET, Steven

XXV. FABLES DES ANIMAVX. VRAY MIROIR EXEMPLAIRE, PAR LEQVEL TOVTE PERSONNE RAISONnable pourra voir & comprendre . . . la conformite & similitude de la personne ignorante . . . aux animaux & bestes brutes: COMPOSE' ET MIS EN LVMIERE PAR ESTIENNE PERRET . . . Imprime à DELF, chez ADRIEN GERARDS . . . 1621. fol. pl.I-XXIIII; illus.

635.m.19.

The engravings after Marcus Gheeraerts, some as in the 1578 Plantin edition, some reversed. With a new frontispiece preceding pl.I, showing a different version of man as king of the animals.

P71 PERS, Dirck Pietersz

BELLEROPHON, OF LVST TOT VVYSHEYD. Begrijpende veel zeedighe, stichtelijcke en leerlijcke Sinne-beelden met haere verklaringhen. T'AMSTELREDAM. By Dirck Pietersz. . . . 1614. 4° sig.A-I^4; illus.

11556.cc.64(1).

The author's prefatory poem signed: Dorotheos a Bembda, pseudonym of Dirck Pietersz Pers. The first and last of the engraved emblems signed: Joos de Bosscher. With: Register der sinne-beelden H. Dammani; i.e. of the original author of the Latin mottoes inscribed on the emblems?

P72 PERSANT, Leonhartus

DISPVTATIO INAVGVRALIS DE COLICA PASSIONE Quam . . . PRO GRADV DOCTORATVS In MEDICINA Consequendo Publicè tuebitur LEONHARTVS PERSANT . . . LVGDVNI BATAVORVM, Ex Officina Thomæ Basson, 1608. 4° sig.A^4

1185.g.1(33).

P73 PERSONS, Robert

AN ANSVVERE TO THE FIFTH PART OF REPORTES Lately set forth BY Sir EDVVARD COOKE . . . CONCERNING The ancient & moderne Municipall lawes of England vvhich do apperteyne to Spirituall Power & Iurisdiction. By occasion vvherof . . . there is laid forth an euident . . . demonstration of the continuance of Catholicke Religion in England . . . By a Catholicke Deuyne . . . 1606. 4° pp.386

883.i.1.

Anonymous and without imprint; published by François Bellet at St. Omer. The titlepage in the first setting with line 7 ending with 'Kinges', mounted. Ownership inscriptions: Hameles (?); Francis Hargrave; Jacob Grenewood.

PERSONS, Robert. Apologia pro hierarchia ecclesiastica. 1601. *See* below: A briefe apologie.

P74 PERSONS, Robert

[An appendix to the Apologie . . . for defence of the hierarchie.] APPENDIX AD APOLOGIAM PRO HIERARCHIA ECCLESIASTICA A S.^{mo} D.N. CLEMENTE PAPA VIII. Apud Anglos instituta. Qua Latinus eiusdem Apologiæ interpres R.G. iudicium suum censuramq; fert de octo libellis famosis sub inquietorum presbyterorum nomine recens . . . editis . . . M.DCII. 8° pp.195

847.c.19; 4103.aa.49.

Anonymous and without imprint; published by Arnout Coninx at Antwerp. Translated by Richard Walpole. The copy at 4103.aa.49 with the bookplate of Henry Francis Lyte.

PERSONS, Robert. A brief, and cleere confutation. 1603. [Sometimes wrongly attributed to Robert Persons.] *See* WALPOLE, Richard

P75 PERSONS, Robert

[A brief discours contayning certayne reasons.] A BRIEFE DISCOVRSE containing certaine reasons, Why Catholikes refuse to goe to Church. Written by a learned . . . man . . . And dedicated by I.H. to the Queenes . . . Maiestie. Printed at Doway. 1601. 12° sig.A-G[12]; illus.

3932.a.7.

The dedication signed: IHON HOVVLET, pseudonym of Robert Persons. The imprint is false; printed secretly in England.

P76 PERSONS, Robert

[A brief discours contayning certayne reasons.] QVÆSTIONES DVÆ De Sacris alienis non adeundis, Ad vsum praximq; ANGLIÆ breuiter explicatæ: QVARVM PRIMA EST, An liceat Catholicis Anglicanis . . . Protestantium Ecclesias, vel preces adire. SECVNDA, Vtrum, si non precibus, at concionibus saltem haereticis . . . licitè possint interesse, eas͗que audire. In vtraque Quæstione pars negatiua . . . asseritur: Et in Secunda, scripto . . . cuidam Anonymo in contrarium edito respondetur . . . 1607. 12° pp.144

697.a.43(3).

Anonymous and without imprint; printed by François Bellet at St. Omer? The anonymous work is referred to as 'De audiendis concionibus'.

P77 PERSONS, Robert

[A briefe apologie.] APOLOGIA PRO HIERARCHIA ECCLESIASTICA A . . . Clemente PP.VIII. his annis apud Anglos instituta. Qua sacerdotum quorundam, eandem libellis . . . contentiosis impugnantium, temeritas coargitur, & legitimi Superioris Authoritas defenditur [etc.] 8° ff.157

G.11704.

Anonymous. Translated by Thomas Stevenson. An answer to 'Declaratio motuum' by John Mush and 'The copies of certaine discourses'. Without imprint; published by Arnout Coninx at Antwerp in 1601, who also published the original English edition.

P78 PERSONS, Robert

THE CHRISTIAN DIRECTORY Guiding men to eternall saluation, Deuided into three Bookes . . . In this volume is only contayned the first Booke . . . 1607. 12° pp.684

C.111.f.6.

Anonymous. Including 'The preface . . . conteyning certaine notes vpon a false edition of the same booke by M. Edmund Buny'. Without imprint; published by François Bellet at St. Omer. Ownership inscriptions: Robert Blackwall; Sara Blackwall; Candy.

P79 PERSONS, Robert

A DISCVSSION OF THE ANSVVERE OF M. VVILLIAM BARLOVV . . . to the Booke intituled: The iudgment of a Catholike Englishman . . . CONCERNING The Apology of the new Oath of Allegiance. VVRITTEN By . . . Robert Persons . . . M.DC.XII. 4° pp.543

860.i.8.

Edited by Edward Coffin. Without imprint; published by the English College press at St. Omer. From the library of John Morris.

P80 PERSONS, Robert

THE IVDGMENT OF A CATHOLICKE ENGLISH-MAN, LIVING IN BANISHMENT FOR HIS RELIGION: VVritten to his priuate friend in England. Concerning A late BOOKE set

forth, and entituled: Triplici nodo, triplex cuneus, Or, An Apologie for the Oath of Allegiance . . . 1608. 4° pp.128
C.45.d.23(2).
Anonymous and without imprint; published by the English College press at St. Omer. Bound after a copy of 'Triplici nodo' of 1607 with James I's manuscript corrections.

P81 PERSONS, Robert
A MANIFESTATION OF THE GREAT FOLLY AND BAD SPIRIT OF certayne in England calling themselues secular priestes. VVho set forth dayly most infamous . . . libels against worthy men of their owne religion . . . of which libels sundry are heer examined and refuted. By priestes lyuing in obedience . . . 1602. 4° ff.114
3935.cc.18.
Anonymous and without imprint; published by Arnout Coninx at Antwerp.

PERSONS, Robert. Quaestiones duae de sacris alienis non adeundis. 1607. *See* above: A brief discours.

P82 PERSONS, Robert
A QVIET AND SOBER RECKONING VVITH M. THOMAS MORTON somewhat set in choler by his adversary P.R. . . . There is also adioyned a piece of Reckoning with Sir Edward Cooke . . . M.DC.IX. 4° pp.688
860.e.24.
Anonymous and without imprint; published by the English College press at St. Omer.

PERSONS, Robert. A relation of the triall made before the King of France. 1603. 1604. *See* below: A treatise of three conversions

PERSONS, Robert. A review of ten publike disputations. 1604. *See* below: A treatise of three conversions

P83 PERSONS, Robert
(tp.1) A TREA[TIS]E OF THREE CONVERSIONS OF ENGLAND from Paganisme to Christian Religion . . . DIVIDED Into three partes . . . The former two whereof are handled in this booke . . . By N.D. author of the VVard-vvord . . . Imprinted with licence . . . 1603.
(tp.2) [THE T]HIRD PART OF A TREATISE, Intituled: of three Conuersions of England: conteyninge. An examen of the Calendar or Catalogue of Protestant Saints, Martyrs and Confessors, diuised by Iohn Fox . . . VVith a Pararell [*sic*] or Comparison therof to the Catholike Roman Calendar . . . THE FIRST SIX MONETHS. Whereunto . . . is annexed a defence of a certaine Triall, made before the King of France . . . betweene Monsieur Peron Bishop of Eureux, and Monsieur Plessis Mornay . . . about sundry points of Religion. By N.D. . . . Imprinted vvith licence . . . 1604.
(tp.3) A RELATION OF THE TRIALL Made before the King of France . . . betvvene the Bishop of Eureux, and the L. Plessis Mornay . . . By N.D. . . . M.DC.III.
(tp.4) THE THIRD PART OF A TREATISE Intituled OF THREE CONVERSIONS OF ENGLAND . . . THE LAST SIX MONETHES. VVhervnto is annexed . . . another seuerall Treatise, called: A re-view of ten publike Disputations, or Conferences, held in England about matters of Religion . . . vnder King Edward and Queene Mary. By N.D. . . . Imprinted with licence . . . 1604.
(tp.5) A REVIEVV OF TEN PVBLIKE DISPVTATIONS . . . By N.D. . . . M.DC.IIII. 8° 3 tom.: pp.658; 530,237; 465,370
296.h.31+296.h.31,31*+296.h.32.
Anonymous and without imprint; printed by François Bellet at St. Omer. The titlepages of tom.1 and tom.2. pt.1 are mutilated. Separate issues of tom.2. pt.2 and tom.3 pt.2 are entered below.

P84 PERSONS, Robert

[A treatise of three conversions.] A RELATION OF THE TRIALL Made before the King of France, vpon the yeare 1600. betvvene the Bishop of Eureux, and the L. Plessis Mornay. About certayne pointes of corrupting . . . authors, wherof the said Plessis was openly conuicted. Newly reuewed . . . with a defence therof, against the impugnations both of the L. Plessis . . . & of O.E. in England. By N.D. . . . Imprinted with licence . . . M.DC.IIII. 8° pp.237

853.e.2(2).

Anonymous. A separate issue of tom.2. pt.2 of 'A treatise of three conversions'. The initials O.E. stand for Matthew Sutcliffe. Without imprint; printed by François Bellet at St. Omer.

P85 PERSONS, Robert

[A treatise of three conversions.] A REVIEVV OF TEN PVBLIKE DISPVTATIONS Or Conferences held vvithin the compasse of foure yeares, vnder K. Edward & Qu. Mary, concerning some principall points in Religion, especially of the Sacrament & sacrifice of the Altar . . . By N.D. . . . Imprinted vvith licence . . . M.DC.IIII. 8° pp.370

853.e.2(1).

Anonymous. A separate issue of tom.3. pt.2 of 'A treatise of three conversions'. Without imprint; printed by François Bellet at St. Omer.

P86 PERSONS, Robert

A TREATISE TENDING TO MITIGATION tovvardes Catholicke-Subiectes in England . . . AGAINST the seditious wrytings of THOMAS MORTON . . . Dedicated to the learned Schoole-Deuines . . . of the tvvo Vniuersities of England. By P.R. . . . 1607. 8° pp.556

698.c.23; 1019.i.19.

Anonymous and without imprint; printed by François Bellet at St. Omer.

P87 PERSONS, Robert

THE WARN-WORD TO SIR FRANCIS HASTINGES WAST-WORD: Conteyning the issue of three former Treateses, the Watch-word, the Ward-word and the Wast-word . . . togeather with certaine admonitions & warnings . . . Wherunto is adioyned a breif reiection of an insolent . . . minister masked with the letters O. E. . . . By N.D. author of the Ward-word . . . 1602. 8° 2 pt.: ff.131[133],138

698.b.13.

Anonymous and without imprint; published by Arnout Coninx at Antwerp. The initials O.E. stand for Matthew Sutcliffe.

PERTH Assembly. 1619. *See* CALDERWOOD, David

P88 PETER Canisius; Saint

Daghelicxe Meditatien/ende Oeffeninghen/naer den eysch van elcke daghen binnen der weke/seer schoon ende profijtelijck om eenen mensch tot der kennisse ende liefde Godts te verweckene. Eerst ghemaect by Petrum Canisium . . . Ende ouerghesedt in Duytsche, by H. Peeter Calentijn. TOT LOVEN, By Jan Maes . . . 1602. 8° sig.AB^8; illus.

4407.bb.11(3).

The titlepage woodcut shows the crucifixion, that on the titlepage verso shows the celebration of Mass under the title 'Fulget Crucis Mysterium'.

P89 [*PETER Canisius; Saint

Daghelijcxe Meditatien/ende Oeffeninghen . . . om eenen mensch tot der kennisse ende liefde Godts te verwecken. Eerst ghemaect by Petrum Canisium . . . Ende ouerghesedt in Duytsche, By H. Peeter Calentijn. TOT LOVEN, By Jan Maes . . . 1606. 8° sig.A-C^8; illus.

3395.d.8(3).]

*Destroyed. Described from the General Catalogue and the copy in the library of the Institutum Berchmanianum, Nijmegen, at 465 CAN. The illustrations are as in the preceding.

P90 PETER Canisius; Saint

SVMMA DOCTRINÆ CHRISTIANÆ, EX POSTREMA RECOGNITIONE . . . PETRI CANISII . . . ANTVERPIÆ, EX OFFICINA PLANTINIANA, Apud Ioannem Moretum. M.D.CI. (col.) ANTVERPIÆ, EX OFFICINA PLANTINIANA, Apud Ioannem Moretum. M.D.CI. 16° pp.367

3505.a.25.

P91 PETITION

A PETITION APOLOGETICALL, PRESENTED TO THE KINGES MOST EXCELLENT MAIESTY, BY THE LAY CATHOLIKES OF ENGLAND, in Iuly last . . . Printed at Doway by IOHN MOGAR . . . 1604. 4° pp.40

3935.b.14; C.26.l.7.

The editor's dedication signed: Io. Lecey. The imprint is false; printed secretly in England.

P92 PETITION

[A petition apologeticall.] Der Catholijcken SVPPLICATIE aen de Coninckliјcke Majesteyt, tot Toelatinghe vande Catholijcke Religie in ENGLAND. Met weynighe ende corte aenwysinghen op de canten ghestelt. Waer by noch ghevoecht is . . . Een Supplicerende Teghen-ghewichte, ghedaen by de Protestanten aende selve Conincklicke MAIESTEYT. Tsamen met de redenen van beyde zijden . . . Wt den Enghelschen overgheset door Richard Schilders. MIDDELBVRCH, Ghedruct by Richard Schilders . . . 1602. 4° pp.39[40]

T.2417(13).

The editor's preface signed: Gabriel Powel.

P93 PETITION

[A petition apologeticall.] Requeste, Ghepresenteert by die vande Catholijcke Religie in Enghelant aen den . . . Coninck IACOB den eersten. Ghedruckt . . . 1603. 8° sig.A^4

8050.aa.15(10).

Signed: De Catholijcken van Enghelant.

P94 PETITION

[A petition apologeticall.] VERTOOCH ende Versoek der genaemder Catholiken aende Coninclicke Majesteyt/om te hebben toelatinghe van haerlieden Religie in Enghelandt. Met korte aenmerckinghen op den kant. Midtsgaders een Teghen-ghewicht der Protestanten/by forme van Vertooch ghestelt teghen t'Vertooch der Catholiken/mede aende selve Conincklicke Majesteyt. Tsamen met de redenen van beyden zijden . . . Wt het Engelsch origineel . . . overgheset. IN S'GRAVEN-HAGHE, By Hillebrandt Jacobsz. . . . 1603. 4° pp.38

573.f.40.

The editor's preface signed: Gabriel Powel.

P95 PETRARCA, Francesco

[Canzoniere. French] LE PETRARQVE EN RIME FRANCOISE AVECQ SES COMMENTAIRES, TRADVICT PAR PHILIPPE DE MALDEGHEM . . . A DOVAY, Chez FRANÇOIS FABRY . . . M.DC.VI. [etc.] 8° pp.547; illus., ports.

11431.de.21.

A reissue of the edition printed by Rutger Velpius at Brussels in 1600, with a new titlepage bearing the engraved portrait of Petrarch. On sig.†4v a woodcut double portrait of Petrarch and Laura.

PETREIUS, Nicolaus. Disputatio medica de arthritide. 1614. *See* PAAUW, Petrus

PETRI, Johannes; of Ansbach. Disputatio theologica de coena Domini. 1604. *See* LINDEN, Henricus Antonides van der

P96 PETRI, Nicolaus

(tp.1) PRACTICQVE, Om te leeren Rekenen, Cypheren ende Boeckhouden: met de Reghel Coss ende Geometrie . . . Van nieus gecorrigeert ende vermeerdert/door Nicolaum Petri . . . A°1603. t'Amsterdam/by Cornelis Claesz. . . . 1605.
(tp.2=f.129) Hier Volghet eene corte ende claere Instructie/van de alder cunstrijcksten Regulen d'Algebre ofte Coss. Het tweede deel. ANNO. M.D.XCVI.
(tp.3=f.194) Hier volghet d'Instructie vande Geometrye, verciert met vele Lustighe Vraeghen/ende Mathematischen Exempelen. Het derde deel. ANNO M.VJC. ende V.
(tp.4=f.287) Het vierde deel deses Boecx/leerende t'Boeckhouwen met twee Boecken/van nieuws gecomponeert op de maniere Italiane. Anno 1606.
(tp.5=Pp1r) 1591. Iournael Boeck ghetekent met die Letter A Anno. M.DC.VI.
(tp.6=Qq4r) 1591. Schult-boeck gheteeckent met die Letter A ANNO M.VIC.VI.
(tp.7=Ss2v) 1591. Oncost-Boec voor den handel t'vvelcke van sommighe gheheetem [*sic*] vvort Cassa Boeck. A ANNO M.VIC.VI.
(tp.8=Ss6r) 1592. Schult-boeck gheteeckent met die Letter B ANNO M.VIC.VI.
8° ff.289, sig.Pp-Tt[8]: plates; illus.; port.
C.133.b.1.

Sig.Pp-Tt are irregularly paginated. The engraved portrait on the titlepage is by Hendrik Goltzius and is dated 1603.

P97 PETRI, Suffridus

APOLOGIA SVFFRIDI PETRI . . . PRO Antiquitate & Origine FRISIORVM, CUM BERNARDI GERBRANDI FVRMERII . . . PERORATIONE CONTRA VBBONEM EMMIVM . . . FRANEKERAE TYPIS AEGIDII RADAEI . . . 1603. 4° pp.158: plate
154.m.12; 590.c.23(2); C.61.b.9.

Edited by Bernardus Furmerius. All three copies are imperfect: that at 154.m.12 wants the illustration of an inscription intended for p.143; that at 590.c.23(2) wants pp.137-144 and the plate; that at C.61.b.9 lacks the plate and has p.143 also blank. The copy at C.61.b.9 with manuscript notes by Ubbo Emmius.

P98 PETRONIUS ARBITER, Titus

PETRONII ARBITRI Satyricon: Cum vberioribus, COMMENTARII instar, Notis; concinniùs . . . & commodiùs quàm antè dispositis. EX OFFICINA PLANTINIANA Raphelengii. M.D.C.IIII. 16° pp.384
1067.a.14.

The editor's dedication signed: Ioan. a Wouweren. With an additional preface to the reader, preceding the notes, by the printer. Published at Leiden.

P99 PETRONIUS ARBITER, Titus

PETRONII ARBITRI Satyricon. EX OFFICINA PLANTINIANA RAPHELENGII, M.D.CXIV. 32° pp.135
C.20.f.35.

With the 'Fragmenta ex editione Ioannis à Wouweren'. Published at Leiden. From the travelling library of Sir Julius Caesar.

PETRUS, Bartholomaeus. *See* PEETERS, Bartholomaeus

P100 PEVERNAGE, Andreas

(tp.1) CHANSONS D'ANDRE PEVERNAGE A SIX, SEPT, ET HVICT PARTIES. SVPERIVS. EN ANVERS De l'Imprimerie de Pierre Phalese 1607.
(tp.2) CHANSONS D'ANDRE PEVERNAGE . . . TENOR. EN ANVERS De l'Imprimerie de Pierre Phalese 1607.
(tp.3) CHANSONS D'ANDRE PEVERNAGE . . . CONTRATENOR. EN ANVERS De l'Imprimerie de Pierre Phalese 1607.

PRACTICQVE,

Om te Leeren Rekenen/Cypheren ende Boeckhouden:

met de Reghel Coſs ende Geometrie/ ſeer profitelijcken voor alle Coopluyden. Van nieus gecorrigeert ende vermeerdert/ door

Nicolaum Petri Daventrienſem.

t'Amſterdam/ by Cornelis Claesz. opt Water int Schrijf-boeck. Anno 1605.

P96

(tp.4) CHANSONS D'ANDRE PEVERNAGE . . . BASSVS. EN ANVERS De l'Imprimerie de Pierre Phalese 1607.
(tp.5) CHANSONS D'ANDRE PEVERNAGE . . . QVINTA PARS. EN ANVERS De l'Imprimerie de Pierre Phalese 1607. obl.4° 5 pt.: pp.28; 28; 29; 28 [29]; 29 [32]
Music A.259.b.
The pagination of pt.4, 5 is irregular. The signatures are continuous.

P101 PEVERNAGE, Andreas
(tp.1) HARMONIA CELESTE DE DIVERSI ECCELLENTISSIMI MVSICI A IV. V. VI. ET VIII. VOCI RACCOLTA PER ANDREA PEVERNAGE . . . NOVAMENTE RISTAMPATA. CANTO. IN ANVERSA Appresso Pietro Phalesio. M.DCV.
(tp.2) HARMONIA CELESTE . . . RACCOLTA PER ANDREA PEVERNAGE . . . ALTO. IN ANVERSA Appresso Pietro Phalesio. M.DCV.
(tp.3) HARMONIA CELESTE . . . RACCOLTA PER ANDREA PEVERNAGE . . . TENORE. IN ANVERSA Appresso Pietro Phalesio. M.DCV.
(tp.4) HARMONIA CELESTE . . . RACCOLTA PER ANDREA PEVERNAGE . . . BASSO. IN ANVERSA Appresso Pietro Phalesio. M.DCV. obl.4° 6 pt.: ff.35; 35; 35; 35; 10-36; 23-36
Music A.259.a.
Pt.5,6 containing the Quinto and Sesto parts begin with the songs in 5, respectively 6 parts and have no titlepages.

P102 PEVERNAGE, Andreas
(tp.1) MISSÆ V. VI. ET VII. VOCVM AVCTORE M. ANDREA PEVERNAGIO . . . TENOR. ANTVERPIÆ Apud Petrum Phalesium. M.DCII.
(tp.2) MISSÆ . . . AVCTORE M. ANDREA PEVERNAGIO . . . ALTVS. ANTVERPIÆ Apud Petrum Phalesium. M.DCII.
(tp.3) MISSÆ . . . AVCTORE M. ANDREA PEVERNAGIO . . . BASSVS. ANTVERPIÆ Apud Petrum Phalesium. M.DCII.
(tp.4) MISSÆ . . . AVCTORE M. ANDREA PEVERNAGIO . . . SEXTVS. ANTVERPIÆ Apud Petrum Phalesium. M.DCII. 4° 4 pt.: ff.24; 25; 21; 19
Music C.257
The signatures run G-M^4; N-S^{4}T^2; V-Z^4, Aa^{4}B^1; Ii-Nn^4.

P103 PHAEDRUS
[Latin] PHÆDRI . . . Fabularum Aesopiarum LIBRI V. IOANNES MEVRSIVS . . . denuo recensuit, & ANIMADVERSIONES addidit. EX OFFICINA PLANTINIANA RAPHELENGII, M.D.CX. 8° pp.213, 55
637.c.7; 1068.h.11; 244.h.32.
With 'Aenigmata Symposii . . . cum scholiis Josephi Castalionis', 'In Phædri fabulas Cunradi Rittershusii notæ', 'Gasperis Schoppii . . . Spicilegium in Phædri fabulas', 'Fabellæ & ænigmata veterum poetarum'. Published at Leiden. The copy at 244.h.32 has the added gathering signed EE bound in at the end instead of its usual place following sig.E. The copy at 1068.h.11 bears the manuscript dedication of Meursius to Grotius and has manuscript notes by Grotius. Ownership inscription of that copy: Ex libris Iohan ab Oldenbarnevelt . . . fuimus Troes [etc.]

P104 PHALÈSE, Pierre
[Chansons.] LIVRE SEPTIEME DES CHANSONS VVLGAIRES, DE DIVERSES AVTHEVRS A QVATRE PARTIES, CONVENABLES ET VTILES A LA IEVNESSE, TOVTES MISES EN ORDRE SELON LEVRS TONS. Auec vne brieue & facile Instruction pour bien apprendre la musique. SVPERIVS. EN ANVERS. Chez Pierre Phalese Libraire Iuré. M.D.CI. obl.4°
Music A 315.c(1).
The titlepage only, with the 'Brieve instruction' on the verso. The work was compiled by Pierre Phalèse.

P105 PHALESE, Pierre
[Chansons.] LIVR[E] SEPTIEM[E DES] CHANSONS VVL[GAIRES . . .] Auec vne Brieue & facil[e Instruction . . .] TEN[OR] EN ANVE[RS] Chez Pierre Phalese [. . .] M.DCV. obl.4° ff.[28]
Music A.315a.
Compiled by Pierre Phalèse. Texts in French, Latin, Italian or Spanish. Mutilated, with loss of pagination; the titlepage torn in half.

P106 PHALÈSE, Pierre
[Chansons.] (tp.1) LIVRE SEPTIEME DES CHANSONS VVLGAIRES. DE DIVERSES AVTHEVRS A QVATRE PARTIES, CONVENABLES ET VLTILES [*sic*] A LA IEVNESSE, TOVTES MISES EN ORDRE SELON LEVRS TONS. A la requeste d'aucuns amateurs avons adiousté certaines chansons, comme de Maistre Iean Pietersen Swellinck . . . Iacques Vredeman . . . Gerard Iansen Schagen . . . Auec vne . . . Instruction pour bien apprendre la Musique. TENOR. On les trouve chez Cornille Claessen, Imprimeur des livres á Amsterdam. M.DCVIII.
(tp.2) LIVRE SEPTIEME DES CHANSONS VVLGAIRES . . . A QVATRE PARTIES . . . BASSVS. On les trouve chez Cornille Claessen . . . á Amsterdam. M.DCVIII. obl.4° 2 pt.: ff.36; 29-35
Music A.315.b.
Compiled by Pierre Phalèse. The texts in French, Italian, Spanish, or Dutch. The Bassus part is imperfect; wanting all before p.29 and after p.35.

P107 PHALÈSE, Pierre
[Chansons.] (tp.1) LIVRE SEPTIEME DES CHANSONS VVLGAIRES . . . Auec vne Brieue & facile Instruction pour bien apprendre la Musicque. TENOR. EN ANVERS De l'Imprimerie de Pierre Phalese au Roy Dauid M.DCIX.
(tp.2) LIVRE SEPTIEME DES CHANSONS VVLGAIRES . . . BASSVS. EN ANVERS De l'Imprimerie de Pierre Phalese . . . M.DCIX.
(tp.3) LIVRE SEPTIEME DES CHANSONS VVLGAIRES . . . SVPERIVS. EN ANVERS De l'Imprimerie de Pierre Phalese . . . M.DCIX.
(tp.4) LIVRE SEPTIEME DES CHANSONS VVLGAIRES . . . CONTRATENOR. EN ANVERS De l'Imprimerie de Pierre Phalese . . M.DCIX. obl.4° 4 pt.: ff.28; 28; 28; 28
Music. K.7.b.1.
Compiled by Pierre Phalese. The texts in French, Latin, Italian or Spanish

P108 PHALESE, Pierre
[Chansons.] LIVRE SEPTIEME DES CHANSONS VVLGAIRES . . . Auec vne Brieue & facile Instruction pour bien apprendre la Musicque. TENOR. EN ANVERS De l'Imprimerie de Pierre Phalese au Roy Dauid M.DCXIII. obl.4° 4 pt.: ff.28; 28; 28; 28
Music. A.315.
Compiled by Pierre Phalese. Texts in French, Latin, Italian or Spanish. The parts containing the Bassus, Superior and Contratenor have no titlepages. The Tenor part has an index listing songs in Dutch, not present in the text.

P109 PHALÈSE, Pierre
(tp.1) FLORILEGIVM SACRARVM CANTIONVM QVINQVE VOCVM Pro diebus Dominicis & Festis totius Anni, E CELEBERRIMIS NOSTRI TEMPORIS MVSICIS . . . CANTVS. ANTVERPIÆ Ex Typographia Petri Phalesij ad insigne Dauidis Regis. M.DCIX. [etc.]
(tp.2) FLORILEGIVM SACRARVM CANTIONVM QVINQVE VOCVM . . . TENOR. ANTVERPIÆ Ex Typographia Petri Phalesij . . . M.DCIX. [etc.]
(tp.3) FLORILEGIVM SACRARVM CANTIONVM QVINQVE VOCVM . . . ALTVS. ANTVERPIÆ Ex Typographia Petri Phalesij . . . M.DCIX. [etc.]
(tp.4) FLORILEGIVM SACRARVM CANTIONVM QVINQVE VOCVM . . . BASSVS. ANTVERPIÆ Ex Typographia Petri Phalesij . . . M.DCIX. [etc.]
(tp.5) FLORILEGIVM SACRARVM CANTIONVM QVINQVE VOCVM . . . QVINTVS.

ANTVERPIÆ Ex Typographia Petri Phalesij . . . M.DCIX. [etc.] 4° 5 pt.: sig. A-K4L6; A-K4L8; A-K4L6; A-K4L8; A-K4L6
Music R.M.15.d.1(2); Music C.298
The compiler's dedication signed: Petrus Phalesius. Some of the leaves in those parts having eight leaves in sig. L are signed: A. These additional leaves are wanting in the copy at Music C.298 which consists of the Tenor, Altus and Bassus parts only. The approbation is printed at the end of the Bassus part only.

P110 PHALÈSE, Pierre
(tp.1) GHIRLANDA DI MADRIGALI A SEI VOCI, DI DIVERSI ECCELLENTISSIMI AVTORI DE NOSTRI TEMPI. Raccolta di Giardini di Fiori odoriferi Musicali. NVOVAMENTE POSTA IN LVCE. CANTO. IN ANVERSA. Appresso Pietro Phalesio. M.D.CI.
(tp.2) GHIRLANDA DI MADRIGALI A SEI VOCI . . . TENORE. IN ANVERSA. Appresso Pietro Phalesio. M.D.CI.
(tp.3) GHIRLANDA DI MADRIGALI A SEI VOCI . . . ALTO. IN ANVERSA. Appresso Pietro Phalesio. M.D.CI.
(tp.4) GHIRLANDA DI MADRIGALI A SEI VOCI . . . BASSO. IN ANVERSA. Appresso Pietro Phalesio. M.D.CI. 4° 4 pt.: pp.24; 24; 24; 24
Music A.232
The compiler's dedication signed: Pietro Phalesio.

P111 PHALÈSE, Pierre
MADRIGALI PASTORALI A SEI VOCI DESCRITTI DA DIVERSI Et posti in Musica da altri tanti Auttori DI NOVO STAMPATI. TENORE. IN ANVERSA Appresso Pietro Phalesio. M.DCIV. obl.4° pp.21
Music A.277.e.
Compiled by Pierre Phalèse. The signatures run G[D]–F.

P112 PHALÈSE, Pierre
[MVSICA DIVINA A III. V. VI. ET VII. VOCI DI XIX. AVTORI ILLVSTRI RACCOLTA DA PIETRO PHALESIO Nella quale si contegono [*sic*] i più eccellenti Madrigali che hoggidi si cantono [*sic*] NOVAMENTE RISTAMPATA. SESTO. IN ANVERSA. Appresso Pietro Phalesio . . . M.DCXIII.] obl.4° ff.23–36
Music A.324.a.
Wanting all before f.23. The title is in manuscript, evidently copied from a complete copy. The approbation at the end refers to: Quadrigæ hæc Musicales seu quatuor hi Libri Musici intitulati Musica Diuina, Harmonia Celeste, [etc.]

P113 PHALÈSE, Pierre
(tp.1) NOVI FRVTTI MVSICALI MADRIGALI A CINQVE VOCI DI DIVERSI ECCELLENTISSIMI MVSICI Nouamente augmentati & dati in luce. TENORE. IN ANVERSA Appresso Pietro Phalesio al Re Dauid M.DCX.
(tp.2) NOVI FRVTTI MVSICALI . . . BASSO. IN ANVERSA Appresso Pietro Phalesio . . . M.DCX. obl.4° 2 pt.: pp.37; 37
Music A.231.
The dedication, signed: Pietro Phalesio, describes the work as based on a Venetian collection, with additions. The book contains works by Sweelinck, Verdonck, Pruenen and others.

P114 PHALÈSE, Pierre
(tp.1) IL TRIONFO DI DORI, DESCRITTO DA DIVERSI, Et posti in Musica, da altretanti Autori. CANTO. IN ANVERSA Appresso Pietro Phalesio . . . M.DCXIII.
(tp.2) IL TRIONFO DI DORI . . . TENORE. IN ANVERSA Appresso Pietro Phalesio . . . M.DCXIII.
(tp.3) IL TRIONFO DI DORI . . . ALTO. IN ANVERSA Appresso Pietro Phalesio . . . M.DCXIII. obl.4° 3 pt.: pp.29; 29; 29
Music A.258.
Edited by Pierre Phalèse.

P115 PHALÈSE, Pierre

(tp.1) IL VAGO ALBORETO DE MADRIGALI ET CANZONI A QVATTRO VOCI DE DIVERSI ECCELLENTISSIMI AVTHORI, NOVAMENTE RISTAMPATO. CANTO. IN ANVERSA Appresso PETRO PHALESIO . . . M.D.C.XX.

(tp.2) IL VAGO ALBORETO DE MADRIGALI ET CANZONI . . . ALTO. IN ANVERSA Appresso PETRO PHALESIO . . . M.D.C.XX.

(tp.3) IL VAGO ALBORETO DE MADRIGALI ET CANZONI . . . TENORE. IN ANVERSA Appresso PETRO PHALESIO . . . M.D.C.XX.

(tp.4) IL VAGO ALBORETO DE MADRIGALI ET CANZONI . . . BASSO. [I]N ANVERSA [Appresso PETRO PHAL]ESIO . . . M.D.C.XX. obl.4° 4 pt.: ff.27; 27; 27; 27

Music A.230.

Compiled by Pierre Phalèse. The titlepage of the Basso part is slightly mutilated.

PHILALETHIUS, Ireneus; pseudonym of Ewout Teellinck. *See* TEELLINCK, Ewout

P116 PHILALETHUS, Desiderius

EEN Ootmoedige supplicatie Aen den Paus voor D. OLIVIER VAN HATTEM die om sijne onverdraechlijcke wijsheyt eñ hooghmoedighe kennisse sijn swerende hooft gheleyt heeft/in de schoot des Roomschen stoels/op hoope dat het selve soetelijck verbonden werde/met een gulden plaester . . . BESCHREVEN door DESIDERIVM PHILALETHVM. Ghedruckt . . . M.DJ^{C}.IX. 8° sig.⁂[8]

T.2420(25).

The pseudonym has remained unsolved.

P117 PHILALETIUS, Eusebius; pseudonym of Vincent van Drielenburch?

Antwoordt OP Seecker Laster-Schrift gheintituleert/Zeedich (in der daet onzedich) Onder-soeck van eenighe Handelinghen in Ghelder-Landt in de Maent Februarius, ter oorsaecke van seecker verschil tusschen de Predicanten voor-ghevallen . . . DOOR EVSEBIVM PHILALETIVM . . . GHEDRVCKT In de Mater Salem . . . 1617. 4° pp.83

T.2247(32).

With a refutation of the 'Tafereel' by Reinier Telle. 'In de Mater Salem' is an anagram of Amsterdam.

PHILALETIUS, Galenus; pseudonym of Mathias Damius. *See* DAMIUS, Mathias

PHILALETIUS, Ireneus; pseudonym of Ewout Teellinck. *See* TEELLINCK, Ewout

PHILIATROS, Philologus; pseudonym of Jacobus Viverius. *See* VIVERIUS, Jacobus

P118 PHILIPPUS de Liam; King of Sierra Leone

BRIEF, Van HEER PHILIPPVS Koningh van Sierra Leona, AEN DE Majesteyt van Spaengien. Vermeldende vande Goudt-ende-Zilverrijcke Koninghrijcken/ aldaer . . . ghelegen/met de overvloedighe bruchtbaerheyt [*sic*] van dien . . . In Spaensch beschreven by Bartholomeus Andriesz . . . Overghezet uyt de Spaensche in de Nederlandsche tale/Door Isaac Iansz Bijl . . . TOT ROTTERDAM, Ghedruct voor Jzaac Jansz Bijl . . . 1621. 4° sig.A[6]

1295.c.18.

The letter, which was translated from a captured manuscript, is dated 25 February 1606. The binding is stamped with a rams-head and the initials: H T.

P119 PHILIPS, Peter

(tp.1) CANTIONES SACRAE PRO PRÆCIPVIS FESTIS TOTIVS ANNI Et Communi Sanctorum QVINIS VOCIBVS, AVTORE R.D. PETRO PHILIPPI . . . CANTVS. ANTVERPIÆ Ex Typographia Petri Phalesij . . . M.D.CXII.

(tp.2) CANTIONES SACRAE . . . AVTORE R.D. PETRO PHILIPPI . . . TENOR. ANTVERPIÆ Ex Typographia Petri Phalesij . . . M.D.CXII.

(tp.3) CANTIONES SACRAE . . . AVTORE R.D. PETRO PHILIPPI . . . ALTVS. ANTVERPIÆ Ex Typographia Petri Phalesij . . . M.D.CXII.
(tp.4) CANTIONES SACRAE . . . AVTORE R.D. PETRO PHILIPPI . . . BASSVS. ANTVERPIÆ Ex Typographia Petri Phalesij . . . M.D.CXII.
(tp.5) CANTIONES SACRAE . . . AVTORE R.D. PETRO PHILIPPI . . . QVINTVS. ANTVERPIÆ Ex Typographia Petri Phalesij . . . M.D.CXII.
(tp.6) CANTIONES SACRAE . . . AVTORE R.D. PETRO PHILIPPI . . . BASSO CONTINVO. ANTVERPIÆ Ex Typographia Petri Phalesij . . . M.D.CXII. 4° 6 pt.: sig. A-K^4; A-I^4K^3; A-I^4K^3; A-I^4K^2; A-K^4; A-K^4
Music K.7.a.7; Music R.M.15.d.1(2).
The blank leaves at the end of some of the parts are missing. The copy at Music R.M.15.d.1(2) is without the Basso continuo part.

P120 PHILIPS, Peter
[Cantiones sacrae.] (tp.1) PRIMVS CHORVS. CANTIONES SACRAE, OCTONIS VOCIBVS, AVCTORE R.D. PETRO PHILIPPI . . . CANTVS. ANTVERPIÆ Ex Typographia Petri Phalesij . . . M.D.C XIII.
(tp.2) PRIMVS CHORVS. CANTIONES SACRAE . . . AVCTORE R.D. PETRO PHILIPPI . . . ALTVS. ANTVERPIÆ Ex Typographia Petri Phalesij . . . M.D.C XIII.
(tp.3) PRIMVS CHORVS. CANTIONES SACRAE . . . AVCTORE R.D. PETRO PHILIPPI . . . TENOR. ANTVERPIÆ Ex Typographia Petri Phalesij . . . M.D.C XIII.
(tp.4) PRIMVS CHORVS. CANTIONES SACRAE . . . AVCTORE R.D. PETRO PHILIPPI . . . BASSVS. ANTVERPIÆ Ex Typographia Petri Phalesij . . . M.D.C XIII.
(tp.5) SECVNDVS CHORVS. CANTIONES SACRAE, OCTONIS VOCIBVS. AVCTORE R.D. PETRO PHILIPPI . . . CANTVS. ANTVERPIÆ Ex Typographia Petri Phalesij . . . M.D.C XIII.
(tp.6) SECVNDVS CHORVS. CANTIONES SACRAE . . . AVCTORE R.D. PETRO PHILIPPI . . . ALTVS. ANTVERPIÆ Ex Typographia Petri Phalesij . . . M.D.C XIII.
(tp.7) SECVNDVS CHORVS. CANTIONES SACRAE . . . AVCTORE R.D. PETRO PHILIPPI . . . TENOR. ANTVERPIÆ Ex Typographia Petri Phalesij . . . M.D.C XIII.
(tp.8) SECVNDVS CHORVS. CANTIONES SACRAE . . . AVCTORE R.D. PETRO PHILIPPI . . . BASSVS. ANTVERPIÆ Ex Typographia Petri Phalesij . . . M.D.C XIII 4° 8 pt.: sig. A-E^4 (each part)
Music K.4.f.4; Music C.57.c.
The copy at Music C.57.c. consists of Primus Chorus Altus, Tenor, Bassus and Secundus chorus Tenor only.

P121 PHILIPS, Peter
(tp.1) GEMMVLAE SACRÆ BINIS ET TERNIS VOCIBVS Cum Basso Continuo ad Organum, AVCTORE R.D. PETRO PHILIPPI . . . EDITIO ALTERA. BASSVS. ANTVERPIÆ, Excudebat Petrus Phalesius M.D.C XXI.
(tp.2) GEMMVLAE SACRÆ AVCTORE R.D. PETRO PHILIPPO . . . EDITIO ALTERA. CANTVS II. ANTVERPIÆ, Excudebat Petrus Phalesius M.D.C XXI. 4° 2 pt.: sig. Aa-Ff^4G^2; AA,BB^4
Music C.57.d.

P122 PHILIPS, Peter
[Madrigali a 6.] (tp.1) DI PIETRO PHILIPPI . . . Il Primo Libro DE MADRIGALI A SEI VOCI Nuouamente Ristampati & Corretti. CANTO. IN ANVERSA Appresso Pietro Phalesio M.DCIV.
(tp.2) DI PIETRO PHILIPPI . . . Il Primo Libro DE MADRIGALI A SEI VOCI . . . TENORE. IN ANVERSA Appresso Pietro Phalesio M.DCIV.
(tp.3) DI PIETRO PHILIPPI . . . Il Primo Libro DE MADRIGALI A SEI VOCI . . . ALTO. IN ANVERSA Appresso Pietro Phalesio M.DCIV.

(tp.4) DI PIETRO PHILIPPI . . . Il Primo Libro DE MADRIGALI A SEI VOCI . . . BASSO. IN ANVERSA Appresso Pietro Phalesio M.DCIV.
(tp.5) DI PIETRO PHILIPPI . . . Il Primo Libro DE MADRIGALI A SEI VOCI . . . SESTO. IN ANVERSA Appresso Pietro Phalesio M.DCIV. obl.4° 5 pt.: sig. A-C^4D^2; E-G^4H^2; I-L^4M^2; N-P^4Q^2; X-Z^4Aa^2
Music A.344a; Music A.344.d.
Wanting the 'Quinto' which would have sig. R-V. The copy at Music A.344.d consists of the Tenore part only.

P123 PHILIPS, Peter
[Madrigali a 6.] (tp.1) DI PIETRO PHILIPPI . . . Il Secondo Libro DE MADRIGALI A SEI VOCI Nouamente Composto & dato in luce. CANTO. IN ANVERSA. Appresso Pietro Phalesio M D C III.
(tp.2) DI PIETRO PHILIPPI . . . Il Secondo Libro DE MADRIGALI A SEI VOCI . . . TENORE. IN ANVERSA. Appresso Pietro Phalesio M D C III.
(tp.3) DI PIETRO PHILIPPI . . . Il Secondo Libro DE MADRIGALI A SEI VOCI . . . BASSO. IN ANVERSA. Appresso Pietro Phalesio M D C III.
(tp.4) DI PIETRO PHILIPPI . . . Il Secondo Libro DE MADRIGALI A SEI VOCI . . . SESTO. IN ANVERSA. Appresso Pietro Phalesio M D C III. obl.4° 4 pt.: pp.29; 32; 29; 29
Music A.344.i.
With an index at the end of the Tenore part.

P124 PHILIPS, Peter
[Madrigali a 6.] (tp.1) DI PIETRO PHILIPPI . . . Il Secondo Libro DE MADRIGALI A SEI VOCI NOVAMENTE RISTAMPATI. CANTO. IN ANVERSA. Appresso Pietro Phalesio M DC XV.
(tp.2) DI PIETRO PHILIPPI . . . Il Secondo Libro DE MADRIGALI A SEI VOCI . . . TENORE. IN ANVERSA. Appresso Pietro Phalesio M DC XV.
(tp.3) DI PIETRO PHILIPPI . . . Il Secondo Libro DE MADRIGALI A SEI VOCI . . . ALTO. IN ANVERSA. Appresso Pietro Phalesio M DC XV.
(tp.4) DI PIETRO PHILIPPI . . . Il Secondo Libro DE MADRIGALI A SEI VOCI . . . BASSO. IN ANVERSA. Appresso Pietro Phalesio M DC XV.
(tp.5) DI PIETRO PHILIPPI . . . Il Secondo Libro DE MADRIGALI A SEI VOCI . . . SESTO. IN ANVERSA. Appresso Pietro Phalesio M DC XV. obl.4° 5 pt.: pp.32; 32; 32; 32; 32; illus.
Music A.344.b; Music A.344.e.
The titlepage verso of the Canto part bears the engraved arms of Albert and Isabella, surrounded by four musical emblems. The copy at Music A.344.e consists of the Tenore part only.

P125 PHILIPS, Peter
[Madrigali a 8.] (tp.1) DI PIETRO PHILIPPI . . . MADRIGALI A OTTO VOCI. Nouamente Ristampati. CANTO. IN ANVERSA Appresso Pietro Phalesio. M.DCXV.
(tp.2) DI PIETRO PHILIPPI . . . MADRIGALI A OTTO VOCI . . . CANTO SE. IN ANVERSA Appresso Pietro Phalesio. M.DCXV.
(tp.3) DI PIETRO PHILIPPI . . . MADRIGALI A OTTO VOCI . . . ALTO. IN ANVERSA Appresso Pietro Phalesio. M.DCXV.
(tp.4) DI PIETRO PHILIPPI . . . MADRIGALI A OTTO VOCI . . . ALTO SE. IN ANVERSA Appresso Pietro Phalesio. M.DCXV.
(tp.5) DI PIETRO PHILIPPI . . . MADRIGALI A OTTO VOCI . . . TENORE SE. IN ANVERSA Appresso Pietro Phalesio. M.DCXV.
(tp.6) DI PIETRO PHILIPPI . . . MADRIGALI A OTTO VOCI . . . BASSO. IN ANVERSA Appresso Pietro Phalesio. M.DCXV.
(tp.7) DI PIETRO PHILIPPI . . . MADRIGALI A OTTO VOCI . . . BASSO SE. IN ANVERSA

Appresso Pietro Phalesio. M.DCXV. obl.4° 7 pt.: sig.A-C^4D^2 (each part)
Music A.344; Music A.344.h.
With an index at the end of the Basso secondo part, followed by the approbation. The copy at Music A.344.h consists of the Tenore secondo part only.

PHILODUSUS, Janus; pseudonym of Daniel Heinsius. *See* HEINSIUS, Daniel

P126 PHILOMETOR
PHILOMETOR, Ofte Christelijcke 'tsamen-sprekinghe/van 't recht der Kercke in Kerckelijcke saken . . . TOT MIDDELBVRGH, By Adriaen vande Vivere . . . M.DC.XVJ. 4° pp.53[54]
T.2246(3).
Variously attributed to Ewout Teellinck or Adriaen vande Vivere.

PHILOPATOR, Alexius; pseudonym of Ewout Teellinck. *See* TEELLINCK, Ewout

P127 PHILOSTRATUS, Flavius
PHILOSTRATI LEMNII SOPHISTæ Epistolæ quædam, partim nunquam, partim auctiores editæ. IOANNES MEVRSIVS Primus vulgavit, & adjunxit, DE PHILOSTRATIS Dissertatiunculam. LUGDUNI BATAVORUM. Ex Officinâ LVDOVICI ELZEVIRII. Typis GODEFRIDI BASSON . . . M.DC.XVI. 4° pp.24
519.b.27(2).

P128 PHLEGON of Tralles
PHLEGONTIS TRALLIANI, Quæ exstant, Opuscula. IOANNES MEVRSIVS Recensuit, & NOTAS Addidit. LVGDVNI BATAVORVM, Apud ISAACVM ELZEVIRIVM . . . M D CXX. 4° pp.190
235.e.32(3).

P129 PHRASES
PHRASES, ELEGANTIÆ P[O]ETICÆ, EPITHETA, ANTITHETA, Ex claßicis Auctoribus diligenti studio selecta. ANTVERPIÆ APVD I. TROGNÆSIVM, M.DCVI. [etc.] 12° pp.349
1509/3047.
The titlepage is slightly mutilated. Ownership inscriptions: Joannes van wyninghen maior; John Gray 1702; P. Blair. The binding is stamped with the initials: FMA.

P130 PICKFORD, John
THE SAFEGUARDE FROM SHIP-WRECKE, OR HEAVENS HAVEN . . . Compiled by I.P. Priest. PRINTED AT DOVAY, BY PETER TELV . . . 1618. [etc.] 8° pp.285
3936.aa.30.
Anonymous. Sometimes wrongly attributed to John Price. Ownership inscriptions: Richard Stacy; Joseph Tasker.

PICTORUM aliquot celebrium . . . effigies. 1610. *See* HONDIUS, Henricus; the Elder

P131 PIERCY, JOHN
A REPLY MADE VNTO Mr. ANTHONY WOTTON AND Mr. IOHN WHITE MINISTERS. VVHERIN It is shewed, that they haue not sufficiently answered the Treatise of Faith . . . By A.D. Student in Diuinity . . . Imprinted with Licence, M.DC.XII. 4° pp.325
C.26.i.3; C.26.k.2(1).
Anonymous and without imprint; published by the English College press at St. Omer.

P132 PIERCY, John
[A reply made unto Mr. Anthony Wotton.] A CATALOGVE OF DIVERS VISIBLE PROFESSORS OF the Catholike Faith . . . Taken out of the Appendix to the Reply of A.D. vnto M. Ant. Wotton, and M. Ioh. White Ministers . . . M.DC.XIV. 8° ff.15
C.26.k.4(2).
Anonymous and without imprint; published by the English College press at St. Omer.

P133 PIERCY, John

[Tractatus de fide.] A TREATISE OF FAITH. WHEREIN Is briefly . . . shewed, a direct Way, by which euery man may resolue . . . all Doubts . . . concerning matters of Faith. REVIEVVED corrected, and augmented with marginall notes. By A.D. Student in Diuinity . . . M.DC.XIV. 8° pp.188

C.26.k.4(1).

Anonymous and without imprint; published by the English College press at St. Omer.

P134 PIGHIUS, Stephanus Vinandus

[Annales magistratuum et provinciar. S.P.Q.R. ab urbe condita.] (tp.1) STEPHANI VINANDI PIGHII . . . ANNALES ROMANORVM: QVI COMMENTARII vicem supplent in omnes veteres HISTORIAE ROMANAE Scriptores; TRIBVS TOMIS DISTINCTI: E quibus duo posteriores POSTVMI, nunc primùm in lucem exeunt, recensiti, aucti, & illustrati operâ & studio ANDREAE SCHOTTI . . . ANTVERPIÆ, EX OFFICINA PLANTINIANA, Apud Viduam & Filios Ioannis Moreti. M.DC.XV. (col.1) ANTVERPIAE, EX OFFICINA PLANTINIANA, APVD IOANNEM MORETVM. M.DXCVIII.

(tp.2) STEPHANI VINANDI PIGHII . . . ANNALES ROMANORVM . . . TOMVS SECVNDVS, POSTVMVS, Opera & studio ANDREAE SCHOTTI . . . recensitus, auctus, & illustratus . . . ANTVERPIÆ, EX OFFICINA PLANTINIANA, Apud Viduam & Filios Ioannis Moreti. M.DC.XV. (col.2) [device only].

(tp.3) STEPHANI VINANDI PIGHII . . . ANNALES ROMANORVM . . . TOMVS TERTIVS . . . ANTVERPIÆ, EX OFFICINA PLANTINIANA, Apud Viduam & Filios Ioannis Moreti. M.DC.XV. (col.3) ANTVERPIÆ, EX OFFICINA PLANTINIANA, APVD VIDVAM ET FILIOS IOANNIS MORETI. M.DC.XV. fol. 3 tom.: pp.469; xl,494[510]; 735; illus.

664.h.2–4; 198.f.3,4.

With 'Vita Stephani Vinandi Pighii . . . Per Ioannem Winterum' added to tom.2. With the original, engraved, titlepage of the first edition of 1599 in tom.1 which is a reissue of that edition and has the colophon of 1598. The engraved illustrations in tom.1 are by Pieter van der Borcht. The copy at 664.h.2–4 bears the ownership inscription: Domus Prof. Romanæ Soc. Iesu Bib. Comm., and what seems to be its library stamp.

P135 PIGHIUS, Stephanus Vinandus

[Annales magistratuum et provinciar. S.P.Q.R. ab urbe condita.] STEPHANI VINANDI PIGHII . . . ANNALES ROMANORVM . . . ANTVERPIÆ, EX OFFICINA PLANTINIANA, Apud Viduam & Filios Ioannis Moreti. M.DC.XV. fol. 3 tom.: pp.469; xl,494[510]; 735; illus.

587.l.2–4.

Tom.1 is a reprint of the corresponding part of the preceding, retaining the 1599 engraved titlepage and the 1598 colophon. tom.2,3 are other copies of the preceding. The 'Præfatio . . . ad lectorem' has been omitted from tom.1.

P136 PILLETERIUS, Caspar

PLANTARVM TVM PATRIARVM TVM EXOTICARVM, IN WALACHRIA, ZEELANDIÆ INSVLA, NASCENTIVM SYNONYMIA. authore CASPARO PILLETERIO . . . MIDDELBVRGI, Excudebat Richardus Schilders . . . 1610. 8° pp.398

448.a.7.

Mainly in Latin, with some Dutch. From the library of Sir Joseph Banks. Ownership inscription: Tournefort.

P137 PINELLI, Lucas

[Gersone della perfettione religiosa.] THE MIRROVR OF RELIGIOVS PERFECTION . . . Written in Italian by the R.F. Lucas Pinelli, of the Society of IESVS. And translated into English by a Father of the same Society . . . M.DC.XVIII. 8° pp.560

C.110.b.12.

Translated by Thomas Everard. Without imprint; published by the English College press at St. Omer.

P138 PISANELLI, Baldassare
[Trattato della natura de' cibi et del bere.] TRAICTÉ DE LA NATVRE DES VIANDES, ET DV BOIRE, AVEC LEVRS VERTVS, VICES, REMEDES, ET histoires naturelles . . . De l'Italien du Docteur Baltazar Pisanelli mis en nostre vulgaire, par A.D.P. A S.OMER, Chez Charles Boscart . . . 1620. 12° pp.225
1606/14.
Translated by Antoine de Pouvillon.

P139 PISANI, Ottavio
OCTAVII PISANI ASTROLOGIA SEV MOTVS, ET LOCA SIDERVM . . . ANTVERPIAE, EX OFFICINA ROBERTI BRVNEAV . . . M.DC.XIII. [etc.] fol. coll.XXXXIIII: plates; illus., maps, port., tables
Maps 187.u.1.
The columns are printed in italics on the verso of the maps and in roman on the verso of the tables. The titlepage engravings show the large arms of Cosimo de' Medici, to whom the work is dedicated, and a small figure of Europa; the portrait is signed: Iean Wiricx fecit. With numerous volvelles.

P140 PISANI, Ottavio
LE LEGGI PER LE QVALI SI FA VERA, ET PRESTA GIVSTITIA, SENZA SPESE, ET TRAVAGLI DE LITIGANTI . . . SENZA LINGVA LATINA . . . RACCOLTE DA OTTAVIO PISANI. IN ANVERSA, Appresso Henrico Aertsio. M.DC.XVIII. [etc.] fol. pp.71; illus., port.
495.k.16.
The engraved portrait on the titlepage verso is the same as in the preceding.

P141 PISTORIUS, Johannes
NAYMAXIA INTER CLASSES VENETORVM, apud Batavos instructam: ET HISPANORVM, in portu Gibraltar hærentem. DVCE . . . CAROLO HVYN ab AMSTENRADE, &C. AMMIRALIO . . . MELCHIORE van den KERCKHOVEN. Descripta à IOHANNE PISTORIO . . . HAGÆ COMITIS Ex Officina Hillebrandi Iacobi . . . 1618. 4° sig.AB[4]
1055.g.38(1).

PLACCAET. Proclamations and other legal documents bearing this title, whether of the original official issue or reprinted or translated, are entered in chronological order under the name of the issuing country, province or city, followed by the original date of the document in square brackets.

A PLAINE demonstration. 1620. *See* LUCULENTA demonstratio

PLAIX, César de. Anti-Cotton. 1610. *See* COTON, Pierre. Brief, dienende tot verclaringe.

PLANCIUS, Daniel. Disputationum theologicarum quarta, de attributis Dei. 1601. *See* DU JON, François; the Elder

P142 PLANCIUS, Daniel
Reden-strijdt van de Ketters gheen gheloove te houden/wt het Decreet van Constantz: Schriftelijck ghehandelt tusschen eenen Antwerpschen Jesuwyt/ENDE Danielem Plancium . . . Door een Lief hebber uyt den Latijne overgheset. t'Amstelredam/by Dirck Pietersz . . . 1609. 4° pp.17; illus.
T.1713(31); T.2239(15).
Directed against Heribertus Rosweydus. The author named in the preface as Daniel Plantius and at the end as Daniel Plancius. There is no p.9. The titlepage woodcut shows the burning of a heretic at the stake. Corresponding to the copy described in *Knuttel* no.1663.

P143 PLANCIUS, Daniel

REDEN-STRYT VAN De Ketters gheen ghelove te houden . . . Schriftelijck ghehandelt tusschen eenen Antwerpschen Jesuwijt/ENDE Danielem Plancium . . . T'AMSTELREDAM, By Dirck Pietersz . . . 1609. 4° pp.17
T.2421(6).

Another issue of the preceding, without the woodcut. Corresponding to the copy described in *Knuttel* no.1664.

P144 PLATO

[Timaeus. Latin] CHALCIDII V.C. TIMÆVS De Platonis Translatus. ITEM Ejusdem in eundem Commentarius. IOANNES MEVRSIVS Recensuit, denuò edidit, & NOTAS addidit. LVGDVNI BATAVORVM, Ex Officinâ IVSTI COLSTERI . . . M D C XVII. 4° pp.42,463
714.e.18.

P145 PLAUTUS, Titus Maccius

[Works. Latin] M.ACCI PLAVTI COMOEDIÆ VIGINTI. EX OFFICINA PLANTINIANA RAPHELENGII. M.D.CIX. 32° pp.719
166.k.17.

Published at Leiden.

P146 PLAUTUS, Titus Maccius

[Works. Latin] M.ACCI PLAVTI COMŒDIÆ Superst: XX. Ad doctiss: virorum editiones repræsentatæ. Amsterodami, Apud Guilj Ianssonium A° M DC XIX. 24° pp.747
11707.a.36.

With 'Marci Accii Plauti Vita, ex Petro Crinito & Lilio Gyraldo desumpta'. The titlepage is engraved. Ownership inscription: Sum Danielis Ebaldi.

P147 PLAUTUS, Titus Maccius

[Amphytruo. Dutch] M.ACCII PLAVTI AMPHITRYO. Overgheset in de Nederduytsche tale Door ISAACVS van DAMME. TOT LEYDEN, Voor Bartholomeus Iacobsz. de Fries . . . 1617. 4° sig.A-F^4G^6
1509/3609.

Dedicated to Jacob van Dijk. With a laudatory poem by Wilhelmus van Nivelle.

Le PLAYDOYER de l'Indien hollandois. 1608. *See* WALERANDE, J.B. de

P148 PLEMP, Cornelis Gysbertszoon

(tp.1) CORNELII GISELBERTI PLEMPII AMSTERODAMVM MONOGRAMMON. AMSTERODAMI Apud Ioannem VValschardum M DC XVI.
(tp.2=p.37) CORNELII GISELBERTI PLEMPII QVISQVILIAE. seu ELEGIARVM LIBER VNVS. AMSTERODAMI Apud Ioannem VValschardum M DC XVI.
(tp.3=p.117) CORNELII GISELBERTI PLEMPII EMBLEMATA QVINQVAGINTA. AMSTERODAMI Apud Ioannem VValschardum. M.DC.XVI. 4° pp.190; illus.
11408.f.38.

The woodcut illustrations in the 'Emblemata' have sometimes been ascribed to Christoffel van Sichem.

P149 PLINIUS SECUNDUS, Caius

[Selections. Dutch] CAII PLINII SECUNDI. Des wijtberoemden . . . Philosophi . . . Boecken ende Schriften/in drie deelen onderscheyden . . . Nu nieuwelijck uyt den Hoochduytsche in onse Nederlantsche sprake overgeset/eñ met schoone Figuyren geciert. TOT ARNHEM. Ghedruckt by Jan Janszen . . . M.DC.X. 4° pp.612; illus.
975.c.13.

Containing also the fourth book, on fishes. With selections also from other writers. The illustrations are woodcuts.

P150 PLINIUS SECUNDUS, Caius

[Selections. Dutch] CAII PLINII SECVNDI . . . Boecken eñ Schriften/in vier deelen onderscheyden . . . Nu nieuwelijck uyt den Hoochduytsche in onse Nederlantsche sprake overgheset, ende met schoone Figuren verciert. TOT ARNHEM, By Jan Jansz. . . . 1617. 4° pp.612; illus.

461.a.1.

Dl. 1–3 are a new edition, ending with p. 512; dl. 4 begins with p. 514 as in the preceding and is a reissue of that part. The index at the end of dl. 4 has not been altered to accord with the new setting of dl. 1–3. The illustrations have been retained in part, others are copies or are completely new. From the library of Sir Joseph Banks.

P151 PLUTARCH

[De educatione puerorum. Greek and Latin] ΠΛΟΥΤΑΡΧΟΥ ΠΕΡΙ ΠΑΙΔΑΓΩΓΗΣ. PLVTARCHI DE LIBERIS EDVCANDIS COMMENTARIVS, IN CERTA CAPITA distinctus, perpetua analysi logica, & sententijs variorum Autorū illustratus: NVNC SECVNDA CVRA MARCI BEVMLERI ITA expolitus, vt analysis planè nova, & innumeris mendis purgata prodeat. ARNHEMIAE, Apud Ioannem Ianssonium. M.DC.VI. 8° pp.135

1030.c.1(2).

Reprinted from the edition published by Bernhard Albin at Speyer in 1593. With some manuscript notes.

P152 PLUTARCH

[Vitae parallelae. Abridgments. Dutch] Tleven ende vrome daden vande Doorluchtige Griecsche ende Romeynsche mannen/met haer figuren. Deur PLVTARCHVS int lange beschreven/ende nu int corte begrepen/ende in Latijn gestelt door DARIVS TIBERTVS . . . Hier by is gevoecht tleven vande excellente Veltheeren, door ÆMILIVS PROBVS beschreven, ende van ander mannen . . . met sommige nieuwe vergelijckingē, die nu eerst int licht zijn wtgecomen. In onse Neerduytsche sprake overgeset, door M. Everart . . . TOT LEYDEN, By Jan Claesz. van Dorp . . . 1601. 8° pp.834; illus.

1607/5572.

The additional lives attributed to Aemilius Probus are in fact by Cornelius Nepos. The illustrations are small woodcut portraits.

A POEME declaring the real presence of Christ in the Blessed Sacrament of the aultar. 1606. *See* SOUTHWELL, Robert

P153 POLITISCH

Politisch vnd Historisch/Auch Christliches vnd getrewhertziges Bedencken/vber vorgestandener ergangener . . . Vnruhe vnd Kriegsgefahr/im loͤblichen Koͤnigreich Boͤheimb . . . Gestellet durch einen getrewen Patrioten. Gedruckt zu Leiden . . . 1619. 4° sig. A-C^4; illus.

1310.c.33(1).

The titlepage woodcut shows a king and a commoner shaking hands. The imprint is false; not printed in the Netherlands, nor translated from a Dutch original.

P154 POLYANDER a Kerckhoven, Johannes

DISPVTE contre L'ADORATION DES RELIQVES DES Saincts trespassés. Par Jehan Polyander. Avec la refutation d'un escrit & indice des Chanoines d'Aix en Allemagne touchant ce subiect. A DORDRECHT. Par François Borsaler [*sic*]. M.D.C.XI. 8° pp.159

873.f.2.

Printed by Joris Waters at Dordrecht?

P155 POLYANDER a Kerckhoven, Johannes

[Dispute contre l'adoration des reliques.] A DISPVTATION against the Adoration of the reliques of Saints departed . . . Together with, The refutation of a Jesuiticall Epistle, and an Index of the reliques, vvhich . . . are shovvne at Avvcon in Germanie . . . compiled by the Canons of S. Maries Church An. 1608. By Iohn Polyander . . . & translated by Henry Hexham, out of French into English. At Dordrecht. Printed by George Walters . . . 1611. 8° pp.156

C.118.a.25(2).

P156 POLYANDER a Kerckhoven, Johannes

DVÆ ORATIONES IOHANNIS POLYANDRI . . . DE SS[æ]. THEOLOGIAE nobis in Verbo Dei revelatæ præstantia & certitudine. Habitæ in auditorio Thologico [*sic*] Academiæ Lugduno-Batavæ, atque in gratiam studiosæ Juventutis evulgatæ. LVGDVNI-BATAVORVM, Apud LUDOVICUM ELZEVIRIUM . . . M D CXIV. 4° sig.A-E^4F^3

491.b.12(3).

P157 POLYANDER a Kerckhoven, Johannes

(tp.1) ORATIO IOHANNIS POLYANDRI . . . De primarijs falsæ Theologiæ auctoribus devitandis, & fidis veræ Doctoribus imitandis: Habita in Collegio Illust. Ordinum Hollandiæ & VVest-Frisiæ, Cùm D. FESTVS HOMMIVS Regens, & M. DANIEL SINAPIVS Subregens, in eo inaugurarentur. Cui præfixus est Catalogus disputationum facultatis Theologicæ, inchoatarum mense Januario, Anni 1620. LVGDVNI BATAVORVM, Ex officina IACOBI MARCI . . . M D C XX.

(tp.2) ORATIO DE SS. THEOLOGIA. Eiusque studio capessendo. Ab ANTONIO THYSIO . . . publicè habita, I. Decemb. . . . M DC XIX. LVGDVNI BATAVORVM, Ex officina IACOBI MARCI . . . M DC XX. 4° 2 pt.: pp.16; 30

491.b.12(7,8).

The two texts form one whole, connected by a catchword.

P158 POLYST-STEEN

(tp.1) POLYST-STEEN. Tot weghneminghe van de vuyle vlecken des Christalijnen Brils . . . Hier is noch by-ghevoeght een korte vvederlegginghe van de Voor-redē gestelt voor het gepretendeerde boeck Castellij, geintituleert, KORTE EN DVYDELICKE WEDERLEGGINGHE . . . Ghedruckt . . . 1614.

(tp.2=p.35) Antwoorde Op de voor-reden en na-reden: GHESTELT Voor en achter dit . . . Boeck Sebastiani Kastellij . . . 1614. 4° pp.68; illus.

T.2244(1).

Directed against Bernardus Dwinglo and Sébastien Châteillon. The titlepage woodcut shows a spectaclemaker's bench.

P159 PONTANUS, Johannes Isacius

(tp.1) DISCEPTATIONES CHOROGRAPHICÆ DE RHENI DIVORTIIS ATQ. OSTIIS EORVMQVE ACCOLIS POPVLIS. in quibus, PRAETER CETERA, GEOGRAPHORVM atque historicorum præstantissimi . . . & omnium maximè CORNELIVS TACITVS, passim vel illustrantur vel explicantur, & à pravis insuper ac sinistris . . . interpretationibus, præsertim PHILIPPI CLUVERI, vindicantur, per IOHANNEM ISACIVM PONTANVM,[*sic*] AMSTELODAMI Ex officinâ HENRICI LAVRENTII . . . 1614.

(tp.2) CORNELII HAEMRODII . . . BATAVIAE Omniumque inter Helium & Flevum gentium atque urbium BREVIS DESCRIPTIO. Cui . . . accedunt . . . DISCEPTATIONES aliquot CHOROGRAPHICAE eòdem spectantes, Cura & studio Viri veritatis studiosi. HARDROVICI, Typis Thomæ Henrici. (col.) HARDROVICI Typis THOMÆ HENRICI. 8° 2 pt.: pp.223; 63

156.b.1(1).

With a revised edition of the work by Cornelis Haemrood and extracts from the 'Anonymus', both first published in 'Rerum et urbis Amstelodamensium historia' by Pontanus. Ownership inscription: H.E.Z. Kunoviz (?).

P160 PONTANUS, Johannes Isacius

IOHANNIS ISACI PONTANI DISCEPTATIONVM CHOROGRAPHICARVM Adversus PHIL. CLVVERVM Nova Sylloge: Complectens . . . confutationem eorum quæ Antiquæ Germaniæ, responsionis quasi vice ad priores Disceptationes, idem Cluverus passim inspersit. HARDERVICI, Typis Thomæ Henrici, Impensis HENRICI LAVRENTII . . . 1617. 8° pp.128

156.b.1(2).

Published at Amsterdam.

P161 PONTANUS, Johannes Isacius

ITINERARIVM GALLIAE NARBONENSIS cum duplici Appendice id est vniuersæ fere Galliæ descriptione Philologica ac Politica. Cui accedit GLOSSARIVM PRISCO-GALLICVM seu de Lingua Gallorum veteri DISSERTATIO: Authore IOHANNE ISACIO Pontano. LVGDVNI BATAVORVM, Ex officina Thomæ Basson, impensis Commelinorum. M.D.C.VI. 24° pp.354

576.a.3.

Consisting of a short poem and long prose commentary. With the Lord's Prayer in French and British Celtic and in Latin. Published at Leiden and/or Amsterdam. From the library of John Morris.

P162 PONTANUS, Johannes Isacius

ORIGINVM FRANCICARVM LIBRI VI. in quibus PRAETER GERMANIAE AC RHENI CHOrographiam, FRANCORVM Origines ac primæ sedes aliaque ad gentis in Gallias transitum variasque victorias, instituta ac mores pertinentia, ordine deducuntur, Authore IOHANNE ISACIO PONTANO. HARDERVICI, Ex Officinâ Thomæ Henrici, Impensis HENRICI LAVRENCII . . . MD XVI [*sic*]. 4° pp.618: plate; illus.

C.81.c.9; 286.d.41.

The number C missing in the date on the titlepage has been supplied in manuscript. The titlepage woodcut shows the portrait of 'Chlodovicus Rex Francorum'. Published at Amsterdam. The copy at C.81.d.41 bears the cypher of Charles II on the spine.

P163 PONTANUS, Johannes Isacius

RERUM ET URBIS AMSTELODAMENSIUM HISTORIA . . . Auctore IOH. ISACIO PONTANO. Accedunt sub calcem Auctores vetustiores duo numquam editi: Quorum nomina & seriem versa pagella indicabit. AMSTERODAMI . . . excudit Judocus Hondius . . . 1611. fol. pp.292,38: plates; illus., maps

794.i.6; 153.g.4.

The titlepage is engraved, showing an allegory of Amsterdam, including the initials I.H. as tradesman's monogram on a barrel. The additional works are described on the titlepage verso as by 'Anonymus' and Cornelius Haemrodius. The titlepage of the copy at 794.i.6 has been laminated, making the verso illegible. The cartouche on 'fol.228' is left blank.

P164 PONTANUS, Johannes Isacius

[Rerum et urbis Amstelodamensium historia.] HISTORISCHE Beschrijvinghe der seer wijt beroemde Coop-stadt AMSTERDAM . . . Eerst int Latijn ghestelt ende beschreven Door IOH. ISACIVM PONTANVM. Ende by den selven . . . oversien ende . . . vermeerdert ende verbetert . . . in Nederduyts overgheset Door PETRVM MONTANVM . . . TOT AMSTERDAM, Ghedruckt by IUDOCUM HONDIUM . . . 1614. [etc.] (col.) TOT AMSTERDAM, Ghedruckt by IVDOCVM HONDIVM . . . M DCXIV. 4° pp.360: plates; illus., maps

795.i.7; 802.k.38.

Both copies are imperfect; that at 795.i.7 wanting the titlepage and all plates except three and leaf ⋆2 is mutilated; that at 802.k.38 wanting all the plates except one. Some of the maps are signed: BW or: Beniamin Wrght [*sic*], celator.

POPMA, Ausonius. Ausonii Popmae . . . De instrumento fundi liber. 1620. *See* CATO, Marcus Porcius; the Censor. [Works] M. PorcI Catonis De re rustica liber.

P165 POPMA, Ausonius

AVSONII POPMÆ . . . DE ORDINE, ET VSV IVDICIORVM, LIBRI TRES . . . LEOVARDIÆ, EXCVDEBAT ABRAHAMVS RADÆVS . . . M.D.CXVII. 4° pp.255

1570/973.

Ownership inscription: Johannes Colyckius, Dordra. 1652.

P166 POPMA, Ausonius

AVSONI POPMÆ . . . DE VSV ANTIQVÆ LOCVTIONIS LIBRI DVO. EX OFFICINA PLANTINIANA RAPHELENGIJ, M.D.CVI. 8° pp.158

1568/3734.

Published at Leiden.

P167 POPMA, Ausonius

FRAGMENTA HISTORICORVM VETERVM LATINORVM, AB AVSONIO POPMA . . . Collecta, emendata & SCHOLIIS illustrata. AMSTELODAMI, Sumptibus IOHANNIS COMMELINI Viduæ . . . 1620. (col.) HARDERVICI, Impensis Commelini, typis THOMAE HENRICI Viduæ . . . 1620. 8° pp.193

246.c.9(4).

P168 POPPIUS, Eduardus

[Letters] Eduardi Poppij TVVEE BRIEVEN D'eene aen BARTHOLOMÆVM NICOLAI Contra-Remonstrantsch-Predikant binnen ter Goude: daer op een swaer Vonnisse vande E. Magistraet der selver Stede op den 18. Novemb. teghen Poppium ghevolght is: D'ander aen De Remonstrantsche Ghemeynte binnen ter Goude . . . Ghedruckt . . . 1621. 4° pp.48

T.2251(10).

P169 POPPIUS, Eduardus

ANTWOORDT op de Malitieuse Calumnie der Contra-Remonstranten in de Vereenighde Nederlanden. Daer mede sy/oorsake nemende . . . uyt de schandelijcke Afval Petri Bertii, de Remonstrantsche Predicanten . . . valschelijck beschuldighen, dat sy Papisten zijn/ofte na't Pausdom hellen/ende 'tselve in de Ghemeynten hares Vaderlandts soecken in te voeren . . . 1620. 4° pp.52

T.2250(13).

Anonymous.

P170 POPPIUS, Eduardus

DE ENGE POORTE, ofte, PREDICATIEN Over eenighe . . . Texten/ofte Spreucken der heyligher Schrifture . . . Gepredickt/ende . . . in druck uytghegheven Door Eduardum Poppium . . . Ghedruckt ter Goude, By Jasper Tournay/voor Andries Burier . . . 1616. 4° pp.538

1578/1222.

The titlepage is slightly mutilated.

P171 POPPIUS, Eduardus

NIEVWE-IAER Vervatende STOFFE tot Goede ende vreedsame bedenckingen ende raetpleginghen over Religions saken in dese bedroefde tijden: Voor Magistraten, Leeraers, ende gemeene Ingesetene vande vereenighde Nederlanden . . . 1621. 4° pp.80

T.2251(23).

Anonymous.

PORTA, Johann a. Over-Rhetische ofte Grysonsche acten. 1619. [Sometimes attributed to Johann a Porta.] *See* GRISONS

P172 PORTUGAL

[31.10.1605] Placcaet des Conincx van Spaengien/ghepubliceert in Portugael/ teghens de Ingeboorne Nederlanders/residerende in Portugael ende andere Zee-steden vanden Coningh. Wt den Portugesche overgeset in onse Nederlantsche tale. Naede Copye ghedruckt in Portugael . . . 1605. 4° sig.A^4

T.1713(9); T.1717(39).

Issued at Lisbon, 31 October 1605.

P173 POSSEVINO, Giovanni Battista Bernardino

[Praxis curae pastoralis.] DE OFFICIO CVRATI, ET QVORVMLIBET PRESBYTERORVM, ad praxim . . . LIBER IOAN. BAPT. BERNARDINI Posseuini . . . Hac postrema editione emendatus, Auctoris Additionibus, Notisque ANDR. VICTORELLI . . . auctus Accessêre Sacræ Congregationis . . . de Matrimonio Declarationes . . . In hac editione recognitus, & à mendis . . . repurgatus . . . Per W. de Kerchoue . . . AVDOMARI, Ex Typographia Caroli Boscardi . . . 1617. 12° pp.556

1568/5483.

POST-BODE. 1616. *See* TAURINUS, Jacobus

P174 POSTHUMUM

POSTHVMVM CALVINI STIGMA IN TRIA LILIA, SIVE TRES LIBROS DISPERTITVM. A Rhetoribus Collegij Societatis IESV Bruxellis. Anno 1611. Nieusgierige coopt myn . . . BRVXELLÆ, Ex Officinâ RVTGERI VELPII, & HVBERTI ANTONII . . . 1611. [etc.] 8° pp.172 [271]; illus.

1212.h.13; 1474.aaa.23(1).

The last number of the pagination has been printed upside down. The titlepage illustration is an allegorical engraving. Some Greek laudatory poems are added at the end, perhaps printed at the Officina Plantiniana at Antwerp? The copy at 1474.aaa.23(1) is imperfect; wanting pp.3-14, for which other pages have been substituted.

P175 POSTILLIOEN

POSTILLIOEN VVtghesonden Om te soecken den veriaegdē Coninck van Praghe. Eerst ghedruckt den 18. Januarius. 1621. T'Hantwerpen/by Abraham Verhoeven/ [etc.] 4° 4 unsigned leaves; illus.

P.P.3444.af(176); 1471.aa.9.

In verse. The titlepage headed: Ianuarius 1621.7. The titlepage woodcut shows a courier on horseback. The copy at 1471.aa.9 is imperfect; wanting the titlepage.

P176 POSTILLIOEN

[Postillioen wtghesonden om te soecken den . . . Coninck van Praghe.] POSTILLION, Depesché du Conte de Bucquoy pour chercher le Palatin Roy de Boheme. Traduict de Flameng en François, l'An M.DC.XXI. A Anuers, Chez Abraham Verhoeuen . . . 1621. fol. a single sheet; illus., port.

1750.c.1(44).

The sheet is made up of two pieces glued together, one for the engravings, the other the text. The engraved part consists of two sections, the upper showing the portraits of Frederick and Bethlem Gabor on either side of a view of Heidelberg, the lower showing the great tun and the postillion. The upper has inscriptions in Latin and German, the lower in Dutch and French. The text part contains the 'Postillioen' poem in French translation, another poem entitled 'Le Catechisme du Palatin', and a prose piece entitled 'Claire & vraye pourtraicture du grand tonneau à vin de Heydelberch'. A German version of 'Le Catechisme du Palatin', entitled 'Palatinischer Catechismus' is placed at 1750.c.1(30).

POSTILLION, depesché du Conte de Bucquoy. 1621. *See* POSTILLIOEN

P177 PRACTYCKE

PRACTYCKE VAN DEN SPAENSCHEN RAEDT, Dat is: Clare vertooninghe dat den Raedt door I. Lipsium, Er. Puteanum, ende Fran. Campanellam ghegeven/om de vereenighde Nederlanden wederom te brenghen onder 'tgebiedt van den Coningh van Spangjen . . . ofte alreede in't werck gestelt is/ofte noch daghelijcks in't werck ghestelt wordt . . . Ghedruckt uyt kracht vande Privilegien der Vrije Nederlanders . . . 1618. 4° pp.54; illus.
T.2422(6).

Sometimes said to have been written by or with the assistance of François van Aerssen. The titlepage woodcut shows an allegory of the Dutch lion in his garden defending it against Spain and the Pope who are offering an olive branch.

P178 PRACTYCKE

[Practycke van den Spaenschen Raedt.] PRACTIICKE VAN DEN SPAENSCHEN RAET . . . Ghedruckt uyt kracht vande Privilegien der Vrye Nederlanders . . . 1618. 4° pp.52
T.2248(55*).

Another edition of the preceding.

P179 PRAGUE

[1621] EXECVTIE ende banne gepubliceert, Inde dry Pragher Steden/Teghens de gevluchte Directeurs, ende andere persoonen. Ouerghesedt wt de Hooch-Duytsche sprake in onse Nederlantsche Tale. Eerst ghedruckt den 27. Appril. 1621. T'Hantwerpen/By Abraham Verhoeuen/[etc.] 4° pp.8; illus. sig. ¶[4];
P.P.3444.af(224).

Headed: Appril 1621. 65. The titlepage woodcuts show a man on horseback holding a staff of office, with attendants, and a court in session.

PRATEOLUS, Gabriel. *See* DU PRÉAU, Gabriel

Het PRIEEL der gheestelicker melodiie. 1617. *See* TOLLENAER, Jean de

PRIERIO, Silvestro de. *See* MAZZOLINI, Silvestro; da Prierio

P180 PRIMALEON of Greece

Het tweedde Boec van Primaleon vā Griecken/Sone van Palmerin van Olijve/ Keyser van Constantinopelen . . . In Nederduytsch ghestelt door Samuel Min-el. TOT ROTTERDAM. By Jan van Waesberghe . . . 1621. 4° sig.A-L[8]; illus.
12450.d.14.

With the Amadis woodcuts, including that of the ships signed: 'A', i.e. Arnold Nicolai on sig.I6v, and one on sig.C3v signed: I.L.

P181 PRINCIPALE

Principale puncten/die inde voorder handelinghe vanden Vrede van weghen de . . . Staten Generael . . . onbegrijpelick sullen geproponeert werden/ onvermindert t'gene naermaels/eñ buyten besoigne sonde [*sic*] moghen voorcomen. Hier zijn oock mede by ghevoeght de voorghestelde Artijckelen by de gecommitteerde vande Majesteyt van Spaengien/ende Eerts-hertoghen van Brabandt . . . M.VIC.VIII. 4° 2 unsigned leaves; illus.
T.2420(4); 106.d.24.

The titlepage woodcut shows the Dutch lion in his garden.

P182 PRISE

[Prise et reduction de la ville de S. Iean d'Angely.] Articulen/ende inneminghe/ofte Reductie der Stadt van S. Ian d'Angely. Midtsgaders oock den Missief-Brieff die zijne Majesteydt, heeft gheschreuen aen . . den Hertoch van Montbazon, Gouverneur van Parijs. Ende d'Articulen by zyne Majesteydt gheaccordeert, soo vvel aende Soldaeten als aende Invvoonders der seluer Stadt. Eerst ghedruct den

16. Iulij. 1621. T'Hantwerpen/by Abraham Verhoeuen/[etc.] 4° pp.11; sig.M⁴N+²; illus.
P.P.3444.af(260).

Headed: Iulius. 1621. 103, to which a pencil note 'bis' has been added, perhaps referring to the entry in *Bibliotheca Belgica* V197, p.516: 103 (103*). The letter is dated 25.6.1621 and the piece is a translation of the fullest version of several entitled 'Prise et reduction de la ville de S. Iean d'Angely', cf. *Catalogue de l'histoire de France,* I 1671. The titlepage woodcut shows the arms of Louis XIII.

P183 PROCESSUS

[Processus in coronando rege Bohemiae Friderico I.] Corte ende warachtige beschrijvinge Van de Crooninge des Conincx van Bohemen/FRIDERICI Den eersten . . . Overgheset uyt de Latijnsche spraecke . . . Door M. D. S. Hier achter is noch byghevoecht t'extrackt van eenen sekeren brief . . . uyt Heydelberch . . . aengaende de geschiedenissen des Oorlooghs tusschen . . . FRIDERICVM Coninck van Bohemen ende den Keyser van Roomen. Ghedruct nae de Latijnsche copie . . . 1619. 4° sig.A⁴B²
T.2423(25).

The original was published at Prague, 'Typis Danielis Carolidæ à Carlspergka'.

P184 PROCEZ

PROCEZ, EXAMENT, CONFESSIONS ET negations du meschant & execrable parricide François Rauaillac sur la mort de HENRY LE GRAND . . . Iouxte la coppie Imprimee, A PARIS, chez IEAN RICHER. 1611. [etc.] 8° pp.63: plate; port.
C.38.a.26.

The plate signed: Christoffel van Sichem Inuentor et fecit. Without imprint; printed in the Netherlands?

PROCLAMATIE ende wederlegginghe byden Hartoch van Venetien gedaen. 1606. *See* VENICE [6.5.1606]

P185 PROCLUS; Saint, Patriarch of Constantinople

ΠΡΟΚΛΟΥ ΑΡΧΙΕΠΙΣΚΟΠΟΥ ΚΩΝΣΤΑΝΤΙΝΟΥ Πόλεως Τα ἑυρισκόμενα. B. PROCLI . . . Opuscula, quæ reperiri potuerunt omnia. Nunc primum Græcè & Latinè junctim edita & recensita, Ex Bibliotheca GEVERHARTI ELMENHORST[I]. LVGDVNI BATAVORVM, Apud IACOBVM MARCI . . . M.D.CXVII. 8° pp.167
845.a.17.

Two extra leaves (cancels? cancellands?) bearing pp.7-10 have been inserted between sig.**1 and **2; pp.7-10 occur in their correct place.

P186 PROCOPIUS of Gaza

PROCOPII GAZÆI IN LIBROS REGVM, ET PARALIPOMENOV, Scholia. IOANNES MEVRSIVS Nunc primus Græcè edidit, & Latinam interpretationem adiecit. LVGDVNI BATAVORVM, Typis ISAACI ELZEVIRII . . . M D C XX. 4° pp.346 [396]
1016.i.6.

P.393 has been misprinted 343.

P187 PROCURATIE

PROCVRATIE ENDE VERBANDT. By de Remonstrantsche Steden malcander toeghesonden/ende elcx hare Ghedeputeerde/ten dachvaert gaende/mede-gegeven. GHEDRVCKT Om te kennen te gheven het onderlinghe verdraechsaem ghemoet ende t'samen-rottinghe der Remonstrants-ghesinde . . . 1618. 4° sig.A²
T.2248(50).

Two leaves belonging to the following tract in the volume have by mistake been bound between the two leaves of this.

PROPHETIE dewelcke ghevonden is tot Saumeurs. 1620. *See* JOHN of Capistrano; Saint

PROPOSITIE, ghedaen by de Gesanten van de . . . Ceurfursten . . . aen Maximiliaen, Paltzgrave aen den Rijn. 1620. *See* GERMANY. Union of Halle, 1610 [19-29.12.1619]

PROTEST des autheurs vanden Christalijnen bril. 1614. *See* DWINGLO, Bernardus

PROVISIONELE ontdeckinge eeniger misslaghen, de welcke Adolphus Venator . . . heeft begaen. 1611. *See* HILLE, Cornelis van; the Younger

P188 PROVISIONELE

Provisionele Openinghe. Van verscheyden saecken/ghestelt in de Remonstrantie van den . . . Advocaet van Hollandt ende West-vrieslandt. Tot naerder Onderrechtinghe/so van hare Ed. Mog. als van alle ghetrouwe Patriotten . . . Waerinne oock/de Nulliteyt van de ghenaemde Ontdeckinghe van de Valsche Spaensche ende Jesuytische Practijcquen . . . wort aenghewesen. GHEDRVCT Wt cracht van de Privilegien der Vrye Nederlanders . . . 1618. 4° pp.59
T.2422(9).

Sometimes attributed to François van Aerssen. Directed against Johan van Oldenbarnevelt and Cornelis van der Myle.

The PRUDENTIAL ballance of religion. 1619. *See* SMITH, Richard; Bishop of Chalcedon

P189 PRUDENTIUS CLEMENS, Aurelius

AVRELII PRVDENTII CLEMENTIS . . . OPERA, Ex recensione VICTORIS GISELINI. EX OFFICINA PLANTINIANA RAPHELENGII, 1610. 32° pp.281
1069.a.43; C.20.f.54.

Published at Leiden. The copy at 1069.a.43 is slightly mutilated throughout; that at C.20.f.54, from the travelling library of Sir Julius Caesar, has the titlepage slightly mutilated.

PSALMI Vesperarum et Magnificat quatuor vocum. 1615. *See* TERZAGHI, Angelo

P190 PTOLEMAEUS, Claudius

CLAUDII PTOLEMÆI . . . GEOGRAPHIAE LIBRI OCTO GRÆCO-LATINI. Latinè primùm recogniti & emendati, cum tabulis geographicis ad mentem auctoris restitutis per Gerardum Mercatorem: Jam verò ad Græca & Latina exemplaria à Petro Montano iterum recogniti, et . . . castigati. Adjecta insuper ab eodem nomina recentia et æquipollentia . . . Sumptibus Cornelij Nicolai & Iudoci Hondij Amsterodammi [*sic*] . . . 1605. fol. pl.A-Z, Zz, Aa, Bb; pp.215; illus.; port.
215.f.7.

The titlepage is engraved. The engraved portrait of Mercator signed: F. Hog, i.e. Frans Hogenberg; the illustrations in the text are woodcuts. Hondius named as the editor of the maps in a poem by Daniel Heinsius. The titlepage, first preliminary leaf and last leaf are mounted.

PUBLICATIE ende verbodt ghedaen by Iacobus den sesten. 1603. *See* ENGLAND [23.6.1603]

P191 PUCCINI, Vincenzo

[Vita della veneranda Madre Suor Maria Maddalena de' Pazzi.] THE LIFE OF THE HOLY AND VENERABLE MOTHER Suor Maria Maddalena DE PATSI . . . WRITTEN In Italian by . . . Vincentio Puccini . . . And now translated into English . . . Published . . . M.DC.XIX. 8° pp.292
1370.c.11.

The translator's dedication signed: G.B., i.e. Sir Toby Matthew. Without imprint; published by the English College press at St. Omer. Imperfect; wanting the table of chapters.

P192 PUENTE, Luis de la
[Meditaciones de los mysterios de nuestra santa fe.] (tp.1) MEDITATIONS VPPON THE MYSTERIES OF OVR HOLY FAITH WITH the practice of mental praier touching the same, Composed in Spanish by . . . LVYS DE LA PVENTE . . . AND Translated into English by F. RICH. GIBBONS . . . THE FIRST PART . . . M.DCX.
(tp.2) MEDITATIONS VPPON THE MYSTERIES OF OVR HOLY FAITH . . . Composed in Spanish by . . . LVYS DE LA PVENTE . . . AND Translated . . . by F. RICH. GIBBONS . . . THE SECOND PART . . . M.DCX. 8° 2 pt.: pp.359; 306
C.26.l.10.
Without imprint; printed, the first part by Charles Boscard, the second part by Pierre Auroi, both at Douai. Ownership inscription: Dom[9] Prof. Rom. S.I. Bibl. comm.

P193 PUENTE, Luis de la
[Meditaciones de los mysterios de nuestra santa fe.] (tp.1) MEDITATIONS VPON THE MYSTERIES OF OVR HOLIE FAITH . . . COMPOSED In Spanish, by . . . Lewis of Puente . . . And translated out of Spanish into English, by IOHN HEIGHAM. THE FIRST TOME . . . AT S. OMERS . . . 1619. [etc.]
(tp.2) MEDITATIONS VPON THE MYSTERIES OF OVR HOLIE FAITH . . . COMPOSED In Spanish, by . . . Lewis of Puente . . . And translated . . . by IOHN HEIGHAM. THE SECOND TOME . . . AT S. OMERS . . . 1619. [etc.] 4° 2 tom.: pp.784; 936
4403.i.25.
With additional parts not found in the earlier translation. Printed by Charles Boscard at St. Omer. Ownership inscription: Eliza: More.

PURGATORIES triumph over Hell. 1613. *See* FLOYD, John

P194 PUTEANUS, Erycius
[Collections] ERYCI PVTEANI AMOENITATVM HVMANARVM DIATRIBAE XII. Quæ partim Philologiam, partim Philosophiam spectant. LOVANI, Typis CHRISTOPH. FLAVI. Francofurti, apud LVD. ELZEVIR. M.DC.XV. 8° pp.845
816.b.32.
Described on the titlepage verso as tom.II pt.1 of the works of Puteanus. The Frankfurt imprint is misleading; published at Leiden.

P195 PUTEANUS, Erycius
[Letters] (tp.1) ERYCI PVTEANI EPISTOLARVM PROMVLSIS. CENTVRIA I. & innovata. LOVANII, EX OFFICINA FLAVIANA. M.DC.XI. [etc.]
(tp.2) ERYCI PVTEANI EPISTOLARVM FERCVLA SECVNDA. CENTVRIA II. & innovata. LOVANII, EX OFFICINA FLAVIANA. M.DC.XIII.
(tp.3) ERYCI PVTEANI EPISTOLARVM BELLARIA. CENTVRIA III. & Nova. LOVANII, EX OFFICINA FLAVIANA. M.DC.XII. [etc.]
(tp.4) ERYCI PVTEANI EPISTOLARVM APOPHORETA. CENTVRIA IV. & Recens. LOVANII, EX OFFICINA FLAVIANA. M.DC.XII. [etc.]
(tp.5) ERYCI PVTEANI EPISTOLARVM RELIQVIÆ. CENTVRIA V. & Postrema. LOVANII, EX OFFICINA FLAVIANA. M.DC.XII. [etc.] 4° 5 pt.: pp.120; 234; 152; 115; 143; illus.
636.h.6.
Tp.1, 3-5 have engraved borders; an engraved portrait of Epicurus after Pieter de Jode occurs in pt.5. p.142. With an essay on writing in cypher at the end of pt.5.

P196 PUTEANUS, Erycius
[Letters] ERYCI PVTEANI EPISTOLARVM ATTICARVM PROMVLSIS, IN CENTVRIAS TRES DISTRIBVTA. COLONIÆ, Sumptibus LVDOVICI ELZEVIRII, M.DC.XVI. [etc.] 8° pp.632
1083.k.1.
The imprint is false; printed by the Officina Flaviana at Louvain and published by Louis Elzevier at Leiden. Ownership inscription: Robertus Clayton.

P197 PUTEANUS, Erycius

[Letters] ERYCI PVTEANI EPISTOLARVM ATTICARVM MISSVS SECVNDI, IN CENTVRIAS TRES DIVISI. Operum omnium TOMVS IV. COLONIÆ, Prostant in Officinâ ELZEVIRIANA, M DCXVII [etc.] 8° pp.432,171

1083.k.2.

The imprint is false; published at Leiden. Printed by the Officina Flaviana at Louvain.

P198 PUTEANUS, Erycius

ERYCI PVTEANI ÆNIGMA HISTORICVM REGIVMQVE, AD IACOBVM PVTZIVM . . . Iurisconsulto titulo recèns donatum. 4° 4 unsigned leaves

534.f.32(2).

Without imprint; printed by the Officina Flaviana at Louvain in 1617. Leaves 2 and 3 are transposed, leaf 2 is cropped.

P199 PUTEANUS, Eerycius

ERYCI PVTEANI ARX LOVANIENSIS A PRINCIPIBVS LVSTRATA: Eorum quæ hîc dicta & facta Διηγημάτιον. LOVANII, Apud BERNARDINVM MASIVM. M.DC.XIX. 12° pp.33

1055.a.25(4).

An account of the visit of Albert and Isabella to the author's house, i.e. the castle of Louvain. With the device of the Louvain printer Gerardus Rivius on the titlepage.

PUTEANUS, Erycius. Burgerlijck discours. 1617. *See* below: De induciis Belgicis.

P200 PUTEANUS, Erycius

ERYCI PUTEANI COMVS, SIVE PHAGESIPOSIA CIMMERIA. SOMNIVM: Secundò jam & accuratiùs editum. LOVANII, Typis GERARDI RIVII. M.DC.X. [etc.] 8° pp.204

1084.d.26.

A school prize copy, inscribed 'Ex liberali munificentiâ D.D. Juratorum 1620 Præmio Catechistico Donatum Carolus Henricus Grammaticus Nundliensis (?)'.

P201 PUTEANUS, Erycius

ERYCI PVTEANI COMVS . . . SOMNIVM: Secundò jam & accuratiùs editum. LOVANII, Typis GERARDI RIVII. M.DC.XI. [etc.] 8° pp.204

1079.d.5.

P202 PUTEANUS, Erycius

(tp.1) ERYCI PVTEANI DE ANNVNCIATIONE VIRGINIS-MATRIS ORATIO: Louanij, in Æde Sodalitatis habita, VII. Kal. April. M.DC.XVIII. ANTVERPIÆ, EX OFFICINA PLANTINIANA, Apud Balthasarem Moretum & Viduam Io. Moreti. M.DC.XVIII. (tp.2) CAROLI SCRIBANI . . . IN ANNVNCIATIONEM DEI MATRIS VOTIVA GRATVLATIO. ANTVERPIÆ, EX OFFICINA PLANTINIANA, Apud Balthasarem Moretum & Viduam Io. Moreti. M.DC.XVIII. 4° 2 pt.: pp.37; 29

1124.g.10(2,3).

The work of Scribani is a new edition of bk.1. ch.3 of his 'Amor Divinus', requested by Puteanus for joint publication in a letter to Scribani of 7 April 1618. Its signatures are AA-Cc^{4}Dd^3, therefore clearly supplementary to those of the text by Puteanus, i.e. A-E^4.

P203 PUTEANUS, Erycius

ERYCI PVTEANI DE COMETA ANNI M.DC.XVIII. Novo Mundi Spectaculo, LIBRI DVO. PARADOXOLOGIA. LOVANII, Apud BERNARDINVM MASIVM. M.DC.XIX. 12° pp.167

8560.aa.22.

With the device of the Louvain printer Gerardus Rivius on the titlepage. Author's presentation copy to 'Raph. Hentorfano [or Mentorfano] [?] suo'.

P204 PUTEANUS, Erycius

ERYCI PVTEANI . . . DE INDVCIIS BELGICIS DISSERTATIO POLITICA. Hactenus ab

Auctore Suppressa, sed nunc bono publico in Lucem emissa. Adjecta est IVSTI LIPSII, ob argumenti similitudinem, de Induciis Epistola . . . 1617. 4° pp.38[39]
1055.a.26(1).
Without imprint; printed by the Officina Flaviana at Louvain. Imperfect; Wanting sig.D3=pp.29,30, bearing the titlepage 'Iusti Lipsii Epistola . . . 1608'.

P205 PUTEANUS, Erycius
[De induciis Belgicis.] (tp.1) ERYCI PUTEANI . . . Burgerlijck Discours over de Nederlandsche TREVES . . . Noch is hier by ghevoegt, om de gelijckheid der verhandelinge IUSTI LIPSII brief, vande TREVES. Wt t'Latijn in onse Nederduytsche Tale overgheset door E.M.F.L. Ghedruckt . . . 1617.
(tp.2) IVSTI LIPSII Sendtbrief, IN WELCKE Hy Antwoorde geeft aen een seker groot Heere/Op de Vrage: Welcke van drien den Koninck van Hispagnien best geraden ware . . . Geschreven den derden Ianuarij M.D.XCV. Ghedruckt . . . 1617.
4° 2 pt.: sig.AB^4; C^2
T.2422(1,2).
Without imprint; printed by the Officina Flaviana at Louvain?

P206 PUTEANUS, Erycius
ERYCI PVTEANI DE OFFICIO IVDICIS DISSERTATTIO. Ex officinâ ELZEVIRIANA. M D C XIX. 8° pp.28
1053.a.13(3).
Published at Leiden.

P207 PUTEANUS, Erycius
ERYCI PVTEANI DE PVRIFICATIONE VIRGINIS-MATRIS ORATIO, Lovanii, in Æde Sodalitatis habita, Postridie Kalend. Februarii, M.DC.XII. LOVANII Typis IO. CHRISTOPH. FLAVI. [etc.] 4° pp.21; illus.
522.d.33(2).
With the author's tribute to the printer. The titlepage engraving shows the Virgin and Child. Published in 1612.

P208 PUTEANUS, Erycius
ERYCI PVTEANI DEMOCRITVS, SIVE DE RISV DISSERTATIO SATVRNALIS . . . LOVANII, Apud IO. CHRISTOPH. ELAVIVM [*sic*] . . . M D C XII. [etc.] 8° pp.22
8406.aaa.20(2).
The publisher's name is Flavius.

P209 PUTEANUS, Erycius
ERYCI PUTEANI FACULA DISTINCTIONVM: Ad omnem LECTIONEM, & SCRIPTIONEM necessaria. EIVSDEM De eisdem SYNTAGMA . . . In tertiâ hac editione correctum. LOVANII, Typis GERARDI RIVII. MDC.X. 12° pp.43
1089.a.1(1).

P210 PUTEANUS, Erycius
ERYCI PVTEANI HISTORIÆ CISALPINÆ LIBRI DVO: Res potissimùm circa LACVM LARIVM à IO. IACOBO MEDICÆO gestæ. ACCEDIT GALEATI CAPELLÆ De Bello Mussiano Liber . . . LOVANII, Apud PHIL. DORMALIVM & IO. SASSENVM. M.DC.XIV. 4° pp.160: plates; illus., ports.; genealogical tables
592.e.1; C.47.f.8.
The titlepage engraving shows a trophy. The portraits of Puteanus and Giovanni Giacomo de' Medici are by Pieter de Jode. Printed by Joannes Christophorus Flavius. The copy at C.47.f.8 is bound in blue silk bearing the arms of Philip William of Orange to whom the book is dedicated and contains a coloured emblematic drawing of the ship 'Progredior'.

P211 PUTEANUS, Erycius

ERYCI PVTEANI HISTORIAE INSVBRICAE LIBRI VI. Qui IRRVPTIONES BARBARORVM In ITALIAM continent: Rerum ab Origine gentis ad Othonem M. EPITOME. LOVANII, Typis IO. CHRISTOPH. FLAVII. Apud LVD. ELZEVIRIVM. M D CXIV. (col.) IO. CHRISTOPHORVS FLAVIVS EXCVDEBAT LOVANII M.DC.XIV. MENSE SEPTEMBRI. 8° pp.221
1053.a.13(2).

Pp.145–162: 'Additiuncula ex And. Alciati De formula R. imperii libello'. Published at Leiden.

P212 PUTEANUS, Erycius

ERYCI PVTEANI IN IS. CASAVBONI AD FRONT. DVCÆVM . . . EPISTOLAM STRICTVRAE. LIBER PRODROMVS. LOVANII, Apud IO. CHRISTOPH. FLAVIVM. M.D C.XII. [etc.] 4° pp.60
522.d.33(3).

The pagination is erratic. With a contemporary manuscript note on an additional leaf, defending Casaubon.

P213 PUTEANUS, Erycius

ERYCI PVTEANI IN IS. CASAVBONI AD FRONT. DVCAEVM . . . EPISTOLAM STRICTVRAE. LIBER PRODROMVS. LOVANII, Apud IACOBVM HVLZIVM, M.DC.XII. [etc.] 4° pp.39
4071.c.42; G.5590(2).

Reprinted from the preceding.

P214 PUTEANUS, Erycius

ERYCI PVTEANI LIPSIOMNEMA ANNIVERSARIVM, SIVE IVSTI LIPSI V.C. Laudatio Funebris, Die anniversario habita. ITEM NICOLAI OVDARTI In Manes LIPSI Secundi Adfectus. ANTVERPIÆ, EX OFFICINA PLANTINIANA, Apud Ioannem Moretum. M.DC.VII. (col.) ANTVERPIÆ, EX OFFICINA PLANTINIANA, Apud Ioannem Moretum. M.DC.VII. 4° pp.28
1562/115.

The contribution by Oudaert is in verse.

P215 PUTEANUS, Erycius

ERYCI PVTEANI MARTYREMATA ACADEMICA, SIVE Doctrinæ & Probitatis TESTIMONIA: A IVSTO ET FAVSTO PVTEANIS E. FILIIS In Librum vnum collecta. LVGDVNI-BATAVORVM, Prostant in Officinâ Elzeviriana . . . M.DC.XVIII. 8° pp.60
1020.g.11(1).

A collection of testimonials given by Puteanus to his students, mainly at Louvain.

P216 PUTEANUS, Erycius

ERYCI PUTEANI PALÆSTRA BONÆ MENTIS Auctoritate Sereniss.um Principum in Atheneo Louaniensi instituta. In quâ ad Civilem Litteraturam et Eloquentiam Iuventus ducitur. LOVANII, E Bibliopolio Flaviano . . . M.DC.XI. 4° pp.152
522.d.33(1).

The titlepage is engraved.

P217 PUTEANUS, Erycius

ERYCI PVTEANI PIETATIS THAVMATA IN BERNARDI BAVHVSI . . . PROTEVM PARTHENIVM, vnius Libri VERSVM, vnius VERSVS Librum, Stellarum numero, siue formis M.XXII. variatum. ANTVERPIÆ, EX OFFICINA PLANTINIANA, Apud Balthasarem & Ioannem Moretos. M.DC.XVII. 4° pp.116; illus.
837.i.4; 1124.g.10(1).

Consisting of variations on a line of Bauhusius, a poem by Puteanus and prose meditations. The titlepage engraving shows the Virgin and Child on a cloud against the starry sky.

[Illustrations of **Q1** overleaf]

Q1 (frontispiece)

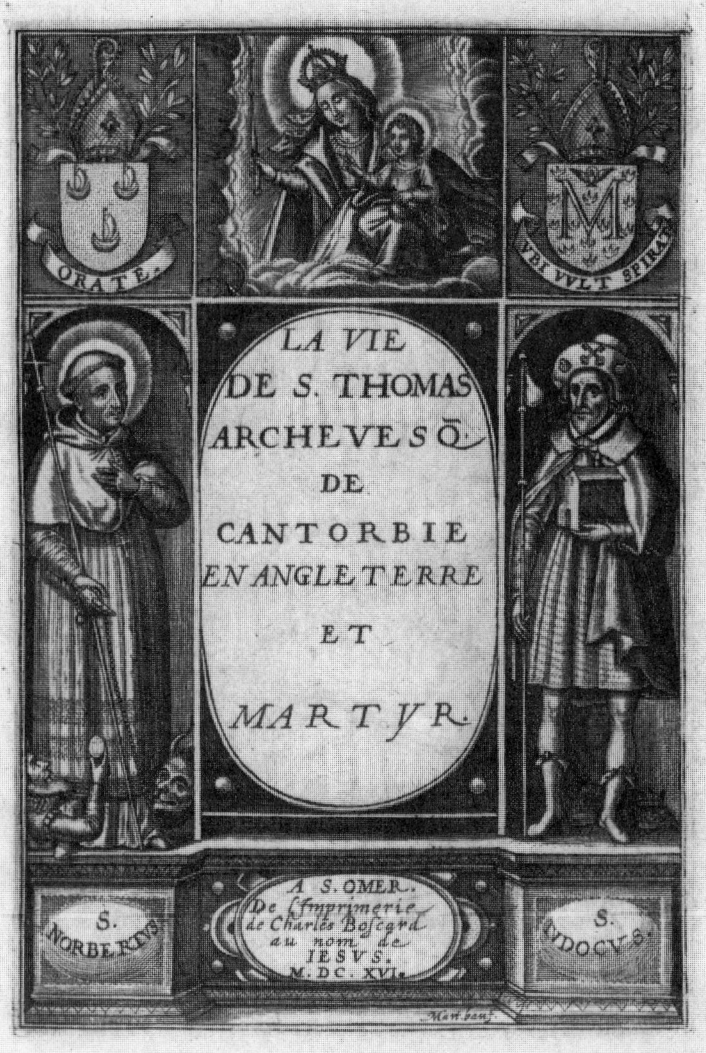
ORATE.
VBI VVLT SPIRAT
LA VIE
DE S. THOMAS
ARCHEVESQ.
DE
CANTORBIE
EN ANGLETERRE
ET
MARTYR.
S.
NORBERTVS
A S. OMER.
De l'Imprimerie
de Charles Boscard
au nom de
IESVS.
M.DC.XVI.
S.
IVDOCVS.

P218 PUTEANUS, Erycius

ERYCI PUTEANI STIMVLVS LITTERARVM. ORATIO PARÆNETICA: Habita ex tempore, In Collegio Trilingui Buslidiano. LOVANII, Typis GERARDI RIVII. M.ICↃ.X [*sic*] 8° pp.20

1089.a.1(2).

Proposing Federico Borromeo and Jean Richardot as examples to follow in study. Bound after the same author's 'Facula', with a poem on that work in this.

Den PYL der liefden. 1609. *See* COBBAULT, Arnoldus

PYLKOKER der dwaesheyt. 1612. *See* BROECK, Hubrecht wten

Q

Q1 QUADRILOGUS

[Vita & processus sancti Thome.] LA VIE DE S. THOMAS ARCHEVESQVE DE CANTORBIE . . . Ensemble les Miracles aduenues par son intercession en l'Abbaye de Domp-Martin . . . Par F. Charles du Canda . . . À S. OMER, De l'Imprimerie de CHARLES BOSCARD . . . 1615. 4° pp.276: plate; port.

G.1343; 488.a.12.

Translated by Charles du Canda from the Old French version of the 'Vita & processus sancti Thome' known as the 'Quadrilogus'. With an additional engraved titlepage, reading: LA VIE DE S. THOMAS ARCHEVESQ̄ DE CANTORBIE EN ANGLETERRE ET MARTYR. A S. OMER De l'Imprimerie de Charles Boscard . . . M.DC.XVI. The additional titlepage and the frontispiece signed: M.,resp. Mart., Baes. The copy at 488.a.12 is imperfect; wanting the engraved titlepage and frontispiece.

t QUAEDT syn meester loondt. 1618. *See* AGUILAR, Gaspar

QUAESTIONES duae de sacris alienis non adeundis. 1607. *See* PERSONS, Robert

Q2 QUEL-GEEST

QVEL-GEEST, Vervaetende ettelijcke Vragen aen de CONTRA-REMONSTRANTEN, van de Praedestinatie der onmondige kinderen, in haere kintsheyt stervende; OM Daer op te hebben ronde eñ eenvoudige antwoort, conform t'ghevoelen dat in desen . . . beleden hebben die Theologanten, welcke sy in haer TEGEN-VERTOOCH . . . verclaeren . . . 1618. 4° pp.27

700.h.25(15).

A QUIET and sober reckoning. 1609. *See* PERSONS, Robert

R

Le RABELAIS reformé par les ministres. 1619. *See* GARASSE, François

R1 RABELAIS, François

[Works] (tp.1) LES OEVVRES DE M. FRANÇOIS RABELAIS . . . Derniere edition de nouueau reueuë & corrigee. A ANVERS Par IEAN FVET. 1605.

(tp.2) LE CINQVIEME LIVRE DES FAITS ET DITS Heroïques du bon Pantagruel . . . Auec la visitation de l'Oracle de la diue Bacbuc, & le mot de la Bouteille . . . Lę tout composé par M. François Rabelais : . . 1608. 12° 2 pt.: pp.347,469; 166; illus.

1081.k.4.

The illustration, a woodcut, occurs in pt.2. p.157. The signatures are continuous through both parts. The imprint appears false; printed in France? Imperfect; wanting pt.1. pp.105–112, with other leaves mutilated.

RADAEUS, Adrianus. Theses theologicae de aeterna deitate Domini Nostri Iesu Christi. 1612. *See* LINDEN, Henricus Antonides van der

R2 RADZIWIŁŁ, Mikołaj Krzysztof; Prince

[Peregrynacja do Ziemi Świętej.] IEROSOLYMITANA PEREGRINATIO . . . NICOLAI CHRISTOPHORI RADZIVILI DVCIS OLICÆ ET NIESVISII PALATINI VILNENSIS . . . Primùm à THOMA TRETERO . . . ex Polonico sermone in Latinum translata. Nunc variè aucta, et correctius . . . edita. ANTVERPIÆ EX OFFICINA PLANTINIANA Apud Viduam et Filios Ioannis Moreti. M.DC.XIV. fol. pp.308; illus.

566.i.15; 985.h.13; 148.f.7; G.1782.

The titlepage and the illustrations are engraved. The copy at G.1782 bears the ownership inscriptions: Collegii S.J. Nouesii 1627; R.P. Johanni Holdthausen D.D.Joha: Carol9 Erlenwein 1627.

R3 RAEDT

Raedt teghen DE Kerckelijcke Svvaricheden, Ofte, Advys van een Treflick/Geleert Man/buyten dese Landen/over het Middel/waer door dese Kerckelijcke swarichedē aller bequaemst souden connen affgedaen worden. Gheextraheert uyt sijnen Brief gheschreven uyt N. den 7. Novemb. Anno 1617. Ende . . . uyt Liefde tot de Vrede overgheset ende uyt-gegeven . . . TOT LEYDEN, By David Jansz. van Ilpendam . . . 1618. 4° sig.AB^{4}

700.h.25(23).

RAEDTSEL. 1608. *See* ADAMS, Yemant

R4 RAEMOND, Florimond de

L'ANTIPAPESSE OV ERREVR POPVLAIRE DE LA PAPESSE Ieanne. Par FLORIMOND DE RÆMOND . . . A CAMBRAY, De l'Imprimerie de Iean de la Riuiere. M.DC.XIII. [etc.] 8° pp.304

4571.a.28.

With the exlibris of Henry Spencer Ashbee, 1895.

R5 RAEMOND, Florimond de

(tp.1) L'ANTI-PAPESSE . . . Par FLORIMOND DE RÆMOND . . . A ARRAS, Chez GILLES BAVDVYN . . . M.DC.XIII.

(tp.2) DE LA COVRONNE DV SOLDAT. Traduict du Latin de Q. SEPTIM. TERTVLLIAN. Par FLORIMOND DE RAEMOND . . . A CAMBRAY, De l'Imprimerie de Iean de la Riuiere. M.DC.XIII. [etc.] 8° 2 pt.: pp.304; 67

4570.a.30.

Pt.1 is another issue of the preceding; pt.2 has its own signatures, but concludes with an index to pt.1. Pt.2 also contains the translation of Tertullian's 'Ad martyres'.

R6 RAEMOND, François de

FRANCISCI REMONDI . . . EPIGRAMMATA ET ELEGIÆ. ANTVERPIAE Apud Ioachimum Trognæsium. M.DCVI. [etc.] 12° pp.349

11408.a.41.

With 'Andreæ Frusii . . . Epigrammata in haereticos' and 'Crispus. Tragoedia Bernardini Stephonii'. The date of the privilege is 1607.

RAINOLDS, John. An answere to a sermon . . . by George Downame. 1609. [Sometimes wrongly attributed to John Rainolds]. *See* ANSWERE

R7 RAINOLDS, John

A DEFENCE OF THE IVDGMENT OF THE REformed churches. That a man may lawfullie not onelie put awaie his wife for her adulterie, but also marrie another. Wherin both Robert Bellarmin the Iesuites Latin treatise, and an English pamphlet of a

ECCLESIASTICI CAP. XLIII.
In ſermone eius ſiluit ventus, et cogitatione ſua placauit abyſſum.
PSALMO CVI.
Et clamauerunt ad Dominum cum tribularentur: et de
neceſsitatibus eorum eduxit eos.
Et ſtatuit procellam eius in auram: et ſiluerunt fluctus eius.
Et lætati ſunt quia ſiluerunt: et deduxit eos in portum
voluntatis eorum.

Ee 3

R2 (p.221)

namelesse author . . . are cōfuted by Iohn Raynolds . . . Printed ANNO 1609. 4° pp.94
860.k.15(1).
Without imprint; printed by Joris Waters at Dordrecht.

R8 RAINOLDS, John
A DEFENCE OF THE IVDGMENT OF THE Reformed churches . . . Wherin both Robert Bellarmin the Jesuits Latin treatise, and an English pamphlet of a namelesse author . . . are confuted by Iohn Raynolds . . . The faultes escaped in the first impression, are here in this carefully corrected by the Printer . . . Printed by George Walters, 1610. 4° pp.78
1608/1146.
Printed at Dordrecht.

RAINOLDS, John. A replye answering a Defence of the sermon . . . by George Downame. 1613,14. [Sometimes wrongly attributed to John Rainolds.] *See* REPLYE

R9 RALEIGH, Sir Walter
[The discoverie of . . . Guiana.] (tp.1) VVarachtighe ende grondighe beschryvinghe van het groot en Gout-rijck Coningrijck van Guiana . . . ontdeckt ende beschreven . . . Door . . . Walter Raleigh . . . ende Laurens Keymis. t'Amstelredam/by Cornelis Claesz . . . 1605.
(tp.2=sig.I1) VVarachtighe ende grondighe beschryvinghe vande tweede Zeevaert der Engelschen nae Guiana . . . beschreven . . . Door . . . Laurentium Keymis. t'Amstelredam/by Cornelis Claesz . . . 1605. obl.4° ff.47; illus., map
1858.a.1(7).
A new edition of the one published by Claesz in 1598. For the edition by Michiel Colijn at Amsterdam, 1617, *see* COLIJN, Michiel. Oost-Indische ende West-Indische voyagien.

R10 RAMIREZ DE PRADO, Lorenço
ΠΕΝΤΗΚΟΝΤΑΡΧΟΣ SIVE QVINQVAGINTA MILITVM DVCTOR D. LAVRENTI RAMIREZ DE PRADO STIPENDIIS CONDVCTVS: Cujus auspicijs varia in omni litterarum ditione monstra profligantur, abdita panduntur, latebræ ac tenebræ pervestigantur, & illustrantur. ANTVERPIÆ, Apud Ioannem Keerbergium . . . M.DC.XII. 4° pp.357: plates; illus., tables
C.79.b.2.
The tables are lists of virtues and vices. Some of the engravings signed: Guilielm, hanius fecit; the engraved device on the titlepage signed: W D Hà. Imperfect; wanting leaf B2, containing a portrait. Sometimes said to be the work of Francisco Sánchez de las Brozas whose manuscript Ramirez acquired and published as his own.

R11 RAPHELENGIUS, Franciscus; the Elder
FRANCISCI RAPHELENGII LEXICON ARABICVM. LEIDÆ, Ex Officinâ Auctoris, 1613. fol. pp.648,LXVIII; illus., port.
622.l.5.
Edited by Franciscus the Younger and Justus Raphelengius, with notes by Thomas Erpenius, who printed this book with the Arabic type of Rapehelengius. With manuscript notes.

RATELWACHTS Roeprecht. 1611. *See* LE CANU, Robbert Robbertsen

R12 RAUCHENSTEIN, Berchtoldus à
CONSTANTIVS PEREGRINVS CASTIGATVS seu RELECTIO ITINERIS QVADRIMESTRIS BVQVOI. Authore BERCHTOLDO à RAVCHENSTEIN. BRVGGÆ Apud HENRICVM LEPORARIVM . . . M.DC.XXI. 4° pp.95
1054.a.7(2).
The author's name is a pseudonym, as is that of Constantius Peregrinus whose real name is Boudewijn de Jonge, (or, as claimed here, Candidus Eblanus, i.e. Joannes Labenus?). The imprint is false; published at Munich.

R13 RAVENSPERGER, Hermann

IOSEPHVS PRÆSVL SIVE DE Præsulatu seu principatu IOSEPHI IN ÆGYPTO sacra disputatio QVAM . . . Sub Præsidio . . . D. HERM. RAVENSPERGERI . . . tueri conabitur IOHANNES HACHTINGIVS . . . GRONINGAE Typis Ioannis Sassij . . . 1617. 12° pp.[143]–166
T.495(7).

The leaves bear a mixture of signatures G and H and were no doubt intended to form part of a collection of similar exercises.

R14 RAYMAKER, Jean

COMPTES POVR LES CASSIERS. Tres-vtils à tous Marchands & autres menants train de Marchandise. Par IEAN RAYMAKER. A ANVERS. Chez Hierosme Verdussen . . . 1603. 8° sig. A-F^8; illus.
1606/46.

The titlepage woodcut shows a mathematician-astronomer. Bound in a piece of manuscript on vellum.

R15 RAYMAKER, Jean

COMPTES pour les Cassiers. Tres-vtils à tous Marchands . . . Par IEAN RAYMAKER. A ROTTERDAM, Chez Iean VVaesbergue . . . 1605. 8° sig. A-F^8
1607/155(4).

R16 RAYMAKER, Jean

TRAICTE D'ARITHMETIQVE, contenant les cinc Especes . . . Tresproufitable & vtile à la Ieunesse & autres . . . Par IEAN RAYMAKER, A ROTTERDAM, Chez Iean VVaesbergue . . . 1610. 8° sig. A-C^8
1607/155(3).

RAYNOLDS, John. *See* RAINOLDS, John

REASONS taken of Gods word. 1604. *See* JACOB, Henry

R17 REBBE, Nicolaus de

OPVS DE DIGNITATIBVS ET OFFICIIS ECCLESIASTICIS . . . AVCTORE NICOLAO DE REBBE . . . DVACI, Ex Officina BALTAZARIS BELLERI . . . 1612. [etc.] 4° pp.72,83
484.a.30(1).

With a combined index for this work, the 'Tractatus de utilitate' and the 'Tractatus theologicus'. Printed for Bellère by Laurence Kellam at Douai as shown by the ornament bearing the initials LK. With the arms of Jacques Auguste de Thou on the binding and with the library stamp of Richard Heber.

REBBE, Nicolaus de. Tractatus theologicus. 1612. *See* infra: Tractatus de utilitate.

R18 REBBE, Nicolaus de

(tp. 1) TRACTATVS DE VTILITATE LECTVRÆ THEOLOGICÆ IN ECCLESIIS METROPOLITANIS, CATHEDRALIBVS, COLLEGIAT. ET REGVLARIBVS. ET DE PRÆBENDÆ THEOLOGALIS ORIGINE . . . Auctore NICOLAO DE REBBE . . . DVACI, Ex Officina BALTAZARIS BELLERI . . . 1611. [etc.]
(tp. 2) TRACTATVS THEOLOGICVS DE RESIDENTIA BENEFICIATORVM QVORVMLIBET, ET LECTVRA S. SCRIPTVRÆ IN ECCLESIIS CANONICORVM ET REGVLARIVM. Auctore NICOLAO DE REBBE . . . DVACI, Ex Officina BALTAZARIS BELLERI . . . 1612. [etc.] 4° 2 pt.: pp.32; 32
484.a.30(2,3).

Both works have a joint approbation and privilege and their signatures run through from A-H. Pt. 2 appears to have been published also with the date 1611; perhaps at the end of the year? Printed for Bellère by Laurence Kellam at Douai.

R19 REBREVIETTES, Guillaume de; Sieur d'Escoeuvre

LE PHILARET Diuise en deux parties, Erres Et Ombre. De l'inuention de Guillaume

de Rebreuiettes . . . A Monseigneur le Prince d'Orange. A ARRAS de l'imprimerie de Guillaume de la Riuiere . . . 1611. [etc.] 8° pp.240,88
4407.de.37.
The titlepage, which is engraved, shows Philaret and L'Ombre with devices below the arms of Philip William of Orange. This edition has no separate titlepages for the two parts as sometimes described and has a combined 'table' at the end.

RECHT ghebruyck ende misbruyck van tydlicke have. 1620. *See* FURMERIUS, Bernardus

R20 RECHTE

De rechte Spore ende Aenvvijsinghe, Dat de . . . Prince van Orangien hoochloflicker Memorie/de bescherminghe der Nederlanden heeft aenghenomen voor de warachtige Religie/tegen de tyrannije der Spagniaerden . . . Dienende (by maniere van een Voor-loper) tot de wederlegginghe van de . . . Nasporinge . . . Metter spoet by-ghebracht door T.G.B.V.A.P.L. . . . IN 'SGRAVEN-HAGHE, By Aert Meuris . . . 1617. 4° pp.26
T.2247(52).
Directed against the 'Na-sporingh' by Jacobus Taurinus.

R21 RÉCIT

[Récit véritable de ce qui s'est passé en la défaite des ennemis rebelles au roi.] Waerachtich Verhael Vā de Victorie en den slach gheschiet teghen de Hughenotten die den Stadt Montalbaen meyndē te comē ontsetten. Met den Nombre van allen de dooden ende Ghequetsten, met de Namen van de Cappiteynen, ende Ghevangenen . . . Eerst ghedruckt den 16. October 1621. T'Hantwerpen/By Abraham Verhoeuen/[etc.] 4° pp.8; sig.Vvv^4; illus.
P.P.3444.af(298).
Headed: October, 1621. 151. Described internally as 'Articulen vvt eenen Brieff vanden 28. September 1621. vvten Legher voor Mont Albaen', i.e. translated from 'Récit véritable de ce qui s'est passé en la défaite des ennemis rebelles au roi, venant au secours de Montauban'. The titlepage woodcut shows an attack on a castle.

R22 RÉCIT

[Récit véritable de la prise par force de la ville d'Albiac.] Verhael vant' Innemen met ghevvelt van de Stadt van Albiac, gheleghen by Mont'Alban . . . Eerst Ghedruckt den 3. September. T'Hantwerpen, [*sic*] Abraham Verhoeuen, [etc.] 4° pp.8; sig.Mm^4; illus.
P.P.3444(278).
Headed: September, 1621. 123. A translation of 'Récit véritable de la prise par force de la ville d'Albiac près Montauban'. The large titlepage woodcut shows fighting in a burning city.

De REDENEN die de Staten van Bohemen beweecht hebben. 1619. *See* BOHEMIA. States [1-7.11.1619]

REDENEN ende oorsaken. 1616. *See* LANGIUS, Johannes

R23 REDENEN

REDENEN VVaerom die Invvoonders van Valtellina hebben de Wapenen aen genomen teghen die Caluinische Grisons: ENDE Cort Relaes vanden Voort-ghanck des Oorloghe aldaer . . . Ghedruckt int Iaer . . . 1620. 4° pp.8; sig.A^4
P.P.3444.af(92).
Pp.1–6: 'Tot den Leser', printed in roman, refers to the situation of Calvinists in various countries, including Switzerland; pp.6–8 deals with the Valtellina and is described as 'Wt Genoua den 22 Augusti 1620'. Without imprint; published by Abraham Verhoeven at Antwerp as part of his regular news reports. Pt.1 refers to the 'Manifest hier naer volgende', i.e. the item entered under MANIFEST.

REDENEN, waerom men in goede conscientie metten . . . Contra-Remonstranten gheen geestelijcke gemeenschap houden . . . mach. 1620. *See* WTENBOGAERT, Jan

R24 REDEN-RIJCKE

Der Reden-rijcke Rijnschen Helicon/Betreft inden Dorpe van Leyder-Dorp, onder t'woort Liefd' Bliift Sonder Endt, opt beroep der Rhijnlandtsche Dorp-Cameren-ghehouden . . . den 22. Julij. 1616. TOT LEYDEN By Iohannis Sol . . . 1617. 4° sig. A^6A-D^8E^4; illus.

11555.d.46(1).

The dedication signed: H.V. Berch, I. Sol. The repeated illustration shows the device of the Chamber.

Der REDEN-RIJCKEN springh-ader. 1614. *See* NOOTWENDICH vertoogh der alleen-suyverende springh-ader aller kinderen Gods.

R25 REDEN-RYCKERS

Der REDEN-RYCKERS stichtighe tsamenkomste/op t'ontsluyt der Vraghe: VVat tnoodichst' is om d'arme VVeesen t'onderhouvvē? Ghehouden binnen Schiedam/ A° XVJ^c.JJJ. opten vj^{en} July ende de navolghende dagen: Vervatende zeven Spelen . . . Noch eenighe andere wercken/op den zelven zin ende reghel/ voorghestelt by de Roode Roosen/tot SCHIEDAM. (col.) Tot Rotterdam/by Jan van Waesberghe. 4° sig. A-Bb^4; illus., music

11555.d.46(2); 11556.ccc.6(2).

The titlepage woodcut, repeated on sig. A4, shows the emblem of the Chamber. Published in 1603.

REEFSENUS, Jacobus. Tractatio thetica de anima separata. 1607. *See* JACCHAEUS, Gilbertus

R26 REFEREYNEN

REFEREYNEN Ghemaeckt op een vraghe/Of in Christum te gheloven in aller menschen macht is . . . Ende noch op een Reghel, Sy prediken alle in den Naem des Heeren. Tot AMSTERDAM Voor Abraham Huybrechtsz. . . . 1611. (col.) Tot AMSTELREDAM Ghedruckt by Paulus van Ravesteyn . . . 1611. 4° sig. A-F^4

11557.f.13.

The invitation issued by the Chamber 'De Goudsbloem' and signed: Michiel Vlack.

A REFUTATION of Mr. Ioseph Hall his Apologeticall discourse. 1619. *See* COFFIN, Edward

REGISTER van allen den schouten/burghermeesteren/schepenen . . . der stede Amstelredamme. 1613. *See* AMSTERDAM [1613]

REGNERUS Antverpianus. De tribus præceptis. 1602. [Sometimes tentatively attributed to Regnerus Antverpianus.] *See* DE tribus iuris praeceptis.

RELACION de la iornada del exc^{mo} Condestable de Castilla. 1604. *See* FERNANDEZ DE VELASCO, Juan

R27 RELAES

RELAES Ende cort verhael van t'ghene nv lestmael is gheschiedt int comen eñ retireren vanden Leger vanden Pfaltz-Graeff wt het Landt vanden Vorst van Darmstadt eñ Berghstraete. Ghetranslateert wt het Spaens in onse Nederlandtsche spraecke. Eerst Ghedrnckt [*sic*] den 22. Junij. 1622. T'Hantwerpen/By Abraham Verhoeuen/[etc.] 4° pp.7; sig. N^4; illus.

P.P.3444.af(335).

Headed: Iunius, 1622. 90. The titlepage woodcut shows a battle between Christians and Turks, using artillery, under a castle.

R28 RELAES

Relaes van het innemen/van het stercke Slodt Steyen, int Palsgrauen Lant . . . Eerst Ghedruckt den 15. September. T'Hantwerpen, by Abraham Verhoeuen, [etc.] 4° pp.8; sig.Ss[4]; illus.

P.P.3444.af(282).

Headed: September, 1621. 127. With news from Italy and Bohemia. The titlepage woodcut shows a fortified town and marching armies.

Het RELAES van syne Majesteyt in dese leste sessie van t'Parlamente. 1606. *See* JAMES I; King

RELATION authentique, envoyee par les prelats . . . de l'Estat des Indes. 1607. *See* PEREIRA, Francisco; Bishop

A RELATION of some speciall points concerning the state of Holland. 1621. *See* Den COMPAIGNON vanden verre-sienden waerschouwer.

A RELATION of the death, of . . . Troilo Sauelli. 1620. *See* BIONDI, Giuseppe

A RELATION of the triall made before the King of France. 1604. *See* PERSONS, Robert. A treatise of three conversions.

REMONDUS, Franciscus. *See* RAEMOND, François de

Der REMONSTRANTEN kerck-gangh. 1619. *See* GREVINCHOVEN, Nicolaas

Secunda REMONSTRANTIA. 1617. *See* WTENBOGAERT, Jan. Copye van seker vertooch.

REMONSTRANTIE by de zes colloquenten. 1618. *See* WTENBOGAERT, Jan

R29 REMOOVALL

The Remoouall Of certaine Imputations laid vpon the Ministers of Deuon: and Cornwall by one M.T.H. and in them, vpon all other Ministers els-where, refusing to subscribe . . . 1606. 4° pp.66

T.499(5); 111.a.52.

Directed against Thomas Hutton. Without imprint; published by Richard Schilders at Middelburg.

R30 RENNECHERUS, Hermannus

ORATIO BREVIS ET SVCCINCTA, In Laudem Sanctæ & reuerendæ HEBRAEAE LINGVAE . . . habita AB HERMANNO RENNECHERO. LVGDVNI BATAVORVM, Apud Thomam Basson, 1603. 4° pp.37

825.a.9.

A REPLY made unto Mr. Anthony Wotton and Mr. John White. 1612. *See* PIERCY, John

R31 REPLYE

(tp.1) A REPLYE ANSWERING A DEFENCE OF the Sermon, preached at the Consecration of the Bishop of Bathe and Welles, by George Downame . . . In defence of an Answere to the foresayd Sermon Imprinted anno 1609 . . . Imprinted Anno 1613. (tp.2) THE SECOND PARTE OF A REPLY, Answering A DEFENCE OF A SERMON PREACHED AT THE Consecration of the Bishop of Bathe and Welles, by George Downame . . . Imprinted Anno 1614. 4° 2 pt.: pp.293; 164

4135.a.28; 4355.a.29.

Sometimes wrongly attributed to John Rainolds. Without imprint; printed by Giles Thorp at Amsterdam. The copy at 4355.a.29 is imperfect; wanting pt.1 and with its last leaf mutilated, with loss of pagination.

R32 REQUEST

Request Aen de Eedele . . . HEEREN . . . De Staten van Hollant ende West-Vrieslandt. Van weghen de Huysvrouwe ende Kinderen vanden Heere van Olden-Barnevelt . . . Door een Liefhebber der Nederlandtsche Regeeringhe, maer niet des Paus. Ghedruckt . . . 1619. 4° pp.7
T.2422(18).

REQUESTE, Ghepresenteert by die vande Catholijcke Religie in Enghelant aen den . . . Coninck. 1603. *See* PETITION

R33 REQUESTE

REQUESTE Vande Dolerende Kercke van HAERLEM, Aende . . . Magistraet der selver Stadt: MET den Deductie, Ghestelt tot justificatie van d'onder-teeckeninghe/die tot het overleveren van het . . . Request . . . aldaer is gheschiedt . . . Neffens het provisioneel Accoort 't Voorleden jaer aldaer ghemaeckt . . . t'AMSTERDAM, By Marten Jansz. Brandt . . . 1617. 4° pp.15
T.2247(41).

With the large device signed: P-S, i.e. P. or Ph. [C.] van Sichem? and the monogram W I C I Æ or I W C Æ I at the end.

R34 REQUESTE

REQVESTE Vande Studenten in de H. Theologie/ghelevert inde handen van . . . de Heeren Curateuren van de Universiteyt tot Leyden/den derden Octob. Anno 1610. ende den sesthienden des selfden maents inden Hage aende . . . Heeren de Gedeputeerde Staten van Hollant ende West-Vrieslandt. Aengaende de beroepinghe Conrardi Vorstij tot de Professie der H. Theologie inde Vniversiteydt tot Leyden . . . 1611. 4° sig. A-C^4
1568/8453.

RESOLUTION. The first part of the resolution of religion. 1603. *See* BROUGHTON, Richard

RESPONCE ou solution, sur une lettre des Estatz de Hollande. 1602. *See* NETHERLANDS. United Provinces. Staten Generaal [7.6.1602]

R35 RESPONSE

RESPONSE DV ROY au soldat François, qui demande la guerre: & au soldat Espagnol qui demande la paix. Qu'il ne fera ni la guerre ni la paix. (col.) A DOVAY. 1604. 12° pp.47
596.a.22(4).

Without titlepage; the above title as it appears on p.1. Bound with 'Le soldat français' by Pierre l'Hostel and related works, all published in France. The Douai imprint given in the colophon may be false. From the library of John Morris.

A RESTITUTION of decayed intelligence. 1605. *See* VERSTEGAN, Richard

R36 RETORTIE

RETORTIE OFTE VVEDER-STEECK, Ghegheven met de smadelijcke Sift by eenighe bittere Calvinisten . . . in Figuren af-ghebeeldet . . . MET Noch twee bygaende Rijmen . . . uyt-ghegheven/door een Lief-hebber der waere Christelijcke Vryheyt. Ghedruckt . . . 1619. 4° sig. A^4B^1
T.2249(44).

Sometimes attributed to Reinier Telle.

REUCK-APPEL. 1618. *See* TAURINUS, Jacobus

A REVIEW of ten publike disputations. 1604. *See* PERSONS, Robert. A treatise of three conversions.

R37 REYD, Everard van

Trouhertighe vermaninghe aen het vereenichde Nederlandt/om niet te luysteren na eenighe ghestroyde ende versierde vreed-Articulen/nu onlangs wtghegaen ende int gheschrifte van hant tot hant wtghecopyeert/eñ . . . inden Druck ghebracht. Dienende tot eene waerschouwinghe van alle vrome Christenen/ende beminders vande Nederlantsche vryheyt. Beschreven door een lief-hebber der selve vryheyt. Ghedruckt int Jaer . . . M.DC.V. 4° sig.A-C^4; illus.

T.1713(10).

Anonymous and without imprint. *Knuttel* no.1300 suggests Dirck Cornelisz Troost as the printer on the strength of the titlepage woodcut representing the figures of a soldier, a scholar, a woman on a pedestal holding a document, i.e lawful freedom, and another woman with snakes on her head, i.e. discord, and below them the sword 'Slaverni' impaling the cap of freedom. The editor's preface signed: Ireneus Ammonius, pseudonym of Johan van der Sande.

R38 RHAETIAE

RHAETIAE Dat is: 't Lant vande Grisons ende Veltolijn. Waer in te sien is/hare Regieringhe met de opbouwinghe der bloedighe forten met de Justitie over de Verraders des selven Landts/oock de leste Moorden ende Tyrannijen/tot beter bewijs is hier neffens eẽ Landtkaert by-gevoecht. TOT LEYDEN, By Joris Abrahamsz. vander Marsce/1621. Voor Nicolaes Geel-kerck. 4° pp.39: plate; illus., map

C.175.b.16.

The map entitled: Helvetiæ conterminarumqꝫ terrarum antiqua descriptio auctore Phil. Cluverio. The titlepage engraving shows a scene of murder, arson, etc., with the inscription 'Maeckt vrede'.

R39 RIBADENEIRA, Pedro de

ILLVSTRIVM SCRIPTORVM RELIGIONIS SOCIETATIS IESV CATALOGVS: Auctore P. PETRO RIBADENEIRA . . . ANTVERPIÆ, EX OFFICINA PLANTINIANA, Apud Ioannem Moretum. M.DC.VIII. 8° pp.287

4999.a.16.

With indices and other additions by Joannes Moretus. Ownership inscription: Matthias Hornius.

R40 RIBADENEIRA, Pedro de

[Illustrium scriptorum religionis Societatis Iesu catalogus.] CATALOGVS SCRIPTORVM RELIGIONIS SOCIETATIS IESV: Auctore P. PETRO RIBADENEIRA . . . SECVNDA EDITIO . . . locupletior. ANTVERPIÆ, EX OFFICINA PLANTINIANA, Apud Viduam & Filios Io. Moreti. M.DC.XIII. [etc.] 8° pp.380

610.b.7.

With the indices and other additions of Joannes Moretus.

R41 RIBADENEIRA, Pedro de

[Relacion de lo que ha sucedido en el negocio de la canonizacion del bienauenturado P. Ignacio de Loyola.] NARRÉ DE CE QVI S'EST PASSÉ EN LA POVRSVITE DE la Canonisation du Bien-heureux P. IGNACE DE LOYOLA . . . ET DE CE QVE . . . PAPE PAVL V. a ordonné l'an 1609. touchant sa beatification. Traduit de l'Espagnol du R. Pere PIERRE DE RIBADENEYRA . . . Par . . . ANTOINE BALINGHEM . . . A TOVRNAY, Chez NICOLAS LAVRENT . . . 1610. [etc.] (col.) A TOVRNAY, De l'Imprimerie de CHARLES MARTIN, & de IOSEPH DV HAMEL . . . M.DC.X. 12° pp.139

859.a.14; 4824.b.42.

With 'La lettre du P. Antoine Laubegeois, escrite de Coimbre . . . au R. P. François Fleron'. The copy at 4824.b.42 with the ownership inscription: Carm. Discalc. Conv. Antw.

R42 RIBADENEIRA, Pedro de
[Vida del P. Ignacio de Loyola.] THE LIFE OF B. FATHER IGNATIVS OF LOYOLA . . . Translated out of Spanish into English, by W.M. . . . M.DC.XVI. 8° pp.358
G.14364.
The author named in the dedication. Translated anonymously by Michael Walpole. Without imprint; published by the English College press at St. Omer. Ownership inscription: George Wrenn.

R43 RIBADENEIRA, Pedro de
[Vida del P. Ignacio de Loyola.] VITA B.P. IGNATII . . . Nuper à R. P Petro Ribadeneira . . . Hispanicè conscripta, Et ab eodem rebus memorabilibus illustribusque miraculis ita locupletata, vt alia ab illa priore . . . videri possit; A P. GASPARE QVARTEMONT . . . latiné conuersa. IPRIS FLANDRORVM, Apud FRANCISCVM BELLETVN [*sic*], M.DC.XII. [etc.] (col.) IPRIS, EX TYPOGRAPHIA FRNCISCI BELLETI M.DC.XII. 12° pp.199
859.a.8(2).
Pp.193, 194 are slightly mutilated.

R44 RIBADENEIRA, Pedro de
[Vida del P. Ignacio de Loyola. Pictorial illustrations] VITA BEATI PATRIS IGNATII LOYOLÆ . . . AD VIVVM EXPRESSA EX EA QVAM P. PETRVS RIBADENEYRA . . . SCRIPSIT: DEINDE MADRITI PINGI, POSTEA IN ÆS INCIDI ET NVNC DEMVM TYPIS EXCVDI CVRAVIT ANTVERPIÆ . . . M.DC.X. fol. pl.15; ports.
C.128.h.4.
From the Galle workshop at Antwerp: the titlepage and pl.2, 5, 10 signed: Corn. Galle sculpsit; pl.1, 6 signed: Theodorus Gallæus fecit et excudit; pl.3, 7, 14 signed: Adrianus Collaert fecit; pl.4, 8, 9, 11, 13 signed: C. de Mallery fecit, et ex.; pl.15 signed: Ioan. Collaert sculp.; pl.12, a view of Rome, unsigned. All engravings are double-spread, without text. Ownership inscription: Wentworth House Library; with the exlibris of William Charles de Meuron, Earl Fitzwilliam.

RIBERA, Francisco de. R. P. Francisci Riberae . . . in librum Duodecim Prophetarum commentarii. 1612. *See* BIBLE. Minor Prophets. Latin

R45 RIBERA, Francisco de
[In sacram . . . Apocalypsim commentarii.] FRANCISCI RIBERÆ . . . De templo, & de iis quæ ad templum pertinent, libri quinque . . . ANTVERPIÆ, Apud Martinum Nutium . . . M.DC.II. 8° pp.446
481.a.26.
Originally published as pt.4 of Ribera's 'In sacram . . . Apocalypsim commentarii'.

R46 RIBERA, Francisco de
[La vida de la Madre Teresa de Jesus.] (tp.1) HET LEVEN DER H. MOEDER TERESE VAN IESVS FVNDATERSE VANDE BARVOETSCHE CARMELITEN ENDE CARMELITESSEN. DOOR P. FRANCOIS VAN RIBERA . . . Het eerste deel. T'HANDTVVERPEN BY IOACH. TROGNESIVS. M.DC.XX.
(tp.2 = leaf ⋆1 between pp.463/464) HET LEVEN DER H. MOEDER TERESE VAN IESVS . . . DOOR P. FRANCOIS VAN RIBERA . . . Het tvveede deel. T'HANDTVVERPEN BY IOACH. TROGNESIVS. M.DC.XX. 8° pp.870; illus., port.
4823.bbb.6.
With a dedication to Isabella in Spanish by Trognesius, who has been thought to be the translator. The engraved portrait of St. Theresa unsigned. Ownership inscription: Theresiæ van Peteghem.

R47 RICCI, Bartholomaeus; Jesuit
TRIVMPHVS IESV CHRISTI CRVCIFIXI per R. P. Bartholomæū Riccium . . . ANTVERPIÆ Adrianus Collaert figuras sculpsit . . . Narrationem Historicam, qua TRIVMPHVS

illustratur, typis Plantinianis excudit Ioannes Moretus. M.DC.VIII. (col.) ANTVERPIÆ, EX OFFICINA PLANTINIANA, Apud Ioannem Moretum. M.DC.VIII. 8° ff.70
554.b.43.
Each leaf bears an engraving and is faced by a page of narrative and contemplative text. The engraved titlepage bears the manuscript inscription: Car Collaert ex.

R48 RICCI, Matteo; Jesuit
[Annua della Cina.] HISTOIRE DE L'EXPEDITION CHRESTIENNE AV ROYAVME DE LA CHINE ENTREPRINSE PAR LES PERES DE LA COMPAGNIE DE IESVS . . . TIREE DES MEMOIRES DV R. P. MATTHIEV RICCI . . . par le R. P. NICOLAS TRIGAVLT . . . ET NOVVELLEMENT TRADVITE EN FRANCOIS PAR LE S.D.F. DE RIQVEBOURG-TRIGAVLT. A LILLE, De l'Imprimerie de PIERRE DE RACHE . . . 1617. [etc.] (col.) A LILLE, De l'Imprimerie de PIERRE DE RACHE . . . M.DC.XVII. 4° pp.559
1369.d.27.
Translated from the Latin version of Nicolas Trigault, 'De Christiana expeditione apud Sinas'.

R49 RICHEOME, Louis
[Consolation envoyée à la Royne mère du Roy.] IVSTA ANNIVERSARIA HENRICO MAGNO SEV CONSOLATIO AD REGINAM GALLIÆ Regis matrem regnique moderatricem. IN FVNESTAM MORTEM HENRICI IV. . . . Ex Gallico R. P. Richeomij . . . ANTVERPIÆ, Ex Officina HIERONYMI VERDVSSI, M.DC.XIII. [etc.] 4° pp.74; illus., port.
10660.ff.23.
The translator's dedicatory letter to Richeome signed: Nicolaus Caussinus. The titlepage engraving shows the effigy of Henry IV on his tomb.

R50 RICHEOME, Louis
LE PANTHEON HVGVENOT decouuert et ruiné contre l'Aucteur de l'Idolatrie papistique Ministre de Vauuert, cy deuant d'Aigues:mortes . . . Par Louis Richeome . . . A VALENCHIENNE Chez Iean Veruliet 1610. [etc.] 8° pp.328
850.d.11.
A reply to the work by Jean Basilion, itself a reply to Richeome's 'L'idolatrie huguenote'. The titlepage is engraved, signed: Martinus Bas. Printed by Guillaume de la Rivière at Arras.

R51 RICHER, Edmond; Syndic de la Faculté de Théologie de Paris
[Libellus de ecclesiastica et politica potestate.] VANDE KERCKELICKE ENDE POLITIICKE MACHT. De Kercke is een Monarcklicke Politie . . . beleyt door een Aristocratijcksche Regieringhe . . . VVt het Francoys int Nederduytsch overgheset. IN S'GRAVEN-HAGHE, By Hillebrant Jacobsz . . . 1612. 4° pp.21
T.2242(8).
Anonymous.

RIDDERUS, Jacobus. Theses logicae. 1614. *See* BAERLE, Caspar van

The RIGHT and jurisdiction of the prelate. 1617; 1621. *See* KELLISON, Matthew

R52 RIJNLAND. Hoogheemraadschap
Keuren ende Ordonnantien vant Heemraetschap van Rijnlandt/ende den ghevolghe. Ghemaeckt by Dijckgrave ende Hogheheemraden des selfs Lants. TOT LEYDEN, Ghedruckt ten bevele vande voornomde Dijckgrave/ende Hogheheemraden/by Jan Paedts Jacobszoon . . . 1610. 4° 87; illus.
1560/3688.
The titlepage engraving shows the arms of 'Wilhelmus Rex Romanorum Anno MCCLV Die v. Octob.', with dolphins, shells, etc., signed: W.S., i.e. Willem van Swanenburgh.

R53 RIMONTE, Pietro

(tp.1) MISSAE SEX IV. V. ET VI. VOCVM AVCTORE PETRO RIMONTE . . . CANTVS. ANTVERPIÆ Apud Petrum Phalesium. M.DCIV.

(tp.2) MISSAE SEX . . . AVCTORE PETRO RIMONTE . . . ALTVS. ANTVERPIÆ Apud Petrum Phalesium. M.DCIV.

(tp.3) MISSAE SEX . . . AVCTORE PETRO RIMONTE . . . TENOR. ANTVERPIÆ Apud Petrum Phalesium. M.DCIV.

(tp.4) MISSAE SEX . . . AVCTORE PETRO RIMONTE . . . BASSVS. ANTVERPIÆ Apud Petrum Phalesium. M.DCIV.

(tp.5) MISSAE SEX . . . AVCTORE PETRO RIMONTE . . . QVINTVS. ANTVERPIÆ Apud Petrum Phalesium. M.DCIV.

(tp.6) MISSAE SEX . . . AVCTORE PETRO RIMONTE . . . SEXTVS. ANTVERPIÆ Apud Petrum Phalesium. M.DCIV. 4° 6 pt.: ff.25; 26; 24; 24; 27; 26

Music D.218; Music D.218a.

The copy at Music D.218a consists of the Bassus part only.

RIO, Martinus Antonius del. *See* DEL RIO, Martinus Antonius

R54 RIVET, André

CRITICI SACRI SPECIMEN. Hoc est, CENSVRÆ DOCTORVM tam ex Orthodoxis quam ex Pontificiis, IN SCRIPTA QVÆ PATRIBUS PLERISQUE . . . vel affinxit incogitantia, vel supposuit impostura: Collectæ . . . studio & operâ ANDREÆ RIVETI . . . DORDRECHTI, Apud IOHANNEM BEREWOUT . . . M.DC.XIX. 8° pp.504

845.a.8.

R55 RIVET, André

ORATIO DE Bono Pacis & Concordiæ in Ecclesia. HABITA AB ANDREA RIVETO . . . Jn Auditorio Theologico . . . 12. Octob. 1620. LVGDVNI BATAVORVM, Apud ISAACVM ELZEVIRIVM . . . M D CXX. 4° pp.46

491.b.33; 700.h.7(5).

In the copy at 491.b.33 the first letter of the title is badly printed.

R56 RIVET, André

[Sommaire et abbregé des controverses de nostre temps.] SCHAT-BOECK Der Roomscher dwalinghen . . . Al waer Het gevoelen ende redenen vande Papisten trouwelijck werden voor-ghesteldt uyt den Catechismus van Guilliam Baile . . . Ende wederom. De belijdenisse vande Gereformeerde Kercke . . . wort verandtwoort/door . . . Andreas Rivet . . Over-geset door Godefridum Vdemans . . . TOT MIDDELBVRCH, By Symon Moulert . . . 1617. 4° pp.78 [821]

3925.c.77.

The title of Guillaume Baile's book, published in 1607, is 'Catéchisme et abbrege des controverses de nostre temps'. The French edition of Rivet's refutation was published in 1608.

RIVETUS, Guilielmus. Theses theologicae, de foederibus, & Testamentis divinis. 1602. *See* DU JON, François; the Elder

R57 RIVIUS, Gaugericus

IVSTI LIPSI PRINCIPATVS LITTERARIVS, à GAVGERICO RIVIO . . . scriptus ad ritum priscum. ANTVERPIAE, EX OFFICINA PLANTINIANA, Apud Ioannem Moretum. M.DC.VII. 4° pp.30

631.k.4(9).

ROBBERTSEN, Robbert. *See* LE CANU, Robbert Robbertsen

ROBBERTSZ, Robbert. *See* LE CANU, Robbert Robbertsen

R58 ROBERT Bellarmino; Saint

APOLOGIA ROBERTI . . . BELLARMINI, PRO RESPONSIONE SVA AD LIBRVM IACOBI MAGNÆ BRITANNIÆ REGIS, CVIVS TITVLVS EST, Triplici nodo, triplex cuneus, IN QVA APOLOGIA refellitur Præfatio Monitoria Regis eiusdem. EDITIO ALTERA. ROMÆ, Apud Bartholomæum Zannettum. M.DC.X. [etc.] 4° pp.220
860.c.28(3); 860.f.14(2).

The imprint is false; printed by the English College press at St. Omer.

R59 ROBERT Bellarmino; Saint

DE ÆTERNA FELICITATE SANCTORVM LIBRI QVINQVE . . . AVCTORE ROBERTO Card. BELLARMINO . . . ANTVERPIÆ, EX OFFICINA PLANTINIANA, Apud Balthasarem & Ioannem Moretos. M.DC.XVI. 8° pp.298
4257.aaa.3.

Ownership inscriptions: Michaël Ghyssens; J. W. Newett.

R60 ROBERT Bellarmino; Saint

[De ascensione mentis.] A MOST LEARNED AND PIOVS TREATISE, full of Diuine and Humane Philosophy, framing a Ladder, WHERBY OVR MINDES May Ascend to God . . . Written in Latine by . . . Cardinal Bellarmine . . . 1615. Translated into English, By T. B. Gent . . . Printed at Douay . . . 1616. 12° pp.575
Cup.403.l.4.

Translated by Francis Young. The imprint is false; printed secretly in England.

R61 ROBERT Bellarmino; Saint

DE GEMITV COLVMBÆ, siue De bono lacrymarum, LIBRI TRES: Auctore ROBERTO BELLARMINO . . . ANTVERPIÆ, EX OFFICINA PLANTINIANA, Apud Balthasarem & Ioannem Moretos. M.DC.XVII. (col.) ANTVERPIÆ, EX OFFICINA PLANTINIANA, Apud Balthasarem & Ioannem Moretos. M.DC.XVII. 8° pp.346
860.f.16.

R62 ROBERT Bellarmino; Saint

[Dichiarazione più copiosa della dottrina christiana. English] [An ample] DECLARATION OF THE CHRISTIAN DOCTRINE. COMPOSED IN ITAlian, by . . . Card. BELLARMIN. &c. Translated into English, by Richard Hadock . . . Printed at Dovvay, by Laurence Kellam. 1605. 12° pp.302
Cup.403.a.2.

The imprint is false; printed secretly in England. The titlepage is mutilated. Ownership inscription: Robert Simpson.

R63 ROBERT Bellarmino; Saint

[Dichiarazione più copiosa della dottrina christiana. English] AN AMPLE DECLARATION OF THE CHRISTIAN DOCTRIN. Composed in Italian by . . . Card. Bellarmin. &c. Translated into English by R. A. Doctor of Diuinitie. AT DOVAY, 1617. By IOHN HEIGHAM [etc.] 12° pp.406
C.122.a.46.

Translated by Richard Hadock. Printed by Pierre Auroi at Douai. With a manuscript index said in a manuscript note signed: J. B. W. to be in the handwriting of the Rev. John Pointer. With the torn bookplate of Sir John Bicke[l] . . . at W[itham?].

R64 ROBERT Bellarmino; Saint

[Dichiarazione più copiosa della dottrina christiana. Welsh] EGLVRHAD HELAETHLAWN O'R ATHRAWAETH GRISTNOGAVVL. A gyfansodhwyd y tro cyntaf yn Italaeg, trwy waith yr Ardherchoccaf a'r Hybarchaf Gardinal RHOBERT BELLARMIN . . . Ag

o'r Italaeg a gymreigwyd er budh Yspridol i'r Cymru, drwy . . . V.R. . . . M.DC.XVIII. 8° pp.348
C.26.h.10; 1018.h.27.

The pagination omits p.288. Without imprint; printed by the English College press at St. Omer. The copy at 1018.h.27 is imperfect; wanting p.348 and the errata. With an interlined manuscript English translation in that copy.

R65 ROBERT Bellarmino; Saint
[Disputationes de controversiis Christianae fidei. Selections] (tp.1) ROBERTI BELLARMINI . . . Solida Christianæ Fidei DEMONSTRATIO. OPERA . . . BALDVINI IVNII . . . Ex eius operibus controuersiarum desumpta. ANTVERPIÆ, Sumptibus Hæredum MARTINI NVTII. M.DC.XI. [etc.]
(tp.2=p.393) ROBERTI BELLARMINI . . . Fundamenti Christianæ Fidei, PARS SECVNDA. OPERA . . . BALDVINI IVNII . . . Ex controuersijs desumpta. ANTVERPIAE, Sumptibus Hæredum MARTINI NVTII. M.DC.XI. [etc.]
(tp.3=p.669) ROBERTI BELLARMINI . . . Fundamenti Christianæ Fidei, PARS TERTIA. OPERA . . . BALDVINI IVNII . . . Ex controuersijs desumpta. ANTVERPIAE, Sumptibus Hæredum MARTINI NVTII. M.DC.XI. [etc.] (col.) ANTVERPIÆ, Excudebat Andreas Bacx, Sumptibus Hæredum Martini Nutij. 1611. 4° pp.942
1509/3301.

The first titlepage is engraved. Ownership inscriptions: Wm Constable; J. H. Pavillion.

R66 ROBERT Bellarmino; Saint
INSTITVTIONES LINGVÆ HEBRAICÆ, EX OPTIMO QVOQVE AVCTORE COLLECTÆ, Et ad quantam maximam fieri potuit breuitatem . . . reuocatæ: vnà cum exercitatione Grammatica in Psalmum XXXIII. ROBERTO BELLARMINO . . . Auctore. Accessit in hac noua editione commodior . . . rerum . . . distinctio. ANTVERPIÆ, EX OFFICINA PLANTINIANA, Apud Ioannem Moretum. M.DC.VI. [etc.] 8° pp.206
621.d.17.

R67 ROBERT Bellarmino; Saint
INSTITVTIONES LINGVÆ HEBRAICÆ . . . vnà cum Exercitatione Grammatica in Psalmum XXXIII. AVCTORE ROBERTO BELLARMINO . . . Accessit in hac noua editione commodior . . . rerum . . . distinctio. ANTVERPIÆ, EX OFFICINA PLANTINIANA, Apud Viduam & Filios Ioannis Moreti. M.DC.XVI. 8° pp.206
1507/311.

With a bookplate reading: Bib. S^i. F^i. X^ii. Hereford:

R68 ROBERT Bellarmino, Saint
MATTHÆI TORTI . . . RESPONSIO AD LIBRVM INSCRIPTVM, Triplici nodo, triplex cuneus, SIVE Apologia pro Iuramento fidelitatis: aduersus duo Breuia Papæ PAVLI V. & recentes litteras CARDINALIS BELLARMINI AD GEORGIVM BLACVELLIVM Angliæ Archipresbyterum . . . EDITIO ALTERA . . . 1608. 4° pp.139
860.c.28(2).

Pseudonymous and without imprint; printed by the English College press at St. Omer.

ROBERT Bellarmino; Saint. A most learned and pious treatise. 1616. *See* above: De ascensione mentis.

R69 ROBERTI, Johannes
CVRATIONIS MAGNETICÆ, & VNGVENTI ARMARII MAGICA IMPOSTVRA clarè demonstrata à IOHANNE ROBERTI . . . MODESTA RESPONSIO Ad perniciosam Disputationem Io. BAPTISTÆ ab HELMONT . . . contra eumdem Roberti acerbè conscriptam. LVXEMBVRGI Excudebat Hubertus Reuland . . . 1621. 8° pp.100
1033.e.26.

Ownership inscription: Joseph Fenton.

R70 ROBERTI, Johannes

GOCLENIVS HEAVTONTIMORVMENOS: id est, CVRATIONIS MAGNETICÆ, & VNGVENTI ARMARII RVINA. IPSO RODOLPHO GOCLENIO Iuniore, nuper Parente, & Patrono; nunc Cum SIGILLIS, & CHARACTERIB. Magicis, vltro PRORVENTE, ET PRAECIPITANTE. IOHAN. ROBERTI . . . DESCRIPSIT. ET GOCLENII MAGNETICAM SYNARTHROSIN meram Αναρθρωσιν esse ostendit . . . LVXEMBVRGI Excudebat HVBERTVS REVLANDT . . . M.DC.XVIII. 8° pp.356

1034.e.10(1).

R71 ROBERTI, Johannes

HISTORIA S. HVBERTI . . . Conscripta A IOHANNE ROBERTI . . . LVXEMBVRGI, Excudebat HVBERTVS REVLANDT. Sumtibus Monasterij S. HVBERTI in Arduennâ . . . XXI. [etc.] 4° pp.576; illus.

205.c.28(1); 486.c.13.

Pp.513-530: De nomine, Hubertus . . . Epistola R. P. Arnoldi a Boecop . . . ad P. Iohannem Roberti. On p.576 an advertisement for a French edition which was not published. The illustrations are woodcuts. The copy at 486.c.13 is imperfect; wanting all after p.332.

R72 ROBERTI, Johannes

METAMORPHOSIS MAGNETICA CALVINO-GOCLENIANA, QVA CALVINO-DOGMATISTÆ, ET IN PRIMIS D. RODOLPHVS GOCLENIVS, Stupendo MAGNETISMO, in GIEZITAS migrant. ET ALIA MYSTERIA MAGNETICA MIRIFICISSIMA: Vi, & nouâ . . . arte ipsius D. GOCLENII. Descripta à R. P. IOHANNE ROBERTI . . . Ex occasione intexuntur CONSIDERATIONES aliquot ad Marcum Antonium de Dominis . . . super Consilio . . . Profectionis . . . suæ. LEODII, Ex Officina IOANNIS OUVVERX . . . M.DC.XVIII. 8° pp.140

860.d.26.

R73 ROBINSON, John; Pastor at Leiden

APOLOGIA IVSTA, ET NECESSARIA QVORVNDAM Christianorum, æque contumeliose ac communiter dictorum Brownistarum sive Barowistarum. per IOHANNEM ROBINSONVM . . . 1619. 8° pp.96

1607/2847(1).

Without imprint; the attribution once made to the press of William Brewster at Leiden is rejected in *Harris & Jones (1)* no.20† where that of Giles Thorp at Amsterdam is tentatively suggested.

R74 ROBINSON, John; Pastor at Leiden

A IVSTIFICATION OF SEPARATION from the Church of England. Against Mr. Richard Bernard his invective, INTITVLED: The Separatists schisme. By Iohn Robinson . . . 1610. 4° pp.479 [483]

4135.b.71.

Without imprint; printed by Giles Thorp at Amsterdam. Ownership inscription: ex lib Cosmi Alisonii.

R75 ROBINSON, John; Pastor at Leiden

A MANVMISSION TO A MANVDVCTION, OR ANSWER TO A LETTER INFERRING PUBlique communion in the parrish assemblies upon private with godly persons there . . . By Iohn Robinson . . . 1615. 4° pp.24

C.53.c.43.

A reply to William Bradshaw's 'A manudiction for Mr. Robinson'. Without imprint; printed by Giles Thorp at Amsterdam. Ownership inscription: Nich[s] Mint; R. W. D.

R76 ROBINSON, John; Pastor at Leiden

Of Religious COMMVNION Private, & Publique. With the silenceing of the clamours raysed by M[r] Thomas Helvvisse against our reteyning the Baptism receaved in

Engl: & administering of Bapt: vnto Infants. As also a Survey of the confession of fayth published in certayn Conclusions by the remaynders of Mr. Smithes company . . . By IOHN ROBINSON. Printed . . . 1614. 4° pp.131
4323.b.69.

Without imprint. Sometimes tentatively assigned to an unidentified printer at Amsterdam, but on the strength of the device and other typographical material clearly from the press of Henrick van Haestens at Leiden. With manuscript notes in English. Ownership inscription: Randall Thickins.

R77 RODENBURGH, Theodore

[Alexander.] Treur-bly-eynde-spel Van ALEXANDER. In vier en veertich uuren gerymt . . . t'AMSTERDAM, Voor Jan Evertsz. Cloppenburch . . . 1618. (col.) t'AMSTERDAM, Ghedruckt by Paulus van Ravesteyn . . . 1618. 4° pp.77; illus.
11755.bb.83(9).

With Rodenburgh's 'Nobilitas' emblem in woodcut on the titlepage and the signature: Theodore Rodenburgh under the dedication. With another woodcut entitled 'In lieft bloeiiende 1528' on the titlepage verso.

R78 RODENBURGH, Theodore

[Amstels Eglentier.] Tweede deel. AMSTELS EGLENTIER. GERYMT Door . . . THEODORE RODENBVRG . . . T'AMSTELREDAM, Ghedruckt by Paulus van Ravesteyn, 1618. 4° 2 unsigned leaves; illus.
11755.bb.83(10).

A fragment, consisting of the titlepage and one preliminary leaf bearing a poem entitled 'Poësis Amstelo-Belgica . . . Theodoro Rodenburgio . . . poëtae suo', signed: I. F. With Rodenburgh's 'Nobilitas' emblem in woodcut on the titlepage.

RODENBURGH, Theodore. Anna Rodenburghs trouwen Batavier. 1617. *See* GUARINI, Giovanni Battista

R79 RODENBURGH, Theodore

CASANDRA Hertoginne van Borgonie/EN KAREL BALDEUS Treur eu [*sic*] Bly-eynde-Spel . . . t'AMSTERDAM, Voor Cornelis Lodewijcksz. vander Plasse . . . 1617. 4° sig.A^2A-$I^4$$K^2$; illus.
11755.bb.83(3).

With Rodenburgh's 'Nobilitas' emblem as titlepage woodcut and the dedication signed: Chi sara sara, the motto of Theodore Rodenburgh. Adapted from Lope de Vega's 'El perseguido'.

R80 RODENBURGH, Theodore

EGLENTIERS Nieuwe-Jaers-Gift/IN LIEFD BLOEYENDE OP 'T IAER M.DC.XIX. t'AMSTELREDAM, Voor Nicolaes Ellertsen Verbergh . . . 1619. 4° sig.AB^4; illus.
11556.cc.77.

Anonymous, but with Rodenburgh's 'Nobilitas' emblem, signed: CVS, i.e. Christoffel van Sichem, as titlepage woodcut. With the oval device of the Chamber in woodcut on the titlepage verso. Printed by Paulus van Ravesteyn.

R81 RODENBURGH, Theodore

[Eglentiers nieuwe-jaers-gift . . . M.DC.XIX.] OP DE COMEET Oft Ster met de Staert EGLENTIERS Nieuwe-Jaers-gift/IN LIEFD BLOEYENDE OP 'T IAER M.DC.XIX. T'AMSTELREDAM, Voor Nicolaus Ellertsz. Verbergh . . . 1619. 4° sig.AB^4; illus.
T.2423(8).

Anonymous, but with Rodenburgh's 'Nobilitas' emblem as titlepage woodcut, signed CVS, i.e. Christoffel van Sichem. Printed by Paulus van Ravesteyn. Another issue of the preceding.

R82 RODENBURGH, Theodore

EGLENTIERS POËTENS Borst-weringh. DOOR THEODORE RODENBVRGH . . . T'AMSTERDAM, Ghedruckt by Paulus van Ravesteyn, Voor Ian Evertsz. Cloppenburgh, 1619. 4° pp.440: plate; illus.

C.108.d.28.

Poems and plays in Dutch, with occasional Latin captions. With numerous laudatory poems. With Rodenburgh's 'Nobilitas' emblem, signed: CVS, i.e. Christoffel van Sichem, on the titlepage. The plate shows a portrait of Prince Maurice, dated 1616. Printed with much use of civilité. Bound in vellum, gold-tooled, cut, and decorated on all the edges.

R83 RODENBURGH, Theodore

Hertoginne CELIA En Grave PROSPERO Bly-eynde-spel . . . t'AMSTERDAM, Voor Jacob Pietersz. Wachter . . . M.DC.XVII. 4° sig.⋆A-F⁴; illus.

11755.b.81(1).

Anonymous, but with Rodenburgh's 'Nobilitas' emblem in woodcut on the titlepage and his motto 'Chi sara sara' as signature of the dedication. Adapted from Lope de Vega's 'El molino'. Printed by Paulus van Ravesteyn.

R84 RODENBURGH, Theodore

Jalourse STVDENTIN BLY-EYNDE-SPEL . . . t'Amstelredam, Voor Willem Jansz. Stam . . . 1617. (col.) t'Amstelredam, By Nicolaes Biestkens . . . 1617. 4° sig.A-G⁴; illus.

11755.bb.83(5).

Anonymous, but with Rodenburgh's 'Nobilitas' emblem in woodcut on the titlepage and his motto 'Chi sara sara' as signature of the dedication. Adapted from Lope de Vega's 'La escolástica zelosa'.

R85 RODENBURGH, Theodore

[Jalourse studentin.] IALOERSCHE STVDENTEN [*sic*] . . . TOT LEYDEN, By Bartholomeeus Jacobsz. de Fries . . . 1617. 4° sig.A-G⁴; illus.

11755.bb.83(6).

Anonymous, but with Rodenburgh's 'Nobilitas' emblem engraved on the titlepage. Another edition of the preceding, without the dedication.

R86 RODENBURGH, Theodore

(tp.1) KEYSER OTTO DEN DERDEN, EN GALDRADA BLY-EYNDE-SPEL. HET EERSTE DEEL . . . tAMSTELREDAM. By Porcevant Morgan Boeckdrucker . . . 1616.

(tp.2) KEYSER OTTO Den derden/En GALDRADA . . . Tvveede deel . . . tAmsterdam, Voor Abraham de Coningh . . . 1617. (col.2) t'Amsterdam, By Nicolaes Biestkens . . . 1617.

(tp.3) KEYSER OTTO Den derden/En GALDRADA . . . Derde deel . . . t'Amsterdam, By Nicolaes Biestkens . . . 1617. (col.3) T'AMSTERDAM, By Nicolaes Biestkens . . . M.DC.XVIII. 4° 3 pt.: sig.A-I⁴; A-F⁴; A-E⁴; illus.

11755.bb.83(4).

Anonymous, but with Rodenburgh's 'Nobilitas' emblem in different woodcuts on the titlepages. With other, astrological, illustrations. Adapted from Lope de Vega's 'La mayor victoria', itself derived from Bandello. Part 1 has no colophon.

R87 RODENBURGH, Theodore

[Melibéa.] (tp.1) Eerste deel/MELIBÉA Treur-bly-eynde-spel. t'AMSTELREDAM, Voor Jan Evertsz. Cloppenburch . . . 1618. (col.1) 'TAMSTELREDAM, Ghedruckt by Paulus van Ravesteyn . . . 1617.

(tp.2) Tweede deel MELIBÉA . . . 'TAMSTELREDAM, Voor Jan Evertsz. Cloppenburch . . . 1617. (col.2) t'AMSTELREDAM, Ghedruckt by Paulus van Ravesteyn . . . 1618.

(tp.3) Derde deel MELIBÉA . . . ț'AMSTELREDAM, Voor Jan Evertsz. Cloppenburch . . . 1617. (col.3) 'TAMSTERDAM, Ghedruckt by Paulus van Ravesteyn . . . 1618. 4° 3 pt.: sig.1,★★,★★, A-H4; A-H4; A-G4; illus.
11755.bb.81(2).

The author named in laudatory poems, which are in Latin, Italian, Spanish, French, Portuguese, English and are matched by interludes in the text in these languages, and with his 'Nobilitas' emblem in woodcut on the titlepages. With the device of the Chamber 'De Eglentier' in woodcut on sig.★★1r.

RODENBURGH, Theodore. 't Quaedt syn meester loondt. 1618. *See* AGUILAR, Gaspar

R88 RODENBURGH, Theordore

RODOMONT EN ISABELLA Treur-spel . . . t'AMSTERDAM, Voor Jan Evertsz. Cloppenburch . . . 1618. (col.) t'AMSTERDAM, Ghedruckt by Paulus van Ravesteyn . . . 1618. 4° pp.70; illus.
11755.bb.83(2).

The dedication signed: Theodore Rodenburgh. With his 'Nobilitas' emblem in woodcut on the titlepage and the device of the Chamber 'In lieft bloeiende. 1528' in woodcut on sig.★3r. It has been suggested that this play is adapted from Lope de Vega's lost 'Zelos de Rodamonte'.

RODENBURGH, Theodore. Treur-bly-eynde-spel, vande trouwe liefd van Cypriaen en Orania. 1618. *See* GUARINI, Giovanni Battista. Il pastor fido.

RODENBURGH, Theodore. Wraeck-gierigers treurspel. 1618. *See* TOURNEUR, Cyril

RODERICUS, Emanuel. *See* RODRIGUEZ, Manuel; Franciscan

RODOMONT en Isabella. 1618. RODENBURGH, Theodore

R89 RODRIGUES GIRAÕ, Joaõ

LITTERÆ IAPONICÆ ANNI M.DC.VI. CHINENSES ANNI M.DC.VI. & M.DC.VII. Illæ à R. P. IOANNE RODRIGVEZ, hæ à R. P. MATTHÆO RICCI . . . transmissæ ad . . . CLAVDIVM AQVAVIVAM . . . Latinè redditæ à Rhetoribus Collegij Soc. IESV Antuerpie. ANTVERPIÆ, EX OFFICINA PLANTINIANA, Apud Viduam & Filios Io. Moreti. M.DC.XI. 12° pp.201
867.e.27; 4767.b.39.

Translated under the direction of Hermannus Hugo. With a dedication by Jacobus de Cater on the controversy with Leiden and with a laudatory poem by him. The copy at 4767.b.39 is imperfect; wanting the colophon which consists of a device without text.

R90 RODRIGUES GIRAÕ, Joaõ

[Lettera annua del Giappone.] Litteræ Iaponicæ A R. P. PROVINCIALI SOCIETATIS IESV IN IAPONE, AD . . . CLAVDIVM AQVAVIVA . . . nuperrimè transmissæ. Anno s.1609. & 1610. mense Martio . . . Vertit ex Italico Romæ impresso in Latinum sermonem P. PETRVS HALLOIX . . . DVACI, Typis BALTAZARIS BELLERI . . . M.DC.XII. 12° pp.136
866.a.8.

The title describes Joaõ Rodrigues Giraõ by his office.

R91 RODRIGUES GIRAÕ, Joaõ

[Lettera annua del Giappone.] LITTERÆ IAPONICÆ ANNORVM M.DC.IX. ET X. AD . . . CLAVDIVM AQVAVIVAM . . . GENERALEM PRÆPOSITVM SOCIETATIS IESV A R.P. Prouinciali eiusdem in IAPONE Societ. missæ. Ex Italicis Latinæ factæ ab AND. SCHOTTO . . . ANTVERPIÆ, Apud PETRVM & IOANNEM BELLEROS. M.DC.XV. [etc.] 8° pp.111
867.f.5(1).

Signed: Ioannes Rodrigues Girand. Ownership inscription: Isaacus Gruterus.

R92 RODRIGUES GIRAÕ, Joaõ
[Relationi della gloriosa morte di nove Christiani Giaponesi.] LA GLORIEVSE MORT DE NEVF CHRESTIENS IAPPONOIS MARTYRIZEZ POVR LA FOY CATHOLIQVE AVX ROYAVMES DE FINGO, SASSVMA, ET FIRANDO: Envoyée du Iapon l'an 1609. & 1610 au mois de Mars, par le R.P. PROVINCIAL de la Societé de IESVS, au R.P. CLAVDE AQVAVIVA . . . A DOVAY, De l'Imprimerie de PIERRE AVROY . . . 1612. 8° pp.160
4766.a.7.
The title describes Joaõ Rodrigues Giraõ by his office. The dedication signed: I.F.D.S. Ownership inscription: Domus Prob. Soc. Jesu. Torn. Cas.Inf.

R93 RODRIGUEZ, Manuel; Franciscan
(tp.1) QVÆSTIONES REGVLARES ET CANONICÆ . . . Autore P.F. EMANVELE RODERICO . . . TOMVS PRIMVS, Nunc de nouo per . . . Autorem recognitus; correctus; & additus . . . Editio vltima prioribus . . . auctior, & distinctior. ANTVERPIÆ, Apud Petrum & Ioannem Belleros. M.DC.xvj. [etc.]
(tp.2) QVÆSTIONES REGVLARES ET CANONICÆ . . . Autore P.F. EMANVELE RODERICO . . . TOMVS SECVNDVS . . . Editio vltima . . . ANTVERPIÆ, Apud Petrum & Ioannem Belleros. M.DC.xvj. [etc.]
(tp.3) QVÆSTIONES REGVLARES ET CANONICÆ . . . Autore P.F. EMANVELE RODERICO . . . TOMVS TERTIVS . . . Editio vltima . . . ANTVERPIÆ, Apud Petrum & Ioannem Belleros. M.DC.xvj. [etc.]
(tp.4) PRAXIS CRIMINALIS REGVLARIVM, SÆCVLARIVMQVE OMNIVM ABSOLVTISSIMA ex antiquioribus . . . & recentioribus autoribus . . . in vnum collecta, & . . . in Titulos . . . digesta. A Patre F. Paulino Berti . . . NVNCVPATA QVÆSTIONVM REGVLARIVM TOMVS QVARTVS . . . Antverpiæ, Apud Petrum & Ioannem Belleros. M.DC.XVI. [etc.] fol. 4 tom.: pp.368; 322; 243; 346; illus.
L.20.gg.5.
The engraving on the verso of tp.1, showing the Virgin and Child flanked by Saints Norbert and Adrian, inscribed: 'Crux arida nutrit' and signed: G. D. Mortien f.

R94 RODRIGUEZ, Manuel; Franciscan
[Summa de casos de conciencia.] SVMMA CASVVM CONSCIENTIÆ, OMNIVM . . . COPIOSISSIMA . . . Composita per . . . EMANVELEM RODRIQVEZ . . . Hispano idiomate . . . Hac postrema editione ab authore . . . aucta . . . Translata nunc primum in Latinum . . . opera BALTAZARIS DE CANIZAL . . . DVACI, Ex Typographia BALTAZARIS BELLERI . . . 1614. [etc.] 4° pp.916
499.aa.16.
Printed by Laurence Kellam at Douai.

R95 ROELANDS, David
T'MAGAZIN Oft Pac-huys der Loffelycker Penn-const; vol Subtyle ende Lustighe Trecken . . . Figuren . . . ende . . . Onderscheyden Gheschriften. Verciert met . . . Gulden Sententien . . . Ghepractizeert Door DAVID ROELANDS . . . Fransoyschen School-M^r^. binnen Vlissingen . . . 1616. obl. fol. 44 plates; port.
559*.d.29; 1268.e.16.
Engraved throughout. The texts in Dutch, English, French, German or Latin. With illustrations of the technique of calligraphy. The portrait signed: F. Sechelemans, better known as Schillemans, with a verse signed: Simon Frisius. Both copies are imperfect; wanting the letterpress preliminary text obviously printed by Richard Schilders at Middelburg for the author and dating the work as 1617. The copy at 1268.e.16 also wanting two of the plates, one of them bearing the portrait.

ROGIERS, Pieter. Triumphante ende blijde incomste. 1609. [Sometimes tentatively attributed to Pieter Rogiers.] *See* TRIUMPHANTE

R96 ROJAS, Fernando de

[Calisto. Dutch] Celestina, Tragicomedie van Calisto ende Melibea . . . Getranslateert wt de Spaensche in onse Nederduytsche sprake: Ende met vele figueren verciert. t'Hantwerpen, By Heyndric Heyndricz. 1616. 8° sig. A-R^{8}S^7; illus.

11725.a.7.

Anonymous. The original generally attributed to Fernando de Rojas. The imprint is false. A close reprint of the genuine edition by Heyndricz of ca.1580; printed in the Northern Netherlands? The illustrations are woodcuts.

R97 ROLLENHAGEN, Gabriel

NVCLEVS EMBLEMATVM SELECTISSIMORVM, QVÆ VVLGO IMPRESAS vocant priuata industria studio singulari, vndiqꝫ conquisitus, non paucis venustis inuentionibus auctus, additis carminibꝰ illustratus etc. A GABRIELE ROLLENHAGIO . . . E Musæo cœlatorio CRISPIANI PASSÆI. PROSTANT Apud Ioānē Iansoniū Bibliopolā Arnhemiēsē 4° sig. A^4; port.: pl. 100

636.g.29.

The titlepage, which is slightly mutilated, is engraved and in this copy is not mounted. The letterpress text consists of verses added to the portrait and of the unsigned preface, sometimes attributed to Crispijn van der Passe. The letterpress may have been printed by Jansz at Arnhem while the artist was still at Cologne. Published ca.1610?

R98 ROLLENHAGEN, Gabriel

(tp. 1) NVCLEVS EMBLEMATVM . . . A GABRIELE ROLLENHAGIO . . . COLONIÆ E Musæo cœlatorio CRISPIANI PASSÆI. PROSTANT Apud Ioānē Iansoniū Bibliopolā Arnhemiēsē (tp. 2) LES EMBLEMES DE MAISTRE GABRIEL ROLLENHAGVE, MIS EN VERS FRANCOIS par vn professeur de la langue Françoise a Colongne. COLONIÆ, Excudebat Seruatius Erffens: Prostant Apud Ioannem Iansonium bibliopolam Arnheimensem . . . MDCXI. 4° sig. AB^4; port; A-D^4: pl. 100

C.57.b.24(1).

The first titlepage is engraved. In the Latin preliminaries sig. B has been bound in between A1, i.e. the title, and A2. Leaf A3 is cropped with loss of the numeration in the signature. In relation to the preceding the word 'Coloniae' appears to have been added to the earlier engraved imprint on the titlepage, a dedication has been added and the preface and text of the portrait have been reset with such changes as u to v and the correction of 'landem' to 'laudem' on A4r. The second set of signatures contains the French text. With the bookplate of Syston Park.

R99 ROLLENHAGEN, Gabriel

NVCLEVS EMBLEMATVM . . . A GABRIELE ROLLENHAGIO . . . E Musæo cœlatorio CRISPIANI PASSÆI. Zeelando Excussori. 4° pl. 100

90.i.26.

The word 'Coloniae' on the engraved titlepage has been deleted and the Jansz imprint removed and substituted with 'Zeelando excussori' and a flourish. This copy is without letterpress or portrait. The titlepage and some of the plates are mounted. Probably produced at Utrecht ca.1615.

R100 ROLLENHAGEN, Gabriel

GABRIELIS ROLLENHAGEN selectorum Emblematum CENTVRIA SECVNDA. A° M D C XIII. Vltraiecti ex officina Crispiani Passæi, Prostant apud Joan. Janssoniū Bibli: Arnh. 4° pl. 100; port.

90.i.27; 554.b.4.

The titlepage is engraved. The emblems have text in Latin, with verses in Greek or Italian. The portrait is the same as in the 'Nucleus', but without letterpress. Without the dedication on the verso of the portrait found in some copies and without the additional French texts and the Cologne imprint. The copy at 554.b.4 is imperfect; wanting the titlepage, portrait and pl.20, 22, 39–42, 50, 76, 77.

R101 ROLLENHAGEN, Gabriel

[Selections from 'Nucleus' and 'Emblematum centuria secunda'.] 4° pl. [100]
637.d.19.

A made-up copy consisting of plates from both series of emblems, without titlepage or portrait and without letterpress. The plates are in poor state, their numbers have been added in manuscript. This may be a remnant of two complete series or compiled from the start as a selection. Imperfect; wanting pl.2, 4, 24, 31–33, 36, 50, 51, 64, 76, 81–84, 93. Manuscript notes and scribbles in English have been added to plates and endpapers.

R102 ROLWAGHEN, Jan Claessen

Tsamenspreeckinghe van drie Persoonen/over het regireus Placcaet van Groninghen/ghekondicht den 7. September . . . Sesthien-hondert ende een . . . Door welcke . . . verthoont wort/dat die van Groninghen . . . in voeren tot onderdrukkinge . . . Opt nieuwe ouersien ende verbetert . . . Ghedruckt . . . M.VJC.II. 4° sig.A–G^4
T.2239(5).

Anonymous. By Jan Claessen Rolwaghen and Caspar Coolhaes, perhaps with the assistance of Jacob Pietersz Vermeulen. On the suppression of the Anabaptists at Groningen and directed mainly against Johannes Bogerman.

R103 ROMANUS, Adrianus

[Ideae mathematicæ pars . . .] SPECVLVM ASTRONOMICVM, SIVE ORGANVM FORMA MAPPÆ EXPRESSVM: In qvo licet immobili qvi in Primo cælo, Primoq̃ve mobili spectari solent motus, planissimè . . . repræsentantur. AVTHORE A. ROMANO . . . LOVANII, Ex officina Ioannis Masij . . . 1606. Sumptibus Authoris. Prostat Francofurti apud Levinum Hulsium. 4° pp.151; illus.
8560.c.49.

The privilege, dated 7 November 1590, gives the work's title as 'Idea mathematica'; the Royal Library Albert I at Brussels has an edition dated 1591, entitled: 'Ideae mathematicae pars prima', dealing with geometry. The woodcut illustrations show diagrams.

R104 ROME

[Collections of laws. Justinian. Institutiones.] GERARDI TVNINGI . . . IN QVATVOR LIBROS INSTITVTIONVM IVRIS CIVILIS Divi Iustiniani COMMENTARIVS: ex adversarijs Auctoris . . . collectus ac nunc primùm editus Ab ARNOLDO VINNIO . . . LVGDVNI BATAVORVM, Ex Officinâ ELZEVIRIANA . . . M.D.CXVIII. 4° pp.928
5255.c.26.

With the original text and with a life of Tuningius by Daniel Heinsius.

R105 ROME. Church of Rome. Cancelleria Apostolica

TAXE DES PARTIES CASVELLES DE LA BOVTIQVE DV PAPE, En Latin & en François. Avec annotations . . . Par A. D. P. A LEYDEN. 1607. Suivant la copie imprimé à Lion, l'an mil cinq cens soixante & quatre. 8° pp.140; illus.
861.b.19; 1375.b.10.

The titlepage woodcut is a copy of that of the original edition published by Jean Saugrain at Lyon in 1564. Edited by Antoine du Pinet. The copy at 861.b.19 with the bookplate of Iacob Asselin.

R106 ROME. Church of Rome. Popes

[14.1.1620] BRIEF van Interdictie vande ses tienden over alle vruchten ende Kerckelijcke pensioenen van Italien. Van . . . H. H. Paulus . . . Paus den vijfden. VVt den welcken blijckt het eynde, vvaerom dese tienden gheboden zijn. Herdruckt naer 't Exemplaer, gedruckt tot Rome . . . 1620 uyt-gegaen. 4° sig. A^4B^2; illus.

T.2423(37).

The titlepage woodcut shows the pope receiving the taxes.

ROMPEL, J. For publications under the pseudonym of Yemand van Waer-mond, sometimes identified as J. Rompel, *see* WAER-MOND, Yemand van

R107 RONSSEUS, Balduinus

BALDVINI RONSSEI . . . OPVSCVLA Medica . . . Accesserunt quidam aliorum . . . Medicorum DE SCORBVTO Tractatus. LVGDVNI BATAVORVM, Apud IOHANNEM MAIRE, M DC.XVIII. 8° pp.4, 3–257; 236; 107; 90; illus.

1165.b.8.

The first 4 pages are preliminaries on sig. (·.·) 1, 2, the titlepage, i.e. sig. A1, is intended to precede p.3=A2. The illustrations belong to the part of pp.236, entitled 'De morbis muliebribus'. The part consisting of pp.107 contains the verse composition 'Balduini Ronssei De venatione medica'.

ROSAEUS, Clemens. Theses medicae de convulsione. 1621. *See* VORSTIUS, Aelius Everardus

ROSAEUS, Clemens. Theses medicae de dysenteria. 1621. *See* HEURNIUS, Otto

R108 ROSIER, Jean

Poëmes François CONTENANS PLVSIEVRS EPITHALAMES, EPIGRAMMES, EPITAPHES, ELEGIES, COMEDIES, ET AVTRES DISCOVRS . . . PAR M. IEAN ROSIER . . . A DOVAY, De l'Imprimerie de PIERRE AVROY . . . M.DCXVI. 8° pp.327

11475.aa.37.

Ownership inscription: Ex libris Dennareux[?] org modulatoris.

R109 ROSWEYDUS, Heribertus

HERIBERTI ROS-VVEYDI . . . ANTI-CAPELLVS SIVE EXPLOSIO NAENIARVM IACOBI CAPELLI Quas funeri ISAACI CASAVBONI ad LEGEM XII. TABVLARVM, in VINDICIIS suis accinuit. ACCEDIT COROLLARIVM contra coccysmos CAPELLI De fide hæreticis seruandâ, ad lucem historiæ HVSSI. ANTVERPIÆ, EX OFFICINA PLANTINIANA, Apud Balthasarem Moretum, & Viduam Ioannis Moreti, & Io. Meursium. M.DC XIX. 8° pp.250

1007.b.17.

Ownership inscription: Ex legato . . . Decani Holvoet.

R110 ROSWEYDUS, Heribertus

HERIBERTI ROS-VVEYDI . . . DE FIDE HAERETICIS SERVANDA ex decreto Concilij Constantiensis DISSERTATIO Cum DANIELE PLANCIO . . . In quâ, quæ de HVSSO historia est, excutitur. ANTVERPIÆ, EX OFFICINA PLANTINIANA, Apud Viduam & Filios Io. Moreti. M.DC.X. 8° pp.236

4377.aaa.42.

R111 ROSWEYDUS, Heribertus

LEX TALIONIS XII. TABVLARVM CARDINALI BARONIO AB ISAACO CASAVBONO DICTA: RETALIANTE HERIBERTO ROS-VVEYDO . . . ANTVERPIÆ, EX OFFICINA PLANTINIANA, Apud Viduam & Filios Io. Moreti. M.DC.XIV. 8° pp.227

877.h.14.

ROSWEYDUS, Heribertus. Martini Antonii Del-Rio . . . vita. 1609. [Sometimes attributed to Heribertus Rosweydus.] *See* SUSIUS, Nicolaus

R112 ROSWEYDUS, Heribertus

HERIBERTI ROS-VVEYDI . . . SYLLABVS MALÆ FIDEI CAPELLIANÆ EXCERPTVS ex IACOBI CAPELLI mendaci Assertione BONÆ FIDEI, & fictis Artibus ROMANÆ SEDIS pro ANTI-CAPELLO suo & Dissertatione DE FIDE HÆRETICIS SERVANDA. ANTVERPIÆ, EX OFFICINA PLANTINIANA, Apud Balthasarem Moretum, & Viduam Ioannis Moreti, & Io. Meursium. M.DC.XXI. (col.) ANTVERPIÆ, EX OFFICINA BALTHASARIS MORETI. M.DC.XX. 8° pp.344

847.d.16.

The final figure 'I' in the date on the titlepage has apparently been added after printing.

ROSWEYDUS, Heribertus. Vitae patrum. 1615. *See* VITAE

ROTHE, David. Hiberniae . . . vindiciae. 1621. [Sometimes wrongly attributed to David Rothe.] *See* FLEMING, Richard

R113 ROTTERDAM

[18.2.1612] CORT BERICHT Van de Redenen Om de welcke de . . . Burghemeesteren/Raden ende Vroetschappen der stede Rotterdam Cornelium Geselium . . . van zijnen Dienst gedeporteert . . . en . . . wt hare stadt hebben doen leyden. Begrepen in een seeckere Missive van de Heeren . . . Mitsgaders CORNELII GESELII Teghenbericht op de selve redenen . . . 1612. 4° pp.21

T.2242(5).

The official declaration dated 18 February 1612.

R114 ROTTERDAM

[5.3.1612–11.2.1617] PRESENTATIEN ghedaen/Soo by de Heeren Magistraten/als by den Kercken-Raedt tot Rotterdam/aen de Af-ghezonderde Lidtmaten vande Ghereformeerde Kercke aldaer. TOT ROTTERDAM, By Matthijs Bastiaensz . . . 1618. 4° pp.16

T.2248(8).

The documents dated between 5 March 1612 and 11 February 1617.

R115 ROTTERDAMSCHE

Rotterdamsche Moort/begaen door den Dijckgraef Duyn Claessen/op de ghevanckenisse des Eerw: ende Godtsalighen Symon Lucas Bysterus op de Kermisse des dyngsdaechs/den 24 Augusti Anno 1621. Ghedruckt . . . 1621. 4° sig.A^2

T.2251(9).

R116 ROTTERDAMSCHE

Rotterdamsche nieuwe Tijdinghen/hoemen daer de Arminianen om haer Predicken vervolght/plundert/slaet ende . . . mis-handelt. Nv eerst Ghedruckt den 3 Junij 1620. T'Hantwerpen/By Abraham Verhoeuen . . . 1620. [etc.] 4° pp.8; sig.Aa^4; illus.

P.P.3444.af(56).

The titlepage woodcut shows a magistrate and soldiers.

R117 ROUZAEUS, Ludovicus

PROBLEMATVM MISCELLANEORVM, ANTARISTOTELICORVM, centuria dimidiata, ad DOMINOS STVDIOSOS in Academia Leydensi, A LVDOVICO ROVZÆO DIRECTA. LVGDVNI BATAVORVM, Ex Officina GODEFRIDI BASSON . . . 1616. 12° pp.90

518.a.44.

From the library of John Morris.

R118 ROVERIUS, Petrus

(tp.1) [Henrico IIII Franciæ et Navarræ regi . . . in instauratione Godranii Societatis Iesu Collegii, Panegyricus, dictus Divione a P. Petro Roverio . . . Additæ notæ et primigeniæ, ac Reuertentis Fortunæ Characteres . . . Editio altera

auctior et emendatior. Antverpiæ, ex Officina Plantiniana, apud Ioannem Moretum, M.D.CX.]
(tp.2) ELOGIVM HISTORICVM HENRICI IV. . . . ANTVERPIÆ, EX OFFICINA PLANTINIANA, Apud Ioannem Moretum. M.DC.X. 8° 2 pt.: pp.165; 15
12301.aaa.23(2, 3).
Imperfect; wanting tp.1. The two parts normally found together and listed under pt.1 only, but with the complete number of gatherings for both, in the manuscript catalogue of Plantin-Moretus editions (Ms. 321) at the Plantin-Moretus Museum at Antwerp, from whose copy the title has been described above. The preface on tp.2 verso says the work is the translation from the French by a 'Belga doctissimus', tentatively identified as Joannes Woverius. Another, separate, illustrated issue of pt.2 is entered under ELOGIUM.

R119 ROYAL
[The royal entertainment of . . . the Earle of Nottingham.] VVaeractich [*sic*] verhael vAn de Reyse van den Ambassadeur van Engelant nae Spaignen/ mitsgaders wat hem op de selve reyse wedervaren is . . . Ghemaect by een Engelsman die mede gevveest is in Engelsch, ende uyt het Engelsch overgheset in Duyts. Tot Antvverpen By Anthoni Ballo . . . 1605. 4° sig.A^4
597.d.27.
A translation of 'The royal entertainment of . . . the Earle of Nottingham', with additions from other sources. The mistranslation 'Luinborow' on A1v as the port of embarcation is due to the italic 'Q' in 'Quynborow' on the English titlepage of Robert Treswell's 'A relation of such things as were observed in the journey of Charles earle of Nottingham, to Spaine', which is easily misread as 'L'.

R120 RUBENS, Philips
PHILIPPI RVBENI Electorvm Libri II. In quibus antiqui Ritus, Emendationes, Censuræ. EIVSDEM ad IVSTVM LIPSIVM Poëmatia. ANTVERPIAE, EX OFFICINA PLANTINIANA, Apud Ioannem Moretum. M.DC.VIII. (col.) ANTVERPIAE, EX OFFICINA PLANTINIANA, Apud Ioannem Moretum. M.DC.VIII. 4° pp.124: plates; illus.
589.h.4(2).
The engravings, some signed: Corn. Galle, after designs made by Pieter Paul Rubens at Rome.

R121 RUISCHIUS, Nicolaus
THESES MEDICÆ ΠΕΡΙ ΑΙΜΑΤΟΣ ΠΤΥΣΕΩΣ DE SANGVINIS PER OS REIECTATIONE, Quas . . . Pro summo in Medicinâ Gradu consequendo, Tueri conabor NICOLAVS RVISCHIVS . . . LUGDUNI BATAVORUM, Ex Officinâ Ioannis Patii . . . M.D.CII. 4° sig.A^6
7306.f.6(10).

R122 RUTGERS, Joannes
IANI RVTGERSII VARIARVM LECTIONVM LIBRI SEX . . . LVGDVNI BATAVORVM, Ex Officinâ ELZEVIRIANA . . . M.DC.XVIII. (col.) LVGDVNI BATAVORVM, Typis ISAACI ELZEVIRI . . . M.DC.XVIII. 4° pp.636
630.k.24; 11350.f.1.
The copy at 11350.f.1, with the ownership inscription: Joannis de Witt, has the author's corrections and additions for a second edition, transcribed from the original, added in manuscript in the handwriting of Jan de Witt.

R123 RUYCKER
Ruycker T'samen-ghevlochten/Wt vijf-ende-twintich BLOEMKENS, Die gelesen . . . syn wt seeckeren Boeck van Fredericus Broeckerus nu ter tijdt predicant der Contra-Remonstrantscher ghemeente binnen Rotterdam. Anderzints/Aenspraecke/gestelt in forme van een Missive der Rotterdamscher Contra-Remonstranten/aen haren Herder Fred. Broeckerum/ter oorsaecke van

eenighe vreemde stucken die in syn Antidotum tegens D. Vorstius syn te vinden. Gedruckt . . . 1619. By my/Beminder der alghemeyner Vryheydt. 4° pp.18
T.2249(45).

R124 RUYTINCK, Symeon
GVLDEN LEGENDE vande Roomsche Kercke: Mitsgaders Hare Heylighdommen, Ende Aflaten, Aenden Toet-steen der Waerheyd beproeft. DOOR Symeon Ruytinck . . . TOT LONDEN, By Thomas Snodham. 1612. 4° pp.225, 62
4827.c.33.
In verse, including 'Historisch-lied' on the Gunpowder plot, with a prose commentary.

R125 RUYTINCK, Symeon
[Harmonia synodorum Belgicarum.] HARMONIE, Dat is OVEREENSTEMMINGE der Nederlandtsche Synoden, Ofte REGVLEN Naer de welcke de Kercken worden gheregiert . . . Cortelick by den anderen ghestelt, Door S. R. TOT LEYDEN, Voor David Jansz. van Ilpendam . . . 1618. 4° sig.RS[4]
T.2248(18).
Anonymous. Intended to be published as part of 'Monster vande Nederlantsche verschillen' by Festus Hommius, for which *see* HOMMIUS, Festus.

R126 RYCKEWAERT, Carel; the Younger
BRIEF Aen de verdruckte Ghemeynte Jesu Christi binnen der Stadt Vtrecht. Ghedruckt int Jaer sesthienhondert ende neghenthien. 4° pp.38
T.2249(49).
Anonymous. Printed with use of civilité type.

RYCKEWAERT, Carel; the Younger. Disputationum theologicarum trigesima-secunda, de resurrectione carnis. 1604. *See* GOMARUS, Franciscus

RYCKEWARDUS, Carolus; the Younger. *See* RYCKEWAERT, Carel

R127 RYCQUIUS, Justus
IVSTI RYCQVI DE CAPITOLIO ROMANO COMMENTARIVS . . . GANDAVI, Apud Cornelium Marium . . . M.DC.XVII. 4° pp.179; illus.
C.74.d.10; 140.c.5.
The engraved printer's device with a monogram identified in the *Bibliographie gantoise* no.734 as that of Christoffel van Sichem. Both copies wanting the plate described there. The illustrations are woodcuts showing coins.

R128 RYCQUIUS, Justus
IVSTI RYCQVII . . . PIETAS, IN FVNERE PHILIPPI III. AVSTRIACI, HISPANIAR. INDIARVMQ. REGIS POTENTISS. (col.) ANTVERPIÆ, EX OFFICINA PLANTINIANA BALTHASARIS MORETI. M.DC.XXI. 4° pp.16
1199.f.3(8).

S

S. MARY MAGDALENS pilgrimage. 1617. *See* SWEETNAM, John

S. PETERS complaint. 1616. *See* SOUTHWELL, Robert

S1 SACKVILLE, Edward; Earl of Dorset
ORATIE Van . . . S^r^. Eduard Sakfield, Ghehouden Int Opper-huys vanden PARLAMENTE, Omtrent den 20. May Ouden Styl/Omme het selve Parlament te beweghen tot Contributie van middelen/omme den Coninck van Bohemen wederomme te stellen in Possessie van den Pals, ende andere af-ghenomen Landen. Na de Copy, Ghedruckt te Londen by Bonham Norton ende Iohan Bill . . . 1621. 4° pp.7
T.2424(18).

S2 SACRAE

SACRÆ LITANIÆ VARIÆ, Cum breui piaque quotidiana exercitatione . . . ANTVERPIÆ, EX OFFICINA PLANTINIANA, Apud Ioannem Moretum. M.DC.VII. (col.) ANTVERPIÆ, EX OFFICINA PLANTINIANA, Apud Ioannem Moretum. M.DC.VII. 8° pp.257; illus.
845.a.35.

The illustration, on p.15, is an engraving of the Cross and the instruments of the Passion. With additional prayers in Latin and French in manuscript at the end, signed: Phil. Rooper.

S3 SACROBOSCO, Christophorus a

DE INVESTIGANDA VERA AC VISIBILI CHRISTI ECCLESIA TRACTATVS: Auctore CHRISTOPHORO A SACROBOSCO . . . Noua editio ab ipso auctore recognita & aucta. ANTVERPIÆ Apud Heredes MARTINI NVTII. M.DC.XIX. 8° pp.119
1352.b.3.

S4 SACROBOSCO, Christophorus a

(tp.1) DEFENSIO DECRETI TRIDENTINI ET SENTENTIAE ROBERTI BELLARMINI . . . De authoritate vulgatæ editionis Latinæ aduersus sectarios, maximè VVHITAKERVM . . . AVTHORE CHRISTOPHORO A SACROBOSCO . . . Accessit eiusdem De inuestiganda vera ac visibili Christi Ecclesia libellus. ANTVERPIAE, Apud Ioannem Keerbergium . . . M.D.C.IIII. [etc.]
(tp.2) DE INVESTIGANDA VERA AC VISIBILI CHRISTI ECCLESIA, Libellus. AVTHORE CHRISTOPHORO A SACROBOSCO . . . ANTVERPIAE, Apud Ioannem Keerbergium . . . M.D.C.IIII. [etc.] 8° 2 pt.: pp.413; 32
697.c.39.

SACROSANCTI . . . Concilii Tridentini . . . canones et decreta. 1615. *See* TRENT. Council of Trent

The SAFEGARDE from ship-wreck. 1618. *See* PICKFORD, John

S5 SAILLY, Thomas

DEN NIEVWEN MORGHEN-VVECKER, Wijsende de Natuere, voort-ganck, vruchten, remedien, der Ketterije; Te Voor-schyne ghebracht, Tot het Welvaert der Gheunieerde, ende andere Nederlandtsche Provincien: DOOR THOMAS SAILLY . . . Ghedruckt tot LOVEN, BY IO. CHRISTOPH. FLAVIVS. M.DC.XII. [etc.] 4° pp.329; illus.
1578/6750.

The titlepage engraving shows an alarm clock, inscribed 'Vigilate et Orate'. A reply to Willem Baudaert's 'Morghen-wecker'.

S6 SAILLY, Thomas

THESAVRVS PRECVM ET EXERCITIORVM SPIRITVALIVM, In vsum pręsertim SODALITATIS PARTHENIÆ: Auctore THOMA SAILLIO . . . Additæ breues APOLOGIÆ, eidem subseruientes. ANTVERPIÆ, EX OFFICINA PLANTINIANA, Apud Ioannem Moretum. M.DC.IX. 8° pp.551; illus.
1607/3956.

The titlepage and illustrations are engraved, the latter variously attributed to Theodoor Galle after Adam van Noort and Pieter de Jode or to the Wiericx brothers.

S7 SAINT JULIEN, Antoine de; Knight of Malta

LA FORGE DE VULCAIN, OU L'APPAREIL DES MACHINES DE GUERRE. TRAITE' CURIEUX, Dans lequel on fait voir comme en racourci quels sont les Instrumens Militaires . . . Par le Chevalier de SAINT JULIEN. A LA HAYE, Chez GUILLAUME DE VOYS . . . M.DCVI. 8° pp.144: plate
1568/1877; 58.f.25.

The date is a misprint for 1706.

SAKFIELD, Eduard. *See* SACKVILLE, Edward; Earl of Dorset

S8 SALA, Angelo

ANATOMIA ANTIMONII: ID EST DISSECTIO tam DOGMATICA quàm HERMETICA ANTIMONII . . . AVCTORE ANGELO SALA . . . LVGDVNI BATAVORVM, Ex Officina GODEFRIDI BASSON. M.D.C.XVII. 8° pp.145

1034.b.5(2).

Imperfect; wanting pp.17-32. Ownership as for following entry.

S9 SALA, Angelo

(tp.1) ANGELI SALÆ . . . ANATOMIA VITRIOLI in duos Tractatus divisa . . . Accedit arcanorum complurium . . . SYLVA. Omnia ex Italicâ in Latinam linguam translata, studio & operâ I.P.C.R. EDITIO TERTIA, ab Authore recognita. LVGDVNI BATAVORVM, Ex Officinâ GODEFRIDI BASSON. M.D.C.XVII.

(tp.2=p.27) ANGELI SALÆ . . . ANATOMIÆ VITRIOLI TRACTATVS ALTER . . . Ex Italica in Latinam linguam translatus, studio & operâ I.P.C.R. LVGDVNI BATAVORVM, Ex Officinâ GODEFRIDI BASSON. M.D.C.XVII. 8° pp.107

1034.b.5(1).

Ownership inscription: Est Alberti O. Fabri.

S10 SALA, Angelo

EMETOLOGIA OV Enarration du naturel et vsage des Vomitoires . . . Par Angelus Sala . . . DELPHIS. Apud Joannem Andreæ . . . 1613. 8° pp.101

547.a.19.

The dedication to Prince Maurice and the running title name the book 'Triomphe des medicamens vomitifs'.

S11 SALA, Angelo

SEPTEM PLANETARVM terrestrium Spagirica recensio. QVA . . . DECLAratur ratio nominis Hermetici, analogia metallorum cum microcosmo, eorum præparatio . . . proprietates, & vsus medicinales. Authore Angelo Sala . . . AMSTERODAMI, Apud Wilhelmum Ianssonium. M.DC.XIV. 12° pp.98

1035.a.5(2).

S12 SALA, Angelo

TERNARIUS BEZOARTICORUM OU TROIS SOUVERAINS MEDICAMENTS BEZOARDIQUES, Contre tous venins et empoisonnements . . . Par ANGELUS SALA . . . A. [*sic*] LEYDEN Chez. Godefroy. Basson. 1616. 4° pp.91

546.d.20; 42.d.15.

The titlepage is engraved, showing a scene in a laboratory and the figures of 'Mithridates Rex' and 'Andromachus Medic.' Ownership inscription in the copy at 42.d.15: Est Alb. Otton. Fabri.

S13 SALLAEUS, Andreas; Pastor

INDEX AMPLISSIMVS MATERIAM PRÆCIPVARVM, Quæ sparsim in Concionibus de Tempore & Sanctorum Festis solemnibus, à R. P. F. LVDOVICO GRANATENSI in lucem editis, continentur . . . D. ANDREÆ SALLÆI . . . INDVSTRIA CONCINNATVS, Nunc emendatus, & . . . locupletatus . . . ANTVERPIÆ, EX OFFICINA PLANTINIANA, Apud Ioannem Moretum. M.D.CII. [etc.] (col.) ANTVERPIÆ, EX OFFICINA PLANTINIANA, APVD IOANNEM MORETVM. M.D.CIII. 8° pp.106; illus.

3834.de.1.

The illustration shows the engraved emblem used by the author, 'Sole et sale', by Theodoor Galle? Ownership inscription: Ad usum Martini Hermannutij Cartusiæ Brixiæ.

S14 SALLUSTIUS CRISPUS, Caius

[Works. Latin] C. CRISPI SALLVSTII OPERA OMNIA QVÆ EXSTANT. HELIAS PVTSCHIVS ex fide vetustiss. cod. correxit, & NOTAS addidit: idem FRAGMENTA . . . auxit & interpolauit. Adiectæ . . . PETRI CIACCONII . . . NOTÆ. EX OFFICINA PLANTINIANA RAPHELENGII. M.D.CII. 8° pp.299

587.b.18(1).

Contents: Catilina, Jugurtha, Histories fragments; letters and speeches. Published at Leiden.

S15 SALLUSTIUS CRISPUS, Caius

[Works. Latin] C. CRISPI SALLVSTII OPERA OMNIA QVÆ EXTANT, Ad PETRI CIACCONI, HELIÆ PVTSCHII, aliorumq́ue Notas & Obseruationes recognita. EX OFFICINA PLANTINIANA RAPHELENGII, M.D.CXII. 8° pp.226

587.b.19.

Contents as in the preceding. Published at Leiden.

S16 SALLUSTIUS CRISPUS, Caius

[Works. Latin] CAII SALLVSTII OPERA OMNIA QVÆ EXSTANT. EX OFFICINA PLANTINIANA RAPHELENGII, M.D.CXIII. 16° pp.205

C.20.f.29.

Contents as in the preceding. Published at Leiden. From the travelling library of Sir Julius Caesar.

S17 SALLUSTIUS CRISPUS, Caius

[Works. Latin] C. SALLVSTII CRISPI OPERA QVÆ EXSTANT ET, L. CORNELII SISENNAE HISTORIARVM FRAGMENTA. AVSONIVS POPMA . . . recensuit, & SCHOLIIS illustravit. FRANEKERAE, Excudebat Ioannes Lamrinck . . . M DC XIX. (col.) FRANEKERAE, Excudebat Ioannes Lamrinck . . . 1619. 8° pp.471

587.b.20.

With additional notes by Cyprianus Popma. From the library of John Morris.

S18 SALLUSTIUS CRISPUS, Caius

[Works. Spanish] OBRAS DE CAIO CRISPO SALLVSTIO: Traducidos por EMANVEL SVEIRO . . . En Anuers en casa de Iuan Keerberghio M.DC.XV. (col.) ANTVERPIÆ, Typis G. WOLSCHATI, & H. ÆRTSI. M.DC.XV. 8° pp.235

803.b.3.

The titlepage is engraved, containing the arms of Juan de Mendoça, Duque del Infantado. Contents: Jugurtha, Catilina. Ownership indication: initials HT on the binding.

S19 SALOMO

SALOMO, Dat is/VERMANINghe aen die Christenen/die wt eenen eenvoudigen yver zich aende syde vande genaemde Remonstranten houden/tot vereeninghe mette openbare Ghereformeerde Kercken/inde vereenichde Landen . . . Door I.V.H. Een liefhebber der warer Christelijcker vrede. TOT ROTTERDAM, By Jan van waesberghe . . . 1621. 4° sig.A-D^4E^1

T.2251(13).

S20 SALSMAN, Guilhelmus

PSALMO LXXXIV. Barmhertzigkeit vnd warheit seind einander begegnet: Gerechtigkeit vnd Frid haben sich geküsset . . . PPALMO [*sic*] LXXXIV. Misericordia & veritas obuiauerunt sibi: Iustitia & Pax osculatæ sunt. fol. a single sheet; illus.

1750.c.1(20).

The text, in Latin and German, signed: Guilhelmus Salsman. The title of the engraving, signed: Helias vanden Bossche fecit, is 'Conflabunt gladios suos in vomeres [etc.]' The date of publication is given in a chronogram: aVrea MeDIoCrItas, i.e. 1607. Dealing with the negotiations for a truce. Published in the Netherlands.

PSALMO LXXXIV.

Barmhertzigkeit vnd warheit seind einander begegnet: Gerechtigkeit vnd Frid haben sich geküsset.

Ertzhertzog Albert Keyserlich
Geboren/ vnd auch Königlich/
Sampt sein Gemahl die Infantin
Erhalte Gott von anbegin/
In jhrem hochfürstlichem standt/
In ruw vnd ehren der Niderland/
Biß auff des lebens endliche zil/
Das wunschen wir so Gottes will.
Graff Mauritz der auch Edel Held/
Erweist sein manheit in dem feld/
Erhalten hat auch manchen sig/
In schlachten vnd sturmen zuglich.
Der Printz Graff Heinrich Friderich
Versucht hat auch vil stich/
Das junge blut vnd manliche hertz
Treib mit den Waffen keine schertz.
Das hat beiden groß ehr gebracht
Zum friden ist man mehr bedacht.
Ambros Spinola der Marquis
Bekommen hat Heldischen preis/
Fürsichtig vnd dapffer gemut/
Sucht doch nit verderben vnd blut/
Wie man an jm jetzt spüren kan/
Das er ist ein frid lebend Man.
Carl Graff von Buquoi genant
Hat seinen feiand vbermant/
Gantz ritterlich gehandelt hat/
Gibt auch zum friden guten raht.
Die Herren Staten in gemein
Beiderseits schicken sich gar fein
In einem fridlichen verstand:
In hoffnung steht das gantze land.
Der fridmacher Johan de Ney
Spart kein arbeit/ vnd wagt es frei.
Der ist fürwar ein Gottes man/
Der als zum besten kehren kan.
Der Frid/ die gutte Pax kompt her
Mit ölzweiglin gezieret sehr:
Helkräntzlin führet auff dem haar/
Das ist ein fridens Zeichen zwar.
Daher kompt wolfart alles gut/
Das man von hertzen wunschen thut.
Justitia Gerechtigkeit
Das Schwert fürt mit bescheidenheit/
Ein wäglin in der lincken hand:
Erwagt alles recht/ schont niemand.
Ein Königin der Tugend fron
Tragt auff dem haupt ein Keysers Kron.
Geseller disse Nymphen zwo
Auf einem Triumpfwagen fro
Fahren zu einem Tempel schon/
Des namen heist Religion.
An iren füssen zwo Kranichen
In irer gestalt seind zu sehen/
Fahren in ihren schnebelen
Ingebunden zwey hertzlein.
Disse vögel fliegen samptlich/
Also auffen wider finden sich:
Die geben euch den alberen
Ein warzeichen der Einigkeit.
Ihr Niderlanden diß betracht/
So werd ihr brechen alle macht.
Der wagen wol gezogen wird
Von Pferden aller schonst geziert.
Die führ Nymphen vnd Wagnerin
(Die nim wol zu hertzen vnd sin)
Seind/ warheit, welche ist ein licht/
Wie man das auff jhrem haupt sicht.
In ewigkeit bleibet warheit/
Das zeigt das buch alse bescheidt.
Barmhertzigkeit ist ihr gespan/
Die nimt sich jhres negsten an/
Vnd soll sie mittheilen ihr hertz/
Des armen leid ist auch ihr schmertz.
Darumb ist der Himmel ihr lohn/
Den sie auff dem haupt tragen schon.
Von den vier Tugenden ... icht
Im achtzig vierten Psalmen gedicht.
Als dan wirdt Mars gefangen sein/
Auff wapffen wird man schmiden fein/
Des fridens gutte Instrument/
Gott helff vns all zu dissem end.

PSALMO LXXXIV.

Misericordia [illegible]eritas obuiauerunt sibi: Iustitia & Pax osculatæ sunt.

Inuicte sanguis Cæsarum, ac Diuum genus
ALBERTE cum ter maxima PHILIPPIDE,
Manete Belgis paterno sospites.
Fulua micare secula orbis incipit,
NASSAVidæ fratres, Gradiui fulmina,
Belli satis: vacationem vult Deus.
Admira MAVRITI tua est adorea;
E ferculo tibi exige palmarium
Robur, quod in tuo ferunt emblemate.
Henrice sat fratrem æmularis est satis.
Victrix est SPINA satis, Dux SPINVLA;
Nam te reminicit vellus aureum Colchicum.
Depulsus esto terminum tot prælijs.
Sit dulcem AMBROSIA palato Belgij.
BVCOIDE expugnator vrbium potens
TE CAROLE iam lam saturum aurium facit
Summe coite in fœdus ORDINES nouum.
Viri graues amor REIpubLICAE &
Impensius huic labor celebres efficit.
Vobis ducibus agri carebunt horridis
Armis & impij fora rigida litibus.
Quies sat empta sit cruento iam lytro.
Consul quietis, & genus pacis nouæ
DENEIde IANNES, fis auctor consili
Sit optime, ne post triumphent sanguine,
Nepos eueni & ciuium vires duces.
Indissolubili vinciat pacem bonam
Auspex fidelitatis arcto robore.
Tunc illa PAX alumna mundi, & omnium
Rerum redibit vitemue à fluibus
Mundi saeuaque oliuam dextera feret.
Corolla pacalis vire sit incomis,
Innexa ceruice redimita cui
Erunt Amalthea ferace brachia
Cornu beata copiæque, hanc comes
Astræa dabitur casta multum vindice
Curas, sciamente hac librat æquo pondere?
Regina virtutum, sijs amplexibus
Iungentur hæ Nymphæ, osculis haud antibus:
Sic pollice meditatum est Lyricen omans
Iessæus, præcentor aureus.
Has efferet quadriga sublimes Deas
Voluentibus rotis, bonis iugalibus,
Quarum ad pedes Thracum volucres se dua
Sistendo cor præsident nouum concordibus
Rostris, quod illigabunt vincla mutua:
Produnt nam hic est auibus, vt segregent
Se nenti quam, seu passibus demittere
Se sine circumscribere volunt nobile,
Pennis: id ergo symbolum est concordiæ.
Vos inter ergo congruat BELGAE optimi;
Sitis GRVES, vobis malum quid ne ingruat;
Sic iura congrue, bona tuta fieri erunt.
PAX, IVSTITIA triumphum agent hic VERITAS
Prodibit, & comat a radijs afferet
Diem micare diam, vti alma filia
Dei, manet quæ seculis firma omnibus.
Huic obuiam alma MISERICORDIA fiet, &
Ad proximi miseriam habens cor mobile,
Quod in sinum eius funderet cum viscere
Tot, repenit huic Deus tot præmia.
Quot sidera emicant superne, quot faces
Cælo coitionis huius est memor
Quest patris, Deique moderatum cauid.
Stat sacra moles, æmulans fastigio
Cælum profanus non ferens per limina:
Hinc inferent gressum beata hæc numina,
Tunc vinctus ibit Mars, suique complices.
Vulcanus arma Martis aptabit bona
Frugum parenti falx erit pro cuspide,
Pro lancea comis reddit merx sua
Terris & æquor pari cum fœnore
Prouinciales ergo Nympha vos decem,
Tres quatuorque dexteras et pectora
Iungeris: immortale fœdus hoc erit.
Rumpatur ctsi Laurel Furor crepet.
Fati parentum ergo nostram prosperis,
Regatque nostrum Deus clementior.

ANNO

aVrea MeDIoCrItas.

Guilhelmus Salman.

S20

S21 SALUSTE DU BARTAS, Guillaume de
[Works. Dutch] (pt.1. tp.) W. S Heere van BARTAS Wercken door Zacharias Heijns. (pt.2.tp.1) TWEEDE WEKE Van . . . WILLEM VAN SALVSTE, HEERE VAN BARTAS. Vertaelt Door ZACHARIAS HEYNS. TOT ZWOL . . . 1621.
(pt.2.tp.2=sig.★2r) BARTASSI ADAM, OFTE EERSTE DAGH VANDE TWEEDE WEKE . . . Vertaelt Door ZACHARIAS HEYNS. Tot ZWOL. T'AMSTELDAM, Gedruckt by Paulus van Ravesteyn . . . 1621.
(pt.2.tp.3=p.135) BARTASSI NOAH, OFTE TWEEDE DAGH VANDE TVVEEDE VVEKE . . . Vertaelt Door ZACHARIAS HEYNS, Tot ZWOL. T'AMSTELDAM, Gedruckt by Paulus van Ravesteyn . . . 1621.
(pt.2.tp.4=p.267) BARTASSI ABRAHAM ENDE MOYSES, OFTE DERDE DAGH VANDE TVVEEDE VVEKE . . . Vertaelt Door ZACHARIAS HEYNS, Tot ZWOL. T'AMSTELDAM, Gedruckt by Paulus van Ravesteyn . . . 1621.
(pt.2.tp.5=p.451) BARTASSI DAVID, EN DE NACOMELINGEN . . . Vertaelt Door ZACHARIAS HEYNS, Tot ZWOL. T'AMSTELDAM, Gedruckt by Paulus van Ravesteyn . . . 1621.
(pt.3.tp.) II. Weke VYFDE DAG . . . Door Zacharias Heyns. Tot Rotterdam. By Pieter van Waesberge . . . 1628. 4° 3 vol.: pp.313; 634; 150, 231: plates; illus., port.
Cup.403.w.1.
The titlepages of pt.1, 3 are engraved. Vol.1 is the second edition of 'De weke', first published at Zwolle in 1616, without the prose paraphrase and with different engravings. The portrait of Heyns may be by Hendrik Goltzius. The commentary is based on that of Simon Goulart de Senlis. Vol.3, which has a half-title reading 'Vervolgh vande Weken van Bartas. Door Z. Heyns' is original work by Heyns. The second set of pagination in that volume contains translations of other works by Du Bartas and of a poem by James I which Du Bartas had translated into French, but which is published here in a translation from the original English by Abraham vander Myl. Two of the cantos in vol.2 are translated by Joost van den Vondel. Vol.1 of this copy belongs to the variant which contains the privilege and the dedication to the Admiralty.

S22 SALUSTE DU BARTAS, Guillaume de
[Première sepmaine.] DE EERSTE VVEKE DER SCHEPPINGE DER WERELT. Eerst gheuonden/ende in Francoische Dicht ghestelt door . . . Wilhelm de Saluste, Heere van Bartas, Vertaelt in Nederlantschen Ryme door T.V.L.B. TOT BRVESSEL, By Rutgeert Velpius . . . 1609. [etc.] (col.) TOT BRVESSEL, IN DE DRVCKERYE VAN RVTGEERT VELPIVS . . . M.DC.IX. 4° pp.166
11557.ee.28.
The translator's name printed in the dedication as Theoderick van Liefvelt, in the approbation as Theodore van Lieffvelt.

S23 SALVIANUS Massiliensis
[Adversus avaritiam.] Quis Diues Saluus. HOW A RICH MAN MAY BE SAVED. WRITTEN . . . by Saluianus . . . Translated into English by N.T. . . . M.DC.XVIII. 8° pp.314
3627.aa.30.
Translated by Joseph Creswell? Without imprint; published by the English College press at St. Omer.

S24 SAMBUCUS, Joannes
[Icones veterum . . . medicorum.] Veterum aliquot ac recentium MEDICORVM PHILOSOPHORVMQV. Icones; Ex Bibliothecâ IOHANNIS SAMBVCI: cum eiusdem ad singulas ELOGIIS. Præmisso hac editione, VITÆ singulorum & SCRIPTORVM Indiculo;

Additis . . . diuersorum de eisdem ENCOMIIS. Ex Officinâ Plantinianâ RAPHELENGII, 1603. fol. sig.A^{6}: pl.67; sig.N2-6; port.
551.e.12.
With a biographical sketch of the author. The titlepage has an engraved border. The engravings are by Pieter vander Borcht. Published at Leiden.

S25 SAMERIUS, Henricus
SACRA CHRONOLOGIA A MVNDO CONDITO AD CHRISTVM. R.P. HENRICO SAMERIO . . . Authore. ANTVERPIÆ, Apud Hieronymum Verdussen. M.DC.VIII. [etc.] fol. pp.67; tables
3906.m.9(2).
Ownership inscription: Conventus Augustani Fr. Fr. Prædicatorum. Also with the bookplate of the same. The binding bearing the initials: F.M.A.D.P. and the date: 1609.

S26 SANCHEZ, Thomas
(tp.1) DISPVTATIONVM DE SANCTO MATRIMONII SACRAMENTO, TOMI TRES. Auctore THOMA SANCHEZ . . . Editio hæc postrema . . . correcta: in qua, præter vitam Auctoris, locorum . . . citationes . . . distinctæ sunt . . . ANTVERPIÆ, Apud Heredes MARTINI NVTII & IOANNEM MEVRSIVM . . . M.DC.XVII. [etc.]
(tp.2) TOMVS SECVNDVS DISPVTATIONVM DE SANCTO MATRIMONII SACRAMENTO. Auctore THOMA SANCHEZ . . . ANTVERPIÆ, Apud Heredes MARTINI NVTII & IOANNEM MEVRSIVM . . . MDC.XVII.
(tp.3) TOMVS TERTIVS DISPVTATIONVM DE SANCTO MATRIMONII SACRAMENTO. Auctore THOMA SANCHEZ . . . ANTVERPIÆ, Apud Heredes MARTINI NVTII & IOANNEM MEVRSIVM . . . MDC.XVII. fol. 3 tom.: pp.500; 404; 408
497.i.6.
The biographical sketch based on the accounts of Pedro de Ribadeneira and Joannes van Crombeeck.

S27 SANCHEZ, Thomas
(tp.1) DISPVTATIONVM DE SANCTO MATRIMONII SACRAMENTO, TOMI TRES, Auctore THOMA SANCHEZ . . . ANTVERPIÆ Ex officina Heredum MARTINI NVTII . . . M.DC.XX. [etc.]
(tp.2) TOMVS SECVNDVS DISPVTATIONVM DE SANCTO MATRIMONII SACRAMENTO, Auctore THOMA SANCHEZ . . . ANTVERPIÆ Ex officina Heredum MARTINI NVTII . . . M.DC.XX.
(tp.3) TOMVS TERTIVS DISPVTATIONVM DE SANCTO MATRIMONII SACRAMENTO, Auctore THOMA SANCHEZ . . . ANTVERPIÆ Ex officina Heredum MARTINI NVTII . . . M.DC.XX. fol. 3 tom.: pp.500; 404; 408
497.i.7.
A reprint of the edition of 1617, but without the last leaf of the index bearing the printer's device.

S28 SANCTI
SANCTI LVDOVICI CAROLI II. REGIS SICILIÆ FILII, EX ORDINE MINORVM EPISCOPI TOLOSANI VITA. F. Henricus Sedulius ex tenebris eruit, stilo & Commentario illustrauit. ANTVERPIÆ, EX OFFICINA PLANTINIANA, Apud Ioannem Moretum. M.DCII. 8° pp.115
486.a.11.
An anonymous life found in a manuscript, edited earlier by Henricus Willot. From the library of John Morris.

S29 SANDERUS, Antonius
DIRÆ IN ICONOCLASTAS, Sacrosanctæ Redemptoris è Cruce pendentis imagini nuper

iniurios. Scripsit, & euulgauit ANTONIVS SANDERVS . . . GANDAVI, Apud Gualtérum Manilium . . . 1618. 4° sig. AB^4
1461.d.18.

In verse, with a long prose dedication to Carolus a Burgundia and others. The titlepage is a separate leaf. Author's presentation copy to Franciscus Borlutius.

S30 SANDERUS, Antonius
(tp.1) ANTONI SANDERI PRIMITIÆ. VARIORVM POEMATVM. DVACI, Typis LAVRENTII KELLAMI . . . M.CD.XII [*sic*].
(tp.2=p.51) ANTONI SANDERI VARIORVM POEMATVM LIBER SECVNDVS . . . 1612.
(tp.3=p.93) ANTONI SANDERI VARIORVM POEMATVM LIBER TERTIVS . . . 1612.
8° pp.144
11409.aaa.25.

SANDRA, Melchisedec. Positiones philosophicae ex logica de definitione. 1608. *See* JACCHAEUS, Gilbertus

S31 SANFORD, Hugh
DE DESCENSV DOMINI NOSTRI IESV CHRISTI ad Inferos. LIBRI QVATVOR. Ab auctore . . . HVGONE SANFORDO . . . Inchoati. Opera veró et studio ROBERTI PARKERI, ad umbilicum perducti, ac . . . In Lucem editi . . . AMSTELODAMI. In ædibus Ægidij Thorpij . . . 1611. 4° pp.51, 165, 249, 213
4226.cc.40.

SANGA VERINUS, Liberius; Cantaber, pseudonym of Martinus Antonius Delrio. *See* DELRIO, Martinus Antonius

S32 SANTA CRUZ DE DUEÑAS, Melchior de
FLORESTA ESPANOLA De Apotehgmas [*sic*] o Sententias sabia y graciosamente dichas, de algunos Españoles. COLEGIDAS POR MELchior de Santa Cruz, de Dueñas . . . EN BRVCELLAS, En casa de Roger Velpius . . . 1605. 12° pp.194
G.17622.

S33 SANTA CRUZ DE DUEÑAS, Melchior de
FLORESTA ESPAÑOLA, De Apotehgmas [*sic*] . . . COLEGIDAS POR MELCHIOR DE Santa Cruz, de Dueñas . . . LA FLORESTA SPAGNOLA, OV LE PLAISANT BOCAGE. Contenant plusieurs comptes, gosseries, brocards, cassades, & graues sentences de personnes de tous estats. A BRVXELLES, Par Rutger Velpius, & Hubert Anthoine . . . 1614. 8° pp.509
12315.b.1.

In Spanish and French. Ownership inscription: S. Engl [?] a Wagram.

S34 SANTEN, Gerard Cornelisz van
G. C. van SANTENS LICHTE VVIGGER . . . TOT LEYDEN, Voor David Jansz. van Ilpendam . . . 1617. 4° sig. $A\text{-}F^4G^3$
11754.bb.22.

S35 SANTEN, Gerard Cornelisz van
G. C. van SANTENS SNAPPENDE SIITGEN . . . TOT LEYDEN, Voor Bartholomeus vander Bild . . . 1620. 4° sig. $A\text{-}D^4E^2$
11754.bb.23.

S36 SAPMA, Dominicus
[Letters] Droeve Ghevanckenisse/ende Blijde Uytkomst van DOMINICVS SAPMA . . . Vervaet in seeckere Brieven . . . mitsgaders Een Remonstrantie ofte Supplicatie des selven Gevanghen aende H. H. Burghemeesteren/Schout/ende Schepenen der Stadt Amsterdam. Ghedruckt . . . 1621. 4° pp.46
T.2251(7).

S37 SAPMA, Dominicus

BESPRECK, Ofte Onder-handelinge ghehouden over eenige Huydendaechsche Kerckelijcke verschillen . . . Tusschen Dominicum Sapma . . . Ende Rippertum Sixti . . . Ghedruckt tot Hoorn, By Jan Joachimsz. Byvanck/voor Hendrick Gaerman . . . 1617. 4° pp.792 [279]
T.2247(17).
Edited also by Dominicus Sapma.

S38 SAPMA, Dominicus

LEVGEN-STRICK, OFTE Praetjen vande onderteijckeninghe tot Waelwijck/kortelijck wederleydt tot verantwoordinghe vande uytghesettede Predikanten aldaer . . . GHEDRVCKT . . . 1619. [etc.] 4° pp.10
T.2249(34).
Anonymous.

SATIRAE duae Hercules tuam fidem. 1617. *See* HEINSIUS, Daniel

S39 SAUMAISE, Claude de

AMICI AD AMICVM DE SVBVRBICARIIS REGIONIB. ET ECCLESIIS SVBVRBICARIIS EPISTOLA. M.DC.XIX. 8° pp.118
1474.a.38(1).
Anonymous. A reply to Jacques Sirmond's 'Censura coniecturae anonymi scriptoris de suburbicariis regionibus et ecclesiis', a work written by Jacques Godefroy. Presumably published at Leiden.

S40 SAUTERIUS, Daniel

De Officijs MERCATORVM, Sive DIATRIBAE, quæ præcipua Mercatorum Pietatis inter Negociandum continent officia, Auctore DANIELE SAVTERIO. LVGDVNI BATAVORVM, Ex Officina Ioannis à Dorp, 1615. Prostant apud Iohannem Maire. 8° ff.70
877.b.6; 877.f.10(2).
The copy at 877.b.6 contains a long contemporary manuscript note in Latin.

S41 SAUTERIUS, Daniel

Mastix FALLITORVM, SIVE CÆSARVM, REVM, PRINCIPVM, AC MAGISTRATVVM VARIORVM Huius superiorisque ævi Senatusconsulta & Edicta DE POENIS MERCATORVM NEQVITER FORO CEDENTIVM: Summâ diligentiâ collecta, utilibusq; exemplis . . . illustrata, A DANIELE SAVTERIO. LVGDVNI BATAVORVM, Ex Officina Iacobi Marci, M D C XIX. 4° pp.148
884.h.26(2).

S42 SAUTERIUS, Daniel

PRAXIS Banccæ-ruptorum huius seculi . . . Auctore DANIELE SAVTERIO. LUGDUNI BATAVORUM Excudebat GODEFRIDUS BASSON, M D CXV. 8° pp.94
877.f.10(1).
P.46 has been left blank.

S43 SAXONY

[6.4.1620] Verclaringe eñ Patente die den Cheur-Vorst van Saxen heeft laten publiceren. By de welcke de Ghepubliceerde Mandaten de Anno 1618. ende 1619. worden nv vernieuwt 1620. Ende alle vremde wervinghe . . . van krijsch-volck zijn verboden/met aendieninge . . . dat de Leen-mannen ende Ondersaten hen niet en souden begheuen in eenighen vremden krijsch-dienst . . . Overghesedt wt den Hooch-Duytsch in onse Nederlantsche sprake. Nv eerst Ghedruckt den 29. Mey 1620. T'Hantwerpen/By Abraham Verhoeuen . . . 1620. [etc.] 4° pp.8; sig. Y^4; illus.
P.P.3444.af(53).

Issued 6 April 1620. The titlepage woodcut shows the arms of Saxony, rather blurred and poor. The variant corresponds to the copy in the Museum Meermanno-Westreenianum at The Hague, described in the *Bibliotheca Belgica* no. V196.

S44 SAXONY. Nobility

[12/22.9.1620] COPIE Der Resolutie, vvelcke de Cheursachsische Ridderschap laestleden in de Vergaderinghe te Meissen, den $\frac{12}{22}$ Septembris Sijn Cheurvorst. Ghenade, aengaende de Krijchsexpeditie, ghegheven hebben. TOT LEYDEN, By Iacob Marcusz . . . 1620. 4° sig. A^4

T.2423(44).

S45 SAYER, Robert; name in religion: Gregorius Sayrus

(tp. 1) REVERENDI P. D. GREGORII SAYRI . . . OPERVM THEOLOGICORVM TOMVS PRIMVS, QVI DE SACRAMENTIS IN CŌMVNI . . . NOVISSIMA EDITIO COMMODA characterum varietate distinctius & emendatius elaborata . . . DVACI, Ex Officina Typographica BALTAZARIS BELLERI . . . M.DC.XX.

(tp. 2) REVERENDI P. D. GREGORII SAYRI . . . OPERVM THEOLOGICORVM TOMVS SECVNDVS, QVI CASVVM CONSCIENTIÆ, SIVE THEOLOGIÆ MORALIS THESAVRVS, DE CENSVRIS ECCLESIASTICIS . . . DVACI, EX OFFICINA TYPOGRAPHICA BALTAZARIS BELLERI.

(tp. 3) PATRIS D. GREGORII SAYRI . . .OPERVM THEOLOGICORVM TOMVS TERTIVS, IN QVO FLORES DECISIONVM SIVE CASVVM CONSCIENTIÆ, Ex Doctrina Consiliorum Martini ab Azpilcueta Doctoris Nauarri collecti, & iuxta librorum iuris Canonici dispositionem in suos Titulos distributi . . . Nouissima editio, castigatior & distinctior præcedentibus. DVACI, EX OFFICINA TYPOGRAPHICA BALTAZARIS BELLERI. fol. tom. 1-3: pp. 318; 642; 187

C.81.k.5.

Preceded by a half-title reading 'R.P.D. GREGORII SAYRI . . . OPERA THEOLOGICA. MORALIS DOCTRINÆ . . . THESAVRVS PLENISSIMVS. QVATVOR TOMIS DISTINCTVS . . . Nouissimam hanc editionem recensuit, & castigauit . . . Pater D. LEANDER DE S. MARTINO [etc.]'. Imperfect; wanting tom. 4. From the library of James I.

S46 SAYON, A.

CONGRATVLATIE Aenden Grooten Capiteyn . . . MAVRITIVS VAN NASSAV: Op sijne arbeydelijcke/periculeuse ende grootdadighe Krijgh-Tocht/Vanden Iare, M. VI^{c}. V. Door A. Sayon. B. TOT DELF, By Ian Andriesz [etc.] 4° sig. AB^4

11555.e.32.

In verse. The 'B' after the author's name on the titlepage, perhaps indicating his native place, is printed in a different type and is not part of the author's signature at the end of the text. A marginal note with poem II: 'Int voorleden jaer 1604' confirms the date of publication as 1605.

SCABAELJE, Dierick. *See* SCHABALJE, Dierick

SCAGEN, Cornelius. Theses medicae de febre pestilenti. 1619. *See* VORSTIUS, Everardus Aelius

S47 SCALIGER, Joseph Juste

[Collections] (tp. 1) IOSEPHI SCALIGERI . . . POEMATA omnia, Ex museio PETRI SCRIVERII. Ex Officina Plantiniana RAPHELENGII, M.D.CXV.

(tp. 2) IOSEPHI SCALIGERI . . . POEMATA PROPRIA, Latina & Græca. LVGDVNI BATAVORVM Ex Officina Plantiniana RAPHELENGII M D C XV.

(tp.3) IOS. SCALIGERI . . . POEMATA GRÆCA, VERSA Ex Lat. Ital. & Gall. PETRVS SCRIVERIVS publicabat. LVGDVNI BATAVORVM Ex Officina Plantiniana RAPHELENGII M D C XV.
(tp.4) IOSEPHI SCALIGERI . . . POEMATA LATINA versa è Græco. LVGDVNI BATAVORVM Ex Officina Plantiniana RAPHELENGII M D C XV. 16° 3 pt.: pp.166; 144; 184
1213.b.6.
Tp.1 is a collective titlepage.

S48 SCALIGER, Joseph Juste
CATALECTA VIR GILII [*sic*] & aliorum Poëtarum Latinorum veterum POEMATIA: Cum Commentariis IOSEPHI SCALIGERI . . . LVGDVNI BATAVORVM, Apud Ioannem Maire. 1617. 8° pp.264, 348
1067.e.28; 237.a.12(1).
With 'Notæ Friderici Linden-Bruch in Appendicem P. Virgilii Maronis et veterum poetarum catalecta' and with Scaliger's defence of his edition of Priapeia etc. in a letter to Sebastianus Sennetonius. The copy at 1067.e.28 with the ownership inscription: Joannis Mensinga and the exlibris of Henry Spencer Ashbee 1895.

S49 SCALIGER, Joseph Juste
IOSEPHI SCALIGERI . . . DE RE NVMMARIA Dissertatio, LIBER POSTHVMVS: Ex Bibliotheca Academiæ Lugd. Bat. EX OFFICINA PLANTINIANA RAPHELENGIJ, 1616. 8° pp.112
602.a.10.
The editor's dedication signed: Willebrordus Snellius. Published at Leiden.

S50 SCALIGER, Joseph Juste
IOSEPHI SCALIGERI . . . Elenchus Trihæresii NICOLAI SERARII. Ejus in ipsum Scaligerum animadversiones confutatæ. EIVSDEM delirium fanaticum . . . quo Essenos Monachos Christianos fuisse contendit . . . elusum. FRANEKERAE, Excudebat AEGIDIVS RADAEVS . . . M.DC.V. 8° pp.272
C.79.a.21.

S51 SCALIGER, Joseph Juste
(tp.1) IOSEPHI SCALIGERI . . . ELENCHVS Vtriusque Orationis Chronologicæ D. DAVIDIS PAREI: Quarum secunda operis calci addita: Prior vero Commentariis auctoris in Hoseam Heydelbergæ excusis prostat. LVGDVNI BATAVORVM, Ex Officina Henrici Ludovici ab Haestens, Jmpensis Ludovici Elzevierii . . . 1607.
(tp.2) DAVIDIS PAREI ORATIO CHRONOLOGICA ALTERA DE QVÆSTIONE: Vtrum Chronologia integra ab Adam ad Christum ex sola historia sacra haberi possit . . . LVGDVNI-BATAVORVM Ex Officina Henrici Ludovici ab Haestens, Impensis Ludovici Elzevirij . . . 1607.
(tp.3) IOSEPHI SCALIGERI . . . Elenchus Primæ ORATIONIS Chronologicæ DAVIDIS PAREI. LVGDVNI BATAVORVM Ex Officinâ Ioannis Patii . . . M.D.C.VII. Impensis Ludovici Elzevierii. 4° 3 pt.: pp.103: plate; sig.A-E^4; A-E^4
C.75.b.16(1,2).
The editor's prefatory letter signed: Franciscus Gomarus. Author's presentation copy to Isaac Casaubon.

S52 SCALIGER, Joseph Juste
IOSEPHI SCALIGERI . . . IAMBI GNOMICI nunc primum editi à DANIELE HEINSIO. LVGDVNI BATAVORVM Ex officinâ Henrici ab Haestens. jmpensis Ioannis à Maire. M.D.C.VII. 8° pp.44
C.83.a.19(2).
Printed in italics throughout.

S53 SCALIGER, Joseph Juste

IOSEPHI SCALIGERI LOCI CVIVSDAM GALENI DIFFICILLIMI EXPLICATIO DOCTISSIMA, Nunc primum in lucem edita, Ex Musæo IOACHIMI MORSI. LVGDVNI BATAVORVM Excudebat IACOBVS MARCI. M DC XIX. 4° pp.8

543.b.19(2).

Leaf A4 is mutilated.

S54 SCHABALJE, Dierick

Corte ende clare aenwysinghe van den sin/meeninghe/ende het ooghemerck des H. Apostels Pauli/in het neghende Capittel zynes Briefs tot den Romeynen . . . Door Dierick Scabaelje . . . t'Amstelredam, By Nicolaes Biestkens . . . 1616. 4° pp.18

T.2246(2).

S55 SCHABALJE, Dierick

KORTE Verclaringhe eener Vraech Stucken/aengaende DE VERKIESINGE Ten dienste van yder in rijme ghestelt/DOOR DIRICK SCHABALIE . . . Ghedruckt tot Haerlem, By my Iacob Houwaert, Voor Daniel de Keyser . . . 1614. 4° pp.16

11555.e.44(2).

S56 SCHABALJE, Dierick

Spel des gheschils tot ATHENEN, Ghenomen uyt het 17 Cap. van de Handelinghen der Apostelen: Ende in Rijm ghesteldt door Dierick Scabaelje. t'Amsterdam, By Nicolaes Biestkens . . . 1617. 4° sig.A-E^4

11754.bbb.51.

De SCHADT-KISTE der philosophen ende poeten. 1621. *See* THIEULLIER, Jan

S57 SCHAGHEN, Cornelis Pieterszoon

C. P. SCHAGHENS ALCKMAAR LOF-DICHT. Tot ALCKMAER. Ghedruckt by Pieter de Meester . . . 1621. Ende men vintse te coop by Thomas Pietersz. Baert [etc.] 4° sig.A-E^4

11556.dd.46.

SCHALICHIUS, Theodorus. Disputationum physicarum secunda de principiis physicis. 1607. *See* JACCHAEUS, Gilbertus

SCHEEL-HANS. *See* GERSDORFF, Hans von; called Schylhans

S58 SCHERER, Georg; Jesuit

PRECES AC MEDITATIONES PIAE In Mysteria Passionis ac Resurrectionis D. N. Iesu Xp̄i collectæ Per GEORGIVM SCHERER . . . Figuris Æneis ab Alberto Durero olim artificiose sculptis, ornatæ. BRVXELLÆ Apud Rutger. Velpium et Hub. Anthoniū . . . M.DC.XII. [etc.] 12° pp.228: plate; illus.

3457.cc.24.

Originally published as part of Dominicus Mengin's 'Enchiridium Christianarum precationum', Ingolstadt, 1586. The titlepage signed: G. Hani. fecit; other engravings signed: WDH, i.e. Willem de Haen; one plate signed: C. de Mallery ex.

S59 SCHERMUTSELINGHEN

SCHERMVTSELINGHEN VAN SOMMIGHE LICHT-GEWAPENDE CRYGHSKNECHTEN DAT IS, Aenvvysinghe vande bedriegelicke ende onbehoorlicke vvyse van doen, int verbreyden der gevaerlicker van outs begraevener nieuvvicheden, ghepleecht by de voorstanders van D. ARMINIVS . . . ENDE D. CONRADVS VORSTIVS. Getrocken uyt

diversche Schriften die van beyde sijden . . . uytghegaen zijn Per H.I. ad honorem Dei . . . M.D.C.XIII. 4° pp.98
T.2243(1).
Sometimes attributed to Franciscus Gomarus. Apparently an earlier issue of the copy in the Koninklijke Bibliotheek, The Hague (*Knuttel* no.2070) which has a correction in the pagination, but is otherwise in the same setting, bearing the imprint: MIDDELBVRGH, Voor Adriaen vanden Vivere, M.D.C.XIII.

SCHIEDAMS Rood Roosjens spel. 1619. *See* WAEL, Job A. van de

Het SCHILT der verdructer ghemoederen. 1619. *See* CAMPHUYSEN, Dirck Raphaelsz

S60 SCHLAAFF, Ludovicus
DE NATIVITATE CHRISTI, ORATIO QVAM . . . Publicè recitavit. LVDOVICVS SCHLAAFF . . . FRANEKERÆ, EXCVDEBAT AEGIDIUS RADAEUS . . . 1607. 4° sig.AB[4]
480.a.7(4).

S61 SCHNEEBERGER, Anton
CATALOGUS MEDICAMENTORUM simplicium & facilè parabilium PESTILENTIÆ Veneno adversantium, ANTONII SNEEBERGERI TIGVRINI, Recognitus & multorum remediorum accessione adauctus Opera & studio HENRICI à BRA . . . FRANEKERÆ, APVD AEGIDIVM RADAEVM . . . M.D.CV. 8° pp.186
1168.e.11(2).

A SCHOLASTICALL discourse. 1607. *See* PARKER, Robert

S62 [*SCHOLIER, Peter
KOOCBOEC OFT FAMILIEREN KEKENBOEC [*sic*]. Bequaem voor alle Jouffrouwen/die hun van keuken-handel oft backen van Toertkens ende Taertkens willen verstaen. GEMAECT Door M. Antonius Magirus. TOT LOVEN. By CHRISTOPH. FLAVIVS . . . 1612. [etc.] 8° pp.137
07944.de.8.]
*Destroyed. Pseudonymous. The description is taken from the General Catalogue and the copy in the Royal Library Albert I, Brussels (III 17.312 A).

S63 SCHONAEUS, Cornelius
FABVLA COMICA, In commendationem ædificij, egenis senibus HARLEMI extruendi: scripta, aut lusa potius A CORNELIO SCHONAEO . . . ZVVOLLÆ, Apud ZACHARIAM HEYNS . . . M.D.CVII. 4° sig.A-$D^4E^2E^6$; illus.
C.175.ff.13(3); G.18275(3).
Partly in Latin and partly in Dutch. The illustration shows an engraved emblem matching the blazons of chambers of Rhetoric, with the motto 'Diligentia parit artis [*sic*] Anno 1607'. The copy at G.18275(3) is imperfect; wanting all before sig.E. Both copies wanting the plate described in *Bibliotheca Belgica* no.J37.

S64 SCHONAEUS, Cornelius
FABVLA COMICA . . . scripta . . . A CORNELIO SCHONAEO . . . ZVVOLLAE Apud ZACHARIAM HEYNS, M.D.CVII. 4° sig.A-D^4E^2; illus.
11712.c.58.
Another edition of the Latin text of the preceding.

S65 SCHOON
EEN Schoon ende Heerlijke VER TROOSTINGE [*sic*], aen alle Lief-hebbers der Waere ende suyvere Religie/onder de Ghemeynte der Remonstrants-ghezinde/hoe zy haer in dese verdruckinghe . . . sullen dulden ende draghen . . . GHEDRVCKT . . . 1619. [etc.] 4° pp.22
T.2249(33).

Een SCHOONE heerlicke ende warachtige aenwysinge. 1614. *See* JOSEPHI, Joannes

S66 SCHOONHOVEN

[8.9.1618] PVBLICATIE Van de E. Vroedtschap der Stede Schoonhoven, van weghen de ware Ghereformeerde Religie. Ghedaen den 8. September. Anno 1618 . . . TOT AMSTERDAM, By Marten Jansz. Brandt . . . 1618. fol. a single sheet
T.2248(10).

S67 SCHOONHOVIUS, Florentius

Emblemata FLORENTII SCHOONHOVII . . . Partim Moralia partim etiam Civilia. Cum latiori eorundem ejusdem Auctoris interpretatione. Accedunt et alia quædam Poëmatia in alijs Poëmatum suorum libris non contenta. GOUDÆ. Apud Andream Burier. M.D.C.XVIII. 4° pp.251; illus., port.
C.76.b.10.

The titlepage is engraved. All the engravings are by Crispin van de Passe the Younger.

S68 SCHOONHOVIUS, Florentius

FLOR. SCHOONHOVII . . . POEMATA ANTEHAC NON edita . . . LVGDVNI BATAVORVM Ex Officina GODEFRIDI BASSON. M.D.C.XIII. 8° pp.204
11403.a.32.

S69 SCHOPPE, Caspar

[Classicum belli sacri.] Des Duyvels Alarm-slagh Van CASPARI SHIOPPI . . . teghen alle Euangelische C. Wt den Hoochduyschen ghetranslateert door W. Baud. Tot Leyden, By Zacharias de Smit/Voor Isack de Beer. 4° sig.AB^{4}C^2; illus.
T.2248(53); T.2424(11).

A translation by Willem Baudaert of 'Extract auss Gasparis Scioppii . . . Bůchlein, dessen Titul: Classicum belli sacri'. The titlepage woodcut shows a devil riding an eagle and beating drums. Published in 1619.

S70 SCHOPPE, Caspar

[Classicum belli sacri.] NIEV Veldt-gheschrey/van Roomen. Tot Bestorminghe der Ghereformeerden . . . NIMMEGHEN, Ghedruckt by Henderick van Holt . . . 1619. 4° sig.A^{4}B^2; illus.
T.2249(41); T.2423(21).

Translated from what the titlepage verso describes as 'Boecxken Caspari Scioppij . . . Wiens Tytel is: Classicum belli sacri', i.e. the same original as in the preceding. The titlepage woodcut shows a trumpet.

S71 SCHOTTUS, Andreas

AND. SCHOTTI . . . DE BONO SILENTII RELIGIOSORVM ET SAECVLARIVM LIBRI II. ANTVERPIAE Apud Petrum & Ioannem Belleros fratres. M.DC.XIX. [etc.] 12° pp.307
1568/9203(2).

In a contemporary German blind-tooled white pigskin binding.

S72 SCHOTTUS, Andreas

NODI CICERONIS VARIORVMQ. LIBRIS IIII. ENODATI. AB. AND. SCHOTTO . . . ANTVERPIAE, Apud heredes Martini Nutij. Typis HENRICI ÆRTSI. M.DC.XII. [etc.] 8° pp.192, 1-32; illus.
835.d.19.

With 'Favonii Eulogii . . . in Cicer. Somnium Scipionis disputatio . . . Typis nunc primùm edita', edited by Andreas Schottus. Imperfect; wanting all after p.32 of the second pagination. Author's presentation copy to Isaac Casaubon.

S73 SCHOTTUS, Andreas

ΠΑΡΟΙΜΙΑΙ ΕΛΛΗΝΙΚΑΙ. ADAGIA SIVE PROVERBIA GRAECORVM EX ZENOBIO seu

ZENODOTO DIOGENIANO & SVIDAE COLLECTANEIS. Partim edita nunc primùm, partim Latinè reddita, SCHOLIISQVE parallelis illustrata, ab ANDREA SCHOTTO . . . ANTVERPIAE, EX OFFICINA PLANTINIANA, Apud Viduam & Filios Ioannis Moreti. M.DC.XII. [etc.] 4° pp.702
635.k.7; 635.k.8; 679.e.4; 87.k.12; 681.f.16(1); G.8292.
Ownership inscriptions in the copy at 635.k.7: Gilbert Wakefield; James Collings.

S74 SCHOTTUS, Andreas
TABVLAE REI NVMMARIAE ROMANORVM GRAECORVMQ. Ad Belgicam, Gallicam, Hispanicam & Italicam monetam reuocatæ . . . EX GVL. BVDÆO AGRICOLA ET CIACCONIO. ANTVERPIÆ. Apud Gerardum Wolsschatium. M.DC.XV. (col.) ANTVERPIÆ Apud Gerardum Wolsschatium. M.DC.XVI. 8° pp.22, 16, 14, 24, 24
811.c.1; 975.b.26.
The compiler's dedicatory letter signed: Andreas Schottus, 1616. With 'Tabula mensium Romanorum et Atticorum', 'Tabula anomalorum verborum graecorum', 'Geometrica et gromatica vetusti scriptoris' and 'Index auctorum Plinii Maioris', all edited by Andreas Schottus. Ownership inscription in the copy at 811.c.1, p.1: John Morris or Norris. The copy at 975.b.26 is imperfect; wanting all except the 'Index auctorum Plinii Maioris'.

S75 SCHOTTUS, Andreas
AND. SCHOTTI . . . TVLLIANARVM QVÆSTIONVM De instauranda CICERONIS Imitatione LIBRI IIII. ANTVERPIÆ, EX OFFICINA PLANTINIANA, Apud Ioannem Moretum. M.DC.X. [etc.] (col.) ANTVERPIÆ, EX OFFICINA PLANTINIANA, Apud Ioannem Moretum. M.DC.X. 8° pp.383
11312.bb.3.
Partly in Greek.

S76 SCHOUTEN, Willem Cornelisz
IOVRNAL OV DESCRIPTION DE L'ADMIRABLE VOYAGE de Guillaume Schouten . . . Illustré de belles Cartes & Figures taillez en cuivre. A AMSTERDAM. Imprimé ches Guilliaume Iansen. 4° pp.88: plates; illus., maps, port.
1045.e.17(1).
The authorship is doubtful, but generally attributed to Willem Schouten, probably with additional material from the diary of Jacob Le Maire. In this copy the titlepage engraving was not yet available, nor were the poems by Vondel due to be printed on leaf A4. There is no world map and there are only 4 plates instead of the nine described in the literature. Published in 1618.

S77 SCHOUTEN, Willem Cornelisz
JOVRNAL Ou DESCRIPTION DV MERVEILLEVX VOYAGE DE GVILLAVME SCHOVTEN . . . A AMSTREDAM, Chez Pierre du Keere . . . 1619. 4° pp.88: plates; illus., maps, port.
1045.e.17(3).
A reprint by Johannes Janssonius of the edition of W. J. Blaeu. In this copy the large map of the 'Zuijdzee' is included twice, once as frontispiece in place of the world map. The titlepage engraving shows the ships in the port of Hoorn. With Vondel's epigrams in French.

S78 SCHOUTEN, Willem Cornelisz
JOVRNAL Ou DESCRIPTION DV MERVEILLEVX VOYAGE DE GVILLAVME SCHOVTEN . . . fait es années 1615. 1616. & 1617 . . . A AMSTERDAM, Chez Harman Ianson . . . 1619. 4° pp.88: plates; illus., maps, port.
980.e.30; G.6736.
Another issue of the edition printed by Johannes Janssonius, using the name of the printer Harmen Jansz Muller who had died in 1617. With Vondel's epigrams in French. In the copy at 980.e.30 the plates have been strengthened, to the detriment of the text on their versos which is still legible in the copy at G.6736. The copy at 980.e.30 from the library of Sir Joseph Banks.

S79 SCHOUTEN, Willem Cornelisz

[Journal ou description du merveilleux voyage.] DIARIVM VEL Descriptio laboriosissimi, & Molestissimi Jtineris, facti à GVILIELMO CORNELII SCHOVTENIO . . . Annis 1615. 1616. & 1617 . . . AMSTERDAMI, Apud Petrum Kærium . . . 1619. 4° pp. 1–24, 17–71: plates; illus., maps., port.

1045.e.17(2); G.6735.

Printed by Johannes Janssonius. With the view of the port of Hoorn on the titlepage. Without the poems by Vondel. The copy at 1045.e.17(2) is without the view of the 'Hoornse Eijlandt', that at G.6735 is without the world map, the maps of the 'Zuijdzee' and the 'Nieuwe Passage' and the view of 'Cocos Eylandt'.

S80 SCHOUTEN, Willem Cornelisz

[Journal ou description du merveilleux voyage.] NOVI FRETI, A PARTE MERIDIONALI FRETI Magellanici, in Magnum Mare Australe DETECTIO: Facta laboriosissimo & periculosissimo itinere à Guilielmo Cornelij Schoutenio . . . Annis 1615. 1616, & 1617, totum Orbem circumnavigante. AMSTERODAMI, Apud Guilielmum Iansonium. 1619. 4° pp. 87: plates; illus., maps, port.

981.a.8.

Translated and with a laudatory poem by Nicolaes van Wassenaer. Ownership inscription: Dionys. Pauli Cimb: Husumiensi 1640 signed: Disce pati; from the library of Sir Joseph Banks.

SCHOUWE, over D. Francisci Gomari Proeve. 1610. *See* CORVINUS, Joannes Arnoldi

S81 SCHRICKELICKE

Schrickelicke ende grouwelijcke verraderije/ghepracktiseert by den Paus, den Coninck van Spaengien, Huys Oostenrijck, Florensen, Lottringhen, ende Papistische Zvvitsers, om de Evangelische Zvvitsers op den 1. Novembris, 1618. ouden stijl van alle kanten te overvallen . . . Ontdect . . . van den Hartoch van Savoyen . . . die daer van de verbintenissen en contracten . . . aen de Republijcke van Bern heeft over-ghesonden/ende watter voorts gevolcht is . . . VVt den Hoochduytschen, van een Professor van Zurich gheschreven . . . verduyscht [*sic*]. t'Amsterdam, by Broer Iansz. 4° sig. A^4

T.2423(13).

Translated from manuscript? Published in 1619?

S82 SCHRIECK, Adriaen van

ADRIANI SCHRIECKI . . . ADVERSARIORVM LIBRI IIII . . . IPRIS FLANDRORVM Ex Officina typographica Francisci Belletti. M.DC.XX. (col.) IPRIS FLANDRORVM. APVD FRANCISCVM BELLETTVM . . . M.DC.XX. fol. pp. 112

155.a.13(2); 621.l.12(1).

On the Hebrew and Dutch languages, but not a new edition of part of 'Van t'beghin'. The titlepage of the copy at 621.l.12(1) is mutilated.

SCHRIECK, Adriaen van. Monitorum secundarum libri V. 1615. *See* below: Van t'beghin.

S83 SCHRIECK, Adriaen van

VAN T'BEGHIN DER EERSTER VOLCKEN VAN EVROPEN, IN-SONDERHEYT VANDEN OORSPRONCK ENDE SAECKEN DER NEDER-LANDREN, XXIII BOECKEN . . . BESCHREVEN DOOR ADRIAEN VAN SCHRIECK . . . T'YPRE, BY FRANÇOIS BELLET . . . M.DC.XIV. [etc.] (col.) IPRIS FLANDRORVM, EX TYPOGRAPHIA FRANCISCI BELLETTI . . . M.DC.XIV. fol. pp. 560; illus.

9405.h.10.

With an additional, engraved titlepage reading: ADRIANI SCRIECKI . . . ORIGINVM RERVMQ.

CELTICARVM ET BELGICARVM LIBRI XXIII., signed: G.D.T. fe. Ip., i.e. Guillaume du Tielt fecit Ipris. The dedication and introduction are in Latin, the privilege is in French and Dutch. The illustration on the last leaf of the prelims is an engraving of a coat of arms. Imperfect; wanting pp.481-492.

S84 SCHRIECK, Adriaen van

(tp.1) VAN T'BEGHIN DER EERSTER VOLCKEN VAN EVROPEN . . . BESCHREVEN DOOR ADRIAEN VAN SCHRIECK . . . T'YPRE, By FRANCOIS BELLET . . . M.DC.XIV. [etc.] (col.1) IPRIS FLANDRORVM, EX TYPOGRAPHIA FRANCISCI BELLETTI . . . M.DC.XIV. (tp.2) ADRIANI SCRIECKI . . . MONITORVM SECVNDORVM LIBRI V. Quibus Originum rerumq́ȝ Celticarum & Belgicarum OPVS nuper editum, altiùs & auctius . . . probat, firmatq́ȝ . . . YPRIS FLANDRORVM, Ex Officina typographica Francisci Belletti. M.DC.XV. [etc.] (col.2) IPRIS FLANDRORVM, Ex Officina Typographica FRANCISCI BELLETTI . . . M.DC.XV. fol. 2 pt.: pp.560; 63; illus.

C.77.g.8(1, 2); 155.a.13(1, 3); 9005.g.11.

Pt.1 is a reissue of the preceding, with a printer's preface describing the whole as an enlarged edition and specifying its parts as does the author in his preface 'In editionem hanc auctam quædam Præmonita'. The numbered pages of pt.2 are followed by an 'Index tertius', sig.I-O^4P^6. In the copy at 155.a.13(1,3) the leaves bearing the new prefaces are bound immediately after the engraved titlepage, preceding tp.1. The copy at 9005.g.11 has had two leaves inserted, both bearing the same portrait signed: G.T., i.e. Guillaume du Tielt, and with a Latin distich by C. Torrius. This copy is imperfect; its titlepage is mutilated and it wants all of pt.2 except the 'Index tertius'.

S85 SCHRIFTELICKE

Schriftelicke CONFERENTIE, GEHOVDEN IN s'Gravenhaghe inden Iare 1611.tusschen sommighe Kercken-dienaren: Aengaende de Godlicke Prædestinatie metten aencleven van dien. Ter Ordonnantie vande . . . Staten van Hollandt ende West-Vrieslandt Ghedruckt IN S'GRAVEN-HAGE, By Hillebrandt Jacobsz . . . 1612. 4° pp.440

1609/5508.

Edited by Jan Wtenbogaert. Sometimes wrongly attributed to Joannes Arnoldi Corvinus.

S86 SCHRIFTELICKE

[Schriftelicke Conferentie, gehouden in s'Gravenhaghe . . . 1611.] Schriftelijcke CONFERENTIE, GEHOVDEN IN s'Gravenhaghe inden Iare 1611. tusschen sommighe Kercken-dienaren: Aengaende de Godlicke Prædestinatie . . . IN S'GRAVEN-HAGE, By Hillebrant Jacobsz . . . 1617. 4° pp.440

T.2241(21).

A new edition of the preceding.

S87 SCHRIFTELICKE

[Schriftelicke Conferentie, gehouden in s'Gravenhaghe . . . 1611.] (tp.1) Collatio SCRIPTO HABITA HAGAE comitis [*sic*] anno . . . 1611. inter quosdam Ecclesiastas de divina Prædestinatione, & ejus appendicibus . . . Ex sermone vernaculo Latina facta interprete HENRICO BRANDIO . . . Huic est etiam subiecta Collatio inter sex Ecclesiastas Delphis habita anno 1613. ZIRIZÆÆ, Typis Ioannis Hellenij. Impensis Hadriani Vivarij Bibliopolæ apud MIDDELBVRGENSES M.DC.XV.

(tp.2) Collatio SCRIPTO INTER SEX ECCLESIAstas Delphis Batavorum vicesimâ sexta & septima Februarij anni 1613. Præsentibus Deputatis Ordinum Hollandiæ & Frisiæ Occidentalis Habita . . . Ex sermone vernaculo Latina facta interprete HENRICO BRANDIO . . . Excusa impensis Hadriani Viverij Bibliopolæ apud Middelburgenses . . . typis Ioannis Hellenij. M.D.C.XV. 4° 2 pt.: pp.18; 524

701.h.53.

For the original Dutch text of the Delft conference *see* below: SCHRIFTELICKE Conferentie, ghehouden tot Delff. In this copy the Latin text of the Delft conference is bound before that of the Hague Conference, following the dedication of the whole volume.

S88 SCHRIFTELICKE

Schriftelicke CONFERENTIE, GHEHOVDEN tot Delff, den 26$^{en.}$ ende 27$^{en.}$ Februarij 1613. tusschen ses Kercken-dienaren. Om te beramen eenighe bequaeme middelen/waer door de swaricheden . . . in de Kercken hier te Lande ontstaen . . . af-gedaen/ende voort-aen goede vrede . . . onder houden soude connen werden . . . TOT DELF, Ghedruckt by Ian Andriesz. . . . 1613. 4° pp.36
T.2243(15).

The expositions of the two sides signed respectively: Iohannes Wtenbogaert, Adrianus vanden Borre, Nicolaus Grevinchovius, and: Iohannes Bogardus, Iohannes Becius, Festus Hommius. With annotations and with an extract from a letter by David Pareus in Latin and Dutch. For the Latin translation *see* above: Schriftelicke Conferentie, gehouden in s'Gravenhaghe . . . 1611. Collatio.

S89 SCHRIFTELICKE

Schriftelicke CONFERENTIE Tusschen de Kercken-Dienaren des Vorstendoms Geldre ende Graef-schap Zutphen, Aenghevangen Anno 1617. ende in hare Provinciale Synode in Iunio 1618. volbracht: Aengaende de vyff Artijculen . . . Hier is noch by-ghedaen eene Voor-reden vervatende den oorspronck ende voort-gangh der Kerckelijcke svvaricheden. TOT DELF. Ghedruckt by Ian Andriesz . . . 1618. 4° pp.72
T.2248(43).

SCHRIFTELIJCKE Conferentie, gehouden in s'Gravenhaghe . . . 1611. 1617. *See* SCHRIFTELICKE.

SCHRIFTELIJCKE insinuatie ghedaen by . . . Hertoch Maximiliaen van Beyeren. 1620. *See* MAXIMILIAN I; Elector of Bavaria [Letters. 25.8.1620]

SCHRIJVER, Pieter. *See* SCRIVERIUS, Petrus

SCHUYL[L]IUS, Winandus. Disputationum theologicarum decima-tertia, de peccatis in universum. 1603. *See* GOMARUS, Franciscus

SCHUYL LOOSLEVER, Everhardus Hermanni F. Disputationum physicarum prima de constitutione physicae. 1607. *See* JACCHAEUS, Gilbertus

SCHUYL LOOSLEVER, Everhardus Hermanni F. Disputationum physicarum duodecima, de meteoris. 1608. *See* JACCHAEUS, Gilbertus

SCHUYL LOOSLEVER, Everhardus Hermanni F. Disputationum physicarum decima-quinta, de sensibus externis. 1608. *See* JACCHAEUS, Gilbertus

S90 SCHUYT-PRAETGENS

Schuyt-praetgens, Op de Vaert naer Amsterdam/tusschen een Lantman, een Hovelinck, een Borger, ende Schipper. 4° sig. A^4
T.1713(18).

Sometimes attributed to Willem Usselincx. Published in 1608. This edition corresponds to that described in *Knuttel* no.1451.

S91 SCHUYT-PRAETGENS

Schuyt-praetgens Op de Vaert naer Amsterdam/Tusschen een Lantman, een Hovelinck, een Borgher, ende Schipper. 4° sig. A^4
11517.c.8(2); T.2420(5); 106.b.44.

Another edition of the preceding, corresponding to that described in *Knuttel* no.1452. Published in 1608.

S92 SCOTLAND. Church of Scotland

[Books of Discipline] THE FIRST AND SECOND BOOKE OF DISCIPLINE. Together with some ACTS OF THE GENERALL ASSEMBLIES, Clearing and confirming the same: And AN ACT OF PARLIAMENT . . . 1621. 4° pp.92

1230.a.2; 1492.m.4.

Possibly edited by David Calderwood. Without imprint; printed by Giles Thorp at Amsterdam.

SCHYLHANS. *See* GERSDORFF, Hans von; called Schylhans

SCOTT, Thomas; B.D., Minister at Utrecht. Den compaignon vanden verre-sienden waerschouwer. 1621. [Sometimes wrongly attributed to Thomas Scott.] *See* COMPAIGNON

SCOTT, Thomas; B.D., Minister at Utrecht. A relation of some speciall points concerning the state of Holland. 1621. *See* Den COMPAIGNON vanden verre-sienden waerschouwer.

S93 SCOTT, Thomas; B.D., Minister at Utrecht

VOX POPVLI. OR NEWES FROM SPAYNE, translated according to the Spanish coppie. Which may serve to forewarn both England and the United Provinces how farre to trust to Spanish pretences. Imprinted in the yeare 1620. 4° sig.A-C^4D^2

100.c.4.

Anonymous and without imprint. Sometimes believed to have been printed in the Netherlands, but more probably printed in London. Described in *STC* no.22098.

S94 SCOTT, Thomas, B.D., Minister at Utrecht

[Vox populi. Or newes from Spayne. 1620.] 4° sig.A-C^4D^2

8012.aaa.15.

A different edition from that at 100.c.4. Probably printed in London in 1620. Imperfect; wanting the titlepage. Described in *STC* no.22098.5.

S95 SCOTT, Thomas; B.D., Minister at Utrecht

VOX POPVLI. OR NEVVES FROM SPAYNE, translated according to the Spanish coppie. Which may serve to forewarn both England and the Vnited Provinces how farre to trust to Spanish pretences. Imprinted in the yeare 1620. 4° pp.60; port.

1103.e.12(1).

The preface signed: Thomas Scott, signed at the end: T.S. Without imprint and sometimes believed to have been printed in London, but more probably printed in the Netherlands, perhaps at Utrecht. The preliminaries are derived from an edition definitely printed in the Netherlands. The portrait after Crispin van de Passe? In spite of the date on the titlepage printed in 1624. For a description *see STC* no.22100, 22101.

S96 SCOTT, Thomas; B.D., Minister at Utrecht

VOX POPVLI OR NEVVES FROM SPAYNE . . . Imprinted in the yeare 1620. 4°

590.b.5(2).

A made-up edition, wanting the titlepage and consisting of sig.A-C of the same edition as the preceding copy at 1103.e.12(1), without the portrait, and sig.D of the edition of the copy at 100.c.4. With manuscript notes, that on the titlepage reading: 'A Tho: Scot. A relation of him murthered. pr. Lond: 1628. 4to.' Cropped. Probably made up at London, certainly after 1624. Described in *STC* no.22099.

S97 SCOTT, Thomas; B.D., Minister at Utrecht

[Vox populi.] Nieuwe Tydingen Wt den CONSEIO, Ofte Secreten Raedt VAN SPANGIEN. Waer-inne men . . . kan sien/hoe dat de Spangiaert steedts swanger gaet met de op-richtinge van syne gepretendeerde Monarchie . . . Dienende tot waerschouwinge voor Groot Bretangien/de Vereenigde Nederlanden/en andere

Princen . . . sich te wachten voor den Spangiaert . . . T'AMSTELDAM, Voor Iacob Pietersz. Wachter . . . 1621. [etc.] 4° pp.50
T.2422(33); T.2424(13); 106.d.55.
Printed by Paulus van Ravesteyn.

S98 SCRIBANI, Carolus
CAROLI SCRIBANI . . . ADOLESCENS PRODIGVS. Succumbit vitiis. redit ad se. & in omnem ætatem ac fortunam à Virtute instruitur. ANTVERPIÆ Apud Martinum Nutium & Fratres . . . M.DC.XXI. 8° pp.336 [338]
1608/5342.
With poems preceding and following the text. Ownership inscriptions: Hieronymi Winghij can°: Tor.; Biblioth. Eccles. Cathed. Torn.

S99 SCRIBANI, Carolus
CLARI BONARSCII AMPHITHEATRVM HONORIS in quo Caluinistarum in SOCIETATEM IESV criminationes iugulatæ. PALÆOPOLI ADVATICORVM APVD ALEXANDRVM VERHEYDEN. M.DCV. 4° pp.376; illus.
4091.g.9.
In prose and verse. Pseudonymous and with a fictitious imprint. Printed at Antwerp, but not, as has been suggested, at the Plantin press. The engraved illustration shows Truth triumphant over her enemies. Printed by Joachim Trognaesius?

S100 SCRIBANI, Carolus
CLARI BONARSCII AMPHITHEATRVM HONORIS . . . EDITIO ALTERA IV. libro auctior. PALÆOPOLI ADVATICORVM APVD ALEXANDRVM VERHEYDEN. M.DCVI. 4° pp.427; illus.
487.h.15.
A new edition of the preceding. Also printed at Antwerp, probably by Joachim Trognaesius.

S101 SCRIBANI, Carolus
CAROLI SCRIBANI . . . ANTVERPIA. ANTVERPIÆ, EX OFFICINA PLANTINIANA, Apud Ioannem Moretum. M.DC.X. [etc.] 4° pp.146, 24
153.e.6(2).
The additional 24 pages, signed A-Γ, contain poems in Greek or Hebrew and Greek, preceded by a prose piece, ' Ἡ πρωτογενεια και ἐπιστρεφομενη τυχη της 'Ανβερσης', signed: G.S., i.e. Gilles Schoondonck.

SCRIBANI, Carolus. In annunciationem Dei Matris. 1618. *See* PUTEANUS, Erycius. De annunciatione Virginis-Matris.

S102 SCRIBANI, Carolus
IVSTI LIPSI DEFENSIO POSTVMA. C. B. Amico benè merenti posuit. ANTVERPIÆ, EX OFFICINA PLANTINIANA, Apud Ioannem Moretum. M.DC.IIX. (col.) ANTVERPIÆ, EX OFFICINA PLANTINIANA, APVD IOANNEM MORETVM. M.DC.VIII. 16° pp.110
1088.c.15(1).
The initials C.B. are those of Carolus Bonarscius, pseudonym of Carolus Scribani.

S103 SCRIBANI, Carolus
CAROLI SCRIBANI . . . MEDICVS RELIGIOSVS DE ANIMORVM MORBIS ET CVRATIONIBVS. ANTVERPIÆ Apud Heredes MARTINI NVTII . . . M.DC.XVIII. 8° pp.677
848.d.18.

S104 SCRIBANI, Carolus
CAROLI SCRIBANI . . . ORIGINES ANTVERPIENSIVM. ANTVERPIÆ, EX OFFICINA PLANTINIANA, Apud Ioannem Moretum. M.DC.X. [etc.] 4° pp.172: plates
749.h.29; 153.e.6(1).
The signatures are in double letters and the approbation and privilege name this work after Scribani's 'Antverpia', which indicates that the two works were intended to be bound together as they are here in the copy at 153.e.6, though in the wrong order. The plates are

derived from Guicciardini's description of Antwerp, reworked by Theodoor Galle. Ownership inscription in the copy at 794.h.29: Bibliotheca Collegij S. Antonij de Padua ff. Minor. Hibern. Lovanij 1762.

SCRIECKIUS, Adrianus. *See* SCHRIECK, Adriaen van

S105 SCRIVERIUS, Petrus

(tp.1) P. SCRIVERII ANIMADVERSIONES IN MARTIALEM . . . LVGDVNI BATAVORVM, APVD IOANNEM MAIRE . . . M.DC.XVIII.

(tp.2) CL. VV. IVSTI LIPSII, IANI RVTGERSII, I. ISACI PONTANI NOTæ IN MARTIALEM. Ad Petrum Scriverium. Lugduni Batavorum, APVD IOANNEM MAIRE . . . M D CXIX. 16° 2 pt.: pp.285; 24

1001.a.16.

With the device of the Officina Plantiniana Raphelengii on the first titlepage.

S106 SCRIVERIUS, Petrus

BATAVIA ILLVSTRATA, seu DE BATAVORVM INSVLA, HOLLANDIA, ZELANDIA, FRISIA, TERRITORIO TRAIECTENSI ET GELRIA, Scriptores varij notæ melioris, nunc primùm collecti, simulqúe editi. Ex Musæo PETRI SCRIVERII. LVGDVNI BATAVORVM, Apud Ludovicum Elzevirium. M.D.C.IX. 4° pp.232, 184, 56, 40; illus.

10271.c.12; 154.l.8(2).

Containing the 'Antiquitatum Batavicarum tabularium' by Scriverius and the 'Illustrissimorum Hollandiae Zelandiaeque Comitum ac Dominorum Frisiae icones et historia'. The illustrations are woodcuts. Printed by Jan Paedts at Leiden? The copy at 154.l.8.(2) is imperfect; wanting all after the first set of pagination.

S107 SCRIVERIUS, Petrus

[Batavia illustrata.] Beschrijvinghe van OVT BATAVIEN, met de ANTIQVITEYTEN van dien: Mitsgaders D'Afkomst ende Historie der . . . Graven van HOLLAND, ZEELAND, ende VRIESLANDT . . . Alles . . . met Anteyckeninghen [*sic*] ende Waerschouwinghen, uyt . . . gheloof-waerdige Schryvers ende oude stucken . . . opgesocht/by een nieuwe Vader-lands-lievende Schrijver nieuwelickx uytgegeven. TOT ARNHEM, By Jan Janssoon . . . 1612. 8° pp.608; illus.

1436.c.24(1).

The half-title inscribed: Saxo Grammaticus ad lectorem, using a pseudonym of Petrus Scriverius. The preface signed: Petrus Scriverius. Printed by Henrick Lodewijcxz van Haestens at Leiden. The illustrations include woodcut portraits with five line verses.

SCRIVERIUS, Petrus. Collectanea veterum tragicorum. 1620. *See* SENECA, Lucius Annaeus. L. Annæus Seneca tragicus. 1621.

S108 SCRIVERIUS, Petrus

INFERIORIS GERMANIAE PROVINCIARVM VNITARVM ANTQVITATES. Scilicet; De RHENI tribus alveis ostijsque, & de TOXANDRIS, BATAVIS, CANINEFATIBVS, FRISIIS, MARSACIS, alijsque Populis. Adjectæ tabulæ geographicæ. Item Picturæ operum ac monumentorum veterum, nec non COMITVM HOLLANDIÆ, ZELANDIÆ, & FRISIÆ Eicones, eorundemque HISTORIA. Ex Musæo PETRI SCRIVERII. LVGDVNI BATAVORVM, Apud Ludovicum Elzevirium. M.DC.XI. 4° pp.232, 232, 184, 56, 40: plate; illus., maps

1054.h.7; 154.l.8(1).

A combined reissue of Philippus Cluverius, 'Commentarius de tribus Rheni alveis' and Scriverius, 'Batavia illustrata'. The dedication of the latter, together with all the preliminaries, has been reprinted, by Henrick van Haestens at Leiden and prefixed to the whole. Printing of the whole has been attributed by *Rahir* no.50 to J. J. Paedts and J. Bouwensz at Leiden. Neither copy contains the portraits described by *Willems* no.68 and both are imperfect; the copy at 1054.h.7 wanting the 'Comitum . . . eicones', that at 154.l.8(1) wanting the plate with two maps. The latter copy has manuscript annotations.

S109 SECREET

Het Secreet des Conings van Spangien/Philippus den tweden/achter-gelaten aen synen Zoone . . . vervatende hoe hy hem reguleren sal nae zijns Vaders doodt. In't licht gebracht door . . . Rodrigo D. A. Ende nu over-gheset uyt den Spaenschen. Door P.A.P. 4° sig. A^4

T.1724(59).

Published in 1608? Corresponding to the copy described in *Knuttel* no.1059.

S110 SECREET

Het Secreet des CONINGS van Spangien . . . achter-gelaten aen zijnen lieven Sone . . . In't licht gebracht door . . . Rodrigo D. A. Ende nu over-gheset uyt den Spaenschen. Door P.A.P. 4° sig. A^2

T.1713(3*); T.1713(4*).

Published in 1608? Corresponding to the copy described in *Knuttel* no.1063.

S111 SECREET

Het Secreet des Conings van Spangien . . . achter-ghelaten aen zijnen lieven Soone . . . In't licht ghebracht door . . . Rodrigo D. A. Ende nu over-gheset uyt den Spaenschen Door P.A.P. 4° sig. A^2

T.1713(4).

Published in 1608? Corresponding to the copy described in *Knuttel* no.1061.

S112 SECREET-BOECK

Secreet-Boeck Waer in vele diversche Secreten/ende heerlicke Consten/in veelderley verscheyden materien/wt seker Latijnsche/ Fransoysche/ Hoochduytsche/ende Nederlandtsche Authoren/te samen . . . ghebracht zijn . . . Tot Dordrecht. By Abraham Canin . . . 1601. 8° pp.419

1036.c.3(2).

Ownership inscription: Charles Massonet 1662 London.

S113 SECRETISSIMA

SECRETISSIMA INSTRVCTIO, GALLO-BRITANNA-BATAVA, FRIDERICO V. COMITI PALATINO ELECTORI DATA. EX GALLICO CONVERSA, ac bono publico, in lucem evulgata. M.DC.XX. 8° sig. A^8B^7

8073.aa.11.

Possibly published by Huybert Antoon Velpius at Brussels. For other editions in the British Library, but so far found impossible to assign to any place or printer, *see* the General Catalogue s.v. FREDERICK I., *Elector Palatine, King of Bohemia*

S114 SECRETISSIMA

[Secretissima instructio . . . Friderico V. . . . data.] Verre-kijcker. Ofte, SECRETE Fransch-Engelsch-Hollandtsche INSTRVCTIE Ghegheven aen FREDERICVS DE VYFDE . . . Overgheset uyt het Latijn . . . 1620. 4° sig. A-D^4E^2

T.2250(29).

An enlarged translation of 'Secretissima instructio'. *Knuttel* no.3037 suggests this may have been printed by Abraham Verhoeven at Antwerp.

S115 SECUNDUS, Joannes

IOANNIS SECVNDI . . . OPERA QVÆ REPERIRI POTVERVNT OMNIA. Curante atque edente PETRO SCRIVERIO. LVGDVNI BATAVORVM. Typis IACOBI MARCI M D C XIX. (col.) LVGDVNI BATAVORVM, M D C XIX. 8° pp.301; illus., port.

11409.aa.36.

A woodcut showing a basket of flowers, cut out of a separate piece of paper, has been inserted on the titlepage above the imprint in place of part of the original titlepage.

S116 SEDULIUS, Henricus

F. HENRICI SEDVLI . . . APOLOGETICVS aduersus Alcoranum Franciscanorum, pro Libro Conformitatum. LIBRI TRES. De sancto Francisco. De Ordine & Regulâ S. Francisci. De pietate & moribus Franciscanorum. ANTVERPIAE, EX OFFICINA PLANTINIANA, Apud Ioannem Moretum. M.DC.VII. (col.) ANTVERPIÆ, EX OFFICINA PLANTINIANA, APVD IOANNEM MORETVM. M.DC.VII. 4° pp.287
1601/440.

With manuscript notes and corrections. Ownership inscription: Bibliothecae Missionis Amstelead. [*sic*] Ord. FF. Min. Prov. Germ. jnferioris. With stamps reading 'Algemene Provincie Kataloog Minderbroedersklooster Alverna Gld.'; 'Bibliotheca Conventus Woerdensis'.

S117 SEDULIUS, Henricus

F. HENRICI SEDVLI . . . DIVA VIRGO MOSÆ-TRAIECTENSIS. De Ciuitate Mosæ-Traiectensi, & Diuæ Virginis Imagine . . . ANTVERPIÆ, EX OFFICINA PLANTINIANA, Apud Ioannem Moretum. M.DC.IX. 8° pp.201; illus.
862.g.6(2).

The titlepage engraving relates to the devotion to the Virgin Mary. Ownership inscription: Ioh. Mauritius.

S118 SEDULIUS, Henricus

HISTORIA SERAPHICA VITÆ B.MI P. FRANCISCI ASSISIATIS, ILLVSTRIVMQ. VIRORVM ET FEMINARVM, QVI EX TRIBVS EIVS ORDINIBVS RELATI SVNT INTER SANCTOS. Item Illustria Martyria FF. Minorum Prouinciæ inferioris Germaniæ, ab hæreticis . . . crudeliter interfectorum. F. HENRICVS SEDVLIVS . . . concinnauit, Commentarijs et Notis illustrauit. ANTVERPIÆ Sumptibus Hæredum Martini Nutij. M.DC.XIII. (col.) ANTVERPIA [*sic*] Typis HENRICI ÆRTSI . . . M.DC.XIII. fol. pp.696
1605/760.

The titlepage is engraved; signed: C. de Mallery sculpsit.

S119 SEDULIUS, Henricus

IMAGINES SANCTORVM FRANCISCI, ET QVI EX TRIBVS EIVS ORDINIBVS RELATI SVNT INTER DIVOS, CVM ELOGIIS. Auct. F. Henrico Sedulio . . . ANTVERPIÆ Apud Philippum Gallæum. M.DCII. 4° pp.31; illus.
4828.aaa.22(1).

The titlepage is engraved, as are the thirteen illustrations, by Philips or Theodoor Galle. Ownership inscriptions: Margarita de Huth; John Wesley Hall Clifton 1856.

S120 SEDULIUS, Henricus

F. HENRICI SEDVLI . . . PRÆSCRIPTIONES ADVERSVS HÆRESES. ANTVERPIÆ, EX OFFICINA PLANTINIANA, Apud Ioannem Moretum. M.DC.VI. 4° pp.257
1200.cc.20.

S121 SEECKERE

Seeckere Particulariteyt ende Conditien van de Stadt Praghe/soo de selve ghebracht is onder de Ghehoorsaemheyt van zijne KEYSERLYCKE MAIESTEYT. Overghesedt wt de Hooch-Duytsche sprake in onse Nederlantsche Tale. Nv eerst Ghedruckt den 2. December. 1620. T'Hantwerpen/By Abraham Verhoeuen . . . 1620.[etc.] 4° pp.14; sig.Cc Dd^4; illus.
P.P.3444.af(151).

Pp.13, 14 contain Latin chronograms. The titlepage woodcut shows artillery attacking a castle.

S122 SEER

Een seer schoon Klach-dicht/Gemaeckt ter eeren Gods Tegen de grouwelijcke

verzierde PREDESTINATIE. Item noch een schoon Liedeken . . . Met noch twee schoone Refereynen . . . 1613. 4° sig. A[6]
T.2243(10).

Een SEER schoone ende ghenoechelicke historie vanden ridder Palmerijn van Olijve. 1602; 1613. *See* PALMERIN de Oliva

SEKER vraghen ende antwoorden: belanghende de leere vande Predestinatie. 1611. *See* CERTAIN questions

SEKERE missive wt den Raet vande . . . Staten, aende Classis van Rotterdam. 1612. *See* HOLLAND. Staten [11.3.1610]

S123 SEKEREN

SEKEREN Brieff gheschreuen aen mijnen seer goeden Vriendt N N. tot Amsterdam/ hoe dat Sijn Excellentie den MARQVIS SPINOLA zieck vvas, Maer Godt loff nv vvel te passe is . . . Overghesedt in onse Nederlantsche Tale. Ghedruct . . . M.DC.XX. 4° pp. 7; sig. ★[4]
1193.l.34; 10631.a.39; P.P.3444.af(130).

Without imprint; printed by Abraham Verhoeven at Antwerp. The date of the letter given in the text as October 1620. Referring to a satire on Spinola showing him as vomiting Wesel and Hulst and claiming his victories to be the cure for this illness. With 'Antwoorde geschreuen aen mijnen ghoeden Vriendt' and a satirical poem entitled 'Den troost vanden Pals-graue'.

S124 SENECA, Lucius Annaeus

[Works. Latin] L. ANNÆI SENECÆ PHILOSOPHI OPERA, QVÆ EXSTANT OMNIA: A IVSTO LIPSIO emendata, et Scholijs illustrata. ANTVERPIÆ, EX OFFICINA PLANTINIANA, apud Ioannem Moretum, M.DC.V. [etc.] fol. pp. 798, 53: plate; illus., ports.
31.k.12.

The titlepage is engraved. The portrait of Lipsius signed: Theod. Galle fecit.

S125 SENECA, Lucius Annaeus

[Works. Latin] L. ANNÆI SENECÆ PHILOSOPHI OPERA, QVÆ EXSTANT OMNIA: A IVSTO LIPSIO emendata et scholijs illustrata. Editio secunda, atque ab vltimâ LIPSI manu. ANTVERPIÆ, EX OFFICINA PLANTINIANA, apud Viduam et Filios Io, Moreti. M.DC.XV. [etc.] (col.) ANTVERPIÆ, EX OFFICINA PLANTINIANA, APVD VIDVAM ET FILIOS IOANNIS MORETI. M.DC.XIV. fol. pp. 795, 53; illus., ports.
8461.h.7.

The titlepage is engraved, copied from that of the earlier edition, with different portraits of Seneca and Epictetus. The new portrait of Lipsius and the engraving of Seneca committing suicide signed: Corn. Galle sculp. The preface names Rubens as the designer of the portraits of Seneca. The titlepage is slightly mutilated.

S126 SENECA, Lucius Annaeus

[Works. Latin] (tp. 1) L. ANNÆI SENECAE M.F. PHILOSOPHI, ET M. ANNÆI SENECÆ RHETORIS PATRIS: Opera quæ exstant omnia, Variorum NOTIS illustrata. LVGDVNI BATAVORVM, Apud HARMANNVM à WESTERHVSEN . . . M D.C XIX.
(tp. 2) L. ANNÆI SENECAE M.F. Philosphi OPERVM PARS ALTERA . . . LVGDVNI BATAVORVM, Apud HARMANNVM à WESTERHVSEN . . . M DXIX [*sic*]. (pt. 2 col.) LVGDVNI BATAVORVM Excudebat Georgius Abrahami a Marsce. M.D.C.XIX.
(tp. 3) M. ANNÆI SENECAE RHETORIS Suasoriæ, Controuersiæ; & Declamationum excerpta. ab ANDREA SCHOTTO . . . castigata . . . Præterea IVSTI LIPSII ET IOANNIS ISAACI PONTANI Notis Emendationibusque explicata & aucta. LVGDVNI BATAVORVM, Apud HARMANNVM à WESTERHVSEN, M.DC.XIX. 8° 3 pt.: pp. xlviii, 847; 498; 320; illus., port.
8462.b.9.

Tp. 1, 2 show the same portrait of Seneca.

S127 SENECA, Lucius Annaeus
[Tragedies] DECEM TRAGOEDIÆ, Quæ LVCIO ANNAEO SENECAE tribuuntur: Operâ FRANCISCI RAPHELENGII FR. F. PLANTINIANI, Ope . . . IVSTI LIPSI emendatiores: Cum vtriusque . . . Animadversionibus & Notis. ANTVERPIÆ, Apud Martinum Nutium . . . M.DCI. 16° pp.502
1000.a.7.
Ownership inscription: Ioh. Mauritius.

S128 SENECA, Lucius Annaeus
[Tragedies] L. ANNÆI SENECAE ET ALIORVM TRAGOEDIÆ SERIO EMENDATAE. Cum IOSEPHI SCALIGERI, nunc primum . . . editis, & DANIELIS HEINSII Animadversionibus & Notis. LVGDVNI BATAVORVM, Ex Typographia Henrici ab Haestens. Impensis Iohannis Orlers, And. Cloucq, & Iohannis Maire, 1611. 8° pp.584
1000.d.10.
Ownership inscriptions: John Bemister; Thomas Tyro.

S129 SENECA, Lucius Annaeus
[Tragedies] LVCII ANNÆI SENECÆ Tragœdiæ: Ad doctorum virorum emendationes recognitæ. EX OFFICINA PLANTINIANA RAPHELENGII, M.D.CXII. 32° pp.288
C.20.f.52.
Published at Leiden. From the travelling library of Sir Julius Caesar.

S130 SENECA, Lucius Annaeus
[Tragedies] (tp.1) L. ANNÆVS SENECA, TRAGICVS: Ex Recensione & Muséo PETRI SCRIVERII . . . LVGDVNI BATAVORVM, Apud Iohannem Maire. M.D.C.XXI.
(tp.2) PETRI SCRIVERII COLLECTANEA Veterum TRAGICORVM, L. LIVII ANDRONICI, Q. ENNII . . . aliorumque FRAGMENTA: Et . . . Notæ breves. QVIBVS ACCEDVNT SINGVLARI LIBELLO Castigationes & Notæ vberiores GERARDI IOANNIS VOSSII. LVGDVNI BATAVORVM, Apud Iohannem Maire M DC.XX.
(tp.3) GERARDI IOANNIS VOSSII in Fragmenta L. LIVII ANDRONICI, Q. ENNII . . . Castigationes & Notæ. LVGDVNI BATAVORVM, Apud Iohannem Maire, M D C XX. (col.) Excudebat HENRICVS AB HAESTENS, M D C XX. 8° 3 pt.: pp.384; 190; 192, 413
1000.d.11; 1000.d.12; 1000.d.1; 160.c.8; G.9075.
With additional commentaries by Justus Lipsius and others. In the copy at 1000.d.11 tp.3 has been inserted after the preliminaries of pt.2. The copy at 1000.d.12 is made up of pt.3 pt.2, pt.2, pt.3 pt.1; wanting pt.1. The copy at 160.c.8 consists of pt.2, 3. The copies at 1000.d.1 and G.9075 consist of pt.2, pt.3 pt.1. Ownership inscription in the copy at 1000.d.12: Aegidius Menagius, Domus Professa Parisiensis; in the copy at 160.c.8: Steevens's catalogue no.471.

S131 SENECA, Lucius Annaeus
[De tranquillitate animi.] L. ANNAEI SENECÆ DE TRANQVILLITATE ANIMI Ad Serenum LIBER. Ex officina RAPHELENGII. M.DCI. 128° pp.249
C.17.b.10/39.
Printed in italics. Pp.209-249 contain extracts from the tragedies. Published at Leiden.

SENECA, Marcus Annaeus. Suasoriae, Controversiae; & Declamationum excerpta. 1619. *See* SENECA, Lucius Annaeus [Works. Latin]

SENTENTIA lata et pronuntiata adversus Aegidium Ledenbergium. 1619. *See* NETHERLANDS. United Provinces. Staten Generaal [15.5.1619]

SENTENTIA lata et pronuntiata adversus Hugonem Grotium. 1619. *See* NETHERLANDS. United Provinces. Staten Generaal [18.5.1619]

SENTENTIA lata & pronuntiata adversus Ioannem ab Oldenbarnevelt. 1619. *See* NETHERLANDS. United Provinces. Staten Generaal [13.5.1619]

SENTENTIA lata & pronuntiata adversus Rumoldum Hogerbetium. 1619. *See* NETHERLANDS. United Provinces. Staten Generaal [18.5.1619]

SENTENTIE Iohannis Grevii, ghewesen Predicant tot Heusden. 1620. *See* NETHERLANDS. United Provinces. Staten Generaal [16.5.1620]

SENTENTIE, uyt-ghesproocken . . . over Gielis van Ledenberch. 1619. *See* NETHERLANDS. United Provinces. Staten Generaal [15.5.1619]

SENTENTIE, uyt-ghesproocken . . . over Hugo de Groot. 1619. *See* NETHERLANDS. United Provinces. Staten Generaal [18.5.1619]

SENTENTIE, uyt-ghesproocken . . . over Iohan van Oldenbarnevelt. 1619. *See* NETHERLANDS. United Provinces. Staten Generaal [13.5.1619]

SENTENTIE, uyt-ghesproocken . . . over Rombout Hoogerbeetz. 1619. *See* NETHERLANDS. United Provinces. Staten Generaal [18.5.1619]

S132 SERENISSIMI

SERENISSIMI ALBERTI AVSTRIACI BELGARVM PRINCIPIS CENOTAPHIVM. ANTVERPIÆ, EX OFFICINA PLANTINIANA. M.DC.XXI. 4° 4 unsigned leaves; illus.
1199.f.3(2).

Various epitaphs. The titlepage engraving shows the arms of Albert, supported by angels. Issued in 1622 with Aubert Le Mire's 'De vita Alberti'.

S133 SERVETUS, Michael

[De Trinitatis erroribus.] Van de Dolinghe inde DRIEVVLDIGHEYD, Seven Boecken . . . in Latijn beschreven Door MICHIEL SERVETVS . . . Ende Nu ghetrouvvelijck overgeset in onse Nederlandsche tale, Door R.T. Hier sijn noch byghevoegt eenige andere kleyne tractaetjens van den selven Auteur . . . Ghedruckt In't jaer . . . 1620. 4° ff.100
479.a.6.

Translated by Reinier Telle. Without imprint; printed by Pieter Arentsz at Norden. Without the additional texts which are not found in any recorded copy.

S134 SES

Ses vragen by de E, [*sic*] Heeren Burghermeesteren voor-ghestelt/dienende tot naerder openinghe over het houden eens Nationalen Synode. Met de antwoorde der Kercke. Gedruckt . . . M.DC.XVJJJ. 4° sig.A[4]
T.2248(17).

S135 SEVERINUS Cracoviensis

[De vita, miraculis, et actis Canonizationis S. Hyacinthi.] HISTOIRE DE LA VIE, MIRACLES ET CANONIZATION DE S. Hyacinthe Polonois . . . COMPOSEE EN LATIN PAR LE R.P. Frere Seuerin . . . Depuis traduicte en François, par Frere Estienne le Clou . . . A ARRAS, Chez Gilles Bauduyn . . . M.D.C.II. 8° pp.336; illus.
1578/8150.

The engraving on the titlepage verso shows St. Hyacinth in prayer before the Virgin Mary.

S136 SEVERUS, Sulpicius

SVLPICII SEVERI . . . HISTORIA SACRA. Edente & emendante I. DRVSIO, cum commentario libro sive notis ejusdem . . . FRANEKERÆ, Ex Officina AEGIDII RADAEI . . . M.D.CVII. (col.) EXCVDEBAT FRANEKERÆ FRISIORVM ÆGIDIVS RADÆVS . . . ANNO MILLESIMO SEXCENTESIMO SEPTIMO MENSE AVGVSTO. 8° pp.172, 280
856.e.4.

S137 SEYNDT-BRIEF

SEYNDT-BRIEF vant' ghene den MARQVIS AMBROSIVS SPINOLA int Palsgrauen Landt in de maent September 1620. vvtgerecht heeft, Ende van den teghenwoordighen staet van Duytslandt/ende d'Omligghende Landen. Gheschreuen vvt Ceulen den 28. September 1620. T'hantwerpen/By Abraham verhoeven . . . 1620. [etc.] 4° pp.7; sig. Nom.X^4
P.P.3444.af(108).

A Latin edition, entitled 'De rebus ab Ambrosio Spinola gestis', is dated 30 September 1620 and was published in several variants, with the signature A. The copy in the British Library is entered under DE. Both versions are probably derived from a German original which has not been identified.

S138 SHERWODUS, Joannes

THESES INAVGVRALES DE Humoribus crudis in Morborum principijs expurgandis. QVAS . . . Pro Doctorali Laurea in Medica facultate consequenda . . . exagitandas proponit, IOANNES SHERWODVS . . . LVGDVNI BATAVORVM, Ex Officinâ GODEFRIDI BASSON, 1620. 4° sig.A^4
1185.g.1(69).

A SHORT relation of the departure of . . . Prince Frederick. 1619. *See* HARRISON, John

A SHORTE treatise, of the crosse in baptisme. 1604. *See* BRADSHAW, William

S139 SICCAMA, Sibrandus

LEX FRISIONVM SIVE ANTIQVÆ FRISIORVM LEGES, A reliquis Veterum Germanorum Legibus separatim æditæ & NOTIS Illustratæ A SIBRANDO SICCAMA IC^TO^. FRANEKERÆ apud IOANNEM LAMRINCK . . . M DCXVII. (col.) FRANEKERÆ Apud IOANNEM LAMRINCK . . . 1617. 4° pp.151
590.c.24(2).

S140 SICHEM, Christoffel van

Afbeeldinghe/van David Joris zijner Leer/ende leuen int cort verclaert. obl. fol. a single sheet
10759.l.1 (insert 65).

An engraved portrait, inscribed 'David Georgivs Delphis in Batavia natus. Añ.° M.D.' with another two lines in Latin and Dutch verse, the latter beginning 'Onder t'schijnsel van lieflijck wesen', printed in letterpress below. Dutch letterpress text is printed on either side of the portrait. The engraving signed: C. V. Sichem sculpsit, and: J. C. Wou:, i.e. J. C. Woudanus, the designer. The engraved date of David Joris's birth is followed by overprinted numerals reading 'CVIJ'; making this the date of publication? Published by Christoffel van Sichem at Amsterdam. Another edition of the portrait with German text is described in *Van Someren Portretten* no.2815a*, which is dated 1606.

S141 SICHEM, Christoffel van

BERNHARD KNIPPERDOLLING fol. a single sheet
10759.l.1 (insert 57).

A portrait, engraved after J. C. Woudanus, inscribed 'Bernhard Knipperdollinck' and signed: C.V.Sichem scul: et excud: The title used above has been superimposed in letterpress at the top of the engraving and Dutch letterpress descriptive text has been printed below the portrait, the whole within a typographical border. There are traces of further engraved text, perhaps verses, after the engraved inscription, cut off to shorten the plate before the addition of the letterpress text. Possibly also cut back at the top. Printed between 1606 and 1607, at Leiden or Amsterdam.

S142 SICHEM, Christoffel van
DIEDERICK SNYDER NAECTLOPER. fol. a single sheet
10759.l.1 (insert 59).

An engraved portrait, inscribed: DIEDERICK SNYDER DEN EERSTEN ADAMYT ENDE NAECTLOOPER, and signed: [C.] V. Sichem fe excudit. The above title is superimposed in letterpress at the top and Dutch letterpress descriptive text is printed below the portrait, the whole within a typographical border. Printed between 1606 and 1607, at Leiden or Amsterdam. *Van Someren Portretten* no. 5188*[*] describes a different edition.

S143 SICHEM, Christoffel van
[Historische beschrijvinge ende afbeeldinge der voornaemste hooft-ketteren.] Grouwelen der voornaemster Hooft-Ketteren Die haer in dese laeste tijden soo in Duytslandt/als oock in dese Nederlanden/opgheworpen hebben/haer Leven/ Leere/Begin/ende Eynde . . . Mits-gaders Haere af-beeldingen . . . TOT LEYDEN By Henrick Lod. van Haestens . . . 1607. 8° sig. A^{10} B-F^8G^7; illus.
698.a.45(2).

Anonymous. The portraits copied and the text taken from the engravings of Christoffel van Sichem, with or without additional text, first published separately in 1606/7 and then in bookform in 1608 as 'Historische beschrijvinge'. The portraits of Müntzer and Matthesius have been accidentally transposed in this and all later 8° editions. The device 'Godt bewaert in noot' is one used by David van Ilpendam at Leiden. Sig. B7, 8 are mutilated.

S144 SICHEM, Christoffel van
[Historische beschrijvinge ende afbeeldinge der voornaemste hooft-ketteren.] Greuwel der vornahmsten Haupt-ketzeren/So wohl Wiedertauffer/als auch andern . . . Zugleich Mitt ihrer Abcontrafaitung/ihrem Leben/Lher [*sic*]/Anfang vnnd Ende . . . beschrieben. Gedruckt zu Leyden Durch Henrichen von Haestens . . . 1608. 8° sig. A-F^8; illus.
698.a.45(3).

Anonymous. The portraits copied and the text translated from the engravings by Christoffel van Sichem of 1606 and published in 1608 in bookform as 'Historische beschrijvinge, etc.' Cropped.

S145 SICHEM, Christoffel van
[Historische beschrijvinge ende afbeeldinge der voornaemste hooft-ketteren.] SPECVLVM ANABAPTISTICI FVRORIS, Vivis quorundam Enthysiastarum . . . iconibus variega[t]um, & historicis descriptionibus i[l]lustratum. Addita Michaelis Serv[e]ti effigies . . . LVGDVNI BATAVORVM Ex Typographio Henrici ab Haestens. M D CVIII. 8° sig. A-G^8; illus.
G.19547.

Anonymous. The portraits copied and the text translated from the engravings by Christoffel van Sichem of 1606 and published in 1608 in bookform as 'Historische beschrijvinge, etc.' The titlepage has been cut and subsequently mended, with damage to some of the text. The translator named in the other issue entered below: H.S.F.D.M.D., i.e. Henricus Salamonis Filius Delmanhorstius Medicinae Doctor.

S146 SICHEM, Christoffel van
[Historische beschrijvinge ende afbeeldinge der voornaemste hooft-ketteren.] APOCALYPSIS insignium aliquot HÆRESIARCHARVM, QVA Visiones & insomnia ipsis per somnia patefacta . . . revelantur, vnaq́ue opera vitæ ac mortes Cœlo Latino donantur: Superadditæ septendecim [*sic*] eorum . . . Icones æreis expressæ Interprete [H.S.F.]D.M.D. LVGDVNI-BATAVORVM Ex Typographio Henrici ab Haestens. M.D.C.VIII. 8° sig. A-G^8; illus.
1114.a.3.

Another issue of the preceding. The titlepage is a cancel, very worn and the intitials H.S.F. almost rubbed off.

S147 SICHEM, Christoffel van

[Historische beschrijvinge ende afbeeldinge der voornaemste hooft-ketteren.] ICONICA & HISTORICA DESCRIPTIO PRAECIpuorum Hæresiarcharùm . . . in qua eorum dogmata non minus, quam vitæ initium & Finis breuiter perstringuntur: Cuìusmodi antehac nunquam, sed nunc primúm in lucem prodijt. Per C.V.S. ARNHEMY. Apud Ioan. Iansonium Bibliocop [*sic*], &c. 1609. fol.° 18 unnumbered leaves

696.l.14.

The laudatory poem on the titlepage verso, signed: R. Lubbaeus, provides the author's name in the lines: Manus . . . Zichemi horum sculpsit imagines; most plates signed: C.V. Sichem, the portrait of Beuckels signed: Christof: van Sichem sculp: et exc:. Printed on one side of the leaf only and assembled in random order. The translation differs from that by Henricus Delmanhorstius. The engraved captions are in Dutch.

S148 SICHEM, Christoffel van

IOAN MATHYS VAN HAERLEM fol. a single sheet

10759.l.1 (insert 58).

An engraved portrait inscribed 'IOHAN MATHYS VAN HAERLEEM [*sic*] EEN PROPHEET DER GEESTDRYVERS' and signed: C.V. Sich: excu. With the above title superimposed in letterpress at the top and Dutch letterpress descriptive text underneath, the whole within a typographical border. The plate appears to have been shortened at the top and bottom. Published at Leiden or Amsterdam in 1606 or 1607. *Van Someren Portretten* no.3540 describes a different edition.

S149 SICHEM, Christoffel van

[Waerachtighe afbeeldinghe des Conincks van Munster.] JAN BEUCKELS VAN LEYDEN. fol. a single sheet

10759.l.1 (insert 56).

An engraved portrait after J. C. Woudanus, inscribed: JOHAN BEUCKELS VON LEYDEN and signed: Christof van Sichem sculp. et exc. With the above title superimposed in letterpress at the top of the engraving and Dutch letterpress descriptive text underneath, the whole within a typographical border. Some engraved text at the foot of the portrait has been deleted to shorten the plate, but traces remain. Published at Leiden or Amsterdam in 1606 or 1607. Adapted from an issue of 1606 described in *Van Someren Portretten* no.2746. Also cropped at the top?

S150 SICHEM, Christoffel van

[E]in wunderkunstig Schiff/welches vber die gefrohren Wasser vnnd Landt fahret/mit Leüt geladen/vnnd mitten Windt gantz schnelligklich vber weg fahrt . . . Zu Leyden, durch Christoffel von Sichem . . . 1605. obl. fol. a single sheet

C.18.e.2(106).

An engraving, signed: CVSichem sculp, above an unsigned poem by Christoffel van Sichem beginning: [W]ah findt man doch ein Landt, wie Hollandt desgeleich [etc.], the text printed by Henrick van Haestens at Leiden? Cropped.

S151 SICKINGHE, Joannes

DECLAMATIO SCHOLASTICA, Quâ ostenditur quanta sit in utramvis partem vis EDVCATIONIS atq; disciplinæ, quantæq; gratiæ fidelibus morum & studiorum architectis debeantur. Habita in maximo scholæ auditorio A IOANNE SICKINGHE, Iun. . . . GRONINGÆ, Excudebat Ioannes Sassius . . . 1619. 4° pp.50

1031.g.3(6).

Printed in italics.

S152 SILESIA
[1.10.1619]. Des Fursten-daghs RESOLVTIE. Soo deselve van den . . . Fursten ende Stenden in Over ende Neder-Slesien/de Augsburchsche Confessie toeghedaen zijnde/by een alghemeene ghehoudene Vergaderinghe/op den eersten dach des maendts Octobris/tot Breslau; gheresolveert ende besloten is. Inden Iare M.DC.XIX. Eerst in Hoochduytsch Ghedruckt tot Prage . . . Ende nu IN 'SGRAVEN-HAGE. By Aert Meuris . . . M.DC.XJX. 4° sig.AB[4]
T.2249(51); T.2423(22).

S153 SILESIA
[2.1621] ARTYCKELEN, Waer op de Vorsten ende Standen van Slesien/met de Keyserlicke ende Conincklijcke Majesteyt van Hungeren/ende Bohemē begheeren te accorderen/beneffens de Conditiē ende voorslach vanden Ceurvorst van Sacxen daer teghens ghedaen. Overghesedt vvt de hooch-Duytsche sprake in onse Nederlandtsche Tale. Eerst ghedruckt den 12. Meert/1621. T'Hantwerpen/By Abraham Verhoeuen/[etc.] 4° pp.8; sig.C[4]; illus.
P.P.3444.af(203).
Headed: Martius 1621. 37. With other news, and with an advertisement for issues 38-40. All the news in this issue relates to February 1621. The titlepage woodcuts show (a) a portrait of the Elector of Saxony in a typographical border, and (b) three men seated in an assembly.

S154 SILESIA
[3.1621] Puncten ende Articulē van het Accoort tusschen de Princen ende . . . Staten van Slesien/soo die van Slesiē zijn ghecomen onder de ghe [*sic*] hoorsaemheyt ende Obedientie van zijne Keyserlijcke Majesteyt. Eerst ghedruckt den 23. Appril. 1621. T'Hantwerpen by Abraham Verhoeven/[etc.] 4° pp.8; sig.A[4]; illus.
P.P.3444.af(222).
Headed: Appril 1621. 63. With the reply of the Elector of Saxony and other news, all relating to March 1621. The titlepage woodcut shows a commander (Spinola?), with his long staff of office and his helmet on a table.

S155 SILIUS ITALICUS, Caius
SILIVS ITALICVS DE SECVNDO Bello Punico. EX OFFICINA PLANTINIANA RAPHELENGII, M.D.CXI. long 24° pp.286
C.20.f.57; 1068.b.28.
Published at Leiden. With the exlibris of Thomas Birch dated 1723 in the copy at 1068.b.28. In that copy sig.B2v, B3r and C1r are poorly inked and illegible. The copy at C.20.f.57 from the travelling library of Sir Julius Caesar.

S156 SILIUS ITALICUS, Caius
SILIVS ITALICVS DE SECVNDO Bello Punico. Amsterodami Apud Guiljel: Janssonium . . . M DC XX. long 24° pp.164 [264]
1069.a.15.
The titlepage is engraved.

S157 SILIUS ITALICUS, Caius
SILIVS ITALICVS DE SECVNDO Bello Punico. Amsterodami Apud Guiljel: Janssonium . . . M DC XX. long 24° pp.279
1471.a.12(3).
With the same engraved titlepage as in the preceding.

S158 SILVA, Marcos da; Bishop
[Primeira parte das chronicas da ordem dos Frades Menores.] THE CHRONICLE AND INSTITVTION OF THE ORDER OF . . . S. FRANCIS. CONTEYNING His life, his death, and his miracles, and of all his holie disciples and companions. SET FOORTH First in the

Portugall, next in the Spanish, then in the Italian, lastlie in the French, and now in the English tongue. THE FIRST TOME. AT S. OMERS, By IOHN HEIGHAM . . . 1618. [etc.] 4° pp.747
C.25.h.13.
The running title is 'The Chronicles of the Frier Minors'. The translator named in the approbation as Guilielmus Cape. Printed by Charles Boscard at St. Omer. No more published.

S159 SILVA Y FIGUEROA, Garcia de
GARCIÆ SILVA FIGVEROA . . . DE REBVS PERSARVM EPISTOLA . . . AD MARCHIONEM BEDMARI . . . ANTVERPIÆ, EX OFFICINA PLANTINIANA, M.DC.XX. 8° pp.16
804.a.43(3); 1313.c.19.
Described as a translation from the Spanish; probably translated from manuscript.

S160 SIMON, Richard; Hebraist
RÉPONSE au Livre entitulé SENTIMENS de quelques Théologiens de Hollande sur l'Histoire critique du Vieux Testament. Par LE PRIEUR DE BOLLEVILLE . . . A AMSTERDAM, Chez PIERRE DE COUP. M DCXXI. 4° pp.256
4.a.4(4).
The date is false, as is the author's name given on the titlepage. The 'Sentimens' are the work of Jean Le Clerc. Signed: A Bolleville . . . le 15. Septembre 1685. An edition is recorded with the imprint: Rotterdam, Reinier Leers, 1686.

SIMONIDES, Simon. *See* SZYMONOWICZ, Szymon

S161 SIMONS, Menno
Dat Fundament der Christelycker leere. Door Menno Simons op dat alder correckste geschreven/ende wt ghegheven/Anno M.D.XXXIX. Ende nu nae het alder outste exemplaer wederom herdruckt . . . 1616. 8° ff.133
3906.d.1(1).
Without imprint; printed by Jan Theunisz at Amsterdam.

S162 SIMONS, Menno
Een Lieffelijcke Vermaninge oft Onderwijsinghe uyt Gods Woort/Door Men. Sy. Hoe dat een Christen sal gheschickt zijn/eñ van dat schouwen ofte afsnijden der valscher Broederen eñ Susteren/ofte die met Kettersche Leeringen verleyt zijn/ofte die een Vleyschelijcke schandighe Leven voeren . . . Ghedruckt tot Amstelredam by Jan Theunisz. . . . 1605. 8° sig. AB^8C^4
3906.d.1(2).
The author's name is given in full in the text.

S163 SIMONS, Pierre; Bishop
PETRI SIMONIS . . . DE VERITATE LIBRI SEX: Et reliqua eius . . . OPERA. Collegit & recensuit . . . P. Ioannes David . . . ANTVERPIÆ, EX OFFICINA PLANTINIANA, Apud Ioannem Moretum. M.DC.IX. fol. pp.654; illus., port.
473.e.14.
The portrait engraved by Theodoor Galle? From the library of Prince Henry.

SIMSONS treurspel. 1618. *See* KONING, Abraham de

S164 SINAPIUS, Daniel
DECADES. ALIQVOT PROPOSITIONVM PHILOSOPHICARVM Quarum veritatem . . . Pro gradu MAGISTERII in Philosophiâ consequendo . . . Publicè asserere adnitat DANIEL SINAPIVS . . . LEYDÆ in BATAVIS Ex Typographeio Thomæ Basson . . . M.D.C.VIII. 4° sig.) (^{4}
7306.f.6(48).

S165 SINAPIUS, Daniel

DANIELIS SINAPII ORATIO in laudem Philosophiæ . . . Habita Lugduni Batavorum 22. Octobris Anno 1619. LVGDVNI BATAVORVM Ex officina IACOBI MARCI . . . M D C XX. 4° pp.20

536.e.8(3).

S166 SISMUS, Paulus

PAULI SISMI . . . TRACTATUS DE DIÆTÂ . . . HAGÆ-COMITIS. Apud ÆGIDIUS [*sic*] à LIMBURG . . . M.DƆ.IV [*sic*]. 8° pp.68

1038.f.31(1).

The date is a misprint for 1704.

S167 SKYTTE, Johannes; the Elder

ILLVSTRISS. VIRI IOHANNIS SKYTTE . . . ORATIONES TRES: Habitæ Ad Sereniss. MAGNÆ BRITANNIÆ Regem. In quarum primâ, caussæ ob quas SIGISMVNDVS . . . III. ab Ordinibus Sueciæ ejectus, in ejusq; locum . . . CAROLVS . . . IX. substitutus est, redduntur: In alterâ, gratiæ pro composito Sueco-Danico & Sueco-Moscovitico bello aguntur; & eorum caussæ exponuntur: In tertiâ, Sueco-Polonici belli caussæ recensuntur . . . M D C. XVIII. 4° pp.70

8092.de.62.

Without imprint. According to *Warmholtz* no.3412 this edition was seen through the press by Daniel Heinsius and if so, it may have been printed at Leiden. With manuscript notes.

S168 SLADUS, Matthaeus

[(tp.1) M. Sladi . . . cum C. Vorstio . . . de blasphemiis, Haeresibus & atheismis, a . . . Magnae Britanniae . . . rege Iacobo . . . in ejusdem Vorstii de Deo tractatu, & Exegesi apologetica, nigro Theta notatis, scholasticae disceptationis pars prima . . . in qua fides orthodoxa de vera immensitate & infinitate Trin-uni Dei, opponitur heterodoxiae A. Steuchi . . . & Vorstii . . . statuentium Deum . . . finitum esse . . . ostenditurque . . . regem gravissimas ob causas Vorstii doctrinam . . . condemnasse . . . Addita est . . . D. Parei ad Vorstium epistola, nuper scripta . . . Amstelodami, 1615.]

(tp.2) MATTHAEI SLADI . . . DISCEPTATIONIS CVM CONRADO VORSTIO . . . PARS ALTERA. De immutabilitate & simplicitate Dei. QVA DOCETVR . . . Magnæ Britanniæ . . . Regem IACOBVM . . . justè ac meritò notâsse blasphemum VORSTI dogma, Deum esse mutabilem & accidentibus subjectum adserentis . . . AMSTELODAMI, Apud IUDOCVM. HONDIUM I.F. . . . MDCXIV. 4° 2 pt.: –;137

[4373.h.8;] 1009.d.16.

The perfect copy at 4373.h.8 has been mislaid and a different work given this pressmark, to be readjusted if and when the missing book has been found. The copy at 1009.d.16 is imperfect; wanting pt.1. The title for the whole work and simultaneously for pt.1 has been taken from the General Catalogue.

S169 SLATIUS, Henricus

Amsterdamsche Nouvelles, dat is/Nieuwe Tydinghen/Van 'tghene datter onlancx is ghepasseert in Bohemen/Hongarien/Weenen/Polen/Slesien/ Meeren/Ceulen/ Venetien/Neaples/Heydelberch/Vranckeryck/Enghelandt / Brabandt/Vrieslandt/ ende Hollandt/rc. Wt ghegeven ende in 'tlicht ghebrocht tot troost der Calvinisten. Door A.R.E.S. Ghedruckt tot Herders-wyck/door Authoriteyt van de Kercke/ ende de Synode van Dordrecht . . . 1620. 4° pp.12

11555.e.41(7).

Anonymous and with a false imprint; printed by Abraham Verhoeven at Antwerp?

S170 SLATIUS, Henricus

HENRICI SLATII BEWIIS, Dat de Schuer-Predicanten zijn Vrienden ende Toe-standers van deese Leere: Dat Godt on-mondighe jonge Kinderkens/die . . . sterven/zelfs der Gheloovighen van eeuwigheyt heeft verworpen/ende . . . verdoemt . . . TOT ROTTERDAM, By Matthijs Bastiaensz. . . . 1617. 4° pp.20
T.2247(9).

S171 SLATIUS, Henricus

Christalijnen SPIEGEL, Vvaer in men . . . kan zien/wie t'zedert eenige Jaren herwaerts inde Provintie van Hollandt/de Hoogheydt Rechten/Privilegien en vrij heden [*sic*] hebben gevioleert . . . Of wie de rechte Autheurs zyn van alle divisie Scheuringe/twist/tweedracht en andere ongevallen in dese . . . Provintie opgeresen . . . 1619. 4° pp.40
T.2249(35).

Anonymous. Corresponding to the copy described in *Knuttel* no.2980. Followed by a manuscript entitled 'Copie van sekere requeste Aende . . . Burghemeesteren ende Gerechte der Stadt Leyden ouergegeven den 3 Julij 1619'.

S172 SLATIUS, Henricus

Christalijnen SPIEGEL, Vvaer in men . . . kan zien/wie t'zedert eenighe Jaren herwaerts inde Provintie van Hollandt/de Hoogheydt/Rechten/Privilegien en Vry heden [*sic*] hebben gevioleert . . . Of wie de Rechte Autheurs zijn van alle divisie Scheuringe/twist/tweedracht en andere onghevallen in dese . . . Provintie opgheresen . . . 1619. 4° pp.40
106.d.52.

Anonymous. Corresponding to the copy described in *Knuttel* no.2981.

S173 SLATIUS, Henricus

DEN Gepredestineerden Dief/OFTE EEN T'AMEN-SPREKINGE [*sic*] ghehouden TVSSCHEN EEN PREDICANT DER CALVINVS-GHESINDE ENDE EEN DIEF, die ghesententieert was om te sterven. Waer in Levendigh wert voor ooghen ghestelt . . . hoe de Leere der Contraremonstranten . . . dē mensche . . . oorsake geeft om Godlooselick te leven . . . GHEDRVCKT . . . 1619. 4° pp.38
4255.bb.21.

Anonymous and without imprint; according to *Tiele* no.1677 printed at Antwerp. Corresponding to the copy described in *Knuttel* no.2978.

S174 SLATIUS, Henricus

DEN Gepredestineerden Dief/OFTE EEN SAMEN-SPREKINGE, ghehouden TVSSCHEN EEN PREDICANT DER CALVINVS-GHESINDE ENDE EEN Dief, die ghesententieert was om te sterven. Waer in Levendigh werdt voor ooghen ghestelt . . . hoe de Leere der Contraremonstranten . . . den mensche . . . oorsake gheeft om godlooselick te leven . . . GHEDRVCT . . . 1619. 4° pp.38
4255.bb.19.

Anonymous and without imprint; according to *Tiele* no.1678 printed at Antwerp, but the printer's ornaments point to the Northern Netherlands. Corresponding to the copy described in *Tiele*.

S175 SLATIUS, Henricus

DEN Ghepredestineerden DIEF, OFTE EEN T'SAMEN-SPREKINGE ghehouden Tusschen een Predicant der Calvinus-gezinde/ende een dief/die gesententieert was om te sterven. Waer in Levendigh wert voor ooghen gestelt . . . hoe de Leere der Contra-Remonstranten . . . den mensche . . . oorsaeke gheeft om Godlooselijck te Leven . . . GHEDRVCKT . . . 1619. 4° pp.35
4255.bb.22(1).

Anonymous and without imprint. Corresponding to the copy described in *Knuttel* no.2977.

S176 SLATIUS, Henricus

DEN Ghepredestineerden DIEF, OFTE Een t'Samen-sprekinge/gehouden tusschen een Predicant der Calvinus-ghesinde ende een Dief, die gesententieert was om te sterven. GHEDRUCKT Nae de Copye tot Frederickstadt. 4° sig. A-C^4; illus.
4255.bb.20(1).

Anonymous and without imprint or date and with a fictitious copy imprint. Could be an edition of 1619, but is sometimes dated 1622 because the attached 'Bekeringe' of that year refers to it in the preface as the 'preceding dialogue' — which does not exclude a date between 1619 and 1621. Also variously dated 1641 or 1657. The titlepage engraving shows the thief behind bars, with the jailer and the preacher on the outside. Corresponding to the copy described in *Tiele* no. 1679.

S177 SLATIUS, Henricus

[Joannis Calvini Tyrannien.] IOANNES CALVINVS Vreedt, bitter, vals. Dat is: Corte . . . verbeldinghe [*sic*] Vanden Aert of Gheest IOANNIS CALVINI HEM VERTOONENDE In sijne Tyrannie . . . GHETROCKEN wt Joannis Calvini leere . . . Eerst gheteeckent Door eenen liefhebber der nederlantsche vryheyt in Schielandt. Naermaels door drie woorden dienaers in Hollant in drucke ghestelt. Anno M.DC.XVJ. Nu sonder . . . veranderinghe door Liefhebbers der Catholijcke waerheydt wtghegheven. t'HANTWERPEN, By Guilliam Lesteens . . . M.DC.XJX. 4° pp. 36
T.2249(39).

Anonymous. Originally edited by Jacobus Bontebal, Henricus Slatius and Matthijs Verburg (=Burgius). With a new preface by the printer.

S178 SLATIUS, Henricus

Monsterkens VAN DE NIEVWE HOLLANDSCHE INQVISITIE Ghelijck die nu/zedert ontrent een jaer herwaerts/inde Gheunieerde Provincien/teghen de Arminianen is Ghepractiseert: Ten thoone ghestelt door eenen Hollander, in sekere Brief aen synen Vriendt. GHEDRVCKT . . . 1620. 4° pp. 24
T.2249(37).

Anonymous; signed: F.P.Z.V'FF.

SMALLEGANGE, Hieronymus. Disputatio medica de angina. 1606. *See* VORSTIUS, Aelius Everardus

S179 SMALLEGANGE, Hieronymus

EXAMEN QVAESTIONIS MEDICAE. An puerperæ suffocationi uterinæ obnoxiæ, febri acuta laboranti, in morbi principio, tuto & ex arte possit exhiberi Moschus. Authore HIERONYMO SMALLEGANGE . . . MIDDELBVRGI Apud Symonem Moulert . . . 1613. 8° pp. 45
1176.b.4(1).

S180 SMARAGDUS; Abbas Verdunensis

DIADEMA MONACHORVM R.[DI] IN CHRISTO P. SMARAGDI . . . Iussu Reuerendi D. D. PETRI LOYERS Monasterij S. Martini Tornaci Abbatis, ex M.S. Codicibus bibliothecæ Monasterij eiusdem plurimùm ab alijs editionibus emendatum, & marginum citationibus & notis adauctum. Operâ F. IACOBI LE LOVCHIER . . . TORNACI, Ex Officina LAVRENTIANA . . . 1610. 12° pp. 391
4071.aa.44.

Printed by Charles Martin and Joseph Duhamel at Tournai. Ownership inscription: Monasterij Elchingensis.

S181 SMET, Peeter de
Voor-bereydinghe Totter doot: om eenen siecken mensch tot zijnder salicheyt te vermanen/ende in zijn wterste by te staen. Ghemaeckt by . . . Peeter de Smet . . . TOT BRVSSEL, By Jan Mommaert . . . 1616. 12° ff.47; illus.
4402.e.9(1).
The author's name given in the author's preface as: Petrus Faber, in the editor's preface as: Peeter de Smit. Edited by Petrus Calentinus. The prayers for the dead are in Latin. The illustrations on the titlepage and titlepage verso are woodcuts. Bought at the Serrure sale.

S182 SMITH, Richard; Bishop of Chalcedon
AN ANSWER TO THOMAS BELS LATE CHALLENG NAMED BY HIM THE DOVVNFAL OF POPERY WHERIN AL HIS ARGVMENTS are answered . . . By S. R. . . . AT DOWAY, Imprinted by LAVRENCE KELLAM . . . M.DC.V. 8° pp.446
3932.aaa.9.
Anonymous.

S183 [*SMITH, Richard; Bishop of Chalcedon
An answer to Thomas Bels late challeng named by him The downfall of popery . . . By S. R. . . . At Doway, Imprinted by Laurence Kellam . . . M.DC.VI. 8° pp.446
3935.a.38.]
*Destroyed. Anonymous. A reprint or reissue of the preceding. The title is that of the General Catalogue.

S184 SMITH, Richard; Bishop of Chalcedon
[De auctore et essentia Protestanticae ecclesiae.] OF THE AVTHOR AND SVBSTANCE OF THE PROTESTANT CHVRCH AND RELIGION . . . Written first in Latin by R. S. Doctour of Diuinity, AND Now reuiewed by the Author, and translated into English by VV. Bas. . . . M.DC.XXI. 8° pp.329
3935.b.37.
Anonymous and without imprint; published by the English College press at st. Omer. Translated by Richard White of Basingstoke. Ownership inscriptions: Mr. Herberts book; Thos. Brindle; Bp Baines.

S185 SMITH, Richard; Bishop of Chalcedon
THE PRVDENTIALL BALLANCE OF RELIGION Wherein the Catholike and Protestant religion are weighed together . . . THE FIRST PART . . . Printed . . . 1609. 8° pp.598
3936.aa.34; 3936.b.42.
Anonymous and without imprint; printed by François Bellet at St. Omer. The titlepage of the copy at 3936.aa.34 is mutilated; the copy at 3936.b.42 is cropped. The second part, 'Collatio Doctrinae Catholicorum ac Protestantium cum expressis S. Scripturae verbis', was published in Paris in 1622 (1009.c.14) and in English at Douai in 1631 (3935.dd.4).

S186 SMOUT, Adriaen Jorisz
Eendracht Van over de vijftich menigherley Schriften/die Teghen 't Pelaghiaensdom . . . door de Treffelicste ghereformeerde Kercken ende School-Leeraren . . . Gheschreven . . . zijn . . . Metter tijt by een ghebracht . . . overgheset// ende . . . wtghegheven/door HADRIANVM GEORGIVM SMOVTIVM . . . TOT ROTTERDAM, By Jan van Waesberghe . . . M.DC.JX. 4° sig.a–i^4, ff.195, sig.Aa^4; illus.
T.2239(12).
The woodcut on f.162v shows Faith carrying the Cross, stepping on an orb.

S187 SMOUT, Adriaen Jorisz
Onschuldt ende Afwijsinge ADRIANI SMOUTII over 'tghene hem Van weghen de

t'onrecht-verdachte Predikanten toeghewesen is/iu [*sic*] hun Aenvvijsinge van de onbehoorlijcke vvijse van doen, &c. onder den name P. Cupi ende de letteren C.S.a.G. binnens maendts wtghegheven . . . Voor Felix van Sambeec/TOT DELFT . . . 1610. 4° pp.59
1608/4413.
The writer of the preface of the 'Aenwijsinge', signing himself C.S.a.G., was Nicolaas Grevinchoven.

S188 SMOUT, Adriaen Jorisz
ADRIANI SMOVTII Onse Vader: Dat is, Verklaringhe hoe God de Vader des Heeren Jesu Christi Onse Vader mede is/ende wy zyne Kinderen zijn . . . Bekentenisghewyse . . . in vier Artijckelen vervatet ende ghestelt teghen de vijf Remonstrantsche . . . nu den Ghereformeerden Kercken-raedt van de Nederlandtsche Natie/binnen Dordrecht . . . vergadert . . . opghedraghen ende toe-gheeyghent . . . T'AMSTERDAM, Voor Marten Jansz. Brandt . . . M DC XVIII. 4° pp.135
T.2248(35).
Printed by Paulus van Ravesteyn at Amsterdam?

S189 SMOUT, Adriaen Jorisz
SCHRIFTELIC IA Over de Vraghe/Of de leer-pointen, die ten huydighen daghe in gheschil ghetrocken vvorden, het Fondament der salicheyt raken ofte niet. Teghen het onschriftmatich Neen ende zegghen van zommighe Dat d'opinien van beyde partijen . . . bestaen konnen . . . Bevesticht . . . Door Adriaen Iorisz. Smout . . . TOT SCHIEDAM, By Adriaen Cornelisz van Delf . . . 1613. 4° pp.154
T.2243(9).

S190 SMOUT, Adriaen Jorisz
Toetse ADRIANI SMOVTII, Van sekere Antwoorde ende Bericht/in December 1611. uytgekomen/met desen Titel: Conradi Vorstij . . . Teghen-bericht/Op sekere Artikelen onlangs onder de ghemeyne man . . . ghestroyt . . . Ghedruckt . . . 1612. 4° pp.230
T.2242(27).

S191 SMYTERS, Anthoni
EPITHETA, Dat zijn Bynamen oft Toenamen, Beschreven door ANTHONI SMYTERS . . . TOT ROTTERDAM, By Jan van Waesberghe . . . 1620. 8° sig.(.?.) A-Bb^{8}Cc^4
827.d.42.

S192 SMYTH, John; the Se-Baptist
THE CHARACTER OF THE BEAST: OR THE FALSE CONSTITVTION OF THE CHVRCH. Discovered IN CERTAYNE PASSAGES BETWIXT Mr. R. CLIFTON & Iohn Smyth, concerning true Christian baptisme of New Creatures, or New borne Babes in Christ: &nd [*sic*] false Baptisme of infants borne after the Flesh . . . 1609. 4° pp.71
4139.aaa.26.
The preface signed: John Smyth. Without imprint; printed by Richard Schilders at Middelburg.

S193 SMYTH, John; the Se-Baptist
THE DIFFERENCES OF THE Churches of the seperation: Contayning, A DESCRIPTION OF THE LEITOVRGIE AND Ministerie of the visible Church . . . BY IOHN SMYTH . . . 1608. 4° pp.22[31]
C.53.b.28.
Without imprint; printed by Richard Schilders at Middelburg.

S194 SNELLIUS, Willebrordus

WILEBRORDI SNELLII APOLLONIVS BATAVVS, Seu, Exsuscitata APOLLONII PERGAEI ΠΕΡΙ ΔΙΩΡΙΣΜΕΝΗΣ ΤΟΜΗΣ Geometria. LVGODINI [*sic*], Excudebat Iohannes a Dorp, 1608. Prostant apud Iohannem Maire. 4° pp.37; illus.

A reconstruction by Snellius of a lost work by Apollonius Pergaeus.

S195 SNELLIUS, Willebrordus

Cœli & siderum in eo errantium OBSERVATIONES HASSIACÆ . . . PRINCIPIS WILHELMI HASSIÆ LANTGRAVII auspicijs quondam institutæ. ET Spicilegium biennale EX OBSERVATIONIBVS BOHEMICIS . . . Tychonis BRAHE. Nunc primum publicante WILLEBRORDO SNELLIO . . . Quibus accesserunt, IOANNIS REGIOMONTANI & BERNARDI WALTERI Observationes Noribergicæ. LVGDVNI BATAVORVM. Apud IVSTVM COLSTERVM . . . M D C XVIII. 4° pp.116; ff.68; illus.

531.k.13(1); 8563.aa.35.

The illustrations are woodcuts.

S196 SNELLIUS, Willebrordus

VVILLEBRORDI SNELLII . . . CYCLOMETRICVS, De circuli dimensione . . . LVGDVNI BATAVORVM, Ex Officinâ ELZEVIRIANA . . . M D CXXI. 4° pp.102; illus.

530.i.12.

With the arms of Marie Auguste de Sultzbach, wife of Charles Philippe Théodore de Sultzbach, Count Palatine and Duke of Bavaria, 1724–1765, on the binding.

S197 SNELLIUS, Willebrordus

WILLEBRORDI SNELLII R. F. DE RE NVMMARIA Liber singularis. EX OFFICINA PLANTINIANA RAPHELENGII, M.D.CXIII. 8° pp.72

602.a.9(1).

Dedicated to Hugo Grotius. Published at Leiden. Some pages badly cut.

S198 SNELLIUS, Willebrordus

VVILLEBRORDI SNELLII DESCRIPTIO COMETÆ, qui anno 1618 mense Novembri primùm effulsit. Huc accessit CHRISTOPHORI RHOTMANNI . . . descriptio accurata cometæ anni 1585. Nunc primum à WILL. SN. R. F. in lucem edita. LVGDVNI BATAVORVM, Ex Officinâ ELZEVIRIANA . . . MD.C.XIX. 4° pp.156; illus.

C.76.b.15.

The illustrations are woodcuts.

S199 SNELLIUS, Willebrordus

ERATOSTHENES BATAVVS De Terræ ambitus vera quantitate, A WILLEBRORDO SNELLIO . . . Suscitatus. LVGDVNI BATAVORVM, Apud IODOCVM à COLSTER . . . M D CXVII. (col.) Excudebat GEORGIVS ABRAHAMI A MARSSE . . .M DCXVII. 4° pp.263; illus.

793.f.10.

With modern manuscript annotations. Presented by Wibrandus Suysius to John Greaves, Leiden, 6 November 1633.

S200 SNOUCKAERT VAN SCHAUBURG, Maerten

(tp.1) PROCRIS En AIAX Treur-spelen. Door M. Snouckaert van Schauwenburg. Ghedruckt voor Ian Tomassz. . . . 1621. TOT AMSTERDAM, [*sic*]
(tp.2=sig.B1) PROCRIS Treur-spel. Door M. Snouckaert van Schauwenburg . . . Ghedruckt voor Ian Tomassz. . . 1621. TOT AMSTERDAM, [*sic*] 4° sig.A-H^4I^1

11754.bbb.57.

The 'Ajax' begins halfway down leaf E1r, without a separate titlepage.

S201 SOHN, Georg

Een treffelijcke Oratie, Leerende hoe sich een Christen mensche schuldich is te

draghen int onderzoecken der waerheyt/wanneer inde Kercke over de Leere verschillen . . . op-rijsen. Eertijts by . . . Georgium Sohnium . . . ghedaen . . . Hier is byghevoeght een Voor-reden, vervatende . . . een korte Historie, vanden oorspronc ende voortganc der oneenicheden . . . ooc der swaricheden in onse Hollantsche Kercken op-gheresen door N.I.R. TOT SCHIEDAM, By Adriaen Cornelisz van Delf . . . M.D.C.XI. 4° pp.32
T.2241(16).
Edited by Richard Jean de Nerée. The preface was also published separately in 1612, as 'Corte beschrijvinghe [etc.]', for which see *Knuttel* no.2012.

SOLUTION of Doctor Resolutus. 1619. *See* CALDERWOOD, David

S202 SOMMATIE
SOMMATIE Ghedaen van wegen des Conincx, aen Monsieur de Soubise, Hooft der Rebellen van S. Ian d'Angely, door eenen Franschen Herault. d'Antvvoorde vanden . . . Heere de Soubise ende de Replicque vanden . . . Herault. Ende t'ghene datter inden Legher ghepasseert is/t'sedert den 28. Mey tot nv toe. Ouerghesedt vvt het Fransoys, in onse Nederlantsche sprake. Nv eerst Ghedruckt den 25. Junij. T'Hantwerpen/By Abraham Verhoeuen/[etc.] 4° pp.8; sig.C^4; illus.
P.P.3444.af(251).
Headed: Iunij, 2621 [*sic*]. 95. The titlepage woodcut shows two armorial shields.

S203 SOMMIER
Sommier verhael van de wreede handelinghe der Bloed-dorstighe Calvinisten/ ghepleeght teghen de Remonstranten buyten Rotterdam/op Sondagh voorleden deu [*sic*] xx. October. 1619. Men vintse ce [*sic*] coope daerse veyl zijn. Ghedruckt . . . M.DC.XJX. 4° pp.8; unsigned
P.P.3444.af(22).
Without imprint; printed by Abraham Verhoeven at Antwerp. With a typical Verhoeven ornament on the titlepage and another in the text.

S204 SOMMIER
Sommier verhael van de wreede handelinghe der Bloet-dorstighe Calvinisten/ ghepleeght tegen de Remonstranten buyten Rotterdam/op Sondagh . . . den xx. October. 1619. Mitsgaders, Vande groote Tierannije ende . . . Wreetheden/ die . . . van dese Suyvere Ghepredestineerde Broeders bedreven zijn. Hier is noch by gevoeght/Een nieu Liedeken/hoe dat het Dortsche Sinode/de Remonstranten soecken uyt te roeyen . . . GHEDRVCKT . . . M.DC.XJX. Ende men vinse [*sic*] te Coope daerse veyl zijn. 4° pp.16
T.2249(38).
Another edition of the preceding, with additional matter, probably printed in the United Provinces.

SOMMIGHE ghebeden. 1602. *See* BIBLE. Selections. Dutch

Den SOO-VEELSTEN Vraegh-Al. 1618. *See* VRAEGH-AL

S205 SOTO, Andres de
[De la verdadera soledad.] DE SCHOLE VAN DE EENICHEYDT DES MENSCHS MET GODT DOOR P.F. ANDREAS A SOTO . . . T'ANTWERPEN By Ioachim Trognæsius . . . 1616. [etc.] 8° pp.274
1578/1628.
The titlepage is engraved; signed: P. Serwouters. The translator named in the approbation as Jacobus Farcinius. With the exlibris of Gustave Charles Antoine van Havre.

S206 SOTO, Andres de

[Dos dialogos.] TWEE T'SAMENSPREKINGEN BEHANDELENDE DE LEEringe ende materie vanden mirakelen . . . Door . . . Andreas de Soto . . . Ende onlancx ouergheset vuyter Spaensche tale int Franchois/ende daer naer int Nederlants/door Philips Numan . . . TOT BRVESSEL, By Rutgeert Velpius eñ Huybrecht Antoon . . . 1614. [etc.] 8° pp.xliii
1568/9275(4).

SOUTER liedekens. 1613. *See* BIBLE. Psalms. Latin and Dutch

S207 SOUTHWELL, Robert

AN EPISTLE OF COMFORT, TO THE Reuerend Priests, and to the Honourable, Worshipfull, & other of the Lay sort, restrayned in durance for the Catholike Faith. By R.S. of the Society of IESVS . . . M.DC.XVI. 8° pp.419
C.26.h.15.

Signed at the end: Ro. Southwell. Without imprint; printed by the English College press at St. Omer. Ownership inscription: Bibl. [C]oll. F.Fr. Pr. Lo: Anglo-Lovanij apposuit infrascript. Ad usum F. Ambrosij Burgis. With the exlibris of Henry Francis Lyte.

S208 SOUTHWELL, Robert

A POEME DECLARING THE REAL PRESENCE OF CHRIST IN THE BLESSED SACRAMENT OF THE AVLTAR. (col.) Printed at Doway, by Laurence Kellam . . . 1606. 4° a single sheet
1865.c.10(48).

Anonymous. The poem begins: 'In Paschal feast, the end of ancient rite [etc.]'.

S209 SOUTHWELL, Robert

S. PETERS COMPLAINT. AND SAINT MARY MAGDALENS FVNERALL TEARES. With sundry other . . . Poems. By R.S. of the Society of IESVS . . . M.DC.XVI. 8° pp.170
C.26.gg.5.

Anonymous and without imprint; printed by the English College press at St. Omer. Partly in prose.

S210 SOUTHWELL, Robert

S. PETERS COMPLAINT AND SAINT MARY MAGDALENS FVNERALL TEARES. With sundry other selected, and deuout POEMES. By . . . Robert Southwell . . . M.DC.XX. 8° pp.170
C.26.h.11.

Another edition of the preceding. Without imprint; printed by the English College press at St. Omer. Ownership inscription: John Griffithe his book.

De SPAENSCHE gheboode ingestelt door, Paulus V. 1615. *See* VISIOEN

De SPAENSCHE tiranije. Dienende tot een morghen-wecker. 1620. *See* BAUDAERT, Willem

S211 SPAENSCHE

SPAENSCHE TIRANNYE IN NEDERLANDT. 4° pl.16
1609/5514.

Plates, all mounted — originally loose —, printed on one side of the leaf only, with engraved 16-line verses under the engravings, divided into two columns, with the plate numbers between the columns. Similar sets described in the literature as having 18 plates, but also ending with the death of William of Orange or continuing until 1597. One set is described as having a separate titlepage in folio, reading 'tyrannye der Spanj.'. Usually dated 1620. The plates based on those of Frans Hogenberg.

S212 SPAENSCHEN

SPAENSCHEN RAEDT, Hoemen de vereenichde Nederlanden alderbest wederom sal konnen brengen onder t'gebiedt van den Coninc vā Spagnien. Tot waerschouwinghe van alle vroome Nederlanders . . . uyt de uytgegevene schriften van eenige Spaensche Raetsluyden . . . door een Liefhebber des Vaderlandts uytghetrocken/ende t'samen ghestelt. Ghedruckt int Jaer . . . 1617. 4° pp.13

T.2422(4).

The 'Spanish councillors' named on the titlepage verso as Justus Lipsius, Erycius Puteanus and Franciscus Campanella. A copy of the edition described in *Knuttel* no.2458.

S213 SPAENSCHEN

SPAENSCHEN RAEDT, Hoemen de vereenichde Nederlanden alderbest wederom sal konnen brenghen onder 'tghebiedt van den Koninck van Spagnien . . . 1617. 4° pp.8

700.h.25(6).

Another edition of the preceding, corresponding to that described in *Knuttel* no.2459.

S214 SPAIN

[11.12.1604] PLACCAET Des Conincks van Spaegnien: Wtgegheven in Valladolid/ den 11. der Maent van December . . . 1604. Ghetrouwelijcken uyt het Spaensch in onse Nederlandtsche Spraecke overgheset . . . 1605. 4° sig.A^2

T.1717(36).

Concerning trade between Spain and the Netherlands.

S215 SPAIN

[3.9.1606] Verclaringhe oft uytroep in Spaengien/van weghen het handelen der Hoochduytscher Coopmanschappen/comende uyt het Rijcke van groot Britangien ende Vranckrijck in Spangien. Insghelijcx het teghendeel ghemaeckt teghen die Stadt van Rochelle . . . Ghegheven tot Lorenzo den 3. September 1606. Ghetrouwelijck overgheset uyt den Spaensche in onse Nederlandtsche tale . . . 1606. 4° sig.A^2

T.1717(40).

S216 SPAIN

[11.11.1607] verclaringhe [*sic*] ghedaen uyt den naem des Conincx van Spaengnien/tot waerschouwinghe aen alle de Cooplieden ende Negotianten in zijne Rijcken ende Landen van Spaengnien/ende Portugael/van . . . den elfsten November/1607. Tot Middelburgh by Richard Schilders/nae het Spaensche exemplaer. 4° sig.A^2

T.1717(41).

SPAIN [9.4.1609]. For documents issued in Spain relating to the Truce in the Netherlands and published there, *see* NETHERLANDS. Southern Provinces

S217 SPAIN

[11.9.1609] MISSIVE OFTE PLACCAET Van den Coninck van Spangien ghesonden aenden Hartoch van Lerma. aengaende het bannen ende verjaghen van de Moriscos . . . Van dato den 11. September . . . 1609, Wt den Spaenschen in onse Nederduytsche tale overgheset/DOOR I.H. VAN LINSCHOTEN. Ghedruckt tot Enchuysen/by Jacob Lenaertsz. Meyn . . . 1609. 4° sig.A^4

T.1717(44).

The last leaf is blank.

S218 SPAIN

[15.6.1617] PACTORVM De perpetua Successione in Regnis Hungariæ & Bohemiæ ac Provinciarum ad ea pertinentium, INSTRVMENTA VI. & XV. Mensis junij, Anno DCXVII. Pragæ confecta. PHILIPPO III. Hispaniarum Rege, Iuri suo renunciante . . . FERDINANDO, Austriæ Archiduce, hæc acceptante . . . MATTHIA II. Rom. Imp. Pacta hæc . . . confirmante. [etc.] 4° sig. A^4B^2
1054.h.9(4).

Without imprint; printed by Richard Schilders at Middelburg in 1617. Cropped.

S219 SPAIN

[17.1.1622] Copije van een Decret, oft Ordonnantie ons Heeren des Conincx/ Onderteeckent by de eyghen handt van zijne Majesteydt, voor den Heere President van Castillien/Ghedepescheert int Pardo [*sic*], den veerthienden Januarij van desen . . . Jaere 1622. Ghetranslateert Wt het Spaens, in onse Nederlantsche sprake. T'Hantwerpen/By Abraham Verhoeven/[etc.] 4° pp.8; sig.G; illus.
P.P.3444.af(334).

Headed: Februarius, 1622. 25. Demanding that all officials shall declare their property. The 'Copy' signed at Madrid on 17 January 1622. The titlepage woodcut shows the aegis.

The SPEACH of the Kirk of Scotland. 1620. *See* CALDERWOOD, David

SPECULUM Anabaptistici furoris. 1608. *See* SICHEM, Christoffel van. Historische beschrijvinge.

SPECULUM tragicum. 1601–1605. *See* DICKENSONUS, Joannes

S220 SPECULUM

SPECVLVM VITÆ B. FRANCISCI ET SOCIORVM EIVS . . . A mendis expurgatum, in meliorem ordinem ac stilum, & notis breuibus illustratum Operâ & studio GVILIELMI SPOELBERCH . . . ANTVERPIÆ, Ex Officina Gerardi Wolsschatij. M.DC.XX. [etc.] 8° 2 pt.: pp.208; 191
861.f.6.

Ownership inscription: Sōctis Jesv Antwerp. D.D.

SPEILBERGHEN, Joris van. *See* SPILBERGEN, Joris van

't SPEL van sinne, vertoont op de tweede lotery. 1616. *See* KONING, Abraham de

SPEL van Tiisken vander Schilden. 1615. *See* COSTER, Samuel

SPEL vande Rijcke-man. 1615. *See* COSTER, Samuel

SPELBERGH, Joris van. *See* SPILBERGEN, Joris van

S221 SPELEN

(tp.1) Spelen van Sinne vol schoone allegatien/loflijcke leeringhen ende Schriftuerlijcke onderwijsinghen. Op de vraghe: VVie den meesten troost oyt quam te baten Die schenen te zijn van Godt verlaten. Ghespeelt ende vertoont binnen der Stadt Rotterdam/by de neghen Kameren van Rethorijken/die hen daer ghepresenteert hebben den xx dach in Julio/Anno 1561. TOT ROTTERDAM, By Jan van Waesberghe de Jonghe . . . 1614.
(tp.2) Dryderley Refereynen ghepronunceert opte Rethorijck-feest der blauvve Acoleyen van Rotterdam/Anno 1561 . . . TOT ROTTERDAM, By Jan van Waesberghe de Jonghe . . . 1614. 8° 2 pt.: sig.⁂, $A–S^8T^2$; $A–E^8F^4$; illus.
11754.aa.57(1).

Reprinted from the edition by Willem Silvius at Antwerp, 1564, with a new verse dedication to the Rotterdam Admiralty by Jan van Waesberghe de Jonghe preceding the preface of Willem Silvius. The illustrations are woodcuts showing the blazons of the Chambers.

S222 SPELEN

[Spelen van sinne . . . Rotterdam . . . 1561.] Dryderley Refereynen ghepronunceert opte Rethorijck-feest der blauvve Acoleyen van Rotterdam . . . 1561 . . . TOT ROTTERDAM, By Jan van Waesberghe de Jonghe . . . 1614. 8° sig. A-E^{8}F^4; illus.

11754.aa.57(2).

Another issue of pt.2 of the preceding, with the blazon of the Blauwe Acoleyen on the titlepage in place of Jan van Waesberghe's device.

S223 SPEUY, Hendrick

De Psalmen Davids/gestelt op het Tabulatuer van het Orghel ende Clavecymmel [*sic*]/met 2. Partijen/door HENDERICK SPEVY . . . Les Pseaumes de David, mis en Tableture sur l'Instrument des Orgues & de l'Espinette, a 2. parties, composés par Henri Speuy . . . TOT DORDRECHT. Ghedruckt by Peeter Verhaghen . . . Voor den Autheur. 1610. fol. pp.49

Music K.1.i.14.

With a dedication to James I in French, although the poem by G. J. Vossius states that it was dedicated to the States General. A poem by the composer is printed in civilité.

De SPIEGEL der Nederlandsche elenden. 1621. *See* VERSTEGAN, Richard

SPIEGEL vande doorluchtige . . . vrouwen. 1606. *See* HEINSIUS, Daniel

S224 SPIEGEL, Hendrick Laurensz

H. L. SPIEGHELS. HART-SPIEGHEL . . . t'AMSTERDAM, Voor Cornelis Dirckxz. Cooll . . . 161 . (col.) 't AMSTERDAM Ghedruckt by Paulus van Ravesteyn . . . 1614. 16° pp.137; illus., port.

1155.a.39.

The date on the titlepage has been left open. The titlepage woodcut shows Arion riding the dolphin, symbolizing Spiegel's motto; the engraved portrait on the titlepage verso after a portrait of 1579 signed: JMuller sculp. A note on p.[138] states that this small pocket edition is to be followed by a large one with plates. On pp.[139-142]: 'H.L. Spieghels Wterste-wil'. Cropped.

S225 SPIEGEL, Hendrick Laurensz

H. L. SPIEGHELS HART-SPIEGHEL . . . t'AMSTERDAM, Voor Cornelis Dirckxz. Cooll . . . 1615. (col.) t'AMSTERDAM, Ghedruckt by Paulus van Ravesteyn . . . M.DC.XV. 8° pp.86; illus., port.

11555.c.37(1).

With a similar titlepage woodcut as in the preceding. The woodcut portrait on the titlepage verso signed: CVS, i.e. Christoffel van Sichem, and dated 1579. With 'H.L. Spieghels Uyterste-Wil . . . Mitsgaders A.B.C. Kettinglied'.

S226 SPIEGEL, Hendrick Laurensz

(tp.1) Twe-spraack vande Nederduitsche Letterkunst/ofte Vant spellen ende eyghenscap des Nederduitschen taals; uytghegheven by de Kamer IN LIEFDE BLOEYENDE, t'Amstelredam. TOT AMSTELREDAM. By Hendrick Barentsz. . . . 1614.

(tp.2=p.93) Ruygh-bewerp vande Redenkaveling/ofte Nederduytsche Dialectike . . . uytghegheven by de Kamer IN LIEFD BLOEYENDE, t'Amstelredam. TOT AMSTELREDAM, By Hendrick Barentsz. . . . 1614.

(tp.3=p.239) Kort begrip Des Redenkavelings: in slechten Rym vervat/om des zelfs voorneemste hoofdpunten te beter inde ghedachten te hechten. TOT AMSTERDAM, By Hendrick Barentsz. . . . 1614.

(tp.4=p.257) Rederijck-kunst/in Rijm opt kortst vervat, Hier by ghevoeght de REDENKAVELING ENDE LETTER-KUNSTS GRONDVESTEN. uytghegheven by de Kamer in Liefd' Bloeyende t'AMSTELREDAM. TOT AMSTELREDAM By Hendrick Barentsz. 1614.

(col.) Tot Amstelredam by Hendrick Barentsz. . . . 1614. 8° pp.283: tables; illus. Cup.402.k.26.

Anonymous. Reprinted from the edition published at Leiden, 1584-87, with correction of misprints. The preface signed: D.V. Koornhert. With the Chamber's emblem on the versos of all titlepages. The three tables at the end are misbound, with that bearing the colophon here in second place.

SPIEGHEL ende sonderlinghe exempel. 1618. *See* JOANNIS, Adrianus

S227 SPIEGHEL

DEN SPIEGHEL Voor Den Pfalts-Graeff/Gheschreven wt Bohemen in de Stadt Prage. Eerst Ghedruckt in Januarius/1621. T'Hantwerpen/by Abraham Verhoeven/[etc.] 4° pp.8; sig.A^4; illus., port.
P.P.3444.af(180); 1471.aa.6.

Headed: Ianuarius 1621. 11. In verse. The titlepage woodcut shows a mirror reflecting the head of Frederick losing the crown.

S228 SPILBERGEN, Joris van

Copye Van een Brief/geschreven door Joris van Spelbergh/Commijs Generael/ende Capiteyn over de Zeeusche Soldaten . . . tracterende van't veroveren der Spaensche Armade . . . in dato 9 Mey, 1607. 4° sig.A^2
T.1713(12).

Published in 1607.

S229 SPILBERGEN, Joris van

[Copye van een brief.] Historie ende generale beschrijvinge Van die heerlicke victorie die God verleent heeft den kloucken ende stouten Heldt . . . Iacob van Heemskercke . . . voor die stadt Gibaltar [*sic*] inde Strate/Anno 1607. Door I.S. 4° 2 unsigned leaves
1578/335.

Anonymous. Another edition of the preceding. Published in 1607.

S230 SPILBERGEN, Joris van

['t Historiael journael.] Het Journael van Joris van Speilberghen . . . Desē Journalē . . . heeft geordineert eñ tzijnen costen doen drucken Floris Balthazar . . . tot Delff/alwaermen de selve te coope vint. 1605. obl.4° pp.67: plates; maps
1858.a.1(3).

The running title is: Reyse van Ioris van Spilberghen naer Oost-Indien.

S231 SPILBERGEN, Joris van

t'Historiael Journael/van tghene ghepasseert is van weghen drie Schepen/ghenaemt den Ram, Schaep ende het Lam, ghevaren uyt Zeelandt . . . naer d'Oost-Indien/onder t'beleyt van Ioris van Speilberghen . . . 1601 . . . tot in't Eylant Celon . . . Dese Historie is verciert met seventhien . . . platen . . . Ghecorrigeert verbetert ende vermeerdert. 't AMSTERDAM, By Michiel Colijn . . . 1617. obl.4° ff.41: plates; illus., maps
983.ff.5.

A separate issue of the copy included as pt.4 in 'Oost-Indische ende West-Indische voyagien' compiled by Michiel Colijn. The leaves in sig.C have had the text printed on in a wrong order. One of the plates signed: Balt[9]. Florentii F. Delphi. The dedication on the map on the plate facing f.18v, signed: Florentius Balthazari F. Delph: editor., is mutilated.

S232 SPILBERGEN, Joris van

Oost ende West-Indische SPIEGEL Der 2. leste Navigatien/ghedaen inden Jaeren

1614. 15. 16. 17. ende 18. daer in vertoont woort/in wat gestalt Ioris van Speilbergen door de Magellanes de werelt rontom geseylt heeft/met eenighe Battalien . . . ende 2 Historien de een van Oost ende de ander van West-Indien . . . Met de Australische Navigatien, van Iacob le Maire, die int suyden door een nieuwe Straet ghepasseert is . . . in 26 coperen platen afghebeelt. TOT LEYDEN, By Nicolaes van Geelkercken . . . 1619. obl.4° pp.192: pl.25; maps
10028.df.17.

A copy of the reissue of the edition first published earlier the same year. Probably written according to Spilbergen's instructions by Jan Cornelisz May. With 'Beschrijvinghe vande regheringhe van Pera' by Pedro de Madriga, with additional, anonymous, notes on Chile by Jacob Dirickszoon van Purmerlant, 'Discours' by Apollonius Schot, and 'Corte beschrijvinghe . . . vande forten . . . inde Indien ten dienste vande Gheneraele Compaignie'. The 26th plate mentioned in the title is the titlepage illustration, showing a naval engagement. Corresponding to *Tiele Mémoire* p.65 no.5b with additional information pp.69–73.

S233 SPILBERGEN, Joris van
Oost ende West-Indische SPIEGHEL Waer in Beschreven werden de Twee laetste Navigatien/ghedaen inde Jaeren 1614. 1615–1616. 1617. ende 1618. De eene door den vermaerden Zee-Heldt IORIS van SPILBERGEN . . . Hier syn mede by ghevoecht tvvee Historien, de eene vande OOST ende de andere vande WEST-INDIEN . . . De andere ghedaen by IACOB LE MAIRE, de welcke in't Zuyden . . . een nieuwe Straet ontdeckt heeft . . . Alles verciert met schoone Caerten ende Figueren . . . 'TAMSTELREDAM, By Ian Ianssz . . . M.DC.XXI. obl.4° pp.192: pl.25; maps
1486.gg.28.

A reprint of the preceding, without a titlepage engraving. Imperfect; wanting sig.A4. Ownership inscription: David Goubaud. Corresponding to *Tiele Mémoire* p.68 no.5e.

S234 SPILBERGEN, Joris van
[Oost ende West-Indische spiegel.] MIROIR Oost & VVest-Indical, Auquel sont descriptes les deux dernieres Navigations, faictes es Années 1614. 1615. 1616. 1617. & 1618. l'une par . . . GEORGE de SPILBERGEN, par le Destroict de Magellan . . . Icy sont aussi adiouestées deux Histoires, l'une des Indes Orientales, l'autre des Indes Occidentales . . . l'autre faicte par JACOB LE MAIRE, lequel . . . a descouvert un nouveau Destroict . . . Le tout embelli de . . . Cartes & Figures . . . A AMSTELREDAM, Chez IAN IANSZ. . . . 1621. obl.4° pp.172: pl.25; maps
436.b.19; 216.a.20; G.6792.

The copy at 436.b.19 is from the library of Sir Joseph Banks. Corresponding to *Tiele Mémoire* p.70 no.5g.

S235 SPILBERGEN, Joris van
[Oost ende West-Indische spiegel.] SPECVLVM ORIENTALIS OCCIDENTALISQVE INDIÆ NAVIGATIONVM: Quarum una Georgij à Spilbergen classis cum potestate Præfecti, altera Iacobi le Maire auspicijs imperioque directa, Annis 1614,15,16,17,18. Exhibens Noui in mare Australe transitus . . . inuentionē: prælia . . . commissa . . . vna cum duabus nouis utriusque Indiæ Historijs, Catalogo munitionum Hollandicarum . . . Fretisque quatuor: suis quæque figuris ac imaginibus illustrata. Lugduni Batauorum apud Nicolaum à Geelkercken . . . MDCXIX. obl.4° pp.175: pl.25; maps
1486.gg.27; 682.b.14.

The copy at 682.b.14 from the library of Clayton Mordaunt Cracherode. Corresponding to *Tiele Mémoire* p.66 no.5c.

S236 SPILBERGEN, Joris van

[Oost ende West-Indische spiegel.] SPECVLVM ORIENTALIS OCCIDENTALISQVE INDIÆ NAVIGATIONVM . . . Lugduni Batauorum apud Nicolaum à Geelkercken . . . M D CXIX. Sumptibus IVDOCI HONDII. obl.4° pp.175: pl.25; maps

G.6909.

Another issue of the preceding, published at Amsterdam. Corresponding to *Tiele Mémoire* p.67 no.5d.

S237 SPINOLA, Ambrogio; Marquis

Ambrosius Spinola/Marquis van Cesto . . . Overghesedt wt het Fransoys d'welck ghepubliceert is int Legher/ende in Pfaltz-Landt. Eerst ghedruckt in Februarius/ 1621. T'Hantwerpen/by Abraham Verhoeven/[etc.] 4° pp.8; sig. A^4; illus., port.

P.P.3444.af(187).

Headed: Februarius 1621. 18. The titlepage woodcut shows the portrait of Spinola. The order, not defined in the title, declares protection for travellers on the highways. With other news.

S238 SPINOLA, Ambrogio; Marquis

Wy AMBROSIO SPINOLA . . . Ontbieden den . . . Hooftlieden/Raden/ commissarissen/ende . . . alle Ghevreyte Rijcx/Ridderschap/aenden Rijnstroom ende Wetterau . . . onse vriendelijcke Groetenisse. Overghesedt wt den Hooch-Duytsche/in onse Nederlantsche Tale. T'Hantwerpen/By Abraham Verhoeven . . . 1620 [etc.] 4° pp.6; sig.P^4; illus., port.

P.P.3444.af(107); 1480.aa.15(27).

With the text of the letter from the 'Ritterschaft' to accompany further transmission of Spinola's letter. Originally issued as part of 'Waerachtighe coppyen'. The titlepage woodcut shows the portrait of Spinola. The privilege is printed on p.[8], after p.[7] which is blank.

S239 SPOELBERCH, Willem van

DEN SPIEGHEL DER CONSCIENTIEN, Inhoudende de principale punten daermen mede misdoet tegen Godt/sijn seluen/oft sijnen naesten . . . Ghemaeckt deur . . . VVillem Spoelberch . . . T'ANTVVERPEN, By Gheleyn Janssens . . . 1607. [etc.] 8° pp.154; illus.

1509/3601.

The titlepage woodcut shows a scene of confession. The preface is printed in civilité.

SPRAECK ende woord-boeck, inde Maleysche ende Madagaskarsche talen. 1603. *See* HOUTMAN, Frederick de

S240 SPRANCKHUYSEN, Dionysius

D. SPRANCKHVSY IVSTIFICATIE Teghen Alle Calumnien ende lasteren/die hem van sijnen Kerckendienst tot Haerlem opgheticht sijn. Mitsgaders De redenen, vvaerom hy goet ghevonden hebbe te versoeken ontslaginghe van sijnen Dienst tot Haerlem . . . GHEDRVCKT t'HAERLEM. By Adriaen Rooman . . . 1617. 4° pp.44

T.2247(45).

Den STANDT van Jerusalem. 1610. *See* KEERE, Pieter van de

S241 STANEY, William

A Treatise of Penance, VVITH AN EXPLICATION of the Rule, and manner of liuing, of the Brethren and Sisters, of the third Order of S. FRAVNCIS: commonly called, of the Order of PENANCE . . . By F.W.S. . . . WHEREVNTO IS ADDED, THE EPIstle and Annotations vpon this Rule, of . . . PETER GONZALES . . . With a Catalogue made by him, of the names of the chiefe persons of this Order . . . At Douay by IOHN HEIGHAM . . . 1617. 8° pp.498

1111.b.10; C.65.hh.17.

The author's full name given in the approbations. With an additional, engraved titlepage, reading: A treatise of the Third Order of S. Francis. Printed by Pierre Auroi at Douai. The copy at 1111.b.10 has the exlibris of Thomas, Duke of Norfolk and one of the library bequeathed to his family by Edward, Duke of Norfolk; ownership inscription in the copy at C.65.hh.17: John Edwards. Parts of the original binding of the copy at C.65.hh.17 are preserved, bearing the initials: I.H. The copy at C.65.hh.17 is imperfect; wanting the additional, engraved titlepage.

S242 STANIHURST, Richard
RICHARDI STANIHVRSTI . . . BREVIS PRÆMVNITIO Pro futurâ concertatione cum IACOBO VSSERIO . . . Qui in suâ historicâ explicatione conatur probare, Pontificem Romanum . . . verum & germanum esse Antichristum. DVACI, Ex Typographia BALTAZARIS Belleri . . . 1615. 8° pp.38
G.5493.
Badly cropped, with occasional loss of pagination, catchwords, signatures and some text.

S243 STANIHURST, Richard
HEBDOMADA EVCHARISTICA EX SACRIS LITTERIS ATQVE ORTHODOXIS CATHOLICÆ ROMANÆ Ecclesiæ Patribus collecta. Auctore RICHARDO STANIHVRSTO . . . DVACI Ex Officina BALTAZARIS BELLERI . . . 1614. 12° pp.201
1650/3(1).
Ownership inscription: Conuentûs Ratisbonensis In vsum R×P. Esaie Augustiniani.

S244 STANIHURST, Richard
HEBDOMADA MARIANA, Ex Orthodoxis Catholicę Romanę Ecclesiæ Patribus collecta: In memoriam festorum . . . Virginis MARIÆ, per singulos hebdomadæ dies distributa. Auctore Richardo Stanihursto . . . ANTVERPIÆ, EX OFFICINA PLANTINIANA, Apud Ioannem Moretum. M.DC.IX. (col.) ANTVERPIÆ, EX OFFICINA PLANTINIANA, Apud Ioannem Moretum. M.DC.IX. 16° pp.208; illus.
C.52.b.11.
The illustrations are engravings. The text pages are rubricated.

S245 STAPLETON, Thomas
PROMPTVARIVM MORALE SVPER EVANGELIA DOMINICALIA TOTIVS ANNI . . . Authore THOMA STAPLETONO . . . Editio altera, ab ipso Authore aucta & recognita. PARS ÆSTIVALIS . . . MOGVNTIÆ, Apud Balthasarum Lippium. Sumptibus Ioannis Moreti, & Hermanni Mylii. M.DC.X. [etc.] 8° pp.640
1507/433.
The publication costs borne by Joannes Moretus at Antwerp and Hermann Mylius at Cologne. With the 1565 and 1590 Antwerp privileges, made out for six years to Plantin and Moretus respectively. Wanting the Pars hiemalis.

S246 STAPLETON, Thomas
(tp.1) PROMPTVARIVM MORALE SVPER EVANGELIA DOMINICALIA TOTIVS ANNI . . . Ex Sacris Scipturis, SS. Patribus, & optimis quibusque Auctoribus . . . collectum: Auctore THOMA STAPLETONO . . . Nouissima editio, ab Auctore aucta & recognita. PARS HIEMALIS . . . ANTVERPIÆ, EX OFFICINA PLANTINIANA, Apud Viduam & Filios Io. Moreti. M.DC.XIII. (col.1) ANTVERPIÆ, EX OFFICINA PLANTINIANA, APVD VIDVAM ET FILIOS IOANNIS MORETI. M.DC.XIII.
(tp.2) PROMPTVARIVM MORALE . . . Auctore THOMA STAPLETONO . . . PARS AESTIVALIS . . . ANTVERPIÆ, EX OFFICINA PLANTINIANA, Apud Viduam & Filios Io. Moreti. M.DC.XIII. 8° 2 pt.: pp.692; 592
1216.b.13,14.
The colophon of pt.2 consists of a device only. Ownership inscription: Ioēs M: Gaethoffs 1796.

S247 STARTER, Jan Jansz
[Collections] FRIESCHE LUST-HOF, Beplant met verscheyde stichtelyke Minne-Liedekens/Gedichten/ende Boertige Kluchten. DOR IAN IANSZ. STARTER . . . Met . . . kopere Figueren verçierd; ende by alle onbekende VVysen, de Noten, ofte Musycke gevoeght, Door M$^{r.}$ IACQVES VREDEMAN . . . T'AMSTELREDAM, Gedruckt by Paulus van Ravesteyn . . . 1621. Voor Dirck Pietersz: Voscuyl . . . 1621. obl.4° pp.201, sig.A-C^4: plate; illus., music, port.
11556.bbb.55; C.34.a.18.

The plates are by Jan vande Velde. The pagination jumps from p.152 to p.163, without loss of text. Both copies are imperfect; that at 11556.bbb.55 wanting leaf ★4, bearing the poem by Theodore Rodenburgh and the portrait; that at C.34.a.18 wanting pp.179-201. Ownership inscription in the copy at 11556.bbb.55: G. Lamberts Amst. 1831.

S248 STARTER, Jan Jansz
I. I. STARTERS Blyeyndich-Truyrspel/VAN TIMBRE DE CARDONE ENDE FENICIE VAN MESSINE, Met een Vermaecklijck Sotte-Clucht van een Advocaet ende een Boer op't plat Friesch. TOT LEEVWARDEN, Voor Jan Jansen Starter . . . 1618. 4° sig.★★^{6}A-I^4
11755.bbb.80.

The comedy is an interlude. The plot of the main work is derived from Bandello. Without the titlepage engraving mentioned in *Kleerkoper Starters werken* no.AII, 1.

S249 STARTER, Jan Jansz
I. STARTERS DARAIDE . . . 't AMSTELREDAM, Voor Dirck Pietersz. Voskuyl . . . 1621. (col.) T'AMSTELDAM, Ghedruckt by Paulus van Ravesteyn . . . 1621. 4° sig.★, A-I^4; music
11754.bb.24; 11755.bb.71(1).

The last leaf is blank. Printed with some use of civilité.

STARTER, Jan Jansz. Lyck-klachte. 1620. *See* FEDDES, Pieter. Uytvaert.

S250 STATIUS, Publius Papinius
[Works] (tp.1) P. STATII PAPINII OPERA QVÆ EXTANT, IOH. BERNARTIVS AD LIBROS VETERES RECENSVIT, ET SCHOLIIS illustrauit. ANTVERPIAE, Ex Officina Typographica Martini Nutii . . . M.DC.VII.
(tp.2) IO. BERNARTII AD P. STATII PAPINII THEBAIDOS ET ACHILLEIDOS SCHOLIA, AD SYLVARVM LIBROS NOTAE . . . ANTVERPIÆ, Ex Officina Typographica Martini Nutii . . . M.DC.VII. 8° 2 pt.: pp.510; 181
1068.i.12; 1068.i.13.

The texts are printed in italics, the notes in roman. Ownership inscription in the copy at 1068.i.13: Mgr Markland.

S251 STATIUS, Publius Papinius
[Works] PVBLII PAPINII STATII OPERA OMNIA. IANVS CASPERIVS GEVARTIVS Recensuit, et, PAPINIARVM LECTIONVM LIB. V. Illustravit. Accessit nunc primum Copiosissimus INDEX. LVGDVN. BATAVOR APVD IACOB. MARCVM MDCXVI (col.=sig.Gg4r, p.[471]) LVGDVNI BATAVORVM, Excudebat Vlricus Honthorstius . . . MDCXVI. 8° pp.460,238
C.45.b.16.

The titlepage is engraved. Sig.P2 of pt.2, p.227 reading: '[Ad Abascant.]'; the catchword on p.227 is 'tripode' but the word is omitted on p.228; the catchword on p.238 reads 'Eer' leading to 'Errata' on p.[239]. With Richard Porson's manuscript annotations. Ownership inscription: Sum Fra: St John Mitford 1809 (Bib: Porson:).

S252 STATIUS, Publius Papinius
[Works] PVBLII. PAPINII STATII OPERA OMNIA. Ianvs Casperivs Gevartivs recensuit,

ET, PAPINIARVM LECTIONVM LIB.V. illustravit. Accedit nunc primum copiosissimus INDEX. LVGDVNI BATAVORVM, Ex Officina IACOBI MARCI MD CXVIII. (col.) LVGDVNI BATAVORVM, Excudebat Georgius Abrahami a Marsse, MDCXVI. 8° pp.460,238
687.c.11.

A reissue, published in 1618, of the corrected issue of the edition of 1616 in which the engraved titlepage has been substituted by a cancel letterpress title. Imperfect; wanting the preliminary leaves sig.)?(2–8; accidentally removed with the engraved title and not reattached?, and pp.433–448.

S253 STATIUS, Publius Papinius

[Works] PVBLII PAPINII STATII OPERA OMNIA. IANVS CASPERIVS GEVARTIVS Recensuit . . . LVGDVN. BATAVOR APVD IACOB. MARCVM MDCXVI (col.) LVGDVNI BATAVORVM, Excudebat Georgius Abrahami a Marsse, M D C XVI. 8° pp.460,238
687.c.10.

Another issue of the preceding, published in 1618, in which sig.P of pt.2 has been reset. P.227 reads: '[Ad Abscantij pietatem.]'; the catchword at the foot is 'diva-'; p.238 ends with 'FINIS.' and has the catchword 'Erra-'. The colophon occurs on the verso of the last leaf. Ownership inscription: R. Bentley.

S254 STATIUS, Publius Papinius

[Works] [Publii Papinii Statii opera omnia.] (col.) LVGDVNI BATAVORVM, Excudebat Georgius Abrahami a Marsse, M D C XVI. 8° pp.238
1001.d.16.

Another copy of pt.2, 'Iani Casperii Gevartii . . . commentarius' in the corrected issue. It is not possible to establish whether it formed part of the corrected edition of 1616 or of the reissue of 1618. It is bound separately in its original vellum. With the bookplate of Charles Burney.

STATUTEN, Ordonnantien, ende Costumen van Frieslandt. 1602. *See* FRIESLAND

STELLA, Didacus. Rdi Patris Fratris Didaci Stellae . . . in sacrosanctum Iesu Christi . . . Euangelium secundum Lucam enarrationum tomus primus. 1608. *See* BIBLE. Luke [Latin]

S255 STEMPEL, Gerhardus

VTRIVSQVE ASTROLABII TAM PARTICVLARIS QVAM VNIVERSALIS FABRICA ET VSVS. Sine vllius Retis, aut Dorsi adminiculo . . . Studio . . . & industria D. Gerardi Stempelij . . . & M. Adriani Zelstij, in lucem . . . emissa. LEODII, Typis Christiani Ouvverx . . . M.D.CII. [etc.] (col.) Exemplaria prostant Coloniæ, apud hæredes Francisci Hoghenbergii. 4° pp.40,40,99: plate; map
532.f.25.

S256 STERVEN

HET STERVEN DER WARE Hollandtsche Eendracht/Phenix der gantscher Werelt . . . 1617. 4° sig.A^4B^2
700.h.25(4).

In verse. Leaf B2 wrongly signed: B3.

S257 STEVIN, Simon

CASTRAMETATIO, Dat is LEGERMETING, Beschreven door Symon Stevin . . . Na d'oordening en 'tghebruyc VANDEN . . . Heere MAVRITS PRINCE van Oraengien . . . TOT ROTTERDAM, By Ian van VVaesberghe . . . 1617. fol. pp.55; illus.
1605/218(2).

Without the laudatory poems and the portrait and arms of Prince Maurice mentioned by *Dijksterhuis* p.53 no.XIIA. With the dedication to the States General as described by Dijksterhuis, whereas *Ledeboer* p.62 describes a dedication to the city of Rotterdam. The illustrations are woodcuts.

S258 STEVIN, Simon

[Castrametatio.] LA CASTRAMETATION, Descrite par Symon Stevin . . . selon l'ordonnance & vsage DE TRES-ILLVSTRE . . . PRINCE . . . MAVRICE . . . PRINCE d'Orange . . . A ROTTERDAM, Chez Iean VVaesbergue . . . 1618. fol. pp. 54; illus.
534.m.18(3).

With 'Sonet auquel est fait jugement de ceux qui ont bien campé' on the verso of the portrait of Maurice and 'Sonet A Monsieur Stevin' on the verso of the arms of Maurice, both signed: De Neree. The illustrations are woodcuts.

S259 STEVIN, Simon

[Castrametatio.] LA CASTRAMETATION, Descrite par Symon Stevin . . . selon l'ordonnance & vsage DE TRES-ILLVSTRE . . . PRINCE . . . MAVRICE . . . Seconde Edition reueuë & corrigée. A LEYDEN, Chez Matthieu & Bonaventure Elzevier. 1618. fol. pp. 54; illus.
534.m.18(1); 61.f.15(2).

There are few changes in the text, e.g. 'Henryson' for 'Hindersham' on p. 18. The laudatory poems are transposed. In the copy at 61.f.15(2) the leaves bearing the engravings and sonnets are bound in reverse order. The illustrations are woodcuts.

S260 STEVIN, Simon

NIEVVVE MANIERE VAN STERCTEBOV, door SPILSLUYSEN. Beschreven door Symon Stevin . . . TOT ROTTERDAM, By Ian van VVaesberghe . . . 1617. fol. pp. 59; illus.
1605/218(1).

Without the portrait and arms of Prince Maurice mentioned by *Ledeboer* p. 62 as belonging to this work, though *Dijksterhuis* pp. 53, 54 no. XIIB assigns these to the 'Castrametatio' for which see above. The illustrations are woodcuts.

S261 STEVIN, Simon

[Nieuwe maniere van sterctebou.] NOVVELLE MANIERE DE FORTIFICATION PAR ESCLVSES. Descrite par Symon Stevin . . . A LEYDEN. Chez Matthieu & Bonaventure Elzevier . . . 1618. fol. pp. 61; illus.
534.m.18(2); 61.f.15(2).

With the woodcuts of the Dutch edition. The running title on pp. 6, 8, 14, 16 has the spelling 'NOVELLE', i.e. both copies belong to the second edition. The illustrations are woodcuts.

S262 STEVIN, Simon

[Wiskonstighe gedachtenissen.] (tp. 1) HYPOMNEMATA MATHEMATICA . . . A SIMONE STEVINO conscripta, & e Belgico in Latinum á VVIL. SN. conversa. LVDGVNI BATAVORVM, Ex Officinâ Ioannis Patii . . . M.D.C.VIII.
(tp. 2) TOMVS PRIMVS MATHEMATICORVM HYPOMNEMATVM DE COSMOGRAPHIA . . . Conscriptus à SIMONE STEVINO . . . LVGDVNI BATAVORVM, Ex Officinâ Ioannis Patii . . . M.D.C.VIII.
(tp. 3) SECVNDA PARS COSMOGRAPHIAE, DE GEOGRAPHIA . . . Conscripta à SIMONE STEVINO . . . LVGODINI BATAVORVM, Ex Officinâ Ioannis Patii . . . MDCV.
(tp. 4) TOMVS SECVNDVS MATHEMATICORVM HYPOMNEMATVM DE GEOMETRIAE PRAXI . . . Conscriptus à SIMONE STEVINO . . . LVGODINI BATAVORVM, Ex Officinâ Ioannis Patii . . . MDCV.
(tp. 5) TOMVS TERTIVS MATHEMATICORVM HYPOMNEMATVM DE OPTICA . . . Conscriptus à SIMONE STEVINO . . . LVGODINI BATAVORVM, Ex Officinâ Ioannis Patii . . . MDCV.
(tp. 6) TOMVS QVARTVS MATHEMATICORVM HYPOMNEMATVM DE STATICA . . . Conscriptus à SIMONE STEVINO . . . LVGODINI BATAVORVM, Ex Officinâ Ioannis Patii . . . MDCV.
(tp. 7) TOMVS QVINTVS MATHEMATICORVM HYPOMNEMATVM, DE MISCELLANEIS . . . Conscriptus à SIMONE STEVINO . . . LVGDVNI BATAVORVM, Ex Officinâ Ioannis

Patii . . . M.D.C.VIII. fol. 5 tom.: pp.343, 188, 335; 184; 100; 196; 9, 14[24], 19, 51–88, 8, 39, 139–214; illus.
L.35/33; C.80.e.10.
The translator is Willebrordus Snellius. The copy at L.35/33 has been transferred from the old Patent Office Library.

S263 STOKE, Melis
[Rijmkroniek.] HOLLANDTSCHE RIIM-KRONIIK Inhoudende de gheschiedenissen der Graven van Hollandt tot het iaer M.CCC.V. Door eenen wiens naeme noch onbekent is voor 319. Iaren beschreven. Met een Voorrede des Edelen E. Ionkh. Ian vander Does . . . Hier is noch by gevoecht een vvaerachtige deductie vande gelegentheyt van Graef Floris ende Gerrit van Velsen . . . IN S'GRAVEN-HAGHE, By Hillebrant Iacobssz . . . 1620. fol. pp.99,6; illus.
85.l.3(2).
Anonymous. The titlepage engraving shows 'Dederick de Eerste Graue van Hollandt', by Jacob Matham?

S264 STRADA, Famianus
PROLVSIONES ACADEMICÆ, ORATORIÆ, HISTORICÆ, POETICÆ: R.P. FAMIANI STRADÆ . . . AVDOMARI, Apud CAROLVM BOSCARDVM . . . M.DC.XIX. 12° pp.501
11826.a.20.
Ownership inscriptions: Carolus Niciæ Daviesius me jure tenet 1833; Prou[æ] Angliæ Soc[tis] JESV pro Reperentibus; B R.

STRATENUS, Gulielmus. Disputatio medica de calculo renum. 1612. *See* PAAUW, Petrus

STRANDE. 1614. *See* BORSSELEN, Philibert van

S265 STRUZZI, Alberto
IMAGO MILITIÆ AVSPICIIS AMBROSII SPINOLÆ . . . STATARIA ACIE ADVMBRATA. Industria & opera ALBERTI STRVZZI . . . coacta & concinnata. Cui adiutricem manum adiunxit IOANNES VANDER ELST . . . BRVXELLÆ, Ex Officina Rutgeri Velpii & Huberti Antonij . . . 1614. fol. sig.[A]-C[2]: plate
1197.i.4(3).
The elaborate emblematic plate is not signed. Cropped.

S266 STUCKEN
STVCKEN Gemencioneert in den Bycorff die byde . . . Staten Generael der vereenichde Nederlanden toeghestaen ende niet verboden worden/volghende den Placcate vanden xxvij[en]. Augusti Anno sesthien-hondert ende acht/Soo raeckende de vredehandelinghe als anderssints. IN S'GRAVEN-HAGHE, By Hillebrant Iacobsz. . . . 1608. 4° sig.A-D[4]
D.N.2/8.
Contains the texts of 'Offres ende presentatien van haere Hoocheden', 'Antwoordt vande . . . Staten . . . ', 'Brief van verbande . . . ', 'Aggreatie vanden Coninck van Hispaignien', 'Antwoorde vande . . . Staten Generael', 'Brief des Keyserlijcke Majest.', 'Sendbrief in forme van supplicatie . . . '.

S267 STURMIUS, Joannes; Mechlinianus
DE ROSA HIERICHVNTINA LIBER VNVS . . . Auctore IO. STVRMIO . . . LOVANII Ex Typographia GERARDI RIVII . . . 1608. 8° pp.96
966.b.39(1); B.226(5).

S268 SUAREZ, Franciscus; S.J.
TRACTATVS DE LEGIBVS, AC DEO LEGISLATORE, In decem libros distributus. AVTHORE P. D. FRANCISCO SVAREZ GRANATENSI . . . ANTVERPIÆ APVD IOANNEM KEERBERGIVM . . . M.DC.XIII. fol. pp.835
1605/294.

S269 SUCQUET, Antoine

ANTONI SVQVET . . . VIA VITÆ ÆTERNÆ ICONIBVS ILLVSTRATA per Boëtium A Bolswert. ANTVERPIÆ Typis Martini Nutij. M.DC.XX. 8° pp.875: pl.32
4408.e.1.

The titlepage is engraved. pl.15 is handcoloured.

S270 SUETONIUS TRANQUILLUS, Caius

[Collections] C. SVETONII TRANQVILLI Duodecim Cæsares: ET De illustribus GRAMMATICIS, & claris RHETORIBVS, Libelli duo. EX OFFICINA PLANTINIANA RAPHELENGII, M.D.CXI. 32° pp.336
C.20.f.33.

Published at Leiden. From the travelling library of Sir Julius Caesar.

S271 SUETONIUS TRANQUILLUS, Caius

[Collections] CAIVS SVETONIVS Tranquillus. Amsterodami, Apud G: Ianssoniū. M DC XIII. long 24° pp.288[287]
C.46.a.25.

The titlepage is engraved, showing the portraits of the emperors.

SUPPLICATIE der Neder-Oostenrijcksche Lant-Stenden. 1620. *See* AUSTRIA. Lower Austria. Landtag

S272 SURIUS, Joannes

MORATÆ POESEOS VOLVMEN. I. AVCTORE R.P. IOANNE SVRIO . . . ATREBATI. REGIACORVM. TYPIS GVILIELMI RIVERII. 1617. 8° 2 pt.: pp.318; 318
11405.aaa.39.

The titlepage is engraved, signed: MB.f., i.e. Martin Baes. The two parts have a half-title each, reading respectively 'R.P. Ioannis Surii . . . Moratæ poesis volumen primum. M.D.C.XVII' and 'R.P. Ioannis Surii . . . Moratæ poesis volumen secundum. M.D.C.XVIII'. The dedication is dated 1618. The binding shows the emblem of the city of Brussels with the date 1754.

S273 SUSIUS, Nicolaus

NICOLAI SVSII . . . OPVSCVLA LITTERARIA: LIMA CICERONIANA, siue DE STYLO LIBER SINGVLARIS, DE PVLCRITVDINE B. MARIÆ VIRG. DISCEPTATIO QVODLIBETICA, POEMATA: ELEGIÆ MARIANÆ, LVSVS ANACREONTEI, DRAMA COMICVM. ANTVERPIÆ Apud Heredes MARTINI NVTII . . . M.DC.XX. 8° pp.276[275]
630.b.2(3).

The comedy is entitled 'Pendularia'. The editor's preface signed: H.O. Ownership inscription: Sum Johañis Morris.

S274 SUSIUS, Nicolaus

MARTINI ANTONII DEL-RIO . . . VITA Breui Commentariolo expressa. ANTVERPIAE, EX OFFICINA PLANTINIANA, Apud Ioannem Moretum. M.DC.IX. 4° pp.46
4866.e.32(1).

Anonymous. Sometimes attributed to Heribertus Rosweydus. The editor's dedication signed: Hermannus Lange-veltius. Ownership inscription; Soc.tis Jesu Louanij.

SUYSIUS, Vincentius Adriani. Disputatio medica de purgatione. 1607. *See* VORSTIUS, Aelius Everhardus

S275 SWANENBURGH, Willem van

IANVS HAVTENVS REIPVBL. LVGDVNO-BATAVÆ A SECRETIS NATVS ANNO MD XLII. DIE XIV DECEMBRIS 4° a single sheet; port.
Maps C.9.d.4(82v).

The engraved portrait of Jan van Hout, signed: WSwanenb. sculp. Anno 1608, with Latin verses, beginning 'Inclyta Lugdunum, manibus seruata tuorum', signed: DH., i.e. Daniel Heinsius. Part of the Beudeker Collection.

S276 SWART, Willem

DEN LVST-HOF DER NIEVWE MVSYCKE, MIT ALLER VVELRIECKENDE BLOEMEN VERCIERT, SEER LIEFLICK OM SINGEN ENDE SPEELEN OP ALLE Musicale Instrumenten, in vier eñ vijf partyen . . . Waerin begrepen zijn tseventich stucken van Hemel ende Aerde tracterende, in onse Nederduytsche tale . . . Gheinventeert, ghecomponeert ende gestelt in Rime, door WILLEM SWART van Arnhem . . . SVPERIVS. Gedruckt t'Amstelredam ten huyse van Willem Swart . . . 1603. [etc.] obl.4° ff.55; music
Music K.3.b.16.

Dedicated to James I. With the exlibris: J M Grypt als't rypt.

S277 SWARTIUS, Eustathius

EVSTATHI SWARTI ANALECTORVM LIBRI III. In quibus innumera Auctorum, quà GRÆCORVM quà LATINORVM, loca emendantur, dilucidantur, illustrantur, notantur . . . LVGDVNI BATAVORVM, Apud LVDOVICVM ELZEVIRIVM . . . M D C XVI. 4° pp.144
11825.cc.4.

Ownership inscription: Ex libris Francisci Petri 1733.

S278 SWEDEN

[1.12.1608] Placcaet van Carolus de negende/Coningh van Sweden . . . Waer by toeghelaten werdt te moghen varen op de Stadt Riga . . . Overgheset uyt den Hoogduytsche in onse Nederlandtsche Tale. Ghedruckt . . . 1609. 4° 2 unsigned leaves
T.1729(14).

S279 SWEELINCK, Jan Pietersz

(tp.1) CINQVANTE PSEAVMES DE DAVID, mis en musique à 4,5,6,&7 parties, par Ian Swelinck . . . CANTVS. A AMSTERLEDAM [*sic*], M.DC.IIII.
(tp.2) CINQVANTE PSEAVMES DE DAVID, mis en musique . . . par Ian Swelinck . . . ALTVS. A AMSTERLEDAM, M.DC.IIII.
(tp.3) CINQVANTE PSEAVMES DE DAVID, mis en musique . . . par Ian Swelinck . . . TENOR. A AMSTERLEDAM, M.DC.IIII.
(tp.4) CINQVANTE PSEAVMES DE DAVID, mis en musique . . . par Ian Swelinck . . . BASSVS. A AMSTERLEDAM, M.DC.IIII.
(tp.5) CINQVANTE PSEAVMES DE DAVID, mis en musique . . . par Ian Swelinck . . . QVINTVS. A AMSTERLEDAM, M.DC.IIII.
(tp.6) CINQVANTE PSEAVMES DE DAVID, mis en musique . . . par Ian Swelinck . . . SEXTVS. A AMSTERLEDAM, M.DC.IIII. obl.4° 6 pt.: pp.68; 74; 64; 56; 54; 24
Music K.2.e.1(1).

Printed (for the composer?) by Jean de Tournes at Geneva, with use of some civilité. Ownership inscription: De la Cour.

S280 SWEELINCK, Jan Pietersz

(tp.1) LIVRE SECOND DES PSEAVMES DE DAVID, NOVVELLEMENT MIS EN Musique, à 4, 5, 6, 7, 8, parties, Par IAN P. SWEELINCK . . . Contenant XXX. Pseaumes . . . CANTVS. A AMSTELREDAM, Aux despens de HENDRIC BARENTSEN. M.DC.XIII. On les vend à Francfort chez Christoffle van Hartichuelt.
(tp.2) LIVRE SECOND DES PSEAVMES DE DAVID . . . MIS EN Musique . . . Par IAN P. SWEELINCK . . . ALTVS. A AMSTELREDAM, Aux despens de HENDRIC BARENTSEN. M.DC.XIII. On les vend à Francfort chez Christoffle van Hartichuelt.
(tp.3) LIVRE SECOND DES PSEAVMES DE DAVID . . . MIS EN Musique . . . Par IAN P. SWEELINCK . . . TENOR. A AMSTELREDAM, Aux despens de HENDRIC BARENTSEN. M.DC.XIII. On les vend à Francfort chez Christoffle van Hartichuelt.
(tp.4) LIVRE SECOND DES PSEAVMES DE DAVID . . . MIS EN Musique . . . Par IAN P. SWEELINCK . . . BASSVS. A AMSTELREDAM, Aux despens de HENDRIC BARENTSEN. M.DC.XIII. On les vend à Francfort chez Christoffle van Hartichuelt.

(tp.5) SECOND LIVRE DES PSEAVMES DE DAVID . . . MIS EN Musique . . . Par IAN P. SWEELINCK . . . QVINTVS. A AMSTELREDAM, Aux despens de HENDRIC BARENTSEN. M.DC.XIII. On les vend à Francfort chez Christoffle van Hartichuelt.
(tp.6) LIVRE SECOND DES PSEAVMES DE DAVID . . . MIS EN Musique . . . Par IAN P. SWEELINCK . . . SEXTVS. A AMSTELREDAM, Aux despens de HENDRIC BARENTSEN. M.DC.XIII. On les vend à Francfort chez Christoffle van Hartichuelt. (col.1,2,4,6) De l'Jmprimerie de Jean de Tournes. obl.4° 6 pt.: sig. $\cdot J^2A-L^4M^2$; $\cdot J^2A-M^4N^2$; $\cdot J^2A-K^4L^2$; $\cdot J^2A-K^4$; $\cdot J^2A-I^4K^2$; $\cdot J^2A-E^4$
Music K.2.e.1(2).
Printed at Geneva. Ownership inscription: De La Cour.

S281 SWEELINCK, Jan Pietersz
(tp.1) LIVRE TROISIEME DES PSEAVMES DE DAVID, NOVVELLEMENT MIS EN Musique, à 4,5,6,7,8 parties, Par IAN P. SWEELINCK . . . contenant XXX. Pseaumes . . . CANTVS. A AMSTELREDAM, Aux despens de HENDRIC BARENTSEN. M.DC.XIIII. On les vend à Francfort chez Christoffle van Hartichuelt.
(tp.2) LIVRE TROISIEME DES PSEAVMES DE DAVID . . . MIS EN Musique . . . Par IAN P. SWEELINCK . . . ALTVS. A AMSTELREDAM, Aux despens de HENDRIC BARENTSEN. M.DC.XIIII. On les vend à Francfort chez Christoffle van Hartichuelt.
(tp.3) LIVRE TROISIEME DES PSEAVMES DE DAVID . . . MIS EN Musique . . . Par IAN P. SWEELINCK . . . TENOR. A AMSTELREDAM, Aux despens de HENDRIC BARENTSEN. M.DC.XIIII. On les vend à Francfort chez Christoffle van Hartichuelt.
(tp.4) LIVRE TROISIEME DES PSEAVMES DE DAVID . . . MIS EN Musique . . . Par IAN P. SWEELINCK . . . BASSVS. A AMSTELREDAM, Aux despens de HENDRIC BARENTSEN. M.DC.XIIII. On les vend à Francfort chez Christoffle van Hartichuelt.
(tp.5) LIVRE TROISIEME DES PSEAVMES DE DAVID . . . MIS EN Musique . . . Par IAN P. SWEELINCK . . . QVINTVS. A AMSTELREDAM, Aux despens de HENDRIC BARENTSEN. M.DC.XIIII. On les vend à Francfort chez Christoffle van Hartichuelt.
(tp.6) LIVRE TROISIEME DES PSEAVMES DE DAVID . . . MIS EN Musique . . . Par IAN P. SWEELINCK . . . SEXTVS. A AMSTELREDAM, Aux despens de HENDRIC BARENTSEN. M.DC.XIIII. On les vend à Francfort chez Christoffle van Hartichuelt.
(tp.7) LIVRE TROISIEME DES PSEAVMES DE DAVID . . . MIS EN Musique . . . Par IAN P. SWEELINCK . . . SEPTIMVS. A AMSTELREDAM, Aux despens de HENDRIC BARENTSEN. M.DC.XIIII. On les vend à Francfort chez Christoffle van Hartichuelt.
(tp.8) LIVRE TROISIEME DES PSEAVMES DE DAVID . . . MIS EN Musique . . . Par IAN P. SWEELINCK . . . OCTAVVS. A AMSTELREDAM, Aux despens de HENDRIC BARENTSEN. M.DC.XIIII. On les vend à Francfort chez Christoffle van Hartichuelt. (col.1–8) De l'Jmprimerie de Jean de Tournes. obl.4° 8 pt.: sig. $\cdot J,A-P^4$; $\cdot J,A-Q^4$; $\cdot J,A-P^4$; $\cdot J,A-N^4O^3$; $\cdot J,A-M^4$; $\cdot J,A-I^4$ $\cdot J,A-D^4E^3$; $\cdot J,A-C^4$
Music K.2.e.1(3).
Printed at Geneva. Ownership inscription: De La Cour.

SWEERTIUS, Franciscus. Deorum deorumque capita. 1602. *See* ORTELIUS, Abraham

S282 SWEERTIVS, Franciscus
XII CAESARVM ROMANORVM IMAGINES E numismatibus expressae, et historica narratione illustratæ. Ex museio FRANC. SWEERTI F. . . . ANTVERPIÆ, Apud Ioannem Baptistam Vrintivm . . . M.D.CIII. [etc.] (col.) ANTVERPIÆ, TYPIS ROBERTI BRVNEAV . . . M.DCIII. 4° sig. $A-C^4D^3$; illus.
602.e.10(3).
Engravings, by Philips Galle? The text compiled by Sweertius, with verses by Joannes Bochius and Balthasar Moretus. Dedicated to Emanuel Sueyro. The titlepage is engraved, with the imprint only in letterpress.

S283 SWEERTIUS, Franciscus
XII CAESARVM ROMANOVM IMAGINES . . . Ex museio FRANC. SWEERTI F. . . .

ANTVERPIAE, Exstant in OFFICINA PLANTINIANA, apud Viduam & Filios Io. Moreti. M.DC.XII. (col.) ANTVERPIÆ, TYPIS ROBERTI BRVNEAV . . . M.DCIII. 4° sig.A-D^4; illus.
C.132.b.30.
A reissue of another issue of the edition of 1603, with a new letterpress imprint on the titlepage. Dedicated to Aubert Le Mire, with the date 1602. With the exlibris of Sir Paul Methuen.

S284 SWEERTIUS, Franciscus
MONVMENTA SEPVLCRALIA ET INSCRIPTIONES PVBLICÆ PRIVATÆQ. DVCATVS BRABANTIAE. FRANCISCVS SWEERTIVS F. posteritati collegit. ANTVERPIAE, Apud GASPAREM BELLERVM . . . M.DC.XIII. 8° pp.394
277.a.5.
With inscriptions to Plantin on p.65, Ortelius on p.140, Philips Rubens on p.144 and the house of Bellère on p.194, but without an index.

S285 SWEERTIUS, Robertus
DE FIDE HAERETICIS SERVANDA Dissertatio ROBERTI SWEERTI . . . Aduersus Elenchum DANIELIS PLANCI . . . ANTVERPIÆ, EX OFFICINA PLANTINIANA, Apud Viduam & Filios Io. Moreti. M.DC.XII. 8° pp.71
857.f.17.

S286 SWEERTIUS, Robertus
DEN ERENTFESTEN/ACHTbaren . . . Heeren, Balieu, Borgemeesteren eñ Schepenen der Stede van Rotterdam. 4° 2 unsigned leaves
T.2240(19*).
A letter, signed: Robertus Sweertius and dated 4 October 1610, in defence of Roman Catholicism and protesting against 'Ghespreck over de leere vande transubstantiatie' by Franciscus Lansbergius. Published in 1610.

S287 SWEET, John; S.J.
Monsig.^{r} fate voi. OR A DISCOVERY OF THE DALMATIAN APOSTATA, M. ANTONIVS DE DOMINIS, AND HIS BOOKES. By C.A. to his friend P.R. Student of the Lawes in the Middle Temple . . . M.DC.XVII. 4° pp.294
C.26.k.2(2).
Anonymous and without imprint; published by the English College press at St. Omer.

S288 SWEETNAM, John
THE PARADISE OF DELIGHTS. OR The B. Virgins Garden of Loreto . . . By I.S. of the Society of IESVS . . . M.DC.XX. 8° pp.217
C.26.k.9.
Anonymous and without imprint; published by the English College press at St. Omer. Ownership inscription: Dom. Prof. Rom. S.J. Bibl. Com.

S289 SWEETNAM, John
S. MARY MAGDALENS PILGRIMAGE TO PARADISE . . . By I.S. of the Society of IESVS . . . M.DC.XVII. 8° pp.142
C.26.h.9.
Anonymous and without imprint; published by the English College press at St. Omer. Including various poems. With a manuscript poem on a separate leaf added to precede the titlepage, by John Smeaton? Ownership inscription: Liber Monasterij Lambspringensis Ordinis S. Benedicti. Congregat: Anglicanæ Joannes Smeaton.

SYBILLA, Bartholomaeus. Speculum. 1621. *See* LEANDER de Sancto Martino. Otium.

SYLVA anachoretica Aegypti et Palaestinae. 1619. *See* VITAE patrum.

S290 SYMONSZ, Adriaen
EEN SPONCIE vanden Donckeren Spiegel van Petrus Wassenburgh . . . daer-in dat oogen-schijnelijcken ontdect worden de . . . ontrouwigheden ende onwaerheden/die hy in syn schrift heeft begaen: Ghestelt Door ADRIAEN SYMONSZ . . . Ghedruckt By Philips Philipsz. . . . 1618. 4° pp.43
T.2248(40).
Published at Rotterdam.

SYNOPSIS Reipublicae Venetae. 1619. *See* COTOVICUS, Joannes. Itinerarium.

SYNTAGMA herbarum encomiasticum. 1614. *See* COLIUS, Jacobus

S291 SZYMONOWICZ, Szymon; Bendoński
SIMONIS SIMONIDÆ POEMATA AVREA . . . edita ex Bibliotheca IOACHIMI MORSI Accedit VITA ET OBITVS MAGNI IOANNIS SAMOSCHI PATRONI SIMONIDIS. LVGD. BATAV. Typis Iacobi Marci, M D C XIX. 8° pp.126
11409.d.33.
With letters by or about Szymonowicz. The 'Vita et obitus . . . Ioannis Samoscii' is by Adam Bursius.

T

TABULAE rei nummariae. 1615 [1616]. *See* SCHOTTUS, Andreas

T1 TACITUS, Publius Cornelius
[Works. Latin]
(tp.1) C. CORNELII TACITI OPERA QVAE EXSTANT. IVSTVS LIPSIVS postremùm recensuit. Additi COMMENTARII aucti emendatíque ab vltima manu. Accessit C. VELLEIVS PATERCVLVS cum eiusdem LIPSI auctioribus NOTIS. ANTVERPIAE, EX OFFICINA PLANTINIANA, Apud Ioannem Moretum. M.DC.VII. [etc.]
(tp.2) IVSTI LIPSI DISPVNCTIO NOTARVM MIRANDVLANI CODICIS AD CORN. TACITVM. Editio secunda. ANTVERPIAE, EX OFFICINA PLANTINIANA, APVD IOANNEM MORETVM. M.DC.VII.
(tp.3) C. VELLEIVS PATERCVLVS CVM ANIMADVERSIONIBVS IVSTI LIPSI, Quas postremùm auxit & emendauit. ANTVERPIAE, EX OFFICINA PLANTINIANA, Apud Ioannem Moretum. M.DC.VII. [etc.] (col.) ANTVERPIÆ, EX OFFICINA PLANTINIANA, APVD IOANNEM MORETVM, M.DC.VII. fol. 3 pt.: pp.547; 36; 84
587.l.12.
The editor's preface signed: Joannes Wouerius Antuerpiensis. The variant readings to Velleius Paterculus compiled by Franciscus Raphelengius. Ownership inscription: Comparavit C. Casimirus A° 1723.

T2 TACITUS, Publius Cornelius
[Works. Latin] C. CORNELII TACITI Opera omnia Ex recensione Iusti Lipsij. Lugduni Batauorum Apud IOANNEM MAIRE M.D.C.XIX. (col.) Typis Henrici ab Haestens. 16° pp.620
588.a.29; C.20.f.30.
A reissue of an edition of 1618. The titlepage of the copy at 588.a.29 is slightly mutilated. Ownership inscription in the copy at 588.a.29: Hoffmann[9]. The copy at C.20.f.30 from the travelling library of Sir Julius Caesar.

T3 TACITUS, Publius Cornelius
[Works. Latin] C. COR. TACITI quæ extant OPERA. Ex recensione I. LIPSII. LVGD [*sic*] BATAVORVM Ex Officina ELZEVIRIANA . . . M.D.C.XXI. 16° pp.789
9040.aaa.10.
The titlepage is engraved. This copy has been divided into two volumes. Ownership inscription: Pleffort or Preffort.

[Illustration of ***T6*** overleaf]

PHILIPPICA.

Ou haras de cheuaux,

DE

IEAN TACQVET,

ESCVIER,

Seigneur de Lechene, de Helst &c.

A ANVERS,

Chez ROBERT BRVNEAV, M. DC. XIV.

T4 TACITUS, Publius Cornelius

[Historiae. Extracts. Latin] BATAVORVM CVM ROMANIS BELLVM, à Corn. Tacito lib. IV. & V. Hist. olim descriptum, figuris nunc æneis expressum, Auctore OTHONE VÆNIO . . . DE BATAVISCHE Oft OVDE HOLLANDTSCHE OORLOGHE teghen de Romeynen. ANTVERPIÆ, Apud Auctorem væneunt. M.DC.XII. [etc.] obl.4° pl.36

198.c.4.

Plates, with explanatory captions in Latin and Dutch engraved on the recto and extracts from the Histories in Latin only printed in letterpress on the verso. The preface is in Latin and Dutch. The first plate signed: Ant. Tempesta f. Printed by David Mertens at Antwerp?

T5 TACITUS, Publius Cornelius

[Historiae. Extracts. Latin] BATAVORVM CVM ROMANIS BELLVM, à Corn. Tacito lib. IV. & V. Hist. olim descriptum, figuris nunc æneis expressum, Auctore OTHONE VÆNIO . . . ANTVERPIÆ, Apud Auctorem væneunt. M.DC.XII. [etc.] (col.) Typis Dauidis Martinij. obl.4° pl.36; pp.xxvii: map

557*.c.29.

Another issue of the preceding, with a map added before pl. I and additional explanatory text in Dutch added after the plates. The titlepage and the preface on its verso are differently set from the corresponding pages in the preceding. Printed at Antwerp.

T6 TACQUET, Jean

PHILIPPICA. Ou haras de cheuaux, de IEAN TACQVET . . . A ANVERS, Chez ROBERT BRVNEAV, M.DC.XIV. 4° pp.276: plate; illus., port.

C.130.c.30.

The titlepage is engraved. The titlepage engraving and the plate signed: CB, i.e. Cornelis Boel; the final engraved illustration signed: SV, i.e. Sebastiaen Vrancx, and: E.v.P. scul., i.e. Egbert van Panderen. The portrait is also known to be by Egbert van Panderen. Author's presentation copy to: Charles de Bourgogne, Baron de Wackere, et Monsieur de Lembeke, son frere.

T7 TAFEL

TAFEL, Begrijpende kortelijck het groot ende merckelijc verschil datter is tusschen de Leere des Goddelijcken woordts/ende de H. Schriftuere/die in de rechsinnige [*sic*] Gereformeerde Kercken van Vranckrijc/Engelandt/Schotlandt/Savoyen/Zwitserlandt/Duytslandt ende Nederlandt/gheleert . . . wordt: ENDE De Leere van de Drijvers der nieuwigheden/die men Remonstranten en Arminianen ofte Vorstianen noemt. t'AMSTERDAM, By Marten Jansz. Brandt . . . 1616. 4° pp.24

T.2247(28).

Extracts from the Bible and the Catechism parallelled with passages from Remonstrant writers. Sometimes attributed to Jacobus Trigland. For a similar compilation from the other side *see:* TELLE, Reiner. Tafereel.

TAFEREEL, begrijpende cortelijck het . . . verschil. 1618. *See* TELLE, Reinier

Een TAFEREELKEN . . . Door H.V.D. 1609. *See* DANTZIG, Hans van

TAFFIN, Jean. Claire exposition de l'Apocalypse. 1609. *See* BIBLE. Revelation. French

TAFFIN, Jean. L'estat de l'église. 1605. *See* CRESPIN, Jean

T8 TAURELLUS, Nicolaus

PHILOSOPHIÆ TRIVMPHVS, hoc est, METAPHYSICA PHILOSOPHANDI METHODVS, QVA . . . humanæ rationes eò deducuntur, ut . . . quæ diu Philosophorum sepulta fuit authoritate, PHILOSOPHIA uictrix erumpat . . . AVTORE, NICOLAO TAVRELLO . . . ARNHEMI Apud Ioannem Iansonij . . . 1617. 8° pp.305

1387.d.35.

TAURINUS, Jacobus. Balance. 1618. *See* below: Weegh-schael.

T9 TAURINUS, Jacobus
Cleynen VVECH-WYSER, Ghestelt tot ONDER-RICHTINGHE der Een-voudighen, Om de Harten/Die in desen tijdt . . . nauwlicks en weten hoe sy haer draghen sullen/Claerlijck aen te wijsen, wat wegh sy moeten in-gaen, om . . . recht te oordeelen . . . Wt-ghegheven door GEER-AARD VAN VRI-BVRCH . . . Ghedruckt . . . 1612. 4° sig. A-E^4
T.2242(30).
Pseudonymous. On the Vorstius affair.

T10 TAURINUS, Jacobus
Copye van sekeren brief, Daer inne beantwoort wort De losse en on-tijdige Na-Reden die FESTVS HOMMIVS, Tot verantwoordinghe (van t'ghene hem inde Naemscherminghe jeghens zijne hevighe Predicatie vanden 16. October te laste was gheleyt) terstont na de Predicatie op den 6. November heeft ghedaen in de Hoogh-landsche Kercke . . . Ghedruckt in DE MATER SALEM. 4° sig. A-C^4D^2
T.2246(17).
Anonymous. The imprint is an anagram of 'Amsterdam'; the printer's device is a variant of that of Joachim Trognaesius of Antwerp. Published in 1616. For the 'Naemscherminghe' *see* CORVINUS, Joannes Arnoldi. Verantwoordinge.

T11 TAURINUS, Jacobus
Corte ende naecte ondeckinghe van den LVEGEN-GEEST, onlangx verschenen in de uytgegevene Antwoordt tot wederlegginghe van het Discours over de Amsterdamsche beroerten . . . Ghedruckt . . . 1617. 4° pp.35
T.2247(23).
Anonymous. For the 'Discours' *see* below 'In-houdt van eenighe Brieven'. For the 'Antwoordt' *see* ANTWOORT.

T12 TAURINUS, Jacobus
Ernstighe Aen-spraeck Aen de MAEGHDT VAN HOLLANDT, Tot VVaerschouwinghe van alle goede Liefhebbers der Oude Vaderlijcke Vrijheydt. En Vertellingh van een DROOM. Ghedruckt . . . 1617. 4° pp.8
T.2247(53,54); T.2247(56).
Anonymous. In verse. The copy at T.2247(53) has had two leaves separated from it which have been bound after the pamphlet numbered (54). The copy at (56) is complete and correctly bound. In this issue which corresponds to the copy described in *Knuttel* no. 2470, the last two leaves forming sig. B contain 'Droom-gesicht op rommel-dicht', beginning 'Hoort toe trouwe me-ghesellen'.

T13 TAURINUS, Jacobus
Ernstighe Aen-spraeck Aen de Maeghd van Hollandt, Tot VVaerschouvvinghe van alle goede Lief-hebbers der Oude Vaderlijcke Vrijheydt. En Vertellingh van een DROOM. Ghedruckt . . . 1617. 4° pp.8
11555.e.44(5).
Another issue of the preceding, also anonymous. In this issue the two unsigned leaves after p. 8 contain 'DROOM-GHEDICHT', beginning 'Alsoo een mensche van twee deel is gheschapen'. The last page is blank.

TAURINUS, Jacobus. Een kort Monickendammer discours. 1618. [Sometimes attributed to Jacobus Taurinus.] *See* KORT

T14 TAURINUS, Jacobus
In-houdt Van eenighe Brieven, aengaende de BEROERTEN BINNEN AMSTERDAM onlangs voor-gevallen. Met een DISCOVRS aen ALLE GOEDE PATRIOTTEN . . . Ghedruckt . . . 1617. 4° pp.26
T.2247(20).
Anonymous.

T15 TAURINUS, Jacobus
NAARDER OPENINGE Dienende tot Grondige Aan-wijsinge van eenige Manieren van spreken gebruykt by IACOBVM TAVRINVM in zijn Eerste Deel Van de ONDERLINGE VERDRAAGSAAMHEYDT: Gestelt Aan de . . . Schouth, Burger-Meesteren, Schepenen, ende Vroedtschap . . . van AMSTERDAM . . . T'VTRECHT. Voor Ian Everdsen van Doorn; [etc.] 4° sig. A-F^4G^2
T.2246(19).
Signed: Jacobus Taurinus. Published in 1616.

T16 TAURINUS, Jacobus
Na-Sporingh/Hoe ende in vvat manieren . . . DE PRINCE VAN ORANGIEN . . . De Bescherminghe deser Landen heeft aenghenomen, Om de Nederlandtsche Belijdenisse . . . te mainteneren: En t'Gevoelen der Contra-Remonstranten, in't stuck vande PREDESTINATIE . . . over al in te voeren. Ghedruckt . . . 1617. 4° pp. 15
T.2247(26).
Anonymous. Cropped.

T17 TAURINUS, Jacobus
NOTVLEN, Ofte Aen-merckingen/Op het AF-SCHEYDT Der Predicanten van Nimmegen, ghegeven by den E. Raedt der selver Stadt op den 8. April. 1618. Ghedruckt . . . 1618. 4° sig. AB^4
T.2248(26).
Anonymous.

T18 TAURINUS, Jacobus
POST-BODE. 4° sig. Bb^4
700.h.25(31*).
Anonymous. A separate issue of sig. Bb of dl. 2 of 'Van-de onderlinge verdraagsaamheydt'. Printed for Jan Everdsen van Doorn at Utrecht in 1616. Here attached to 'Den Opwecker der oude . . . Bataviers', 1619.

T19 TAURINUS, Jacobus
Reuck-Appel/Af-ghevende den lieffelijcken Geur van de Daden des . . . Vorsts, den PRINCE VAN ORANGIEN . . . Tegen de quade Lucht/onlanghs . . . veroorsaeckt/ door het Op-doen ende Aenwijsen van een Valsche/Fenijnighe SPORE, tot verdedingh [*sic*] vande Op-rechte NA-SPORINGH . . . Met een Cort Historisch Verhael/Van den Grondt ende Aen-vangh der Neder-lantsche Oorloge . . . Gestelt door een Lief-hebber der Neder-Landtsche VRIIHEYDT. Ghedruckt te PHILADELPHI. M.DC.XVIII. 4° pp. 88
T.2248(2).
Anonymous. The imprint is false. For the 'Na-sporingh' *see* above. For the 'Spore' *see* De RECHTE spore.

T20 TAURINUS, Jacobus
(tp. 1) VAN-DE ONDERLINGE VERDRAAGSAAMHEYDT, Die soo wel Predicanten als gemeyne Lidt-maten/niet tegenstaande Verscheydenheyt van Gevoelen in eenige Leer-poincten, Met malcanderen in Lieffde behooren te onder-houden; Tegen IACOBI TRIGLANDI (t'onrecht genaamden) Recht-gematigden Christen. Gestelt Door IACOBUS TAURINUS . . . 'T EERSTE DEEL . . . T'VTRECHT. Voor Ian Everdsen van Doorn; [etc.]
(tp. 2) VAN-DE ONDERLINGE VERDRAAGSAAMHEYDT . . . Gestelt Door IACOBUS TAURINUS . . . HET TWEEDE DEEL . . . T'VTRECHT, Voor Ian Everdsen van Doorn; [etc.] 4° 2 pt.: sig. ( ), ( ) ( ), A-X^4Y^2; ( ), ( ) ( ), A-Z, $AaBb^4$; illus.
T.2246(18, 19*).
Published in 1616. Each titlepage has a woodcut showing two clasped hands under a heart pierced by an arrow, the whole within a floral wreath.

T21 TAURINUS, Jacobus
DEN VRAEGH-AL, In-houdende ettelijcke Questien ofte Vraghen/Om Daer op te hebben een bondighe Antwoorde van de Theologanten, Politijcken, Rechts-geleerden, Chrijs-luyden, ende anderen . . . Ghedruckt in't Jaer 1618. 4° sig. A^6
700.h.25(24); T.2248(15).
Anonymous.

T22 TAURINUS, Jacobus
Wat Vvonder-Oudt-Nieuws: Dienende Tot claer on-vveder-leggelijck Bewijs, Hoe DE REMONSTRANTSCHE PREDICANTEN Reysen en rotsen/om de IESVITEN, CAPVCIINEN, Ende andere Gheestelijcken by den Vyandt/te besoecken: ende met wat Courtoisijen zy malcanderen ont-halen. Ghedruckt . . . 1618. 4° sig. A-C^4D^2
T.2248(49).
Anonymous. A refutation of Fabrice de la Bassecourt's 'A l'encontre'.

T23 TAURINUS, Jacobus
Weegh-Schael, Om . . . te over-vveghen DE ORATIE Vanden . . . Heere . . . DVDLEY CARLETON . . . Onlanghs ghedaen inde Vergaderinghe der . . . Staten Generael . . . Ghedruckt . . . 1617. 4° pp.65 [71]
T.2247(24).
Anonymous. Without imprint; printed by Abraham van Herwijck for Jan Everdsen van Doorn, both at Utrecht. Corresponding to the copy described in *Knuttel* no.2368.

T24 TAURINUS, Jacobus
[Weegh-schael.] BALANCE Pour Peser . . . la HARANGVE Du . . . Seigneur . . . DVDLEY CARLETON . . . Faite . . . en l'assemblée des . . . Estats generaux des Provinces Vnies du païs bas . . . 1618. 4° pp.79
476.a.27.
Anonymous. Translated by Charles de Nielles? With the text of Sir Dudley Carleton's speech in French. Printed in the Netherlands.

T25 TAURINUS, Jacobus
Zedich Onder-soeck Van EENIGE HANDElingen in Gelderlandt inde Maent Februarius ter oorsaecke van seecker Verschil tusschen de Predicanten voorghevallen . . . 1617. 4° pp.24
T.2247(31).
Anonymous. Directed against the decision of the States of Gelderland issued on 5 February 1617 and with Reinier Telle's anonymous 'Tafereel, leere der Contra-Remonstranten', extracted from his 'Tafereel, begrijpende . . . het . . . verschil', first published in 1616.

TAXATIE vande salarissen. 1616. *See* ANTWERP [26.1.1616]

T26 TEELLINCK, Ewout
ANDERDE Clachte der Kercke/Aen Eenighe . . . Overheden des Landts: Over Den Grouwel tot Alckmaer uytghebroet/Ende eenighe andere verwerringhen tot verstoringhe vande Kerckelijcke Vrede/onlancx voorghevallen. Door IRENVM [*sic*] PHILALETHIVM . . . t'AMSTELREDAM, By Marten Jansz. Brandt . . . 1617. 4° pp.61
T.2247(35).
Pseudonymous. For the first 'Clachte' *see* below: Querela ecclesiae.

T27 TEELLINCK, Ewout
BABYLON, Ofte naeckte ontdeckinge ende Verthooninge van het huydigh Antechristische Ryck . . . Door PHILALETHIVM ZERVBAAL . . . T'AMSTELREDAM, Voor Marten Iansz Brandt . . . 1621. 4° pp.48; illus.
T.2424(12).
Pseudonymous. The titlepage woodcut shows crowned archers and soldiers armed with

guns attacking a castle on which sits the Babylonian Whore on the Apocalyptic Beast. Printed by Paulus van Ravesteyn.

T28 TEELLINCK, Ewout

BOHEEMSCH GELVYT Ofte Christelyck Gespreck/Over het teghenwoordich Boheemsche wesen/ende de Oorloge daer ontrent ontstaen . . . Door IRENEUM PHILALETHIUM . . . T'AMSTELREDAM, Voor Marten Iansz Brandt . . . 1620. [etc.] (col.) T'AMSTELDAM, Gedruckt by Paulus van Ravesteyn . . . 1620. 4° pp.58; illus.

T.2423(42).

Pseudonymous. The titlepage woodcut shows the Lion of Holland.

T29 TEELLINCK, Ewout

CLEOPHAS Ofte Christelijck Ghespreck/Van twee Disciplen gaende nae Emaus. Waer in gehandelt wert/Van het oochmerck deser Kerckelijcke gheschillen/ende van de middelen om de selve te stillen. Door IRENEVM PHILALETIVM . . . t'Amsterdam, Voor Marten Jansz. Brandt . . . 1617. 4° pp.34

T.2247(4).

Pseudonymous. Printed by Paulus van Ravesteyn at Amsterdam? With the large oblong device, signed: PS, identified by *Nagler* no.3040 mas P.[C.] van Sichem.

T30 TEELLINCK, Ewout

DE CREVPELE BODE, Brengende seeckere tydinge UYT BOËMEN, Met een Christelycke waerschouwinge daer over. Door IRENEUM PHILALETHIUM . . . T'AMSTELREDAM, Voor Marten Iansz Brandt . . . 1621. [etc.] 4° pp.27

T.2249(48); T.2424(2).

Pseudonymous. Printed by Paulus van Ravesteyn, with use of civilité.

T31 TEELLINCK, Ewout

EEN HARDT BODE, Brengende quade tydinge Wt BOËMEN, Met een Geestelycke Hert-Sterckinge daer tegens. Door IRENEUM PHILALETHIUM . . . T'AMSTELREDAM, Voor Marten Iansz Brandt . . . 1621. [etc.] 4° pp.27

T.2251(2); T.2424(1).

Pseudonymous. Printed by Paulus van Ravesteyn at Amsterdam. The large oblong device with a double scene signed: PS, i.e. P. or Ph. [C.] van Sichem?

T32 TEELLINCK, Ewout

KLAUWE Vande Beeste/Ofte/Blyckelijcke teeckenen des Antichrists . . . DOOR IRENEUM PHILALETIUM . . . t'AMSTELREDAM, Voor Marten Jansz Brant . . . 1619. [etc.] (col.) t'AMSTELDAM, Ghedruckt by Paulus van Ravesteyn . . . 1619. 4° pp.40; illus.

T.2249(42).

Pseudonymous. The titlepage woodcut shows the Babylonian Whore. Printed with use of civilité.

T33 TEELLINCK, Ewout

MIZPA, Ofte Christelyck Gespreck/Van het rechte gebruyck des algemeenen vasten-biddaghs . . . Door IRENEUM PHILALETHIUM . . . T'AMSTELREDAM, Voor Marten Iansz Brandt . . . 1620. [etc.] 4° pp.37 [47]

T.2423(43).

Pseudonymous. Printed by Paulus van Ravesteyn at Amsterdam.

T34 TEELLINCK, Ewout

QUERELA ECCLESIAE. Ofte Clachte der Kercke Aende Overheden des Lants/ende Dienaren des Goddelycken Woorts/over hare . . . swaricheden. Door IRENEUM PHILALETIVM . . . t'Amsterdam, Voor Marten Jansz. Brandt . . . 1617. 4° pp.31 [47]

T.2247(34).

Pseudonymous. Printed by Paulus van Ravesteyn at Amsterdam. The large device signed: PS, i.e. according to *Nagler* no. 3040 P. or Ph. [C.] van Sichem.

T35 TEELLINCK, Ewout

QUERELA PATRIAE: Dat is/Klachte des Vaderlants Over de teghenwoordighe swaricheden/door ettelijcke . . . Nieus-ghesinde Leeraers/inden Lande van Hollandt verweckt. Claegs-wijse gestelt, Door ALEXIUS PHILOPATOR. Den derden Druck. t'AMSTERDAM, Voor Marten Jansz. Brandt . . . 1617. 4° pp. 24

T. 2247(33).

Pseudonymous. Printed by Paulus van Ravesteyn at Amsterdam. The large device signed: P-S, i.e. P. or Ph. [C.] van Sichem?

T36 TEELLINCK, Ewout

SVLAMITH, Ofte Baniere des Vredes/Opgeworpen Om Japhet te locken/dat hy weder kome wonen in de Hutten Sems. Dat is: Om d'afgewekene Remonstranten weder te brengen tot de gemeenschap vande Gereformeerde Kercke . . . Door IRENEUM PHILALETIUM . . . T'AMSTELREDAM, Voor Marten Iansz Brandt . . . 1621. 4° pp. 69

T. 2251(14).

Pseudonymous. Printed by Paulus van Ravesteyn at Amsterdam, with use of civilité.

T37 TEELLINCK, Willem

Philopatris, Ofte Christelijck bericht hoemen Staets saecken soude moghen gheluckelick uytvoeren: Dienende tot desen jeghenwoordighen Vredehandel. Door Willem Teellinck, Dienaer des Woordts. MIDDELBVRCH, Voor Adriaen vanden Vivre . . . 1608. 4° pp. 25

T. 1713(27); T. 2420(20).

Printed by Richard Schilders at Middelburg.

TEGHEN-BERICHT jeghens D. Francisci Gomari Waerschouwinge. 1610. *See* CORVINUS, Joannes Arnoldi

T38 TEGHEN-VRAECH-AL

Den Teghen=Vraech=al, Inhoudende Ettelicke questien of vraghen/Om Daer mede den mondt te stoppen aen den dwasen Vraech-al . . . dienende om den anderen Vraech-al te verstercken . . . GHEDRVCKT, By't recht voorstant in Hollandt . . . 1618. 4° pp. 14

700. h. 25(30).

For the original 'Vraegh-al' *see* TAURINUS, Jacobus. For the 'Anderen Vraech-al' *see* VRAEGH-AL

TEIONIS, Phocaeus. Disputatio theologica, de creatione. 1613. *See* LINDEN, Henricus Antonides van der

T39 TEIXEIRA, José

[Exegesis genealogica . . . regis Henrici . . . IIII.] STEMMATA FRANCIÆ ITEM NAVARRÆ REGVM, A prima utriusque gentis origine usque ad . . . HENRICVM MAGNVM AVGVSTVM. Authore R.P.F. IOSEPHO TEXERA . . . LVGDVNI BATAVORVM, Apud IOANNEM MAIRE, M.D.C.XIX. 4° pp. 192: plate; illus., genealogical tables, port.

C. 77. b. 2.

A reissue of the edition by Franciscus Raphelengius of 1592, without the Errata, Addenda or privilege, with a new titlepage and dedication. The folding plate has the portrait of Henry IV in the centre. In a binding bearing the initials of Jacques Auguste de Thou.

TEIXEIRA, Pedro. Relaciones. 1610. *See* MUḤAMMAD IBN KHĀVAND SHĀH

T40 TELLE, Reinier

DER Contraremonstranten KERF-STOCK . . . Aen de Roomsche Catholijcken . . .

Door een Lief-hebber van de vrye Waerheydt. Ghedruckt in de groote onbekende Werelt. 4° 6 unsigned leaves

11555.e.27(3).

Anonymous. In verse, with 'Vande sichtbare Ghemeynte ons Heeren Iesu Christi' in prose. Published in 1617.

T41 TELLE, Reinier

GAL-BRAECKE, Teweghe ghebracht door een Leydtsche Purgatie, Aen den Persoon van Vincent van Drielenburgh . . . 1617. 4° sig. A^4

T.2247(55).

Signed: R.T. In verse.

TELLE, Reinier. Retortie ofte weder-steeck. 1619. [Sometimes attributed to Reinier Telle.] *See* RETORTIE

T42 TELLE, Reinier

TAFEREEL, Begrijpende cortelijck het . . . verschil datter is tusschen de Leere der heyligher Schriftuere, ende der Ghereformeerde Kercken aen d'eene/ende der Contra-Remonstranten aen d'ander zijde . . . Den derden Druck, Vermeerdert met een Na-reden aen die uytvercorenen Kinderen Godts . . . Ghedruckt . . . 1618. 4° sig. AB^4

T.2248(29).

Anonymous, with a postscript refutation. An earlier edition consisting of extracts is printed at the end of TAURINUS, Jacobus. 'Zedich onder-soeck', 1617.

T43 TELLE, Reinier

REINIER TELLES Tweede Vrede-sang: OFTE Jaerliedt op de vol-eyndinge van de eerste hondert jaren na de aengevangene Reformatie der Kercken . . . t'AMSTERDAM Gedruckt by Porcevant Morgan . . . 1617. 4° 4 unsigned leaves

T.2247(1).

Cropped.

T44 TELLE, Reinier

[Tweede vrede-sang.] REYNIER TELLES VREDE-ZANGH: Ofte JAER-LIEDT. Op de voleyndinge van de eerste hondert Jaren, na de aengevangene Reformatie der Kercken 1617. Met noch een Nieuw-Jaer Liedeken voor den Jare 1615 . . . t'AMSTERDAM, Voor een Liefhebber van Vrede. 4° sig. AB^4

115555.e.42(1).

An enlarged edition of the preceding, published in 1617.

T45 TERENTIUS AFER, Publius

[Works. Latin] PVB. TERENTII AFRI COMOEDIÆ SEX. EX OFFICINA PLANTINIANA RAPHELENGII, M.D.CXIII. 32° pp. 214

C.20.f.50.

Published at Leiden. From the travelling library of Sir Julius Caesar.

TERTULLIANUS, Quintus Septimius Florens. [De corona militis. Ad martyres. French] De la couronne du soldat. 1613. *See* RAEMOND, Florimond de. L'anti-papesse. Arras, 1613.

T46 TERZAGHI, Angelo

(tp. 1) R.P. ANGELI TERZACHI . . . PSALMI VESPERARVM ET MAGNIFICAT QVATVOR VOCVM Cum Basso Continuo ad Organum, Et in fine aliquot FALSI BORDONI cum Versu Venerabilis Sacramenti. ALTVS. ANTVERPIÆ Apud Petrum Phalesium M.D.CXV.

(tp. 2) R.P. ANGELI TERZACHI . . . PSALMI VESPERARVM ET MAGNIFICAT . . . TENOR. ANTVERPIÆ Apud Petrum Phalesium M.D.CXV.

(tp. 3) R.P. ANGELI TERZACHI . . . PSALMI VESPERARVM ET MAGNIFICAT . . . BASSVS

CONTINVVS. ANTVERPIÆ Apud Petrum Phalesium M.D.CXV. 4° 3 pt.: pp.33; 33; 32
Music C.113.

The form 'Terzaghi' occurs at the foot of all pages beginning a new signature.

T47 TESTAMENT

TESTAMENT van den Coninck Philippus den III. Coninck van Hispanien/ende Indien/&c. Met zijne vvterste vvoorden, ende vermaninghen ghesproken tot zijne kinderen. Eerst Ghedruckt den 28. Mey 1621. T'Hantwerpen/By Abraham Verhoeven/[etc.] 4° pp.8; sig.A^4; illus.
P.P.3444.af(236); 1193.f.31.

Headed: Mey 1621.80. The titlepage woodcut shows Philip III on his deathbed. Some letters which in the copy at 1193.f.31 have failed to print, have been supplied in manuscript.

T48 TESTAMENT

HET TESTAMENT vande Oorloghe. Het Testament vande Oorloghe wort hier vertelt/Deur Selden tijt// sonder strijt//in Baladen gestelt. Noch is hier bygevoecht, de COPYE Vanden Brief gheschreven van syn Hoogheyt/aen Graef Herman vandē Berg . . . Noch vint ghy hier achter by gevoecht/een warachtig ende genoechlick discours/van D.D. Nicolaum Mulerium . . . van wegen der stadt Groeninghen ende de omme-landen . . . ANNO 1608. 4° sig.A^4
T.2420(10).

The first piece only is in verse.

TEXERA, Josephus. *See* TEIXEIRA, José

TEXTOR, Johannes. Disputationum theologicarum duodecima, de officiis filii Dei incarnati. 1601. *See* GOMARUS, Franciscus

TEXTOR, Johannes. Disputationum theologicarum decima-sexta, de Evangelio. 1603. *See* GOMARUS, Franciscus

TEXTOR, Johannes. Theses theologicae de fide iustificante. 1603. *See* TRELCATIUS, Lucas

TEXTOR, Renatus. Disputationum theologicarum decima-nona, de officio Christi. 1603. *See* GOMARUS, Franciscus

THEATRE d'histoire. 1613. *See* BELLEVILLE, Philippe de

THEATRE des cruautez des heretiques de nostre temps. 1607. *See* VERSTEGAN, Richard

The THEATRE of Catholique and Protestant religion. 1620. *See* COPINGER, John

THEATRUM crudelitatum haereticorum nostri temporis. 1604. *See* VERSTEGAN, Richard

T49 THEMISTIUS Euphrada

THEMISTII EVPHRADÆ ORATIONES ALIQVOT non editæ Cum interpretatione PETRI PANTINI: & viri eruditi Notis. LVGDVNI BATAVORVM Excudit Ioannes Patius . . . M.D.C.XIV. 8° pp.127
834.b.21.

The editor is Daniel Heinsius. Cropped.

THEOCRITUS a Ganda; pseudonym of Daniel Heinsius. *See* HEINSIUS, Daniel

T50 THEODORET; Bishop

['Εκκλησιαστικὴ ἱστορία.] THE ECCLESIASTICALL HISTORY OF THEODORET BISHOP OF CYRVS . . . VVritten in Greeke . . . AND Now translated into our English tongue . . . Imprinted . . . M.DC.XII. 4° pp.405
1364.b.8.

Translated by Roger Cadwallader. The preface signed: G.E. Without imprint; published by the English College press at St. Omer. Ownership inscription: Jon[a] Robinson 1745.

T51 THEODORICUS

THEODORICVS TRAGEDIE A represēter par la Ieunesse du College de la Societé de IESVS à Malines le [11] de Septembre l'an 1618 . . . A MALINES, Imprimé par HENRI IAEY . . . 1618. 4° sig. A^4
11735.e.2.
The programme of a play said in the 'Sommaire' to be on a subject drawn from Cesare Baronius's 'Annales ecclesiastici' and abridged from a play of the same title by Nicolaus Vernulaeus. The precise date has been inserted in manuscript.

THEOLOGIA vera et mera. 1617. *See* WTENBOGAERT, Jan

T52 THEOPHRASTUS

ΘΕΟΦΡΑΣΤΟΥ ΤΟΥ ΕΡΕΣΙΟΥ ῞ΑΠΑΝΤΑ. THEOPHRASTI ERESII Græce & Latine opera omnia. DANIEL HEINSIVS Textum Græcum . . . emendauit: hiulca suppleuit, male concepta recensuit: interpretationem passim interpolauit . . . LVGDVNI BATAVORVM, Ex Typographio HENRICI ab HAESTENS. IMPENSIS Iohannis Orlers, And. Cloucq, & Ioh. Maire . . . M.D CXIII. fol. pp. 508
985.h.5; C.79.e.7; 35.g.19.
The 'Concordia' device signed: ₵, i.e. Jan Cornelis Woudanus or, less probably, Christoph Jeghers? The copy at 985.h.5 from the library of Sir Joseph Banks.

T53 THEOPHYLACTUS

THEOPHYLACTI, ARCHIEPISCOPI BVLGARIÆ, Epistolæ. IOANNES MEVRSIVS Nunc primùm è tenebris erutas edidit. LVGDVNI BATAUORVM, Ex Officinâ GODEFRIDI BASSON . . . M.D.C.XVII. 4° pp. 118
1125.g.6; 92.c.5.
In Greek only. The copy at 92.c.5 is on large paper. Ownership inscription: Bequeathed by Thos Tyrwhitt Esqr 1786.

T54 THERESA de Cepeda, de Jesús; Saint

LIBRO de las FVNDACIONES DE LAS HERMANAS DEScalças Carmelitas, que escriuio la Madre Fundadora Teresa de IESVS. EN BRVSELAS, En casa de Roger Velpio, y Huberto Antonio . . . 1610. [etc.] 8° pp. 371; illus.
4785.aa.33.
With 'Litterae S[mi] D.N. Pauli PP. V. ad Henricum IIII. Regem Galliae, pro constructione Conuentuum Ordinis Fratrum Carmelitarum Discalceatorum in suo regno'. The titlepage woodcut shows a Nativity scene. The binding stamped: J. Gomez de la Cortina et amicorum, and with the exlibris: Bibliotheca Cortiniana.

T55 THERESA de Cepeda, de Jesús; Saint

[Vida de Santa Teresa de Jesús.] THE LYF OF THE MOTHER TERESA OF IESVS . . . Written by her self . . . and now translated into English, out of Spanish. By W.M. of the Society of Iesus . . . Imprinted in Antwerp for HENRIE IAYE . . . M.DC.XI. 4° pp. 364
4829.cc.17.
The translator is Michael Walpole. Published at Mechelen. The unnamed Antwerp printer is Arnout Coninx.

T56 THIELMANS, Cornelis

CORT VERHAEL, VAN HET LEVEN Der Heylighen van S Franciscus Oirden Met HAER LEVENDE FIGVREN Wt Diuersche historie Scriuers genomen DEVR . . . Cornelis Thielmans . . . GEDRVCKT TSHERTOGENBOSCH, By Ian Scheffer . . . M.D.CVI. 4° sig. X, $A\text{-}T^2V^6$; illus.
4828.aaa.22(2).

Based on the 'Imagines sanctorum' of Henricus Sedulius, with the engravings in reverse and additional ones. The titlepage, originally belonging to an edition of 1606, has had a label pasted over the text inside its engraved border, reading: 'CORTE LEGENDE DER HEYLIGHEN van S. Franciscus Oorden met haer Figuren, Aflaet van Portiunckel, [etc.]'. The original title is legible from the verso. Another label, known from copies elsewhere, bearing the imprint of Jan van Turnhout and the date 1610, has been removed. Sigg. A-P,X are printed on one side of the leaf only. The illustration on sig. V1v is signed: Joan: Berwinckel sculp. The approbations are dated 1610. Sig. X follows the titlepage. Imperfect; wanting the leaf bearing the illustration belonging to sig. P.

T57 THIELMANS, Cornelis

CORT VERHAEL, VAN HET LEVEN Der Heylighen . . . M.DC.VI. 4° sig.X, A-T^2V^6
1578/3235.

Another copy or issue of the preceding in which the label over the title has also been removed and the text, damaged in the process, poorly emended in manuscript. The illustration belonging to sig. P is of a different size and style from the other engravings and may be a later substitution. Imperfect; wanting all of sig. O.

THIEN Contra-Remonstrantsche positien. 1618. *See* GREVINCHOVEN, Nicolaas

T58 THIEULLIER, Jan

(tp.1) DE SCHADT-KISTE DER PHILOSOPHEN ENDE POETEN WAER INNE TE VINDEN SYN VEEL . . . BLASOENEN, REFEREYNEN ENDE LIEDEKENS Gebracht ende gesonden op de PEOEN-CAMERE binnen Mechelen van d'omliggende steden in Brabant, Vlaenderen, Hollandt ende Zeelandt: Gepprononciert ende gesonghen op henlieder Feeste den 3. Mey . . . 1620 . . . Gedruckt tot Mechelen by Hendrick Iaye. A°. 1621.
(tp.2) PORPHYRE EN CYPRINE TREVR-SPEL VERTHOONT By . . . die PEOEN binnen Mechelen . . . TOT MECHELEN, Gedruckt by HENDRICK IAYE . . . M.DC.XXI. fol. 2 pt.: pp.321; lxxij: plates; illus.
1489.m.45; Cup.401.k.10.

The author of the play in pt.2 named in a poem on p.lii as Ian Thieullier, who is also the compiler and editor of pt.1. The 'Esbatement' on pp.liij-lx is stated to be 'Ghecomponeert . . . by . . . Henrick Fay-d'Herbe'. Tp.1 is engraved, tp.2 bears a large engraved illustration.

T59 THIOFRIDUS; Abbas Epternacensis

D. THIOFRIDI . . . FLORES EPITAPHII SANCTORVM, LIBRI QUATUOR . . . IOHANNES ROBERTI . . . Ex duobus MSS. Biblioth. EFTERNACENSIS S. CLEMENTIS WILLIBRORDI, Descripsit, recensuit, distinxit, & NOTIS illustrauit. Floruit THIOFRIDVS ante annos fere DL. cuius & VITA ab eodem ROBERTI addita. LVXEMBVRGI, Excudebat HVBERTVS REVLANDT . . . M.DC.XIX. 4° pp.214
486.c.8(1).

THOMAEUS, Jacobus. Disputationum anatomicarum sexta . . . de ossibus. 1618. *See* WINSEMIUS, Menelaus

THOMAEUS, Jacobus. Disputationum anatomicarum duodecima, de cute. 1619. *See* WINSEMIUS, Menelaus

THOMAEUS, Jacobus. Disputationum anatomicarum decima-septima . . . de partibus urinariis. 1619. *See* WINSEMIUS, Menelaus

T60 THOMAS a Jesu; name in religion of Diego de Avila

DE PROCVRANDA SALVTE OMNIVM GENTIVM, SCHISMATICORVM, HÆRETICORVM, Iudæorum, Sarracenorum, cæterorumq; Infidelium LIBRI XII . . . Accedit . . . pro conuersis CATECHISMVS . . . Auctore R.P. THOMA à IESV, Biatensi, Ordinis Carmelitarum Discalceatorum in Belgio superiore. ANTVERPIÆ, Sumptibus Viduæ & hæredum Petri Belleri . . . 1613. [etc.] (col.) ANTVERPIÆ, Excudebat Andreas Bacx, sumptibus Viduæ & hæredum Petri Belleri . . . 1613. 4° pp.926
475.b.8.

T61 THOMAS a Kempis
[Works] (tp.1) THOMAE A KEMPIS . . . Opera omnia. AD AVTOGRAPHA EIVSDEM EMENdata, atque . . . aucta . . . in tres Tomos distributa: OPERA AC STVDIO HENRICI Sommalij . . . ANTVERPIAE, Ex Officina Typographica Martini Nutij . . . M.DCI. (tp.2) TOMVS SECVNDVS operum THOMAE A KEMPIS . . . PARS PRIMA. ANTVERPIAE, Ex Officina Typographica Martini Nutij . . . M.DC.
(tp.3) TOMVS TERTIVS Operum THOMAE A KEMPIS . . . PARS PRIMA. ANTVERPIAE, Ex Officina Typographica Martini Nutij . . . M.DCI. 8° 3 tom.: pp.713; 203; illus.
IX.App.10.
Tom.1, 2 have continuous pagination, with tp.2 on p.275. The second parts of tom.2, 3 have no separate titlepages. The engraving shows the arms of the dedicatee. Ownership inscriptions: Joannes de Wolfswinckel; T. J. Wright 1720; Miles Martindale 1813; Albertus Eufrenius; Edmund Waterton.

T62 THOMAS a Kempis
[Works] (tp.1) THOMÆ MALLEOLI A KEMPIS . . . Opera omnia . . . EMENdata . . . OPERA AC STVDIO R.P. HENRICI SOMMALII . . . EDITIO SECVNDA. ANTVERPIÆ, Ex Officina Typographica MARTINI NVTII . . . M.DC.VII.
(tp.2=p.257) OPERVM THOMAE MALLEOLI A KEMPIS . . . THOMVS [*sic*] SECVNDVS. EDITIO SECVNDA. Jterum correcta & auctior facta. OPERA AC STVDIO R.P. HENRICI Sommalii . . . ANTVERPIAE, Ex Officina Typographica Martini Nutii . . . M.DC.VII.
(tp.3=p.613) OPERVM THOMAE MALLEOLI A KEMPIS . . . TOMVS TERTIVS. EDITIO SECVNDA. Jterum correcta & auctior facta. OPERA AC STVDIO R.P. HENRICI Sommalii . . . ANTVERPIAE, Ex Officina Typographica Martini Nutii . . . M.DC.VII. 4° pp.879: plate; port.
3845.de.1.

T63 THOMAS a Kempis
[Works] VEN. VIRI THOMÆ MALLEOLI A KEMPIS . . . OPERA OMNIA . . . emendata . . . Opera ac studio R.P. HENRICI SOMMALII . . . EDITIO TERTIA. ANTVERPIÆ, Apud Heredes MART. NVTII ET JOANN. MEVRSIVM. M.DC.XV. 8° pp.1040
IX.App.11.

T64 THOMAS a Kempis
[De imitatione Christi. Latin] DE IMITATIONE CHRISTI LIBRI QVATVOR, AVTHORE THOMA A KEMPIS . . . Ad Autographum emendati, opera . . . HENRICI SOMMALII . . . Editio tertia, prioribus castigatior. ANTVERPIÆ, EX OFFICINA PLANTINIANA, Apud Ioannem Moretum. M.DCVII. [etc.] 12° pp.321
IX.Lat.267.

T65 THOMAS a Kempis
[De imitatione Christi. Latin] DE IMITATIONE CHRISTI LIBRI QVATVOR, AVTHORE THOMA A KEMPIS . . . Ad Autographum emendati, opera ac studio HENRICI SOMMALII . . . Editio vltima prioribus castigatior. DVACI Ex Typographia BALTAZARIS BELLERI . . . 1608. (col.) IN ACADEMIA DVACENA Excudebat BALTAZAR BELLERVS . . . 1608. 32° pp.452: plates
IX.Lat.98.
The plates are engraved. Pp.99, 100 are mutilated. With 'Peritia libelli De imitatione Christi' by Sommalius on separate signatures A^8B^4.

T66 THOMAS a Kempis
[De imitatione Christi. Latin] DE IMITATIONE CHRISTI LIBRI QVATVOR, AVTHORE THOMA A KEMPIS . . . opera ac studio HENRICI SOMMALII . . . Editio vltima prioribus castigatior. DVACI, Ex Typographia BALTAZARIS BELLERI . . . 1612. [etc.] 32° pp.409
C.20.f.18.

With 'Peritia libelli De imitatione Christi' by Sommalius. From the travelling library of Sir Julius Caesar.

T67 THOMAS a Kempis
[De imitatione Christi. Latin] VEN. P.F. THOMÆ A KEMPIS . . . DE IMITATIONE CHRISTI LIBRI QVATVOR Ad Autographum . . . iterum recensiti. ANTVERPIAE Apud Gasparum Bellerum M.DC.XVI. [etc.] 32° pp.458: plates; illus.
IX.Lat.97.
The titlepage engraving shows Christ with saints. The editor named in the preface as Georgius Duras. Ownership inscription: Edmund Waterton.

T68 THOMAS a Kempis
[De imitatione Christi. Latin] THOMÆ A KEMPIS . . . DE IMITATIONE CHRISTI LIBRI QVATVOR: Nunc postremò ad autographorum fidem recensiti. Cum VINDICIIS KEMPENSIBVS Heriberti Ros-vveydi . . . Aduersus C. Caietanum . . . ANTVERPIÆ, EX OFFICINA PLANTINIANA, Apud Balthasarem & Ioannem Moretos. M.DC.XVII. 12° pp.516; illus.
IX.Lat.268.
The titleage engraving shows Christ bearing the Cross. A full-page engraving of the Virgin appearing to Thomas a Kempis is signed: Hieronymus Wierx fecit. Ownership inscriptions: J. P. Gasser; Edmundus Waterton.

T69 THOMAS a Kempis
[De imitatione Christi. Latin] DE IMITATIONE CHRISTI LIBRI QVATVOR, AVTHORE THOMA A KEMPIS . . . Ad Autographum emendati, operâ ac studio HENRICI SOMMALII . . . Editio vltima prioribus castigatior. DVACI, Ex Typogr. BALTAZARIS BELLERI . . . 1618. [etc.] 32° pp.428
C.106.a.33.
With 'Peritia libelli De imitatione Christi' by Sommalius.

T70 THOMAS a Kempis
[De imitatione Christi. Latin] THOMAE A KEMPIS . . . De Imitatione Christi. LIBRI QVATVOR. Ex POSTREMA RECognitione R.P. Heriberti Ros-weydi . . . LVXEMBVRGI. Excudebat Hubertus Reuland . . . M.DC.XX. 32° pp.495
IX.Lat.3.
With 'Peritia libelli De imitatione Christi' by Henricus Sommalius.

T71 THOMAS a Kempis
[De imitatione Christi. English] THE FOLLOWING OF CHRIST. Deuided into foure Bookes. Written in Latin by . . . THOMAS à KEMPIS . . . AND Translated into English by F.B. . . . 1620. 12° pp.396
C.123.a.6.
Translated by Anthony Hoskins. Without imprint; published by the English College press at St. Omer.

T72 THOMAS a Kempis
[De imitatione Christi. Dutch] QVI SEQVITVR ME, DAT IS: Die Navolghinghe Christi: bedeylt in vier Boecken. Door . . . Thomas Hamerken van Campen . . . Ouerghestelt wten Latijne in Brabants Duytsch door Heer Nicolaus van Winghe . . . Tot Louen/by Jan Maes . . . 1601. [etc.] (col.) TOT LOVEN By Jan Maes . . . M.CCCCCC.i. 8° ff.180; illus.
IX.Dut.59(1).
The titlepage woodcut shows Christ and his followers bearing crosses. Ownership inscription: Monasterij Ochsenhusani 1650.

T73 THOMAS a Kempis
[De imitatione Christi. Dutch] QVI SEQVITVR ME, DAT IS. Die Navolginghe Christi: bedeylt in vier Boecken. Door . . . Thomas Hamerken vā Campen . . .

Ouerghestelt vvten Latijne in Brabants Duytsch door Heer NICOLAVS VAN VVINGE . . . T'HANTVVERPEN. By Jan van Keerbergen . . . 1606.[etc.] 12° ff.260; illus.
IX.Dut.34.
The titlepage engraving shows Christ and his followers bearing crosses.

T74 THOMAS a Kempis
[De imitatione Christi. Dutch] DE NAVOLGINGE CHRISTI, in vier Boecken bedeelt, Door . . . THOMAS VAN KEMPEN . . . Van nieus oversien na het Latijnsch exemplaer, [v]erbetert na de gheschreven copije vanden Autheur door P. Heribertus Rosvveydus . . . T'HANTVVERPEN, [By] Hieronymus Verdussen . . . 1617. 12° pp.475; illus.
IX.Dut.45.
With the life of Thomas a Kempis by Rosweyde. The titlepage engraving shows Christ and his followers bearing crosses. The titlepage is slightly mutilated.

T75 THOMAS a Kempis
[De imitatione Christi. French] L'internelle consolation, OV THOMAS A KEMPIS DE L'IMITATION DE IESVS CHRIST LIVRES IIII. De nou[u]eau reueú, cōferé auec le Latin, corrigé & a[diou]sté de beaucoup de lieux de la saincte Escr[iptu]re par gēs scauans . . . Et amplifié de la Practique d'iceluy . . . A DOVAY, De l'Imprimerie de BALTAZAR BELLERE . . . 1619. 12° pp.462; illus.
IX.Fren.80.
Translated by Antoine Vivien. With 'Sommaire des choses principales de la religion chrestienne' and 'La practique du livret' by Henricus Sommalius. The titlepage engraving shows Christ and his followers bearing crosses, unusually facing left. The titlepage is mutilated. Imperfect; wanting pp.347–350. Ownership inscription: Religieuses penitentes à Oudenarde.

T76 THOMAS a Kempis
[De imitatione Christi. French] IIII. LIVRES DE L'IMITATION DE IESVS-CHRIST. PAR THOMAS DES CHAMPS . . . NOVVELLEMENT MIS EN Francois par M.R. Gaultier A. Et reueu par luy mesme en ceste derniere Edition. A CAMBRAY, De l'Imprimerie de IEAN DE LA RIVIERE. M.DC.XIX. 12° pp.448; illus.
IX. Fren.95.
With 'La practique du livret' by Henricus Sommalius. The woodcut at the end of the book shows the Resurrection of Christ. Ownership inscriptions: J.P. Gasser; Edmund Waterton.

T77 THOMAS a Kempis
[De imitatione Christi. French] QVATRE LIVRES DE L'IMITATION DE IESVS-CHRIST. De Thomas de Champs . . . Mis en meilleur françois en l'an 1608. par vn scauant homme de S. Omer. A S.OMER. De l'Imprimerie de Pierre Geubels . . . 1619. 12° pp.430; illus.
IX.Fren.81.
The illustrations are woodcuts. Ownership inscriptions: Carmelitersse tot Boxmeer; Maria Carmeliterssen te Boxmeer Elzendaal.

T78 THOMAS a Kempis
[De imitatione Christi. Spanish] CONTEMTVS MVNDI, O DE LA IMITACION DE CHRISTO, Libros Quatro, Compuestos en Latin por Thomas de Kempis . . . Traduzidos en Español por . . . Luys de Granada. De nueuo corregidos por vn Padre de la Compañia de IESVS. Se venden en Anueres en casa de Gusleno Iansenio, 1612. 12° pp.384
IX.Span.9.
Revised by Franciscus Smidt? Ownership inscriptions: Ex libris Conuent, Coloniensis SS Carmel. Discal:; Edmund Waterton; F.F. Tils. 1814.

T79 THOMAS a Kempis
[Soliloquium animae. Dutch] DIE Alleen-sprake der ZIELEN MET GODT. Door . . . Thomas Hamerken van Campen . . . Onlancx wt het Latijns exemplaer . . . ghecorrigeert/ende verbetert door . . . P.I.V.S. Priester der Societeyt IESV. TOT LOVEN, By Ian Maes . . . M.D.CI. 8° pp.175; illus.
4407.bb.11(1); IX.Dut.59(2).

Edited by Jacobus Stratius. The illustrations are woodcuts; that on the titlepage shows the Virgin and Child with angels playing musical instruments. The 'Prologhe des autheurs' is printed in civilité.

T80 THOMAS Aquinas; Saint
[De regimine principum.] D. THOMAS AQUINAS De rebuspublicis, ET Principum institutione, LIBRI IV. LUGDUNI BATAVORUM, Ex Officinâ IOANNIS MAIRE, M DCII. 16° pp.444
527.a.5.

T81 THOMAS Aquinas; Saint
[Summa theologica. Prima.] (tp.1) COMMENTARIORVM, AC DISPVTATIONVM IN PRIMAM PARTEM S. THOMÆ TOMVS PRIMVS . . . AVCTORE P. GABRIELE VAZQVEZ . . . Nunc primùm in Germania excusus . . . M.DC.IX. INGOLSTADII . . . Excudebat ANDREAS ANGERMARIVS. Impensis Hæredum MARTINI NVTII, & IOANNIS HERTSROY. (tp.2) COMMENTARIORVM . . . IN PRIMAM PARTEM S. THOMÆ TOMVS SECVNDVS. AVCTORE P. GABRIELE VAZQVEZ . . . M.DCIX. INGOLSTADII . . . Excudebat ANDREAS ANGERMARIVS. Impensis Hæredum MARTINI NVTII, & IOANNIS HERTSROY. (col.) Excudebat ANDREAS ANGERMARIVS . . . M.DC.IX. fol. 2 tom.: pp.800; 828
697.m.2,3.

Published jointly by Hertzroy then at Ingolstadt and the Heirs of M. Nutius at Antwerp. Another edition forms part of the works of G. Vasquez. Ownership inscription: Monasterij Sancti Georgij in Prüuening. With the text.

T82 THOMAS Aquinas; Saint
[Summa theologica. Prima Secundae.] (tp.1) COMMENTARIORVM . . . IN PRIMAM SECVNDAE S. THOMAE, TOMVS PRIMVS . . . AVCTORE P. GABRIELE VAZQVEZ . . . Nunc primum in Germania excusus . . . M.DC.VI. INGOLSTADII . . . EX OFFICINA TYPOGRAPHICA EDERIANA, IMPENSIS IOANNIS HERTSROY, & ANDREÆ ANGERMARII. [etc.]
(tp.2) COMMENTARIORVM, AC DISPVTATIONVM IN PRIMAM SECVNDAE S. THOMÆ, Tomus Secundus . . . AVCTORE P. GRABRIELE VAZQVEZ . . . Nunc secundò in Germania excusus. ADDITVM EST . . . INTEGRVM EXEMPLAR CONCILII PALÆSTINI . . . M.DC.XII. INGOLSTADII . . . EX OFFICINA TYPOGRAPHICA EDERIANA, JMPENSIS MARTINI NVTII, ET JOANNIS HERTSROY. fol. 2 tom.: pp.960; 964[946]
697.m.4,5.

A made-up set, with tom.1 of the wholly German edition of 1606 and tom.2 of the 1612 edition, published jointly by Joannes Hertzroy then at Munich and Martinus Nutius at Antwerp. Ownership inscription: Monasterij Sancti Georgij in Prüuening.

T83 THOMAS Aquinas; Saint
[Summa theologica. Summaries. Latin] TOTA THEOLOGIA SANCTI TH. ABBREVIATA. Per modū conclusionum, responsalium ad singulos articulos Sūmæ Theologiæ eiusdē Sancti Doctoris, quasi Summam Sūmando, pro veritatum prōptiori memoria & intellectu. Authore R.P.F. Seraphino Capponi à Porrecta . . . ANTVERPIÆ. Apud GASPAREM BELLERVM . . . 1614. 32° pp.762
C.20.f.16.

From the travelling library of Sir Julius Caesar.

T84 THOMAS Aquinas; Saint
[Supposititious and doubtful works] SECRETA ALCHIMIÆ MAGNALIA D. THOMÆ AQVINATIS . . . Item Thesaurus Alchimiæ secretissimus . . . ACCESSIT ET IOANNIS DE RVPESCISSA Liber lucis, ac Raymundi Lullij opus . . . quod inscribitur Clavicula & Apertorium . . . Opera DANIELIS BROUCHUISII . . . Cum Præfatione D. Ioannis Heurnij. EDITIO TERTIA. LUGDUNI BATAVORUM, Ex Officinâ Thomæ Basson. M.D.CII. 8° pp.71: plate
1509/1908.
The plate consists of one woodcut each on recto and verso showing alchemical installations. They are from the original edition published by Niclaes Bohmbargen at Cologne in 1579. From the old Patent Office Library.

T85 THOMAS Cantimpratensis
[Bonum universale de apibus.] THOMÆ CANTIPRATANI . . . MIRACVLORVM, ET EXEMPLORVM MEmorabilium sui temporis LIBRI DVO. In quibus præterea, ex mirifica APVM Repub. vniuersa vitæ bene & Christiane instituendæ ratio . . . traditur, & . . . pertractatur. Ad exemplaria complura cùm mss. tum excusa, collati . . . expurgati, aucti, & notis illustrati. Opera & studio GEORGII COLVENERII . . . DVACI, Ex typographia BALTAZARIS BELLERI . . . 1605. [etc.] 8° pp.597,86; illus.
4827.b.37.
The titlepage engraving shows clerics watching a beekeeper with a swarm of bees. Printed by Laurence Kellam at Douai.

T86 THOMSON, George; of St. Andrews
VINDEX VERITATIS, Adversus IVSTVM LIPSIVM Libri duo. Prior insanam ejus religionem politicam . . . refellit. Posterior Sichemiensis . . . miracula convellit . . . Auctore GEORGIO THOMSONO . . . ALCMARIÆ, Excudebat Iacobus Meesterus, secundum exemplar Nortonianum. M.DC.VI. 8° pp.141
1020.d.2(2).
The original London edition was also in Latin.

T87 THOMSON, Richard; M.A., of Clare Hall, Cambridge
RICHARDI THOMSONIS . . . DIATRIBA DE AMISSIONE ET INTERCISIONE GRATIÆ, ET IVSTIFICATIONIS . . . LVGDVNI BATAVORVM. Excudit Iohannes Patius . . . MDCXVI. 8° pp.126
4255.cc.64.

T88 THOMSON, Richard; M.A., of Clare Hall, Cambridge
RICHARDI THOMSONIS . . . DIATRIBA DE AMISSIONE ET INTERCISIONE GRATIÆ, ET IVSTIFICATIONIS . . . LVGDVNI BATAVORVM, Excudit Ioannis [*sic*] Patius . . . MDCXVIII. 8° pp.166
702.a.46.

T89 THORIUS, Raphael
MEDICI LONDINENSIS EXIMII. EPISTOLA de Viri Celeberrimi ISAACI CASAVBONI MORBI MORTISQVE CAVSA. Edita ex Museo IOACHIMI MORSI. LVGDVNI BATAVORVM Excudebat IACOBVS MARCI. M D C XIX. 8° sig.A^2
1169.h.36(1).
Anonymous. The printer's preface contains the author's initials: R.T.

T90 THRONUS
P.T.L. THRONVS CVPIDINIS. Editio altera; priori emendatior, & multo auctior. AMSTERODAMI, Apud Wilhelmum Iansonium. 1618. obl.32° sig.A-G^8; illus.
11556.a.28.
Poems by various authors and emblems, based on Pieter van der Borcht's illustrations to Ovid's 'Metamorphoses', engraved by Crispin de Passe and Cri le Blon. The editor's initials

have been variously interpreted as those of the probable compiler Crispin de Passe and the translators I.A. Timmermans and de Lalaing, or as those of Petri Theodorus Librarius, i.e. Dirck Pietersz Pers. With an additional titlepage, engraved. Imperfect; wanting sig.H-M.

T91 THRONUS

THRONVS IVSTITIÆ. HOC EST de optimo judice TRACTATVS electissimis quibusque exemplis iudiciarijs æri . . . incisis illustratus. Addita tabularum brevi explicatione tam soluta oratione quam vincta. PICTORE IOACHIMO VVTENVVALIO . . . ET SCVLPTORE VVILHELMO SVVANENBVRGIO . . . AMSTELREDAMI, Excudebat Christophorus a Sichem . . . M.D.C.VII (col.) LVGDVNI BATAVORVM, Typis Henrici Ludovici ab Haestens . . . 1607. fol. sig.A-C^4: pl.13
C.80.i.7.

With verses by Hugo Grotius for Cicero's translation of Aratus and with texts by Libanius and Philo Judaeus. The date on the titlepage has been altered from an original M.D.C.VI. to M.D.C.VII, without full stop; pl.13 is dated 1606. The engraved device 'Oculi Domini super iustos spalm [*sic*] 34' bears the monogram HXH; the emblem of Justice signed: ZDL Inu., i.e. Zacharias Dolendo; the whole signed: CVSichem excud.

THURYN, Johannes. *See* TORINO, Giovanni

T92 THYRAEUS, Guillielmus

DISCVRSVS PANEGYRICI DE NOMINIBVS, TRIBVLATIONIBVS, ET MIRACVLIS S. PATRICII IBERNORVM APOSTOLI, CVM EXHORTATIONE AD persecutiones pro fide patienter ferendas, & Apostrophe ad Iberniam, qui, Auctore . . . GVILLIELMO THYRÆO . . . habiti sunt in Collegio Ibernorum Duaci, anno 1616. DVACI, Ex Officina BALTAZARIS BELLERI . . . 1617. 8° pp.213
862.f.1; 1122.a.37.

The editor's dedication signed: Patricius Donovanus. In the copy at 862.f.1 the last line on p.4, part of the dedication, has had one word deleted between 'Anglicanæ' and 'cuneos'; in the copy at 1122.a.37 the whole phrase 'per medios Anglicanæ . . . cuneos' has been deleted. Printed by the widow of Laurence Kellam at Douai.

T93 THYRAEUS, Guillielmus

DISCVRSVS PANEGYRICI . . . qui, Auctore . . . GVILLIELMO THYRÆO . . . habiti sunt . . . DVACI, Ex Officina BALTAZARIS BELLERI . . . 1617. 8° pp.213
G.5721.

Another issue of the preceding. The dedication on pp.3–6 has been re-set, the offending phrase 'per medios Anglicanæ . . . cuneos' being omitted. Printed by the widow of Laurence Kellam at Douai.

THYSIUS, Antonius; the Elder. Oratio de SS. Theologia. 1620. *See* POLYANDER, Joannes. Oratio . . . de primarijs falsæ theologiæ auctoribus devitandis.

T94 THYSIUS, Antonius; the Elder

THESES THEOLOGICÆ DE SESSIONE CHRISTI, ad dextram Patris. QVAS . . . SVB TVTELA . . . D. Antonij Thysij . . . Publicè discutiendas proponit THOMAS CUMINGIUS . . . HARDROVICI Excudebat Thomas Henrici . . . 1611. 4° sig.A^4B^2
479.a.19(2).

T95 TIJDINGE

Tijdinge van duytslãt/ende andere Quartieren/Met Tijdinghe van Amsterdam in Hollandt. Ouerghesedt wt het Hoochduyts/in onse Nederlantsche sprake. Eerst Ghedruckt den 13. Augusti. 1621. T'Hantvverpen, by Abraham Verhoeuen [etc.] 4° pp.8; sig.Z^4; illus.
P.P.3444.af(270).

Headed: Augustus, 1621. 113. The news from Amsterdam is that trade is bad, businesses are about to fail and people are praying for peace. The titlepage woodcut shows a battle between Christians and Turks outside a castle.

T96 TIJDINGE

Tijdinge vvt Duytslant, ende Hongarijen, ende de Stadt Praghe. Met het verhael vanden kloecken Heldt ende vromen Cappiten [*sic*] Generael Graeff van Bucquoy. Ouerghesedt wwt het Hoochduyts/in onse Nederlantsche sprake. Eerst Ghedruckt den 6. Augusti. 1621. T'Hantvverpen, by Abraham Verhoeuen, [etc.] 4° pp.8; sig.T[4]; illus.

P.P.3444.af(267).

Headed: Augustus, 1621. 110. News of the death in battle of Bucquoy, with other news. P.8 contains a Latin verse epitaph in praise of Bucquoy. The titlepage illustration shows an artillery attack on a town.

T97 TIJDINGE

Tijdinge wt Duytslāt ende Hongharijen/met t'ghene aldaer ghepasseert is. Overghesedt wt de Hooch-Duytsche sprake/in onse Nederlantsche Tale. Eerst Ghedruckt den 24. Julij 1621. T'Hantwerpen/By Abraham Verhoeuen/[etc.] 4° pp.8; sig.O[4]; illus.

P.P.3444.af(262).

Headed: Iulius 1621. 105. With news from Italy and France. The titlepage woodcut shows the rout of an army into a river.

T98 TIJDINGE

Tijdinge wt Pfaltz-grauen Landt. Ende vvt den Legher van zijn Excellentie den Marquis Spinola. Nv Eerst Ghedruct den 30. December 1620. T'Hantwerpen/By Abraham Verhoeuen . . . 1620. 4° pp.7; sig.¶[4]; illus., port.

1193.l.31; P.P.3444.af(167).

The titlepage woodcuts show a portrait of Spinola and a Gorgon shield.

TIJDINGHE. *See* also TYDINGHE

T99 TIJDINGHE

Tijdinghe van den Hertoch van Saxen/hoe dat hy het Landt vander Lausnitz gebrocht heeft onder de gehoorsaemheyt vande Roomsche Keyserlijcke Majesteyt. Overghesedt Wt de Hooch-Duytsche sprake in onse Nederlantsche Tale. Nu eerst ghedruckt den xj. December. 1620. T'Hantwerpen/By Abraham Verhoeuen/[etc.] 4° pp.8; sig.Mm[4]; illus.

P.P.3444.af(158); 1193.f.25; 1480.15(55).

The titlepage woodcut shows the portrait of John George I, Duke of Saxony, holding a sword.

T100 TIJDINGHE

Tijdinghe Van den Rhijnstroom eñ der Protestanten Vorsten. Met het Placcaet oft Mandaet vande Keys. Majest. Overghesedt wt de Hooch-Duytsche sprake in onse Nederlantsche Tale. Eerst ghedruckt den 8. Ianuarius 1621. T'Hantwerpen/by Abraham Verhoeven/[etc.] 4° pp.8; not signed; illus.

P.P.3444.af(172).

Headed: Ianuarius 1621. 3. The titlepage woodcut shows the arms of Ferdinand II. With an extract from a decree on taxation dated 20 December 1620.

T101 TIJDINGHE

Tijdinghe van Duytslandt/ende Bethlehem Gabor die de Croone van Hongheren mede heeft. Noch hoe den Eerts-Hertoch Leopoldus de stadt Straesborch heeft doen berennen . . . Gedruckt den 30. december/By Abraham Verhoeven. 1620. 4° pp.9; sig.Zz[4]; illus.

P.P.3444.af(166); 1480.aa.15(50).

The large titlepage woodcut shows an army with packhorses, a group of civilians, including a woman and a dog, mountains and a city in the background, with Bethlen Gabor (?) as a fugitive and beggar. Published at Antwerp.

T102 TIJDINGHE
Tijdinghe van Duytslandt, van Mansfeldt, ende wt Hongharijen/ende van Jtalien. Ouerghesedt vvt het Hoochduyts, in onse Nederlantsche sprake. Eerst ghedruckt den 3. September. 1621. T'Hantwerpen/By Abraham Verhoeuen/[etc.] 4° pp.8; sig.Nn4; illus.
P.P.3444.af(279).
Headed: September, 1621. 124. With news also from Spain and Turkey. The titlepage woodcut shows a landscape with villages, and a seaport with ships.

T103 TIJDINGHE
Tijdinghe van weenen in Oostenrijc met t'ghene in Duytslandt passeert/ende in Bohemen/en Praghe. Ouerghesedt vvt het Hoochduyts, in onse Nederlantsche sprake. Eerst gedruckt den 10. September. 1621. T'Hantwerpen/By Abraham Verhoeuen/[etc.] 4° pp.8; sig.Pp4; illus.
P.P.3444.af(280).
Headed: September, 1621. 125. With news from Italy. The titlepage woodcut shows a city being burnt by enemy troops.

T104 TIJDINGHE
Tijdinghe wt Brussel/Ende oock den Legher in Vlaenderen wat daer ghepasseert is. Eerst Ghedruckt den 29. Julij. 1621. T'Hantwerpen/by Abraham Verhoeuen, [etc.] 4° pp.8; sig.Q4; illus.
P.P.3444.af(264); 1193.f.34.
Headed: Iulius, 1621. 107. On the death of the Archduke Albert and on a military parade at Beveren. The titlepage woodcut shows the Pope and two bishops at prayer.

T105 TIJDINGHE
Tijdinghe wt de Stadt Praghe/Weenen in Oostenrijck/ende Moravien. Overghesedt wt de Hooch-Duytsche sprake in onse Nederlantsche Tale. Eerst Ghedruckt in Januarius 1621. T'Hantwerpen/By Abraham Verhoeven/[etc.] 4° pp.8; sig.A4; illus.
P.P.3444.af(182).
Headed: Ianuarius 1621. 13. The titlepage woodcut shows Maximilian of Bavaria and Bucquoy or Spinola on horseback.

T106 TIJDINGHE
Tijdinghe wt den Coninckliјcken Leger voor de stadt van Gulick. Met noch Tijdinghe wt den Legher voor Montalbaen in Vranckrijck. Eerst Ghedruckt den 3. December. 1621. T'Hantwerpen/By Abraham Verhoeuen/[etc.] 4° pp.7; sig.B4; illus.
P.P.3444.af(323).
Headed: December. 1621. 178. The titlepage woodcut shows a fortified town and marching armies.

T107 TIJDINGHE
Tijdinghe wt den Leger voor Sluys, ende Brugge in Vlaanderen/Met noch Tijdinge wt Duytslandt . . . Overghesedt wt het Hoochduyts in onse Nederlandtsche sprake. Eerst Ghedruckt den 1. December 1621. T'hantwerpen/By Abraham Verhoeuen/[etc.] 4° pp.8; sig.Zzzz4; illus.
P.P.3444.af(321).
Headed: December, 1621. 176. The titlepage woodcut shows an army in a tented camp.

T108 TIJDINGHE
Tijdinghe wt der Slesien/hoe dat dē Marc-Graeff van Iagherendorp, heeft ontboden aen de Heeren Staten des Lants in Slesien/allē t'ghene hy doet is wt volle macht van Fredericus Pfaltz-Graue. Met het Placcaet daer teghen ghedaen van den

Hertoch van Saxen. Eerst Ghedruckt den 13. Augusti. 1621. T'Hantwerpen/By Abraham Verhoeuen/[etc.] 4° pp.8; sig. Aa^4; illus.
P.P.3444.af(271).

Headed: Augustus. 1621. 114. The titlepage woodcut shows a portrait of Frederick on horseback, losing his crown and sceptre. The titlepage was folded while in the press.

T109 TIJDINGHE
Tijdinghe wt Hollandt ende Pfaltz-Graven Landt. Met Nieuvve Tijdinghe van de stadt Rochelle . . . Nv eerst Ghedruckt den 17. Iunij. 1621. T'Hantwerpen/By Abraham Verhoeuen/[etc.] 4° pp.8; unsigned: illus.
P.P.3444.af(247).

Headed: Iunij, 1621. 91. With other news, including a report of the difficulties caused to the Dutch textile industry because of the war with Spain. The titlepage woodcut shows a ship at sea.

T110 TIJDINGHE
Tijdinghe wt Italien/ende Polen/ende hoe dat de Cosacken den Turck int Lant zijn ghevallen. Overghesedt uyt de Hooch-Duytsche sprake in onse Nederlantsche sprake. Eerst ghedruckt den 14. Mey/1621. T'Hantwerpen by Abraham Verhoeven/[etc.] 4° pp.8; sig. ¶^{4}; illus.
P.P.3444.af(230).

Headed: Mey 1621. 74. With more news of other events than about the Turks. The titlepage woodcut shows a troop of cavalry under clouds, sun and stars.

T111 TIJDINGHE
Tijdinghe wt Parijs/ende wt den legher voor Montalbaen/hoe dat die van binnen eenen wt-val hebben ghedaen in des Conincx Legher. Ouerghesedt wt het Fransoys in onse Nederlantsche sprake. Eerst ghedruckt den 2. Nouember 1621. T'Hantwerpen/By Abraham Verhoeuen/[etc.] 4° pp.7; sig. Eeee^4; illus.
P.P.3444.af(306).

Headed: Nouember. 1621. 159. The titlepage woodcut shows a cavalry skirmish.

T112 TIJDINGHE
Tijdinghe wt Praghe ende Verklaringhe van het beghinsel tot den Eynde/hoe . . . de dry Pragher steden met het Casteel sijn verouert gheworden/van s'Keysers volck/ende den Hertoch van Beyeren/met den Grave van Bucquoy als Generaels ouer de Legers . . . Nv eerst ghedruckt den 9. December. T'Hantwerpen/By Abraham Verhoeuen [etc.] 4° pp.14; sig.: IiKk^4; illus.
P.P.3444.af(156); 1480.aa.15(53).

With the privilege dated 1620 on p.[15]. The titlepage woodcut shows an assault on a walled city. Published in 1620. The copy at P.P.3444.af(156) has the censor's initials 'Vidit C.D.W.A.' added between the end of the text and the word 'Finis' on p.14. where they are wanting in that at 1480.aa.15(53).

T113 TIJDINGHE
Tijdinghe wt Praghe hoe dat den Procureur Fruvvein, een vande principaelste Rebellen, die daer Ghevanghen sitten/is ter vensteren van eenen Toren wt gesprongen ende is doot ghevallen/is daer naer ghevierendeelt gheworden . . . Eerst Ghedruckt den 30. Junij. 1621. T'Hantwerpen/By Abraham Verhoeuen/[etc.] 4° pp.8; sig.: E^4; illus.
P.P.3444.af(253).

Headed: Iunij, 1621. 97. With other news. The titlepage woodcut shows the body of Fruwein being quartered.

T114 TIJDINGHE

Tijdinghe wt s'Graven-Haghe vande PROPOSITIE aldaer ghedaen vanden Ambassadeur vanden Coninck van Vranck-rijck/Inde Vergaderinghe vande . . . Staten Generael der Ghev-nieerde Provincien. Eerst Ghedruckt den v. October. 1621. T'Hantwerpen/By Abraham Verhoeuen/[etc.] 4° pp.8; sig.Kkk^4; illus.
P.P.3444.af(292).

Headed: October, 1621. 143. With other news from Holland. The 'Proposition' is a complaint against moral and military support accorded to the Huguenots. The titlepage woodcut shows a court scene.

T115 TIJDINGHE

Tijdinghe wt weenen/ende hoe dat het Doodt Lichaem vanden kloecken Heldt/den Graue van Bucquoy, binnen de stadt vā Weenen . . . is ghebrocht/ende in Baren ghestelt/inde Kercke vande Minimen. Ouerghesedt vvt het Hoochduyts, in onse Nederlantsche sprake. Eerst Ghedruckt den 13. Augusti 1621. T'Hantwerpen, By Abraham Verhoeuen, [etc.] 4° pp.8; sig.X^4; illus.
P.P.3444.af(269).

Mainly consisting of other news from Italy, Spain, etc. The titlepage woodcut shows a fortress.

T116 TIJDINGHE

Tijdinghe wt weenen ende Praghe/met den Nombre van de principaelste Heeren/die in den Slach ghebleuen zijn/van d'een zijde ende d'ander . . . Eerst Ghedruckt den 16. December 1620. Chronographicum . . . T'Hantwerpen/By Abraham Verhoeuen, [etc.] 4° pp.8; sig.Pp^4; illus.
P.P.3444.af(161); 1480.aa.15(58).

With a satirical poem on Frederick said to have been sent from Amsterdam. The titlepage woodcut shows the assault on 'Het Casteel de Sterre ★ daer den Slach was'.

T117 TIJDINGHE

Tijdinghe wt weenen in Oostenrijck/hoe dat den Boheemschen Legher is op ghebroken by Kockezan/met den nieuwen Ghepretendeerden Coninck/door de aencompste van s'Keysers volck. Ende hoe dat den Grave van Bucquoy de stadt Plan . . . heeft inghenomen . . . Nv eerst Ghedruckt den xx. November. 1620. T'Hantwerpen/By Abraham Verhoeven . . . 1620, [etc.] 4° pp.8; sig.X^4; illus.
P.P.3444.af(140); 1480.aa.15(45).

The titlepage woodcuts show the portraits of Ferdinand II and Bucquoy.

T118 TIJDINGHEN

Tijdinghen uyt verscheyde quartieren. VVt Romen den 26. October. 1619. (col.) Gedruct by Broer Iansz. . . . den 22. Nov. 1619. fol. a single sheet
T.2423(23).

On the verso: Hoe de Crooninge den 4. deses in Prage geschiet is. Mutilated.

T119 TIJDINGHEN

Tijdinghen wt Vranckrijck eñ Duytslandt van t'ghene daer passeert. Met tydinghen vvt Hollant. Eerst Ghedruckt den 10. Meert 1621. T'Hantwerpen/by Abraham Verhoeven/[etc.] 4° pp.8; sig. (.·.)^4; illus.
P.P.3444.af(199).

Headed: Martius 1621. 33. The titlepage woodcut shows a ring and three feathers.

T120 TILENUS, Daniel

[Consideratio sententiae Jacobi Arminii de praedestinatione.] Overlegginghe Ofte proeve Van t'ghevoelen Jacobi Arminij/van de predestinatie/van de ghenade Gods/ende van de vryen wille des menschen aen de Staten van Hollant ende

West-vrieslandt van hem verclaert. Door Danielem Tilenum . . . Wt de Latijnsche sprake . . . overgheset . . . 1612. 4° sig. A-G^4
T.2242(2).

TIMANNI, Hermannus. Theses theologicae de invocatione sanctorum. 1614. *See* LINDEN, Henricus Antonides van der

TO the right high and mightie Prince, James . . . An humble supplication. 1609. *See* JACOB, Henry

T121 TOETSTEEN

Toetsteen, Waer aen mē waerlick beproeuē mach/hoe valsch ende ongefondeert/ dat zijn de leugenachtighe calumnieuse Libellen, Pasquillen ende faemroouische schriften/die door eenige Spaensche oft Iesuits gesinde/in Brabant, vlaenderen oft elders versiert/ende alhier in onse Landen gestroyt/ende in Druck ouer ghesonden werden. Midtsgaders oock onlanckx door haren fenijnighen Domphoren, haer vergift . . . teghen ons wtspouwen . . . Ghedruct . . . 1603. 4° pp.66; illus.
1608/1717.

In verse. Anonymous and without imprint; printed by Richard Schilders at Middelburg. The titlepage woodcut represents a fable which is explained in a poem on the verso. With the exlibris of V. de la Montagne.

T122 TOLL, Adrianus

DISPVTATIO INAVGVRALIS. DE PALPITATIONE CORDIS QVAM . . . Pro Gradu Doctoratus in Medicina consequendo Publice examinandam suspendit ADRIANVS TOLL . . . LVGDVNI BATAVORVM, Ex Officina Iacobi Patij . . . 1615. 4° sig. AB^4; illus.
1185.g.1(60).

With a device inscribed: Cor rectum inquirit scientiam.

T123 TOLLENAER, Jean de

HET PRIEEL DER GHEESTELICKER MELODIIE, Inhoudende veel schoone Leysenen . . . Van nieuvvs ouer-sien vermeerdert ende verbetert . . . T'HANTVVERPEN, By Hieronymus Verdussen . . . 1617. 8° pp.290; music
Music A.649.t.

Anonymous. The words are in Dutch, French or Latin. Intended for school use at Bruges. The approbation is dated 1611, the privilege 1614. A plate has been added to serve as a frontispiece, bearing the imprint of Auguste Goubaud at Brussels, ca. 1825.

T124 TONEEL

Toneel der Arminianen . . . Loopt toe loop toe 'tis boven 't mallen. [etc.] 4° pp.20; illus.
T.2422(26).

In verse. Signed: 'k Sal vvilt Godt. The titlepage is engraved and larger than the text pages. Published in 1618. With the readings 'VVagen' in l.4, 'O' Lants' in l.15, etc. on the titlepage verso, corresponding to the copy described in *Knuttel* no.2774.

T125 TORINO, Giovanni

[Ausszug der Spanischen Busspsalmen.] Den uyt-toght VAN SPINOLA, Met een PATER NOSTER Voor zijnen God met drie kroonen. Eerst in 't Hoog-duytsch beschreven Door IOHANNIS THVRYN . . . Ende nu . . . over gheset. Ghedruckt Buyten Romen in't Jaer 1620. sonder consent van den Paus. 4° sig. A^4; illus.
T.2423(29).

The titlepage woodcut shows a man, probably Spinola, in conversation with the Pope. One of the copies of the issue from which the one described in *Knuttel* no.3127 has been copied. The imprint of the German original is 'getruckt zu Rom . . . 1619'.

T126 TORNIELLUS, Augustinus

(tp.1) ANNALES SACRI, ET EX PRÆCIPVI, AB ORBE CONDITO AD EVMDEM CHRISTI PASSIONE REDEMPTVM: AVCTORE AVGVSTINO TORNIELLO . . . Ab eodem Quarta hac editione recogniti . . . aucti et locupletati. TOMVS I. ANTVERPIÆ, EX OFFICINA PLANTINIANA, Apud Balthasarem Moretum, et Viduam, Ioannis Moreti, et Io. Meursium. M.DC.XX. [etc.]
(tp.2) ANNALES SACRI . . . AVCTORE AVGVSTINO TORNIELLO . . . TOMVS II. ANTVERPIÆ, EX OFFICINA PLANTINIANA, Apud Balthasarem Moretum, et Viduam Ioannis Moreti, et Io. Meursium. M.DC.XX. [etc.] (col.1,2) ANTVERPIÆ, EX OFFICINA BALTHASARIS MORETI. M.DC.XX. fol. 2 tom.: pp.769; 720; illus., maps
3105.f.10.
The titlepages are engraved by Theodoor Galle after Rubens. Ownership inscription: Seminarium Sancti Irenaei Lugdunense.

T127 TORRES BOLLO, Diego de

[Relatione breve.] DE REBVS PERVANIS . . . DIEGHI DE TORRES . . . Commentarius, à Ioanne Hayo . . . ex Italo in Latinum conuersus. ANTVERPIAE, Ex Officina Typographica Martini Nutij . . . M.DC.IIII. 8° pp.99
867.i.36.
With additional letters by other missionaries. Ownership inscription: Sylvester Kundtmann.

T128 TORSELLINO, Orazio

DE PARTICVLIS LATINÆ ORATIONIS. HORATIO TVRSELLINO . . . Authore. Accessit recens eorum, quæ indigere videbantur, explanatio in gratiam iuuentutis Gallicanæ. DVACI, Typis BALTAZARIS BELLERI . . . 1615. 12° pp.299
1471.de.17.
Printed by the widow of Laurence Kellam at Douai?

T129 TORSELLINO, Orazio

DE VITA B. FRANCISCI XAVERII . . . LIBRI SEX. HORATII TVRSELLINI . . . AB EODEM AVCTI ET RECOGNITI, in hac vltima editione. CAMERACI, Ex Officina IOANNIS RIVERII . . . M.DC.XXI. [etc.] 12° pp.550
863.b.21.

T130 TORSELLINO, Orazio

[Historiae Lauretanae libri quinque.] THE HISTORY OF OVR B. LADY OF LORETO. TRĀSLATED out of Latyn into English. Imprinted . . . 1608. 8° pp.540[541]; illus.
1482.a.39; C.26.h.6.
The author's dedication superscribed: Horatius Tursellinus. The translator's dedication and preface signed: T.P., i.e. Thomas Price. The titlepage is engraved. It and the illustration signed: Guil. du Tielt fe. The page numeration 153 is used on both recto and verso of the leaf. Without imprint; published by the English College press at St. Omer. The copy at 1482.a.39 with the exlibris of the Guildhall Library, London. In it a plate has been inserted, signed: Mich. Snyders excud. The copy at C.26.h.6 has manuscript notes and is cropped.

TORTUS, Matthaeus; pseudonym of Roberto Bellarmino. *See* ROBERT Bellarmino; Saint

TOSTATO RIBERA, Alfonso, de Madrigal; Bishop. Aenigmatum sacrorum pentas. 1621. *See* LEANDER de Sancto Martino. Otium.

T131 TOURNEUR, Cyril

[The revenger's tragedy.] WRAECK-GIERIGERS Treur-spel. Op de Reghel. De dulle woeste mensch . . . blijft . . . ellendelijcke steken. t'AMSTELREDAM, Ghedruckt by Paulus van Ravesteyn . . . 1618. 4° pp.62; illus.
11755.bb.81(3).

Anonymous. Translated by Theodore Rodenburgh, with his 'Nobilitas' device as titlepage woodcut and his motto 'Chi sara sara' at the end of the dedication. With a full-page woodcut showing the emblem of the 'Eglentier' chamber of rhetoric.

T132 TRAGEDIE

TRAGEDIE De L'empereur Anastase EXTRAICTE DV 3. TOME DE Baronius aux Annales Ecclesiasticques. Que sera representes par les estudians de la grande Escole mardy prochain le 3. de Iuilet 1618 . . . au Seminaire le Monseig. de Reuerendiss. & Illust. Archeuesque. A MALINES, Imprime par HENRY IAEY . . . 1618. 4° sig. A^4
11735.e.3.
A synopsis.

T133 TRAGICOMEDIE

TRAGICOMEDIE DE L'EMPEREVR HENRY ET KVNEGVNDE, Representée par les estudiants de la Compagnie de IESVS, à Malines, le 5. Iuillet. 1616. EN ANVERS, Chez les heritiers de feu MARTINVS NVTIVS, & IEAN DE MEVRS . . . MDC.XVI. 4° sig. A^4
11735.e.1.
A synopsis.

T134 TRAGICOMEDIE

TRAGICOMEDIE SACREE, Intitulée LE BIEN-HEVREVX IGNACE DE LOYOLA, OU ANTI-LVTHERE. En laquelle se declarent le conseil & prouidence de Dieu, selon laquelle il a excité vne nouuelle milice de IESVS, soubs la banniere du Capitaine Ignace: & plus outre si represente le miserable estat de la Saincte Eglise Catholicque Romaine, du Christianisme, & siecle corrompu . . . Sera representée au College de la Compagnie de IESVS, par les Escolliers dudit College en Bruxelles, deuant noz Princes serenissimes, le 2. iour d'Aougst, pour la premiere fois, & pour la seconde, le 3. du mesme mois, anno 1610. A BRVXELLES, Chez Rutger Velpius & Hubert Antoon . . . 1610. 4° sig. AB^4
860.f.19(2).
A synopsis.

T135 TRAGICOMEDIE

[Tragicomedie sacrée, intitulée Le bien-heureux Ignace de Loyola.] Mera DeLIratIo Ies VItaLIs, EENE H. TRAGI-COMEDIE Ge-Intituleert Den Salighen Ignatius de Loyola, OFT ANTI-LVTHER . . . Vertoont in t'Collegie der Iesuyten door de Scholieren desselfs tot Bruessel . . . Ende nu Overgheset uyt den Fransoyschen Exemplare, ghedruckt tot Bruessel, by Rutgeert Velpius, ende Huybrecht Antoni . . . 1610. Gedruct buyten Roomen sonder Privilegie der Iesuyten . . . 1610. 4° sig. A^4B^2
T.2421(14).
A translation of the preceding, with an anti-Jesuit commentary and an additional 'refrain', not found in the French text. Published in the United Provinces.

TRANSLAET uyt den Hoochduytsche van de Ligue . . . die de Catholijcke vorsten van Duytslandt . . . ghemaeckt . . . hebben. 1610. *See* GERMANY. League of Würzburg, 1610. Newe Zeitung.

TRANSLAET vanden brief des Conincks van groot Britaengien. 1611. *See* JAMES I, King [Speeches and letters]

TRANSLAET vanden brief gheschreuen by de . . . Borgher-meesteren ende Raedt der stadt van Franckfort. 1620. *See* FRANKFURT ON THE MAIN [21.8.1620]

T136 TRANSYLVANIA

[24.8.1620] Den Eedt met dē welcken Bethlem Gabor . . . hem verplicht oft verbonden heeft aen dē Turc tot Cassouw . . . Met de Belofte die den Turck ghedaen heeft aen Bethlem Gabor. Ouergesedt vvt de Poolsche sprake, in onse Nederlantsche Tale. Nv eerst Ghedruckt den 9. Iunij 1621. T'Hantwerpen/By Abraham Verhoeuen/[etc.] 4° pp.8; sig.A[4]; illus.
P.P.3444.af(242).
Headed: Iunij, 1621. 86. The titlepage woodcut shows an imaginary portrait of 'Soliman'.

T137 TRAVERS, Walter

[Ecclesiasticae disciplinae, et Anglicanae Ecclesiae ab illa aberrationis, plena . . . explicatio.] A FVLL AND PLAINE DECLARATION OF ECCLESIASTICAL DISCIPLINE OVT OF the word of God, and of the declining of the Church of England from the same. Reprinted . . . 1617. 4° pp.109[106]
4106.b.46.
Anonymous and anonymously translated by Thomas Cartwright. Without imprint; printed by William Brewster at Leiden.

A TREATISE of divine worship. 1604. *See* BRADSHAW, William

A TREATISE of faith. 1614. *See* PIERCY, John

A TREATISE of penance. 1617. *See* STANEY, William

A TREATISE of the Third Order of S. Francis. 1617. *See* STANEY, William. A treatise of penance.

A TREATISE of three conversions of England. 1603,04. *See* PERSONS, Robert

A TREATISE tending to mitigation. 1607. *See* PERSONS, Robert

Een TREFFELIJCK ende wonderlijck vrouwen-lof. 1611. *See* AGRIPPA, Henricus Cornelius

T138 TREFFELIJCKE

Eene treffelijcke tsamensprekinghe tusschen den Paus ende Coninck van Spangien/belanghende den Pays met ons Lieden aen te gaene. 4° sig.A[4]
T.1713(20).
Published in the United Provinces, probably in 1607.

T139 TRELCATIUS, Lucas

DISPVTATIONVM THEOLOGICARVM VIGESIMA, DE LEGE ET EVANGELIO, Quam . . . Sub Præsidio . . . DD. LUCÆ TRELCATII . . . suscipiet IACOBVS VIOLATIVS . . . LVGDVNI BATAVORVM, Ex Officinâ Ioannis Patii . . . D.M.CII. 4° sig.V[6]
4376.de.16(32).
Cropped.

T140 TRELCATIUS, Lucas

DISPVTATIONVM THEOLOGICARVM VIGESIMA-OCTAVA, DE ORATIONE, Quam . . . Præside . . . D. LUCA TRELCATIO . . . publicè examinandam proponit IOANNES FELIX . . . LUGDUNI BATAVORVM, Ex Officinâ Ioannis Patii . . . M.D.CIV. 4° sig.Ee[4]
4376.de.16(41).

T141 TRELCATIUS, Lucas

THESES THEOLOGICÆ DE FIDE IVSTIFICANTE, ET FIDEI IVSTIFICATIONE, Quas . . . Sub Præsidio . . . D. LUCÆ TRELCATII . . . Publicè tuebitur IOHANNES TEXTOR . . . LUGDUNI BATAVORVM, Ex Officinâ Ioannis Patii . . . M.D.CIII. 4° sig.AB[4]
4376.de.16(64).
Cropped.

T142 TRELCATIUS, Lucas

THESES THEOLOGICÆ DE Iugi Christianorum sacrificio contra Missam Papalem, quas . . . Sub Præsidio . . . D. LUCÆ TRELCATII . . . defendere conabitur IOANNES GODETVS . . . LVGDVNI BATAVORVM, Ex Officinâ Ioannis Patii . . . M.D.CIII. 4° sig.A[4]

4376.de.16(58).

Cropped.

T143 TRENT. Council of Trent

SACROSANCTI ET OECVMENICI CONCILII TRIDENTINI . . . CANONES ET DECRETA. Recèns accesserunt . . . D. IOANNIS SOTEALLI . . . & HORATII LVTII . . . vtilissimæ . . . annotationes . . . Additæ . . . sunt . . . PII IIII. Pontificis Maximi Bullæ, vnà cum . . . Indice. ANTVERPIÆ, EX OFFICINA PLANTINIANA, Apud Viduam & Filios Io. Moreti. M.DC.XV. 8° pp.269

1568/8644.

T144 TRENT. Council of Trent

DECISIONES ET DECLARATIONES Illustrissimorum CARDINALIVM sacri CONCILII TRIDENTINI Interpretum, Quæ in quarto volumine Decisionum ROTÆ ROMANÆ habentur . . . ab infinitis mendis repurgatæ . . . secundum correctionem factam per . . . PETRVM DE MARZYLLA . . . Cum indice . . . Opera & studio D. IOANNIS DE GALLEMART. DVACI Ex Typographia BALTAZARIS BELLERI . . . 1615. [etc.] 8° pp.427

C.48.c.14(1).

In a binding bearing the arms of Jacques Auguste de Thou.

T145 TRES-GENTIL

Tres-gentil Traicté DE LA CVRE, OV GVERISON DE l'Apostume, laquelle infecte les Cœurs & Sens de l'Homme. Nouvellement mis en Lumiere, Par G.D.T. A Amsterdam Imprimé par Paul de Ravesteyn . . . 1611. 4° sig.A[4]B[2]

440.l.37.

On love.

TREUR-BLY-EYNDE-SPEL van Alexander. 1618. *See* RODENBURGH, Theodore

TREUR-BLY-EYNDE-SPEL vande trouwe liefd van Cypriaen en Oriana. 1618. *See* GUARINI, Giovanni Battista [Il pastor fido. Dutch]

A TREVVE description of the nobill race of the Stewards. 1603. *See* JONSTONUS, Johannes; Abredoniensis

T146 TRIGAULT, Élie Philippe

PETIT DISCOVRS ESCRIT PAR ELIE TRIGAVLT . . . Contenant plusieurs belles particularitez de son voyage aux Indes Orientales. A VALENCIENNE, De l'Imprimerie de IAN VERVLIET . . . M.DC.XX. 8° pp.44

4767.aaa.13(2).

Edited by Nicolas Trigault.

T147 TRIGAULT, Nicolas

COPYE DES BRIEFS GHESCHREVEN VANDEN E.P. NICOLAES TRIGAVLT . . . Aenden E.P. FRANCISCVM FLERON . . . Wt Goa in Oost-Indien op Kersmis-auont. 1607. VVAER IN VERHAELT VVORT de vermeerderinghe des Christen gheloofs in Indien, Chinen, Iaponien, &c. MITSGADERS, Het belech van Mozambic, Malaca, Amboin . . . door de Hollantsche Vlote. T'HANTVVERPEN, By Daniel Vervliet . . . 1609. [etc.] 8° pp.79

4766.aaa.3.

T148 TRIGAULT, Nicolas

[Due lettere annue della Cina.] LITTERÆ SOCIETATIS IESV E REGNO SINARVM AD R.P. CLAVDIVM AQVAVIVAM . . . Annorum M.DC.X. & M.DC.XI. A. R.P. NICOLAO TRIGAVTIO . . . conscriptæ. ANTVERPIÆ, Apud PETRVM & IOANNEM BELLEROS. M.DC.XV. 8° pp.227

4767.e.11; 867.f.15(2); 867.f.5(2).

The translation sometimes, probably wrongly, attributed to Andreas Schottus. None of the copies contains the plate described in *Sommervogel* s.v. Trigault, Nicolas no.3, as occurring on p.iii. Ownership inscription in the copy at 867.f.5(2): Isaacus Gruterus.

T149 TRIGAULT, Nicolas

VITA GASPARIS BARZÆI . . . AVCTORE P.NIC. TRIGAVLT . . . ANTVERPIÆ Ex Officina Ioach. Trognæsij . . . M.DC.X. 8° pp.338

862.h.7.

T150 TRIGLAND, Jacobus; the Elder

CHRISTELYCKE Ende nootwendighe verclaringhe, Waerinne . . . verclaert wordt/ wat in seecker formulier van eenicheyt/uyt gegheven onder den tydel [*sic*] van Resolutie vande Doorluchtige &c. Met Godes Woort ende met de Leere der Ghereformeerde Kercken over een compt/ofte daer van verschilt. Versterckt Met d'Authoriteyt der H. Schrift . . . GEDRUCKT, Voor een lief-hebber der Waerheydt . . . M.DC.XV. 4° pp.451

T.2245(2).

Anonymous and without imprint. The republication in 1616 of pp.24–29 with the text of the 'Resolutie' refers to their earlier publication 'at The Hague', referring to the official issue there of the text, not its inclusion in this work. Printed by Nicolaas Biestkens at Amsterdam?

T151 TRIGLAND, Jacobus; the Elder

CLARE AENVVYSINGE HOE Iohannes Utenbogaert hem gheensins en suyvert noch verontschuldight in sijn . . . Clare Justificatie/van die ontrouwigheyt ende onbehoorlijcke maniere van doen die Iacobus Triglandius . . . in sijn boeck Verdediginghe . . . hem naecktelijck hadde verthoont . . . Ghemaeckt: Door IACOBVM TRIGLANDIVM . . . t'AMSTERDAM, By Marten Jansz. Brandt . . . 1616. 4° pp.80

T.2246(10).

T152 TRIGLAND, Jacobus; the Elder

Geessel Om uyt te dryven den ARMINIAENSCHEN Quel-Gheest. By een ghebracht om te bedwinghen de vermetene curieusheyt van eenen onbekenden Vrager/ noopende de Predestinatie . . . in een boecxken dat hy den Quel-gheest gheintituleert heeft . . . t'AMSTELREDAM, Voor Marten Jansz. Brant . . . 1618. 4° pp.32

T.2248(46).

Anonymous. Printed by Paulus van Ravesteyn at Amsterdam.

TRIGLAND, Jacobus; the Elder. Klaer ende grondich teghen-vertoogh. 1617. [Sometimes attributed to Jacobus Trigland.] *See* KLAER

T153 TRIGLAND, Jacobus; the Elder

ONTMOETER Bejeghenende DEN Voor-bode van de Antwoordt op seker boecxken gheintituleert Ontrouwe des Valschen Waerschouwers . . . GESTELT By forme van t'samen-sprekinghe . . . t'AMSTERDAM, By Marten Jansz. Brandt . . . 1617. 4° pp.32

T.2247(51).

Anonymous. For the 'Voor-bode' *see* DWINGLO, Bernardus. With the large device signed P-S, identified by *Nagler* no.3040 as P. [C.] van Sichem. Printed by Nicolaas Biestkens at Amsterdam?

T154 TRIGLAND, Jacobus; the Elder

ONTROUVVE Des valschen Vvaerschouwers/Die teghen een seker boecxken/ ghenaemt Stant vande hedendaeghsche Gheschillen/als tegen een Malitieus . . . gheschrift . . . is uytghevaren. Waer by oock is ghevoeght een Claer Bewijs vande dvvalinghen Grevinchovii. MIDTSGADERS De Handelinghe D. Festi ende M. Episcopij, voor de Curateuren ende Heeren tot Leyden. t'AMSTERDAM, By Marten Jansz. Brandt . . . 1616. 4° pp.54
1608/4403.

Partly in verse. Anonymous. With the large device, signed: P-S; i.e. P. or Ph. van Sichem?

T155 TRIGLAND, Jacobus; the Elder

OORSPRONCK VANDE Swarigheden/ende Voor-slagh tot reddinghe in de Kercken van Hollandt. DOOR EVBVLVM EIRENEPHILVM . . . t'AMSTERDAM, By Marten Jansz. Brandt . . . 1617. 4° pp.16
T.2247(37).

Pseudonymous. With the large device, signed: P-S, i.e. P. or Ph. [C.] van Sichem? Printed by Nicolaas Biestkens at Amsterdam?

T156 TRIGLAND, Jacobus; the Elder

Den Recht-gematichden CHRISTEN. Ofte Vande Moderatie/ende verdrachsaemheyt . . . Door IACOBUM TRIGLANDIUM . . . Uytgegeven door een Liefhebber der Waerheyt . . . t'AMSTELDAM Ghedruckt by Paulus van Ravesteyn . . . 1615. 4° pp.67
T.2245(17).

TRIGLAND, Jacobus; the Elder. Tafel, begrijpende kortelijck het groot . . . verschil. 1616. [Sometimes attributed to Jacobus Trigland.] *See* TAFEL

TRIGLAND, Jacobus; the Elder. Verdediging Van den Recht-gematichden Christen. 1616. [Sometimes attributed to Jacobus Trigland.] *See* VERDEDIGING

T157 TRIOMFE

Triomfe vande Doorluchtige Pr. van ORANGIEN, ende het gheheele huys van Nassau, so vvel overleden als teghenwoordigh. Met bewijs van de schandelicke daden ende schriften/in wat Balans ofte Weeghschael de Lasteraers/dese Doorluchtige Pr . . . omspringen . . . By C.Ar.G. . . . 1618. 4° pp.24[32]; illus.
11555.e.40(1).

Partly in verse. The titlepage woodcut shows an emblem of the House of Orange with the mottoes 'Honi soit qui mali [*sic*] pense', 'Concordie res parvae crescunt' and 'Een goet Orangien . . . Boom/Wast Weder [etc.]', also used in a cut back version for 'TRIUMPHE tot Amsterdam' of the same year, published by Uldrick Cornelisz Honthorst at Leiden, and therefore possibly also published by him? *Knuttel* no.2508 reads the initials of the imprint as C.Az.G.

Il TRIONFO di Dori. 1614. *See* PHALÈSE, Pierre

TRIPLICI nodo, triplex cuneus. 1608. *See* JAMES I; King

TRITHEIM, Johann. Curiositas regia. 1621. *See* LEANDER de Sancto Martino. Otium.

T158 TRIUM

Trium Linguarum DICTIONARIVM TEUTONICAE, LATINAE, GALLICAE. Omnibus aliis, hujus formæ Dictionariis multò locupletius, & majori hactenus diligentia castigatum & correctum . . . FRANEKERÆ, APVD AEGIDIVM RADAEVM . . . M.D.CIIII. 8° sig.$\star^4$A-Y^8Z^4
628.c.1.

Preface printed in civilité. Ownership inscription: Jōhes Morris empt. Lugd. Batauorū.

T159 TRIUMPH

DEN TRIVMPH Vanden Oorloch/ende de Mis-prijsinghe Vanden Peys. Seer ghenoechlijck ende corts-wijlich om te lesen. Dit Iaer sesthienhondert en acht, Wort den Oorloch bouen den Peys gheacht. Int Jaer ons Heere Jesu Christi. 1608. 4° sig.(∴)^4

T.2420(9).

Printed in columns. With a quotation from Petrarch in Dutch. Corresponding to the copy described in *Knuttel* no. 1479.

T160 TRIUMPHANTE

Triumphante ende Blijde Incomste binnen ANTVVERPEN, Vande Ambassadeurs/ van wegen de Coninghen van Vranckrijck ende Enghelant. Opt stuck vande Vrede-handel . . . Gheschiet den negensten February. 1609. Na de Copije: t'Hantwerpen. By Anthoni Ballo . . . 1609. Men vintse te coop: tot Dordrecht/By Philips Jansz. [etc.] 4° 2 unsigned leaves

T.2421(7).

Sometimes tentatively attributed to Pieter Rogiers.

T161 TRIUMPHE

TRIUMPHE Tot Amsterdam/Over het Incomen vanden . . . Vorst Mauritius Prince van Orangien, Met een . . . uytlegginghe op de verthooninge van alle Camers/ gheschiet den 23. 24. 25. May . . . 1618 . . . Tot Leyden, By Uldrick Cornelisz. Honthorst. 4° sig. A^4; illus.

T.2248(61).

The titlepage woodcut shows an emblem of the house of Orange in woodcut, with the motto 'Tandem fit surculus arbor' in letterpress, cut back from the original as used in 'TRIOMFE vande . . . Pr. van Orangien' which is entered above.

T162 TROGNAESIUS, Alexander Carolus

VETERVM POETARVM COMPARATIONES In vsum Studiosæ Iuuentutis collectæ. ANTVERPIÆ Ex Officina Ioach. Trognæsij. M.DC.X. [etc.] 8° pp. 512

11824.b.31.

The compiler's dedication signed: Alex. Carol. Trognaesius.

T163 TROGUS POMPEIUS

IVSTINI EPITOMA HISTORIARVM PHILIPPICARVM TROGI POMPEII. EX OFFICINA PLANTINIANA RAPHELENGII, M.D.CXIII. 32° pp. 284

C.20.f.31.

Published at Leiden. From the travelling library of Sir Julius Caesar.

T164 TROUHERTIGE

Trouhertige waerschouwinghe aen alle Christelijcke Potentaten ende Overicheden: teghens de t'samenspreeckinghe ende het discours des Paus Pauli/ Philippi Coninc van Spaengien/ende d'Ertshertoghe Ferdinandus/hoemen Duytslant overvallen ende bedwinghen mochten/Van der societeyt Iesu tot Munchen ende Inghelstadt . . . uytghegaen . . . Overgheset uyt den Hoochduytsche in onser Nederlandtsche Tale. Nae de Copie van Mayborgh/1608. 4° sig. A^4

T.2420(7).

T165 TROUHERTIGE

Trouhertige waerschouwinghe aen alle Christelijcke Potentaten . . . Nae de Copie van Magdeburgh/1608. 4° sig. A^4

T.2420(17); T.2420(18).

Another issue of the preceding, with only the copy imprint in different spelling and the last word of the text and the word 'Finis' in a different setting from the preceding.

T166 TROUHERTIGHE

TROVHERTIGHE VERMANINGHE aen alle Swangere ende Barende Vroutgens: aen alle Ouders die kinderen teelen ende ter Doope presenteren . . . mitsgaeders aen alle Predikanten als Festum, Colonium, Hermannum, &c. wanneer zy kinderkens krijghen/om den H. Doop aen de selfde te verrichten . . . Anno 1618. 4° pp.14
T.2248(45).

Wrongly attributed to Festus Hommius in *Knuttel* no.2525. With quotations in Latin, French, Dutch and English.

TROUHERTIGHE vermaninghe aen het vereenichde Nederlandt. 1605. *See* REYD, Everard van

T167 TRUE

A TRVE, MODEST, AND IVST DEFENCE OF THE PETITION FOR REFORMATION, EXHIBITED TO THE KINGS MOST EXCELLENT MAIESTIE . . . Imprinted 1618. 8° pp.240; tables
3935.a.15.

Without imprint; printed by William Brewster at Leiden. A copy with the last leaf of the preliminaries in the setting with 'bi regis fides' at the beginning of the sixth line from the bottom, cf. *STC* no.6469. With the exlibris of Henry Francis Lyte.

T168 TRUE

[A true relation of a wonderfull sea fight.] A notable And wonderfull SEA-FIGHT Betweene Two great and vvel-mounted SPANISH SHIPPS, And a Small and not very well provyded ENGLISH SHIPP. VVho par force vvas constreyned to enter into this conflict. AT AMSTERDAM, Printed by George Veseler . . . 1621. 4° sig.A[4]
1093.b.84.

An abridgment of the edition entitled 'A true relation of a wonderfull sea fight', published at London.

T169 TRUER-DICHTEN

TRVER-DICHTEN Over het iammerlijck Om-brenghen DES Edelen ende vvijdtberoemden Helds IOHAN VAN OLDENBARNEVELT . . . Gedruckt . . . 1620. 4° sig.A[4]
T.2422(37).

The 'Liedeken' on sig.A3v-A4r signed: By my,, die ick zy. The 'Iaar-dicht' on sig. A4r signed: D.O.M. Without imprint; printed by Abraham Verhoeven at Antwerp?

TRY before you trust. 1609. *See* HIGGONS, Theophilus. The first motive.

TSAMENSPREECKINGHE van drie persoonen. 1602. *See* ROLWAGHEN, Jan Claessen

T'SAMEN-SPREKINGHE tusschen dry princen. 1621. *See* COLLOQUIUM trium principum.

Een TSAMENSPREKINGHE van twee boersche persoonen. 1609. *See* HICHTUM, Johan van

T170 TUKE, Thomas

[The high-way to heaven.] DE Conincklicke wech tot den Hemel . . . Tsamen ghevoecht . . . eerst in de Enghelsche tale door Thomam Tuke, ende nu . . . over-geset door Henricum Hexham. Tot Dordrecht. By Joris Waters . . . 1611. 4° pp.87
T.2241(17).

T171 TULDENUS, Diodorus

DIODORI TVLDENI . . . DE PRINCIPIIS IVRISPRVDENTIÆ LIBRI IV . . . LOVANII, Apud Philippum Dormalium 1621. 8° pp.189
500.b.26.

T172 TUNINGIUS, Gerardus

APOPHTHEGMATA GRÆCA, LATINA, ITALICA, GALLICA, HISPANICA: collecta à GERÆRDO TVNINGIO . . . EX OFFICINA PLANTINIANA RAPHELENGII, M.D.CIX. 8° pp.95, 100, 136, 116, 104
G.8901.
Published at Leiden.

TURSELLINUS, Horatius. *See* TORSELLINO, Orazio

TWELVE generall arguments, proving that the ceremonies imposed upon the ministers of the Gospell in England . . . are unlawfull. 1605. *See* BRADSHAW, William

TWE-SPRAACK vande Nederduitsche letterkunst. 1614. *See* SPIEGEL, Hendrick Laurensz

TWO letters or embassies. 1620. *See* BOHEMIA. States [1620]

TYDINGHE. *See* also TIJDINGHE

T173 TYDINGHE

Tydinghe wt Dresden/hoe dat die van Hooch ende Neder Slesien hun als Ghetrouwe Ondersaeten aende Roomsche Keyserlijcke Majesteyt hebben over ghegheven. Met tijdinghe wt den Paltz/hoe dat die van Worms hebben in brandt ghesteken Westhouen ende Oosthoeven. Ouergeset vvt den Hooch-Duytsche in onse Nederlantsche Tale. Eerst ghedruckt den 26. Meert. 1621. T'Hantwerpen/By Abraham Verhoeuen/[etc.] 4° pp.8; sig.(?)^4; illus.
P.P.3444.af(211).
Headed: Martius. 1621. 47. With other news. The titlepage woodcut shows a burning city with fighting troops.

TYPOGRAPHIA PLANTINIANA. *See* OFFICINA PLANTINIANA

T174 TYPUS

TYPVS ÆNIGMATICVS TEMPORIS. Vorbildung von der Zeit. obl. fol. a single sheet
Cup.651.e(58).
An engraving, unsigned, but sometimes tentatively attributed to Claes Jansz Visscher. Inscriptions are in Latin, Dutch or German. With explanatory text in German. The whole a satire on the various princes claiming Jülich. Published, if by Visscher, at Amsterdam, in 1610?

TYPUS occasionis. 1603. *See* DAVID, Jan

T175 T'ZAMEN-SPREKINGE

T'ZAMEN-SPREKINGE Tusschen Eenen Predikant ende Leerlingh/over de huydensdaegsche Verschillen/ende de heftige Procedueren die ter oorzake van dese verschillen/van de ghene diemen Gomaristen of Schuerganghers naemt/woorden [*sic*] by-der-handt ghenomen. Ghedruct . . . 1617. (col.) Ghedruct by Philips Philipsz. 1617. 4° pp.43
T.2247(7).
Published at Rotterdam.

U

UBEDA, Francisco de; pseudonym of Andres Perez. *See* PEREZ, Andres

U1 UFANO, Diego

TRATADO DELA ARTILLERIA YVSO [*sic*] DELLA PLATICADO POR EL CAPITAN diego ufano

TRATADO
DELA ARTILLERIA
YVSO DELLA
PLATICADO POR EL CAPITAN
diego usano
En las Guerras de flandes
EN BRVSSELAS
EN CASA DE IVAN MOMARTE
IMPRESOR IVRADO AÑO DEL
SEÑOR
1612
CON PRIVILEGIO

En las Guerras de flandes. EN BRVSSELAS EN CASA DE IVAN MOMARTE . . . 161Z [*sic*] [etc.] 4° pp.423: plates; illus.
1480.bb.33.

The titlepage is engraved, obviously by an engraver who did not know Spanish. The engraved view of Hulst above the dedication has inscriptions in Latin, Dutch and French. P.[424] bears the engraved emblem of the author. With woodcuts dated 'Deziembre 1612'. With three exlibris, one armorial bearing the motto 'Nemo me impune lacessit'; one bearing the motto 'Sero sed serio'; the third of Newbattle Abbey Library.

U2 UFANO, Diego

[Tratado dela artilleria.] ARTILLERIE, C'est a dire: VRAYE INSTRVCTION DE L'ARTILLERIE ET DE TOVTES SES APPARTENANCES . . . Avec vn enseignement de preparer toutes sortes des feux artificiels . . . Le tout recueilly de l'experience, es guerres du Pays-bas & publié en langue Espagnolle. PAR DIEGO UFANO . . . Mais maintenant traduit en langue Françoise, & orné de belles & necessaires figures. A ZVTPHEN, Chez ANDRE D'AELST . . . 1621. fol. pp.144,6: plates; illus.
M.L.f.10.

The text is that of the French Frankfurt edition of 1614, for which Theodor de Bry copied the original plates, now copied from these for this edition, bearing the same French and German inscriptions. The catchword 'Indice' at the foot of the last text page is not followed by an index, but by a supplement which has been inserted in its place. Printed by Paulus van Ravesteyn at Amsterdam, with the 'Nobilitas' device of Theodore Rodenburgh on the titlepage as used by this printer and with some use of civilité.

U3 ULTRALAEUS, David

TRACTATVS MEDICVS PER-BREVIS. In quo succinctè . . . disputatur an puerperæ liceat exhibere moschum. A DAVIDE VLTRALÆO conscriptus. MIDDELBVRGI, Excudebat Isaacus Schilders, 1613. 8° sig.A^8B^4
1176.b.4(2).

U4 UNIVERSEL

Vniversel GAZETTE Des Christendoms, Jnde Maent van December 1621. Eerst Ghedruckt den 3. December 1621. T'Hantwerpen/By Abraham Verhoeuen/[etc.] 4° pp.8; sig.A^4; illus.
P.P.3444.af(322).

Headed: December, 1621. 177. Dealing with Polish-Turkish affairs, Spain, Switzerland and Germany. The titlepage woodcuts show a framed portrait of the Emperor Ferdinand II and a somewhat larger unframed view of a fort by a river.

The UNREASONABLENESSE of the separation. 1614. *See* BRADSHAW, William

USSELINCX, Willem. For those books issued under the pseudonym Yemant Adams which have sometimes been tentatively attributed to Willem Usselincx, *see* ADAMS, Yemant

U5 USSELINCX, Willem

Bedenckinghen Over den staet vande vereenichde Nederlanden: Nopende de Zee-vaert/Coop-handel/ende de gemeyne Neeringe inde selve. Ingevalle den Peys met de Aerts-hertogen inde aen-staende Vrede-handelinge getroffen wert. Door een lief-hebber eenes oprechten ende bestandighen Vredes voorghestelt. Gedruckt . . . 1608. 4° sig.AB^4
1568/9165.

Anonymous. With a device showing the figure of Fortune with her hair at the back, but the motto 'Post occasio calva'. Corresponding to the copy described in *Knuttel* no.1438.

U6 USSELINCX, Willem

[Bedenckinghen over den staet vande vereenichde Nederlanden.] Grondich discours over desen aen-staenden Vrede-handel. 4° sig. AB^4

T.1729(9); 106.b.17.

Anonymous. Another edition of the preceding, differently set, with different spellings. The first line of the text begins 'Alzo' and ends 'vrem-'; the last line of A1r ends 'werden', with a full stop below 's' in 'dese'; without titlepage and without a catchword after the final words 'zouden komen' on B1r, corresponding to the copy described in *Knuttel* no.1439a. Published in 1608.

U7 USSELINCX, Willem

[Bedenckinghen over den staet vande vereenichde Nederlanden.] Grondich discours [etc.] 4° sig. AB^4

T.1713(21).

Anonymous. A variant of the preceding. B1 ends 'zoudē komen' and has the catchword 'te', corresponding to the copy described in *Knuttel* no.1439b. Published in 1608.

U8 USSELINCX, Willem

[Bedenckinghen over den staet vande vereenichde Nederlanden.] Grondich discours [etc.] 4° sig. AB^4

1485.h.6.

Anonymous. Another edition of the preceding, with different spelling and setting, the first line of the text beginning 'Alzoo' and ending 'vele ende', the last line of A1r ends 'werden', with a full stop below 'L' in 'Landen'; B1 ends 'zouden komen', without catchword. Corresponding to the copy described in *Knuttel* no.1440. Published in 1608.

U9 USSELINCX, Willem

Naerder Bedenckinghen, Over de zee-vaerdt/Coophandel ende Neeringhe/als mede de versekeringhe vanden Staet deser vereenichde Landen/inde teghenwoordighe Vrede-handelinghe met den Coninck van Spangnien ende de Aerts-hertoghen. Door een lies-hebber [*sic*] eenes oprechten, ende bestandighen vredes voorghestelt. Ghedruckt . . . 1608. 4° sig. A-D^{4}E^2

1486.df.2; 106.d.22.

Anonymous. In both copies the word 'verliesende' on E2v has been corrected in manuscript to 'verkiesende'.

U10 USSELINCX, Willem

Den Nederlandtschen BYE-CORF: Waer in Ghy beschreven vint/al het gene dat nu wtgegaen is/op den stilstant ofte Vrede . . . beginnende in Mey 1607 ende noch en hebben wy niet het eynde. Ende is ghestelt op een tsamen-sprekinghe/tusschen een Vlamyng ende Hollander. Noch is hier by ghevoecht/een GHEDICHT. Ter eeren des begonnen Peys . . . Jnt Iaer sesthien hondert en acht/Jeghelick na een goede Vrede wacht. 4° sig. A^4

106.d.12.

Anonymous. The poem signed: Iemant Adams.

USSELINCX, Willem. Schuyt-praetgens, op de vaert naer Amsterdam. 1608. [Sometimes attributed to Willem Usselincx.] *See* SCHUYT-PRAETGENS

U11 USSELINCX, Willem

Vertoogh, hoe nootwendich, nut ende profitelick het sy voor de vereenighde Nederlanden te behouden de Vryheyt van te handelen op West-Indien, Inden vrede metten Coninck van Spaignen. 4° sig. AB^{4}C^2

8244.bb.21.

Anonymous. The date '1608' has been added in manuscript to this title at the head of A1r.

UTENBOGAERT, Jan. *See* WTENBOGAERT, Jan

U12 UTRECHT
[31.3.1617] Publicatie/ende Interdictie Vande E. MAGISTRAET DER STADT VTRECHT, Tegens De ghenen die, onder decksel vande Gereformeerde Religie, In de Christelijcke Gemeynte ende Republijcke der selver Stadt poogen Scheuringe ende Onrust aen te rechten. T'VTRECHT, By Salomon de Roy . . . 1617. 4° sig. A^4
T.2247(19).
Issued 31 March 1617.

U13 UTRECHT
[28.10.1619] PLACCAET, Ghepubliceert binnen Vytrecht, den 28 October, 1619. 4° sig.∴^{2}; illus.
T.2249(27).
An extract, ending with the catchword 'PLAC'. Dealing with the Remonstrants at Utrecht. The titlepage woodcut shows the arms of Utrecht.

U14 UTRECHT. Province of Utrecht. Staten
[28.8.1612] Christelijcke KERCKEN-ORDENINGE Der Stadt, Steden, ende Landen van VTRECHT. Ghearresteert binnen Vtrecht den XXVIII Augusti XVI$^{C.}$XII. 4° ff.27
T.2242(15).

U15 UTRECHT. Province of Utrecht. Staten
[17.9.1617] ANTVVOORDT Van de . . . Staten van Uytrecht/op de Propositien/ ghedaen van weghen de . . . Staten Generael . . . sijne Ex^{cie}. ende den Raedt van Staten/in September lestleden. Binnen de Stadt van Uytrecht . . . 1617. 4° sig. A^4
700.h.25(8); T.2247(19*).
Issued 17 September 1617. Printed by Salomon de Roy at Utrecht?

UYTTOCH van t'ghevoelen der Predicanten tot Campen. 1618. *See* GOSWINIUS, Thomas

UYTVAERT van Willem Ludwigh Grave tot Nassau. 1620. *See* FEDDES, Pieter

V

V1 VAECK-VERDRYVER
DEN Vaeck-verdryver van de Swaermoedighe Gheesten. Vertellende Vermakelijcke Kluchtjens . . . Ghedruckt t'Haerlem by Adriaen Rooman, Voor Ian Evertsz. Kloppenburgh . . . 1620. (col.) Ghedruckt t'HAERLEM, by Adriaen Rooman . . . 1621. 8° pp.340
12304.c.39.
Partly in verse. Published at Amsterdam.

VAENIUS, Otho. *See* VEEN, Otto van

V2 VAERNEWYCK, Marcus van
[Den spieghel der Nederlandscher audheyt.] DE HISTORIE VAN BELGIS diemen anders noemen mach: den SPIEGHEL DER NEderlantscher oudheyt. Waer inne men sien mach . . . veel wonderlijcke gheschiedenissen/die van alle oude tijden/over al die weerelt gheschiet zyn: maer bysonder in die Nederlanden . . . oock van Enghelandt/Schotlandt/Vranckerijcke/Duytschlandt . . . Ghemaeckt deur MARCVS VAN VAERNEWIICK . . . Nu van nieus in veel plaetsen ghecorrigeert/ verbetert/ende met noch een . . . Tafel verciert. TOT BRVSSEL, By Fernande de

Hoeymaker . . . M.DC.XIX. [etc.] (col.=sig.★★7v) Typis Hierônymi Verdussen. fol. ff.CXLV: plate; illus., port.
1312.k.16.
The editor's dedication signed: Ioannes Schepperus. The engraved portrait of the author signed: Petrus de Jode. The woodcut illustrations include the arms of cities. Printed at Antwerp.

Il VAGO alboreto de madrigali. 1620. *See* PHALÈSE, Pierre

V3 VALERIUS MAXIMUS
VALERIVS MAXIMVS, Editionis Pighianæ. EX OFFICINA PLANTINIANA RAPHELENGII, M.D.CXII. 16° pp.399
C.20.f.82; 588.a.30.
Published at Leiden. Printed in italics throughout. The copy at 588.a.30 is imperfect; wanting the titlepage. The copy at C.20.f.82 from the travelling library of Sir Julius Caesar.

V4 VALERIUS MAXIMUS
VALERII MAXIMI. DICTORVM FACTORVMQVE MEMORABILIVM. LIBRI IX. INFINITIS MENDIS EX VETERVM exemplarium fide repurgati, atque in meliorem ordinem restituti, per STEPHANVM PIGHIVM . . . Accessêre in fine IVSTI LIPSI Notæ. ANTVERPIÆ, Apud Ioannem Keerbergium . . . M.DC.XV. 12° pp.474
1136.b.2.
The initials in this copy have been illuminated. Ownership inscriptions: Sum N: Mulerii 1684; Petrus Mulerius 1681; Sum Petri Mulerii 1691; W.W.N.; W. Macqueen.

V5 VALERIUS MAXIMUS
VALERII MAXIMI DICTORVM FACTORVMQVE MEMORABILIVM LIBRI IX . . . repurgati, atque . . . restituti, per STEPHANVM PIGHIVM . . . Breues Notæ IVSTI LIPSI [*sic*]. ANTVERPIÆ, Apud MARTINVM NVTIVM, & FRATRES . . . 1621. (col.) ANTVERPIÆ, Ex Typographiâ Henrici Ærtssij. M.DC.XXI. 8° pp.41 [411]
588.b.23.
Another issue of one bearing the imprint and device of Aertssius on the titlepage recorded in the *Bibliographia Belgica* no. V166.

V6 VALIGNANO, Alessandro
[Lettera de' 10 ottobre 1599.] (tp.1) DISCOVRS DES CHOSES REMARQVABLES ADVENVES AV ROYAVME du Iappon . . . EN DEVX LETTRES ENVOYEES au R.P. Claude Aquauiua . . . DV X. d'Octobre . . . M.D.XCIX. ET XXV. Feburier . . . M.DCI. A ARRAS, De l'Imprimerie de Robert Maudhuy . . . M.D.C.IIII. [etc.]
(tp.2=p.85) SVPPLEMENT DE LA LETTRE DE L'AN MIL SIX CENS . . . Escript . . . Par . . . Valentin Carauaille . . . Et nouuellement tourné d'Italien en François PAR . . . FRANÇOIS SOLIER . . . De l'Imprimerie de Robert Maudhuy. 12° pp.211
866.a.1.
The first letter signed: Alexandre Valignan.

V7 VALIGNANO, Alessandro
[Lettera de' 10 d'Ottobre del 1599.] LITTERÆ R.P. ALEXANDRI VALIGNANO Visitatoris Societatis IESV in Iapponia & China, Scriptæ 10. Octobris 1599. Ad R.P. CLAVDIVM AQVAVIVA . . . A IOANNE HAYO . . . ex Italico in Latinum conuersæ. ANTVERPIÆ Apud Ioachimum Trognæsium. M.DCIII. 12° pp.65
1366.b.27.

V8 VALLA, Laurentius
LAVRENTII VALLÆ . . . de falso credita & ementita CONSTANTINI M. IMP. RO.

donatione DECLAMATIO . . . Nunc iterum . . . in lucem edita. Addita est ipsa Constantini Imp. Donatio. LVGDVNI BATAVORVM Ex officina JACOBI MARCI. M DC XX. 4° pp. 104
700.h.27.
With Ulrich von Hutten's preface and other documents.

V9 VALLET, Nicolas
PIETÉ ROYALLE C'EST A DIRE: LES CENT CINQVANTE PSEAVMES DE DAVID, ACCOMMODEZ POVR IOVER SVR LE LVTH, D'UNE NOVVELLE ET TRES-FAcile mode, non encor veüe ny oüye par cy devant. Par NICOLAS VALLET. A AMSTREDAM, On les vend chez l'Autheur demeurant sur le Lely-Graft, à l'enseigne de la Bastille. 1620. [etc.] obl. 4° pp. 169: plates; music
Music K.4.b.14; Music K.4.b.15.
With an additional, engraved, titlepage, reading 'REGIA PIETAS HOC EST Psalmi Dauidici concinné aptati ad modulantes fides. Authore Nicolao Vallotto', showing David at prayer with musicians and music, signed: DvB.1619, i.e. David Vinckboons?, P.S.Schulp., i.e. Philips Serwouter? The music engraved by Rafael Drappentier, the preliminaries printed by Paulus van Ravesteyn at Amsterdam. Additional plates of music bearing the names, mottoes and arms of their donors: Jacomo pauw; Guillaume Bartolot le Jeune; Jeronimus Jorisz Waephelier, Libertus van Axele; Michiel van Eyck, signed: Le Blond, Blond or Nic. Blondus fecit. The copy at Music K.4.b.14 with the ownership inscription: Jñ Prince Dorchester This Book wase gave me By Mr. Manvill Aprill 7:1787. The copy at Music K.4.b.15 is imperfect; wanting all before sig. XXI and all the additional music plates.

V10 VALLET, Nicolas
[Le secret des Muses.] Le second Livre DE Tablature de Luth, Intitulé LE SECRET DES MVSES: Contenant plusieurs belles pieces . . . Ensemble plusieurs autres pieces mises en Tablature . . . entr' autres quelques pieces mises: pour iouër a quatre Luts differemment accordez. Par NICOLAS VALET [*sic*]. A AMSTERDAM, Chez Ian Ianssz . . . M.D.XIX. [etc.] obl. 4° pp. 50; music
Music K.4.b.13(2).
The music is engraved, p. 1 signed: Rafel Drappentier fe.

V11 VALLET, Nicolas
[Le secret des Muses.] PARADISUS MUSICUS TESTUDINIS, in quo Multæ insignes et ante hunc diem inauditæ, Gallicæ, Germanicæ, Anglicæ, Hispanicæ, Polonicæ, cantiones; Nec non Varia Præludia, Fantasiæ, Tripudia continentur: Præterea punctis suprà tum̃ [*sic*] ad latus singulis cuiusque tactus literis adscriptis, eorumque præmissa explicatione, docetur quibus tum dextræ tum sinistræ manus digitis chorda tangenda pulsandaque sit, Auctore Nicolao Valletto. Omnia in æs incisa. AMSTELODAMI; Apud Joannem Janssonium . . . 1618. obl. 4° pp. 94; music, port.
Music K.4.b.13(1).
Beginning with 'Petit discours, contenant la maniere dese bien seruir . . . du present liure Intitulè, LE SECRET DES MVSES', which is also the running title. The titlepage is engraved, showing Apollo and Hermes, musical scenes and snippets, signed: Dauit Vinckeboons inuentor; Ioan. Berwinckel sculpsit. Engraved throughout, except for table of contents. The music engraved by Rafael Drappentier.

V12 VALUATION
Valuation de la monnoye d'or, du 22. de Mars l'An 1611. A Anuers, chez Hierosme Verdussen, [etc.] obl. 4° a single sheet
107.g.12(2).
Printed on half a leaf, in civilité, within typographical borders.

VAN Godes verkiesinghe. 1611. *See* COORNHERT, Dirck Volckertsz. Vande predestinatie.

VANDE kerckelicke ende politijcke macht. 1612. *See* RICHER, Edmond

V13 VANDE
Vande Neghen Chooren der Ingelen/vande H. Drijvuldicheyt/ende vande seuen Bloetstortinghen ons liefs Heeren Jesu Christi . . . TOT LOVEN, By Jan Maes . . . 1602. 8° sig. AB^8; illus.
4407.bb.11(4).
Another edition of 'Een devote oeffeninge tot eenen yegeliken choor der enghelen'. The titlepage woodcut shows the celebration of Mass, that on the last leaf is another full-page illustration of the Mass, with the caption 'Door v heylighe vijff wonden/Vergheeft ons alle onse sonden'.

VANDE trouwe liefd van Cypriaen en Orania. 1618. *See* GUARINI, Giovanni Battista [Il pastor fido.] Treur-bly-eynde-spel [etc.]

VANDE verworpelinghen. 1611. *See* COORNHERT, Dirck Volckertsz. Vande predestinatie.

V14 VANDEN
Vanden Spinnekop ende t'Bieken ofte Droom-ghedicht. 4° 2 unsigned leaves
107.g.1(2).
A poem satirising Spinola, found also at the end of Lipsius, Heylige Maghet van Hall, Delff, 1605. Published in 1607 or 1608?

VANDEN vroomen . . . ridder Amadis van Gaula. 1613. *See* AMADIS de Gaula

VANDER-VOORT, Isaacus. Theses physicae de anima vegetativa. 1606. *See* JACCHAEUS, Gilbertus

VARRERIUS, Caspar. *See* BARREIROS, Gaspar

V15 VARRO, Marcus Terentius
[Works] M. TERENTII VARRONIS OPERA OMNIA QVÆ EXTANT. Cum Notis IOSEPHI SCALIGERI, ADRIANI TURNEBI, PETRI VICTORII, & ANTONII AVGVSTINI. His accedunt TABVLÆ NAVFRAGII, seu FRAGMENTA ejusdem auctiora & meliora . . . DURDRECHTI, Ex Officinâ IOANNIS BEREVVOUT . . . M D C XIX. 8° pp. 143, sig. K-O^5; 129, sig. I1-K1; 255, sig. qq8-ss2; 48; 77; 142 [242], sig. QQ2
687.f.18; G.8949; 159.m.17; 827.d.4.
The copy at 159.m.17 is imperfect; wanting the second section; that at 827.d.4 has been missing since 1962.

V16 VASQUEZ, Gabriel
[Works] (tp.1) COMMENTARIORVM, AC DISPVTATIONVM IN PRIMAM PARTEM SANCTI THOMÆ TOMVS PRIMVS . . . AVCTORE R.P. Gabriele Vazquez . . . ANTVERPIÆ, Apud Petrum & Ioannem Belleros. M.DC.XXI.
(tp.2) COMMENTARIORVM . . . IN PRIMAM PARTEM SANCTI THOMÆ TOMVS SECVNDVS . . . AVCTORE R.P. GABRIELE VAZQVEZ . . . ANTVERPIÆ, Apud Petrum & Ioannem Belleros. M.DC.XXI.
(tp.3) COMMENTARIORVM, AC DISPVTATIONVM IN PRIMAM SECVNDÆ SANCTI THOMÆ TOMVS PRIMVS . . . AVCTORE R.P. Gabriele Vazquez . . . ANTVERPIÆ, Apud Petrum & Ioannem Belleros. MDC.XXI.
(tp.4) COMMENTARIORVM . . . IN PRIMAM SECVNDÆ SANCTI THOMÆ TOMVS SECVNDVS . . . AVCTORE R.P. Gabriele Vazquez . . . ANTVERPIÆ, Apud Petrum & Ioannem Belleros. MDC.XXI. (col. 1-4) ANTVERPIÆ, Ex Typographiâ Henrici Ærtssij. M.DC.XX.

(tp.5) COMMENTARIORVM, AC DISPVTATIONVM IN TERTIAM PARTEM SANCTI THOMÆ TOMVS PRIMVS AVCTORE R.P. GABRIELE VAZQUEZ . . . ANTVERPIÆ, Apud Petrum & Ioannem Belleros. M.DC.XXI.
(tp.6) COMMENTARIORVM . . . IN TERTIAM PARTEM SANCTI THOMÆ TOMVS SECVNDVS AVCTORE R.P. GABRIELE VAZQUEZ . . . ANTVERPIÆ, Apud Petrum & Ioannem Belleros. M.DC.XXI.
(tp.7) COMMENTARIORVM . . . IN TERTIAM PARTEM SANCTI THOMÆ TOMVS TERTIVS AVCTORE R.P. GABRIELE VAZQUEZ . . . ANTVERPIÆ, Apud Petrum & Ioannem Belleros. M.DC.XXI.
(tp.8) COMMENTARIORVM . . . IN TERTIAM PARTEM SANCTI THOMÆ TOMVS QVARTVS AVCTORE R.P. Gabriele Vazquez . . . ANTVERPIÆ, Apud Petrum & Ioannem Belleros. M.DC.XXI.
(tp.9) PATRIS GABRIELIS VAZQVEZ . . . Opuscula Moralia . . . ANTVERPIÆ, Apud Petrum & Ioannem Belleros . . . M.DC.XXI. fol. 9 tom.: pp.708; 739; 894; 882; 500 [890]; 567; 794; 441; 605
3675.f.1.
The half-title to tom.1 reads: R.P. Gabrielis Vazquez Opera omnia. Ownership inscriptions: Da Livraria do Coll° de S. Agostinho dos Conegos Regularg⁹; do Collegio de S^to Aug°; Do D^tor Dom Gaspar. For other volumes of Vasquez's commentaries on Thomas Aquinas, containing the text, *see* THOMAS Aquinas; Saint. Summa theologica.

V17 VASQUEZ, Gabriel
COMMENTARIORUM, AC DISPVTATIONVM IN TERTIAM PARTEM S. THOMÆ, TOMVS PRIMVS. AVCTORE P. GABRIELE VAZQVEZ . . . Nunc primum in Germania excusus . . . M.DC.X. . . . INGOLSTADII, Excudebat ANDREAS ANGERMARIVS. Impensis IOANNIS HERTSROY.
(tp.2) COMMENTARIORVM, AC DISPVTATIONVM IN TERTIAM PARTEM S. THOMÆ, Tomus Secundus. AVCTORE P. GABRIELE VAZQVEZ . . . Nunc primum in Germania excusus . . . M.DC.XII. INGOLSTADII . . . EX OFFICINA TYPOGRAPHICA EDERIANA, JMPENSIS MARTINI NVTII, ET JOANNIS HERTSROY.
(tp.3) COMMENTARIORVM AC DISPVTATIONVM IN TERTIAM PARTEM S. Thomæ. TOMVS TERTIVS . . . AVTHORE PATRE GABRIELE VAZQVEZ . . . ANTVERPIÆ, Apud Ioannem Keerbergium . . . M.DC.XIV.
(tp.4) COMMENTARIORVM AC DISPVTATIONVM IN TERTIAM PARTEM SANCTI THOMÆ TOMVS QVARTVS. AVCTORE P. GABRIELE VAZQVEZ . . . ANTVERPIÆ, Sumptibus Ioannis Hasrey, & Ioannis Meursij . . . MDCXV. [etc.] fol. 4 tom.: pp.1101; 618; 879; 500
697.m.6-9.
Tom.1,2 published by Joannes Hertsroy at Munich; tom.2 also published by Martinus Nutius at Antwerp; tom.3,4 printed by Henricus Aertssius at Antwerp? Ownership inscription: Mon. St. Georgij Prüuening.

V18 VASQUEZ, Gabriel
[Selections] R.P. GABRIELIS VAZQVEZ . . . DISPVTATIONES METAPHYSICAE DESVMPTÆ EX VARIIS LOCIS SVORVM OPERVM. ANTVERPIÆ, Apud Ioannem Keerbergium. M.DC.XVIII. 8° pp.623
1488.ff.8.
From the library of Aberdeen University.

V19 VAUX, Laurence
A CATECHISM OR CHRISTIAN DOCTRINE, NEcessary for Children and ignorant People. By Laurence Vaux . . . At S. Omers . . . 1620. [etc.] 24° pp.332
Cup.403.l.2.
A reprint, probably done in England ca.1670, of the genuine St. Omer edition of 1620,

revised by John Heigham and printed by Charles Boscard. The signatures are in twelves, the chainlines indicate 24°, the watermarks are irregular. Ownership inscription: Dorothy Worthington.

V20 VEEN, Otto van

AMORIS DIVINI EMBLEMATA STVDIO ET AERE OTHONIS VÆNI CONCINNATA . . . ANTVERPIÆ, Ex officina Martini NutI & Ioannis MeursI . . . MDCXV. [etc.] 4° pp.127; illus.

C.104.dd.26.

The recto pages bear the emblems; the verso pages opposite bear Latin quotations from the Bible and the early Christian authors, Spanish verse mottoes by Alphonso de Ledesma and Dutch and French poems by Otto van Veen and Carolus Hattronius respectively.

V21 VEEN, Otto van

AMORVM EMBLEMATA, FIGVRIS ÆNEIS INCISA STVDIO OTHONIS VÆNI . . . ANTVERPIÆ, Venalia apud Auctorem. M.DC.IIX. (col.) Typis Henrici Swingenij. obl.4° pp.247; illus.

11556.bbb.60.

The introductory poem is in Dutch and French; the verses accompanying the emblems are in Latin, Dutch and French. The first emblem signed: C. Boel fecit. The pagination is correct; p.6 has the reading '*Puer & net*'; p.36 has the spelling 'ATLATE'; p.120 has the reading 'Podaleiria'; p.244 reads 'Exemploq́ue'; a simple rule divides the text on the last, unnumbered, page.

V22 VEEN, Otto van

AMORVM EMBLEMATA, FIGVRIS ÆNEIS INCISA STVDIO OTHONIS VÆNI . . . ANTVERPIÆ, Venalia apud Auctorem. M.DC.IIX. (col.) Typis Henrici Swingenij. obl.4° pp.747[247]; illus.

11556.bbb.59.

The introductory poem is in Italian and French; the other verses are in Latin, Italian and French. The pagination of the last page is misprinted; p.6 reads 'Pur & net'; p.36 'ATLANTE'; p.120 'Podaleiria'; p.244 'Exemploq́ʒ'; the dividing line on the last page consists of two double rules with oblique hatching between these.

V23 VEEN, Otto van

AMORVM EMBLEMATA, FIGVRIS ÆNEIS INCISA STVDIO OTHONIS VÆNI . . . ANTVERPIÆ, Venalia apud Auctorem. M.DC.IIX. (col.) Typis Henrici Swingenij. obl.4° pp.247; illus.

96.a.26.

Another edition of the preceding, newly set. p.120 reads 'Megaleiria'; p.244 'Exemploq́ue'; the last page is divided by a simple rule.

V24 VEEN, Otto van

AMORVM EMBLEMATA, FIGVRIS ÆNEIS INCISA STVDIO OTHONIS VÆNI . . . Emblemes of Loue. with verses in Latin, English, and Italian. ANTVERPIÆ, Venalia apud Auctorem. M.DC.IIX. (col.) Typis Henrici Swingenij. obl.4° pp.747[247]; illus.

11556.bbb.58.

The English verses are by Richard Verstegan. The introductory poem is in English and Italian. p.36 reads 'ATLATE'; p.120 'Podaleiria'; p.244 'Exemploq́ʒ'; the last leaf has the double, hatched rule.

V25 VEEN, Otto van

HISTORIA SEPTEM INFANTIVM DE LARA Authore Ott. Vænio. HISTORIA DE LOS SIETE INFANTES DE LARA . . . ANTVERPIÆ. Prostant apud Philippum Lisaert . . . M.DC.XII. obl. fol. pl.40

G.992; 551.e.9.

Plates, engraved by Antonio Tempesta, with text in Spanish and Latin engraved underneath. In the copy at 551.e.9 the text has been cut off from the plates which have been mounted, lacking a titlepage. English text in manuscript has been supplied instead.

V26 VEEN, Otto van

PHYSICAE ET THEOLOGICAE conclusiones, NOTIS ET FIGVRIS DISPOSITÆ AC DEMONSTRATÆ, De primariis fidei capitibus, Atque imprimis DE PRÆDESTINATIONE, Quomodo effectus illius superetur à LIBERO ARBITRIO. AVTHORE OTTHONE VÆNIO . . . ORSELLIS . . . M.DC.XXI. 4° ff.43; illus.

1009.d.21(2).

Consisting of 43 unsigned numbered engravings on the rectos of the leaves with accompanying texts on the preceding versos. In a prefatory note the printer claims that he received the manuscript from a friend of the author's and decided to publish it without the author's knowledge, getting the engravings made from the author's drawings. There is no known place with the Latin name of Orsellae, although both Oberursel in Germany and a village by the name of Ursel (or Urselle) near Ghent have been suggested. There seems to have been no printer capable of producing this elaborate and finely printed work at Oberursel at this time, while no printer at all is known at the village of Ursel near Ghent. It is possible that this may be the Leiden edition allegedly mentioned by Rubens in a letter to Petrus Vaenius, the author's brother, written in Italian, as quoted by F.M. Haberditzl in *Jahrbuch der Kunsthistorischen Sammlungen,* Vienna, vol.27 (1908), p.230, in which case the date given by Rubens for the edition (which he only knew from hearsay) as 1620 could have been communicated to him in 'old style'. Rubens is also quoted by Haberditzl as enquiring after this as 'operetta anonima', and again, this description would have had originally to refer to the printer or publisher rather than to the author. There is no record of an earlier edition which did or did not name the author.

V27 VEER, Gerrit de

Waerachtighe Beschryvinghe Van drie seylagien/ter weerelt noyt soo ghehoort/drie jaeren achter malcanderen deur de Hollandtsche ende Zeelandtsche schepen by noorden Noorweghen/Moscovia ende Tartaria/na . . . Catthai ende China . . . Ghedaen deur Gerrit de Veer . . . Ghedruckt t'Amstelredam, by Cornelis Claesz. . . . 1605. obl.4° ff.61: plates; maps

983.ff.7; 1858.a.1(5).

The maps signed: Baptista a Doetechum. The foliation is erratic. The running title is 'Het eerste (-derde) deel vande Navigatie om den Noorden'. According to *Tiele Land- en Volkenkunde* no.1129 n. the third edition of the Dutch text.

V28 VEER, Gerrit de

[Waerachtighe beschryvinghe.] VRAYE DESCRIPTION DE TROIS VOYAGES DE MER TRES ADMIRABLES . . . Par GIRARD LE VEER. Imprimé à Amsterdam, chez Cornille Nicolas . . . 1609. fol. ff.44; illus., maps

566.k.15(6).

The engravings are by Baptista van Doetechum. F.8v wrongly headed 'Premiere partie'. *Tiele Mémoire* no.99 and *Tiele Land- en Volkenkunde* no.1131n. do not refer to this error and therefore do not distinguish this from the following.

V29 VEER, Gerrit de

[Waerachtighe beschryvinghe.] VRAYE DESCRIPTION DE TROIS VOYAGES DE MER . . . Par GIRARD LE VEER. Imprimé à Amsterdam, chez Cornille Nicolas . . . 1609. fol. ff.44; illus., maps

C.73.g.2(3); G.6620(4).

A different edition from the preceding, with the same engravings. F.8v is correctly headed 'Seconde partie'.

V30 VEGA CARPIO, Lope Felix de
[Plays. Collections] LAS COMEDIAS DEL FAMOSO POETA LOPE DE VEGA CARPIO. RECOPILADAS POR BERNARDO GRASSA. AGORA NVEVAMENTE IMPRESSAS Y EMENDADAS. Dirigidas al Licenciado don Antonio Ramirez de Prado . . . EN AMBERES, EN CASA DE MARTIN NVCIO . . . M.DCVII. 8° pp.622
11725.aa.19.

V31 VEGA CARPIO, Lope Felix de
[Plays. Collections] SEGVNDA PARTE DE LAS COMEDIAS DE LOPE DE VEGA CARPIO, Que contiene otras doze . . . Dirigidas a doña Casilda da Gauna Varona, muger de Don Alonso de Guevara, Alcalde mayor de la ciudad de Burgos. EN BRVSSELAS, Por Roger Velpio, y Huberto Antonio . . . 1611. [etc.] (col.) ANTVERPIAE, Excudebat Andreas Bacx. 1611. 8° pp.645
11725.aaa.18.
The privilege, printed at the end, is made out to Rutgeert Velpius and Hubert Anthoon. The titlepage has an ornament.

V32 VEGA CARPIO, Lope Felix de
[Plays. Collections] SEGVNDA PARTE DE LAS COMEDIAS DE LOPE DE VEGA CARPIO . . . EN AMBERES En casa de la biuda y herederos de Pedro Bellero 1611. [etc.] (col.) ANTVERPIAE, Excudebat Andreas Bacx, 1611. 8° pp.645
1072.f.4.
Another issue of the preceding, with the same privilege made out to Rutgeert Velpius and Hubert Anthoon. With the device of the Bellère publishing firm on the titlepage. With the exlibris of J. Wilkinson; W. Combes.

V33 VEGA CARPIO, Lope Felix de
[Other works] ARCADIA PROSAS Y VERSOS, DE LOPE DE VEGA CARPIO . . . EN ANVERES, En casa de Martin Nucio . . . M.DC.V. [etc.] 12° pp.471
243.a.35.

V34 VEGA CARPIO, Lope Felix de
[Other works] ARCADIA PROSAS Y VERSOS, DE LOPE DE VEGA CARPIO . . . EN ANVERS. En casa de Pedro y Iuan Bellero . . . 1617. [etc.] 12° pp.471
243.a.33.
A word for word reprint of the preceding, but with the misprint '496' in the pagination for '469'.

V35 VEGA CARPIO, Lope Felix de
[Other works] PASTORES DE BELEN, PROSAS Y VERSOS DIVINOS, DE LOPE DE VEGA CARPIO . . . EN BRVSSELAS, Por Roger Velpio y Huberto Antonio . . . 1614. [etc.] 12° pp.636
1072.a.17; 243.a.24.

V36 VEGA CARPIO, Lope Felix de
[Other works] EL PEREGRINO EN SV PATRIA De Lope de Vega Carpio . . . EN BRVSSELAS, En casa de Roger Velpius . . . 1608. 12° pp.587
1072.f.25; 11450.aa.74.
With a list of Lope de Vega's plays on sig.⁎⁎1r-3v. Ownership inscription in the copy at 1072.f.25: L. Tieck.

V37 VEGETIUS RENATUS, Flavius
(tp.1) V. INL. FL. VEGETII RENATI COMITIS, ALIORVMQVE VETERVM De Re Militari LIBRI. Accedunt FRONTINI Stratagematibus [*sic*] eiusdem auctoris alia opuscula. Omnia emendatiùs, quædam nunc primùm edita à PETRO SCRIVERIO. Cum

Commentariis aut Notis GOD. STEWECHII & FR. MODII. EX OFFICINA PLANTINIANA RAPHELENGIJ. M.D.CVII.
(tp.2) GODESCHALCI STEWECHII COMMENTARIVS AD FLAVI VEGETI RENATI DE RE MILITARI LIBROS. EX OFFICINA PLANTINIANA RAPHELENGIJ. M.D.CVI. 4° pp.102, 123, 208; 347, 24; illus.
C.78.b.7.
Also containing: Claudii Aeliani Tactica . . . ex interpretatione Theodori Gazae; Polybii Tractatio de militia et castrametatione Romanorum: ex interpretatione Andreae Iani Lascaris; Anonymi de rebus bellicis liber; Sexti Iulii Frontini Strategematicωn . . . libri quatuor, De aquaeductibus urbis Romae commentarius, De re agraria . . . liber unus: cum Aggeni Urbici commentario; Francisci Modii notæ in Flavii Vegetii Renati De re militari libros; Godeschalci Stewechii coniectanea ad Sexti Iulii Frontini libros Stratagematicon. The illustrations are woodcuts. Published at Leiden. From the library of John Morris.

VELASCIUS, Joannes Fer. *See* FERNANDEZ DE VELASCO, Juan

VELASCO, Juan Fernandez de. *See* FERNANDEZ DE VELASCO, Juan

V38 VELDE, Jan van den
Duytsche Exemplaren VAN Alderhande Gheschriften, Seer nut ende bequaem voor de duytsche Schoolmeesters ende alle beminders der Pennen. Int licht gebracht DOOR JAN VANDEN VELDE . . . 1620. D. V. Horenbeeck Excudebat. Gerardus Gauw. Haerlemensis Sculpt. fol. 12 unnumbered plates
1269.h.33.
The plates consist of the titlepage, the dedication to David van Horenbeeck and Laurens Serweytius, 24 examples on 8 plates and 'fondamenten' on 2 plates. Published at Haarlem.

V39 VELDE, Jan van den
[Duytsche exemplaren.] HET DERDE DEEL Der Duytscher ende Franscher Scholen Exemplaer-boeck. Inhoudende Verscheyden Brieven van alderhande Gheschriften, so in Duytsch als Fransch. GHESCHREVEN Door Jan Vanden Velde . . . Ende int licht ghestelt By M. David van Horenbeeck . . . Gerardus Gau Haerlemensis Sculptor. fol. 12 unnumbered(?) plates
1269.h.34.
Consisting of the engraved titlepage and 11 examples of calligraphy. The first and ninth plates are thus numbered in contemporary manuscript; other plates are mutilated in this corner. Published at Haarlem, probably in 1621. Ownership inscription: Sibrandus Valckenaer.

V40 VELDE, Jan van den
EXEMPLAER-BOEC Inhoudende Alderhande Gheschriften zeer bequaem ende dienstelyck voor de Joncheydt ende allen Lief-hebbers der Pennen: Int licht ghestelt Door Jan vanden Velde . . . M.DC.VII. obl.4° 24 unnumbered plates
1256.kk.35.
The engraved titlepage signed: Gerardus Gauw Haerlemensis scalp. The examples are in Dutch, French, German, Italian and English. Some of the plates have also been used in other works by Jan van den Velde. Probably published at Haarlem.

V41 VELDE, Jan van den
MIROIR literaire. Auquel se void [*sic*] plusieurs sortes d'Escritures, tant Latines, Romaines, Italienes et Espaignoles, que Flamandes Françoises, Angloises et Alemandes. Avec une ample Instruction des Fondemens d'icelles. Mis en lumiere par Jan vanden Velde . . . M.DC.VIII. obl. fol. 12 unnumbered plates
C.119.h.12(3).
Engraved throughout by Simon Frisius. Published by Jan van Waesberghe at Rotterdam. The texts are in French, Dutch, English, German, Latin, Spanish and Italian.

V42 VELDE, Jan van den

(tp. 1) SPIEGHEL Der Schrijfkonste, Inden welcken ghesien worden veelderhande Gheschriften met hare Fondementen ende onderrichtinghe Wtghegeven DOOR Jan vanden Velde . . . 1605.

(tp. 2) Artificiosissimum Grammatices Verum nobilissimumq; speculum . . . Auctore Johanne Veldio . . . Rotterdami . . . 1605. obl. fol. 50 unnumbered plates

C. 119. h. 12(2).

Engraved throughout by Simon Frisius. The allegorical titlepage border signed: KMander inue., IMaetham sculp. The two plates showing a hand holding a pen signed: Frysius. Two plates containing letters to Petrus Carpenterius and Philippus vande Veken dated 1609. The texts are in Dutch, French, English, German, Latin, Italian and Spanish. Published by Jan van Waesberghe at Rotterdam in 1609.

V43 VELDE, Jan van den

SPIEGHEL Der Schrijfkonste . . . Door Jan vanden Velde . . . 1605. Ghedruckt tot Amsterdam, Bij Willem Iansz. [etc.] obl. fol. 51 unnumbered plates

1268. g. 3.

A new edition of the preceding, with the addition of the new imprint to the original titlepage. The two 'Frysius' plates, the two plates showing circles and the plate beginning 'Alle goede' have been omitted and six others added in their place. The order is not strictly repeated, but long sequences are left as in the original edition. The last two plates of ornamental capitals, one of them signed, the other unsigned, were originally used in the 'Miroir'. Published in 1610?

V44 VELDE, Jan van den

Thresor Literaire, CONTENANT Plusieurs diverses Escritures, les plus usitées és Escoles Francoyses des Provinces unies du Pays-bas. Escrit et mis en Lumiere PAR Jean Vanden Velde . . . POUR M. D. V. HORENBEECK . . . 1621. fol. 12 unnumbered plates

1269. h. 32.

The titlepage signed: Gerardus Gauw sculp. Harlemens. Published at Haarlem.

V45 VELSIUS, Joannes

PROGNOSTICATIE VAN DIE Nieuwe . . . Comeet ofte Harige Ster Anno 1618. verschenen/DOOR D^r. IOANNEM VELSIVM . . . Tot Franeker/Ghedruckt by Jan Lamrinck . . . 1618. 4° sig. A^4; illus.

T. 2423(5).

The titlepage woodcut shows a comet.

V46 VELTLINISCHE

[Veltlinische Tyranney.] VOLTOLYNSCHE TYRANNYE, Dat is: Volcomen ende waerachtige Beschrijvinghe vanden schrickelijcken . . . Moort . . . aende Evangelische Inghesetenen . . . ghedaen door de Barbarische Spaensche macht . . . den 9. ende 10. Iul. Anno 1620 . . . Eerstelijck beschreven int Hoochduytsch/ende tot Zurich ghedruckt . . . Ende nu . . . vertaelt. TOT ARNHEM, By Ian Ianssen . . . 1621. 4° sig. A-C^4

T. 2424(7); T. 2424(25).

Sometimes attributed to Caspar Waser.

V47 VENATOR, Adolf Tectander

EEN Claer ende Doorluchtich Vertooch van d'Alckmaersche kerckelicke gheschillen . . . insonderheyt int Iaer 1608 ende 1609. Rijms-vvyse als een Spel van sinnen ghestelt. Wtghegheven tot contentement van allen Liefhebbers/die Cornelius Hillenius tot het lesen des selven . . . begeerich mocht hebben

ghemaeckt . . . Ghelijck . . . tot zijnder ontlastinghe gheschiedt . . . Ghedruckt . . . 1611. 4° sig.∴, A-E⁸, F⁷
T.2241(5).

Anonymous. The allusion is to criticism made on the play before its publication. Printed by Jacob de Meester at Alkmaar?

V48 VENATOR, Adolf Tectander

NOOTVVENDIGH Historisch Verhael/van allen Swaricheyden/verschillen/ende Proceduren/soo wel in Kercklijcken, als Politijcken saken, etlijcke Jaren herwaerts binnen der Stadt Alckmaer voorghevallen. VVtghegheven by Burgmeesteren, Vroetschappen, ende Kerckenraedt, der voorsz Stede . . . Teghens het Lasterboeck Cornelij Hillenij . . . TOT ALCKMAER, Ghedruckt by Jacob de Meester . . . 1611. Ende men vindtse te koop by Willem Jansz. . . . tot Amsterdam. 4° pp.271
T.2241(1).

Anonymous. With an official letter from the city of Alkmaar to the States of Holland. With the arms of Alkmaar on the titlepage and in the colophon. Partly printed in civilité.

V49 VENATOR, Adolf Tectander

[Nootwendigh historisch verhael.] Kopije/Van de Remonstrantie by Adolphum Venatorem . . . ontworpen: Anno/1610. in Januario. Om aen de . . . Staten van Hollant ende West-Vrieslant ghepresenteert te worden: Daer in het voornaemste is de belijdenis van syn ghevoelen inde Leere. Ghetrocken wt het Boec genaemt, NOOTVVENDICH [*sic*] HISTORISCH VERHAEL, Wt-ghegeven by Burghemeesteren, Vroetschappen ende Kercken-raet, der voorsz. Stede . . . Na de Kopije, Tot Alcmaer/by Jacob de Meester . . . M.D.C.XJ. 4° sig.A-D⁴
T.2241(2).

With the device of Matthijs Bastiaensz of Rotterdam on the titlepage. Published in 1611.

V50 VENATOR, Adolf Tectander

REDEN-VREVCHT Der Wijsen in haer wel-lust/Ende Belachen der dwasen quel-lust/ In't lachen Democriti door Persoon-tooningh. Ghemaeckt van . . . Adolpho Tectandro Venatore . . . TOT ALCMAER, Ghedruckt by Jacob de Meester . . . M.VI^{C}.III. Ende men vindtse te coop by den Autheur/ende den Drucker. 4° sig.A-F⁴G²
11755.bb.59.

V51 VENATOR, Adolf Tectander

THEOLOGIA VERA ET MERA. Lactentium & infantium in Christo. Een Suyver/Claar/ Alghemeyn FONDAMENT-BOECK. Door naacte Schriftueren des O. Ende . . . des N. Testaments alle kinderen Gods . . . in de Hooft-stucken der Christelijcken Religie onderwijsende. Met een DEVOTIE-BOEC . . . 'Twelck de Christenheyt wel veerthien-hondert Jaren gemist heeft/ende nu eerst te voorschijn wort gebracht door een Lief-hebber van de Vrije Eenigheyt aller Godt-lievenden herten . . . Ghedruckt by de Weduwe van Jacob de Meester. 1617. 4° pp.38, 58
T.2247(46).

The dedication signed: A.T.V.T.F.D., i.e. Adolf Tectander Venator. Published at Alkmaar.

V52 VENATOR, Adolphus

THESES MEDICÆ INAVGVRALES De Triplici MELANCHOLIA, Quas . . . Pro lauro doctorali consequendâ, disputatione publicâ excutiendas proponit ADOLPHVS VENATOR . . . LVGDVNI BATAVORVM, Excudit IACOBVS PATIVS . . . 1618. 4° sig.A⁴B⁶
1185.g.1(66).

VENER, Wilhelmus. *See* FENNOR, William

V53 VENICE

[6.5.1606] PROCLAMATIE ende VVederlegginghe byden Hartoch van Venetien gedaen/op ende teghen den onbehoorlijcken Ban door den Paus Paulus de vijfste teghen hem/teghen zynen Raet/ende teghen zyne ondersaten uytgegeven . . . 1606. Door een Liefhebber int nederduytsch vertaelt. Tot Amstelredam Ghedruckt by Hendrick Barentsz. . . . 1606. 4° sig. A^2
T.2417(12).
Issued 6 May 1606.

V54 VENO, Henricus de

DISPUTATIONUM PHYSICARUM PRIMA, DE PHYSICA, QUAM . . . PRÆSIDE . . . D. HENRICO DE VENO . . . discutiendam exhibet BERNARDUS PALUDANUS . . . FRANEKERÆ. Ex Officina AEGIDII RADAEI . . . MDCIII. 4° sig. A^4
7306.f.6(38).

V55 VENO, Henricus de

DISPUTATIONUM PHYSICARVM NONA, DE Misti Generatione & ejus Interitu, QUAM . . . SUB PRAESIDIO . . . D. HENRICI DE VENO . . . Excutiendam proponit BERNARDUS PALUDANUS . . . FRANEKERÆ, EXCUDEBAT AEGIDIUS RADAEUS . . . 1604. 4° sig.F1,2,G3,4
7306.f.6(46).

VERANTWOORDINGE des Eerweerdighen . . . D. Jacobi Arminii. 1612. *See* WTENBOGAERT, Jan

VERANTWOORDINGE teghens de hevige predicatie Festi Hommii. 1616. *See* CORVINUS, Joannes Arnoldi

De VERANTWOORDINGHE des Princen van Orangien. 1610. *See* JUSTIFICATION. La justification du Prince d'Orange.

V56 VERBORGENTHEYT

Verborgentheyt Der Ongherechticheydt Ofte Conscientie-Dwangh Schuylende inden boesem der Contra-remonstranten/ondeckt in een seker Boeck ghenaemt EVBVLVS, ende ghemaeckt/door Willem Teelinck . . . Ghedruckt . . . By een Lief-hebber des Algemeynen Vader-Landts . . . 1619. 4° pp.7
T.2249(36).

VERCLAERINGHE. *See* also VERCLARINGE; VERCLARINGHE; VERKLARINGE; VERKLARINGHE

VERCLAERINGHE van den ghedenckweerdighen scheeps-strijdt, gheschiet tusschen vijf Hollandtsche schepen, ende de groote Armade der Portugesen . . . 1601; 1603. *See* WARACHTIGHE afbeeldinghe vanden wonderbaren ende ghedenckweerdighen scheeps strijdt.

V57 VERCLAERINGHE

Verclaeringhe van het ghene nv onlanckx in Italien is ghepasseert. Overghesedt wt de Hooch-Duytsche sprake in onse Nederlantsche Tale. Eerst Ghedruckt den xvij. Julij. T'Hantwerpen/By Abraham Verhoeuen . . . 1620. [etc.] 4° pp.8; sig. Pp^4; illus.
P.P.3444.af(67).
Including reports on Turkish, Tunisian, Maltese matters, etc., also news from Vienna and Prague. The titlepage illustration shows Time.

VERCLARINGE. *See* also VERCLAERINGHE; VERCLARINGHE; VERKLARINGE; VERKLARINGHE

VERCLARINGE eñ patente die den Cheur-vorst van Saxen heeft laten publiceren. 1620. *See* SAXONY [6.4.1620]

VERCLARINGE ende verhael hoe de heere Wouter Raleighe . . . hem ghedreghen heeft. 1619. *See* DECLARATION. A declaration of the demeanour and cariage of sir Walter Raleigh.

VERCLARINGE ghedaen by de Ghemeynte in Engelandt. 1621. *See* ENGLAND [4.6.1621]

V58 VERCLARINGE
Verclaringe van Gout Silver/Realen/ende Coopmanschappen/ghecomen met dese Vlote wt Nieu Spagnien. 1621. Met noch Tijdinge wt Vranck-rijck. Eerst Ghedruckt den 1. December. 1621. T'Hantwerpen/By Abraham Verhoeuen/ [etc.] 4° pp.8; sig.Yyyy^4; illus.
P.P.3444.af(320).
Headed: December. 1621. 175. With news from Spain of miracles in India. The titlepage illustration consists of five woodcuts showing six ships, one of them about to sink.

VERCLARINGHE. *See* also VERCLARINGE; VERCLAERINGHE; VERKLAERINGE; VERKLARINGHE

V59 VERCLARINGHE
Verclaringhe der Kercken-Dienaers tot Leeuwarden/over D. VORSTII volcomener antvvoordt op de Naeder-VVaerschuvvinghe . . . Gedruckt Tot Leeuvvarden By Abraham vanden Rade . . . 1612. 4° pp.104
T.2242(28).
Drawn up by Johannes Bogerman and others.

VERCLARINGHE, ghedaen by den Raedt ende principale Heeren ende Edelen van Engelant. 1603. *See* ENGLAND [24.3.1603]

VERCLARINGHE ghedaen by den Raedt ende principalen Adel van Enghelandt. 1603. *See* ENGLAND [24.3.1603]

V60 VERCLARINGHE
Verclaringhe/oft bedietsel vande verthooninghen die ghedaen sullen worden in den OMMEGANC diemen tot Antvverpen sal houden op den xvj. Augusti 1615. Noch hoe ende in wat manieren elcken Waghen sal verciert wesen met zijn Personagien. T'HANTVVERPEN, By Abraham Verhoeuen, [etc.] 4° 4 unsigned leaves; illus.
106.a.51.
The titlepage woodcut shows the arms of Antwerp. Published in 1615.

V61 VERCLARINGHE
Verclaringhe van den Gouden Blaes-balck/Van den Spaenschen Schalck. Om Signoors Practijcken t'ontdecken//en te sien/Is dit Gedruckt sonder gecken/ /sesthien hondert achtien. 4° sig.A^{4}B^2; illus.
T.2422(24*).
Sig.A is in prose, sig.B in verse. Accusing Oldenbarnevelt of being in the pay of the Spaniards. The titlepage engraving showing Oldenbarnevelt receiving Spanish money appears to have been cut on the right side. Corresponding to the copy described in *Knuttel* no.2764.

V62 VERCLARINGHE

Verclaringhe van den Gouden Blaes-balck/Van den Spaenschen Schalck. Om Signoors Practijcken t'ontdecken//en te sien/Is dit Gedruckt sonder gecken//sesthien hondert achtien. 4° sig. A^4; illus.
T.2248(63).

In prose and verse. A different edition from the preceding, with a copy of its titlepage engraving. The 'refereyn' ends on A3r. Corresponding to the copy described in *Knuttel* no.2765.

VERCLARINGHE vande uyterlijcke ende innerlijcke religie. 1612. *See* COORNHERT, Dirck Volckertsz. Vre-reden.

V63 VERDEDIGING

Verdediging Van Den Recht-gematichden CHRISTEN Iacobi Triglandij, Tot voorstant van de rechtsinnighe onderlinghe verdraeghsaemheyt/teghens de vermomde onderlinghe verdraeghsaemheyt Iacobi Taurini, ende sijn verwart boeck vande selve. DOOR Een Ghetrouvven, Godtsalighen Dienaer des Goddelijcken woordts inde Ghemeynte Iesu Christi. Met een Voor-reden Iacobi Triglandij . . . t'AMSTELDAM, By Marten Jansz. Brandt . . . 1616. 4° pp.123
1608/1650.

The author's preface signed: P.N.P.S. Not included in the early edition of Trigland's collected works, but could be by him. Printed by Paulus van Ravesteyn?

V64 VERDEDINGHE

VERDEDINGHE Voor die Edele Mogende Heeren Staten vande ghevnieerde Provintien/teghens de lasteringhe der ghener Diese t'onrechte beschuldighen van Inbreuke ende onrechtveerdighe besittinghe des Rijcx. Wt het Latijn, door een Liefhebber des Vaderlants/overgeset ANNO M.DC.IX. 4° sig. A-F^4
T.1713(31); T.1723(9); T.2420(22); 106.d.30.

Printed by Richard Schilders at Middelburg.

V65 VERDONCK, Cornelius

(tp.1) DI CORNELIO VERDONCH MADRIGALI A SEI VOCI NOVAMENTE POSTI IN LVCE . . . CANTO. IN ANVERSA. Appresso Pietro Phalesio. M DCIII.
(tp.2) DI CORNELIO VERDONCH MADRIGALI A SEI VOCI . . . ALTO. IN ANVERSA. Appresso Pietro Phalesio. M DCIII.
(tp.3) DI CORNELIO VERDONCH MADRIGALI A SEI VOCI . . . TENOR. IN ANVERSA. Appresso Pietro Phalesio. M DCIII.
(tp.4) DI CORNELIO VERDONCH MADRIGALI A SEI VOCI . . . SESTO. IN ANVERSA. Appresso Pietro Phalesio. M DCIII. obl.4° 4 pt.: ff.16; 16; 16; 16
Music A.439.

Among the named authors of the words, all in Italian, is Ambrogio Spinola.

V66 VEREPAEUS, Simon

[Precationum piarum enchiridion.] CATHOLICVM PRECATIONVM SELECTISSIMARVM ENCHIRIDION. EX SANCTORVM PATRVM, ET ILlustrium tum veterum, tum Recentium Auctorum scriptis, & PRECATIONVM LIBELLIS, concinnatum: per M. SIMONEM VEREPÆVM. Editio vltima, & superioribus castigatior, & pulcherrimis Imaginibus illustrior. ANTVERPIÆ, Sumptibus Viduæ & Heredum Io. BELLERI . . . 1603 [etc.] 16° pp.538; illus.
1018.b.12.

The illustrations are small engravings. For an English work in part derived from this, *see* FLINTON, George

V67 VERGILIUS, Polydorus

HISTORIA ANGLICA POLYDORI VERGILII LIBRIS VIGINTI SEX COMPREHENSA. Ab ipso autore postremùm iam recognita, emaculata, & . . . expolita. Nouo corollario Anglorum Regum Chronices Epitome aucta per GEORGIVM LILIVM . . . DVACI, Typis BALTAZARIS BELLERI . . . 1603. 8° 2 tom.: pp.1742

9510.a.11.

A division between the two volumes is indicated on p.815: Ne non commodè Polydorus noster Anglicus circumferri possit, visum est expedire ut eum in duas omnino scindamus partes: quarum prior hos sedecim, posterior verò reliquos complectetur libros. Ownership inscription: Mr. George Stokes, Cheltenham.

V68 VERHAEL

Verhael der Vrome Feyten/ende wercken van . . . Carolus Longueval, Graeff van Bucquoy . . . vande Maent Februarij Anno 1620. tot des Jaers 1621. Des Maents April/inde welcke maent alsoomē verstaedt/de Principaelste Stadt van Hongheren . . . Presburch tot de ghehoorsaemheydt des Keysers is ghebrocht. Eerst Ghedruckt den 21. Mey 1621. T'hantwerpen/By Abraham Verhoeuen/[etc.] 4° pp.8; sig.A^4; illus.

P.P.3444.af(232).

Headed: Mey 1621. 76. The titlepage woodcut shows a city under siege.

V69 VERHAEL

Verhael hoe dat de Cosaggen wederom in Moravien ghevallen zijn/ende vijf hondert Ruyteren vande Boheemsche gheslagen hebben . . . Nu eerst Ghedruckt/ den xv. Mey 1620. T'Hantwerpen/By Abraham Verhoeven . . . 1620. [etc.] 4° pp.8; sig.R^4; illus.

P.P.3444.af(50).

With news from Alsace and Venice. The titlepage woodcut shows a battle outside a fortress.

V70 VERHAEL

Verhael hoe dat de Cosagghen met thien Duysent mannen in Hungheren zijn ghevallen . . . Overghesedt wt de Hoochduytsche sprake in onse Nederlantsche Tale. Eerst Ghedruckt den xxi. Augusti 1620. T'Hantwerpen/By Abraham Verhoeuen . . . 1620, [etc.] 4° pp.8; sig.Eee^4; illus.

1480.aa.15(18); P.P.3444.af(81).

The titlepage woodcut shows cavalry cutting down infantry.

V71 VERHAEL

Verhael Hoe dat de Polacken/den Grooten Turck ouer de vijftich Duysendt Turcken hebben af gheslaghen. Ouerghesedt vvt het Hooch-duyts in onse Nederlantsche Taele. Eerst Ghedruckt den 1. October. 1621. T'Hantwerpen/by Abraham Verhoeuen/[etc.] 4° pp.8; sig.Ggg^4; illus.

P.P.3444.af(289).

With other news. The titlepage woodcut shows a cavalry battle between Christians and Turks.

V72 VERHAEL

Verhael hoe dat den Boheemschen Legher/beghint te Muytineren/ende willen ghelt hebbē waer ouer den Ghepretendeerden Coninck met zijn Huysvrouwe den 6. Augusti wt Praghe vertrocken is. Overghesedt wt de Hooch-duytsche sprake in onse Nederlantsche Tale. Eerst Ghedruckt den xxj. Augusti 1620. t'Hantwerpen/ by Abraham Verhoeuen . . . 1620. 4° pp.7; sig.Fff^4; illus.

1480.aa.15(7); P.P.3444.af(82); P.P.3444.af(82*).

The titlepage woodcuts show (a) the portrait of a young king (Louis XIII?) and (b) a cavalry battle.

V73 VERHAEL
Verhael hoe dat den Cheur-Vorst Hertoch van Saxen is in Bohemen ghevallen-met xij. duysent Voedtknechten/ende dry duysent Peerdē . . . Eerst Gedruckt den xxvj. Augusti 1620. T'Hantwerpen/By Abraham Verhoeuen . . . 1620. [etc.] 4° pp.7; sig.Ggg[4]; illus.
1193.f.24; 1480.aa.15(20); P.P.3444.af(83).
The titlepage woodcut shows the Elector John George I of Saxony in front of his army pointing to a city in the mountains.

V74 VERHAEL
Verhael hoe dat den Coninck van Polen is ghefaellieert gheweest vermoort te wesen van een groot Edelman ghenaempt Pisckarsky/binnen de Stadt Warsouien . . . Eerst ghedruckt den 3. Meert/1621. T'hantwerpen/By Abraham Verhoeuen/[etc.] 4° pp.8; sig.A[4]; illus., port.
P.P.3444.af(194).
Headed: Martius 1621. 26. With other news. The titlepage woodcut shows the portrait of King Sigismund III.

V75 VERHAEL
Verhael hoe dat den Hertoch van Beyerens Volck den Oversten Artillery Meester met 5000. mannen Slackenwaldt in Bohemen heeft in ghenomen . . . Overghesedt vvt de hooch-Duytsche sprake in onse Nederlantsche Tale. Eerst ghedruckt den 24. Meert/1621. T'Hantwerpen/By Abraham Verhoeuen [etc.] 4° pp.8; sig.C[4]; illus.
P.P.3444.af(210).
Headed: Martius 1621. 46. The titlepage woodcut shows troops moving in a city.

V76 VERHAEL
Verhael hoe dat den Nieuvven Ghepretendeerden, Coninck in Bohemen/den thienden man binnen Praghe op ontboden heeft/met allen de Boeren ende wilt seluer te velde comen. Overghesedt wt den Hoochduytsche in onse Nederlantsche sprake. Eerst Ghedruckt den xxiij. September 1620. T'Hantwerpen/By Abraham Verhoeven . . . 1620. [etc.] 4° pp.7; sig.Lll[4]; illus.
1480.aa.15(25); P.P.3444.af(103).
The titlepage woodcuts show (a) a portrait of a young king (Louis XIII?) and (b) a monument of a ball [of wool?] cut by a sword.

V77 VERHAEL
Verhael hoe dat Den Pfaltz-Graef nieuwē Ghepretendeerden Coninck van Bohemen wilt te velde comen/ende heeft zijnen Sone naer Enghelant gesondē. Overghesedt wt den Hooch-Duytsche in onse Nederlantsche sprake. Nv eerst Ghedruckt den vij. October . . . 1620. T'Hantwerpen/By Abraham Verhoeven . . . 1620. [etc.] 4° pp.8; sig.Qqq[4]; illus.
1193.f.13; 1480.aa.15(31); P.P.3444.af(113).
The titlepage woodcut shows troops storming a city.

V78 VERHAEL
Verhael hoe dat den Protestanten Legher van Franckfort op ghebroken is. Ghedruckt den iiij. Sept. 1620. 4° pp.7; sig.Nombre JJJJ.[4]; illus.
P.P.3444.af(89).
Without imprint or colophon, but with the privilege made out to Abraham Verhoeven at Antwerp. The titlepage woodcut shows an army abandoning the siege of a city as relief approaches.

V79 VERHAEL
Verhael hoe dat der Protestanten Legher opghebroken is/ende hebben by Franckfort thien Dorpen geplundert/ende eenich in brant ghestoken.

T'Hantwerpen/by Abraham Verhoeuen. 4° pp.8; sig.Nomb.V.[4]; illus.
P.P.3444.af(90).

News from Frankfurt and Bonn, dated 31 August 1620. The titlepage woodcut shows Gideon (Judges 7:5). At the end an advertisement for news from the Valtellina to be published shortly. Published in 1620.

V80 VERHAEL

(tp.1) Verhael hoe dat in Hollant binnen de stadt van Leyden/de Arminianen zijn vergaert geweest in een Huys om te Preken/op den xxi. April 1619 Waer ouer de Gomaristen met het Grau zijn ghecomen/ende hebben de Predicatie verstoordt/het Huys berooft/ende geplundert/ende den Predicant is int water ghespronghen. Noch met het verhael vant Placcaet ghepubliceert binnen Rotterdam/teghen d'Arminiaenen . . . Ende is eerst Ghedruckt tot Rotterdam/Voor Cornelis Maertens . . . 1619.
(tp.2=p.5) Coppije van het Placcaet dat nv lest in Hollant teghen d'Arminianen is Ghepubliceert. PLACCAET gepubliceert den 8 April 1619. By . . . Schout, Burghemeesteren/ende Schepenen der Stadt ROTTERDAM. Eerst Gedruckt, Tot ROTTERDAM, Voor Cornelis Maertens, 1619. 4° pp.8; sig.A[4]; illus.
P.P.3444.af(6).

Without imprint; published by Abraham Verhoeven at Antwerp in 1619. The titlepage woodcut shows branches, that on p.5 shows what appears to be intended as the Dutch lion, cut back from an originally larger woodcut.

V81 VERHAEL

Verhael hoe Dat Keysers volck de Stadt Mareck . . . hebben in ghenomen . . . Nv eerst Gedruckt den 12. Junij 1620. T'Hantwerpen/By Abraham Verhoeuen . . . 1620. [etc.] 4° pp.7; sig.Dd[4]; illus.
P.P.3444.af(58).

The titlepage woodcut shows a town by a river with troops moving into it. The *Bibliotheca Belgica* no.V196 records an issue dated 5 June 1620.

V82 VERHAEL

Verhael hoe dat s'Keysers volck met den Generael Graeff vā Bucquoy het stercke Casteel Ratsenbergh met stormender hant heeft in ghenomen . . . 1620. Nu eerst Ghedruckt/den 8. Mey 1620. T'Hantwerpen/By Abraham Verhoeuen . . . 1620. [etc.] 4° pp.7; sig.Q[4]; illus.
P.P.3444.af(49).

The titlepage woodcut shows a castle in which a woman is addressing a meeting while cavalry is moving about outside.

V83 VERHAEL

Verhael hoe dat sijn EX. MARQVIS SPINOL[A] is met den gheheelen Legher naer de stadt Worms ghetrocken[/]Ende hoe dat der Protestanten Legher oft Ghevnieerde Vorsten met hunnen Legher ghescheyden zijn . . . Eerst Ghedruckt den 6. Nouember 1620. T'Hantwerpen/By Abraham Verhoeuen . . . 1620. 4° pp.7; sig.Q[4]; illus.
P.P.3444.af(131).

The news is dated 24 October and 1 November. This is an earlier issue than the two recorded in the *Bibliographia Belgica* no.V 196 which are dated 12 November 1620. The titlepage woodcut shows a town under artillery attack. The titlepage is mutilated.

V84 VERHAEL

Verhael hoe dat sijn EX. MARQVIS SPINOL[A] is met den gheheelen Legher naer . . . Worms ghetrocken . . . Eerst Ghedruckt 12 Nouember 1620. T'Hantwerpen/By Abraham Verhoeuen . . . 1620. 4° pp.7; sig.Q[4]; illus.
P.P.3444.af(132).

A reissue of the preceding. The titlepage is slightly mutilated.

V85 VERHAEL

Verhael hoe dat sijn EX. MARQVIS SPINOLA is met den gheheelen Legher naer . . . Worms ghetrocken . . . Eerst Ghedruckt in Nouember 1620. T'Hantwerpen/By Abraham Verhoeuen . . . 1620. 4° pp.7; sig.Q^4; illus.
P.P.3444.af(133).

A variant reissue of the one dated 6 November.

V86 VERHAEL

Verhael hoe de Boheemsche den Churvorst Frederick Pfaltz-graff etc. Tot Coninck van Bohemen hebben ghekosen. Noch van d'Orloghe in Duytslandt/met het innemen der steden/ghedaen door Conte Bucquoy. Eerst Gheprint den 27. September. T'Hantwerpen/By Abraham Verhoeven/[etc.] 4° pp.8; sig.A^4; illus.
P.P.3444.af(19).

The titlepage woodcuts show (a) a trophy; (b) a siege; (c) the storming of a city.

V87 VERHAEL

Verhael hoe de Kosagghen wederom in Moravien ende Slesien gevallen ziin . . . Ende hoe dat den Pfaltz-Grave noch tijdt ghegheuen is om de Croone van Bohemen af te legghen tot den 1. Junij 1620. t'Hantwerpen/By Abraham Verhoeuen . . . 1620. [etc.] 4° pp.7; sig.X^4; illus.
P.P.3444.af(55).

With other news of the war. The titlepage woodcuts show (a) a cavalry skirmish; (b) a portrait inscribed 'Ismael Sophi'; (c) a tiny castle inscribed 'Antwer'.

V88 VERHAEL

Verhael hoe den CONINCK VAN VRANC-RYCK in Bearn, den geluckigen voortganck heeft gedaen 1620. Alwaer hy wederom de Catholijcke Apostolijcke Roomsche Religie heeft inghestelt . . . Ouerghesedt vvt het Fransoys in onse Nederlantsche sprake. Nu eerst ghedruckt den 22. December. 1620. T'Hantwerpen/By Abraham Verhoeuen/[etc.] 4° pp.16; sig.$QqRr^4$; illus.
1193.f.9; P.P.3444.af(162).

The titlepage woodcuts show (a) the royal arms of Louis XIII with a single crowned L; (b) his cypher inscribed 'Duo protegit unus', bearing two crowned Ls.

V89 VERHAEL

Verhael hoe den CONINCK VAN VRANC-RIICK in Bearn den geluckigen voortganck heeft gedaen 1620 . . . T'Hantwerpen/By Abraham Verhoeuen/[etc.] 4° pp.16; sig.$QqRr^4$; illus.
P.P.3444.af(163).

A reissue of the preceding, without date of publication. The single titlepage woodcut shows the arms of Louis XIII with the single crowned L.

V90 VERHAEL

Verhael hoe den Hertoch vā Beyeren in hooch Oosten-rijck met zijnen Legher ghevallen is/eñ de stadt Lints tot ghehoorsaemheyt heeft/ende vier steden . . . in ghenomen heeft . . . Eerst Ghedruckt den xviij. Augusti 1620. T'Hantwerpen/By Abraham Verhoeuen . . . 1620. 4° pp.7; sig.Ccc^4; illus.
1480.aa.15(16); P.P.3444.af(79).

With other news. The titlepage woodcut shows fighting in a burning city.

V91 VERHAEL

Verhael hoe den Hertoch van Beyeren/met zijnen Legher opghetrocken is/naer dat hy met de Rijckx Stadt Vlm is veraccordeert/ende getrocken met zijne macht naer Hooch-Oostenrijck ende . . . de stadt Linctx belegert heeft/ende den Hertoch van

Saxen volck . . . Eerst Ghedruckt den vij. Augusti 1620. T'Hantwerpen/by Abraham Verhoeuen . . . 1620. 4° pp. 7; sig. Zz[4]; illus.
P.P.3444.af(77).

With other news. The titlepage woodcut shows a city under attack.

V92 VERHAEL

Verhael hoe den Marquis Spinola den Legher by Cobelentz heeft doen monsteren den xx. Augusti . . . ende heeft een brugge ouer den Rhijn gheslagen/ende is met zijn volck ouer ghetrockē ende verouert met Accoort Rectz/ende Brabach . . . Eerst Ghedruckt den xxviij. Augusti 1620. t'Hantwerpen/by Abraham Verhoeuen . . . 1620. [etc.] 4° pp. 8; sig. Nombre JJ.[4]; illus.
P.P.3444.af(86).

V93 VERHAEL

Verhael hoe den Marquis Spinola naer Franckfort ghetrocken is/Nv eerst Ghedruckt den iiij. september 1620. (col.) T'hantwerpen/By Abraham verhoeven . . . 1620. 4° pp. 8; sig. Nomb. JJJ.[4]; illus.
P.P.3444.af(87).

Containing army lists. The large titlepage woodcut shows a general (Spinola?), surrounded by various places: a fortress, a river, a town, tents, soldiers, the general shown again in combat; in the left top corner arms with two lions rampant, a ducal crown and a cardinal's hat.

V94 VERHAEL

Verhael hoe den Marquis Spinola naer Franckfort ghetrocken [is/] Nv eerst Ghedruckt den v. september 1620. (col.) T'hantwerpen/By Abraham verhoeven . . . 1620. 4° pp. 7; sig. Nomb. JJJ.[4]; illus.
P.P.3444.af(88).

Another edition of the preceding. Without army lists, but with additional news. The titlepage woodcut is the same, but in this copy slightly cropped.

V95 VERHAEL

Verhael hoe ende in wat manieren den Heere M. Johan Van Olden-Barneveldt . . . is Onthalst gheworden smaendaechs voor noen den xiij. Mey Anno duysent ses hondert negen-thien. T'Hantwerpen/By Abraham Verhoeuen . . . 1619. 4° pp. 8; sig. A[4]; illus.
P.P.3444.af(9).

A biographical sketch of Oldenbarnevelt, with an eyewitness account of his execution. The titlepage woodcut shows that scene.

V96 VERHAEL

Verhael hoe ende in wat manieren/die van Neder Oostenrijck/De Keyserlijcke Majesteydt/hebben ghesworen . . . den Eedt van ghetrouwicheydt biddende verghiffenisse/van hare Rebellicheyt . . . Eerst Ghedruckt den v. Augusti 1620. T'Hantwerpen/By Abraham Verhoeuen . . . 1620. [etc.] 4° pp. 7; sig. Xx[4]; illus.
1480.aa.15(13); P.P.3444.af(76).

The titlepage woodcut shows the portrait of the Emperor, surrounded by Electors.

V97 VERHAEL

Verhael van de AMBASSADEVRS Vanden Coninck van Spagnien/Vranck-rijck/ende Italien . . . aen zijne Keyserlijcke Majesteyt/ende hoe datse tot Weenē ghearriveert zijn. Eerst ghedruckt den xviij. Augusti 1620. t'Hantwerpen/by Abraham Verhoeuen . . . 1620. 4° pp. 7; sig. Ddd[4]; illus.
1480.aa.15(15); P.P.3444.af(80).

With an account of the clothes worn by the ambassadors and their entourages. The titlepage woodcut shows soldiers embarking.

V98 VERHAEL
Verhael van de groote Aertbeuinghe/De welcke gheschiedt is nv onlanckx in Julio 1619. in Italien binnen de stadt van Mantua. Gheprint t'Hantwerpen/By Abraham Verhoeuen/[etc.] 4° pp.8; sig.A^4; illus.
1480.aa.15(2); P.P.3444.af(14).

Published in 1619. The titlepage woodcuts show (a) a walled city attacked by bees (?); (b) a knight on horseback jumping over a moat.

V99 VERHAEL
Verhael van de Groote Victorie eñ slach die den Graef van Bucquoy heeft vercreghen met de Cosagghen/teghen de Hunghersche . . . Ouerghesedt vvt den Hooch-Duytsche in onse Nederlantsche Tale. Eerst Ghedruckt den 31. Meert. 1621. T'Hantwerpen/By Abraham Verhoeuen/[etc.] 4° pp.8; sig.(?)^4; illus.
P.P.3444.af(214).

Headed: Martius 1621. 50. With other news. The titlepage woodcut shows a battle between Turkish and Christian cavalry.

V100 VERHAEL
Verhael van de groote Victorie in Pfalts-Grauē Landt/de welcke ons volck daer vercregen heeft/ende hebben twee Steden in ghenomen/met een Casteel/te weten/de steden Bensheym, Heppenheym, en t'Casteel sterckenberch, met de Berchstraete. Met Tijdinghe Wtden Legher van . . . den Marquis Spinola. Eerst Ghedruckt den 4. October, 1621. T'Hantwerpen, By Abraham Verhoeuen, [etc.] 4° pp.8; sig.Hhh^4; illus.
P.P.3444.af(290).

Headed: October, 1621. 141. The three titlepage woodcuts show (a) troops with wagons; (b) a fortress; (c) a city under siege.

V101 VERHAEL
Verhael van de groote Victorie vercregen door't volc van sijne Catholijcke Majesteyt van Spagnien, de welcke de Stadt Chiauenna, hebben in ghenomen/van de Graubontenaers in de Valtellina. Eerst Ghedruckt den 10. December 1621. T'hantwerpen/By Abraham Verhoeuen/[etc.] 4° pp.8; sig.D^4; illus.
P.P.3444.af(325).

Headed: December, 1621. 180. With news from France. The titlepage woodcut shows a fight in a burning city.

V102 VERHAEL
Verhael van de Leghers in Duytslandt/ende innemen der steden. Overghesedt wt den Hooch-Duytsche in onse Nederlantsche sprake. Nv eerst Ghedruckt den vij. October . . . 1620. T'Hantwerpen/By Abraham Verhoeven . . . 1620, [etc.] 4° pp.7; sig.Ppp^4; illus.
1480.aa.15(30); P.P.3444.af(112).

The titlepage woodcuts show (a) a cavalry skirmish; (b) a fortified camp by a river.

V103 VERHAEL
Verhael van de Puncten ende Articulē de welcke den Transilvaen Bethlin Gabor/versocht heeft aen den nieuwen Boheemschen Coninck/ende aen de Standen van Bohemen/Slesien/ende Moravien. Eerst ghedruckt int Hoochduytsche, nv ouer ghesedt in onse Nederlantsche sprake den x. December 1619. T'Hantvverpen, By Abraham Verhoeuen, [etc.] 4° pp.8; sig.A^4; illus., ports.
1480.aa.15(6); P.P. 3444.af(26).

The titlepage woodcuts show portraits of Frederick and Bethlen Gabor.

[Illustration of ***V105*** overleaf]

Verhael vande Victorie vanden Marquis Spinola/hoe dat hy twee steden in Pfaltz-Graven Lant in ghenomen heeft.

Gedruckt den xix. Sept. 1620. Nom. VII.

T'Hantwerpen/ By Abraham Verhoeuen.

V104 VERHAEL

Verhael van De Schermutseringhe gheschiedt int wt trecken wt de Vrijheyt vā Scādeck, den elffsten van September/Anno 1620 . . . tusschen een Deel van de Coronelsche Compaignie van den Prince van Espinoy/ende twee Compaignien Harquebusiers van den vyant/van de welcke d'eene was de Garde van den Marquis van Ansbach/ende d'andere die van Stakenbroeck Hollander. Volghens . . . Brieven . . . vvt het Legher van sijne Catholijcke Majesteyt . . . Ghedruct int Iaer . . . 1620. 4° pp.7; sig.A^4

P.P.3444.af(99).

Printed by Abraham Verhoeven at Antwerp.

V105 VERHAEL

Verhael van de Victorie vanden Marquis Spinola/hoe dat hy twee steden in Pfaltz-Graven Lant in ghenomen heeft. Gedruckt den XIX. Sept. 1620 . . . T'Hantwerpen/By Abraham Verhoeuen. 4° pp.7; sig.Nom.VIJ^4; illus.

P.P.3444.af(101).

The titlepage woodcut shows an army mustering outside a city. A reissue of the copy described in the *Bibliographia Belgica* no.V196, dated 18 September 1620. [See ERRATUM, p.719.]

V106 VERHAEL

Verhael van den Hertoch van Beyeren/hoe dat hy tot Munichen heeft doen stellen 130. Vendelen soo Cornetten vā Peerdē als Infanterie die hy in dē slach voor Praeg heeft gewonnē. Met noch den costelijcken Spieghel die gheschoncken was van die van Amsterdam aen de Pfalts-gravinne met eenen costelickē Bijbel van de Pfalts-gravinne ende andere Juweelen . . . Eerst ghedruckt den 15 Ianuarius 1621. T'Hantwerpen/By Abraham Verhoeven/[etc.] 4° pp.8; 4 unsigned leaves; illus.

P.P.3444.af(175).

Headed: Ianuarius. 6. The titlepage woodcuts show a portrait of a general; a trophy.

V107 VERHAEL

Verhael van den Oproer binnen Rotterdam in Hollant/hoe dat de Arminianen zijn vergaert geweest om te Preken op de Visch-marckt Sondach . . . den xxi. Julij. Alwaer een lanck Hollants wijf/in plaetse vā den Predicant haer verthoonden/ende de Salmen ophief diemen daer singhden . . . Gheprint t'Hantwerpen/By Abraham Verhoeuen/[etc.] 4° pp.8; sig.A^4; illus.

P.P.3444.af(12).

Published in 1619. The titlepage woodcuts show (a) the woman; (b) soldiers.

V108 VERHAEL

Verhael van den Rijcx-dagh ghehouden tot Mulhausen/tusschen de Catholijcke Cheur-Vorsten/ende de Lutersche. Ende hoe de Rebellen in Bohemen . . . met den Turc tracteren . . . Nu eerst ghedruckt den 30. April. 1620. T'Hantwerpen/op de Lombaerde Veste/inde gulde Sonne 1620. 4° pp.8; sig.N^4; illus.

P.P.3444.af(45).

Without the printer's name, but with the address of Abraham Verhoeven. The titlepage woodcut shows Turkish cavalry.

V109 VERHAEL

Verhael van der Protestanten Legher/ende op breken der seluer. Gedruc[t] den xxv. Sept 1620. T'hantwerpen/by Abraham Verhoeuē. 4° pp.8; sig.IX^4; illus.

P.P.3444.af(105).

The large titlepage woodcut shows Spinola crowned by angels, handing keys to the Emperor and Empress on a throne in a military landscape, with the three virtues and the Holy Ghost in the form of a dove in a cloud above them.

V110 VERHAEL

Verhael Van des Keysers Legher/de welcke de stadt ende Casteel Schitnauvv, in Hongharijen belegert heeft/door den Generael Graeff van Bucquoy. Ouergesedt vvt de Hooch-duytsche sprake, in onse Nederlantsche Tale. Nv eerst Ghedruckt den 11. Iunij 1621. T'Hantwerpen/By Abraham Verhoeuen/[etc.] 4° pp.8; 4 unsigned leaves; illus.

P.P.3444.af(244).

Headed: Iunij, 1621. 88. The titlepage woodcut shows the plan of a fortified town under siege.

V111 VERHAEL

Verhael van Duytslandt met het innemē der stercten ende Casteelen. Overghesedt wt de Hoochduytsche sprake 1620. Geprint den 27. Meert. T'Hantwerpen/By Abraham Verhoeuen/1620. 4° pp.8; sig.F^4; illus.

P.P.3444.af(38).

With news from Malta. The privilege includes the following issue, 'Edictale cassatie'. The titlepage woodcut shows the bird's-eye view of a fortified place by a river under artillery attack.

V112 VERHAEL

Verhael van Duytslant ende Bohemen. Van t'ghene daer nv ghepasseert is/van de Legers daer ontrent ligghende. Nv eerst Ghedruckt den 27. Junij 1620. T'Hantwerpen/By Abraham Verhoeuen . . . 1620. 4° pp.7; sig.Hh^4; illus.

P.P.3444.af(61).

Political and military news. The titlepage woodcuts show (a) the portrait of the Emperor; (b) a bird's-eye view of a fortified town with a windmill.

V113 VERHAEL

Verhael vā Duytslant hoe dat den Grave van Bucquoy op ghetrocken is/ende de Boheemsche in hun Quartier ouer vallen heeft . . . Overghesedt wt den Hoochduytsche in onse Nederlantsche sprake. Eerst Ghedruckt den xij. September 1620. T'Hantwerpen/By Abraham verhoeven . . . 1620. [etc.] 4° pp.8; sig.Hhh^4; illus.

1480.aa.15(24); P.P.3444.af(98).

The titlepage woodcut shows a battle scene. The copy at 1480.aa.15(24) is without approbation, that at P.P.3444.af(98) is with approbation.

V114 VERHAEL

Verhael vā Duytslant, hoe de Boheemsche tot Praghe hebben Raedt ghehouden om een groote somme Gheldts op te brenghen/tot den Oorloch/ende Soldaten te betalen. Noch hoe dat s'Keysers volck wederom wt Budweysz sijn ghevallen ende veel Dorpen in Bohemen hebben verbrandt. T'Hantwerpen/By Abraham Verhoeven . . . 1620. 4° pp.8; sig.B^4; illus.

P.P.3444.af(30).

A copy of the alternative issue ending with 'Finis' in place of the approbation, as described in the *Bibliographia Belgica* no.V196, vol.V, p.473. The large titlepage woodcut shows the outskirts of a city on fire.

V115 VERHAEL

Verhael van eenige Articulen van Bethlin Gabor Transilvaen. Ouerghesedt wt den Hooch Duytsche in onse Nederlantsche sprake. t'Hantwerpen/By Abraham Verhoeuen . . . 1620. 4° pp.8; sig.A^4; illus.

P.P.3444.af(31).

The articles preceded by news from Naples and Savoy. For another account of the Articles *see* above: Verhael van de Puncten ende Articulē . . . ouer ghesedt . . . den x. December 1619', P.P.3444.af(26). The titlepage illustration shows an encampment of oriental tents by a river, inscribed 'Boristius ad neper fl.', with cavalry.

V116 VERHAEL

Verhael van het Beleg der stercke stadt Gulick, ende het innemen van het stercke Casteel Rede, door Graeff Hendrick vanden Berghe. Eerst Ghedruckt den 15. September. T'Hantwerpen/By Abraham Verhoeuen/[etc.] 8° pp.8; sig.Tt^4; illus.

P.P.3444.af(283).

Headed: September, 1621. 128. With other news. The titlepage woodcut shows a fortified village with a windmill.

V117 VERHAEL

Verhael van het innemen der Steden in Bohemen/vā des Keysers volck/ende den Grave van Bucquoy/den Hertoch van Beyeren/ende den Cheur-Vorst van Saxen. Overghesedt wt de Hoochduytsche sprake in onse Nederlantsche Tale. Eerst Ghedruckt den xx. November. 1620 . . . T'Hantwerpen/By Abraham Verhoeuen . . . 1620. [etc.] 4° pp.8; sig.V^4; illus., ports.

P.P.3444.af(138).

The titlepage woodcuts show two portraits inscribed respectively 'Den Hertoch van Beyeren', 'Den Hertoch van Saxen'. The titlepage is cropped.

V118 VERHAEL

Verhael van het innemen der Steden in Bohemen/vā des Keysers volck . . . Eerst Ghedruckt den xxiij. November. 1620 . . . T'Hantwerpen/By Abraham Verhoeuen . . . 1620. [etc.] 4° pp.8; sig.V^4; illus., ports.

P.P.3444.af(139).

A reissue of the preceding. The titlepage woodcuts are the same.

V119 VERHAEL

Verhael van het Ouergheuen der Stadt Thabor, in Bohemen aen den Keyser. Met verscheyden Tijdinge wt Hongerijen/Duytslandt/Enghelandt/Vranck-rijck/ende andere Landen. Eerst Gedruckt den 17. December. 1621. T'Hantwerpen/By Abraham Verhoeuen/[etc.] 4° pp.7; sig.L^4; illus.

P.P.3444.af(332).

Headed: December. 1621. 187. In fact, without news from England. The titlepage illustration shows a fortified town with marching armies.

V120 VERHAEL

Verhael van het vertreck ende grooten Tocht vā . . . Marquis Spinola/de welcke vertrocken is wt Brussel/met eenen Legher naer Duytslandt. Eerst Ghedruckt den xxviij. Augusti 1620 . . . T'Hantwerpen/By Abraham Verhoeuen . . . 1620. [etc.] 4° pp.7; sig.Nomb.$J.^4$; illus., port.

P.P.3444.af(85).

An earlier issue than the copy described in the *Bibliographia Belgica* no.V196, dated 31 August 1620. The titlepage woodcut shows the portrait of Spinola with military symbols and a city on a river, with his full name and titles printed above it.

V121 VERHAEL

Verhael van Praghe/met t'ghene datter ghepasseert is. Overghesedt wt de Hooch-Duytsche sprake in onse Nederlantsche Tale. Eerst Ghedruckt den xxi. Julij. T'Hantwerpen/By Abraham Verhoeuen . . . 1620. [etc.] 4° pp.7; sig.Qq^4; illus.

P.P.3444.af(68).

With other news. Containing advertisements for the following issues to be signed Ss and Tt. According to the *Bibliographia Belgica* a variant of this issue is known, signed Rr on the titlepage. The titlepage woodcut shows the portrait of a general with only one hand.

V122 VERHAEL

Verhael van t'gene nv tot weenen ghepasseert is/Ende hoe de Polacken ende Hongersche malcanderen dapper hebben gheslaghen . . . Eerst Ghedruckt den xv. Mey 1620. t'Hantwerpen/By Abraham Verhoeuen. [etc.] 4° pp. 8; sig. S^4; illus.
P.P.3444.af(51).

Mostly political and military news from Austria. The large titlepage woodcut shows a fight between knights in armour.

V123 VERHAEL

Verhael van t'Ghene Nu in Duytslant ghepasseert is/ende wat t'sedert de leste Schermutseringhe gheschiet is ontrent Weenen. Ende hoe de Cosagghen een van de principaelste Rebellen van Bohemen/vermoordt hebben in sijn Casteel . . . Overghesedt uyt de Hoochduytsche sprake, in onse Nederlantsche Tale. Nu eerst Ghedruckt/den 28. April 1620. T'Hantwerpen/op de Lombaerde veste/inde gulde Sonne. 1620. [etc.] 4° pp. 8; sig. M^4; illus.
P.P.3444.af(44).

Without a name in the imprint; the address is that of Abraham Verhoeven. The large titlepage woodcut shows infantry fighting in a burning city.

V124 VERHAEL

Verhael van t'ghene nv in Hollant is ghepasseert, tot Rotterdam/wtrecht en Dort/ende hoe dat de Gommaristen hebben verboden aen de Arminiaenen niet meer te mogē Preken/op Lijff-straffinghe als volcht 1619. Ghy Arme Haenen, staet nv cloeck als mannen, Vvant de Synode tot Dort, begint v vvt Hollandt te Bannen. T'Hantvverpen, By Abraham Verhoeuen, [etc.] 4° pp. 6; 3 unsigned leaves; illus.
P.P.3444.af(3).

The three titlepage woodcuts all show ships, the largest one on the left has its flag inscribed: REINVT.

V125 VERHAEL

Verhael van t'ghene nv tot weenen/ende Praghe ghepasseert is. Nu eerst Ghedruckt/den 8. Mey 1620. T'Hantwerpen/op de Lombaerde Veste/inde gulde Sonne 1620. [etc.] 4° pp. 8; sig. O^4; illus.
P.P.3444.af(47).

With news from Alsace. Without a name in the imprint; the address is that of Abraham Verhoeven. The titlepage woodcut shows a full-length portrait of Maximilian I, Duke of Bavaria.

V126 VERHAEL

Verhael van weenen/ende Legher in Oosten-rijck. Overghesedt wt de Hooch-Duytsche sprake in onse Nederlantsche Tale. Eerst Ghedruckt den xvij. Julij. T'Hantwerpen/By Abraham Verhoeven . . . 1620. [etc.] 4° pp. 8; sig. Oo^4; illus.
P.P.3444.af(66).

Containing various items of news. The titlepage woodcut shows the bird's-eye view of a city with a windmill.

VERHAEL vande articulen ende conditien vanden peyse, eñ verbont, gesloten tusschen onsen . . . Keyser . . . ende den Turck. 1607. *See* GERMANY [1.1.1607]

V127 VERHAEL

Verhael vande Belegheringe vande stadt MONT-ALBAEN, Door den Legher vanden Coninck van Vranc-rijck. Ende hoe dat Monsieur Duc d'Vmena, duysendt vier hondert soldaten heeft gheslagen vande Huguenotten . . . Eerst Ghedruckt den 1. September, 1621. t'hantvverpen, by Abraham Verhoeuen, [etc.] 4° pp. 8; sig. Ll^4; illus.
P.P.3444.af(277).

Headed: September, 1621. 122. The titlepage woodcuts show (a) an execution scene; (b) a fight in a moat.

V128 VERHAEL

Verhael vande Crooninghe/geschiet binnen Franckfort den ix. September 1619. Aen . . . Ferdinandus Roomsch Keyser . . . Nu eerst Gheprint den xxvij. September. T'hantwerpen/By Abraham Verhoeven/[etc.] 4° pp.7; sig.A[4]; illus. P.P.3444.af(18).

Published in 1619. The titlepage shows the Emperor with the Electors and their arms.

V129 VERHAEL

Verhael vande EXECVTIE ende Iustitie ghegaen tegens den Boos-wicht Pierskarski . . . Eerst ghedruckt den 3. Meert. 1621. T'Hantwerpen/by Abraham Verhoeven/[etc.] 4° pp.8; sig.A[4]; illus.
P.P.3444.af(195).

Headed: Martius 1621. 27. The titlepage woodcut shows the scene of execution. With other news.

V130 VERHAEL

Verhael vande groote Victorie, die den Grave van Bucquoy vercreghen heeft in Hungharijen/teghen t'volck van Bethlem Gabor, die quamen . . . om de belegherde stadt Neuheusel, te ontsettē de welcke zijn alles geslagen geworden . . . Noch hoe de Polacken de Rijcke stadt Trebisonda hebben inghenomen ende verbrandt. Nv eerst Ghedruckt den 30. Iunij. 1621. T'Hantwerpen, By Abraham Verhoeuen, [etc.] 4° pp.8; sig.D[4]; illus.
P.P.3444.af(252).

Headed: Iunij, 1621. 96. The titlepage woodcut shows a battle outside a burning city.

V131 VERHAEL

Verhael vande groote Victorie ende slach/gheschiet in Duytslant/vercreghen teghen de Rebellen van den Keyser/ende Bethlehem Gabor. Ende hoe dat de Cosacken xiij. Vendelen hebben ghenomen vanden Vyandt . . . ende veel duysent vyanden hebben doot gheslaghen. Eerst ghedruckt den xxvij. October. 1620. T'Hantwerpen/By Abraham Verhoeuen . . . 1620. [etc.] 4° pp.7; sig.J[4]; illus.
P.P.3444.af(127).

An earlier issue than the copy described in the *Bibliographia Belgica* no.V196 which is dated end of October. The titlepage woodcut shows a battle between Christians and Turks below a castle.

V132 VERHAEL

Verhael vande groote Victorie ende slach/gheschiet in Duytslant/vercreghen teghen de Rebellen van den Keyser/ende Bethlehem Gabor . . . Eerst ghedruct int lest van October. T'Hantwerpen/By Abraham Verhoeuen . . . 1620. 4° pp.7; sig.J[4]; illus.
1193.f.11; P.P.3444.af(128).

A copy of the same issue as that described in the *Bibliographia Belgica* no. V196 as 'derniers jours d'octobre 1620'. The titlepage woodcut is the same as in the preceding.

V133 VERHAEL

Verhael vande groote Victorie ende Slach hoe dat de Polacken acht Duyzent Turcken hebben verslaghen/Ende den Oppersten van de Cosagghen/heeft noch verstroyt ende gheslaghen xv. Duysendt Tartaren. Ouerghesedt vvt het Hoochduyts, in onse Nederlantsche sprake. Eerst gedruckt den 15. September. 1621. T'Hantwerpen/By Abraham Verhoeuen/[etc.] 8° pp.8; sig.Tt[4]; illus.
P.P.3444.af(284).

Headed: September, 1621. 129. With news from France. The titlepage woodcut shows a cavalry skirmish.

VERHAEL vande heeren . . . Adrian van Mathenes . . . Hugo de Groot . . . gedeputeert, om Amsterdam te onderrichten. 1616. *See* HOLLAND. Staten [29.6.1616]

V134 VERHAEL

Verhael vande Leghers in Duytslandt. Ende hoe datter den thienden Junij/voor den Keyser twee duysent twee hondert Peerden/ende vijf duysent ses hondert voedt-knechten ouer den Rhijn ghepasseert zijn . . . Eerst Ghedruckt den xxvj. Junij. T'Hantwerpen/By Abraham Verhoeven . . . 1620. [etc.] 4° pp.7; sig.Ji[4]; illus.

P.P.3444.af(62).

The titlepage woodcut shows a cavalry skirmish between Christians and Turks.

V135 VERHAEL

Verhael Vande Occasie eñ Oorsaeck waer door de Nederlanden gecomen zijn aenden Vreede handel. 4° sig.A[4]

T.1713(15).

Consisting of three poems, i.e. 'Te comen tot onser meininge', an anonymous version into verse of the prose 'Ghenoechlich discours' by Nicolaus Mulerius; 'Fida admonitio'; 'Getrouwe waerschouwinge', translation of 'Fida admonitio'. Published in 1608.

V136 VERHAEL

Verhael vande Puncten ende Articulen van het ouergaen van Graitze/door den Generael Conte de Busquoy [sic]. Met noch het innemen vant slodt ende Stadt Weitragh . . . Noch met den Marckt Weisal . . . Overghesedt wt de Hooch-Duytsche sprake/Ende nv in onse Nederlantsche Tale den xxvj. Julij 1619 . . . T'Hantwerpen, by Abraham Verhoeuen . . . 1619. 4° pp.8; sig.A[4]; illus.

1480.aa.15(3); P.P.3444.af(13).

The titlepage woodcuts show (a) troops storming a city; (b) a cavalry skirmish. The woodcut at the end shows the Habsburg arms.

V137 VERHAEL

Verhael vãde Solemniteyt gehouden tot Madril in Spagnien 1620. int gheuen vanden Cardinaels Hoedt aen . . . Don Fernando/den tweedē Sone des . . . Conincx van Spagnien/etc. t'Hantwerpen/By Abraham Verhoeuen . . . 1620. 4° pp.8; sig.K[4]; illus.

P.P.3444.af(43).

The titlepage woodcut shows the Spanish arms.

V138 VERHAEL

Verhael vande Victorie die den Grave van Bucquoy vercreghen heeft in Hungarijen, naer dat hy de Stadt Presborch ende Casteel heeft verovert/is voorts ghetrocken met den Legher naer Bethlehem Gabor. Ouerghesedt wt de Hooch-Duytsche sprake in onse Nederlantsche Tale. Eerst Ghedruckt den 5. Junij. 1621. T'Hantwerpen, By Abraham Verhoeuen, [etc.] 4° pp.8; sig.C[4]; illus.

P.P.3444.af(241).

Headed: Iunij. 1621. 85. With other news. The titlepage woodcut shows a battlefield.

V139 VERHAEL

Verhael vande Victorie/ende in nemen der steden in Hongharijen, die s'Keysers volck heeft gecreghen/onder t'beleydt vanden Generael Graeff van Bucquoy. Overghesedt wt het Hooch-duyts in onse Nederlantsche sprake. Nv eerst Ghedruckt den 4. Iunij. 1621. T'Hantwerpen/By Abraham Verhoeuen/[etc.] 4° pp.8; sig.A[4]; illus.

P.P.3444.af(239).

Headed: Iunij. 1621. 83. With other news. The titlepage woodcut shows a cavalry skirmish between Turks and Christians.

V140 VERHAEL

Verhael vande Victorie/in Bohemen/ghedaen door des Keysers volck/ende innemen der steden/alwaer den Grave van Bucquoy/selver de stadt Pis-ka heeft

helpen beclimmen . . . Gedruct den 21. October 1620. T'Hantwerpen/By Abraham Verhoeven. 4° pp.7; sig.E[4]; illus.
1480.aa.15(40); P.P.3444.af(123).
With 'Anagramma in nomen falsi Regis Bohemiæ'. The large titlepage woodcut shows a Roman general surrounded by prostrate soldiers with a background scene of battle and a figure kneeling before God in a cloud.

V141 VERHAEL
Verhael vande Victorie in Bohemen/vā het in nemen der steden . . . door het Crijsvolck vande Keyserlijcke Majesteyt/ende den Legher vanden . . . Hertoch van Beyeren/ende den Legher vanden . . . Hertoch vā Saxen . . . Nv eerst Ghedruckt den xiij. November 1620. T'Hantwerpen/By Abraham Verhoeven . . . 1620. [etc.] 4° pp.7; sig.T[4]; illus.
1480.aa.15(44); P.P.3444.af(137).
The titlepage woodcut shows a cavalry fight between Christians and Turks.

V142 VERHAEL
Verhael vande Vrome Feyten/vanden . . . Veldt-Heer AMBROSIVS SPINOLA . . . Eerst Ghedruckt den 29. Appril 1621. T'Hantwerpen/By Abraham Verhoeuen/ [etc.] 4° pp.8; sig.(??)[4]; illus., port.
P.P.3444.af(226).
Headed: Appril 1621. 67. The titlepage woodcut shows the portrait of Spinola.

V143 VERHAEL
Verhael vanden Afgrijselijcken ende Bloedighen Slach gheschiet in Bohemen/ teghen de Rebellen/eer dat s'Keysers Volck de Stadt praghe heeft inghenomen . . . Eerst Ghedruckt den xxvij. Nouember. T'Hantwerpen/By Abraham Verhoeuen, [etc.] 4° pp.6; sig.Aa[4]; illus.
1480.aa.15(47); P.P.3444.af(144).
The last leaf recto is blank, the verso bears the privilege. The titlepage woodcut shows a fight between Christians and Turks. Published in 1620.

V144 VERHAEL
Verhael vanden Boheemschē krijch wat datter nv onlanckx ghepasseert is. Overghesedt wt de Hooch-duytsche sprake in onse Nederlantsche Tale. Eerst Ghedruckt den xij. Junij. T'Hantwerpen/By Abraham Verhoeven . . . 1620. [etc.] 4° pp.7; sig.S[4]; illus.
P.P.3444.af(59).
The titlepage woodcut shows a cavalry battle.

V145 VERHAEL
Verhael vandē Bohemschen [*sic*] krijch/by Prage. Ende hebben den Chur-Vorst Pfaltz, Fredrich voor Coninck van Bohemen ghekosen, maer en is noch niet ghekroont. Ghedruckt den xj. October. T'Hantwerpen/By Abraham Verhoeven/ [etc.] 4° pp.8; sig.A[4]; illus., port.
1480.aa.15(4); P.P.3444.af(20).
The titlepage woodcuts show (a) an army camped by a river; (b) a portrait of Frederick. Published in 1619.

V146 VERHAEL
Verhael vandē Crijch in Duytslandt/ende hoe den Hertoch van Beyeren voor de stadt Lintz ghecomen is. Overghesedt wt de Hoochduytsche Tale in onse Nederlantsche sprake. Eerst Ghedruckt den xiiij. Augusti 1620. t'Hantwerpen/by Abraham Verhoeuen . . . 1620. 4° pp.7; sig.Bbb[4]; illus.
1480.aa.15(14); P.P.3444.af(78).
The titlepage woodcut shows the imperial arms.

V147 VERHAEL

Verhael vanden doodt des Advocaets van Hollandt/Johan van Olden-Barnevelt/ hoe hy op den 13. Mey 1619. inden Haghe onthooft is/alsoo ick't selve ghesien hebbe. Ghedruckt tot Amsterdam, by Broer Iansz. . . . 1619. fol. a single sheet T.2422(27).

V148 VERHAEL

Verhael vanden Gefaillieerden Aēslach van den Hertoghe van Buillion op de Rijcxstadt van Besanzon . . . Met Relaes van verscheydē victorien in Bemerlandt, vercreghen door dē Hertoghe van Beyeren, ende den Graue vā Bucquoy. Eerst Ghedruckt den xxiij. October 1620. T'Hantwerpen/By Abraham Verhoevē . . . 1620, [etc.] 4° pp.7; sig.F^4; illus.
1480.aa.15(41); P.P.3444.af(124).

The titlepage woodcut shows the portrait of Maximilian I, Duke of Bavaria.

V149 VERHAEL

Verhael vanden grooten slach in Duytslandt, Hoe den Generael Graeff van Bucquoy/wederom een groote Victorie heeft ghecreghen ende vande Boheemsche gheslagen heeft duysendt vijf hondert Peerden/vijf Cornetten ghenomen . . . ende den oppersten Luytenandt vanden Vyandt/vanden Graeff de La Tour ghevanghen ghenomen. T'Hantwerpen/By Abraham Verhoeven . . . Den 27. Februarij. 4° pp.8; sig.C^4; illus.
P.P.3444.af(34).

With other war news. The titlepage woodcut shows a cavalry battle between Turks and Christians. Published in 1620.

V150 VERHAEL

Verhael vanden Grouwelijcken eñ Bloedigen Slach ende Victorie die de Cosacken van Polen hebben ghehadt teghen de Turcken ende Tartaren/ende hebben twee Steden van den Turck in ghenomen . . . Bolagrat ende . . . Chilien . . . Nv eerst Ghedruct den 12. Meert. 1621. T'Hantwerpen/By Abraham Verhoeven/[etc.] 4° pp.8; sig.(∴)^4; illus.
P.P.3444.af(202).

Headed: Martius 1621. 36. With other news. The titlepage woodcut shows a cavalry battle between Turks and Christians.

V151 VERHAEL

Verhael vanden Slach ghewonnen teghen die Rebellen van Bohemen/de welcke meynden den Legher van den Keyser/met den Grave van Bucquoy by Langhenlois op te lichten. Eerst Ghedruckt den x. Julij. T'Hantwerpen/By Abraham Verhoeuen . . . 1620. [etc.] 4° pp.7; sig.Nn^4; illus.
P.P.3444.af(65).

The report from Langenlois dated 17 June 1620. The titlepage woodcut shows an army attacking a fortress with artillery and cavalry, with gallows and wheel in the background.

V152 VERHAEL

Verhael vanden slach in Duytslandt/nv lest gheschiedt. Eerst Ghedruckt den x. April 1620. T'Hantwerpen/By Abraham Verhoeven . . . 1620. [etc.] 4° pp.8; sig.J^4; illus.
P.P.3444.af(42).

The titlepage is printed sideways. The woodcuts show (a) infantry and artillery before a castle on a hilltop, with Turkish and Christian flags; (b) an army camp, by a river; (c) a city.

V153 VERHAEL

Verhael vant innemen der steden in Duytslāt Door den Generael Graeff van Bucquoy/ende den Graeff van Tampier in Moravien. Overghesedt wt den

Hooch-Duytsche in onse Nederlantsche sprake. Nv eerst Ghedruckt den xxv. October. T'Hantwerpen/By Abraham Verhoeuen . . . 1619. 4° pp.8; sig.A[4]; illus.
P.P.3444.af(23).
The titlepage woodcut shows a battle scene with a windmill.

VERHAEL vant' innemen met ghewelt van de stadt van Albiac. 1621. *See* RÉCIT véritable de la prise . . . de la ville d'Albiac.

V154 VERHAEL
Verhael vant' T'ghene ghebeurdt is tot Parijs, met t'Vonnis vant' Hoff vant' Parlement/van Parijs/op den Oproer ghebeurt den 26. September 1621. Jnt wedercomen van die vande Ghepretendeerde Ghereformeerde Religie vā Charenton. Ouerghesedt vvt het Fransoys in onse Nederlantsche Tale. Eerst Ghedruckt den 6. October. 1621. T'Hantwerpen/By Abraham Verhoeven/[etc.] 4° pp.8; sig.Ll[4]; illus.
P.P.3444.af(293).
An account of the riot preceding the proclamation itself. The titlepage woodcut shows the arms of Louis XIII. The *Bibliographia Belgica* no.V197 records an issue of 8 October 1621.

VERHANDELING vande Unie. 1618. *See* NETHERLANDS. United Provinces [1579]

VERHANDELINGHE vande Unie . . . binnen . . . Utrecht ghesloten. 1607. *See* NETHERLANDS. United Provinces [1579]

V155 VERHEIDEN, Jacob
OP EEN PENNINGH Vande Staten der Vereenichde Nederlandtsche Provincien/ gheslagen ANNO 1590 . . . Aende . . . Heeren Ghedeputeerde op den Landt-dach van Nieumeghen . . . 1615. [etc.] fol. a single sheet; illus.
1889.d.3(300).
A poem, signed: I. Verheyden. The engraving shows both sides of the medal.

V156 VERHEIDEN, Jacob
PRÆSTANTIUM aliquot THEOLOGORUM, qui ROM. ANTICHRISTUM præcipuè oppugnarunt, EFFIGIES: quibus addita E'LOGIA [*sic*], LIBRORUMQ. CATALOGI: Operâ IAC. VERHEIDEN. HAGÆ-COMITIS. M.D.C.II. [etc.] (col.) EX OFFICINA Bucoldi Cornelii Nieulandii. fol. pp.226; illus.
203.e.15; G.1456.
Engraved portraits, ending with an emblem, signed H, Hh,Hhon,HAB. The engraved titlepage signed: sculpebat, et excud. henricus hondius. The copy at G.1456 has a device of Martinus Nutius of Antwerp pasted on the inside of the cover.

V157 VERHEIDEN, Jacob
PRÆSTANTIUM . . . THEOLOGORUM . . . EFFIGIES . . . Operâ IAC. VERHEIDEN. HAGÆ-COMITIS. M.D.C.II. [etc.] (col.) EX OFFICINA Bucoldi Cornelii Nieulandii. fol. pp.226; illus.
491.i.6(1); C.80.b.6.
Another issue of the preceding; with the addition of two leaves, signed: (?)1,2 and bearing the portrait of Berengarius on (?)1r and his biography on (?)1v-(?)2v, inserted between leaves ★5 and ★6.

V158 VERHEIDEN, Jacob
[Praestantium aliquot theologorum . . . effigies.] AF-BEELDINGEN Van sommighe in Godts-Woort ervarene MANNEN, die bestreden hebben den ROOMSCHEN ANTICHRIST. Waer by ghevoecht zijn de LOF-SPREVCKEN ende Registers harer Boecken. Eerst int Latijn uytghegeven door IAC. VERHEIDEN: Ende nu in Neer-Duijtsch overgheset door P.d.K. In s'Graven-Haghe, By Beuckel

Corneliszoon Nieulandt. M.D.C.III. (col.) IN S'GRAVEN-HAGHE, By Beuckel Corneliszoon Nieulandt . . . M.D.C.III. 4° ff.147; illus.
487.f.16.

The engraved titlepage has had the centre removed, with loss of the signature of Henricus Hondius, to allow insertion of the letterpress title. The translator's 'Sonnet' signed: Kamp-en-eere, motto of Paulus de Kempenaer. With additional verses by this author. The engravings as in the preceding. Ownership inscription: J. Wolffers (?) 1614.

V159 VERHEIDEN, Willem
[De iure belli Belgici.] ORATIE, of VVtspraecke van het Recht der Nederlandsche Oorloge tegen Philippum Coning van Spaengien . . . van eenen Nederlandschen Edelman ghedaen. In Nederlandsche ghetrouvvelick vertalet. t'AMSTELREDAM. By Michiel Colijn . . . M.DC.VIII. 4° pp.48
T.1723(5).

Anonymous. Corresponding to the copy described in *Knuttel* no.1491.

V160 VERHEIDEN, Willem
[De iure belli Belgici.] ORATIE, OF VVtspraecke van het Recht der Nederlandtsche Oorloge teghen Philippum Coningh van Spaengien . . . t'AMSTELREDAM, By Michiel Colijn . . . M.DC.VIII. 4° pp.48
106.d.23.

Anonymous. Another edition of the preceding, corresponding to the copy described in *Knuttel* no.1490.

V161 VERHEIDEN, Willem
GVILLELMI VERHEIDEN ORATIONES DVÆ: VNA AD NOVOS BATAVOS, ALTERA IN DISCESSVM SVVM. AD ACADEMICOS: Quibus accessit IACOBI fratris DE PROGNOSTICIS POLITICIS ORATIO: Ante Annos XXVII habitæ IN ACADEMIA LEIDENSI. ARNHEMII, Apud IOANNEM IANSONIVM. M.D.C.XVII. 4° sig.A^6C-F^4G^6; illus.
610.k.17(11).

The editor's dedication signed: Jacobus Verheiden. The titlepage engraving shows the device of Willem Verheiden, the Dutch lion with the motto 'animo et virtute'.

VERHEYDEN, Jacob. *See* VERHEIDEN, Jacob

VERIFICATION de la bonne foy de M. Fabrice de la Bassecourt. 1618. *See* NIELLE, Charles de

V162 VERITABLE
[Veritable discours de la descouverte de l'entreprise de Loys de Camboursier.] Een Vvaerachtich verhael van het Ontdecken des aenslachs op de stadt Geneve ende het Landt van Berne. Voorgenomen by . . . Loijs de Combousier Du Tarrail ende sijnen knecht la Bastide/beyde daer over ter doot ghebracht. VVt Geneven In eenen brief herwaerts overgheschreven inde Fransche tale/ende in de Nederlandtsche tale ghestelt. Ghedruckt na het Geneefsche exemplaer/voor Michiel Colijn . . . tot Amsterdam. 1609. 4° sig.A^4
T.1729(6); T.2420(39).

The copy at T.2420(39) is imperfect; wanting sig.A3,4.

VERKLAERINGE. *See* also VERCLAERINGHE; VERCLARINGE; VERCLARINGHE; VERKLARINGHE

VERKLARINGE vande sententie ghepronuncieert jeghens Johan Oldenbarnevelt. 1620. *See* NETHERLANDS. United Provinces. Staten Generaal [6.6.1620]

VERKLARINGHE. *See* also VERCLAERINGHE; VERCLARINGE; VERCLARINGHE; VERKLARINGE

V163 VERKLARINGHE
Een Verklaringhe/over den 133. Psalm. Met eē zeker onderscheyt inde Voorredē vant verscheel/dwelc is onder onse Predickanten/belanghende vande Predestinatie ende het aenkleven van dien . . . samen ghestelt/door een Lief-hebber des Vreedts . . . By my wel te vreden . . . 1611. 4° sig. A-D^4
T.2241(18).
Sometimes tentatively attributed to Franciscus Lansbergius. Without imprint; printed by Matthijs Bastiaensz or Jan van Waesberghe at Rotterdam? The imprint is part of the woodcut titlepage border which has been handcoloured.

VERKLARINGHE van de . . . Staten van Hollandt . . . op de Ordonnantie vande successien. 1617. *See* HOLLAND. Staten [13.5.1594]

VERKLARINGHE Van den . . . Koning van groot Britannien. 1612. *See* JAMES I, King [Speeches and letters]

V164 VERKLARINGHE
Verklaringhe van een Monnincks Cap, hare cracht/macht/deucht ende virtuyten. Item een Ghedicht van't Bestandt. Tot Middelburch, By Jasper de Craeyer. 1609. 4° sig. (⁎⁎⁎)^4
T.2421(2).

VERRE-KIJCKER. 1620. *See* SECRETISSIMA Instructio.

V165 VERSTEGAN, Richard
CHARACTEREN OFT Scherpsinnighe Beschrijvinghe van de Proprieteyten, oft eygendommen van verscheyde personen. DOOR R.V. t'HANTWERPEN, By Guilliam Lesteens . . . 1619. [etc.] (col.) By Guilliam Lesteens . . . 1619. 8° sig. A-H^{8}I^4
012330.de.25.
Anonymous. The signatures of the first gathering are irregular.

VERSTEGAN, Richard. Een cluchtich verhael, van eenen gepredestineerden cappuyn. 1619. [Sometimes tentatively attributed to Richard Verstegan.] *See* CLUCHTICH

V166 VERSTEGAN, Richard
IAN Josepsens droom Gheschreven Door sijnen goeden vriendt aen den welcken hy het selvér verhaelt heeft. Gheprent te Drucken-dorp, door t'bestier, Van swerten inct, en vvit pampier . . . 1619. Men vintse te coop daerse veyl zijn. 8° sig. A^{8}B^7
3925.a.2.
Anonymous. Signed: I.I.*s*., i.e. Jan Josepsen. A defence of Arminians and Catholics, made by the ghost of Oldenbarnevelt, with named attacks on Luther and Johannes Bogerman. Although set in the environs of The Hague Arminius is said to have been seen 'here at Leiden'. *Sabbe Moretussen* p.124 describes an edition or issue with the address of Abraham Verhoeven of Antwerp added to the title. Could this have been on sig. B8? If not, this copy corresponds to that described in *Van der Wulp* no.1671.

V167 VERSTEGAN, Richard
NEDER-DVYTSCHE EPIGRAMMEN Op verscheyden saecken, Soo wel om te stichten, als den geest te vermaecken. MET Genuchlycke EPITAPHIEN op d'ouerledene gedicht, waer deur dat de leuende worden oock gesticht. Ghecomponeert deur R.V. TOT MECHELEN. By Henrick Iaey, 1617. [etc.] 8° sig. A-G^{8}H^4
11555.aa.36.
The dedication signed: Richardus Versteganus. The poems numbered in two series of a hundred each, preceded by an apologetic preface.

V168 VERSTEGAN, Richard

NEDERLANTSCHE ANTIQVITEYTEN met de bekeeringhe van eenighe der selue landen tot het kersten ghelooue, DEVR S. WILLIBRORDVS . . . T'HANTWERPEN, By GASPAR BELLERVS . . . 1613. [etc.] 8° pp.112; illus.

1606/277(1).

The dedication signed: Richardus Versteganus. With an engraving of St. Willibrord on the titlepage and engravings of heathen gods in the text.

V169 VERSTEGAN, Richard

ODES IN IMITATION OF THE SEAVEN PENITENTIAL PSALMES, VVith Sundry other Poemes and ditties tending to deuotion and pietie. IMPRINTED . . . M.D.CI. 8° pp.115; illus.

C.38.b.29.

Anonymous. The dedication signed: R.V. Without imprint; printed by Arnout Conincx at Antwerp. With the exlibris of Lea Wilson.

V170 VERSTEGAN, Richard

A RESTITVTION of DECAYED INTELLIGENCE: In antiquities. Concerning the . . . English nation. By the studie and trauaile of R.V. . . . Printed at Antvverp by Robert Bruney. 1605. And to be sold at London . . . by Iohn Norton and Iohn Bill. 4° pp.338; illus.

687.e.33; G.5940; 598.d.13.

The dedication signed by the author in full. The engraved illustrations include Verstegan's(?) arms on p.[339]. The copy at 598.d.13, with the ownership inscription: Rob. Parkhurst, is imperfect; wanting sig. Vv3-Xx4, containing the index.

V171 VERSTEGAN, Richard

DE SPIEGEL DER NEDERLANDSCHE ELENDEN. Getoont Door een Lief-hebber der Waerheyt ende der Nederlanden weluaert. TOT MECHELEN, By HENRICK IAYE 1621. 8° pp.174

12315.aaa.10.

Anonymous. The dedication signed: R.V. Ownership inscription: Coll. S.J. Bruxellæ.

V172 VERSTEGAN, Richard

DE SPIEGEL DER NEDERLANDSCHE ELENDEN . . . TOT MECHELEN, By HENDRICK IAYE 1621. 8° pp.174

1193.d.25.

Another issue of the preceding, with the publisher's device on the titlepage where the preceding has an ornament. Imperfect; wanting the last leaf bearing the approbation and errata.

V173 VERSTEGAN, Richard

THEATRVM Crudelitatum Hæreticorum Nostri Temporis. Editio altera emendatior. ANTVERPIÆ, Apud Hadrianum Huberti . . . M.DCIIII. [etc.] 4° pp.95; illus.

489.g.27.

Anonymous; the dedication signed: R.V. The engravings at least in part attributed to the Wierix brothers. The anonymous verses describing them are by Joannes Bochius. Badly mutilated.

V174 VERSTEGAN, Richard

[Theatrum crudelitatum.] THEATRE des Cruautez des Hereticques de nostre temps. Traduit du Latin en François. La seconde edition, augmentée & plus correcte. EN ANVERS, Chez Adrien Hubert. 1607. [etc.] 4° pp.95; illus.

858.h.17; G.20236.

Anonymous; the dedication signed: R.V. Illustrated as the preceding, with the verses by Joannes Bochius.

V175 VERTHOONINGHEN

Verthooninghen. Ghedaan by die vande Nederduytsche Academi. Door bevel van de E. Heeren deser Stede Amsterdam: tot onthaal van zyne Koninglijcke Majesteyt van BOHEMEN. In't Iaar 1621, den 6 Iunij. T'AMSTERDAM, Voor Antony van Salinghen. 1621. (col.) t'Amsterdam, by Nicolaas Biestkens/[etc.] 4° sig.A^4; illus.

11555.d.2.

An additional unsigned leaf, conjugate with the title-leaf, occurs between sig.A1 and A2. An engraved portrait of Frederick of Bohemia and his family, signed: CJVisscher excudebat and dated 1621, has been added to this copy. The titlepage woodcut shows the emblem of the 'Academie'.

V176 VERTOIG

T'Vertoig der Zeeuscher Nymphen, aende onverwinnelicke Nassausche Helden, voirstanderen der Nederlandsche vrijheyd, ende Vaderen des Vaderlands. Fistula dulce canit, volucrem DVM deCIpIt. 4° sig.AB^4; illus.

T.1713(3).

The chronogram reads 1607; the illustration on the last leaf, showing a pair of spectacles with Latin inscriptions around them and Dutch and Latin inscriptions below, bears the date 1609.

V177 VERTOOCH

Vertooch Aen myne Heeren vant Hof van Parlemente/op de Vader-moort begaen in den persoon des Conincks Hendrick de Groote. Ghedruckt . . . 1610. 4° sig.AB^{4}C^2

T.1731(2).

Translated from an unidentified French original.

VERTOOCH ende Versoeck der genaemder Catholiken. 1603. *See* PETITION

V178 VERTOOCH

VERTOOCH Vande wreetheyt der Calvinisten bewesen aen den Rhijn tusschen Bacherach ende Coub. Eerst ghedruckt int Latijn, nv ghetrouvvelijck ouergesedt in onse Nederlantsche Tale. Eerst Ghedruckt den 1. Appril 1621. T.'Hantwerpen by Abraham Verhoeven/[etc.] 4° pp.8; sig.A^4; illus.

P.P.3444.af(215).

Headed: April. 1621. 51. On the murder of Godefridus Thelen S.J. and others on 25 September 1620. The titlepage woodcuts show (a) a fortress; (b) a ship with one sail.

V179 VERTOOGH

Vertoogh/BY DE REMONSTRANTEN gheciteert ende ghedeputeert, op het Synodes Nationnael tot Dordrecht. Affghesonden naer den Haghe/met eenen expressen den 26. Januarij/Anno 1619. AEN DE . . . STATEN GENERAEL Der Vereenichde Neder-Landen. Door een Liefhebber der Nederlantsche vrijheyt/die van herten den welstant deser Landen bemint. Ao. 1619. 4° pp.24

T.2249(4).

V180 VERTOOGH

Verroogh [*sic*] ende Supplicatie, By de Remonstranten gecitteerde ende Ghedeputeerde/op het Synodes Nationnael tot Dordrecht, Door eenen expressen den 26. Januarij 1619. afghesonden: Aen den . . . PRINCE VAN ORAIGNEN, &c. In Druck uyt laten gaen/door een Liefhebber der Vrijheyt vande Gheunieerde Provintien. Ghedruct . . . 1619. 4° pp.13

T.2249(3).

Ascribed in a manuscript note on the titlepage to Caspar Barlaeus. Another edition described in *Knuttel* no.2839 has the correct spelling 'Vertoogh'.

VERTOOGH, hoe nootwendich, nut ende profijtelick het sy. 1608. *See* USSELINCX, Willem

VERTOOGH van verscheiden nieuwigheden. 1617. *See* GREVINCHOVEN, Nicolaas

VERTROOSTINGHE aen de Remonstrantsche kercken. 1619. *See* BAERLE, Caspar van

VERUS, Lucius; pseudonym of Mathias Damius. *See* DAMIUS, Mathias

V181 VERVLIET, Jean

(tp.1) HISTOIRE DV MASSACRE DE PLVSIEVRS RELIGIEVX, DE S. DOMINIQVE, DE S. FRANÇOIS, Et de la Compagnie de IESVS, Et d'autres Chrestiens, aduenu en la rebellion de quelques Indois de l'Occident contre les Espagnols. ITEM Diuerses Lettres escrites par aucuns de ladite Compagnie, qui du Païs-bas ont esté enuoyez aux Indes Occidentales en l'An 1615. ET Vne du P. NICOLAS TRIGAVLT, enuoyée depuis son retour aux Indes Orientales. A VALENCIENNE. De l'Imprimerie de IEAN VERVLIET . . . M.DC.XX.

(tp.2=p.1) HISTOIRE DV MASSACRE DE PLVSIEVRS RELIGIEVX . . . aduenue en la rebellion . . . contre les Espagnols. Le tout tiré du memorial presenté au Roy d'Espagne, iouxte la Copie imprimée à Barcelonne, 1616. ITEM Diuerses extraicts des Lettres escrites par aucuns de ladicte Compagnie, qui du Païs-bas ont esté enuoyez aux Indes Occidentales en l'an 1615. A VALENCIENNE, De l'Imprimerie de IAN VERVLIET . . . M.DC.XX. 8° pp.31,80,59

4767.aaa.13(1).

Anonymous. Compiled by the publisher, Jean Vervliet. Pt.1 by Francisco Figueroa. Published on behalf of the Belgian Province of the Jesuits. There has as yet been no trace of the Memorial published at Barcelona in 1616 of which the 'Histoire' itself is said to be an abridged translation. Tp.1v bears an advertisement for the work of Elie Trigault, 'to be published shortly' and not, as sometimes assumed, part of this work. It is followed by a conjugate but unsigned leaf bearing the privilege. Tp.2, signed A1, bears on the verso a list of Jesuits sent to the Indies. The last leaf bears on p.59 parts of the Salve Regina in Mexican and on the verso the Lord's Prayer in Peruvian. For the work of Elie Trigault, edited by Nicolas Trigault and referred to as by him on this titlepage, *see* TRIGAULT, Elie

V182 VERVOORT, Frans

Bruydegoms Mantelken/vanden inwendigen nauolghen des leuens ende des Cruycen . . . Jesu Christi . . . Door Petrum Godefridi . . . T'HANTVVERPEN. By Marten Huyssens . . . 1607. [etc.] 12° ff.113[111]; illus.

1606/224.

Anonymous. Based on two sermons of Johann Tauler and on Alijt Bake's 'Merkelijke leeringhe', edited by Petrus Godefridi. The illustrations are woodcuts.

V183 VERZET

VERZET, Teghen den Schutterlicken Scherm-slach, ghegheven na de vrome Borghers, die den lossen Dicht-maker zeydt, haer zelven ontschuttert te hebben . . . 1618. 4° a single sheet

1889.d.3(302).

Two poems, signed respectively: ES.R.BE.DN.IE.S.BW.EN. and R.G.SB.M.I.VBI. H.G;G.S.S.D.D.M.S.G.E.S.S., directed against 'Schutterlicke scherm-slach', on the Leiden militia.

V184 VESALIUS, Andreas

ANDREÆ VESALII . . . EPITOME ANATOMICA. Opus redivivum. cui accessere, NOTÆ AC COMMENTARIA P. PAAW . . . LVGDVNI BATAVORVM. Ex Officina IVSTI à COLSTER . . . M D CXVI. (col.) LVGDVNI BATAVORVM, Ex Officina typographica Ulrici Corn: Honthorstij . . . M.D.CXVI. 4° pp.226: plate; illus.

548.g.4.

The plate and illustrations are engraved. Ownership inscription: Joseph Fenton.

VETERUM poetarum comparationes. 1610. *See* TROGNAESIUS, Alexander Carolus

VIC, Franciscus de. Disquisitio . . . de humani corporis partibus. 1621. *See* WINSEMIUS, Menelaus

VICTORIA victis. Dat is, den waren zeghen Gods. 1620. *See* CAMPHUYSEN, Dirck Raphaëlsz

La VIDA de Lazarillo de Tormes. 1602. *See* LAZARILLO de Tormes

La VIE de S. Thomas Archevesque de Cantorbie. 1615[1616]. *See* QUADRILOGUS

VIGERIUS, Marcus; Cardinal. Decachordum Christianum. 1616. *See* PALEOTTI, Alfonso. Historia. tom.2.

V185 VIGNIER, Nicolas; the Elder
RECVEIL DE L'HISTOIRE DE L'EGLISE, Depuis le Baptesme de nostre Seigneur IESVS CHRIST, iusques à ce temps: Par NICOLAS VIGNIER DE BAR SVR SEINE . . . A LEYDEN, Aux despends de CHRISTOFFLE DE RAPHELENGIEN. 1601. (col.) Acheué d'imprimer au mois de Decembre . . . M.DCI. fol. pp.638
C.73.f.4.
Edited by Nicolas Vignier the Younger and Jean Vignier, with additions to the original text. Probably not printed in the Netherlands; perhaps at Geneva? The copy at Leiden University Library is in a tract volume with Vignier's 'Sommaire de l'histoire des François' which has a colophon by Henry Thierry for Seb. Nivelle, Paris 1579. From the library of Henry, Prince of Wales.

V186 VIGNIER, Nicolas; the Younger
LEGENDE DOREE OV Sommaire de l'histiore [*sic*] des freres Mendians de l'Ordre de Dominique, & de François, comprenant briefuement . . . l'origine, le progrez, la doctrine & les combats d'iceux: tant contre l'Eglise Gallicane . . . que cõtre les Papes & entr'eux mesmes depuis quatre cens ans. A LEYDEN: Pour Iean le Maire, 1608. 8° pp.155; illus.
698.a.48.
Anonymous. On the titlepage verso: 'Anagramme sur le nom de l'autheur: NVL GAIN I RECOIS'. The titlepage woodcut shows an armed man attacking a woman and child.

V187 VILLAMONT, Jacques de
LES VOYAGES DV S[R]. DE VILLAMONT . . . A ARRAS, De l'Imprimerie de Guillaume de la Riuiere . . . M.D.C.V. 8° pp.641; illus., port.
G.7059.
The titlepage bears the engraved portrait of the author.

V188 VILLEGAS, Alfonso
[Flos sanctorum.] FLOS SANCTORVM. THE LIVES OF THE SAINTS. Written in Spanish by . . . ALFONSO VILLEGAS . . . Translated out of Italian into English, and compared with the Spanish by W. & E.K.B. THE FIRST TOME. [etc] 4° pp.218
487.f.29.
The translators' initials stand for William and Edward Kinsman Brothers. No more published. A note on p.218, signed: K.E., explains that an accident prevented the publication of more. The preface is dated 1609. Without imprint; printed by Pierre Auroi at Douai.

V189 VILLEGAS, Alfonso
[Flos sanctorum.] THE LIVES OF THE SAINTS Written in Spanish, by . . . ALFONSO VILLEGAS . . . Translated out of Italian into English, and conferred with the Spanish. By W. & E.K.B. . . . Printed at DOWAY, By the Widow of LAVRENCE KELLAM . . . M.DC.XIV. 8° pp.665[655]
1607/2693.
Containing the saints for September to December only. Translated by William and Edward Kinsman Brothers.

V190 VILLEGAS, Alfonso
[Flos sanctorum.] (tp.1) THE LIVES OF SAINTS Written in Spanish, by . . . ALFONSO VILLEGAS . . . The First Part . . . Translated out of Italian into English, and conferred with the Spanish. by W. & E.K.B. . . . Printed at DOWAY, By the Widow of LAVRENCE KELLAM . . . M.DC.XV.
(tp.2) THE LIVES OF SAINTS . . . The Second Part . . . Printed at DOWAY, By the Widow of LAVRENCE KELLAM . . . M.DC.XV. 8° 2 pt.: pp.464,326; 506[505],665[655]
4823.cc.10.
Translated by William and Edward Kinsman Brothers. P.200 of the second part of pt.1 is blank; the verso of p.506[505] bears a preface to the following part, signed: E.K. Pt.1 with the exlibris of Stephen White and of Alfred White Presbyter; pt.2 with the ownership inscriptions: G.E. Corrie; Alexander Duncan 1752.

V191 VILLEGAS, Alfonso
[Flos sanctorum.] THE LIVES OF SAINTS. Written in Spanish by . . . ALFONSO VILLEGAS . . . Translated out of Italian into English, and diligentlie compared with the Spanish. Wherunto are added the liues of sundrie other Saints . . . Extracted out of F. Ribadeniera [*sic*], Surius, and out of other approued authors. The second edition, set forth by IOHN HEIGHAM . . . 1621. 4° pp.1050,86
C.127.d.20.
The translation is that by William and Edward Kinsman. With 'An appendix of the saints lately canonized, and Beatified, by Paul the fifth, and Gregorie the fifteenth, and first', which has an approbation dated 27 May 1623, attributing the translation of this part to Edward Kinsman only. Without imprint; printed by Charles Boscard at St. Omer. Ownership inscription: Mary Naddings her Book 1743.

V192 VINAC, Hugo de; de Prato Florido
[Sermones de sanctis.] PRATI FLORIDISSIMI CONCIONVM DE SANCTIS . . . Editi olim à præstantissimo TH. HVGONE DE PRATO FLORIDO . . . Operâ ac studio . . . GVILIELMI OONSELII . . . restituti . . . Cum indicibus diuersis . . . ANTVERPIÆ Apud Petrum & Ioannem Belleros. M.DC.XVII. 8° 2 pt.: pp.1116
1578/1949.

VINCENTIUS Hollandus, Liberius; pseudonym of Niccolò Crasso. *See* CRASSO, Niccolò

VINEA, Daniel Hochedaeus a. Theses philosophicae de materia prima. 1606. *See* JACCHAEUS, Gilbertus

V193 VINEIS, Raymundus de; de Capua
[Vita Sanctae Catharinae Senensis.] THE LIFE OF THE BLESSED VIRGIN, SAINCT CATHARINE OF SIENA. Drawne out of all them that had written it from the beginning. And written in Italian by the reuerend Father, Doctor Caterinus Senensis. And now translated into Englishe . . . by Iohn Fen . . . 1609. 8° pp.455
1482.a.32.
Anonymous, or rather, erroneously ascribed to Ambrosius Catharinus, name in religion of Lancelotto Politi, Bishop of Minou and Archbishop of Conza, who had translated the Latin text by Raymundus de Vineis into Italian. With a dedication by John Heigham. Without imprint, printed by Charles Boscard, for John Heigham?, at Douai.

V194 VINSEMIUS, Dominicus
CONTRA TRAGICOS ECCLESIASTES LIBELLVS defensandæ veritatis APOLOGIAM, Atque ad Ecclesiasticam concordiam exhortationem complectens. Auctore DOMINICO VINSEMIO Bonarum literarum & eloquentiæ studio operam dante Leidæ

Batavorum. Excusus Anno Domini . . . 1610. 4° pp.73
1019.e.7(1).
P.1: 'Contra M. Petrum Bertium & nonnullos alios Ecclesiæ Dei perturbatores . . . Apologia'. The address to the reader states that the book was printed 'in extera Provincia', presumably meaning outside the province of Holland. Dedicated to the States of Zeeland; therefore printed in that province? Other copies known with a dedication to the States of Friesland; therefore printed in that province?

V195 VINSEMIUS, Dominicus
Een kleene Heldere ende klaere Spieghel der THEOLOGIE Waer inne . . . verthoont . . . wordt/hoe dat der Contra-Remonstranten Leere niet uyt der Joden/Turcken/Saracijnen/ende Jesuwijten/etc. Slijck-borne, maer uyt de springhende Fonteyne des Godtlijcken woorts gheschept ende gheput sy/teghen het . . . Calumnieren van Ioannes Wtenbogaert, Taurinus, ende andere Remonstranten . . . In't licht uyt ghegheven door DOMINICVM VINSEMIVM . . . T'AMSTERDAM, Ghedruckt voor Titus Roelandus . . . 1618. (col.) t'AMSTERDAM, Ghedruckt by Paulus van Ravesteyn . . . 1618. 4° pp.184
T.2248(31).
Imperfect; wanting sig.Aa bearing the index.

VINSHEMIUS, Menelaus. *See* WINSEMIUS, Menelaus

VIOLATIUS, Jacob. Disputationum theologicarum vigesima, de lege et Evangelio. 1602. *See* TRELCATIUS, Lucas

V196 VIOLIERE
ORDONNANTIE vande Gulde vande VIOLIERE, ghevoeght by de Gulde van Sinte LVCAS, in het iaer M.CCCC.LXXX. alsdoen den selven naem ghekreghen hebbende, met den vvoorde WT IONSTEN VERSAEMT. 4° pp.8
107.g.13(3).
Issued 7 June 1619. Without imprint; printed at Antwerp not before 1619, but could be considerably later.

V197 VIRGILIUS MARO, Publius
[Aeneis. Dutch] De twaelf boecken Aeneas/ghenaemt int Latijn AEneidos, beschreven door den gheleerden ende vermaerden Poëte VIRGILIVS MARO: In Duytscher talen door Cornelis van Ghistele overghezet . . . TOT ROTTERDAM, By Jan van Waesberghe . . . 1609. 8° ff.264; illus.
11375.a.2.
The illustrations are woodcuts, including a 'portrait' of Virgil on the titlepage.

V198 VIRINGUS, Joannes Walterius
DE TRIPLICI COENA CHRISTI AGNI, VVLGARI, EVCHARISTICA. Auctore R.P. IOANNE WALTERIO VIRINGO . . . ANTVERPIÆ, Apud Heredes Martini Nutij, et Ioannem Meursium. M.DC.XVII. [etc.] 4° pp.280
4325.ee.31.
The titlepage is engraved. Author's presentation copy to Gabriel de Succa 'in domu Liranesi'. Ownership inscriptions: Soc Jesu Liris; J.F. van de Velde . . . Lovanii.

V199 VISCHERUS, Augustus
DISCVRSVS HISTORICO-POLITICO-IVRIDICVS DE ELECTIONE REGIS ET IMPERATORIS ROMANORVM, EIVSQVE SOLEMNITATIBVS AD AVREÆ BULLÆ CAROLI IV. Romani Imperatoris LEGES IMPERII FVNDAMENTALES Methodicè conscriptus ET . . . censuræ expositus AB AVGVSTO VISCHERO . . . Luxemburgi, Typis Huberti Reulandt. Sumptibus IOANNIS NICOLAI ZECH . . . M.DC.XX. 4° pp.128
1055.a.26(2).
The place of publication is Cologne. Slightly cropped.

V200 VISIOEN

[Een visioen in den droom.] (tp.1) A VISION OR DREAME CONTAYNING THE whole State of the Netherland warres . . . Imprinted at London for Edward Marchant. 1615.
(tp.2=sig.E1=p.1) A SHORT And faithfull Narration from certaine Citizens of note of the Towne of Goch . . . At London Printed 1615.
(tp.3=p.7) Corten [*sic*] waerachtich verhael wt de mont van eenighe loffweerdige Borgers van Goch, vant abominabel . . . verraet by seeckere achthien persoonen geintenteert . . . op de Steden Goch, Cleef, Emmerick ende Rees . . . op lesten Februwarie . . . 1615. TOT VTRECHT Ghedruckt by Ian Amelissz. . . . 1615. 4° 2 pt.: pp.30,16; sig.A-D^4; E-F^4; illus.
1314.g.16(3,4).
A collection of pieces, the English translation of each preceding its Dutch text. Pt.1 consists of the 'Visioen' and 'Ghy patriotten', pt.2 of the 'Verhael' and 'De Spaensche gheboode ingestelt door, Paus Paulus V'. The last piece is in verse. The titlepage woodcut shows the riderless horse of the vision, symbolising the United Provinces, turning away from a monk. The Utrecht imprint is copied from the original. Printed by George Purslowe and Nicholas Okes at London.

VISIOEN, ofte vertreckinghe der zinnen. 1616. *See* DRIELENBURCH, Vincent van

A VISION or dreame. 1615. *See* VISIOEN

VISSCHER, Claes Jansz. Typus aenigmaticus temporis. 1610? [Sometimes tentatively attributed to Claes Jansz Visscher.] *See* TYPUS

V201 VISSCHER, Roemer

BRABBELING Van Roemer Visscher. By hemselven oversien, en meer als de helft vermeerdert. t'Amsterdam, By Willem Jansz. . . . 1614. 16° pp.220; illus.
11557.a.8.
With 'Volghen sommighe ghedichten van Hendrick Laurentsz. Spieghel' on pp.195–220. The titlepage woodcut shows a jug of wine, a jug of beer or water and a goblet, with the motto 'Elck wat wils'. Without the 'plates' mentioned in *UBA CNL* p.62 no.253. The first edition was part of 't'Loff vande mutse'. Ownership inscription: Melchior Van Hems . . . nay(?).

V202 VISSCHER, Roemer

T'LOFF VANDE MVTSE, ende van EEN BLAEVVVE SCHEEN: Met noch ander GHENOEGHELICKE BOERTEN ende QVICKEN, Soo uyt het Grieckx, Latijn, en Franchoys in rijm overgheset, als selfss Poeetelick ghedicht . . . TOT LEYDEN, By Ian Paets Iacobszoon . . . 1612. obl.4° pp.148
Cup.403.z.36.
Anonymous. The first and second poems described as 'Door R.V.', the name 'Roemer' given in the printer's preface and elsewhere. Printed in civilité throughout.

VITAE patrum. For editions naming St. Jerome as the author *see* JEROME, Saint

V203 VITAE

VITÆ PATRVM. DE VITA ET VERBIS SENIORVM LIBRI X. HISTORIAM EREMITICAM COMPLECTENTES: AVCTORIBVS suis et NITORI pristino restituti, ac NOTATIONIBVS illustrati, Operâ et studio HERIBERTI ROSWEYDI . . . accedit ONOMASTICON rerum et Verborum difficiliorum, cum multiplici INDICE. ANTVERPIÆ EX OFFICINA PLANTINIANA Apud Viduam et Filios Io. Moreti M.DC.XV. [etc.] fol. pp.lxxix,1008: plate; maps
1230.i.1.
The titlepage is engraved, by Theodoor Galle. The double-spread plate containing two maps

signed: Fran. Haraeus delineauit. Ownership inscription: M.P. Drake, PeterHouse 1837; with the bookplate of The Hon. Shute Barrington, LL.D., Bishop of Durham.

V204 VITAE
[Vitae patrum. Extracts] 'T BOSCH DER EREMYTEN ENDE EREMYTINNEN VAN ÆGYPTEN ENDE PALESTINEN MET FIGVREN VAN ABRAHAM BLOMMAERT. in coper ghesneden DOOR BOETIVS A BOLSWERT. Met cort verhael van eens yders leven ghetrocken uyt het VADERS-BOECK. 'THANTVVERPEN, By Hieronymus Verdussen. M.DC.XIX. 4° ff.51: illus.
C.68.c.4.
The dedication signed: H.R., i.e. Heribertus Rosweydus. Three engravings unnumbered, the rest printed on versos of leaves, numbered in two series, each 1–25, with Latin inscriptions, faced by text on rectos, each pair numbered equally.

V205 VITAE
[Vitae patrum. Extracts] LA FOREST DES HERMITES ET HERMITESSES D'EGYPTE, ET DE LA PALESTINE, Representee en figures de cuivre de l'inuention d'ABRAHAM BLOMMAERT, taillees par BOECE BOLSWERT. Et de plus illustré d'vn succinct recueil de leur vies tiré de la vie des Peres. A ANVERS, De l'imprimerie de HIEROSME VERDVSSEN. M.DC.XIX. 4° ff.51; illus.
564.e.16.
The dedication signed: H.R., i.e. Heribertus Rosweydus. The engravings as in the above, though in a much poorer condition, the first showing signs of reworking.

V206 VITAE
[Vitae patrum. Extracts] SYLVA ANACHORETICA ÆGYPTI ET PALÆSTINÆ. Figuris æneis ET BREVIBVS VITARVM ELOGIIS EXPRESSA. ABRAHAMO BLOMMAERT Inuentore. BOETIO A BOLSWERT Sculptore. ANTVERPIÆ, Ex Typographiâ Henrici Ærtssij. Sumptibus Auctoris. M.DC.XIX. 4° ff.51; illus.
563.b.27.
The text taken from the 'Vitae patrum', edited by Heribertus Rosweydus. The dedication signed: IR.S.I. (in error for H.R.?). The engravings as in the Dutch edition above. Imperfect; wanting sig.C bearing ff.8r–12v.

VITELLIUS, Regnerus. *See* TELLE, Reinier

VITUS, Richardus. *See* WHITE, Richard

V207 VIVERIUS, Jacobus
Claegh-ghedicht Op het overlyden Vanden Wysen/Vromen ende Welgheleerden D. WARNERUS HELMICHIUS Ghetrouwen Dienaer des Godelijcken Woordes in de Kercke tot Amstelredam. Ontslapen . . . den xxix Augusti M.DC.VIII. 't Amstelredam, By Cornelis Claesz. . . . 1608. 4° sig.A^4
T.2417(21).
Signed: De doodt doet leven, motto of Jacobus Viverius.

V208 VIVERIUS, Jacobus
Eene ELEGIA, Of Christen Klagh-reden over den Doodt des wijd-beroemden ende hoogh-gheleerden D. IOANNES HEVRNIVS . . . Ghedaen . . . van IACOBVS VIVERIVS . . . t'Amsterdam by Herman de Buck, Voor Laurens Jacobsz . . . 1601. 4° sig.A^4
11555.e.44(1).
Printed with use of civilité.

V209 VIVERIUS, Jacobus
DE Wintersche Avonden/OF Nederlandtsche vertellingen van PHILOLOGVS PHILIATROS, a Ganda. Waer in verscheydene vremdigheden/dese lest voorledene

hondert iaeren ghebeurt . . . worden verhaelt. Verbeterde druck. TOT AMSTERDAM, By Dirck Pietersz . . . 1617. (col.) Ghedruckt tot Leyden. By Joris Abrahamsz. vander Marsse . . . 1617. 8° pp.377
12350.aa.21.
Pseudonymous.

V210 VLACQ, Michiel
(tp.1) DEN NIEVWEN VERBETERDEN Lust-hof/Gheplant vol uytgelesene/eerlijcke/ Amoreuse ende vrolijcke ghesanghen . . . Verciert met seeckere Copere Figueren . . . Item is noch hier achter . . . by ghevoeght/een Bruylofts Bancket, versien . . . met stichtelijcke . . . Liedekens . . . Den derden druck gebetert en veel vermeerdert. t'Amstelredam, By Dirck Pietersz . . . 1607.
(tp.2) BRVYLOFTS BANCKET . . . Van nieus in druck ghebracht ende ghemaeckt door M.V. binnen ter Goude. Daer by noch andere Liedekens . . . ghevoecht zijn . . . t'Amstelredam, by Dirck Pietersz. [etc.] obl.4° 2 pt.: pp.96; 24; illus.
11555.ee.22; 11556.bbb.8.
The compiler's second dedicatory poem signed: Wie kant ontvlien?, motto of Michiel Vlacq. In pt.2 one of the laudatory poems addresses him by name: Vlack. Two poems preceding p.1 of pt.1 signed: Liefd, respectively: Liefde, verwinnet al. I.V. Vondelen. The titlepage engravings, both the same, signed: DVB, i.e. David Vinckboons or Daniel van den Bremden. Printed largely in civilité; by Paulus van Ravesteyn? The copy at 11556.bbb.8 is followed by 28 leaves bearing another collection of poems in manuscript.

V211 VLACQ, Michiel
(tp.1) DEN NIEVWEN VERBETERDEN Lust-hof . . . Den vierden druck ghebetert. t'Amstelredam, by Dirck Pietersz. [etc.]
(tp.2) BRVYLOFTS Bancket . . . Van nieus in druck ghebracht ende ghemaeckt door M.V. binnen der Goude . . . t'Amstelredam, by Dirck Pieterss. [etc.] obl.4° 2 pt.: pp.96; 24; illus.
11555.aaa.60(3).
A different edition of the preceding, the compiler and the engraver of the titlepage identified as above, but without Vondel's name at the foot of his poems. Printed in a different civilité type from the 1607 edition; by Paulus van Ravesteyn? Dated 1610 by *Scheurleer* p.137; the latest edition quoted by *Carter & Vervliet* p.108 no.309 dated 1608.

VLAERDINGS Redenrijck-bergh. 1617. *See* WAEL, Job A. van de

VLIET, Abrahamus. Disputationum theologicarum vigesima-prima, de exaltatione Christi. 1603. *See* GOMARUS, Franciscus

VOETIUS, Gisbertus. Disputationum physicarum quinta de motu. 1607. *See* JACCHAEUS, Gilbertus

Een VOLCOMEN ontdeckinghe van de Roomsche leere. 1609? *See* MORTON, Thomas; Bishop. An exact discoverie

VOLMAER, Jonas. Disputationum theologicarum tertio-repetitarum quadragesima-quarta de Missa. 1604. *See* GOMARUS, Franciscus

VOLTOLYNSCHE tyrannye. 1621. *See* VELTLINISCHE Tyranney

V212 VONDEL, Joost van den
[Single plays] HIERVSALEM Verwoest. TREVRSPEL . . . Door I. V. VONDELEN . . . T'AMSTELREDAM, Voor Dirck Pietersz. . . . 1620. 4° pp.80
11754.e.31.
With 'Davids Lofzangh van Hierusalem' on pp.75–80. Printed by Paulus van Ravesteyn, with some use of civilité.

V213 VONDEL, Joost van den
[Single plays] Het PASCHA ofte DE VERLOSSINge Israels wt Egypten. TRAGECOMEDischer vvyse een yeder tot leeringh opt tonneel gestelt . . . TOT SCHIEDAM, BY ADRIAEN CORNELISON BOECKDRVCKER 1612. (col.) TOT SCHIEDAM, Voor Jan Wolffertsz . . . 1612. 8° sig. A-E^8F^4; illus.
11755.a.95(1).
The preface signed: I.V. Vondelen. The dedicatory poem is in French. The titlepage woodcut shows Moses and Aaron holding a shield bearing the title.

V214 VONDEL, Joost van den
[Other works] Den Gulden Winckel der Konstlievende Nederlanders Gestoffeert met veel treffelycke historische, Philosophische, Poeetische morale ende schrifturelijcke leeringen. Geciert met schoone kunst platen . . . t'Amsterdam. By Dirck Pietersz. [etc.] (col.) TOT AMSTELREDAM, By Dirck Pietersz. . . . 1613. 4° ff. 78; illus.
11556.e.12(1).
The dedicatory poem signed: I.V. Vondelen. Emblems, using plates attributed to Gerard de Jode, previously known as 'Microcosmos. Parvus mundus'. The engraved titlepage signed: P. Serwout. fe. f.23 lacks an engraving. The engraving on f.60 repeats that on f.54 where it was correct. The text is in verse. Printed by Paulus van Ravesteyn at Amsterdam.

V215 VONDEL, Joost van den
[Other works] DE HELDEN GODES DES Ouwden Verbonds/Met kunstige beeldenissen vertoont, en Poeetelijck verklaert. Midsgaders: een Hymnus of Lofzangh van de Christelijcke RIDDER, de Heerlijckheyd van SALOMON, en HIERVSALEM Verwoest. Gerijmt door I. V. VONDELEN. T'AMSTELDAM, Voor Dirck Pietersz. . . . 1620. 4° sig. A^6 ff. 1–36; illus.
11555.ee.29(2).
Separate editions of 'De Heerlijckheyd van Salomon' and of 'Hierusalem verwoest' are entered respectively under SALUSTE DU BARTAS, Guillaume de, and under Vondel's 'single plays' above. The engravings signed: J.S. or Johan' Sadeler fe'; Crispine, or CVB, inv. i.e. Crispijn van den Broeck. Imperfect; wanting ff. 37, 38 and the unnumbered leaves containing the 'Hymnus' and the colophon quoted in *Unger Vondel* no.99 and *Schuytvlot* no.59 for leaf M2v, as 't' Amsteldam, Ghedruckt by Paulus van Ravesteyn'. With the visiting card of J.R.D. Romyn used as bookplate.

V216 [*VONDEL, Joost van den
[Other works.] Op de WAEG-SCHAEL. fol. or 4° a single sheet; illus.
1750.b.28(11).]
*Destroyed. Anonymous. An engraving on the defeat of the Remonstrants at the Synod of Dort. With an accompanying poem beginning 'Gommar en Armijn te Hoof', by Vondel, in three columns. Published in 1618. This copy seems to have been of the issue described in *Muller* no.1333c (= *Schuytvlot* no.272). Described after the copy in the Royal Library, The Hague, Pamfl. 2770b. For another version of the plate, without text, *see* NETHERLANDS. United Provinces. Staten Generaal [3.7.1619].

V217 VONDEL, Joost van den
[Other works] VORSTELIICKE WARANDE DER DIEREN: Waer in Zeden-rijcke Philosphie, Poëtisch, Morael, en Historiael . . . wort voorghestelt . . . Oock met aerdige Afbeeldingen geciert, ende çonstich in coper gesneden, door MARCVS GERARDS . . . AMSTELREDAM, Bij DIRCK PIETERSZ. . . . 1617. 4° ff. 125; illus.
12305.ccc.8(1).
Emblems. The introductory poem signed: I.V. Vondelen. The plates first published in Eduard de Dene's 'Waerachtighe fabulen der dieren', retouched as required, with additional engravings, by Philips Galle?

V218 VOOCHT, Nicolaas
Lof-ghedicht/Ter eeren Den . . . VORST MAVRITS . . . PRINCE VAN ORANGIEN . . . T'AMSTELDAM, Voor Jan Benningh . . . 1620. 4° sig. A^4B^2; port.
1568/8868.
Signed: N. Voocht. With the engraved portrait of the Prince of Orange on the titlepage. Printed by Paulus van Ravesteyn, partly in civilité.

VOORBODE vande antwoort op seker boecxken gheintituleert Ontrouwe des valschen waerschouwers. 1616. *See* DWINGLO, Bernardus

VOORBURCH, Joannes. Disputatio medica de paralysi. 1609. *See* PAAUW, Petrus

VOORDRAGINGHE, hoe de Roomsche Keyserlijcke Maiesteyt . . . tot Norrenbergh . . . gedaen. 1620. *See* GERMANY [11.1619]

V219 VOORLOOPER
Voorlooper, Over Adriani Smoutij Schriftuerlyck jae, dienende tot openinge ende recht verstandt van synen Toe-eyghen-Brief aen de . . . Staten/aengaende de questie: Of de vyf verschillighe poincten de Salicheyt raecken of niet. Ghestelt door eenen Lief-hebber der waerheyt . . . TOT ROTTERDAM. By Matijs Bastiaensz. [etc.] 4° sig. A-D^4
T.2243(11).
With a manuscript attribution to Jan Wtenbogaert on the titlepage. Published in 1613.

VOORT, Isaacus van der. Theses physicae de anima vegetativa. 1604. *See* JACCHAEUS, Gilbertus

V220 VORSTELIJCK
Vorstelijck gheschenck. Dat is: Een MEDECYN-BOECK. Inhoudende vele geproefde . . . Medecijn-stucken: Om alderhande Sieckten . . . te ghenesen . . . Alles in grooter weerden . . . ghehouden in den Vorstelycken Huyse van die van Nassouwen . . . Wt den Hoochduytsche/in de Nederlantsche Tale overgheset/ ende in dese tweede druck verbetert. TOT AMSTERDAM. By Hendrick Barentsz . . . 1621. 8° pp. 232
1038.d.15.
Possibly translated from manuscript. Interleaved.

VORSTELIJCKE warande der dieren. 1617. *See* VONDEL, Joost van den [Other works]

V221 VORSTIUS, Aelius Everardus
DISPVTATIO MEDICA DE ANGINA, Quam . . . Præside . . . D.D. ÆLIO EVERHARDO VORSTIO . . . exercitii gratia, sustinere adnitar HIERONYMVS SMALLEGANGE . . . LVGDVNI BATAVORVM, Ex Officinâ Ioannis Patii . . . M.D.C.VI. 4° sig. A^4
1185.g.1(26).

V222 VORSTIUS, Aelius Everardus
DISPVTATIO MEDICA, DE ANGINA VERA. Quam . . . PRÆSIDE . . . D. ÆLIO EVERHARDO VORSTIO . . . Publicè examinandam proponit FRANCISCVS LANSBERGIVS. F. . . . LVGDVNI BATAVORVM, Ex Officina Vlrici Cornelij, & Georgij Abrahami . . . M.D.CXV. 4° sig. A^4
1185.g.1(57).

V223 VORSTIUS, Aelius Everardus
DISPVTATIO MEDICA DE APOPLEXIA. Quam . . . PRÆSIDE . . . D. AELIO EVERHARDO VORSTIO . . . Publico examini subijcit BENEDICTVS à CASTRO . . . Lugduni Batavorum, Ex officinâ ZACHARIAE SMETII. M.D.C.XXI. 4° sig. K^4
1185.g.2(13).

V224 VORSTIUS, Aelius Everardus

DISPVTATIO MEDICA DE FEBRIBVS PVTRIDIS, earumq̃ue differentijs & curandi ratione, Quam . . . SVB . . . D.D. ÆLIO EVERHARDO VORSTIO . . . publice discutiendam proponit VLRICVS à GROENESCHEI . . . LVGDVNI BATAVORVM, Ex Officina V.C. Honthorstij . . . 1619. 4° sig. A^6
1185.g.1(67).

V225 VORSTIUS, Aelius Everardus

DISPVTATIO MEDICA DE HEPATIS OBSTRVCTIONE Quam . . . Sub Præsidio . . . D.D. ÆLY EVERHARDI VORSTII . . . Defendere conabitur IOHANNES ALTENA . . . LVGDVNI BATAVORVM, Ex officina Ulrici Cornelii & Georgii Abrahami . . . 1613. 4° sig. A^4
7306.f.6(15).

V226 VORSTIUS, Aelius Everardus

DISPVTATIO MEDICA DE HVMORIBVS ALIMENTARIIS ET EXCREMENTIIS, Quam . . . Præside . . . D.D. ÆLIO EVERHARDO VORSTIO . . . Exercitij gratia publicè discutiendam proponit IACOBVS A MVYLWIICK . . . LVGDVNI BATAVORVM, Ex Officina Thomæ Basson, 1607. 4° sig. A^4
1185.g.1(28).

V227 VORSTIUS, Aelius Everardus

DISPVTATIO MEDICA DE LVE VENEREA Quam . . . PRÆSIDE . . . D. AELIO EVERHARDO VORSTIO . . . Publicè defendendam proponit GVILIELMVS LIBERGEN . . . Lugduni Batavorum, Ex officinâ ZACHARIÆ SMETII. M.D.C.XXI. 4° sig. I^4
1185.g.2(12).

V228 VORSTIUS, Aelius Everardus

DISPVTATIO MEDICA DE PVRGATIONE, Quam . . . Præside . . . D.D. ÆLIO EVERHARDO VORSTIO . . . Asserere conabitur VINCENTIVS A. SVYSIVS . . . LVGDVNI BATAVORVM, Ex Officinâ Ioannis Patii . . . M.D.C.VII. 4° sig. A^6
1185.g.1(27).

V229 VORSTIUS, Aelius Everardus

DISPVTATIO MEDICA DE REGIO MORBO Quam . . . PRÆSIDE . . . D. AELIO EVERHARDO VORSTIO . . . ad publicam συζητησιν proponit ANCHISES ANDLA . . . Lugduni Batavorum, Ex officinâ ZACHARIAE SMETII. M.D.C.XXI. 4° sig. G^4
1185.g.2(10).

V230 VORSTIUS, Aelius Everardus

EVERARDI VORSTII . . . Oratio funebris IN OBITVM . . . CAROLI CLVSII . . . Accesserunt VARIORVM EPICEDIA. IN OFFICINA PLANTINIANA RAPHELENGII, 1611. 4° pp. 39
835.f.16(14).

With a biographical sketch of Charles de l'Écluse by Jean Jacques Boissard. Published at Leiden. From the library of John Morris.

V231 VORSTIUS, Aelius Everardus

THESES DE PESTE, QVAS . . . SVB PRÆSIDIO . . . D.D. ÆLII EVERHARDI VORSTII . . . Publice defendendas suscipiet GVLIELMVS MERVLA . . . LVGDVNI BATAVORVM, Ex Officina GODEFRIDI BASSON, 1614. 4° sig. A^4
1185.g.1(56).

V232 VORSTIUS, Aelius Everardus

THESES MEDICÆ DE APOPLEXIA, Quas . . . Præside . . . Dn. ÆLIO EVERHARDO VORSTIO . . . publicè defendere conabor ADOLPHVS NANSIVS . . . Lvgdvni Batavorvm, Ex Officinâ Ioannis Patii . . . M.D.C.V. 4° sig. A^4
1185.g.1(24).

V233 VORSTIUS, Aelius Everardus

THESES MEDICÆ DE CONVVLSIONE QUAS . . . PRÆSIDE . . . D. ÆLIO EVERHARDO VORSTIO . . . Publicè defendere conabitur CLEMENS ROSÆVS . . . Lugduni Batavorum, Ex officinâ ZACHARIÆ SMETII, M.D.C XXI. 4° sig. A^4
1185.g.2(3).

V234 VORSTIUS, Aelius Everardus

THESES MEDICÆ DE FEBRE PESTILENTI Quas . . . Præsidió . . . D. Ælij Everhardi Vorctij [*sic*] . . . Defendet CORNELIVS SCAGEN . . . Lugduni Batavorum Excudebat Georgius Abrahami a Marsce, 1619. 4° sig. A^4
1185.g.1(68).

V235 VORSTIUS, Aelius Everardus

THESES MEDICÆ DE FEBRI HECTICA, Quas . . . PRÆSIDE . . . D. AELIO EVERHARDO VORSTIO . . . publicè discutiendas proponit THOMAS CARBASIVS . . . LVGDVNI BATAVORVM, Ex Officina Thomæ Basson, 1608. 4° sig. A^4
1185.g.1(32).

V236 VORSTIUS, Aelius Everardus

THESES MEDICÆ DE INTESTIN. VERMIBVS, Quas . . . Præside . . . D. ÆLIO EVERHARDO VORSTIO . . . publicé defendere suscipit MARTINVS HERCVLANVS . . . LVGDVNI BATAVORVM, Ex Officinâ Ioannis Patii . . . M.D.C.V. 4° sig. A^4
1185.g.1(25).

V237 VORSTIUS, Aelius Everardus

THESES MEDICÆ DE MELANCHOLIA HYPOCHONDRIACA. Quarum . . . Præside . . . Dn. D. AELIO EVERHARDO VORSTIO . . . defensionem experiar IACOBVS ANRAET . . . Lugduni Batavorum, Ex Officinâ THOMÆ BASSON. 1612. 4° sig. A^4
1185.g.1(48); 7306.f.6(19).

V238 VORSTIUS, Aelius Everardus

THESES MEDICÆ DE MELANCHOLIA QUAS . . . PRÆSIDE . . . D. ÆLIO EVERHARDO VORSTIO . . . Publicè defendere conabitur IOHANNES LE PIPER . . . Lugduni Batavorum, Ex officinâ ZACHARIÆ SMETII. M.D.C.XXI. 4° sig. C^4
1185.g.2(5).

V239 VORSTIUS, Aelius Everardus

THESES MEDICÆ DE PHTHISI QUAS . . . PRÆSIDE . . . D. ÆLIO EVERHARDO VORSTIO . . . Publicè examinandas proponit THEODORVS BERNH. AGNÆUS . . . Lugduni Batavorum, Ex officinâ ZACHARIÆ SMETII. M.D.CXXI. 4° sig. E^4
1185.g.2(7).

V240 VORSTIUS, Conrad

Conradi Vorstij AMICA COLLATIO, Cum Clariss°. Theologo D. Iohanne Piscatore . . . Super Notis hujus . . . ad illius Tractatum de DEO, & Exegesin Apologeticam . . . GOVDÆ, Typis Caspari Tournæi. Impensis Andreæ Burier . . . 1613. 4° pp. 278
4255.cc.65.

Without the errata described as provided as needed 'in quibusdam exemplaribus'.

V241 VORSTIUS, Conrad

(tp. 1) CONRADI VORSTII AMICA DVPLICATIO AD IOHANNIS PISCATORIS . . . Apologeticam Responsionem, & Notas ejusdem, Amicæ Collationi oppositas. PARS OPERIS PRIMA, In qua de Prædestinatione Dei . . . videl. de morte Christi pro omnibus, de modo conversionis restibili, deq; possibili justorum defectione &c. copiosè disseritur. Addita sunt seorsim PARALIPOMENA hujus partis . . . GOVDÆ, Apud Andream Burier. M.DC.XVII.

(tp.2) APPENDIX DVPLICATIONIS, SEV PARALIPOMENA PRIMÆ PARTIS. In quibus Notæ IOH. PISCATORIS, Amicæ Collationi oppositæ, quatenus Prædestinatione Dei . . . pleniùs refutantur. Authore Conrado Vorstio . . . GOVDÆ, Apud Andream Burier. M.DC.XVII. 4° 2 pt.: pp.612; 127
848.g.3.
With the printer's device of Jaspar Tournay of Gouda on the second titlepage. No more published.

VORSTIUS, Conrad. Antwoordt . . . aen de Curateuren. 1611. *See* WTENBOGAERT, Jan. Twee sendtbrieven.

V242 VORSTIUS, Conrad
[Apologetica exegesis sive plenior declaratio locorum aliquot . . . ex libro De Deo . . . excerpta.] Seeckere gheextraheerde Articulen uyt het Tractaet D. Vorstij de Deo: mitsgaders een corte naerder verclaringhe daer op. 4° pp.[20]
T.2241(29).
Imperfect; wanting the titlepage and any preliminaries; the title here given is taken from p.1. Sig.C is mutilated, with loss of pagination. Published by Jan Paedts Jacobszoon at Leiden in 1611?

V243 VORSTIUS, Conrad
Conr. Vorstij . . . BREVIS REFVTATIO Speciminis, à Leowardiensibus Ecclesiastis adversum ipsum editi . . . LVGDVNI BATAVORVM, Ex Officina Ioannis Patij . . . 1612. 4° sig.A^4
1010.a.7(3).
Directed against Johannes Bogerman's 'Specimen conscientiæ . . . D. Vorstii'.

V244 VORSTIUS, Conrad
[Christiana et modesta responsio.] BRIEF D. CONRADI VORSTII. AENDE . . . STATEN GENERAEL der Vereenichde Nederlanden. Ghestelt Voor desselven VORSTII Latijnsche antvvoorde, op de Articulen ghesonden vvt Enghelandt. Wt het Latijn int Nederduytsche overgeset. TOT DELFT, By Harmen Bruynssz Schinckel . . . 1612. 8° sig.AB^4
T.2242(24).
A translation of the preface to 'Christiana et modesta responsio'.

V245 VORSTIUS, Conrad
[Christiana et modesta responsio.] CONRADI VORSTII . . . Teghen-bericht. Op seeckere articulen onlangs by openbare druck onder de ghemeene man . . . ghestroyt. TOT LEYDEN. By Ian Paedts Iacobszoon . . . 1611. 4° sig.a,$\star^4$
T.2241(31).
Imperfect; wanting all after the translator's preface, sometimes attributed to — Pervinius[?].

V246 VORSTIUS, Conrad
GHEWISSEN DOODT-STEECK Der Calviniaenscher Predestinatie/Met haren ghevolge. Ghegheven door een der vernaemster Leeraren onder de uytghebannen Remonstranten . . . Ende in Druck vervaerdicht door een onpartydich Liefhebber der waerheydt . . . Tot Harders-wijck/Door authoriteyt vande Kerck/ende Synode van Dordrecht . . . 162[0]. 4° pp.123
1568/6247.
Anonymous. The imprint is false; printed at Antwerp? The titlepage is slightly mutilated, with loss of the last figure of the date.

V247 VORSTIUS, Conrad
ORATIE TOT VERANTWOORDINGHE. Ghedaan Inde volle Vergaderinghe der . . . Staten van Hollandt ende West-Vrieslandt. In s'Graven-Haghe den 22ten. Martij

stilo novo. Van CONRADO VORSTIO . . . IN S'GRAVEN-HAGHE, By Hillebrant Iacobssz . . . 1612. 4° pp.75
T.2242(25).

Translated from the German manuscript. The Latin version is entered immediately below.

V248 VORSTIUS, Conrad

ORATIO APOLOGETICA HABITA PLENO CONCESSV ILLVstrium Præpotentium Hollandiæ & VVestfrisiæ Ordinum. Hagæ Comitis 22. Martij Stilo Novo: A CONRADO VORSTIO . . . LVGDVNI BATAVORVM, Ex Officina Ioannis Patij . . . 1612. 4° pp.93
1090.m.6(3).

According to the preface the speech, made in German, was translated into both Dutch and Latin and published at the request of the States of Holland. The Dutch version is entered immediately above.

V249 VORSTIUS, Conrad

Conradi Vorstij . . . PRODROMVS Plenioris responsi, suo tempore . . . secuturi, Ad Declarationem D. Sibrandi Lubberti, & iteratam Ministrorum Leowardiensium Cautionem, aliaque plura . . . Eristica scripta, recenter in lucem adversus ipsum emissa . . . LVGDVNI BATAVORVM. Ex Officina Ioannis Patij . . . 1612. 4° pp.56
1010.a.7(1); 3837.a.44.

V250 VORSTIUS, Conrad

[Prodromus plenioris responsi.] Conradi Vorstij . . . VOORLOPER Van een volcomene antvvoort . . . TEGHEN DE VERCLARINGHE D. SIBRANDI LVBBERTI, mitsgaders de naerder vvaerschouvvinge der Predicanten tot Leeuvvaerden . . . TOT LEYDEN. By Ian Paedts Iacobszoon . . . 1611. 4° sig.★,A,★★,★★★,A-E^4
T.2241(32).

Printed partly in civilité.

V251 VORSTIUS, Conrad

Conradi Vorstij . . . RESPONSVM PLENIVS Ad scripta quædam eristica, non ita pridem . . . contra ipsum edicta, præsertim verò ad scriptum illud nuperum Ministrorum Leowardiensium quod Commonefactionem ampliorem vocant . . . LVGDVNI BATAVORVM, Ex officina Ioannis Patij . . . M.DC.XII. 4° pp.77[67]
1010.a.7(2).

Directed mainly against Sibrandus Lubbertus and Johannes Bogerman. The original catchword 'Plenius' at the end of the preface has been pasted over and 'Resp.' printed beside it.

V252 VORSTIUS, Conrad

[Responsum plenius.] CONRADI VORSTII . . . VOLCOMENDER ANTVVOORT Op eenighe tvvist-schriften, onlangs by verscheyden Broederen teghens hem uytgegheven, voornemelick op de verclaringe D. Sibrandi Lubberti, mitsgaders de naerder vvaerschouvvinge der Predicanten tot Leeuvvaerden . . . TOT LEYDEN, By Ian Paedts Iacobszoon . . . 1612. 8° sig.★,★★,A-K,A-D^4E^6
T.2242(26).

VORSTIUS, Conrad. Seeckere gheextraheerde articulen. 1611? *See* above: Apologetica exegesis.

VORSTIUS, Conrad. Teghen-bericht. 1611. *See* above: Christiana et modesta responsio.

V253 VORSTIUS, Conrad

[Theses theologicae et apologeticae de persona et officio Christi.] Vertaelde Theses. Vande Persoon ende Ampt Christi. Tot verantwoordinghe ende Christlicke ondersoeckinghe ghedisputeert inde . . . Schole tot Steinfort . . . den

17. Aug. 1611. Door D. Gerardum Grimerium. Onder de beschermingh des . . . D. Conrad. Vorstij . . . Nae de Copye Ghedruct tot Steinfort, by Theophilus Cæsar . . . 1611. 4° sig. AB^4C^2
T.2241(33).
The translator's note signed: A.V.H.

V254 VORSTIUS, Conrad
Verantvvordinghe D. CONRADI VORSTII . . . Ghestelt teghen de Waerschouwinghe onlangs van de . . . Ghecommitteerde Raeden van Vrieslant vuyt-gegeven/ende aende . . . Curateuren der Universiteyt/ende Burghemeesteren der Stadt Leyden Schriftelick over-ghesonden. TOT DELF Ghedruckt by Ian Andriessz . . . 1611. 8° sig. $A\text{-}C^4D^2$
T.2242(22).
Edited by Jan Wtenbogaert. Another edition is found in WTENBOGAERT, Jan. Twee sendtbrieven.

VORSTIUS, Conrad. Vertaelde theses. 1611. *See* above: Theses theologicae.

VORSTIUS, Conrad. Volcomender antwoort. 1612. *See* above: Responsum plenius.

VORSTIUS, Conrad. Voorloper van een volcomene antwoort. 1611. *See* above: Prodromus plenioris responsi.

VORSTIUS, Conrad. Wt-legginghe, Coenradi Vorstii, over sommighe Schriftuer-plaetsen, vergheleken. Met de verklaringhe der Socinianen. 1611. *See* WAERSCHOUWINGHE, aen alle Gereformeerde Kercken.

V255 VORSTIUS, Conrad
[Selections] Bekentenisse. D.D. CONRADI VORSTII Over sommighe voornaemste Hooftpoincten der Christelijcker Religie. Ten deele uyt zijne eyghene Handtschriften. Ten deele uyt zijne Private Disputatien. Ten deele uyt zijne gedicteerde Lessen/getrouwelic uytgetogen. Hier zijn byghevoecht twee Brieven eene D.D. Parei aen D.D. Vorstium, de andere der Theologanten van Basel/aen de Pastooren des Graefschaps van Benthem over de saecke D.D. Vorstij. Tot Franeker by Uldrick Balck . . . 1612. 4° pp. 79
T.2242(23).
Probably compiled and translated by Sibrandus Lubbertus.

VORSTIUS, Everardus. *See* VORSTIUS, Aelius Everardus

V256 VOSKUYL, Everaert
Medicijn-meester Voor t'Verwonde Nederlandt/Ontdeckende, Aen een daer over bedroefde inwoonder/d'oorsake van de wonde/ende middel om te ghenesen . . . Door Everart Voscuyl . . . 1620. 4° sig. A^4B^3
T.2250(16).

V257 VOSSIUS, Gerardus Johannis
GERARDI JOHANNIS VOSSII HISTORIÆ, De CONTROVERSIIS, Quas PELAGIUS EJUSQUE reliquiæ moverunt, LIBRI SEPTEM. Iuxta Exemplar quod LUGDUNI BATAVORUM, Excudit Joannes Patius . . . 1618. 4° pp. 791
1010.a.11.
A reprint, made in the Netherlands, after 1618 and before 1655. Ownership inscription: Tho. Birch.

VOX populi. Or newes from Spayne. 1620. *See* SCOTT, Thomas

VRAECH-AL (VRAEGH-AL) Den VRAEGH-AL. 1618. *See* TAURINUS, Jacobus. For 'Den Teghen-vraech-al' *see* TEGHEN-VRAECH-AL

V258 VRAECH-AL (VRAEGH-AL)

ANDERE VRAECH-AL, In der haest ghestelt/om met des eersten Vraegh-als Vraegh-stucken beantwoort te worden/ist moghelijck, Ghedruckt voor een Lief-hebber der waerheydt . . . M.D.XJJX. 4° pp.16
T.2248(16).

A reply to the 'Vraegh-al' of Jacobus Taurinus. Variously attributed to François van Aerssen or Cornelis Boogaert. Corresponding to the copy described in *Knuttel* no.2599.

V259 VRAECH-AL (VRAEGH-AL)

ANDERE VRAECH-AL. In der haest ghestelt/om met des eersten Vraegh-als Vraegh-stukken beantwoordt te worden/ist moghelijck. Den derden Druck. GHEDRVCKT, By 't recht voorstant in Hollandt/Anno 1618. 4° pp.16
700.h.25(25).

Another edition of the preceding. *Knuttel* no.2597 describes 'Den tweeden Druck'.

V260 VRAECH-AL (VRAEGH-AL)

Den Derden VRAEGH-AL Aen de Heeren Pensionarissen van Leyden en Rotterdam/om van hun beantwoort te werden; ende hier uyt te amplieren de instructie aen haere Borgemeesteren respective/op't stuck van de Waert-gelders. 4° sig.A^2
700.h.25(26).

On events at Heusden. Published in 1618. Printed by Paulus van Ravesteyn at Amsterdam. Corresponding to the copy described in *Knuttel* no.2603.

V261 VRAECH-AL (VRAEGH-AL)

Den vierden VRAEGH-AL Pour tailler des besoignes Aen den derden Vraegh-al die soo heus den standt van een Frontier-plaetse overweeget. Ghedruckt int Jaer 1618. 4° pp.12
700.h.25(27).

Corresponding to the copy described in *Knuttel* no.2605.

V262 VRAECH-AL (VRAEGH-AL)

VYFDE VRAECH-AL, Tot ampliatie van het derde Vraech-altjen, ende rescriptie op des grooten Vraech-als tegen-vraghe. GHEDRVCKT, By 't recht voorstant in Hollandt. Anno 1618. 4° pp.16
700.h.25(28).

P.13 wrongly signed A3. Corresponding to the copy described in *Knuttel* no.2606.

V263 VRAECH-AL (VRAEGH-AL)

DEN SESTEN VRAEGH-AL: In alder ijl by den anderen ghestelt. ANNO M.DC.XVIII. 4° pp.7
700.h.25(29).

Corresponding to the copy described in *Knuttel* no.2607.

V264 VRAECH-AL (VRAEGH-AL)

DEN SOO-VEELSTEN Vraegh-Al: In alder ijl by den anderen ghestelt . . . M.DC.XVIII. 4° pp.7
T.2248(59).

Another edition of the preceding. Corresponding to the copy described in *Knuttel* no.2609, although the inscription relating to the second ornamental woodcut portrait on the titlepage reads 'ARIS', where *Knuttel* apparently wrongly describes it as 'Paris'.

V265 VRAGHE

VRAGHE Oft den Christenen oft Lidtmaten der Kercken/nae dat de waerheyt die welck sy . . . belyden . . . is/verdoemt/ende de Leeraers . . . uytgeworpen ende afgeset/in conscientie vry staet ghemeenschap in den wettelijcken Godsdienst te houden met den genē die men nu Contra-Remonstranten noemt/ofte die de

voorsz. condemnatie . . . ghedaen ofte toeghestaen hebben? Ghedruckt int't Jaer 1619. 4° sig. AB^4
1568/1334.

V266 VRANCK, Franchois
[Wederlegghinge van seker boeksken, uitghegheven by François Verhaer.] PRO LIBERTATE ORDINVM BELGII VINDICIAE SIVE REFVTATIO LIBRI FRANCISCI VERHAER . . . cui titulum fecit Sincera declaratio causarum Belli Belgici scripta iam pridem Belgico sermone A FRANCISCO FRANCK . . . nunc vero Latinitati donata A DANIELE IOHANNIDE . . . FRANEKERÆ, Apud Ioannem Lamrinck . . . 1620. Prostant Apud Danielem Iohannidem Bibliopolam Franekeranum. 4° sig. A-G^4
1193.k.6(1).
With a device showing the figure of Justice and the motto 'Oculi Domini super iustos Spalm [*sic*] 34', sometimes used by Ulderick Balck at Franeker.

V267 VRANCKEN, Godefridus
VÆ VICTIS. LVSVS RHETORVM ADVATICORVM ADVERSVS LEYDENSES ERVCTATIONES MVNERARIO GODEFRIDO VRANCKEN. EXCVDEBAT MECASTOR AEDEPOL 1609. 8° pp.64, 15
11409.ee.26(1,2).
The name of the author is probably fictitious. The text written possibly by students at the Jesuit College, Antwerp. Edited by Gaspar Maximiliaan van Habbeke. Directed against Dominicus Baudius and other anti-Jesuit authors at Leiden University. The second part, entitled 'Epicitharisma' is printed on leaves wrongly signed F instead of E. Printed by Joachim Trognaesius at Antwerp.

VRAY pourtraict de la trefforte . . . ville de Grave. 1602. *See* DOETECHUM, Baptista van

VREDEPUNCTEN tusschen den Evangelische ende Catholijcke gheunieerde standen tot Ulm besloten. *See* GERMANY. Union of Halle, 1610 [3.7.1620]

VREEDS-TRIUMPH-GEDICHT. 1609. *See* MUYR, Hendrick van der

VRE-REDEN of onderwijs tot eendracht. 1612. *See* COORNHERT, Dirck Volckertsz

V268 VREUGHDEN-GHESANCK
VREVGHDEN-GHESANCK OVER DE Schoone veranderinghen in't Vrye Nederlandt/ DOOR Het kloeck beleyt der STATEN GENERAEL, Met het Eedele Huys van NASSOVWE. ENDE Antwoort in dicht/OP HET Schandich . . . Libel/'tonrecht genaemt: Eenvuldige vvaerschouvvinge aende vreemdelinge . . . TOT AMSTELREDAM. Voor Lauris Hemling . . . 1618. 4° sig. AB^4
11555.e.44(6).
The two poems signed respectively: G.R.S.V. and 'Omhelst de deucht'. The 'Eenvuldige waerschouwinge' was written by Marijn de Brauwer.

VRIBURCH, Geerard; pseudonym of Jacobus Taurinus. *See* TAURINUS, Jacobus

V269 VRIENTIUS, Maximus Aemilianus
MAXÆMYLIANI VRIENTI . . . EPIGRAMMATVM LIBRI IX. ANTVERPIÆ Apud Ioachimum Trognæsium. M.DCIII. 8° pp.230
1481.d.3(2); 11408.aa.44.

V270 VRIENTIUS, Maximus Aemilianus
VRBES FLANDRIÆ ET BRABANTIÆ Auctore MAXÆMILIANO VRIENTIO . . . LOVANII, In Officinâ GERARDI RIVII . . . M.DC.XIV. (col.) LOVANII; TYPIS GERARDI RIVII . . . M.DC.XIV. 8° sig. A-C, A-C^8 D^4
1481.d.3(1).
With contributions by other poets and verse inscriptions written by Vrientius for public occasions.

VRIES, Jan Vredeman de. Les cinq rangs de l'architecture. 1617. *See* HONDIUS, Henrik; the Elder

V271 VRIES, Jan Vredeman de

[Perspective, dat is de . . . conste.] (tp. 1) PERSPECTIVE C'est a dire, le tresrenommé art du poinct oculaire d'vne veuë dedans où travers regardante, estant sur vne muraille vnie, sur vn tableau, ou sur dela toile, en laquelle il y ayt quelques edifices . . . le tout posé sur les lignes fondamentales, & le fondement d'icelles clairement expliquées . . . Jnventé par Joan Vredeman Frison. HENRIC. HONDIVS SCVLPS. ET EXCVD. . . . LVGDVNI BATAVORVM. (col. 1) A LA HAYE, Chez Beuckel Nieulandt. pour Henry Hondius demeurant a Leyden. 1604.

(tp. 2) PERSPECTIVE LA SECONDE PARTIE, DE LA TRES-EXCELLENTE SCIENCE . . . Inuenté par Iean Vredeman Frison. HENRIC. HONDIVS SCVLPS. ET EXCVD. . . . LVGDVNI BATAVORVM. (col. 2) A LEYDEN, CHEZ HENRI HONDIVS, TAILLEVR en cuyure . . . 1605. obl. fol. 2 pt.: sig. â, A-H[1]: pl. 49; pl. 24; illus.

L.35/12.

The titlepages are engraved, with spaces left for the letterpress titles. Pl. 33, 34 of pt. 1 are on one leaf, pl. 49 of pt. 1 and pl. 13 of pt. 2 have been cut out and mounted on blank sheets. The dedication of pt. 2 is dated 5 mars 1605. Some plates bear the initials BD = BD i.e. Bartolomeus Dolendo, or P.V., i.e. Paulus Vredeman de Vries. Sig. â of pt. 1 bears the portrait of Prince Maurice with dedicatory verses on the recto and a verse address to Leeuwarden on the verso. From the old Patent Office Library.

VRIES, Paulus Vredeman de. Les cinq rangs de l'architecture. 1617. *See* HONDIUS, Henrik; the Elder

VRIJMOEDIGH ondersoeck. 1620. *See* WTENBOGAERT, Jan

V272 VRY, Frederick de

HISTORIA SIVE Brevis & vera Narratio. Initii & progressus turbarum Ecclesiasticarum in Hollandiâ. Ex Bibliothecâ FREDERICI DE VRY . . . AMSTELODAMI, Apud IOANNEM EVERARDI Cloppenburgium. M.D.C.XXI. [etc.] 4° pp. 97

698.i.45.

Based on an account of the Synod of Dordrecht, with other matter. It is not clear whether the Latin edition was published before the Dutch edition described below or is a translation of it.

V273 VRY, Frederick de

HISTORIE OFTE Kort ende waerachtich Verhael van den Oorspronck ende Voortganck der kerckelijcke Beroerten in Hollandt. VVtghegheven door Frederick de Vry . . . 't AMSTERDAM, Ghedruckt by Ian Evertsz. Kloppenburgh . . . 1621. [etc.] 4° pp. 120

T.2250.(15); 106.d.58.

The parallel Latin version is entered above.

VRYE aenwysing van de onwaerheden . . . in de ghenaemde Historie van Frederick de Vry. 1621. *See* WTENBOGAERT, Jan

VRYHEDEN ende privilegien van des Keurvorsts van Brandenburgh . . . en vrou Anne . . . verleent. 1612. *See* JÜLICH, KLEVE AND BERGE

V274 VULCANIUS, Bonaventura

GOTHICARVM ET LANGOBARDICARVM RERVM Scriptores aliquot veteres; Ex Bibliotheca Bon. Vulcanii & aliorum . . . LVGDVNI BATAVORVM, Apud Ioannem Maire. 1617. 8° pp. 264; 191; 337; 109

G.15166.

Containing works by Jornandes, Isidorus, Paulus Diaconus and others, edited by Bonaventura Vulcanius.

V275 VULCANIUS, Bonaventura

GOTHICARVM ET LANGOBARDORUM RERVM Scriptores . . . Ex Bibliotheca Bon. Vulcanii & aliorum . . . LVGDVNI BATAVORVM. Apud Ioannem Maire. 1618. 8° pp.264; 191; 337; 109

C.61.d.1; 171.d.14.

A reissue of the preceding. The copy at C.61.d.1 is bound in a different order and inscribed: Bequeathed by Thos Tyrwhitt. Esqr 1786.

V276 VULCANIUS, Bonaventura

POEMATA [& EFFI]GIES Trium fratrum Belgarum NICOLAI GRVDII NIC: . . . HADRIANI MARII NIC.: . . . IOANNIS SECVNDI NIC. . . . AD Ioannis Secundi Reginæ Pecuniæ Regiam ACCESSIT LVSCHI ANTONII VICENTINI Domus Pudicitiæ ET DOMINICI LAMPSONII BRVGENSIS Typus vitæ humanæ. Vœneunt LVGDVNI BATAVORVM Apud LVDOVICVM ELSEVIRIVM. AMNO [*sic*] M.DC.XII. 8° pp.191; 96; 37: plates; ports.

1070.c.19.

Edited by Bonaventura Vulcanius. The plates signed: J. Mul. sculp. Printed by Henrick van Haestens at Leiden. The titlepage is mutilated. Described in *Willems* no.75 note.

V277 VULCANIUS, Bonaventura

POEMATA & EFFIGIES Trium fratrum Belgarum . . . Vœneunt LVGDVNI BATAVORVM Apud LVDOVICVM ELSEVIRIVM. AMNO M.DC.XII. 8° pp.191; 96; 37: plates; ports.

1213.h.38.

Another issue of the preceding. The text of the last page of the preliminaries has been re-set and somewhat changed. An extra leaf has been added bearing epigrams by Bonaventura Vulcanius and the errata, transferred from sig.★8v. *Willems* no.75 describes this leaf, but not the changed text at the end of the preliminaries. Printed by Henrick van Haestens at Leiden.

V278 VUYLSTEKE, Dionysius

DIONYSII UVYLSTEKII . . . Elegiarum, & epigrammatum Liber. MIDDELBVRGI, Excudebat Isacus Schilders. 1612. 8° pp.72

11409.aa.13.

There is no signature A; the titlepage is conjugate with an additional leaf numbered 49 on the verso, inserted between p.48 and the original p.49, between sig.E and D. Could a dedication have been removed during printing?

VYTTOCH van t'ghevoelen. 1618. *See* GOSWINIUS, Thomas

W

W1 WAEL, Job A. van de

SCHIEDAMS Rood Roosjens SPEL, Van David ende Goliath, Op de Vraghe; VVat eer den PRINS behoort, die syn vyandt bestrede, met Waep'nen overwon', en braght' tghemeent' tot vrede? TOT ROTTERDAM, By Matthijs Bastiaensz . . . 1619. 4° sig.A-E^{4}F^2

11754.bbb.71.

Signed: J. van Wael. With added poems. The dedication to Prince Maurice by the Schiedam Chamber of Rhetoric declares that this play won the first prize at the competition at Haastrecht.

W2 WAEL, Job A. van de

(tp.1) Vlaerdings Redenrijck-bergh, met middelen beplant Die noodigh sijn 't Gemeen, en voorderlijck het Landt. t'AMSTERDAM, Gedruckt by Kornelis Fransz . . . 1617. [etc.]

(tp.2=sig.Lll1v) DER KAMEREN PROEF-STVCK VVaer in dat vvordt verklaert, Hoe dat onvrede vree, en vree onvrede baert. t'AMSTERDAM, Gedruckt by Kornelis Fransz. . . . 1617. 4° sig.a^6b-d^4A-Ooo^4; illus.
1490.s.14.
The compiler's introductory poem signed: Job A. van de Wael. The illustrations are woodcuts showing the blazons of the chambers of rhetoric taking part.

W3 WAELRANT, Hubert
(tp.1) SYMPHONIA ANGELICA DE DIVERSI ECCELLENTISSIMI AVTHORI A QVATRO, CINQVE ET SEI VOCI RACCOLTA DA HVBERTO WAELRANT Nella quale si contengono i più Eccellenti Madrigali che hoggi si cantino NOVAMENTE RISTAMPATA. CANTO. IN ANVERSA Appresso Pietro Phalesio . . . M.dcxi.
(tp.2) SYMPHONIA ANGELICA . . . RACCOLTA DA HVBERTO WAELRANT . . . ALTO. IN ANVERSA Appresso Pietro Phalesio . . . M.DCXI.
(tp.3) SYMPHONIA ANGELICA . . . RACCOLTA DA HVBERTO WAELRANT . . . TENORE. IN ANVERSA Appresso Pietro Phalesio . . . M.DCXI.
(tp.4) SYMPHONIA ANGELICA . . . RACCOLTA DA HVBERTO WAELRANT . . . BASSO. IN ANVERSA Appresso Pietro Phalesio . . . M.DCXI. obl.4° 4 pt.: ff.36; 36; 36; 36
Music A.559.c.

WAERACHTICH. *See* also WAERACHTIG(H); WARACHTICH; WARACHTIG(H)

W4 WAERACHTICH
VVaerachtich verhael, Belanghende de aenkomste tot Constantinoplen/van den Ambassadeur der . . . Staten Generael van de Vereenighde Nederlanden: Midtsgaders het goede tractement ende onthael den selven Heere Ambassadeur Cornelis Haga . . . aldaer ten Hove aengedaen . . . By Jacob Harmansz Verblack/ 1612. 4° sig.A^6B^4
1312.b.42.
Published at Alkmaar.

W5 WAERACHTICH
Waerachtich verhael ende Beschrijvinghe vanden Afgrijsselijcken ende Bloedigen slach hoe die begost ende vergaen is voor Praghe/met allen de Particulariteyten. Ghetrocken wt de Brieuen van den Secretaris van . . . den Grave van Bucquoy. Nv eerst Ghedruckt . . . T'Hantwerpen/By Abraham Verhoeuen . . . 1620. 4° pp.16; sig.VvXx^4; illus.
1480.aa.15(61); P.P.3444.af(147); 1193.f.32.
The titlepage is printed sideways. The titlepage woodcuts show (a) Frederick in flight on horseback, the crown falling off his head, inscribed: 'Addieu/Coninck sonder Landt'; (b) a battle scene between Christian and Turkish troops near a castle. Without the map referred to in the text which was separately published. The copy at P.P.3444.af(147) is cropped; that at 1193.f.32 is imperfect; wanting the titlepage.

W6 WAERACHTICH
VVaerachtich Verhael hoe dat de Justicie gheschiet is binnen Madril in Spagnien/ ouer Don Rodrigo Calderon. Ouerghesedt vvt het Spaens in onse Nederlantsche Tale. Eerst ghedruckt den 19. Nouember 1621. T'Hantwerpen/By Abraham Verhoeuen/[etc.] 4° pp.7; sig.$Oooo^4$; illus.
P.P.3444.af(313).
Headed: Nouember, 1621.168. The titlepage woodcuts show (a) a sheriff on horseback accompanied by soldiers; (b) a court of law. Not translated from Fernando Manojo's 'Relacion'.

W7 WAERACHTICH

Waerachtich verhael Hoe dat dē Prince Gratiaē ouer ghelevert heeft het Lant de Walachy/ende Moldauia/aen den Coninck van Polen/ende veel duysent Turcken heeft verslaghen. Noch hoe dat de Tarteren in Podolien sijn ghevallen met 80.duysent mannen, ende 20.duysent Ianitserē oft Turcken, waer van de Cosagghen hebben over de 30 duysent . . . doot geslagen. Nv eerst ghedruckt den 12. December. T'Hantwerpen/By Abraham Verhoeuen/[etc.] 4° pp.7; sig.Oo^4; illus.

1480.aa.15(57); P.P.3444.af(160).

The titlepage woodcut shows the portrait of a ruler with sceptre and flag, i.e. Caspar Gratianus, Woiwode of Walachia? Published in 1620.

W8 WAERACHTICH

waerachtich [*sic*] verhael van de Aflijuinghe van den . . . Eerts-Hertoch . . . ALBERTVS binnen Brusselen gheschiedt/Anno 1621. Nv eerst Ghedruckt den 6. Augusti 1621. T'Hantwerpen, By Abraham Verhoeuen, [etc.] 4° pp.8; sig.V^4; illus.

P.P.3444.af(268).

Headed: Augustus, 1621. 111. Mainly in Dutch, but with a Latin poem 'Apostrophe ad Belgicam super morte . . . Alberti', beginning 'Revolve clades, & Grauem sortem tuam'. The titlepage woodcut shows the Archduke lying in state.

W9 WAERACHTICH

Waerachtich verhael van de seer Heerlicke eñ triumphante Crooninghe/des . . . Coninck IACOBVS, Coninck van Schotlant . . . als Coninck van Enghelant/ende Yrlandt . . . Gedruckt tot Leyden/By Jan Claesz. van Dorp . . . 1603. 4° sig.A^4

573.f.34.

WAERACHTICH verhael vā de victorie en den slach gheschiet teghen de Hughenotten. 1621. *See* RÉCIT véritable de ce qui s'est passé en la défaite des ennemis rebelles au roi.

WAERAC[H]TICH verhael van de reyse van den Ambassadeur van Engelant nae Spaignen. 1605. *See* ROYAL entertainment.

WAERACHTICH verhael van het ontdecken des aenslachs op de stadt Geneve. 1609. *See* VERITABLE discours.

W10 WAERACHTICH

Waerachtich verhael van Het optrecken te velde/van . . . den Generael Marquis Spinola, met de Crijgschmacht van Oorloghe/soo te voet als te Peerde/1621. Met de ghereetschappe daer toe dienende. Eerst ghedruckt den 2. September. T'Hantwerpen/By Abraham Verhoeuen/[etc.] 4° pp.16; sig.$GgHh^4$; illus.

P.P.3444.af(274).

Headed: Augustus, 1621.119. With news from France. The titlepage woodcuts show (a) Spinola on horseback among his army; (b) a cart with multiple cannon. Leaf Gg4 has been badly damaged in the press.

W11 WAERACHTICH

Waerachtich verhael vande Groote Victorie vercregē in Duytslandt/teghen die van Bohemen/de welcke dē slach hebben verloren teghen . . . den Graue van Busquoy [*sic*]/begost den 8. Junij eñ voleynt den 10. ditto . . . T'Hantwerpen/By Abraham Verhoeuen . . . 1619. 4° pp.8; sig.A^4; illus.

P.P.3444.af(10).

The report stated to have been written by a German. The titlepage woodcut shows a cavalry battle.

W12 WAERACHTICH

Waerachtich Verhael vande Victorie van sijn Excellentie den MARQVIS SPINOLA, Van het innemen der steden in Pfaltz-Grauen Lant. Eerst Ghedruckt den xxvj. November. 1620. T'Hantwerpen/By Abraham Verhoeuen . . . 1620. [etc.] 4° pp.8; sig.Y^4; illus., port.

P.P.3444.af(140a).

The titlepage woodcut shows the portrait of Spinola with military emblems.

W13 WAERACHTICH

Waerachtich verhael vande Victorie van sijn Excellentie den MARQVIS SPINOLA, Van het innemen der steden in Pfaltz-Grauen Lant. Eerst Ghedruckt den xxvij. November. 1620. T'Hantwerpen/By Abraham Verhoeuen . . . 1620. [etc.] 4° pp.8; sig.Y^4; illus., port.

1193.l.21; P.P.3444.af(143).

A reissue of the preceding, with a new date.

W14 WAERACHTICH

Waerachtich verhael vanden grooten Slach ende Victorie vā Duytslandt vercreghen teghen de Rebellen van Bohemen/Slesien/Moravien eñ Hongersche. Alwaer den Generael Graeff van Bucquoy dē Vyant heeft geslagen ouer de 1500. doot, eñ veel verdroncken, ende noch 1500. gevangē ghenomen. T'Hantwerpen/By Abraham Verhoeven [etc.] 4° pp.7; sig.A^4; illus.

1480.aa.15(5); P.P.3444.af(25).

p.7: Wt Luxemburch den III. Nouember. Coppije; p.8: Wt weenen. The titlepage woodcut shows an infantry battle between Christians and Turks. Published in 1619.

W15 WAERACHTICH

VVaerachtich verhael vanden grooten Slach/ende Victorie verkreghen teghen de Rebellen van Bohemen/door den Generael Graeff van Bucquoy/gheschiedt op Palmsondach . . . Nu eerst Ghedruckt den 8. Mey 1620. T'Hantwerpen/By Abraham Verhoeven . . . 1620. [etc.] 4° pp.8; sig.P^4; illus.

P.P.3444.af(48).

The titlepage woodcut shows a cavalry battle.

W16 WAERACHTIGE

waerachtige [*sic*] verclaringhe/hoe ende in wat manieren de Keyserlijcke Executie, reghens [*sic*] de Gevangene Rebellen Directeurs, ende andere . . . tot Praghe voor t'Sadthuys [*sic*] vande Oude Stadt/is gheschiedt . . . Eerst ghedruct den 10. Iulij. T'Hantwerpen/by Abraham Verhoeuen/[etc.] 4° pp.14; sig.JK^4; illus.

P.P.3444.af(258).

Headed: Iulius, 1621.102. With a list of the names of the victims. The titlepage woodcut shows the place of execution with the event; a small woodcut on p.3 shows one man at the block and another at the gallows; p.[16] has a woodcut printed sideways of soldiers and prisoners, entitled 'De Justitie ghedaen tot Praghe/ouer sommighe Rebellen'. p.[15] is blank. A statement on p.3 reads '. . . Alles wel . . . t'samen ghevoecht, ende naer de Boheemsche Praechsche Coppije in Druck ghestelt'.

W17 WAERACHTIGH

VVAERACHTIGH Ende Cort verhael vande groote Ambitie ende Wreede Tyrannye des Conings van Hispaengien/Philips den tweeden van dier Namen. Ende hoe Godt Almachtich alle syne voorghenomen aenslaghen vernietighet heeft. Ende wat voorder bedenckinge dat in d'onderhandelinghe van dese aenstaende Vrede is. Door een Liefhebber, synes Vaderlandschen vrijheydts by een vergadert. Anno 1608. 4° sig.A^6

T.2420(3); 106.d.18.

The description of the author known to have been used sometimes by Adriaen van Nierop. Printed by Hillebrant Jacobsz van Wouw at The Hague?

W18 WAERACHTIGH

VVaerachtigh Relaes OFT Verhael van het innemen Der twee Steden BRALOGARD ende CHILIA, gheleghen in Turckijen/de welcke den iongen Koninck van Polen verouert heeft . . . ghetrocken vvt seeckere Brievē van Cracau, Constantinopoli, ende van Venetien gheschreven, ende vvt de Hooch-Duytsche sprake in onse Nederlantsche Tael overghesedt. Nv eerst Ghedruct den 31. Meert, 1621. T'Hantwerpen/By Abraham Verhoeuen/[etc.] 4° pp.8; sig.☞[4]; illus.
P.P.3444.af(213).

Headed: Martius 1621. 49. The titlepage woodcut shows knights in combat.

W19 WAERACHTIGHE

[Waerachtighe affbeeldinge der Stadt Oostēde.] Warhafftige vnd eygentliche abbildung der stercke Stadt Ostende samptlich mit dem ietz nieu erfundenen sturm-wagen oder brucken wie deselbige Stadt von . . . Hern Alberto Ertzhertigen [*sic*] van Ostenreich . . . vom dritten Julio 1601. bis auf den heutigen dach den 6. Martij . . . 1604. ist belegert. fol. a single sheet; illus.
1750.c.1(13).

The German text has been pasted on at the top and bottom of the engraving which bears the inscription in Dutch 'Waerachtighe affbeeldinge der Stadt Oostēde [etc.]' and is dated 16. Feb. 1604.

WAERACHTIGHE beschrijvinge des gherichtlicken Proces gehouden tot Sursee. 1609. *See* HERMANN, Gabriel

W20 WAERACHTIGHE

Waerachtighe beschrijvinghe/Vande treffelijcke ende vermaerde Disputatie/ Ghehouden tot Poissi in . . . 1561 . . . Tusschen de Cardinalen van Lorayne ende Tournoy, ende de Prelaten ter eener/ende Theodorum Bezam, Petrus Martyr ende syne mede-hulpers ter ander zijden. Over het verschil vande Merck-teeckenen der Kercke/ende de Leere des heylighen Avontmaels. Ghetrouwelijck overgheset uyt de Fransoysche tale. TOT DELF, By Adriaen Gerritz . . . 1610. 4° pp.92
1578/337.

WAERACHTIGHE coppyen van sommighe placcaten eñ brieven by de Roomsche Keyserlijcke Majesteyt . . . gepubliceert. 1620. *See* GERMANY [3.9.1620]

W21 WAERACHTIGHE

Waerachtighe goede ende Nieuwe Tijdinge vanden Afgrijsselijcken Slach gheslaghen in Hungharijen/teghen den Luytenant Generael van Bethlin Gabor/ ghenaempt Ragazi/de welcke verloren heeft ouer de xij. duysent Mannen/ende den Omenay wesende voor de keyserlijcke Mayesteyt/heeft den Ragazi Ghevangen ghenomen. t'Hantwerpen/By Abraham Verhoeuen . . . Gheprint den 8. Januarij . . . 1620. 4° pp.8; sig.A^4; illus., port.
P.P.3444.af(28).

With news from Germany. The titlepage is printed sideways; the titlepage woodcuts show (a) a cavalry battle by a river; (b) an infantry and artillery battle outside a castle flying the Turkish flag. On p.3 a woodcut portrait, intended to represent George I, Rákóczy, Prince of Transylvania?

WAERACHTIGHE legende van Ian de Witte. 1609. *See* LEGENDE veritable de Iean le blanc.

W22 WAERACHTIGHE

Waerachtighe nieuwe Tijdinge van Duytslandt/hoe ende in wat manieren de Boeren in Bohemē beginnen te Rebelleren tegen den Pfaltz-Grave om de groote schattinghen diese moeten gheuen. Nv eerst Gedruct 1620. in Julij. T'Hantwerpen/by Abraham Verhoeuen . . . 1620. 4° pp.7; sig.Ss^4; illus.
P.P.3444.af(70).

With other news, including news from Friesland. The titlepage woodcut shows Mucius Scaevola.

W23 WAERACHTIGHE

VVaerachtighe onderrechtinghe van de goede meyninge ende intentie/die de Ghereformeerden altijdt gehadt/ende noch hebben/om de vryheydt van de Conscientie voor te staen/en niemandt in sijn ghemoet of Religie/eenich leedt aen te doen. Ghedruckt buyten Romen. 4° sig.A^4
T.2246(12).

Extracts from various documents restricting religious freedom, compiled in defence of the Remonstrants. Published in 1616.

W24 WAERACHTIGHE

Waerachtighe Tijdinge vande groote Victorie/ende slach gheslaghen teghen de Rebellē in Bohemen/alwaer den Graeff Bucquoy met den Hertoch van Beyeren vier duysent voetvolc ende xxiiij. Cornetten Peerden vanden vyāt hebben verslaghen . . . Waer ouer den Grave van Bucquoy zijne Victorie heeft vervolcht/ ende de stadt van Praghe inghenomen. Nv eerst Ghedruckt den xxvj. November. 1620. T'Hantwerpen/By Abraham Verhoeven . . . 1620. [etc.] 4° pp.5; sig.Z^4; illus.
P.P.3444.af(141).

A letter from an employee of the Spanish (?) ambassador, signed: G.I., to the 'Regeerders van mijn Vaderlant', telling of the battle of the White Mountain on 9 November 1620, the flight of Frederick and of the English ambassadors and of the finding of the Garter. Dated Brussels, 23 November 1620. The titlepage woodcut shows a battle between Christian and Turkish troops below a castle. A large woodcut on p.[8] shows an army mustering outside a city inscribed 'Praghe', with other troops inside.

W25 WAERACHTIGHE

Waerachtighe Tijdinge vande groote Victorie/ende slach gheslaghen teghen de Rebellē in Bohemen . . . Nv eerst Ghedruckt den xxvij. November. 1620. T'Hantwerpen/By Abraham Verhoeven . . . 1620. [etc.] 4° pp.5; sig.Z^4; illus.
P.P.3444.af(142).

A reissue of the preceding, with a new date.

W26 WAERACHTIGHE

Waerachtighe Tijdinghe Hoe die vande Hooftstadt Praghe/den Eedt van ghetrouwicheyt hebben ghesworen/aen den Hertoch van Beyeren den Keyser ghetrouw te blijven/ende den Pfalts Graef hebben afghesworen. Nu eerst ghedruckt den 9. December. 1620. T'Hantwerpen/By Abraham Verhoeuen/[etc.] 4° pp.8; sig.Ll^4; illus., port.
1480.aa.15(54).

Without approbation. The titlepage woodcut shows the portrait of Maximilian of Bavaria.

W27 WAERACHTIGHE

Waerachtighe Tijdinghe hoe die vande Hooftstadt Praghe/den Eedt van ghetrouwicheyt hebben ghesworen . . . Nu eerst ghedruckt den 9. December. 1620. T'Hantwerpen/By Abraham Verhoeuen/[etc.] 4° pp.8; sig.Ll^4; illus., port.
1193.k.31; P.P.3444.af(157).

Another issue of the preceding, with approbation.

W28 WAERACHTIGHE

VVaerachtighe Tijdinghe wt den Leger van zijn Ex. MARQVIS SPINOLA, in October wt Oppenheim. Ende hoe dat de Ghev-nieerde Vorsten met den heelen Legher van Worms sijn op ghebroken/met de Cavaillerie van Graef Hendrick van Nassouw/ende meynende de Stadt Altseym te surprenderen oft in te nemen. Eerst Ghedruckt den xxvij. October 1620. T'Hantwerpen/By Abraham Verhoeven . . . 1620. [etc.] 4° sig.KL[4]; illus.

1193.l.25; P.P.3444.af(129).

With 'Tijdinghe wt Besanzon'. The titlepage woodcut shows a town under siege. A copy of the corrected issue described in the *Bibliotheca Belgica* no. V196, vol.5 p.491, note.

W29 WAERACHTIGHE

Waerachtighe Tijdinghe wt Vranckrijck/ende Parijs/van den Afgrijsselijcken Brandt die daer gheschiet is/ende van den Legher van den Coninck voor Montalbaen. Ouerghesedt wt het Fransoys in onse Nederlantsche sprake. T'Hantwerpen/By Abraham Verhoeuen/[etc.] 4° pp.8; sig.Gggg[4]; illus.

P.P.3444.af(308).

Headed: Nouember. 1621.161. The titlepage woodcut shows soldiers setting a town on fire.

W30 WAERACHTIGHE

Waerachtighe Tijdinghe wt weenen/Hoe dat gheheel Moravien is veraccordeert met zijne Keyserlijcke Majesteydt/ende ghecomen in Onderdanicheyt ende Obedientie. Overghesedt wt de Hooch-Duytsche sprake in onse Nederlantsche Tale. Eerst ghedruckt den 29. Januarius/1621. T'Hantwerpen/by Abraham Verhoeven/[etc.] 4° pp.8; sig.A[4]; illus., ports.

P.P.3444.af(184).

Headed: Ianuarius 1621.15. The titlepage woodcuts show (a) a general with keys, i.e. Bucquoy; (b) an emperor with sword.

W31 WAERACHTIGHE

Waerachtighe Tijdinghen Gheschreven wt den legher/hoe datse teghen den vyant gevochten hebben/ende eenighe doot gheslaghen/ende 25. ghevanghen/met 20. waghenen geladen met meel . . . Overghesedt wt de Hooch-Duytsche sprake in onse Nederlantsche Tale. Nv eerst Gedruckt den 30. Julij. 1620. T'Hantwerpen/by Abraham Verhoeuen . . . 1620. [etc.] 4° pp.7; sig.Vv[4]; illus.

P.P.3444.af(72).

The titlepage woodcut shows a mobile mill driven by a horse and a donkey.

WAERACTICH. *See* WAERACHTICH

W32 WAER-MOND, Yemand van

HET TESTAMENT OFTE VVtersten wille vande Nederlandsche Oorloghe. Ghelijc als sy, liggende op haer Dood-bedde in den Hage, dien verclaert, onderteeckent, doen schrijven ende bezegelen heeft den tvveeden Februarij deses Iaers 1609. Door YEMAND VAN VVAER-MOND. Tot Franc end al By Frede-rijck de Vrije. 4° sig.AB[4]

T.2420(11).

In verse. The pseudonym is known to have been used by Simon van Middelgeest in 1622, but cannot be so identified with certainty for this and the following items. The titlepage verso bears several poems, one, entitled 'Anagramma ende Wensch des Dichters' contains the apparent anagram 'HELP' ONS BLY RVSTE BAREN', which I have been unable to solve. The main poem is signed with the motto 'Denckt op't EYNDE', for which *De Kempenaer* gives the name J. Rompel. It is not clear whether this identification applies to the pieces under the pseudonym Yemand van Waer-mond = Someone of True-Speech which lends itself to multiple use. The same can be said for the fictitious imprint. This copy corresponds to the one described in *Knuttel* no.1581.

W33　WAER-MOND, Yemand van

HET TESTAMENT OFTE VVtersten wille vande Nederlandtsche Oorloghe. Ghelijck als sy, ligghende op haer Dood-bedde in den Haghe dien verclaert . . . heeft den tvveeden Februarij deses Iaers 1609. DOOR YEMAND VAN VVAER-MOND. Tot Franc end al By Frede-rijck de Vrije. 4° sig. AB^4
161.n.67.

Another edition of the preceding, with different spelling, but with all the signatures and mottoes as there and an additional motto or signature, 'Dies en attulit ultro', under the final additional poem, 'Versus musicus', which is unsigned in the preceding. This copy does not correspond to those described in *Knuttel* no. 1582 or 1583 or *Van der Wulp* no.1131, which either show a comma on the titlepage between 'al' and 'By' in the imprint, not found in this copy, or are differently set altogether,

W34　WAER-MOND, Yemand van

[Het testament . . . vande Nederlandsche oorloghe.] CODICILLE van de Nederlandsche Oorloghe/Waer in Sy eenighe Vrienden, VVel-doenders ende Dienaren, in haer principael Testament van date den tvveeden Februarij 1609. vergheten zynde, van haer overighe goederen yet-vvat tot een Testament beset . . . heeft op den 12. Martij des selven Iaers. NOCH Een Wellecom-Dicht van het Bestandt. NOCH Andere Ghedichten van Bestandighe Vrede. Alle door YEMAND VAN VVAER-MOND. Tot Franc end al By Frederijck de Vrije. 4° sig. A^6
T.2420(12); 161.n.68.

All in verse. Signed: De Tijt brengt Eer-en-prijs. See preceding entries for authorship and imprint.

W35　WAER-MOND, Yemand van

HET TESTAMENT Van Me-Vrouvve van Treues. Door YEMAND VAN VVAER-MOND. Tot Franc end al By Frede-rijck de Vrije. 4° sig. A^2; illus.
161.n.69.

In verse. See preceding entries for authorship and imprint. The titlepage woodcut shows a sick woman in bed upstairs, her maid admitting (or refusing?) a would-be visitor at the door downstairs. Mention in the text of the dispute concerning Cleves and reference to the death of Henry IV and accession of Louis XIII point to a publication date of 1610 or 1611.

WAERSCHOUWINGE, tegen het malitieus . . . gheschrift. 1616. *See* WTENBOGAERT, Jan

W36　WAERSCHOUWINGHE

Vvaerschouvvinghe, Aen alle Gereformeerde Kercken ende vrome inghesetene vande vereenichde Nederlanden. By consent vande . . . Staten van Vrieslandt, in druck uytghegheven . . . Tot Delff. By Jan Andriessz. . . . Na de Copie/ Ghedruckt tot Leeuwaerden/By Abraham van den Rade . . . 1611. 4° sig. A-C,$A\text{-}G^4$
T.2241(27).

The preface signed: De Bedienaers des H. Euangely . . . tot Leevvvaerden. Drawn up by Johannes Bogerman and others to oppose the appointment of Conrad Vorstius as Professor of Theology at Leiden. With Latin 'evidence' in the appendix.

W37　WAERSCHOUWINGHE

[Waerschouwinghe, aen alle Gereformeerde Kercken.] WT-LEGGHINGHE, COENRADII VORSTII, Over sommighe Schriftuerplaetsen, vergheleken. Met de verklaringhe der Socinianen: Mitsgaders De kettersche Practijcken Pauli Samosateni ende Arij. Wt de kerckelijcke Historien. Alles in de waerschouwinghe/ by konsent der . . . Staten van Vrieslandt, onlancx wtghegeven: Int Latyn

ghestelt: Ende nu . . . int Nederduytsche overghebracht. Nae de kopije/Gedruct in Vrieslant . . . M.VJ^C.XJ. 4° sig. A-C^4
T.2241(34).

A translation of the 'evidence', originally attached in Latin to the 'Waerschouwinghe' issued by the Leeuwarden ministers Johannes Bogerman and others. Printed by Jan Andriesz Cloeting at Delft?

W38 WAGHEN-PRAETJEN

Waghen-Praetjen, Nopende die Hedendaechsche strydige saken/zoo die Religie aengaende/als oock eenighe manieren van handelingen by den Contra/ Remonstranten ghebruyckt/betreffende. Ghehouden tusschen eenen Theologum ende Liefhebber der Waerheijdt . . . Gedruct . . . 1613. 4° sig. A-F^4G^3
T.2243(18).

W39 WALAEUS, Antonius

HET AMPT DER KERCKENDIENAREN: Midtsgaders de authoriteyt, ende opsicht, die een Hooghe Christelicke Overheydt daer over toecompt. Waerin sekere nader bedenckingen . . . worden ghestelt . . . insonderheyt over het tractaet des E.I. Wtenbogaerts, van het ampt ende authoriteyt eener Hoogher Christelicker Overheyt in Kerckelicke saecken. door ANTONIVM WALÆVM . . . TOT MIDDELBVRCH, By Adriaen vanden Vivere . . . M.DC.XV. 4° pp.215
T.2245(10).

W40 WALAEUS, Antonius

ORATIO de studij Theologici recta institutione, habita ab ANTONIO WALÆO cum professionem SS. Theologiæ in Academia Leidensi Publice inchoaret, 21. Octobris 1619. LVGDVNI BATAVORVM Ex officina MARCIANA. M D CXX. 4° pp.35
491.b.12(6).

With a poem to Joannes Polyander.

W41 WALERANDE, J. B. de

LE PLAYDOYER DE L'INDIEN HOLLANDOIS, CONTRE LE PRETENDV PACIFICATEVR ESPAGNOL . . . Imprimé l'an 1608. 4° sig. A^4
8245.c.71; T.2420(15).

Signed: I.B. de Walerande. A decorative border with birds and putti has been pasted onto the titlepage of the copy at T.2420(15), partially covering the text.

W42 WALPOLE, Michael

A BRIEFE ADMONITION TO ALL ENGLISH CATHOLIKES, CONCERNING A late Proclamation set forth against them . . . Togeather with the Confutation of a Pamphlet . . . cōcerning a Decree of the Sorbon . . . AND An Epistle to Doctor King, in the behalfe of the Iesuites. By M.C.P. . . . M.DC.X. 4° pp.135
3936.d.16.

The author's initials stand for Michael Christopherson Priest, pseudonym of Michael Walpole. Without imprint; published by the English College press at St. Omer. The last leaf is mutilated.

W43 WALPOLE, Richard

A BRIEF, AND CLEERE CONFVTATION, OF A NEW, VAINE, and vaunting Chalenge, made by O.E. Minister, vnto N.D. Author of the Wardword . . . BY W.R. . . . 1603. 8° ff.218
3935.aa.19.

Anonymous, with the author's initials in reverse order. Sometimes wrongly attributed to Robert Persons. The initials O.E. stand for Matthew Sutcliffe, N.D. for Robert Persons. Without imprint; printed by Arnout Conincx at Antwerp. Ownership inscription: ex libris Roberti Noodham (or: Nordham?) 1688.

WALRAVEN, Guilielmus. Disputationum theologicarum vicesima octava, de libero arbitrio. 1605. *See* LINDEN, Henricus Antonides van der

W44 WALSINGHAM, Francis; Jesuit

A SEARCH MADE INTO MATTERS OF RELIGION, BY FRANCIS WALSINGHAM Deacon of the Protestants Church, before his change to the Catholicke. VV HEREIN [*sic*] Is related, how first he fell into his doubts: And how for finall resolution therof he repayred vnto his Maiesty . . . And what the issue was . . . M.DC.IX. 4° pp.512

698.d.26.

Without imprint; published by the English College press at St. Omer. Ownership inscriptions: Tho: Bedford 1630; G. Chambers.

W45 WALSINGHAM, Francis; Jesuit

A SEARCH MADE INTO MATTERS OF RELIGION, BY FRANCIS VVALSINGHAM . . . THE SECOND EDITION . . . M.DC.XV. 4° pp.504

3935.c.29.

Without imprint; published by the English College press at St. Omer. With the exlibris of William Fermor, Tusmore, and ownership inscriptions: S.I. Oxon.; F.N.

W46 WALTHER, Rudolf; the Elder

[Selections] Vande Christelijcke Disciplijne ende Excommunicatie: vanden Kercken Raedt ende Ouderlinghen . . . het ghevoelen der Kercken Christi tot Zurich/tot Bern/ende anderen . . . steden . . . in Zwitzerlant/door . . . Rodolphum Gwalterum, in verscheyden zijnen Sermoonen int Latijn beschreven/ende int jaer 1582. . . . in onse Tale . . . Overgheset ende in Druck ghegheven door Casparum Coolhaes . . . Nu . . . oversien/ende . . . in Druck ghegheven . . . Tot Amstelredam. Voor Willem Adriaenssz Ocker . . . 1611. 4° pp.34[35]

T.2241(19).

WARACHTICH. *See* also WAERACHTICH; WAERACHTIG(H); WARACHTIG(H)

W47 WARACHTICH

Warachtich verhael Hoe dat de . . . Staten der vereenichde Provintien/onder het beleyt van zijne Princelicke Excellentie/met een . . . Schips Armade van Zeelandt ghetoghen zijn/op de 25^{en}. April 1604. na het Eylandt van Casant, Alwaer de . . . Heeren verovert hebben de Schansse van Coxie . . . met noch ettelicke . . . Schanssen ende Redouten . . . MIDDELBVRGH, By Richard Schilders . . . 1604. 4° sig. A^4

T.2417(20).

W48 WARACHTICH

Warachtich Verhael van de Ceremonien gheschiet in Engelandt in't Installeren van zijne Princelijcke Excellentie/nevens sijne Hoocheyt den Cheurfurst Paltz in de Coninghlycke Ordre van den Cousebant. Midtsgaders Ghelijck Warachtich Verhael van de Triumphen/ende Ceremonien ghepleecht in't Celebreren van't Houwelijck tussen . . . den Cheurfurst Paltz-grave . . . Ende de Princesse van groot Britangien. IN S'GRAVEN-HAGE, By Hillebrandt Jacobssz . . . 1613. 4° sig. A^4

9930.c.31.

W49 WARACHTICH

Een Vvarachtich verhael van den treffelijcken Zee-slach/gheschiet inde Baye ende onder't Gheschut vande Stadt ende Sterckten van Gibraltar in Spaengien: Onder het . . . beleydt vande . . . Heere/Iacob van Heems-kerke . . . T'AMSTELREDAM, By Cornelis Claesz. . . . M.DC.VII. 4° 2 unsigned leaves; illus.

1578/334.

The titlepage woodcut shows a man-of-war.

WARACHTICH verhael van tgene datter ghebeurt is in Ingelant. 1601. *See* ENGLAND [9.2.1601]

W50 WARACHTIGE
Warachtige afconterfeictinge van het belegh van Sluys. fol. a single sheet; illus.
Maps C.9.e.10(21).
An engraving consisting of a map of the siege of Sluis in 1604, with a picture of one of the covered assault bridges underneath, entitled 'Waere afbeeldinge vande stormbruggen gemaeckt by Syne Excellentie voor de Stadt van Sluys waer van de verclaringe hier ter syden int lange is gestelt'. The engraved text on the left, by Broer Jansz?, contains the key to numbers on the map and a description of the bridges which the writer claims to have seen on 1 July, ready for use. Without artists' names or imprint; published by Broer Jansz at Amsterdam in 1604? The engraving by Floris Balthasarsz van Berckenrode? Part of the Beudeker collection.

W51 WARACHTIGE
EEN VVarachtige Beschrijvinge, Vande heerlijcke Ende Triomfante In-komste, vanden Marquis Spinola; ende zijne Bont-genooten in wat maniere eũ [*sic*] in wat Staet hij ontfangen is gheweest daer hy deur is gepasseert tot in Schraven Haage . . . Gedruckt tot ROTTERDAM voor Jan Gillissoon . . . 1608. long 8° pp.7
9405.a.31.
Van der Wulp no.1109 describes the format as 12°, *Petit* no.855 as 8°.

W52 [*WARACHTIGE
Warachtige ende sekere beschryvinge van die groote grouwelijcke ende vreeselijcke verraderie die nu geschiet is in Engelant . . . over eenen edelen Ridder Sir Thomas Overberry genaemt, welck verraet . . . is gestelt door den Grave van Somerset eñ sijn huysvrou, met haer medehulpers, eñ hoe wonderlyck dese verraderie int openbaer is gecomen staet in dit boecxken verhaelt . . . wt den Enghelschen in onse Nederduytsche Tale ghetrouwelijck over-gheset . . . Haerlem . . . 1616. 4°
6006.ee.12(1).]
*Destroyed. Described from the General Catalogue. The copy described in *Knuttel* no.2236 is a different translation. *Van der Wulp* no.1412 corresponds to *Knuttel* no.2236.

W53 WARACHTIGHE
[Warachtighe afbeeldinghe vanden wonderbaren ende ghedenckwaerdighen scheeps strijdt ende slagh, welcke in Oost-Indien, int ghesicht van de vermaerde coopstadt Bantam gheschiet is, tusschen vijf Molucksche soo schepen als jachten van Amstelredam: ende de Armade vanden . . . Coningh van Spaegnien, etc.] obl. fol. 3 unsigned leaves, sig.B^2: plate
440.i.1(3).
Lacking a titlepage; the title supplied by the Rijksprentenkabinet at Amsterdam from their copy of a related work which bears the signature of C.J. Visscher on the plate and has the accompanying text printed on strips surrounding the engraving. No such signature is found on the plate belonging to the British Library copy which has the text printed on both sides of the leaf. The dedication of the engraving to the directors of the Dutch East India Company in Holland and Zeeland is signed by the publishers: Hermãnus Alardi et Johannes Everardj Cloppenburgius, both of Amsterdam, and dated: 1603. [A2r] headed: Verclaeringhe van den ghedenckweerdighen Scheeps-strijdt/gheschiet tusschen vijf Hollandtsche schepen/ende de groote Armade der Portugesen/int ghesicht der stadt Bantam/1601. in December. B2r contains a key to the plate. The text is bound between copies of other voyages published at various dates, the plate is bound before the first item in the volume.

W54 WARE

VVARE VERTHOONING Ende afbeeldinghe van eenen dooden en meest half verrotten Vis/door die Zee aen der strande op gheworpen/den 20. . . . September . . . 1608 . . . tusschen Catwijk ende Schevelingen . . . Aenwijsende den Standt ende conditie des Conincx van Spaignien ende sijn bedroch inden wtganck van desen Vrede-handel gheopenbaert . . . TOT MIDDELBVRGH, Voor Adriaen vande Vivere . . . M.DC.VIII. 4° sig. AB^4C^2; illus.

1560/4445.

The illustration consists of a woodcut on the titlepage verso, with verses.

W55 WARFORD, William

A BRIEFE INSTRVCTION. BY VVAY OF DIALOGVE, CONCERNINGE THE PRINCIPALL poyntes of Christian Religiō, gathered out of the holy Scriptures, Fathers, and Councels. By . . . George Doulye . . . Imprinted at Louaine by Laurence Kellam . . . 1604. 8° ff. 134, sig. R5–T8; illus.

3504.a.70.

Pseudonymous. The titlepage woodcut shows Christ among the doctors. The imprint is false; printed by Francisco Perez at Seville? Leaf T2 is mutilated.

W56 WARFORD, William

(tp. 1) A BRIEFE INSTRVCTION BY WAY OF A DIALOGVE . . . Gathered out of the holy Scriptures, ancient Fathers, & Councells. By George Douley . . . M.DC.XVI. (tp. 2=p. 275) A BRIEFE AND COMPENDIOVS METHODE, For the better . . . examination of our Conscience, for a Generall Confession. Newly reuiewed, & augmented BY George Douley . . . M.DC.XVI. 8° pp. 345

C.26.gg.6.

Pseudonymous. Without imprint; published by the English College press at St. Omer. Ownership inscriptions: Ignatius Thorpe; Rev. Patrick Walsh, Dublin; James Weale, Dublin.

W57 WARHAFFTIGE

Eine Warhafftige beschreibung EInes Wunderzeichens oder Offenbahrung/welche geschehen ist binnen Lier/Daselbst ist ein Engel des Herrn zu einem Man gekommen/vnd hat . . . gesagt: das alle Menschen solten Busse thun . . . geschehen im Jahr M.DC.XII. Gedruckt zu Antwerpen bey Paulus Strobandt. 4° sig. A^2

1609/806(3).

Concerning Peter Danielsen and Gerhart Gerhartsen. The woodcut illustration shows the angel appearing to Peter Danielsen. Published in 1612? The imprint may be only that of an unidentified original serving as copy for a German publication.

WARHAFFTIGE und eygentliche abbildung der . . . Stadt Ostende. 1604. *See* WAERACHTIGHE affbeeldinge der Stadt Oostēde.

W58 WARMINIAEN

WARMINIAEN. De nieusgierige hoop t'veelhoofdich Wonder-dier . . . 1618 exc. fol. a single sheet

1889.d.3(308).

An engraving, the figure inscribed: WARMINIAEN, its parts and attributes described in Latin and Dutch, with Dutch verses satirising the Remonstrants,

W59 WARMONDT, Johannes Rulandi

THESES MEDICÆ DE Crisibus ac diebus decretorijs. quas . . . Pro GRADV DOCTORATVS in MEDICINA consequendo, publicè tuebitur IOHANNES R. WARMONDT . . . Lugduni Batavorum, Excudebat THOMAS BASSON, 1611. 4° sig. AB^4

1185.g.1(46).

The WARN-WORD to Sir Francis Hastinges Wast-word. 1602. *See* PERSONS, Robert

W60 WASER, Caspar

GRAMMATICA SYRA, Duobus libris methodice explicata à CASPARO VVASERO . . . Editio posterior, priori ita emendatior & locupletior, ut nova videri posssit. LEIDAE, Typis RAPHELENGIANIS . . . 1619. 4° pp.178

1568/2958.

In Latin, with Greek and Syriac. With Latin manuscript notes.

WASER, Caspar. Voltolynsche tyrannye. 1621. [Sometimes attributed to Caspar Waser.] *See* VELTLINISCHE Tyranney.

W61 WASSENAER, Nicolaes Jansz. van

ΑΡΛΕΜΙΑΣ Η ΕΞΗΓΗΣΙΣ ΤΗΣ ΠΟΛΙΟΡΚΙΑΣ ΤΗΣ ΠΟΛΕΩΣ ΑΡΛΕΜΙΗΣ, HARLEMIAS SIVE ENARRATIO OBSIDIONIS VRBIS HARLEMI, Quæ accidit Anno 1572. Græco carmine conscripta A NICOLAO IOHAN. à WASSENAER . . . LVGDVNI BATAVORVM, Ex Officinâ Ioannis Patii . . . M.D.C.V. 4° sig.★,★★, A-K^4, L^6

837.g.21(1).

In Greek and Latin, with additional matter in either language. With laudatory poems by Daniel Heinsius and Petrus Scriverius.

W62 WASSENBURCH, Petrus

SPIEGHEL Waer inne cortelijck Doch claerlijck wert aenghewesen/hoe de Gereforde [*sic*] Leeraers ende leere van Adriaen Symontsen ende den remonstranten/met openbare onwaerheden ende tastelicke lasteringen/beswaert ende verdacht ghemaeckt werden . . . Door Petrum Wassenburch . . . Ghedruct tot Leyden, Voor Davidt Jacopsz. . . . 1618. 4° pp.89

T.2248(39).

W63 WASSENBURGH, I. I. van

HISTORIAALSPEL van Koningh Reynier van Norwegen ende de schoone Langerta, ghetrocken Wt het vyfde deel der Tragischer Historien/Het derde. Speel-wys in rijm ghestelt. Door I. I. van VVassenburgh. By Abraham Migoen [etc.] 4° sig.A-E^4; illus.

11754.bb.28.

Dramatised from François de Belleforest's French version of Matteo Bandello's novella. With the blazon of the Rotterdam Chamber of Rhetoric 'De Blaeu Acoleyen' as a device on the titlepage. Published at Rotterdam ca.1615.

W64 WAT

VUat wonder oudt nieuws. fol. a single sheet; illus.

T.2423(11).

Consisting of three square engravings at the top of the sheet, showing: the Tower of Babel; Pope Hadrian VI; views of Rome and Utrecht; each surrounded by two lines of verse on all four sides, all engraved, and signed: Vincenti Mey 1618. Corresponding to the copy described in the *Atlas van Stolk* no.1335. Published at Utrecht?

WAT wonder-oudt-nieuws. 1618. *See* TAURINUS, Jacobus

WAT wonders wat nieuws. 1617. *See* DRIELENBURCH, Vincent van

W65 WEDER-KLAGHE

WEDER-KLAGHE Vande ware CHRISTELIICKE Gereformeerde Kercke/teghens de Bloed-klachte vande woeddende Kerc: AENDE OVERHEDEN DES LANDTS . . . 1617. 4° sig.AB^4

T.2247(36).

In verse. Directed against the 'Querela Ecclesiae' of Ewout Teellinck. Published by Mathijs Bastiaensz at Rotterdam?

WEEGH-SCHAEL. 1617. *See* TAURINUS, Jacobus

W66 WEERDT, Jodocus de
CONCORDIÆ BELGICÆ Panegyricus Parnassicus, A IODOCO DE VVEERDT . . . decantatus. ANTVERPIÆ, EX OFFICINA PLANTINIANA, Apud Ioannem Moretum. M.DC.IX. (col.) ANTVERPIÆ, EX OFFICINA PLANTINIANA, Apud Ioannem Moretum. M.DC.IX. 4° pp.55
11403.dd.2.
With chronograms and other games. Ownership inscriptions: J. Upland (?) 1834; Guil. Hen. Niger 1835.

WEIERSTRASS, Segerus. Disputatio medica de pleuritide. 1610. *See* HEURNIUS, Otto

W67 WELLENS, Boudewijn Jansen
[T' VERMAECK DER IEVGHT, Waer in ghevōden worden veel Schoone . . . Ghesanghen . . . by een vergadert . . . door BOUDEWIJN IANSEN WELLENS. Gedruct t'Franeker. By Thomas Lamberts Salwaada [*sic*]. 1612] (col.) Men vintse te coop, tot FRANEKER, By Thomas Lamberts, [*sic*] Salwaarda. obl.4° pp.139
11555.aaa.60(4).
Imperfect; wanting the titlepage and any other preliminaries before sig. A2, p.3. The text of the titlepage has been supplied from the reproduction of the engraved titlepage in *UBA CNL* no.303 p.75, signed: Jac Matham sculp.

WERNERIUS, Franciscus. Theses theologicae de peccato originali. 1613. *See* LINDEN, Henricus Antonides van der

W68 WERVE, Jan van den
[Het tresoor der Duytscher talen.] Den Schat der Duytscher Talen: Een seer profijtelick Boeck/voor alle de ghene die de Latijnsche sprake . . . niet en connen/ende bysonder die de Rechten hanteren. Ghemaeckt vanden . . . Heer Ian van den Werve . . . TOT DELF, By Bruyn Harmansz Schinckel . . . 1614. 8° sig. A-I^8K^7
1568/3589.
The earliest surviving edition, published at Antwerp in 1552/3, was anonymous.

W69 WESEMBEECK, Jacob van
[La description de l'estat, succes et occurrences, advenues au Pais Bas, au faict de la religion.] Beschryvinghe Vanden Staet ende voortganck der Religie in Nederlant/ende saecken daer over ontstaen/van den Jare 1500. aff/ende principalick . . . inde Jaren 1565. ende 1566. Beschreven int Franchois, door M[r]. Iacob van VVesembeeck . . . Ende nu . . . overgheset door een Liefhebber der waerheyt. TOT BREDA, Gedruct by Isaac Schilders . . . 1616. 4° pp.187
T.2419(7).
The translator identified in the preface as Isaac Schilders. Corresponding to the copy described in *Knuttel* no.148 note as a new translation of the work originally published in both languages in 1569.

W70 WESEMBEECK, Jacob van
[La description de l'estat . . . au faict de la religion.] Beschryvinghe Vanden Staet . . . der Religie in Nederlant . . . Beschreven . . . door Mr. Iacob van VVesembeeck . . . MIDDELBVRGH, Voor Adriaan vanden Vivere . . . 1616. 4° pp.187
1123.a.21.
Another issue of the preceding. Printed by Isaac Schilders at Breda, with the correction in the preface, as described in *Knuttel* no.148 note, i.e. the insertion of the omitted word 'tale' in line 6 on sig.⋆3v.

W71 WESTON, Edward

DE TRIPLICI HOMINIS OFFICIO, ex notione ipsius Naturali, Morali, ac Theologica; Institutiones orthodoxæ, contra Atheos, Politicos, Sectarios. AVTHORE ODOVARDO WESTONO . . . ANTVERPIÆ Apud Ioanem Keerbergium . . . M.DC.II. 4° pp.248, 424, 436

849.k.6.

The titlepage is engraved, the border signed: Anton. wierx fecit. In a probably Flemish or West German contemporary black stained pigskin binding. With an exlibris reading 'Ex Electorali Bibliotheca Sereniss. Vtriusq; Bavariae Ducum'.

W72 WESTON, Edward

IVRIS PONTIFICII SANCTVARIVM. Defensum ac propugnatum contra ROGERII WIDDRINGTONI in Apologia & Responso Apologetico Impietatem. Authore ODOVARDO WESTONO . . . 1613. 8° pp.465 [481]

1020.h.12.

Without imprint; printed by Laurence Kellam at Douai.

W73 WESTON, Edward

THE TRIALL OF CHRISTIAN TRVTH BY THE RVLES OF THE VERTVES . . . FAITH, HOPE, CHARITIE, AND RELIGION: SERVING FOR THE DISCOVERIE OF HERESIE . . . The first parte, Entreating of Faith . . . By EDWARD VVESTON . . . At Douay . . . 1614. 4° pp.200

3938.bb.81.

Printed by the Widow of Laurence Kellam.

WESTONUS, Odovardus. *See* WESTON, Edward

W74 WHEELER, John; Secretary to the Society of Merchant Adventurers

A TREATISE OF COMMERCE, WHERIN ARE SHEWED THE COMMODIES [*sic*] ARISING BY A WELL ORDERED, AND RVLED TRADE, Such as that of the Societie of Merchantes Adventurers is proved to bee, written . . . BY IOHN WHEELER . . . MIDDELBVRGH, By Richard Schilders . . . 1601. 4° pp.178

1029.e.3.

W75 WHETENHALL, Thomas

A DISCOVRSE of the Abuses novv in Question in the CHVRCHES of CHRIST, OF THEIR CREEPING IN, GROWING vp, and flourishing in the Babilonish Church of Rome . . . By THOMAS WHETENHALL . . . Now distinguished into Chapters, and Enlarged in the Index . . . Reprinted. 1617. 8° pp.231

4103.aa.57.

Without imprint; assigned in *Harris & Jones (2)* p.78, no.2a, to the press of William Brewster at Leiden.

W76 WHITE, Richard; of Basingstoke

AELIA LAELIA CRISPIS. EPITAPHIVM ANTQVVM. QVOD IN AGRO BONONIENSI ADHVC VIDETVR, À DIVERSIS HACtenus interpretatum variè: novissimè autem à Richardo Vito . . . explicatum . . . DVRDRECHTI. Typis IOANNIS LEONARDI BEREWOVT . . . M.D.C.XVIII. 8° pp.83

590.a.4(3).

Pp.61–83: 'Nicolai Barnaudi . . . Commentariolum in aenigmaticum . . . epitaphium' and other interpretations.

W77 WHITE, Richard; of Basingstoke

BREVIS EXPLICATIO MARTYRII SANCTÆ VRSVLÆ ET VNDECIM MILLIVM VIRGINVM BRITANNARVM, PER R.V.B. DVACI, Ex Typographia PETRI AVROI . . . M.DC.X. 8° pp.79

862.g.31(1); G.2491(2).

The dedication names the author as Ricardus Vitus.

W78 WHITE, Richard; of Basingstoke

BREVIS EXPLICATIO PRIVILEGIORVM IVRIS, ET CONSVETVDINIS, CIRCA VENERABILE SACRAMENTVM EVCHARISTIÆ. PER R.V.B. DVACI, Apud CAROLVM BOSCARDVM . . . M.DC.IX. 8° pp.44. G.2496.

P.1 headed: Richardi Viti Basinstochii, votiva lectio. The running title is 'Richard Vitus de reliquijs et veneratione sanctorum', which by rights belongs to a book of that title of the same date, recorded in the *BCNI* no.5522.

W79 WHITE, Richard; of Basingstoke

(tp.1) RICARDI VÏTI . . . HISTORIARVM BRITANNIAE INSVLAE . . . Libri Nouem Priores, AD SENATVM, POPVLVMQ: BRITANNVM . . . Apud CAROLVM BOSCARDVM . . . M.D.CII.

(tp.2) HISTORIARVM BRITANNIÆ LIBER SEXTVS . . . A R. VITO . . . conscriptus. DVACI, Apud Carolum Boscardum . . . M.D.XCVIII. (col.) ATTREBATI, EX TYPOGRAPHIA GVLLIELMI RIVERII . . . M.D.XCVIII.

(tp.3) HISTORIARVM BRITANNIÆ LIBER SEPTIMVS . . . A. R. VITO . . . conscriptus. DVACI, Apud Carolum Boscardum . . . M.D.C.

(tp.5) HISTORIARVM BRITANNIÆ LIBER NONVS . . . A. R. VITO . . . conscriptus. DVACI, Apud Carolvm Boscardvm . . . M.D.C. 8° 5 pt.: pp.469; 123; 96; 108; 174; illus., port.

598.c.24.

Edited by Thomas White. The titlepage and preliminaries to bk.6 precede bk.7; those to bk.7 precede bk.8. There is no titlepage (tp.4?) specifying bk.8. Bk.1–8 are reissues of the edition of 1597–1600, but with new titlepage and dedication for bk.1–5. The original dedication to Archduke Albert is retained. The original titlepage had the imprint 'Atrebati, Ex Officina Gulielmi Riuerij; M.D.XCVII'. The engraved portrait and arms signed: H. Mortier F. The portrait was a plate in some copies of the earlier edition; here it is printed on the titlepage verso and accompanied by verses.

W80 WHITE, Richard; of Basingstoke

(tp.1) RICARDI VITI . . . HISTORIARVM LIBRI . . . CVM NOTIS ANTIquitatum Britannicarum. ATREBATI, Ex Officina Gulielmi Riuerij, M.D.XCVII.

(tp.2) HISTORIARVM BRITANNIÆ LIBER SEXTVS . . . A R. VITO . . . conscriptus. DVACI, Apud Carolum Boscardum . . . M.D.XCVIII.

(tp.3) HISTORIARVM BRITANNIÆ LIBER SEPTIMVS . . . A. R. VITO . . . conscriptus. DVACI, Apud Carolum Boscardum . . . M.D.C.

(tp.4) HISTORIARVM BRITANNIÆ LIBER OCTAVVS . . . A. R. VITO . . . conscriptus. DVACI, Apud CAROLVM BOSCARDVM . . . M.D.C.

(tp.5) HISTORIARVM BRITANNIÆ LIBER NONVS . . . A. R. VITO . . . conscriptus. DVACI, Apud CAROLVM BOSCARDVM . . . M.D.CII.

(tp.6) HISTORIARVM BRITANNIÆ LIBER DECIMVS . . . A. R. VITO . . . cōscriptus. DVACI, Apud CAROLVM BOSCARDVM . . . M.D.C.VI.

(tp.7) HISTORIARVM BRITANNIÆ LIBER VNDECIMVS . . . A. R. VITO . . . conscriptus. DVACI, Apud CAROLVM BOSCARDVM . . . M.D.C.VII. 8° 7 pt.: pp.469; 123; 96; 108; 174; 142; 110: plate; port.

G.2492,93; C.16.e.10.

Edited by Thomas White. Bk.1–8 are reissues of the earlier edition. bk.9 is another copy of the corresponding volume of the preceding. In bk.6 the page reserved for the approbation and colophon has been left blank. Instead, this page and the errata leaf bear woodcut blocks and Hebrew letters. The portrait is printed on a plate, not on the titlepage verso, without verses; signed: H. Mortier f. The copy at C.16.e.10 has no titlepage to bk.8 and no portrait.

W81 WHITE, Richard; of Basingstoke

RICARDI VITI . . . HISTORIARVM BRITANNIAE . . . Libri Nouem Priores . . . Apud CAROLVM BOSCARDVM . . . M.D.CII. 8° 7 pt.

G.2494.

W79 (Sig.a2v.)

A combined edition of volumes of both preceding sets. Bk. 1–9 as in the copy at 598.c.24, but with a titlepage to bk. 8 and all titlepages and preliminaries correctly bound; bk. 10, 11 as in the copy at G.2492.

W82 WILHELM

. . . (*begin:*) WILHELM GRAEF'T wijt en breet, t'is niet LEGIER om winnen [etc.] fol. or 4°? a single sheet, lower half only

T.2420(30).

Verses, perhaps accompanying an engraving, or following on earlier text. A chronogram on the siege of Sluis reads 1604. Signed: Fecit, Peyst om d'eewich. If this motto was used exclusively by the author signing himself elsewhere 'D.M. Peyst om d'eeuwigh', it could stand for Daniel Mostaert, then aged 14. Attempts at locating a complete copy have proved unsuccessful.

W83 WILLIAM I; Prince of Orange

[Letters and documents] APOLOGIE, Ofte Verantwoordinghe des . . . Vorsts . . . Wilhelms . . . Prince van Orangien . . . Teghen den Ban ofte Edict by forme van Proscriptie . . . Hier is oock byg hevoecht [*sic*]den voorsz. Ban ofte Proscriptie. TOT LEYDEN, By Jan Paedts Jacobsz . . . M.DC.VII. 4° pp.119; illus.

T.1723(3).

A new edition of the Dutch text, first published in French, Latin, English and Dutch at Delft in 1581, presumed to have been written on behalf of William by Pierre de Loyseleur and revised by Hubert Languet. With the woodcut arms of William I on the titlepage verso and in the colophon.

W84 WILLIAM I; Prince of Orange

[Letters and documents] De verantvvoordinghe Des Princen van Orangien/ Teghen de valsche leughenen/daer mede zijn Wedersprekers hem soecken . . . te beschuldighen . . . Amsterdam/voor Michiel Colijn . . . 1610. 4° pp.84; illus.

T.1721(3); T.2419(2).

A new edition of the Dutch text, first published without imprint in French and Dutch in 1568. The titlepage woodcut of the arms of William I is the same as that used in the preceding.

W85 WILSON, John; Priest

THE ENGLISH MARTYROLOGE CONTEYNING A SVMMARY OF THE LIVES of the . . . Saintes of . . . ENGLAND, SCOTLAND, AND IRELAND. COLLECTED AND DISTRIBVTED into Moneths, after the forme of a Calendar, according to euery Saintes festiuity. WHERVNTO Is annexed . . . a Catalogue of those, who haue suffered death in England for defence of the Catholicke Cause . . . By a Catholicke Priest . . . 1608. 8° pp.356

1125.a.14; C.26.h.5.

The preface signed: I.W. Without imprint; published by the English College press at St. Omer.

WINCHESTER, Bisschop van (1603). *See* BILSON, Thomas

W86 WING, John

THE CROWNE CONIVGALL OR, THE SPOVSE ROYALL. A Discovery of the true honor and happines of CHRISTIAN MATRIMONY . . . By IOHN WING . . . PRINTED AT MIDDELBVRGH, By Iohn Hellenius . . . 1620. 4° pp.146; illus.

8415.cc.11.

Sermons. The titlepage woodcut shows an emblem of marriage.

W87 WING, John

IACOBS STAFFE. TO BEARE VP, THE Faithfull. AND TO BEATE DOWNE, THE Profane . . . Formerly preachcd [*sic*] at Hamburgh by IOHN VVING . . . as his farewell to the famous followship [*sic*] of Merchant Adventurers of England resident in that City. And now published, and dedicated, to the honor and vse, of that . . . Society, there, or wheresoever being . . . AT FLVSHING, Printed by Martin Abraham vander Nolck . . . 1621. 4° pp.216; illus.

4455.de.8.

The woodcut shows the arms of the Merchant Adventurers. With an initial 'T' formerly belonging to Richard Schilders at Middelburg. Ownership inscription: Samuel Brooking.

W88 WINSEMIUS, Menelaus

DISPVTATIO INAVGVRALIS, DE HYDROPE, QVAM . . . Pro Gradu & Priuilegijs Doctoratus in Medicinâ consequendis, Publicè sine Præside defendet, MENELAVS VINSHEMIVS . . . LVGDVNI BATAVORVM, Excudebat Henricus Ludouici ab Haestens . . . M.D CXII. 4° sig.A^4

1185.g.1(51).

WINSEMIUS, Menelaus. Disputatio medica de variolis. 1612. *See* PAAUW, Petrus

W89 WINSEMIUS, Menelaus

[Disputationum anatomicarum prima etc.] (tp.1) Adspirante Archiatro Opt. Max. Disputationum Anatomicarum PRIMAM, Quæ est DE ANATOME, SVB PRÆSIDIO . . . D. MENELAI WINSEMII . . . publice propugnabit GERHARDVS DE LEEW . . . FRANEKERAE, Ex officina Ioannis Lamrinck . . . 1618.

(tp.2) Disputationum Anatomicarum SECVNDA, DE HVMANI CORPORIS Divisione, & partium differentiis, QVAM . . . SVB PRÆSIDIO . . . D. MENELAI WINSEMII . . . Publice defendere conabitur IOHANNES HOBBII ANSTA . . . FRANEKERAE, Ex officina Ioannis Lamrinck . . . 1618.

(tp.3) Disputationum Anatomicarum TERTIA, Quæ est prima DE OSSIBVS Humani Corporis, QVAM . . . SVB PRÆSIDIO . . . D. MENELAI WINSEMII . . . ad publicam συζητησιν proponit ANCHISES ANDLA . . . FRANEKERAE, Ex officina Ioannis Lamrinck . . . 1618.

(tp.4) Disputationum Anatomicarum QVARTA, Quæ est secunda DE OSSIBVS Humani Corporis, QVAM . . . SVB PRÆSIDIO . . . D. MENELAI WINSEMII . . . publicè propugnandam suscipiet PAVLVS BERGIVS . . . FRANEKERAE, Ex officina Ioannis Lamrinck . . . 1618.

(tp.5) Disputationum Anatomicarum QVINTA, Quæ est tertia, DE OSSIBVS Humani Corporis, QVAM . . . SVB PRÆSIDIO . . . D. MENELAI WINSEMII . . . publice defendere conabitur IOHANNES le PIPER . . . FRANEKERAE, Ex officina Ioannis Lamrinck . . . 1618.

(tp.6) Disputationum Anatomicarum SEXTA, Quæ est quarta, DE OSSIBVS Humani Corporis, QVAM . . . SVB CLYPEO . . . D. MENELAI WINSEMII . . . publicè discutiendam suscipiet IACOBVS THOMÆVS . . . FRANEKERÆ, Ex officina Ioannis Lamrinck . . . 1618.

(tp.7) Disputationum Anatomicarum SEPTIMA, Quæ est DE CARTILAGINIBVS, LIGAMENTIS, &C. QVAM . . . SVB PRÆSIDIO . . . D. MENELAI WINSEMII . . . publicè ventilandam exhibet GERHARDVS de LEEW . . . FRANEKERAE, Ex officina Ioannis Lamrinck . . . 1618.

(tp.8) Disputationum Anatomicarum OCTAVA, Quæ est DE VENIS ET ARTERIIS, QVAM . . . SVB PRÆSIDIO . . . D. MENELAI WINSEMII . . . publicè exagitandam adfert IOANNES HOBBII ANSTA . . . FRANEKERAE, Ex officina Ioannis Lamrinck . . . 1618.

(tp.9) Disputationum Anatomicarum NONA, Quæ est DE NERVIS HUMANI CORPORIS, QVAM . . . SVB PRÆSIDIO . . . D. MENELAI WINSEMII . . . publicè discutiendam proponit ANCHISES ANDLA . . . FRANEKARAE, Ex officina Ioannis Lamrinck . . . 1618.

(tp.10) Summo adspirante Archiatro Disputationum Anatomicarum DECIMAM, DE CARNIBVS, PRÆSIDE . . . D. MENELAO WINSEMIO . . . publicè proponit PAVLVS BERGIVS . . . FRANEKARAE Ex officina Ioannis Lamrinck . . . 1619.
(tp.11) Summo adspirante Archiatro Disputationum Anatomicarum VNDECIMAM, DE MVSCVLIS, PRÆSIDE . . . D. MENELAO WINSEMIO . . . Publicè proponit IOHANNES le PIPER . . . FRANEKARAE, Ex officina Ioannis Lamrinck . . . 1619.
(tp.12) Disputationum Anatomicarum DVODECIMA, DE CVTE, PINGVEDINE &c. QVAM . . . SVB CLYPEO . . . D. MENELAI WINSEMII . . . publice ventilandam exhibet IACOBVS THOMÆUS . . . FRANEKARAE, Ex officina Ioannis Lamrinck . . . 1619.
(tp.13) Disputationum Anatomicarum DECIMAM-TERTIAM, DE ORGANIS Chylificationi inservientibus PRIMAM . . . PRÆSIDENTE . . . D. MENELAO WINSEMIO . . . Publicè disputandam proponit GERHARDVS de LEEW . . . FRANEKARAE, Ex officina Ioannis Lamrinck . . . 1619.
(tp.14) Disputationum Anatomicarum DECIMA-QVARTA, Quæ est secunda DE ORGANIS Chylificationi inservientibus, Quam . . . SVB . . . D. MENELAO WINSEMIO . . . Publicè disputandam proponit IOANNES HOBBII ANSTA . . . FRANEKARAE, Ex officina Ioannis Lamrinck . . . 1619.
(tp.15) Disputationum Anatomicarum DECIMA-QVINTA, Quæ est, DE PARTIBVS Chyli distributioni inservientibus, QVAM . . . PRÆSIDENTE . . . D. MENELAO WINSEMIO . . . Publicè disputandam proponit ANCHISES ANDLA . . . FRANEKARAE, Ex officina Ioannis Lamrinck . . . 1619.
(tp.16) Summo Adspirante Archiatro Disputationum Anatomicarum DECIMAM-SEXTAM, DE ORGANIS Sanguificationis Præside . . . D. MENELAO WINSEMIO . . . publicè proponit PAVLVS von BERGEN . . . FRANEKARAE, Ex officina Ioannis Lamrinck . . . 1619.
(tp.17) Disputationum Anatomicarum DECIMA-SEPTIMA, QVAE EST DE PARTIBVS VRINARIIS, &C. QVAM . . . PRÆSIDE . . . D. MENELAO WINSEMIO . . . Publice disputandam proponit IACOBUS THOMAEUS. FRANEKARÆ, Ex officina Ioannis Lamrinck . . . 1619.
(tp.18) Disputationum Anatomicarum DECIMA-OCTAVA, DE ORGANIS GENERATIONIS in utroque Sexu, Ad Quam . . . PRÆSIDE . . . D. MENELAO WINSEMIO . . . Respondebit GERARDVS de LEEW. FRANEKARAE, Ex officina Ioannis Lamrinck . . . 1619.
(tp.19) Disputationum Anatomicarum DECIMA-NONA, Quæ est Prima DE PROCREATIONE HOMINIS Quam . . . PRÆSIDE . . . D. MENELAO WINSEMIO . . . publicè disputandam proponit IOANNES HOBBII ANSTA . . . FRANEKERAE, Ex officina Ioannis Lamrinck . . . 1619.
(tp.20) Disputationum Anatomicarum VICESIMA, Quæ est secunda DE PROCREATIONE HOMINIS. Ad quam . . . PRÆSIDE . . . D. MENELAO WINSEMIO . . . Resp. ANCHISES ANDLA. FRANEKARAE, Ex officina Ioannis Lamrinck . . . 1620.
4° sig. A-C⁴D⁵EF⁶G⁴H⁶I⁴I³L-V⁴; illus.
548.f.28(1–20).
The illustrations are woodcuts on the titlepage versos of the 13th and 14th disputations, showing the arms of Friesland, surrounded by those of the Frisian cities. Ownership inscription: Le Moyne.

W90 WINSEMIUS, Menelaus
DISQUISITIO Physiologico-Anatomica DE HVMANI CORPORIS PARTIBVS, earumq; præcipuis differentiis, QVAM . . . PRÆSIDE . . . D. MENELAO WINSEMIO . . . Defendere annitar FRANCISCVS DE VIC . . . Ad diem [-] Ianuarij. FRANEKERÆ, Excudebat Fredericus Heynsius . . . 1621. 4° sig. A⁴
1185.i.13(1).
The precise date has been left blank to be supplied in manuscript.

W91 WINSEMIUS, Pierius

PIERII VVINSEMII . . . ORATIO FVNEBRIS IN OBITVM . . . FREDERICI de VERVOV . . . Habita . . . FRANEKERÆ, Ex officina Ioannis Lamrinck . . . 1621. 4° sig.(∴)^{2}A-C^4; illus.

835.g.16(2).

With 'Carmina funebria D.D. Professorum Acad. Franeq.', signed: Sixtinus Amama; Tim. Faber; M. Winsemius; S. Arcerius. The titlepage woodcut shows the arms of Friesland, surrounded by those of the Frisian cities.

W92 WINWOOD, Sir Ralph

DE TWEEDE ORATIE Ghedaen door . . . Rodolphus Winwood Ridder/Ambassadeur van weghen syne Majesteydt van groot Brittannien/etc. aende . . . Staten Generael vande vereenichde Nederlanden/Aengaende de beroepinghe Conradi Vorstij, tot de professie der H. Theologie inde Vniversiteyt tot Leyden. Item vande Leere ende Discipulen Arminij, ende anders. Anno M.DC.XI. 4° sig.A^4

106.d.37.

Partly in both Latin and Dutch. Corresponding to the copy described in *Knuttel* no.1873.

W93 WITTENHORST, Walraven van

PROPOSITIE vanden Heere vander Horst/Ghedaen ende ghepresenteert ter vergaderinge vande . . . Staten der Vereenighde Nederlanden den xiij^{en} Januarij 1607. MIDTSGADERS d'Antvvoort vande . . . Staten opte . . . Propisitie [*sic*] gedaen. ENDE NOCH Het uyt-schrift vande . . . Staten, ghesonden aen allen Provintien ende Steden opte aenstaende Vrede-handelinghe. Ghedruckt . . . 1608. 4° sig.A^4

T.2420(2); 107.g.1(9).

The 'Propositie' signed: VValraven van VVitten-horst. The copy at 107.g.1(9) is imperfect; wanting sig.A3,4.

W94 WITTIUS, Daniel

DANIELIS WITTII . . . Super Religione & vita Pontificiorum ORATIO: Habita . . . 7. Idus Decembr. Anno 1600. LVGDVNI BATAVORVM, Ex Typographeio Christophori Guyotij . . . M.D.CI. 4° pp.57

491.b.42(1).

W95 WOLRATH, Fridericus; Veritat. Stud.

Vertrawliches Gespräch etlicher Personen/Nemlich eines Bäyers/Sachssens/Böhmens vnd vnparteyischen ausländischen Peregrinaten/Welche sich/wegen des jetzigen Zustands im heiligen Römischen Reich/vnd sonderlichen der Böhmischen Vnruhe halben/Politicè vnd Theologicè vnterreden . . . Allen getrewen Patriotten . . . zu guter nachrichtung in Druck verfertiget/Durch Fridericum Wolrath/Veritat. Stud. . . . Gedruckt zu Leyden . . . 1621. 4° sig.A-D^{4}E^3

8074.c.19(14).

Pseudonymous and with a false imprint; printed in Germany.

W96 WONDERBAERLICKE

VVōderbaerlicke vertooninghe/gheschiet ontrendt Marcilien/by claren daghe/alwaer groote menichte van Ruyters ende voetvolck gepasseert is . . . die eyntlijck in een bosschagie verdwenen zijn . . . Hier is mede by ghevoecht een . . . Historie/die Godt . . . de stadt Jerusalem . . . voor de destructie heeft verthoont. Voor Cornelis Adriaensz. . . . 1609. 4° 2 unsigned leaves

T.2420(31).

Published at Vlissingen.

W97 WONDERLIJCKE

EEN Wonderlijcke/dogh ghenoechlijcke T'samen-sprekinghe/Van een Esel ende

Nacht-uyl: VVaer in het Vrouwen-praetjen gheexamineert vverdt. GHEDRVCKT . . . 1618. 4° pp.32
T.2248(58).

A reply to 'Een lieffelijck vrouwen-praet' by H.S., sometimes identified as Dionysius Spranckhuysen, published in 1617.

W98 WONDERLIJCKE

Een wonderlijcke ende waerachtighe Historie/van t'Heylich Bloet van Mirakel. GHESCHIET INT BOSCH VAN HEER Isaac int Bisdom van Camerijk, by Nijuel, int Iaer . . . duysent vier hondert en vijue . . . Gheschreuen door sommighe Religiosen der seluer plaetse. T'HANTVVERPEN, By Marten Huyssens . . . M.D.CII. (col.) Typis Antonij de Ballo. 8° pp.70; illus.
4807.aa.16.

Printed at Antwerp.

W99 WONDERLIJCKE

Wonderlijcke nieuwe Tijdinghe van Duytslandt/van Jtalien/ende Vranckrijck/met t'ghene daer ghepasseert is. Ouerghesedt wt het Hoochduyts/in onse Nederlantsche sprake. Eerst Ghedruckt den 8. October. 1621. T'Hantwerpen/By Abraham Verhoeuen/[etc.] 4° pp.8; sig.Nnn[4]; illus.
P.P.3444.af(295).

Headed: October, 1621. 146. The titlepage woodcuts show (a) a view of Prague(?); (b) a portrait of a general.

W100 WONDERLIJCKEN

Wonderlijcken Droom Vande School-houdinghe van M[r]. Ian van Oldenbarnevelt. Met de verclaringhe van dien. Wy leeren lustich voort/[etc.] 4° sig.AB[4]; illus.
T.2248(62); T.2422(25).

In prose and verse. Signed: Beminder van Nassou. The titlepage engraving shows Oldenbarnevelt and his supporters in a school setting. Published in 1618.

W101 WONDERLYCKE

VVonderlycke Tydinghen, Op den dagh van den slagh ontrent Praghe/wesende Sondagh viij. Nouemb. 1620 waer van 't Evangelie was in houdende . . . datmen de keyser soude gheuen dat hem toekomt/ende God dat God toekomt. Aen den Pals-Graeff. Loffdicht ouer de Heerlijcke ouerwinninghe vande Stadt Prage. Eerst Ghedruckt den 30. December 1620. T'Hantwerpen/By Abraham Verhoeuen/ [etc.] 4° pp.8; sig.Yy[4]; illus.
1480.aa.15(59); P.P.3444.af(164).

In verse. The titlepage woodcut shows Frederick and Elizabeth on either side of a tree in a landscape.

W102 WONDER-MAER

DEes wonder-Maer end' Prophetsije wis/[etc.] 4° sig.A[B][4]
106.b.11.

Consisting of two unrelated stories, one about the murder of a Frenchman by his former friend, an Italian, dated 22 May 1607, the other a dream warning against peace with Spain, interspersed with verses. With the manuscript date '1608' inserted on sig.A1.

W103 WOODWARD, Philip

THE DOLEFVLL KNELL, OF THOMAS BELL. THAT IS A full and sounde ansvver, to his Pamphlet, Intituled, THE POPES FVNERAL. VVhich he published, against a Treatise of myne, called. THE FORE-RVNNER OF BELS DOVVNFALL . . . By B.C. Student in Diuinitye . . . Printed at Roane. 1607. 8° pp.414; illus.
3936.bb.42.

Anonymous and with a false imprint; printed, the preliminaries by Pierre Auroi, the text by Laurence Kellam, both at Douai. The illustration is a woodcut showing the Crucifixion, at the end of the book.

W104 WORTHINGTON, Thomas

AN ANKER OF CHRISTIAN DOCTRINE . . . Printed at Doway by Thomas Kellam . . . 1618. 4° pt.1: pp.495 [496]

3936.bbb.41(1).

The preface signed: Th.W. The imprint is false; printed by the Birchley Hall press in Lancashire or elsewhere secretly in England. Pt.2-4 of this edition were published in 1622. The last page has probably lost its pagination by being cropped.

W105 WORTHINGTON, Thomas

AN ANKER OF CHRISTIAN DOCTRINE . . . Printed at Doway by Thomas Kellam . . . 1618. 4° pp.496

3936.bbb.34.

Another issue of the preceding, with a reset titlepage which now has a rule after 'DOCTRINE', not present on the titlepage of the preceding; the last page is definitely numbered and begins 'You may please' where the preceding reads 'Tou may please'. Also printed secretly in England, probably at the Birchley Hall press in Lancashire.

W106 WORTHINGTON, Thomas

[An anker of Christian doctrine.] THE SECOND PART OF AN ANKER OF CHRISTIAN DOCTRINE. WHEREIN, THE MOST PRINCIPAL POINTES of Catholique Religion, are proued: By the onlie written word of God . . . AVCTORE T.VV.S.T.D.P.A. . . . AT MACKLINE, Printed by HENRY IAEY, M.DC.XX. [etc.] 4° pp.318

Cup.401.d.15.

The preface signed: T.W.Sem. Pr. Ownership inscription: Alexander Hudsonis book 1693; 1692.

W107 WOVERIUS, Joannes; of Antwerp

ASSERTIO LIPSIANI DONARI ADVERSVS GELASTORVM SVGGILLATIONES. ANTVERPIÆ, EX OFFICINA PLANTINIANA, Apud Ioannem Moretum. M.DC.VII. 4° pp.30

631.k.4(8).

The dedication signed: Ioannes VVouerius Antuerpiensis. A defence of the work by Lipsius on miracles. The Plantinian device as reproduced in the *Bibliographia Belgica*, no.L548b and s.v. Marques typographiques, vol.5 p.114, no.89, but signed: G.

W108 WOVERIUS, Joannes; of Antwerp

IOANNIS WOVERI . . . PANEGYRICVS AVSTRIÆ SERENISSIMIS ARCHIDVCIBVS BELGICÆ . . . PRINCIPIBVS scriptus. ANTVERPIÆ, EX OFFICINA PLANTINIANA, Apud Ioannem Moretum. M.DC.IX. (col.) ANTVERPIÆ, EX OFFICINA PLANTINIANA, Apud Ioannem Moretum. M.DC.IX. 8° pp.73

12301.aaa.23(1).

W109 WOVERIUS, Joannes; of Antwerp

VITA B. SIMONIS VALENTINI Sacerdotis A IOANNE WOVERIO . . . descripta . . . ANTVERPIÆ, EX OFFICINA PLANTINIANA, Apud Viduam & Filios Io. Moreti. M.DC.XIV. 8° pp.59

C.77.a.10(2).

No such saint or beatified person is known.

WRAECK-GIERIGERS treurspel. 1618. *See* TOURNEUR, Cyril

W110 WRIGHT, Thomas

QVATVOR COLLOQVIA INTER R^dvm DOMINVM THOMAM WRIGHTVM . . . & illustrem Dominum THOMAM ROE . . . ad aquas Spadanas habita, anno Domini 1613. Opera . . . IACOBI de NIXON . . . collecta, & typis mandata. MECHLINIÆ, Apud HENRICVM IEAY. 1614. 8° pp.52

1366.c.7.

Edited by Thomas Wright.

W111 WRIGHT, William; Jesuit

A DISCOVERY OF CERTAINE NOTORIOVS SHIFTS, EVASIONS, AND VNTRVTHES VTTERED BY M. IOHN VVHITE MINISTER, In a Booke of his lately set forth, and intituled, A Defence of the Way &c. . . . By W. G. Professour in Diuinity, in manner of a Dialogue. THE SECOND EDITION . . . M.DC.XIX. 4° pp.120

117.g.36.

Anonymous and without imprint; published by the English College press at St. Omer.

W112 WRIGHT, William; Jesuit

A TREATISE OF THE CHVRCH. IN VVHICH Is proued M. Iohn White his Way to the true Church to be indeed no way at all to any Church, true or false . . . VVRITTEN By VV.G. Professour in Diuinity: in manner of Dialogue . . . M.DC.XVI. 4° pp.96

117.g.35.

Anonymous and without imprint; published by the English College press at St. Omer.

W113 WTENBOGAERT, Jan

Achabs Biddagh/Dat is Schriftuerlijck ende Politijck Discours van den Biddagh ghehouden in Aprili Anno 1619. Voor d'VVtspraeck van de Kerckelijcke ende Politijcke Oordeelen ofte Sententien over de Remonstranten ende Ghevanghene Heeren. Midtsgaders Van't MIZPA, de HARDT- ende CREVPELE-BODE . . . Ghedruckt . . . 1621. 4° pp.127

T.2251(3).

Anonymous. Directed against Ewout Teellinck.

W114 WTENBOGAERT, Jan

Acht voorstellinghen, Uytghegheven van die van het Pausdom/om te bevestighen de waerheydt . . . hares gheloofs/teghens alle nieuwe (gelijck syse noemen) Sectarissen: Mitsgaders oock Acht teghenstellinghen, Der Gereformeerde: dienende tot antwoort . . . Wtghegheven . . . door I.W. . . . In het Iaer . . . sesthien hondert neghen. 4° sig.A^6

T.2417(23).

Anonymous. Signed: Science et Conscience.

W115 WTENBOGAERT, Jan

Advertissement, ofte Vvaerschouwingh/Over het Oordeel/uyt-spraeck/ende den Eedt van't Synodus Nationael der ghenaemde Ghereformeerde Kercken van Vranckrijck/ghehouden tot ALEZ inde CEVENNES, besloten ende gearresteert den 6. Octobris 1620. Nopende De vijf Artijckelen der Remonstranten in Nederlandt. ghedruckt . . . 1621. 4° pp.40

T.2251(16).

Anonymous.

WTENBOGAERT, Jan. Aenhangsel van der kercken-dienaren Remonstranten Naerder bericht. 1612. *See* below: Naerder bericht.

W116 WTENBOGERT, Jan

BRIEF aen de . . . Staten Generael der Vereenighde Nederlanden ghesonden door . . . IOHANNES VVTENBOGAERT . . . Nopende 'Tuytgheven van seecker Libel Gheintituleert Morghen-vvecker, &c. Ghedruckt . . . 1621. 4° pp.6

T.2251(6).

W117 WTENBOGAERT, Jan

BRIEF AENDE . . . STATEN GENERAEL. OVER DE SENTENTIE IOH. GREVII GHEBANNEN INT TVCHTHVYS T'AMSTERDAM. Mitsgaders Over eenighe saecken roerende 't Examen SAMVELIS PRINCII ende BERNHERI VESEKII Die versonden is in't Rasphuys tot HAERLEM. In't Jaer 1620. 4° pp.22

T.2250(6).

Signed: IWtenbogaert, S. Episcopius, N. Grevinchovius.

W118 WTENBOGAERT, Jan
CONTRA-DISCOVRS kerckelic ende Politijck Dat is: ANTWOORDT Op de Glosen ende 't Discours/met Consent van de Heeren Regierders der Stadt Amsterdam aldaer uytghegheven op . . . M. Simonis Episcopij Brief: Daer in voornemelijck gehandelt wort vande Ghesepareerde vergaderingh der Remonstranten . . . Tweede Druck, verrijckt ende verbetert. Ghedruckt . . . 1621. 4° pp.73
T.2250(11).
Anonymous and without imprint. The 'Glosen ende Discours' were by Jacobus Trigland. According to evidence quoted in *Knuttel* no.3087 possibly printed by Joris Veseler at Amsterdam.

W119 WTENBOGAERT, Jan
COPYE, Van een Missive den ij. Aprilis 1619, aen eenen particulieren ende oudt-bekenden vrient afgeveerdicht Door . . . JOHANNEM WTEN BOGAERT, Waer in Hy zijnen staet ende oorsaeck van zijne . . . noncomparatie . . . te kennen gheeft . . . Ghedruckt . . . 1619. 4° pp.22
T.2249(8).

W120 WTENBOGAERT, Jan
Copye van seker Vertooch Onlanghs by eenighe Predicanten der Ghereformeerde Kercke ghedaen aende . . . Staten van Hollandt ende West-Vrieslandt. Roerende de oudtheyt vande Gereformeerde Leere, ende de nieuwicheden die daer teghens werden ghepleecht. TOT DELF, By Bruyn Schinckel . . . 1617. 4° sig.AB[4]
T.2247(38).
Anonymous.

W121 WTENBOGAERT, Jan
[Copye van seker vertooch.] SECVNDA REMONSTRANTIA Ministrorum Ecclesiarum Hollandicarum & West-Frisicarum qui REMONSTRANTES vocantur . . . ORDINIBVS Hollandiæ & West-Frisiæ tradita in Aprili, ANNO 1617. CVM SECVNDA CONTRA-REMONSTRANTIA, seu Responsio ad eam . . . iisdem . . . Ordinibvs tradita in Augusto Anno 1617. Ex Belgicis in Latinam linguam . . . translata . . . LVGDVNI-BATAVORVM, Apud IOHANNEM ORLERS, 1617. 4° pp.128
697.c.15(1).
Anonymous. The 'Secunda remonstrantia' is a translation of the 'Seker vertooch', drawn up by Jan Wtenbogaert, the 'Secunda contra-remonstrantia' is a translation of 'Klaer ende grondich teghen-vertoogh', sometimes attributed to Jacobus Trigland.

W122 WTENBOGAERT, Jan
CORT BERECHT. Nopende seeckere Copije van een REMONSTRANTIE, die (soo men voor-gheeft) in den Druck van de CONFERENTIE in den Haghe ghehouden, naghelaten oft vergheten is. Vervatet in eenen Seynt-brief des . . . D. Ioannis Wten-bogaert aen synen Vrient N.G. gheschreven/ende door den selven in Druck wtghegheven. TOT ROTTERDAM By Mattijs Bastiaensz . . . 1612. 4° sig.AB[4]
T.2244(3).
The text of the letter, addressed to and edited by Nicolaas Grevinchoven.

W123 WTENBOGAERT, Jan
Den eenigen ende rechten WAEROM, Vande uytvoeringhe der Remonstrantsche Leeraers uyt de Gheunieerde PROVINTIEN. Tot Onderrichtinghe vande Eenvoudighe Christenen ende goede Patriotten des Landts . . . 1619. 4° sig.A[4]
T.2249(28).
Anonymous.

W124 WTENBOGAERT, Jan
Naerder-Bericht ENDE OPENINGE VANDE PROCEDVREN BY DEN KERCKEN-DIEnaren Remonstranten ghehouden inde teghenvvoordighe Verschillen. Dienende tot nodighe Verantwoordinge op de Beschuldigingen vervat inde Remonstrantie tegens hun over ghegeven/Gedruckt int 13. ende eenige volgende bladeren vande schriftelicke Conferentie . . . Aende . . . Staten van Hollandt ende West-vrieslandt. IN S'GRAVEN-HAGE, By Hillebrandt Jacobsz . . . 1612. 4° pp.116
T.2242(13).
Anonymous.

W125 WTENBOGAERT, Jan
[Naerder-bericht.] Aenhangsel Van der Kercken-dienarē Remonstranten Naerder bericht: Vervatende klaer bewijs dat d'Artikelen by hun verworpen/niet en zijn ter quader trouwen voorghedraghen/maer dat d'inhouden van dien . . . inde Schriften van verscheyden Leeraren der Ghereformeerde Kercke bevonden wordt . . . TOT ROTTERDAM, By Matthijs Bastiaensz . . . 1612. 4° sig.a-d, A-K[4]
T.2242(14,14*).
Anonymous.

W126 WTENBOGAERT, Jan
(tp.1) Noodighe Antwoordt OP DER Contra-Remonstranten TEGEN-VERTOOCH, Vervatende eene clare . . . wederlegginghe van t'selve: MET VAST BEVVYS Dat de Leere der Remonstranten . . . niet Nieu/maer Oudt is. Met eene Voor-Rede . . . roerende mede d'Anderde klachte der Kercke . . . IN S'GRAVEN-HAGE, By Hillebrant Jacobsz. . . . 1617.
(tp.2) TVVEEDE DEEL Van de Noodighe Antwoorde op der Contra-Remonst. Teghen-Vertooch . . . IN S'GRAVEN-HAGHE, By Hillebrant Jacobssen . . . 1618. 4° 2 dl.: pp.208; 164
T.2247(40).
Anonymous. Directed against the 'Klaer ende grondich teghen-vertooch', sometimes attributed to Jacobus Trigland, and 'Anderde klachte' by Ewout Teellinck.

W127 WTENBOGAERT, Jan
Noodighe ontschuldiginghe IOANNIS VVTENBOGAERT Over 'tChartabel van Grove Lasteringen ende Beschuldigingen, Niet getogen uyt sijn Tractaet/maer uyt sijne wel-ghestelde Redenen verkeerdelijck aen-gewesen . . . IN 'SGRAVEN-HAGHE, By Hillebrandt Iacobsz . . . M.DC.XVI. 4° pp.31
T.2246(9*).
Directed against Vincent van Drielenburch.

W128 WTENBOGAERT, Jan
ON-deckinghe Van Verscheyden On-vvaerheyden, ende Ontrouvvicheyden, begaen in een seecker Schrift t'AMSTERDAM Wtghegheven, met den Titel, TAFEL, Begrijpende t'Verschil tusschen de Leere des Goddelijcken VVoordts ende der Remonstranten. Den tweeden Druck . . . 1617. 4° pp.32
T.2247(29).
Anonymous. The 'Tafel', published in 1616, sometimes attributed to Jacobus Trigland.

W129 WTENBOGAERT, Jan
Oprecht ende Noodt-wendigh Bericht IOANNIS VVTENBOGAERT Op een bitter Schrift nu versch t'Enckhuysen uyt-ghegeven, metten Titel van Naerder Advis over de Conferentie tot Delf/&c. . . . IN 'SGRAVEN-HAGHE, Ghedruckt by Hillebrandt Iacobsz. . . . 1615. 4° pp.70
T.2245(4).
The 'Naerder advijs' was by Festus Hommius.

W130 WTENBOGAERT, Jan

PREDICATIE, Door IOHANNEM WTENBOGART bearbeydet/in welcke hy de voornaemste gronden syns laetsten Boecx/handelende vande macht der Politiker Overheydt in Kerckelijcke Zaken . . . betoont/gheensins syn ghevoelen te bevestighen. Door RVARDVM ACRONIVM . . . inden Druck verveerdicht. TOT SCHIEDAM, by Adriaen Cornelisz . . . M.D.C.X. 4° pp.26
T.2240(12).

W131 WTENBOGAERT, Jan

Redenen, Vvaerom men in goede Conscientie metten Nederlandtschen Contra-Remonstranten/die haer den naem van Ghereformeerde toe-eyghenen/gheen geestelijcke gemeenschap houden/of den uyterlijcken Godes-dienst langher met hun pleghen en mach . . . Ghedruckt tot Friburch [etc.] 4° sig.A-E^4
T.2250(17).

Anonymous and with a false imprint; printed at Antwerp? Published in 1620.

WTENBOGAERT, Jan. Secunda remonstrantia ministrorum ecclesiarum Hollandicarum . . . qui Remonstrantes vocantur. 1617. *See* above: Copye van seker vertooch.

W132 WTENBOGAERT, Jan

REMONSTRANTIE By de zes Colloquenten Vander Remonstranten weghen in de Haechsche Conferente [*sic*] bekent/overghegheven aen de . . . Staten van Hollandt ende West-Vrieslandt in September lest-leden. Waer in Sy haere bedenckinghen openen over het houden der Synoden, ende billijcke conditien voorslaen/op de welcke zy bereydt zyn in de zelve Synoden te verschijnen. TOT ROTTERDAM, By Matthijs Bastiaensz . . . 1618. 4° pp.48
T.2248(20).

Anonymous. At the end: 'Met consent van de Heeren Burghemeesteren der Stede Rotterdam'.

W133 WTENBOGAERT, Jan

REMONSTRANTIE van IOANNES VVTENBOGAERT ghepresenteert in Novembri . . . 1618. Aen de . . . Staten Generael vande Ge-Unieerde Provincien . . . Nopende het presenteren van sijne verantwoordinge tegens seeckere beschuldingen Festi Hommij, aen den Synodum Nationalem/mitsgaders ronde verclaringhe over verscheyden geruchten t'onrecht hem nagestroyt. Tot Leyden/By Govert Basson. 1618. 4° sig.A^4
T.2248(21).

W134 WTENBOGAERT, Jan

IOANN. WTENBOGARDI RESPONSIO, ad ea, Quæ illi speciatim impegit FESTVS HOMMIVS, libro non ita pridem edito . . . cum Titulo SPECIMINIS CONTROVERSIARVM BELGICARVM. LVGDVNI BATAVORVM, Ex Officinâ GODEFRIDI BASSON . . . 1618. 4° sig.AB^4
3504.bb.30(3); 697.c.15(2).

The titlepage of the copy at 697.c.15(2) is mutilated, with loss of some letters in the imprint.

W135 WTENBOGAERT, Jan

Schriftelijcke Verantwoordinghe/Van . . . IOHANNIS UYT DEN BOGAERT . . . Op de openbaere Klock in luydinghe ende Edicte, den 19. Martij, Ao' 1619. over syn Persoon gedaen. Ghedruckt . . . 1619. 4° pp.21
T.2249(1).

W136 WTENBOGAERT, Jan

Tweede Schriftelijcke Verantwoordinghe/Van . . . IOHANNIS UYT DEN BOGAERT . . . Aen den . . . PRINCE van ORAIGNEN. Op de openbaere Klock-

inluydinghe ende Edicte/den 19. Martij/Ao. 1619. over syn Persoon ghedaen. Ghedruckt . . . 1619. 4° sig.A^4
T.2249(2); 106.a.54.

W137 WTENBOGAERT, Jan
Treffelijcke ende bundige VERANTWOORDINGE, gheschreven Aen de . . . Burghemeesters ende Vroedtschap der stadt Vtrecht/door . . . IOHANNES VVTENBOGAERT . . . over De valsche beschuldinghen ende verzierde leughenen/ door Nicolaes Berck Burgemeester: t'Vtrecht ghepractiseert . . . Ghedruckt . . . 1620. 4° pp.40
T.2250(4).

W138 WTENBOGAERT, Jan
TWEE Sendtbrieven/eene des . . . D. IOHANNIS wt den Bogaert/ende d'andere DD. COENRADI VORSTII. Tot waerschouwinghe voor de Jnghesetene deses Landts/ teghen de onghefondeerde beschuldinghen . . . onlancx teghen de persoonen voorsz in druc ghegheven . . . Gedruct voor Hillebrandt Gerritsz. 1611. 4° sig.$\star AB^4C^2$
T.2241(25).
No place is known for this printer; the imprint is probably fictitious. Another edition of the letter of Conrad Vorstius, entitled 'Verantwoordinghe D. Conradi Vorstii', is entered under VORSTIUS, Conrad.

W139 WTENBOGAERT, Jan
Verantwoordinge des Eerweerdighen . . . D. IACOBI ARMINII . . . Teghen de grove calumnie . . . zijns Naems/begaen byden vertaelder vande Theses roerende de regieringhe der Kercken . . . onlancx tot Delft ghedruckt/ende met louter onwaerheyt onder zijnen Naem uytghegeven. In druck vervaerdicht by des voorsz. Arminij Weduwe. TOT LEYDEN, Ghedruckt by Godefridus Basson . . . 1612. 4° pp.20
T.2242(4).
In fact written by Jan Wtenbogaert.

W140 WTENBOGAERT, Jan
Verdedigingh vande RESOLVTIE Der . . . Staten van Hollant ende VVest-Vrieslant, Totten VREDE DER KERCKEN, Teghen seker Libel, gheintituleert Antwoort op drie Vraghen/dienende tot advijs in de huyden-daeghsche zwarigheyden. EERSTE DEEL. Ghestelt door Iohannem Wtenbogaert . . . IN 'SGRAVEN-HAGHE, By Hillebrant Iacobsz. . . . M.DC.XV. 4° pp.205
T.2244(6).
The book referred to as 'Antwoort' is the translation of Fabrice de la Bassecourt's 'Response' by Jacobus Trigland, entitled 'Antwoorde'. No more published. Imperfect; wanting sig.★2,3.

WTENBOGAERT, Jan. Voorlooper, over Adriani Smoutij Schriftuerlyck jae. 1613. [Sometimes attributed to Jan Wtenbogaert.] *See* VOORLOOPER

W141 WTENBOGAERT, Jan
VOOR-LOOPER. Tegen het Libel fameus oft Pasquil Van IA ende NEEN, Wt gegeven tegen Johannē Wten bogaert. Met eenen Brief desselven I. VVtenbogaerts, Aende Christelicke Ghemeynte ende Borgherschap der Stadt VTRECHT . . . TOT VTRECHT. By Jan Melissz . . . 1610. 4° sig.A-E^4
T.2240(14).
The whole by Jan Wtenbogaert. The preface printed in civilité. Directed against the selections from works by Jan Wtenbogaert compiled by Festus Hommius, entered below under: Selections.

W142 WTENBOGAERT, Jan

Vrijmoedigh Ondersoeck van verscheyden Placcaten/inde Gheunieerde Prouincien/binnen twee iaerē herwaerts/gepubliceert teghen de Christenen ingheborenen ende inwoonders der seluer Landen diemen REMONSTRANTEN noemt. DIENENDE MEDE tot Justificatie vande selue Remonstranten ende . . . van wijlen den Heer . . . Iohan van Oldenbarnevelt . . . ende de ghevanghenen Heeren Rombout Hogherbeetz ende Hugo de Groot. TOT VRYBVRCH By Adelaert Waermont 1620. 4° pp.188

T.2250(14).

Anonymous and with a false imprint; printed at Antwerp?

W143 WTENBOGAERT, Jan

Vrye AENVVYSING VAN de Onwaerheyden/trou-loose verdrayinghen/calumnien/ ende andere grove mis-slaghen/bevonden in de ghenaemde Historie Van FREDERICK DE VRY Burghemeester der Stadt Amstelredam/aengaende de Kerckelijcke beroerten van Hollandt. Ghestelt By Forme van 'tSamen-spraeck tusschen den selven De Vry ende den Aenvvijser . . . Ghedruckt . . . 1621. 4° pp.131

T.2251(25).

The preface signed: Nicolaus Bonifacius, pseudonym of Jan Wtenbogaert.

W144 WTENBOGAERT, Jan

WAERSCHOUWINGE, Teghen het Malitieus ende Valsch Gheschrift . . . Met den Titul: Den staet van de voornaemste Quæstien ende Gheschillen, die ten huydighen daghe Ghedisputeert worden, &c. IN S'GRAVEN-HAGHE, By Hillebrant Jacobsz . . . 1616. 4° pp.31

T.2246(14).

Anonymous. The book referred to is by Johannes Polyander.

W145 WTENBOGAERT, Jan

[Selections] Van de BEROEPINGHE Der Kercken-Dienaren/IA ende NEEN, Van IOHANNES VVTENBOGAERT . . . Wt zijn Boeck van't Ampt der Overheyt in Kercklijcke saecken/ende uyt zyne ghedruckte Predicatie over Joan 10/vers.3. Cortelijck ende ghetrouwelijck . . . by een ende teghen malcander ghestelt . . . Ghedruckt in't Jaer ons Heeren/1610. 4° sig.A-D^4E^3

T.2240(13).

Edited by Festus Hommius, though also sometimes attributed to Ruardus Acronius.

WTLEGGINGHE, Coenradi Vorstii, over sommighe Schriftuer-plaetsen. 1611. *See* WAERSCHOUWINGHE, aen alle Gereformeerde Kercken.

Ein WUNDERKUNSTIG Schiff. 1605. *See* SICHEM, Christoffel van

W146 WYTFLIET, Cornelius

DESCRIPTIONIS PTOLEMAICÆ AVGMENTVM. siue OCCIDENTIS Notitia Breui commentario illustrata, et hac secunda editione magna sui parte aucta Cornelio Wytfliet . . . auctore. DVACI Apud franciscum fabri . . . 1603. fol. pp.191: plates; maps

G.7209.

There had in fact been two previous editions, dated 1597 and 1598, but the latter is practically a reissue of the former and may therefore not have been counted as 'second' edition. The present edition printed by the same printer as the earlier one, therefore by Jan Bogard at Louvain. Several of the maps are dated 1597. The titlepage is engraved.

W147 WYTFLIET, Cornelius

[Descriptionis Ptolemaicae augmentum.] HISTOIRE VNIVERSELLE DES INDES, ORIENTALES ET OCCIDENTALES, DIVISÉE EN DEVX LIVRES LE PREMIER PAR CORNILLE

*[Illustration of **Y1** overleaf]*

CONSTITVTIONES
ET DECRETA

SYNODI

DIOECESANÆ IPRENSIS

Celebratæ die quarta mensis Nouembris anno CIↃ DC. IX.

Præsidente in ea R^mo *in* CHRISTO *Patre ac Domino*, D. CAROLO MASIO *Episcopo Iprensi.*

IPRIS,
Typis FRANCISCI BELLETI
M. DC. X.

Cum Priuilegio.

2/

WYTFLIET: LE SECOND PAR ANT. M. & AVTRES HISTORIENS. A Douay, aux despens de François Fabri. fol. 2 pt.: pp.126; 52 [56]: plates; maps.
601.l.23.

The titlepage is engraved. The chief source for bk.2 is Giovanni Antonio Magini. Printed by Pierre Auroi at Douai. In a binding bearing the arms of Jean Jacques de Barillon de Morangis, Conseiller au Parlement de Paris. Some of the maps are dated 1597. The publisher's dedicatory letter dated 1605.

W148 WYTFLIET, Cornelius

[Descriptionis Ptolemaicae augmentum.] (tp.1) HISTOIRE VNIVERSELLE DES INDES OCCIDENTALES, Diuisée en deux liures, faicte en latin par Monsieur WYTFLIET: Nouuellement traduicte: Où il est traicté de leur descouuerte, description, & conqueste faicte tant par les Castillans que Portugais, ensemble de leurs mœurs, religion, gouuernemens, & loix. A DOVAY, Chez FRANÇOIS FABRI . . . 1607.
(tp.2) HISTOIRE VNIVERSELLE DES INDES ORIENTALES, Diuisée en deux liures, faicte en Latin par ANTOINE MAGIN. Nouuellement traduicte. Contenant la descouuerte, nauigation, situation & conqueste, faicte tant par les Portugais que par les Castillans. Ensemble leurs mœurs, ceremonies, loix, gouuernemens, & reduction à la foy Catholique. A DOVAY, Chez FRANÇOIS FABRI . . . 1607.
(tp.3) [La suite de l'Histoire des Indes Orientales . . . A Douay. Chez François Fabry. 1607.] (col.) A DOVAY, De l'Imprimerie de PIERRE AVROY . . . 1607. Aux despens de FRANCOIS FABRI [etc.] fol. 3 pt.: pp.136; 72 [=1-42, 35-72], ff.7 [8]; pp.9-66 [72]: plates; maps
787.l.48(1,2); 800.l.25.

The titlepages are engraved; the titlepage to pt.3 is wanting. The titlepages are in a revised state; maps in pt.1, 2 only, of the 1597 edition. The half-title at the end of pt.1 should precede p.77. The copy at 800.l.25 has long been mislaid.

W149 WYTFLIET, Cornelius

[Descriptionis Ptolemaicae augmentum.] (tp.1) HISTOIRE VNIVERSELLE DES INDES OCCIDENTALES ET ORIENTALES, ET DE LA CONVERSION DES INDIENS. Diuisee en trois Parties, par Cornille VVytfliet, & Anthoine Magin, & autres Historiens. PREMIERE PARTIE. A DOVAY, Chez FRANÇOIS FABRI . . . 1611.
(tp.2) HISTOIRE VNIVERSELLE DES INDES ORIENTALES. Diuisée en deux liures, faicte en Latin par ANTOINE MAGIN. Nouuellement traduicte . . . SECONDE PARTIE. A DOVAY, Chez FRANÇOIS FABRI . . . 1611.
(tp.3) LA SVITE DE L'HISTOIRE DES INDES ORIENTALES. DE LA CONVERSION DES INDIENS. LA TROISIEME PARTIE. A DOVAY. Chez FRANÇOIS FABRY . . . 1611. fol. 3 pt.: pp.108; 66; 54: plates; maps
146.e.8; G.4311.

The engraved titlepage has been greatly reworked and the title printed in letterpress. The maps are those of the earlier editions. Ownership inscription in the copy at 146.e.8: Collegij Soc[tis] Jesv Louany Dono M. Remigij du lo Roy.

X —

Y

Y1 YPRES. Diocese

CONSTITVTIONES ET DECRETA SYNODI DIOECESANÆ IPRENSIS Celebratæ die quarta mensis Nouembris anno M DC.IX. Præsidente in ea . . . D. CAROLO MASIO Episcopo Iprense. IPRIS, Typis FRANCISCI BELLETTI M.DC.X. [etc.] 8° pp.123; illus.
1606/455.

The titlepage engraving showing the arms of the Bishop signed: G.D.T., i.e. Guillaume du Tielt.

Y2 YSELVEER, Willem Jansz

BALADE, Op en teghen den partialen Domp-hoorn, onlancks by eenen . . . Iesuwijt (ofte sijns ghesinde) met den Leugen-hamer . . . ghesmedet/op . . . straet-rijm ghestelt/ende in druk wt-ghegheven: Waerinne den Autheur . . . te vergeefs pooght te dompen de kracht des . . . Missijfs der . . . Staten generael (dien hy de Hollantsche Fackel noemt) . . . den vij^{en}. Junij 1602. wt-ghezonden . . . In s'Graven-Haghe. By Hillebrandt Iacobsz. 1603. 4° sig. AB^4
T.2417(19).

Signed: Liefd' baert Peys, motto of Willem Jansz Yselveer. Directed against Jan David's 'Domp-hooren'.

YSERMANS, Joan. Aen zijn Hoocheyt. (A son Alteze.) 1620. [By Joan Ysermans?] *See* AEN

Z

ZEDICH onder-soeck. 1617. *See* TAURINUS, Jacobus

Z1 ZEELAND. Staten

[19.2.1609] Placcaet Vanden Staten van Zeelandt/Daer by verboden wort dat egheen Jesuyten/vreemde Papen/noch andere Geestelicke persoonen/jnde Provintie van Zeelandt en mogen commen: Midtsgaders niemanden der selver Ingheseten hen begeven ter scholen by de Jesuyten/noch oock inde Universiteyten oft Scholen onder den Coninck van Spaignen oft Eertzhertogen behoorende. MIDDELBVRGH, By Richard Schilders . . . 1609. 4° sig. A^4
T.1727(14).

Issued 19 February 1609.

Z2 ZEPPER, Wilhelm

Schriftuerlijcke Onderwijsinghe/In de Leere van de Goddelijcke PREDESTINATIE. Eertijdts in Hoochduytsch beschreven/door . . . VVilhelmum Zepperum . . . Ende alsnu vvt den Latijne, in onse Nederduytsche tale overghezet door I.G.O. . . . TOT ROTTERDAM, By Felix van Sambix . . . 1612. 4° pp.28
T.2242(34).

Translated by Joannes Gysius 'Ostendanus' from 'Institutiones de omnibus controversiis Capp. inter Protestantes'. The original German title has not been identified.

ZERUBAAL, Philalethius; pseudonym of Ewout Teellinck. *See* TEELLINCK, Ewout. Babylon. 1621.

Z3 ZONHOVEN, Reynier Olivier van

Blyeindig-Treurspel/Van 'tGevecht Der dry Horatien ende Curiatien, ende der Zuster-moord Horatij . . . Genomen Wt Tito Livio . . . Door REYNIER OLIVIER van Zonhoven. TOT FRANEKER, Gedruckt by Vldrick Balck . . . 1616. 4° pp.52
11755.b.78.

An engraved titlepage belonging to 'Zonhovens, van Gesperdens, en Wevelinchovens Spelen', dated 1747, has been added to this copy.

Z4 ZUALLART, Jean

LA DESCRIPTION DE LA VILLE D'ATH . . . A ATH, Chez Iean Maes . . . 1610. 8° sig. $A\text{-}E^8F^3$
10270.aaa.34.

In fact an imitation of the original edition published by François Foppens at Brussels ca. 1720.

Z5 ZUALLART, Jean

[Il devotissimo viaggio di Gerusalemme.] LE TRESDE VOT [*sic*] VOYAGE DE IERVSALEM, Auecq les Figures des lieux saincts, & plusieurs autres, tirées au naturel.

Du Sainct mont de Caluaire.

Chapitre XXII.

A La premiere chapelle
B La seconde
C La creucure du mont
D Ou se garde la teste de Adam
E Le sepulchre de Godefroy
F Celuy du Roy Baudouyn
G La pierre de l'onction
H La montee du mont
I La retraicte des Abyssins
K L'entree de l'Eglise

Passant

Faict & descript par IEAN ZVALLART . . . EN ANVERS, Chez ARNOVLD S'CONINCX, M.DC.VIII. 4° pp.191, 235 [237]; illus., maps, plans
1046.i.1; 280.d.29; G.15705.

Translated by the author. The privilege is made out to Jan van Keerberghen. The illustrations, including maps and plans, are engraved.

ZUERIUS, JACOBUS. Disputationum theologicarum decima-octava, de incarnatione filii Dei. 1603. *See* GOMARUS, Franciscus

ZUTPHEN. For laws of Zutphen issued by the States of Gelderland. *See* GELDERLAND

Z6 ZYPE, Henricus vanden

SANCTVS GREGORIVS MAGNVS, Ecclesiæ Doctor, primus eius Pontifex Romanus, Ex . . . familia Benedictina oriundus. Multus hîc etiam sermo de laudibus S.P.N. Benedicti, de prȩstantia Regulæ ab ipso conscriptæ, deq́ue . . . Ordinis eius incremento in ipsa sua origine . . . AVCTORE D. HENRICO VANDEN ZYPE. IPRIS, Ex typographia Francisci Belletti 1610. [etc.] 8° pp.233; illus.
862.c.19.

The titlepage engraving signed: G.D.T., i.e. Guillaume du Tielt.

ADDENDUM

J79a JONGE, Boudewijn de

T'Huys Der VVijsheyt/waer in gesproken wort vande kennisse Godts/de H. Schrifture/de nature Godts/de Predestinatie/ende vande H.Dryvuldicheyt. GHEMAECKT Door den E.P.F. BALDVINVS IVNIVS . . . T'ANTVVERPEN, By Marten Huyssens . . . M.DC.XIII. [etc.] 8° pp.666; illus.
R.B.23.a.3143.

The dedication to Cornelius Junius is in Latin. The titlepage engraving shows a church built like a Roman temple with the papal emblems above it. Ownership inscriptions: Desen boeck hoordt toe Melchjor Hasaerdt . . . ijnde scheepstraet bijde waterschap. 1619; W. Schwartz 1821, Harlemensis.

ERRATUM

V105 For: Verhael van de, read: Verhael vande.

APPENDIX
Chronological list of news reports

This list contains publications which form part or are assumed to form part of regularly published reports, regardless of variable titles. Its purpose is to allow the easiest possible identification of an issue and a quick grasp of its contents. To this end titles are shortened and adapted, e.g. misprints are silently corrected, I/J, U/V shown according to modern usage as is capitalisation, numerals are represented by arabic numbers, contractions resolved, suppressed letters added in italics. Catalogue numbers are supplied for full descriptions and references which do not claim to be exhaustive to existing literature provided. Entries are arranged alphabetically by towns and printers or assumed printers, then chronologically numbered separately under each of these. They feature all or some of the following elements:

Date = date of publication (in round brackets if derived from internal evidence), with serial numeration as applicable after oblique stroke
Signature = signature(s) if present; single sheets described as 's.sh.'
Title = simplified title
Genre = genre, e.g. D for dialogue or drama, P for prose, V for verse
Illustration = illustration(s)
Contents = additional information from within the item
References = references (cf. list of abbreviations below)
Shelfmark = British Library shelfmark
Catalogue No = number in this catalogue
Notes = additional information from outside the item, including headings in this catalogue where not immediately apparent, indicated by 's.v.'

Abbreviations used under *References* above:
BB: *Bibliotheca Belgica. Fondée par Ferdinand van der Haeghen. Rééditée sous la direction de Marie-Thérèse Lenger*. Bruxelles, 1964–75. (References to numbers which themselves comprise a large number of issues, such as V196 & 197 for Verhoeven news reports 1620 & 1621, have had further specifications, such as precise date descriptions or page numbers, added in round brackets.)

Dahl: Folke Dahl, *A bibliography of English corantos and periodical newsbooks, 1620–1642*. London, 1952.

H-F: Paul Hohenemser, *Flugschriftensammlung Gustav Freytag*. Frankfurt, 1925.

Kn: W.P.C. Knuttel, *Catalogus der pamfletten-verzameling berustende in de Koninklijke Bibliotheek te 'sGravenhage*. 'sGravenhage, 1889–1920.

LFV: Herman de la Fontaine Verwey, *Uit de geschiedenis van het boek*. Amsterdam, 1976–9.

M: Frederik Muller, *De Nederlandsche geschiedenis in platen*. (S = Supplement) Amsterdam, 1863–82.

M-D: J. ter Meulen & P.J.J. Diermanse, *Bibliographie des écrits sur Hugo Grotius, imprimés au XVIIe siècle*. La Haye, 1961.

Pt: Louis D. Petit, *Bibliotheek van Nederlandsche pamfletten. Verzamelingen van de Bibliotheek van Joannes Thysius en de Bibliotheek der Rijks-Universiteit te Leiden*. 's-Gravenhage, 1882-Leiden, 1934.

S: Maurits Sabbe, *Brabant in't verweer*. Antwerpen, 1933.

S Mor: Maurits Sabbe, *De Moretussen en hun kring*. Antwerpen, 1928.

Sim: A.E.C. Simoni, 'Poems, pictures and the press. Observations on some Verhoeven newsletters (1620–1621)' in: *Liber amicorum Leon Voet. Ed. F. de Nave*. Antwerpen, 1985, pp.353–74.

St: *Katalogus der historie-, spot- en zinneprenten betrekkelijk de geschiedenis van Nederland, verzameld door A. van Stolk. Beschreven door G. van Rijn*. Amsterdam, 1895–1923.

STC: A.W. Pollard & G.R. Redgrave, *A short-title catalogue of books printed in England, Scotland, & Ireland and of English books printed abroad 1475–1640. Ed.2*, revised & enlarged, begun by W.A. Jackson & F.S. Ferguson. Completed by Katharine F. Pantzer. London, 1976–86.

T: P.A. Tiele, *Bibliotheek van Nederlandsche pamfletten. Verzameling van Frederik Muller te Amsterdam. Naar tijdsorde gerangschikt en beschreven*. Amsterdam, 1858–61.

W: J.K. van der Wulp, *Catalogus van de tractaten, pamfletten, enz. over de geschiedenis van Nederland, aanwezig in de bibliotheek van Isaac Meulman*. Amsterdam, 1866–8.

Abbreviations for locations of other copies mentioned:
MPM: Museum Plantin-Moretus, Antwerp
M-W: Rijksmuseum Meermanno-Westreenianum, The Hague
RLB: Royal Library Albert I, Brussels
St Ant: Stadsbibliotheek, Antwerp

ALTMORE (suggesting **ALKMAAR**). MH (false imprint)

1
Date: 29 July 1621
Signature: s.sh.
Title: Newes from the Low Countries.
Genre: P
References: STC 18507.26; Dahl 25
Shelfmark: C.55.l.2(12)
Catalogue No: N193
Notes: printed in London

AMSTERDAM. BROER JANSZ

1
Date: 20 February 1606
Title: Nieuwe tydinghe uyt Engelandt. Van het executeren van 8 verraders.
Genre: P
References: Kn 1323
Shelfmark: 1568/8638
Catalogue No: N294
Notes: the attribution to Broer Jansz is tentative

2
Date: (September 1610)
Title: Nieuwe tydinghe van het overgheven der stadt Gulich, den 31. Augustij. Midtsgaders het over gheven vant huys Bredenbent.
References: Kn 1746
Shelfmark: T.1729(3)
Catalogue No: N295
Notes: a forerunner of Broer Jansz's regular newspapers?

3
Date: 22 November 1619
Signature: s.sh.
Title: Tijdinghen uyt verscheide quartieren.
Genre: P
Contents: with an account of the coronation of Frederick I of Bohemia
Shelfmark: T.2423(23)
Catalogue No: T118

4
Date: 9 April 1621
Signature: s.sh.
Title: Courante, or, newes from Italy and Germany.
Genre: P
References: STC 18507.18; Dahl 17
Shelfmark: Harl.Ms.389(56)
Catalogue No: C249
Notes: said to be printed either by Broer Jansz at Amsterdam or for Thomas Archer at London

5
Date: 22 April 1621
Signature: s.sh.
Title: Courante, or, newes from Italy and Germany, &c.
Genre: P
References: STC 18507.19; Dahl 18
Shelfmark: Harl.Ms.389(68)
Catalogue No: C250
Notes: said to be printed either by Broer Jansz at Amsterdam or for Thomas Archer at London

6
Date: 6 June 1621
Signature: s.sh.
Title: Corante, or, newes from Italy and Germanie.
Genre: P
References: STC 18507.20; Dahl 19
Shelfmark: Harl.Ms.389(87)
Catalogue No: C176
Notes: with Broer Jansz's imprint, but said possibly to have been printed for Thomas Archer at London

7
Date: (June 1621)
Signature: s.sh.
Title: Letters patents graunted by the States of the United Netherland Provinces, to the West Indian Company of Merchants, resident in those countries.
Genre: P
References: STC 18459.5
Shelfmark: Harl.Ms.389(81)
Catalogue No: N188
Notes: tentatively attributed to the press of Broer Jansz at Amsterdam
Notes: S.V. NETHERLANDS. United Provinces. Staten Generaal [9.6.1621]

8
Date: 25 June 1621
Signature: s.sh.
Title: Corante, or, newes from Italy, Germanie, Hungarie and Spaine.
Genre: P
References: STC 18507.21; Dahl 20
Shelfmark: Harl.Ms.389(82)
Catalogue No: C178

9
Date: 3 July 1621
Signature: s.sh.
Title: Corante, or, newes from Italy, Germanie, Hungarie, Spaine and France.
Genre: P
References: STC 18507.22; Dahl 21
Shelfmark: Harl.Ms.389(83)
Catalogue No: C180

10
Date: 9 July 1621
Signature: s.sh.
Title: Corante, or, newes from Italy, Germanie, Hungarie, Spaine and France.
Genre: P
References: STC 18507.23; Dahl 22
Shelfmark: C.55.l.2(9); Harl.Ms.389(84)
Catalogue No: C181

11
Date: 20 July 1621
Signature: s.sh.
Title: Corante, or, Newes from Italy, Germanie, Hungarie, Poland, Bohemia and France.
Genre: P
References: STC 18507.24; Dahl 23
Shelfmark: C.55.l.2(11); Harl.Ms.389(104)
Catalogue No: C179

12
Date: 2 August 1621
Signature: s.sh.
Title: Corante, or, newes from Italy, Germany, Hungaria, Bohemia, Spaine and Dutchland.
Genre: P
References: STC 18507.25; Dahl 24
Shelfmark: C.55.l.2.(13)
Catalogue No: C182
Notes: with Broer Jansz's imprint, but said possibly to have been printed for Thomas Archer at London

AMSTERDAM. JORIS VESELER

1
Date: 25 November 1619
Signature: s.sh.
Title: Courante uyt Italien, Duytslandt, &c.
Genre: P
Shelfmark: T.2423(24)
Catalogue No: C251

2
Date: 2 December 1620
Signature: s.sh.
Title: The new tydings out of Italie are not yet com.
Genre: P
Contents: 'to be soulde by Petrus Keerius'
References: STC 18507.1; Dahl 1
Shelfmark: C.55.l.2(1)
Catalogue No: N192

3
Date: 23 December 1620
Signature: s.sh.
Title: Corrant out of Italy, Germany, &c.
Genre: P
Contents: 'to be soulde by Petrus Keerius'
References: STC 18507.2; Dahl 2
Shelfmark: C.55.l.2(2)
Catalogue No: C184

4
Date: 4 January 1621
Signature: s.sh.
Title: Corrant out of Italy, Germany, &c.
Genre: P
Contents: 'to be soulde by Petrus Keerius'
References: STC 18507.3; Dahl 3
Shelfmark: C.55.l.2(3)
Catalogue No: C185

5
Date: 21 January 1621
Signature: s.sh.
Title: Corrant out of Italy, Germany, &c.
Genre: P
Contents: 'to be soulde by Petrus Keerius'
References: STC 18507.4; Dahl 4
Shelfmark: C.55.l.2(4)
Catalogue No: C186

6
Date: 12 February 1621
Signature: s.sh.
Title: Courante uyt Italien, Duytslandt, &c
Genre: P
Contents: 'voor Caspar van Hilten'
Shelfmark: T.2424(5)
Catalogue No: C252

7
Date: 31 March 1621
Signature: s.sh.
Title: Courant out of Italy, Germany, &c.
Genre: P
Contents: 'to be soulde by Petrus Keerius'
References: STC 18507.5; Dahl 5

Shelfmark: C.55.l.2(5)
Catalogue No: C246

8
Date: 9 April 1621
Signature: s.sh.
Title: Courant out of Italy, Germany, &c.
Genre: P
Contents: 'to be soulde by Petrus Keerius'
References: STC 18507.6; Dahl 6
Shelfmark: C.55.l.2(6)
Catalogue No: C247

9
Date: 25 May 1621
Signature: s.sh.
Title: Courant newes out of Italy, Germany, Bohemia, Poland, &c.
Genre: P
References: STC 18507.7; Dahl 7
Shelfmark: Harl.Ms.389(79)
Catalogue No: C238
Notes: STC: 'sold by P. Keerius'

10
Date: 5 June 1621
Signature: s.sh.
Title: Courant newes out of Italy, Germany, Bohemia, Poland, &c.
Genre: P
References: STC 18507.10; Dahl 9
Shelfmark: C.55.l.2(7)
Notes: STC: 'sold by P. Keerius'

11
Date: 12 June 1621
Signature: s.sh.
Title: Courant newes out of Italy, Germany, Bohemia, Poland, &c.
References: STC 18507.11; Dahl 10
Shelfmark: C.55.l.2(8)
Catalogue No: C240
Notes: STC: 'sold by P. Keerius'

12
Date: 20 June 1621
Signature: s.sh.
Title: Corante, or, newes from Italy and Germanie.
Genre: P
References: STC 18507.9; Dahl 8
Shelfmark: Harl.Ms.389(106)
Catalogue No: C177

13
Date: 25 June 1621
Signature: s.sh.
Title: Courant newes out of Italy, Germany, Bohemia, Poland, &c.
Genre: P
References: STC 18507.12; Dahl 11
Shelfmark: C.55.l.2(10)
Catalogue No: C241
Notes: STC: 'sold by P. Keerius'

14
Date: 9 August 1621
Signature: s.sh.
Title: Newes from the Low Countries, or a courant out of Bohemia, Poland, Germanie, &c.
References: STC 18507.13; Dahl 12
Shelfmark: C.55.l.2(15)
Catalogue No: N194
Notes: probably printed in England with a false imprint

15
Date: 6 September 1621
Signature: s.sh.
Title: The courant out of Italy and Germany, &c.
Genre: P
References: STC 18507.14; Dahl 13
Shelfmark: C.55.l.2(16)
Catalogue No: C242
Notes: STC: 'sold by P. Keerius'

16
Date: 12 September 1621
Signature: s.sh.
Title: The courant out of Italy and Germany, &c.
Genre: P
Contents: begin: 'From Rome, the 7. August. We have from Palermo [etc.]'
References: STC 18507.15; Dahl 14
Shelfmark: C.55.l.2(17)
Catalogue No: C243

17
Date: 12 September 1621
Signature: s.sh.
Title: The courant out of Italy and Germany, &c.
Genre: P
Contents: begin: 'From Roome the 7 August. Wehere from Palermo [etc.]'
References: STC 18507.16; Dahl 15
Shelfmark: C.55.l.2(18)
Catalogue No: C244

18
Date: 18 September 1621
Signature: s.sh.
Title: The courant out of Italy and Germany, &c.
Genre: P
References: STC 18507.17; Dahl 16
Shelfmark: C.55.l.2(19)
Catalogue No: C245
Notes: STC: 'sold by P. Keerius'

AMSTERDAM? UNIDENTIFIED PRINTER

1
Date: (1621)
Signature: s.sh.
Title: Copije vande brieff door den Marckgrave van Jaghersdorp aende Vorsten ende Standen in Slesien.
Genre: P
References: T1807
Shelfmark: T.2424(21)
Catalogue No: J62
Notes: s.v. JOHN GEORGE; Margrave of Jägerndorf

ANTWERP. ABRAHAM VERHOEVEN

1
Date: (January) 1607
Signature: A
Title: Verhael vande articulen vanden peyse gesloten tussen Keyser Rudolphus ende den Turck, ende Hongherijen.
Genre: P
Shelfmark: 1193.a.30(2)
Catalogue No: G42
Notes: s.v. GERMANY [1.1.1607]

2
Date: (August) 1615
Title: Verclaringhe vande verthooninghen in den ommeganc tot Antwerpen op den xvj. Augusti 1615.
Genre: P
Shelfmark: 106.a.51
Catalogue No: V60

3
Date: 1619
Signature: A
Title: Naemregister van alle de ghecommitteerde opt Nationael Synode van de Nederlantsche Ghereformeerde Kercken binnen Dordrecht.
Genre: P
Illustration: fireball
References: Kn 2832
Shelfmark: P.P.3444.af(1)
Catalogue No: N2

4
Date: 1619
Signature: A
Title: Een cort verhael van die principaelste puncten, die tot Dort, in die Synode ghetrackteert worden.
Genre: V
Illustration: devil
References: Kn 2859
Shelfmark: P.P.3444.af(2)
Catalogue No: C194

5
Date: 1619
Title: Een cort verhael, hoe die Gommarissen van Hollant, hemel en eerde willen innemen met eene slach, nae die leere van Plancius en Calvinus.
Genre: V
Illustration: 'Plancius'
References: Kn 2860; Pt 1228
Shelfmark: P.P.3444.af(4)
Catalogue No: L102
Notes: s.v. LIEFF-HEBBER

6
Date: 1619
Title: Verhael van t'ghene nu in Hollant is ghepasseert, tot Rotterdam, Wtrecht en Dort . . . hoe dat de Gommaristen hebben verboden aen de Arminiaenen niet meer te moge*n* preken.
Genre: P
Illustration: ships
References: Kn 2866
Shelfmark: P.P.3444.af(3)
Catalogue No: V124

7
Date: 1619
Signature: AB
Title: Een cluchtich verhael, van eenen gepredestineerden cappuyn.
Genre: PV
Illustration: cook chasing dog stealing chicken
References: Pt 1229, S pp.49–54
Shelfmark: P.P.3444.af(8)
Catalogue No: C126
Notes: by R. Verstegan?

8
Date: (April) 1619
Signature: A
Title: Cort verhael vanden slach tegen de*n* Turck ende hoe dat den Primo Visier is ghecomen int coninck-rijck va*n* Persien.
Genre: P
Illustration: battle scene
Shelfmark: P.P.3444.af(5)
Catalogue No: C200
Notes: the approbation dated 4.4.1619

9
Date: (April) 1619
Signature: A
Title: Verhael hoe dat binnen Leyden, de Arminianen zijn vergaert geweest op den 21. April 1619 waer over de Gommaristen zijn ghecomen. Noch met het verhael vant Placcaet ghepubliceert binnen Rotterdam, teghen d'Arminiaenen.
Genre: P
Illustration: branches; lion
References: BB V229; Kn 2871
Shelfmark: P.P.3444.af(6)
Catalogue No: V80
Notes: without imprint

10
Date: (May) 1619
Signature: A
Title: Verhael hoe Johan van Olden-Barnevelt is onthalst gheworden den 13. Mey 1619.
Genre: P
Illustration: execution scene
References: Kn 2897
Shelfmark: P.P.3444.af(9)
Catalogue No: V95

11
Date: (June) 1619
Signature: A
Title: Waerachtich verhael vande victorie vercrege*n* in Duytslandt, teghen die van Bohemen den 8. Junij.
Genre: P
Illustration: battle scene
Shelfmark: P.P.3444.af(10)
Catalogue No: W11
Notes: the winning side under Bucquoy

12
Date: 12 July 1619
Signature: A
Title: Beschrijvinghe vant belegh ende verraedt van Weenen. Ende hoe dat ons volck hebben inghenomen Fronsberch, ende Rosenberch, met noch gheplundert Rodolfstadt.
Genre: P
Illustration: battle scene
Shelfmark: P.P.3444.af(11); 1480.aa.15(1)
Catalogue No: B104

13
Date: (July) 1619
Signature: A
Title: Verhael van den oproer binnen Rotterdam hoe dat de Arminianen zijn vergaert geweest den 21. Julij.
Genre: P
Illustration: woman preacher; soldiers
Shelfmark: P.P.3444.af(12)
Catalogue No: V107

14
Date: 26 July 1619
Signature: A
Title: Verhael vande puncten ende articulen van het overgaen van Graitze, door Busquoy. Met noch het innemen vant slodt Weitragh met noch Weisal.
Genre: P
Illustration: storming a city; battle scene
References: BB V234
Shelfmark: P.P.3444.af(13); 1480.aa.15(3)
Catalogue No: V136

15
Date: (July) 1619
Signature: A
Title: Verhael van de aertbeuinghe gheschiedt in Julio 1619. binnen Mantua.
Genre: P
Illustration: crevasse
References: BB V235
Shelfmark: P.P.3444.af(14); 1480.aa.15(2)
Catalogue No: V98

16
Date: (September) 1619
Signature: A
Title: Corte verclaringhe met wat ghestaltenisse Ferdinandus Coninck van Hungharijen tot Roomschen Keyser den 28. Augusti is ghekosen gheworden.

Genre: P
Illustration: portrait of Ferdinand II
Shelfmark: P.P.3444.af(15)
Catalogue No: C208

17a
Date: 30 August 1619
Signature: A
Title: Cort verhael vande oorloghe in Duyts-landt ende hoe ons volck in Marheren Landt ghevallen is.
Genre: P
Illustration: battle scene
Contents: with other news
Shelfmark: P.P.3444.af(16)
Catalogue No: C198
b
Illustration: imperial eagle & arms
Shelfmark: P.P.3444.af(17)
Catalogue No: C199
Notes: variant of no.17a

18
Date: 27 September 1619
Signature: A
Title: Verhael vande crooninghe, gheschiet binnen Franckfort den 9. September 1619. aen Ferdinandus Roomsch Keyser.
Genre: P
Illustration: Emperor & Electors
Shelfmark: P.P.3444.af(18)
Catalogue No: V128

19
Date: 27 September 1619
Signature: A
Title: Verhael hoe de Boheemsche Frederich Pfaltz-graff tot Coninck van Bohemen hebben ghekosen. Noch van d'orloghe in Duytslandt ghedaen door Bucquoy.
Genre: P
Illustration: trophy; siege
Shelfmark: P.P.3444.af(19)
Catalogue No: V86

20
Date: 11 October 1619
Signature: A
Title: Verhael vande*n* Bohemschen krijch, by Prage. Ende hebben Fredrich voor Coninck van Bohemen ghekosen, maer noch niet ghekroont.
Genre: P
Illustration: camp by a river; Frederick
Shelfmark: P.P.3444.af(20); 1480.aa.15(4)
Catalogue No: V145

21
Date: 14 October 1619
Signature: A
Title: Nieuwe tijdinge van tleger in Duytslant.
Genre: P
Illustration: Emperor with sword; battle scene
Shelfmark: P.P.3444.af(21)
Catalogue No: N217

22
Date: (October) 1619
Title: Sommier verhael van de wreede handelinghe der Calvinisten teghen de Remonstranten buyten Rotterdam den 20. October. 1619.
Genre: P
References: Kn 2965
Shelfmark: P.P.3444.af(22)
Catalogue No: S203

23
Date: 25 October 1619
Signature: A
Title: Verhael vant innemen der steden in Duytsla*n*t door Bucquoy, ende Tampier in Moravien.
Genre: P
Illustration: battle scene
Shelfmark: P.P.3444.af(23)
Catalogue No: V153

24
Date: 25 October 1619
Signature: A
Title: Cort verhael vande Heerlijcke Incompste van de*n* Keyser Ferdinandus, binnen Auspurg.
Genre: P
Illustration: Ferdinand II; coin
Contents: with other news
Shelfmark: P.P.3444.af(24)
Catalogue No: C196

25
Date: (November) 1619
Signature: A
Title: Waerachtich verhael vanden slach ende victorie teghen de rebellen van Bohemen, Slesien, Moravien en*de* Hongersche.
Genre: P
Illustration: battle scene

Contents: on Bucquoy; "Wt Luxemburch den 3. November 1619"; "Wt Weenen".
Shelfmark: P.P.3444.af(25); 1480.aa.15(5)
Catalogue No: W14

26
Date: 10 December 1619
Signature: A
Title: Verhael van de puncten ende articul*en* de welcke Bethlin Gabor, versocht heeft aen den nieuwen Boheemschen Coninck, ende aen de Standen van Bohemen.
Genre: P
Illustration: Frederick; Gabriel
Shelfmark: P.P.3444.af(26); 1480.aa.15(6)
Catalogue No: V103
Notes: cf. no.44

27
Date: 1619
Signature: W
Title: Extract wt sekere missive wt Constantinopel*en*. Hoe die gherebelleerde Hongheren trachten den Turck te persuaderen den krijch t'aenveerden teg*en* haere Keyserlijcke Majesteyt.
Genre: P
Illustration: Turk
Shelfmark: P.P.3444.af(27)
Catalogue No: E90

28
Date: 1620
Signature: ¶
Title: Prognostique van Joannes Liechtenberger op die versaminghe van Saturnus ende Jupiter int jaer 1484. Oock op den eclipsis in de sonne int jaer 1485.
Genre: P
Shelfmark: P.P.3444.af(32); 1607/724
Catalogue No: J67
Notes: s.v. JOHANN Lichtenberger

29
Date: 1620
Signature: ¶
Title: Afbeeldinge ende beschrijvinghe vanden dolenden Jode.
Genre: P
Illustration: Passion scene with Jew
Shelfmark: P.P.3444.af(168)
Catalogue No: A30

30
Date: 1620
Signature: A
Title: Jammer-liedekens ende rijmen, voor desen in Hollant gestroyt ende gesongen.
Genre: V
Contents: Laments for Oldenbarnevelt and other Remonstrants
References: LFV III (p.90); Kn 3110; T1778
Shelfmark: 11555.e.27(1)
Catalogue No: J46
Notes: without imprint; compiled by Hendrik Slatius?

31
Date: 8 January 1620
Signature: A
Title: Waerachtighe goede tijdinge vanden slach in Hungharijen, teghen den generael luytenant van Bethlin Gabor, Ragazi.
Genre: P
Illustration: battle scenes; Ragazi?
Contents: with news from Germany
References: BB V196(8.1.1620)
Shelfmark: P.P.3444.af(28)
Catalogue No: W21

32
Date: 17 January 1620
Signature: A
Title: Nieuwe tijdinge van Hungarijen, Polen, ende Duytslandt, alwaer s'Keysers volck 8 steden in Hungarijen hebben in ghenomen. Ende hoe de Polackers in der Slesien zijn ghevallen.
Genre: P
Illustration: battle scene with camels
Contents: with an advertisement for a pamphlet by Heereman Chunradus, i.e. H.C. von Friedenberg
References: BB V196(17.1.1620)
Shelfmark: P.P.3444.af(29)
Catalogue No: N216

33
Date: 19 February 1620
Signature: A
Title: Nieuwe tijdinge va*n*den krijch in Bohemen ende Moravien, hoe de Italianen ende Walen wt Budweysz zijn ghevallen in Bohemen.
Genre: P

Illustration: camp by a river
References: BB V196(19.2.1620)
Shelfmark: P.P.3444.af(33); 1480.aa.15(7)
Catalogue No: N218

34
Date: (February) 1620
Signature: B
Title: Verhael van Duytslant, hoe de Boheemsche tot Praghe hebben raedt ghehouden. Noch hoe dat s'Keysers volck wt Budweysz sijn ghevallen ende veel dorpen hebben verbrandt.
Genre: P
Illustration: burning city
References: BB V196 (p.473) M-W copy
Shelfmark: P.P.3444.af(30)
Catalogue No: V114
Notes: without approbation

35
Date: 27 February 1620
Signature: C
Title: Verhael vanden slach in Duytslandt, hoe Bucquoy een groote victorie heeft ghecreghen.
Genre: P
Illustration: battle scene
Contents: with other war news
References: BB V196(27.2.1620)
Shelfmark: P.P.3444.af(34)
Catalogue No: V149

36
Date: 13 March 1620
Signature: D
Title: Sententie van t'Hoff van t'Parlement den 14. Jan. 1620. tegens het reglement vande vergaderinghe te Loudon.
Genre: P
Illustration: arms in laurel
Contents: with news of the French court
References: BB V196(13.3.1620)
Shelfmark: P.P.3444.af(35)
Catalogue No: P43
Notes: s.v. PARIS. Parlement [14.1.1620]

37
Date: 13 March 1620
Signature: E
Title: Nieu tijdinghe vanden Graeff van Bucquoy die wederom de Bemersche in Oostenrijck gheslaghen heeft.
Genre: P
Illustration: siege
Contents: with news from France
References: BB V196(13.3.1620)
Shelfmark: P.P.3444.af(36)
Catalogue No: N211

38
Date: 27 March 1620
Signature: F
Title: Verhael van Duytslandt met het innemen der stercten ende casteelen.
Genre: P
Illustration: attack on a fortified place
Contents: with news from Malta
References: BB V196(27.3.1620)
Shelfmark: P.P.3444.af(38)
Catalogue No: V111
Notes: with the privilege for no. 40

39
Date: 27 March 1620
Signature: G
Title: Nieuwe tijdinghe vanden krijch in Bohemen.
Genre: P
Illustration: battle scene by a river; storming a city
References: BB V196(27.3.1620)
Shelfmark: P.P.3444.af(40)
Catalogue No: N243

40
Date: (March-April) 1620
Signature: AB
Title: D'edictale cassatie van Ferdinandus II. teghens de electie, ende crooninge in Bohemen.
Genre: P
Illustration: imperial arms
References: [BB V196 (29.3.1620)]
Shelfmark: P.P.3444.af(39)
Catalogue No: G46
Notes: the privilege for this issue included in that of no.38; previously published 29 March; s.v. GERMANY [29.1.1620]

41
Date: 10 April 1620
Signature: H
Title: Nieuwe tijdinghe van Duytslant by Egenburgh, met de slaghen.
Genre: P
Illustration: battle scene
References: BB V196(10.4.1620) M-W copy

Shelfmark: P.P.3444.af(41)
Catalogue No: N234

42
Date: 10 April 1620
Signature: J
Title: Verhael vanden slach in Duytslandt.
Genre: P
Illustration: castle under siege; riverside camp; city
References: BB V196(10.4.1620)
Shelfmark: P.P.3444.af(42)
Catalogue No: V152

43
Date: (April) 1620
Signature: K
Title: Verhael va*n*de solemniteyt gehouden tot Madril int gheven vanden cardinaels hoedt aen Fernando soone des Conincx van Spagnien.
Genre: P
Illustration: Spanish arms
References: BB V196 (p.474)
Shelfmark: P.P.3444.af(43)
Catalogue No: V137
Notes: published after 10 April 1620

44
Date: (April) 1620
Signature: A
Title: Verhael van eenige articulen van Bethlin Gabor.
Genre: P
Illustration: 'Boristius ad Neper fl.'
Contents: with news from Naples & Savoy
References: BB V196(p.473)
Shelfmark: P.P.3444.af(31)
Catalogue No: V115
Notes: cf. no.26

45
Date: 4 May 1620
Signature: L
Title: Extract ende conditien, wt de propositien van den Generalen landtdagh, de welcke de rebellen van Bohemien, binnen Prage ghesloten hebben.
Genre: P
Illustration: 2 Turks
References: BB V196(28.4.1620) M-W copy
Shelfmark: P.P.3444.af(46)
Catalogue No: B219
Notes: previously published 28 April; s.v. BOHEMIA. States [3? 1620]

46
Date: 28 April 1620
Signature: M
Title: Verhael van t'ghene in Duytslant ghepasseert is, ende wat gheschiet is ontrent Weenen. Ende hoe de Cosagghen een van de rebellen van Bohemen vermoordt hebben.
Genre: P
Illustration: battle scene, burning city
References: BB V196 (28.4.1620)
Shelfmark: P.P.3444.af(44)
Catalogue No: V123
Notes: the imprint with Verhoeven's address without his name

47
Date: 30 April 1620
Signature: N
Title: Verhael van den Rijcx-dagh ghehouden tot Mulhausen, tusschen de Catholijcke Cheur-vorsten, ende de Lutersche. Ende hoe de rebellen in Bohemen met den Turc tracteren.
Genre: P
Illustration: Turkish cavalry
References: BB V196 (30.4.1620)
Shelfmark: P.P.3444.af(45)
Catalogue No: V108

48
Date: 8 May 1620
Signature: O
Title: Verhael van t'ghene tot Weenen, ende Praghe ghepasseert is.
Genre: P
Illustration: Maximilian I of Bavaria
References: BB V196 (8.5.1620)
Shelfmark: P.P.3444.af(47)
Catalogue No: V125

49
Date: 8 May 1620
Signature: P
Title: Waerachtich verhael vanden slach, ende victorie teghen de rebellen van Bohemen, door den Graeff van Bucquoy, op Palmsondach.
Genre: P
Illustration: battle scene
References: BB V196 (8.5.1620)
Shelfmark: P.P.3444.af(48)
Catalogue No: W15

50
Date: 8 May 1620

Signature: Q
Title: Verhael hoe dat s'Keysers volck met den Graeff van Bucquoy het casteel Ratsenbergh heeft in ghenomen.
Genre: P
Illustration: castle
References: BB V196 (8.5.1620)
Shelfmark: P.P.3444.af(49)
Catalogue No: V82

51
Date: 15 May 1620
Signature: R
Title: Verhael hoe dat de Cosaggen in Moravien ghevallen zijn, ende ruyteren vande Boheemsche gheslagen hebben.
Genre: P
References: BB V196 (15.5.1620)
Shelfmark: P.P.3444.af(50)
Catalogue No: V69

52
Date: 15 May 1620
Signature: S
Title: Verhael van t'gene tot Weenen ghepasseert is, ende hoe de Polacken ende Honghersche malcanderen hebben gheslaghen.
Genre: P
Illustration: fighting knights
Contents: mostly political and military news from Austria
References: BB V196 (15.5.1620)
Shelfmark: P.P.3444.af(51)
Catalogue No: V122

53
Date: 21 May 1620
Signature: T
Title: Hollandsche nieuwe tijdinghen hoemen in Hollandt de placcaten teghen de Arminianen soeckt in 't werck te stellen.
Genre: P
Illustration: scene of persecution
References: [BB V196 (19.5.1620); Kn 3065: 19.5.1620]
Shelfmark: P.P.3444.af(52); 1480.aa.15(8)
Catalogue No: H153
Notes: previously published 19 May

54
Date: (May) 1620
Signature: X
Title: Verhael hoe de Kosagghen in Moravien ende Slesien gevallen ziin. Ende hoe dat den Pfaltz-Grave tijdt ghegheven is tot 1. Junij.
Genre: P
Illustration: battle scene; 'Ismael Sophi', 'Antwerp' castle
Contents: with other war news
References: BB V196 (1.6.1620)
Shelfmark: P.P.3444.af(55)
Catalogue No: V87
Notes: the date assigned to this issue in BB is obviously anticipated

55
Date: 29 May 1620
Signature: Y
Title: Verclaringe en*de* patente die den Cheur-Vorst van Saxen heeft laten publiceren.
Genre: P
Illustration: Saxon arms
Contents: concerning military service
References: BB V196 (29.5.1620) M-W copy
Shelfmark: P.P.3444.af(53)
Catalogue No: S43

56
Date: (June) 1620
Signature: Z
Title: De Rom. Keys. Majesteyt Ferdinandi II. monotorial mandaten, aen de Cheur Pfaltz, nopende de quitteringhe vant' Coninck-rijck Bohemen.
Genre: P
Illustration: 'Lempereur Ferdinandus'
References: BB V196 (p.478)
Shelfmark: P.P.3444.af(54)
Catalogue No: G47
Notes: s.v. GERMANY [30.4.1620]

57
Date: 13 June 1620
Signature: Aa
Title: Rotterdamsche nieuwe tijdinghen, hoemen de Arminianen om haer predicken vervolght.
Genre: P
Illustration: magistrate
References: BB V196 (3.6.1620); T 1741
Shelfmark: P.P.3444.af(56)
Catalogue No: R116

58
Date: 3 June 1620
Signature: Bb

Title: Nieuwe tijdingen van t'ghene tot Harlinghen, s'Graven-haghe, Leyden, Hoorn, Briel, en Campen is gheschiedt.
Genre: P
Illustration: a dispute in prison
Contents: persecution of Remonstrants
References: BB V196 (3.6.1620)
Shelfmark: P.P.3444.af(57)
Catalogue No: N227

59
Date: 12 June 1620
Signature: Dd
Title: Verhael hoe dat Keysers volck Mareck hebben in ghenomen.
Genre: P
Illustration: troops entering a city
References: [BB V196 (5.6.1620)]
Shelfmark: P.P.3444.af(58)
Catalogue No: V81
Notes: previously published 5 June

60
Date: 12 June 1620
Signature: Ee
Title: Verhael vanden Boheemschen krijch.
Genre: P
Illustration: battle scene
References: BB V196 (12.6.1620)
Shelfmark: P.P.3444.af(59)
Catalogue No: V144

61
Date: (June) 1620
Signature: Ff
Title: Nieuwe placcaten vande Keyserlijcke Majesteyt Ferdinandus den tweeden, aen alle Rijckxsteden, die hun met de Boheemsche rebellen deelachtich ghemaeckt hebben.
Genre: P
Illustration: imperial arms
Contents: decrees joint to those of no.56
References: BB V196 (p.479)
Shelfmark: P.P.3444.af(60)
Catalogue No: G48
Notes: s.v. GERMANY [30.4.1620]

62
Date: 26 June 1620
Signature: Ji
Title: Verhael vande leghers in Duytslandt.
Genre: P
Illustration: battle scene
Contents: imperial troops crossing the Rhine
References: [BB V196 (25.6.1620)]
Shelfmark: P.P.3444.af(62)
Catalogue No: V134
Notes: previously published 25 June

63
Date: 27 June 1620
Signature: Hh
Title: Verhael van Duytslant ende Bohemen. Van de legers daer ontrent ligghende.
Genre: P
Illustration: Emperor; fortified town with windmill
References: BB V196 (27.6.1620)
Shelfmark: P.P.3444.af(61)
Catalogue No: V112
Notes: previously published or intended for publication before no.62?

64
Date: (June/July) 1620
Signature: Kk
Title: Copia des briefs vande Keur-vorsten, ende Vorsten tot Mulhausen, vergadert aenden Cheur-vorst Pfaltzgrave.
Genre: P
Contents: the letter signed: Johan Schweickhard & others; without other documents listed on titlepage
References: BB V196 (p.480)
Shelfmark: P.P.3444.af(37)
Catalogue No: G65
Notes: s.v. GERMANY. Electors [21.3.1620]

65
Date: 3 July 1620
Signature: Ll
Title: Den brieff ghesonden aen de Standen des Coninckrijcx Bohemien.
Genre: P
Contents: sent by the Electors on 21 March 1620; the second document listed on the titlepage of no.64
References: BB V196 (3.7.1620)
Shelfmark: P.P.3444.af(63)
Catalogue No: G66
Notes: s.v. GERMANY. Electors [21.3.1620]

66
Date: 10 July 1620
Signature: Mm
Title: Nieuwe tijdinghe wt des Keysers legher, hoe de Boheemschen met schaden hebben moeten wt trecken.

Genre: P
Illustration: battle scene
Contents: with other news
References: BB V196 (10.7.1620)
Shelfmark: P.P.3444.af(64)
Catalogue No: N257
Notes: a different issue with signature Mm described in BB V196 contains the third document listed on the title-page of no.64

67
Date: 10 July 1620
Signature: Nn
Title: Verhael vanden slach teghen die rebellen van Bohemen by Langhenlois.
Genre: P
Illustration: fortress under attack
Contents: report dated Langenlois 17 June 1620
References: BB V196 (10.7.1620)
Shelfmark: P.P.3444.af(65)
Catalogue No: V151

68
Date: 17 July 1620
Signature: Oo
Title: Verhael van Weenen, ende legher in Oosten-rijck.
Genre: P
Illustration: a town with a windmill
References: BB V196 (17.7.1620)
Shelfmark: P.P.3444.af(66)
Catalogue No: V126

69
Date: 17 July 1620
Signature: Pp
Title: Verclaeringhe van het ghene in Italien is ghepasseert.
Genre: P
Illustration: Time
Contents: including reports on Turkish, Tunisian, Maltese affairs etc., with news from Vienna & Prague
References: BB V196 (17.7.1620)
Shelfmark: P.P.3444.af(67)
Catalogue No: V57

70
Date: 21 July 1620
Signature: Qq
Title: Verhael van Praghe.
Genre: P
Illustration: one-handed commander
Contents: with advertisements for the issues signed Ss & Tt
References: BB V196 (21.7.1620)
Shelfmark: P.P.3444.af(68)
Catalogue No: V121
Notes: evidence in BB V196 of a variant of this issue signed Rr

71
Date: (July) 1620
Signature: Rr
Title: Nieuwe tijdinghe, hoe dat de Cosagghen door Hongherijen, ende Moravien geslage*n* zijn, ende Trenchin in genomen hebben.
Genre: P
Illustration: Gideon
Contents: with other news
References: BB V196 (p.481)
Shelfmark: P.P.3444.af(69)
Catalogue No: N228

72
Date: (July) 1620
Signature: Ss
Title: Waerachtighe nieuwe tijdinge van Duytslandt, hoe de boeren in Boheme*n* beginnen te rebelleren tegen den Pfalts-grave.
Genre: P
Illustration: Mucius Scaevola
Contents: with news from Friesland & elsewhere
References: BB V196 (p.481-2)
Shelfmark: P.P.3444.af(70)
Catalogue No: W22

73
Date: 24 July 1620
Signature: Tt
Title: Nieu tijdinghe wt Ulm, hoe dat de boeren rebelleren in Bohemen teghen haere heeren.
Genre: P
Illustration: Maximilian I of Bavaria
References: BB V196 (24.7.1620); T 1726
Shelfmark: P.P.3444.af(71); 1480.aa.15(10)
Catalogue No: N210

74
Date: 30 July 1620
Signature: Vv
Title: Waerachtighe tijdinghen wt den legher, hoe datse gevochten hebben, ende eenighe ghevanghen, met waghenen geladen met meel.

Genre: P
Illustration: a mobile mill
References: BB V196 (30.7.1620)
Shelfmark: P.P.3444.af(72)
Catalogue No: W31

75
Date: 30 July 1620
Signature: Ww
Title: Nieuwe tijdinge wt Ausburch, hoe dat de Cosacken hebben bereet ghemaeckt 300. schepen.
Genre: P
Illustration: 'Plachta'
Contents: mainly news from Bavaria
References: BB V196 (30.7.1620)
Shelfmark: P.P.3444.af(73); 1480.aa.15(11)
Catalogue No: N214

76
Date: 5 August 1620
Signature: Xx
Title: Verhael hoe die van Neder Oostenrijck, de Keyserlijcke Majesteydt, hebben ghesworen den eedt van ghetrouwicheyt.
Genre: P
Illustration: Emperor & Electors
References: BB V196 (5.8.1620)
Shelfmark: P.P.3444.af(76); 1480.aa.15(13)
Catalogue No: V96

77
Date: 5 August 1620
Signature: Yy
Title: Accoordt ghesloten int overgheven des H. Rijckx-Stadt Ulm in Julij 1620. tusschen den Hertoghe van Beyeren ende den Marck-grave Joachim Ernestus van Brandenborch.
Genre: P
Illustration: siege of a fortified town
Contents: translated from the 'Accord' of 23.6.1620 o.s. = 3.7.1620 n.s.
References: BB V196 (5.8.1620)
Shelfmark: P.P.3444.af(75)
Catalogue No: G61
Notes: S.V. GERMANY. League of Würzburg, 1610 [Accord. 23.6.1620]

78
Date: 7 August 1620
Signature: Zz
Title: Verhael hoe den Hertoch van Beyeren opghetrocken is naer Hooch-Oostenrijck ende Linctx belegert heeft.
Genre: P
Illustration: city under attack
Contents: with other news
References: BB V196 (7.8.1620)
Shelfmark: P.P.3444.af(77)
Catalogue No: V91

79
Date: (August) 1620
Signature: Aaa
Title: Particulier verhael va*n*de magnificentie geschiet tot Weenen, op de huldinghe des Keysers.
Genre: P
Illustration: Ferdinand II as triumphant Roman general
References: BB V196 (p.483)
Shelfmark: P.P.3444.af(74); 1480.aa.15(9)
Catalogue No: P50

80
Date: 14 August 1620
Signature: Bbb
Title: Verhael vande*n* crijch in Duytslandt, ende hoe den Hertoch van Beyeren voor Lintz ghecomen is.
Genre: P
Illustration: imperial arms
References: BB V196 (14.8.1620)
Shelfmark: P.P.3444.af(78); 1480.aa.15(14)
Catalogue No: V146

81
Date: 18 August 1620
Signature: Ccc
Title: Verhael hoe den Hertoch va*n* Beyeren met zijnen legher de stadt Lints tot ghehoorsaemheyt ghebrocht heeft, ende vier steden in ghenomen heeft.
Genre: P
Illustration: a fight in a burning town
Contents: with other news
References: BB V196 (18.8.1620)
Shelfmark: P.P.3444.af(79); 1480.aa.15(16)
Catalogue No: V90

82
Date: 18 August 1620
Signature: Ddd
Title: Verhael van de ambassadeurs vanden Coninck van Spagnien, Vranckrijck, ende Italien aen zijne Keyserlijcke Majesteyt, ende hoe datse tot Weene*n* ghearriveert sijn.

Genre: P
Illustration: soldiers embarking [from *Amadis?*]
Contents: with an account of the clothes worn
References: BB V196 (18.8.1620)
Shelfmark: P.P.3444.af(80); 1480.aa.15(15)
Catalogue No: V97

83
Date: 21 August 1620
Signature: Eee
Title: Verhael hoe dat de Cosagghen in Hungheren zijn ghevallen.
Genre: P
Illustration: battle scene
References: BB V196 (21.8.1620)
Shelfmark: P.P.3444.af(81); 1480.aa.15(18)
Catalogue No: V70

84
Date: 21 August 1620
Signature: Fff
Title: Verhael hoe dat den Boheemschen legher, beghint te muytineren waer over den ghepretendeerden Coninck met zijn huysvrouwe den 6. Augusti wt Praghe vertrocken is.
Genre: P
Illustration: Louis XIII; battle scene
References: BB V196 (21.8.1620)
Shelfmark: P.P.3444.af(82); P.P.3444.af(82*); 1480.aa.15(7)

85
Date: 26 August 1620
Signature: Ggg
Title: Verhael hoe dat den Cheur-vorst Hertoch van Saxen is in Bohemen ghevallen.
Genre: P
Illustration: the Elector leading his army
References: BB V196 (26.8.1620)
Shelfmark: P.P.3444.af(83); 1480.aa.15(20); 1193.f.24
Catalogue No: V73

86
Date: 28 August 1620
Signature: No.I
Title: Verhael van het vertreck va*n* Spinola, wt Brussel, met eenen legher naer Duytslandt.
Genre: P
Illustration: Spinola; city on a river
References: [BB V196 (31.8.1620)]
Shelfmark: P.P.3444.af(85)
Catalogue No: V120
Notes: reissued 31 August

87
Date: 28 August 1620
Signature: No.II
Title: Verhael hoe Spinola den legher by Cobelentz heeft doen monsteren den 20. Augusti ende heeft een brugge over den Rhijn gheslagen ende is over ghetrocke*n* ende verovert Rectz, ende Brabach.
Genre: P
Illustration: siege of a town; bakery; mobile mill
References: BB V196 (28.8.1620) M-W copy
Shelfmark: P.P.3444.af(86)
Catalogue No: V92

88
Date: 4 September 1620
Signature: No.III
Title: Verhael hoe Spinola naer Franckfort ghetrocken is.
Genre: P
Illustration: Spinola as Roman general
References: BB V196 (4.9.1620)
Shelfmark: P.P.3444.af(87)
Catalogue No: V93
Notes: with imprint in colophon; another edition described below in no.90

89
Date: 4 September 1620
Signature: No.IIII
Title: Verhael hoe dat den Protestanten legher van Franckfort op ghebroken is.
Genre: P
Illustration: army leaving a city
References: BB V196 (4.9.1620)
Shelfmark: P.P.3444.af(89)
Catalogue No: V78
Notes: without imprint

90
Date: 5 September 1620
Signature: No.III
Title: Verhael hoe Spinola naer Franckfort ghetrocken is.
Shelfmark: P.P.3444.af(88)
Catalogue No: V94
Notes: another edition of no.88, with other news instead of the army lists printed there

91
Date: (September) 1620
Signature: No.V
Title: Verhael hoe dat der Protestanten legher opghebroken is, ende hebben thien dorpen geplundert, ende in brant ghesteken.
Genre: P
Illustration: Gideon
Contents: news from Frankfurt & Bonn dated 31 August 1620; with advertisement of news from Valtellina, probably no.97
References: BB V196 (p.485)
Shelfmark: P.P.3444.af(90)
Catalogue No: V79

92a
Date: 12 September 1620
Signature: Hhh
Title: Verhael va*n* Duytslant hoe dat Bucquoy op ghetrocken is, ende de Boheemsche over vallen heeft.
Genre: P
Illustration: battle scene
Shelfmark: 1480.aa.15(24)
Catalogue No: V113
Notes: without approbation; this issue not recorded in BB

b
Contents: with approbation
References: BB V196 (12.9.1620)
Shelfmark: P.P.3444.af(98)
Catalogue No: V113

93
Date: (September) 1620
Signature: M
Title: Waerachtighe coppyen van placcaten en*de* brieven by de Roomsche Keyserlijcke Majesteyt als oock by Spinola gepubliceert ende geschreven aen de Staten van de*n* Rijnstroom raeckende de verseeckeringhe vande sauvegarde.
Genre: P
Illustration: Spinola(?) with keys
Contents: the first document only
References: BB V196 (p.491)
Shelfmark: P.P.3444.af(95); 1480.aa.15(21)
Catalogue No: G50
Notes: s.v. GERMANY [3.9.1620]

94
Date: (September) 1620
Signature: N
Title: B. Copia. Keyserlijck schrijven ae*n* Spinola, pro bescherminghe voor de Ridderschap aenden Rijnstroom.
Genre: P
Illustration: messenger
Contents: the second document listed in no.93
References: BB V196 (p.492)
Shelfmark: P.P.3444.af(96); 1480.aa.15(22); 1193.f.19
Catalogue No: G51
Notes: s.v. GERMANY [3.9.1620]

95
Date: (September) 1620
Signature: O
Title: Onse ende des Rijckx Hooftlieden, Raden, Commissarissen, der Ridderschap aenden Rijnstroom . . . Ferdinandus de 2.
Genre: P
Illustration: Spinola
Contents: the third document listed in no.93
References: BB V196 (p.492)
Shelfmark: P.P.3444.af(97); 1480.aa.15(23); 1193.i.29
Catalogue No: G52
Notes: s.v. GERMANY [3.9.1620]

96
Date: (September) 1620
Signature: P
Title: Wy Ambrosio Spinola ontbieden den Hooftlieden, Raden, Commissarissen, ende alle Ridderschap, aenden Rijnstroom onse groetenisse.
Genre: P
Illustration: Spinola
Contents: with the letter of the Nobility transmitting Spinola's letter; the fourth document belonging to no.93
References: BB V196 (p.492)
Shelfmark: P.P.3444.af(107); 1480.aa.15(27)
Catalogue No: S238
Notes: s.v. SPINOLA, Ambrogio; Marquis

97
Date: (September) 1620
Signature: A
Title: Redenen waerom die inwoonders van Valtellina hebben de wapenen aen genomen teghen die Calvinische Grisons.
Genre: P

Contents: on Calvinism throughout Switzerland and elsewhere; pp.6-8: 'Wt Genova den 22 Augusti 1622' on Valtellina; reference to 'Manifest hier naer volgende', i.e. no.98
References: BB R101; W 1699
Shelfmark: P.P.3444.af(92)
Catalogue No: R23
Notes: probably the piece advertised in no.91; without imprint

98
Date: (September) 1620
Signature: JBC
Title: Het Manifest van t'ghene bestaen is van de Valtellinoisen, teghen d'overtollighe handelinghe van de Grisons.
Genre: P
Contents: with 'Artyckelen des verbondts tusschen den Bischop van Coira, ende de dry Liguen der Grisons, ende de Valtellinoisen' of 1513
References: BB V196 (p.486); W1698
Shelfmark: P.P.3444.af(93)
Catalogue No: M24

99
Date: 18 September 1620
Signature: No.VI
Title: Cort verhael hoe dat Spinola met den legher in Pfaltz-graven Landt ghetrocken is.
Genre: P
Illustration: battle scene below castle
References: BB V196 (18.9.1620)
Shelfmark: P.P.3444.af(100)
Catalogue No: C189
Notes: a reprint is described in no.104

100
Date: (September) 1620
Signature: No.VI
Title: Translaet vanden brief gheschreven by de Borgher-meesteren, ende Raedt der stadt van Franckfort aende Borgher-meesteren, ende Schepenen deser stadt van Antwerpen.
Genre: P
Contents: dated 21.8.1620, declaring that both armies will observe non-interference with the autumn fair
Shelfmark: P.P.3444.af(94)
Catalogue No: F68
Notes: S.V. FRANKFURT ON THE MAIN [21.8.1620]

101
Date: 19 September 1620
Signature: No.VII
Title: Verhael vande victorie van Spinola, hoe dat hy twee steden in Pfaltz-graven Lant in ghenomen heeft.
Genre: P
Illustration: army outside a city
References: BB V196 (18.9.1620) M-W copy
Shelfmark: P.P.3444.af(101)
Catalogue No: V105
Notes: previously published 18 September

102
Date: 23 September 1620
Signature: Kkk
Title: Nieuwe tijdinghe wt Weenen, ende het legher van Bucquoy.
Genre: P
Illustration: 2 portraits, one of them Bucquoy
References: BB V196 (23.9.1620)
Shelfmark: P.P.3444.af(102); 1480.aa.15(26)
Catalogue No: N292

103
Date: 23 September 1620
Signature: Lll
Title: Verhael hoe dat den Coninck in Bohemen, den thienden man binnen Praghe op ontboden heeft, met allen de boeren ende wilt selver te velde comen.
Genre: P
Illustration: Louis XIII; sword cutting a crowned ball on monument
References: BB V196 (23.9.1620)
Shelfmark: P.P.3444.af(103); 1480.aa.15(25)
Catalogue No: V76

104
Date: 24 September 1620
Signature: No.VI
Title: Cort verhael hoe dat Spinola in Pfaltz-graven Landt ghetrocken is.
Shelfmark: P.P.3444.af(104)
Catalogue No: C190
Notes: a reissue of no.99

105
Date: 25 September 1620
Signature: Mmm
Title: Copye vande antwoorde geschreven byden Keurvorst van Saxen, aenden Pfaltz-graeff Jan tot Heydelberch.
Genre: P

Illustration: Frederick
Contents: the letter dated 9.8.1620
References: BB V196 (25.9.1620)
Shelfmark: P.P.3444.af(106)
Catalogue No: J75
Notes: S.V. JOHN GEORGE; Elector of Saxony

106
Date: 25 September 1620
Signature: No.IX
Title: Verhael van der Protestanten legher, ende op breken der selver.
Genre: P
Illustration: Spinola in allegorical setting
References: BB V196 (25.9.1620)
Shelfmark: P.P.3444.af(105)
Catalogue No: V109

107
Date: (September/October) 1620
Signature: A
Title: Verhael van de schermutseringhe gheschiedt int wt trecken wt de Vrijheyt va*n* Sca*n*deck, den 11. September tussen de Coronelsche Compaignie van den Prince van Espinoy, ende twee compaignien van den vyant.
Genre: P
Shelfmark: P.P.3444.af(99)
Catalogue No: V104
Notes: without imprint

108
Date: 2 October 1620
Signature: Nnn
Title: Nieuwe tijdinghe wt Oostenrijck, Hongharijen, Bohemen, Palslandt, Grysons, Italien.
Genre: P
Illustration: fortress under siege
References: BB V196 (2.10.1620)
Shelfmark: P.P.3444.af(110); 1480.aa.15(28); 1193.f.23
Catalogue No: N276

109
Date: 2 October 1620
Signature: Ooo
Title: Articulen ghesloten int overgheven van Oppenheim, aen Spinola.
Genre: P
Illustration: Spinola's army on the Rhine
References: BB V196 (2.10.1620)
Shelfmark: P.P.3444.af(111); 1480.aa.15(29); 1193.f.28
Catalogue No: O22
Notes: S.V. OPPENHEIM

110
Date: 7 October 1620
Signature: Ppp
Title: Verhael van de leghers in Duytslandt, ende innemen der steden.
Genre: P
Illustration: battle scene; camp by a river
References: BB V196 (7.10.1620)
Shelfmark: P.P.3444.af(112); 1480.aa.15(30)
Catalogue No: V102

111
Date: 7 October 1620
Signature: Qqq
Title: Verhael hoe dat den Pfaltz-graef nieuwe*n* Coninck van Bohemen wilt te velde comen, ende heeft zijnen Sone naer Enghelant gesonde*n*.
Genre: P
Illustration: assault on a city
References: BB V196 (7.10.1620)
Shelfmark: P.P.3444.af(113); 1480.aa.15(31); 1193.f.13
Catalogue No: V77

112
Date: 9 October 1620
Signature: Rrr
Title: Nieuwe tijdinghe hoe dat Bucquoy heeft in ghenomen Hooren, Rees, ende Egghenburgh.
Genre: P
Illustration: city under siege
References: BB V196 (9.10.1620)
Shelfmark: P.P.3444.af(114); 1480.aa.15(32)
Catalogue No: N229

113
Date: 9 October 1620
Signature: Sss
Title: Copya van diversche schriftelijcke commissien ende placcaten by de Roomsche Keyserlijcke Majesteyt aen den Hertoge van Beyeren over gesonden, raecke*n*de de gerebelleerde Bohemen.
Genre: P
Contents: the first message only
References: BB V196 (9.10.1620)
Shelfmark: P.P.3444.af(115); 1480.aa.15(33)
Catalogue No: G49
Notes: S.V. GERMANY [30.6.1620]

114
Date: 9 October 1620
Signature: Ttt
Title: De resolutie die Maximilianus van Beyeren aende drije Standen in Oostenrijck, ende d'Landt op der Ens, op haere ontschuldinghe ghegeven heeft.
Genre: P
Contents: the second message listed for no.113
References: BB V196 (9.10.1620)
Shelfmark: P.P.3444.af(116); 1480.aa.15(34)
Catalogue No: M61
Notes: s.v. MAXIMILIAN I; Elector of Bavaria [Letters. 17.8.1620]

115
Date: 9 October 1620
Signature: Vvv
Title: Sekeren brief aende Staten, ende ondersaten van Bohemen, by Maximilianus van Beyeren, oock de Keyserlijcke Patente in originael.
Genre: P
Contents: the third message listed for no.113
References: BB V196 (9.10.1620)
Shelfmark: P.P.3444.af(117); 1480.aa.15(35)
Catalogue No: M63
Notes: s.v. MAXIMILIAN I; Elector of Bavaria [Letters. 25.8.1620]

116
Date: (October) 1620
Signature: Xxx
Title: Schriftelijcke insinuatie ghedaen by Maximiliaen van Beyeren, aenden Pfaltz-grave belanghende de Keyserlijcke Commissie, aende Staten van Bohemen.
Genre: P
References: BB V196 (p.488)
Shelfmark: P.P.3444.af(84); 1480.aa.15(19)
Catalogue No: M62
Notes: s.v. MAXIMILIAN I; Elector of Bavaria [Letters. 25.8.1620]

117
Date: 14 October 1620
Signature: Yyy
Title: Nieuwe tijdinghe van Bohemen met de belegheringhe van Wittingau. Met den slach ende verlies van den Turck in de Golfo van Venetien.
Genre: P
Illustration: naval battle
References: BB V196 (14.10.1620)
Shelfmark: P.P.3444.af(118); 1480.aa.15(36); 1193.f.22
Catalogue No: N231

118
Date: 14 October 1620
Signature: Zzz
Title: Nieuwe tijdinghe wt legher van Spinola. Hoe Bacharach is inghenomen.
Genre: P
Illustration: fortified city by a river
References: BB V196 (14.10.1620)
Shelfmark: P.P.3444.af(119); 1480.aa.15(37); 1193.l.30
Catalogue No: N275

119
Date: (October) 1620
Signature: No. X
Title: Seyndt-brief vant' ghene Spinola int Pals-graven Landt in September 1620. wtgerecht heeft, ende van den staet van Duytslandt, ende d'omligghende landen. Gheschreven wt Ceulen den 28. September 1620.
Genre: P
References: BB V196 (28.9.1620)
Shelfmark: P.P.3444.af(108)
Catalogue No: S137
Notes: probably derived from a German original as may be the Latin version, dated 30 September, described in no.120

120
Date: (October) 1620
Signature: A
Title: De rebus ab Ambrosio Spinola gestis in Palatinatu, mense Septembri 1620. Et de rerum statu in Germania, vicinisque provincijs, epistola Coloniae data 30 Sept. 1620.
Genre: P
References: BB R105; W1714
Shelfmark: P.P.3444.af(109)
Catalogue No: D31
Notes: probably derived from the same German original as no.119, dated 28 September

121
Date: 16 October 1620
Signature: A
Title: Gazette universele des maents Octo-

ber 1620. Waer inne verhaelt wort den gheluckighen voortganck der Keyserlijcke leghers in Duytslandt.
Genre: P
References: BB V196 (16.10.1620)
Shelfmark: P.P.3444.af(120); 1480.aa.15(38)
Catalogue No: G23

122
Date: 16 October 1620
Signature: B
Title: Nieuwe tijdinghe vanden grooten slach inde Grysons, tegens de Calvinische Cantons.
Genre: P
Illustration: battle scene by a river
References: BB V196 (16.10.1620)
Shelfmark: P.P.3444.af(121); 1480.aa.15(39)
Catalogue No: N242

123
Date: 17 October 1620
Signature: C
Title: Nieuwe tijdinghe wt Duytslant, ende Bohemen hoe dat s'Keysers volck Praga-ditz heeft in ghenomen. Noch hoe dat Spinola Kirberch heeft in ghenomen in Pfaltz-graven Landt.
Genre: P
Illustration: siege of a city
Contents: with other news
References: BB V196 (17.10.1620)
Shelfmark: P.P.3444.af(122)
Catalogue No: N263

124
Date: (October) 1620
Signature: D
Title: Grisonsche historie des iaers 1620. waer inne verhaelt worden de oorsaken, ende redenen, die de inwoonders van Valtellina hebben bedwonghen die waepenen aen te nemen teghen die Calvinische Grisons.
Genre: P
Contents: with a reference to the 'Manifest', i.e. no.98
Contents: BB V196 (p.490)
Shelfmark: P.P.3444.af(91); 1480.aa.15(12)
Catalogue No: G160

125
Date: 21 October 1620
Signature: E
Title: Verhael vande victorie, in Bohemen, ende innemen der steden, alwaer Bucquoy Pis-ka heeft helpen beclimmen.
Genre: P
Illustration: allegory of triumphant general
Contents: with 'Anagramma in nomen falsi Regis Bohemiae'
References: BB V196 (21.10.1620)
Shelfmark: P.P.3444.af(123); 1480.aa.15(40)
Catalogue No: V140

126
Date: 23 October 1620
Signature: F
Title: Verhael vanden gefaillieerden aenslach van den Hertoghe van Buillion op Besanzon. Met relaes van victorien in Bemerlandt, vercreghen door den Hertoghe van Beyeren, ende Bucquoy.
Genre: P
Illustration: Maximilian I of Bavaria
References: BB V196 (23.10.1620)
Shelfmark: P.P.3444.af(124); 1480.aa.15(41)
Catalogue No: V148

127
Date: (23 October) 1620
Signature: G
Title: Copy van een boecxken, trackterende van een miraeckel, dat te Amsterdam gheschiet is van eenen linden boom, voor het huys van Reynier Paeu.
Genre: V
Illustration: a dead tree
Contents: in defence of Oldenbarnevelt
References: [BB V196 (Oct. 1620)]
Shelfmark: P.P.3444.af(125); 1480.aa.15(60)
Catalogue No: C172
Notes: without imprint; reissued without precise date

128
Date: 23 October 1620
Signature: H
Title: Nieuwe tijdinghe hoe dat den Hertoch van Beyeren Budna heeft doen beschieten, ende daer na in ghenade ontfanghen, met het innemen der stadt Bautzen.
Genre: P
Illustration: attack on a townhall
References: BB V196 (23.10.1620)
Shelfmark: P.P.3444.af(126); 1480.aa.15(42)
Catalogue No: N230

129a
Date: 27 October 1620
Signature: I
Title: Verhael vande victorie, gheschiet in Duytslant, vercreghen teghen de rebellen van den Keyser, ende Bethlehem Gabor. Ende hoe dat de Cosacken 14. vendelen hebben ghenomen vanden vyandt.
Genre: P
Illustration: battle scene
Shelfmark: P.P.3444.af(127)
Catalogue No: V131
Notes: the earlier issue of no.129b, not recorded in BB

b
Date: late October 1620
References: BB V196 (derniers jours octobre 1620)
Shelfmark: P.P.3444.af(128); 1193.f.11
Catalogue No: V132
Notes: a reissue of no.129a, dated 'int lest van October'

130
Date: 27 October 1620
Signature: KL
Title: Waerachtighe tijdinghe wt den leger van Spinola, in October wt Oppenheim. Ende hoe dat de Vorsten met den legher van Worms sijn op ghebroken meynende Altseym in te nemen.
Genre: P
Illustration: siege of a town
Contents: with 'Tijdinghe wt Besanzon'
References: BB V196 (p.491) MPM copy
Shelfmark: P.P.3444.af(129); 1193.l.25
Catalogue No: W28

131
Date: (October/November) 1620
Signature: *
Title: Sekeren brieff gheschreven aen NN. tot Amsterdam, hoe dat Spinola sieck was, maer nu wel te passe is.
Genre: PV
Contents: referring to a satire on Spinola shown as vomiting Wesel & Hulst, the remedies mentioned now in the shape of his victories; with a second 'Antwoorde' & a satirical poem on Frederick, 'Den troost vanden Palsgrave'
References: BB B308
Shelfmark: P.P.3444.af(130); 1193.l.34; 10631.a.39
Catalogue No: S123

132
Date: 6 November 1620
Signature: Q
Title: Verhael hoe dat Spinola is met den legher naer Worms ghetrocken.
Genre: P
Illustration: attack on a town
Shelfmark: P.P.3444.af(131)
Catalogue No: V83
Notes: reissues described in no.134a,b

133
Date: 6 November 1620
Signature: R
Title: Nieuwe tijdinghe vande Spaensche vlote, met het Accoort, van Bautsen.
Genre: P
Illustration: embarcation of troops [from *Amadis*?]
References: BB V196 (6.11.1620)
Shelfmark: P.P.3444.af(134); 1480.aa.15(43)
Catalogue No: N240

134a
Date: 12 November 1620
Signature: Q
Title: Verhael hoe dat Spinola is naer Worms ghetrocken.
References: BB V196 (12.11.1620) M-W copy
Shelfmark: P.P.3444.af(132)
Catalogue No: V84
Notes: a reissue of no.132

b
Date: November 1620
References: BB V196 (12.11.1620) main description
Shelfmark: P.P.3444.af(133)
Catalogue No: V85
Notes: a reissue of no.132 or no.134a

135
Date: 13 November 1620
Signature: S
Title: Nieuwe tijdinghe wt den legher van Spinola ende hoe dat Lans-berch int Pfaltz Graven Lant overgegeven is.
Genre: P
Illustration: Spinola; attack on a castle
References: BB V196 (13.11.1620)
Shelfmark: P.P.3444.af(135); 1193.l.28

Catalogue No: N247
Notes: a reissue is described in no. 137

136
Date: 13 November 1620
Signature: T
Title: Verhael vande victorie in Bohemen van het in nemen der steden, ende vanden Hertoch van Beyeren, ende vanden Hertoch van Saxen.
Genre: P
Illustration: battle scene
Contents: with news from Valtellina
References: BB V196 (13.11.1620)
Shelfmark: P.P.3444.af(137); 1480.aa.15(44)
Catalogue No: V141

137
Date: 19 November 1620
Signature: S
Title: Nieuwe tijdinghe wt den legher van Spinola.
Shelfmark: P.P.3444.af(136)
Catalogue No: N248
Notes: a reissue of no. 135

138
Date: 20 November 1620
Signature: V
Title: Verhael van het innemen der steden in Bohemen, van des Keysers volck, Bucquoy, den Hertoch van Beyeren, ende den Cheurvorst van Saxen.
Genre: P
Illustration: 'Den Hertoch van Beyeren'; 'Den Hertoch van Saxen'
References: BB V196 (20.11.1620)
Shelfmark: P.P.3444.af(138)
Catalogue No: V117
Notes: a reissue is described in no. 140

139
Date: 20 November 1620
Signature: X
Title: Tijdinghe wt Weenen, hoe dat den Boheemschen legher is op ghebroken by Kockezan. Ende hoe dat Buquoy Plan heeft inghenomen.
Genre: P
Illustration: Ferdinand II; Bucquoy
References: BB V196 (20.11.1620)
Shelfmark: P.P.3444.af(140); 1480.aa.15(45)
Catalogue No: T117

140
Date: 23 November 1620
Signature: V
Title: Verhael van het innemen der steden.
Shelfmark: P.P.3444.af(139)
Catalogue No: V118
Notes: a reissue of no. 138

141
Date: 26 November 1620
Signature: Y
Title: Waerachtich verhael vande victorie van Spinola, van het innemen der steden in Pfaltz-graven Lant.
Genre: P
Illustration: Spinola
References: BB V196 (26.11.1620)
Shelfmark: P.P.3444.af(140a)
Catalogue No: W12
Notes: a reissue is described in no. 143

142a
Date: 26 November 1620
Signature: Z
Title: Waerachtighe tijdinge vande victorie teghen de rebellen in Bohemen, alwaer Bucquoy met den Hertoch van Beyeren voetvolc ende peerden vanden vyant hebben verslaghen, waer over Bucquoy zijne victorie heeft vervolcht, ende Praghe inghenomen.
Genre: P
Illustration: battle scene; army mustering outside 'Praghe'
Contents: with the letter from an employee of an ambassador to the 'Regeerders van mijn vaderlant', telling of the battle of the White Mountain and its aftermath, dated Brussels 23.11.1620
References: BB V196 (26.11.1620)
Shelfmark: P.P.3444.af(141)
Catalogue No: W24
b
Date: 27 November 1620
References: BB V196 (26.11.1620) M-W copy
Shelfmark: P.P.3444.af(142)
Catalogue No: W25
Notes: a reissue of no. 142a

143
Date: 27 November 1620
Signature: Y
Title: Waerachtich verhael vande victorie van Spinola.
References: BB V196 (26.11.1620) St Ant copy

Shelfmark: P.P.3444.af(143); 1193.l.21
Catalogue No: W13
Notes: a reissue of no.141

144
Date: 27 November 1620
Signature: Aa
Title: Verhael vanden slach gheschiet in Bohemen, teghen de rebellen, eer dat s'Keysers volck Praghe heeft inghenomen.
Genre: P
Illustration: battle scene
References: BB V196 (27.11.1620)
Shelfmark: P.P.3444.af(144); 1480.aa.15(47)
Catalogue No: V143

145
Date: 28 November 1620
Signature: Bb
Title: Gazette van blyschap wt Prage, Brussel, Parijs, ende andere plaetsen.
Genre: P
Illustration: arms of Louis XIII
Contents: with promise of further report on the occupation of Prague in issue of 1 December, i.e. no.146
References: BB V196 (28.11.1620)
Shelfmark: P.P.3444.af(145); 1480.aa.15(48)
Catalogue No: G28

146
Date: 2 December 1620
Signature: CcDd
Title: Seeckere particulariteyt van de stadt Praghe, soo de selve ghebracht is onder de ghehoorsaemheyt van zijne Keyserlijcke Majesteyt.
Genre: P
Illustration: artillery assault on a castle
Contents: with Latin chronograms
References: BB V196 (1.12.1620) M-W copy
Shelfmark: P.P.3444.af(151)
Catalogue No: S121
Notes: previously published on 1.12.1620

147
Date: (December) 1620
Signature: Ee
Title: Particulier relaes vande groote victorie, ende het innemen der heele stadt van Praghe.
Genre: P
References: BB V196 (pp.494-5)
Shelfmark: P.P.3444.af(152); 1480.aa.15(49)
Catalogue No: P49

148
Date: 5 December 1620
Signature: Ff
Title: Aen zijn Hoocheyt op de nieuwe tydinghen ghecomen int leste van November.
Genre: VP
Contents: verses & inscriptions in celebration of the victory over Frederick, largely addressed to Archduke Albert, the inscriptions signed with the motto of Joan Ysermans
References: BB V196 (5.12.1620); S pp.80-81; Sim no.3 (pp.358-60)
Shelfmark: P.P.3444.af(153); 1480.aa.15(51)
Catalogue No: A21
Notes: a French version of the poems is described in no.150

149
Date: 5 December 1620
Signature: Gg
Title: Cataloge vande coningen, princen, graven ende andere vorsten, met Ferdinandus II. opentlijck houdende teghen de Unie der Calvinisten ende adherende Protestanten.
Genre: P
Illustration: imperial emblems
Contents: with 'Naemen vande Protestante princen van Duytslandt'
References: BB V196 (5.12.1620) MPM copy
Shelfmark: P.P.3444.af(155); 1480.aa.15(52)
Catalogue No: C49

150
Date: (5? December 1620)
Signature: Hh
Title: A son Alteze. Sur les nouvelles venues le 23, Novembre 1620.
Genre: VP
Illustration: Albert & Isabella
Contents: the French version of most of the poems in no.148
References: BB V196 (5.12.1620); S pp.80-81; Sim no.3 (pp.358-360)
Shelfmark: P.P.3444.af(154); 1480.aa.15(46)
Catalogue No: A22

151a
Date: 9 December 1620
Signature: Kk
Title: Tijdinghe wt Praghe hoe de 3 Pragher steden met het Casteel sijn verovert gheworden.

Genre: P
Illustration: assault on a walled city
References: BB V196 (9.12.1620) MPM copy
Shelfmark: 1480.aa.15(53)
Catalogue No: T112
Notes: without approbation
b
Contents: with approbation
References: BB V 196 (9.12.1620) main description
Shelfmark: P.P.3444.af(156)
Catalogue No: T112n

152a
Date: 9 December 1620
Signature: Ll
Title: Waerachtighe tijdinghe hoe die vande hooftstadt Praghe, den eedt van ghetrouwicheyt hebben ghesworen, aen den Hertoch van Beyeren, ende den Pfalts Graef hebben afghesworen.
Genre: P
Illustration: Maximilian I of Bavaria
References: BB V196 (9.12.1620) M-W copy
Shelfmark: 1480.aa.15(54)
Catalogue No: W26
Notes: without approbation
b
Contents: with approbation
References: BB V196 (9.12.1620) main description
Shelfmark: P.P.3444.af(157); 193.k.3
Catalogue No: W27

153
Date: 11 December 1620
Signature: Mm
Title: Tijdinghe van den Hertoch van Saxen, hoe dat hy het landt vander Lausnitz gebrocht heeft onder de gehoorsaemheyt vande Roomsche Keyserlijcke Majesteyt.
Genre: P
Illustration: John George of Saxony
References: BB V196 (11.12.1620)
Shelfmark: P.P.3444.af(158); 1480.aa.15(55); 1193.f.25
Catalogue No: T99

154a
Date: 11 December 1620
Signature: Nn
Title: Keyserlijck decreet teghens eenighe agenten.
Genre: P
Illustration: the Aegis
Shelfmark: 1480.aa.15(56)
Catalogue No: G53n.
Notes: without approbation; s.v. GERMANY [19.10.1620]
b
Contents: with approbation & additional text 'Ad mandatum-Bucher' on p.7
References: BB V196 (11.12.1620)
Shelfmark: P.P.3444.af(159)
Catalogue No: G53

155
Date: 12 December 1620
Signature: Oo
Title: Waerachtich verhael hoe dat de*n* Prince Gratiae*n* over ghelevert heeft de Walachy, ende Moldavia, aen den Coninck van Polen. Noch hoe dat de Tarteren in Podolien sijn ghevallen met 80. duysent mannen, waer van de Cosagghen hebben over de 30 duysent doot geslagen.
Genre: P
Illustration: Gratianus? or Turkish ruler?
References: BB V196 (12.12.1620)
Shelfmark: P.P.3444.af(160); 1480.aa.15(57)
Catalogue No: W7

156
Date: 16 December 1620
Signature: Pp
Title: Tijdinghe wt Weenen ende Praghe, met den nombre van de heeren, die in den slach ghebleven zijn.
Genre: PV
Illustration: 'Het Casteel de Sterre * daer den slach was'
Contents: with a satirical poem on Frederick
References: [BB V196 (pp.496-7): December 1620]
Shelfmark: P.P.3444.af(161); 1480.aa.15(58)
Catalogue No: T116
Notes: apparently reissued later

157
Date: (December) 1620
Signature: Pp
Title: Dresdani praedicantis epistola, ad N. Francofurtensem, de Calvinistis bello persequendis. Scripta Dresdae die 20. Novembris 1620.
Genre: P
Contents: with reference to Frankfurt Fair catalogues

References: BB D205
Shelfmark: P.P.3444.af(148)
Catalogue No: D101
Notes: without imprint

158
Date: 22 December 1620
Signature: QqRr
Title: Verhael hoe den Coninck van Vrancryck in Bearn, den geluckigen voortganck heeft gedaen 1620.
Genre: P
Illustration: arms of Louis XIII with single crowned L; cypher with 2 crowned Ls, inscribed 'Duo protegit unus'
References: BB V196 (22.12.1620) M-W copy
Shelfmark: P.P.3444.af(162)
Catalogue No: V89

159
Date: December 1621
Signature: QqRr
Title: Verhael hoe den Coninck van Vrancriick in Bearn den geluckigen voortganck heeft gedaen 1620.
Genre: P
Illustration: arms of Louis XIII with single crowned L
References: BB V196 (22.12.1620) main description
Shelfmark: P.P.3444.af(163)
Catalogue No: V90
Notes: a reissue of no.158

160a
Date: December 1620
Signature: Ss
Title: Lamentatie des Pfaltz Graeff over syn gepretendeer-croon van Bohemen.
Genre: P
Illustration: crown & three rings
Contents: with Latin & Dutch chronograms on 8 November
Shelfmark: P.P.3444.af(146)
Catalogue No: L9

b
Date: December 1620
Signature: Ss
Title: Lamentatie des Pfaltz Graeff over syn gepretendeer-decroon van Bohemen
References: BB V196 (p.497)
Shelfmark: P.P.3444.af(165)
Catalogue No: L10
Notes: reissue of no.160a with attempted correction in the title

161
Date: (December) 1620
Signature: VvXx
Title: Waerachtich verhael vanden slach voor Praghe, met allen particulariteyten. Ghetrocken wt de brieven van den secretaris van Bucquoy.
Genre: P
Illustration: Frederick in flight, 'Adieu, Coninck sonder landt'; battle scene
Contents: with reference to a separately published map
References: BB V196 (p.497)
Shelfmark: P.P.3444.af(147); 1480.aa.15(61); 1193.f.32
Catalogue No: W5

162
Date: 30 December 1620
Signature: Yy
Title: Wonderlycke tydinghen, op den dagh van den slagh ontrent Praghe. Aen den Pals-graeff. Loffdicht over de overwinninghe vande stadt Prage.
Genre: V
Illustration: Frederick & Elizabeth on either side of a tree in a landscape
References: BB V196 (30.12.1620)
Shelfmark: P.P.3444.af(164); 1480.aa.15(59)
Catalogue No: W101

163
Date: 30 December 1620
Signature: Zz
Title: Tijdinghe van Duytslandt, ende Bethlehem Gabor. Noch hoe den Eerts-hertoch Leopoldus Straesborch heeft doen berennen.
Genre: P
Illustration: army on the march
References: BB V196 (p.498)
Shelfmark: P.P.3444.af(166); 1480.aa.15(50)
Catalogue No: T101

164
Date: 30 December 1620
Signature: ¶
Title: Tijdinge wt Pfaltz-graven Landt. ende wt den legher van Spinola.
Genre: P
Illustration: Spinola
References: BB V196 (p.498): Mansfeld?
Shelfmark: P.P.3444.af(167); 1193.l.31
Catalogue No: T98

165
Date: (December) 1620
Signature: A
Title: Epinicium ad duces Caesarianos fortissimos recuperata Praga.
Genre: P
References: BB E275
Shelfmark: P.P.3444.af(150)
Catalogue No: E48

166
Date: (December) 1620
Signature: B
Title: Belli Bohemici origo, progressus, & finis.
Genre: P
Illustration: 'Arx Pragensis'
References: BB B312
Shelfmark: P.P.3444.af(149)
Catalogue No: B77

167
Date: (early) 1621
Signature: A
Title: Beclach gedaen vanden Praechschen hoff-kock over den verdreven Coninck van Bohemen.
Genre: V
Illustration: cook in kitchen
References: BB B303; M S1431C; Sim no.2 (pp.357–8); St 1487
Shelfmark: P.P.3444.af(169)
Catalogue No: B72
Notes: 1621 date in colophon

168
Date: 8 January 1621/1
Title: Diversche tijdinghen wt Weenen ende andere quartieren.
Genre: P
Illustration: battle scene with mill
References: BB V197 (p.498)
Shelfmark: P.P.3444.af(170)
Catalogue No: D65

169
Date: 8 January 1621/2
Title: Cort verhael van t'gene passeert binnen Praghe.
Genre: P
Illustration: Prague Castle under attack
References: BB V197 (p.498)
Shelfmark: P.P.3444.af(171)
Catalogue No: C195

170
Date: 8 January 1621/3
Title: Tijdinghe van den Rhijnstroom en*de* der Protestanten vorsten. Met het placcaet vande Keys. Majest.
Genre: P
Illustration: imperial arms
References: BB V197 (p.498)
Shelfmark: P.P.3444.af(172)
Catalogue No: T100

171
Date: 15 January 1621/4
Signature: [A]B
Title: Een cort verhael van eenen nieuwen draeck ende afgoden van Hollant. Ende van die victorie in den slach van Bohemen.
Genre: VP
Illustration: the dragon
Contents: with reference to Spinola
References: BB V197 (p.499); M S1431D; S (pp.85–6); Sim no.10 (pp.372–3)
Shelfmark: P.P.3444.af(173); P.P.3444.af(173*)
Catalogue No: L103
Notes: S.V.LIEFHEBBER

172
Date: 15 January 1621/5
Title: Gazette universele des maents Januarij 1621. Met de doot va*n*de Palsgravinne ende innemen der stadt Hanau door Spinola.
Genre: P
Illustration: Elizabeth supposedly on her deathbed
References: BB V197 (p.499)
Shelfmark: P.P.3444.af(174)
Catalogue No: G22

173
Date: 15 January 1621/6
Title: Verhael van den Hertoch van Beyeren, hoe dat hy heeft doen stellen 130 vendelen die hy in de*n* slach voor Praeg heeft gewonne*n*.
Genre: P
Illustration: Spinola; trophy
Contents: also on other booty
References: BB V197 (p.499)
Shelfmark: P.P.3444.af(175)
Catalogue No: V106

174
Date: 18 January 1621/7
Signature: A
Title: Postillioen wtghesonden om te soecken den verjaegden Coninck van Praghe.
Genre: V
Illustration: messenger
References: BB V197 (7.1.1621) RLB copy; [Kn 3147: Postillon pour chercher le roy dechassé de Prague]; Sim no.4 (pp.360-3)
Shelfmark: P.P.3444.af(176); 1471.aa.9
Catalogue No: P175

175
Date: 18 January 1621/8
Title: Coninck feest vanden Palatin 1621.
Genre: D
Illustration: Frederick losing his crown
References: BB V197 (p.500); S (p.77); Sim no.5 (pp.363-5); St 1492
Shelfmark: P.P.3444.af(177); P.P.3444.af(177*)
Catalogue No: C154

176
Date: 20 January 1621/9
Title: Nieuwe tijdinghe van s'Hertogenbos, hoe Grobbendonck is wt ghetrocken naer Heusden, ende hoe dat den gouverneur van Heusden Kessel, is te ghemoet ghecomen Grobbendonc.
Genre: P
Illustration: siege
Contents: with other news
References: BB V197 (p.500)
Shelfmark: P.P.3444.af(178)
Catalogue No: N238

177
Date: January 1621/10
Signature: A
Title: Aenslagen vanden Prince Hendric Frederic inden Unions krijch. Met tijdinghe wt Vranckrijck van de Hughenotten.
Genre: VP
Illustration: siege of a fortress
References: BB V197 (p.500)
Shelfmark: P.P.3444.af(179)
Catalogue No: A25

178
Date: January 1621/11
Signature: A
Title: Den spieghel voor den Pfalts-graeff.
Genre: V
Illustration: mirror image of Frederick losing his crown
References: BB V197 (p.500)
Shelfmark: P.P.3444.af(180); 1471.aa.6
Catalogue No: S227

179
Date: January 1621/12
Signature: A
Title: Nieuwe tijdinghe wt Italien, ende Weenen.
Genre: P
Illustration: ship
References: BB V197 (p.500)
Shelfmark: P.P.3444.af(181)
Catalogue No: N273

180
Date: January 1621/13
Signature: A
Title: Tijdinghe wt Praghe, Weenen, ende Moravien.
Genre: P
Illustration: Maximilian I of Bavaria & Bucquoy (?) on horseback
References: BB V197 (p.501)
Shelfmark: P.P.3444.af(182)
Catalogue No: T105

181
Date: January 1621/14
Signature: A
Title: De tweede gazette universele des maents januarij, 1621. hoe dat Moravia is ghereconcilieert met den Keyser, ende Bucquoy is ghetrocken naer Hongheren.
Genre: P
Illustration: 'L'Empereur Ferdinandu [*sic*]'
Contents: with advertisement for a print of the Heidelberg Tun dated 27.1.1621
References: BB V197 (p.501)
Shelfmark: P.P.3444.af(183)
Catalogue No: G21
Notes: for the print cf. Sim no.4 (p.362)

182
Date: 29 January 1621/15
Signature: A
Title: Waerachtighe tijdinghe wt Weenen, hoe dat Moravien is veraccordeert met zijne Keyserlijcke Majesteyt.
Genre: P

Illustration: Bucquoy(?); emperor with sword
References: BB V197 (p.501)
Shelfmark: P.P.3444.af(184)
Catalogue No: W30

183
Date: February 1621/16
Title: T'samen-sprekinghe tusschen 3 princen, gehouden tot Worms.
Genre: V
Illustration: court scene
Contents: translated from 'Colloquium trium principum'
References: BB V197 (p.501); Sim no.6 (pp.365-8)
Shelfmark: P.P.3444.af(185); 1193.f.29
Catalogue No: C145
Notes: s.v. COLLOQUIUM

184
Date: February 1621/17
Signature: A
Title: Nieuwe tijdinghe van den slach, hoe Bucquoy 900. Hongheren heeft gheslaghen.
Genre: P
Illustration: battle scene
Contents: with news from Valtellina
References: BB V197 (p.501)
Shelfmark: P.P.3444.af(186)
Catalogue No: N233

185
Date: February 1621/18
Signature: A
Title: Ambrosius Spinola [etc.]
Genre: P
Illustration: Spinola
Contents: ordering protection of travellers; with other news
References: BB V197 (p.501)
Shelfmark: P.P.3444.af(187)
Catalogue No: S237
Notes: s.v. SPINOLA, Ambrogio; Marquis

186
Date: February 1621/19
Signature: A
Title: Dat s'Pals-graven dwaesheydt niet en is te verschoonen sullen wy den vromen leser int cort gaen verthoonen.
Genre: V
Illustration: fable scene
Contents: with another poem in praise of Ferdinand II
References: Sim no.7 (pp.369-70)
Shelfmark: P.P.3444.af(188)
Catalogue No: L104
Notes: s.v. LIEFHEBBER

187
Date: February 1621/20
Signature: A
Title: Godt ter eeren, en den Marquis Spinola vaillant.
Genre: V
Illustration: Spinola
References: Sim no.8 (p.370)
Shelfmark: P.P.3444.af(189); 1471.aa.8
Catalogue No: L105
Notes: s.v. LIEFHEBBER

188
Date: February 1621/21
Signature: A
Title: Een nieu liedeken vande wilde vogelen strijt.
Genre: V
Illustration: stork
Contents: satire on the rebellious Protestants
References: S (pp.83-5, 430-3); Sim no.9 (pp.370-2)
Shelfmark: P.P.3444.af(190)
Catalogue No: L106
Notes: s.v. LIEFHEBBER

189
Date: [February 1621/22]
Signature: A
Title: [Die Calvinische predestinatie, tusschen eenen Gommarist ende Arminiaen.]
Genre: VD
Illustration: [disputation]
References: BB V197 (2.1621)
Shelfmark: P.P.3444.af(7)
Catalogue No: C15
Notes: wanting titlepage

190
Date: 26 February 1621/23
Signature: A
Title: Nieuwe tijdinghe wt Italien ende Romen met de namen der cardinalen. Noch van Venetien, Constantinopelen ende andere plaetsen.
Genre: P
Illustration: papal symbols
References: BB V197 (p.502)
Shelfmark: P.P.3444.af(191)
Catalogue No: N270

191
Date: 26 February 1621/24
Signature: A
Title: Nieuwe tijdinghe wt Duytslant ende Vrancrijck.
Genre: P
Illustration: imperial arms
References: BB V197 (p.502)
Shelfmark: P.P.3444.af(192)
Catalogue No: N264

192
Date: 26 February 1621/25
Signature: A
Title: Nieuwe tijdinghe wt Hollant, van Amsterdam, ende Weenen.
Genre: P
Illustration: arms of Amsterdam
Contents: with references to controversial pamphlets
References: BB V197 (p.502)
Shelfmark: P.P.3444.af(193)
Catalogue No: N268

193
Date: 3 March 1621/26
Signature: A
Title: Verhael hoe dat den Coninck van Polen is ghefaellieert gheweest vermoort te wesen.
Genre: P
Illustration: Sigismund III
Contents: the attempt by Marek Piekarski; with other news
References: BB V197 (p.502)
Shelfmark: P.P.3444.af(194)
Catalogue No: V74

194
Date: 3 March 1621/27
Signature: A
Title: Verhael vande executie ghegaen tegens Pierskarski.
Genre: P
Illustration: execution scene
Contents: with other news
References: BB V197 (p.502)
Shelfmark: P.P.3444.af(195)
Catalogue No: V129

195
Date: 3 March 1621/28
Signature: A
Title: Articulen besloten op den Neder-Oostenrijckschen Landtdach.
Genre: P
Illustration: assembly
Contents: with other news
References: BB V197 (p.502)
Shelfmark: P.P.3444.af(196)
Catalogue No: A180
Notes: S.V. AUSTRIA. Lower Austria. Landtag [1.1621]

196
Date: 5 March 1621/30
Signature: A
Title: Liste van alle de nieuwe capiteynen ghemaeckt in Februarius 1621.
Genre: P
Illustration: Albert & Isabella; officer with pike
References: BB V197 (p.503) variant "HOOCHEYT"
Shelfmark: P.P.3444.af(197)
Catalogue No: N130
Notes: S.V. NETHERLANDS. Southern Provinces. Army

197
Date: 5 March 1621/30
Signature: A
Title: Liste van alle de nieuwe capiteynen.
Contents: a new edition of the preceding, with some substitute text and corrections
Shelfmark: P.P.3444.af(197*)
Catalogue No: N131
Notes: as no.196

198
Date: 10 March 1621/32
Signature: (-)
Title: Copia vande brieven gheschreven van Frederick Pfaltzgraeff aen de Standen van Slesien. Met noch eenen aen den ouden Grave van Thouren.
Genre: P
Illustration: a queen & child
References: BB V197 (p.503)
Shelfmark: P.P.3444.af(198)
Catalogue No: B209*
Notes: BOHEMIA [12.1620-1.1621]

199
Date: 10 March 1621/33
Signature: (.·.)
Title: Tijdinghen wt Vranckrijck ende Duytslandt.
Genre: P
Illustration: ring & three feathers
References: BB V197 (p.503)

Shelfmark: P.P.3444.af(199)
Catalogue No: T119

200
Date: 10 March 1621/34
Signature: ¶
Title: Nieuwe tijdinghen wt Engelant met het placcaet vanden Coninck verbiedende, dat zijn ondersaten niet en souden spreecken van matterie van staet.
Genre: P
Illustration: arms of James I
Contents: with other English news
References: BB V197 (p.504)
Shelfmark: P.P.3444.af(200)
Catalogue No: E38
Notes: S.V. ENGLAND [24.12.1620]

201
Date: 10 March 1621/35
Signature: A
Title: Nieuwe tijdinghe wt Switzerlandt ende Valtellina. Met tijdinghe wt Hollandt ende andere quartieren.
Genre: P
Illustration: fortified town
References: BB V197 (p.504)
Shelfmark: P.P.3444.af(201)
Catalogue No: N285

202
Date: 12 March 1621/36
Signature: (·.·)
Title: Verhael vanden slach ende victorie die de Cosacken hebben ghehadt teghen de Turcken ende hebben in ghenomen Bolagrat ende Chilien.
Genre: P
Illustration: battle scene
References: BB V197 (p.504)
Shelfmark: P.P.3444.af(202)
Catalogue No: V150
Notes: cf. no.213

203
Date: 12 March 1621/37
Signature: ¶
Title: Artyckelen, waer op de Vorsten ende Standen van Slesien, met de Keyserlicke ende Conincklijcke Majesteyt van Hungeren, ende Bohemen begheeren te accorderen, beneffens de conditien vanden Ceurvorst van Sacxen daer teghens ghedaen.
Genre: P
Illustration: Elector of Saxony; assembly
Contents: with other news
References: BB V197 (p.504)
Shelfmark: P.P.3444.af(203)
Catalogue No: S153
Notes: S.V. SILESIA [2.1621]

204
Date: 17 March 1621/38
Signature: A-C
Title: Der H. Keyserlycker Maiesteyt edictale cassatie vande onwettelijcke verkiesinghe Gabriel Bethlens in't Coninck-rijck van Hungharijen: ende annullatie van alle acten inde Landtdaghen van Presborgh ende Nieuwen-zol.
Genre: P
Illustration: Gabriel
References: BB V197 (p.504)
Shelfmark: P.P.3444.af(204)
Catalogue No: G54
Notes: S.V. GERMANY [10.12.1620]; this is dated later than following serial numbers: was there an earlier issue?

205
Date: 16 March 1621/39
Signature: (.·.) ☞ (.·.)
Title: Copia vanden keyserlycken ban, ghedeclareert teghens Hans Georgen den Ouden, Marck-grave van Brandenborch, met Christiaen Vorst van Anhalt, ende George Frederick Grave van Hohenloe.
Genre: P
References: BB V197 (pp.504-5)
Shelfmark: P.P.3444.af(205)
Catalogue No: G55
Notes: S.V. GERMANY [29.1.1621]

206
Date: 16 March 1621/40
Signature: A-C
Title: Copia vande achts-verclaringhe, gedaen teghen Fredericus Pfaltzgrave Ceur-vorst.
Genre: P
Illustration: imperial eagle
References: BB V197 (p.505)
Shelfmark: P.P.3444.af(206)
Catalogue No: G56
Notes: S.V. GERMANY [29.1.1621]

207
Date: 19 March 1621/42

Signature: +
Title: Antwoorde vande Hertoghe Desdiguieres, op de klachten aen hem ghesonden by die vande verghaderinghe van Rochelle.
Genre: P
Illustration: Louis XIII
References: BB V197 (p.505)
Shelfmark: P.P.3444.af(207)
Catalogue No: B229
Notes: s.v. BONNE, François de; Duke de Lesdiguières

208
Date: 19 March 1621/43
Signature: (??)
Title: Nieuwe tijdinghe wt Roomen, Venetien, Milanen, Spagnien, ende andere plaetsen.
Genre: P
Illustration: a general
References: BB V197 (p.505)
Shelfmark: P.P.3444.af(208)
Catalogue No: N281

209
Date: 24 March 1621/45
Signature: (.·.)
Title: Onbegrijpelijcke post couranten, met de ceremonien gehouden tot Roomen in het verkiesen van zijn Heyligheyt. Met tydinghen wt Duytslant.
Genre: P
Illustration: amphora
References: BB V197 (p.506)
Shelfmark: P.P.3444.af(209)
Catalogue No: O12

210
Date: 24 March 1621/46
Signature: ¶
Title: Verhael hoe dat den Hertoch van Beyerens volck den Oversten Artillery Meester met 5000. mannen Slackenwaldt in Bohemen heeft in ghenomen.
Genre: P
Illustration: fortified city with troops
References: BB V197 (p.506)
Shelfmark: P.P.3444.af(210)
Catalogue No: V75

211
Date: 26 March 1621/47
Signature: (?)
Title: Tydinghe wt Dresden, hoe dat die van Slesien hun als ghetrouwe ondersaeten aende Roomsche Keyserlijcke Majesteyt hebben over ghegheven.
Genre: P
Illustration: burning city with troops fighting
References: BB V197 (p.506)
Shelfmark: P.P.3444.af(211)
Catalogue No: T173

212
Date: 26 March 1621/48
Signature: (??)
Title: Nieuwe tijdinghe wt Prage, ende van den Rhijnstroom.
Genre: P
Illustration: greyhound under a tree
Contents: with other news
References: BB V197 (p.506)
Shelfmark: P.P.3444.af(212)
Catalogue No: N279

213
Date: 31 March 1621/49
Signature: ☞
Title: Waerachtigh relaes van het innemen der steden Bralogard ende Chilia in Turckijen.
Genre: P
Illustration: knights fighting
References: BB V197 (p.506)
Shelfmark: P.P.3444.af(213)
Catalogue No: W18
Notes: cf. no.202

214
Date: 31 March 1621/50
Signature: (?)
Title: Verhael van de victorie die Bucquoy heeft vercreghen met de Cosagghen, teghen de Hunghersche.
Genre: P
Illustration: battle scene
Contents: with other news
References: BB V197 (p.507)
Shelfmark: P.P.3444.af(214)
Catalogue No: V99

215
Date: 1 April 1621/51
Signature: A
Title: Vertooch vande wreetheyt der Calvinisten bewesen tusschen Bacherach ende Coub.

Genre: P
Illustration: a fortress; a ship
Contents: on the murder of Godefridus Thelen S.J.
References: BB V197 (p.507)
Shelfmark: P.P.3444.af(215)
Catalogue No: V178

216
Date: 1 April 1621/52
Signature: A
Title: Cort verhael hoe Mr. Hugo Grotius met een koffer wt zijne ghevanckenisse ghedraghen, ende ontkomen is.
Genre: P
Illustration: the open chest
References: BB V197 (p.507); Kn 3186a; M-D no.13; S Mor p.125–6; St 1515
Shelfmark: P.P.3444.af(216)
Catalogue No: C191

217
Date: 5 April 1621/53
Signature: (??)
Title: Nieuwe tijdinghe wt Praghe. Met verhael van de verraders welcke daer ghevanghen zijn.
Genre: P
Illustration: Prague Castle
Contents: mainly other news
References: BB V197 (p.507)
Shelfmark: P.P.3444.af(217)
Catalogue No: N244

218
Date: 5 April 1621/54
Signature: (?)
Title: Nieuwe tijdinghe van Weenen ende hoe dat Bucquoy Thyrna in Hungarijen wilt belegheren.
Genre: P
Illustration: siege of a town
Contents: with other news
References: BB V197 (p.507)
Shelfmark: P.P.3444.af(218)
Catalogue No: N239

219
Date: April 1621/58
Signature: (.·.)
Title: Het leven ende sterven van Philippus den III., Coninck van Hispanien.
Genre: P
Illustration: Pilip III with family
References: BB V197 (p.508)
Shelfmark: P.P.3444.af(219); 1193.f.33
Catalogue No: L97

220
Date: 19 April 1621/59
Signature: A
Title: Gazette van blijschap des maents Aprilis, 1621. Van het overgheven van Hungherijen, Slesien, Pfaltzlandt, Pilsen, ende andere plaetsen.
Genre: P
Illustration: musical instruments
Contents: with other news
References: BB V197 (p.508)
Shelfmark: P.P.3444.af(220)
Catalogue No: G25

221
Date: 23 April 1621/62
Signature: ¶
Title: Artijculen va*n* t'verdrach tusschen Spinola ter eenre, ende Joachim Ernest Marquis va*n* Brandenborch ende Jean Fredericq Hertoghe van Wirtenberch.
Genre: P
References: BB V197 (p.508–9); H-F 5042 (cf. BB A208–9; Kn 3136a; W1760)
Shelfmark: P.P.3444.af(221)
Catalogue No: G59
Notes: s.v. GERMANY [12.4.1621]

222
Date: 23 April 1621/63
Signature: A
Title: Puncten van het accoort tusschen de Princen ende Staten van Slesien, soo die zijn ghecomen onder de ghehoorsaemheyt van zijne Keyserlijcke Majesteyt.
Genre: P
Illustration: Spinola(?)
Contents: with the reply of the Elector of Saxony and other news
References: BB V197 (p.509)
Shelfmark: P.P.3444.af(222)
Catalogue No: S154
Notes: s.v. SILESIA [3.1621]

223
Date: 26 April 1621/64
Signature: (??)
Title: Nieuwe tijdinghe wt Venetien, Prage, ende Weenen.
Genre: P
Illustration: 'Ismael Sophi'; 'Answen' Castle

Contents: with news of Algerian pirates and other matters
References: BB V197 (p.509)
Shelfmark: P.P.3444.af(223)
Catalogue No: N287

224
Date: 27 April 1621/65
Signature: C
Title: Executie ende banne gepubliceert, inde dry Pragher steden, teghens de gevluchte directeurs, ende andere persoonen.
Genre: P
Illustration: Magistrate on horseback; court of law
References: BB V197 (p.509)
Shelfmark: P.P.3444.af(224)
Catalogue No: P179
Notes: s.v. PRAGUE [1621]

225
Date: 27 April 1621/66
Signature: A
Title: De tweede gazette van blyschap des maents April 1621. Met tijdingen wt diversche quartier*en*.
Genre: P
Illustration: Arion
Contents: On Spinola's entry into Brussels, events in Holland and other news
References: BB V197 (p.509)
Shelfmark: P.P.3444.af(225)
Catalogue No: G24

226
Date: 29 April 1621/67
Signature: (??)
Title: Verhael vande vrome feyten, vanden Veldt-heer Spinola.
Genre: P
Illustration: Spinola
References: BB V197 (p.509)
Shelfmark: P.P.3444.af(226)
Catalogue No: V142

227
Date: 30 April 1621/68
Signature: (.·.)
Title: Nieuwe tijdinghe wt Weenen ende Polen, hoe dat de Polacken over de 150.duysent mannen ghereet hebben, ende zijn gheresolveert de Turcken int lant te vallen.
Genre: P
Illustration: a camel; 3 turbaned bowmen
Contents: with other news
References: BB V197 (pp.509-10)
Shelfmark: P.P.3444.af(227)
Catalogue No: N293

228
Date: 7 May 1621/71
Signature: A
Title: Gazette des maents Mey, 1621, verhalende verscheyden tijdinghen wt Palslandt, Oostenrijck, Spanien, Hollant, ende andere landen.
Genre: P
Illustration: basket of flowers
References: BB V197 (p.510)
Shelfmark: P.P.3444.af(228)
Catalogue No: G19

229
Date: 14 May 1621/73
Signature: A
Title: Nieuwe tijdinghe, wt Duytslandt, van Weenen, ende Praghe.
Genre: P
Illustration: garden urn
References: BB V197 (p.510)
Shelfmark: P.P.3444.af(229)
Catalogue No: N261

230
Date: 14 May 1621/74
Signature: ¶
Title: Tijdinghe wt Italien, ende Polen, hoe dat de Cosacken den Turck int lant zijn ghevallen.
Genre: P
Illustration: battle scene
Contents: with other news
References: BB V197 (pp.510-11)
Shelfmark: P.P.3444.af(230)
Catalogue No: T110

231
Date: 21 May 1621/75
Signature: A
Title: Accoordt gemaeckt tusschen Spinola ter eendre, ende Mauritius, Lant Grave van Hessen ter andere zyden, inde stadt Binghen.
Genre: P
References: BB V197 (p.511)
Shelfmark: P.P.3444.af(231)
Catalogue No: G58
Notes: s.v. GERMANY [5.4.1621]

232
Date: 21 May 1621/76
Signature: A
Title: Verhael der vrome feyten, ende wercken van Bucquoy vande maent Februarij anno 1620. tot des jaers 1621. des maents April, inde welcke Presburch tot de ghehoorsaemheydt des Keysers is ghebrocht.
Genre: P
Illustration: siege
References: BB V197 (p.511)
Shelfmark: P.P.3444.af(232)
Catalogue No: V68

233
Date: 26 May 1621/77
Signature: A
Title: Nieuwe tijdinghe wt Prage, met de naemen der ghevluchte rebellen.
Genre: P
Illustration: magistrate with attendants
Contents: with the sentence on the rebels
References: BB V197 (p.511)
Shelfmark: P.P.3444.af(233)
Catalogue No: N280

234
Date: 26 May 1621/78
Signature: A
Title: Nieuwe tijdinghe wt Italien, Spanien, ende Duytslandt.
Genre: P
Illustration: a seal
Contents: with advertisement of map of new Antwerp-Milan route
References: BB V197 (p.511)
Shelfmark: P.P.3444.af(234)
Catalogue No: N274

235
Date: 28 May 1621/79
Signature: A
Title: Nieuwe tijdinge wt Spagnie*n* wt Madril, zedert de doot vanden Coninck Philippus, den derden.
Genre: P
Illustration: Philip IV
References: BB V197 (p.512)
Shelfmark: P.P.3444.af(235)
Catalogue No: N223

236
Date: 28 May 1621/80
Signature: A
Title: Testament van Philippus den III. Met zijne wterste woorden tot zijne kinderen.
Genre: P
Illustration: Philip III on his deathbed
References: BB V197 (p.512)
Shelfmark: P.P.3444.af(236); 1193.f.31
Catalogue No: T47

237
Date: 29 May 1621/81
Signature: A
Title: Die tweede gazette van blyschap des maents Mey, over verscheyde victorien der Catholijcken in Hungharijen, Vranckrijck, ende andere landen.
Genre: P
Illustration: Arion
References: [BB V197 (p.512; 2.6.1621)]
Shelfmark: P.P.3444.af(237)
Catalogue No: G26
Notes: the issue recorded in BB is entitled 'Gazette van blyschap des maents Junij' and has an approbation not found in that of 29 May

238
Date: 2 June 1621/82
Signature: A
Title: De exploicten va*n* oorloghe door den Hertoch van Espernon int landt van Bearn.
Genre: P
Illustration: Louis XIII
References: BB V197 (p.512)
Shelfmark: P.P.3444.af(238)
Catalogue No: E87

239
Date: 4 June 1621/83
Signature: A
Title: Verhael vande victorie, ende in nemen der steden in Hongharijen onder Bucquoy.
Genre: P
Illustration: battle scene
Contents: with other news
References: BB V197 (p.512)
Shelfmark: P.P.3444.af(239)
Catalogue No: V139

240
Date: 4 June 1621/84
Signature: B

Title: Puncten, wat die van Ellenboghen vanden Generael vanden Beyerschen leger hebben begheert, ende wat puncten men hun heeft gheaccordeert.
Genre: P
Illustration: fortified town with troops
Contents: with news from Prague
References: BB V192 (p. 512)
Shelfmark: P.P.3444.af(240)
Catalogue No: E8
Notes: s.v. ELBOGEN [1621]

241
Date: 5 June 1621/85
Signature: C
Title: Verhael vande victorie die Bucquoy vercreghen heeft in Hungarijen, naer dat hy Presborch heeft verovert.
Genre: P
Illustration: battlefield
Contents: with other news
References: BB V197 (p. 513)
Shelfmark: P.P.3444.af(241)
Catalogue No: V138

242
Date: 9 June 1621
Signature: A
Title: Den eedt met de*n* welcken Bethlem Gabor hem verplicht heeft aen de*n* Turc tot Cassouw. Met de belofte die den Turck ghedaen heeft aen Bethlem Gabor.
Genre: P
Illustration: Soliman
References: BB V197 (p. 513)
Shelfmark: P.P.3444.af(242)
Catalogue No: T136
Notes: s.v. TRANSYLVANIA [24.8.1620]

243
Date: 11 June 1621/87
Signature: D
Title: Nieuwe tijdinge wt Roomen, Duytslandt, Hongharijen, ende Pfaltzgraven landt.
Genre: P
Illustration: battle scene
Contents: with news from France
References: BB V197 (p. 513)
Shelfmark: P.P.3444.af(243)
Catalogue No: N222

244
Date: 11 June 1621/88
Title: Verhael van des Keysers legher, de welcke Schitnauw belegert heeft, door Bucquoy.
Genre: P
Illustration: plan of fortified town under siege
References: BB V197 (p. 513)
Shelfmark: P.P.3444.af(244)
Catalogue No: V110

245
Date: 16 June 1621/89
Signature: A
Title: Nieuwe tijdinge wt Vranckrijck, van t'ghene passeert tusschen de Catholijcken ende Hughenotten, met andere tijdinge wt Duytslant.
Genre: P
Illustration: French arms
References: BB V197 (p. 513)
Shelfmark: P.P.3444.af(245)
Catalogue No: N225

246
Date: 17 June 1621/90
Signature: A
Title: Nieuwe tijdinghe wt Surich, ende Weenen, met Praghe.
Genre: P
Illustration: Maximilian I; Elector of Bavaria
References: BB V197 (p. 513)
Shelfmark: P.P.3444.af(246)
Catalogue No: N284

247
Date: 17 June 1621/91
Title: Tijdinghe wt Hollandt ende Pfaltzgraven landt. Met tijdinghe van Rochelle.
Genre: P
Illustration: ship
Contents: with other news
References: BB V197 (pp. 513-4)
Shelfmark: P.P.3444.af(247)
Catalogue No: T109

248
Date: 17 June 1621/92
Signature: A
Title: De tweede gazette des maendts Juny 1621, van gheschiedenisse in Hongheren, Bemen, Engelandt, Vranckrijck, Nederlant, Italie, Spanie, &c.
Genre: P
Illustration: battle scene with windmill
References: BB V197 (p. 514)

Shelfmark: P.P.3444.af(248)
Catalogue No: G16

249
Date: 25 June 1621/93
Signature: A
Title: Gheschreven brieff van Gabriel Bethlen, aen Galga Zulthan, 1621.
Genre: P
Illustration: Gabriel
References: BB V197 (p.514)
Shelfmark: P.P.3444.af(249)
Catalogue No: G4
Notes: s.v. GABRIEL Bethlen; Prince of Transylvania [Letters]

250
Date: 25 June 1621/94
Signature: AB
Title: Declaratie vanden Coninck van Vranckrijck, daer by alle de inwoonders inde steden van Rochelle ende S. Jan d'Angely zijn ghedeclareert crimineels van laese majesteyt.
Genre: P
Illustration: French arms
References: BB V197 (p.514)
Shelfmark: P.P.3444.af(250)
Catalogue No: F61
Notes: s.v. FRANCE [27.5.1621]

251
Date: 25 June 1621/95
Signature: C
Title: Sommatie ghedaen van wegen des Conincx, aen Monsieur de Soubise, door eenen herault. D'antwoorde vanden Heere de Soubise ende de replicque vanden herault. Ende t'ghene datter inden legher ghepasseert is, t'sedert den 28. Mey tot nu toe.
Genre: P
Illustration: arms of two cities
References: BB V197 (p.514)
Shelfmark: P.P.3444.af(251)
Catalogue No: S202

252
Date: 30 June 1621/96
Signature: D
Title: Verhael vande groote victorie, die Bucquoy vercreghen heeft in Hungharijen, teghen t'volck van Bethlem Gabor, die quamen om Neuheusel te ontsetten. Noch hoe de Polacken Trebisonda hebben inghenomen.
Genre: P
Illustration: battle scene with burning city
References: BB V197 (p.514)
Shelfmark: P.P.3444.af(252)
Catalogue No: V130

253
Date: 30 June 1621/97
Signature: E
Title: Tijdinghe wt Praghe hoe dat Fruwein is ter vensteren ghesprongen ende doot ghevallen.
Genre: P
Illustration: Fruwein's body quartered
References: BB V197 (p.515)
Shelfmark: P.P.3444.af(253)
Catalogue No: T113

254
Date: 30 June 1621/98
Signature: E
Title: Nieuwe tijdinghe wt den Haghe Dort, ende Amsterdam, van t'ghene daer ghepasseert is. Met wat vrempts wt Enghelandt.
Genre: P
Illustration: a ship
Contents: with news from Germany
References: BB V197 (p.515) Sim no.1 (p.357)
Shelfmark: P.P.3444.af(254)
Catalogue No: N266

255
Date: 3 July 1621/99
Signature: F
Title: Nieuwe tijdinghe wt des Conincx van Vrancrijckx legher, voor S. Jan d'Angely.
Genre: P
Illustration: Queen Regent & Louis XIII; French arms
Contents: with news from Germany and advertisement for a print of the siege of S. Jean d'Angély
References: BB V197 (p.515)
Shelfmark: P.P.3444.af(255)
Catalogue No: N256

256
Date: 9 July 1621/100
Signature: G
Title: Nieuwe tijdinghe wt Spagnien, met het verhael, hoe dat de Hollantsche

schepen, met de zeerovers schepen, gheslaghen zijn van de Spaensche gallioenen, ende galleyen, soo sy Mamorra hadden beleghert.
Genre: P
Illustration: naval battle
References: BB V197 (p.515)
Shelfmark: P.P.3444.af(256)
Catalogue No: N283

257
Date: 10 July 1621/101
Signature: Hh
Title: Gazette des maents Julij. 1621, met tijdinghe wt Vranck-rijck, Duytslant, Hongharijen ende Polen.
Genre: P
Illustration: siege of a town
Contents: with news of Louis XIII's entry into S. Jean d'Angély
References: [not same as BB V197 (p.515) entry for no.101, signed: H]
Shelfmark: P.P.3444.af(257)
Catalogue No: G18

258
Date: 10 July 1621/102
Signature: IK
Title: Waerachtige verclaringhe, hoe de keyserlijcke executie, teghens de gevangene rebellen directeurs tot Praghe is gheschiedt.
Genre: P
Illustration: various execution scenes
Contents: with the names of the victims
References: BB V197 (p.516) [one imperfect copy]
Shelfmark: P.P.3444.af(258)
Catalogue No: W15

259
Date: 16 July 1621/103
Signature: L
Title: Nieuwe tijdinghe wt Vrancrijck, van ettelijcke groote heeren die ghebleven zijn voor S. Jan d'Angely.
Genre: P
Illustration: armorial shields
Contents: with other French news
References: BB V197 (p.516)
Shelfmark: P.P.3444.af(259)
Catalogue No: N291

260
Date: 16 July 1621/103
Signature: MN+
Title: Articulen, ende inneminghe, van S. Ian d'Angely. Midtsgaders den missief-brieff die zijne Majesteydt, heeft gheschreven aen den Hertoch van Montbazon.
Genre: P
Illustration: French arms
References: BB V197 (p.516, no.103 (103*))
Shelfmark: P.P.3444.af(260)
Catalogue No: P182
Notes: translated from 'Prise et reduction de la ville de S Iean d'Angely'; s.v. PRISE

261
Date: 16 July 1621/104
Signature: N
Title: Nieuwe tijdinghe wt Hongharijen, hoe Bucquoy Nieuheusel belegert heeft.
Genre: P
Illustration: siege of a city and an island
Contents: with news from Austria
References: BB V197 (p.516)
Shelfmark: P.P.3444.af(261)
Catalogue No: N269

262
Date: 24 July 1621/105
Signature: O
Title: Tijdinge wt Duytslant ende Hongharijen.
Genre: P
Illustration: an army driven into a river
Contents: with news from Italy and France
References: BB V197 (p.516)
Shelfmark: P.P.3444.af(262)
Catalogue No: T97

263
Date: 24 July 1621/106
Signature: P
Title: Nieuwe tijdinghe wt des Coninckx van Vranckrijckx legher, met de steden die den Coninck ghewonnen heeft vande Hughenotten.
Genre: P
Illustration: defence of a town
References: BB V197 (p.516)
Shelfmark: P.P.3444.af(263)
Catalogue No: N255

264
Date: 29 July 1621/107
Signature: Q
Title: Tijdinghe wt Brussel, ende den legher in Vlaenderen.

Genre: P
Illustration: Pope & 2 bishops praying
Contents: on the death of the Archduke Albert & on a parade at Beveren
References: BB V197 (p.516–7)
Shelfmark: P.P.3444.af(264); 1193.f.34
Catalogue No: T104

265
Date: 30 July 1621/108
Signature: R
Title: Nieuwe tijdinghe wt Duytslandt, ende Polen, hoe dat den oorloghe is begost, tusschen den Coninck van Polen, ende den Turck, ende hoe dat de Polacken 12. duysent Tarteren, hebben verslaghen.
Genre: P
Illustration: battle scene
Contents: with news from France
References: BB V197 (p.517)
Shelfmark: P.P.3444.af(265)
Catalogue No: N260

266
Date: 6 August 1621/109
Signature: S
Title: Nieuwe tijdinghe wt Italien, ende Vranckrijck, ende hoe datse de Hughenotten in Champagne ghedisarmeert hebben.
Genre: P
Illustration: naval battle
References: BB V197 (p.517)
Shelfmark: P.P.3444.af(266)
Catalogue No: N272

267
Date: 6 August 1621/110
Signature: T
Title: Tijdinge wt Duytslant, ende Hongarijen, ende Praghe. Met het verhael vanden kloecken heldt Bucquoy.
Genre: P
Illustration: a town under attack
Contents: on Bucquoy's death in battle, with other news
References: BB V197 (p.517)
Shelfmark: P.P.3444.af(267)
Catalogue No: T96

268
Date: 6 August 1621/111
Signature: V
Title: Waerachtich verhael van de aflijvinghe van Albertus binnen Brusselen gheschiedt, 1621.
Genre: P
Illustration: Albert lying in state
References: BB V197 (p.517)
Shelfmark: P.P.3444.af(268)
Catalogue No: W8

269
Date: 13 August 1621/112
Signature: X
Title: Tijdinghe wt Weenen, ende hoe het lichaem vanden kloecken heldt, Bucquoy, binnen Weenen is ghebrocht, ende ghestelt, inde Kercke vande Minimen.
Genre: P
Illustration: a fortress
Contents: with other news
References: BB V197 (p.517)
Shelfmark: P.P.3444.af(269)
Catalogue No: T115

270
Date: 13 August 1621/113
Signature: Z
Title: Tijdinge van Duytslant, ende andere quartieren, met tijdinghe van Amsterdam.
Genre: P
Illustration: battle scene with castle
References: BB V197 (p.517)
Shelfmark: P.P.3444.af(270)
Catalogue No: T95

271
Date: 13 August 1621/114
Signature: Aa
Title: Tijdinghe wt der Slesien, hoe dat den Marc-graeff van Jagherendorp, heeft ontboden, allen t'ghene hy doet is wt volle macht van Fredericus Pfaltzgrave. Met het placcaet daer teghen ghedaen van den Hertoch van Saxen.
Genre: P
Illustration: Frederick losing crown & sceptre
References: BB V197 (p.518)
Shelfmark: P.P.3444.af(271)
Catalogue No: T108

272
Date: 18 August 1621/115
Signature: Bb

Title: Gazette universele des maents Augusti, vanden staedt der oorloghe in Nederlandt, Palslandt, Bemen, Hongherijen, Vranck-rijck, Polen, ende andere landen.

Genre: P

Illustration: Ferdinand II; Turkish ruler

Contents: news on Spanish pay for the army in the Netherlands, news from London on Anglo-Dutch relations

References: BB V197 (p.518)

Shelfmark: P.P.3444.af(272)

Catalogue No: G20

273

Date: 18 August 1621/116

Signature: CcDd

Title: Nederlantsche traenen over die doot vanden Prince Albert. Met het beclach soo wel die van Hollandt, Zeelandt, Vrieslant ende Over-Yssel, &c.

Genre: V

Illustration: Albert lying in state

References: BB V197 (p.518)

Shelfmark: P.P.3444.af(273)

Catalogue No: N14

274

Date: 2 September 1621/119

Signature: GgHh

Title: Waerachtich verhael van het optrecken te velde, van Spinola, 1621.

Genre: P

Illustration: Spinola with his army; cart with multiple cannon

References: BB V197 (p.519)

Shelfmark: P.P.3444.af(274)

Catalogue No: W10

275

Date: 27 August 1621/120

Signature: Ii

Title: De tweede gazette des maents Augusti, 1621, waer in verhaelt wordt de victorie van de Polacken, teghen den Turck, ende den staet van Hollandt, &c.

Genre: P

Illustration: 2 armies in battle order

Contents: with news from Spain, England, Italy, etc.; news from Holland on publication of a pamphlet

References: BB V197 (p.519)

Shelfmark: P.P.3444.af(275)

Catalogue No: G17

276

Date: 27 August 1621/121

Signature: Kk

Title: Nieuwe tijdinge wt Duytslandt, vanden legher vanden Hertoch van Beyeren, teghen Mansveldt. Met tijdinge wt Vranck-rijck, ende het innemen der stadt Clerac.

Genre: P

Illustration: troops entering a town

Contents: with news from Scandinavia & Holland

References: BB V197 (p.519)

Shelfmark: P.P.3444.af(276)

Catalogue No: N220

277

Date: 1 September 1621/122

Signature: Ll

Title: Verhael vande belegheringe vande stadt Mont-albaen, door het legher vanden Coninck van Vranc-rijck. Ende hoe dat Duc d'Umena, 1400 soldaten heeft gheslagen vande Huguenotten.

Genre: P

Illustration: execution scene; fight in a moat

References: BB V197 (p.519)

Shelfmark: P.P.3444.af(277)

Catalogue No: V127

278

Date: 3 September 1621/123

Signature: Mm

Title: Verhael vant' innemen de stadt van Albiac.

Genre: P

Illustration: fight in a burning city

Contents: translated from 'Récit véritable de la prise de la ville d'Albiac'

References: BB V197 (p.519)

Shelfmark: P.P.3444.af(278)

Catalogue No: R22

Notes: s.v. RÉCIT

279

Date: 3 September 1621/124

Signature: Nn

Title: Tijdinghe van Duytslandt, van Mansfeldt, ende wt Hongharijen, ende van Italien.

Genre: P

Illustration: view of a coastal scene

Contents: with news from Spain & Turkey
References: BB V197 (p.520)
Shelfmark: P.P.3444.af(279)
Catalogue No: T102

280
Date: 10 September 1621/125
Signature: Pp
Title: Tijdinghe van Weenen met t'ghene in Duytslandt passeert, ende in Bohemen, en Praghe.
Genre: P
Illustration: fight in a burning city
Contents: with news from Italy
References: BB V197 (p.520)
Shelfmark: P.P.3444.af(280)
Catalogue No: T103

281
Date: 10 September 1621/126
Signature: QqRr
Title: Generale beschrijvinghe van de steden, ende plaetsen die den Coninc heeft gewonnen, vande Huguenotten t'sedert den 28. April lestleden tot nu toe 1621.
Genre: P
Illustration: Louis XIII
References: BB V197 (p.520)
Catalogue No: G38

282
Date: 15 September 1621/127
Signature: Ss
Title: Relaes van het innemen, van het slodt Steyen.
Genre: P
Illustration: fortified town with troops
Contents: with news from Italy & Bohemia
References: BB V197 (p.520)
Shelfmark: P.P.3444.af(282)
Catalogue No: R28

283
Date: 15 September 1621/128
Signature: Tt
Title: Verhael van het beleg der stadt Gulick, ende het innemen van het casteel Rede, door Hendrick vanden Berghe.
Genre: P
Illustration: fortified village with windmill
Contents: with other news
References: BB V197 (p.520)
Shelfmark: P.P.3444.af(283)
Catalogue No: V116

284
Date: 15 September 1621/129
Signature: Tt
Title: Verhael vande victorie hoe dat de Polacken acht duyzent Turcken hebben verslaghen, ende noch verstroyt ende gheslaghen 15.000 Tartaren.
Genre: P
Illustration: battle scene
Contents: with news from France
References: BB V197(p.520)
Shelfmark: P.P.3444.af(284)
Catalogue No: V133

285
Date: 28 September 1621/136
Signature: Ccc
Title: Nieuwe tijdinge van Duytslant, Hongarijen, ende Presborch. Ende hoe datter 3 regimenten. va*n* Mansvelt, zijn aen den Hertoch van Beyeren overgevallen.
Genre: P
Illustration: battle scene with castle
References: [BB V197 (p.522:27 September)]
Shelfmark: P.P.3444.af(285)
Catalogue No: N215
Notes: previously published 27 September

286
Date: 28 September 1621/137
Signature: Ddd
Title: Nieuwe tijdinge wt den legher by Wesel, van Spinola, met het innemen der steden, ende casteelen.
Genre: P
Illustration: a city under attack
References: [BB V197 (p.522: 27 September)]
Shelfmark: P.P.3444.af(286)
Catalogue No: N219
Notes: previously published 27 September

287
Date: 27 September 1621/138
Signature: Eee
Title: Nieuwe tijdinghe wt s'Gravenhage, ende Amsterdam, met de naemen vande Hollantsche schepen, ende schippers die ghenomen ende ghebleven zijn inden slach teghen de Spaegniaerden.
Genre: P
Illustration: Philip IV(?); 2 ships

References: [BB V197 (p.522: 24 September)]
Shelfmark: P.P.3444.af(287)
Catalogue No: N282
Notes: previously published 24 September

288
Date: 1 October 1621/139
Signature: Fff
Title: Nieuwe tijdinghe wt Italien ende Spagnien.
Genre: P
Illustration: ship
Contents: with news from Algiers, Constantinople & France
References: BB V197 (p.522)
Shelfmark: P.P.3444.af(288)
Catalogue No: N271

289
Date: 1 October 1621/140
Signature: Ggg
Title: Verhael hoe dat de Polacken, over de 50.000 Turcken hebben gheslaghen.
Genre: P
Illustration: battle scene
Contents: with other news
References: BB V197 (p.522)
Shelfmark: P.P.3444.af(289)
Catalogue No: V71

290
Date: 4 October 1621/141
Signature: Hhh
Title: Verhael van de victorie in Pfaltsgraven landt, ende hebben in ghenomen, Bensheym, Heppenheym, en t'casteel Sterckenberch, met de Berchstraete. Met tijdinghe wtden legher van Spinola.
Genre: P
Illustration: army with wagons; fortress under siege
References: [BB V197 (p.522): "Wt den", "4 October"]
Shelfmark: P.P.3444.af(290)
Catalogue No: V100
Notes: the different readings in BB may be accidental

291
Date: 4 October 1621/142
Signature: Iii
Title: Nieuwe tijdinge wt Vranckrijck, ende hoe dat den Duc de Mayne, doot geschoten is, voor Montalbaen.
Genre: P
Illustration: French arms within trophy
References: BB V197 (pp.522-3)
Shelfmark: P.P.3444.af(291)
Catalogue No: N224

292
Date: 5 October 1621/143
Signature: Kkk
Title: Tijdinghe wt s'Graven Haghe vande propositie ghedaen vanden ambassadeur vanden Coninck van Vranckrijck, inde vergaderinghe vande Staten Generael.
Genre: P
Illustration: assembly
Contents: objecting against support for the Huguenots; with other news from Holland
References: [BB V197 (p.523: 8 October)]
Shelfmark: P.P.3444.af(292)
Catalogue No: T114
Notes: reissued 8 October

293
Date: 6 October 1621/144
Signature: Lll
Title: Verhael vant' t'ghene ghebeurdt is tot Parijs, met t' vonnis op den oproer ghebeurt den 26. September 1621, int wedercomen van die van Charenton.
Genre: P
Illustration: French arms; armorial shields
Shelfmark: [BB V197 (p.523: 8 October)]
Shelfmark: P.P.3444.af(293)
Catalogue No: V154
Notes: reissued 8 October

294
Date: 8 October 1621/145
Signature: Mmm
Title: Nieuwe tijdingen van politijcke saecken gepasseert in Hollandt.
Genre: P
Illustration: arms of Amsterdam
Contents: on Remonstrants, escapes from prison, etc.
References: BB V197 (p.523)
Shelfmark: P.P.3444.af(294)
Catalogue No: N226

295
Date: 8 October 1621/146
Signature: Nnn
Title: Wonderlijcke nieuwe tijdinghe van

Duytslandt, Italien ende Vranckrijck.
Genre: P
Illustration: Prague(?); a general
References: BB V197 (p.523)
Shelfmark: P.P.3444.af(295)
Catalogue No: W99

296
Date: 15 October 1621/149
Signature: Sss
Title: Nieuwe tijdinghe van Duytslant met de steden die den Hertoch van Beyeren in den Over-Pfalts heeft in ghenomen.
Genre: P
Illustration: Prague(?); battle scene
Contents: with news from Italy & elsewhere
References: BB V197 (p.524)
Shelfmark: P.P.3444.af(196)
Catalogue No: N235

297
Date: 15 October 1621/150
Signature: Ttt
Title: Nieuwe tijdinghe wt den legher voor Gulick.
Genre: P
Illustration: fortified village & island under siege
Contents: with advertisement for a map of Jülich
References: BB V197 (p.524)
Shelfmark: P.P.3444.af(297)
Catalogue No: N251

298
Date: 16 October 1621/151
Signature: Vvv
Title: Waerachtich verhael va*n* de victorie gheschiet teghen de Hughenotten die Montalbaen meynde*n* te come*n* ontsetten. Met den nombre van de dooden ende ghequetsten, met de namen van de cappiteynen, ende ghevangenen.
Genre: P
Illustration: castle under attack
Contents: translated from 'Récit véritable de la defaite des ennemis rebelles au roi, venant au secours de Montauban'
References: BB V197 (p.524)
Shelfmark: P.P.3444.af(298)
Catalogue No: R21
Notes: s.v. RÉCIT

299
Date: 20 October 1621/152
Signature: Xxx
Title: Nieuwe tijdinghe wt de*n* legher in Pfaltz-graven lant met het in-nemen van steden ende veroveringhe der stadt Keysers Louter.
Genre: P
Illustration: battle scene with river
Contents: with advertisement for a map of Sluis
References: BB V197 (p.524)
Shelfmark: P.P.3444.af(299)
Catalogue No: N246

300
Date: 22 October 1621/153
Signature: Yyy
Title: Nieuwe tijdinghe wt Polen, Duytslandt, Italien, ende Brussel
Illustration: battle scene
Contents: from Brussels: beatification of Thomas de Villanova; with news from Antwerp
References: BB V197 (p.524)
Shelfmark: P.P.3444.af(300)
Catalogue No: N277

301
Date: 22 October 1621/154
Signature: Zzz
Title: Nieuwe tijdinghe van Prage vant' accoort ghedaen met Mansveldt. Met noch tijdinghe wt Pfaltz-graven landt van den leger aldaer.
Genre: P
Illustration: fortress under siege; a general
Contents: with news from Switzerland & Turkey
References: BB V197 (p.525)
Shelfmark: P.P.3444.af(301)
Catalogue No. N237

302
Date: 29 October 1621/155
Signature: Aaaa
Title: Nieuwe tijdinghe wt Vranckrijck, hoe dat Mo*n*sieur le Connestable is ghetrocken naer Monsieur de Rohan 3 mijlen van Montalbaen, om te sien oftmen tot eenich accoort soude moghen comen.
Genre: P
Illustration: fighting in burning city
Contents: with other Franch news up to 14 October

References: BB V197 (p.525)
Shelfmark: P.P.3444.af(302)
Catalogue No: N290

303
Date: 29 October 1621/156
Signature: Bbbb
Title: Nieuwe tijdinghe wt Polen, ende Italien.
Genre: P
Illustration: castle taken by army; Turkish ruler
Contents: with news from Switzerland
References: BB V197 (p.525)
Shelfmark: P.P.3444.af(303)
Catalogue No: N278

304
Date: 29 October 1621/157
Signature: Cccc
Title: Nieuwe tijdinghe wt de*n* legher voor Franckendael, hoe dat ons volck 3. halve manen in hebben ghenomen.
Genre: P
Illustration: fortified village with island under siege
References: BB V197 (p.525)
Shelfmark: P.P.3444.af(304)
Catalogue No: N252

305
Date: 2 November 1621/158
Signature: Dddd
Title: Gazette van blyschap, over het overcomen van Mansfelt. Item over een victorie by Franckendael.
Genre: P
Illustration: Maximilian I of Bavaria & Spinola(?)
References: BB V197 (p.525)
Shelfmark: P.P.3444.af(305)
Catalogue No: G27

306
Date: 2 November 1621/159
Signature: Eeee
Title: Tijdinghe wt Parijs, ende wt den legher voor Montalbaen, hoe dat die van binnen eenen wt-val hebben ghedaen.
Genre: P
Illustration: battle scene
References: BB V197 (p.525)
Shelfmark: P.P.3444.af(306)
Catalogue No: T111

307
Date: 5 November 1621/160
Signature: Ffff
Title: Nieuwe tijdinghe wt Duytslant, va*n* Weenen, ende noch wt den legher voor Gulick.
Genre: P
Illustration: fortified village & troops
Contents: with news from Italy
References: BB V197 (pp.525–6)
Shelfmark: P.P.3444.af(307)
Catalogue No: N265

308
Date: November 1621/161
Signature: Gggg
Title: Waerachtighe tijdinghe wt Vranckrijck, ende Parijs, van den brandt die daer gheschiet is, ende van den legher voor Montalbaen.
Genre: P
Illustration: troops burning a city
References: BB V197 (p.526)
Shelfmark: P.P.3444.af(308)
Catalogue No: W29

309
Date: 10 November 1621/162
Signature: Hhhh
Title: Nieuwe tijdinghe van de victorie, gheschiet teghen den Turck ende hoe dat de*n* Coninck van Polen 80000. Turcken heeft verslaghen.
Genre: P
Illustration: battle scene
Contents: with news from Italy & Holland
References: BB V197 (p.526)
Shelfmark: P.P.3444.af(309)
Catalogue No: N232

310
Date: 10 November 1621/163
Signature: Iiii
Title: Nieuwe tijdinghe wt Duytslandt, ende Praghe.
Genre: P
Illustration: attack on a castle; battle scene
Contents: with news from France
References: BB V197 (p.526)
Shelfmark: P.P.3444.af(310)
Catalogue No: N258

311
Date: 16 November 1621/166
Signature: Mmmm

Title: Nieuwe tijdinghe wt den leger voor Montalbaen.
Genre: P
Illustration: artillery attack on fortified city
Contents: based on letters dated 15.10–2.11.1621
References: BB V197 (p.526)
Shelfmark: P.P.3444.af(311)
Catalogue No: N245

312
Date: 16 November 1621/167
Signature: Nnnn
Title: Nieuwe tijdinghe wt den Marquis Spinola legher, ende wt Pfaltsgraven landt, van November.
Genre: P
Illustration: map of siege of Jülich
References: BB V197 (p.527)
Shelfmark: P.P.3444.af(312)
Catalogue No: N254

313
Date: 19 November 1621/168
Signature: Oooo
Title: Waerachtich verhael hoe dat de justitie gheschiet is binnen Madril, over Rodrigo Calderon.
Genre: P
Illustration: sheriff with attendants; court of law
References: BB V197 (p.527)
Shelfmark: P.P.3444.af(313)
Catalogue No: W6

314
Date: 19 November 1621/169
Signature: Pppp
Title: Nieuwe tijdinghe wt Venetien ende Turckijen, hoe dat Emerido van Sorida, Tripoli heeft ghenomen.
Genre: P
Illustration: Turkish ruler
Contents: with news from Spain & Switzerland
References: BB V197 (p.527)
Shelfmark: P.P.3444.af(314)
Catalogue No: N286

315
Date: 19 November 1621/170
Signature: Qqqq
Title: Nieuwe tijdinghe wt den legher voor Sluys, hoe dat die van Sluys eenen wt-val hebben ghedaen. Met noch tijdinghe wt Hollant, ende wt den legher voor Gulick.
Genre: P
Illustration: map of Sluis
References: [BB V197 (p.527: with advertisement for map of Jülich)]
Shelfmark: P.P.3444.af(315)
Catalogue No: N250

316
Date: 23 November 1621/171
Signature: RrrrSsss
Title: Journael, ende beschrijvinghe, wat in den slach, teghen den Turck, met de Polacken, ghepasseert is.
Genre: P
Illustration: soldiers with camels in village; battle scene
Contents: also on false news in Holland
References: BB V197 (p.527)
Shelfmark: P.P.3444.af(316)
Catalogue No: J89

317
Date: 24 November 1621/172
Signature: Tttt
Title: Nieuwe tijdinghe wt Vranck-rijc ende wt den legher voor Montalbaen. Ende hoe datter rebellen in Normandien hun hadden op gheworpen.
Genre: P
Illustration: king with sword; battle scene
References: BB V197 (p.527)
Shelfmark: P.P.3444.af(317)
Catalogue No: N288

318
Date: 26 November 1621/173
Signature: Vvvv
Title: Nieuwe tijdinghe van Mansfeldt, ende de belegheringhe vande stadt Heydelbergh.
Genre: P
Illustration: Mansfeld; fight in a ditch
References: BB V197 (p.528)
Shelfmark: P.P.3444.af(318)
Catalogue No: N241

319
Date: 19 November 1621/174
Signature: Xxxx
Title: Nieuwe tijdinghe wt Duytslandt, van Weenen. Noch hoe dat den Coninck van Vranck-rijckx oorlochsschepen, hebben 9 schepen genomen

van die van Rochelle, waer onder was een Hollandts, oorlochs schip.
Genre: P
Illustration: ship
References: [BB V197 (p.528: 26.11.1621)]
Shelfmark: P.P.3444.af(319)
Catalogue No: N262
Notes: reissued 26 November

320
Date: 1 December 1621/175
Signature: Yyyy
Title: Verclaringe van gout silver, realen, ende coopmanschappen, ghecomen wt Nieu Spagnien. 1621. Met noch tijdinge wt Vranck-rijck.
Genre: P
Illustration: 6 ships
Contents: with news of miracles in India
References: BB V197 (p.528)
Shelfmark: P.P.3444.af(320)
Catalogue No: V58

321
Date: 1 December 1621/176
Signature: Zzzz
Title: Tijdinghe wt den leger voor Sluys, ende Brugge. Met noch tijdinge wt Duytslandt.
Genre: P
Illustration: army camp
References: BB V197 (p.528)
Shelfmark: P.P.3444.af(321)
Catalogue No: T107

322
Date: 3 December 1621/177
Signature: A
Title: Universel gazette des Christendoms, inde maent December 1621.
Genre: P
Illustration: Ferdinand II; fort by a river
Contents: on Polish-Turkish affairs, Spain, Switzerland & Germany
References: BB V197 (p.528)
Shelfmark: P.P.3444.af(322)
Catalogue No: U4

323
Date: 3 December 1621/178
Signature: B
Title: Tijdinghe wt den Coninckliijcken leger voor Gulick. Met noch tijdinghe wt den legher voor Montalbaen.
Genre: P
Illustration: fortified city with troops
References: BB V197 (p.528)
Shelfmark: P.P.3444.af(323)
Catalogue No: T106

324
Date: 10 December 1621/179
Signature: C
Title: Nieuwe tijdinghe wt Vranckrijck, ende des Coninckx legher.
Genre: P
Illustration: battle scene
Contents: the news dated 25 November
References: BB V197 (p.528)
Shelfmark: P.P.3444.af(324)
Catalogue No: N289

325
Date: 10 December 1621/180
Signature: D
Title: Verhael van de victorie vercregen doort' volc van sijne Catholijcke Majesteyt van Spagnien, de welcke Chiavenna, hebben in ghenomen.
Genre: P
Illustration: fight in burning city
Contents: with news from France
References: BB V197 (p.529)
Shelfmark: P.P.3444.af(325)
Catalogue No: V101

326
Date: 10 December 1621/181
Signature: E
Title: Nieuwe tijdinghe wt Duytslandt, ende hoe dat 50 000 Cossagghen, zijn over den Donauw ghepasseert.
Genre: P
Illustration: battle scene
Contents: with news from Italy about the Spanish Marriage, from Switzerland, on shipping
References: BB V197 (p.529)
Shelfmark: P.P.3444.af(326)
Catalogue No: N259

327
Date: 10 December 1621/182
Signature: F
Title: Nieuwe tijdinge wt Engelant met noch het relaes vande victorie, die de Grisons hebben vercreghen teghen die ketters, met het innemen van Chiavenna, item Engedina.
Genre: P
Illustration: a king; ship

Contents: with news from Spain & Germany
References: BB V197 (p.529)
Shelfmark: P.P.3444.af(327)
Catalogue No: N221

328
Date: 15 December 1621/183
Signature: G
Title: Nieuwe tijdinghe wt den legher voor Gulick, met tijdinghe van Mansfeldt.
Genre: P
Illustration: Ferdinand II; Spinola; Mansfeld
Contents: with news from Spain
References: BB V197 (p.529)
Shelfmark: P.P.3444.af(328)
Catalogue No: N253

329
Date: [15 December 1621/184]
Signature: H Hh
Title: [Discours op het leven ende doodt vanden Marquis ende Marquise van Ancre. Item van Rodrigo Calderon. Ende van Barneveldt, ende andere favoriten.]
Genre: P
Illustration: [a ghost appearing to a sleeper]; Spanish arms
References: BB V197 (p.529)
Shelfmark: P.P.3444.af(329); 1471.aa.7
Catalogue No: D62
Notes: both copies wanting titlepage

330
Date: 17 December 1621/185
Signature: I
Title: Nieuwe tijdinghe wt Hollandt, ende hoe dat de Soldaten van s'Hertogenbossche in den Bommeleren-weerdt hebben gheweest, ende ghevanghenen ghehaelt.
Genre: P
Illustration: attack on a fort; ship
Contents: with news from Germany
References: BB V197 (p.529)
Shelfmark: P.P.3444.af(330)
Catalogue No: N267

331
Date: 15 December 1621/186
Signature: K
Title: Nieuwe tijdinghe wt den legher vanden Marquis Spinola. Noch hoe dat 20. van onse ruyters, hebben geslaghen teghen 43. ruyters vanden vyant by Meurs.
Genre: P
Illustration: Spinola
Contents: with news from France
References: BB V197 (pp.529-30)
Shelfmark: P.P.3444.af(331)
Catalogue No: N249

332
Date: 17 December 1621/187
Signature: L
Title: Verhael van het overgheven der stadt Thabor aen den Keyser. Met tijdinge wt Hongerijen, Duytslandt, Enghelandt, Vranck-rijck, ende andere landen.
Genre: P
Illustration: fortified city with troops
Contents: no English news
References: BB V197 (p.530)
Shelfmark: P.P.3444.af(332)
Catalogue No: V119

333
Date: February 1622/25
Signature: G
Title: Copije van een decret ons heeren, des Conincx, ghedepescheert den veerthienden Januarij 1622.
Genre: P
Illustration: the Aegis
Contents: officials to declare their property
References: BB V198 (p.535)
Shelfmark: P.P.3444.af(334)
Catalogue No: S219
Notes: s.v. SPAIN [17.1.1622]

334
Date: [June 1622/83]
Signature: EF
Title: [Discours aengaende Christianus Hertoch van Bruyns-wijck, tusschen Jan ende Andries.]
Genre: D
Illustration: [?]
Shelfmark: P.P.3444.af(333)
Catalogue No: D60
Notes: wanting titlepage and all after p.14; numeration deduced from signatures for this issue otherwise left open in BB V198 (p.545)

335
Date. 22 June 1622/90
Signature: N
Title: Relaes van t'ghene is gheschiedt int comen en*de* retireren vanden leger vanden Pfaltz-graeff wt het landt vanden Vorst van Darmstadt.
Genre: P
Illustration: battle scene with castle
References: BB V198 (p.546)
Shelfmark: P.P.3444.af(335)
Catalogue No: R27

The HAGUE. ADRIAN CLARKE (false imprint)

Date: 10 August 1621
Signature: s.sh.
Title: Corante, or, newes from Italy, Germany, Hungaria, Polonia, France, and Dutchland.
Genre: P
References: STC 18507.28; Dahl 27
Shelfmark: C.55.l.2(14)
Catalogue No: C183
Notes: printed in London

INDEX OF PRINTERS AND PUBLISHERS

Part A of this index consists of an alphabetical list of names, including alternative forms, referring to the towns of their activity, followed where necessary by the standard form of the name. The main part, B, is then arranged under the towns, including towns outside the Netherlands connected with the publication of some of the books in this catalogue, or, failing a name of a town, the countries, in alphabetical order. Made-up names of towns or those whose names are used in imprints in order to mislead are listed in their correct place, qualified as 'false' and the true place or country is added where known or presumed.

The names of printers/publishers within each town or country are again arranged in alphabetical order, including falsely used or fictitious names. Under each name the relevant books are arranged by number in chronological order, those spanning more than one year being entered under the earliest, with the difference that an *oblique stroke* between dates indicates a discrepancy within a single volume, while a *hyphen* refers to varying dates over several parts of a book. A date followed by a plus sign means this year or after; one preceded by a minus sign correspondingly means this year or before. A query following an entry denotes a doubt relating to the precise date or to the attribution of the particular book to this printer, more fully explained in the main catalogue entry. The word 'copy' following an entry indicates that the imprint occurs in the book in the form of a reference to an earlier edition used as printer's copy, either in the same language as now or in some other language from which the present text has been translated. The terms 'false', 'reprint' and 'reissue', as well as alternative dates given in brackets, are self-explanatory.

At the end of the entries for individual printers/publishers under some towns will be found references to those books bearing only the place-name, whether true or false, in their imprint or presumed to have been printed or published there. Imprints giving a place-name preceded by 'buyten', i.e. 'outside', or which imply the name of a town by means of an adjective in their imprint are added at the end of the town concerned.

Two further groups of references follow on those under towns. The first is an alphabetical list of names without place, with the solutions of pseudonyms where known or presumed, the relevant books being entered under these imprints as before. The second is a purely numerical list of those books for which no printer/publisher has been identified or presumed: scope for further research!

A. Alphabetical list of printers and publishers with reference to towns

('No place' refers to the section 'Printers and Publishers without place-name')

B. Index by place of publication

CALAIS

CAMBRAI

COLOGNE

DELFT

1620: A84;
1621: W90
JOHANNIDES, Daniel
1620: A84, V266
KETEL, Gerard
1601: L133
LAMRINCK, Jan
1617: S139;
1618: A106, C18, N208;
1618–20: W89;
1619: S17;
1620: C57, H18, V266;
1621: W91
RADE, Gillis van den
1601: N302;
1602: D130, F73, L117;
1603: D127, 128, P97, V54;
1604: D134, L113, T158, V55;
1604–6: D129;
1605: D133, L118, S50, 61;
1605–8: M89;
1606: D123;
1607: F79, S60, 136;
1608: L239, N303;
1608–9: D118;
1609: D135, F80, L211, 213;
1611: L210, 212;
1612: D125, 126, 131, L121;
1613: L120;
1614: L119
SALWARDA, Thomas Lamberts
1612: W67?
VERHAL, Jelis Claesz (false?)
1616: D114

FRANKENTHAL
FLAMAND, Jacques
1615: M132

FRANKFURT ON THE MAIN
BASSON, Govert (false, = Leiden)
1616: P46
BRY, Theodor de
1610: L130
ELZEVIER, Louis (false, = Leiden)
1615: P194
HARTICHVELT, Christoph von
1613: S280;
1614: S281
HOFFMANN, Nicolaus
1611: J92
HULSIUS, Levinus
1606: R103
HULSIUS, Widow of Levinus
1610: C33
ROSA, Jonas
1611: J92
UNCKEL, Johann Carl
1619: M136, 137
Frankfurt unspecified
1621: A3 (copy)

FREDERICKSTADT (false)
1619+: S176 (copy)

FRIBURCH (false, = Antwerp?)
1620: W131

GDANSK
VERMEULEN, Crijn; de Jonge (false)
1610: B34, 44;
1620: B45 (copy)?

GENEVA
BERJON, Mathieu
1608–10: M57
DOREAU, Jehan (false?)
1602: M133
STOER, Jacob
1619: J93
TOURNES, Jean de
1604: S279;
1613: S280;
1614: S281
Geneva unspecified & tentative
1601: V185;
1609: V162 (copy);
1619: F66?

GENFF IN HOLLAND (false, = Germany?)
GUMPERLE, Niclas
1621: C16

GERMANY
unspecified
1601: A164;
1612+: W57;
1620: B15;
1621: C16?, W95

GHENT
KERCHOVE, Jan vanden
1620: H20
MANILIUS, Gautier
1606: N43;
1608: C91, N55;
1610: F29–31 (all copy);
1614: G79;
1618: S29
MARIUS, Cornelius
1617: L236, R127
STEENE, Jan van den
1606: N43;
1608: N55;

1610: F28;
1613: C45;
1616: F32

GOES
NACHTEGAEL, Yemannus Joannis
1619: L21

GORINCHEM
HELMICHSZ, Adriaen
1608: B190;
1609: M155

GOUDA
BURIER, Andreas
1613: C95, V240;
1616: C161, 215, P170;
1617: V241;
1618: S67
MIGOEN, Jacobus
1607/8: B268?, M111?;
1609: B269?
TOURNAY, Jasper
1609: M20?;
1610: C268;
1611: C162–164;
1612: C97?, 98?, 165, 166;
1613: C95, D157, V240;
1616: C161, 215, P170;
1617: V241;
1621: B136

GRAS-RIJCK BUYTEN AMSTERDAM (false, = Abraham Verhoeven at Antwerp)
1620: C172

GRONINGEN
KETEL, Gerard
1603: E14
RADE, Jan van den
1608: E12;
1610: A63
SAS, Johannes
1608: E12;
1611: M149;
1613: K14;
1616: H207;
1617: R13;
1619: E16, S151;
1621: E7, 15

HAARLEM
ARENTS, Pieter
1613: C96
BEYTS, François
1617: J95;
1618: J96
BOGAERT, Salomon
1616: A91
CASTELEYN, Vincent; the Elder
1613: C96;
1614: N312;
1615: G77;
1621: D99
HORENBEECK, David van
1620: V38;
1621: V39, 44
HOUWAERT, Jacob
1614: S55
KEYSER, Daniel de
1611: H157;
1612–13: F48;
1613: F47;
1614: N312, S55
ROMAN, Adriaen
1611: H157;
1612–13: F48;
1613: F47;
1615: H26;
1616: A91;
1617: H1, J95, S240;
1618: H3–6, J96;
1620/21: V1;
1621: A92
ROOMAN, Gillis
1604: C125
WACHTENDONCK, David
1613: C96;
1614: N312
WESBUSCH, Paschier van
1602: B168;
1603–4: M21;
1609: D15, E58, M20;
1610: B80, M19
Haarlem unspecified & doubtful
1606: J49;
1607: V40;
1616: W52;
1618: K28

The HAGUE
CLARKE, Adrian (false, = London)
1621: C183
ELZEVIER, Lowijs; the Younger
1610: H21
GHEYN, Jacob de; the Younger
1607: G83;
1608: G84, 86, 87?
HEYNDRICKSZ, Aelbrecht

1601: G162, H134;
1602: H135, N35;
1603: E22, 23, H136;
1604: H137;
1608: L156 (copy 1595)?;
1616: N135 (copy 1591)
HONDIUS, Henricus; the Elder
1608: H164;
1610: H167?;
1615: H165
LIMBURG, Aegidius a
1604(=1704): S166
MEURIS, Aert
1609: L55;
1617: B234, R20;
1618: A26, B214, M112?, 113?;
1619: B206, 211, 216, 316, D34, E1, F49, G1, 2, 96, 158, 166, M71, 140, N168, 170, 173, 175, 177, S152;
1620: B87, 220, C225, D44, G62, 159?, J1, O16 (copy);
1621: C150, 151 (false, = Edward Allde in London), D9, 36 (false, = London), E2, 40, 41, K9, L171, M60, 121, O54, P62
NIEULANDT, Beuckel Cornelisz
1602: V156, 157;
1603: D94, V158;
1604–5: V271;
1605: N23;
1606: M144 (copy)
OFFICINA HILLEBRANDI IACOBI (= Hillebrant Jacobsz van Wouw)
1613: B20
VOYS, Guillaume de
1606(=1706): S7
WOUW, Hillebrant Jacobsz van
1602: D32;
1603: E27, P94, Y2;
1604: M91;
1605: H86?, L13, M93;
1606: N137–140;
1607: C188 (copy), N56, 132;
1608: C175? L157?, N145, S266, W17?;
1609: A153, B103, 204, C210, J43, N64–66 (copy), 146, 149, 150;
1610: A162, C232, G60, J90, N87, 88, 151–156;
1612: N158, R51, S85, V247, W124;
1613: B20, G178, H195, L18, W48;
1614: B256, H142, M86;
1615: H209, N159, 160, W129, 140;
1616: B313, D73, 75, H145, W127, 144;
1617: F58, H130, 132, 146, N161, S86;
1617–18: W126;
1618: B270, H133, 148, M87, 116–118, N163, O8, 9, P141;
1619: A179?, D88, H129, 147, N164–167, 169, 172, 174, 176, 178, 179, O7;
1620: B208, 209, E50, G63?, 64?, 159 (copy), H149, J70?, N180–184, S263;
1621: C171, D37 (copy), H150, 151, N186, 187, 189
The Hague unspecified
1620: L229 (false)

HANAU
MARNE, Claudius de & Heirs of Jean Aubry, Typis Wechelianis
1610: N306 (1605 reissue)

HARDERWIJK
HENDRICKSZ, Thomas
1611: T94;
1613: H208;
1614: P159;
1616: P162;
1617: L5, P160
HENDRICKSZ, Widow of Thomas
1620: P167

HERDERS-WIJCK (false, = Antwerp?)
Typographia Synodalis
1620: D90, 91, E52, S169, V246

HEIDELBERG
"buyten Heydelberch" (false)
1620: C172 (copy)

's-HERTOGENBOSCH
SCHEFFER, Anthoni
1614: B314;
1621: L232
SCHEFFER, Jan; the Younger
1606(=1610): T56, 57;
1611: G121
TURNHOUT, Jan van; Third of the Name
1610: T56, 57

HOLLAND
't RECHT VOORSTANT IN HOLLANDT
1618: N307, 308, T38, V259, 262

HOORN
ANDRIESZ, Willem
1606: H125;
1614: L45;
1617: B277

BYVANCK, Jan Jochimsz
1617: O52, S37
CORNELISZ, Zacharias
1617: O52
GAERMAN, Hendrick
1617: S37

INGOLSTADT
ANGERMARIUS, Andreas
1606: T82;
1609: T81;
1610: V17
HERTZROY, Johann
1606: T82;
1609: T81;
1610: V17?
OFFICINA TYPOGRAPHICA EDERIANA
1606–12: T82;
1612: V17

KAMPEN
BERENDSZ, Willem
1617: G131;
1618: G132

LANCASHIRE
BIRCHLEY HALL PRESS
1618: W104, 105?

LAND-UIT (false)
BACHARACH, Colophon van (false)
1602: D22

LA ROCHELLE
PIÉ DE DIEU, Pierre (false)
1621: M25, 26 (copy)

LEEUWARDEN
BERENTSMA, Barent Adriaensz
1609: H109;
1614: H193
FEDDES, Pieter
1620: F6, 7
KNOOP, Isaac
1612: A64
RADE, Abraham van den
1608: P51;
1611: N1, W36 (copy), 37 (copy)?;
1612: A64, V59;
1612–17: F80;
1614: H193, 196;
1616: F76 (copy?);
1617: P165
STARTER, Jan Jansz
1615: B241;
1617: J32;
1618: D72, H18, S248

LEIDEN
BASSON, Govert
1612: A155, 158, B21, 309, F36, W139;
1613: B230, H92, 197, S68;
1614: A12, P3, 4, 7, 8, V231;
1615: B48, E64, G135, P15, S42;
1616: A144, B2, 3 (copy), 60, 61, F44, H50, M94, P26, 31, 46, 127, R117, S12;
1617: B156, 232, F45, S8, 9, T53;
1618: B6, C70, H51, M105, O24, W133, 134;
1619: M90;
1620: B49; S138;
1621–26: B233
BASSON, Thomas
1601: B22, 23, G149;
1602: T84;
1603: H35, 69, M84, R30;
1604: H170;
1605: H65, M110;
1606: C71, D51, E35, 85, J23, P161;
1607: B59, 62 (false), D40, E63, J25, M123, O11, P13, 37, V226;
1608: P72, S164, V235;
1609: B53?, D95, 98, E29, 30 (copy), H27, J45, P11;
1610: A98, 150, 161, B26, 278, C51, G97, H99, M96, P9;
1611: A151, B34, 320, J1, W59;
1612: P5, V237
BEER, Isaac de
1619: P41, S69
BILDT, Bartholomaeus van der
1619: D13, 14, G198, L31;
1620: S35
BONAVENTURE, Corneille (false, = Mathieu Berjon at Geneva)
1608: M57
BOUWENS, Jan
1608: B123;
1610: C160;
1611: A142, B124, C127, 157, S108?;
1612: L73;
1613: A19 (1612 reissue), C122;
1614: B131;
1621: A89 (use of device)?
BREWSTER, William
1617: A5, 85, B155, D66, F13, T137, W75;
1618: C8, 35?, T167;
1619: C9, R73 (false)

CAILLOU, Pierc (false)
1603: L95
CLOUCQ, Andries
1601: F1, M92;
1602: H47;
1607: D97;
1609: B54, 58, H58, M100;
1610: L243;
1611: H67, S128;
1613: M101, T52;
1617(=1616): G163;
1617: M104
COLSTER, Joost van
1614: 102, 103;
1615: C85, 86, P20;
1616: H118, V184;
1617: P144, S199;
1618: S195;
1619: C87
COMMELINI. Bibliopolium Commelinianum; Officina Commeliniana
1606: E85, P161?;
1612: M157;
1613: H91;
1616: C122
DIEPHORST, Joannes
1621: A89, N327
DOREAU, Jehan (false, = Geneva)
1602: M133
DORP, Jan Claesz van
1601: P152;
1603: W9;
1604: M82;
1607: C50, 52;
1608: S194;
1613/14: M83;
1615: S40;
1616: B273, E60;
1618: A28
ELZEVIER, Isaac
1617: B51, 91, 102, C156, H54, 115;
1618: A86, H96, R122;
1618/19: B101;
1619: A105, 134, C129, F3, H55, 155, M98;
1620: A133, C265, D82, H156, P128, 186, R55;
1620/21: M80;
1621: A143, H45, 48, 49, M99
ELZEVIER, Lowijs; the Elder
1602: D53;
1603: D55;
1604: M81;
1605: D56;
1606: D51;
1607: S51;
1609; B58, G174, H58, J80, S106;
1610: C264, M96, N306;
1611: A142, C127, 157, S108;
1612: H40, 182, L73, V276, 277;
1613: A18, 19, B50, 91?, C122, H57, 59, 71, M28;
1614: H68, L79, M97, 107, P156, 211;
1615: F2, H13, 41, M108, 132, P194;
1616: A144, C128, D163, E13, M94, P31, 127, 196, S277;
1617; B51, 92, H52
ELZEVIER, Matthijs & Bonaventura *See* OFFICINA ELZEVIRIANA
ERPENIUS, Thomas
1613: R11;
1615: L234;
1617: K24, M148;
1620: E71;
1621: E70
FRANSZ, Frans
1619: O18
FRIES, Bartholomeus Jacobsz de
1617: P147, R85
GANNE, Johannes
1612: B55;
1620: G129
GEELKERCK, Niclaes van
1618: A32, C248, H6;
1619: S232, 235, 236;
1621: J39, R38
GUYOT, Christoffel
1601: E84, J94, W94;
1602: D145, G92, 116;
1603: E79, 80, H46, J81;
–1605: E82, 83
HAAK, Theodoor
1612(=1712): C253
HAESTENS, Henrick Lodewijcxsoon van
1605: S150?;
1606: D155;
1607: B189, S51, 52, 143, T91;
1608: D100, G29, J19, S144–146;
1609: B54, 56, G30?, 119, J80, P42;
1610: B258, D151, H100, J28, 29?, P2?;
1611: D78 (copy), E92, H67?, S108, 128;
1612: D156, H40, J82?, O31, P16, 17, S107, V276, 277, W88;
1613: H11, 75, 199, T52;
1614: H12, 68?, L79, M97, 107, O28,

P14, R76;
1615: H13, 41, M108, O29, P21;
1616: C128, E13, G196;
1617: A7?, C146, L237;
1619: G198, T2;
1620: B196;
1620–21: S130
HONDIUS, Henricus; the Elder
1604–5: V271
HONTHORST, Uldrick Cornelissz
1612: B55, 223, J82, M157;
1613: V225;
1614: C85;
1615: B133, V222;
1616: S251, V184;
1618: T157?, 161;
1619: V224
HOUT, Jan van
1602: H188;
1604: L56
ILPENDAM, Daniel Jansz van
1607: S143?;
1617: S34;
1618: A4, H163, R3, 125
JACOPSZ, Davidt
1618: W62
LE FEVRE, Jean (false, = France?)
1608: J44
MAIRE, Antoine
1602: B163
MAIRE, Joannes
1602: T80;
1603: H35, 69;
1607: C50, 52, E45;
1608: S194, V186;
1611: H67, S128;
1613: H43, T52;
1614: O28;
1615: S40;
1616: B318;
1617: A7, G171, H44, N18, S48, 52, V274;
1618: C110, R107, S105, V275;
1619: A90, H97, M48, T2, 39;
1620: D12;
1620–21: S130;
1621: B159, E69, H45, L33, 34
MARCUS, Jacob
1610: J29?;
1611: D78 (copy);
1614: D38?, M102, 103;
1615: C85;
1616: S251;
1616/18: S252, 253, 254?;
1617: B46, P185;
1618: E61, M82, N5;
1619: B16, 47, 98, C203, D13, 154, L52, S41, 53, 115, 291, T89;
1620: B81, 319, H161, P157, S44, 165, V8, W40;
1621: H120, O21
MARSCE, Joris Abrahamsz van der
1612: B55, 223, J82, M157;
1613: V225;
1614: B237?;
1615: B24, C85, 86, P6, V222;
1616: O30;
1616/18: S252, 253, 254?;
1617: B46, M52, S199, V209;
1619: C87, D13, 14, 93, S126, V234;
1621: H168, R38
MOLINAEUS, Petrus
1621: L33
MORSIUS, Joachimus
1618: L32, M82
OFFICINA ELZEVIRIANA (= Matthijs & Bonaventura Elzevier)
1617: B156, C156, L238, P197;
1618: A86, G175, H96, 162, P215, R104, 122, S259, 261;
1619: A134, C129, E16, M95, 98, 106, P206, S198;
1620: H42, N21, 22;
1621: A143, H45, 48, 49, S196, T3
OFFICINA PLANTINIANA. Christophorus Raphelengius
1601: B161, D96, H116, P18, V186
OFFICINA PLANTINIANA. Franciscus Raphelengius; the Elder
1610: H179 (1594 reissue);
1613: T39 (1592 reissued)
1621: L34 (1592 reissue)
OFFICINA PLANTINIANA. Franciscus Raphelengius; the Younger
1601: G126?, S131;
1602: L39, H64, 66, S14;
1603: C67, H56, 91, 202, S24;
1604: P98;
1605: B289?, 290?, C111, F55, G189, L49, 166, 216, M79;
1606: C4, M46, P166;
1606–7: V37;
1607: A29, C120, H94;
1608: A58, 176, B141, D68, H70, 95;
1609: B146, H58, J99, P145, T172;
1609–11: H93;
1610: C108, G169, 170, H179 (1594 reissue), P103, 189;
1610–13: B139;
1610–15: B116;

DOORN, Jan Everdsen van
1611: N157;
1616: G180, T15, 18, 20;
1617: T23;
1621: A20
HENRICKSZ, Coenraedt
1607: N132 (1579 copy)
HERWIJCK, Abraham van
1617: T23;
1620: B245
JANSZ, Melis
1618: B213
PASSE, Crispijn van de; the Elder
1612: P53;
1613: H158, R100;
1614: P54, 58?;
1614/16: P57?;
1614–17: P56;
1615: P59, R99?; 101?;
1620: H152
RHENEN, Jan Willemsz van
1612: H198
ROY, Salomon de
1601: F56;
1609: L75;
1610: N190, 191 (copy);
1612: H198;
1614: H141;
1615: P59;
1617: U12, 15?;
1618: N133
VOET, Pieter
1610: N190, 191 (copy)
Utrecht unspecified & doubtful
1612: U14;
1618: W64;
1619: U13
"BUYTEN UTRECHT" (false, = Nicolaes Biestkens at Amsterdam)
1616: D109

VALENCIENNES
VERVLIET, Jean
1609: C74;
1610: R50;
1614: G15;
1619: L41;
1620: T146, V181

VENICE
LE CAILLER, Corneille (false, = in the Netherlands?)
1609: B37

VLISSINGEN
ADRIAENSZ, Cornelis
1609: W96
NOL(IJ)CK, Marten Abrahamsz vander
1609: B176;
1621: W87
Vlissingen unspecified (false, = London)
1620: L94

VRYBURCH (false, = Antwerp)
WAERMONT, Adelaert
1620: W142

YPRES
BELLET, François
1610: Y1, Z6;
1612: R43;
1614: C2, S83;
1614–15: S84;
1620: S82

ZIERIKZEE
HELLEN, Hans van der
1614: L108, 109;
1615: S87

ZUTPHEN
AELST, Andries Jansz van
1611: D5 (copy);
1616: D7;
1619: G89;
1621: U2

ZWOLLE
HENDRICKSZ, Thomas
1609: C131
HEYNS, Zacharias
1607: H104, S63, 64;
1608: B327, H106, 107;
1609: C131?;
1621: S21

PRINTERS & PUBLISHERS WITHOUT PLACE-NAME
A.P.C.
1618: G194
AEDEPOL, Mecastor (= Joachim Trognaesius at Antwerp?)
1609: V267
AUREUS, Dammanus, sive Isaacus Goutius (= Paulus van Ravesteyn & Marten Jansz Brandt at Amsterdam?)
1616: D110
BEMINDER DER ALGHEMEYNER VRYHEYDT
1619: R123

GENERAL INDEX

This index contains the names of additional authors, editors, artists, translators and where known identifies initials, pseudonyms and mottoes. Initials are given in the sequence in which they appear in the book; no attempt is made at finding the initial of the surname, nor are those of titles like D for Doctor, M for Monsieur, etc., excluded. Previous owners are distinguished by asterisks preceding their names or the individual numbers or groups of numbers given at the end of references, e.g. s.v. GROOT, Hugo de, references from B5 to W142 are followed by an asterisked reference to P103. Subject headings, on the whole based on the system applied in the series of Subject Index volumes published by the British Museum/British Library, also include entries for genres such as Drama, Poetry, Prose, Orations, Sermons, etc. Subject references are necessarily approximate and will at times seem arbitrary; nevertheless they may prove useful. Round brackets indicate alternative or additional forms of names. Mottoes are put between double, anonymous works between single quotation marks. References to NEWS REPORTS relate to that section of the Catalogue. The Alphabetical Catalogue should always be consulted for entries under authors or corporate bodies which are not repeated in this index.

B

C

D

M

N

T